THE BEST PUBS OF GREAT BRITAIN

SIXTEENTH EDITION

THE BEST PUBS OF GREAT BRITAIN

SIXTEENTH EDITION

Edited by Andrea Gillies

Chester, Connecticut

©1989 by Campaign for Real Ale Limited (CAMRA)
Published in the United States by The Globe Pequot Press, 138 West Main Street, Chester, Connecticut 06412, with permission from CAMRA, Campaign for Real Ale, Limited, 34 Alma Road, St. Albans, Herts., ALI 3BW, UK. British editions are entitled *The Good Beer Guide*. All rights reserved. No parts of this publication may be reproduced, stored in retrieval systems, or transmitted in any form or by any means, electronic, mechanical, photocopying or otherwise, without the prior permission of the publisher.

Library of Congress Catalog Card Number 87-640216
ISBN 0-87106-608-4

Contents

For Yankees Only   1

Introduction   4

The Disappearing Pub   6
Can the Great British Pub survive attempts to improve it? Virginia Matthews investigates

Behind the Velvet Curtains   9
Roz Morris on the increasingly computerised world of pub interior design

Keg Beer, Keg Food   11
Drew Smith, editor of the *Good Food Guide* asks why we're squandering two great national assets

Real Fire Pub of the Year   14
Join our search for the pub with the warmest welcome

Godfrey Smith   16
The *Sunday Times* columnist recalls his first pint

But I Don't Like Beer . . .   18
Michael Jackson takes on the lager drinkers

The Breweries Section: Introduction **21**; The Independents **23**; Home Brew Pubs **43**; The Voracious Eight (née the Big Seven) **46**; Beers Index **52**

GOOD BEER GUIDE 1989   57
England, Wales, Scotland, Isle of Man, Channel Islands, Northern Ireland: 5000 pub listings begin here

Glossary   67
Also 113, 241, 273, 288 . . . the essential terminology

Contents

The Advertising Hype   165
Don Steele, Director of *Action on Alcohol Abuse*, watches the commercials

Campaigning: Why Bother?   167
Danny Blyth, CAMRA's Research Officer

Women And The Pub: the bitter truth   170
Katherine Adams muses on the terrors of drinking alone

A Taste of London   190
Roger Protz on how a quiet drink turned into an epic

Licensing Act: a layman's guide   227

Small Towns, Big Trouble   261
by Tim Webb

Letters Page   297

Business File   311

Death of a Young Conservative   325

Editor: Andrea Gillies. **Deputy Editor**: Jill Adam. **Additional Research**: Iain Dobson, Brian Glover, Tim Webb. **Special thanks for Production Assistance to**: Jo Bates, Carol Couch, Jenny Mellors. **Additional Production Assistance**: Danny Blyth, Malcolm Harding, Susan Oakes, Clare Stevens. **Cartoons** by Ken Pyne. **Line Drawings** of Michael Jackson, Peter Martin, Rob Walker, and those accompanying A Taste of London by Phil Evans. **Maps** David Perrott.

The editor gratefully acknowledges the help of several thousand CAMRA members in the compiling of the Good Beer Guide.

For Yankees Only

AMERICAN visitors to Britain who have not been deterred by the unlikely perils of Libyan terrorism have an additional peril to face—British beer! The image most Americans have of our national drink is that it is weak, warm, flat as last week's bathwater ... and just about as inviting. The strange thing is that once you have given our beer a fair chance, you tend to come away rather liking it.

You can't generalise too much about our beer, because wherever you are in Britain, there are different ones to try. Though, like the USA, we have a handful of giant companies trying to dominate the market, we also have a host of smaller companies ranging from breweries supplying 100 or so pubs, down to pubs brewing their own beer on the premises. As a result, British beers, like British pubs, are as different and full of character as the people who drink them.

It is true that our beer tends to be served warmer and flatter than beer in the US. This is partly because of custom, partly because of our not-always-excellent weather and partly because excessive cooling and carbonation kill the flavour and character of beer. If you're old enough to remember Britain during the Second World War, don't make the mistake of thinking that the weak, watery stuff that passed for beer then was typical.

While you're in Britain, you probably will hear a good deal of talk about "real ale" and you may wonder what on earth that is. Real ale is traditional British beer, brewed only from pure natural ingredients—malted barley, hops, yeast and pure water—and cask-conditioned (it continues to mature and improve in flavour in the pub cellar until the moment it is served, either straight from the cask or through the traditional hand-pump).

Our other type of beer we call "keg" or brewery-conditioned beer. It may be made from the same ingredients, but it usually has

1

For Yankees Only

cheaper adjuncts replacing part of the barley malt and often has several chemical additives included. They are there to improve the eye appeal or shelf life of the product, but they do nothing for its taste. Before the beer leaves the brewery, it is chilled, filtered and pasteurised. It is kept under a blanket of carbon dioxide and served under CO_2 pressure. The result is beer that keeps well, but is cold, gassy and tasteless . . . just like a lot of American beer, in fact!

At its best, British beer has a character and flavour that compares with any in the world. If you want to try proper British beer—the real thing—avoid our keg beers and our fake "foreign" lagers (all brewed in Britain and about as foreign as fish and chips) and stick to real ale. Its flavour will shock you first, surprise you second, and may well finish up by delighting you. Wherever you go in Britain, you'll find new beers to enjoy. Each region has its own brewers and its own outstanding ales, but let me influence you a little.

Though there are well over 1000 different beers, there are four basic beer styles—mild, bitter, strong ale and stout. Mild refers to the flavour. Mild beers have less hops in them than the other styles so they are less bitter-tasting, although also usually weaker. While mild drinking is declining in Britain, it is still strong in the heartlands of the Midlands and the North West. Try a pint (or even two) of Thwaites rich, dark mild or Ansells or Banks's, frequent winners of the Best Mild award at the Campaign for Real Ale's annual Great British Beer Festival.

Bitter is the typical British beer, a bit stronger than mild, with the extra hop bitterness that gives the style its name. Every region has its own superb variations. Try to sample as many as you can of Adnams's, Bateman's, Brain's, Brakspear's, Donnington's, Fuller's, Holt's, Home's, Hook Norton's, Robinson's, Shepherd Neame's, Taylor's, Tetley's and Young's, and you'll be well on the way to understanding why the normally placid British can be roused to fury at threats to their traditional ales.

Further up the strength scale, although too potent for all-night sessions, are the best bitters. These include some of the finest British beers. Marstons Pedigree and my nominee as the best British beer of all, Timothy Taylors Landlord, are two that no serious student should miss.

At the top of the scale are the strong ales, brewed to mind-boggling alcoholic strength, often with a delicious flavour to match. Theakston's rich, dark Old Peculier (with its peculiar spelling) and Fuller's pale, hoppy ESB are the two leading examples of the genre, but nearly every small brewery has its own variant, often with outlandish, descriptive names such as Dogbolter or Moonraker. Silly young men often try to prove their manhood by drinking several pints of these strong ales; unless you, too, want to end your evening in the horizontal position, approach with care!

The last of the great beer styles is stout, synonymous to most British people with Guinness, black as night, bitter as a Chicago winter and one of the world's great beers. "Proper" Guinness is available only on draught in Ireland. British drinkers consume an imitation of the real stuff. Either stick to bottled (bottle-conditioned) Guinness or try two of the refreshing British alternatives, Timothy Taylor's Porter or Strathalbyn's superlative Beardmore Stout.

This quick tour of the beers of the British Isles should be enough to get you started. The true joy is in making your own discoveries . . . round every bend in the road there could be another superb pub with a range of distinctive local beers to offer. If you're not sure what to try, ask the landlord. If his pub is in this book, it means he takes a pride in his beer and should be pleased to offer some advice.

Delicious as our beer can be, it wouldn't be half the drink without our pubs in which to drink it. British pubs have evolved over thousands of years, and they have always been at the heart of our

For Yankees Only

social life. No one can define what makes a good British pub something special, while anywhere else, it might be just a bar. There's a wealth of tradition, a character and an atmosphere in a good pub that can't be pinned down—it should just be enjoyed!

One warning before I leave you: Britain's licensing magistrates have not yet discovered that the First World War has ended. As a result, pubs in England and Wales are still controlled by laws introduced in 1915 to stop munitions workers spending too much time in the pub. Scotland and Ireland are relatively civilised, but in England and Wales, all pubs close for at least two hours in the afternoon, and evening closing time is either 10:30 or 11. Once the landlord has called "Time" you are allowed ten minutes to finish your drink. Luckily, not all licensees enforce this law with the energy our magistrates would no doubt like to see, especially in country areas.

In the following pages you'll find well over 5000 examples of the Great British pub. If you don't manage to fit them all in this year, don't worry, you can always come back next year to visit the rest! Cheers and good hunting!

Neil Hanson

INTRODUCTION

The Campaign for Real Ale is still perceived by some people, and unfortunately most of the media, as an organisation trapped in a mid 1970s timewarp; a drinking club populated exclusively by large, round (and exceptionally hirsute) men with a really rather peculiar obsession. Active CAMRA members can encounter the view that in the troubled '80s, there are many more important things to worry about than whether ale is 'real' or not.

We're often portrayed as an outdated minority interest, and this goes some way to explaining why CAMRA is lumped in with all things hippy in the popular tabloid imagination. (Save the ale, and save the whale while you're at it, right?)

Well, ecologically speaking, the Real Ale Food Chain looks something like this:

Big national brewers **gobble** up the independents:

➤ Keg beers and lagers are easier and cheaper to make. Products are sold on image rather than quality (wave bye bye to a bit of British history).

➤ Big companies are **eaten** by even bigger ones (wave bye bye to consumer choice).

➤ The **dinosaurs** remaining own most of the breweries, and most of the pubs. Remaining pubs are tied with cheap deals. Pubs become Leisure Venues designed by Brewery Marketing Departments (wave bye bye to a Great British Institution).

That's why the 1989 Good Beer Guide is concerned with the fate of the Great British Pub.

The perpetrators of change are unrepentant. "We're just falling in line with consumer-led change" is the cry of brewery PRs across the land, "and if the customers didn't like they'd vote with their feet."

It's a great argument, until you consider that if all the pubs in your area have been tarted up; if all the beers in your area are the same, there's very little opportunity for voting at all. That's what marketing-led change is all about – do it across the board, and the consumer will get used to it. Train them, with the aid of glossy advertising, to choose between X and Y, and they'll forget about Z altogether. At the end of the day, you can rely on the fact that your customer would rather go to any old pub than not go to the pub at all.

We put up with a lot, we Brits. We don't complain enough, and we don't complain loudly enough. Silent customers are always presumed to be happy customers.

Entirely coincidentally, three of the articles commissioned for this year's Good Beer Guide begin by comparing our brewing industry with the wines of France. A significant coincidence.

France values its wine styles, and the way of life of which they have long been a part. If the wines of France disappeared into several bland national brands; if the cafe-bars of France became as distinct from each other as international airport hotels, there would be a national outcry.

Not only in France, but by people in Britain apparently unaware of the irony of this sudden concern.

Andrea Gillies

Pub Listings
Pub listings are arranged alphabetically by county in England and Wales, and by region in Scotland. Greater London appears under L; Greater Manchester under M, and the three counties of Yorkshire under Y. West Midlands appears under W.

Maps
Each county or region has its own map, with beer mugs marking the site of a listed pub. This year for the first time, we have also marked the locations of Independent Breweries in each county, so you can see at a glance whether the pint you're offered is a local brew or not.

Opening Hours
The 1989 Good Beer Guide was compiled at a time when the liberalisation of the licensing laws was finally becoming a reality. Unfortunately, despite being the best-researched pub guide in Britain, or indeed the world, even *we* couldn't then predict how each of the 5000 pubs listed in these pages would apply the new freedom to its own opening hours.

For this reason, old style pubs opening hours are still listed. For an explanation of the Licensing Act, see our Layman's Guide on page 227.

Surveys
Surveys for the pubs to be listed in the Good Beer Guide are done from scratch each year by volunteers from CAMRA's 20,000 membership. Unlike some other pub guides we could mention, all our reports are done by people who know their area, its pubs and beers intimately. We also welcome reports from non-members; fill in the form on page 381, or drop a line to the editor, and your suggestion will be passed on to local surveyors for consideration.

Sponsorship
CAMRA does not seek nor accept sponsorship of the Good Beer Guide from breweries, drinks companies, tobacco companies, or any others whose involvement might compromise the independence and integrity of the Guide. We accept sponsorship only from companies whose products we can endorse as contributing to the character of the Great British Pub. The 1989 Good Beer Guide is again sponsored by the Solid Fuel Advisory Service; our thanks to them for their continuing support.

The Disappearing Pub

Virginia Matthews

Back in the days of yore, when men were men and women were stuck at home doing all the work, seventeenth century yokels would gather at the Jolly Hangman or The Ploughman's Revenge for a bit of a moan.

Hunched over their brimming yards of ale, always within striking distance of ye olde worlde spittoon, the gnarled peasants would mutter about the quality of the fayre, the irascible nature of the lunatic guvnor and the general incompetence of James I. By the late eighteenth century, the brewers were attracting a better class of tap-room philosopher. Bar bores such as Doctor Johnson would demand no more than a flagon of wine and some hearty victuals in return for their relentlessly witty observations.

It is little known that Dr J had something to say about targeted drinking: "Claret is the liquor for boys, port for men; but he who aspires to be a hero . . . must drink brandy", as well as his more famous "There is nothing which has yet been contrived by man, by which so much happiness is produced as by a good tavern or inn." The (anonymous) customers' lament "This tankard, sir, I was wont to kiss, until I heard that you serve gnat's piss" was not really his style.

The history of the pub is, say its devotees, a colourful chronicle of changing times, and of course rising prices. Its imminent demise has been predicted by wiser generations than our own; if the gripe a decade ago was the grubby squalor of so many boozers, today's moan concerns pathetic attempts to tart them up, but still the local survives. It is no accident that top-rated soap EastEnders includes in its cast a drinking churchman. Maligned for centuries, yet still able to retain the loyalty of a dwindling number, the Church and the pub share the same key problem. Once focal points for a community, now second fiddle to the building society and estate agent, reverends and publicans are fighting against redundancy.

The church, like the public house, has with varying degrees of success cleaned up the shop. But the big task is to transform the clientele – both Sunday worshippers and regular drinkers being largely an ageing and dying breed. Trendy vicars and trendy wine-bars are the obvious pitches to the young and affluent. But at what cost?

The big brewers are spending £2 million every day on transforming the local pub. On the assumption that the spit 'n' sawdust watering hole of yesteryear is no longer acceptable to today's discerning drinker, they are pressing on with the wholesale slaughter of moose heads and pickled eggs.

If pub-goers had one overriding complaint a decade ago, it was that every pub was beginning to look the same. Spurred on by what it's no exaggeration to call Operation Soulless, the brewers had an orgy of redecoration; replacing dingy, if familiar, carpets, bars and lighting with polished floors, chrome and chintz. The Cheese & Pickle in Grimsby was by now beginning to look indistinguishable from the Ham & Cheese in Guildford. The industry hit on a solution.

Targeting and Niche Marketing are the watchwords of the

1980s and Operation Soulless goes on apace. Instead of indistinguishable pubs in just one style, we are now seeing the development of indistinguishable pubs in a variety of styles. Fin de Siecle, Tudor, Victorian, Disco, Art Deco, Bistro, American Diner, Sports and Greek Taverna are the new decors. The complaints, and the drinking, go on.

Whether your local watering hole is being transformed into turn of the century or disco can depend largely on a computer; a dastardly mixture of pseudo sociology and smart number crunching.

I live in a run down, but increasingly gentrified area that appears to pose great problems for the Computer Solution. The majority of residents and pub-goers here are white, middle-aged, slightly down at heel beer drinkers. Moving into the area at a rate of knots are white, young, affluent wine drinkers. Add to this a third cultural mix, a large population of young West Indians who in this case don't tend to drink in 'white' pubs, and you have a situation destined to confuse and unsettle the breweries.

The majority of pubs in my area appear to have remained unchanged for centuries. Friend to neither wine-drinker nor microwave, they are depressing pits of nicotine stained ceilings and coughing old men. The guttural cries of the miserable customers and the ear-shattering volume of the feature film size tellies do nothing for me, but I am quite prepared to believe that to many, they are heaven.

Then there are those pubs that have been trying for years, unsuccessfully, pitifully, to attract the yuppie pound. In a bid to move upmarket they have a blitz on the interior roughly every three years. Installing instant wine bar "areas" or covering the walls in cutesy prints usually results in an instant influx of fresh-faced Golf owners that lasts approximately . . . three weeks. The old men know that if they stick it out long enough, they will recapture the old look, the old smell, and they have yet to be proved wrong.

There is just one pub that qualifies as yuppie in my tiny cosmos. It has the requisite prints, 1930s piped music, chilled wine by the glass or bottle, pink curtains, No Dogs and No

Working Boots, clean loos, an affluent Mine Host and all the ambience of a particularly boring dinner party. The small, select clientele are Italian antiques dealers, BMW-owning designers, local entrepreneurs and estate agents. The old men, who used to pack it to the gills of a Saturday night, just know by osmosis that they are no longer welcomed across its portals. The odd three or four still use it for their regular injection of light and bitter, or mild, but painfully aware that their custom is merely tolerated – "Goodness, Rupert, aren't those flat caps simply super?" – they scuttle off into the night well before closing time.

The big brewers already have a theme pub for people like me I suppose. It's full of ridiculous potted ferns, ruffled curtains, sexually frustrated 20 year olds, a nauseating decor of mint green and dusky pink, toilet signs called "Todeloo" and warm Liebfraumilch and Muscadet. It's called the Wine Bar.

Just about the only thing the brewers haven't tinkered with are the pub names. Once the faithful reflection of a nation's eating habits, (The Haunch of Venison, The Shoulder of Mutton), heroes, (The Walpole, The Wat Tyler), and crafts (The Yarnspinners, The Hatters) the majority of names are now laughably out of date. Where pray is the Jolly Poll Tax Inspector, The One-Cal and Perrier or The Claimant's Arms?

The brews may have changed and the lager may be disgusting, but the pub as an institution is still very much alive. It may no longer be the focal point of the community, and it may make you cringe with the tastelessness of the decor, but the pub retains a unique, if chequered, position in British life. Where we can, just like the old days, expect a snarling welcome from the local Dirty Den, a brew that tastes like liquid feet, and a meal of raw pigeon.

So farewell to the wine bar, adieu to the disco pub. I'm off to Ye Olde Beer Mat for a yard of ale and an articulate ploughman.

BEHIND THE VELVET CURTAINS

Roz Morris

Working in the pub industry used to mean being a publican, a salesman, a barmaid or a brewer. Nowadays there are new breeds of pub workers, and the ones with the most clout are the designers and the marketing managers.

No longer is it enough just to open a pub and see who comes in. Perish the thought, banish such heresy from your mind. Today's pub, however olde worlde it may appear, has been meticulously designed and market-researched in a thoroughly modern manner, right down to the style of the ashtrays and the exact mood of the pictures on the wall.

This is the era of the computerised customer, where you may think *you* are choosing your pub, but really *They* are choosing you.

It's a sign of the times that Valerie Jackson, appointed marketing and development director at Ind Coope in March 1988, was previously marketing research director at Habitat.

"All of my background is lifestyle and leisure, and trying to find a balance between being led by the market and trying to lead it as well", she says.

Valerie started in marketing with Fisons, moved from garden products to holidays, with Wings, and then to Taylor Walker, and Allied Bakeries, before reaching Habitat, a company that epitomises the successful marketing of a lifestyle.

At Ind Coope, with its two and a half thousand outlets, Valerie has a computerised system called the Pub Categorisation Scheme, to help her and her colleagues get their market segments sorted out and their customer targetting spot on.

Or in other words, to try and sell beer. However, as is well known, beer sales are at best static, at worst slightly declining. "But lager is growing steadily and compensating for the static beer sales" Valerie says. "And I think there will definitely be growth too in low-alcohol beers. The market is changing fast, as the leisure market as a whole continues to grow, especially with all day opening.

"Basically we're a large company with a large number of sites, and we have decided that the best way to keep ahead of the game is to use a computerised system which analyses the character of each pub. The Pub Categorisation Scheme is a guide to help us decide how best to target each outlet.

"The factors we feed in are: the characteristics of the site – is it on a high street, a housing estate, a traffic island with lots of passing traffic, a country road? What sort of people live in the area, and very important indeed, what is the competition in the area and what type of outlet do they have?"

All this information produces a profile of each pub and the products most likely to sell there. "For instance" says Valerie, "a traditional pub in town may have a higher proportion of beer to lager sales because older men prefer beer. Meanwhile in a young persons pub there'll be more lager consumption.

"In a town centre and in a country venue there will be a strong food element, whereas in a local, people will want drinks and snacks, not full meals. But it's not just the product mix, it's the ambience and feel of a pub which encourages people to go there."

Ambience and feel used to be created by the publican and his or her regular customers. Remember when the plates on the wall and the Toby jugs, the horse brasses, even the vase of flowers used to actually *belong* to the landlord? Nowadays many brewers call their managers and tenants "retailers" and talk about "customer targetting to find the retail proposition".

And all this marketing jargon means that it's the designers who create the ambience, select the Toby jugs (but only if necessary to their detailed designs) and work out exactly how to get the chosen prey into their predestined watering holes.

Small wonder that one pub designer told me she believed the public would be "really amazed" if they knew the extent of categorisation of customers by the beer companies. "Designers are now given very tight design briefs, much more specific than even five years ago, and it's not just the style of the furniture and the wallpaper that is important.

"For example, older people won't go near flashing blue lights, mirrors and not many seats. But younger people want exactly that, lots of mirrors and raised areas, so they can eye each other up on a night out. In a family style local, on the other hand, you can arrange the furniture to discourage singles. You can intimidate people you don't want, just by the style of the furniture and fittings and the atmosphere you create."

It's all a long way from the era of "Bass for Men" when the only people intimidated in pubs were women, put off by the masculine drinking den tradition.

Now, not only are more women going into pubs, they are running them, designing them, and as Valerie Jackson's appointment shows, taking on key positions in the brewing industry. And that doesn't just mean pubs. In fact, the number of pubs is going down, while the total of licensed outlets is rising. No wonder more and more pubs are offering pizzas and white wine, and the acquisitions departments of the major breweries are not only branching out by buying up high street shops and turning them into pubs, but also developing chains of cafe bars.

But Valerie Jackson doesn't think these new trends mean the end of the traditional British pub. "There's room in an expanding leisure market for both pub and cafe style outlets" she says. "The growing market is very much the family pub, that broadly meets the needs of a range of customers. But people's expectations are much higher than they used to be. They want good quality service in a clean and pleasant environment. Even the loos are a vital part of good presentation. Women are very perceptive about this. They see a tatty loo and they begin to wonder about the state of the kitchen."

According to some pub designers, women are also the worst offenders in causing damage to loos and generally lowering the tone of the designer's carefully created ambience. For this reason, marketing strategies now extend right into the Ladies and the Gents. In a high quality Ladies, there are full-length mirrors, makeup shelves and elegant lighting. At the rougher end of the market, everything is deliberately thiefproof and immovable. Cisterns and lights are behind panels; there are no shelves or ashtrays to rip out, and often no mirrors at all. "In the Gents" one pub designer says, "the age range is the key. The younger they are, the faster you whip everything away behind panels." So now you know. The next time your pub selects you as a customer, you can always tell what type of "target" you are, and what the brewing company and its designers really think of you, by inspecting the Ladies or Gents.

KEG BEER, KEG FOOD

Drew Smith

Just for a moment, let us compare the beer industry in this country with the wine industry in France.

For the best part of the last 150 years, the small farmers of France who have planted their hillsides with vines have struggled, fought and litigated until they got their product properly labelled. Not just as le vin, but le vin du region, and not just to the region but to the town and not just to the town but to the actual hectares. And not just that, he also puts on the label what sort of grapes he uses.

The result is that even the average Sainsbury's customer now knows the difference between a Chardonnay and a Shiraz. The farmer is selling his produce to people hundreds, sometimes thousands of miles away, at prices so high that governments are taxing it at more than £1 a bottle. The farmer is supported in his work by the government through the much maligned EEC Agricultural Policy – indeed it might have been invented for him.

And he is very successful, sometimes selling his most prized bottles for £100 and more. He contributes a lot to the French economy each year and to boot he often has not a bad lifestyle.

It almost begins to bend the mind to compare this brilliantly conceived, backed and marketed industry developed over the century with our own short term, stop and start equivalent. Does the average Sainsbury's shopper know the names of any kind of hops?

What support did the government give to the farmers in this country to carry on growing hops at all? What consumer protection has there ever been in this country for beers so that anyone might tell the difference between real ales and keg? What are the export figures for real ales compared to the import figures to this country alone of wine? Why does an average vin ordinaire sell for three times as much as the same amount of the finest real ale?

The question the beer industry should be asking itself is not whether or not people prefer real ale or keg or lager, but why is it the figures for wine consumption are rocketing? How is it that it is more marketable to bring a drink from another country than to sell the local brew?

The answer to this is simple and well known. The big brewers are stupid. The French are running rings around them and will go on doing so, just as they do with food. The difference is that the French are committed and proud not just of their wines, but the lifestyle that allows their farmers to go on producing these wines. The big breweries are run by people who palpably do not give a toss about such things, in fact probably regard them as liabilities.

What is of concern in investing so heavily in lager is this. If you make a lot of lager, and develop a lot of lager expertise to sell it abroad, in the short term you will succeed. The quality of advertising and promotion for lager is nothing short of superb, quite the match for the French. It is possible to buy a stake in the market. But as with the whole value-added-foods argument so beloved of politicians suddenly, and lager is a very highly value added product, this leaves the back door open. Britain may well be able to sell some of its lager to the rest of the world, but having converted the UK market place to lager, the rest of the world is free, willing and quite able to sell lager to the UK. And there are more of them than there are of us.

The only protection either commercial or for the consumer from this inevitable state of affairs is to maintain a domestic market in which home grown produce occupies a major footing. This is done by deliberately fostering and supporting trades and industries indigenous to this country and at which we excel.

Real ale is the perfect example. It is a product unique to this country. It is unquestionably of a quality that rivals the best wines; a product that could carry a premium. And its relationship with the English pub is as crucial to our national image for tourism as the red gingham cloth of the French bistro. The two are a national asset.

The brewers folly is twofold: first, that without the help of this book the average consumer no longer has any means of finding these superb beers because all the avenues and supply lines have been blocked off by the keg and lager brewers.

Secondly, that a national resource is being destroyed, quite systematically in the name of commerce and progress, when anyone can see that it is neither good commerce nor real progress. Lagers and keg beers are cuckoos in the nest. In fact more than that – they are commercial grey squirrels and threaten to wipe out the entire red squirrel population.

Of course brewers should develop into new markets and products, but not to the extent of undermining their own bread and butter, which effectively is what has happened, only it is disguised by property values.

If that sounds unduly pessimistic, look at other indigenous foods that have suffered the fateful value added philosophy.

Cheese is a good example. The farmhouse industry has been almost exterminated by factory production. Of course we eat more cheese as a result, but we eat more foreign imported cheese too.

And what confidence is there to be taken from the promise of the brewers moving in to the food arena? Precious little. Pubs are going to be fitted up into outlets for highly processed, highly valued added, fast profit moving foods. These will be made in factories, injected with high dosages of additives to ensure they travel well, and distributed through chains. One suspects, also, that there will be a high level of pub casualties, with more conversions to lounge diners, fake haciendas and tapas bars, and restaurants with horrible romantic names.

The first effect of all these operations will be to undermine the local food economy.

The pub is the hub on which a lot of local traders rely – butchers, bakers, fishmongers, grocers etc. This trade, which is often enough pretty scant anyway, will be snapped off. I am no great enthusiast for the current state of pub food, nor for the quasi restaurant that leeches on to pubs. But what seems fairly certain is that more pubs are going to go over to food in the next few years, and the real ale campaign is going to be fighting increasingly on the same ground as the real food campaign.

And the real ale cause is a lot more advanced than the food lobby.

Any landlord using fresh food is now likely to have a reputation for serving good food. Just by the simple act of making the soups on the premises – and by that I do not mean opening a tin can as some of the scandalous hoardings advertising Home Cooked food suggest; the simple act of serving hot roast meat sandwiches, of buying proper bread twice a day and getting farmhouse cheddar, surely the prime accompaniment to real ales; of baking a whole ham for salads, having a stew or a hot pie or perhaps a good fish, will set his pub apart from the rest.

For all the hundreds of thousands the brewers are spending tarting up pubs, I would only ask for £2,200, which is the cost of a new four door Aga cooker. It does not have to be an Aga of course, any old cooker would do, even a secondhand one, but, in these design-conscious days, you need image.

13

Quest for the winter – find *your* 'real fire' pub

For members of CAMRA nominating their annual pub entries for the 'Good Beer Guide' the prime consideration, not unnaturally, is the beer. What is its brewing pedigree? How well is it kept? With what degree of style and bonhomie is it sold and served?

People within the Solid Fuel Advisory Service, another consumer minded organisation with special interest in the Guide (witness its front cover), have a different priority. Their main concern is with a pub's fire, or preferably, fires. Do they burn coal or smokeless fuel? Are they caringly tended from opening to closing time? Is the central heating based on them? And do they constitute an instant invitation to the incoming customer and then make him reluctant to leave the premises? These are important criteria when it is remembered that for the domestic solid fuel industry pubs constitute some of its most influential product 'shop windows'.

The patron who lingers over his pint, captivated by a cheerily glowing fire in his favourite local, is a man likely to seek the same degree of comfort when relaxing in his own living room at home.

And what a wonderful variety of solid fuel fires and stoves are on display in the bars and lounges of Britain's pubs, today. Not to mention the coal-fired boilers and cookers playing their essential part behind the scenes. Because of their pronounced visual appeal, real open fires are the natural choice for welcoming licensed premises, whether they be quaint country pubs with centuries of history or trendy contemporary taverns, designed and built to serve new housing estates. More than 100 approved, up-to-date models of varying sizes and styles are currently available on the market, in addition to many decorative, if less sophisticated, dog grates and fire baskets, so suited to traditional inns bent on preserving authentic period atmosphere.

Ancient or modern, an added bonus is that fires ensure a good rate of air change in rooms where they are alight, which is useful for clearing tobacco smoke and maintaining a healthy environment for customers and staff. Both modern open fires and stoves – or roomheaters as the latest versions are termed – can be installed with back boilers to supply ample hot water for bar and kitchen use and still provide an element of central heating through radiators in other rooms. The continuing popularity of real fire heating can be gauged from the fact that more than 1,000 pubs listed in this year's Guide are solid fuel users. Covered by the identifying 'fire' symbol are a whole range of options from simple grates in cosy snug bars to giant inglenook fireplaces in which up to half a dozen customers can roast on cold evenings. From coal-fired cookers, producing appetising hot snacks to order, to the latest fully automated Coalflow boilers giving trouble-free, temperature controlled central heating on a year-round basis.

The SFAS is currently assessing them to choose its 'real fire pub of the year'. A near impossible selection task which Guide readers may care to try for themselves this winter when hearths are alight and aglow throughout the land.

To get going and set a standard, we've dipped into the county entries and come up with two cracking contenders, north and south of Watford.

The **Malt Shovel** at Brearton in the Yorkshire Dales is a 16th

Century village inn set in James Herriot country. Focus of the local community, it draws customers from miles around, lured by the promise of a perfect pint in an atmosphere of stone walls, oak beams and a welcoming fire. A choice of five real beers and tasty home-cooked food are on offer from landlord Leigh Parsons, who acknowledges: "I wouldn't dream of running a pub without a coal fire".

Two hundred and fifty miles south his sentiments would find an echo in East Sussex, where another gem of a country inn, **The Peacock** at Piltdown is equally worth seeking out. A dated cast iron back plate to the massive inglenook dog grate in the lounge bar authenticates the house as mid-17th Century and uneven floors and ancient beams help make the interior as appealing as its 'chocolate box' facade.

New owners of this splendid, five ale Free House, partners Matthew Arnold and Keith Western, even claim it has a female ghost, who sensibly likes to take up a fireside seat after the last customer has departed. Other attractions of the showplace pub are its one-acre beer garden – a popular venue with summer evening drinkers, a cold buffet luncheon table sporting 18 varieties of cheese and a small stove-heated restaurant with an enterprising menu featuring such delicacies as Peacock Chicken and Steak Marilyn Monroe.

Two 'real fire' pubs getting close to perfection. But maybe you know better? **John Plowman**

Above and left: The Peacock

Below and right: The Malt Shovel

15

The Godfrey Smith Column

I've always loved the smell of a brewery. Even today, belting out of town on the M4, and coming up to turning 12, I get a Proustian throwback from the pervasive aroma of malt wafted across the road by the Courage plant outside Reading. It brings back with a thump the delicious smell of the Courage brewery at Alton where I spent all my holidays as a boy. It stood for hearts at peace under an English heaven. I put that brewery – and the town – into a novel called *The Business of Loving*. The beer was transmuted to Margrave, the place to Aylsbourn, the river (in reality the Wey) to the Cressbrook. I still get letters every now and then from readers who've enjoyed it. They don't brew beer in Alton any more, alas; they bottle lager there now.

The first beer I ever tasted was in a ginger beer shandy bought for me by my father. He was a bit of a connoisseur of beer, and knew a lot about breweries; but was exceedingly modest in his intake. I doubt if he ever weighed as much as ten stone. I wish to heaven I had his metabolism. The shandy was very drinkable on a hot day; but soon after that I noticed serious drinkers looking at my glass askance if I ordered one. They were not sure if it was shandy or beer long past its best; and rather than cause dismay I gave up shandy therewith. The first real beer I drank, on the other hand, was at Rosslyn Park Football Club. Not rugby football, note; Rosslyn Park is one of those very few rugby clubs so old (Bath is another) that it has pre-empted the word football, since it began life when the two codes had still not yet divided. It had long and romantic traditions; and one, unknown to me as an innocent 17-year-old, was dispensing beer out of an old jug for players as they came off the field. I had never played for the Park before (it was the colts XV, let me hasten to add) and I had never been offered real beer before. I felt I had reached man's estate.

The best pint I ever drank was in Winchester. I had walked there one morning from Alton with my old friend Bob Dumper. The church of St Lawrence was striking seven in the morning as we walked out of Alton; we came down the hill into Winchester at 20 minutes past noon; in between we had walked nigh on 20 miles. Well, we were 18 then, and it came easier. Many people have walked further in a morning; no-one enjoyed their first pint afterwards (from Strong's I think) more than we did.

Whatever happened to mild? I know it's still drunk but I would guess that in far less quantities than formerly. And what about mild and bitter? Maybe it's a function of age or milieu, but I don't hear people order it any more. Yet I suppose the four most enjoyable pints I ever drank were mild, put away one summer evening just after the war. I was stationed at some disused airfield – rather like the one Terence Rattigan portrayed in *The Way to the Stars* – and nearby was a tiny, unreconstructed ale-house with a single barrel of mild on offer. We were about nineteen, all aircrew cadets made useless, thank God, by the war's end, and we sat in the sun supping mild and swapping the stories of our lives. I should love to find that place again; but of course it would be a hideous anti-climax if I ever did: probably a theme pub with a juke box – and no mild whatsoever.

I always enjoyed drinking my beer out of a jug with a handle. Still do, for that matter. I know this puts me in a minority among real ale men, who believe the dimples obscure a close inspection of the ale's clarity. True; but the straight glass or sleeve can slide from uncaring hands as the night advances. I know a slight bulge has been built into the straight glass to give a better grip; I still feel uncomfortable with it. Yet my nephews and godsons all swear by the straight glass; they say it's neater. I suppose the jug earmarks me for what I am; a middle-aged, middle-class southron with rugby and Air Force connections. Not a real ale man at all, some would say.

When I was an undergraduate the sconce was still in nightly use. This was the ornate silver three-pint tankard which was called for when anyone transgressed one of the unwritten rules at dinner in hall – mentioning a woman's name, using a foreign word, and so on. Dear innocent, male chauvinist days! You either tried to drink the sconce straight down or, if you had any sense, took a swig, passed it round the table, and paid for it. There was also a 7-pint tankard brought out when the college went head of the river. Whatever has happened to sconces, I wonder, in our brave new world? Can you sconce someone for mentioning a woman's name when half your fellow undergraduates are women themselves?

My father tried to interest me in Guinness; but I could never take to the stuff. On the other hand, I took to Simonds Milk Stout, served in our college buttery, as if it were in fact mother's milk. Now, alas, it has gone for ever; swallowed up by one of the brewing giants. It's daft to try to re-live old drinking delights; but I do miss it.

In the same way, it's daft to try to drink beer in America, our kind of beer, that is. You can find plenty of so-called English pubs in America and indeed round the world; none of them looks or feels quite right. When I was working on an American newspaper, my buddies asked what I thought of their beer. I said it was all right; but not like the stuff we got out of a barrel back home. But, they protested, we have draught beer too; and they took me off to try some. And it still tasted like gnat's pee.

In our local pub in the country, our excellent young landlord keeps careful barrels of Wadworth 6X, Mole's, and Archer's. All have their adherents, though I hear Mole's is pulling ahead. All are brewed in Wiltshire. All are honest English ales. I enjoy each one, but none half as much as the one I sank that day I walked down the hill into Winchester.

"BUT I DON'T LIKE BEER . . ."
Michael Jackson

Could you imagine a Frenchman, on his own turf, ordering a German wine? Worse still, a French wine pretending to be German? If you could, perhaps you should put your belief to the test. Go to Bordeaux, sit yourself down in a café, bar or restaurant, and say that you fancy a real Blue Nun, so to speak.

Sacre Bleu Soeur! That's fixed you, hasn't it? You have just been on the receiving end of the reaction I suppress every time I see someone who otherwise appears to be British go into his or her local and order something vaguely described as "a lager". I keep my thoughts to myself because a broken nose would interfere with my appreciation of my superbly aromatic pint of Burton Ale.

Lager has its place. Let us not be niggardly; it has its places. There are at least three of them: Czechoslovakia, if you would like to try the golden-coloured, dry, flowery style of lager that was first made in the town of Pilsen, Bohemia; or Vienna, if you think you might prefer a fuller-coloured, spicier, lager; or Bavaria, if your taste could run to a lager that is sweetly malty and sometimes in the original, dark brown, style.

Real lager is dark? I never knew that.

Not many people do, but you won't learn much about lager from drinking the British stuff.

I drink Ersatzenbräu. That's German.

German-ish. It's brewed under licence in a place you thought was nothing more sinister than a missile silo, at a convenient intersection of trucking routes between three major centres of population.

It's modern then, isn't it?

The Bavarians were brewing lager in the 1400s.

It's refreshing. That's really why I drink it.

Ever tried Fuller's Chiswick Bitter, in London? Or Jennings', in Cumbria?

Those are beers. I don't like beer.

Lager is beer, too. It is a Bohemian-Austrian-Bavarian style of beer. Ale is a British (and Belgian) style.

Ale? You mean Bitter?

Mild Ale, Bitter Ale, Brown Ale, Pale Ale, Light Ale, Heavy Ale, Old Ale, Barley Wine. Not to mention Porter and Stout.

I like lager better because it is less fattening.

Only if you don't drink any.

I like lager better because it is less/more alcoholic.

Sometimes. The regular version of Carlsberg, to take a well-known British-brewed lager, is weaker than many Mild Ales. Carlsberg Special Brew, on the other hand, is stronger than many Barley Wines (though not half as tasty). In general, lagers and ales in Britain have similar strengths, according to price-range.

I like lager better because I am a lady/gentleman. People like me are too prissy to drink beer. We don't do that kind of thing.

Neither do football hooligans. These days, they represent the vanguard of lager-drinking. The super-patriot who wears a Union Jack tee-shirt and strives so tirelessly to elevate Britain's name abroad can be relied upon to drink fake German lager. The Queen Mother, on the other hand, enjoys Young's Special Bitter, and has been photographed doing so. When she is at Balmoral, I bet she drinks Belhaven.

So is this a question of patriotism?

One reason the French are so keen on their wines is that they have good taste (the people and the claret). Another is that they are proud of the products their country makes best, and put their mouth where their money is.

What does Britain make best?

In the world of beer, we are by far the biggest ale-brewers. With its characteristic fruitiness, fullness of palate, and complexity, ale is to the world of beer what claret and burgundy are to the universe of wine. Our ales are the clarets of the beer world.

Can you really talk of ale in those terms?

The Belgians put theirs in Champagne bottles, wrap them in tissue paper, lay them down in the cellar, and serve it in Burgundy samplers. The Americans are trying furiously to emulate British ale. Ever come across Ballard Bitter, from Seattle, Washington? Or Big Foot Barley Wine, from Chico, California?

Let's be British about this – and no tissue paper, please. Let's go to a pub. Where do we start?

Gently. We begin with something low in alcohol but full of fruity flavour. We will set out in London, with the apple-tinged dark Mild they brew at the Greyhound pub, in Streatham. Then we will head for Hertfordshire to try some of the wonderfully complex pale Mild made by the McMullen brewery. After that, go to the real Mild Ale regions: the West Midlands and Manchester.

In the Midlands, we will make a point of sampling an unusually strong rich "ruby" Mild made by John Hughes in a tiny tower brewery behind his grandmother's pub at Dudley. There are so many home-brew pubs around Dudley that we might have to stay the weekend.

I didn't know anyone made Mild these days.

You have to look for it. That's half the fun.

In home-brew pubs? I thought all the small breweries had closed.

There are more small breweries in Britain today than there have been for 25 years. They might even stay in business if you could bring yourself to lay off the Ersatzenbräu.

You've persuaded me. Where can we get a good pint of Bitter?

Depends on what takes your fancy. For a really dry, hoppy Bitter, let's stay in the South: Shepherd Neame's brewery at Faversham is set among the hop-gardens of East Kent, the region that grows the Golding, the world's most aromatic ale hop.

Michael Jackson on the job.

Young's and Fuller's in London both make hoppy Bitter. Brakspear's, of Henley, produces classic examples.

For drily fruity Bitter, the East. Ridleys, of Chelmsford; the splendidly tart Greene King, of Bury St Edmunds; the more complex, salty Adnams Bitter from Southwold; fruity-hoppy, big-bodied, Bitter from Ruddles, of Rutland.

For creamy Bitter, Yorkshire and the adjoining counties. The new real ales from the Mansfield Brewery; the Bitter from the small Old Mill Brewery, and from Tetley's, Timothy Taylor's and Samuel Smith's, of Yorkshire. Even John Smith's have a real ale these days. Across the Durham border, Strongarm, from Cameron's.

For firm-bodied, acidic Bitter, the North-West. The malty-dry Lees; the deceptively soft Hyde's; the austere Holt's; the gentle, subtle Robinson's; all from Greater Manchester. For really chewy Bitter, Wales: the big, rounded Bitter from Felinfoel; the dry, profound Special Ale from Brain's. For softly fruity Bitter, the West. Fruity-nutty ales from Palmer's thatched brewery; tasty Badger beers from Hall and Woodhouse, both in Dorset; deeply fruity Bitter from Wadworth's, in Devizes; assertive ales from Arkell's and beautifully clean, fresh Bitter from the small Archer's brewery, both in Swindon.

You're mentioning every Bitter in Britain.

On the contrary, I've missed out half of my favourites.

What about Pale Ale, then?

Certainly, we'll have to go to Burton for that. We'll have an elegant Marston's Pedigree in the pub, as an aperitif, and take home a bottle of sedimented Worthington White Shield to have with our roast beef dinner.

A Barley Wine? An Old Ale?

After dinner, and from the South Coast. A Cognac-like Harvey's Elizabethan, from Sussex; a Calvados-tasting Prize Old Ale, with a drawn cork, from Gale's of Hampshire; a Madeira-ish, vintage-dated (but make sure it's at least five years old) Thomas Hardy's Ale from Dorset; or a sweet, warming Domesday from Cornwall.

Isn't Porter the oldest style of all?

An old London style, made by the new breweries all over the country. In Pimlico, the Orange Pub brewery has an appropriately chocolatey example; in Essex, Crouch Vale's porter has more of a licorice note; in Cheshire, Oak Porter is on the syrupy side; in North Yorkshire, Malton's Porter is coffee-ish and intense. We shouldn't forget Stouts, either. A "Russian" Stout, with a hint of Christmas pudding, from Courage; an Anglo-Irish one, with an espresso roastiness, from Guinness . . .

What about Scotland?

Full-bodied, warming ales – especially the strong, Export style from Belhaven and Maclay's. Or a beautifully clean and malty, extra strong, "90 Shilling" from Caledonian, a magnificent brewery that has regained its independence. Its 90/- is a classic pale Scotch Ale, the beer world's answer to a Lowland Malt. Traquair House is the classic dark Scotch Ale, oaky-tasting from its fermentation in wood, and almost "Chateau-bottled".

What would your man in the bar in Bordeaux think of all these comparisons with French wines?

He'd drink his bottle of Traquair House, and toast the Auld Alliance. That's what he'd do.

---

* Michael Jackson is the author of the "World Guide to Beer" (Bloomsbury), "Pocket Guide to Beer" (Mitchell Beazley) and Chairman of the British Guild of Beer-Writers. He was among the winners in both the Glenfiddich and Wine Magazine/Deinhard Awards, 1988.

The Breweries Section

INTRODUCTION

The French are proud of their wines. You cannot imagine them ignoring the merits of a fine claret or a rich Burgundy, in order to concentrate all their efforts on producing a poor copy of a German Liebfraumilch.

Yet that is exactly what is happening in the British brewing industry.

We are the only country in the world brewing mild and bitter ales, stouts and barley wines. We should be boasting about this unique range of beers. Instead our major brewers neglect this heady heritage, and foolishly commit all their resources to marketing pale imitations of foreign lagers.

First came the brands with the Scandinavian or Germanic-sounding names, like Skol and Hofmeister, to compete at the bar with lagers brewed under licence from leading Continental companies – but to much weaker recipes – like Carlsberg or Heineken.

Then came the flood of Aussie brews from Down Under, Fosters and Castlemaine XXXX, coupled with the bland tide from across the Atlantic of tasteless American beers, Budweiser and Miller Lite. All, despite the emphasis on their foreign origins, brewed under licence in this country.

The latest invasion sees Labatts of Ontario being pumped out across the North of England from such unlikely Canadian cities as Warrington, Sunderland and Hartlepool. Ironically, one of the first lager brands, Carling Black Label, was also brewed under agreement with Canada. The next step was obvious. Once brewers from abroad saw the success of their beers in Britain, they wanted more than a small sip of the profits. They wanted full control. So Elders IXL, the owners of Fosters, bounded in to buy Courage. And soon the sweet smell of the 'amber nectar' was penetrating over 10,000 pubs.

It was the first leap in a lager-led landslide that could see the bulk of the British brewing industry swept into foreign ownership in the next decade.

Already another ambitious Australian company, the Bond Corporation, brewers of Castlemaine XXXX, have taken a significant share stake in Allied Breweries. While Anheuser Busch of the United States, the brewers of Budweiser, so huge that they brew more than the whole of the British brewing industry put together, could easily swallow one of Britain's major breweries.

This stampede towards a global brewing industry, with international brands, is an inevitable extension of the rationalisation process that has been squeezing the life out of the British brewing industry for years.

In 1960 there were 360 breweries in Britain. Then along came the 'Big is Better' brigade and hung 150 companies during the Swinging Sixties. A handful of national combines sprang to

21

prominence and swiftly tightened the beer tap, turning the choice flow of traditional ales into a trickle.

Ten years ago there were still 100 established independent breweries. Today there are barely 50 surviving with more being lost each year. If the trend continues, none will be left at all by the end of the century.

Breweries butchered within the last two years include Rayments of Hertfordshire, Paines of St. Neots, Wem of Shropshire and Oldham Brewery – often in the teeth of bitter local opposition organised by CAMRA. Two of Theakston's breweries, Carlisle and Workington, vanished during the sad saga which saw Scottish & Newcastle finally seize control of Matthew Brown of Blackburn in 1987, against the wishes of Brown's board, many shareholders and local drinkers.

Plants in the tender grasp of other national combines have fared no better. Whitbread top the hit list. Having already axed eight other breweries in this decade, they chopped down a further two in 1988 – Wethereds of Marlow, Buckinghamshire, and Chesters of Salford, Manchester.

The major combines are not only intent on reducing the number of breweries, they also want to cut our choice of beers. National brands are the order of the day.

This dire drive to conformity across the country is best illustrated by Watney. Most of their pubs, from Ushers in the West Country to Norwich in the East, offer the same three real ales: Webster's Yorkshire Bitter, Ruddles Best and Ruddles County. Local beers like Combes Bitter in London have been poured away. The only shaky step towards improving quality and variety has been the welcome appearance of over 300 new small breweries during the past 15 years. But over half of these have already disappeared; most of Britain's bars are bolted shut against their beers, either because the big boys own the pubs or because they have tied them up through financial deals.

In recent months popular breweries like Titanic in the Potteries or Rockside of Barnsley have brewed their last. While Scotland has lost significant ventures in Strathalbyn of Glasgow and Alice of Inverness. The Alice plant was shipped across the Atlantic to North America, as was Herald of Northern Ireland. So at least these breweries are still making real ale – even if it's in another country.

The year also saw the retirement of the father of the new brewery revolution, Peter Austin of Hampshire's Ringwood Brewery, who has set up over 40 breweries at home and abroad. While the cheeky individual who made home-brew pubs front-page news, David Bruce, sold his London chain of Firkin pubs to Midsummer Leisure for £6.5 million.

But the news is not all gloom. In 1987, 20 pint-size breweries dried up, compared to half that number rolling out their first barrel. But in 1988, the tide turned and more new ventures appeared than closed down. The largest was Premier Midland Ales, which has set up a sizeable plant at Stourbridge, with two home-brew houses to follow. The most welcome, despite producing mainly keg beer, was the Orkney Brewery, the first brewery in the far northern isles for over 50 years.

Brian Glover

Brian Glover is the author of the **New Beer Guide**, *the CAMRA* **Dictionary of Beer**, *and ex-editor of CAMRA's newspaper,* **What's Brewing**.

Independent Breweries

ADNAMS, Sole Bay Brewery, Southwold, Suffolk. ☎ 0502 722424.
E. Anglia's famous seaside brewery, with real ale in all 65 pubs and 1,900 free trade accounts in Southern England. Expanding steadily in free trade. Launched Broadside in 1988 to compete in free trade with Greene King's Abbot.
Mild (1034) – dark dry ale.
Bitter (1036) – well hopped.
Extra (1044) – crisp and full-bodied.
Old (1042) dark malty winter brew.
Broadside (1049) – vigorous full-flavoured new strong beer.
Tally-Ho (1075) – classic sweet barley wine for Christmas.

ALLOA Brewery, Scotland. See Allied Breweries, page 46.

ANSELLS, Birmingham. See Allied Breweries, page 46.

ARCHERS, London Street, Swindon, Wilts. ☎ 0793 467789.
Successful small brewery, set up in 1979, which in 1985 doubled its brewing capacity. Serves 100 free trade outlets from Oxford to Bath plus three tied houses.
Village Bitter (1035) – light and refreshing.
Best Bitter (1040) – well-hopped bitter.
A.S.B. (1048) – full-flavoured and smooth.
Headbanger (1065) – dark, strong and malty.

ARKELL, Kingsdown Brewery, Swindon, Wilts. ☎ 0793 823026.
Family brewery, established in 1843, with real ale in 59 of its 68 pubs and three off-licences. Now has free trade in the Thames Valley and London. Beware of brewery-conditioned (keg) 3B on handpump.
John Arkell Bitter (BB) (1033) – light and hoppy.
Arkells Best (3B) (1038) – fuller bodied, distinctive nutty bitter.
Kingsdown Ale (1052) – stronger malty version of 3B.

ASH VINE Brewery, The White Hart, Trudoxhill, Frome, Somerset.
☎ 0373 84324
Ted Bishop, who originally set up Cotleigh Brewery, has now sold his Bishop's Brewery to Rob Viney, although he has stayed on as brewer. The new brewery will be moved to the tied house, the White Hart during 1988. Around 20 free trade customers are supplied.
Ash Vine Bitter (1039) – medium dry bitter; well-hopped and full-bodied.

ASTON MANOR, 173 Thimblemill Lane, Aston, Birmingham. ☎ 021 328 4336.
Concentrates on bottled beer; produces the occasional cask ale for special events.

AXMINSTER, Fordwater, Axminster, Devon. ☎ 0460 20257.
The former Hardington brewery in Somerset was taken over in 1988 and moved to its new site at Axminster. Brewing is now the responsibility of manager, David McCaig, who will continue with Hardington beers, plus a new Axminster brew.
Axminster Bitter (1036) – new bitter, for the Devon area.
Hardington Bitter (1037) – well-hopped and fruity.
Somerset Best Bitter (1043) – full-bodied, dark and smooth.
Horrors (1050-55) – dark and deadly. Brewed for Bank Holidays.

AYLESBURY Brewery Co. (ABC), Bucks. See Allied Breweries page 46.

BALLARDS, Elsted, Midhurst, W. Sussex. ☎ 073 081 4936.
Begun in 1980 at Cumbers Farm, Trotton, and in 1985 moved to their first tied house, the Ballards (formerly the Railway Inn), Elsted. It is intended to move the brewery to Nyewood during 1988. Supplies some 45 free trade outlets.
Best Bitter (1042) – well balanced and nutty.
Wassail (1060) – strong, malty brew.

23

Independent Breweries

BANKS'S, Park Brewery, Lovatt Street, Wolverhampton. ☎ 0902 711811.
With Hanson's makes up Wolverhampton and Dudley Breweries, the largest surviving independent 'family brewers' in the country. Traditional (cask-conditioned) ales served in nearly all 650 tied houses, virtually all through electric metered dispense. Beware of keg (brewery-conditioned) beers in clubs and free houses.
Mild Ale (1035) – smooth and malty.
Banks's Bitter (1038) – full-bodied and well-hopped.

BANKS & TAYLOR, The Brewery, Shefford, Beds. ☎ 0462 815080.
Set up in 1982 and now serving some 50 outlets including 12 tied houses. SOD often sold under house names.
Dark Mild (1032) – occasional brew.
Shefford Bitter (1038) – clean and hoppy.
Eastcote Ale or **SPA** (1041) – smooth, full-flavoured.
Shefford Old Strong (SOS) (1050) – full-bodied and fruity.
Shefford Old Dark (SOD) (1050) – rich brew, dark version of SOS.

BARRON, Land Farm, Silverton, Devon. ☎ 0392 860406.
Farm brewery set up in 1984 supplying outlets around Exeter. Beers brewed using the farm's spring water, without the use of additives.
Barron's Delight (1039) – smooth and malty.
Exe Valley Bitter (1042) – full-bodied and well-hopped.
Devon Glory (1050) – new strong ale.

BATEMAN, Salem Bridge Brewery, Wainfleet, Skegness, Lincs. ☎ 0754 880317.
A small family brewery which produced a Victory Ale to celebrate its hard-fought battle for independence in 1987. Its XXXB was voted CAMRA's 1986 Beer of the Year. All 85 tied houses sell "Good Honest Ales" in traditional form. A vigorously expanding free trade includes a high gravity ale to the USA.
Mild (1033) – robust, creamy and dark.
XB (1036) – excellent, distinctive, well-hopped bitter.
XXXB (1048) – powerful, malty ale.
Victory Ale (1056) – very strong ale with deceptively mellow palate.

BATHAM, Delph Brewery, Brierley Hill, W. Midlands. ☎ 0384 77229.
Hidden behind one of the Black Country's most famous pubs, the 'Bull and Bladder', this small family firm has managed to survive since 1877, brewing excellent beer for its eight pubs and free trade, which accounts for 40% of its output. Now bottling, its own beer again after a lapse of 30 years.
Mild (1036) – dark and tasty.
Bitter (1043) – distinctive and full-bodied.
Delph Strong Ale (1054) – a Christmas ale.

BEARDS, Stella House, Diplocks Way, Hailsham, Sussex. ☎ 0323 847888.
No longer brews. Takes Harvey's range of ales under its own name for its 23 pubs and wholesales other beers like King & Barnes.

BELHAVEN Brewery, Dunbar, East Lothian, Scotland. ☎ 0368 62734.
Scotland's oldest and best-known independent brewery, which has had a turbulent but colourful history, now controlled by Perth-based Belhaven PLC. Primarily free trade, with a third of its 600 accounts taking real ale. 70% of its 40 pubs and hotels serve real ale.
60/- Light (1031) – dark and malty.
70/- Heavy (1035) – light and hoppy.
80/- Export (1041) – heavy, full-bodied ale.
90/- Strong Ale (1070) – occasional rich brew (not for the faint-hearted!)

BENSKINS, Watford, Herts. See Allied Breweries, page 46.

24

Independent Breweries

BERKHAMSTED, Bourne End Lane, Bourne End, Herts. ☎ 04427 73781.
Brewery inside premises of Inn Brewing brewing equipment manufacturers. Beer chiefly sold 'through the door'. Varies between malt extract and full mash.
Castle Bitter (1035) – medium "party" brew.
Best Bitter (1041) – a hoppy brew.
Premium (1055) – dry strong ale.

BERROW, Coast Road, Berrow, Burnham-on-Sea, Somerset. ☎ 027 875 345.
Begun in 1982 and now supplying about 20 pubs and clubs in Somerset and Avon.
BBBB (1038) – full-tasting bitter.
Topsy Turvy (1055) – distinctive, pale strong ale.

BIG LAMP, Summerhill Street, Newcastle-upon-Tyne. ☎ 091 261 4227.
Set up in 1982, now the longest-established independent real ale brewery in the north-east! Now serves two tied houses and several free trade outlets.
Big Lamp Bitter (1038) – hoppy and distinctive.
Stout (1044) – rich, black, and creamy.
Prince Bishop Ale (1044) – full-bodied pale ale – very hoppy.
Old Genie (1070) – powerful dark brew.
Blackout (1100) – very powerful, brewed for festivals only.

BLACKAWTON, Washbourne, Totnes, Devon. ☎ 080 423 339.
One of the earliest new small breweries, dating from 1977, and now the oldest brewery in Devon. Serves 75 free trade outlets.
Blackawton Bitter (1037) – hoppy and well-rounded.
Forty-Four (1044) – premium, full-flavoured bitter.
Headstrong (1049) – like a strong mild.

BLEZARDS, Liverpool. See Tetley-Walker, Allied Breweries, page 47.

BODDINGTONS', Strangeways, Manchester. ☎ 061 831 7881.
Manchester's most ambitious brewing son; also owns Higsons Brewery in Liverpool and now brews OB beers at Strangeways, after closing Oldham brewery in 1988. All 280 tied houses serve real ale (either Boddingtons, Higsons or OB). Free trade accounts for approximately a quarter of the volume business.
OB Mild (1031) – malty and dark.
Mild (1032) – dark and full flavoured.
Bitter (1035) – popular, straw coloured bitter.
OB Bitter (1037.2) – pale and full flavoured

BRAIN, Old Brewery, St. Mary Street, Cardiff. ☎ 0222 399022.
A fiercely independent brewery established in 1713 and as much a part of Wales as Rugby Union. These good value, distinctive beers are served traditionally in all their 128 pubs. Extensive free trade.
Dark (1034) – smooth and malty mild.
Bitter (1035) – light and well-flavoured.
SA (1042) – full-bodied, malty bitter.

BRAKSPEAR, The Brewery, Henley-on-Thames, Oxfordshire. ☎ 0491 573636.
Popular country brewery with many superb, unspoilt pubs. All 117 tied houses serve traditional ales. Also have a substantial involvement in the free trade.
Mild (1031) – thin but hoppy.
Bitter (1035) – distinctively flavoured.
Special (1043) – full-bodied premium bitter.
Old or **XXXX** (1043) – Special with caramel.

BROUGHTON Brewery, Broughton, Peeblesshire. ☎ 08994 345.
One of the most significant new breweries set up in 1980 by former S & N executive, David Younger; supplying their own and Theakston's draught ales to some 200 outlets in Scotland, as well as a considerable bottled beer trade to off-licences.
Greenmantle Ale (1038) – bitter-sweet beer.
Broughton Special Bitter (1038) – dry-hopped version of Greenmantle.
Merlin's Ale (1044) – magical golden brew.
Old Jock (1070) – bottled strong ale occasionally on draught.

25

Independent Breweries

MATTHEW BROWN, Blackburn. See Scottish and Newcastle, page 49.

BUCKLEY, Gilbert Road, Llanelli, Dyfed. ☎ 0554 758441.
Wales's oldest brewery dating back to 1767, with cask beer in majority of its 130 pubs in S. West Wales. Taken over by new owners, Brodian in 1987. Also has a major stake in Llanelli neighbours Felinfoel. Has expanded tied trade by pub swaps with Whitbread. XXXX Mild sold as Ansell's Dark by Ansells.
XXXX Mild (1032) – dark and fruity.
XD Mild (1032) – extra dark mild for Swansea area.
Best Bitter (1036) – full-flavoured.

BULLMASTIFF, 5 Anchor Way, Penarth, South Glamorgan ☎ 0222 702985.
A small brewery set up in late 1987 by a fanatical home-brewer. Now supplies some 20 outlets – a welcome addition to the free trade choice in S.E. Wales.
Bitter (1035) – light, clean-tasting beer.
Ebony Dark (1042) – Very smooth, malty strong dark mild.
Best Bitter (1043) – full-bodied and well-balanced.
Son Of A Bitch (1062) – rich, sweetish, strong ale.

BUNCES, The Old Mill, Netheravon, Salisbury, Wilts. ☎ 0980 70631.
Set up in 1984 on the Wiltshire Avon; brews two cask-conditioned beers for the free trade from Avon to Surrey. A Great Western Beer Festival winner in 1986. Visits to the brewery, a listed building, are welcome, by prior arrangement.
Benchmark (1035) – robust flavour for its gravity.
Best Bitter (1042) – full-bodied, hoppy bitter.

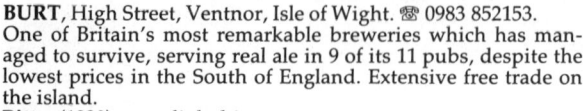

BURT, High Street, Ventnor, Isle of Wight. ☎ 0983 852153.
One of Britain's most remarkable breweries which has managed to survive, serving real ale in 9 of its 11 pubs, despite the lowest prices in the South of England. Extensive free trade on the island.
Bitter (1030) – rare light bitter.
Mild (1030) – dark nutty mild.
VPA (1040) – hoppy, distinctive bitter.
4X (1040) – winter old ale.

BURTON BRIDGE, Bridge Street, Burton-upon-Trent, Staffs. ☎ 0283 36596
Started in 1982 with one tied outlet at the front of the brewery and selling to local free trade. This has now extended to a radius of 150 miles, serving around 200 outlets with guest beers. Specialises in commemorative bottled beers.
XL Bitter (1040) – light hoppy beer.
Bridge Bitter (1042) – distinctive fruity beer.
Burton Porter (1045) – dark and bitter (also bottle-conditioned).
Burton Festival Ale (1055) – strong smooth ale.
Old Expensive or **OX** (1066) – dark winter warmer.

BURTONWOOD, Bold Lane, Burtonwood, Warrington, Cheshire. ☎ 09252 5131.
Family brewery with 282 scattered pubs including several in N. Wales. 242 offer real ale. Widespread and increasing free trade in clubs. Beware a few remaining houses selling keg beer (usually mild) through handpumps.
Dark Mild (1032) – pleasant, nutty flavour.
Bitter (1036.5) – light and creamy.

BUTCOMBE, Butcombe, Bristol. ☎ 027 587 2240.
One of the most successful new breweries, set up in 1978 by a former Courage Western managing director. Extensive penetration of the free trade, particularly in Avon and Somerset. Owns three pubs, all serving real ale.
Butcombe Bitter (1039) – dry, well-hopped and clean tasting.

Independent Breweries

CALEDONIAN, Slateford Road, Edinburgh. ☎ 031 337 1286.
After Vaux closed the famous Lorimer & Clark brewery in May 1987, a management team aquired it. They now operate from the old brewery with the last direct fired open coppers in Britain, brewing traditional Scottish beer.
70/- Ale (1036) – soft, malty flavour.
Porter (1036) – dry, nutty flavour.
80/- Ale (1043) – malty, flavoursome with good hop balance.
Merman XXX (1052) – dark, heavy beer.
Strong Ale (1080) – rich and deceptively strong.

CAMERON, Lion Brewery, Hartlepool, Cleveland. ☎ 0429 66666.
The N. East's major brewers of real ale, who narrowly escaped being taken over by Scottish & Newcastle Breweries in 1984. In 1986 they bought 78 pubs from Mansfield Brewery, particularly in Hull, and in 1987 took over Melbourn's 32 pubs around Stamford, Lincolnshire.
Traditional Bitter (1036) – tasty, hoppy brew.
Strongarm (1040) – fine malty bitter.

CANTERBURY, 28 St. Radigunds Street, Canterbury, Kent.
☎ 0227 456057.
Non-brewing company with three pubs and two restaurants. Draught beers brewed by Mansfield Brewery.
Canterbury Ale (1037) – light, fruity bitter.
Buffs Bitter (1047) – strong pale ale, brewed occasionally.

CASTLETOWN, Isle of Man. See Isle of Man Breweries, page 33.

CHARRINGTON, London. See Bass, page 48.

CHESTERS, Manchester. See Whitbread, page 51.

CHILTERN, Nash Lee Road, Terrick, Aylesbury, Bucks. ☎ 029 661 3647.
Begun in 1980. Now supplying 30 mainly local outlets including some Aylesbury Brewery pubs.
Chiltern Ale (1036) – distinctive, light bitter.
Beechwood Bitter (1043) – full-bodied and nutty.

CLARK, Westgate Brewery, Wakefield, W. Yorks. ☎ 0924 373328.
Drinks wholesale company which began brewing again in 1982, and now brews Clark's Traditional Bitter for 27 free trade accounts. The other three beers are chiefly sold at their three 'Boon' pubs, named after founder, Henry Boon Clark.
Clark's HB (1033) – light, refreshing bitter.
Garthwaite Special (1036) – refreshing bitter with distinctive aroma.
Traditional Bitter (1038) – well-hopped brew.
BBB or **Burglar Bill's** (1044) – dark, well-rounded brew.
Hammerhead (1050) – rich, warming ale.

CORNISH BREWERY CO., The Brewery, Redruth, Cornwall.
☎ 0209 213591.
A wholly owned subsidiary of J A. Devenish PLC. Devenish's old Weymouth brewery closed at the end of 1985, with all production transferred to Redruth. A subsequent merger with Inn Leisure increased their tied estate by 45 houses. Now all 380 pubs sell real ale, many still under the name of Devenish.
JD Dry Hop Bitter (1032) – pleasant light brew.
Cornish Original (1038) – new bitter.
Wessex Royal (1042) – fuller-bodied bitter formerly Wessex Stud.
Great British Heavy or **GBH** (1050) – strong ale.

COTLEIGH, Ford Road, Wiveliscombe, Somerset. ☎ 0984 24086.
Begun in Devon in 1979. Moved into new, purpose-built premises in 1985. Serves 75 outlets, mostly in Devon and Somerset, but beers are becoming increasingly available across the country.
Kingfisher Ale (1036) – light and refreshing.
Tawny Bitter (1040) – smooth and hoppy.
Old Buzzard (1048) – smooth, dark, distinctive strong brew.

Independent Breweries

CROPTON, New Inn, Cropton, Pickering, North Yorkshire. ☏ 07515 330.
A former home-brew pub, established in 1984, at the New Inn. The brewery was expanded in 1987 to supply its additive-free beers to a free trade whose customers are adapting to ordering "Two Pints" instead of one!
Two Pints (1038) – full flavoured and distinctive.
Special Strong Bitter (1058) – strong winter ale.

CROUCH VALE, 12 Redhills Road, S. Woodham Ferrers, Chelmsford, Essex. ☏ (0245) 322744.
Founded in 1981 by CAMRA enthusiasts. One tied house serving real ale and supplies 65–70 free trade outlets in Essex and Greater London.
Woodham Bitter (1035.5) – light bitter.
Best Bitter (1039) – distinctive and consistent.
Strong Anglian Special or **SAS** (1048) – deceptively powerful.
Essex Porter (1050) – rich, dark old ale.
Willie Warmer (1060) – rude dark winter ale.

CROWN Brewery Plc. Pontyclun, Mid Glamorgan. ☏ 0443 225453.
Former South Wales Clubs Brewery, specialising in the club trade where most of the beer is pressurised. Now also supplies some free trade pubs using traditional dispense. Also owns four pubs.
SBB or **Special Best Bitter** (1037) – smooth and tasty bitter.
Black Prince or **Dark** (1037) – full-flavoured dark mild.
1041 (1041) – Malty, full-bodied bitter, "Special" renamed.

DARLEY, S. Yorks. See Ward, page 00.

DAVENPORTS, Birmingham. See Greenall Whitley, page 00.

DEVENISH. See Cornish Brewery Co., page 00.

DONNINGTON Brewery, Stow-on-the-Wold, Glos. ☏ 0451 30603.
Britain's most picturesque brewery, set in an old mill alongside a lake. At its best the taste of the beer, served by handpump in their 16 Cotswold stone pubs, matches the beauty of the buildings.
XXX (1035) – rare dark mild.
BB (1036) – beautiful light bitter.
SBA (1042) – full-bodied bitter.

ELDRIDGE POPE, Dorchester Brewery, Dorchester, Dorset. ☏ 0305 251251.
Boasts Britain's strongest naturally-conditioned, bottled beer, **Thomas Hardy's Ale** (1125). However, the award-winning draught beers are served using a caskbreather device in most 180 tied houses, resulting in a lack of Eldridge Pope pubs in the Guide.
Dorchester Bitter (1033) – light but well-balanced.
Dorset Original IPA (1041) – well-hopped beer.
Royal Oak (1048) – full-bodied malty brew.

ELGOOD's, North Brink Brewery, Wisbech, Cambs. ☏ 0945 583160.
Tucked-away brewery in the fenlands near the Wash, selling real ale in around 30 of its 54 pubs. Beware of keg beer through handpumps in some houses.
Bitter (1036) – refreshing, well-regarded brew.
G.S.B. Strong Bitter (1045) – a hoppy, full-bodied ale.

EVERARDS, Castle Acres, Narborough, Leicester. ☏ 0553 891010.
A small, family-owned brewery, producing Old Original and Beacon Bitter at their Leicester brewery. Mild and Tiger are brewed at Everard's old brewery, now the Heritage Brewery, in Burton-on-Trent. 98 of its 138 tied houses sell real ale, many offering guest beers. Approx. 450 free trade outlets.
Burton Mild (1033) – dryish dark mild.
Beacon Bitter (1036) – well-balanced, light bitter.
Tiger (1041) – tasty best bitter.
Old Original (1050) – malty, finely hopped ale.

Independent Breweries

FEDERATION, Lancaster Road, Dunston, Tyne & Wear. ☎ 091 460 9023.
A co-operative, founded in 1919 which expanded to supply pubs and clubs, mainly through wholesalers. Resumed brewing cask-conditioned ales in 1986.
Best Bitter (1036) – clean, well-balanced bitter.
Federation Special Ale (1041) – premium ale, lightly coloured and delicately hopped.

FELINFOEL, Brewery, Felinfoel, Llanelli, Dyfed. ☎ 0554 773356.
Britain's champion brewers in the past, this famous Welsh brewery serves its beers without pressure in 30 of its 76 pubs.
XXXX Mild (1031) – dark, nutty beer.
Bitter Ale (1033) – light, refreshing bitter.
Double Dragon (1040) – stronger, malty bitter.

FLOWERS, Gloucester. See Whitbread, page 51.

FORBES ALES, The Brewery, Harbour Road Industrial Estate, Oulton Broad, Lowestoft, Suffolk. ☎ 0502 87905.
In March 1988 Derek Longman took over the former Oulton Broad Brewery to brew additive-free beers for the free trade. He also sells direct to the public from the brewery.
Forbes Bitter (1040) – smooth and hoppy.

FRANKLINS, Bilton Lane, Bilton, Harrogate, N. Yorks. ☎ 0423 74328.
Small brewery behind the Gardeners Arms, since 1980. Serves three permanent and 25 guest outlets, but not the Gardeners.
Franklin's Bitter (1038) – a full, fruity Dales brew.

FREMLINS, Kent. See Whitbread, page 51.

FRIARY MEUX, Surrey. See Allied Breweries, page 46.

FULLER, Smith and Turner, Griffin Brewery, Chiswick, London W4. ☎ 01 994 3691.
One of only two independent brewers in the capital to survive the takeovers of the Sixties. Now buying up pubs in and around London. Has won more awards at CAMRA's Great British Beer Festival than any other brewery. Real ale in all but nine of their 145 tied houses.
Chiswick Bitter (1035.5) – pleasant session beer.
London Pride (1041.5) – fruity, rounded best bitter.
ESB (1055.75) – Extra Special Bitter in every sense.

GALES, Horndean, Portsmouth, Hants. ☎ 0705 594050.
Hampshire's largest independent brewery with real ale in all its 92 pubs, and extensive free trade. Produces the only naturally-conditioned beer sold in a corked bottle – **Prize Old Ale** (1095).
XXXL (1030) – light mild.
XXXD (1031) – rare dark mild.
BBB or **Butser Brew Bitter** (1037) – light, well-flavoured and hoppy.
XXXXX (1044) – dark, sweet winter brew.
HSB (1051) – Horndean's special, full-bodied bitter.

GIBBS MEW Anchor Brewery, Milford Street, Salisbury, Wilts. ☎ 0722 411911.
A family brewery, established in 1866. It has been brewing Godson Chudley beers under licence since the latter brewery closed in 1987. Has recently acquired more than 100 tenancies from Watney and serves real ale in all but a few of their 160-odd pubs. Extensive free trade, partly through Coopers of Wessex in which they now have a 50% stake.
Wiltshire Traditional Bitter (1036) – light and hoppy.
Chudley Local Line (1036) – well-balanced bitter.
Premium Bitter (1042) – malty brew, linked with Best.
Salisbury Best (1042) – full-bodied, hoppy bitter.
GBH (1047) – dark and malty.
The Bishop's Tipple (1066) – distinctive barley wine.

29

Independent Breweries

GLENNY, The Two Rivers Brewery, Station Lane, Witney, Oxon. ☎ 0993 2574.
Set up in 1983 in part of the old Clinch's brewery, Glenny now have their own premises, from which they supply roughly 70 free trade outlets.
Witney Bitter (1037) – tasty session beer.
Wychwood Best (1044) – full-flavoured bitter, a CAMRA prize-winner.
Hobgoblin (1058) – dry, ruby-red strong ale.

GOACHER'S, Hayle Mill Cottages, Bockingford, Maidstone, Kent. ☎ 0622 682112.
Kent's most successful small independent brewer, producing ales from only malted barley and Kentish hops for the free trade in the Maidstone area.
Light Maidstone Ale (1036) – clean, fruity with mid-Kent Golding hops.
Dark Maidstone Ale (1040) – original ale with black and chocolate malts.
Old Maidstone Ale (1066) – dark barley wine from pure Golding hops.

GODSON CHUDLEY. See Gibbs Mew, page 29.

GOLDEN HILL, Wiveliscombe, Somerset. ☎ 0984 23798.
Has the unique distinction of winning the Best Bitter award at CAMRA's Great British Beer Festival only months after starting in 1980. Exmoor Ale is now served in over 100 pubs in the south-west and can be found throughout the south.
Exmoor Ale (1039) – malty, well-balanced beer.
Exmoor Dark (1039) – darker, hoppier brew.
Exmoor Gold (1045) – strong, smooth golden ale (also bottled).

GOOSE EYE, Turkey Mills, Goose Eye, Keighley, W. Yorks. ☎ 0535 605807.
Brewers since 1978, now chiefly for their bars in the mill. Also brews occasional, experimental beers.
White Rose Bitter (1036) – smooth session beer.
Goose Eye Bitter (1038) – tangy, straw-coloured bitter.
Pommie's Revenge (1058) – pale, fruity and dangerously drinkable.

GREENE KING, Westgate Brewery, Bury St. Edmunds, Suffolk. ☎ 0284 763222 and The Brewery, Biggleswade, Beds. ☎ 0767 313935.
East Anglia's largest regional brewery. Run by take-over conscious accountants to the detriment of the customer; closed Rayments of Hertfordshire in 1987. From October 1989, the Biggleswade brewery is scheduled to produce lager only.
KK Mild (1031) – pleasant light mild (brewed at Biggleswade, but not for much longer).
XX Mild (1031) – innocuous dark mild; occasionally delicious.
IPA (1035) – well-hopped bitter of variable quality.
Rayments BBA (1037) – experimental brew to replace extinct original.
Abbot Ale (1048) – robust, distinctive brand leader.

GUERNSEY Brewery, South Esplanade, St. Peter Port, Guernsey. ☎ 0481 20143.
One of two breweries on this Channel island, serving stronger than usual real ales in 15 of their 35 tied houses, as excise duty is uniquely levied on quantity not strength. Trades under the name 'Pony Ales'. Free trade covers Alderney and Herm. Taken over by Ann Street Brewery, Jersey in 1988.
LBA Mild (1037.7) – dark and sweet.
Draught Bitter (1045) – full-flavoured and hoppy.

HADRIAN, Unit 7, Foundry Lane Industrial Estate, Byker, Newcastle-upon-Tyne. ☎ 091 2765302.
New brewery set up in 1987 to serve the free trade in an area dominated by the giants, such as Scottish and Newcastle. The Emperor fights back!
Gladiator Bitter (1039) – smooth, mellow beer.
Centurion Best Bitter – (1045) – well-hopped but smooth.
Emperor Ale (1060) – strong winter warmer.

Independent Breweries

HALLS, Oxford. See Allied Breweries, page 46.

HANCOCKS. See Bass, Welsh Brewers, page 48.

HALL & WOODHOUSE, Blandford Forum, Dorset. ☎ 0258 52141. More usually known as 'Badger Beer', the brewery serves cask beer in 150 of its 154 houses, though a quarter of the pubs use the cask breather device on Tanglefoot. This beer won the 1987 Championship Trophy for cask-conditioned beer at the Brewing Industry International Awards. Discontinued Hector's Bitter in 1988 and replaced it with Gales BBB.
Badger Best Bitter (1041) – well-hopped and full-bodied.
Tanglefoot (1048) – lightish-coloured strong ale.

HANSON'S, High Street, Dudley, W. Midlands. ☎ 0902 711811. The other half of Wolverhampton and Dudley Breweries (see Banks's). The Black Country Bitter is brewed by Banks's at Wolverhampton. Real ale in most of the 153 tied houses.
Mild (1035) – medium dark and malty.
Black Country Bitter (1035) – session beer.

HARDINGTON. See Axminster, page 23.

HARDYS & HANSONS, Kimberley Brewery, Nottingham. ☎ 0602 383611. Nottingham's last independent brewery, arising from a merger in 1930 between two neighbouring Kimberley breweries. Noted for good value beers. Serves cask beers in 174 of its 205 houses, but increasingly uses top pressure to dispense.
Best Mild (1035) – dark, malty brew.
Best Bitter (1039) – distinctive beer.

HARTLEYS, Old Brewery, Ulverston, Cumbria. ☎ 0229 53269. Brewery famous for its 'Beers from the Wood', which was taken over by Robinsons of Stockport in 1982. Still brewing for its 57 pubs.
Mild (1031) – smooth and dark.
Bitter (1031) – smooth and light.
XB (1040) – strong, well-flavoured bitter.

HARVEY, Bridge Wharf Brewery, Cliffe High Street, Lewes, E. Sussex. ☎ 0273 480209.
Traditional family brewery with real ale in all 34 pubs. New brewing tower completed in 1985 to match the original Gothic design. A growing Home Counties free trade. Frequent commemorative beers – some available on draught.
XX (1030) – pleasant dark mild.
Pale Ale (1032) – well-hopped light bitter.
BB (1038) – stronger, slightly sweet bitter.
XXXX (1040) – tasty, dark, winter brew.
Elizabethan (1088) – occasional draught barley wine.

HARVIESTOUN, Dollar, Clackmannanshire, Scotland. ☎ 02594 2141. One of Scotland's few remaining small breweries, operating from a former dairy at the foot of the Ochil Hills near Stirling. Serves 15 outlets in Central Scotland; beer also available by the pint from the brewery.
Harviestoun 80/- (1040) – straw-coloured, full-bodied beer.
Old Manor (1050) – dark beer with roast malt flavour.

HERITAGE, Anglesey Road, Burton-on-Trent, Staffs. ☎ 0283 63563. The brewing company of the new Heritage Brewery Museum (☎ 0283 69226). Brewing beers under licence in the former Everard's Tiger Brewery. Primarily brews Burton Mild and Tiger for Everards.

HERMITAGE, Emsworth, W. Sussex. See Sussex Brewery, page 39.

HIGHGATE, Walsall, W. Midlands. See Bass, page 47.

31

Independent Breweries

HIGSONS, Stanhope Street, Liverpool L8. ☎ 051 709 8734.
Merseyside's only remaining brewery, taken over in 1985 by Boddingtons, chiefly for its lager-brewing capacity. Higsons own cask ales' survival depends on their retaining or improving their market share. Boddies have invested considerably in upgrading the pubs – all managed houses now serve real ale.
Mild (1033) – well balanced dark ale. Good value.
Bitter (1038) – excellent hoppy bitter.

HILDEN Brewery, Hilden House, Lisburn, Co. Antrim. ☎ 0846 663863.
N. Ireland's brave new brewery, the first to brew traditional beer in Ulster for decades when it began in 1981. Hilden Ale now naturally conditioned in bottle.
Hilden Ale (1040) – hoppy, straw-coloured bitter.
Special Reserve (1044) – a rich, tawny ale.

HOLDEN, George St., Woodsetton, Dudley, W. Midlands. ☎ 0902 880051.
One of the long-established family breweries of the Black Country, producing a good range of real ales for their 18 tied houses and over 100 free trade customers.
Black Country Mild (1038) – dark and mellow.
Black Country Bitter (1039) – distinctive palate.
Special Bitter (1050) – full-bodied, sweetish ale.
XL Old Ale (1092) – powerful winter warmer.

HOLT, Derby Brewery, Empire St., Cheetham, Manchester 3. ☎ 061 834 3285.
Traditional family firm, which brews one of Britain's true bitters of character. Real ale (including mild!) in all 92 tied houses, often delivered in huge hogsheads (54 gallon barrels) such is its enthusiastic following and amazingly low price.
Mild (1033) – dark, malty and bitter.
Bitter (1039) – famous bitter of distinction.

HOLT, PLANT & DEAKIN (H P & D), Oldbury, W. Midlands. See Allied, page 46.

HOME, Nottingham. See Scottish & Newcastle, page 49.

HOOK NORTON Brewery, Hook Norton, Banbury, Oxon. ☎ 0608 737210.
One of the most delightful traditional tower breweries in Britain, with all 35 country pubs serving real ale. Also extensive free trade.
Mild (1032) – light and fruity.
Best Bitter (1036) – distinctive and hoppy.
Old Hookey (1049) – genuine dark old ale.

HOSKINS, The Beaumanor Brewery, Beaumanor Road, Leicester. ☎ 0533 661122.
The smallest remaining old (pre-WWI) brewery. Now has 12 tied houses and is still seeking to expand.
Mild (1033) – smooth and dark.
Beaumanor Bitter (1039) – dry and hoppy.
Penn's Ale (1045) – stronger, nutty, copper-coloured bitter.
Premium (1050) – strong bitter, summer version of Old Nigel.
Old Nigel (1060) – pale winter brew.

HOSKINS & OLDFIELD, North Mills, Frog Island, Leicester. ☎ 0533 532191.
Set up by two members of Leicester's famous brewing family, Philip and Stephen Hoskins, in 1984, after the sale of the old Hoskins Brewery. They produce a wide range of beers for a scattered free trade.
HOB Mild (1033) – dark and sweet.
HOB Bitter (1041) – distinctive, hoppy brew.
Little Matty (1041) – darker version of HOB.
Tom Kelly's Stout (1043) – dry 'Irish' brew.
EXS Bitter (1051) – full-bodied beer.
Old Navigation (1071) – strong, dark and sweet.
Christmas Noggin (1100) – powerful festive ale.

Independent Breweries

HYDES Anvil Brewery, 46 Moss Lane West, Manchester M15. ☎ 061 226 1317.
The smallest of the long-established Manchester breweries, serving real ales in all 48 tied houses, largely in the south of the city. The only Manchester brewery still producing two milds.
Anvil Mild (1032) – dark and malty.
Anvil Light (1034) – light and hoppy (formerly Best Mild).
Anvil Bitter (1036.6) – full-flavoured bitter.
Anvil Strong Ale (1080) – rich winter brew.

IND COOPE, Burton and Romford. See Allied Breweries, page 46.

ISLE OF MAN BREWERIES Ltd., Falcon Brewery, Douglas, Isle of Man. ☎ 0624 73034.
The island's sole brewery, following the merger in 1986 of the Okell and Castletown breweries. Real ale is produced under the unique Manx Pure Beer Act (permitted ingredients: malt, sugar and hops only). Operates from an impressive Victorian brewhouse, serving 102 tied houses.
Okells Mild (1035.2) – dark and smooth.
Okells Bitter (1035.9) – nicely hopped and full-bodied.
Castletown Bitter (1036) – well-hopped, dry and sharp.

JENNINGS, Castle Brewery, Cockermouth, Cumbria. ☎ 0900 823214.
Traditional brewery in the far N. West whose real ales are not only available in all 79 tied houses, but also in an increasing number of Tetley houses.
Mild (1034) – dark and mellow.
Bitter (1034) – hoppier brew.
Marathon (1041) – strong bitter.

KING & BARNES, 18 Bishopric, Horsham, W. Sussex. ☎ 0403 69344.
Sussex family brewery which serves real ale in all its 65 country houses. In 1988 gained 11 former Watney pubs in Sussex. Runs a popular 'Ale Trail' passport scheme. Extensive free trade in 40 mile radius.
Sussex Mild (1034) – smooth, rare dark mild.
Sussex Bitter (1034) – well-hopped bitter – voted CAMRA's Best Standard Bitter in 1987.
Old Ale (1046) – malty, winter ale.
Draught Festive (1050) – strong, full-flavoured bitter.

LARKINS Brewery Ltd., Grange Road, Rusthall, Tunbridge Wells, Kent. ☎ 0892 49919.
At present operating from the premises formerly occupied by the Royal Tunbridge Wells and then the Kentish Ales breweries, with plans to move to the owners' farm. Additive-free beers using partly their own hops. Supplies 40 outlets in and around Tunbridge Wells.
Traditional Ale (1035) – a well-hopped ordinary bitter.
Sovereign Bitter (1040) – drinkable, lighter than Best.
Best Bitter (1045) – a fruity, well-bodied best bitter.
Porter (1055) – a rich, bitter-sweet winter brew.

LEES, Greengate Brewery, Middleton Junction, Manchester. ☎ 061 643 2487.
One of Manchester's clutch of surviving family-owned independent breweries, serving real ale in all 150 of the tied houses and clubs (mostly in N. Manchester), and supplying free trade customers in the North West.
GB Mild (1032) – smooth, medium-dark mild.
Bitter (1038) – full-flavoured and malty.
Moonraker (1073) – rich, dark and sweet.

LLOYDS, John Thompson Inn, Ingleby, Derbyshire. ☎ 03316 3426/2469.
Set up as a home-brew operation in 1977 at the inn, Lloyds is now a separate business, serving five regular customers and several free trade outlets for guest beers
JTS XXX or **Bitter** (1042) – full and fruity.
Skullcrusher (1065) – heavy Christmas brew.

LORIMER, Edinburgh. See Vaux, page 41, and Caledonian Brewery page 27.

Independent Breweries

McEWAN, Edinburgh. See Scottish a Newcastle, page 49.

MACLAY, Thistle Brewery, Alloa, Scotland. ☎ 0259 723387.
One of Scotland's two remaining independent breweries after the takeover typhoon swept through the country. Supplies real ale to 13 of its 28 houses and an appreciative free trade.
60/- Light (1030) – flavoursome dark beer.
70/- Heavy (1035) – well-hopped brew.
80/- Export (1040) – well-balanced beer.
Porter (1040) – dark, tasty brew.

McMULLEN, 26 Old Cross, Hertford. ☎ 0992 584911.
Hertfordshire's oldest independent family brewery. Serves the 'real McCoy' in 137 of its 163 pubs.
AK Mild (1033) – popular brew, more of a light bitter.
Country Bitter (1041) – malty and distinctive.
Christmas Ale (1070) – seasonal warmer.

MALTON, Crown Hotel, Wheelgate, Malton, N. Yorks. ☎ 0653 697580.
Set up in 1985 behind a pub by former Russells and Wrangham brewer, to revive Malton's proud brewing heritage. Limited free trade.
Malton Pale Ale (1033.8) – light, session beer.
Double Chance (1037.8) – well-hopped bitter.
Pickwick's Porter (1041.8) – new dry stout.
Owd Bob (1054.8) – dark, dry winter warmer.

MANNS, Northampton. See Watney, pages 00–00.

MANSFIELD, Littleworth, Mansfield, Notts. ☎ 0623 25691.
Took over North Country Breweries of Hull in 1985, subsequently selling some 80 pubs from the enlarged estate to Camerons. 1987 saw a much more positive commitment to real ale with the introduction of two new cask beers, Old Baily being a replacement for 4XXXX. Real ales can be found in 140 of their 330 houses. Extensive free trade.
Riding Traditional Bitter (1035) – distinctive, dry, hoppy palate.
Old Baily (1045) – well-balanced, rich and creamy.

MARSTON, PO Box 26, Shobnall Road, Burton-upon-Trent, Staffs. ☎ 0283 31131.
One of Britain's great traditional breweries with real ale in most of their 856 pubs, stretching from Cumbria to Hampshire. 37% of their production goes to the free trade. The only brewery using the unique Burton Union system of fermentation for their stronger ales. In 1984 took over Border Brewery of Wrexham.
Border Mild (1031) – a dark and full-flavoured mild.
Mercian Mild (1032) – dark and fruity.
Border Exhibition (1034) – light and flavourful.
Border Bitter (1034) – a soft, smooth bitter.
Burton Bitter (1036) – well-balanced bitter, with hop bouquet.
Pedigree (1043) – full-bodied and smooth bitter.
Merrie Monk (1043) – powerful, dark brewed mild.
Owd Rodger (1080) – strong barley wine.

MARSTON MOOR, c/o Crown Inn, Kirk Hammerton, York. ☎ 0423 330341.
Small brewery set up in 1984, brewing 7–8 barrels a week.
Cromwell Bitter (1037) – distinctive bitter beer.
Brewers Droop (1050) – strong ale.

MARTIN ALES, Martin, nr. Dover, Kent. ☎ 0304 852488.
A small E. Kent brewery established in 1983, producing real ale in an original eighteenth-century brewhouse which had lain idle for over 70 years. Only traditional methods and materials are used.
Johnson's Bitter (1042) – dark and full-bodied, but mild in flavour.
College Ale (1080) – rich and powerful, but not too heavy.

Independent Breweries

MAULDON, 7 Addison Road, Chilton Industrial Estate, Sudbury, Suffolk. ☎ 0787 311055.
The head brewer at Watney's Mortlake plant revived the name of his former family brewery in 1982. Supplies over 100 free trade outlets in Suffolk, S. Norfolk, Essex and Cambridge.
F.A. Mild (1034) – good Suffolk dark mild.
Bitter (1037) – full-flavoured, regular Ipswich CAMRA festival award-winner.
Porter (1042) – dark, bitter ale.
Old XXXX (1042) – new, dark winter brew.
Special (1044) – premium, hoppy ale.
Suffolk Punch (1050) – new strong brew with growing popularity.
Christmas Reserve (1065) – festive beer.

MELBOURNS, Stamford, Lincs. See Camerons, page 27.

MILL, Unit 18C, Bradley Lane, Newton Abbot, Devon. ☎ 0626 63322.
Begun in 1983 on the site of an old water mill, to supply free trade in S. Devon and Torbay. Janner's Old Original is often sold under local pub names; "Janner" being the local term for a Devonian.
Janner's Ale (1038) – well-hopped bitter.
Janner's Old Dark Ale (1040) – dark, malty brew.
Janner's Old Original (1045) – light, hoppy strong bitter.
Christmas Ale (1050) – winter brew.

MINERA, Wrexham. See Allied Breweries, pages 00–00.

MINERS ARMS, Westbury-sub-Mendip, Somerset. ☎ 0749 870719.
Home-brew house set up in 1973 in Priddy, producing naturally-conditioned bottled beer, which in 1981 moved site and switched to brewing draught beer for the free trade under the same name. Now serves 35 outlets and one tied house, with beers becoming increasingly available throughout the country.
Own Ale (1040) – well-balanced with hoppy aroma.
Guvnor's Special Brew (1048) – stronger ale, slightly less hoppy.

MITCHELLS 11 Moor Lane, Lancaster. ☎ 0524 63773/66580/60000.
Lancaster's last independent brewery, now brewing in Yates and Jackson's former brewery for their 50 pubs and expanding free trade.
Mild (1034.8) – dark and smooth.
Bitter (1036) – malty brew.
ESB (1050) – round and full-bodied.

MITCHELLS & BUTLERS, Birmingham. See Bass, page 47.

MOLE'S, Merlin Way, Bowerhill, Melksham, Wilts. ☎ 0225 704734.
Established in 1982 by a former Usher's brewer. The brewery name came from his nickname. Now serves around 50 outlets in the Wilts/Avon area and one tied house.
Mole's PA (1035) – tasty, lunchtime bitter.
Mole's Cask Bitter (1040) – light and well-hopped.
Mole's 97 (1050) – premium strong ale.

MOORHOUSE'S Burnley Brewery, Moorhouse St., Burnley, Lancs. ☎ 0282 22864.
Long-established producer of hop bitters which in 1979 began brewing beer. Has since had several new owners. Now has one tied house. Bitter gained silver medal at Brewex in 1983.
Premier Bitter (1036) – smooth and full-flavoured.
Pendle Witches Brew (1050) – potent, malty bitter.

MORLAND, PO Box 5, Ock Street, Abingdon, Oxon. ☎ 0235 553377.
Thames Valley brewery with handpumps in more than half the 209 tied houses, but many of these use a cask breather. Also has a considerable clubs trade.
Mild (1032) – refreshing dark ale.
Bitter (1035) – dry and bitter.
Old Masters (1040) – well-hopped bitter, replaces Best Bitter.

35

Independent Breweries

MORRELLS, Lion Brewery, St. Thomas Street, Oxford. ☎ 0865 792013.
The famous university city's last surviving brewery produces one of the widest ranges of real ales in the country for over 120 of its 133 pubs, though a few use blanket pressure. Free trade expanding to London, Bristol, Coventry and Northampton. Recently made trading agreement to supply Federation outlets.
Light Ale (1032) – lightly hopped beer.
Dark Mild (1033) – rare malty ale.
Bitter (1036) – subtle well-balanced beer.
Varsity (1041) – full-bodied malty bitter.
Celebration (1066) – occasional strong pale brew.
College (1072) – sweeter, heavy ale.

NETHERGATE, 11–13 High Street, Clare, Suffolk. ☎ 0787 277244.
Purpose-built brewery, set up in 1986. Its single beer won the Best Bitter award at Cambridge Beer Festival in 1986 and 1987 when it was also voted champion beer. Now available in 60 outlets in W. Suffolk, Essex and S. Cambridgeshire. A Christmas Ale (1055) should be available October–March.
Nethergate Bitter (1039) – distinctive bitter brew.

NEWCASTLE. See Scottish & Newcastle, page 49.

NEW FOREST, Old Lyndhurst Road, Cadnam, Hants. ☎ 0703 812766.
Set up in 1979, the brewery concentrates on supplying keg beers to the club trade in Hampshire and Bournemouth, but also produces two real ales for 16 outlets.
New Forest Real Ale (1035) – well-balanced beer.
Kingswood Cask Bitter (1039) – fuller-bodied bitter.

NORTH & EAST RIDING BREWERS, Hotel Stresa, 15–16 Esplanade, South Cliff, Scarborough, N. Yorks. ☎ 0723 365627.
A family-run independent brewery, set up behind a Victorian hotel to brew Scotch-style beers for the Highlander bar. The beers are now finding their way into a widespread free trade.
William Clark's Thistle Mild (1034) – dark, medium mild.
William Clark's Thistle Bitter (1040) – traditional scotch bitter.
William Clark's EXB (1040) – a bitter with scotch overtones.
William Clark's 68 (1050) – strong premium bitter.

NORWICH Brewery. See Watney, page 50.

OAK, 59 Merseyton Road, Ellesmere Port, South Wirral. ☎ 051 356 0950.
Brewery established in 1982 by former Bass engineer. Supplies W. Cheshire, the Wirral, Liverpool, Gtr Manchester and W. Yorkshire.
Oak Best Bitter (1038) – hoppy and light.
Tyke Bitter (1041) – West Riding bitter, brewed under licence.
Old Oak Ale (1044) – Burton-style brew.
Double Dagger (1050) – special strong bitter.
Porter (1050) – dark winter brew.
Wobbly Bob (1060) – strong, hoppy and fruity.

OAKHILL, Old Brewery, High Street, Oakhill, Somerset. ☎ 0749 840134.
Set up by a farmer in 1984 and now serves 65 outlets, within a 35 mile radius, in Avon, Dorset, Somerset and Wiltshire.
Farmers Ale (1038) – all-malt bitter.

OKELL, Isle of Man. See Isle of Man Breweries, page 33.

OLDHAM, Manchester. See Boddingtons, page 25.

OLD MILL, Mill Street, Snaith, Goole. ☎ 0405 861813.
Brewery set up in 1983 by a former Wilson's production director. Now has three tied houses and 75 free trade customers.
Traditional Mild (1034) – full flavoured.
Traditional Bitter (1037) – distinctive hoppy brew.
Bullion Bitter (1044) – award-winning beer.

OULTON BROAD. See Forbes Ales, page 29.

36

Independent Breweries

ORKNEY, Sandwick, Orkney. ☎ 0856 84 802.
The Orkneys have gained their first brewery in living memory – set up in 1988 by a former licensee, Roger White. A real ale addict, he had to brew keg "to appease local palates," but hopes to entice the islanders onto the real thing soon.
Raven Ale (1038.5) – keg, apart from an occasional cask.

RAVEN ALE

JAMES PAINE, St. Neots. See Tolly Cobbold. page 40.

PALMER, West Bay Road, Bridport, Dorset. ☎ 0308 22396.
The only thatched brewery in the country, in a delightful seaside setting. Now most of the 70 houses serve the beers without pressure.
BB (1030.4) – refreshing, light, pleasant bitter.
IPA (1039.5) – well-balanced, hoppy bitter.
Tally Ho (1046) – strong, nutty brew which commands respect.

PARADISE Brewery, Paradise Park, Hayle, Cornwall. ☎ 0736 753365.
Unusual brewery set up in a bird park in 1981. The brewery is behind the one tied house, the Bird in Hand.
Paradise Bitter (1040) – pleasant beer.
Artist Ale (1055) – smooth and full-bodied.

PARADISE BITTER
Real Cornish Ale

PEMBROKESHIRE OWN ALES, Llanteglos Brewery, Llanteg, nr. Amroth. ☎ 083 483 677.
The only full-mash brewery in Dyfed, set up in 1985 at the Llanteglos Hamlet holiday complex. Beers marketed by Ansells in South and West Wales. Up for sale at time of going to press.
Benfro Bitter (1037) – light and hoppy.
Benfro Extra (1042) – fuller-bodied brew.

PHOENIX, Brighton. See Watney, page 50.

PILGRIM Brewery, West Street, Reigate, Surrey. ☎ 07372 22651.
Surrey's only free trade brewery supplying London, Surrey and Sussex and, through wholesalers, Midlands and the North.
Surrey Bitter (1038) – hoppy, light bitter.
Dark XXXX (1040) – mild ale.
Progress (1041) – malty, dark beer.
Talisman (1048) – strong ale (mainly winter).

PITFIELD, The Beer Shop, 8 Pitfield Street, London N1. ☎ 01 739 3701.
Britain's first new brewery in an off-licence, set up in 1981 and later moved its brewery to a new site in Hoxton Square to cope with increased demand. No unnatural additives or preservatives are used in the beers. Serves 40–50 outlets in London, Sussex and the Black Country. Dark Star voted Champion Beer at 1987 Great British Beer Festival.
Pitfield Bitter (1038) – dry and hoppy.
Hoxton Best (1048) – strong malty brew (formerly "Heavy").
Dark Star (1050) – dark old ale (bottled version now pasteurised).
London Porter (1058) – strong dark beer, brewed to an 1850s recipe.
Christmas Ale (1065) – strong, festive brew.

LONDON BOROUGH OF HACKNEY
PITFIELD BREWERY

PLASSEY, Eyton, Wrexham, Clwyd. ☎ 0978 780922.
Following the closure of Border Brewery in Wrexham, brewer Alan Beresford set up his own brewery in an old dairy on a working farm and caravan site, whose bars serve the beer.
Farmhouse Bitter (1039) – light, all-malt brew.

PLASSEY BREWERY
FARMHOUSE BITTER

PLYMPTON BREWERY, Plymouth. See Allied Breweries, page 46.

POOLE, rear of 38 Sandbanks Avenue, Poole, Dorset. ☎ 0202 715161.
Set up in 1980 – Dorset's first independent brewery for 100 years, moved premises in 1987. In 1983 added a home-brew pub called the Brewhouse in Poole High Street (where beers are kept under blanket pressure). Supplies 20 free trade outlets.
Dolphin Best Bitter (1038) – hoppy session brew.
Bosun Best (1046) – rich and smooth.

POOLE BREWERY

37

Independent Breweries

POWELL, Mochdre Ind. Estate, Newtown, Powys. ☎ 0686 28021.
Central Wales beer wholesale company which took over the plant and premises of the neighbouring Powys Brewery in 1983 in order to supply its own beer again. Serves 60 outlets.
Sam Powell B.B. (1035) – session beer.
Sam Powell Original Bitter (1038) – full-bodied bitter.
Samson (1050) – smooth and malty strong ale.

PREMIER ALES, Mill Race Lane, Stourbridge Industrial Estate, Stourbridge, W. Midlands. ☎ 0384 442040.
New brewery, set up in 1988 by Graeme and Eddie Perks of the traditional pub chain, Premier Midland Ales. They serve the free trade and their five tied houses, one of which, the Paget Arms is due to start brewing on the premises.
Knightly Brew (1044) – light, full malt brew, pleasantly bitter.
Dark Knight (1050) – stout.
Once a Knight (1075) – evil brew.

RANDALL, Vauxlaurens Brewery, St. Julians Avenue, St. Peter Port, Guernsey. ☎ 0481 20134.
Guernsey's smaller brewery, operating under the 'Bobby Ales' sign. Seven of the 20 tied houses sell real ale.
Best Mild (1037) – dark, full-bodied brew.
Best Bitter (1047) – light and well flavoured.

RAYMENT, Furneux Pelham, Herts. See Greene King, page 30.

REEPHAM, 1 Collers Way, Reepham, Norfolk. ☎ 0603 871091.
Family brewery, started in 1983 with purpose-built plant in a small industrial unit. Now supplying 45 outlets in Norfolk and bottled Rapier Pale Ale to supermarkets.
Granary Bitter (1038) – hoppy and well-balanced.
Rapier Pale Ale (1044) – award-winning, dry premium bitter.
Reepham Gold (1048) – pale, full-flavoured, strong ale.
Reepham Stout (1048) – strong, dry winter stout.
Brewhouse Ale (1055) – full-bodied bitter.

RIDLEY, 88 Broomfield Road, Chelmsford, Essex. ☎ 0245 353513.
Traditional Essex brewery, selling real ale in all 65 houses and to an expanding free trade, at the lowest prices in the S. East. Beware of handpumped Old Bob, a brewery-conditioned beer of a lower O.G. than its bottled namesake in free trade outlets.
XXX (1034) – a pleasant dark mild.
PA (1034) – light, bitter brew.

RINGWOOD, 138 Christchurch Road, Ringwood, Hants. ☎ 0425 471177.
Begun by a pioneer of the new brewery revolution, Peter Austin, who has helped many others to start brewing. Moved to new premises in 1985. Two tied houses and 80 free trade outlets in the Wessex region.
Ringwood Best Bitter (1038) – hoppy and full-bodied.
Fortyniner (1048) – heavy, malty brew.
4X (1048) – tasty winter porter.
Old Thumper (1058) – well-hopped, strong bitter.

ROBINSON, Unicorn Brewery, Stockport, Cheshire. ☎ 061 480 6571.
Major family brewery with all 320-odd tied houses selling real ale. Also own Hartleys of Ulverston. Pubs mainly concentrated in S. Manchester and Cheshire. Dark Best Mild in danger of disappearing. Tied estate currently suffering from bland, unimaginative refurbishment programme.
Best Mild (1032) – light and well-balanced.
Dark Best Mild (1032) – best mild with added caramel, only found in 8 pubs.
Bitter (1035) – hoppy and refreshing, only sold in 20 pubs.
Best Bitter (1041) – full-bodied and well hopped.
Old Tom (1080) – strong, smooth barley wine.

RUDDLES, Rutland, Leics. See Watneys, page 50.

Independent Breweries

ST. AUSTELL, 63 Trevarthian Road, St. Austell, Cornwall. ☎ 0726 74444.
Popular 'holiday' brewery in Cornwall, which in recent years has widened its range of real ales by adding two stronger brews. The majority of the 133 houses now sell real ale; free trade in Cornwall and W. Devon.
Bosun's Bitter (1035) – stimulating session beer.
XXXX (1038) – rare dark mild.
Tinners Bitter (1038) – well-hopped malty bitter.
Hicks Special (1050) – a rich distinctive brew.

SELBY, 131 Millgate, Selby, N. Yorks. ☎ 0757 702826.
Old family brewery that began brewing again in 1972 after a gap of 18 years. Only a few free trade outlets and one tied house.
Best Bitter (1039) – a hoppy brew bottled as No.1.
Old Tom (1069) – strong Christmas brew.

SHEPHERD NEAME, 17 Court Street, Faversham, Kent. ☎ 0795 532206.
The oldest (1698) independent brewery in the country, using only East Kent hops. Real ale in all 250 tied houses and free trade throughout the South-East.
Master Brew Bitter (1036) – fine, hoppy brew.
Master Brew Best Bitter (1039) – fruity premium bitter.
Stock Ale (1039) – full dark ale.

SHIPSTONE, Nottingham. See Greenall Whitley, page 49.

SMILES, Colston Yard, Colston Street, Bristol. ☎ 0272 297350.
Avon's first new brewery, dating from 1977, now supplying over 120 free trade outlets and four tied houses, from its city centre site. Growing slowly and pleasurably.
Brewery Bitter (1037) – well-balanced, golden, dry bitter.
Best Bitter (1041) – smooth, well-rounded, malty beer.
Exhibition (1052) – dark ruby, rich, full-bodied bitter.
Old Vic (1065) – occasional dark, rich, malty winter brew.

JOHN SMITH, Tadcaster, N. Yorks. See Courage, page 48.

SAMUEL SMITH, Old Brewery, Tadcaster, N. Yorks. ☎ 0937 832225.
Yorkshire's oldest and most traditional brewery brews its ales without the use of any adjuncts. Cask beer is fermented only in Yorkshire Squares and racked to wooden casks. Operates the only brewery-based manufacturing cooperage in the U.K. 300 tied houses include 26 in London, which offer good value for the capital.
Old Brewery Bitter or BBB (1038.9) – full-bodied and malty.
Museum Ale (1047) – rich full-flavoured and warming.

SPRINGFIELD, Wolverhampton. See Bass, page 47.

STOCKS Brewery, 33–34 Hallgate, Doncaster, S. Yorks. ☎ 0302 328213.
Originated as a brew-pub; now has two tied houses and supplies an expanding free trade.
Best Bitter (1037) – well-hopped brew.
Select (1044) – malty beer.
Old Horizontal (1054) – good, strong, all-round beer.

STONES, Sheffield. See Bass, page 47.

SUSSEX BREWERY, Main Road, Hermitage, Emsworth, W. Sussex ☎ 02433 71533.
Small, traditional brewery (formerly Hermitage Brewery), attached to a pub and serving a small number of free trade outlets.
Sussex Pale Ale (1034) – golden coloured, creamy taste (summer only).
Wyndhams Bitter (1036) – well-balanced bitter with barley taste.
Hermitage Best Bitter (1048) – strong, slightly sweet bitter.
Lumley Old Ale (1056) – malty, dark winter brew.
Warrior Ale (1058) – strong, resolute ale.

Independent Breweries

TAYLOR, Knowle Spring Brewery, Keighley, W. Yorks. ☎ 0535 603139.
The fame of Timothy Taylor's quality ales – which have won a barrel full of Championship medals – stretches far beyond W. Yorkshire and their 29 pubs. One of the widest ranges of real ales, with Landlord the pride of the pack.
Golden Best or **Bitter Ale** (1033) – light and malty.
Best Dark Mild (1033) – Golden Best with caramel.
Best Bitter (1037) – well-hopped bitter.
Landlord (1042) – distinctive, full-bodied bitter.
Porter (1043) – occasional rich brew.
Ram Tam (1043) – Landlord with caramel.

TAYLOR WALKER, London. See Allied Breweries, page 47.

TENNENT-CALEDONIAN, Scotland. See Bass, page 48.

JOSHUA TETLEY, Leeds. See Allied Breweries, page 47.

THEAKSTON, Masham, N. Yorks. See Scottish & Newcastle, page 50.

THOMPSONS, London Inn, 11 West Street, Ashburton, Devon. ☎ 0364 52478.
Began brewing in 1981 for their own pub, but now supplying three tied houses and 20 outlets around Dartmoor and S. Devon.
Bitter (1040) – malty premium bitter.
IPA (1045) – strong and hoppy.

THWAITES, PO Box 50, Star Brewery, Blackburn, Lancs. ☎ 0254 54431.
Traditional Lancashire brewery, providing its award-winning real ales, including two fine milds, in 399 of its 413 houses. In 1984 took over Yates & Jackson's pubs in Lancaster, closing the brewery.
Mild (1032) – nutty and dark.
Best Mild (1034) – excellent malty brew.
Bitter (1036) – creamy and hoppy.

TOLLY COBBOLD, Cliff Brewery, PO Box 5, Ipswich, Suffolk. ☎ 0473 231723.
Ipswich brewery which has considerably improved the range of real ales in 300 of its 340 pubs. Like Camerons, owned by the Barclay Brothers hotel group. Extensive free trade. In 1987 took over Paines of St. Neots where brewing has since ceased; some Paines beers now brewed by Tolly.
Mild (1031) – sweet and malty.
Bitter (1034) – subtle and pleasantly dry.
Paine's XXX (1036) – smooth, medium bitter.
Original (1037) – well-hopped, flavoursome bitter.
Old Strong (1046) – rich, fruity winter brew.
XXXX (1046) – smooth, strong cask ale.
Paine's EG (1047) – full-bodied and malty.

TRAQUAIR HOUSE, Innerleithen, Peeblesshire, Borders, Scotland.
☎ 0896 830323.
Eighteenth-century Scottish brewery in an ancient fortified manor house, revived by the Laird of Traquair in 1965. Previously known for his widely exported rich strong bottled beer, Peter Maxwell Stuart also brews a draught beer for the free trade.
Bear Ale (1050) – strong draught ale.
House Ale (1075) – usually bottled but occasionally on draught.

TROUGH Brewery, Louisa Street, Idle, Bradford, W. Yorks. ☎ 0274 613450.
Established in 1981 to serve seven tied houses, the free and club trade. A take-over in 1988 has seen an injection of funds and the future seems assured with expansion likely.
Trough Bitter (1035.5) – smooth, refreshing bitter.
Wild Boar Bitter (1039.5) – full-bodied and distinctive.

TRUMAN, London. See Watney, page 50.

Independent Breweries

ULEY, Old Brewery, Uley, Dursley, Glos. ☎ 0453 860120.
Victorian village brewery, re-opened in 1985 to serve the free trade in Gloucestershire and neighbouring counties.
Hogshead (1037) – light bitter.
Uley Bitter (1040) – well-hopped and malty.
Old Spot Ale (1050) – smooth, malty ale.
Pig's Ear (1050) – very pale, brewed with lager malt.

USHER, Trowbridge, Wilts. See Watney, page 50.

VAUX, The Brewery, Sunderland, Tyne & Wear. ☎ 091 567 6277.
The country's second largest independent regional brewer (founded 1806) believes that retaining independence is the key to preserving jobs in the region, although Vaux itself closed Darley's in Yorkshire and sold off Lorimer & Clark in Edinburgh in 1986 and 1987 respectively. Darley's beers are now brewed by Vaux subsidiary Wards. Out of 410 tied houses, 179 serve real ale; free trade extends from Leeds to Newcastle.
Lorimers Best Scotch (1036) – scotch ale, brewed in Sunderland.
Vaux Bitter (1038) – thin session beer.
Samson (1041) – full-bodied and flavoursome.

WADWORTH, Northgate Brewery, Northgate, Devizes, Wilts. ☎0380 3361.
Delightful market town brewery whose excellent 6X is popular in the free trade throughout the South. Solidly traditional, with all of the 155 houses selling real ale.
Devizes Bitter (1030) – a light bitter.
Henry Wadworth IPA (1034) – hoppier brew.
6X (1040) – a splendid, malty bitter.
Farmer's Glory (1046) – dark and distinctive.
Old Timer (1055) – heavy and fruity.

PETER WALKER, Liverpool. See Allied Breweries, page 47.

WARD, Sheaf Brewery, Ecclesall Road, Sheffield S11. ☎ 0742 755155.
South Yorkshire subsidiary of Vaux of Sunderland which since the closure of the neighbouring Thorne brewery in September, 1986 also produces Darley's beers. Extensive free trade from London to the north east. Total Ward and Darley estate is 170 houses with real ale in 130 of them.
Darley Dark Mild (1032) – smooth and well-rounded.
Darley Thorne Best Bitter (1037) – distinctive and full-flavoured.
Sheffield Best Bitter (1038) – malty bitter.

WEBSTER, Halifax, W. Yorks. See Watney, page 50.

WELLS, Havelock Street, Bedford. ☎ 0234 65100.
This regional company completely rebuilt its brewery on a new site and is now building up its tied estate, even in London. Almost all of the 280 pubs serve cask beer without pressure. In 1984 opened a home-brew pub, the Ancient Druids, in Cambridge.
Eagle Bitter (1035) – consistent bitter beer.
Bombardier (1042) – full-bodied best bitter.

WELSH BREWERS, Cardiff. See Bass, page 48.

WEM, Shropshire. See Greenall Whitley, page 48.

WETHEREDS, Marlow, Bucks. See Whitbread, page 51.

WHITBY'S OWN BREWERY, Saint Hilda's, The Ropery, Whitby, N. Yorks.
New brewery set up in a former workhouse in this famous Yorkshire fishing port in 1988. James and Joan Evans intend to supply the local free trade with 'good pure beer'.

41

Independent Breweries

WILSONS, Manchester. See Watney, page 50.

WILTSHIRE, Stonehenge Brewery, Church Street, Tisbury, Wilts. ☎ 0747 870666.
This brewery, set up in 1985, was completely restructured in late 1987: the 15 tied managed houses were sold and replaced with nine tenanted pubs, all serving real ale. The range of beers was also completely revised.
Local Bitter (1035) – well-balanced refreshing session beer.
Stonehenge Best Bitter (1041) – full-bodied with strong malty flavour.
Old Grumble (1049) – top of the range bitter.
Old Devil (1057–61) – dark ale, easily drunk but deceptively strong.

WOOD, Wistanstow, Craven Arms, Shropshire. ☎ 05882 2523.
Begun in 1980 next to the Plough Inn. Supplies over 50 outlets.
Parish Bitter (1040) – refreshing, light bitter.
Wood's Special (1043) – full-flavoured, sweetish bitter.
Christmas Cracker (1060) – dark winter warmer.
Wood's Wonderful (1050) – strong, dark beer.

WOODFORDE'S NORFOLK ALES, Spread Eagle Brewery, Erpingham, Norfolk. ☎ 0263 768152.
Begun in 1981 in Norwich, bringing much-needed choice to this Watney dominated region. Supplies 70 free trade outlets plus own pub at the brewery. Wide range of beers occasionally augmented by special brews. Brewery due to move late 1988 to Broadland Brewery, The Street, Woodbastwick, Norfolk.
Norfolk Pride (1036) – light but full-flavoured.
Broadsman Bitter (1036) – light, hoppy bitter.
Wherry Best Bitter (1039) – pale and malty.
Norfolk Porter (1041) – distinctive, dark and hoppy.
Phoenix XXX (1047) – full-bodied, malty bitter.
Norfolk Nog (1049) – strong dark ale.
Head Cracker (1069) – pale winter ale.

WORTHINGTON. See Bass, page 47.

WYE VALLEY, 69 St. Owens Street, Hereford. ☎ 0432 274 968.
The only home-brew pub in the county of Hereford. Also serves some 20 free trade outlets.
Hereford Bitter (1038) – clean, hoppy beer.
Hereford Supreme (1043) – malty, smooth ale.
Brew 69 (1055) – pale, strong and hoppy.

YATES, Ghyll Farm, Westnewton, Cumbria. ☎ 0965 21081.
Small, traditional brewery set up in 1986 in a converted barn by former Jennings' brewer, Peter Yates and his wife. Probably the only brewery in the country to own a herd of pedigree goats! Bottled Premium (1048) occasionally available on draught.
Bitter (1035) – beautiful straw-coloured, delicately hopped beer.
Best Cellar (1052) – occasional brew; rich and smooth.

YOUNG & CO., Ram Brewery, Wandsworth, London SW18. ☎ 01 870 0141.
Last but not least is one of the most warmly regarded breweries in the country, which stood alone against the keg tide in the Capital in the early Seventies. All 150 houses offer real ale, some delivered by horse-drawn drays. Are currently buying pubs.
Bitter (1036) – light and bitter.
Special (1046) – full-flavoured and distinctive.
Winter Warmer (1055) – strong old ale.

YOUNGER, Edinburgh. See Scottish & Newcastle, page 49.

Home-Brew Pubs

ABINGTON PARK, Wellingborough Road, Northampton. ☎ 0604 31240.
Cobblers Ale (1038)
Abington Extra (1048)
Celebration Ale (1050)
One of five Clifton Inns 'in-house breweries'. Blanket pressure.

ALE HOUSE, 79 Raglan Road, Leeds. ☎ 0532 455447.
Monster Mash (1038)
Real ale off-licence next to Leeds University which started brewing in late 1987. Organically-grown malt.

ALFORD ARMS, Frithsden, Herts. ☎ 044 27 4480.
Cherrypicker's Bitter (1036)
Pickled Squirrel (1044)
Rudolf's Revenge (1053)
Whitbread's first home-brew pub, founded in 1981. The three beers are available in rotation. Malt extract.

ALL NATIONS, (Mrs Lewis's), Coalport Road, Madeley, Shropshire. ☎ 0952 585747.
Pale Ale (1032)
One of four home-brew pubs left before the new wave arrived. The others are the Blue Anchor, Old Swan and Three Tuns. Still known as Mrs Lewis's despite her death in 1988.

ANCIENT DRUIDS, Napier Street, Cambridge. ☎ 0223 324514.
Kite Bitter (1040)
Druid's Special (1047)
Merlin (1055)
Charles Wells home-brew pub set up in 1984. Malt extract. Seasonal and occasional brews.

BAKERY & BREWHOUSE, 14 Gloucester Street, Oxford. ☎ 0865 727265.
Tapper (1038)
Best (1044)
Porter (1045)
Oxbow (1059)
Old Wrot (1072)
Hall's home-brew pub, uniquely linked with a bakery. Blanket pressure.

BATTERSEA Brewery (Prince of Wales), 339 Battersea Park Road, London SW11. ☎ 01 622 2112
Battersea Bitter (1036)
Best Bitter (1040)
Power House (1050)
Watney's brew-pub run by Conway Taverns.

BEER ENGINE, Newton St. Cyres, Exeter, Devon EX5 5AX. ☎ 0392 851202.
Rail Ale (1037)
Piston Bitter (1044)
Sleeper (1055)
'Rail' home-brew established 1983; now supplying a few local free houses.

BLUE ANCHOR, Coinagehall Street, Helston, Cornwall. ☎ 032 65 62821.
Medium (1050)
BB (1053)
Special (1066)
Extra Special (1070)
Historic thatched home brewery producing powerful ales.

BODICOTE BREWERY, Plough Inn, Bodicote, Banbury, Oxon. ☎ 0295 62327.
Bodicote Bitter (1035)
Old English Porter (1045)
No.9 (1045)
Triple XXX (1050)
Brews from its own well for the pub-restaurant and free trade.

BREWERY TAP & BREWERY, 50 Lowesmoor, Worcester. ☎ 0905 21540.
Jolly Roger Quaff Ale (1038)
Jolly Roger Severn Bore Special (1048)
Jolly Roger Georgian Ale (1050)
Old Lowesmoor (1058)
Worcester Winter Wobbler (1088)
Prize-winning ales and regular special brews. Georgian Ale brewed for their new pub, Upstairs Downstairs at No. 54.

BREWHOUSE, High Street, Poole, Dorset.
Poole Bitter (1039)
Bosun Bitter (1048)
Purbeck Lager (1036)
Owned by Poole Brewery. Blanket pressure.

BRIDGEWATER BREWERY, Little Gaddesden, Herts. ☎ 044 284 2717.
Triple BBB (1034)
BSB (1042)
Earl's Bitter (1048)
Old Santa (1066)
Blanket pressure. Developing free trade.

BRITISH OAK BREWERY, Salop Street, Eve Hill, Dudley, W. Midlands DY1 3AX. ☎ 0384 236297.
Castle Ruin (1037)
Eve'ill Bitter (1042)
Ian Skitt started brewing behind his parents' free house in May 1988.

BUSHY'S BREWPUB, Victoria Street, Douglas, Isle of Man. ☎ 0624 75139.
Bushy's Bitter (1037)
Old Bushy Tail (1045)
Piston Brew (1045) – brewed for T.T. races only.
Strongest draught Manx ale from the island's only pub brewery, established 1986.

DOG & PARROT, Clayton Street West, Newcastle-upon-Tyne. ☎ 0632 616998.
Mirandinha Mild (1034.5)
Scotswood Ale (1036)
Alfies Special Bitter (1040)
Wallop (1046)
Christmas Cracker (1090)
Whitbread – malt extract.

EARL SOHAM BREWERY, The Victoria, Earl Soham, Suffolk. ☎ 072 882 758.
Gannet Mild (1030–35)
Victoria Bitter (1034–39)
Albert Ale (1042–47)
Jolabrugg (OG varies)
Also supplies other pubs.

FALCON & FIRKIN 360 Victoria Park Road, London E9. ☎ 01 985 0693.
Falcon Ale (1038)
Hackney Bitter (1045)
Dogbolter (1060)
Former Bruce's 'Firkin' pub brewery. Taken over, along with all the other pubs, by Midsummer Leisure in 1988, with the assurance that no radical changes would be made. Blanket pressure.

FELLOWS, MORTON & CLAYTON, Canal St., Nottingham.
☎ 0602 506795.
Fellow's Bitter (1041)
Clayton's Original (1048)
Whitbread – malt extract.

FERRET & FIRKIN, 114 Lots Road, London SW10. ☎ 01 352 6645.
Stoat Bitter (1038)
Ferret Ale (1045)
Dogbolter (1060)
Full name 'Ferret & Firkin in the Balloon up the Creek'. Blanket pressure.

FIRST IN LAST OUT, 14 High Street, Hastings, Sussex. ☎ 0424 425079.
Old Crofters (1040)
Cardinal Sussex Ale (1048)
St. Clements Brewery established 1985.

FLAMINGO & FIRKIN, 88 London Road, Kingston-upon-Thames.
☎ 01 541 3717.
Flamin' Ale (1036)
Royal Borough Bitter (1045)
Dogbolter (1060)
Opened in 1987, David Bruce's last pub before he sold up. Good family room.

FLEECE & FIRKIN, 12 St. Thomas Street, Bristol. ☎ 0272 277150.
Brunel Bitter (1036–38)
Bristol Best (1043)
Coal Porter (1050)
Rambo (1058–60)
Old Woolly (1087–88) – winter only.
Firkinstein Lager (1044)
Former Bruce's pub in old

43

Home-Brew Pubs

wool market, sold to Halls in 1983. Blanket pressure.

FLOUNDER & FIRKIN, 54 Holloway Road, London N7. ☎ 01 609 9574.
Fish T'ale (1038)
Whale Ale (1045)
Dogbolter (1060)
Guest beers and ciders. Blanket pressure.

FOX & FIRKIN, 316 Lewisham High Street, London SE13. ☎ 01 690 8925.
Vixen Ale (1038)
Fox's Bitter (1045)
Dogbolter (1060)
Blanket pressure. Home-cooked food.

FOX & HOUNDS, Barley, Royston, Herts. ☎ 076 384 459.
Nathaniel's Special (1036)
14th century pub with rare 'gallows' sign across the road.

FOX & HOUNDS, Stottesdon, Shropshire. ☎ 074 6323 222.
Dasher's Draught (1040)
Christmas Special (1070)
Also available in other pubs.

FOX & NEWT, Burley Road, Leeds 3. ☎ 0532 432612.
Rutland (1032)
Burley Bitter (1036)
Old Willow (1046)
Kirkstall Ruin (1066)
Monthly guest beers. Whitbread-malt extract.

FROG & FIRKIN, 41 Tavistock Crescent, London W11. ☎ 01 727 9250.
Tavistock Ale (1045)
Bullfrog (1050)
Dogbolter (1060)
Blanket pressure. Viewing panel in the floor to the brewery. Hat collection.

FROG & FRIGATE, 33 Canute Road, Southampton, Hants. ☎ 0703 332231.
Frog's Original (1038)
Croaker (1050)
Captain Frigate (1078) – winter
Brewing again after brief closure. Supplies other Frog & Frigate in Portsmouth.

FROG & PARROT, Division Street, Sheffield. ☎ 0742 21280.
Old Croak Ale (1035)
Reckless Bitter (1046)
Roger's Old Fashioned Porter (1054–60)
Roger's Conqueror (1066)
Roger's Specials (1080 +)
Roger & Out (1125)
Whitbread – malt extract.

GOLDEN LION, Market Place, Leyburn, N. Yorks. ☎ 0969 22161.

Oliver John's Bitter (1037)
Brewery behind the hotel.

GOOSE & FIRKIN, 47 Borough Road, Southwark, London SE1. ☎ 01 403 3590.
Goose Bitter (1038)
Borough Bitter (1045)
Dogbolter (1060)
London's first pub to revive home-brewing in 1979. Malt extract. Blanket pressure.

GREYHOUND, 151 Greyhound Lane, Streatham, London SW16. ☎ 01 677 9962.
XXX Pedigree (1036)
Greyhound Special (1038)
Streatham Strong (1048)
Streatham Dynamite (1056)
Clifton Inns. XXX Pedigree is the only real mild brewed in London. Cask breathers.

GRIBBLE INN, Oving, Nr. Chichester, W. Sussex. ☎ 0243 786893.
Gribble Ale (1042)
Reg's Tipple (1050)
Beers brewed at Madam Green Farm near the pub, marketed in free trade under the Bosham Brewery name.

HOP BACK BREWERY, Wyndham Arms, Estcourt Road, Salisbury, Wilts. ☎ 0722 28594.
GFB (1034–7)
Hop Back Special (1040)
Entire Stout (1042) – winter
Wiltshire's only pub-brewery. Home-cooked food.

JOLLY FENMAN, 64 Blackfen Road, Sidcup, Kent. ☎ 01 850 6664.
Blackfen Bitter (1037)
Fenman Fortune (1047)
Fenman Dynamite (1056)
Clifton Inns. Blanket pressure.

LASS O'GOWRIE, Charles Street, Manchester. ☎ 061 273 6932.
Bitter (1035)
Strong (1042)
Whitbread – malt extract.

MARISCO TAVERN, Lundy Island, Bristol Channel. ☎ 0271 870870.
John O's Bitter (1037)
John O's Special (1055)
Malt extract island brewery.

MARKET PORTER, 9 Stoney St., Borough Market, London SE1. ☎ 01 407 2495.
Market Bitter (1038)
Market Special (1048)
Malt extract brewery supplying the pub and one other 'Market Tavern'.

McDONNELL'S FREEHOUSE, 428 Woolwich Road, Charlton, London SE7. ☎ 01 853 0143.
Country Bitter (1036)

Sidekick (1047)
Also supplies the Queen Victoria, Wellington St.

MIN PIN INN, Tintagel, Cornwall. ☎ 0840 770241.
Legend Bitter (1036)
Brown Willy (1055)
A converted farmhouse, using a tiny 1½ barrel plant. Malt extract.

MINERVA, Nelson Street, Hull, Humberside.
Pilot's Pride (1040)
The only surviving Joshua Tetley home-brew pub, established in 1985.

NEW FERMOR ARMS, Station Road, Rufford, Lancs. ☎ 0704 821713.
Fettlers Bitter (1037)
Owned by Tetley-Walker for four years but now back with original owners. Malt extract.

NIX WINCOTT BREWERY, Ye Three Fyshes, Bridge Street, Turvey, Beds MK43 8ER. ☎ 023 064 264.
Two Henrys Bitter (1040)
Brewing began in December 1987 by licensee Charles Wincott with partner, Martin Nix. Also supply eight other pubs.

OLDE BULL & BUSH, 9 Hartshill Road, Stoke-on-Trent. ☎ 0782 49782.
Potters Bitter (1039)
Saggars Special (1052)
Rough (1070)
Victorian-style home-brew pub selling natural beer.

OLD CROWN INN, Hesket Newmarket, Wigton, Cumbria CA7 8JG. ☎ 06998 288.
Blencathra Bitter (1035)
Cumbrian brewery, opened in April '88 by telex message from Chris Bonnington (an Old Crown regular) from Kathmandu!

OLD SWAN (Ma Pardoe's), Halesowen Road, Netherton, Dudley, W. Midlands. ☎ 0384 53075.
Bitter (1034)
One of the great institutions of Black Country drinking, re-opened after refitting and enlargement into neighbouring premises, now under Hoskins management.

ORANGE Brewery, 37 Pimlico Road, London SW1. ☎ 01 730 5378.
Pimlico Light (1036)
SW1 (1040)
SW2 (1050)
Pimlico Porter (1046)
Clifton Inns' oldest in-house brewery, since early 1983. Blanket pressure.

Home-Brew Pubs

PHANTOM & FIRKIN, 140 Balaam Street, Plaistow, London E13. ☎ 01 472 2024.
Phantom (1037)
Spook (1044)
Dogbolter (1059)
Ex-Bruce's pub. Opened in February 1987. Malt extract. Blanket pressure.

PHEASANT & FIRKIN, 166 Goswell Road, London EC1. ☎ 01 253 7429.
Barbarian Bitter (1038)
Pheasant Bitter (1045)
Dogbolter (1060)
Blanket pressure. Guest beers and ciders.

PHOENIX & FIRKIN, Windsor Walk, London SE5. ☎ 01 701 8282.
Rail Ale (1038)
Phoenix Bitter (1045)
Dogbolter (1060)
Part of former Denmark Hill station. Blanket pressure.

RAISDALE HOTEL, Raisdale Road, Penarth, S. Glamorgan. ☎ 0222 707317.
Eight-Bore Special (1041)
'Vegetarian' beer, only served to hotel residents. Bottled beers also available.

REINDEER FREEHOUSE & BREWERY, 10 Dereham Road, Norwich, Norfolk. ☎ 0603 666821.
Bill's Bevy (1037)
Reindeer (1047)
Red Nose (1057)
Home-brew free house in Watney-dominated Norwich. Blanket pressure.

ROBINWOOD BREWERY, Staff of Life, Burnley Road, Todmorden, W. Yorks. ☎ 0706 818160.
Robinwood Bitter (1036)
Robinwood XB (1044)
Old Fart (1055)
Additive-free beers from a new brewery, set up in Spring '88.

ROSE STREET Brewery, Rose Street, Edinburgh. ☎ 031 220 1227.
Auld Reekie 80/- (1043)
Auld Reekie 90/- (1052)
Scotland's first home-brew pub, run by Alloa Brewery. Malt extract.

ROYAL CLARENCE, The Esplanade, Burnham-on-Sea, Somerset. ☎ 0278 783138.
Clarence Bitter (1036)
Seaside hotel brewery.

ROYAL INN, Horsebridge, Tavistock, Devon. ☎ 082 287 214.
Tamar Ale (1039)
Horsebridge Best (1045)
Right Royal (1050) – occasional
Heller (1060)
15th-century country pub – a former nunnery!

SAIR, Lane Top, Linthwaite, Huddersfield, W. Yorks. ☎ 0484 842370.
Linfit Mild (1032)
Linfit Bitter (1035)
Linfit Special (1041)
English Guineas Stout (1041)
Old Eli (1050)
Leadboiler (1063)
Enoch's Hammer (1080)
Xmas Ale (1082)
A brew-pub in the 19th century, recommenced in 1982 as Linfit Brewery with impressive range of beers. Supplies three other outlets.

SARAH HUGHES BREWERY, Beacon Hotel, Bilston Street, Sedgley, Dudley, W. Midlands. ☎ 09073 3380.
Sarah Hughes Original Mild (1058)
Mr Hughes has re-opened the brewery his grandmother ran at the village pub from 1921 to 1958. Heavy demand from free trade; supplying a few outlets.

STAG & HOUNDS, Burrough on the Hill, Melton Mowbray, Leics. ☎ 066 477 375.
Parish Mild (1033)
Parish Special or **PSB** (1036)
Poachers Ale (1066)
Baz's Bonce Blower (1105–1110)
Probably Britain's smallest commercial brewery. Tiny half-barrel plant. Brews the strongest full-mash beer in England; supplying 15 other pubs.

STEAMBOAT INN, Trent Lock, Sawley, Nottingham NG10 2FY. ☎ 0602 732606.
Seaman's Bitter (1025) – summer
Seaman's Mild (1034)
Frigate Bitter (1038)
Bosun's Bitter (1050)
Destroyer Bitter (1080)
Set up in June 1987 in a tiny brewery. Also produce the Strongest Beer in Britain (1150.5), sold in 1/3 pint measures, Dec–Feb only.

THREE CROWNS, Hammerwood Road, Ashurstwood, E. Grinstead, Sussex. ☎ 0342 21597.
Session Bitter (1038)
The (Watney) Phoenix Brewer's only brewery, originally set up in an outside toilet! Blanket pressure.

THREE TUNS, Bishop's Castle, Shropshire. ☎ 0588 638797.
Mild (1035)
XXX (1042)
Castle Steamer (1045)
Old Scrooge (1054) – Xmas
Historic home-brew pub.

TOM BROWN'S (Goldfinch Brewery), 47 High East Street, Dorchester, Dorset. ☎ 0305 64020.
Tom Brown's Best (1038)
Flashman's Clout (1042)
A former freehouse, Buffer's Inn, now a scene from Tom Brown's Schooldays.

UNICORN INN, Holyhead Road, Ketley, Shropshire. ☎ 0952 617250.
Wrekin Bitter (1038)
Heavengate Ale (1043)
Potters Black Porter (1045)
Hellgate Special Bitter (1048)
Old Horny (1056)
Old Needle's Eye Strong Ale (1068) – winter
Shropshire's smallest brewery, set up in January 1986. Supplies 10 other pubs.

WARRIOR, Coldharbour Lane, London SW9.
Brixton Bitter (1036)
Brixton Best (1040)
Warrior Strong Ale (1050)
Winter Warmer (1056–60)
Owned by Conway Taverns and supplies other Conway pubs in London with local beers like Balmoral Bitter (1040), Castle Bitter (1040) and Anchor Strong Ale (1050).

YORKSHIRE GREY, 2 Theobalds Road, London WC1. ☎ 01 405 2519.
City Bitter (1035)
Headline Bitter (1037)
Holborn Best (1047)
Regiment Bitter (1054)
Clifton Inns. Malt extract. Blanket pressure.

Help keep real ale alive by joining CAMRA. Your voice helps encourage brewers big and small to brew cask beer and offer all beer drinkers a better choice.

The Voracious Eight

ALLIED BREWERIES

Head Office: 107 Station Street, Burton-on-Trent, Staffs. ☎ 0283 45320.

Part of the vast Allied-Lyons group, Allied Breweries was formed in 1961 by the merger of Ansells, Ind Coope and Tetley Walker. The group has 7,300 pubs and includes many non-brewing companies, using "traditional" names, such as Benskins. There has been some rationalisation in the last twelve months, particularly at Ansells who have taken over Ind Coope's East Midlands' pubs, and Ind Coope, who have taken control of Halls brewery in Oxford and are phasing out its Harvest Bitter from managed houses, despite good sales, to replace it with national brands, such as Tetleys.

ALLOA Brewery Company, Craigmillar, Edinburgh EH16 6AT. ☎ 031 661 6161.
Allied's Scottish arm, which increased its standing north of the border early in 1987 by taking over Drybroughs from Watney, with its 155 pubs. Real ale in 90 out of 400 houses.
Archibald Arrols 70/- (1037) – hoppy, session beer.
Archibald Arrols 80/- (1042) – export strength ale.

ANSELLS Ltd., PO Box 379, Tamebridge House, Aldridge Road, Perry Barr, Birmingham B42 2TZ. ☎ 021 356 9177.
Allied's Midlands and South Wales company which now has responsibility for over 1600 pubs, of which 75% serve real ale. The company is divided into a retail company and Ansells Sales Ltd., controlling the tenanted and free trade business. Ansells beers are brewed at Allied's main Burton brewery (see Ind Coope); Ansells also distributes Draught Burton Ale and Tetley Bitter.
Ansells Mild (1035.5) – dark and malty.
Ansells Best Bitter (1037) – light and sweet.

HOLT, PLANT & DEAKIN, 91 Station Road, Oldbury, W. Midlands. ☎ 021 552 1788.
Traditional Black Country company set up in 1984, now running 26 pubs, all serving real ale. Mild and bitter brewed by Tetley-Walker in Warrington; Entire and Deakin's Downfall on their own small plant at Oldbury.
H P & D Mild (1036) – smooth and creamy.
H P & D Bitter (1036) – dry and hoppy.
H P & D Entire (1043) – full-bodied, hoppy brew.
Deakin's Downfall (1060) – warming winter ale.

AYLESBURY Brewery (ABC), Walton Street, Aylesbury, Bucks. ☎ 0296 20541.
Ceased brewing in 1935 and merged with Allied in 1972. Serves real ale in 171 of its 187 pubs. Besides Burton-brewed ABC Best Bitter and Ind Coope Burton Ale, offers Chiltern Beechwood, Draught Bass and Everard's Tiger in some pubs. Fine example of an 'independent' company within a national giant.
ABC Bitter (1037) – well-balanced.

IND COOPE, Allied House, 160 St. John Street, London EC1.
☎ 01 253 9911. The company controlling Allied's southern operations also includes two major breweries: Romford, which no longer brews real ale, and Burton which brews cask ales for the whole Allied group. Ind Coope's name is disappearing as a pub company, to come under the Ansell's banner in the East Midlands.

IND COOPE BURTON BREWERY, 107 Station Street, Burton-on-Trent, Staffs. ☎ 0283 31111.
Allied's major cask beer brewery for the South and Midlands, supplying Ansells and Aylesbury (see above) besides the Ind Coope companies (see below). Altogether brews ten real ales including Allied's national premium cask beer Burton Ale. For details of the other brews see the relevant trading companies. Runs no pubs.
Ind Coope Best Bitter (1037) – reformulated in 1987 – now much hoppier.
Burton Ale (1047.5) – a powerful smack of malt and hops.

IND COOPE BENSKINS, PO Box 105, Station Road, Watford, Herts. ☎ 0923 28585.
Has absorbed the group's East Anglian pubs on the closure of Ind Coope & Allsopps. Runs 1165 pubs in the northern home counties, and E. Anglia, almost 85% of which serve real ale.
Benskins Best (1037) – refreshing brew.

FRIARY MEUX, Station Road, Godalming, Surrey. ☎ 04868 25955.
Around 560 of the 600 pubs in the southern Home Counties and on the South Coast serve real ale.
Friary Meux Best (1037) – improved bitter.

HALLS (Oxford & West), 34 Park End Street, Oxford. ☎ 0865 722433. (Due to move to Eynsham.)
Previously separate Allied company, now part of Ind Coope who are gradually phasing out Harvest Bitter. 292 scattered pubs, 240 serving real ale. Also runs 4 wholesalers and south coast brewery (see below).
Harvest Bitter (1037) – sweet caramel-tasting bitter.

PLYMPTON BREWERY, Valley Road, Plympton, Plymouth. ☎ 0752 347171.
Set up in Hall's Plympton depot in 1984. Real ale in 34 of 39 local tied houses.
Plympton Best (1039) – malty, darkish.
Plympton Pride (1045) – fuller-bodied.

The Voracious Eight

TAYLOR WALKER, 77 Muswell Hill, London N10. ☎ 01 883 6431.
Runs over 700 pubs in Greater London, including the Nicholsons free house chain, and the former 73 Romford Brewery pubs in Essex.
Taylor Walker Best (1037) – malty brew.

JOSHUA TETLEY, PO Box 142, Hunslet Road, Leeds. ☎ 0532 435282.
Yorkshire's favourite brewing son, with real ale in an impressive 950 of the 1,100 pubs.
Tetley Mild (1032) – dark and malty.
Falstaff Best (1032) – local light mild.
Tetley Bitter (1035.5) – creamy and distinctive.
Imperial (1042) – premium cask beer.

TETLEY-WALKER, Dallam Lane, Warrington, Cheshire. ☎ 0925 31231.
Still lagging behind its brother across the Pennines, though over 50% of its 800 pubs serve real ale; 52 pubs sell Jennings Bitter from Cumbria. In 1987 sold 68 pubs on Merseyside, which will operate under the **Blezards** name, with Tetley-Walker brewing the beer.
Tetley Mild (1032) – excellent ale.
Tetley Bitter (1035.5) – sharp and clean-tasting.

PETER WALKER, 85–89 Duke Street, Liverpool. ☎ 051 708 5224.
Fine Merseyside-based chain of 76 traditional pubs, all serving their own Warrington-brewed range of real ales at popular prices.
Walker Mild (1032) – dark and fruity.
Walker Bitter (1033) – refreshing brew.
Walker Best Bitter (1035.5) – hoppier version of Tetley Bitter.
Walker Winter Warmer (1060) – dark seasonal ale.

WREXHAM LAGER BREWERY, East Parade, Llandudno, Gwynedd.
☎ 0492 86011.
Having absorbed the former Lloyd & Trouncer company, now runs 130 pubs in North Wales, half of which serve real ale, plus a small brewery.
MINERA BREWERY, City Arms, Minera, Wrexham, Clwyd.
☎ 0978 758890.
Serves around a dozen Allied pubs and a small free trade.
Minera Bitter (1037) – malt extract.
Minera Premium (1043) – stronger version of bitter, sold under house names.
Minera Winter Warmer (1060) – seasonal brew.

BASS

Head Office: 30 Portland Place, London W1. ☎ 01 637 5499.

The UK's largest brewer, which it is encouraging to note still maintains 13 breweries although sadly, none in the south east. It runs over 7000 pubs. Bass have recently seen beer sales rise in a declining market, maybe because they believe (unlike the other giants) that local breweries are cost efficient and local brands successful. **Bass Ireland**, the Belfast brewery produces no real ale.

BASS BREWING, 137 Station Street, Burton-on-Trent, Staffs. ☎ 0283 45301.
The original home of Bass, producing national brands.
Draught Bass (1044) – a once great ale, still better than other national brands.
Worthington White Shield (1052) – classic naturally-conditioned bottled pale ale.

BASS, MITCHELLS & BUTLERS, Cape Hill Brewery, PO Box 27, Birmingham 16. ☎ 021 558 1481.
One of the largest producers of cask beer in Britain, but the range leaves much to be desired. Bass's Midland division runs two other breweries and four trading companies; 70% of the 2,230 pubs sell cask beer.
M & B Mild (1036) – dark and pleasant.
B & B Mild (1036) – sweet, uninspiring beer.

HIGHGATE BREWERY, Sandymount Road, Walsall, Staffs. ☎ 0922 23168.
Unique mild-only brewery, producing only cask beer.
Highgate Mild (1036) – dark and fruity.

SPRINGFIELD BREWERY (M & B West), Grimstone Street, Wolverhampton. ☎ 0902 54551.

M & B's Wolverhampton brewery which also brews for Charrington. Springfield beers under threat; likely to be replaced by Butler's Bitter.
Springfield Bitter (1036) – refreshing brew.
Springfield Original (1050) – new full-bodied ale.

BASS NORTH, Headingley Office Park, 8 Victoria Road, Leeds.
☎ 0532 744444.
With over 2000 pubs under its control, Bass North is due to be totally reorganised. At the moment it runs four breweries, one of which, Preston Brook in Cheshire, is keg-only. The pubs are currently run through five trading companies. The real ale breweries are:

BASS THE CASTLE, Tower Brewery, Wetherby Road, Tadcaster, Yorks.
☎ 0937 832361.
Bass Mild XXXX (1031) – unassuming but underrated dark mild.
Bass Light 5 Star (1031) – quaffing light mild.
Bass Special Bitter (1036) – not special but much improved.

WILLIAM STONES, Hope Brewery, Wadsley Bridge, Sheffield.

47

The Voracious Eight

☎ 0742 349433.
Bass's specialist bottle beer brewery. 466 pubs. Cask Stones is brewed at the neighbouring:
CANNON BREWERY, 43 Rutland Road, Sheffield. ☎ 0742 349433.
Famous bitter brewery since 1865.
Stones Best Bitter (1038) – fine, well-hopped pale beer.

BASS WALES & WEST, Maes-y-Coed Road, PO Box 116 NDO, Cardiff. ☎ 0222 615831.
Covers a huge area from Hampshire to Cornwall plus Mid and West Wales, with two-thirds of the pubs serving real ale. Operates through five trading companies and runs two breweries; one at Alton, Hants is keg-only, the other is:

WELSH BREWERS, Crawshay Street, Cardiff. ☎ 0222 33071.
Former Hancock's brewery taken over by Bass in 1968. Most of the 500 pubs in S. Wales serve some real ale.
Worthington PA (1033) – light pale ale.
Hancock's PA (1033) – medium pale ale.
Worthington M (1033) – local pale ale.
Worthington Dark (1034) – delicate, creamy mild.
Hancock's HB (1037) – smooth, well-balanced bitter.
Worthington BB (1037) – lightly hopped but tasty bitter.

CHARRINGTON, Anchor House, 129 Mile End Road, London E1. ☎ 01 790 1860.
No longer brews, Charrington IPA being produced by M & B in Wolverhampton. Three-quarters of the 1440 pubs sell real ale. Trades from Norfolk and Kent to Oxfordshire through four regional companies. Some houses have been taking Adnams and Youngs.
Charrington IPA (1039) – uninspiring bitter.

TENNENT CALEDONIAN, 110 Bath Street, Glasgow. ☎ 041 552 6552.
Bass's Scottish beer division with 175 managed houses and extensive free trade. Predominantly lager brewers with little interest in cask beer – the Wellpark brewery, Glasgow, brews no real ale.

HERIOT BREWERY Roseburn Terrace, Edinburgh. ☎ 031 377 1361.
Tennent's 80/- (1042) – rare cask ale, much more widely available in keg. Subject of a contracting out experiment with Maclay.

COURAGE

Head Office: Ashby House, Bridge Street, Staines, Middlesex, TW18 4XH. ☎ 0748 66199.

Courage, established over 200 years ago, is now owned by the Australian giant, Elders IXL, who are keen to use their new acquisition to launch Foster's lager into Europe. The company moved its head office in February 1988 from Southwark to a new home on the site of the former Ashby's brewery at Staines. Runs 5000 pubs – since Elders' takeover, 926 managed houses have been transferred to tenancy, leaving just over 400 as managed houses. These are administered from three regional offices. Courage has three breweries, but the massive Berkshire brewery in Reading is keg-only.

BRISTOL BREWERY, Counterslip, Bristol. ☎ 0272 297222
Courage's only real ale brewery in the South following the closure of traditional breweries in London, Plymouth and Reading. Has recently been substantially expanded to meet the growing demand for cask beer which is heavily promoted, apart from the neglected Bitter Ale.
Bitter Ale (1030) – light and flavoursome.
Best Bitter (1039) – malty, rounded brew.
Directors (1046) – full-bodied and distinctive.

JOHN SMITH, Tadcaster Brewery, Tadcaster, N. Yorks. ☎ 0937 832091.
Extensively modernised brewery. Since the re-introduction of cask bitter in 1984, the handpumped beer has gained an extensive presence in the tenanted estate – most of the 1437 pubs now offer real ale. Courage Directors has recently been introduced into some houses. John Smiths also occasionally brew the powerful bottle-conditioned **Imperial Russian Stout** (1104). The last batch was in 1985, with the next brew expected in 1988.
Bitter (1036) – good drinking beer.

GREENALL WHITLEY

Head Office: Wilderspool Brewery, PO Box 2, Warrington, Cheshire. ☎ 0925 51234.

Controls three breweries and 1700 pubs. The **Wem** brewery was closed early in 1988, despite a hard fight by CAMRA and local townspeople. After further rationalisation within the company, Greenalls still faces difficulties with falling beer sales. Part of their survival plan has been entry into the

The Voracious Eight

international lager market by producing the Canadian Labatt lager under licence.

GREENALL'S, Wilderspool Brewery (as above).
Now with a new image to separate the brewery from the parent company, somewhat marred by the use of fake handpumps (check the pumpclip): "**Local Bitter** and **Mild**" are brewery-conditioned beers. Despite a new commitment to cask beer, it is only available in roughly half their 1050 pubs, with mild increasingly hard to find. Some pubs sell Davenports Bitter.
Cask Mild (1033.7) – dark, sweet, inoffensive brew.
Cask Bitter (1036.5) – pleasant and undistinguished session ale.
Original (1038.5) – unextraordinary best bitter.

DAVENPORTS, PO Box 353, Bath Row, Birmingham. ☎ 021 631 3388.
Award-winning brewery with real ale in most of its 331 scattered houses. Now also brews and distributes Wem beers, but not Wem Mild, which has been deleted. Note that the Wem beers may have lost some of their previous character.
Mild (1035) – dark and smooth.
Wem Best Bitter (1037.5) – once a distinctive bitter.
Bitter (1037.7) – popular and refreshing.
Wem Special Bitter (1042.5) – dark and sweet.

SHIPSTONE, Star Brewery, New Basford, Nottingham. ☎ 0602 785074.
Real ale in nearly all the 260 pubs, many heavily modernised since Greenall's takeover in 1978.
Mild (1034.9) – dark and well-hopped.
Bitter (1037.7) – popular and refreshing.

GUINNESS

Head Office: Park Royal Brewery, London NW10 7RR. ☎ 01 965 7700.

Runs 13 breweries. Besides the well known ones in Dublin (St. James's Gate) and London, it operates seven other stout plants around the world in Nigeria (4), Ghana, Cameroun and Malaysia. There are also contracts to brew Guinness in 22 other countries. Guinness also operates specialist Harp lager keg breweries and three breweries in Eire under the **Irish Ale Breweries** company name.

ARTHUR GUINNESS, St James's Gate, Dublin 8, Eire. ☎ 536700.
The birthplace of Guinness, founded in 1759. Also produces a heavier Foreign Extra Stout (8% alcohol) and Export Stout for sale overseas. Supplies part of the British market besides Ireland.
Draught Guinness (1038) – creamy and distinctive. Unlike England, the draught is not pasteurised.
Guinness Extra (1042) – superb stout, naturally-conditioned in the bottle.

ARTHUR GUINNESS, Park Royal (as above).
Guinness Extra (1042) – superb, bitter-sweet stout, naturally-conditioned in the bottle. Provides a welcome friend in every bar – except in Scotland where all bottled Guinness is pasteurised. All non-returnable bottles and canned Guinness from supermarkets and off-licences are also pasteurised. All Draught Guinness in Britain is keg.

SCOTTISH & NEWCASTLE

Head Office: Abbey Brewery, Holyrood Road, Edinburgh. ☎ 031 556 2591.

Having retained its independence for another 12 months, S&N have now taken over Matthew Brown in Blackburn and with it, Theakston. S&N closed Theakston's Workington brewery in Cumbria in 1988 and are transferring the bulk of production to their Tyne Brewery in Newcastle, while expanding Theakston's original brewery in Masham. S&N's tied estate has now increased to some 2400 pubs. These are operated through five regional trading companies. One brewery, the Royal in Manchester, is keg-only.

FOUNTAIN BREWERY, Fountainbridge, Edinburgh. ☎ 031 556 2591.
These beers are sold under either McEwan or Younger names depending on the area.
McEwan 70/- or **Younger Scotch** (1036.5) – well-balanced, sweetish brew.
McEwan 80/- or **Younger IPA** (1042) – heavy and full-flavoured.
Younger No. 3 (1043) – a rich, dark ale

TYNE BREWERY, Gallowgate, Newcastle. ☎ 0632 325091.
Theakston Best Bitter (1037) – light beer.

MATTHEW BROWN, PO Box 5, Lion Brewery, Blackburn, Lancs. ☎ 0254 52471.
Large N. West brewery which took over Theakston's in 1984, converting some of its "Lion" pubs to Theakstons. 230 out

49

The Voracious Eight

of 550 pubs serve real ale. S&N discontinued **John Peel Bitter** in 1988, following their takeover.
Mild (1031) – dark and nutty.
Bitter (1036) – well-balanced and malty.

HOME Brewery, Daybrook, Nottingham. ☎ 0602 269741.
Taken over in 1986. Runs 450 pubs in the Midlands, and expanding as S&N's Midlands trading company. 75% of the pubs serve real ale, although there are fears that more will be converted to keg.
Mild (1036) – dark and malty.

Bitter (1038) – still hoppy and refreshing, but not the same taste since the takeover.

THEAKSTON, Wellgarth, Masham, Ripon, N. Yorks. ☎ 0765 89544.
Yorkshire Dales brewery renowned for its Old Peculier, which sprang to prominence with the real ale revival.
Best Bitter (1037) – light but distinctive.
XB (1044) – strong, full-bodied bitter.
Old Peculier (1057) – notorious, rich and heavy.

WATNEY, MANN & TRUMAN

Head Office: Grand Metropolitan Brewing Ltd., 91 Brick Lane, London E1. ☎ 01 377 0020.

Brewing arm of the hotel and leisure group, Grand Metropolitan, running five breweries and 3700 tenanted pubs. Manns & Norwich, based in Northampton no longer brews, but is responsible for 900 of these from the W. Midlands to East Anglia. Similarly, the non-brewing company, Phoenix of Brighton controls 410 pubs on the south coast. A further 1640 managed houses, branded restaurants and hotels (including Chef & Brewer, Berni Inns and Open House) are operated by Grand Metropolitan Retailing Ltd., whose Clifton Inns division is responsible for specialist pubs, wine bars and home-brew houses. In 1988 sold off 700 low-barrelage pubs in three large blocks.

RUDDLES, Langham, Oakham, Rutland, Leics. ☎ 0572 56911.
Britain's most famous real ale brewers were taken over by Watneys in 1986, and the brewery is now being considerably expanded, as the beers are developed into national brands.
Best Bitter (1037) – light and tasty.
County (1050) – fine, full-flavoured ale.

USHERS, Parade House, Trowbridge, Wilts. ☎ 02214 63171.
West Country company with 420 pubs whose trading area stretches from Lands End to Oxford. Subsidiary, Watney Truman Wales, is responsible for S. Wales. Over 85 per cent of the pubs serve real ale, 105 pubs having been sold to Salisbury independent brewers, Gibbs Mew, in 1988.
Best Bitter (1036) – sweetish, rounded beer.

WATNEY TRUMAN LTD, 14 Mortlake High Street, London SW14. ☎ 01 876 3434.
The company operates the group's two London breweries, although Mortlake's Stag brewery ceased brewing real ale early in 1988. It runs some 1260 pubs split about 2:1 between Watney and Truman. 85% of the houses offer real ale, generally 'selected' from national brands – Webster's Yorkshire Bitter, Ruddles Best Bitter and County; plus Truman's Best Bitter. Truman ceased brewing its strong ale, Sampson, in 1988.

TRUMAN, Black Eagle Brewery, 91 Brick Lane, London E1. ☎ 01 377 0020.
Best Bitter (1044) – hoppy and full-bodied, a.k.a. 'Red'.

SAMUEL WEBSTER & WILSONS, Monsall Road, Newton Heath, Manchester. ☎ 061 205 2345.
Combined company of Websters in Yorkshire and Wilsons, with all beers brewed by Websters in Halifax following the closure of Wilson's Manchester brewery in 1986. Two-thirds of the 690 pubs serve cask beer.

WEBSTER, Fountain Head Brewery, Ovenden Wood, Halifax. ☎ 0422 57188.
Heavily committed to the northern club trade.
Wilson's Original Mild (1032) – malty brew.
Webster's Green Label (1033) – bitter light mild.
Wilson's Original Bitter (1036) – well-balanced.
Webster's Yorkshire Bitter (1036) – bland brew.
Webster's Choice (1045) – fuller-bodied.

WHITBREAD

Head Office: The Brewery, Chiswell Street, London EC1. ☎ 01 606 4455.

Whitbread have really surpassed themselves this year, by closing the much-loved **Wethereds** brewery at Marlow in Buckinghamshire as well as

The Voracious Eight

Chesters in Manchester. The beers have been transferred to other breweries, but Samuel Whitbread Strong Ale has been deleted completely. This brings the number of breweries Whitbread controls down to six. Its 6400 pubs are run by Whitbread Trading (tenanted pubs), currently based at Chiswell Street, but likely to move to Luton to join Whitbread Inns, which is responsible for the managed houses.

WHITBREAD BREWERIES at Park Street West, Luton, Beds. ☎ 0582 424000 runs two massive modern breweries at Salmesbury in Lancashire and Magor in South Wales, neither of which brew real ale, plus the four traditional breweries which now remain from Whitbread's heavy rationalisation programme.

CASTLE EDEN, PO Box 13, Castle Eden, Hartlepool, Cleveland. ☎ 0429 836431
N. East brewery whose one cask ale is sold throughout the U.K. Durham Mild, brewed for the Midlands, was withdrawn early in 1987.
Castle Eden Ale (1040) – rich, sweetish bitter.

CHELTENHAM, Monson Avenue, Cheltenham, Glos. ☎ 0242 521401.
Whitbread's only remaining traditional brewery serving the S. West, Wales and the W. Midlands. Now also brewing Wethered beers.
West Country Pale Ale (1030) – light session beer.
Wethered Bitter (1035) – well-balanced brew, widely available in the S. East.
Flowers IPA (1036) – hoppy bitter.
Strong Country Bitter (1037) – refreshing brew for Wessex.
Wethered SPA (1040) – special, full-bodied bitter.
Flowers Original (1044) – full-bodied.
Wethered Winter Royal (1055) – warming dark ale.

FREMLINS, Court Street, Faversham, Kent. ☎ 0795 533311.
Whitbread's rival brewery to the independent Shepherd Neame in Kent, with more than 600 tied houses, most of which serve real ale.
Fremlins Bitter (1035) – well-balanced and drinkable.
Pompey Royal (1043) – strong bitter with loyal Portsmouth following.
Flowers Original (1044) – full-bodied ale

SHEFFIELD, Exchange Brewery, Sheffield, S. Yorks. ☎ 0742 761101.
Whitbread's remaining Yorkshire brewery, now producing Chester's beers. 300 of its 800 tied houses serve real ale.
Chester's Best Mild (1032) – thin and dark.
Chester's Best Bitter (1033) – dry and pale.
Trophy (1036) – real version of the widespread keg bitter.

51

The Beers Index

This index is intended to help you track down the brewer of that memorable beer you drank on that distant summer holiday. That is to say, it lists the names of all beers not known by their brewery prefix. For example, you will find Little Matty, brewed by Hoskins & Oldfield, but not Best Bitter, brewed by Ballards *et al*. The latter are all easily found by consulting the relevant part of the brewery section (pages 23-51).

Beer	Brewery

A

ABC Bitter	Aylesbury,	p46
AK Mild	McMullen,	p34
ASB	Archers,	p23
Abbot Ale	Greene King,	p30
Anvil Mild, Light, Bitter, Strong Ale	Hydes,	p33
Albert Ale	Earl Soham,	p43
Alfie's Special Bitter	Dog & Parrot,	p43
Archibald Arrols 70/-, 80/-	Alloa,	p46
Artist Ale	Paradise,	p37

B

BBB/Burglar Bill's	Clark,	p27
BBB/Butser Brew Bitter	Gales,	p29
BBBB	Berrow,	p25
BSB	Bridgewater,	p43
Badger Best Bitter	Hall & Woodhouse,	p31
Barbarian Bitter	Pheasant & Firkin,	p45
Baz's Bonce Blower	Stag & Hounds,	p45
Beacon Bitter	Everards,	p28
Bear Ale	Traquair House,	p40
Beaumanor Bitter	Hoskins,	p32
Beechwood Bitter	Chiltern,	p27
Benchmark	Bunces,	p26
Benfro Bitter, Extra	Pembrokeshire Own Ales,	p37
Best Cellar	Yates,	p42
Bill's Bevy	Reindeer,	p45
Bishop's Tipple	Gibbs Mew,	p29
Blackfen Bitter	Jolly Fenman,	p44
Blackout	Big Lamp,	p25
Black Country Bitter	Hansons, p31; Holden,	p32
Black Country Mild	Holden,	p32
Blencathra Bitter	Old Crown Inn,	p44
Black Prince/Dark	Crown,	p28
Bombardier	Wells,	p41
Border Mild, Exhibition, Bitter	Marston,	p34
Borough Bitter	Goose & Firkin,	p44
Bosun Bitter	Brewhouse,	p43
Bosun's Best	Poole,	p37
Bosun's Bitter	St Austell, p39; Steamboat Inn,	p45
Brew 69	Wye Valley,	p42
Brewer's Droop	Marston Moor,	p34
Brewhouse Ale	Reepham,	p38
Bridge Bitter	Burton Bridge,	p26
Bristol Best	Fleece & Firkin,	p43
Brixton Best, Bitter	Warrior,	p45
Broadside	Adnams,	p23
Broadsman Bitter	Woodforde's,	p42
Brown Willy	Min Pin Inn,	p44
Brunel Bitter	Fleece & Firkin,	p43
Buff's Bitter	Canterbury,	p27
Bullfrog	Frog & Firkin,	p44
Bullion Bitter	Old Mill,	p36
Burley Bitter	Fox & Newt,	p44
Burton Ale	Ind Coope,	p46
Burton Bitter	Marston,	p34
Burton Festival Ale, Porter	Burton Bridge,	p27
Burton Mild	Everards,	p28

C

Captain Frigate	Frog & Frigate,	p44
Cardinal Sussex Ale	First In Last Out,	p43
Castle Bitter	Berkhamsted,	p25
Castle Ruin	British Oak,	p43
Castle Steamer	Three Tuns,	p45
Castletown Bitter	Isle of Man,	p33
Celebration	Morrells,	p36
Celebration Ale	Abington Park,	p43
Centurion Best Bitter	Hadrian,	p30
Cherrypicker's Bitter	Alford Arms,	p43
Chiswick Bitter	Fuller,	p29
Chudley Local Line	Gibbs Mew,	p29
City Bitter	Yorkshire Grey,	p45
Coal Porter	Fleece & Firkin,	p43
Cobblers Ale	Abington Park,	p43
College	Morrells,	p36
College Ale	Martin,	p34
County	Ruddles,	p50
Country Bitter	McMullen, p34; McDonnells,	p44
Croaker	Fleece & Firkin,	p44
Cromwell Bitter	Marston Moor,	p34

D

Dark Knight	Premier Ales,	p38
Dark Maidstone Ale	Goachers,	p30
Dark Star	Pitfield,	p37
Dasher's Draught	Fox & Hounds,	p44
Delph Strong Ale	Batham,	p24
Destroyer Bitter	Steamboat Inn,	p45
Devizes Bitter	Wadworth,	p41
Devon Glory	Barron,	p24

The Beers Index

Beer	Brewery	
Directors	Courage,	p48
Dogbolter	Firkin Group,	p43–45
Dolphin Best Bitter	Poole,	p37
Dorchester Bitter	Eldridge Pope,	p28
Dorset Original IPA	Eldridge Pope,	p28
Double Chance	Malton,	p34
Double Dagger	Oak,	p36
Double Dragon	Felinfoel,	p29
Draught Festive	King & Barnes,	p33

E

Beer	Brewery	
ESB	Fuller, p29; Mitchells,	p35
EXS Bitter	Hoskins & Oldfield,	p32
Eagle Bitter	Wells,	p41
Earl's Bitter	Bridgewater,	p43
Eastcote Ale (SPA)	Banks & Taylor,	p24
Ebony Dark	Bullmastiff,	p26
Elizabethan	Harvey,	p31
Emperor Ale	Hadrian,	p30
English Guineas Stout	Sair,	p45
Enoch's Hammer	Sair,	p45
Entire Stout	Hop Back,	p44
Essex Porter	Crouch Vale,	p28
Eve'ill Bitter	British Oak,	p43
Exe Valley Bitter	Barron,	p24
Exhibition	Smiles,	p39
Exmoor Ale, Dark, Gold	Golden Hill,	p30

F

Beer	Brewery	
FA Mild	Mauldon,	p35
Falstaff Best	Joshua Tetley,	p47
Farmhouse Bitter	Plassey,	p37
Farmers Ale	Oakhill,	p36
Farmer's Glory	Wadworth,	p41
Fettler's Bitter	New Fermor Arms,	p44
Firkinstein Lager	Fleece & Firkin,	p43
Fish T'Ale	Flounder & Firkin,	p44
Flamin' Ale	Flamingo & Firkin,	p43
Flashman's Clout	Tom Brown's,	p45
Forty-four	Blackawton,	p25
Fortyniner	Ringwood,	p38
Frigate Bitter	Steamboat Inn,	p45

G

Beer	Brewery	
GB Bitter, Mild	Lees,	p33
GBH	Gibbs Mew,	p29
GBH/Great British Heavy	Cornish,	p27
GFB	Hop Back,	p44
GSB Strong Bitter	Elgoods,	p28
Gannet Mild	Earl Soham,	p43
Garthwaite Special	Clark,	p27
Gladiator Bitter	Hadrian,	p30
Gold	Reepham,	p38
Golden Best	Taylor,	p40
Granary Bitter	Reepham,	p38
Greenmantle Ale	Broughton,	p25
Guvnor's Special Brew	Miners Arms,	p35

H

Beer	Brewery	
HOB Bitter, Mild	Hoskins & Oldfield,	p32
HSB	Gales,	p29
Hackney	Falcon & Firkin,	p43
Hammerhead	Clark,	p27
Hancock's PA, BB	Bass,	p48
Hardington Bitter	Axminster,	p23
Harvest Bitter	Halls,	p46
Head Cracker	Woodforde's,	p42
Headbanger	Archers,	p23
Headline Bitter	Yorkshire Grey,	p45
Headstrong	Blackawton,	p25
Heavengate Ale	Unicorn,	p45
Heller	Royal Inn,	p45
Hellgate Special Bitter	Unicorn,	p45
Hereford Bitter, Supreme	Wye Valley,	p42
Hermitage Best Bitter	Sussex,	p39
Hick's Special	St Austell,	p39
Hobgoblin	Glenny,	p30
Hogshead	Uley,	p41
Holborn Best	Yorkshire Grey,	p45
Horrors	Axminster,	p23
Horsebridge Best	Royal Inn,	p45
House Ale	Traquair House,	p40
Hoxton Best	Pitfield,	p37

I

Beer	Brewery	
Imperial	Joshua Tetley,	p47

J

Beer	Brewery	
JD Dry Hop Bitter	Cornish,	p27
JTS XXX Bitter	Lloyds,	p33
Janner's Ale, Old Dark Ale, Old Original	Mill,	p35
John O's Bitter, Special	Marisco Tavern,	p44
Johnson's Bitter	Martin,	p34
Jolabrugg	Earl Soham,	p43
Jolly Roger Quaff Ale, Severn Bore Special, Georgian Ale	Brewery Tap,	p43

K

Beer	Brewery	
KK Mild	Greene King,	p30
Kingfisher Ale	Cutleigh,	p27
Kingsdown Ale	Arkell,	p23
Kingswood Cask Bitter	New Forest,	p36

53

The Beers Index

Beer	Brewery	
Kite Bitter	Ancient Druids,	p43
Knightly Brew	Premier Ales,	p38

L

LBA Mild	Guernsey,	p30
Landlord	Taylor,	p40
Leadboiler	Sair,	p45
Legend Bitter	Min Pin Inn,	p44
Light Maidstone Ale	Goacher's,	p30
Linfit Bitter, Mild, Special	Sair,	p45
Little Matty	Hoskins & Oldfield,	p32
Local Bitter	Wiltshire,	p42
London Porter	Pitfield,	p37
London Pride	Fuller,	p29
Lorimers Best Scotch	Vaux,	p41
Lumley Old Ale	Sussex,	p39

M

Marathon	Jennings,	p33
Master Brew Best Bitter, Bitter	Shepherd Neame,	p39
Mercian Mild	Marston,	p34
Merlin	Ancient Druids,	p43
Merlin's Ale	Broughton,	p25
Merrie Monk	Marston,	p34
Merman XXX	Caledonian,	p27
Mirandinha Mild	Dog & Parrot,	p43
Moonraker	Lees,	p33
Monster Mash	Ale House,	p43
Museum Ale	Samuel Smith,	p39

N

Nathaniel's Special	Fox & Hounds,	p44
Norfolk Nog, Porter, Pride	Woodforde's,	p42

O

OB Bitter, Mild	Boddingtons,	p25
OBB/Old Brewery Bitter	Samuel Smith,	p39
Okells Bitter, Mild	Isle of Man,	p33
Old Baily	Mansfield,	p34
Old Bushy Tail	Bushy's,	p43
Old Buzzard	Cotleigh,	p27
Old Croak Ale	Frog & Parrot,	p44
Old Crofters	First In Last Out,	p44
Old Devil	Wiltshire,	p42
Old Eli	Sair,	p45
Old Expensive	Burton Bridge,	p26
Old Fart	Robinwood,	p45
Old Genie	Big Lamp,	p25
Old Grumble	Wiltshire,	p42
Old Hookey	Hook Norton,	p32
Old Horizontal	Stocks,	p39
Old Horny	Unicorn,	p45
Old Jock	Broughton,	p25
Old Lowesmoor	Brewery Tap,	p43
Old Maidstone Ale	Goachers,	p30
Old Manor	Harviestoun,	p31
Old Masters	Morland,	p35
Old Navigation	Hoskins & Oldfield,	p32
Old Needle's Eye Strong Ale	Unicorn,	p45
Old Nigel	Hoskins,	p32
Old Oak Ale	Oak,	p36
Old Peculier	Theakston,	p50
Old Santa	Bridgewater,	p43
Old Scrooge	Sair,	p45
Old Spot Ale	Uley,	p41
Old Thumper	Ringwood,	p38
Old Timer	Wadworth,	p41
Old Tom	Robinson, p38; Selby,	p39
Old Vic	Smiles,	p39
Old Willow	Fox & Newt,	p44
Old Woolly	Fleece & Firkin,	p43
Old Wrot	Bakery & Brewhouse,	p43
Oliver John's Bitter	Golden Lion,	p44
Once a Knight	Premier Ales,	p38
Owd Bob	Malton,	p34
Owd Rodger	Marston,	p34
Oxbow	Bakery & Brewhouse,	p43

P

Paine's EG, XXX	Tolly Cobbold,	p40
Parish Bitter	Wood,	p42
Parish Mild, Special	Stag & Hounds,	p45
Pedigree	Marston,	p34
Pendle Witches Brew	Moorhouse's,	p35
Penn's Ale	Hoskins,	p32
Phoenix XXX	Woodforde's,	p42
Pickled Squirrel	Alford Arms,	p43
Pickwick's Porter	Malton,	p34
Pig's Ear	Uley,	p41
Pilot's Pride	Minerva,	p44
Pimlico Light, Porter	Orange,	p44
Piston Bitter	Beer Engine,	p43
Piston Brew	Bushy's Brewpub,	p43
Poachers Ale	Stag & Hounds,	p45
Pommie's Revenge	Goose Eye,	p30
Pompey Royal	Whitbread,	p51
Poole Bitter	Brewhouse,	p43
Potter's Bitter	Old Bull & Bush,	p44
Potters Black Porter	Stag & Hounds,	p45
Power House	Battersea,	p43
Premier Bitter	Moorhouse's,	p35
Premium	Berkhamsted, p24; Hoskins,	p32

The Beers Index

Beer	Brewery	
Premium Bitter	Gibbs Mew,	p29
Prince Bishop Ale	Big Lamp,	p25
Progress	Pilgrim,	p37
Purbeck Lager	Brewhouse,	p43

R

Rail Ale	Beer Engine, p43; Phoenix & Firkin,	p45
Ram Tam	Taylor,	p40
Rambo	Fleece & Firkin,	p43
Rapier Pale Ale	Reepham,	p38
Raven Ale	Orkney,	p36
Reckless Bitter	Frog & Parrot,	p44
Red Nose	Reindeer,	p45
Regiment Bitter	Yorkshire Grey,	p45
Reg's Tipple	Gribble Inn,	p44
Riding Traditional Bitter	Mansfield,	p34
Right Royal	Royal Inn,	p45
Roger & Out	Frog & Parrot,	p44
Roger's Conqueror, Old Fashioned Porter	Frog & Parrot,	p44
Rough	Olde Bull & Bush,	p44
Royal Borough Bitter	Flamingo & Firkin,	p43
Royal Oak	Eldridge Pope,	p28
Rudolf's Revenge	Alford Arms,	p43
Rutland	Fox & Newt,	p44

S

SA	Brain,	p25
SAS/Strong Anglian Special	Crouch Vale,	p28
SBA	Donnington,	p28
SPA	Wethered,	p??
SW1, SW2	Orange,	p44
Saggar's Special	Olde Bull & Bush,	p44
Salisbury Best	Gibbs Mew,	p29
Samson	Powell, p38; Vaux,	p41
Scotswood Ale	Dog & Parrot,	p43
Seaman's Bitter, Mild	Steamboat Inn,	p45
Select	Stocks,	p39
Session Bitter	Three Crowns,	p45
Sheffield Best Bitter	Ward,	p41
Shefford Bitter, Old Dark/SOD, Old Strong/SOS	Banks & Taylor,	p24
Sidekick	McDonnell's,	p44
Skullcrusher	Lloyds,	p33
Sleeper	Beer Engine,	p43
Somerset Best Bitter	Axminster,	p23
Son of a Bitch	Bullmastiff,	p26
Sovereign Bitter	Larkins,	p33
Spook	Phantom & Firkin,	p45
Stoat Bitter	Ferret & Firkin,	p43
Stock Ale	Shepherd Neame,	p39
Streatham Dynamite, Strong	Greyhound,	p44
Stonehenge Best Bitter	Wiltshire,	p41
Strongarm	Cameron,	p27
Suffolk Punch	Mauldon,	p35
Surrey Bitter	Pilgrim,	p37
Sussex Bitter, Mild	King & Barnes,	p33

T

Talisman	Pilgrim,	p37
Tally Ho	Adnams, p23; Palmer,	p37
Tamar Ale	Royal Inn,	p45
Tanglefoot	Hall & Woodhouse,	p31
Tapper	Bakery & Brewhouse,	p43
Tavistock Ale	Frog & Parrot,	p44
Tawny Bitter	Cotleigh,	p27
Tiger	Everards,	p28
Tinners Bitter	St Austell,	p39
Tom Kelly's Stout	Hoskins & Oldfield,	p32
Topsy Turvy	Berrow,	p25
Trophy	Whitbread,	p51
Two Henry's Bitter	Nix Wincott,	p44
Two Pints	Cropton,	p20
Tyke Bitter	Oak,	p36

V

VPA	Burt,	p26
Varsity	Morrells,	p36
Victoria Bitter	Earl Soham,	p43
Victory Ale	Bateman,	p24
Village Bitter	Archers,	p23
Vixen Ale	Fox & Firkin,	p44

W

Wallop	Dog & Parrot,	p43
Warrior Ale	Sussex,	p39
Wassail	Ballards,	p23
Wessex Royal	Cornish,	p27
Whale Ale	Flounder & Firkin,	p44
Wherry Best Bitter	Woodforde's,	p41
White Rose Bitter	Goose Eye,	p30
Wild Boar Bitter	Trough,	p40
William Clark's Thistle Bitter, EXB, Mild, 68	N & E Riding,	p36
Willie Warmer	Crouch Vale,	p28
Wiltshire Traditional Bitter	Gibbs Mew,	p29
Winter Warmer	Young, p42; Warrior,	p45
Winter Royal	Wethered,	p51
Witney Bitter	Glenny,	p30
Wobbly Bob	Oak,	p36
Woodham Bitter	Crouch Vale,	p28
Worcester Winter Wobbler	Brewery Tap,	p43
Wrekin Bitter	Unicorn,	p45
Wychwood Best	Glenny,	p30
Wyndhams Bitter	Sussex,	p39

55

Good Beer Guide

KEY TO SYMBOLS

- ♨ real fire
- Q quiet pub – no electronic music, TV or obtrusive games
- ☎ indoor room for children
- ⚘ garden or other outdoor drinking area
- ⛵ accommodation
- ◖ lunchtime meals
- ◗ evening meals
- ⚑ public bar
- ⚬ facilities for the disabled
- ▲ camping facilities close to the pub or part of the pub grounds
- ⇌ near British Rail station
- ⊖ near Underground station
- ⊙ real cider

The facilities, beers and pub hours listed in the Good Beer Guide are liable to change but were correct when the Guide went to press.

KEY MAP

Avon

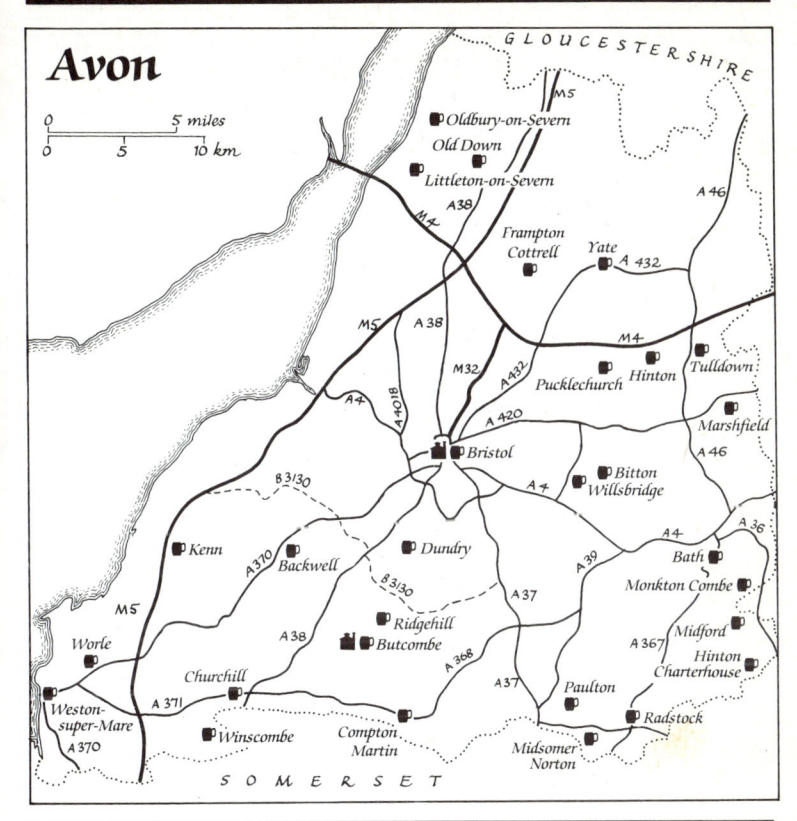

Butcombe Brewery, Butcombe; **Smiles**, Bristol

Bath

10.30–2.30; 5.30–10.30 (11 F, S)

Barley Mow
32 Bathwick Street (by A36 roundabout) ☎ (0225) 330416
Draught Bass; Charrington IPA H
Unpretentious city pub with boisterous, smoky public and more comfortable lounge. Very popular skittles pub ♩ (not Sun) ⌂

12–2.30; 6–10.30 (11 F, S)

Bladud Arms
Gloucester Road, Lower Swainswick (A46)
☎ (0225) 20152
Draught Bass; Butcombe Bitter; Marston Pedigree; Wadworth 6X; Whitbread WCPA H
Named after a local swineherd and prince who cured himself and his pigs of leprosy! Single lounge bar with upstairs pool room, often crowded ⌂ ♩

10.30–2.30; 5.30–10.30 (11 F, S)

Coeur de Lion
17 Northumberland Place
☎ (0225) 65371
Cornish JD Dry Hop Bitter, Original, Wessex Stud, GBH (winter) H
Tiny, intimate pub in city centre passageway. Good conversation, popular with tourists ⌂ ⌂ (limited) ≉

10.30–2.30; 5.30–10.30 (11 F, S)

Devonshire Arms
139 Wellsway ☎ (0225) 28837
Draught Bass; Wadworth 6X H
Spacious and smart local with plush lounge ⌂ ♩ ⌂

10.30–2.30; 5.30–10.30 (11 F, S)

Fairfield Arms
1 Fairfield Park Road
☎ (0225) 310594
Courage Bitter Ale, Best Bitter H
Welcoming local on north-eastern outskirts of city. Darts ⌂ ⌂

10.30–2.30; 5.30–10.30 (11 F, S)

Hatchetts
6–7 Queen Street
☎ (0225) 25045
Marston Pedigree; Miners Arms Own Ale, Guvnors H
Lively bar; upstairs popular with young. Good business lunches. Live music winter Wed nights ♩ ⌂ ≉ (Spa)

10.30–2.30; 5.30–10.30 (11 F, S)

King William
36 Thomas Street (A4)
☎ (0225) 28096
Brain Dark; Marston Burton Bitter, Merrie Monk, Pedigree; Smiles Best Bitter H
Lively street corner free house ⌂

11–2.30; 6–10.30 (11 F, S)

Larkhall Inn
St Saviours Road
☎ (0225) 25710
Courage Bitter Ale, Best Bitter, Directors H
Distinctive pub with unusual brass beer engines ⌂ ⌂ ⌂

11–2.30; 5.30 (6 Sat)–10.30 (11 F, S)

Midland
14 James Street West
☎ (0225) 25029
Courage Bitter Ale, Best Bitter, Directors H
Large central pub opposite the old Green Park station: the decor reflects the railway influence
♩ (not Sun) ⌂ ≉ (Spa)

11–2.30; 5.30–10.30 (11 F, S)

57

Avon

Olde Farmhouse
1 Lansdown Road
☎ (0225) 316162
Butcombe Bitter; Hall & Woodhouse Tanglefoot; Wadworth IPA, 6X H
Lively local of great character. Pub games

11–2.30; 5.30–10.30 (11 F, S)

Old Green Tree
12 Green Street (behind GPO)
☎ (0225) 62357
Ruddles Best Bitter, County; Usher Best Bitter; Webster Yorkshire Bitter H
Small wood-panelled city-centre pub with non-smoking room, no entry after 10.30 Fri and Sat Q (Spa)

11–2.30; 5.30–10.30 (11 F, S)

Pulteney Arms
37 Daniel Street (near Henrietta Park)
☎ (0225) 63923
Ruddles County H**; Usher Best Bitter** H & G**; Webster Yorkshire Bitter** H
Comfortable city pub, a shrine to the glory of Rugby Union. Very popular with 25–35 age group. Enterprising food menu. Darts (until 8.45)

10.30–2.30; 5.30–10.30 (11 F, S)

Ram
20 Claverton Buildings, Widcombe ☎ (0225) 21938
Ruddles Best Bitter, County; Usher Best Bitter; Webster Yorkshire Bitter H
Pleasant pub near first lock on Kennet and Avon canal. Regular live jazz at weekends (Spa)

10.30–2.30; 5.30–10.30 (11 F, S)

Ring of Bells
10 Widcombe Parade, Widcombe ☎ (0225) 336282
Brain Dark; Marston Burton Bitter, Merrie Monk, Pedigree, Owd Rodger; Smiles Best Bitter H
Lively local with regular live rock bands at weekends. Darts (not Sun) (Spa)

10.30–2.30; 5.30–10.30 (11 F, S)

Rose & Crown
6 Brougham Place, St Saviours Road, Larkhall ☎ (0225) 25700
Butcombe Bitter; Charrington IPA; Marston Pedigree H
Friendly out-of-town local; worth finding. Darts

10.30–2.30; 5.30–10.30 (11 F, S)

Royal Oak (Rossiters)
8–10 Summerlays Place, Pulteney Road
☎ (0225) 335587
Gibbs Mew Wiltshire Traditional Bitter, Salisbury Best, Bishops Tipple H
Comfortable split-level lounge bar. Accent on food (Spa)

10.30–2.30; 5.30–10.30 (11 F, S)

Star
23 The Vineyards (A4, by Hedgemead Park)
☎ (0225) 25072
Arkells Kingsdown Ale H**; Draught Bass** G**; Charrington IPA; Wadworth 6X, Old Timer (winter)** H
Enjoy the atmosphere in this old wood-panelled inn Q

11–2.30; 5.30–10.30 (11 F, S)

Victoria
Millmead Road, Oldfield Park
☎ (0225) 25903
Courage Bitter Ale, Best Bitter H
Friendly workingman's local in SW suburbs of city. Children allowed in skittle alley
(Oldfield Park)

Backwell

11–2.30; 6–11

Rising Sun
91 West Town Road (A370)
☎ (027 583) 2215
Draught Bass; Charrington IPA H
Busy bar and quiet lounge. Cheap meals. Pub games

Bitton

11–2.30; 6.30–10.30 (11 F, S)

White Hart
140 High Street (A431)
Courage Bitter Ale, Best Bitter, Directors H
Historic village pub, ½ mile from Bitton Steam Railway. Pub games

Bristol

11–2.30; 5.30–10.30 (11 F, S)

Barley Mow
39 Barton Road, St Philips
☎ (0272) 279946
Wadworth IPA, 6X H**, Old Timer (winter)** G
Comfortable, sociable pub, tucked away in industrial area (as required)
(Temple Meads)

10.30–2.30; 5.30–10.30 (11 F, S)

Duke of Cambridge
82 Seymour Road, Easton (off M32 Jct 3) ☎ (0272) 511031
Marston Burton Bitter, Merrie Monk, Pedigree, Owd Rodger H
Narrow 1-bar, split-level pub in backstreet. Pub games
(Stapleton Rd)

10.30–2.30; 5.30–10.30 (11 F, S)

Farm
Hopetoun Road, Ashley Vale, St Werburghs (near M32 Jct 3)
☎ (0272) 43622
Ruddles County; Ushers Best Bitter H
Popular pub by St Werburghs City Farm. Pleasant garden. Well worth finding. Pub games Q

11–2.30; 5.30 (7 Sat)–10.30 (11 F, S)

Grosvenor Arms
1 Coronation Road, Bedminster (A370/A38)
☎ (0272) 663325
Draught Bass H
Good old-fashioned 1-bar pub. Games
(Temple Meads)

11–2.30; 5.30 (6 Sat)–10.30 (11 F, S)

Highbury Vaults
164 St Michaels Hill, Kingsdown ☎ (0272) 733203
Brain SA; Smiles Brewery Bitter, Best Bitter, Exhibition H
Smiles first tied house; an excellent pub with a small front bar and large rear bar. Very atmospheric. Garden a sun trap. Guest beers. Pub games
Q (Clifton Downs)

10.30–2.30; 6.30–10.30 (11 F, S)

Highwayman
Hill Street, Kingswood (A420)
Halls Harvest Bitter; Ind Coope Burton Ale H
Country pub in town, just outside Kingswood Centre. Pub games

11–2.30; 5.30–10.30 (11 F, S)

Kings Head
60 Victoria Street (B4053)
☎ (0272) 277860
Courage Bitter Ale, Best Bitter H
Splendid, small, narrow bar with unusual lounge in lovely restored Victorian pub. Ornate original fittings. Pub games Q (Mon–Fri)
(Temple Meads)

11–2.30; 6–10.30 (11 F, S)

Kings Head
Whitehall Road, Whitehall (B4465/B4469) ☎ (0272) 517174
Courage Bitter Ale, Best Bitter, Directors H
Smart, rambling pub. Popular both lunchtimes and evenings

11–2.30; 5.30–10.30 (11 F, S)

Knowle Hotel
Leighton Road, Knowle (off A37) ☎ (0272) 777019
Ind Coope Burton Ale; Smiles Best Bitter; Tetley Bitter H
Large and friendly pub. Games

11–2.30; 5.30–10.30 (11 F, S)

Old Castle Green
46 Gloucester Lane, Old Market (off A420)
☎ (0272) 550925
Marston Border Mild, Burton Bitter, Pedigree, Owd Rodger H
Friendly 1-bar local, tucked away at back of old market. Good food
(Temple Meads)

11.30–2.30; 5.30–10.30 (11 F, S)

58

Avon

Phoenix
15 Wellington Road (near A32/A404 Jct) ☎ (0272) 558327
Draught Bass; Halls Harvest Bitter; Miners Arms Own Ale ⊞; Uley Old Spot; Wadworth 6X, Old Timer ⒼG
Pleasant, basic corner local next to swimming baths
Q⊛&⇌ (Temple Meads)

10.30–2.30; 5.30–10.30 (11 F, S)

Plough & Windmill
194 West Street, Bedminster (A38) ☎ (0272) 663460
Courage Bitter Ale, Best Bitter ⊞
Sports-minded, multi-roomed pub. Original fittings enhance atmosphere. Bagatelle table
⊛⊜⇌ (Parson St)

12–2.30; 5.30 (7 Sat)–10.30 (11 F, S)

Pride of the Forest
18 Unity Street, Old Market (off A4044) ☎ (0272) 298109
Wadworth IPA, 6X, Old Timer (winter) ⊞
Convivial cosmopolitan, cosy corner pub where bridge mingles with darts ⊜ (not Sun) ⇌ (Temple Meads)

10.30 (11 Sat)–2.30; 6–10.30 (11 F, S)

Prince of Wales
5 Gloucester Road, Bishopston (A38) ☎ (0272) 45552
Courage Best Bitter, Directors ⊞
Busy pub; popular with young in evening ⊛⊜⇌ (Montpelier)

11–2.30; 6–10.30 (11 F, S)

Queens Head
286 Fishponds Road, Upper Eastville (A432/B4469) ☎ (0272) 518457
Halls Harvest Bitter; Ind Coope Burton Ale ⊞
A distinctive red brick pub facing Eastville Park. Large bar with games area at one end; quiet lounge bar ⊛⊜

11–2.30; 6–10.30 (11 F, S)

Royal George
2 Filton Road, Horfield (A38) ☎ (0272) 519335
Courage Best Bitter ⊞
Comfortable, clean, modernised local, opposite sports centre. Pub games
⊛⊜⊙

10.30–2.30; 7–10.30 (11 F, S)

Sportsmans Arms
20 Wade Street, St Judes ☎ (0272) 559323
Courage Bitter Ale, Best Bitter ⊞
Homely L-shaped, open-plan pub ⊛⊜ (not Sun)

11–2.30; 5.30–10.30 (11 F, S)

Star
4/6 North Street, Bedminster, (B3120) ☎ (0272) 663588
Halls Harvest Bitter; Ind Coope Burton Ale; Smiles Exhibition ⊞
Large, renovated, open-plan pub; very comfortable. Small quaint garden. Pub games
⊛⊜&

10.30–2.30; 5.30–10.30 (11 F, S)

Three Horseshoes
359 Church Road, St George (A420) ☎ (0272) 556818
Draught Bass; Flowers Original; Whitbread WCPA ⊞
Large, popular local on main road. Pub games ⊛⊜⊙

12–2.30; 5.30–10.30 (11 F, S)

Victoria
Southleigh Road, Clifton
Courage Best Bitter, Directors ⊞
Small lively corner pub next to Clifton open air swimming pool. Happy hour at eve opening time ⊜ (not Sun)
⊛⊙ (Clifton Down)

11–2.30; 6–10.30 (11 F, S)

Victoria
20 Chock Lane, Westbury-on-Trym ☎ (0272) 500257
Draught Bass; Wadworth Devizes Bitter, 6X, Farmers Glory, Old Timer (winter) ⊞
Tastefully refurbished pub with gas lighting and unusual garden. Pub games ⊛⊜&

11–2.30; 5.30–10.30 (11 F, S)

White Hart
St James Street (near bus station)
Courage Best Bitter, Directors ⊞
Ancient pub with narrow front bar and separate rear dining area. No meals Sun
⊜⊙&⇌ (Temple Meads)

Butcombe

10.30–2.30; 6–11
Mill Inn
☎ (0761) 62406
Courage Bitter Ale, Best Bitter ⊞
Stone-built, homely local in small village. Large selection of wildfowl outside
Q⊛⊜⊙&♣ (no tap water)

Churchill

11–2.30; 6–11
Crown
The Batch, Skinners Lane, (200 yds from A38) OS447598 ☎ (0934) 852995
Butcombe Bitter; Cotleigh Batch Bitter; Eldridge Pope Royal Oak; Felinfoel Double Dragon; Fuller London Pride; Palmer IPA ⊞
Friendly, well-run pub with best selection of real ale in area. Guest beers
▲Q⊛⊜⊙⊛

Compton Martin

11–2.30; 7–11
Ring O' Bells
On A369 ☎ (0761) 221284
Butcombe Bitter; Marston Pedigree ⊞; Wadworth 6X ⒼG
Cosy locals' bar, large lounge and family room. First class bar meals. Guest beers; pub games ▲⊛⊜⊙⊛

Try also: Bell Inn, Ubley

Dundry

10.30–2.30; 6.30–11
Carpenters Arms
Bristol Road OS565663 ☎ (0272) 640415
Courage Bitter Ale, Best Bitter, Directors ⊞
Stone-built pub with fine views. Friendly and cosy. Pub games ▲⊛⊜⊙

Try also: Dundry Inn

Frampton Cottrell

10.30–2.30; 7–10.30 (11 F, S)
Rising Sun
43 Ryecroft Road (off B4058/A432) ☎ (0454) 772330
Draught Bass; Brakspear Special; Hall & Woodhouse Tanglefoot; Marston Pedigree; Smiles Best Bitter; Wadworth 6X ⊞
Stone-built pub with single bar. A genuine free house. Guest beers. Pub games
▲⊛⊜⊙ (Fri–Sat) &

Hinton

10.30–2.30; 6.30–10.30 (11 F, S)
Bull
Off A46 (1 mile SW of M4 Jct 18) ☎ (027 582) 2332
Wadworth IPA, 6X ⊞
Country local with splendid garden for children. Darts
▲⊛⊜⊙⊛

Hinton Charterhouse

11–2.30; 6–10.30 (11 F, S)
Rose & Crown
On B3110 ☎ (022 122) 2153
Draught Bass; Courage Bitter Ale; Marston Pedigree; Wadworth 6X, Old Timer (winter) ⒼG
Comfortable lounge bar and separate restaurant. Skittles and darts ▲⊛⊜⊙&

Kenn

11–2; 6–11
Drum & Monkey
On B3133 ☎ (0272) 873433
Courage Best Bitter ⊞
Friendly, country 2-bar pub on outskirts of Clevedon. Pub games ⊜⊛⊜⊙ (if eating) ⊛
⊙ (ring) ⊛&♂

Littleton-on-Severn

11.30–2.30; 6–10.30 (11 F, S)
White Hart
☎ (0454) 412275
Hook Norton Bitter; Smiles

59

Avon

Brewery Bitter, Best Bitter, Exhibition H
Very popular 16th-century pub. Regular guest beers, Petanque

Marshfield

12–2.30; 7–10.30 (11 F, S)

Lord Nelson Inn
Hay Street (off A420)
☎ (0225) 891820
Butcombe Bitter; Courage Best Bitter; Marston Pedigree; Smiles Exhibition; Wadworth IPA, 6X H
Old coaching inn with former stables converted into a restaurant where you dine in genuine carriages or reproduction Victorian railway coaches!

Midford

10.30–2.30; 6.30–10.30 (11 F, S)

Hope & Anchor
On B3110 ☎ (0225) 832296
Draught Bass; Butcombe Bitter; Marston Burton Bitter, Pedigree, Owd Rodger; Wadworth 6X H
Nestling between the old Somerset & Dorset Railway line and the disused Somerset coal canal, a 300 year-old pub with restaurant and small family room
(Tue–Sat)

Midsomer Norton

10.30–2.30; 6–11

White Hart
The Island (off B3355)
☎ (0761) 412957
Draught Bass; Charrington IPA G
Deservedly popular, traditional town pub

Monkton Combe

12–2.30; 6–10.30 (11 F, S)

Wheelwrights Arms
½ mile W of A36 at Limpley Stoke viaduct ☎ (022 122) 2287
Adnams Bitter H; **Butcombe Bitter** G; **Wadworth 6X** H
Pleasant village local in picturesque valley. Good food. Darts

Oldbury-on-Severn

11.30–2.30; 6.30–10.30 (11 F, S)

Anchor Inn
Church Road ☎ (0454) 413331
Draught Bass G; **Butcombe Bitter; Marston Pedigree; Theakston Best Bitter** H, **Old Peculier** G
Old local with clean-cut interior; fine food. Near site of Roman fort. Pub games

Old Down

10.30–2.30; 6–10.30 (11 F, S)

Fox Inn
Inner Down off A38
☎ (0454) 412507
Draught Bass; Davenports Bitter; Flowers IPA H
Very popular village local with excellent garden

Paulton

11–2.30; 6–11

Red Lion
High Street (B3355)
☎ (0761) 412157
Halls Harvest Bitter; Ind Coope Burton Ale H
Lively and spacious open-plan bar. Darts

Pucklechurch

11–2.30; 6–10.30 (11 F, S)

Rose & Crown
Parkfield Road
☎ (027 582) 2351
Draught Bass; Wadworth IPA, 6X, Old Timer H
Popular 250 year-old pub, attractively modernised

Radstock

10.30–2.30; 6–11

Waldegrave Arms
Market Place (A367)
☎ (0761) 34359
Courage Best Bitter H
Spacious twin-bar hotel with mainly local, lively custom. Darts and skittles

Ridgehill

10.30–2.30; 6 (7 winter)–11

Crown
Regil Lane ☎ (027 587) 2388
Wadworth IPA, 6X H, **Old Timer** G
Cosy stone pub with dining room. Pub games

Tolldown

11–2.30; 6–10.30 (11 F, S)

Crown
On A46 (½ mile S of M4 Jct 18)
☎ (0225) 891231
Wadworth IPA, 6X, Old Timer (winter) H
16th-century Cotswold stone roadside inn. Darts

Weston-Super-Mare

10.30–2.30; 6–11

Britannia Inn
118 High Street
Courage Best Bitter, Directors H
Old town pub hidden away from street by partially-covered outdoor seating area

10.30–2.30; 6–11

Corner House
Regent Street (near seafront)
Flowers Original H
Comfortable 1-bar pub with modern stained glass windows. A good local, liked by tourists

11–2.30; 6–11

Heron
358–368 Locking Road (A370/A371) ☎ (0934) 22218
Courage Best Bitter H
Spacious roadhouse used as meeting-place for travellers. Pub games
(Milton)

10–2.30; 7–11

Regency
22–24 Lower Church Road
☎ (0934) 33406
Draught Bass; Butcombe Bitter; Wadworth 6X H
Comfortable town pub near college
(lunch) (not Sun)

Try also: Market House Inn

Willsbridge

10.30–2.30; 6–10.30 (11 F, S)

Queens Head
Bath Road (A431)
☎ (0272) 322233
Courage Bitter Ale, Best Bitter H
Small, quiet 16th-century pub near Willsbridge Mill Wildlife Trust and Bitton Steam Preservation Railway. Pub games

Winscombe

10.30–2.30; 6–11

Woodborough
☎ (093 484) 2167
Courage Best Bitter H
Brewers' mock-Tudor pub catering for locals and travellers. Music Thu & Fri. Pub games (lunch, summer)

Worle

11–2.30; 6–11

Nut Tree
Ebdon Road (off B3146)
☎ (0934) 510900
Wadworth 6X; Younger Scotch, IPA H
Cotswold stone ex-farmhouse; a comfortable pub with friendly atmosphere

Yate

11.45–2.30; 6–10.30 (11 F, S)

Cross Keys
North Road (300 yards from A482) ☎ (045 422) 314
Courage Bitter Ale, Best Bitter, Directors H
Picturesque 17th-century pub with stone-floored bar and comfortable lounge. Popular lunchtimes

Bedfordshire

Bedfordshire

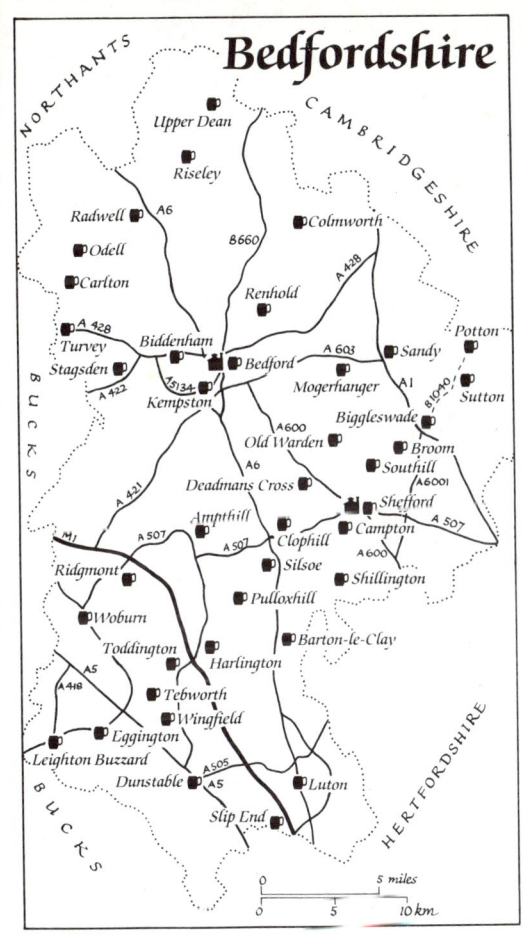

Banks & Taylor, Shefford;
Wells, Bedford

Ampthill

11–2.30; 6–11

Old Sun
87 Dunstable Street (A5120)
☎ (0525) 403101
Flowers Original; Wethered Bitter H
2 small busy bars and separate games room. Prize-winning garden Guest beers
(Mon–Fri)

Barton-le-Clay

10.30–2.30; 6–11

Speed the Plough
Bedford Road (A6 ¼ mile N of village) ☎ (0525) 60205
Tolly Cobbold Bitter, Original H
Large country pub with open-plan bars. Warm friendly atmosphere – log fires and good value home-made lunches

Bedford

11–2.30; 5.30–11

Fleur de Lis
12 Mill Street (off High Street)
☎ (0234) 211004
Wells Eagle Bitter H
Well-run town pub with excellent mix of customers. Good value lunches
(not Sun)

Try also: **Clarence** (Benskins)

Biddenham

11.30–2.30; 6–11

Three Tuns
Main Road (off A428)
☎ (0234) 54847
Greene King IPA, Abbot H
Delightful village inn with excellent range of food (not Sun). Children permitted in dining area

Biggleswade

10.30–2.30; 5.30–11

Crown
34 High Street ☎ (0767) 312228
Greene King IPA, Abbot H
Comfortable old coaching inn backing on to brewery

Broom

10.30–2.30; 6–11

Cock
High Street ☎ (0767) 314411
Greene King IPA, Abbot G
Multi-roomed village local with beer served direct from cellar. Home-cooked cold meats and specialist cheese menu. Separate skittles room

Campton

11.30–2.30; 7–11

White Hart
Mill Lane (off A507)
☎ (0462) 812657
Wells Eagle Bitter H
Fine village pub, lots of games in the bar. Petanque played

Carlton

10.30–2.30; 6–11

Fox
High Street ☎ (0234) 720235
Wells Eagle Bitter H
18th-century, friendly thatched village inn with excellent restaurant. Near a country wildlife park

Clophill

11–2.30; 6–11

Stone Jug
Back Street (2nd right N of A6/A507 roundabout)
☎ (0525) 60526
Banks & Taylor Shefford Bitter; Bateman XB; Courage Directors; John Smith Bitter H
Popular, welcoming free house on edge of village. Sensible prices. Pub games. Guest beers. Children in dining room on request

Try also: **Green Man** (Greene King)

Colmworth

11–2.30; 6–11

Wheatsheaf
Wilden Road (off B660)
☎ (023062) 370
Adnams Bitter; Draught Bass; Everards Old Original; Marston Pedigree H
17th-century country pub

61

Bedfordshire

south of village. Separate restaurant 🏠🍴🍺🍷🚭

Deadmans Cross

11–2.30; 6–11
White Horse
on A600 ☎ (023066) 634
Banks & Taylor Shefford Bitter, SOD, SOS H
Friendly roadside pub with excellent food and book-lined bar 🏠 (eating area)
🍴🍺 (Tue – Sat)

Dunstable

11–3 (10.30–2.30 Sat); 6–11
Bull
115 High Street, North (A5) ☎ (0582) 63443
Courage Best Bitter, Directors H
Enterprising town pub with humorous atmosphere. Pub games 🍴🍺 (Mon–Fri) ♿

11–3 (10.30–2.30 Sat); 5.30–11
Plume of Feathers
6 West Street (near A5 crossroads) ☎ (0582) 61035
Benskins Best Bitter H
Friendly town centre pub with a Celtic atmosphere 🍴🚭

Try also: Highwayman (Wells); Nags Head (Benskins)

Eggington

10.30–2.30; 6–11
Horseshoes
off A4012 ☎ (0525) 210282
Benskins Best Bitter H
Picturesque village local. Delightful wood panelled saloon bar with brass and transport models. Upstairs snug with organ 🏠 (public bar) Q🐕 (ask landlord) 🍴🍺 (not Sun) 🚭

Harlington

11–3 (11–2.30 Sat); 6–11
Old Sun
Sundon Road ☎ (05255) 2417
Flowers IPA, Original H
Pub has split-level interior and small neat garden. Popular with young people; atmosphere is boisterous but friendly. Separate pool room. Guest beers
🐕🍴🍺 (not Sun) ♿🚊

Kempston Green End

10.30–2.30; 5.30–11
Shoulder of Mutton
Green End Road (400 yds W of A5134 at cemetery)
☎ (0234) 853025
Greene King IPA H**, Abbot** G
Honest, no-frills country local. Traditional pub games 🏠Q

Leighton Buzzard

11–2.30; 6–11
Star
230 Heath Road (A418)
☎ (0525) 377294
ABC Best Bitter; Draught Bass; Everards Tiger H
Smart out-of-town 1-bar pub, catering mainly for business lunches and regulars in the evening. Food available at all times except Sun. No fruit machines. Traditional and friendly Q🍴🍺♿

10.30–2.30; 6–11
Sun Inn
42 Lake Street (A4146)
☎ (0525) 379988
Courage Best Bitter, Directors H
Smart pub, close to town centre. One large bar. Office workers at lunchtimes; crowded in evenings. Food recommended 🍴🍺♿

Luton

10.30–2.30; 5.30–11
Gardeners Call
151 High Town Road
☎ (0582) 29037
Greene King KK, IPA, Abbot H
Good locals' pub with pub games. Comfortable lounge and plain public bar
🍴🍺 (Mon–Fri) 🚭🚊 (½ mile)

11–2.30; 5.30 (7 Sat)–11
Two Brewers
43 Dumfries Street (off A6)
☎ (0582) 23777
Banks & Taylor Shefford Bitter, SOD, SOS H
Lively locals' pub, just off town centre. Pub games
🏠🍴🍺 (not Sun) ♿

Moggerhanger

11–2.30; 6–11
Guinea
Bedford Road (A603)
☎ (0767) 40388
Wells Eagle Bitter H**, Bombardier** G
Large comfortable main road pub. Bombardier drawn from cellar 🏠🍴🍺 (not Mon) 🚭

Odell

10.30–2.30; 5.30–11
Mad Dog
Little Odell ☎ (0234) 720221
Greene King IPA, Abbot H
Thatched pub to west of village. Home-cooked food; children's roundabout in garden 🏠🐕🍴🍺

Try also: Bell (Greene King)

Old Warden

11–2.30; 6–11
Hare & Hounds
High Street ☎ (076727) 225
Everards Old Original; Wells Eagle Bitter, Bombardier H
Welcoming 2-bar country pub in picturesque village near Shuttleworth Aircraft Collection and Swiss Garden. Children welcome in restaurant 🏠🐕🍴🍺🚭

Potton

12–2.30; 7–11
Rising Sun
11 Everton Road
☎ (0767) 26023
Adnams Bitter; Courage Best Bitter, Directors H
Busy yet comfortable oak-beamed pub with good food. Games available 🐕🍴🍺

Pulloxhill

10.30–2.30; 6–11
Cross Keys
High Street ☎ (0525) 712442
Wells Eagle Bitter, Bombardier H
15th-century pub and restaurant – popular for good value food. Ballooning and archery. Jazz Sun eves
🏠Q🐕🍴🍺♿⚓

Radwell

11–2.30; 6.30–11
Swan
Felmersham Road (1 mile off A6 at Milton Ernest)
☎ (0234) 781351
Wells Eagle Bitter H
17th-century thatched country pub with restaurant and quiet bar. No food Sun 🏠Q🍴🍺

Renhold

10.30–2.30; 6–11
Three Horseshoes
42 Top End (1 mile N of A428)
☎ (0234) 870218
Greene King XX, IPA, Abbot H
Friendly village inn with good value food – fresh steaks and home-made soup 🏠🍴🍺 (Mon–Fri) 🍺 (Wed–Sat) 🚭

Ridgmont

10–2.30; 6–11
Rose & Crown
89 High Street (A418)
☎ (052528) 245
Wells Eagle Bitter, Bombardier H
Popular, friendly pub and restaurant with separate games room and large grounds. Barbecues in summer. 🏠🐕🍴🏨🍺♿⚓

Riseley

11–2.30; 5.30–11
Fox & Hounds
High Street ☎ (0234) 708240
Wells Eagle Bitter, Bombardier H

62

Bedfordshire

Imposing 16th-century oak-beamed village pub with home-made food. Restaurant/family room and forge grill Q ❧ ⊛ ◐ ▮

Sandy

11–2.30; 5.30–11

Bell
Station Road (off B1042)
☎ (0767) 82067
Greene King IPA, Abbot ⊞
Friendly 1-bar local opposite station. Handy for RSPB HQ at Sandy Warren. No meals Sun ▲⊛ ◐ ▮ ≠

Shillington

10.30–2.30; 6–11

Crown
High Road ☎ (0462) 711667
Flowers IPA, Original; Wethered Bitter, Winter Royal ⊞
Welcoming pub with fine old fireplace in public bar and large garden. Guest beers. No food Sun ▲⊛ ◐ ▮ ⊕

10.30–2.30; 6–11

Musgrave Arms
Apsley End Road
☎ (0462) 711286
Greene King IPA, Abbot ⓖ
2 tiny bars, each with huge fireplace. Lounge has low beams, public has clay tile floor and scrubbed wood tables. Clatter of dominoes is deafening.
▲ Q ❧ ◐ (not Sun) ▮ ⊕

Silsoe

11–2.30; 6–11

Star & Garter
16 High Street (off A6)
☎ (0525) 60250
Flowers IPA, Original ⊞
Friendly village local with lively bar and smart lounge. Pub games ▲⊛ ◐ ▮ ⊕ ▲

Slip End

11–3 (10.30–2.30 Sat); 6–11

Rising Sun
1 Front Street ☎ (0582) 21766
Courage Best Bitter, Directors ⊞
Friendly village pub with busy games-oriented bar and quieter lounge, apart from weekends when live music is featured ⊛ ◐ (not Sun) ⊕ ▲

Southill

11–2.30; 6–11

White Horse
High Road (1 mile W of B658)
☎ (0462) 813364
Flowers IPA; Wethered Bitter ⊞
Large comfortable country inn with restaurant. Miniature steam railway in garden.

Supper licence and live jazz weekly in stables. Near cricket ground ▲ ❧ ⊛ ◐ ▮ ▲

Stagsden

11–2.30; 6 (7 winter)–11

Royal George
High Street (A422)
☎ (02302) 2801
Wells Eagle Bitter ⊞
Friendly pub with huge garden which has animals and children's amusements. Bird gardens nearby. Ale brought to lounge from public bar ▲ ❧ ⊛ ◐ ▮ (Thu/Fri) ⊕ ▲

Sutton

11–2.30; 7–11

John O'Gaunt
High Street ☎ (0767) 260377
Greene King IPA ⊞
Delightful old village pub near John o'Gaunt Golf Club. Pub games ⊛ ◐ ▮

Tebworth

11–3 (10.30–2.30 Sat); 6–11

Queens Head
The Lane ☎ (05255) 4101
Wells Eagle Bitter ⊞, **Bombardier** ⓖ
Popular pub with 2 small bars. Very friendly, hospitable and entertaining. Hosts many friendly darts and dominoes matches. Weekly sing-songs ▲⊛ ◐ (Mon–Sat) ⊕

Toddington

11–3 (10.30–2.30 Sat); 5.30–11

Bedford Arms
64 High Street (A5120)
☎ (0525) 2401
Wells Eagle Bitter ⊞
Attractive both outside and in with magnificent garden at the back; barbecues in summer. 2 warm, comfortable bars ▲⊛

11–3 (10.30–2.30 Sat); 5.30–11

Sow & Pigs
19 Church Square (A5120)
☎ (05255) 3089
Greene King XX, IPA, Abbot ⊞
Unique institution, rich in atmosphere. Attracts colourful characters. Piano, harmonium; separate pool room ▲ Q ⊛ ◐ ▮

Try also: Nags Head (Wells), Oddfellows Arms (Watneys)

Turvey

11–2.30; 6–11

Three Cranes
High Street (off A428)
☎ (023064) 305
Bateman Mild, XXXB, Flowers Original; Hook Norton Best Bitter; Wethered Bitter ⊞
17th-century coaching inn with excellent range of food

and vegetarian dishes both in pub and separate restaurant ▲ ❧ ⊛ ◐ ▮ ▲

11–2.30; 5.30–11

Three Fyshes
Bridge Street (A428)
☎ (023064) 264
Banks & Taylor Shefford Bitter; Draught Bass; Marston Pedigree; Owd Rodger; Two Henry's Bitter ⊞
17th-century riverside inn with good range of food and own mini-brewery. Skittles in public bar and children's room. Guest beers
▲ Q (lounge) ❧ ⊛ ◐ ▮ ⊕ ▲

Upper Dean

12–2.30; 7–11

Prince of Wales
High Street (1½ miles off A45)
☎ (0234) 708551
Greene King IPA; Marston Pedigree ⊞
Bustling village free house and restaurant with a warm welcome. Skittles and darts ▲ ❧ (restaurant) ⊛ ◐ ▮ (not Wed)

Wingfield

11–3 (10.30–2.30 Sat); 6–11

Plough
Tebworth Road (off A5120)
☎ (05255) 3077
Flowers Original; Wethered Bitter ⊞
Thatched pub with a cheerful atmosphere. Genuine farmhouse cooking. Bar billiards, tropical fish, electric organ. Live jazz Wed ▲ ❧ (if eating) ⊛ ◐ ▮ ▲

Woburn

10.30–2.30; 6–11

Black Horse
Market Place (A418)
☎ (0525) 290210
Banks & Taylor Shefford Bitter; Marston Burton Bitter, Pedigree; Tetley Bitter ⊞
Small free house with separate restaurant. 'Upwardly mobile' clientele, but food and drink excellent value for money Q ❧ (restaurant) ⊛ ◐ ▮ ▲ (Woburn Pk)

10.30–2.30; 6–11

Magpie
18 Bedford Street (A418)
☎ (0525) 290219
Ruddles Best Bitter, County; Webster Yorkshire Bitter ⊞
Splendid coaching inn at the centre of an attractive village. Intimate saloon bar adjoins restaurant. Large public bar. Handy for Woburn Safari Park. Skittles and dominoes Q ❧ (restaurant) ⊛ ⋈ ◐ ▮ (not Sun) ⊕ ▲

63

Berkshire

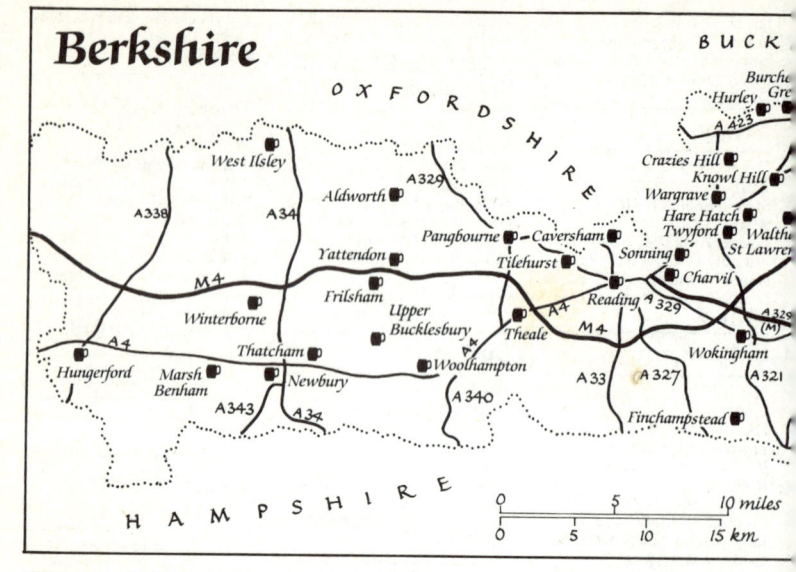

Aldworth

11–2.30; 6–11 (closed Mon)
Bell Inn
OS557797 ☎ (0635) 578272
Arkells BBB; Kingsdown Ale; Hall & Woodhouse Badger Best Bitter; Morland Mild H
Dates from 1340 in parts. Old fashioned hatch bar with wonderful tap room including one-handed clock. Close to the Ridgeway, popular with walkers ♨Q☻❀⊞&

Bracknell

11–3; 5.30–11
Market Inn
Station Road ☎ (0344) 51734
Tetley Bitter; Friary Meux Bitter; Ind Coope Burton Ale H
Friendly town centre pub with live music Fri nights. No meals Sun. Darts, cribbage and pool
☻❀◐⊞ (not Sun) ⇌

Burchetts Green

10–2.30; 5.30–11
Red Lion
Applehouse Hill, Hurley (A423) ☎ (062 882) 4433
Brakspear Bitter, Special, Old H
Excellent country pub. Has been selling Brakspears beers for 200 years ♨Q❀◐

Caversham

10.30–2.30; 5.30–11
Prince of Wales
Prospect Street (A4155/B481 Jct) ☎ (0734) 472267
Brakspear Mild, Bitter, Special, Old H
Good honest local with pool area, dining room and open-plan bar. Extensive menu; food always available ❀◐

Charvil

10–2.30; 6–11
Lands End
Park Lane (1 mile S A3032)
OS781748 ☎ (0734) 340700
Brakspear Bitter, Special, Old H
Popular, friendly local approached by narrow lanes. A good sized play area and small family room
☻❀◐ (not Sun) ⊞

Colnbrook

10.30–2.30; 5.30–11
Red Lion
High Street ☎ (0753) 682685
Courage Best Bitter H
Delightful pub looking more like an antique shop inside. Artefacts of all descriptions adorn the walls
♨❀◐ (Mon–Fri)

Crazies Hill

11–2.30; 6–11
Horns
off A4/A423 nr Warren Row
OS799809 ☎ (073 522) 3226
Brakspear Bitter, Special (summer) Old (winter) H
Picturesque country pub with very unusual menu
♨Q☻❀◐ (Tue-Sat) ⚠

Try also: Old Hatch Gate

Datchet

10.30–2.30; 5.30–11
Royal Stag
Friary Meux Best; Ind Coope Burton Ale; Tetley Bitter H
Classic oak-beamed hostelry on village green. Full of character; superb ale. Pub games ♨Q❀◐⊞&⇌

Fifield

10.30–2.30; 5.30–11
Rising Sun
Forest Green Road (B3024)
☎ (0628) 23639
Morland Mild, Bitter, Best Bitter H
Converted from 2 gamekeepers cottages. Small friendly lounge bar. Children's games in the garden ♨Q❀◐ (Mon–Fri) ⊞&

10.30–2.30; 5.30–11
White Hart
Fifield Road (off B3024)
☎ (0628) 26512
Morland Mild, Bitter, Best Bitter H
Comfortable country pub. Paintings for sale displayed. Children's swings in the garden ♨Q❀◐ (not Sun) ⊞ (games bar) &

Finchampstead

11–3; 6–11
Queens Oak
Church Lane (off B3016)
Brakspear Bitter, Special, Old H
Lovely village pub on the Devil's Highway, an old Roman road, and next to the church in a picturesque village. Large lounge, cosy non-smoking snug. Play area for children in garden
♨Q❀◐ (not winter Sun) ◐ (not Sun) ⚠

64

Berkshire

16th-century pub with stable and paddock still in use – paddock for visitors!
🏠Q✿◐▶ (till 10) ♿🅰

10.30–2.30; 6–11
Dew Drop
Batts Green (off A404)
OS822814 ☎ (062 882) 4327
Brakspear Bitter, Old H
A beer house until 1950s, this 300 year-old pub is situated on a drovers track through the former forest. Not too easy to find, but well worth the effort. Darts 🏠Q✿◐▶ (Tue–Sat) ♿

Knowl Hill

11–2.30; 5.30–11
Seven Stars
Bath Road ☎ (062 882) 2967
Brakspear Mild, Bitter, Special, Old H
Smart 16th-century coaching in with a skittle alley and a warm welcome. Games include Petanque
🏠Q✿❀◐▶◉♿

Langley

10.30–2.30; 5.30–11
Harrow
290 High Street ☎ (0753) 43700
Courage Best Bitter
1642 building, the public bar traditional and basic; the saloon snug and cosy. Each bar is like a different pub. Games ✿◐ (Mon–Fri) ◉♿

Maidenhead

11–2.30; 5.30–11
Hand & Flowers
15 Queen Street
☎ (0628) 23800
Brakspear Mild, Bitter, Special, Old H
Victorian-style pub with brightly painted exterior. Single bar has some wood panelling and stained glass. Pub games ◐ (not Sun)

10.30–2.30; 5.30–11
North Star
North Town Road
☎ (0628) 33511
Wethered Bitter, SPA H
Friendly suburban local pub. Inn sign shows the first GWR locomotive to reach the town. Cyril plays accordion music Fri eves. Pub games
◉♿🚆 (Furze Platt)

10.30–2.30; 5.30–11
Vine
20 Market Street
Brakspear Mild, Bitter, Special, Old (winter) H
Lively town-centre pub. Games include darts, dominoes and cribbage
✿ (forecourt) ◐▶♿

Try also: Jack of Both Sides

Marsh Benham

10.30–2.30; 5.30–11
Red House
½ mile S of A4 ☎ (0635) 41637
Adnams Bitter; Brakspear Bitter, Special; Ringwood Fortyniner H
Smart comfortable country pub with award-winning food. The garden has a summer house and miniature railway – runs every Sunday in summer 🏠Q✿◐▶

Newbury

10.30–2.30; 5.30–11
Blue Ball
2 Greenham Road (just off A34) ☎ (0635) 43564
Halls Harvest Bitter; Ind Coope Burton Ale H
2-bar pub close to racecourse. Quiet saloon with conservatory, livelier public with darts. Pub games
✿◐◉🚆

10.30–2.30 (4 Thu); 5.30 (7 Thu & Sat)–11
Catherine Wheel
Cheap Street (just off Market Place) ☎ (0635) 47471
Courage Best Bitter, Directors H
Popular 1-bar pub with friendly welcome. Unusual castle style frontage. Only real ale pub with market day extension ✿◐♿🚆

Old Windsor

10.30–2.30; 5.30–11
Oxford Blue
Crimp Hill (off A308)
☎ (0735) 861954
Friary Meux Bitter; Tetley Bitter; Ind Coope Burton Ale H
Pub on hillside with verandah and much airline memorabilia. The building is over 300 years old and the name relates to the military. Pub games ❀✿◉◐▶ (not Sun/Tue)♿🅰

Pangbourne

10.30–2.30; 6–11
Cross Keys
Church Road (A340) OS634765
☎ (073 57) 3268
Courage Best Bitter, Directors H
400 year-old inn beside River Pang, with patio view of Chubb. Aviary. Barbecue in summer. Patio can be covered in case of rain. Pub games
🏠Q (lounge) ❀✿◐▶◉🚆

10–2.30; 6–11
Star
Reading Road (A329)
OS637765
Courage Best Bitter, Directors H

Frilsham

12–2.30; 6–11 (11.30 Sat)
Pot Kiln
on Yattendon–Bucklebury road OS553732
☎ (0635) 201366
Arkells Best; Morland Bitter, Best Bitter H
Remote country pub with excellent views – well worth the trouble to find. Folk music Sun eve. No food Sun. Darts; guest beers
🏠Q❀✿◐▶ (not Mon) ◉

Hare Hatch

12–3; 5.30–11
Queen Victoria
Blakes Lane (just off A4)
OS809783 ☎ (073 522) 2477
Brakspear Mild, Bitter, Special, Old H
Convivial low-ceilinged 17th-century country pub – saved some time ago from closing by local CAMRA action. Darts
🏠❀ (if eating) ✿◐▶

Hungerford

11–2.30; 5.30–11
Sun Inn
36 Charnham Street (A4)
☎ (0488) 82162
Morland Mild, Bitter, Best Bitter H
Friendly main road local. Games include pool and unusual solitaire table 🏠✿◉

Hurley

11–2.30; 6–11
Black Boy
on A423 (Henley–Hurley Road) ☎ (062 882) 4212
Brakspear Bitter, Old H

65

Berkshire

Compact village local. Originally 3 cottages – one was a ginger beer factory until 1890. Darts ▲☎✉◐▯⇌

Reading

11–2.30; 5.30 (6 Sat)–11

Butler
85 Chatham Street (off ring road) ☎ (0734) 576289
Fuller Chiswick Bitter, London Pride, ESB H
Former wine merchant and Guinness bottler – now a congenial and popular hostelry. No food Sun. Darts ▲Q☎◐⇌

10.30–2.30; 5.30–11

Eldon Arms
Eldon Terrace
Wadworth IPA, 6X, Farmers Glory, Old Timer H
All a good boozer should be but parking difficult. Pub games ◐▯

10.30–2.30; 5.30–11

Greyhound
4 Mount Pleasant (A33) ☎ (0734) 863023
Courage Best Bitter, Directors H
Comfortable 2-bar pub in old-world style. Live jazz 1st Tue in month ☎◐▶ (pizzas) ▯⇃

10.30–2.30; 5.30–11

Railway Tavern
31 Greyfriars Road ☎ (0734) 590376
Arkells Best Bitter; Ind Coope Burton Ale H
Popular business venue with railway theme. Handy for both bus and train stations. Pub games ◐▶ (till 9) ⇃⇌

11–2.30; 5.30 (6 Sat)–11

Retreat
8 St Johns Street (off Queens Road)
Flowers Original; Wethered Bitter, SPA, Winter Royal H
Excellent back-street local with bar billiards table ◐▯

10.30–2.30; 5.30 (7 Sat)–10.30 (11 F,S)

Sun
Castle Street (near Civic Centre) ☎ (0734) 575106
Courage Best Bitter, Directors; John Smith Bitter H
Historic town pub with split-level drinking areas and collection of hanging jugs and pots. Busy and efficient. Pub games on request ☎◐ (Mon–Sat)

Try also: Horn Castle Street (Courage)

Slough

10.30–2.30; 5.30–11

Alpha Arms
Alpha Street (off High Street) ☎ (0753) 22727
Courage Best Bitter, Directors H

Intimate friendly village pub in a town centre. Recent CAMRA local pub of the year. Street parking difficult. Darts Q☎◐ (Mon–Fri) ⇌

10.30–2.30; 5.30–11

Red Cow
140 Albert Street (A412) ☎ (0753) 22614
Courage Best Bitter, Directors H
16th-century building first licensed in 1730. Was once owned by William Herschel the Astronomer Royal. No food Sun. Darts ☎◐▶ (not Sat) ▯⇃

Sonning

11–3; 6–11

White Hart Hotel
Thames Street ☎ (0734) 692277
Brakspear Bitter H
Very attractive refurbished 15th-century hotel with fine gardens running down to river Q☎✉◐▶ ▯⇃

Sunninghill

11–2.30; 6–11

Carpenters Arms
78 Upper Village Road (off B3020)
Flowers Original; Wethered Bitter, SPA, Winter Royal H
Large pub with very friendly welcome. A number of seating areas create a small pub atmosphere ☎◐▶ ▯⇃

11–2.30; 5.30 (6 Sat)–11

Three Jays
Sunninghill Road (B3020) ☎ (0990) 21359
Courage Best Bitter, Directors H
Pleasant, friendly pub with smashing small public bar. Selection of table top games ▲☎◐▶ (not Sun) ▯⇃

Thatcham

10.30–2.30; 5.30–11

White Hart
2 High Street ☎ (0635) 63251
Courage Best Bitter, Directors; John Smith Bitter H
Elegant but welcoming 1-bar pub – landlady also runs the Kings Head 50 yards away ✉ (dining area) ◐▶ ⇃

Try also: Kings Head (Courage)

Theale

10–2.30; 6–11

Lamb Inn
High Street (old A4)
Courage Best Bitter, Directors H
Friendly village local ▲✉☎◐▯⇌

Tilehurst

11–2.30; 5.30–11

Bear
Park Lane ☎ (0734) 427328
Courage Best Bitter, Directors; John Smith Bitter H
Large estate pub/roadhouse near water tower, which can be seen for miles as you travel east on M4 ✉☎◐▯⇃

11–2.30; 5.30–11

Royal Oak
69 Westwood Glen (off Overdown Road) ☎ (0734) 417300
Ind Coope Burton Ale; Halls Harvest Bitter; Wadworth 6X H
Worth the climb up a steep driveway to escape the rapidly worsening suburban sprawl. Dominoes and cribbage Q✉☎◐ (not Sun) ▯⇃

Twyford

11–3; 5.30 (7 Sat)–11

Duke of Wellington
High Street (A3032) ☎ (0734) 340456
Brakspear Mild, Bitter, Special H
Pleasantly welcoming village-centre local. Popular public bar and small comfortable lounge ☎◐ (Mon–Fri) ▯⇃

Try also: Golden Cross

Upper Bucklebury

10.30–2.30; 6–11

Three Crowns
26 Broad Lane ☎ (0635) 62153
Courage Best Bitter, Directors H
Well-kept pub. Garden has children's playground and pets corner. Bar billiards in public bar ▲☎✉◐▶ ▯

Waltham St Lawrence

11–3; 6–11

Plough
West End (near B3024)
OS824757 ☎ (0734) 340015
Morland Bitter, Best Bitter G
Wonderful low-ceilinged 16th-century thatched country pub ▲Q✉☎▶ (Tue–Sat)

Wargrave

11–3; 6–11

Bull
High Street ☎ (073 522) 3120
Brakspear Bitter, Special H
17th-century village pub with timbered bars and huge open fire. Extensive menu ▲Q☎✉◐▶ (not Sun) ⇃⇌

11–3; 5.30–11

Greyhound
High Street ☎ (073 522) 2556
Courage Best Bitter, Directors H
Cheerful pub, busy public bar and cosy lounge. Darts, dominoes and cribbage.

Berkshire

Family room
♨☺☻◐◑ (not Sun) ⚇⚉

Try also: White Hart

West Ilsley

10.30–2.30; 6–11

Harrow
1 mile W of A34
☎ (063 528) 260
Morland Bitter, Best Bitter H
2-bar pub, well known for its great food. Popular at all times but especially on summer eves, with cricket on the green opposite. Children's play area separate from garden. Pub games ♨☺☻◐◑⚇⚉

Try also: Crown & Horns
East Ilsley (Free)

White Waltham

10.30–2.30; 5.30–11

Beehive
☎ (062 882) 2877
Wethered Bitter, SPA, Winter Royal H
Pleasant village pub opposite cricket pitch. Pub games
♨Q☺☻◐◑⚇⚉

Windsor

10.30–2.30; 5.30–11

Carpenters Arms
Market Street
Draught Bass; Charrington IPA H
Pleasant pub in side street opposite the castle. Everyone made welcome. Pub games
♨◐◑⚇⚉

10.30–2.30; 5.30–11

Horse & Groom
4 Castle Hill
Courage Best Bitter, Directors H
Delightful and welcoming pub, very popular. The absence of music is pure heaven for the local characters
Q◐◑⚇⚉

Prince Christian
11 Kings Road
Brakspear Bitter, King & Barnes Best Bitter; Fuller London Pride H
Superb pub with friendly atmosphere serving good quality ales in pleasant surroundings ☻◐⚇

Winterborne

11–2.30; 6–11

New Inn
☎ (0635) 248200
Eldridge Pope Royal Oak; Flowers Original; Whitbread Castle Eden Ale H
Friendly village pub. Beer range is liable to change
♨☻◐

Wokingham

11–3; 5.30–11

Crooked Billet
Honey Hill (off B3430 2 miles out of town) OS826667
Brakspear Mild, Bitter, Special, Old H
Excellent Victorian country

---

pub with a warm welcome. Small restaurant ♨☻☺◐

11–3; 5.30–11

Queens Head
23 The Terrace
☎ (0734) 781221
Morland Mild, Bitter, Best Bitter H
Unspoilt town pub with real oak beams. Deservedly popular. Darts, Aunt Sally and cribbage
Q☻◐ (not Sun) ◐ (till 9.30)

Woolhampton

11–2.30; 6–11

Angel
Bath Road (A4)
☎ (0734) 713307
Flowers Original; Wethered Bitter, SPA, Winter Royal; Whitbread Castle Eden Ale H
Smart old coaching inn with restaurant and skittle alley
♨☻⚇◐ (not Mon) ⚉
⚉ (Midgham)

Yattendon

11–2.30; 6–11

Royal Oak Hotel
☎ (0635) 201325
Adnams Best Bitter; Draught Bass; Wadworth 6X H
Picturesque high-class hotel in splendid village setting with excellent cuisine and friendly atmosphere. Booking advised for meals
♨Q☺☻◐◑ (not Sun) ⚉

Try also: Nut & Bolt

ON DRINKING . . .
an alternative guide

Straight Glass aka a "sleeve". The sign of real manhood, matched for public bar cred only by an insistence on having every pint from the same dirty glass

Mug aka a "handle/jug/pot" etc etc. A sign of a decadent Southern-based youth. Real beer drinkers forced to drink from same should *not* use the handle for lifting, but rather flaunt it as a knuckle guard

Lady's glass usually an unmarked 12 ounce stunted goblet of a type so useless you can't even get them free with petrol tokens

Lager-Pleezmay(t) mating call of a generation raised on spam and cheeseburgers

Clean Tasting hopless and malt free

Cool served well below room temperature to make the lager in question taste "cool" if not "of something"

Discerning Lager Drinker drinks Carlsberg Special and Barbican mixed, to get drunk while staying below the limit

Refreshing high in water content

Skol Scandinavian drinking toast. Also a Wrexham-brewed lager that tastes like drinking toast

Buckinghamshire

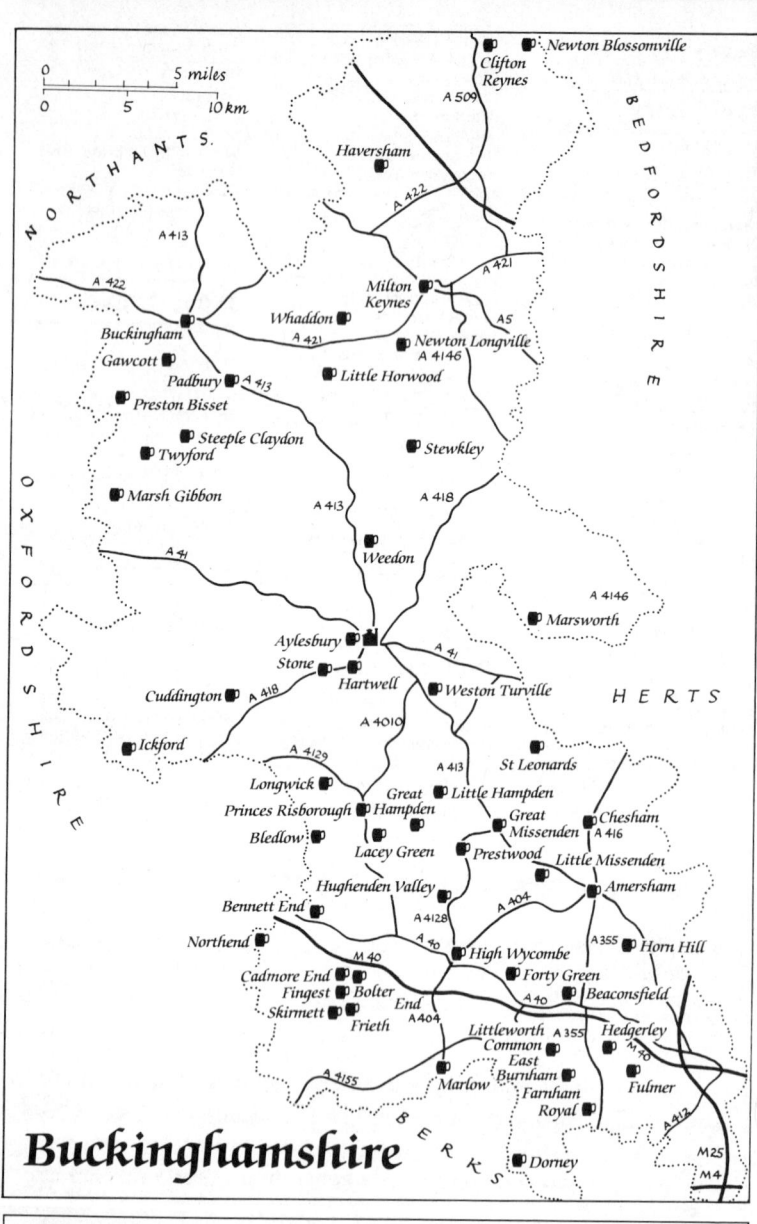

Chiltern, Aylesbury

Amersham

11–2.30; 6–11
Kings Arms
High Street (A413)
☎ (024 03) 6663
Benskins Best Bitter; Ind Coope Bitter H**, Burton Ale** G
Much photographed 15th-century coaching inn. Children's climbing frame in garden. Restaurant closed all day Mon and Sun eve
⌂ Q ✱ (▶ (not Sun) &

11–2.30; 6–11
Queens Head
Whielden Gate (A404)
OS941957 ☎ (024 03) 5240
Benskins Best Bitter; Ind Coope Burton Ale H
Well-run country pub situated below the current road level. Meals always available
⌂ ✤ ✱ (▶ &

Aylesbury

10.30–2.30; 5.30 (6 Sat)–11
White Swan
Walton Street ☎ (0296) 23933
ABC Best Bitter; Draught Bass; Chiltern Beechwood Bitter; Ind Coope Burton Ale H

Buckinghamshire

Excellent town-centre pub with fine good value food. Stable bar to rear reached via award-winning courtyard garden ⛺ 🍴 🍺 (not Sat) &

Try also: Ship (Benskins)

Beaconsfield

10.30–2.30; 5.30–11

Old Hare
41 Aylesbury End (A40)
☎ (049 46) 3380
Benskins Best Bitter; Ind Coope Burton Ale
Highly recommended cosy pub with low beams, stained glass windows and striking exterior. Guest beers
Q 🍴 🍺 (not Sun)

Try also: Prince of Wales (Free)

Bennett End

12–2.30; 7–11

Three Horseshoes
Horseshoe Road (off A40)
OS783973 ☎ (024 026) 3273
Brakspear Bitter; Flowers Original; Wethered SPA
Unspoilt 18th-century inn tucked away in attractive Chiltern Valley
Q ⛺ 🍴 🍺

Bledlow

11–2.30; 6–11

Lions of Bledlow
Church End ☎ (084 44) 3345
Courage Directors; Wadworth 6X; Wethered Bitter; Young Bitter
Rambling old country inn on edge of Chilterns, with pews, oak beams and ghost!
Q ⛺ 🍴 🍺 (not Sun) &

Bolter End

11–2.30; 6–11

Peacock
On B482 ☎ (0494) 881417
ABC Best Bitter; Draught Bass
Popular country pub with good value food
Q 🍴 🍺 (not Sun) &

Buckingham

10.30–2.30; 6–11

Grand Junction
13 High Street ☎ (0280) 813260
ABC Best Bitter; Draught Bass; Everard Tiger
Excellent pub with varied drinking areas, cheerful welcome and large garden. Landlord is town crier
⛺ 🍴 🍺

Try also: Whale (Allied)

10–2.30; 6–11 (all day Tue)

New Inn
18 Bridge Street
☎ (0280) 816219
ABC Best Bitter; Draught

Bass; Chiltern Beechwood Best; Everard Tiger
Sri Lankan curries, belly dancing and pram races in this open-plan pub! ⛺ 🍴 🍺 &

Try also: White Hart (Free)

Cadmore End

10.30–2.30; 6–11

Old Ship
On B482 ☎ (0494) 881404
Brakspear Bitter, Special Bitter, Old
Tiny, totally unspoilt traditional country pub; all beer carried up from cellar. In the same family since 1919
Q 🍴

Chesham

11–2.30; 5.30–11

Queens Head
Church Street (B485)
☎ (0494) 783769
Brakspear Mild, Bitter, Special Bitter
Excellent pub in old part of the town; deservedly popular
Q 🍴 (not Sun)

Clifton Reynes

11–2.30; 5.30–11

Robin Hood
Greene King IPA, Abbot
Hugely improved village pub with 2 cosy bars and extensive garden. Cheese skittles in bar
⛺ 🍴

Cuddington

10.30–2.30; 5.30 6 Sat)–11

Crown
Aylesbury Road
☎ (0844) 292222
ABC Best Bitter; Chiltern Beechwood Bitter; Everard Tiger
Delightful 13th-century thatched building. Low beamed bar has plenty of character, and inglenook fireplaces
Q ⛺ 🍴 🍺 (Thu–Sat)

Dorney

10.30–2.30; 5.30–11

Pineapple
Lake End Road
Friary Meux Best; Ind Coope Burton Ale
Busy local. The first pineapple to be grown in England was cultivated at nearby Dorney Court 🍴 🍺 (not Sun)

East Burnham

10.30–2.30; 5.30–11

Crown
Crown Lane ☎ (028 14) 4125
Courage Best Bitter, Directors
Listed building, with 500 year-old wisteria; used to be the courthouse for local

pound. Ghost!
🍴 🍺 (Fri, Sat) &

Farnham Royal

10.30–2.30; 6–11

Emperor of India
Blackpond Lane
☎ (028 14) 3006
Wethered Bitter, Special, Winter Royal
Named the King of Prussia after Waterloo, described as "well established inn" in 1820. Vincent owners club meets regularly Q 🍴

Fingest

11–2.30; 6–11

Chequers
☎ (049 163) 335
Brakspear Bitter, Special, Old
Friendly 15th-century pub opposite picturesque Norman church. Good restaurant (cold buffet only Sun eve) ⛺ 🍴 🍺

Forty Green

10.30–2.30; 5.30–11

Royal Standard of England
Near B474 OS923919
☎ (049 46) 3382
Brakspear Bitter; Eldridge Pope Royal Oak; Marston Pedigree; Owd Rodger; Royal Standard Bitter
Remarkable rambling historic pub, difficult to find but plenty of people do! Q 🍴 🍺

Frieth

11–2.30; 6–11

Prince Albert
Moor End ☎ (0494) 881683
Brakspear Mild, Bitter, Special, Old
Lovely old-fashioned pub in the country. Friendly service
Q ⛺ 🍴 &

Fulmer

11–2.30; 6–11

Black Horse
Windmill Road
☎ (028 16) 3183
Courage Best Bitter, Directors
One of the few remaining 3-bar pubs in the area. Friendly customers and staff; large garden with summer barbecues
🍴 🍺 (Mon–Fri)

Gawcott

11–2.30; 6–11

Cuckoo's Nest
New Inn Road
☎ (0280) 812092
Glenny Wychwood Bitter; Hook Norton Bitter; Marston Pedigree
Welcoming village pub,

69

Buckinghamshire

formerly called New Inn. Guest beer in summer
▲☎⊛◐&

Great Hampden

12–2.30; 7–11 (closed Sun eve Nov–Apr)

Hampden Arms
Great Hampden OS844015
☎ (024 028)
Brakspear Bitter; Flowers Original; Morland Bitter; Ruddles County H
Small but cosy village pub, popular with ramblers. Good pub meals every day
▲Q⊛◐▶⊟

Great Missenden

11–2.30; 6–11

White Lion
High Street
Benskins Best Bitter; Ind Coope Burton Ale H
Solid Victorian pub popular with locals. Emphasis on pub games ▲≠

Hartwell

10.30–2.30; 6–11

Bugle Horn
On A418 ☎ (0296) 748209
Benskins Best Bitter; Ind Coope Burton Ale H
Smart, well-appointed 17th-century former farmhouse, once part of Hartwell estate. Pleasant garden; conservatory and restaurant. Bar meals at all times ▲⊛☎◐▶&

Haversham

11.30–2.30; 5.30–11

Greyhound
High Street
Greene King IPA, Abbot H
300 year-old local with comfortable lounge and basic public bar. Accent on good value food Q⊛◐▶⊟

Hedgerley

10.30–2.30; 5.30–11

White Horse
☎ (028 14) 3225
Flowers Original; Wethered Bitter, SPA; Whitbread Castle Eden Ale G
Been White Horse since at least 1753. Beautiful country pub with very small bar counter. Stone floor in public bar ▲⊛◐◑ (not Sun) ⊟

High Wycombe

10.30–2.30; 5.30–11

Bell
Frogmore (near viaduct)
Fuller Chiswick Bitter, London Pride, ESB H
Comfortable and friendly oasis amongst Wycombe's run-of-the-mill town centre pubs ☎⊛≠◐◑ (not Sun) ≠

10.30–2.30; 5.30–11

Wendover Arms
Desborough Avenue
☎ (0494) 26476
Brakspear Mild, Bitter, Special, Old H
1930's suburban pub now run by Clifton Inns with carvery restaurant. Only Mild outlet in town ☎⊛◐▶

Try also: Queen (Fuller); Rose & Crown (Courage)

Horn Hill

11–3; 5.30–11

Dumb Bell
Old Shire Lane (off A413) OS018923 ☎ (024 07) 2215
Courage Best Bitter, Directors H
Cosy country pub with games area ⊛◐ (not Sun) &

Hughenden Valley

11–2.30; 6–11

Harrow
Warrendene Road
☎ (024 024) 4105
Courage Best Bitter, Directors G
Traditional 2-bar country pub. Flagstoned public; large garden. No food Sun
▲☎⊛◐▶⊟

Ickford

10.30–2.30; 6–11

Royal Oak
☎ (084 47) 633
Morrell Dark Mild, Light Mild H
Genuine 1-bar village local with good atmosphere and friendly welcome Q☎◐⊖

Lacey Green

11–2.30; 6–11

Pink & Lily
Pink Road, Parslows Hillock
☎ (024 028) 308
Brakspear Bitter, Special; Flowers Original; Greene King IPA; Wadworth 6X; Wethered Bitter G
Lively and friendly pub with snug bar and dining area. Connections with Rupert Brooke ▲Q☎⊛◐▶

Little Hampden

12–2.30; 6 (7 winter)–11

Rising Sun
OS857040
Adnams Bitter; Brakspear Special; Greene King Abbot; Samuel Smith OBB H
Delightful pub in idyllic surroundings. Good bar food Q⊛◐▶⊟

Little Horwood

10.30–2.30; 6–11

Shoulder of Mutton
Church Street

ABC Best Bitter; Everards Tiger H
Pleasingly ramshackle village inn with good food. Beware livestock in adjacent field and low beams inside ⊛▶

Little Missenden

11–2.30; 6–11

Crown
Off A413 OS926989
☎ (024 06) 2571
Hook Norton Bitter; Marston Pedigree; Morrell Varsity H
Excellent village inn in the same family since 1923. Dominoes; shut the box; shove ha'penny ▲Q⊛

10.30–2.30; 5.30–11

Red Lion
Off A413 OS923989
☎ (024 06) 2876
Benskins Best Bitter; Ind Coope Burton Ale H
Small traditional pub; room with pool table leads off main bar. Piano Fri and Sat eves
▲⊛◐&

Littleworth Common

11–2.30; 5.30–11

Beech Tree
Dorney Wood Road OS934860
☎ (062 86) 61328
Wethered Bitter, Special H
Licensed early this century, but the building is older. Still has old bench seating and chairs made by landlord
▲Q⊛&

11–2.30; 5.30–11

Blackwood Arms
Common Lane OS936863
☎ (028 14) 2169
Arkells BBB, Kingsdown Ale; Morrell Mild; Pitfield Bitter, Dark Star; Shepherd Neame Master Brew Bitter; Stock Ale H
Friendly country pub on edge of Burnham Beeches. Beer range varies ▲⊛◐&

Longwick

12–2.30; 6–11

Red Lion
Thame Road ☎ (084 44) 4980
ABC Best Bitter; Hook Norton Best Bitter H
Plain exterior hides spacious comfortable inn. Varied collection of pictures, prints, photos – and robins!
⇌◐▶ (not Sun)

Marlow

10.30–2.30; 5.30–11

Chequers
High Street ☎ (062 84) 2053
Brakspear Bitter, Special H
17th-century inn with 2 bars and a restaurant. Opposite

Buckinghamshire

former Wethered brewery
🏠 Q 🍽 ⌘ ◐ 🚆

10.30–2.30; 6–11

Clayton Arms
Quoiting Square
☎ (062 84) 3037
Brakspear Mild, Bitter, Old H
Town-centre gem with 2 small bars. Landlord has lived in pub for 60 years; the original and genuine local 🏠 Q ⌘ & 🚆

Marsh Gibbon

11–2.30; 6–11

Plough
Church Street ☎ (086 97) 305
Morrell Light Ale, Dark Mild, Bitter H
Pleasant 2-bar 16th century pub with separate dining room and regular live music
🏠 Q ⊕ ⌘ ◐ ⊞ & ♿

Marsworth

11–2.30; 6–11

Red Lion
Vicarage Road (off B489)
ABC Best Bitter; Draught Bass; Everard Tiger H
Superb country pub; popular venue for traditional pub games; information of local interest displayed. Worth finding 🏠 Q ⊕ ⌘ ◐ (not Sun) ⊞

Milton Keynes

11–2.30; 5.30–11

Foresters Arms
Newport Road
☎ (0908) 312348
Wells Eagle Bitter H
Unpretentious local serving good beer; public bar is a trifle boisterous Q ⊞ 🚆 (Wolverton)

11–2.30; 6–11

New Inn
2 Bradwell Road, New Bradwell
Wells Eagle Bitter, Bombardier H
Stone-built canalside pub. Good value bar food, first-floor restaurant. Garden with animals
⊕ ⌘ ◐ ⊞ 🚆 (Wolverton)

11–2.30; 5.30–11

Suffolk Punch
Saxon Street, Heelands
☎ (0908) 311166
Tolly Cobbold Bitter, Original, XXXX, Old Strong H
Fine estate pub, by far Tolly's westernmost outpost. 2 bars, separate carvery. Public bar can get noisy. Family room
⊕ ⌘ ◐ ⊞

Try also: **Cuba** (Wells)

Newton Blossomville

11.30–2.30; 6.30–11

Old Mill Burnt Down

Adnams Bitter; Marston Burton Bitter, Pedigree, Merrie Monk; Younger Scotch, No.3 H
Village local which actually is an old mill that burnt down. Good range of beer, kids welcome, parking a pain
⊕ ⌘ ◐ (not Sun)

Newton Longville

11–2.30; 5.30–11

Crooked Billet
Westbrook End
Benskins Best Bitter H
Convivial low-beamed old thatched pub. Pub games. Thriving ⌘

Northend

11–2.30; 6–11

White Hart
Off B480 ☎ (049 163) 353
Brakspear Bitter, Special, Old H
Attractive, friendly unspoilt pub in beautiful surroundings. Good food, log fires and large garden
🏠 Q ⊕ ⌘ ◐ (not Mon) &

Padbury

11–2.30; 6–11

New Inn (and Filling Station)
On A413
ABC Best Bitter H
Superb village pub which doubles as petrol station. A friendly welcome in a bar full of character 🏠 Q ⌘ ⊞

Preston Bisset

11–2.30; 6 (may open later)–11

Old Hat
Main Street ☎ (028 04) 335
Hook Norton Bitter H
Delightfully individual pub of character, with splendid wooden settle, roaring fire and sleeping dog 🏠 Q ⌘ ⊞

Try also: **White Hart** (ABC)

Prestwood

10.30–2.30; 5.30–11

Kings Head
188 Wycombe Road (A4128)
☎ (024 06) 2392
Brakspear Bitter, Special, Old; Courage Best Bitter; Marston Pedigree G
A permanent beer festival, with choice of up to 10 beers, plus ploughmans' breakfasts. Rivals Hughenden Manor as South Bucks' main tourist attraction 🏠 ⌘ ⊞

Princes Risborough

10.30 (10 Sat)–2.30; 5.30 (6 Sat)–11

Whiteleaf Cross
Market Square ☎ (084 44) 7898

Morland Mild, Bitter, Best Bitter H
Welcoming pub town centre with 1 large bar on 3 different levels. A rare outlet for mild, an oasis amongst the bitter. No food Sun ⌘ ◐ 🚆

St Leonards

11–2.30; 5.30 (6 Sat)–11

White Lion
Jenkins Lane OS918070
☎ (024 029) 387
Benskins Best Bitter; Friary Meux Best; Ind Coope Burton Ale H
Pleasant, low-ceilinged, country pub recently converted to 1 bar. Separate children's room with television
⊕ ⌘ ◐ (limited Sun) ♿

Skirmett

10.30–2.30; 6–11

Old Crown
☎ (049 163) 435
Brakspear Bitter, Special, Old G
Exceptional pub in 1-lane village. Magnificent tap room with quarry tiled floor and full size inglenook fireplace
🏠 Q ⌘ ◐ (not Mon) ⊞ ♿

Steeple Claydon

11–2.30; 6–11

Old Sportsman
North End (off Main Road)
Hook Norton Bitter, Old Hookey E
Commendably individualistic free house with cheap beer and splendidly easygoing approach. Hard to find but a real pleasure Q ⌘ ⊞

Stewkley

10.30 (10 Sat)–2.30; 5.30 (6 Sat)–11

Swan
High Street North
☎ (0525) 240285
Courage Best Bitter, Directors G
Excellent Georgian pub in centre of village. Always a good atmosphere and cheerful log fire. Separate restaurant and unobtrusive bar billiards table. No food Sun
🏠 Q ⌘ ◐ & ♿

Stone

11–2.30; 5.30 (6 Sat)–11

Rose & Crown
2 Oxford Road (A418)
ABC Best Bitter; Chiltern Beechwood Bitter G
Friendly village local. Quiet front parlour can be shut off for families. Take away food in evening
🏠 Q ⊕ ⌘ ◐ (not Sun) ◐ &

Buckinghamshire

Twyford

11–2.30; 6–11

Red Lion
Church End ☎ (029 673) 339
ABC Best Bitter; Ind Coope Burton Ale H
Unique 17th-century pub (and landlord!) an unspoilt gem, well worth a visit. Booking a must for small but renowned restaurant (Tue–Sat only)
🏨 Q ❀ ◐ ▶ 🚲 ♿

Try also: Crown (Free)

Weedon

11–2.30; 6 (7 Sat)–11

Five Elms
Stockaway (off A413)
☎ (0296) 641439
ABC Best Bitter; Draught Bass; Everards Tiger H
Unspoilt country style pub with a warm welcome. Unusual and varying menu (including vegetarian); beware of low beams
🏨 Q ❀ ◐ (Mon–Fri) ▶ ♿

Weston Turville

11.30–2.30; 6–11

Chandos Arms
Main Street ☎ (029 661) 3532
Benskins Best Bitter; Friary Meux Best H
Friendly country pub specialising in German bar food. Aunt Sally; large front garden. No food Mon. Guest beers Q ❀ ❀ ◐ ▶ (not Sun) ♿

Whaddon

10.30–2.30; 6–11

Lowndes Arms
High Street
ABC Best Bitter; Everards Tiger H
Old village pub with original beams, inglenooks and warm atmosphere. Smart motel at rear 🏨 ❀ ❀ ◐ ▶

George Orwell once wrote that his perfect pub, called the Moon Under Water, was so perfect – lacking noisy customers and hated fake inglenook fireplaces – that it couldn't possibly exist. It does now, thanks to the Wetherspoon chain of free houses. The revamped pub in Barnet, North London, is not only called The Moon Under Water but the inn sign carries a rare smiling version of the author's visage. Only problem ... how can the perfect pub possibly sell Scottish and Newcastle beers?

Cambridgeshire

Cambridgeshire

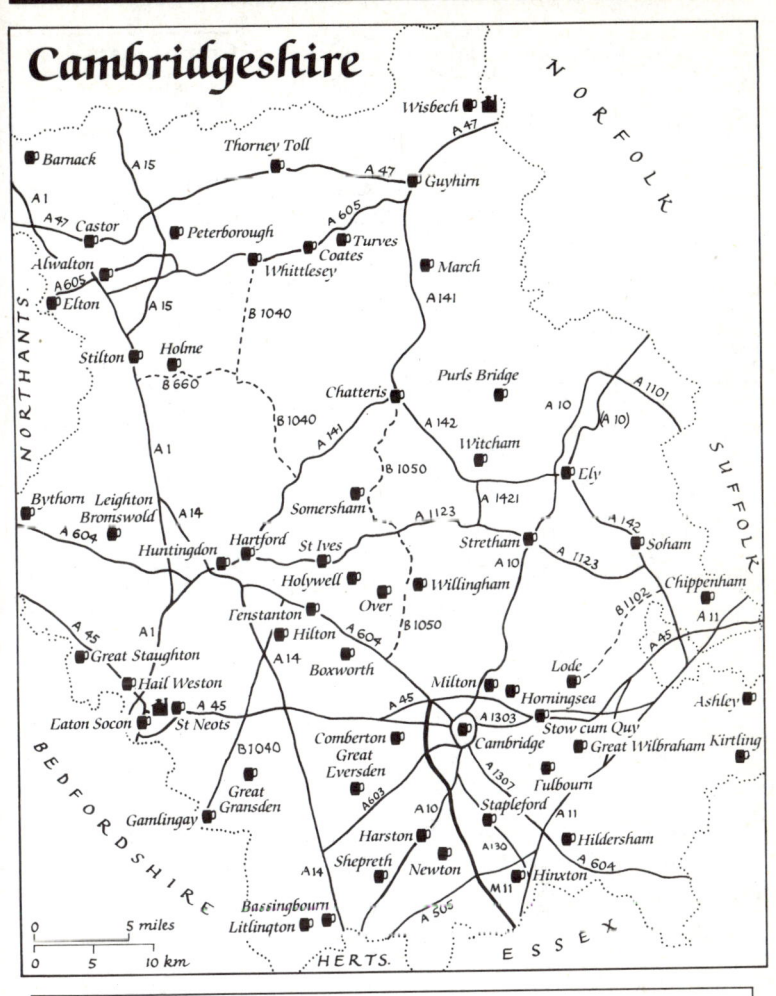

Elgood, Wisbech; **James Paine**, St. Neots

Alwalton

11–2.30; 5.30–11
Wheatsheaf Inn
100 yds off A1 ☎ (0733) 231056
Ind Coope Bitter, Burton Ale
Country pub with good food in a picturesque setting. Near the East of England showground

Ashley

11–2.30; 6 (5 on race days)–11
Crown
Newmarket Road
☎ (0638) 730737
Greene King XX, IPA, Abbot
Friendly pub with colourful local characters. Pool at one end; plenty of room to sit at the other. Book for a fondue in the cosy dining-room. Children's play-tree in the garden. Pub games

Try also: **Red Lion**, Cheveley (Greene King)

Barnack

11–2.30; 6–11
Millstone
Millstone Lane
☎ (0780) 740296
Adnams Bitter; Everards Tiger, Old Original
3-roomed pub serving good food (not Sun)

Bassingbourn

10.30–2.30; 6–11
Pear Tree
61 North End (off A14)
☎ (0763) 44068
Arkells BBB; Flowers IPA; Greene King IPA; Samuel Smith OBB
Village centre pub with social club – discount for OAPs. Lively public bar, separate dining area. Noted for poetry etched on windows. Pub games

Boxworth

12–2.30; 6–11
Golden Ball
High Street ☎ (095 47) 397
Adnams Bitter; Greene King IPA, Abbot; Nethergate Bitter; Theakston Old Peculier
Enterprising free house with up to 16 lovingly tended real

Cambridgeshire

ales at any time. Live music Wed & Fri eves ☞🍴🍺🍷♿

Bythorn

11.30–2.30; 7–11

White Hart
on A604 ☎ (080 14) 226
Flowers IPA; Marston Pedigree H
Main road village pub. Separated into drinking and eating areas catering for local as well as passing trade. Reasonably priced, comfortable accommodation available. Pub games. Guest beers
🛏Q☞ (lunch) 🍴🍽🍺🍷♿A

Cambridge

11–2.30; 6–11

Alma Brewery
Russell Court ☎ (0223) 64965
Marston Pedigree; Tolly Cobbold Mild, Bitter, Original, Old Strong H
Deservedly popular city pub with live music on Sat eves
🍺≈

11–2.30; 5–11

Bird in Hand
Newmarket Road ☎ (0223) 354034
Greene King IPA, Abbot H
Smart, friendly pub next to offices of Cambridge Evening News – so watch what you say! 🛏🍺

11–2.30; 5.30–11

Champion of the Thames
68 King Street ☎ (0223) 352043
Greene King XX, IPA, Abbot G
Smashing little pub with a local's feel – rare in the city centre. The etched windows are worth a look but the enormous sandwiches are equally famous
🛏🍺 (not Sun) ♿

11–2.30; 5–11

Cow & Calf
St Peters Street ☎ (0223) 311919
Tolly Cobbold Bitter, Original, 4X H
Street corner local in improving part of town. Best pub cats in Cambridge 🛏🍺

11–2.30; 5–11

Elm Tree
Orchard Street ☎ (0223) 63005
Wells Eagle Bitter, Bombardier H
Very popular oddly-shaped 1-bar pub. Try the Thai cuisine Q 🍺

11–2.30; 5–11

Green Man
55 High Street, Trumpington ☎ (0223) 844903
Brakspear Bitter; Flowers Original; Wethered Bitter H

A Beefeater where the bar really feels like a pub. Games include shove ha'penny and Devil-among-the-tailors. Guest beers ☞🍴🍺🍷♿

11–2.30; 5–11

Seven Stars
249 Newmarket Road ☎ (0223) 354430
Greene King XX, IPA, Abbot H
Bustling friendly local convenient for the Cambridge Museum of Technology. Pub games Q 🍺🍷

11–2.30; 5–11

Volunteer
Trumpington Road, Trumpington ☎ (0223) 841675
Flowers IPA, Original; Wethered Bitter H
Archways and alcoves lend interest. Hedge acts as pub sign. Ale outsells lager 2-to-1
🍴🍺

11–2.30; 6–11

White Hart
2 Sturton Street ☎ (0223) 66536
Adnams Bitter; Ind Coope Best Bitter, Burton Ale; Tetley Bitter H
Warm and welcoming pub in an area thick with good boozers 🛏🍷♿

11–2.30; 7–11

White Swan
109 Mill Road ☎ (0223) 357144
Greene King XX, IPA, Abbot H
Good old-fashioned local; quiet at lunchtime, lively in the evening 🍴🍷≈

Try also: Free Press (Greene King); Spread Eagle (Whitbread)

Castor

11–2.30; 6–2.30

Royal Oak
24 Peterborough Road (A47) ☎ (073 121) 217
Ind Coope Burton Ale; Tetley Bitter H
Splendid listed building of considerable charm. Low-beamed interior gives cosy atmosphere. Stroke the cat at your peril! Pub games
🛏Q☞🍺

Chatteris

11–2.30; 6–11

Cock
41 London Road (B1050) ☎ (035 43) 2026
Ruddles Best Bitter; Webster's Yorkshire Bitter H
Converted from large town house in 1947 retaining ornate ceilings. Petanque courts at rear 🍴🍺🍷♿

Chippenham

11–2.30; 7–11

Tharp Arms
46 High Street ☎ (0638) 720234
Greene King XX, IPA, Abbot H
Nothing too much trouble at this solid, no-nonsense pub. Jellied eels available. Pub games ☞🍴🍺🍷♿

Coates

10.30–2.30; 6–11 (restaurant licence to midnight)

Carpenters Arms
1 North Green (A605) ☎ (073 120) 431
John Smith Bitter H
Busy and popular, traditional Fenland pub on picturesque village green. Restaurant at rear. Known locally as the "Top House". Darts, dominoes and cribbage
☞ (lounge & restaurant) 🍴🍺🍷

Comberton

12–2.30; 7–11

Three Horseshoes
22 South Street ☎ (022 026) 2252
Flowers IPA; Wethered Bitter H
Good value, sporty village pub
🍴🍺🍷A

Try also: Hoops, Barton (Greene King)

Eaton Socon

10.30–2.30; 5.30–11

Crown
Great North Road (A45, St Neots bypass) ☎ (0480) 212232
Samuel Smith OBB; Tetley Bitter H
Small cottage-style pub, often crowded. Popular for its early evening opening. (Located just inside Bedfordshire). Dining room with a la carte menu. Guest beers 🍴🍺🍷A

10.30–2.30; 5.30–11

White Horse
Great North Road ☎ (0480) 74453
Flowers IPA, Original H
Ivy-clad former coaching inn. Emphasis on food with good bar snacks. Split seating areas create a cosy atmosphere
🛏Q🍴🍺🍷

Elton

11.30–2.30; 6–11

Crown Inn
8 Duck Street (off A605) ☎ (083 24) 232
Greene King IPA; Marston Pedigree H
250 year-old listed building on village green. Upstairs restaurant with good

74

Cambridgeshire

reputation. 50-seat conservatory. Various games. Guest beers ♣Q☎⊛ⓓ♣ ♿

Ely

11–2.30; 6–11

Prince Albert
62 Silver Street ☎ (0353) 3494
Greene King XX, IPA, Abbot Ⓗ
Cosy little pub. An oasis in a Watney dominated town
♣⊛ⓓ

Fenstanton

10.30–2.30; 6–11

King William IV
High Street (off A604)
☎ (0480) 62467
Tolly Cobbold Mild, Bitter, Original, 4X Ⓗ
A typical village pub, separated into drinking and eating areas by beams and settles. Pleasantly situated on the green which is complete with clock tower and pond
⊛ⓓ

Try also: **George** (Whitbread)

Fulbourn

11–2.30; 6–11

Six Bells
9 High Street ☎ (0223) 880244
Tolly Cobbold Mild, Bitter, Old Strong Ⓗ
Bustling village local retaining 2 bars in a timbered listed building. Landscaped garden with summer barbecues. Pub games ♣⊛ⓓ (not Sun)⊞♿

Try also: **Bakers Arms** (Greene King)

Gamlingay

11.30–2.30; 6.30–11

Hardwicke Arms
The Cross ☎ (0767) 50727
Greene King IPA; Marston Pedigree Ⓗ
Comfortable pub on village crossroads. Lounge bar features an impressive inglenook. Guest Beers. Restaurant (book) ♣ⓓ

Great Eversden

11 (12 winter)–2.30; 6 (7 winter)–11

Hoops
High Street ☎ (022 026) 2185
Wells Eagle Bitter, Bombardier Ⓗ
Good home cooking (not Tue) beneath old timber beams. Old part of pub dates from 1680 ♣⊛⇌ⓓ♿

Great Gransden

12–2.30; 6–11

Crown & Cushion
☎ (076 77) 214
Wells Eagle Bitter Ⓗ; **Bombardier** Ⓖ
In a village with some uniquely designed houses, the pub remains traditional in style; split-level floor with single bar. Good, home-cooked food; regular live music ♣⊛ⓓ

Great Staughton

11–2.30; 6–11

White Hart
The Highway (A45)
☎ (0480) 860345
Ruddles Best Bitter; Webster Yorkshire Bitter Ⓗ
An attractive pub styled as a coaching inn. Popular village local which has eating, drinking and games areas ⊛

Great Wilbraham

11.30 (12 winter)–2.30; 6.30 (7 winter)–11

Carpenters Arms
10 High Street ☎ (0223) 880202
Greene King XX, IPA, Abbot Ⓗ
Landlord famous for his ribald ripostes and collection of malt whiskies. Cosy secluded lounge. Petanque and other pub games
♣⊛ⓓ (Wed–Sat) ♿

Guyhirn

10.30–2.30; 5.30–11

Chequers
Main Road (A47)
☎ (094 575) 352
Elgood Bitter Ⓗ
Built 1913. Smart lounge with Ring the Bull; small public bar with pool. Garden has small zoo. Collection of 'decapitated' ties
♣⊛ⓓ⊞♣▲

Hail Weston

10.30–2.30; 6–11

Royal Oak
off A45 ☎ (0480) 72527
Wells Eagle Bitter, Bombardier Ⓗ
A picturesque thatched village pub, which has a huge garden with children's playground and pleasant family room. Pub games ♣Q☎⊛ⓓ♣

Harston

11–2.30; 5–11

Queens Head
48 Royston Road (A10)
☎ (0223) 870693
Greene King IPA, Abbot Ⓗ
Pleasant, friendly pub by village green. Lunches are popular ⊛ⓓ⊞

Hartford

10.30–2.30; 6–11

Barley Mow
Longstaff Way (A141)
☎ (0480) 50557
Wells Eagle Bitter, Bombardier Ⓗ
Stone-built pub unusual for area, converted from derelict ruin into comfortable lounge bar pub. Near Huntingdon Riverside Park ⊛ⓓ▲

Try also: **Black Bull** Godmanchester (Whitbread)

Hildersham

11–2.30; 6–11

Pear Tree
High Street ☎ (0223) 891680
Greene King IPA, Abbot Ⓗ
1-bar pub with hanging tables, stone floor and beer-engine on the wall. Wealth of timbers and exposed brickwork. Barn bar for families in summer. Cream teas on sunny afternoons
♣☎⊛ⓓ

Try also: **Three Hills**, Bartlow

Hilton

11–2.30; 6–11

Prince of Wales
High Street (B1040)
☎ (0480) 830257
Adnams Bitter; Draught Bass; Marston Pedigree Ⓗ
The only pub in the village, welcomes passing trade as well as locals. Occasional live music. Pub games; guest beers
♣⊛ⓓ⊞

Hinxton

11–2.30; 6–11

Red Lion
32 High Street (off A1301)
☎ (0799) 30601
Brakspear Bitter; Flowers IPA; Wethered Bitter; Whitbread Castle Eden Ale Ⓗ
500 year-old village pub with original baker's oven and a parrot. Separate dining area. Watch out for the tarantula!
♣☎⊛ⓓ♿

Try also: **New Inn**, Ickleton (Greene King)

Holme

11–2.30; 6–11

Admiral Wells
Station Road ☎ (0487) 830798
Admiral Wells Bitter; Ind Coope Burton Ale; Tetley Bitter Ⓗ
Claims to be the lowest pub in England. Guest beers. Boules played in large garden
♣☎⊛ⓓ⊞

Holywell

10.30–2.30; 6–11

Olde Ferryboat Inn
☎ (0480) 63227
Draught Bass; Greene King IPA, Abbot; Ruddles Best Bitter Ⓗ
A partly thatched riverside pub, reputedly haunted. Popular with rivergoers in

Cambridgeshire

summer. Good food. In Guinness Book of Records as one of England's oldest pubs 🏠🛏♨🚬 ( )

Horningsea

11.30–2.30; 7–11

Plough & Fleece
High Street ☎ (0223) 860795
Greene King IPA, Abbot H
A fine pub with excellent food. 15 consecutive Good Beer Guide entries must mean something 🏠 Q ⊛ ( ) ▶ ⊕

Try also: **Star**, Waterbeach

Huntingdon

11–2.30; 7–11

Victoria
Ouse Walk ☎ (0480) 53899
James Paine XXX, EG H
A surprising find in this Grand Metropolitan dominated town. A real country pub on the village green! Well worth seeking out. Pub games ⊛ ( ) ▶ ○

Kirtling

11–2.30; 7–11

Queens Head
Cowling Road ☎ (0638)730253
Tolly Cobbold Mild, Bitter, Original, Old Strong
Unspoilt 16th-century inn in delightful surroundings. Reputedly built in the year Elizabeth I became queen. Pub games 🏠⊛♨ ( ) ▶ (not Thu or Sun) ⊕ ▵

Leighton Bromswold

11–2.30; 6.30–11

Green Man
off A604 ☎ (0480) 890238
Tolly Cobbold Original, 4X H
A large rambling rural free house, with a good choice of pub games, like hood skittles. Separate eating area Q ⊛ ▶

Litlington

10.30–2.30; 6–11

Crown
Silver Street ☎ (0763) 852439
Greene King IPA H
Bustling village local with small intimate lounge (jukebox). Beware of village one-way system 🏠⊛ ( ) ⊕

Lode

11–2.30; 7–11

Three Horseshoes
2 Lode Road ☎ (0223) 812098
Greene King XX, IPA H
Smart, friendly village local popular with all ages. One of the few pubs where mild sales equal bitter. Darts and crib popular. Good for local history. No food Wed
🏠🛏⊛ ( ) ▶ ▵

Try also: **Black Horse**, Swaffham Bulbeck (Whitbread); **Kings**, Reach (free)

March

10.30–2.30; 7 (6 Sat)–11 (supper licence)

Ship
1 Nene Parade ☎ (0354) 56999
Greene King XX, IPA, Abbot H
Thatched riverside pub; carved beams in bar. Games include chess
🛏♨ ( ) ▶ (not Tue) ▵

11.30–2.30; 7–11

White Horse
West End ☎ (0354) 53054
Ruddles Best Bitter, County; Webster's Yorkshire Bitter H
Thatched riverside pub. Children's play area and gardens down to river with moorings. Eve meals Fri and Sat or on request
⊛ ( ) (not Sun) ▶ ⊕

Milton

11–2.30; 5–11

Waggon & Horses
39 High Street (off A45) ☎ (0223) 860313
Hall & Woodhouse Tanglefoot; Marston Pedigree; Nethergate Bitter H
Large, comfortable pub with guest beer changing several times a week 🏠🛏⊛ ( ) ▶ ▵

Try also: **King William IV**, Histon

Newton

11.30–2.30; 5–11

Queens Head
Fowlmere Road ☎ (0223) 870436
Adnams Bitter, Old G
Idyllic local. Convivial atmosphere is enjoyed by a wide cross-section of the community Q ⊛ ( ) ⊕

Try also: **Chequers**, Fowlmere (Tolly Cobbold); **Green Man**, Thriplow (Wells)

Over

12–2; 7–11

Exhibition
2 King Street (Long Stanton Road) ☎ (0954) 30790
James Paine XXX; Tolly Cobbold Bitter, Original H
Attractively extended into cottage next door. Difficult to find 🏠⊛ ( )

Peterborough

11–2.30; 6–11

Cherry Tree
Oundle Road (A605) ☎ (0733) 45812
Ind Coope Bitter, Burton Ale; Tetley Bitter H
Refurbished, Victorian-style 1-roomed bar. Games room 🏠🛏⊛ ▵

10.30–2.30; 6–11

Crab & Winkle
Davids Lane (Werrington) (50 yds off A15) ☎ (0733) 322377
Greene King XX, IPA, Abbot H
New village pub. Very friendly. Good food at reasonable prices. Darts Q ( ) ▶ ▵

10.30–2.30; 6–11 (Midnight entertainment licence in lounge)

Crown
749 Lincoln Road, New England (old A15) ☎ (0733) 41366
Adnams Bitter; Draught Bass; Charrington IPA H
Mock-Tudor fronted corner pub with lively atmosphere. 3-rooms: lounge mainly for entertainment. Games include bar skittles 🏠🛏⊛ ( ) ▶ ⊕

10.30–2.30; 6–11

Dragonfly
Herlington Centre, Orton Malborne ☎ (0733) 233130
Tolly Cobbold Bitter, Original, 4X H
Pleasant 2-roomed modern estate pub. Interesting lounge design. Only Tolly Cobbold outlet in the city. Darts ⊛ ( ) ⊕

10.30–2.30; 6–11

Gladstone Arms
124–126 Gladstone Street ☎ (0733) 44388
Bateman XXXB; Fuller London Pride; Marston Pedigree H
Lively terraced pub with a cosmopolitan atmosphere. Live music 3 nights a week. Darts ⊛ ⊕ ⇌ (North) ○

10–2.30; 6–11

Greenkeeper
Thorpe Wood (just off A47) ☎ (0733) 267601
Greene King IPA, Abbot H
Superb outlook across golf course; non-golfers welcome too! Friendly atmosphere Q 🛏⊛ ( )

11–2.30; 6.30–11

White Hart
77 High Street, Old Fletton ☎ (0733) 65088
John Smith Bitter H
Basic public bar and comfortable lounge in typical local on outskirts of city. Darts ⊛ ( ) (Mon–Fri) ⊕

11–2.30; 6.30–11

Woolpack
29 North Street, Stanground ☎ (0733) 54417
Flowers IPA; Whitbread Castle Eden Ale H
Friendly back-street local. Backs onto River Nene; boat moorings available. Pub games Q 🛏⊛ ▵

Cambridgeshire

Purls Bridge

11–2.30; 7–11 (closed Mon)
Ship Inn
☎ (035 478) 578
Greene King IPA H
Isolated Fenland pub popular with ornithologists 🏠Q🍴

St Ives

10–2.30; 6.30–11
Royal Oak
Crown Street ☎ (0480) 69644
Ind Coope Bitter, Burton Ale H
Popular town centre meeting place, dating from early 16th century. Old world atmosphere with beams and settles 🏠🍴🍺

Try also: **Oliver Cromwell** (free)

St Neots

10.30–2.30; 6.30–11
Wheatsheaf
Church Street ☎ (0480) 77435
Greene King XX, IPA, Abbot H
Terraced town-centre locals' pub with friendly atmosphere. Always a welcome here. Thriving darts and quiz teams 🏠🍺

Shepreth

11–2.30; 6–11
Plough
12 High Street ☎ (0763) 60523
Courage Best Bitter, Directors; Wells Eagle Bitter H
Thriving free house with separate pool room and restaurant. Near trout farm and children's zoo. Guest beers 🏠🍴🍺

Soham

12–2.30; 7–11
Carpenters Arms
72 Brook Street
☎ (0353) 721204
Nethergate Bitter; Younger IPA H
Pleasant, timbered pub catering for all tastes 🍴🍺

Somersham

10.30–2.30; 6–11
Windmill
St Ives Road ☎ (0487) 840328
Greene King IPA, Abbot H
Small rural pub in typical Cambridgeshire countryside, near site of secret WWII airfield. Gravity dispense unusual for area. Good public bar. Pub games Q🍴🍺

Stapleford

11–2.30; 5–11
Rose
81 London Road (A1301)
☎ (0223) 843349
Flowers IPA, Original; Wethered Bitter H
Comfortable 16th-century pub. Good food
🏠🍴🍺 (Shelford)

Try also: **University Arms**, Sawston

Stilton

11–2.30; 6–11
Bell Inn
Great North Road
☎ (0733) 242626
Greene King Abbot; Marston Pedigree; Tetley Bitter H
James I, Oliver Cromwell and Daniel Defoe are among the famous guests who have stopped at this 17th-century inn, which is being gradually restored. Pub games; guest beers 🏠Q (upstairs) 🍴 (lunch) 🍺 (not Sun)

Stow Cum Quy

11.30–2.30; 5–11
Prince Albert
Newmarket Road
☎ (0223) 811294
Adnams Bitter; Bateman Mild; Greene King IPA H
Spacious bar with horse-racing flavour. 100 guest beers in last year. Happy Albert family restaurant. Pool room in barn 🏠🍴🍺 (not Mon) ♿

Stretham

11–2.30; 6–11
Lazy Otter
Cambridge Road (1 mile S of village, off A10)
☎ (035 389) 780
Greene King IPA, Abbot; Nethergate Bitter E
Successful new venture in riverside village with preserved Fen pumping engine 🏠🍴🍺♿

Thorney Toll

11–2.30; 6 (7 winter)–11
Black Horse
Wisbech Road (A47)
☎ (073 128) 218
Elgood Bitter H
2-roomed pub with collection of miniatures. Popular stop for east coast traffic. Coaches welcome. Various games 🏠🍺

Turves

11–2.30; 6–11
Three Horseshoes
344 March Road
☎ (073 120) 414
Greene King IPA, Abbot H
Large Fenland pub renowned for its French cuisine, but with a friendly atmosphere and local drinkers. Guest beers. No food Mon. Petanque and other games 🏠🍴🍺♿

Whittlesey

10.30–2.30; 6–11
Bricklayers Arms
9 Station Road
☎ (0733) 202593
Ruddles Best Bitter; Webster Yorkshire Bitter H
Popular town local with large basic bar and modernised lounge. Pub games
🏠🍺 (Sat eve) 🍴♿🚂

Willingham

11–2.30; 5–11
Three Tuns
Church Street ☎ (0954) 60437
Greene King XX, IPA, Abbot H
Unpretentious village local with a welcoming atmosphere. Busy public bar with crib, dominoes, bar billiards and darts. Quiet lounge 🍴🍺

Try also: **New Inn**, Oakington

Wisbech

10.30–2.30; 6–11
Kings Head
13 Old Market (off A47)
☎ (0945) 65402
Elgood Bitter H
200 year-old town centre pub with riverside patio and nautical lounge. Pool and darts 🍴🍺

10.30–2.30; 5.30–11
Wisbech Arms
Exchange Square
☎ (0945) 584387
John Smith Bitter H
1-roomed locals' pub near produce auction rooms. Only pub in Wisbech to open full licensing hours. Darts, cards and dominoes 🍴🍺♿

Try also: **Globe** (Ruddles)

Witcham

12–2.30 (not Mon Wed); 7–11
White Horse
7 Silver Street ☎ (0353) 778298
Bateman XB, XXXB; Greene King IPA G
Fine free house. Licensee's obsession with birds very apparent. Guest beers 🏠🍴🍺

Cheshire

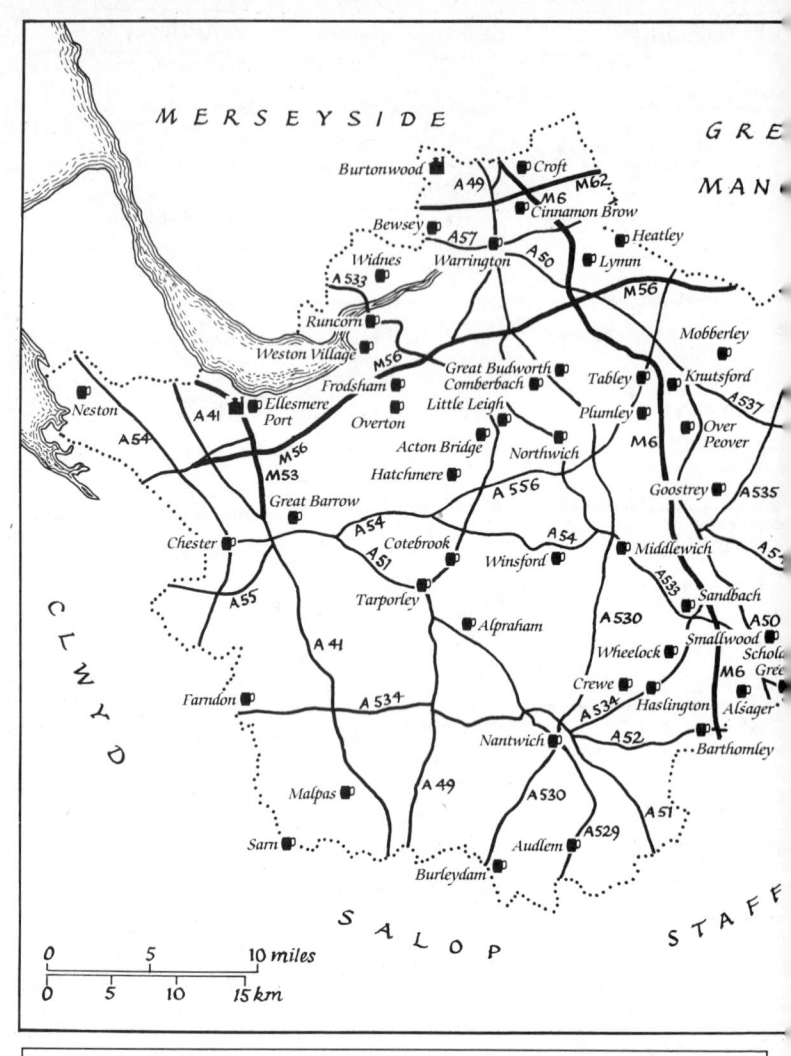

🏭 **Burtonwood**, Burtonwood, Warrington; **Oak**, Ellesmere Port

---

Acton Bridge

11–3; 5.30–11

Maypole
Hilltop Road OS598748
☎ (0606) 583114
Greenall Whitley Mild, Bitter H
Very pleasant country pub with comfortable lounge and busy public bar. Superb floral display in summer. Darts
Q🏠🅿🚻≠

Alpraham

(12–3 Sat only); 6–11

Travellers Rest
on A51
McEwan 70/-; Tetley-Walker Mild, Bitter H
Award-winning locals' pub. Quiet and friendly, but prone to impromptu sing-songs! Darts, dominoes and bowling green ⚓Q🏠🅿♿

Alsager

11–3; 5.30 (7 Sat)–11

Mere
58 Crewe Road (B5077)
☎ (0270) 882019
Greenall Whitley Bitter H
Small pub in centre of town opposite Alsager Mere. Pub games Q🐕🏠♪ (12–2 Tue–Sat) ♿ (help available)

Try also: **Lodge** (Allied)

Audlem

11–3; 7 (5.30 summer)–11

Bridge
Shropshire Street (A525)
Marston Burton Bitter, Pedigree, Merrie Monk H
Locals and boaters pub. A refreshment stop before tackling the Audlem flight of canal locks. Darts, dominoes and table skittles
⚓🐕🏠♪🅿⚓ (nearby)

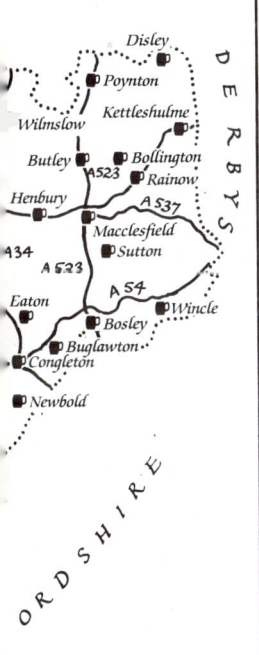

Cheshire

Bollington

Church House
11–3; 5.30–10.30 (11 F, S)
Chapel Street ☎ (0625) 74014
Ruddles County; Tetley-Walker Bitter; Theakston Best Bitter H
Corner terrace pub serving good food in an attractively modernised building. Seating includes renovated church pews ▲Q❀◖▶ (not Mon) ⌐

Holly Bush
11–3; 5.30–10.30 (11 F, S)
Palmerston Street
☎ (0625) 73073
Robinson Best Mild, Best Bitter H
A pleasant and comfortable pub catering for most tastes ▲❀◖▶

Waggon & Horses
11–3; 5.30–10.30 (11 F, S)
Wellington Road
☎ (0625) 74042
Boddingtons Bitter; Higsons Mild H
Large Victorian-style pub on main road, rebuilt in 1907. Lunchtime snacks on request. Pub games ▲❀

Try also: **Meridian** (Boddingtons); **Vale** (Free)

Bosley

Queens Arms
11–3; 5.30–10.30 (11 F, S)
London Road (A523)
☎ (026 03) 267
Boddingtons Bitter H
Attractive, comfortable country pub with small dining room ▲❀◖▶

Buglawton

Church House
11.30–3; 5.30–11
Buxton Road (A54)
☎ (0260) 272466
Robinson Best Mild, Best Bitter E
Roomy pub with excellent bar meals and restaurant. Unusual pub sign combined with pigeon cote ▲❀◖▶ (grill room only Sat) ⌐

Try also: **Robin Hood** (Marston)

Burleydam

Combermere Arms
12–3; 7–11
on A525
Draught Bass; M&B Springfield Bitter (summer); **Marston Pedigree; Younger Scotch Bitter** H
17th-century pub, reputedly haunted. Darts and dominoes ▲Q❀◖▶ ⌐

Butley

Ash Tree
11–3; 5.30–10.30 (11 F, S)
London Road (A523)
☎ (0625) 829207
Boddingtons Bitter H
Comfortable rural pub with excellent choice of food. Pub games ▲❀◖⌐

Chester

Albion
11.30–3; 5.30–11
Albion Street ☎ (0244) 40345
Greenall Whitley Mild, Bitter, Original H
Pub with character near city centre but far enough away from hustle and bustle. Lunchtime menu boasts no chips or fried food
▲☎ (if eating) ◖⌐&

Bouverie Arms
11.30–3; 5.00 (6.30 Sat) 10.45
Garden Lane
Greenall Whitley Mild, Bitter, Original H
Thriving local close to Tower Wharf canal basin. Pub games ❀◖⌐

Bridgewater Arms
11.30–3; 5.30–11
Crewe Street (off City Road)
☎ (0244) 27849
Greenall Whitley Mild, Bitter H
Cosy comfortable 2-roomed urban local handy for the station. Pub games ☎❀⌐≠

Bull & Stirrup
11–3; 5.30–11
Upper Northgate Street (by Crosville bus station)
☎ (0244) 371276
Boddingtons Mild, Bitter, Higsons Mild, Bitter H
Impressive building with modernised interior including 2 video jukebox screens in lounge! ◖▶ ⌐

Little Oak
12–3; 5.30–11
Boughton (A5115)
Greenall Whitley Mild, Bitter, Original H
Warm and cosy pub with intimate atmosphere. Especially popular with law students from local college. Pub games ▲☎❀⌐

Olde Custom House
11–3; 5.30–11
Watergate Street
Marston Border Mild, Border Exhibition, Border Bitter, Pedigree H
Old town pub with 3 rooms opposite original Customs House. Pub games ◖⌐

Try also: **Clavertons Wine Bar** (Lees); **Marlborough** (Whitbread)

Barthomley

White Lion
11–3; 6–11
Audley Road OS768524
Burtonwood Bitter H
Beautiful, thatched and half-timbered pub, dated 1614 and little altered. Landlord of 40 years' standing ▲Q⌐

Bewsey

Bewsey Farm
11–3; 5.30 (6.30 winter)–10.30 (11 F, S)
Bewsey Farm Close, Old Hall (off A57) ☎ (0925) 33705
Boddingtons Bitter; Higsons Mild, Bitter H
Pub built in old barn on farmland in new town. Close to Bewsey Old Hall. Meals summer only Q☎❀◖▶&

Cheshire

Cinnamon Brow

11–3; 5.30–10.30 (11 F, S)
Millhouse
Ballater Drive (off A574)
☎ (0925) 811405
Holt Mild, Bitter H
Large new pub opened early 1987 for new area of residential development. Large basic bar and plush lounge. Justifiably popular. Pub games

Comberbach

12–3; 5.30–11
Drum & Monkey
The Avenue (off A559)
☎ (0606) 891417
Tetley-Walker Mild, Bitter H
Small, cosy pub close to Marbury Country Park. Pub games Q

Congleton

11–3; 5.30–11
Grapes
Willow Street (A54)
☎ (0260) 274863
Tetley-Walker Bitter H
Small terraced pub close to town centre. Beautiful inner door window advertising the North Cheshire Brewery of Macclesfield (lunch)

11–3; 5.30–11
Lion & Swan
Swan Bank, (West Street)
☎ (0260) 273115
Burtonwood Bitter H
Large black and white, half-timbered residential pub. Basic tap room is a sharp contrast to plush lounge/restaurant

11–3; 5.30–11
Wharf
121 Canal Road
☎ (0260) 272809
Greenall Whitley Bitter H
Situated about 1 mile from the town centre, near canal and aqueduct. Busy pub, basic and honest. Much interest in pub games

Cotebrook

10.30–3; 5.30–11
Alvanley Arms
on A49 (near Tarporley)
☎ (082 921) 200
Robinson Best Mild, Best Bitter, Old Tom H
Attractive multi-roomed Georgian pub recently modernised. Accent on food

Crewe

11–3; 5.30–11
British Lion
58 Nantwich Road
Ind Coope Burton Ale; Tetley-Walker Mild, Bitter H
Small, very busy town pub; mainly used by locals. Known as "Pig" because of carving above fireplace. Various games

Try also: Hop Pole, Wistaston Road (Greenall)

11–3; 7–11
Horseshoe
North Street ☎ (0270) 584265
Robinson Best Mild, Best Bitter H, **Old Tom** G
Multi-roomed town pub. Piano Sun nights. Pub games

11–3; 5.30 (7.30 Sun)–11
Kings Arms
56 Earle Street ☎ (0270) 584134
Chesters Best Mild, Best Bitter; Whitbread Trophy H
Town-centre pub. Each of 4 rooms caters for different type of customer. Mild is the most popular pint. Pub games

11–3; 5.30–11
Rising Sun
130 Earle Street
Boddingtons Mild, Bitter H
Extremely popular, 2-roomed pub with wide range of clientele. Landlord famous in Crewe. Plenty of characters. Pub games

Try also: Belle Vue (Walker)

Croft

11.30–3; 5.30–10.30 (11 F, S)
Plough
Heath Lane (off A579 towards Kenyon)
Greenall Whitley Mild, Bitter E
Cosy local: Beer Guide regular. 27 years with same landlord. Don't stand too close to the fire! Q

Disley

11–3; 5.30–10.30 (11 F, S)
Crescent
Buxton Road (A6)
☎ (0663) 62638
Robinson Best Mild, Best Bitter H
Compact, homely pub popular with locals. Room for diners. Varied and excellent menu. Warm and friendly atmosphere (for lunch)

Eaton

11–3 (not Mon–Fri); 5.30–11
Plough
Congleton Road
☎ (0260) 280207
Banks's Mild, Bitter H
A pleasant, low-beamed rural local. Former Winkles Brewery tied house

Ellesmere Port

11–3.; 5.30–10.30 (11 F, S)
Grosvenor Hotel
2 Upper Mersey Street (below M53) ☎ (051) 355 1810
Tetley-Walker Mild, Bitter H
Large dockland pub with kitchen range in lounge and stained glass dome. Handy for nearby National Boat Museum. Pub games

11–3; 5.30–10.30 (11 F, S)
Travellers Rest
14 Ledsham Road, Little Sutton ☎ 051 339 2187
Ind Coope Burton Ale; Walker Dark Mild, Best Bitter, Winter Warmer H
Popular pub on outskirts of Ellesmere Port. Refurbished with large lounge and dining area. Pub games

Try also: Woodland (Bass)

Farndon

11–3; 5.30–11
Greyhound Hotel
High Street (B5130)
☎ (0829) 270244
Greenall Whitley Mild, Bitter, Original H
Smart hotel bar close to River Dee and medieval bridge. A favourite spot for fishermen (not Sun) (not Sat)

Frodsham

11–3; 6–11
Golden Lion
High Street (A56/B5152)
☎ (0928) 32179
Samuel Smith OBB H
Large, open-plan main bar with separate games room. Brewery memorabilia

11–3; 5.30–11
Netherton Hall
Chester Road (A56)
☎ (0928) 32342
Ind Coope Burton Ale; Tetley-Walker Mild, Bitter H
Converted farmhouse replacing demolished Whalebone Inn. Pub history illustrated. Excellent lunches. Pub games Q

Goostrey

11–3; 5.30–10.30 (11 F, S)
Crown
111 Main Road ☎ (0477) 32128
Marston Burton Bitter, Pedigree H
Imposing 16th-century pub in sought-after dormitory village. Homely lounge and traditional tap room. Wide range of food (not Mon) (not Sun)

Cheshire

Great Barrow

12–3; 7–11

White Horse Inn
Main Street (A51)
☎ (0829) 40265
Banks's Mild, Bitter E
Small, friendly village local with country flavour
⊛ ◐ (not Mon) ⊟

Great Budworth

11–3; 5.30–11

George & Dragon
High Street ☎ (0606) 891317
Tetley-Walker Mild, Bitter H
Cosy pub in extremely attractive village, much loved by TV producers looking for an authentic 19th-century setting. Pub games ⌘ ◐ ▶ ⊟

Haslington

11–3; 6.30–11

Hawk
Crewe Road (A534)
Robinson Best Mild, Best Bitter E
15th-century roadside inn with separate restaurant
⌘ ⊛ (patio) ◐ ▶ (Thu–Sat)

Hatchmere

11–3; 5.30–11

Carriers Inn
on B5152 OS554722
Burtonwood Dark Mild, Bitter H
In picturesque countryside next to Hatchmere Lake. Justifiably popular in summer. Pub games
⊅ ⊛ ◐ (Fri–Sun) ⊟ ⚲

Healey

12–3; 5.30–10.30 (11 F, S)

Railway
Mill Lane (B5159)
☎ (092 575) 2742
Boddingtons Mild, Bitter H
Popular multi-roomed pub catering for all tastes. Convenient for visitors to the Lymm area ⊅ ⊛ ◐ ⊟

Henbury

11–3; 5.30–10.30 (11 F, S)

Cock Inn
Chelford Road (A537)
☎ (0625) 25659
Robinson Best Mild, Best Bitter, Old Tom H
Comfortable main road pub, local and passing trade. Just out of Macclesfield. Pub games
⊅ (restaurant) ⊛ ◐ ▶ ⊟

Kettleshulme

11–3 (not winter Mon–Fri); 7–10.30 (11 F, S)

Bulls Head
Macclesfield Road (A5002)
Tetley-Walker Mild, Bitter H
Traditional stone-terraced pub in picturesque Peak National Park village. Quaint unspoilt front lounge a restful retreat, while village gossip is debated in larger vault. Pub games; popular with local farmers
⌘ Q ⊅ (garden) ⊛

Knutsford

11–3; 5.30–10.30 (11 F, S)

Builders Arms
Mobberley Road (off A537)
☎ (0565) 4528
Marston Mercian Mild, Burton Bitter, Pedigree H
Small and busy local with keen games emphasis
Q ⊛ ⊟ ⚲

11–3; 5.30–10.30 (11 F, S)

White Lion
King Street ☎ (0565) 2018
Ind Coope Burton Ale; Tetley-Walker Bitter H
Tasteful pub with extensive range of cheese and paté lunches. Doggie bags provided ⌘ ⊅ ⊛ ◐ (not Sun) ⚲

Little Leigh

11–3; 5.30–11

Holly Bush
on A49 300 yds S of A533 Jct
☎ (0606) 853196
Greenall Whitley Mild, Bitter H
Rustic thatched, local in front of a working farm. The last of a dying breed in this affluent part of the North West
⌘ Q ⊅ ⊛ ⊟ ⌕

Lymm

11–3; 5.30–10.30 (11 F, S)

Spread Eagle
Eagle Brow (A6144)
☎ (092 575) 3139
Lees GB Mild, Bitter H, Moonraker (winter) E
Plush, ornate pub in village centre with small popular snug, large lounge and upstairs ballroom. 200 yards from canal moorings ⌘ ⊟

Macclesfield

11–3 (not Mon–Fri); 5.30–10.30 (11 F, S)

Baths Hotel
Green Street
Boddingtons Mild, Bitter H
Thriving pub named after now defunct public baths. Pub games ⊟ ⚲

11–3; 5.30–10.30 (11 F, S)

Bridgewater Arms
Buxton Road (A537)
☎ (0625) 22660
Wilson's Original Mild, Original Bitter; Webster Yorkshire Bitter H
Next to Macclesfield Canal and named after its builder. Always warm and friendly
⊟ ⚲

11–3; 5.30–10.30 (11 F, S)

Britannia
Hurdsfield Road (100 yds from Macclesfield canal)
☎ (0625) 23954
Greenall Whitley Mild, Bitter H
Small stone built pub that is worth the walk up the hill Q

11–3; 5.30–10.30 (11 F, S)

Evening Star
87 James Street (off Park Lane)
☎ (0625) 24093
Marston Mercian Mild, Burton Bitter, Pedigree E
Former W.A. Smiths house, busy and comfortable pub. Just off the beaten track
Q ⊟ ⚲

11–3; 5.30–10.30 (11 F, S)

Lord Byron
Chapel Street (off Mill Lane)
☎ (0625) 24018
Robinson Best Mild, Best Bitter H
Cosy, friendly local tucked away in a side street. Popular with most ages. Pub games
⌘ ⊟

Malpas

11–3; 5.30–11

Red Lion
1 Old Hall Street (B5395)
☎ (0948) 860368
Draught Bass; Marston Burton Bitter H
Old coaching house with sauna and solarium. Ancient chair with unusual history. Family room. Landlord's own malt whisky on sale. Pub games ⌘ ⊅ ⊛ ⋈ ◐ ▶ ⊟ ⌕

Middlewich

11–3; 5.30–11

Newton Brewery
Webbs Lane (100 yds off A54)
☎ (060 684) 3502
Marston Burton Bitter, Merrie Monk, Pedigree (summer) H
19th century red brick pub. Brewery unfortunately long defunct. A tidy pub, spartan bar and pleasant quiet lounge. Darts and dominoes ⊛ ⊟

Try also: Boars Head (Robinson)

Mobberley

11.30–3; 5.30–10.30 (11 F, S)

Bird in Hand
Knolls Green (B5085)
☎ (056 587) 3149
Samuel Smith OBB, Museum Ale H
Pleasant multi-roomed roadside pub. Good food (Tue–Sat) ⌘ ⊅ ◐ ▶ ⌕

Try also: Chapel House (Boddingtons)

81

Cheshire

Nantwich

11–3; 5.30–11

Bowling Green
The Gullet
Ruddles County; Webster Yorkshire Bitter, Choice; Wilson's Original Bitter H
Smart, multi-levelled pub; popular with younger people, but not swamped by them. Cards and dominoes

11–3; 5.30–11

Rifleman
68 James Hall Street
Robinson Best Mild, Best Bitter E
Back street pub of nooks and crannies, though it has recently lost all its small rooms. Darts, dominoes and cribbage (lunch)

Try also: **Wilbraham Arms** (John Smith)

Neston

11–3; 5.30–10.30 (11 F, S)

Brown Horse
3 The Cross ☎ 051 336 1052
Tetley-Walker Mild, Bitter H
Large village local with 1 long bar; occasional live music. Darts and dominoes

11.30–3; 5.30–10.30 (11 F, S)

Lady Hamilton
Henley Road, Little Neston
☎ 051 336 4632
Boddingtons Bitter; Higsons Mild, Bitter H
Large, comfortable, modern estate pub. New licensee has plans to reinstate public bar. Darts and dominoes (tennis ct)

Newbold

11–3; 5.30–11

Horse Shoe
Fence Lane (2 miles E of Astbury Village) OS863602
☎ (0260) 272205
Robinsons Best Mild, Best Bitter E, **Old Tom (winter)** G
Isolated country pub, recently modernised. Formerly part of a farmhouse

Northwich

11–3 (4 Fri); 5.30–11

Bee Hive
High Street ☎ (0606) 3704
Greenall Whitley Mild, Bitter, Original H
Small, friendly town-centre pub with name in terracotta on front. Popular with shoppers at lunchtime. Pub games

11–3; 5.30–11

Lion & Railway
Station Road ☎ (0606) 6080
Greenall Whitley Mild, Bitter H
Friendly, corner pub opposite station – hence large amount of railway memorabilia. Basic bar and plush larger lounge. Pub games

Over Peover

11–3; 5.30–10.30 (11 F, S)

Whipping Stocks
Stock Lane, Peover Heath (off A50) OS793735
☎ (056 581) 2332
Samuel Smith OBB H
Comfortable, multi-roomed pub just off main road. Good food; children's play area outside; impressive fireplace. Friendly landlord

Overton

11–3; 7 (5.30 summer)–11

Belle Monte
Belle Monte Road (off B5152)
☎ (0928) 32321
Samuel Smith OBB H
Friendly, ornately-decorated pub on hill above Frodsham with fine views over Mersey Estuary, well worth finding

Plumley

11.30–3; 5.30–10.30 (11 F. S)

Golden Pheasant
Plumley Moor Road
☎ (056 581) 2261
Lees GB Mild, Bitter, Moonraker (occasional) H
Comfortable large country pub. Jazz music Tue, C&W Thu. Restaurant; bowling green; pub games

11–3; 5.30–10.30 (11 F, S)

Smoker
Manchester Road (A556)
☎ (056 581) 2338
Robinson Best Mild, Best Bitter E
Old pub with cobbled frontage and thatched roof. Former Elizabethan coaching inn, named after a racehorse owned by a local squire. Restaurant

Poynton

11–3; 5.30–10.30 (11 F, S)

Bulls Head
London Road (A523)
Boddingtons Mild, Bitter E
Traditional, friendly multi-roomed pub. Memorabilia includes sporting photos and trophies in front room vault

Try also: **Boars Head**, Higher Poynton (Boddingtons)

Rainow

11–3; 5.30–10.30 (11 F, S)

Highwayman
A5002, N of Rainow
☎ (0625) 73245
Thwaites Bitter H
400 year-old country pub with magnificent views. Pub games

Runcorn

11–3; 5 (7 Sat)–10.30 (11, F, S)

Barley Mow
56 Church Street
☎ (092 85) 75235
Walker Mild, Bitter H
Comfortable town centre pub near Runcorn–Widnes bridge. Lounge usually used for lunches. Pub games

Sandbach

11–3 (4 Thu); 5.30–11

Lower Chequers
Crown Banks ☎ (0270) 762569
Boddingtons Bitter; Marston Pedigree H
Striking black and white pub, near cobbled market square and Saxon crosses. The oldest in town (1570)

11–3 (4 Thu); 5.30–11

Swan & Chequers
16 Hightown ☎ (0270) 762109
Robinson Best Mild, Best Bitter E
Imposing building, once a corn exchange. Single bar of lounge standard. Pub games

Try also: **Ring o' Bells** (Tetley-Walker)

Sarn

11.30–3; 5–11

Queens Head
off B5069 OS440447
☎ (094 881) 244
Marston Border Mild, Burton Bitter H
Small pub alongside old mill brook in hunting country. Meals served in separate cosy bistro area. Family room. Pub games

Scholar Green

11–3; 7–11 (6.30 F, S)

Globe
12 Drumber Lane OS846579
☎ (0782) 512919
Marston Pedigree H
Pub with 3 small rooms: central bar, lounge and darts room

Smallwood

12–3; 6–11

Bluebell
Spen Green (1 mile W of village on lane towards A34) OS821607
Greenall Whitley Bitter H
300 year-old rural pub, once part of a farm. Low beams, stone floors and antique benches. Pub games

Cheshire

Sutton

11–3; 5.30–10.30 (11 F, S)

Lamb
Hollin Lane ☎ (026 05) 2000
Tetley-Walker Bitter H
Pleasant stone village pub between Macclesfield and Peak National Park. Pub games ⚌ ⛄ ⚽ ◐ ▶ (Thu–Sun) ⚑

Tabley

11–3; 5.30–10.30 (11 F, S)

Windmill
Chester Road (A556)
☎ (0565) 2670
Robinson Best Mild, Bitter, Best Bitter H**, Old Tom** G
Roadside hostelry of 4 rooms each with own special character. A taxidermist's delight! A rare outlet for Robinson's Bitter. Darts ⚌ ◐ ▶ ⚑

Tarporley

11–3; 5.30–11

Rising Sun
High Street ☎ (082 93) 2423
Robinson Best Mild, Best Bitter H
Authentic former coaching inn of character with interesting rooms; Antique furniture and Worthington mirrors. Good value quality meals
⛄ (if dining) ◐ ▶ (not Sun)

Warrington

11–3; 6.30–10.30 (11 F, S)

Lower Angel
Buttermarket Street (near Odeon) ☎ (0925) 33299
Ind Coope Burton Ale; Walker Mild, Bitter, Best Bitter, Winter Warmer H
Small, friendly 2-roomed town-centre pub, with fine Walker's tiled frontage. Comfortable lounge; basic bar. A haven in a town which lacks real ale and good pubs ⚑ ⇌ (Central)

Try also: Lord Rodney (Tetley)

Weston Village

11–3; 5.30–11

Royal Oak
Heath Road South (off A557)
☎ (092 85) 65839
Marston Mercian Mild, Burton Bitter, Pedigree H
Popular at lunchtime with nearby ICI staff. Pool table doubles for food servery Fri lunch. Overlooks Mersey estuary and ICI chemical works. Pub games ⚽ ◐ ▶ ⚑

Wheelock

closed lunchtimes except Sun; 8–11

Commercial
Crewe Road
Boddingtons Bitter; Marston Burton Bitter, Pedigree H
Originally a Georgian house, now a pleasant free house near the canal. Rare outlet for real cider. Pub games ⚌ Q ⚑ ♂

Widnes

11–3; 5–10.30 (11 F, S)

Bradley
Albert Road ☎ (051) 424 3969
Walker Mild, Bitter, Best Bitter, Winter Warmer H
Imposing Victorian town local. Pub games ◐ ⚑

Wilmslow

11–3; 5.30–10.30 (11 F, S)

Farmers Arms
Chapel Lane (off A34)
Boddingtons Mild, Bitter H
Traditional and thriving town local with busy tap room ⚌ Q ⚑ ◐ (not Sun)

11–3; 5.30–10.30 (11 F, S)

Horse & Jockey
Gravel Lane, Davenport Green (just off B5085)
☎ (0625) 582158
Greenall Whitley Mild, Bitter H
Large locals' pub close to Mobberley Road. Big public bar with pool table and darts ⚌ ⚑

Wincle

11–3; 5.30–10.30 (11 F, S)

Wild Boar Inn
on A54 ☎ (026 07) 219
Robinson Best Mild, Best Bitter H
Popular pub on edge of moors. Home of local clay pigeon club. Excellent food
⚌ ⛄ ⚽ ◐ ▶ ♿

Winsford

11–3; 5.30–11

Gate
Chester Road, Over (off A54)
☎ (0606) 592303
Stones Best Bitter H
Welcoming pub with basic bar and cosy lounge. Pub games ⚑

Let's sing a song to the pubs of the land,
With a hey for the nut-brown ale;
The blowsy, the bleary, the brash and the bland
With a hey for the nut-brown ale.

You know 'Ye Smuggler's Cave' will be full
Of polystyrene sloops
A plastic net with a plastic lobster
Caught in its plastic loops;
Where you sit on plastic casks and drink
Warm Watneys from plastic stoups.

The barman caricatures his breed
By calling everyone 'squire';
The barmaid's warmth is slightly less
Than that from the false log-fire;
There's the bluff, suggestive, second-hand smell
Of a distant deep-fat frier.

Let's sing a song to the pubs that we loathe
With a hey for the nut-brown ale.
Where the lampshades are red and the carpet
   is mauve,
With a hey for the nut-brown ale

From "With a Hey for the Nut-Brown Ale", published in *Two Beers, My Friend Will Pay* (order form, p. 381)

Cleveland

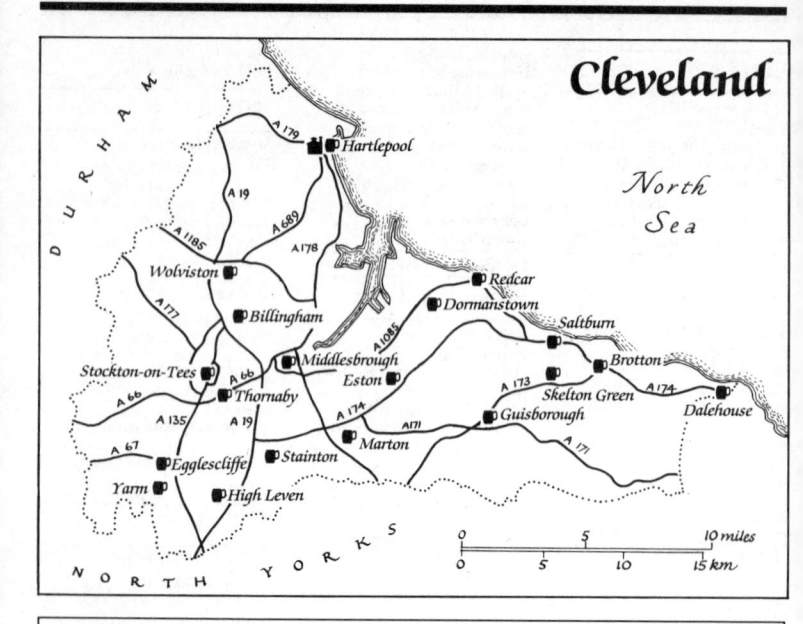

🏠 *Cameron*, Hartlepool

Billingham

11–3; 5.30–10.30 (11 F & S)
Billingham Arms
The Causeway
☎ (0642) 553661
McEwan 80/-; Younger Scotch, No. 3 H
3-star hotel in town centre. Interesting cedar panelling in ward room rescued from luxury liner. Modern lounge bar

11–3; 5.30–10.30 (11 F & S)
Stoney Oak
High Grange Avenue
☎ (0642) 566028
Draught Bass H
Recently built, open-plan pub. Popular with young lager drinkers but do try draught Bass

Brotton

11–3; 7–10.30 (11 F & S)
Green Tree
High Street ☎ (0287) 76377
Cameron Strongarm H
Fine traditional stone-built, street-corner local with several rooms. Originally had a thatched roof

Dalehouse

11.30–3; 6.30–11
Fox & Hounds
4 Dalehouse, Staithes
☎ (0947) 840534
Tetley Bitter; Vaux Samson H
Listed building situated at foot of hill in charming village, half a mile from Staithes. Pleasantly decorated bar and lounge

Dormanstown

11–3; 6–10.30 (11 F & S)
Kingfisher
Farndale Square (off A1042)
☎ (0642) 484815
Samuel Smith OBB H
Estate pub with imposing frontage so typical of Samuel Smith's brewery. Games

Egglescliffe

12–3; 5.30–10.30 (11 F & S)
Pot & Glass
Church Road (off old A19 just N of Yarm Bridge)
☎ (0642) 780145
Draught Bass E
Charming village pub with 2 bars. Whitewashed exterior under pantiled roof. Amazing bar fronts carved from furniture by village carpenter

Eston

11–3; 6–10.30 (11 F & S)
Eston Hotel
Fabian Road ☎ (0642) 453256
Samuel Smith OBB H
Imposing post-war hotel in newer part of Eston

Guisborough

11–3; 5.30–10.30 (11 F & S)
Abbey Inn
35 Redcar Road ☎ (0287) 32802
Samuel Smith OBB, Museum Ale H
Small 2-room pub close to town centre and ancient priory. Locals and travellers can join in sing-song around piano every Saturday night. Varied games

11.30–3; 6.30–10.30 (11 F & S)
Ship
145 Westgate ☎ (0287) 32233
Draught Bass H
A former coaching inn, now a busy town-centre pub with a regular clientele. Friendly and cosy; decorated with genuine maritime relics

11–3; 6.30–10.30 (11 F & S)
Voyager
The Avenue, Hutton Meadows (near Hutton village) ☎ (0287) 34774
Cameron Traditional Bitter, Strongarm H
Large estate pub, imaginatively laid out on 3 levels with partitions. Games

Hartlepool

11–3; 5.30–10.30 (11 F & S)
Causeway
Elwick Road, Stranton (off A689) ☎ (0429) 273954
Cameron Strongarm H
3-roomed, redbrick Victorian pub with long bar room. Close to Cameron's brewery – a true pub in the old style

11–3; 7–10.30 (6–11 F & S)

Cleveland

New Inn
Durham Street (main road to headland) ☎ (0429) 267797
Cameron Strongarm H
Neat and friendly, street-corner pub on headland

High Leven

11.30–3, 7–10.30 (11 F & S)

Fox Covert
Low Lane
Vaux Samson; Ward Sheffield Best Bitter H
A distinctive cluster of brick buildings of obvious farmhouse origin make up this free house beside the A1044. Comfortable, open-plan interior with a warm welcome

Marton

11–3; 5.30–10.30 (11 F & S)

Apple Tree
38 The Derby (off B1380)
☎ (0642) 310564
Draught Bass H
Friendly comfortable pub in a private estate. An example of what can be done with a modern pub

Middlesbrough

11–3; 5.30–10.30 (11 F & S)

Princess Alice
Newport Road (opposite bus station) ☎ (0642) 243838
Draught Bass; Stones Best Bitter H
Victorian pub, modernised in Art Deco style. Single room, but with public bar corner

11.30–3; 5.30–10.30 (11 F & S)

Star & Garter
Southfield Road (behind polytechnic) ☎ (0642) 245307
Draught Bass; Stones Best Bitter; Taylor Landlord; Theakston Best Bitter, XB, Old Peculier H
Former club premises, modernised, but retaining many original features

11.30–3; 5.30–10.30 (11 F & S)

Viking
Broughton Avenue, Easterside (opposite Prissick base on Marton Road) ☎ (0642) 316559
Samuel Smith OBB H
Large pub between council estate and private housing with recently converted Art Deco lounge and upstairs traditional bar. Games

Redcar

12–3; 6.30–10.30 (11 F & S)

Newbigging Hotel
Turner Street ☎ (0642) 482059
Taylor Landlord; Tetley Bitter, Theakston Best Bitter, XB, Old Peculier H
Friendly welcome in old-world style hotel with recommended restaurant (not Sun) (Central)

11.30–3; 6–10.30 (11 F & S)

Yorkshire Coble
West Dyke Road
☎ (0642) 482071
Samuel Smith OBB H
Smart, modern, estate pub beside racecourse – very busy on race days. Pub games (by request)

Saltburn

11–3; 5.30–10.30 (11 F & S)

Victoria
Dundas Street ☎ (0287) 24637
Draught Bass; Theakston Best Bitter, XB, Old Peculier H
Lively, comfortable free house, excellently converted from old warehouse. First true pub in a Quaker town – others are hotels

Skelton Green

12–3; 7–10.30 (11 F & S)

Green Inn
Boosebeck Road
☎ (0287) 50475
Cameron Strongarm H
Terraced, stone-built village local with several rooms. On route of Cleveland Way. Pub games

Stainton

11–3; 5.30–10.30 (11 F & S)

Stainton Inn
off B1380 ☎ (0642) 599902
Cameron Strongarm; Everards Old Original H
Comfortable, 1-room village pub noted for its cuisine

Stockton-on-Tees

11–3 (4.30 Wed); 5.30–10.30 (11 F & S)

Green Dragon
Finkle Street ☎ (0642) 672798
Samuel Smith OBB H
Former coaching house backing on to Green Dragon Yard in the oldest part of Stockton. Cobbled yard for outdoor drinking

11–3; 5.30–10.30 (11 F & S)

Lord Nelson
Bath Lane ☎ (0642) 606450
Cameron Strongarm H
Comfortable town/estate pub with one room and U-shaped bar. Friendly atmosphere

11–3; 5.30–10.30 (11 F & S)

Parkwood Hotel
64–66 Darlington Road, Hartburn (B6541)
☎ (0642) 580800
Ward Sheffield Best Bitter H
Smart conversion of large house in leafy village suburb. Former home of ship-owning Ropner family, now a free house

11–3; 5.30–10.30 (11 F & S)

Stockton Arms Hotel
Darlington Road, Hartburn (B6541) ☎ (0642) 580104
Draught Bass H
Warm and friendly suburban pub with several rooms, some oddly-shaped because pub is on a corner. Deservedly popular Q

11–3 (4.30 Wed); 5.30 (7 Wed)–10.30 (11 F & S)

Sun Inn
Knowle Street (off High Street)
☎ (0642) 615676
Draught Bass H
One of the few unspoilt working men's pubs left on Teesside. A classic and busy pub. Games

11–3; 5.30–10.30 (11 F & S)

Wild Ox
138 Morton Road (opposite Hills timber factory)
☎ (0642) 611655
Cameron Strongarm H
3-roomed local. 2 original rooms retain much of the atmosphere of original Victorian pub. Extension built in last decade

Thornaby

11.30–3; 5.30 (7 Sat)–10.30 (11 F & S)

Cleveland Hotel
Bridge Street
☎ (0642) 676917
Theakston XB; Younger No. 3 H
Warm and friendly local with distinctive façade, opposite station

Wolviston

11–3; 5.30–10.30 (11 F & S)

Wellington
High Street ☎ (074 04) 439
Draught Bass E
Busy village inn on the outskirts of Teesside. Once a stable and forge, named after the Duke himself, who used to stay at nearby Wynyard Hall (Mon to Fri)

Yarm

11–3; 5.30–10.30 (11 F & S)

Black Bull
High Street ☎ (0642) 780299
Draught Bass E & H
Lively and bustling former coaching inn in conservation area. Single deep rambling room full of atmosphere

11–3; 5.30–10.30 (11 F & S)

Ketton Ox
100 High Street
☎ (0642) 788311
Vaux Samson; Ward Sheffield Bitter H
Former coaching inn makes cosy friendly local. Various games (Tue–Sat)

85

Cornwall

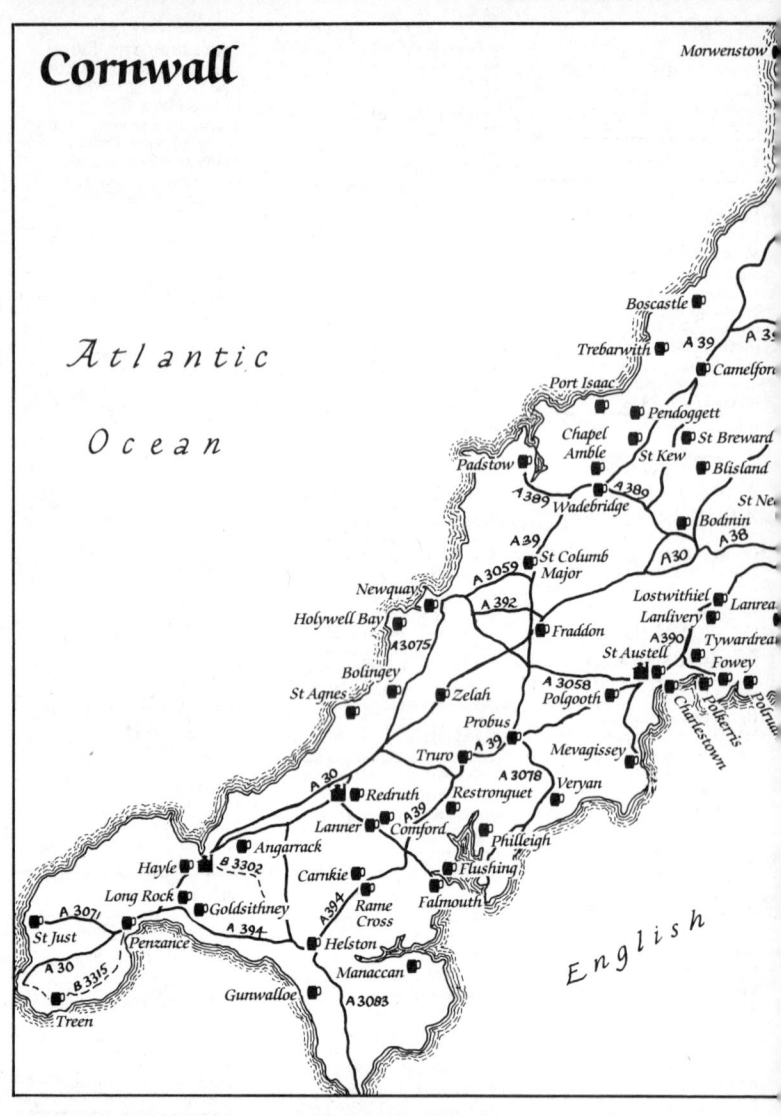

🏭 **Cornish Brewery Co.**, Redruth; **Paradise**, Hayle; **St. Austell**, St. Austell

Altarnun

11–2.30; 5.30–11
Rising Sun
Camelford Road (off A30)
OS825215 ☎ (0566) 86632
Flowers Original H
Excellent 16th-century pub on edge of Bodmin Moor. Popular with locals and visitors. Guest beers 🏠🛏🍴🎵 ()▶ 🚹🅿

Angarrack

11–2.30; 6–10.30 (11 F, S & summer)
Angarrack Inn
Off A30 ☎ (0736) 752380
St Austell Bosun's Bitter, Hicks Special H
Very comfortable and welcoming village pub. Extensive and good value menu 🏠🛏🍴 ()▶ 🚹🅿

Blisland

11.30–3; 6–10.30 (11 F, S & summer)
Royal Oak
1½ miles N of A30
☎ (0208) 850739
Draught Bass H
Friendly inn situated in only Cornish village with a green. Close to Bodmin Moor. Patio and pond. Family room.
🏠Q🛏🍴 ()▶ (not Sun) 🚹🅿

Bodmin

11–3; 6–11
Masons Arms
Higher Bore Street (A389)
Ruddles County; Ushers Best Bitter H

Cornwall

Cornish JD Dry Hop Bitter, Wessex Stud, GBH ⊞ Delightfully unspoilt gem – away from Perranporth's tourist traps
⚐Q😊⬛🍴⦿ 🍴⚐⚑☩ (summer)

Boscastle

11–2.30; 6–10.30 (11 F, S & summer)

Cobweb
B3263, Bude Road
OS102914 ☎ (08405) 278
St Austell Tinners Bitter, Hicks Special; Wadworth 6X ⊞
Dating from the 1700s, this imposing 4-storey building was once a warehouse
⚐Q😊⬛🍴

Try also: Napoleon (Free)

Botus Fleming (Saltash)

12–2.30; 6–11

Rising Sun Inn
½ mile off A388
Ruddles Best Bitter, County ⊞; **Ushers Best Bitter** ⓖ
Unspoilt, basic country pub with friendly atmosphere, on outskirts of Saltash ⚐⬛⚑⦿

Callington

11–3; 6.30–11

Bulls Head
Town centre ☎ (0579) 83387
St Austell Tinners Bitter, Hicks Special ⊞
15th-century town pub with old stone fireplaces and oak beams. Passage once connected the inn to the nearby church 😊⬛⚑⦿

Try also: Coachmakers Arms

Camelford

10.30–3; 6–10.30 (11 F, S & summer)

Masons Arms
Market Place (A39)
☎ (0840) 213009
St Austell Tinners Bitter, Hicks Special ⊞
Over 300 years old, this pub has been flooded several times. Old carved stone fireplace ⚐😊⬛🍴☲ 🍴⚑

Carnkie

10.30–2.30; 6–10.30 (11 F, S & summer)

Wheal Basset Inn
Off B3297, near Redruth
OS688399 ☎ (0209) 216621
Bolsters Bitter; Butcombe Bitter; Hancock's HB ⊞
Friendly village local in former tin mining area. Pub games
⚐Q😊⬛🍴🍴

Chapel Amble

10.30–2.30; 5.30–10.30 (11 F, S & summer)

Maltsters Arms
Off B3314 OS997754
☎ (020 881) 2473
Courage Directors; St Austell Tinners Bitter, Hicks Special ⊞
3 ft thick walls and Delabole slate floor. Busy pub once used by the bargemen. Guest beers ⚐Q😊⬛🍴

Charlestown

11–3; 6–11

Rashleigh Inn
Near harbour ☎ (0726) 73635
Wadworth 6X ⊞
A large village pub and hotel near a tiny port, which is still used for exporting china clay. Family room. Guest beers
⚐Q😊⬛🍴⦿ 🍴⚐⚑

Chilsworthy

12–3; 7–11

White Hart Inn
Latchley Road ☎ (0822) 832307
Courage Best Bitter, Directors; Flowers IPA; Marston Pedigree; Wadworth 6X ⊞
Fine old village inn on the edge of Tamar valley in former mining area. Superb views
⚐😊⬛⚑☩⦿

Try also: Rising Sun, Gunnislake

Comford

11–2.30; 6–10.30 (11 F, S & summer)

Fox & Hounds
A393/B3298 ☎ (0209) 820251
Draught Bass; St Austell Bosuns Bitter, Hicks Special ⓖ
Comfortable country pub with restaurant. Prize-winner in flower and garden competition ⚐😊⬛🍴 🍴☩

Cremyll

11–3; 5.30–11

Edgcumbe Arms
End of B3247 ☎ (0752) 822294
Courage Best Bitter, Directors (summer) ⊞
18th-century inn by the passenger ferry to Admiral's Hard, Plymouth. Near Mount Edgcumbe Country Park and coastal paths ⚐😊⬛⚑

Falmouth

10.30–2.30; 6–10.30 (11 F, S & summer)

Seven Stars
The Moor ☎ (0326) 312111
Draught Bass; Courage Directors, St Austell Hicks Special ⓖ
Totally unspoilt, old-style drinking house, in same

Stratton
Launceston
Tregadillett
Altarnun
A30
A388
Upton Cross
Chilsworthy
A390
Callington
Liskeard
Botus Fleming
Tideford A38
Torpoint
A387
Hessenford
Cremyll
Polperro

D E V O N

C h a n n e l

0 — 10 miles
0 — 10 — 20 km

Comfortable traditional family pub with a warm atmosphere. Pub games ⚐😊⬛🍴⦿

11–3; 6–11

Weavers
11 Honey Street (off A389)
St Austell Tinners Bitter, Hicks Special ⊞
Traditional family pub with lots of antique clocks
😊⬛🍴☩

Try also: Hole in the Wall (Free)

Bolingey

11–2.30; 6–10.30 (11 F, S & summer)

Bolingey Inn
Off B3284 ☎ (0872) 572794

87

Cornwall

family for 5 generations
Q ⊛ ☎ ⑴ ⊕

Try also: Wodehouse (St. Austell)

Flushing

11–2.30; 6–10.30 (11 F, S & summer)

Royal Standard
Off A393 at Penryn
Draught Bass; Cornish JD Dry Hop Bitter; Whitbread IPA H
Pub at the entrance to the village: beware of swans! ⊛ ⑴

Fowey

11–3; 6–11

King of Prussia
Town Quay ☎ (072 683) 2450
St Austell Bosun's Bitter, Tinners Bitter, Hicks Special H
15th-century hotel bar and restaurant; view across the harbour. Pub games
⊛ (restaurant) ~ ⑴ ▶ ☼

Try also: Ship, Lugger & Galleon

Fraddon

11–3; 6–11

Blue Anchor
On A30 ☎ (0726) 860352
St Austell Tinners Bitter, Hicks Special
Popular stop on the busy A30. Regular live groups at weekends; good value meals
⊛ (summer) ⊛ ~ ⑴ ⊕ ☼

Goldsithney

10.30–2.30; 6–10.30 (11 F, S & summer)

Crown
Fore Street (B3280)
St Austell Bosun's Bitter, XXXX, Hicks Special H
Atractive pub with friendly village touch; restaurant serving good food ⚘ ⊛ ⊛ ⑴ ▶ ▲

Try also: Trevelyan Arms

Gunwalloe

11–2.30; 6–10.30 (11 F, S & summer)

Halzephron
Off A3083 OS655225
Cornish Original; Tetley Bitter
Old smugglers' inn. Woodwork in the pub comes from old wrecks ⚘ ⊛ ⊛ ⑴ ▶ ▲

Helston

10.30–2.30; 5.30–10.30 (11 F, S & summer)

Blue Anchor
50 Coinagehall Street
Blue Anchor Medium Bitter, Best Bitter, Special Bitter, Extra Special H
Superb, world-famous 15th-century thatched home-brew pub. Jazz Wed eves
⚘ Q ⊛ ⑴ ▶ ⊕ ☼ ▲

Hessenford

11–3; 5.30–11

Copley Arms
On A387 ☎ (050 34) 209
St Austell Tinners Bitter, Hicks Special H
14th-century country pub. Exposed stone walls, oak beams and fireplaces. Pretty riverside setting. Excellent home cooked food
⚘ Q ⊛ ⊛ ~ ⑴ ▶ ⊕ ☼

Holywell Bay

11–3; 6.30–11

Treguth Inn
Off A3075 ☎ (0637) 830248
Courage Best Bitter, Directors
Real gem with solid walls, low beams and thatched roof. Near acres of fine sandy beach and leisure park ⚘ ⊛ ⊛ ⑴ ▶ ▲

Hayle

11 (12 winter)–2.30; 6–10.30 (11 F, S & summer)

Bird in Hand
Trellisick Road (off B3302)
☎ (0736) 753974
Paradise Bitter, Artist Ale, Victory Ale H
Home-brew pub in a former coach house. Set in grounds of bird park. Food weekends only in winter. Guest beers ⊛ ⊛ ⑴ ▲ ⇌

Lanlivery

11.30–3; 6.30–11

Crown Inn
2 miles W of Lostwithiel
OS080590 ☎ (0208) 872707
Draught Bass H
Comfortable 12th-century inn with excellent food. Guest beers ⚘ Q ⊛ ⊛ ⑴ ▶ ⊕ ▲

Lanner

11–2.30; 6–10.30 (11 F, S & summer)

Coppice Inn
Lanner Moor (off A393)
Ind Coope Burton Ale; Tetley Bitter H
Pleasant pub with spacious grounds and excellent food ⚘ Q ⊛ ⊛ ⑴ ▶ ☼ ▲

Lanreath

11–3; 6–11

Punch Bowl Inn
Off B3359 ☎ (0503) 20218
Draught Bass; Courage Directors; St Austell Punch Bowl Best Bitter H
Famous old coaching inn in pleasant village. Good food. Beer range may vary. Pub games ⚘ ⊛ ⊛ ~ ⑴ ▶ ⊕

Launceston

11–3; 5–11

White Horse Inn
14 Newport Square

Ruddles Best Bitter, County; Ushers Best Bitter; Webster Yorkshire Bitter E
Comfortable 18th-century coaaching inn. Wide selection of home-made meals
⚘ Q ⊛ ⊛ ~ ⑴ ▶ ⊕ ☼ ▲

Try also: Westgate Inn

Liskeard

10.30–3; 5.30–11

Fountain Hotel
The Parade ☎ (0579) 42154
Courage Best Bitter, Directors H
Comfortable, quiet lounge with separate dining area
⚘ ⊛ ⊛ ~ ⑴ ▶ ⊕

Long Rock

11–2.30; 5.30–10.30 (11 F, S & summer)

Mexico Inn
On old A30 ☎ (0736) 710625
Draught Bass; Cornish Original; Courage Directors H
Originally the offices for the Mexico Mine Company. Now an outstanding free house with varied menu. All homemade food
⚘ ⊛ ⊛ ⑴ ▶ ☼ ▲

Lostwithiel

11–3; 6–11

Royal Oak
Duke Street (off A390)
☎ (0208) 872552
Eldridge Pope Royal Oak; Flowers IPA, Original; Fuller London Pride H
Busy, friendly 13th-century inn with a good restaurant. Guest beers. Near Restormel Castle ⊛ ⊛ ~ ⑴ ▶ ⊕ ☼ ▲ ⇌

Try also: Royal Talbot (Free)

Manaccan

11–2.30; 6–10.30 (11 F, S & summer)

New Inn
OS763248 ☎ (032 623) 323
Cornish JD Dry Hop Bitter, Original H
Traditional thatched country pub with peaceful atmosphere, near picturesque Helford River ⚘ Q ⊛ ⊛ ⑴ ▶

Mevagissey

11–3; 6–11

Fountain Inn
Cliff Street ☎ (0726) 842320
St Austell Tinners Bitter H
Cosy, old fashioned pub near the harbour of this still busy fishing village
⚘ Q ⊛ ⊛ ~ ⑴ ▶ ⊕ ☼ ▲ ☼

Try also: Ship Inn; Kings Arms

Morwenstow

12–2.30; 7–10.30 (11 F, S & summer)

Cornwall

Bush Inn
Crosstown OS208151
☎ (028 883) 242
St Austell Tinners Bitter, Hicks Special
Built of slate and stone with cob walls and of monastic origins, parts of this remote pub are 1000 years old

Newlyn

10.30–2.30; 6–10.30 (11 F, S)

Fishermans Arms
Fore Street ☎ (0736) 63399
St Austell Hicks Special
Friendly pub with magnificent view across harbour

Newquay

11–3; 6–11

Fosters
Narrowcliff ☎ (0637) 874037
Courage Best Bitter, Directors; John Smith Bitter
Do not be put off by the name. The interior is traditional and comfortable

Try also: **Harvester** (Courage)

Padstow

10.30–2.30; 5.30–10.30 (11 F, S & summer)

London Inn
6–8 Lanadwell Street
☎ (0841) 532554
St Austell Bosun's Bitter, Tinners Bitter, Hicks Special
Pub with a nautical flavour near the harbour; originally 4 fishing cottages, knocked together and licensed in the 1800s

Pendoggett

10.30–2.30; 6–10.30 (11 F, S & summer)

Cornish Arms
On B3314 ☎ (0208) 880263
Draught Bass; Pendoggett Special
Attractive building with leaded windows. Brewed its own beer in early 1800s

Penzance

10.30–2.30; 5.30–10.30 (11 F, S & summer)

Dolphin
The Quay ☎ (0736) 64106
St Austell Bosun's Bitter, Tinners Bitter, Hicks Special
Quayside tavern still used by seafarers – handy for the Scilly Isles ferry. Good food

10.30–2.30; 6–10.30 (11 F, S & summer)

Turks Head
Chapel Street ☎ (0736) 63093
Cornish JD Dry Hop Bitter, Original, Wessex Stud
Oldest inn in town. Excellent, varied menu; very popular

Try also: **White Lion** (Courage)

Philleigh

11–2.30; 6 (7 winter)–10.30 (11 F, S & summer)

Roseland Inn
Off A3078 at Ruan Highlanes OS870394 ☎ (087 258) 254
Cornish JD Dry Hop Bitter, Original
Superb low-beamed, cob-walled 17th-century unspoilt country inn near King Harry Ferry. Hot toddies in winter

Polgooth

11–3; 6–11

Polgooth Inn
Off A390 and B3273
☎ ((0726) 74689
St Austell Bosun's Bitter, Tinners Bitter, Hicks Special
Village local with family room specialising in food

Polkerris

11–3; 6–11

Rashleigh Inn
Off A3082 ☎ (072 681) 3991
St Austell Tinners Bitter, Hicks Special
Nicely appointed inn above the beach. Good restaurant

Polperro

11–3; 6–11

Crumplehorne Inn
☎ (0503) 72348
St Austell Tinners Bitter, Hicks Special
Pub attractively converted from an old mill. Beer is fined on the premises

Try also: **Blue Peter** (Free)

Polruan

11–3; 6–11

Lugger Inn
The Quay ☎ (072 687) 364
St Austell Tinners Bitter, Hicks Special
A traditional inn beside the water. Best reached by foot passenger ferry from Fowey. Homely, simple nautical decor and friendly atmosphere

Port Isaac

10.30–2.30; 6–10.30 (11 F, S & summer)

Golden Lion
13 Fore Street ☎ (0208) 880336
St Austell Bosun's Bitter (summer), Tinners Bitter, Hicks Special
This pub has a smugglers' tunnel (bricked up by the customs men) leading to the harbour

Probus

11–2.30; 5.30–10.30 (11 F, S & summer)

Hawkins Arms
Fore Street (A390)
☎ (0726) 882208
St Austell Tinners Bitter, Hicks Special
Unpretentious, welcoming village pub. Restaurant offers traditional Sunday lunches and cold buffets. Children's commando course in garden

Rame Cross

10.30–2.30; 5.30–10.30 (11 F, S & summer)

Halfway House
On A394 ☎ (0209) 860222
Cornish JD Dry Hop Bitter, Original, Wessex Stud; Marston Pedigree; Wadworth 6X
Smart roadside pub known for good food (2 miles)

Redruth

10.30–2.30; 5.30–10.30 (11 F, S & summer)

Mount Ambrose
Off A30 ☎ (0209) 215809
St Austell Bosun's Bitter, XXXX, Hicks Special
Lively oasis. Pub games (not Sun) (till 12.30 am)

Restronguet

11–2.30; 6–10.30 (11 F, 3 & summer)

Pandora Inn
Passage Hill, Mylor OS814371
☎ (0326) 72678
Draught Bass; St Austell Bosun's Bitter, Tinners Bitter, Hicks Special
13th-century thatched pub at waterside – reachable from both road and water. Food upstairs

St Agnes

11–2.30; 6 (7 winter)–10.30 (11 F, S & summer)

Railway Inn
10 Vicarage Road
☎ (087 255) 2310
Cornish JD Dry Hop Bitter, GBH
A previous landlady started a collection of shoes. Pub is now crammed with collectors items

St Austell

11–3; 6–11

Queens Head
Fore Street ☎ (0726) 75452

89

Cornwall

Courage Best Bitter, Directors; St Austell Tinners Bitter ⒣
Comfortable town centre bars and hotel

Try also: Duke of Cornwall

St Breward

11–2.30; 6–10.30 (11 F, S & summer)

Old Inn
Church Town ☎ (0208) 850711
Ruddles County; Ushers Best Bitter ⒣
Claimed to be the highest inn in Cornwall, this 11th-century building has large welcoming granite fireplace

St Columb Major

11–3; 6 (7 winter)–11

Ring o'Bells
3 Bank Street ☎ (0637) 880259
Draught Bass; Flowers Original; Ringers Ale
Ancient slate-clad inn. Narrow frontage belies an extensive interior. Guest beers

Try also: Barley Sheaf; other 4 pubs

St Just

11–2.30; 6–10.30 (11 F, S & summer)

'Star Inn
1 Fore Street ☎ (0736) 788767
St Austell Tinners Bitter, Hicks Special ⒢
St Just's oldest inn: fine granite building (no children)

St Kew

11–3; 6–10.30 (11 F, S & summer)

St Kew Inn
Off A39 ☎ (020 884) 259
St Austell Tinners Bitter, Hicks Special ⒣
Comfortable pub with large fireplace, old slate floor and meathooks in the ceiling. New lounge built of old materials. No food Sun

Try also: Red Lion, St Kew Highway

St Neot

11–3; 6–11

London
☎ (0579) 20263
Ruddles County; Usher Best Bitter ⒣
16th-century inn in small village on edge of Bodmin Moor. Adjacent church has famous stained glass windows. Pub games (not Sun)

Stratton

10.30–2.30; 6–10.30 (11 F, S & summer)

Tree Inn
Fore Street ☎ (0288) 2038
Draught Bass; St Austell Tinners Bitter ⒣
Building dates back to the 13th century. Formerly the manor house of the Grenville family, and home of the last Cornish giant, Anthony Payne. 4 bars, restaurant and a skittle alley

Tideford

10.30–2.30; 5.30–11

Rod & Line
Church Road (off A38)
Courage Best Bitter ⒢
Basic, no-frills village pub, with a friendly welcome and good value meals (not Sun)

Torpoint

11–3; 5.30–11

Kings Arms
37 Fore Street (A374 near Plymouth Ferry)
Courage Best Bitter, Directors (summer) ⒣
Former coaching inn. Friendly locals' pub with waterfront views. Darts; children's playroom

Trebarwith Strand

12–2.30; 7–10.30 (11 F, S & summer)

Port William
OS048864 ☎ (0840) 770230
St Austell Tinners Bitter, Hicks Special ⒣
On cliffs overlooking the sea; the bar area was originally stables for working horses in the local slate quarries. Guest beers

Try also: King Arthurs Arms, Tintagel (Free)

Treen

10.30–2.30; 5.30–10.30 (11 F, S & summer)

Logan Rock Inn
Off B3315 ☎ (0736) 810495
St Austell Tinners Bitter, Hicks Special ⒣
Outstanding small country pub near beautiful coastal scenery and Minack Open Air Theatre

Tregadillett

11–2.30; 6–10.30 (11 F, S & summer)

Square & Compass
On A30 OS298838
☎ (0566) 2051
Cornish JD Dry Hop Bitter, Original, Wessex Stud ⒣
Cosy 14th-century inn: old signs and pictures and impressive collection of old clocks

Truro

11–2.30; 5–10.30 (11 F, S & summer)

City Inn
Pydar Street (Perranporth road) ☎ (0872) 72623

Courage Best Bitter, Directors
Excellent town local where the art of conversation is not dead.

11–2.30; 5–10.30 (11 F, S & summer)

Swan Inn
40 Bosvigo Road
Cornish JD Dry Hop Bitter, Original, Wessex Stud ⒣
A local popular with all ages. Original gas lights in bar. Games room. Folk club, in building at rear

Tywardreath

11–3; 6–11

New Inn
Off A390
Draught Bass; St Austell Tinners Bitter ⒣
Popular village bar near Par. Darts and juke box in separate room. Secluded garden off lounge (not Sun) (occasionally) (Par)

Try also: Whych Way Inn

Upton Cross

11–3; 5.30–11

Caradon Inn
On B3254 ☎ (0579) 63391
Flowers Original; St. Austell Hicks Special; Wadworth 6X ⒣
Delightful, welcoming 17th-century country inn. Wellies allowed. Pool room. Guest beers.

Veryan

11–2.30; 6–10.30 (11 F, S & summer)

New Inn
Off A3078 OS916396
☎ (0872) 501362
St Austell Bosun's Bitter, Tinners Bitter ⒣
Traditional, welcoming local in pretty village; home of the Roundhouses. Good bathing beaches nearby and superb countryside

Wadebridge

10.30–2.30; 5.30–10.30 (11 F, S & summer)

Ship Inn
Gonvena Hill (A39)
☎ (020 881) 2839
Cornish Original ⒢
A friendly welcome in this small 16th-century former coaching inn. Note the coloured leaded windows

Zelah

10.30–2.30; 6–10.30 (11 F, S & summer)

Hawkins Arms
On A30 ☎ (087 254) 339
St Austell Bosun's Bitter, Hicks Special ⒣
Pink-washed stone exterior and a cosy atmosphere

Cumbria

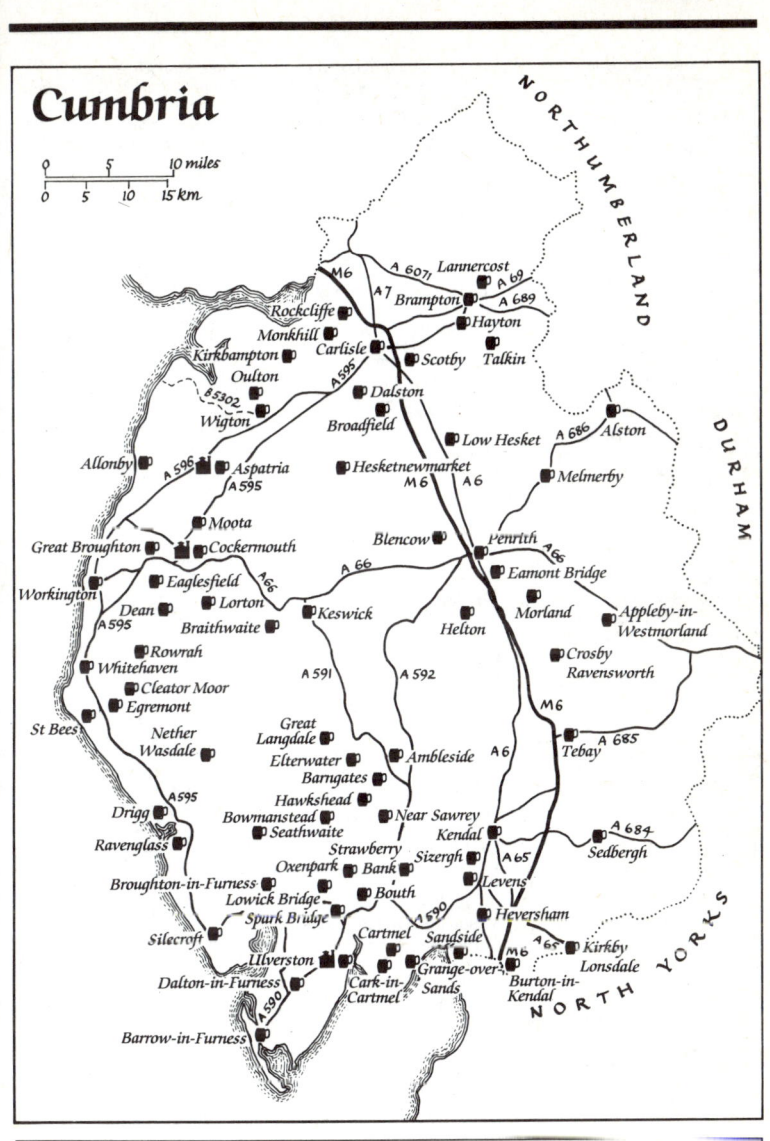

Hartleys, Ulverston; **Jennings**, Cockermouth; **Yates**, Aspatria

Allonby

11–3; 5.30 (7 winter)–10.30 (11 F, S & summer)

Grapes Hotel
☎ (090 084) 344
Jennings Mild, Bitter H
Small friendly local; dominoes and darts Q ☎ ⋈ ◊ ▶ &

Try also: Ship Hotel (Yates)

Alston

11–3; 6.30–11 (winter 11.30–2; 7–11)

Angel Inn
Front Street ☎ (0498) 81363
McEwan 70/-; Tetley Bitter H
Popular 17th-century inn in England's highest market town ⚑ ☎ ⋈ ◊ ▶ ▲

Ambleside

11–3; 6–11

Golden Rule
Smithy Brow (off A591)
Hartleys Mild, XB H
Popular tavern, frequented by climbers, walkers, locals and tourists ⚑ Q ☎ (until 9) ❀ ◊

11–3; 6–11

Waterhead Hotel (Stringers Bar)
On A591 S of town
Mitchells Bitter; Theakston Best Bitter H
Lively and hospitable pub overlooking Lake Windermere ⚑ ☎ ❀ ⋈ ◊ ▶

Try also: Tweedies Bar (Dale Lodge Hotel), Grasmere

Appleby-in-Westmorland

11–3; 6–11

Golden Ball
High Wiend (off Main Street)
Marston Burton Bitter, Pedigree (summer) H
Lively pub, popular with

Cumbria

locals. Worth finding ⛃⊕⇌

11–3; 6–11

Royal Oak
Bongate ☎ (076 83) 51463
Marston Pedigree; Yates Bitter; Younger Scotch Ⓗ
Well-appointed 600 year-old free house. Excellent meals
⛃Q⛃⋈()⊕⇌

Try also: Gate, Midland, Grapes

Aspatria

11–3; 5.30–10.30 (11 F, S)

Grapes Hotel
Market Square (A596)
☎ (0965) 20292
Yates Bitter Ⓗ
Large hotel. Cosy bar, noisy younger persons' lounge
⛃⛃⛃()⊕⇌

Barngates

12–2.30; 7–11 (summer 11.30–3; 6–11)

Drunken Duck
Off B5286 OS351012
☎ (096 66) 347
Jennings Bitter; Marston Pedigree; Tetley Bitter; Theakston XB, Old Peculier Ⓗ
Well-patronised 400 year-old traditional pub with splendid views ⛃Q⛃⛃⋈()⊕&A

Barrow-in-Furness

11.30–3; 5.30–11

Queen Hotel
Duke Street
Hartleys Bitter Ⓗ
Good local pub with a nice friendly atmosphere. Near rugby league ground ⛃()&

11–3; 5.30–11

Wheatsheaf
Anson Street
John Smith Bitter Ⓗ
Traditional pub frequented by navy personnel as well as locals Q⛃⛃⋈()⊕&

Blencow

11–3; 6–11

Clickham Inn
3 miles W of Penrith on B5288
Marston Burton Bitter, Pedigree, Merrie Monk Ⓗ
Attractive roadside inn on old main road to Keswick
⛃⛃⛃()&A

Bouth

summer 11–3; 6–11

White Hart
Thwaites Mild, Bitter Ⓗ
Comfortable oak-beamed village pub with games room
⛃⛃⛃()(until 8)&A

Bowmanstead

11–3; 5.30–11

Ship Inn
Off A593 ☎ (053 94) 224
Hartley XB; Robinson Old Tom Ⓗ

Low-beamed inn, popular with locals ⛃⛃⛃()A

Try also: **Crown**, Coniston

Braithwaite

12–3 (winter variable); 7–10.30 (11 Th, F, S)

Coledale Inn
Signed from bottom of Whinlatter Pass (B5292)
☎ (059 682) 272
Younger Scotch Bitter Ⓗ
Former pencil mill, situated on Coledale Beck. Folk singers welcome ⛃Q⛃⛃⋈()⊕&A

Brampton

11–3; 5.30–11

Nags Head
Market Place ☎ (069 77) 2284
Hartley XB; Whitbread Trophy Ⓗ
Beautiful renovated town pub with original low ceilings and wooden beams. Busy market days ⛃⛃⋈()&⇌

Broadfield

11–3; 5.30–11

Crown Inn
5 miles S of Carlisle racecourse
Matthew Brown Mild, Bitter; Theakston XB Ⓗ
Traditional roadside country inn. 1-roomed pub with the feel of a 3-roomed one! Guest beers ⛃⛃⛃()&A

Broughton-in-Furness

11–3; 6–11 (all day Thu)

Old Kings Head
Station Road ☎ (065 76) 293
Hartley Bitter, XB Ⓗ
Well frequented inn in a very popular Lakeland village. Guest beers Q⛃⛃⋈()

Burton-in-Kendal

11.30–3; 6–11

King's Arms
Main Street ☎ (0524) 781409
Mitchells Mild, Bitter Ⓗ
Old-established coaching inn. Now a village local ⛃⛃⋈() (not winter Mon) &

Try also: **Royal** (Hartleys)

Cark-in-Cartmel

10.30–3; 6–11

Engine Inn
Off B5278
Bass Light 5 Star, Draught Bass, Stones Best Bitter Ⓗ
Cosy village pub, near railway station. Pub games
⛃⛃⛃⋈()⊕A (caravans) ⇌

Carlisle

11–3; 5.30–11

Coach & Horses
Kingstown Road (600 yds S of M6 Jct 44) ☎ (0228) 25535
Matthew Brown Bitter;

Theakston XB Ⓗ
Friendly, popular 2-room pub on northern outskirts of city. Excellent value bar meals ⛃⛃ (for meals) ⛃()(6–8.15)⊕

11–3; 5.30–11

Crown Inn
23 Scotland Road (1 mile N of centre on A6) ☎ (0228) 24725
McEwan 70/-; Younger IPA, No.3 Ⓗ
Popular roadside local designed by Redfern (of State Management fame). Superb wood-panelled smoking room
⛃⊕&

11–3; 6.30–11

Friars Tavern
Devonshire Street (off English Street) ☎ (0228) 23757
Hartleys XB; Whitbread Castle Eden Ale Ⓗ
Lively city-centre local with real ale in downstairs bar. Built on the site of a friary ()(upstairs) ⊕⇌

11–3; 5.30–11

Howard Arms
Lowther Street
Matthew Brown Mild; Theakston Best Bitter, XB Ⓗ
Multi-roomed, city-centre pub with superb tiled frontage. Beer garden ⛃⛃()⇌

11–3; 5.30–11

Woolpack Inn
Milbourne Street (off A595)
☎ (0228) 32459
Jennings Mild, Bitter Ⓗ
Excellent pub with a new plush lounge which features a mural of Carlisle's history
⋈()⊕&⇌

Cartmel

10.30 (11.30 winter)–3; 6 (6.30 winter)–11

Pig & Whistle
Town End
Hartleys Best Bitter Ⓗ
Friendly village pub, popular with farming community. Games ⛃⛃⊕

Cleator Moor

11–3; 5.30–10.30 (11 F, S & summer)

New Crown
Bowthorn Road (B5295)
Hartleys Bitter, XB Ⓗ
Popular town local with friendly atmosphere ⛃⛃⊕

Try also: **Derby Arms**

Cockermouth

11–3; 5.30–10.30 (11 F, S)

Brown Cow
137 Main Street **Theakston Best Bitter, XB, Old Peculier** Ⓗ
Popular corner pub ⛃⛃()⊕

11–3; 5.30–10.30 (11 F, S)

Swan
Kirkgate
Jennings Mild, Bitter Ⓗ

Cumbria

Smart town pub – difficult to find, but worth the effort

Crosby Ravensworth

10.30–3; 6.30–11

Butchers Arms
☎ (093 15) 202
Marston Pedigree; Younger Scotch H
Comfortable village inn, warm and welcoming. Pub games

Dalston

11–3; 6–11

Bridge End Inn
On B5299
Greenall Whitley Original H
Friendly village local at top end of a large popular village

Dalton-in-Furness

11–3; 6–11

Black Bull
Tudor Square (A590)
Hartley Best Bitter; Whitbread Castle Eden Ale H
Good local pub; darts, pool and dominoes

Try also: **Railway**, Lindal-in-Furness

Dean

11–3; 5.30–10.30 (11 F, S)

Royal Yew Inn
1 mile W of A5086 OS074251
Younger Scotch H
Very popular pub for meals

Drigg

11–3; 5.30–10.30 (11 F, S & summer)

Victoria Hotel
Off B5344, next to station
☎ (094 04) 231
Jennings Bitter H
Excellent village pub

Eaglesfield

11–3; 5.30–10.30 (11 F, S)

Black Cock
1 mile W of A5086
☎ (0900) 822989
Jennings Bitter H
Very popular, small village local

Eamont Bridge

11–3; 6–11

Beehive Inn
A6, 1½ miles S of Penrith
Hartleys XB; Whitbread Castle Eden Ale H
Busy pub with interesting sign. Popular with families
(until 9)

Egremont

11–3; 5.30–10.30 (11 F, S & summer)

Blue Bell
Market Place (A595)
Hartleys XB H
1-roomed, modernised town local. Darts

Elterwater

11–3; 6.30–11

Britannia Inn
Off B5343 OS285061
☎ (09667) 210
Bass Special Bitter; Hartleys XB; Jennings Bitter; Tetley Bitter H
Traditional lakeland bar in good setting

Grange-over-Sands

11–3; 6–11

Hardcragg Hall Hotel
Grange Fell Road (near B5277)
☎ (044 84) 3353
John Smith Bitter H
Elegant 16th-century manor house specialising in good food. Wood-panelled bars with large open fireplaces

Try also: **Phoenix**

Great Broughton

11–3; 5.30–10.30 (11 F, S)

Punch Bowl Inn
Main Street (1 mile off A66)
Jennings Bitter H
Friendly village pub with separate entertainments room – singers welcome

Great Langdale

11–3; 6–11

Old Dungeon Ghyll
On A5343 OS285061
☎ (096 67) 272
Theakston Best Bitter; Yates Bitter; Younger No.3 H
Traditional Lakes inn with basic slate-floored bar

11–3; 6–11

Wainwrights Inn
Chapel Stile (B5343)
Theakston Mild, Bitter, XB, Old Peculier H
Large, traditional Lake District pub, popular with tourists. Pub games

Try also: **Hobsons Bar**

Hawkshead

11–3; 6.30 (5.30 summer)–11

Kings Arms
Matthew Brown Mild; Tetley Bitter; Theakston Best Bitter H
Popular pub overlooking village square

Try also: **Queens Head**

Hayton

11–3; 5.30–11

Stone Inn
Hartleys Bitter; Jennings Mild; Tennents 80/-; Theakston Best Bitter H
Attractive and cosy village local; unusual "toasties" (eg Haggis!)

Helton

12–3; 7–11 (closed Tue lunch and midweek winter lunch)

Helton Inn
4 miles S of Penrith (off B5320)
☎ (093 12) 232
Theakston Best Bitter, XB (summer) H
Splendid end of terrace inn. Simple decoration and relaxed atmosphere. Excellent outdoor drinking area
(self catering)

Try also: **Queens Head**
Askham (Vaux)

Hesketnewmarket

11.30–3; 5.30–10.30 (11 F, S)

Old Crown Inn
Take B5299 to Caldbeck
Blencathra Bitter; Thwaites Mild, Bitter H
Very friendly fellside village local. Good "crack" and home cooking. Own brewery at rear, library within pub. Indian cuisine

Heversham

10.30–3; 6–11

Blue Bell
Princes Way (A6)
☎ (044 82) 3159
Draught Bass; Hartleys XB; Tetley Bitter H
Large well-appointed hotel with spartan vault. Pub games
Q (vault)

Kendal

11.30–2.30 (3 Sat); 7.30–11

Brewery Arts Centre
Highgate ☎ (0532) 25133
Vaux Lorimers Scotch, Samson; Ward Sheffield Best Bitter H
Lively arts and community centre in the old Whitwell Mark brewery Q (lunch)
(not winter Sun)

11–3; 6–11

Golden Lion
Market Place ☎ (0539) 24116
Vaux Lorimers Scotch, Bitter, Samson H
Popular homely little bar and dining room (dining room)
(not Sun)

Try also: **Sawyers Arms**

Keswick

11–3; 5.30–10.30 (11 F, S)

Dog & Gun
Lake Road (near Moot Hall)
Theakston Best Bitter, XB, Old Peculier H
Very popular eating place; be early

Cumbria

11–3; 5.30–10.30 (11 F, S)
George Hotel
St John Street (near Moot Hall)
☎ (076 87) 72076
Theakston Best Bitter; Yates Bitter H
Old coaching inn, now a smart hotel ☎⋈ⓇⒹ

11–3; 5.30–10.30 (11 F, S)
Twa Dogs
Penrith Road (A591 towards Ambleside) ☎ (076 87) 72599
Jennings Mild, Bitter H
Bogart Preservation Society HQ, join now!
🏠Q☎⚙⋈ⓇⒹⒺ&

Kirkbampton

12–3 (not winter Mon–Fri); 6.30–10.30 (11 F, S)
Rose & Crown
On B5307 ☎ (0228) 76492
Wilson's Original Bitter H
Genuine Cumbrian village pub, over 200 years old
🏠☎ⓇⒹ

Kirkby Lonsdale

11–3; 6–11
Royal
Market Square, Main Street ☎ (052 42) 71217
Tetley Bitter; Theakston XB; Younger Scotch H
18th-century listed building. Large, rambling hotel with 3 bars 🏠Q☎⋈ⓇⒹⒺ&

Try also: all other pubs in Kirkby

Lanercost

11–3; 5.30–11
Blacksmiths Bar (New Bridge Inn)
2 miles from A69 Jct, E. Brampton ☎ (064 77) 2224
Ruddles Best Bitter H
Old Smithy dating from late 17th century. Excellent food
🏠Q☎⋈ⓇⒹ&

Levens

11–3; 6–11
Hare & Hounds
Off A590 Levens Causeway
Vaux Samson H; **Ward Sheffield Best Bitter** E
Several low-beamed rooms around a single serving area
☎⚙ⓇⒹⒺ

Lorton

11–3; 5.30–10.30 (11 F, S)
Wheatsheaf
On B5289 ☎ (090 085) 268
Jennings Bitter H
Small friendly village local. Games 🏠☎Ⓑ&🅰 (caravans)

Low Hesket

11–3; 6–11
Rose & Crown
A6, 3 miles S of M6 Jct 42
Marston Mercian Mild,
Burton Bitter, Pedigree, Owd Rodger (occasionally) H
Excellent roadside boozer, friendly welcome assured. Cosy lounge and comfortable bar 🏠☎⚙ⓇⒹⒺ&🅰

Lowick Bridge

11–3; 6–11
Red Lion Inn
On A5084 ☎ (022 985) 366
Hartleys Mild, XB H
Always a friendly welcome; a popular local for country folk and farmers. Tasty bar snacks. Pub games 🏠Q☎⚙⋈ⓇⒹ&🅰

Try also: **Farmers Arms**, Lowick Green

Melmerby

11–3; 6–11
Shepherds Inn
8 miles from Penrith on A586
Marston Burton Bitter, Pedigree, Merrie Monk H
Extremely popular pub in attractive fellside village; excellent, good value meals.
Pub games Q☎⚙ⓇⒹ&🅰

Monkhill

12–3; 5.30–11
Drovers Rest
Carlisle–Burgh By Sands road, off B5307 OS343587
Jennings Mild, Bitter H
Friendly local with haaf-netting connections. Clay pigeon's nest. Jennings Lakeland Light is pressurised
🏠☎ (lunch)⚙&

Moota

11–3; 5.30–10.30 (11 F, S)
Laal Moota
On A595 ☎ (0965) 20414
Wilsons Original Mild, Original Bitter H
Only Wilson's house for miles
🏠Q☎⚙ⓇⒹⒺ&🅰

Morland

11–3; 6–11
Kings Arms
Water Street
Marston Burton Bitter, Pedigree H
Small unspoilt village pub
🏠ⓇⒹⒺ

Near Sawrey

11–3; 5.30–11
Towerbank Arms
On B5285 (6 miles S of Ambleside) ☎ (096 66) 334
Matthew Brown Mild; Theakston XB H
Popular country lakeland inn next to Beatrix Potter's cottage
🏠Q☎⚙⋈ⓇⒹ

Nether Wasdale

11–3; 5.30–10.30 (11 summer)
Screes
OS125041 ☎ (094 06) 262
Theakston Best Bitter, Old Peculier; Yates Bitter H
A mile from Wastwater, excellent food and family room 🏠Q☎⚙⋈ⓇⒹ&🅰

Oulton

11–3; 5.30–10.30 (11 F, S)
Bird in Hand
Wigton–Kirkbridge Road OS245515 ☎ (0963) 43363
Jennings Mild, Bitter H
Country local at crossroads to north of village 🏠Ⓔ

Oxenpark

11–3; 6–11
Manor House
N of Greenodd on A590 road to Satterthwaite OS316873
☎ (022 986) 345
Hartleys Mild, XB H
Converted manor house with comfortable beamed lounge, dining area and cosy snug
🏠Q☎⚙⋈ⓇⒹⒺ&🅰

Penrith

11–3 (10–5 Tue and some Mon and Thu); 5.30–11
Agricultural Hotel
Cromwell Road (Castlegate)
☎ (0768) 62622
Marston Burton Bitter, Pedigree, Owd Rodger H
No juke box, no fruit machine. Good ale, good food, good crack 🏠Q☎⚙⋈ⓇⒹ&⇌

11.30–3; 6–11
Beacon Inn
Fell Lane
Whitbread Castle Eden Ale H
Country style pub on eastern edge of the town. Named after nearby Penrith Beacon Q☎ (lunch/early eve)⚙ⓇⒺ&

11–3 (5 Tue); 5.30–11
Museum Inn
17–18 Castlegate
☎ (0768) 63576
Jennings Mild, Bitter; Hartleys XB H
A rare selection of real ales in a Whitbread tied house. Family room 🏠Q☎⋈ⓇⒹ&⇌

11–3 (5 Tue); 6–11
Woolpack
Burrowgate ☎ (0768) 63919
Vaux Samson H
One of the few remaining drinkers' pubs left in town centre Q☎ⓇⒹ&⇌

Ravenglass

11–3; 5.30–10.30 (11 F, S & summer)
Ratty Arms
Hartleys XB; Jennings Bitter; Younger Scotch H
On northbound platform of Victorian railway station.
🏠☎⚙ⓇⒹ&🅰⇌

Rockcliffe

11–3; 5.30–11

Cumbria

Crown & Thistle
Off A74
McEwan 70/-; Younger IPA H
Friendly, comfortable local.
Excellent bar meals
♨ ☎ (not Sat night) ⊕ ◐ ⊕ &

Try also: Metal Bridge, A74

Rowrah
11–3; 5.30–10.30 (11 F, S & summer)

Stork
On A5086 ☎ (0946) 861213
Jennings Mild, Bitter H
Friendly local with numerous hunting and hound trailing trophies ♨ ⊕ ⊕

St Bees
11–3; 5.30–10.30 (11 F, S & summer)

Manor House
Main Street (B5345)
☎ (0946) 822425
Matthew Brown Bitter;
Theakston Best Bitter H
Former coaching inn, cosy bar, plush lounge
♨ ☎ (for meals) ⊕ ◐ ⊕ ≠

Try also: Oddfellows Arms

Sandside
11–3; 6–11

Ship
On B5282 ☎ (044 82) 3113
McEwan 70/-; Younger Scotch Bitter H
Long, low bar – dark woodwork predominates, relieved by nautical knick-knacks, and views of the Kent estuary ☎ ⊕ ◐ &

Scotby
11–3; 5.30–11

Royal Oak
(M6 Jct 43, then A69 for ½ mile) ☎ (0228) 72463
Matthew Brown Mild;
Theakston Best Bitter H
Attractive stone-built village local. Friendly basic bar and comfortable lounge
☎ ◐ (12–2) ⊕ (6–8.30) ⊕ &

Seathwaite
11–3; 6–11

Newfield Inn
N of Broughton-in-Furness on road to Wrynose Pass
OS961229 ☎ (065 76) 208
Younger Scotch Bitter H
Popular pub with walkers and climbers. Slate floor. Non-smoking dining room.
Children welcome ♨ ☎ ⋈ ◐

Sedbergh
11–3; 6–11

Bull
☎ (053 96) 20264
Hartleys XB; Whitbread Trophy H
2 bars; main one knocked through, with beams and leaded windows. Games
☎ ⊕ ⋈ ◐

Try also: Dalesman

Silecroft
11–3; 6–11

Miners Arms
Off A595 ☎ (0657) 2325
Younger Scotch, No.3 H
Listed, 17th-century coaching house ♨ Q ☎ ⊕ ◐ ▶ ⊕ & ▲

Sizergh
11.3; 6–11

Strickland Arms
Off A6 S of A590 Jct OS500873
Theakston Best Bitter, XB, Old Peculier H
Originally the Dower House for Sizergh Castle, also owned by the National Trust
☎ ⊕ ◐ &

Spark Bridge
11–3; 6–11

Royal Oak
Off A5092 ☎ (022 986) 286
Hartleys XB; Thwaites Best Mild, Bitter H
Popular village inn with beer garden leading down to River Crake ♨ ☎ ⊕ ◐ (6–9.30) ⊕ &

Try also: White Hart, Bouth

Strawberry Bank (Cartmel Fell)
11–3; 6–11

Masons Arms
5 miles N of A592 OS413895
☎ (044 88) 486
McEwan 80/-; Theakston Best Bitter; Thwaites Bitter;
Younger No.3 H
Extremely popular old-world inn. Outstanding meals
♨ ☎ ⊕ ⋈ (self-catering) ◐ ▶ ▲

Talkin
12–2.30 (Jul/Aug, bank hols & Sat only); 7–11

Hare & Hounds
From B6413 take village turn-off, not Tarn ☎ (069 77) 3456/7
Hartleys XD, Theakston Best Bitter, XB, Old Peculier H
Charming award-winning village inn near Talkin Tarn.
Intimate atmosphere. No dogs
♨ ☎ ⊕ ⋈ ◐ (until 1.30) ▶ (until 9) ⊕ & ▲

Tebay
11–3; 6–11

Cross Keys
Off M6 Jct 38 on Kendal road
☎ (058 74) 240
Webster Yorkshire Bitter, Choice H
Recently enlarged pub in old railway village, now favoured by fishermen ♨ ☎ ⊕ ⋈ ◐ ▶ & ▲

Ulverston
11–3; 6–11 (all day Thu)

Devonshire
Victoria Road ☎ (0229) 52537
Thwaites Best Mild, Bitter H
Friendly 'workingman's local' near town centre. Popular for darts and doms ☎ ⊕ ◐ ⊕ ≠

11–3; 6–11 (all day Thu)

Kings Head Hotel
Queen Street
Theakston Best Bitter H
Comfortable pub reputed to date from 1670. Bowling green at rear. Very popular with young. Guest beers
♨ ☎ (lunch) ⊕ ⋈ ⊕ & ≠

11–3; 6–11 (all day Thu)

Rose & Crown
Queen Street
Hartleys Mild, XB H
Cosy popular local with old world front parlour and open fire. Good reputation for bar meals ♨ ☎ ⊕ ◐ ▶ ≠

Whitehaven
11–3; 5.30–10.30 (11 F, S & summer)

Central
Duke Street ☎ (0946) 2796
Matthew Brown Mild;
Theakston Best Bitter, XB, Old Peculier H
Quiet locals' bar at back.
Lunches served in popular lounge ☎ (lunch) ◐ ⊕ ≠

Try also: Welsh Arms

11–3; 5.30–10.30 (11 F, S & summer)

Sun Inn
Hensingham Square (A595, 1 mile S of town centre)
Jennings Bitter H
Cosy and relaxed. Parking is difficult Q ⊕

Try also: Sunnyhill

Wigton
11–3; 5.30–10.30 (11 F, S)

Throstles Nest
King Street (A596 next to bus station) ☎ (0963) 43139
Marston Burton Bitter, Pedigree H
One of the last pubs built by State Management. Basic bar and comfortable lounge
♨ ☎ ⊕ ◐ ▶ ⊕ & ≠

Workington
11–3; 5.30–10.30 (11 F, S)

George IV
29 Stanley Street (on quay)
Jennings Bitter H
Cosy back-street local with long-serving landlady ♨ ⊕ ≠

11–3; 5.30–10.30 (11 F, S)

Miners Arms
Guard Street
Matthew Brown Mild;
Theakston Best Bitter, XB H
Small friendly local used as brewery workers' tap-house
☎ (lunch) ◐ ⊕

95

Derbyshire

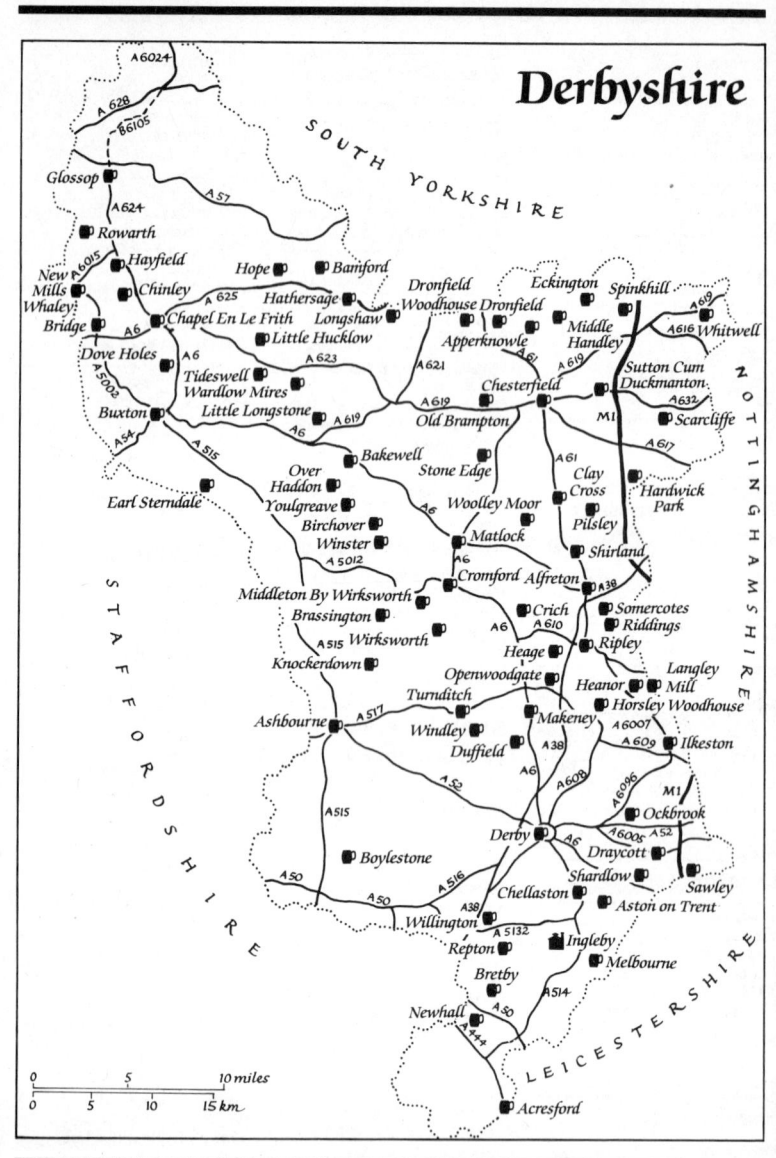

🏠 *Lloyds, Ingleby*

Acresford

10.30–2.30; 6–11
Cricketts Inn
A444 near B5002 Jct
☎ (0283) 760359
Draught Bass H
Popular 18th-century coaching inn near county boundary. Smart lounge; tidy bar. Good food – Bass Welcome Food Award holder ▲⊛◐ ⊞&

Alfreton

11.30–3; 6–11

Robin Hood
26 Nottingham Road (B600)
☎ (0773) 833588
Hardys & Hansons Best Mild, Best Bitter E
Unpretentious, friendly local. Skittle alley in garden ⊱⊛◐&

Try also: Devonshire Arms (Shipstone)

Apperknowle

12–3; 7–11
Yellow Lion
45 High Street ☎ (0246) 413181
Marston Pedigree; Stones Best Bitter; Tetley Bitter H
Busy village local with large lounge and separate restaurant. Extensive menu and good range of bar snacks. Organ played at weekends. Guest beers Q⊱⊛◐&

Ashbourne

10.30–3; 6–11
Bowling Green
Buxton Road (A515)
☎ (0335) 42511
Draught Bass H
Spacious bar and smaller lounge on edge of town. Ideal

Derbyshire

starting point for Tissington Trail. Interesting food

Try also: White Lion (Ind Coope)

Aston on Trent

10–2.30; 6–11

Malt Shovel
The Green (off A6)
☎ (0332) 792256
Ind Coope Best Bitter, Burton Ale
Friendly and popular village local in Victorian mock-Tudor style. Emphasis on meals (not Mon) (Tue–Sat)

Bakewell

11–3; 6–11

Red Lion Hotel
The Square ☎ (062 981) 2054
Marston Pedigree, Owd Rodger (winter); **Ruddles County, Stones Best Bitter**
Originally a 16th-century alehouse. Situated right in the heart of this historic stone-built town and only yards from the original Bakewell Pudding shop

Try also: Peacock (Ward)

Bamford

11–3; 5.30–11

Derwent Hotel
Main Road (A6013)
☎ (0433) 51395
Stones Best Bitter; Ward Sheffield Best Bitter
Country hotel built in 1890 with taproom, 2 lounge areas and dining room. Collection of vintage sewing machines and kitchen gadgets. Guest beers

11–3; 5.30–11

Yorkshire Bridge
Ashopton Road (A6013 ½ mile S of Ladybower Reservoir)
☎ (0433) 51361
Stones Best Bitter
Country pub with 50s and 60s juke box. Brass collection. Popular with ramblers

Birchover

12–3; 6–11

Red Lion
Main Street ☎ (062 988) 229
Marston Pedigree; Tetley Bitter
Classic village pub with old-world atmosphere. Near famous Roter Rocks

Boylestone

11–3 (closed Tues); 7–11

Rose & Crown
Off A515 ☎ (033 523) 518
Marston Pedigree, Owd Rodger (winter)
White-washed pub in pleasant rural setting. 2 small rooms with low-beamed ceilings

Brassington

10.30–3; 6–11

Miners Arms
Off B5035 ☎ (062 985) 222
Marston Pedigree
Smart, stone-built village inn. Pub sign mistakenly depicts coal mining!

10.30–3; 6–11

Olde Gate
Off B5035 ☎ (062 985) 448
Marston Pedigree
Traditional village pub built in 1616. Scrubbed-top tables and black leaded range. Not far from High Peak Trail

Bretby

11–2.30; 6–11

Chesterfield Arms
Ashby Road (A50)
☎ (0283) 211606
Ind Coope Best Bitter, Burton Ale; Tetley Bitter
Former gatehouse to Bretby estate. Comfortable lounge with chesterfield settees; separate dining area. Earls of Chesterfield memorabilia. Children's play area outside (if eating)

Buxton

11–3; 5.30–11

Bakers Arms
West Road (50 yds from A6 Jct)
Draught Bass
Stone-built cottage pub with 2 small cosy bars. A little off the beaten track, but worth the effort

11–3; 5.30–11

Cheshire Cheese
High Street (A6) ☎ (0298) 5371
Hardys & Hansons Best Mild, Best Bitter
Lively market-place pub with interesting façade. Good range of meals

Chapel-en-le-Frith

11–3; 5.30–11

Old Pack Horse
Town End (A6)
☎ (0298) 812135
Robinson Best Dark Mild, Best Mild, Best Bitter
Well-patronised market town pub. One of the few outlets for Dark Mild

11–3; 5.30–11

Roebuck
Market Place
Tetley Mild, Bitter
Pub of great character overlooking small cobbled, market square by village stocks

Chellaston

10–2.30; 6–11

Corner Pin
Swarkestone Road (A514)
Ind Coope Burton Ale
Plush, comfortable roadside inn recently extended into old, adjoining Cruck-framed cottage (not Sun)

Chesterfield

11–3; 5.30–11

Derby Tup
Sheffield Road, Whittington Moor (off A61)
☎ (0246) 454316
Bateman XXXB; Marston Pedigree; Owd Rodger; Ruddles County; Taylor Landlord; Theakston XB, Old Peculier
12 handpulled beers in a friendly unspoilt free house

12–3; 5.30–11

Devonshire Arms
Mansfield Road, Hasland (Off A617) ☎ (0246) 32218
Tetley Bitter
Busy local 30 yards from park. Pool table in public bar (Mon–Fri)

11–3; 5.30–11

Grouse
136 Chatsworth Road, Brampton ☎ (0246) 79632
Draught Bass; Stones Best Bitter
Popular local, just off town centre, on route to Peak District and Chatsworth House. Pub games

11–3; 6–11

Holme Hall
Linacre Road, Holme Hall (Off B6051) ☎ (0246) 39995
Ind Coope Burton Ale; Marston Pedigree; Tetley Bitter
Tastefully converted 18th century farmhouse with large outdoor play area and garden for children. Lively popular pub with separate eating area (meals) (not Sun)

11–3; 6–10.30

Market Hotel
New Square ☎ (0246) 73641
Ind Coope Burton Ale; Tetley Bitter
Popular, town-centre pub frequented by market tradesmen, shoppers and young people in the eves

11–3; 7–10.30

Royal Oake
The Shambles ☎ (0246) 205508
Stones Best Bitter
Superb, half-timbered 13th century inn off small pedestrian way near market. Not to be missed

97

Derbyshire

11–3; 5.30–11
White Hart
Matlock Road, Walton (A632)
☎ (0246) 566392
John Smith Bitter H
Busy pub with emphasis on outdoor facilities for families
⌂☎⊛◐▶◑&

Chinley

11–3; 5.30–11
Old Hall Inn
Whitehough (½ mile from village) ☎ (0663) 50529
Marston Pedigree; Stones Best Bitter H
Comfortable, restaurant-style pub in historic building dating back to 13th century: stone-built, ivy-clad and mullion windowed
⌂⊛◐▶&⇌

Clay Cross

11–3; 7–11
New Inn
Market Street ☎ (0246) 862212
Ind Coope Burton Ale; Tetley Mild, Bitter H
Deceptively large, market town pub with disco Tue and Thu ⊛⊞

Try also: **Royal Oak** (Tetley)

Crich

10.30–3; 6–11
Cliff Inn
Cromford Road (B5035)
☎ (077 385) 2444
Hardys & Hansons Best Mild, Best Bitter H
Small, cosy and popular local very near National Tramway Museum ⊛◐▶

Cromford

11.30–3; 6–11
Bell Inn
47 The Hill (B5023)
Hardys & Hansons Best Mild, Best Bitter H
Stone pub, protected by conservation order ⊞

Derby

10–2.30; 6–11
Brunswick Inn
Railway Terrace
☎ (0332) 290677
Draught Bass H; **Hook Norton Old Hookey** G; **Taylor Landlord** H
The oldest (1842) purpose built railway pub in the world situated in a good drinking area of the city. Guest beers. Pub games ☎◐▶⇌

10–2.30; 6–11
Dolphin Inn
Queen Street
☎ (0332) 49115
Draught Bass; M&B Mild E
Picturesque, timber-framed pub built 1530, near the cathedral. Memorabilia of a former local brewery. The last haven in the city centre Q ◐⊞

10–2.30; 6–11
Furnace
Duke Street
Hardys & Hansons Best Mild, Best Bitter H & E
Victorian foundrymen's slaker, near St. Mary's Bridge chapel. Photographs of bygone Derby. Pub games ⊛

11–2.30; 6–11
Olde Spa Inne
204 Abbey Street
☎ (0332) 43474
Ind Coope Best Bitter, Burton Ale H
Built in 1773 and won the 1985 CAMRA Pub Preservation Award following a refurbishment which retained traditional features. Only genuine garden drinking area in city ⊛◐

10–2.30; 6–11
Strutts
London Road/Traffic Street
☎ (0332) 44421
Mansfield Riding Traditional Bitter, Old Baily H
Large, comfortable pub catering for the younger set. 1920s decor with curved pine bar ⊛◐⇌

Try also: **Maypole** (Home); **New Flower Pot** (Bass)

Dove Holes

11–3; 5.30 (may delay until 6/6.30)–11
Railway
Buxton Road
Hardys & Hansons Best Mild, Best Bitter H
Weather-beaten pub in exposed moorland. Comfortable with a cosy lounge. Pub games ⌂◐⇌

Draycott

11–2.30; 6–11
Travellers Rest
Derby Road (A6005)
☎ (033 17) 2332
Marston Pedigree H
Modernised, double-fronted Victorian local with separate games room and skittle alley. Sing-alongs Sat nights ⊞&

Dronfield

12–3; 5.30–11
Sidings
91 Chesterfield Road (B6057)
☎ (0246) 410023
Boddingtons Bitter; Stones Best Bitter; Theakston Old Peculier; Ward Sheffield Best Bitter H
Lively, spilt-level free house; has wide appeal but mainly attracts younger people in late eve. Wine bar in basement. Guest beers; house ale is "Hair of the Dog"
⌂⊛◐▶ (Fri) ⇌

Dronfield Woodhouse

11–3; 6–11
Gorsey Brigg
Pentland Road (off B6054)
☎ (0246) 418018
Shipstone Mild, Bitter H
Large modern estate pub. Plush comfortable lounge. 2 pool tables in taproom and separate snooker room. Warm and friendly
☎ (lunch) ⊛◐⊞

Duffield

11–3; 6–11
Bridge
Makeney Road (off A6)
☎ (0332) 841073
Home Bitter E
Large, comfortable lounge; lively bar and pleasant terrace overlooking river. Pub games
⊛⊞⇌

Earl Sterndale

11–3; 5.30–11
Quiet Woman
Earl Sterndale (B5053)
☎ (029 883) 211
Marston Mercian Mild; Burton Bitter H
Superb example of a village local on White Peak Way ⊞

Eckington

11.30–3; 7–11
Prince of Wales
11 Church Street
☎ (0246) 432966
Marston Burton Bitter, Pedigree E, **Owd Rodger (winter)** G
2 room village local, popular with young people in evenings. Extensive garden with farm animals. Pub games
☎⊛◐▶ (Fri, Sat until 10) ⊞&

Try also: **White Hart** (Home)

Glossop

11–3; 5.30–11
Crown
Victoria Street (A624)
Samuel Smith OBB H
A true local; comfortable and friendly. Accent on games ◐⊞

11–3; 5.30–11
Friendship
Arundel Street (off A57)
Robinson Best Mild, Best Bitter
Friendly, town-centre pub which attracts a wide range of customers. Pub games ◐⊞⇌

11–3; 5.30–11
Prince of Wales
Milltown (off A57, on road to Snake Pass)

Derbyshire

Marston Mercian Mild, Burton Bitter, Pedigree H
Cosy characterful end of terrace pub. Keeps out the worst of Glossop winters. Pub games 🍴🍺🎯🚃

Try also: **Manor** (Boddingtons)

Hardwick Park

11–3; 6–11

Hardwick Inn
1 mile S of M1 Jct 29
☎ (0246) 850245
Younger Scotch, IPA H
17th century inn in parkland setting 🍴🐾🍺🎯

Hathersage

11.30–3; 7–11

Plough Inn
Leadmill Bridge (B6001, 1 mile from village) ☎ (0433) 50319
Stones Best Bitter E
Comfortable pub near River Derwent. Strong local following but visitors always made welcome. Comfortable split-level lounge
🍴Q🐾 (lunch) 🍺🎯⚲🚃

Try also: **Hathersage Inn** (Free)

Hayfield

11–3; 5.30–11

George Inn
Off A624 ☎ (0663) 43691
Burtonwood Bitter H
Recently renovated pub in historic building. Interesting stained glass windows and old Hayfield photographs 🍴🎯

11–3; 5.30–11

Royal
☎ (0663) 42721
Webster Yorkshire Bitter, Choice; Wilson's Original Bitter H
Comfortable inn formerly an 18th-century parsonage. Village cricket ground and trout stream alongside. Pub games 🍴🍴🎯🏀

Heage

11–3; 6–11

White Hart
2 Church Street
☎ (077 385) 2302
Draught Bass E
17th-century multi-roomed pub with attractive leaded windows, stonework 🍺🎯

Heanor

11–3; 7–11

New Inn
Derby Road ☎ (0773) 719609
Home Mild, Bitter E
Friendly, compact roadside inn at top of Taghill. Keen games players 🍺🎯

Try also: **Crown** (Hardys & Hansons)

Hope

11–3; 6–11

Old Hall
Market Place (A625)
☎ (0433) 20160
Stones Best Bitter H
Large, oak-panelled lounge with separate games area. Next to cattle market; frequented by farmers and tourists 🍴🐾 (lunch) 🍺🎯 (not winter) 🚻⚲🚃

Try also: **Cheshire Cheese** (Free)

Horsley Woodhouse

11–3; 7–11

Jolly Colliers
27 Main Street (A609)
☎ (0332) 880425
Ward Darley Dark Mild, Sheffield Best Bitter E
Friendly village local. Weekend singalongs always end with house anthem. Pub games 🍺🎯🚻

Ilkeston

11–3; 6–11

Durham Ox
Durham Street (off A6007/6096) ☎ (0602) 324570
Ward Darley Dark Mild, Sheffield Best Bitter H & E
Lively back-street local with a comfortable, intimate atmosphere. Has been in every edition of this guide. If not open on time, knock on side window. Guest beers
🍴🐾🍺🏀🎯🚻

Try also: **General Havelock** (Shipstone)

11–3; 7–11

Flowerpot
Chapel Street ☎ (0602) 320484
Shipstone Mild, Bitter H & E
Old traditional, street-corner pub behind Albion shopping centre. Retains character and atmosphere; not to be missed. Try the pizzas. Pub games 🐾🍺🎯🚻

Try also: **Prince of Wales** (Shipstone); **Rutland Cottage**

Knockerdown

11–3; 6–11

Knockerdown Inn
On B5035 near Hognaston
☎ (062 985) 209
Marston Pedigree G
Isolated, modernised roadhouse. Popular and comfortable 🍴🎯

Langley Mill

11–3; 6–11

Railway Tavern
188 Station Road
☎ (0773) 76475

Home Mild, Bitter E
Busy roadside boozer. Pub games 🍺🎯🚻🚃

Little Hucklow

12–3 (not winter Mon–Fri); 7–11

Old Bulls Head
Off B6049 OS163605
☎ (0298) 871097
Ward Sheffield Best Bitter H
Cosy pub in beautiful countryside. Geological collection and displays of African carvings and farm implements. Winner of many pub awards. Isolated, but worth finding 🍴Q🐾🍺🎯🚻⚲

Little Longstone

11–3; 6–11

Packhorse Inn
Off B6465 near Monsal Head
☎ (062 987) 471
Marston Burton Bitter, Pedigree H, **Owd Rodger** (occasionally) G
Unspoilt 2-roomed village local, popular with hikers. First mentioned as a pub in 1787. Garden has animals for children to play with
🍴Q🐾🍺🍴🎯🚻⚲

Longshaw

10.30–3; 6–11

Grouse Inn
B6054, 2 miles N of Calver
☎ (0433) 30423
Younger No.3 H
Former farm building retaining hay loft and barn doors. Comfortable lounge with conservatory (note the grapevine) at rear, leading into taproom 🍴🐾🍺🎯🚻

Makeney

12–3; 7–11

Hollybush
Hollybush Lane (off A6 at Milford) ☎ (0332) 841729
Marston Pedigree, Owd Rodger; Ruddles County; Theakston Old Peculier G & H
Late 17th-century, listed, beamed pub of exceptional character. Limited parking
🍴Q🍺🎯🚻

Matlock

11–3; 6–11

Sycamore
Sycamore Road (¼ mile from A6 up the Dimple)
☎ (0629) 57585
Draught Bass H
Excellent traditional pub away from the busy town centre. Pub games Q🍺🎯🚻

12–3; 0–11

White Lion
195 Starkholmes Road
☎ (0629) 2511
Home Bitter H

99

Derbyshire

Picturesque old coaching inn with superb view over Derwent Valley. Tourists and hikers made welcome. Family room. Pub games

Melbourne

10–2.30; 6–11

Melbourne Hotel
2 Derby Road ☎ (033 16) 2134
Ind Coope Burton Ale; Marston Pedigree; Tetley Bitter H
Imposing 250 year-old hotel in town centre

Try also: **White Swan** (Marston)

Middle Handley

11–3; 7–11

Devonshire Arms
Westfield Lane (200 yds off B6052) ☎ (0246) 432189
Stones Best Bitter H
Friendly and popular village local. Central bar. Pub games

Middleton by Wirksworth

11–3; 6–11

Duke of Wellington
Duke Street (off B5023)
Draught Bass H
Cheery village local. Pub games

Try also: **Nelson's Arms** (Marston)

Newhall

10.30–2.30; 6–11

Jolly Colliers
2 Rose Valley (off B5353) ☎ (0283) 216951
John Smith Bitter H
Friendly village local, one of oldest pubs in area: parts of building date back to 1613

Try also: **Gate Inn**, Stanton (Marston)

New Mills

11–3; 5.30–11

Crescent
Market Street ☎ (0663) 43889
Tetley Mild, Bitter H
Attractive, stone-fronted pub in crescent-shaped terrace (Central)

11–3; 5.30–11

Fox
Brookbottom Hamlet, Strines (up St Mary's Road)
Robinson Best Mild, Best Bitter H
Old whitewashed pub in small hamlet. Can be reached on foot via the woodland cart-track from Strines station. Worth the effort

11–3; 5.30–11

North-Western
Albion Road, Newtown (200 yds from A6/A6015) ☎ (0663) 43107
Robinson Best Mild, Best Bitter E
Stone-built pub close to Peak Forest canal. Doubles as waiting room for station; named after builders of railway (Newtown)

Ockbrook

10.30–3; 6–11

Royal Oak
Green Lane (off A52) ☎ (0332) 662378
Draught Bass H
Characterful village meeting place with 4 small rooms. Pub games Q (not Sun)

Old Brampton

11–3; 7–11

George & Dragon
Off A619
Marston Burton Bitter, Pedigree H
2-room pub with town, village and farm customers. Opposite footpath to local reservoirs in area known as the Gateway to the Peak. No meals Sun (lunch) (until 8.30)

Openwoodgate

11–3; 6–11

Bulls Head
Ilkeston Road (A609)
Hardys & Hansons Best Bitter E
Exceptionally well-run village local with convivial atmosphere

Over Haddon

11–3; 6–11

Lathkill Hotel
South of B5055 ☎ (062 981) 2501
Ward Darley Dark Mild, Thorne Best Bitter, Sheffield Best Bitter H
Fine welcoming hostelry nestling in one of the county's magnificent dales. Near trout streams, and Lathkill Trail. Good walking and camping country. Well worth seeking out Q (lunch)

Pilsley

11–3; 7–11

Gladstone Arms
Morton Road (off B6039) ☎ (0773) 872285
Home Mild, Bitter H
Lively old stone local in centre of former pit village

Repton

10.30–2.30; 6–11

Boot
Boot Hill (off B5008) ☎ (0283) 703327
Draught Bass E
Lively village local, with functional bar and dimly lit lounge

Riddings

11–3; 6–11

Seven Stars
26 Church Street ☎ (0773) 602715
Ward Darley Dark Mild, Sheffield Best Bitter H
Historic house of character dating from 15th century, set in oldest part of village. Pub games

Ripley

11–3; 6–11

George Inn
Lowes Hill (off A61)
Bateman Mild, XB, XXXB H
Open-plan pub; Bateman's most westerly tied house

11–3; 6–11

Hollybush
Brook Lane, Marehay (off A61) ☎ (0773) 42558
Shipstone Bitter H
Spacious pub overlooking cricket ground. Pub games

Rowarth

11–3; 5.30–11

Little Mill
Left off the Marple Bridge to New Mills road at Mellor Moor ☎ (0663) 43178
Hartleys Bitter; Robinson Best Mild, Best Bitter; Ruddles County H
Popular restaurant-style pub in Peak District foothills. Guest beers

Sawley

11.30–2.30; 7–11

Nags Head
Tamworth Road, Old Sawley ☎ (0602) 732983
Marston Pedigree H
A country pub popular with all ages. Comfortable lounge and more traditional bar. Friendly welcome. Pub games

Scarcliffe

11–3; 7–11

Horse & Groom
On B6417 ☎ (0246) 823152
Home Bitter H
Beamed coaching inn with play area at rear Q (Tue–Sat)

Shardlow

10–2.30; 6–11

Canal Tavern
Hoskins Wharf, London Road,

Derbyshire

(A6, in marina complex)
☎ (0332) 792844
Hoskins Beaumanor Bitter, Penn's Ale, Premium H
Excellent conversion of 1780 grade 2 listed, canal side warehouse. Inside, original beams and brick floor survive; mooring facilities. Superb setting ✿

10–2.30; 6–11
Dog & Duck
London Road (A6)
☎ (0332) 79224
Marston Merrie Monk, Pedigree H**, Owd Roger** G
Much extended, cruck-built original with good choice of rooms

---

10–2.30; 6–11
Navigation
London Road (A6)
☎ (0332) 792918
Davenports Bitter; Wem Special Bitter H
Large roadside pub with gas-lit lounge

10–2.30; 6–11
Shakespeare
London Road (A6)
☎ (0332) 792728
Home Mild, Bitter E
Popular roadhouse, old though much modernised, with small garden

Shirland

11–3; 6.30–11
Duke of Wellington
Main Road (A61)
Home Bitter E
Busy 3-room pub in rural surroundings

Somercotes

11–3; 7–11
Horse & Jockey
Leabrooks Road (B6016)
☎ (0773) 602179
Home Mild, Bitter H
A labyrinth of rooms and passageways; a popular, unspoilt local

Spinkhill

12–3, 7–11
Angel
26 College Road
☎ (0246) 432315
Tetley Bitter H
Large, rambling village local. L-shaped lounge around bar. Games room. Friendly, lively atmosphere.

Stone Edge

11–3; 6.30–11
Red Lion
On B5057 400 yds from A632
☎ (0246) 566142
Ward Darley Dark Mild, Thorne Best Bitter, Sheffield Best Bitter H

Renovated inn with restaurant and ballroom, situated on edge of moors near the oldest industrial chimney in Britain

Sutton-cum-Duckmanton

11–3 (not Sat Oct–March); 6–11
Arkwright Arms
Bolsover Road, Duckmanton (A632) ☎ (0246) 32053
Marston Burton Bitter, Pedigree H
Convivial roadside pub with beer garden and donkeys (Mon–Fri)

Tideswell

11–3; 7–11
George Hotel
Commercial Road (B6049)
☎ (0298) 871382
Hardys & Hansons Best Mild, Best Bitter H
Stone hotel at village centre. Large lounge; dining room; small snug leading to taproom with pool table. Warm and friendly

Try also: **Anchor** (Robinson); **Horse & Jockey** (Tetley)

Turnditch

10.30–3; 6–11
Tiger
Belper Road (A517)
☎ (077 389) 200
Ind Coope Best Bitter, Burton Ale H
Smart, modernised country pub

Wardlow Mires

11–3; 6–11
Three Stags Heads
A623/B6465 ☎ (0298) 871251
Younger Scotch Bitter H
Family-run farmhouse pub that time has passed by. Petrified cat in glass case. Home-produced eggs and bacon on sale. Popular with ramblers

Whaley Bridge

11–3; 5.30–11
Board Inn
62 Chapel Road
Robinson Best Mild, Best Bitter H
Comfortable 1-bar pub with good views and pleasant atmosphere. Pub games

11–3; 5.30–11
Shepherds Arms
Old Road (off A6)
Marston Mercian Mild, Burton Bitter, Pedigree H
Excellent, ageless local with a stone-flagged vault

Whitwell

11–3; 6.30–11

Jug & Glass
Portland Street
John Smith Bitter H
Compact, village centre pub

Willington

10–2.30; 6–11
Green Dragon
The Green (A5132)
☎ (0283) 702377
Ind Coope Best Bitter, Burton Ale H
L-shaped single room, formerly part of railway cottages, with low wooden beams. Very popular in summer (Mon–Fri)

Windley

10.30–3; 6–11
Puss in Boots
Nether Lane (B5023)
☎ (077 389) 316
Draught Bass H
An isolated, characterful country pub with low-beamed ceiling. Pub games

Winster

11 (12 winter)–3; 6–11
Miners Standard
On B5056 ☎ (062 988) 279
Marston Pedigree; Theakston XB H
17th-century rambling country inn with dining room and games room. Guest beers

Wirksworth

11–3 (4 Tue); 7–11
Vaults
Coldwell Street (B5035)
☎ (062 982) 2186
Draught Bass H
White-fronted Georgian building with bow windows; crammed with curiosities

Try also: **Hope & Anchor** (Home)

Woolley Moor

12–2.30; 7–11 (winter); 11.30–3; 6.30–11 (summer)
White Horse Inn
White Horse Lane (off B6014)
☎ (0246) 590319
Draught Bass; M&B Springfield Bitter H
Friendly country inn with excellent food, beautiful view and adventure playground (not Sun)

Youlgreave

10.30–3; 6.30–11
George Inn
Church Street (off A6)
☎ (062 986) 292
Home Mild, Bitter H
Large pub in picturesque village. Pub games

101

Devon

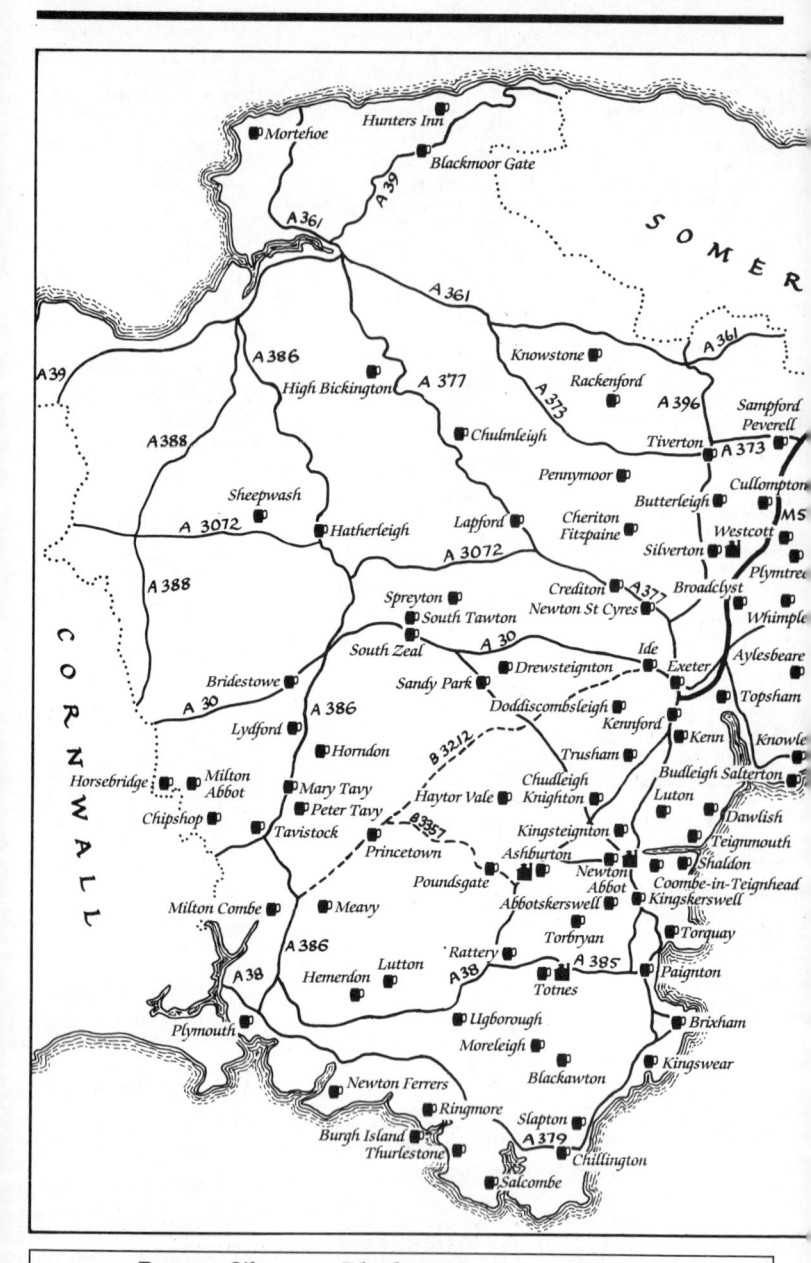

Barron, Silverton; **Blackawton**, Totnes; **Mill**, Newton Abbot; **Thompsons**, Ashburton

Abbotskerswell

11–2.30; 6–11

Two Mile Oak
Totnes Road (A381)
☎ (0803) 812411
Draught Bass; Eldridge Pope Royal Oak 🅶**; Flowers IPA** 🄷
15th-century coaching house. Food dominated lounge but retains an ancient and homely public bar ♨🍴🍺🅿

Ashburton

11–2.30; 5–11

London
11 West Street ☎ (0364) 52478
Thompsons Aysheburton Mild, Bitter, IPA 🄷
Comfortable coaching house with a single enormous meandering lounge. Features traditional pub food ♨🍺

Axmouth

10.30 (11 winter)–2.30;
6 (6.30 winter)–11

Devon

Devon

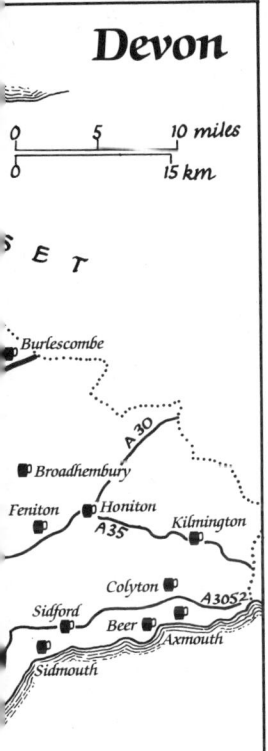

0 5 10 miles
0   15 km

B3052/B3180 ☎ (0395) 32273
Cornish Wessex Stud H
Prosperous country roadhouse, unaffected by Inn Leisure's style council. Locals from nearby millionaires' row. Specialist whisky bar. Pub games

Beer

10.30–2.30; 5.30–11
Anchor Inn
Fore Street ☎ (0297) 20386
Hall & Woodhouse Badger Best Bitter, Tanglefoot; Flowers IPA H
3-bar hotel in appropriately named seaside village. Restaurant features fresh seafood. Pub games

Blackawton

10.30–2.30; 5.30–11
Normandy Arms
2 miles S of B3207
☎ (080 421) 316
Blackawton Bitter, Forty-Four, Ind Coope Burton Ale H
Comfortable 15th-century village pub and restaurant. Caters well for families

Blackmoor Gate

10.30 (11 winter)–2.30; 6.30 (7 winter)–11
Old Station House Inn
A39/A399/B3226 Jct
☎ (059 83) 274
Courage Best Bitter, Directors; Golden Hill Exmoor Ale H
Modern low-lit lounge with a larger bar for families, caters well for restless children. Guest beers

Bridestowe

10.30–2.30; 6–11
Fox & Hounds
A386/B3278 ☎ (082 282) 206
Flowers IPA, Original H
Large pub on edge of Dartmoor. Restaurant and skittle alley

Brixham

11–3; 5.30–11
Burton
23 Burton Street (½ mile from quay) ☎ (080 45)2805
Courage Best Bitter H, **Directors** G
Popular pub with attractive wood-panelled lounge

Broadclyst

11–2.30; 5.30–11
Red Lion
on B3181 ☎ (0392) 61271
Draught Bass; Eldridge Pope Dorset Original IPA, Royal Oak H
Picturesque but pricey 16th-century inn owned by National Trust. Guest beers

Try also: **New Inn**, Whimple Rd

Broadhembury

10.30 2.30; 6–11
Drewe Arms
1 mile off A373
☎ (040 484) 267
Draught Bass; Cotleigh Tawny Bitter G
Fine traditional inn at the heart of a largely unspoilt cob and thatch village. Good food. Pub games

Budleigh Salterton

11–2.30; 6–11
Feathers
Fore Street ☎ (039 54) 2042
Flowers IPA, Original; Whitbread Pompey Royal H
Town centre pub with good value food. Guest beers

Try also: **Salterton Arms**, Chapel St

Burgh Island

11–2.30; 6–11
Pilchard
600 yds off the coast at Bigbury-On-Sea
☎ (0548) 810344
Palmer IPA; Usher Best Bitter H
Small, but strongly atmospheric 14th-century island tavern. Next to the impressively renovated 1930s hotel where several Agatha Christie novels were based. Darts
(summer)

Burlescombe

11–2.30; 6–11
Ayshford Arms
off B3181, 2 miles NE of M5 Jct 27 ☎ (0823) 672429
Cotleigh Tawny Bitter, Buzzard; Theakston Best Bitter H
Spacious, lively pub serving good food

Butterleigh

11–2.30; 6 (6 Fri)–11
Butterleigh Inn
☎ (088 45) 407
Cotleigh Kingfisher Ale, Tawny Bitter, Old Buzzard H
Small, busy pub with stained glass porch; dates back to 1550
(not Sun) (not Tues)

Cheriton Fitzpaine

11–2.30; 7–11
Half Moon
2 miles N of A3072

Ship
on B3172 ☎ (0297) 21838
Cornish Original, Wessex Stud H
Friendly pub in a pretty seaside village. Boasts an aviary, a remarkable collection of dolls and some fine food. Pub games
(not Fri, winter)

Aylesbeare

11–2.30; 6–11
Halfway House

Devon

Flowers IPA, Original ℍ
Friendly traditional village pub. Comfortable lounge. Pub games include skittles and table tennis ≜⊛♿🛏 ◐▶⊖♢

Chillington

12–2.30; 6–11

Chillington Inn
on A379 ☎ (0548) 580244
Palmer IPA 🄶**; Usher Best Bitter** ℍ
Quietly sophisticated village inn with 3 bars. Excellent food and accommodation
≜⊛🛏 ◐ ⊖♢

Chipshop

12–3; 7 (5.30 Sat)–11

Chipshop
1½ miles off A384 OS436752
☎ (0822) 832322
Golden Hill Exmoor Ale; Marston Pedigree; Wadworth 6X ℍ
Bright, welcoming modern pub at a country crossroads. Skittle alley for hire. Guest beers ≜⊛⊛ ◐▶ ♿

Chudleigh Knighton

11–2.30; 6–11

Claycutters Arms
Just off A38
Eldridge Pope Royal Oak; Flowers IPA ℍ
Early 17th-century thatched village pub. Rambling lounge and separate restaurant. Views of Dartmoor. Live music Sat ≜⊛⊛🛏 ◐ ♿ ♿

Chulmleigh

10.30–2.30; 5.30–11

Barnstaple
South Molton Street
☎ (0769) 80388
Draught Bass; Butcombe Bitter; Marston Pedigree ℍ♢
Lovely old village boozer with a friendly welcome for all. Pub games ≜⊛⊛🛏 ◐▶⊖♢

Colyton

11–2.30; 6–11

Kingfisher
Dolphin Street ☎ (0297) 52476
Eldridge Pope Royal Oak; Flowers IPA; Hall & Woodhouse Badger Best Bitter ℍ
Stone-walled pub with partly flagged floor and cartwheel glass store. Darts and skittles; guest beers ⊛⊛🛏 ◐▶ ♢

Coombe-in-Teignhead

11–2.30; 6.30–11

Wild Goose
☎ (0626) 872241
Golden Hill Exmoor Ale; Mill Janner's Ale; Wadworth 6X ℍ 17th-century farmhouse of character. Trad jazz Mon nights. Good food; guest beers ≜⊛⊛ ◐▶

Crediton

11–2.30; 5.30–11

Crediton
28A Mill Street (A3072)
☎ (036 32) 2882
Barron Exe Valley Bitter ℍ
Friendly roadside pub offering above average food. Skittles, dominoes
⊛ ◐▶ ⇌ (Tiverton)

Cullompton

11–2.30; 5–11

Manor House
Fore Street ☎ (0884) 32881
Flowers Original ℍ
16th-century town centre hotel. Good value food ≜⊛⊛🛏 ◐▶ ⊖♢♿

Try also: White Hart

Dawlish

11–2.30; 5–11

Prince Albert
28 The Strand ☎ (0626) 862132
Draught Bass; Flowers IPA ℍ
Cosy and convivial. Also known as Hole in the Wall
Q ◐⇌

Doddiscombsleigh

11–2.30; 6–11

Nobody Inn
2 miles off B3193
☎ (0647) 52394
Eldridge Pope Royal Oak; Hall & Woodhouse Badger Best Bitter 🄶
Atmospheric old inn, noted for food, wine list and exceptional collection of whiskies ≜Q⊛🛏 ◐▶ ♿

Drewsteignton

10.30–2.30; 6–10.30

Drewe Arms
Flowers IPA 🄶
Unspoilt 18th-century village pub with longest-serving licensee in the country
≜Q⊖♢

Exeter

11–2.30; 5–11

Double Locks
Canal Banks, Marsh Barton
☎ (0392) 56947
Eldridge Pope Royal Oak; Everards Old Original; Golden Hill Exmoor Ale; Marston Pedigree; Wadworth 6X 🄶
Extensive, eccentric and extremely successful canalside haunt of discerning drinkers. Caters well for families. Good vegetarian and traditional food. Pub games
≜Q⊛⊛ ◐▶ ⊖♿♢

11–2.30; 5–11

Honiton
Paris Street (opposite coach station)
Draught Bass; Flowers Original ℍ
Recently refurbished pub-bar
⊛ ◐▶ ⇌ (Central)

11–2.30; 6–11

Imperial Hotel
St David's Hill
☎ (0392) 211811
Barron Exe Valley Bitter ℍ
Plush hotel bar
🛏 ◐▶ ⇌ (St David's)

11–2.30; 5–11 (5.30–10.30 winter)

Mill-on-the-Exe
Bonhay Road (Crediton Road)
☎ (0392) 214464
Barron Exe Valley Bitter; Beer Engine Piston Bitter; Cotleigh Old Buzzard; Ind Coope Burton Ale; Plympton Pride 🄶 ℍ & 🄴
Expensive but good converted warehouse on the bank of the Exe especially popular in summer. Terrace overlooks weir. Caters for families
≜⊛⊛ ◐▶ ♿⇌ (St David's)

11–2.30; 5–11

Old Firehouse
New North Road
Flowers IPA; Golden Hill Exmoor Ale; Usher Best Bitter ℍ
City-centre free house that usd to house fire engines. Good value lunches include vegetarian dishes. Guest beers
⊛ ◐⇌ (Central)

11–2.30; 5–11

Welcome
Haven Banks (near Maritime Museum)
Cornish Wessex Stud ℍ
Unspoilt 1-bar riverside pub. Take some bread to feed the ducks. Darts and pool
Q⊛⇌ (St Thomas)

11–2.30; 5–11

Well House
Cathedral Yard ☎ (0392) 58464
Barron Exe Valley Bitter; Flowers IPA; Wiltshire Old Devil ℍ
On site of old city well. Visit the cellar. Good value lunches. Guest beers
🛏 ◐ (not Sun) ⇌ (Central)

Feniton

10.30–2.30; 5.30–11

Nog Inn
Ottery Road ☎ (0404) 850210
Draught Bass; Cotleigh Tawny Bitter ℍ
Cheerful village local with squash court. Guest beers
≜⊛🛏 ♿⇌♢

Hatherleigh

10.30–2.30 (4 Mon); 6–11
(open all day Tue)

104

Devon

George Hotel
Market Street (A386)
☎ (0837) 810454
Draught Bass; Cornish GBH (winter); Marston Pedigree (summer); Wadworth 6X H
Thatched 15th-century small hotel with courtyard; comes alive on market days. Elegant accommodation. Guest beers
⌂☆🐾◐▮🍴🕮

11–2.30 (4 Mon); 6–11; (open all dayTue)

Tally Ho
Market Street (A386)
☎ (0837) 810306
Eldridge Pope Royal Oak; Palmer Tally Ho; Wadworth 6X H
Quaintly furnished 15th-century market town inn. Food recommended ⌂🐾 ◐▮

Haytor Vale

11–2.30; 6–11

Rock Inn
2 miles W of B3344
☎ (036 46) 208
Draught Bass; Eldridge Pope Dorchester Bitter, Dorset Original IPA, Royal Oak H
Superb old Dartmoor village inn: large lounge, tiny public and family room
⌂☆🐾◐▮🍴

Hemerdon

11–2.30; 5.30–11 (10.30 winter)

Miners Arms
☎ (0752) 336040
Draught Bass G & H;
Ruddles County; Wadworth 6X H
Large and expanding village pub with a tin-mining past
⌂Q🐾◐▮🍴🕮

High Bickington

11 (11.30 winter)–2.30; 6 (6.30 winter)–11

Old George Inn
Tucked away off Main Street
☎ (0769) 60513
Hall & Woodhouse Tanglefoot; Usher Best Bitter H
Modernised, but cosy 16th-century thatched village inn. Skittle alley for hire. Summer guest beers ⌂☆🐾◐▮🕮

Honiton

10.30–2.30; 6.30–11

Volunteer
177 High Street ☎ (0404) 2145
Cotleigh Tawny Bitter H
Comfortable, old, traditional town pub. Various games
☆🐾🍴≠🕮

Horndon

11.30–2.30; 6.30–11

Elephant's Nest
off A386. 1½ miles E of Mary Tavy ☎ (082 281) 273

Palmer IPA; St Austell Tinners Bitter; Hicks Special; Wadworth 6X H
Splendid moorland pub named after a former landlord's beard! Guest beers
⌂Q🐾◐▮🍴🕮

Horsebridge

12–2.30; 7–10.30 (11 Sat)

Royal
off A384, 1 mile S of Sydenham Damerel OS402749
☎ (082 287) 214
Draught Bass; Eldridge Pope Royal Oak; Horsebridge Tamar Bitter, Best Bitter, Heller H
Characterful home-brew pub on the banks of the Tamar. Former nunnery. Pub games
⌂Q☆🐾◐▮ (not Sun) 🍴🕮

Hunters Inn

10.30–2.30; 6–11

Hunters Inn
Heddons Mouth, Parracombe (off A39 & A399)
☎ (059 83) 230
Draught Bass; Flowers IPA; Golden Hill Exmoor Ale H
Edwardian country house hotel in a spectacular valley in Exmoor National Park. Caters well for families. Guest beers
⌂☆🐾◐▮🕮

Ide

11–2.30; 5.30–11

Huntsman
2 High Street (½ mile off A30)
☎ (0392) 72779
Cornish JD Dry Hop Bitter, Wessex Stud H
Thatched village inn beside a ford. Boasts longest pub sign in Britain. Bar billiards
⌂Q🐾◐▮ (not Sun)

Kenn

11–2.30; 6–11

Ley Arms
½ mile from A38 (Kennford exit) ☎ (0392) 832341
Draught Bass; Blackawton Bitter, Forty-Four; Flowers IPA H
Thatched village pub with excellent carvery ⌂☆🐾◐▮🕮

Kennford

11–2.30; 6.30–11

Anchor
off A38 ☎ (0392) 832344
Courage Best Bitter, Directors H
Large 1930s roadhouse catering for travellers
🐾◐▮🍴🕮

Kilmington

11–2.30; 7–11

New Inn
The Hill (off A35)
☎ (0297) 33376

Palmer BB, IPA G
Friendly, thatched village local, used to strangers. Food Mon. Pub games ⌂🐾◐▮🕮

Kingskerswell

11–2.30; 6–11

Bickley Mill Inn
Stoneycombe (near quarry)
☎ (080 47) 3201
Draught Bass; Gibbs Mew Bishops Tipple; Wadworth 6X H
Large 13th-century converted mill. Terraced garden with roaming peacocks. Family room and good food. Live music Sat nights
⌂☆🐾◐▮🍴

Kingsteignton

11–2.30; 6–11

Old Rydon
Rydon Lane (off A380)
☎ (0626) 54626
Draught Bass; Mill Devon Special; Wadworth 6X H
Old pub with small bar (cosy corners), upstairs drinking area, and good restaurant
⌂Q◐▮

Kingswear

11–2.30; 6–11

Steam Packet
☎ (080 425) 208
Courage Best Bitter, Directors H
Small friendly local. Good views over River Dart. Meals summer only ⌂ ◐▮

Knowle

7.15–11 (closed lunchtimes and all day Sun & Mon)

Tidwell House
on B3178 ☎ (039 54) 2441
Cotleigh Tawny Bitter; Golden Hill Exmoor Dark H
Family-run hotel, with a cellar bar specialising in good value meals Q☆🐾◐▮

Knowstone

11–2.30; 6–11

Masons Arms
☎ (039 84) 231
Boddingtons Bitter; Hall & Woodhouse Badger Best Bitter; Wadworth 6X G
Delightful, yet simple, thatched village inn. Public bar with large open fire; cosy small lounge. Quiet calm prevails out of season
⌂Q☆🐾◐▮🕮

Lapford

11.30–2.30; 7–11

Old Malt Scoop
½ mile off A377 ☎ (036 35) 330
Draught Bass H; **Eldridge Pope Royal Oak** G; **Marston Pedigree** H; **Wadworth Farmers Glory, Old Timer** G

105

Devon

Rapidly developing pub. Bar dominated by stone fireplace. Pub games
≌Q☎⊛⋈◑▮⊕♿A⇌⌂

Luton

10.30–2.30; 6–11

Elizabethan
½ mile off B3192
☎ (062 67) 5428
Cornish Wessex Stud, GBH; Flowers IPA H
Large lounge and older low-ceilinged area. Emphasis on food ≌☎⊛◑▮⊕A

Lutton

10.30–2.30; 5.30–11 (10.30 winter)

Mountain
☎ (0752) 837 247
Butcombe Bitter; Golden Hill Exmoor Ale; Ind Coope Burton Ale H
Attractive and cosy village pub on a steep incline. Parking requires patience!
≌Q⊛◑▮⌂

Lydford

11–2.30; 6–11

Manor Inn
1½ miles W of village
OS503832 ☎ (082 282) 208
St Austell Tinners Bitter H
Small old-fashioned country hotel with a traditional village bar ≌Q☎⊛⋈◑▮A

Mary Tavy

11–2.30; 7.30–11

Mary Tavy Inn
on A386 ☎ (082 281) 326
St Austell Tinners Bitter, Hicks Special; Usher Best Bitter H
Large roadside inn at edge of the moor. Clock collection. Pub games Q☎⊛⋈◑▮A

Meavy

11–3; 6–11

Royal Oak
☎ (0822) 852944
Draught Bass; Blackawton Bitter, Headstrong (winter) H
15th-century local; lovely slate-floored public bar. Next to an ancient oak on village green ≌Q⊛◑▮⊕A⌂

Milton Abbot

11–2.30; 6–10.30 (11 Sat)

Edgcumbe Arms
on A384 ☎ (082 287) 229
Draught Bass; Flowers Original; Wadworth 6X H
Welcoming, convivial roadside pub with an impressive fireplace. Summer guest beers ≌⊛◑▮⊕A

Milton Combe

11.30–2.30; 6.30–11

Who'd Have Thought It
☎ (0822) 853313
Eldridge Pope Royal Oak; Golden Hill Exmoor Ale; Palmer IPA; Wadworth 6X H
Lovely 16th-century stone pub. The tiny village rests in a hollow off a steep wooded valley. Guest beers
≌Q☎⊛◑▮⌂

Moreleigh

12–2; 6–11

New Inn
1 mile off A381 ☎ (054 882) 326
Palmer IPA G
17th-century village pub with strong local following. Candlelit dining area and boozy bar ≌Q◑▮

Mortehoe

11–2.30; 6–11

Ship Aground
☎ (0271) 870856
Draught Bass; Golden Hill Exmoor Ale, Strong Ale (Wreckers Bitter) H
Modern lounge bar with glimpses of its past showing through. ≌⊛◑▮

Newton Abbot

10.30–2.30; 5–11

Devon Arms
67 East Street ☎ (0626) 68725
Draught Bass; Wadworth 6X H
Lively modern town pub in old building ⊛◑▮⇌

Newton Ferrers

11.30–2.30; 6–11

Dolphin
☎ (0752) 872007
Draught Bass H
Fine old pub in a beautiful creekside setting. Beware of yachty yuppies in high season! Parking requires imagination
≌Q☎⊛◑▮ (not Tue) ⊕⌂

Newton St Cyres

11.30–2.30; 6–11 (midnight Fri Sat with entertainment)

Beer Engine
½ mile off A377
☎ (039 285) 282
Beer Engine Rail Ale, Piston Bitter, Heavy Sleeper H
Railside home-brew house. Brewery on view downstairs. Frequent live music
Q☎⊛◑▮A⇌

Paignton

11–3; 5.30–11

Parkers Arms
343 Totnes Road (A385)
☎ (0803) 551011
Plymouth Best, Pride H
Large pub-cum-small hotel. Skittles ☎⋈◑▮⊕A

Pennymoor

11–2.30; 6–11

Cruwys Arms
1 mile S of A373 ☎ (036 36) 347
Draught Bass H; **Cotleigh Old Buzzard (winter)** G
Unspoilt country pub with splendid open fire. Guest beers ≌☎⊛◑▮A

Peter Tavy

11.30–3; 6.30–11

Peter Tavy
☎ (082 281) 348
Butcombe Bitter; Courage Directors Bitter; Eldridge Pope Royal Oak; Golden Hill Exmoor Ale G
Ancient, low-ceilinged pub with flagstones and settles. Excellent vegetarian food
≌⊛◑▮A⌂

Plymouth

11–2.30; 6–11

Bank
Old George Street
☎ (0752) 672100
Halls Plympton Best, Pride H
Large 2-storey lounge bar in a converted bank next to Theatre Royal. Conservatory area upstairs
☎⊛◑▮ (until 7.30) ⇌

11–2.30; 6–11

Pennycomequick
200 yds from Main Station
☎ (0752) 661412
Halls Plympton Best, Pride H
Plain but friendly 2-bar pub. Games ⊛◑▮⇌

11–3; 6–11

Pym Arms
16 Pym Street, Devonport
☎ (0752) 561823
Eldridge Pope Royal Oak; Marston Pedigree; St Austell XXXX, Hicks Special; Wadworth 6X G
Unashamedly a beer drinker's bar. Single lively room. Only real mild for miles; guest beers
⇌ (Devonport)

12–3; 7–11

Royal Adelaide Arms
9 Adelaide Street, Stonehouse (near Royal Naval Hospital)
☎ (0752) 665348
Golden Hill Exmoor Ale; Wadworth 6X H
1-bar local with a banknote collection. A civilised oasis
☎⋈◑

11–2.30 (3 Sat); 6–11

Stopford Arms
172 Devonport Road, Stoke
☎ (0752) 562915
Courage Best Bitter, Directors H
Clean, smart and well-run traditional 2-bar local. Best of Courage's 112 Plymouth pubs!
◑ (not Sun) ⊕⇌ (Devonport)

106

Devon

12–3; 7–12
Swan
Cornwall Beach, Devonport
☎ (0752) 568761
Gibbs Mew Bishops Tipple; Marston Pedigree; St Austell Hicks Special; Wadworth 6X H
2-tiered, wooden-floored, rough-hewn dockland boozer with plenty of character. Live music till midnight Mon–Sat; no admission after 10.30 pm. Guest beers. Pub games
⛺🐕🍴🍺

12–3; 7–11
Thistle Park Tavern
1 Sutton Road, Coxside (200 yds S of A374) ☎ (0752) 667677
Eldridge Pope Royal Oak; Marston Owd Rodger; St Austell Hick's Special; Wadworth 6X H
Basic beer-drinking pub near the commercial docks. Guest beers ⛺

Plymtree

11–2.30; 6–11
Blacksmiths Arms
☎ (088 47) 322
Draught Bass; Gibbs Mew Salisbury Best; Golden Hill Exmoor Ale H
Friendly village pub. Various games ⛺Q🐕🍴🍺

Poundsgate

11–2.30; 6–11
Tavistock
on A384 ☎ (036 43) 251
Courage Best Bitter H
Traditional granite moorland pub, several hundred years old ⛺🐕🍴🍺

Princetown

11–3; 6.30–11
Prince of Wales
Tavistock Road (100 yds off B3212) ☎ (082 289) 219
Flowers Original; Hall & Woodhouse Tanglefoot; Wadworth 6X H
On the road to H.M. Prison Dartmoor. Popular with walkers and warders alike. Guest beers ⛺🍴🍺

Try also: Devil's Elbow; Plume of Feathers (Free)

Rackenford

11–2.30; 6–11
Stag Inn
400 yds off B3221
☎ (088 488) 369
Cotleigh Tawny Bitter; Wadworth 6X H
Thatched village inn with many rooms ⛺🐕🛏🍴🍺

Rattery

11–2.30; 6–11
Church House

off A38 ☎ (0364) 42220
Courage Best Bitter, Directors H
A victualling house since 1028: one of England's oldest. A mix of ancient and modern. Guest beers ⛺Q🍴🍺♿

Ringmore

11–2.30; 6–11
Journey's End Inn
☎ (0548) 810205
Butcombe Bitter H**; Golden Hill Exmoor Ale; Wadworth 6X (summer), Old Timer (winter)** G
Ancient thatched inn with many original features at the heart of a beautiful village. Car park 400 yards up the hill. Guest beers ⛺🐕🍴🍺🍽

Sampford Peverell

11–2.30; 6–11
Globe
16 Lower Town (A373) ☎ (0884) 821214
Flowers IPA, Original E
Large roadside pub with excellent children's play area. Backs onto Grand Western Canal. Guest beers ⛺🐕🍴🍺🍽♿

Try also: Merriemeade Hotel

Salcombe

10.30–2.30; 5.30–11
Victoria Inn
Fore Street ☎ (054 884) 2604
Draught Bass G
Old yachting pub with traditional public bar and comfortable lounge ⛺🍴🍺🍽

Try also: Ferry Inn (Palmer)

Sandy Park

11–2.30; 7–11
Sandy Park
on A382 ☎ (064 73) 3538
Barron Exe Valley Bitter; Everards Old Original; Marston Pedigree G
Basic country pub with colourful locals ⛺Q🍴

Shaldon

11–2.30; 5–11
Ferry Boat
The Strand ☎ (0626) 872340
Courage Best Bitter, Directors (seasonal) H
1-bar pub on the estuary beach. Home-cooked meals and summer barbecues ⛺🍴🍺

11–2.30; 5–11
Shipwrights Arms
Ringmore Road
Courage Best Bitter, Directors H
2-tier public bar with a

nautical flavour. Views of the estuary. Quiet lounge ⛺🐕🍴🍺

Sheepwash

11–2.30; 6–11
Half Moon
The Square ☎ (040 923) 376
Draught Bass; Courage Best Bitter H
Bright stone-floored fishing hotel in the village square ⛺Q🛏🍴

Sidford

10.30–2.30; 5.30–11
Blue Ball
on A3052 ☎ (039 55) 4062
Cornish JD Dry Hop Bitter, Wessex Stud H
14th-century thatched pub. Stone-flagged floor and inglenook. Family lounge ⛺🐕🍴🍺🍽

Sidmouth

10.30–2.30; 6–11
Old Ship
Old Fore Street
☎ (039 55) 2127
Archers Village Bitter; Boddingtons Bitter; Marston Pedigree H
Attractive 600 year-old pub with strong smuggling connections. Excellent food ⛺Q🍴🍺

Try also: Swan Inn, York Street

Silverton

11.45–2.30; 6–11
Three Tuns
14 Exeter Road
☎ (0392) 860352
Barron Exe Valley Bitter; Beer Engine Piston Bitter; Courage Best Bitter, Directors; Wadworth 6X H
Well-managed pub in a former brewery. Bottle collection. Cheaper drinks on Mon ⛺🐕🍴🍺♿🅿

Slapton

11.30–2.30; 6–11
Tower Inn
☎ (0548) 580216
Blackawton Bitter; Gibbs Mew Bishops Tipple; Golden Hill Exmoor Ale; Wadworth 6X H
Attractive 14th-century inn tucked away up an alley. Catered well for everything except cars. Guest beers ⛺🐕🍴🍺🍽

South Tawton

11–2.30; 6 (7 winter)–11
Seven Stars
☎ (0837) 840292
Flowers IPA; Ind Coope Burton Ale H**; Wadworth 6X,**

107

Devon

Old Timer (winter) G
Solid pub with bar and restaurant (not Sun winter)

South Zeal

11–2.30; 6–11

Oxenham Arms
☎ (0837) 840244
St Austell Tinners Bitter; Hicks Special G
Wonderful stone-built village inn with a genuine old world feel. Strongly recommended. Pub games

Spreyton

11–2.30; 6–11

Tom Cobley Tavern
on main street
Cotleigh Tawny Bitter; Hall & Woodhouse Tanglefoot; Marston Pedigree G
Village pub catering to high standard. First licensed 1598. In 1802 Tom Cobley and friends set out from this inn to Widecombe. Pub games

Tavistock

11–2.30; 6–11

Bedford Hotel
Plymouth Road (A386)
☎ (0822) 61322
Draught Bass; Courage Best Bitter H
THF hotel in centre of town. Real ale in Bedford Bar

Teignmouth

11–2.30; 5–11

Teign Brewery
20 Teign Street
☎ (062 67) 2684
Courage Best Bitter, Directors H
Regular locals' bar and small cosy lounge. Near the estuary

Thurlestone

11–2.30; 6–11

Village Inn
☎ (0548) 560382
Draught Bass; Palmer IPA; Ruddles County; Wadworth 6X H
Stone-fronted, but modern village inn near hotel conference centre

Tiverton

11–2.30; 5–11

Country House
St Andrew Street (400 yds off main street) ☎ (0884) 256473
Draught Bass; Boddingtons Bitter; Wadworth 6X H
Large garden backs onto the river. Excellent children's area indoors

11–2.30; 5–11

Four In Hand
Fore Street ☎ (0884) 252765
Draught Bass H
Busy bar near cinema and bus station. Guest beers

11–2.30; 5–11

Racehorse
Wellbrook Street (W of the river) ☎ (0884) 252606
Usher Best Bitter; Ruddles County H
Popular local

Topsham

11–2; 6.30–11

Bridge
Elm Grove Road (A376)
☎ (0392) 873862
Blackawton Bitter; Golden Hill Exmoor Ale; Marston Pedigree; Wadworth 6X; Wiltshire Old Devil G
Famous riverside alehouse. Many bars including a parlour and downstairs lounge. 12 to 14 beers usually available

Try also: Salutation, Fore Street

Torbryan

11–2.30; 5.30–11

Church House
☎ (0803) 812372
Butcombe Bitter; Cornish GBH; Gibbs Mew Bishops Tipple; Mill Brewery Devon Special; Marston Pedigree; Theakston Old Peculier G & H
Ancient village pub in a lovely hamlet. Wide range of ales may compromise quality

Torquay

11–3; 5.30–11

Clarence Hotel
Newton Road, Torre
☎ (0803) 24417
Draught Bass H
Large pub on main route into Torquay (Torre)

11–3; 5.30–11

Crown & Sceptre
2 Petitor Road, St Marychurch
☎ (0803) 38290
Courage Best Bitter, Directors; John Smith Bitter H
200 year-old, popular local. Folk-oriented; Cockney humour abounds. Family room

11–3; 5.30–11

Saxon Bar (Courtlands Hotel)
Rawlyn Road, Chelston
Draught Bass H
Comfortable hotel bar

Totnes

10.30–2.30; 6–11

Albert
32 Bridgetown (A385 E of river) ☎ (0803) 863214
Courage Best Bitter, Directors H
Lively traditional pub with 2 cosy bars. Folk music Sun eves

Trusham

11–2.30; 6 (7 winter)–11

Cridford Inn
1½ miles off B3193
☎ (0626) 853694
Draught Bass; Cotleigh Old Buzzard G; **Golden Hill Exmoor Ale** H
Converted from an old barn in 1983. Still feels new, but nice atmosphere is developing. Above average food. Pub games; guest beers

Ugborough

11–3; 5.30–11

Anchor
☎ (0752) 892283
Draught Bass; Wadworth 6X G
Lively traditional public bar and bright well-managed "foody" lounge. Hub of village life. Darts

Try also: Ship

Westcott

11–2.30; 6–11

Merry Harriers
on B3181 2 miles S of Cullompton ☎ (0392) 881254
Draught Bass H
Friendly local

Whimple

11–2.30; 6–11

New Fountain
½ mile N of A30
☎ (0404) 822350
Cornish Wessex Stud H
Well managed, high class eating establishment (no food Sun)

10.30–2.30; 6–11

Paddock
London Road (A30)
☎ (0404) 822356
Courage Directors H
Smart, comfortable roadhouse, with selection of over 70 foreign bottled beers. Pub games; guest beers

108

Dorset

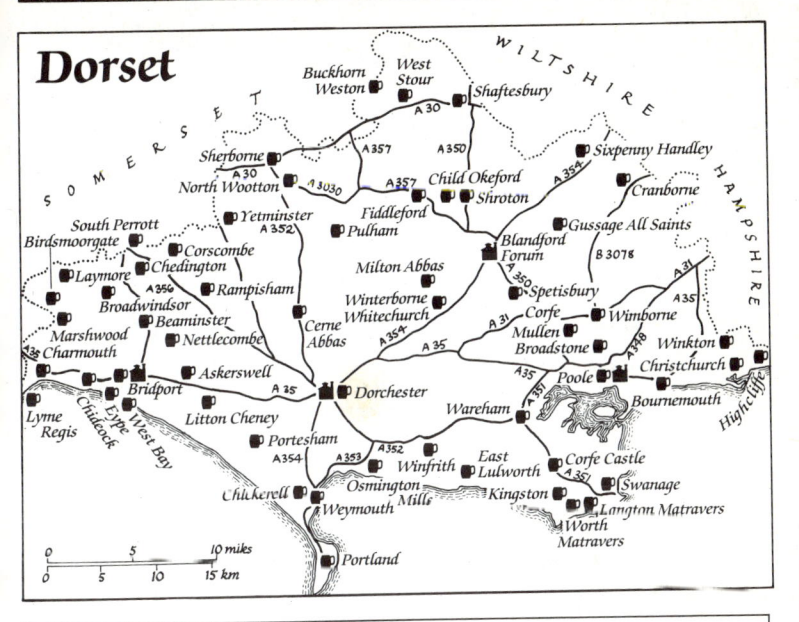

🏠 *Eldridge Pope*, Dorchester; **Hall & Woodhouse**, Blandford Forum; **Palmer**, Bridport; **Poole**, Poole

Askerswell

10–2.30; 6–11

Spyway
1½ miles off A35 OS528934
☎ (030 885) 250
Ruddles County; Usher BB; Webster's Yorkshire Bitter H
Popular pub with large childrens' room, pretty garden and lovely views

Beaminster

10.30–2.30; 7–11

Eight Bells
Church Street ☎ (0308) 863241
Palmer BB, Tally Ho G
Small very old pub in pleasant market town. Pub games played

Birdsmoorgate

10–2.30; 6–11

Rose & Crown
Junction B3164/B3165
OS391009 ☎ (029 77) 527
Cornish Original; Crown House Bitter; Theakston Old Peculier H
Isolated pub in beautiful surroundings. Traditional public bar and separate restaurant. Pub games

Bournemouth

10.30–2.30; 5.30–11

Branswick Hotel
199 Malmesbury Park Road, Charminster (off B3063)
☎ (0202) 290197
Flowers Original; Whitbread Strong Country Bitter; H
Friendly back street local with a folk club on Sat eves and an annual all-day folk festival

11.30–2.30; 5.30 (6 Sat)–11

Cricketers Arms
41 Windham Road, Springbourne (off Holdenhurst Road)
☎ (0202) 24875
Flowers Original; Whitbread Strong Country Bitter H
Splendid Victorian pub (Bournemouth's oldest) with fine mahogany bar fittings. Hub of East Dorset branch of CAMRA. Pub games.
Q (lounge)

10.30–2.30; 5.30 (6 Sat)–11

Old Thumper
113 Poole Road, Westbourne
☎ (0202) 768586
Ringwood Best Bitter, Fortyniner, 4X, Old Thumper; Wadworth 6X H
Friendly, small bar among shops used by students
(Branksome)

Bridport

11–2.30; 6–11

Crown Inn
West Bay Road (on new by-pass B3157) ☎ (0308) 22037
Palmer BB; IPA, Tally Ho H
Popular pub with good food between Bridport and harbour at West Bay

11–2.30; 7–11

Toll House
East Road (A35)
☎ (0308) 23398
Palmer BB, IPA H
Fine road house with genuine welcome. Pub games played

Try also: **White Lion** (Palmer)

Broadstone

10.30–2.30; 6–11

Broadstone Hotel
12–14 Station Approach off B3074 ☎ (0202) 694220
Flowers Original; Whitbread Strong Country Bitter H
100 years-old, ex-railway hotel with patio and skittle alley/function room

Broadwindsor

10.30–2.30; 6–11

White Lion
The Square ☎ (0308) 68855
Palmer BB, IPA, Tally Ho H
Excellent friendly village pub.
Games

Buckhorn Weston

12–2.30; 6–11

Stapleton Arms
2 miles N of A30 OS757247
☎ (0963) 70396
Golden Hill Exmoor Ale; Wadworth 6X H

109

Dorset

2-bar free house. Pool and darts in the public bar, smart lounge with restaurant area. Guest beers 🏠Q☺⊛🎵 ◐ 🏵⇔

Cerne Abbas

11.30 (11 Sat)–2.30; 6.30 (6 Sat)–11

Red Lion
Long Street ☎ (030 03) 441
Adnams Bitter; Wadworth IPA, 6X H
Smart free house in picturesque village, busy in summer. Large bar with dining area. Fine stained glass. Pub games 🏠⊛ ◐ ⇔

Charmouth

10.30–2.30; 6.30–11

Royal Oak
The Street (A35)
☎ (0297) 60277
Palmer IPA H
Small private house-type pub. Very popular with locals. Pub games 🏠☺ ◐ ⇔ 🏵 A

Try also: Star Inn; Coach & Horses

Chedington

11.30–2.30; 7 (6.30 summer)–11

Winyards Gap
A356 ☎ (093 589) 244
Draught Bass; Eldridge Pope Dorchester Bitter; Golden Hill Exmoor Ale H
Welcoming 2-bar pub with splendid views. Guest beers in summer. Pub games Q☺⊛ ◐ 🏵 A

Chickerell

11–2.30; 6.45–11

Fishermans Arms
Lower Putton Lane (off B3157)
OS 651805 ☎ (0305) 785136
Cornish Original G
Hidden away behind restaurant; Home of CAMRA boules team. Bar billiards, and other games available
🏠☺⊛ ◐ (not Tue) 🏵⇔

Chideock

10–2.30; 6–11

George Inn
Main Street (A35)
☎ (0297) 89419
Palmer BB, IPA, Tally Ho H
Welcoming village pub giving good value in all its activities. Pub games 🏠Q☺⊛ ◐ ▶ A

Child Okeford

11.30–2.30; 6.30–11

Baker Arms
The Cross (off A357)
☎ (0258) 860260
Hall & Woodhouse Badger Best Bitter; Wadworth 6X H
Friendly 1-bar pub with pool and darts. Occasional live music Q☺⊛⇔ A

11.30–2.30; 7–11

Saxon Arms
Gold Hill (500 yds NE of Cross) ☎ (0258) 860310
Draught Bass; Charrington IPA H
A quaint old village pub, full of character, tucked away behind cottages. Smart and tidy 🏠☺⊛🎵 ◐ ▶

12–2 (not Mon); 6.30–11

Union Arms
Station Road (off A357)
☎ (0258) 860540
Felinfoel Double Dragon; Hook Norton Best Bitter H
Small village local with new restaurant. Guest beers
🏠Q⊛ ◐ ▶ A ⇔

Christchurch

10.30–2.30; 6–11

Castle Tavern
7 Church Street
☎ (0202) 485199
Draught Bass; Ringwood Best Bitter, Fortyniner, Old Thumper H
Busy lounge bar in town centre. Shove ha'penny and dominoes. Guest beers
☺ (summer lunch) ◐ ⇔ ⇌

10.30–2.30; 6–11

Kings Arms Hotel
Castle Street ☎ (0202) 484117
Draught Bass H
Large town centre hotel bar
🏠☺🎵 ◐ ⇔ ⇌

11–2.30; 6–11

Ship in Distress
66 Stanpit (1 mile S of A35)
☎ (0202) 483867
Flowers Original; Whitbread Pompey Royal H
A splendid inn on the edge of Stanpit Marshes: over 300 years old and a former haunt of smugglers, it takes its name from a local legend. Darts and shove ha'penny
🏠☺⊛ ◐ ▶ (not Tue) 🏵

Try also: George (Whitbread)

Corfe Castle

11–2.30 (3 summer); 7–11

Fox
West Street (off A351)
☎ (0929) 480449
Flowers Original; Whitbread Strong Country Bitter, Pompey Royal G
Homely 16th-century inn which still celebrates the customs of the Purbeck Marblers 🏠Q⊛ ◐ 🏵 A

Corfe Mullen

11–2.30; 6.30–11

Coventry Arms
Mill Street (A31)
☎ (0258) 857284
Cornish Original, Wessex Stud, Great British Heavy G
500 year-old building with low beams, thick walls and stone floors. Bars feature Zodiac signs and Pickwick characters. No smoking bar. Interesting curios include the mummified cat. Pub games
🏠Q☺⊛ ◐ ▶ 🏵⇔

Try also: Lambs Green (Bass)

Corscombe

11.30–2.30 (not Mon); 7–11

Fox
☎ (093 589) 330
Cornish J D Dry Hop Bitter; Eldridge Pope Dorset IPA H
Thatched Dorset gem in centre of a remote village. Darts board 🏠⊛ ◐ ▶ 🏵⇔

Cranborne

11.30–2.30; 6–11

Fleur de Lys
5 Wimborne Street (B3078)
☎ (072 54) 282
Hall & Woodhouse Badger Best Bitter, Tanglefoot H
16th-century coaching inn with restaurant (licensed till 3.30 pm and midnight)
🏠Q☺⊛🎵 ◐ ▶ 🏵⇔ A ⇔

11–2.30; 6–11

Sheaf of Arrows
The Square (off B3078)
☎ (072 54) 456
Wadworth 6X H
Friendly old coaching inn with Victorian frontage; function room
🏠☺⊛🎵 ◐ ▶ 🏵⇔ A ⇔

Dorchester

11.30–2.30; 7–11

Tom Browns
47 High East Street
☎ (0305) 64020
Draught Bass; Goldfinch Tom Browns, Flashmans Clout; H
Simply furnished town pub with tiny brewery upstairs. Pub games 🏠Q🎵⇌

11–2.30; 6–11

White Hart
High East Street
☎ (0305) 63545
Hall & Woodhouse Badger Best Bitter, Tanglefoot H
Friendly local, heavily into pub games. Large lounge bar and small public. Glass-juggling landlord!
🏠Q☺⊛🎵 ◐ 🏵⇌

East Lulworth

11 (11.30 winter)–2.30;
6.30 (7 winter)–11

Weld Arms
on B3070 ☎ (092 941) 211
Cornish JD Dry Hop Bitter, Wessex Stud H
Picturesque 3-bar pub near army ranges on Weld Estate. Deliciously original food. Games include shut-the-box and shove ha'penny
🏠Q☺⊛🎵 ◐ 🏵⇔

110

Dorset

Eype
11–2.30; 6–11
New Inn
off A35 ☎ (0308) 23254
Palmer BB, IPA, Tally Ho H
Very pleasant pub incorporating village post office. A short walk from the beach and the Dorset Coast Path. Pub games

Fiddleford
11–2.30; 6.30–11
Fiddleford Inn
A357 (2 miles S of Sturminster Newton) ☎ (0258) 72489
Bateman XXXB; Wadworth 6X; Wiltshire Old Devil H
Roadside pub in converted brewery. Bar billiards, guest beers

Gussage All Saints
11–2.30; 6–11
Drover's Inn
off B3078 (6 miles N of Wimborne) ☎ (0258) 840084
Butcombe Bitter; Flowers Original; Marston Pedigree; Wadworth 6X H
200 year-old village pub with large brick fireplace. Children's adventure playground in garden

Highcliffe
10.30–2.30; 6–11
Globe Inn
266 Lymington Road (A337)
☎ (04252) 71360
Flowers Original; Whitbread Strong Country Bitter H
Large family pub, a former coaching inn

Kingston
11–2.30; 6.30 (6 summer)–11
Scott Arms
B3069 (1 mile from A351)
☎ (0929) 480270
Cornish Wessex Stud H
Popular pub for day trippers and walkers in picturesque village used in Thomas Hardy film sets. Extensive views over the Purbeck Hills

Langton Matravers
10.30–2.30; 6.30–11
Kings Arms
B3069 ☎ (0929) 422979
Whitbread Strong Country Bitter H
Village local in Purbeck stone and style with many small rooms. Longboard, the unique Purbeck version of shove ha'penny is played

Laymore
11.30–2.30; 6–11
Squirrel Inn
B3162 OS387048
☎ (046 030) 298
Cotleigh Kingfisher; Courage Directors; Wadworth 6X; Wiltshire Old Devil H
Pleasant country free house in remote area. Superb scenery and friendly welcome. Guest beers. Pub games

Litton Cheney
10.30–2.30; 6–11
White Horse
2 miles off A35 ☎ (030 83) 539
Palmer BB, IPA, Tally Ho G
Friendly village local with good value food; wet weather games for children. Occasional garden goat. Next to youth hostel

Lyme Regis
10.30–2.30; 6–11
Angel Inn
Mill Green (down Coombe Street from Square)
☎ (029 74) 3267
Palmer BB, IPA, Tally Ho (summer) G
Locals' pub, tucked away off the tourist beat. Try and find the nearby Lepers Well. Pub games

10.30–2.30; 6–11
Royal Standard
Marine Parade ☎ (029 74) 2637
Palmer BB, IPA, Tally Ho H
Very old pub on beach. Quirky interior design. Pub games

Try also: **Pilot Boat** (Palmer); **Ship; Three Cups Hotel**

Marshwood
11–2.30; 5.30–11
Bottle Inn
Marshwood (B3165)
☎ (029 77) 254
Usher Best Bitter; Wadworth 6X H
Interesting and popular 500 year-old local. Packed with diners in summer. Pub games

Milton Abbas
11–2.30; 6.30–11
Hambro Arms
3 miles N of A354
☎ (0258) 880233
Cornish JD Dry Hop Bitter, Original, Wessex Stud H
Thatched and whitewashed pub in unspoilt model village, built circa 1773. Separate restaurant. Nearby is a brewery farm museum

Nettlecombe
10.30–2.30; 6–11
Marquis of Lorne
off A3066 OS517956
☎ (030 885) 236
Palmer BB, IPA H
Lovely old pub in picturesque setting. Good food, also catering for vegetarians. Close to Powerstock Common and good walking country. Pub games

North Wootton
11–2.30; 6.30–11
Three Elms
A3030 3 miles S E of Sherborne
☎ (0935) 812881
Boddingtons Bitter; Wadworths 6X H
Lively roadside pub. Food taken seriously in comfortable lounge-type bar. Guest beers

Osmington Mills
10.30–2.30; 6–11
Smugglers Inn
off A353 ☎ (0305) 833125
Courage Best Bitter, Directors; Ringwood 4X H
Popular family pub near the sea. Decorated with old beams from Mudeford Quay. Good food. Darts

Poole
11.30–2.30; 6.30–11
Britannia
Britannia Road, Lower Parkstone (off A35)
☎ (0202) 740046
Flowers Original; Whitbread Strong Country Bitter H
2 bar local with music/function room. Games (Parkstone)

10.30–2.30; 6–11
Dorset Knob
162 Alder Road, Parkstone
☎ (0202) 748427
Gales BBB; Hall & Woodhouse Badger Best Bitter, Tanglefoot H
Regulars' pub with various sporting activities. Site of rumoured ghost of girl murdered last century researched by former licensee

11–2.30; 6–11
Inn in the Park
26 Pinewood Road, Branksome Park (60 yds from Branksome Chine car park)
☎ (0202) 761318
Ringwood Best Bitter; Wadworth IPA, 6X H
Plush bar in small hotel – handy for beach

10.30–2.30; 6–11
Lord Nelson
Poole Quay ☎ (0202) 673774

111

Dorset

Gales BBB; Hall & Woodhouse Badger Best Bitter, Tanglefoot ⑪
Lively musical pub with marvellous collection of naval and maritime artefacts from 1800 onwards. Looks towards Brownsea Island and has good view of harbour
🚃🛏️🍴 (Quay) ♿

Portesham

11–2.30; 6–11

Half Moon
Front Street (off B3157)
☎ (0305) 871227
Cornish Original ⑤
Old low-beamed pub in picturesque village. One of few remaining bar billiards tables in area. No food Tue
🚃Q🍴🍺

Portland

10.30–2.30; 6–11

Clifton
50 Grove Road (off A354)
☎ (0305) 820473
Cornish JD Dry Hop Bitter, Wessex Stud ⑪
Busy local off the tourist trail. Popular lunch trade. Skittle alley 🚃🛏️🍴🍺♿

11–2.30; 6–11

Royal Exchange
Weston Road, Weston
☎ (0305) 820291
Cornish JD Dry Hop Bitter, Wessex Stud ⑪
Locals' local. Good value, unpretentious lunches. Skittle alley 🚃🛏️🍴♿

Pulham

10.30–2.30; 6.30–11

Halsey Arms
B3143 ☎ (025 86) 344
Fuller London Pride ⑪
One-bar village free house with dining and family areas. Good children's playground. Pub games. Guest beers
🚃🛏️🍴🍺♿

Rampisham

11–2.30; 7–11

Tiger's Head
1 mile off A356 OS561023
☎ (093 583) 244
Draught Bass; Butcombe Bitter; Wadworth 6X ⑤
Deservedly popular and friendly pub in heart of Dorset. Restaurant serving original food. Skittle alley; comfortable children's room
🚃Q🛏️🍴🍺Å♿

Shaftesbury

11–2.30; 6–11

Old Two Brewers
St James Street ☎ (0747) 2210
Courage Best Bitter, Directors; Wadworth 6X; Young Special ⑪

Fine local with stained glass windows. Nestling beneath the Saxon Hill Town at the bottom of Gold Hill. Guest beers 🛏️🍴🍺♿

Try also: Fountain (Free)

Sherborne

10.30–2.30; 6–11

Britannia
Westbury ☎ (0935) 813300
Boddingtons Bitter; Marston Pedigree; Tetley Bitter ⑪
Friendly 2-bar town local near the Abbey. Once a school for wayward girls! Pub games
🍴🍺

10–2.30; 6–11

Digby Tap
Cooks Lane ☎ (0935) 813148
Hardington Somerset Best Bitter; Smiles Best Bitter ⑪
Splendid side-street tavern close to Abbey. Stone and tile floor. Bikers welcome. Guest beers 🍴 (not Sun) 🍺🚉♿

Shroton

10.30–2.30; 6–11

Cricketers
off A350 (4 miles N of Blandford) ☎ (0258) 860421
Theakston Best Bitter; Hall & Woodhouse Badger Best Bitter; Wadworth 6X ⑪
Friendly L-shaped bar with cricketing memorabilia. Guest beers; pool and darts 🚃🍴🍺

Sixpenny Handley

10.30–2.30; 6–11

Star Inn
14 High Street (B3081)
☎ (0725) 52272
Draught Bass; Marston Pedigree; Wadworth 6X ⑪
Village local with restaurant area, pool and darts
🚃🍴🍺Å

South Perrott

11.30–2.30; 7–11

Coach & Horses
on A356 ☎ (093 589) 270
Draught Bass; Eldridge Pope Dorset Original IPA; Golden Hill Exmoor Ale ⑪
Flagstoned village local with separate games room
🚃Q🛏️🍴 (not Mon) ♿

Spetisbury

11–2.30; 6–11

Drax Arms
High Street (A350)
☎ (0258) 52658
Hall & Woodhouse Badger Best Bitter, Tanglefoot ⑪
Luxurious Victorian pub with cast iron coal-effect fireplace. Rebuilt in 1926. Darts and cribbage Q (lounge) 🛏️🍴

Swanage

10.30–2.30 (3 summer); 6–11

Red Lion
63 High Street ☎ (0929) 423533
Flowers Original; Whitbread Strong Country Bitter ⑤
Popular local, built in Purbeck stone. Handpumps are decorative only. Pub games
🚃🛏️🍴 (Fri & Sat) 🍺♿
Å (nearby) ♿

11–2.30 (10–3 summer); 6–11 (12 disco nights)

White Horse
High Street (near pier)
☎ (0929) 422469
Whitbread Strong Country Bitter, Pompey Royal ⑪
Comfortable friendly atmosphere in large bar with restaurant area. Occasional live music. Pub games
🛏️🍴♿Å

Wareham

11–2.30 (3.30 Thu); 6–11

Antelope
13 West Street ☎ (092 95) 2827
Whitbread Strong Country Bitter ⑪
A genuine town centre local at the gateway to the Purbecks. Friday folk club. Shove ha'penny, dominoes and cribbage 🛏️🍴🍴🍺♿Å🚉

West Bay

11–2.30; 6–11

Bridport Arms Hotel
☎ (0308) 23191
Palmer BB, IPA, Tally Ho ⑪
Fine seaside hotel right on the harbour, close to beach. Good food Q 🛏️🍴🍺Å

Try also: West Bay Hotel; George Hotel

West Stour

11–2.30; 6.30 (6 Sat)–11

Ship Inn
on A30 ☎ (074785) 640
Draught Bass; Marston Pedigree; Wadworth 6X ⑪
Stone-built roadside inn. A traditional bar at one end leads through lounge and family area to a dining room. Pub games 🚃🛏️🍴♿

Weymouth

10–2.30; 6–11

Globe Hotel
24 East Street (off the Quay)
☎ (0305) 785649
Gibbs Mew Wiltshire Bitter ⑪
Street corner local, with pub games 🍴🚉♿

10.30–2.30; 6–11

Sailors Return
1 Nicholas Street (on the Quay) ☎ (0305) 773377

112

Dorset

Cornish JD Dry Hop Bitter, Wessex Stud H
Small pub with wall paintings of Weymouth history. Separate restaurant. Darts
Q ✿ ⊛ ( )

10.30–2.30; 6–11

Ship Inn
Custom House Quay
☎ (0305) 773879
Gales BBB, Hall & Woodhouse Badger Best Bitter, Tanglefoot H
Large quayside steak house with first floor lounge and restaurant overlooking the harbour. Very popular with young people ✿ ( ) ⧉ ⊛

Try also: Portland Railway (Hall & Woodhouse); Waterloo (Gibbs Mew); Weatherbury (Free)

Wimborne

11–2.30; 7–11

Vine
Vine Hill, Pamphill (off B3082 for 800 yds, turn right)
☎ (0202) 882259
Whitbread Strong Country Bitter H
Small friendly country pub with large garden. Darts
✿ ⊛ ( ) ⊟ Å ♢

Winfrith

10–3; 6–11

Red Lion Inn
on A352 ☎ (0305) 852814
Hall & Woodhouse Badger Best Bitter, Tanglefoot H
Large roadside house with 2 contrasting bars. Fine view of nuclear power station! Pub games ⚏ ✿ ⊛ ⋈ ( ) ⊟ ⧉ Å

Winkton

10.30–2.30; 6–11

Fisherman's Haunt
Salisbury Road (B3347)
☎ (0202) 484071
Draught Bass; Ringwood Best Bitter, 4X H
Popular 17th-century country house overlooking River Avon. Good food. Separate restaurant ⚏ ✿ ⊛ ⋈ ( ) ⧉

11–2.30; 6–11

Lamb Inn
Burley Road (off B3347)
☎ (0425) 72427
Gales HSB; Marston Pedigree; Ringwood 4X; Wadworth 6X H
Comfortable and friendly free house in green field setting. Recently extended yet again to provide another bar. Pub games ✿ ⊛ ( ) ⊟ ⧉

Winterborne Whitechurch

10.30–2.30; 6–11

Milton Arms
on A354 ☎ (0258) 880306
Cornish JD Dry Hop Bitter, Wessex Stud H
Warm and comfortable for intellectuals!
⚏ ✿ ⊛ ⋈ ( ) ⊟ ⧉ Å

Worth Matravers

10.30–2.30; 6–11

Square & Compass
off B3069 ☎ (092 943) 229
Whitbread Strong Country Bitter, Pompey Royal G
This stone-built pub is a Purbeck monument, offering views of the sea and a medieval field system. Pub games ⚏ Q ✿ ⊛ ⊟ ⧉ Å (book) ♢

Yetminster

11–2.30; 7–11

White Hart
High Street ☎ (0935) 872338
Draught Bass; Oakhill Farmers Ale H
Smart village free house, popular for food. Pub games
⚏ ⊛ ( ) ⊟ ⧉ ≷

ON PUB DESCRIPTIONS . . .
an alternative guide

Ancient there's an old beam next to the video
Backstreet Local the CAMRA branch drinks here
Basic deemed unsuitable for cleaning
Comfortable probably wrecked
Cosy packed
Estate Pub aircraft hanger with carpets
Family Pub swarming with hyperactive little darlings
Friendly the bar staff can speak
Half-Timbered brewery chairman's local
Heavily Beamed the plywood over the steel girders has been painted mahogany
Lovely Setting awful pub in pretty countryside
Modernised wrecked
Old Fashioned broken
Popular pick-up joint
Quiet frequently raided
Refurbished wrecked
Roadhouse full of bikers
Suburban between the betting shop and the dog track
Tastefully Appointed wrecked
Traditional Public Bar plastic shoe covers recommended
Traditional Village Pub tourists can b . . . . r off
Unspoilt about to be sold to Bass
Welcoming landlord occasionally found on the premises
Wrecked Good Beer Guide inspectors at the end of the annual survey

Durham

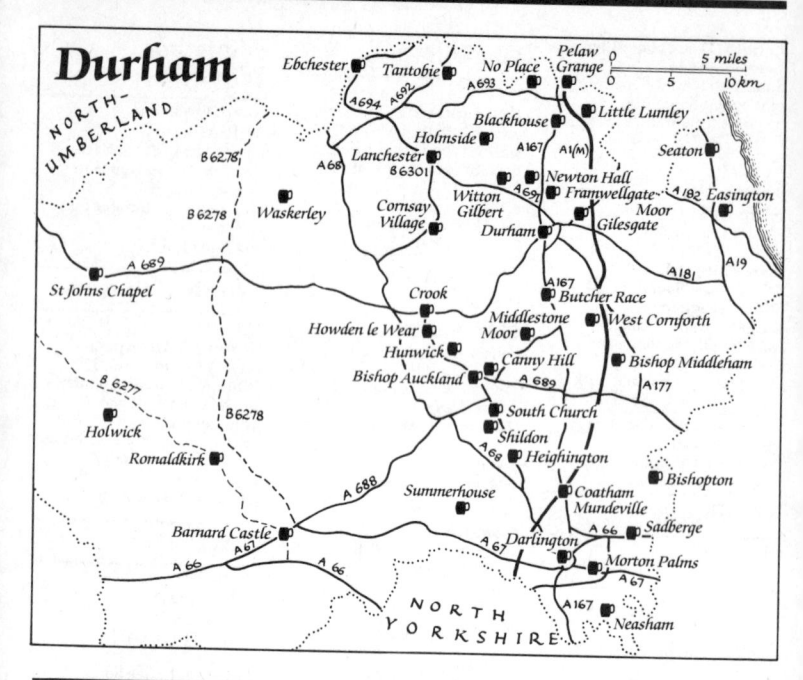

Barnard Castle

12–2; 7–12 (11 Sat, supper licence 12)

Old Well
21 The Bank (nr. Buttermarket)
☎ (0833) 690130
John Smith Bitter; Theakston Best Bitter H
Comfortable family-run hotel with beer garden which backs on to castle walls. Darts
Q🐶⌇()🚊&

11–3; 6.30–10.30 (11 Sat); 11–10.30 Wed, market day

Three Horseshoes
7 Galgate
Draught Bass E
Friendly local situated in town centre. Darts and pool
⌇()▷&

Try also: Cricketers Arms; Kings Head

Bishop Auckland

11–3; 6–10.30 (11 Sat)

Newton Cap
Newton Cap Bank
☎ (0388) 605445
Cameron Strongarm H
Unspoilt local in old part of town; pool room and good old fashioned bar. Dominoes and darts ⌇&🚊

11–3; 6–10.30 (11 Sat)

Sportsman Inn
Market Place ☎ (0388) 607376
Theakston Bitter; Whitbread Castle Eden Ale H
Quiet lunchtimes; busy evenings. In spacious open-plan town pub popular with young. Games ⌇()&🚊⌇

Bishop Middleham

11–3; 6–10.30

Red Lion
3 Bank Top (1 mile from A177)
☎ (0740) 51298
Whitbread Castle Eden Ale H
Traditional country pub overlooking the village green, catering for all tastes
⌇Q⌇⌇()&

Bishopton

11–3; 6–11

Talbot
The Green ☎ (0740) 30371
Cameron Traditional Bitter, Strongarm; Everards Old Original H
Pleasant, popular old local in leafy village. Long lounge, small snug with dartboard. Home base for a Morris side and Talbot FC. Good range of games ⌇⌇⌇()&

Try also: Kings Arms, Gt. Stainton (Whitbread)

Blackhouse

11–3; 6–10.30

Charlaw Inn
Wheatley Green, Edmondsley (B6532) ☎ (0207) 232085
McEwan 80/–; Younger No.3 H
Recently extended country pub with lively bar, lounge and restaurant. Pub games
⌇⌇()⌇

Butcher Race

11–3; 6–10.30

Coach & Horses
1½ miles N of Thinford on A167) ☎ (0388) 814484
Vaux Bitter, Samson H
Single bar/lounge drinking area with separate restaurant. Shove ha'penny and dominoes ⌇⌇⌇()&

Canney Hill

11–3; 6–10.30

Sportsman
Durham Road ☎ (0388) 605160
Cameron Traditional Bitter, Strongarm; Everards Old Original H
A stalwart of the Good Beer Guide, and rightly so. Emphasis on horse racing in the bar but lounge is cosy with an open fire ⌇⌇⌇()&&

Coatham Mundeville

11.30–3; 6–11

Foresters Arms
Brafferton Lane (near A167/A1[M]) ☎ (0325) 320565
John Smith Bitter H
Unspoilt, solidly-traditional old local in a pleasant setting. Choice of 2 comfortable rooms, full of memorabilia
⌇() (not Sun) ⌇

Try also: Stables Bar, Hallgarth

Durham

Cornsay Village

12–2 (Sun only); 7–10.30

Black Horse Inn
2 miles off B6301
☎ (091) 373 4211
Draught Bass H
Lively village pub. Quiz nights (Tue) and good range of games. Home-cooked food Q ☎ ⊛ ((Sun) ▶ ♣ ♠

Crook

7.30–10.30

Dun Cow (Cows Tail)
Old White Lea, Billy Row (1 mile W of B6298)
Theakston Best Bitter H
Last of the old fashioned drinking houses ▲ Q ⊕ ♣

Darlington

11–3 (4 Mon); 5.30–11

Black Swan
Parkgate (A67)
☎ (0325) 466104
Younger No.3 H
Spartan but characterful, with a choice of public bar, pool room, 'commercial room' and mirrored drinking corridor. Fine embossed windows and external tilework. Pool ⊕ ≠

11–3; 5.30–10.30

Britannia
Archer Street (near A68/ring road jct) ☎ (0325) 463787
Cameron Strongarm H
Warm, relaxed, uncomplicated old local just off town centre. A bastion of cask beer throughout its 125 years. Still recognisable as the private house it originally was. The (teetotal) Victorian publisher JM Dent born here Q ⊕ ≠

11–3; 5.30–11

Central Borough
Hopetown Lane (off A167)
☎ (0325) 468490
Cameron Strongarm H
Classic small, street-corner boozer in a mixed housing/industrial area. Very much a locals' pub, with a loyal following. Near the impressive little Railway Museum ⊕ ≠ (North Rd)

11–3; 5.30–11

Cleveland Arms
Cleveland Street, Albert Hill (off A167) ☎ (0325) 463752
Big Lamp Bitter, Prince Bishop Ale H
Simple, small Victorian local surrounded by industry. Retains some fine features – stained glass, floor mosaics, sturdy wooden counter. Pool, TV, juke-box; live acts at weekends. Guest beers ((Mon–Fri) ⊕ ♣

11–3; 6–10.30 (11 F, S)

Falchion

Blackwellgate ☎ (0325) 462541
Cameron Strongarm H
Cosy, friendly little pub in central shopping street. Named after a legendary 'worm'-killing sword. A dominoes stronghold! Q ⊕ ♣

11–3 (4 Mon); 6–11

Pennyweight
Bakehouse Hill, (Market Place)
☎ (0325) 464244
Vaux Lorimer Best Scotch, Bitter; Ward Sheffield Best Bitter H
Smart, busy pub with good value lunches. Can get crowded at weekends. Regular live music. Guest beers (♣

11.30–3; 7–11

Tap & Spile
99 Bondgate ☎ (0325) 463955
Camron Strongarm, Ebor Special H & G
Re-creation of a Victorian ale house, with up to 8 constantly changing real beers. Not cheap but successful. Has its own regular beer festivals ☎ (lunch) (♣

11–3; 5.30–11

Walkers
Parkgate (A67/ring road jct)
☎ (0325) 286117
Theakston Best Bitter, XB, Old Peculier H
Remarkably narrow 1-roomed pub – smart, comfortable and modern. Good value fare; the music (live and juke box) can get noisy. Near theatre ☎ (▶ ♣ ≠

Try also: Turks Head, Bondgate (Camerons)

Durham City

11–3; 6–10.30 (11 F, S & summer)

Colpitts Hotel
Hawthorne Terrace (A690)
☎ (091) 386 9913
Samuel Smith OBB H
2-room old local popular with students and "radicals". Recent panic caused by sighting of paint tin in bar. Folk singing Thu eve; music Mon ▲ Q ⊕ ≠

11–3; 6–10.30 (11 F, S & summer)

Dun Cow
37 Old Elvet ☎ (091) 386 9219
Whitbread Castle Eden Ale H
Cosy, small bar popular with all ages. Busy lounge at weekends. Famous pies and peas ∩ (▶ ⊕ ♣ ≠

11–3; 6–10.30 (11 F, S & summer)

Garden House
North Road (near County Hall just off A691) ☎ (091) 384 3460
Vaux Bitter, Samson; Ward Sheffield Best Bitter H
Tastefully modernised, with conservatory ☎ ⊛ (▶ ♣ ≠

11–3; 6–10.30 (11 F, S & summer)

Half Moon

86 New Elvet
Draught Bass H
Popular city-centre local; name derives from crescent-shaped bar in split-level area ≠

11–3; 6–10.30 (11 F, S & summer)

Old Elm Tree
12 Crossgate ☎ (091) 386 4621
Vaux Samson; Ward Sheffield Best Bitter H
Old pub, popular with all ages; busy bar and quiet lounge ▲ ⋈ (⊕ ≠

11–3; 6–10.30 (11 F, S & summer)

Shakespeare
Saddler Street ☎ (091) 386 9709
McEwan 80/-; Younger No.3 H
Old city pub with tiny snug and 2 small rooms, well worth a visit. Near the cathedral Q ⊕ ≠

11–3; 6–10.30 (11 F, S & summer)

Victoria
86 Hallgarth Street (near Dunelm House on A177)
☎ (091) 386 5269
McEwan 80/-; Younger No.3 H
Listed building; old 3-room pub with collection of Toby jugs in bar Q ⋈ ⊛ ♣ ≠

Try also: Fighting Cocks (Bass); Three Tuns Tudor Bar (Vaux)

Easington

11–3; 6–10.30

Village Inn
Sunderland Road
Theakston Best Bitter H
Only real ale outlet in village of 5 pubs. Friendly landlord ▲ ☎ ⊛ (♣

Ebchester

11–3; 6–10.30

Chelmsford
Front Street (A694)
☎ (0207) 560213
Vaux Samson H
Friendly village local. Pleasant countryside walks nearby ▲ Q ☎ ⊛ (▶ ⊕

Framwellgate Moor

11–3; 6–10.30 (11 F, S & summer)

Marquis of Granby
Front Street (off A167)
☎ (091) 386 9382
Samuel Smith OBB H
14 years in Good Beer Guide. Very popular; 3 rooms with pool and traditional decor ▲ ☎ (lunch) ⊛ (

11–3; 6.30–10.30 (11 F, S & summer)

Tap & Spile
Front Street (off A167)
☎ (091) 386 5451
Cameron Traditional Bitter, Robert Newton Ale,

115

Durham

Strongarm; Everards Old Original H
Third house in the North East's Tap & Spile chain. Wood and brick all round, 1 main bar and 2 back rooms. 4 guest beers ᵹ (lunch) ( ) &

Try also: **Lambton Hounds** (Vaux); **Victoria Bridge** (Cameron)

Gilesgate

11–3; 6–10.30 (11 F, S & summer)

Queens Head Hotel
Sherburn Road Ends (A181)
☎ (091) 386 5649
Cameron Traditional Bitter, Strongarm H
Popular bar and neat lounge with side room featuring live music Thu and Sun. Traditional decor ⌘ ʘ ( ) ⊡ & ⇌

Try also: **Three Horseshoes** (Whitbread)

Heighington

11–3; 5.30–10.30

Locomotion No. 1
Heighington Station (approx. 1 mile W of A167 at Aycliffe)
☎ (0325) 320132
Cameron Strongarm; Everards Old Original; Taylor Landlord; Theakston Best Bitter; Thwaites Bitter H
Historic 1820s railway station converted to inn–restaurant next to branch line
⌘ ᵹ (lunch) ʘ ( ) ⇌

Try also: **Bay Horse**

Holmside

11–3; 6–10.30

Wardles Bridge
Off B6532 ☎ (091) 371 0926
McEwan 70/-, 80/-; Younger No.3 H
Popular 2-room pub, off the beaten track, but well worth the effort. Good, basic bar food and a friendly welcome. Large selection of malt whiskies! Games ⌘ Q ᵹ ( ) ⊡

Holwick

12–3 (not Tue); 7–10.30 (11 Sat)

Strathmore Arms
3½ miles from Middleton in Teesdale, S side of valley
☎ (0833) 40362
John Smith Bitter; Theakston Best Bitter H
Attractive, unspoilt rural pub in heart of upper Teesdale, handy for Pennine Way. Darts and pool ⌘ Q ᵹ ʘ ㉟ ( ) ⊡ ▲

Try also: **Rose & Crown**, Mickleton

Howden Le Wear

11–3; 6–10.30

Australian
Church Street (off A689)
☎ (0388) 762666
Cameron Traditional Bitter, Strongarm H
Good value local; lively bar with games area ⌘ ⊡

Hunwick

11–30; 6–10.30

Wheatsheaf
Lane Ends
Cameron Traditional Bitter, Strongarm H
Good little village local; pool room with jukebox, cosy wood-panelled bar. Games ⊡

Lanchester

11–3; 6–10.30

Blue Bell
Front Street (off A691)
☎ (0207) 520433
Vaux Samson H
Lively drinkers' bar with quiet lounge. Pub games ( ) ⊡

Little Lumley

11–3 (12 Sat); 7–10.30

Smiths Arms
Just off B1284
Stones Best Bitter H
Secluded country local, well furnished in traditional style. Pub games ⌘ ⌘ ⊡ &

Middlestone Moor

11–3; 6–10.30

Masons Arms
Durham Road ☎ (0388) 816169
Cameron Traditional Bitter, Strongarm H
A dour exterior belies a constantly improving interior. Pub games ⌘ ᵹ ⌘ ( ) ⊡ &

Morton Palms

11–3; 5.30–11

Old Farmhouse Inn
Yarm Road (A67)
☎ (0325) 333372
Draught Bass H
New pub in old building, with considerable extensions. Open-plan but with a distinct 'bar' end. Jukebox and TV compete. Emphasis on meals; separate restaurant ᵹ ⌘ ( ) &

Neasham

11–3; 5.30–11

Fox & Hounds
24 Teesway ☎ (0325) 720350
Vaux Samson; Ward Sheffield Best Bitter H
Good village pub near scenic part of river. Busy, friendly bar; enlarged lounge with music and meals. Children's play equipment inside and out. Pub games ᵹ ⌘ ( ) ⊡ &

Newton Hall

11–3; 6–10.30 (11 F, S May–Sept)

Jovial Monk
Canterbury Road
Tetley Bitter H
Busy estate pub. Pub games. Guest beers
⌘ ( ) ⊡ & ▲ (Finchale Abbey)

No Place

11–3; 6–10.30

Beamish Mary
Co-operative Villas
Theakston Best Bitter, XB H
Village pub near Beamish Museum. Small pleasant bar and friendly lounge with dining room tucked round corner. Bar billiards – a rarity in N.E. ⌘ ᵹ ( ) ⊡

Pelaw Grange

11–3; 6–10.30

Wheatsheaf
On A167, Chester-Le-Street–Birtley road
Stones Best Bitter H
New conservatory added to the lounge makes an ideal place for meals and families but the bar remains the hub of local activity. Games
ᵹ ⌘ ( ) ⊡ ▲

Romaldkirk

11–3; 6–10.30 (11 Sat)

Rose & Crown
☎ (0833) 50603
Theakston Best Bitter, Old Peculier H
Popular old-style country hotel near the "Cathedral of the Dales" – St Romalds church ⌘ Q ᵹ ⌘ ( ) ⊡ &
(plus accommodation)

Try also: **Kirk Inn**

Sadberge

11–3; 5.30–11

Buck
Middleton Road
☎ (0325) 332416
Cameron Traditional Bitter H, **Strongarm** E
Thriving village local with its own football team and Leek Club! Named after an 18th-century philanthropist, George Buck, not a deer! 2 comfortable rooms, with good service ᵹ ⌘ ((not Sun) ⊡ &

St Johns Chapel

11–3; 7–10.30 (2am Thu, 11 Sat)

Golden Lion
Alston Road (A689)
☎ (0388) 537231
Whitbread Castle Eden Ale H
Large open-plan pub, near spectacular scenery
⌘ ᵹ ⌘ ( )

Try also: **Bluebell Inn** (Tetley)

Seaton

11–3; 6–10.30

Dun Cow

116

Durham

☎ (091) 813075
Whitbread Castle Eden Ale H
Friendly local, tastefully modernised ▲Q☎❀⊕&

11–3; 6–10.30

Seaton Lane Inn
☎ (091) 581 2038
Marston Pedigree; Theakston Best Bitter, Old Peculier
Long-established real ale pub, basic but friendly ▲Q☎❀⊕&

Shildon

11–3; 6–10.30

King William
1 Cheapside (top of Eldon Bank) ☎ (0388) 772405
Cameron Strongarm H
Large, lively bar and spacious lounge in busy town local ⊕&

11–3; 6–10.30

Timothy Hackworth
107 Main Street (A6072/B6283)
☎ (0388) 772525
Cameron Traditional Bitter, Strongarm H
Small, popular 1-roomed town pub opposite first passenger railway station ⌒≠

Try also: Commercial (Cameron)

South Church

11–3; 6–10.30 (11 Sat)

Red Alligator
Crown Street ☎ (0388) 605644
Vaux Bitter H

Comfortable lounge style pub named after Grand National winner Q❀⌒▶&

Summerhouse

11.30–3; 6.30–11

Raby Hunt
On B6279 ☎ (032 574) 604
Cameron Strongarm; Theakston Best Bitter H
Neat, welcoming old stone free house in a whitewashed hamlet. Comfortably furnished lounge, bustling locals' bar. Excellent home-cooked lunches
▲❀⌒(not Sun) ⊕&

Tantobie

11–3; 7–10.30

Bird Inn
B6311, off A692
☎ (0207) 232416
Bolhaven 80/-; Marston Pedigree, Merrie Monk, Owd Rodger H
Popular village pub with lively bar and comfortable lounge. Regular guest beers make it a welcome oasis
❀⌒▶⊕&

Try also: Commercial (Whitbread)

Waskerley

11–3; 6–10.30

Moorcock
Off A68, 3 miles W of

Castleside OS050487
Marston Pedigree, Merrie Monk H
Welcoming pub in isolated moorland, good quality live music Sat. Fine fire. Well worth the trip
▲Q☎❀⌒▶⊕&▲

West Cornforth

11–3; 7–10.30

Square & Compass
7 The Green (off B6291)
☎ (0740) 54606
Bass Light 5 Star, Draught Bass; Stones Best Bitter H
Hospitable little pub with pictorial history on walls.
Restaurant Q☎❀⌒▶&

Witton Gilbert

11–3; 6–10.30 (11 F, S & summer)

Glendenning Arms
Front Street (A691)
☎ (091) 3710316
Vaux Samson H
Popular pub with horsey decor ▲Q☎❀⊕&

11–3; 6–10.30

Travellers Rest
Front Street (A691)
☎ (091) 3710458
McEwan 70/-, 80/-; Theakston Best Bitter, Old Peculier; Younger No.3 H
Popular village pub with restaurant and non-smoking area ▲Q☎❀⌒▶&

From the campaigning year . . . marching to save Oldham Brewery (May 1988). But they closed it anyway. (Oldham Evening Chronicle)

Essex

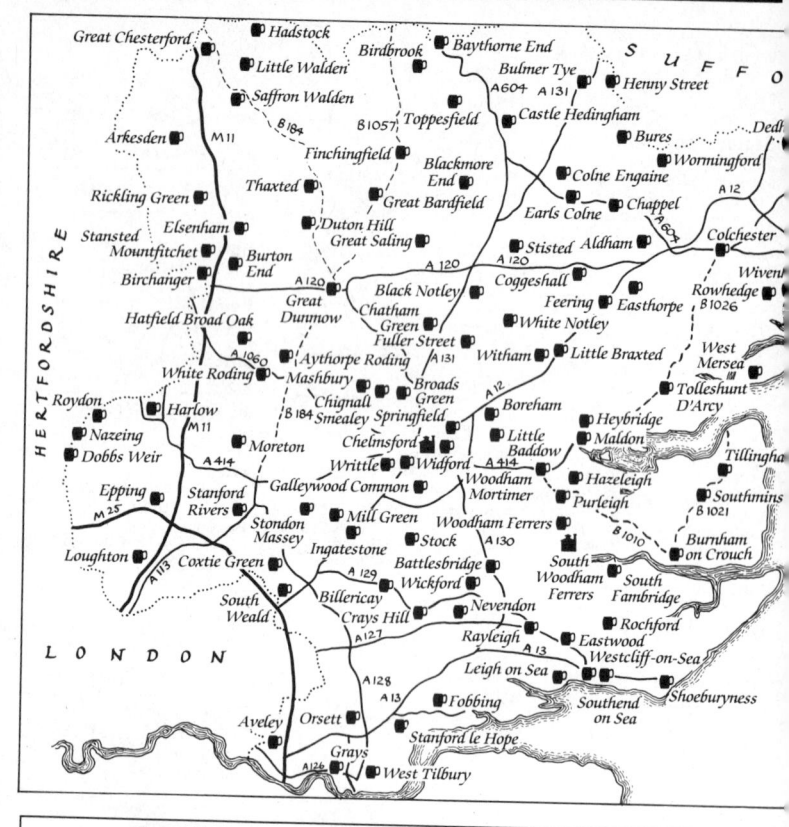

🏭 **Crouch Vale**, South Woodham Ferrers; **Ridley**, Chelmsford

Aldham

11–2.30; 6–11

Queens Head
Ford Street (A604)
☎ (0206) 241291
Adnams Bitter; Greene King XX, IPA, Abbot; Nethergate Bitter H
Timber-framed pub with vast collection of water jugs.
Restaurant Q ☆ ⊛ ( ) 🅱 ᴅ ♿

Arkesden

10.30–2.30; 6–11

Axe & Compasses
2 miles N of B1038 OS483344
☎ (079 985) 272
Greene King Rayment BBA, Abbot H
17th-century traditional local in picturesque village, well worth finding
⌂ Q ⊛ ( ) (Tue–Sat) ♣

Aveley

10.30–2.30; 6–10.30 (11 F, S)

Sir Henry Gurnett
Kennington Farm, Romford Road (near B1335)
☎ (0708) 867009
Courage Directors; Flowers Original; Tolly Cobbold Original H
Historic listed building. Very good steakhouse above main bar. Children's playground in grounds. Aveley Lakes nearby
⌂ ☆ ⊛ ( ) 🖐 (Mon–Sat)

Try also: **Ship**, W Thurrock (Charrington)

Aythorpe Roding

10.30–2.30; 6–11

Axe & Compasses
on B184 ☎ (027 926) 647
Adnams Bitter; Greene King IPA, Abbot H
Old steep-roofed, low-roomed pub with pool and darts
⌂ Q ⊛ ⊞ ~ (B&B) ( )

Battlesbridge

10–2.30; 6–11

Barge
Hawk Hill ☎ (03744) 732622
Taylor Walker Best Bitter; Ind Coope Burton Ale H
Old attractive weather-boarded inn, comfortably furnished. Children's room, dominoes and darts
⌂ ☆ ⊛ (not Sun) ♿ ≠ ↺

Baythorne End

10.30–2.30; 6–11

Swan Inn
A604/A1092 ☎ (0787) 60649
Greene King IPA, Abbot H
Old roadside inn with a welcome for weary travellers
⊛ ( )

Billericay

10–2.30; 6–10.30 (11 F, S)

Coach & Horses
36 Chapel Street (off High Street) ☎ (0277) 622873
Greene King IPA, Abbot H
Friendly 1-bar pub, mainly local trade. Pub games
⊛ ( ) (on request)

10.30–2.30; 6–10.30 (11 F, S)

Railway
1 High Street ☎ (0277) 652173
Greene King IPA, Abbot H
Proper drinkers' pub catering

118

Essex

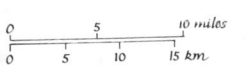

Essex

for all ages. Games room with snooker table 🏨🍺⚏

Birchanger

10.30–2.30; 6–11
Three Willows
off A120/M11 Jct 8
☎ (0279) 815913
Greene King Rayment BBA, Abbot H
Friendly pub in small village; good food (not Sun) 🍺 🍴 🍽️⚓

Birdbrook

11–2.30; 6–11
Plough
1 mile off A604
☎ (044 085) 336
Adnams Bitter; Greene King IPA; Mauldon Special G
Excellent traditional village pub with all the charm of rural Essex 🏨Q🐕🍺 🍴 🍽️⚓

Blackmore End

10.30–3; 7–11
Red Cow
4 miles E of B1053
☎ (0371) 85337
Ridley Bitter H
Comfortable, split-level village pub with games area 🏨🍺 🍴⚓

Black Notley

11–3; 6–11
Green Dragon
Upper London Road (A131)
☎ (0245) 361030
Greene King IPA, Abbot H
Unspoilt public bar.
Restaurant in converted barn.
Smart lounge Q🍺 🍴 🍽️⚓&

Boreham

10–2.30; 6–11
Queens Head
Church Road ☎ (0245) 467298
Greene King IPA, Abbot H
Excellent, friendly and traditional 17th century village pub Q🍺 🍴 🍽️⚓&

Bradfield

11–2.30; 6–11
Village Maid
The Street
Adnams Bitter, Extra H
Timbered village local. Guest beers; pub games
🏨Q🐕🍺 🍴 & ⚓ ≠

Broads Green

11–2.30; 6.30 (6 summer)–11
Walnut Tree
off A130 ☎ (0245) 360222
Ridley Bitter G & H
Traditional Victorian pub overlooking green.
Comfortable lounge and simple public bar with small snug between 🏨🍺 🍴⚓

Bulmer Tye

10.30–2.30; 6–11
Fox
on A131 ☎ (0787) 77505
Greene King IPA, Abbot H
Excellent friendly roadside inn. Passers-by made very welcome 🏨🍺 🍴 🍽️ & ⚓

Bures

11–2.30; 6–11
Swan
1 Station Hill ☎ (0787) 228121
Greene King XX, IPA, Abbot H
Traditional country public bar with dartboard and brick tile floor. Restaurant area in lounge 🏨Q🐕🍺 🍴 🍽️⚓&

Burnham-on-Crouch

10.30–2.30; 6–11
New Welcome Sailor
74 Station Road
☎ (0621) 784778
Greene King IPA, Abbot H
Friendly locals' pub, strong on games; also folk club, pigeon racing and ladies' dancing clubs 🍺 ≠

10.30–3; 6–11
White Harte
The Quay (near Town Hall)
☎ (0621) 782106
Adnams Bitter; Tolly Cobbold Bitter H
Charming, cosy, old red-brick inn. Private jetty and superb views of river. Restaurant.
Dominoes Q🐕 (well-behaved) 🍺🍴 🍽️

Burton End

10.30–2.30; 6–11
Ash
☎ (0279) 814841
Greene King Rayment BBA, Abbot H
Ancient thatched pub on airport perimeter; planes no problem. Children's play-garden, good food (not Sun)
🍺 🍴 🍽️⚓

Castle Hedingham

11–2.30; 6.30–11
Bell
St James Street (B1058)
☎ (0787) 60350
Greene King IPA, Abbot G
Old timbered pub in timeless village, near Norman Castle and Colne Valley Railway.
Good bar meals 🏨🐕🍺 🍴 ⚓

Chappel

11–2.30; 6–11
Swan Inn
100 yds off A604 under viaduct
☎ (078 75) 2353
Greene King IPA, Abbot; Mauldon Bitter H
Friendly riverside pub with 3 bars and restaurant. By viaduct and railway museum
🏨🐕🍺 🍴 🍽️⚓& ≠

Chatham Green

10–2.30; 6–11 (may close early)
Windmill
☎ (0245) 361357
Ridley Bitter H
Small, 1-bar country pub with base of old windmill in garden. Darts 🏨Q🍺

Chelmsford

10–2.30; 6–11
Flyer
Copperfield Road, North Melbourne ☎ (0245) 441242
Tolly Cobbold Bitter, Original, XXXX H
Comfortable, modern local on edge of town estate. The only Tolly tied house in Chelmsford
Q🍺 🍴 (until 9.45) 🍽️&

11–2.30; 6–11
Partners
30 Lower Anchor Street
☎ (0245) 265181
Adnams Bitter; Greene King IPA, Abbot; Marston

Essex

Pedigree; Ridley Bitter
Friendly street corner local with games/family room. New smoke extractor. Guest beer; darts

10.30–2.30; 6–11
Red Lion
147 New London Road
☎ (0245) 354902
Adnams Extra; Ridley Bitter
Basic public with pool table and unusual clear windows. Comfortable saloon

10–2.30; 6–11
Royal Steamer
1–2 Townfield Street
☎ (0245) 358800
Ind Coope Best Bitter; Tetley Bitter
Friendly back street local. Dominoes and shove ha'penny

Chignall Smealey

10.30–2.30; 6–11
Pig & Whistle
Chignal Road ☎ (0245) 440245
Adnams Bitter; Fuller London Pride, ESB; Mauldon Bitter; Young Special
Good value food; try the "Pigs Ear" house beer. No meals Sun. Guest beers

Coggeshall

10–2.30; 6–11
Fleece
27 West Street ☎ (0376) 61412
Greene King IPA, Abbot
Ancient pub with front pargetting; real beams inside. Cards and darts

Colchester

10.30–2.30; 5.30–11
Artilleryman
54–55 Artillery Street
☎ (0206) 578026
Greene King XX, IPA, Abbot
Warm, friendly Victorian backstreet local with charity book shop and angling club. Public bar crowded and basic (St Botolphs/Hythe)

11–2.30; 7–11
Grenadier
67 Military Road
Adnams Bitter, Mild or Old and
Victorian street corner local overlooked by the barracks. Not many military customers. Large public bar has juke box and dartboard; pool in back bar (St Botolphs)

11–2.30; 6–11
Hospital Arms
Crouch Street (opposite county hospital)
☎ (0206) 573572
Tolly Cobbold Bitter, Original, XXXX
Popular pub with strong rugby and cricket connections (not Sun)

11–2.30; 5.30–11
Norfolk
North Station Road
☎ (0206) 45257
Greene King XX, IPA, Abbot
Single large bar with nautical theme. Regular live music (North)

11–2.30 (F, S only); 5.30 (6 Sat)–11
Odd One Out
28 Mersea Road (B1025)
☎ (0206) 578140
Archers Best Bitter; Boddingtons Bitter; Marston Pedigree; Mauldon Bitter
Victorian pub facing the wall of medieval abbey. Central bar with saloon and public bar areas. Guest beers (logs) (St Botolphs)

Colne Engaine

10.30–2.30; 6–11
Five Bells
Mill Lane ☎ (078 75) 4166
Greene King IPA, Rayment BBA, Abbot; Mauldon Special Nethergate Bitter
Large friendly village local with open fire. Exotic bar snacks; adjacent barn converted to restaurant

Coxtie Green

10–2.30; 6–10.30 (11 F, S)
White Horse
173 Coxtie Green Road (1 mile off A128) OS564959
☎ (0277) 72410
Benskins Best Bitter; Ind Coope Burton Ale
Cosy, friendly and traditional country local. Guest beers

Crays Hill

10.30–2.30; 6–10.30 (11 F, S)
Shepherd & Dog
London Road (A129)
☎ (0268) 21967
Benskins Best Bitter; Ind Coope Bitter, Burton Ale
Pleasant and comfortable old pub with separate restaurant. Guest beers

Dedham

11.30–2.30; 5.30–11
Lamb
131 Birchwood Road
☎ (0206) 322216
Tolly Cobbold Mild, Bitter
15th-century ex-monks' residence. 2 small bars; picturesque pub in picturesque village worth looking for (summer)

Try also: Anchor

Dobbs Weir

11–3; 5.30–11
Fish & Eels
☎ (0992) 441385
Benskins Best Bitter; Friary Meux Best; Ind Coope Burton Ale; Tetley Bitter
Old coaching inn on edge of Lee Valley Park. Single room has aquarium above the bar (nearby)

Duton Hill

10–2.30; 6–11
Rising Sun
W of B184 ☎ (037 184) 204
Ridley Bitter
Oak studwork, good food, efficiently run and definitely worth a detour

Earls Colne

11–2.30; 6–11
Drum
21 High Street (A604)
☎ (078 75) 2368
Greene King IPA, Abbot; Mauldon Bitter
Carpeted lounge area with chamber pot collection. Simpler games area at back (summer)

Easthorpe

11–2.30; 6–11
House without a Name
The Street ☎ (0206) 210455
Adnams Bitter; Brakspear Bitter; Flowers IPA; Greene King IPA; Mauldon No Name Bitter
Pleasant and popular split level country local. Interesting menu – busy Sunday lunchtime. Pub games

Eastwood

11–2.30; 6–11
Bell House
321 Rayleigh Road (A1015)
☎ (0702) 524271
Courage Best Bitter, Directors
Old rectory with splendid garden. Harvester Grill Bar upstairs

Elsenham

10.30–2.30; 6–11
Crown
High Street (B1051)
☎ (0279) 812827
Benskins Bitter
Popular, efficient village pub. Excellent food (not Sun)

Epping

10–2.30; 6–11
Forest Gate Inn
Bell Common (just off B1393)
☎ (0378) 72312

Essex

Adnams Bitter ⊞; Greene King Abbot ⒢; Ridley Bitter ⊞
Basic no-frills pub near Epping Forest. Darts. Guest beers ≜Q❀❀❀

Feering

10.30–2.30; 6–11

Bell Inn
The Street ☎ (0376) 70375
Greene King IPA, Abbot ⊞
14th-century inn with large single bar including restaurant area. Lots of nooks and crannies ≜Q❀❀⒧❀&

Finchingfield

10.30–3; 6–11

Red Lion
Church Hill (B1053)
☎ (0371) 810400
Ridley Bitter ⊞
Charming pub in one of the most picturesque villages in Essex ≜❀❀⒧❀

Fobbing

10–2.30; 6–10.30 (11 F, S)

White Lion
Lion Hill (off B1420)
☎ (0375) 673281
Ind Coope Best Bitter, Burton Ale ⊞
300 year-old pub in village that hatched the peasants' revolt Q❀⒧❀

Fuller Street

11–2.30; 6–11

Square & Compasses
OS747161 ☎ (0245) 361427
Ridley Bitter ⒢
Friendly, isolated local, popular with cyclists and walkers. Unusual pitch-penny stool in public bar
≜Q❀❀❀⒧❀❀&Å (on site)

Galleywood Common

11–2.30; 6–11

Horse & Groom
Horse & Groom Lane (off B1007 at Goat Hall Lane)
☎ (0245) 261653
Greene King IPA, Abbot; Ridley Mild ⊞
Off the beaten track. 2 comfortable bars; pool and darts in public. No meals Sun
❀⒧⒧❀&Å

Grays

10.30–2.30; 5.30–10.30 (11 F, S)

Bricklayers Arms
48 Bridge Road (near A126)
☎ (0375) 377265
Draught Bass; Charrington IPA; Fuller ESB (winter) ⊞
Friendly 2-bar, street-corner local on edge of town, opposite football ground. Lunches served in upstairs room. Pleasant enclosed garden
❀ (by appointment) ❀⒧❀❀

Great Bardfield

10.30–3; 6–11

Vine
Vine Street (B1057)
☎ (0371) 810355
Adnams Extra; Ridley Mild, Bitter ⊞
Well-kept, comfortable pub in historic and beautiful village ❀⒧ (not Sun) ⒧❀

Great Bromley

12–2.30; 7–11

Tailors Arms
Frating Road, Balls Green
☎ (0206) 251065
Adnams Bitter; Greene King IPA, Abbot ⊞
Faded country pub with real beams. Games area. Fairly quiet ≜Q❀⒧⒧&

Great Chesterford

10.30–2; 6–11

Plough
High Street (near B1383 and M11 Jct 9) ☎ (0799) 30283
Greene King IPA, Abbot ⒢
Excellent small 18th-century village local ≜❀⒧ (not Sun) ❀

Great Clacton

11–2.30; 6–11

Robin Hood
211 London Road (A133)
☎ (0255) 421519
Draught Bass; Charrington IPA ⊞
Large pub converted from terrace of 16th century cottages. Pool and family room in modern extension. Homely atmosphere; emphasis on food ≜❀❀⒧⒧❀

Great Dunmow

10.30–2.30; 6–11

Cricketers Arms
22 Beaumont Hill (B184)
☎ (0371) 3359
Ridley Bitter ⊞
Popular pub near sports centre. Note the old ovens in saloon bar wall ❀⒧ (not Sun) ⒧ (not Wed) ❀&

Great Saling

11–3; 6–11

White Hart
2 miles N of A120
☎ (0371) 850341
Adnams Extra; Ridley Bitter ⊞
Superb Tudor pub with unusual timbered gallery in saloon ≜❀⒧⒧❀

Hadstock

11–2.30; 6–11

Kings Head
B1052 ☎ (0223) 893473
Tolly Cobbold Bitter, Original ⊞
Well-kept 17th-century village pub. Excellent food ≜❀⒧⒧

Harlow

11–2.30; 6–11

Willow Beauty
Hodings Road ☎ (0279) 37328
Greene King Rayment BBA, Abbot ⊞
Refurbished busy local. Live bands Fri and Sat eve
❀⒧❀❀ (Town)

Try also: Cock, Great Parndon (Courage)

Harwich

10.30–2.30; 6–11

Alma
Kings Head Street
Tolly Cobbold Mild, Original ⊞
Unspoilt turn of century pub with nautical theme. Pub games Q❀&❀

Hatfield Broad Oak

11–2.30; 5.30–11

Cock
High Street (B183)
☎ (0279) 70273
Adnams Bitter; Fuller London Pride ⊞
Basic but comfortable and welcoming. Imaginative menu and wine list. No meals Sun
≜Q❀❀⒧⒧

Hazeleigh

10.30–3; 6–11

Royal Oak
Fambridge Road (1 mile S of Maldon) OS849047
☎ (0621) 53249
Greene King IPA, Abbot ⊞
Friendly, traditional roadside pub; deservedly popular. Piano and sing-songs in saloon; games in public. Garden for children
≜❀ (garden) ❀❀&Å

Henny Street (Great Henny)

11–2.30; 6–11

Swan
Off A131 ☎ (078 729) 238
Greene King IPA, Abbot ⊞
Hamlet pub with large riverside garden – ideal for fishing. Separate tiled restaurant area. Pub games
Q❀❀⒧⒧Å (caravans)

Heybridge

10.30–3; 6–11

Maltsters Arms
Hall Road ☎ (0621) 53880
Greene King IPA, Abbot ⒢
Good no-frills boozer. The only drinkers' pub in Heybridge. Discreetly lit

Essex

Ingatestone

10–2.30; 6–10.30 (11 F, S)
Star
High Street ☎ (0277) 353618
Greene King IPA, Abbot G
Friendly traditional pub with renovated bakehouse at rear, used for meetings. Pub games

Leigh-on-Sea

10.30–2.30; 6–11
Crooked Billet
51 High Street, Old Leigh
☎ (0702) 76128
Ind Coope Best Bitter, Burton Ale; Tetley Bitter H
Unspoilt listed building which shakes when trains go by! Opposite famous cockle sheds. Folk music upstairs Tue

10–2.30; 6–11
Grand Hotel
131 The Broadway
☎ (0702) 76626/78326
Courage Best Bitter, Directors H
Popular 3-bar former Victorian hotel. Live music every eve and Sun lunch
(Chalkwell)

Little Baddow

11.30–2.30; 6–11
Generals Arms
The Ridge ☎ (024 541) 2069
Draught Bass; Charrington IPA H
Friendly roadside pub with 3 bars, in rural surroundings. Pub games

Little Braxted

10.30–2.30; 6–11
Green Man
Kelvedon Road OS849130
☎ (0621) 891659
Ridley Bitter H
Pretty country pub. Flagstone-floored public bar; cosy traditional lounge. Good value food. Pub games

Little Walden

11–2.30; 6–11
Crown
On B1053 ☎ ((0799) 27175
Adnams Bitter; Courage Best Bitter, Directors; Ruddles Best Bitter G
Immaculate village pub – good food (not Sun)

Loughton

10–2.30; 6–11
Wheatsheaf
15 York Hill (off High Road)
Draught Bass; Charrington IPA; Fuller ESB (winter) H
Everything the traditional British pub should be – a real gem. Darts and cribbage

Maldon

10.30–2.30 (3 F, S); 6–11
Blue Boar
Silver Street ☎ (0621) 52681
Adnams Bitter, Old G
Historic hotel with pub. Good mix of drinkers. You can't play darts in every THF hotel!

10.30–3; 6–11
Queens Head
The Hythe ☎ (0621) 54112
Greene King IPA, Abbot H
3 contrasting bars with nautical atmosphere, overlooking the estuary. Darts and cards

Manningtree

10.30–2.30; 5.30–11
Station Buffet
Manningtree Station (Westbound Platform)
Adnams Bitter; Everards Tiger; St Austell Hicks Special; Samuel Smith OBB; Wadworth 6X H
Unaltered, popular watering hole for commuters. Good home-made food

Mashbury

10.30–2.30; 6–11
Fox
Mashbury Road
☎ (0245) 31573
Adnams Extra; Ridley Bitter G
Delightful isolated country pub; well worth finding. Pub games

Mill Green

10–2.30; 6–10.30 (11 F, S)
Viper
Highwood Road (N of village) OS641019 ☎ (0277) 352010
Ruddles Best Bitter; Truman Best Bitter; Webster Yorkshire Bitter H
Unspoilt country pub in quiet woodland setting

Moreton

10.30–2.30; 6–11
White Hart
☎ (027 783) 228
Adnams Bitter; Greene King IPA, Abbot H
Traditional locals' pub in farming community. Good food and friendly atmosphere. Pub games

Try also: Moreton Massey

Nazeing

11–2.30; 6–11
Coach & Horses
Waltham Road (B194)
☎ (099 289) 3151
Ind Coope Bitter H
Saloon was once a 'tearoom'. Christie's Brewery glasswork in public bar. Darts and shove ha'penny

Nevendon

10–2.30; 6–10.30 (11 F, S)
Jolly Cricketers
Arterial Road (off A127;
☎ (0268) 726231
Ind Coope Burton Ale; Taylor Walker Best Bitter H
Oldest pub in Basildon, moved in 1929 to be on tripper route. Games room

Orsett

10.30–2.30; 6–10.30 (11 F, S)
Dog & Partridge
Brentwood Road (A128)
☎ (0375) 891377
Courage Best Bitter, Directors H
Cosy local backing on to windy fen

10–2.30; 6–10.30 (11 F, S)
Foxhound
18 High Road (off A1013)
☎ (0375) 891295
Courage Best Bitter, Directors H
Super pub with unusual games, great atmosphere and noted home-cooking
(by arrangement)

Try also: Kings Arms (Taylor Walker)

Purleigh

10.30–2.30; 6–11
Bell
☎ (0621) 828348
Adnams Bitter; Ind Coope Best Bitter H
Attractive 16th-century pub; friendly and comfortable. Superb views over Blackwater Estuary

Rayleigh

10–2.30; 6–11
Paul Pry
14 High Road (A129)
☎ (0268) 742859
Ruddles Best Bitter, County; Webster Yorkshire Bitter H
Friendly pub with large garden and extensive menu
(6–9 not Sun)

Rickling Green

11–2.30; 6–11
Cricketers Arms
½ mile off B1383 (old A11)
☎ (079 988) 322
Greene King Rayment BBA, Abbot G
Superb Victorian village local, idyllically located on cricket green. Ideal for children. Good food in bar and restaurant

Essex

Rochford

10.30–2.30; 6–11

Golden Lion
35 North Street
☎ (0702) 545487
Crouch Vale Best Bitter G; Fuller London Pride; Greene King Abbot H
Small, popular free house

10.30–2.30; 6–11

Old Ship
12–14 North Street
☎ (0702) 544210
Ind Coope Best Bitter, Burton Ale; Tetley Bitter H
Comfortable former coaching inn with fine stained glass

Rowhedge

11.30–2.30; 6–11

Walnut Tree
Fingeringhoe Road
☎ (0206) 869309
Adnams Old; Felinfoel Double Dragon; Fuller London Pride; Greene King IPA H
Free house at isolated cross roads. Games area with darts and pool

Roydon

11–2.30; 6–11

White Horse
High Street ☎ (027 979) 3131
Courage Best Bitter, Directors; John Smith Bitter H
Known as Top House – pleasant village pub with warm atmosphere. No food Sun. Darts

Saffron Walden

10.30–2.30; 6–11

Railway Arms
Station Road ☎ (0799) 22208
Benskins Bitter; Ind Coope Burton Ale H
Plain, comfortable small-town pub

St Osyth

11–2.30; 6.30–11

White Hart
71 Mill Street ☎ (0255) 820318
Adnams Bitter; Courage Directors; White Hart Tiddles H
Grade II listed 16th-century pub with Victorian frontage. Nice beer garden. Warm friendly atmosphere

Shoeburyness

11–2.30; 6–11

Parsons Barn
Frobisher Way, North Shoebury Village
☎ (0702) 293727
Adnams Bitter G; Greene King IPA, Abbot; Webster Yorkshire Bitter H
Spacious converted 17th-century barn. Excellent food available at all times

Southend-on-Sea

10–2.30; 6–11

Liberty Belle
10 Marine Parade
☎ (0702) 66936
Courage Best Bitter, Directors; John Smith Bitter H
Family-oriented sea front pub with nautical decor. Close to pier and amusement arcades
(Apr–Sept)

South Fambridge

10.30–2.30; 6–11

Anchor Hotel
Fambridge Road
☎ (0702) 203535
Adnams Bitter, Extra; Greene King Abbot H
Splendid Victorian edifice near riverside walk. Excellent range of food; guest beers
(lunch) (not Sun)

Southminster

10.30–3; 6–11

Rose
Burnham Road (B1021)
☎ (0621) 772915
Greene King IPA, Abbot G
Sweet little roadside pub with proper public bar
(not Tue)

South Weald

11–2.30; 6–10.30 (11 F, S)

Tower Arms
Weald Road OS572938
☎ (0277) 210266
Adnams Bitter; Greene King IPA, Abbot; Webster Yorkshire Bitter; Young Special
16th-century listed building, former shooting lodge. Large garden with petanque pitch; summer Sunday barbecues. Guest beers

Springfield

10.30–2.30; 6–11

Endeavour
351 Springfield Road
☎ (0245) 257717
Greene King IPA, Abbot H
Quiet, comfortable 3-room suburban pub with rural atmosphere

Stanford-le-Hope

10.30–2.30; 5.30–10.30 (11 F, S)

Rising Sun
Church Hill (near A1014)
☎ (0375) 671911
Courage Best Bitter, Directors; John Smith Bitter H
Cosy local in shadow of 900 year-old village church. Pub games

Stanford Rivers

10.30–2.30; 6 (7 winter Sat)–11

White Bear
London Road (by A113)
☎ (0277) 362185
Ind Coope Best Bitter, Burton Ale H
Excellent country pub off main road. Large garden overlooks fields. Restaurant Wed–Sat 7–9.30; Sun 12–4

Stansted Mountfitchet

10–2.30; 6–11

Dog & Duck
Lower Street (B1351)
☎ (0279) 812047
Greene King Rayment BBA, Abbot H
Excellent, popular village local, efficient and friendly. Bar billiards
(not Sun)

Try also: Cock (Greene King)

Stisted

11–3; 6–11

Dolphin Inn
Coggeshall Road, Bradwell (A120) ☎ (0376) 21143
Adnams Extra; Ridley Mild, Bitter G
Unspoilt many-beamed pub with log fires. Casks on stillage behind bar. Swings and aviary in garden

Stock

10–2.30; 6–11

Hoop
21 High Street ☎ (0277) 841137
Adnams Mild, Bitter, Old; Marston Pedigree; Owd Rodger H and G; Mauldon Bitter H
Busy free house on village green; large range of guest beers. Outdoor games

Stondon Massey

10.30–2.30; 6–10.30 (11 F, S)

Bricklayers Arms
Ongar Road OS585005
☎ (0277) 821152
Greene King IPA, Abbot H
Friendly and popular split-level pub. Shove ha'penny

Stones Green

10.30–2.30; 6–11

Swan
Off A136 ☎ (025 587) 243
Adnams Bitter; Greene King Abbot H
Friendly village local.

123

Essex

Traditional, simple beer shop

Thaxted

10.30–2.30; 6–11

Star
Mill End ☎ (0371) 830368
Ind Coope Bitter H
Vast fireplaces and exposed beams – an excellent pub in village with splendid church, Guildhall and windmill

Thorpe le Soken

10.30–2.30; 6–11

Bell Hotel
High Street (B1033)
Tolly Cobbold Bitter, XXXX, Old Strong H
Listed 15th-century cosy old-world pub with carved beams. Piano

Tillingham

11.30–3; 6–11

Cap & Feathers
South Street ☎ (062 187) 212
Crouch Vale Mild (May), **Woodham Bitter, Best Bitter, SAS, Essex Porter** (summer), **Willie Warmer** H
Splendid 15th-century village pub. Good value food, family room, fishing trips. Folk music 1st and 3rd Sun of month. No muzak, no fruit machines. Bar billiards

Tolleshunt D'Arcy

11–2.30; 6 (7 Sat)–11

Queens Head
North Street ☎ (0621) 860262
Greene King IPA, Abbot H
Busy village pub with cosy parlour and extensive comfortable saloon

Toppesfield

10.30–2.30; 6–11

Green Man
OS739374 ☎ (0787) 237418
Greene King IPA, Abbot H
Superb, friendly pub in remote village. Worth finding (not Sun)

Walton on Naze

10.30–2.30; 6–11

Royal Marine
Old Pier Street (off sea front)
Adnams Bitter; Greene King IPA, Abbot; Mauldon Suffolk Punch; M&B Mild G
Bar of former large hotel, used by local lifeboat crew. Off licence next door worth a visit. Pub games

Westcliff-on-Sea

10.30–2.30; 6–11

Cricketers
228 London Road (A13)
☎ (0702) 343168
Greene King IPA, Abbot H
3-bars: Sportsmans has projected TV and active darts teams (not Sun)

12–2.30; 6–11

Palace Theatre Centre
430 London Road (A13)
Greene King IPA; Ind Coope Best Bitter, Burton Ale; Ruddles County H
Lively and popular theatre bar. Impromptu live music quite possible. Guest beers. No food Sun

West Mersea

11–2.30; 5.30–11

Fox Inn
East Road ☎ (0206) 383391
Adnams Bitter; Greene King IPA, Abbot H
Friendly modern village pub with large games room and restaurant

West Tilbury

10–2.30; 5.30–10.30 (11 F, S)

Kings Head
The Green OS661780
Charrington IPA H
Much-improved local in pleasant rural setting

White Notley

10.30–2.30; 6–11

Cross Keys
The Street ☎ (0376) 83297
Ridley Mild, Bitter H
Fine village local built in 14th century; formerly Chappells Brewery

White Roding

11–2.30; 6–11 (Sun 7–10.30)

Black Horse
on A1060 ☎ (027 976) 322
Adnams Extra; Ridley PA, XXX (occasional) H
Attractive friendly pub with beer garden; excellent food; pub games

Wickford

11–2.30; 6–10.30 (11 F, S)

Castle
2 The Broadway
Tetley Bitter H
Large lounge opens onto garden. Games room (not Sun)

Widford

10.30–2.30; 6–11

Sir Evelyn Wood
Widford Road (near golf course) ☎ (0245) 269239
Greene King IPA, Abbot H
Lovely, simple back-street pub

Witham

10–2.30; 6–11

George
36 Newland Street
Adnams Extra; Ridley Mild, Bitter H
Welcoming town centre pub with 16th century timber-framed saloon and separate club room. Darts and pool (club room) (Mon–Fri) (public)

11–2.30; 6 (7 Sat)–11

Victoria
Powers Hall End
Ridley Bitter G
Spacious old country house now a local for the nearby housing estate. Large friendly public bar, comfortable lounge. Darts and pool (Mon–Sat) (Thu–Sat)

Wivenhoe

11–2.30; 6–11

Horse & Groom
55 The Cross (B1028)
Adnams Bitter, Old H
Quiet friendly local with utilitarian 60s decor including contemporary Adnams posters

Woodham Ferrers

11–2.30; 6–11

Bell
Main Road ☎ (0245) 320443
Adnams Bitter; Ridley Bitter H
Recently became a free house. Restaurant, saloon, separate games room. Guest beers

Woodham Mortimer

11–3; 6–11

Hurdlemakers Arms
Post Office Road (½ mile off A414) ☎ (024 541) 5169
Greene King IPA, Abbot H
Friendly, traditional pub. Stone-flagged saloon, fine public bar, pleasant garden

Wormingford

11–2.30; 6–11

Queens Head
Bures Road (B1508)
Greene King IPA, Abbot; Mauldon Special H
Old country pub with genuine beams. Keen pool players and other games. Restaurant area with good value meals

Writtle

11–2.30; 6–11

Wheatsheaf
70 The Green ☎ (0245) 420695
Greene King IPA, Abbot G
Friendly local in pleasant village with green. Pub games

Gloucestershire

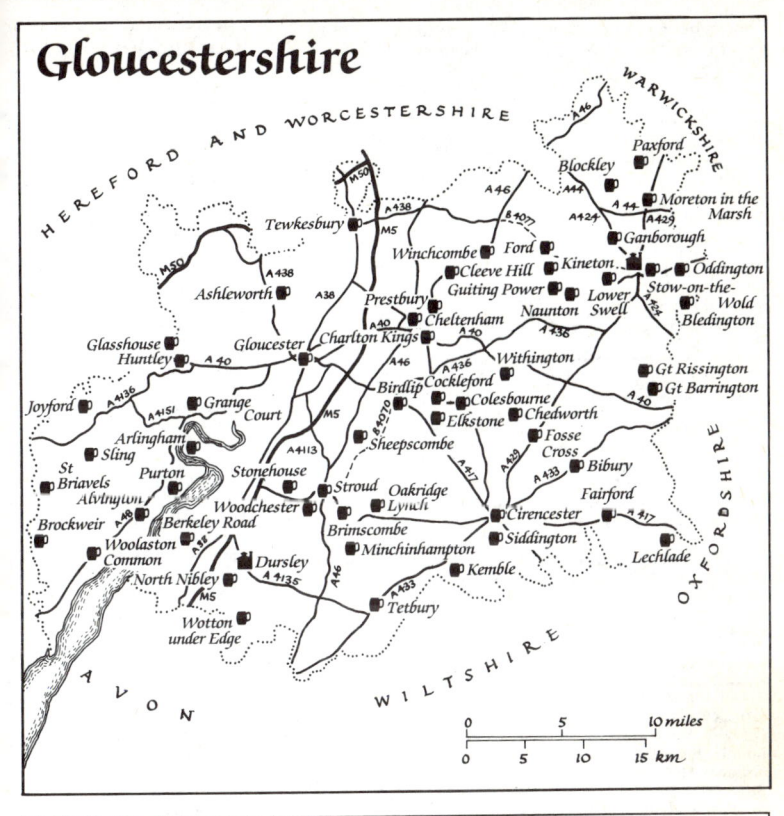

Donnington, Stow-on-the-Wold; **Uley**, Uley, Dursley

Alvington

11–2.30; 6.30–11
Blacksmiths Arms
On A48 ☎ (059452) 657
Wadworth 6X
Very popular drinking and eating place. Good food, good beer, regular guest beers of higher gravity. Friendly landlord. Traditional pub games (not Mon)

Try also: Cross, Aylburton

Arlingham

11.30–2.30; 6.30–11 (11–2.30; 6–11 Sat & summer)
Red Lion
The Cross (off A38)
Marston Pedigree; Smiles Best Bitter; Theakston Best Bitter; Younger Scotch
Real ale paradise, off the beaten track. Spartan bar, lounge has softer seats and no music. Darts, skittles and shove ha'penny

Try also: Bell, Frampton

Ashleworth

11–2.30; 7–11
Arkle
Off A417 ☎ (045 270) 395
Donnington XXX, BB, SBA
Unpretentious, one-bar pub in the village centre on the north bank of the Severn

Berkeley Road

11–2.30; 6–11
Prince of Wales
On A38 ☎ (0453) 810474
Marston Pedigree; Wadworth 6X
Comfortable country hotel with restaurant and function room. Good selection of bar meals
(caravans only)

Bibury

10.30–2.30; 6–11
Catherine Wheel
Arlington village (off A433)
☎ (028 574) 250
Courage Best Bitter,
Directors
Cosy inn oozing with charm. Excellent menu, nice gardens. Bed and breakfast is £25 for a double room

Birdlip

12–2.30; 6–11
Golden Heart
Nettleton Bottom, Coberly (A417)
Adnams Bitter; Draught Bass; Hook Norton Best Bitter; Marston Pedigree; Theakston Old Peculier; Wadworth 6X
Atmospheric old country inn with beer (including guest beers) served straight from the barrels, which are racked behind the bar. Cards and dominoes available. Family room (not Sun)

Bledington

11–2.30; 6.30–11
Kings Head
☎ (060871) 712
Halls Harvest Bitter; Hook Norton Best Bitter; Wadworth 6X

125

Gloucestershire

Popular free house on village green specialising in food 🏠🍺🍴

Try also: New Inn, Nether Westcote

Blockley

11–2.30; 6–11

Crown
High Street (off B4081)
☎ (0386) 700245
Butcombe Best Bitter; Theakston XB; Wadworth 6X H
Comfortable hotel lounge in secluded Cotswold village
🏠🛏🍺🍴🍽 ♿

Brimscombe

11.30–2.30; 6–11

Kings Arms
Bourne Lane ☎ (0453) 885509
Archers Village Bitter; Davenports Bitter; Marston Pedigree; John Smith Bitter; Uley Old Spot; Wadworth 6X H
Village local. Public bar with jukebox and pool table; quieter comfortable saloon bar. Traditional games
🍺🍴🍽 🚭

Brockweir

11.30–2.30; 7–11

Brockweir Country Inn
Off A466 ☎ (029 18) 548
Boddingtons Bitter; Flowers Original; Hook Norton Best Bitter H
Comfortable pub near River Wye in historic village near Tintern Abbey. Traditional games 🏠♿🛏🍺🍴🍽 🚭♿⚽🎵

Charlton Kings

11–2.30; 6–11

Clock Tower
Cirencester Road
Banks's Mild Ale, Bitter; Hansons Black Country Bitter E
Rambling lounge pub with patio under pine trees on edge of town 🍺🍴🍽 (7–10, not Sun)

Chedworth

12–2.30 (closed Mon); 6 (6.30 winter)–11

Seven Tuns
Upper Chedworth
☎ (028 572) 242
Courage Best Bitter, Directors; John Smith Bitter H
Pub of character in delightful village. Good food available 🏠♿ (not games room) 🛏🍺🍴🍽 🚭

Cheltenham

11–2.30; 6–11

Bayshill Inn
85 St Georges Place (near bus station)
Wadworth IPA, 6X,

Farmers Glory H**, Old Timer (winter)** G
Popular town centre pub, threatened with demolition for new road. Good value lunches. Pub games 🍺🍽 🍴

10.30–2.30; 6–11

Beaufort Arms
184 London Road (A40)
☎ (0242) 526038
Hall & Woodhouse Tanglefoot, Wadworth IPA, 6X, Farmers Glory, Old Timer H
Standard public house with a racing theme. Small lounge through sliding door. Limited parking. Metro buses A & B. Skittle alley 🛏🍺🍴🍽 🚭

11–2.30; 6–11

Beehive
1–3 Montpellier Villas (near Eagle Star building)
☎ (0242) 579443
Flowers Original; Whitbread WCPA H
Typical Victorian town pub. Traditional games played
🏠🍺🍴

11–2.30; 6–11

Jolly Brewmaster
35 Painswick Road
Flowers IPA, Original; Whitbread WCPA H
Situated near further education establishment – popular with students and staff 🏠♿🛏 (Sun lunch) 🍺🍽 🍴

Try also: Duck & Pheasant, North Place; **Malvern Inn**, Leckhampton Road

Cirencester

10.30–2.30; 6.30–11

Brewers Arms
70 Cricklade Street
☎ (0285) 3763
Arkells Bitter, Best, Kingsdown Ale H
Busy town pub (public car park nearby). Traditional games ♿🛏🍺🍴🚭

11–2.30; 6–11

Drillmans Arms
Ermin Way, Stratton (A417)
☎ (0285) 3892
Archers Best Bitter, ASB; Wadworth IPA H
Real ale in a real pub just outside town. Warm friendly atmosphere. Darts, dominoes and cribbage 🏠🛏🍺🍴♿

Cleeve Hill

11–3; 6–11

High Roost
Northern end of village
☎ (024267) 2010
Hook Norton Best Bitter, Old Hookey; John Smith Bitter H
Aptly named free house with fine views across Severn Vale to Malvern Hills. Traditional pub games
🏠🛏 (lunch) 🍺🍽 🍴⚽

Cockleford

11–2.30; 6–11

Green Dragon
Off A435 near Cowley
☎ (024 287) 271
Adnams Bitter H**; Draught Bass; Butcombe Bitter** G**; Hook Norton Best Bitter** H**; Theakston Best Bitter; Wadworth 6X** G
Very popular stone-built pub. Jazz on Mondays, folk on Wednesdays. Good food. Guest house next door. Skittles 🏠♿🛏🍺🍴🍽 ♿

Try also: Seven Springs, Jct. A435/A436

Colesbourne

11–2.30; 6–11

Colesbourne Inn
on A435 OS000132
☎ (024 287) 376
Wadworth IPA, 6X, Farmers Glory H
Large roadside inn. Families welcome in restaurant. Pub games played 🏠🍺🍽 🍴🚭 ♿⚽

Elkstone

11–2.30; 6–11

Highwayman
Beech Pike (A417)
☎ (028 582) 221
Arkells Best Bitter; Kingsdown Ale H
Comfortable, character Cotswold stone pub with restaurant, family room and children's play area
🏠♿🛏🍺🍴🍽 ♿

Fairford

12–2.30; 7–11

Marlborough
Cirencester Road (A417)
Butcombe Bitter; Hook Norton Best Bitter H
Friendly local free house. Games include darts, dominoes and cribbage. Guest beers 🏠⚽🚭

Try also: Bull Hotel

Ford

10.30–2.30; 6.30–11

Plough
on B4077 OS088294
☎ (038 673) 215
Donnington BB, SBA H
Famous Cotswold inn. Note the rhyme above the entrance. Part of stocks in lounge bar – formerly used as a court house. Pub games available
🏠🛏🍺🍴🍽 ♿⚽

Fosse Cross

11–2.30; 6–11

Hare & Hounds
Off A429 ☎ (028 572) 288
Hook Norton Best Bitter; Marston Pedigree; Theakston

Gloucestershire

Old Peculier; Wadworth 6X H
Popular country pub serving good beer and good food (vegetarian dishes available)

Ganborough

11–2.30; 6–11

Coach & Horses
On A424, 2 miles N of Stow-on-the-Wold ☎ (0451) 30208
Donnington XXX, BB, SBA H
Pleasant country pub on main road. Not far from brewery. Pub games

Glasshouse

11–2.30; 6–11

Glass House Inn
Glasshouse, Mayhill
☎ (0452) 830529
Butcombe Bitter; Theakston Best Bitter; Whitbread WCPA G
Basic friendly pub of character with quarry tiled floor. Worth a detour. Pub games played

Gloucester

11–2.30; 6.30–11

County Tavern
44 Southgate Street
☎ (0452) 307000
Adnams Bitter; Usher Best Bitter; Wadworth 6X; Whitbread Pompey Royal H
Large single-bar town pub adjoining the new County Hotel, not far south of the Cross. Excellent food

11–2.30; 6–11

Cross Keys
Crosskeys Lane
☎ (0452) 23358
Flowers Original; Whitbread WCPA H
Simple historic pub in a narrow side street near the Cross. Live entertainment most nights

11–3, 0–11

Linden Tree
73–75 Bristol Road (opposite Lloyds Bank) ☎ (0452) 27869
Archers Best Bitter; Butcombe Bitter; Hook Norton Best Bitter H; **Marston Pedigree** G; **Wadworth 6X** H
Friendly pub with a fine range of well-kept beers. A single L-shaped bar in the lower ground floor of a terrace, set back slightly from the main road. No car park

11–2.30; 6–11

Whitesmiths Arms
81 Southgate Street (¼ mile from the Cross)
☎ (0452) 414770
Arkells BBB; Flowers IPA, Original; Whitbread Pompey Royal H
Quiet, unpretentious local

decorated with a strong nautical theme. Wide range of pub games

Grange Court

11–2.30; 7–11

Junction Inn
Off A48 ☎ (045276) 307
Courage Best Bitter; Whitbread WCPA H
Nice country pub with railway theme. Six real ales (including guest beers) always available. Large garden with barbecue. Pub games

Great Barrington

11–2.30; 6–11

Fox
Half mile N of A40 OS204131
☎ (04514) 385
Donnington XXX, BB, SBA H
Traditional stone Cotswold pub next to river. Popular with walkers (and locals). Skittle alley

Great Rissington

11.30–2.30; 6.30–11

Lamb Inn
☎ (0451) 20388
Flowers Original; Marston Pedigree; Wadworth 6X H
Cosy, patriotic village local with a relaxed atmosphere and good service. A clean-air pub

Guiting Power

11.30–2.30; 5.30–11

Olde Inn
OS093249 ☎ (045 15) 392
Hook Norton Best Bitter; Theakston Best Bitter; Wadworth 6X H
Welcoming local; a Cotswold gem. Range of beers may change. No food Mon

Try also: Farmers Arms (Donnington)

Huntley

11–2.30; 6–11

Red Lion Hotel
On A40 ☎ (0452) 830251
Flowers Original; Whitbread WCPA H
Well-appointed hotel with public and lounge bars. Good range of bar meals and snacks. Bed and breakfast

Joyford

11–2.30; 6–11

Dog & Muffler
Near Coleford, off B4432 and off B4228 OS579132
☎ (0594) 32444
Samuel Smith OBB H
Gem of a pub out in the country. Well worth finding. Friendly landlord and plenty

of old world charm. Pub games Q (not bar)

Kemble

11.30–2.30; 6.30–11

Thames Head Inn
Tetbury Road (A433 near railway bridge)
☎ (028 577) 259
Draught Bass; Ruddles Best Bitter, County; Thames Head Bitter H
Friendly free house with games room. Clean air system in public bar. Pub games. Guest beers

Kineton

10.30–2.30; 6–11

Halfway House
Halfway between B4077 and B4068 OS097266
☎ (045 15) 344
Donnington BB, SBA H
Friendly village local; pub games played

Lechlade

11–2.30; 6.30–11

Crown Inn
High Street (A417) **Hook Norton Best Bitter; Wadworth IPA, 6X, Farmers Glory** H
Friendly town free house offering occasional guest beers. Pub games

Try also: Red Lion

Lower Swell

10.30–2.30; 6–11

Golden Ball
B4068 OS175255
☎ (0451) 30247
Donnington XXX, BB, SBA H
Delightful pub with stream close by. Separate dining room recently opened (booking essential). Pub games

Minchinhampton Common

11–2.30; 6 (7 winter)–11

Old Lodge Inn
Box/Nailsworth turn from 'Tom Long's Post' on common OS854006 ☎ (045 383) 2047
Ind Coope Burton Ale; Tetley Bitter; Theakston Best Bitter; Wadworth 6X H
Large former golf club in middle of common. Function room/skittle alley available. Magnificent views. Guest beers
(games room)

Moreton-in-the-Marsh

10.30–2.30; 6–11

Black Bear
High Street ☎ (0603) 50705

127

Gloucestershire

Donnington XX, BB, SBA ⒣
Thriving town centre pub with recently added second bar. Pub games include Aunt Sally ▲🍴🍺 ⓓ 🎯♿⇌

Try also: Wellington (Hook Norton)

Naunton

10.30–2.30; 6–11
Black Horse
off B4068 OS119234
☎ (034 15) 378
Donnington BB, SBA ⒣
Traditional Cotswold pub, retaining 2 bars and pub games
▲🍴🍺 ⓓ 🎯♿ (side door)

North Nibley

12–2.30; 7–11
New Inn
Waterley Bottom OS758963
☎ (0453) 3659
Cotleigh WB, Tawny Bitter; Greene King Abbot; Smiles Best Bitter; Theakston Old Peculier Ⓖ
Popular, friendly free house, but isolated in remote valley. Large garden. Guest beers. Pub games available. Clean air system ▲Q🍴🍺 ⓓ 🎯♿⇌

Oakridge Lynch

11–2.30; 6 (7 winter)–11
Butchers Arms
☎ (028 576) 371
Archers Best Bitter; Butcombe Bitter; Marston Burton Bitter, Pedigree; Uley Old Spot ⒣
Worth the effort to find this thriving and lively village pub. Skittle alley/function room available. Guest beers
▲Q🍺 ⓓ

Oddington

11–2.30; 6–11
Horse & Groom
S of A436; 3 miles W of Stow-on-the-Wold OS223256
☎ (0451) 30584
Wadworth 6X, IPA (occasional) ⒣
Large Cotswold pub with good restaurant. Guest beers
▲🍴🍺 ⓓ ⇌

Paxford

11–2.30; 7–11
Churchill
B4479 ☎ (038 678) 203
Hook Norton Best Bitter, Old Hookey ⒣
Pleasant country local
▲🍺 ⓓ 🎯

Prestbury

10.30–2.30; 6–11
Plough
Mill Street (behind church)
☎ (0242) 44175
Flowers IPA, Original;

Whitbread WCPA Ⓖ
Small, original, unspoilt local with thatched roof. The only gravity-served Whitbread in town. Lovely garden. Quoits played ▲Q🍺♿🎯

Purton

12–2.30; 6.30–11
Old Severnbridge Hotel
Old Severn Bridge (off A48)
☎ (0594) 42454
Flowers Original; Hook Norton Best Bitter; Marston Pedigree ⒣
Attractive setting with lovely views of River Severn. Large garden with children's area. Separate dining room. Worth a detour to find this hotel. Family room ▲Q🍴🍺 ⓓ ♿

St Briavels

11–2.30; 7 (6 summer)–11
George
off A4228 ☎ (0594) 530228
Marston Pedigree; Wadworth 6X ⒣
Pleasant U-shaped, 1-bar free house, near castle. Caters for locals as well as tourists. Pub games played and guest beers on offer ▲Q🍴🍺 ⓓ (not winter Sun or Thu) 🎯

Sheepscombe

11–2.30; 6–11
Butchers Arms
off A46 and B4070
☎ (0452) 812113
Flowers Original; Whitbread WCPA ⒣
Pleasant village local with awards for its hanging baskets. Guest beers. Pub games ▲Q🍴🍺♿

Siddington

11.30–2.30; 6–11
Greyhound
off A419 ☎
Wadworth IPA, 6X, Old Timer (winter) ⒣
Genuine Cotswold stone pub with good food. Popular with the business community. Darts ▲Q🍴🍺 ⓓ ♿

Sling

10.30–2.30; 5.30–11
Orepool Inn
B4228, near Coleford
☎ (0594) 33227
Draught Bass; Hook Norton Best Bitter; Wadworth 6X ⒣
Recently extended and modernised free house. Very popular with the locals. Large bar, pool room, small snug
🍴🍺 ⓓ ♿🎯⇌

Try also: Wyndham Arms, Clearwell

Stonehouse

10–2.30; 6–11

Spa
Old Ends Lane
☎ (045 382) 2327
Flowers Original; Whitbread WCPA ⒣
Comfortable, friendly Whitbread pub near factory estate. Popular at lunchtime. Clean air system in saloon bar. Pub games played
▲ ⓓ (Fri & Sat only) ♿⇌

Stow-on-the-Wold

10–2.30; 6–11
Queens Head
Market Square ☎ (0451) 30563
Donnington XXX, BB, SBA ⒣
Fine old Cotswold pub, popular with tourists and locals alike. Interesting collection of signs in back yard. Pub games
▲🍴🍺 ⓓ ♿

Stroud

11–2.30; 6–11
Clothiers Arms
1 Bath Road ☎ (045 36) 3801
Archers Village Bitter; Ind Coope Burton Ale; Smiles Best Bitter; Tetley Bitter; Wadworth 6X, Farmers Glory ⒣
Very friendly town free house. Signs and windows from old Stroud Brewery. Pub games played. Guest beers ▲ ⓓ

Tetbury

11–2.30; 6–11
Trouble House Inn
A433 (2 miles, on Cirencester road) ☎ (0666) 52206
Wadworth Devizes Bitter, 6X
1680s lovely low-beamed, basic 1-bar pub. Interesting history. Skittles and bar billiards ▲🎯🍺 ⓓ ♿🎯

Tewkesbury

11–2.30; 6–11
Berkeley Arms
Church Street ☎ (0684) 293034
Wadworth Devizes Bitter, 6X, Farmers Glory, Old Timer ⒣
Interesting 17th-century town centre pub with lounge bar at side. Good quality, inexpensive lunchtime snacks. Pub games 🍴 ⓓ ♿

11–2.30; 6–11
Britannia
High Street (A38)
☎ (0684) 294208
Davenports Bitter ⒣
Town centre bar with dartboard ▲ ⓓ

Try also: Albion (Tetley); **Crown,** Shuthonger

Winchcombe

10.30–2.30; 5.30 (6 Sat)–11
White Hart Inn
High Street ☎ (0242) 602359

128

Gloucestershire

Flowers Original; Whitbread WCPA ⓗ
Old coaching inn, popular with locals and tourists alike. Family room and two full-size snooker tables for residents' use. Guest beers
🅿️✉️⊛ ( ) 🄰 (1 mile) ↻

Try also: Corner Cupboard (Whitbread)

Withington

11.30–2.30; 6.30 (6 summer)–11

Mill Inn
off A436 ☏
Samuel Smith OBB, Museum Bitter ⓗ
Cotswold pub with several genuine oak-beam ceilinged rooms. Good food cooked to order (limited menu Sun). Pleasant garden beside stream. Ideal for tourists. Good games selection

includes chess and bar billiards 🅿️🅿️⊛( )♿

Woodchester

11–2.30; 6–11

Ram
South Woodchester (off A46)
☏ (045 387) 3329
Archers Village Bitter; Boddingtons Bitter; Holdens Black Country Bitter; Hook Norton Old Hookey; Uley UB40, Old Spot ⓗ
Welcoming Cotswold stone free house with views across valley. Guest beers. Good food. Pub games 🅿️Q⊛( )

Try also: Royal Oak, Church Road

Woolaston Common

12 (11.30 Sat)–2.30 (closed Wed); 6.30–11

Rising Sun
¾ mile off A48 ☏ (059 452) 282
Hook Norton Best Bitter; Marston Pedigree; Theakston Best Bitter ⓗ
Comfortable pub with good views. Pub games played
🅿️Q⊛( )🄴♿🄰

Wotton-under-Edge

11 (10.30 Sat)–2.30; 6–11

Falcon
20 Church Street
☏ (0453) 842138
Courage Best Bitter, Directors; John Smith Yorkshire Bitter ⓗ
Comfortable town pub. Clean air system. Pub games
🅿️✉️( )

Try also: Swan Hotel (Bass)

TROOPING THE HOP

Many readers of the Good Beer Guide are fascinated by the rituals that have traditionally surrounded the brewing of beer. We are grateful therefore to the New Tyke Taverner, the magazine of CAMRA's Bradford, Keighley and Craven Branches, for bringing to our attention the ancient rite of "Trooping the Hop", held each year at Webster's Yorkshire Brewery.

Researcher Andy Whitley records the following:

The Hop in question is believed originally to have been bought from Joshua Tetley & Co. after they had finished brewing with it. Each year it is fetched from its shrine in a Halifax church by a gaudily clad sorcerer called "The Head Brewer". He carries it on a silk cushion to Ovenden Wood, accompanied by a procession of wailing penitents called "The Shareholders". From here it is taken through the gates of Webster's Brewery to the accompanying sound of Saul's Death March. In olden days this part of the ceremony was performed by a band of locals called "The Drinkers" but this group has almost entirely disappeared from Yorkshire in recent years.

Once inside, the Hop is seized by jubilant workers who may be seen to kiss or embrace it before placing it on a pedestal. In turn they will file past it in the manner of old friends paying their last respects.

At this point, an ornamental guard called "The Board of Directors" will take charge of the Hop and pass it to "The Chairman" who then attaches it to a gold chain that hangs from his waistcoat pocket. In matching pin striped suits this ensemble dance reels in an anticlockwise direction seven times around the mash tun before lowering the Hop into the steaming cauldron.

After one minute's silence the celebration ends with the removal of the Hop, which by now has given the beer its characteristic flavour. It is returned forthwith by trusty messenger to its holy resting place, there to remain until its use in the following year's ceremony.

The congregation then adjourns to the nearest Timothy Taylors pub for a decent pint.

Hampshire

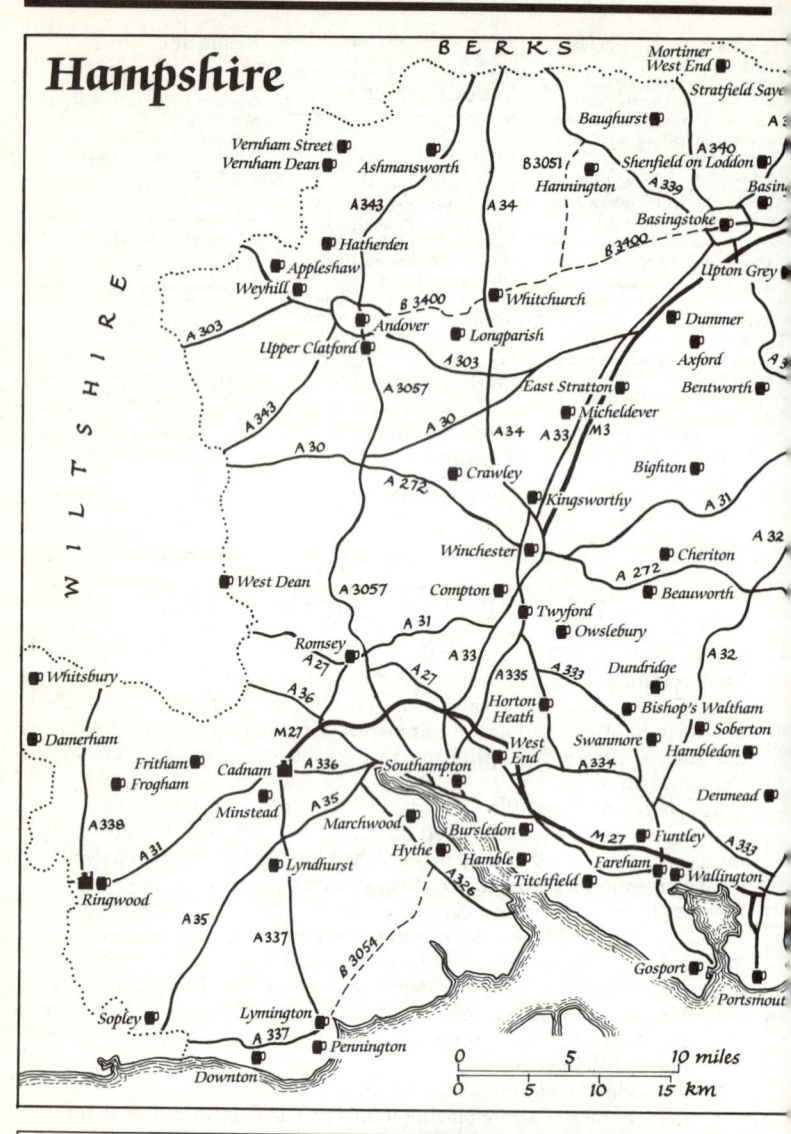

> Gales, Horndean; New Forest, Cadnam; Ringwood, Ringwood

Aldershot

10.30–2.30; 5.30–11
Royal Staff
Staff Road (off A323)
☎ (0252) 22932
Friary Meux Best; Ind Coope Burton Ale H
Well-run, one-bar, community pub in back streets. Good wendy house for the kids! Bar billiards, dominoes, darts and cribbage 🍴🍺🚻

Alton

10.30–2.30; 5.30–10.30 (11 F,S & summer)
Eight Bells
Church Street (off High Street)
☎ (0420) 82417
Charrington IPA; Courage Best Bitter; Fuller London Pride; Hall & Woodhouse Badger Best Bitter; Marston Pedigree H
Dimly-lit free house, full of railway relics, agricultural implements and chamber pots. Excellent food. Guest beers 🍺🍽🚉

10.30–2.30 (3.30 Tue); 6–10.30 (11 F,S & summer)
Kings Head
Market Street (off High Street)
☎ (0420) 82313
Courage Best Bitter; Directors H
Country pub atmosphere in town centre 🍴🍺🍽🚉

Hampshire

☎ (0264) 772626
Flowers Original; Whitbread Strong Country Bitter H
Warm and cosy village pub with inevitable walnut tree in car park. Evening meals for special occasions. Once visited a difficult pub to leave. Ladies keep-fit on Thu mornings! Guest beers
⌂ Q ⌘ ⌥ ⌫ (not Sun)

Ashmansworth

12–2.30; 6–11
Plough
1 mile N of A343
☎ (0635) 253047
Archers Best Bitter, ASB G
Traditional local with warm welcome in county's highest village. Guest beers. Pub games Q ⌘ ⌥ ⌫

Axford

11.30–2.30; 6–11
Candover Crown
on B3046 ☎ (025 687) 492
Hall & Woodhouse Badger Best Bitter; Marston Pedigree; Ringwood Fortyniner H
Pleasant 2-bar country pub in picturesque Candover Valley. Old village photographs displayed ⌂ ⌘ ⌥ ⌫ ▶ ⌫

Basing

10.30–2.30; 6 (5.30 F)–11
Millstone
Bartons Mill, Bartons Lane
☎ (0256) 473560
Fuller London Pride H; **Gales HSB; Wadworth IPA, 6X, Farmers Glory, Old Timer** E
Old mill converted into 1-bar pub. Attractive riverside setting, near ruined Basing House and impressive tithe barn ⌥ ⌫ (not Sun)

Basingstoke

10.30–2.30; 6–11
George (Hole in the Wall)
London Street ☎ (0256) 465168
Courage Best Bitter, Directors H
Value-for-money pub opposite town museum in the older part of the town. Public bar with darts and pool. Lounge decorated in true Victorian style
⌥ ⌫ (not Sun) ⌫

10.30–2.30; 5.30–11
Queens Arms
Bunnian Place (100 yds from station) ☎ (0256) 465488
Courage Best Bitter, Directors; John Smith Bitter H
Friendly pub with crib, darts and dominoes ⌥ ⌫ ▶ ⌫ ⇌

Baughurst

11–2.30; 5.30–11
Badger's Wood
Wolverton Road

☎ (073 56) 4395
Flowers Original; Whitbread Strong Country Bitter H
Large public bar with a strong games influence. Near to 12th-century Pamber Priory, one of the largest priories in Hampshire. Guest beers
⌥ ⌫ (not Sun) ⌫ ⌫

Try also: Wellington Arms

Beauworth

10.30–2.30; 6–10.30 (11 F,S & summer)
Milbury's
Outside village S of A272
OS570246 ☎ (096 279) 248
Flowers Original; Gales XXXD, BBB, HSB; Sussex Hermitage Best Bitter H
Remote old free house with flagstone and beams aplenty. Huge treadwheel and 300 ft well inside! Opens 9.30 am Sunday for brunch (non-alcoholic). Separate restaurant. Guest beers ⌂ Q ⌘ ⌥ ⌫ ▶

Bentworth

10.30–2.30; 6–10.30 (11 summer)
Sun
Sun Hill (off A339)
☎ (0420) 62338
Draught Bass; Bunces Bitter; Courage Best Bitter; Gales HSB H
Genuine 17th-century country pub with blazing log fires in winter. Guest beers; darts and dominoes ⌂ Q ⌥ ⌫ ⌫ ⌫

Bighton

10.30–2.30; 6–10.30 (11 F,S & summer)
Three Horseshoes
off A31 ☎ (0962) 732859
Gales XXXL, BBB, HSB H
Delightful rural local, well off the beaten track, country crafts collection in the bustling locals' bar. Relaxing atmosphere in quiet lounge
⌂ Q ⌘ ⌥ ⌫ ▶ ⌫

Bishop's Waltham

10–2 (2.30 Sat); 6–11
Bunch of Grapes
St Peters Street (off Bank Street) ☎ (048 93) 2935
Courage Best Bitter, Directors (winter) G
Superb, unspoilt alehouse with a very warm welcome, situated in narrow medieval street. Pub has been in same family for over 70 years. Darts Q ⌘

10.30–2.30; 6–11
White Horse
Beeches Hill, Ashton (½ mile off B3035) OS557187
☎ (048 93) 2532
Flowers Original; Fremlins Bitter; Whitbread Strong Country Bitter H, **Pompey Royal** G or H
Attractive and comfortable

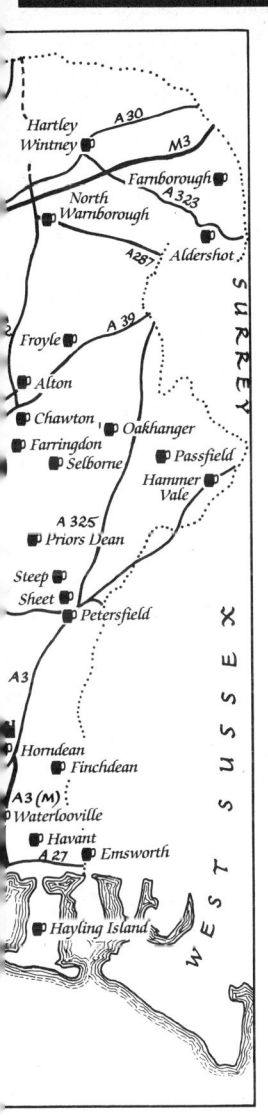

Andover

11 (10.30 Sat)–2.30; 6–11
Railway Tavern
Weyhill Road ☎ (0264) 62474
Flowers Original; Whitbread Strong Country Bitter; Wethered Winter Royal H
Bustling 2-bar pub with darts, crib and quiz teams. Landlord's poodle is closely related to Eastenders star, Roley! Guest beers
⌂ ⌘ ⌥ ⇌ ▶ ⌫

Appleshaw

10 (11 winter)–2.30; 6–11
Walnut Tree
off A342 4 miles N of Andover

131

Hampshire

2-bar cottage pub involved in local community life. Good food. Pub games 🏠🍴🎲🍺 (not Mon or winter Sun) 🚻🏕

Bursledon

11–2.30; 6–11

Linden Tree
School Road, Lowford (400 yds A27/A3025) ☎ (042 121) 2356
Wadworth IPA, 6X, Farmers Glory H Old Timer (winter) G
Comfortable village 1-bar local, with good outside drinking areas and children's play area 🏠🍴🍺 (not Sun)

Chawton

11–2.30; 6–11

Greyfriar
Winchester Road ☎ (0420) 83841
Flowers Original; Whitbread Strong Country Bitter, Pompey Royal H
Superb friendly village pub opposite Jane Austen's house. Good value food. Dominoes 🏠🍴🎲🍺🏕 (Graces Farm)

Cheriton

10.30–2.30; 6–10.30 (11 F,S & summer)

Flower Pots
off A272 ☎ (096 279) 318
Flowers Original; Whitbread Strong Country Bitter G
Fine, unspoilt cosy local where everyone is made to feel welcome. Ideal stop-off when visiting the Watercress Line Steam Railway at Alresford (3 miles). Pub games 🏠🍷🎲🍴🍺🏕

Compton

11–2.30; 6–10.30 (11 F,S & summer)

Captain Barnard
Winchester Road (A31, ¼ mile S Otterbourne Jct of A33) ☎ (0962) 712220
Draught Bass; Gales HSB; Ringwood Best Bitter H
Comfortable cosy village pub full of old artefacts and farm machinery. Named after local roundhead soldier. Pub games 🏠🍷🎲🍴🍺

Crawley

11–2.30; 6–10.30 (11 F,S & summer)

Rack & Manger
Stockbridge Road (A272) ☎ (0962) 72281
Marston Mercian Mild, Burton Bitter, Pedigree, Merrie Monk, Owd Rodger H
Cosmopolitan pub. Large quiet lounge and more vigorous public. Abundance of bric-a-brac. Garden play houses 🏠🍴🎲🍺🏕

Damerham

10.30–2.30; 6–10.30 (11 F,S & summer)

Compasses
B3078 ☎ (072 53) 231
Ind Coope Burton Ale; Wadworth 6X H
Village pub with high standards. Ancient brewery in outbuilding 🏠🍷🎲🍴🍺🏕

Denmead

10.30–2.30; 6–11

Forest of Bere
Hambledon Road ☎ (0705) 263145
Friary Meux Best; Ind Coope Burton Ale; Tetley Bitter H
Old flint-walled pub with lively but friendly public bar, the social centre of village life. Shove-ha'penny, bar billiards 🏠🍷🎲🍴

Downton

11–2.30; 6–10.30 (11 F,S & summer)

Royal Oak
on A337 ☎ (0590) 42297
Flowers Original; Whitbread Strong Country Bitter, Pompey Royal H
18th-century pub in same family for over 100 years. Non-smoking area. Home cooked food 🏠🍷🎲🍴🍺🏕

Dummer

11–2.30; 5.30–11

Sun
Winchester Road (A30, near M3 Jct.7)
Courage Best Bitter, Directors H
Busy roadside pub. Activity garden and family room. Darts. Dummer now famous for its Fergie connections 🏠🍷🎲🍴

Dundridge

11–2.30; 6–11

Hampshire Bowman
Dundridge Lane (1 mile off B3035) OS579185
Gales BBB, XXXXX, HSB; G
Pleasantly situated off the beaten track. 1 traditional stone floored bar, once an abattoir! HQ of the Portuguese Racing Sardine Club! Pub games. Guest beers 🏠🍷🎲🍴

East Stratton

11–2.30; 6–10.30 (11 F,S & summer)

Plough Inn
off A33 ☎ (096 289) 241
Courage Directors; Gales BBB, HSB H
Converted 18th-century farmhouse. Skittle alley. Large outdoor area inhabited by local wildfowl!
🏠🍷🎲🍴🍺🏕

Emsworth

10.30–2.30; 6–10.30 (11 F,S & summer)

Lord Raglan
35 Queen Street ☎ (0243) 372587
Gales XXXD, BBB, HSB H
Listed 16th-century flint pub of unusual design. Small public bar and comfortable lounge. Cribbage, darts and dominoes 🏠🍷🎲🍴🍺🏕

11–2.30; 6–10.30 (11 F,S & summer)

Milkmans
55 North Street ☎ (0243) 373356
Gales XXXL, BBB, HSB H
Traditional 1-bar locals' pub. Popular and lively. Games include Close-the-Box 🍴🍺

Fareham

11–2.30; 6–10.30 (11 F,S & summer)

Golden Lion
28 High Street ☎ (0329) 234061
Gales XXXD, BBB, XXXXX, HSB H
Set in the historic high street this 1-bar pub has a modern interior and appeals to all types. Good range of games. Evening meals and Sun lunch only by request 🍴

Farnborough

11.30–2.30; 6–11

Prince of Wales
184 Rectory Road (off A325) ☎ (0329) 545578
Eldridge Pope Royal Oak; Fuller London Pride; Hall & Woodhouse Badger Best Bitter; Tanglefoot; King & Barnes Sussex Bitter; Wadworth 6X H
Excellent food, comfortable and friendly atmosphere; crowded most of the time especially early evening. Guest beers
Q 🍴🍺🏕 (Farnborough N)

Try also: Monkey Puzzle, Cove

Farringdon

12–2.30; 6–11

Rose & Crown
Crows Lane, Upper Farringdon (off A32) ☎ (042 085) 231
Flowers Original; Marston Owd Rodger; Wethered Winter Royal H
Pleasant village pub with hotel accommodation and restaurant. A number of house beers available
🏠Q🍷🎲🍴🍺

Finchdean

10–2.30; 6–10.30 (11 F,S & summer)

George
☎ (0705) 412257

Hampshire

Friary Meux Best; Ind Coope Bitter, Burton Ale; Tetley Bitter H
Rural pub set in the centre of hamlet. 2 bars and a large garden. Popular with families. Darts, dominoes and shove ha'penny

Fritham

10–2.30; 6–10.30 (11 F, S & summer)

Royal Oak
off B3078 OS242141
☎ (0703) 812606
Flowers Original; Whitbread Strong Country Bitter G
Unspoilt, rustic thatched alehouse deep in the New Forest. Large open hearth with flue still used for smoking hams. A real gem, well worth finding. Darts and dominoes
(1½ miles)

Froyle

10.30–2.30; 6–10.30 (11 F, S & summer)

Anchor
Lower Froyle (off A31)
☎ (0420) 23261
Courage Best Bitter; Eldridge Pope IPA, Royal Oak H
Carefully renovated 14th-century pub with 60-foot well in bar. Small restaurant, cosy snugs; collection of firearms

10.30–2.30; 6–11

Hen & Chicken
Upper Froyle (A31)
☎ (0420) 22115
Brakspear Special; Courage Best Bitter; Flowers Original; Gales HSB; King & Barnes Festive; Ruddles Best Bitter H
Smart upmarket old coaching inn, food oriented, family room; separate restaurant

11–2.30; 6–11

Prince of Wales
Lower Froyle (off A31)
☎ (0420) 23102
Fuller London Pride; King & Barnes Sussex Bitter; Draught Festive; Young Special H
Edwardian country pub in scenic village. Guest beers. Noisy convivial atmosphere

Frogham

11 (11.30 winter)–2.30; 6–10.30 (11 F, S & summer)

Foresters Arms
Abbotswell Road OS173129
☎ (0425) 52294
Hook Norton Best Bitter; Theakston Old Peculier H
Friendly, comfortable free house on fringe of New Forest. Large garden: boules and horseshoes. Family room. Guest beers. Ideal base for 'yomping' in the forest
(not Sun)

Funtley

11–2.30; 6–10.30 (11 F, S & summer)

Miners Arms
112 Funtley Road (2 miles N of Fareham) ☎ (0329) 232065
Gales BBB, XXXXX, HSB H
Everything a village local should be: friendly, cosy, quiet and tucked away. Shove ha'penny and darts (not Tue or Sun)

Gosport

11–2.30; 7–10.30 (11 F, S & summer)

Queens Hotel
143 Queens Road (200 yds off Stoke Road) ☎ (0705) 582645
Archers ASB; Boddingtons Bitter H
A beer drinkers' haven hidden in back streets. Single bar divided into 3 areas. Guest beers. Dominoes, darts, pool and cribbage. No dogs. No food Sun

Hamble

10.45–2.30; 6–11

Olde Whyte Harte
High Street ☎ (0703) 452108
Gales XXXD, BBB, XXXXX, HSB H
Charming 16th-century pub with flagstone floor and excellent log fire situated in famous yachting village. Family room
(until 8pm)

Hambledon

12–2.30; 7–11

New Inn
West Street (off B2150)
☎ (070 132) 466
Eldridge Pope Dorset Original IPA; Gales BBB, HSB; Ringwood Best Bitter H
Best value free house in Hampshire? Pool table. Village is birthplace of cricket

11.30–2.30, 6–11

Vine
West Street (off B2150)
☎ (070 132) 419
Courage Directors Bitter; Gales BBB, HSB; Marston Pedigree; Morland Bitter H
400 year-old pub with friendly locals. Picturesque village setting. Occasional live jazz. Shove ha'penny

Hannington

12–2.30; 6.30–11

Vine
off A339 ☎ (0635) 298525
Gales HSB; Hall & Woodhouse Badger Best Bitter; Ringwood Old Thumper; Ruddles Best Bitter; Wadworth 6X, IPA H
Very popular food-oriented pub in remote location. Small games area. Beer good value for area

Hammer Vale

11–2.30; 6–11

Prince of Wales
Hammer Lane (off A3, sign for Bulmer Hill, turn right at T-Jct) OS868326 ☎ (0428) 52600
Gales XXXD, BBB, HSB G
Unique rural red brick and stained glass building. Bags of atmosphere. Families particularly welcome. Marvellous walking country
(not Sun)

Hartley Wintney

11–2.30; 6–11

Cricketers
Cricket Green (off A30)
☎ (025 126) 2166
Friary Meux Best; Tetley Bitter; Ind Coope Burton Ale H
Friendly locals' pub by village cricket green which is allegedly the oldest in regular use. Cribbage, darts and dominoes (Wed–Sat)

Hatherden

11.30–2.30; 7–11

Hamster
1 mile N of Charlton
☎ (0264) 75321
Courage Best Bitter; Gales HSB; Wadworth 6X H
16th-century thatched coaching inn, with large children's garden, in rural surroundings. Pub games
(not Sun)

Havant

11–2.30; 6–10.30 (11 F, S & summer)

Bear Hotel
East Street ☎ (0705) 486501
Flowers Original H
Comfortable furnished bar in Georgian coaching inn with modern hotel extension
(hotel patio) (hotel restaurant)

10.30–2.30; 6–10.30 (11 F, S & summer)

Robin Hood
6 Homewell ☎ (0705) 482776
Gales XXXL, BBB, HSB G
Recently extended 1-bar pub with welcoming atmosphere

Hayling Island

10–2.30; 6–10.30 (11 F, S & summer)

Maypole
9 Havant Road (A3023)
☎ (0705) 463670
Gales XXXL, BBB, XXXXX, HSB H
Bustling 2-bar pub in typical 1930s style on holiday island. Popular with locals and visitors alike

133

Hampshire

Horndean

11–2.30 (10–2.30 Sat); 6–10.30 (11 F, S & summer)

Ship & Bell Hotel
6 London Road (A3)
☎ (0705) 592107
Gales XXXD, BBB, XXXXX, HSB H
18th-century hotel – the Gales brewery tap. It has 2 modernised bars, good food and live music on Wed. Good range of games ■≈◐ (not Sun) ⊖▲ (Blendworth)

Horton Heath

11–2.30; 6–11

Rising Sun
Botley Road (¼ mile S of Fair Oak on A3051)
☎ (0703) 692377
Flowers Original; Whitbread Strong Country Bitter H
Friendly roadside pub popular with all ages; fresh flowers often adorn the bar. Pub games ℧■◐

Hythe

10.15–2.30; 6–10.30 (11 F, S & summer)

Lord Nelson
High Street (near ferry)
☎ (0703) 842169
Flowers Original; Whitbread Strong Country Bitter; Pompey Royal H
Waterfront pub with quaint bars. Garden area overlooks Southampton Water: spot the ships! Pub games Q■◐⊖▲✿

10.30–2.30; 6–10.30 (11 F, S & summer)

Travellers Rest
Hart Hill, Frost Lane
☎ (0703) 842356
Flowers Original; Whitbread Strong Country Bitter H
Friendly 2-bar pub – off the beaten track; on the Pilgrim Way between Hythe and Bucklers Hard. Pub games ▲Q℧■◐⊖

Kingsworthy

10.30–2.30; 6–10.30 (11 F, S & summer)

Cart & Horses
London Road (A33/A3090 Jct)
☎ (0962) 882360
Marston Burton Bitter, Pedigree H, **Owd Rodger** G
Large rambling roadhouse catering for all needs. Restaurant, skittle alley/function room, children's playground. Family room at weekends ▲Q℧■◐⊖▲&✿

Longparish

11–2.30; 6–11

Cricketers Inn
on B3048 ☎ (0264) 72335
Marston Border Mild, Burton Bitter, Pedigree H

Traditional village pub with cricketing theme in 3 contrasting bars. Good value beer and snacks. Many pub games ℧■◐⊖

Lymington

10–2.30; 6–10.30 (11 F,S & summer)

King's Arms
St Thomas Street (near A337)
☎ (0590) 72594
Flowers Original; Whitbread Strong Country Bitter G
16th-century coaching inn; friendly atmosphere and warm welcome. A rare gravity house. Pub games ▲Q℧ (early eve) ■≈◐⊖&≈ (Town)

Lyndhurst

11–2.30; 6–10.30 (11 F, S & summer)

Mailmans Arms
71 High Street
☎ (042 128) 2257
Marston Burton Bitter, Pedigree, Owd Rodger H
Popular, friendly, comfortable local. Frequent live entertainment; barbecues. Pub games ▲Q℧■◐&

Marchwood

11–2.30; 6–10.30 (11 F, S & summer)

Pilgrim Inn
Hythe Road (off A326)
☎ (0703) 867752
Charrington IPA; Draught Bass; Courage Best Bitter, Directors H
Beautiful thatched inn with immaculate gardens ▲Q■◐&

Micheldever

10.30–2.30; 6–10.30 (11 F, S & summer)

Half Moon & Spread Eagle
Winchester Road (off A33)
Flowers Original; Whitbread Strong Country Bitter H
Hub of village life. Own cricket pitch. Piano singsongs. Pub games ▲Q■◐&

Minstead

10–2.30; 6–10.30 (11 F,S & summer)

Trusty Servant
1 mile W off A337 (Cadnam Lyndhurst Road) OS281110
☎ (0703) 812137
Flowers Original; Fremlins Bitter H
Unspoilt, friendly New Forest village local. Church nearby is resting-place of Sir Arthur Conan Doyle. Darts, draughts and dominoes
▲ (wood stove) ≈◐⊖

Mortimer West End

10.30–2.30; 6–11

Red Lion
Church Road OS633634

☎ (0734) 700169
Brakspear Bitter; Eldridge Pope Royal Oak; Fuller London Pride; Palmer IPA; Wadworth 6X H
15th-century listed building near Silchester Roman town. Popular for food. Restaurant open Tue–Sat ▲■◐&

North Warnborough

10.30–2.30; 6–11

Anchor
The Street (off A287/M3 Jct 5)
☎ (025 671) 2740
Courage Best Bitter, Directors H
Friendly cheerful local with traditional pub games, tucked away in side street. Originally an old brewery serving single pub. Near King John's Castle and Basingstoke Canal. Pub games ▲■◐ (not Sun) &

Oakhanger

10.30–2.30; 6–11

Red Lion
off B3004 ☎ (040 23) 2232
Courage Best Bitter, Directors H
One of the best – all a public bar should be and pleasant lounge with food emphasis. In the shadow of a giant golfball!
▲Q■◐⊖&

Owslebury

11–2.30; 6–10.30 (11 F,S & summer)

Ship
off A333 ☎ (0962) 74358
Marston Mercian Mild, Burton Bitter, Pedigree H
Old, beamed country inn: busy but comfortable bar where the locals meet for banter. Home-cooked food (Not Sun) ▲Q℧■◐

Passfield

10–2.30; 6–10.30 (11 F,S & summer)

Passfield Oak
Passfield Common, Liphook
☎ (0428) 205
Ballards Best Bitter; Bunces Benchmark; Marston Pedigree; Ringwood XXXX, Fortyniner H
Solid village pub with convivial long exposed bar. Children's room and large enclosed garden for families
▲Q℧■◐⊖

Petersfield

11–2.30; 6–10.30 (11 F, S & summer)

Good Intent
40 College Street (A3 one-way northbound) ☎ (0730) 63838
Ballards Best Bitter; Charrington IPA; Eldridge Pope Royal Oak; Hall & Woodhouse Badger Best Bitter, Tanglefoot G

134

Hampshire

16th-century tavern of great character. Don't be confused by the handpumps – the barrels are in a back room. Guest beers. Excellent restaurant ⌂ ( ) (Tue–Sat) ≈

10–2.30; 6–10.30 (11 F, S & summer)
Market Inn
20 The Square ☎ (0730) 63723
Flowers Original; Fremlins Bitter; Whitbread Strong Country Bitter H
Small, listed building in corner of Market Square. Has a basic public bar and a small lounge ( ) ⌂ ≈

10–2.30; 6–10.30 (11 F, S & summer)
Old Drum
16 Chapel Street
☎ (0730) 64159
Friary Meux Best; Ind Coope Burton Ale; Tetley Bitter H
Busy town pub. Won Friary Meux Pub Garden of the Year for its surprisingly large) garden. Relaxing atmosphere ⌂ ( ) (not Sun) ≈

Pennington

11–2.30; 6–10.30 (11 F, S & summer)
Musketeer
26 North Street (250 yds N of A337) ☎ (0590) 76527
Bateman XXXB; Brakspear PA; Felinfoel Double Dragon; Ringwood Best Bitter; Ruddles County H
Attractive 1-bar pub in village centre, originally a coaching inn. A real free house with an interesting choice of beers. No food Sun. Chess, cribbage and dominoes ⌂ Q ⌂ ( ) ≈

Portsmouth

10.30–2.30; 6–10.30 (11 F, S & summer)
Artillery Arms
Hester Road, Milton, Southsea
☎ (0705) 733610
Friary Meux Best; Ind Coope Burton Ale H
Very popular corner local in quiet back street ⌂

10–2.30; 6–10.30 (11 F, S & summer)
Castle Tavern
119 Somers Road, Southsea
(S of ring road)
☎ (0705) 829238
Flowers Original; Whitbread Pompey Royal H
This country pub in the city is a real surprise amongst high rise council flats. Panelled public bar and cosy lounge. Good place for a quiet chat Q (lounge) ⌂ ≈ (Fratton)

10.30–2.30; 6–10.30 (11 F, S & summer)
Compass Rose
Anchorage Road, Anchorage Park (off A2030)
☎ (0705) 673037
Gibbs Mew Wiltshire Traditional Bitter, Salisbury Best, Bishop's Tipple H
Popular pub, especially at lunchtimes, in recent housing and industrial development on site of former airport. Has a quiet corner with leather Chesterfields
⌂ ( ) ⌂ ≈ (Hilsea)

10–2.30; 6–10.30 (11 F, S & summer)
Egremont Arms
82 Crasswell Street
(city centre)
Whitbread Strong Country Bitter, Pompey Royal G
One-time keg-only house but now a "beer-drinkers den" Fri night discos are a contrast to the normally quiet atmosphere. Handy for the shops ≈

10.30–2.30; 6–10.30 (11 F, S & summer)
George
84 Queen Street, Portsea
☎ (0705) 821040
Flowers Original; Fuller London Pride; Glenny Hobgoblin; St Austell Hick's Special; Sussex Warrior Ale; Young Special H
Comfortable 1-bar 18th-century inn with relaxed 'wardroom' atmosphere, close to the Naval Heritage Centre ⌂ Q ⌂ ( ) (not Sun) ≈ (Harbour)

10–2.30; 6–10.30 (11 F, S & summer)
Magpie
66 Fratton Road, Fratton
☎ (0705) 864959
Ind Coope Burton Ale H
Victorian town pub with regular live music. 2 large bars with much passing trade. Pub games ( ) ⌂ ≈ (Fratton)

10–2.30; 6–10.30 (11 F, S & summer)
Mermaid
222 New Road, Copnor
☎ (0705) 824397
Whitbread Strong Country Bitter, Pompey Royal H
Excellent local with Victorian wrought iron canopy outside and figures above public bar. Guest beers (real ale club)
⌂ ( ) ⌂

11–2.30; 6–10.30 (11 F, S & summer)
Old Oyster House
Locksway Road, Milton, Southsea (off Milton Road, A288) ☎ (0705) 827456
Fremlins Bitter; Whitbread Pompey Royal H
2 contrasting bars in pub near Milton Locks on the old Portsmouth to London canal. Good mix of regulars
⌂ ( ) (Mon–Fri) ⌂

10–2.30; 6–10.30 (11 F, S & summer)
Rocket
119 High Street, Cosham
Flowers Original; Whitbread Pompey Royal H
Busy High Street local with car park and garden; opposite popular cinema
⌂ ( ) ⌂ ≈ (Cosham)

10–2.30; 6–10.30 (11 F, S & summer)
St Marys Arms
St Marys Road, Fratton
☎ (0705) 820383
Ind Coope Burton Ale H
1-bar pub with tropical fish. Appeals to locals of all ages. Separate pool room
⌂ ⌂ (B&B) ⌂ ≈ (Fratton)

10–2.30; 6–10.30 (11 F, S & summer)
Scotts Bar
51 King Street, Southsea
☎ (0705) 826018
Courage Best Bitter, Directors; Gales HSB; Marston Pedigree; Ringwood Old Thumper; Wadworth 6X H
Smart town pub with unusual 8-handled beer engine. Good lunchtime atmosphere. Used by local business types. Loud music at night when packed by younger drinkers
( ) (not Sun) ≈

10.30–2.30; 6–10.30 (11 F, S & summer)
Tap
17 London Road, North End (A2047) ☎ (0705) 699943
Fuller London Pride; Gibbs Mew Bishop's Tipple; Glenny Hobgoblin, Tap Special Bitter (TSB) H
Enterprising free house close to North End shops and the continental ferry port. Dogs welcome. Board games
⌂ ( ) ⌂ ⌂

11–2.30; 6–10.30 (11 F, S & summer)
Wellington
62 High Street, Old Portsmouth ☎ (0705) 818965
Friary Meux Best; Ind Coope Burton Ale H
Old hostelry in tourist area: opposite the Square Tower and near the cathedral. Large rambling bar. Pub games
⌂ ( ) ⌂ ≈ (Harbour)

11–2.30; 6.30–10.30 (11 F, S & summer)
Wig & Pen
1 Landport Terrace, Southsea
☎ (0705) 820696
Flowers Original; Whitbread Pompey Royal H
1-bar pub but lounge forms separate area. Bare wood floor. A locals' corner pub situated on the terraces; always a friendly welcome. Picturesque exterior. Good choice of games ( ) (not Sun) ≈

11–2.30; 6–10.30 (11 F, S & summer)
Wine Vaults
43 Albert Road, Southsea (opposite King's Theatre)
☎ (0705) 864712
Ballards Best Bitter; Boddingtons Bitter; Burt VPA; Hook Norton Best Bitter; Palmer IPA; Theakston Old Peculier H
Wood-panelled ale and wine pub with wood floor and 12 hand pumps. Dogs welcome. Seating on former church

135

Hampshire

pews. Guest beers; 1 beer sold cheaply Mon eves
🍴 (vegetarian) ♿

11–2.30; 6–10.30 (11 F, S & summer)
Yorkshire Grey
25 Guildhall Walk
☎ (0705) 822010
Draught Bass; Charrington IPA H
Unspoilt, late Victorian city-centre pub. Impressive oblong bar faces, pew seating and unusual tiled murals 🍴♿≠

Priors Dean

11–2.30; 6–10.30 (11 F, S & summer)
White Horse (Pub with No Name)
NW of Petersfield past Steep
OS714290 ☎ (042 058) 387
Boddingtons Bitter; Gales HSB; King & Barnes Draught Festive; Palmer IPA; Ringwood Fortyniner; Whitbread Pompey Royal H
Remote, traditional pub set in a field. Unsigned, but worth the search. Very popular. Guest beers ▲Q❀❀♿

Ringwood

11–2.30 (10.30–3 Wed); 6–10.30 (11 F, S & summer)
Inn on the Furlong
12 Meeting House Lane
☎ (042 54) 5139
Ringwood Best Bitter, Fortyniner, XXXX, Old Thumper H
Cosy, multi-roomed pub furnished with ex-church wooden furniture. Convenient for local shops. Darts ▲❀❀🍴

Romsey

10–2.30; 6–10.30 (11 F, S & summer)
Tudor Rose
3 The Cornmarket
☎ (0794) 512126
Courage Best Bitter, Directors H
Tiny 15th-century pub in town centre. A convivial haven – always a conversation to join! Outside tables in cobbled court
▲Q❀🍴 (Mon–Fri) ♿

Selborne

11–2.30; 6–11
Selborne Arms
High Street (B3006)
☎ (042 050) 247
Courage Best Bitter, Directors H
Largely unspoilt village pub in historic Gilbert White village. An excellent children's garden includes animals and aviary. Jazz every second Tue. Good choice of games
▲Q❀❀🍴 (not Sun) ❀

Sheet

11–2.30; 6–10.30 (11 F, S & summer)

Queens Head
Off A3 ☎ (0730) 64204
Flowers Original; Fremlins Bitter; Whitbread Strong Country Bitter H
Village local with its own grocer's shop attached, set behind the village green with its spreading chestnut tree. Pub in same family for 3 generations. Darts, dominoes and shove ha'penny ▲❀❀♿

Sherfield on Loddon

10.30–2.30; 6–11
White Hart
Reading Road (off A33)
☎ (0256) 882280
Courage Best Bitter, Directors H
An old coaching inn dating from 1642. 1-bar pub with a separate eating area, popular for good value food ▲❀🍴♿

Soberton

10.30–2.30; 6.30–11
White Lion
School Hill (off A32)
☎ (0489) 877346
Flowers Original; Fremlins Bitter; Wadworth 6X; Whitbread Strong Country Bitter, Pompey Royal H
Unspoilt country pub in lovely setting next to green and church. Restaurant; guest beers; darts and cribbage
▲Q❀❀🍴♿
▲ (Rookesbury Park)

Sopley

10.30–2.30; 6–10.30 (11 F, S & summer)
Woolpack
On B3347 ☎ (0425) 72252
Whitbread Strong Country Bitter, Pompey Royal H
Attractive thatched pub in village centre. Patio by stream. Ducks and geese in paddock; children's playground. Darts ▲❀❀🍴♿

Southampton

11.30–2.30; 6–10.30 (11 F, S & summer)
Bay Tree
10 New Road (opposite Mountbatten Theatre)
☎ (0703) 333187
Draught Bass; Charrington IPA H
Basic but friendly city centre pub. Upstairs bar open for music nights and Fri. Good jazz/blues on Mon and Thu. Darts
Q (lounge) 🍴 (not Sun) ❀≠

11–2.30; 6–10.30 (11 F, S & summer)
Crown & Sceptre
168 Burgess Road, Bassett (on A35 near university)
☎ (0703) 768414
Flowers Original; Whitbread Strong Country Bitter,

Pompey Royal H
Friendly and convivial lounge with oak beams and wood panelled walls. Small but comfortable bar. Good value food. Guest beers ❀❀🍴❀♿

11.30–2.30; 6–10.30 (11 F, S & summer)
Junction Inn
21A Priory Road, St Denys
☎ (0703) 584486
Marston Mercian Mild, Burton Bitter, Pedigree, Merrie Monk, Owd Rodger (winter) H
Excellently preserved Victorian local. Ideal journey break if you are not in a hurry. Darts and bar billiards
Q❀🍴❀≠ (St Denys)

10–2.30; 6–10.30 (11 F, S & summer)
Marsh
42 Canute Road (by Itchen Bridge A2035) ☎ (0703) 635540
Marston Mercian Mild, Burton Bitter, Pedigree H
Friendly, no frills local; one of few remaining docklands pubs retaining its original character. Formerly a lighthouse, which explains its strange shape. Darts and pool room ❀🍴♿

11.30–2.30; 6.30–10.30 (11 F, S & summer)
Mason's Arms
45 St Mary Street (opposite Technical College)
☎ (0703) 632398
Gales XXXD, BBB, XXXXX, HSB H
Unspoilt, cosy town pub convenient for Kingsland Market. Renowned for good value food – especially vegetarian. Restaurant open Thu to Sat eves. Good range of games ▲Q❀❀🍴

11.30–2.30; 6.45–10.30 (11 F, S & summer)
New Inn
16 Bevois Valley Road (A335, near RSH Hospital)
☎ (0703) 228437
Gales XXXD (summer), BBB, XXXXX, HSB H
Small alehouse, busy during University term-time. Congenial barstaff and perspicacious locals combine to make a quintessentially affable atmosphere
❀🍴 (not Sun) ♿

11–2.30; 6.30–10.30 (11 F, S & summer)
Park Inn
37 Carlisle Road, Shirley (off A3057) ☎ (0703) 787835
Wadworth IPA, 6X, Farmer's Glory, Old Timer H
Warm, homely side-street local with friendly regulars and staff. Unobtrusive piped music. Impressive painted mirrors. Darts ▲♿

10–2.30; 6–10.30 (11 F, S & summer)
Richmond Inn
108 Portswood Road, Portswood (A335)

136

Hampshire

☎ (0703) 554523
Marston Mercian Mild, Burton Bitter, Pedigree H
Friendly main road local in a busy suburb. Straightforward public bar and comfortable lounge, with a superb old LSD cash till. Darts
🏠⊕⊛⇌ (St Denys)

10–2.30; 6–10.30 (11 F, S & summer)
Salisbury Arms
126 Shirley High Street, Shirley ☎ (0703) 774624
Marston Mercian Mild, Burton Bitter, Pedigree H
Genuine working-class local. Single bar with separate areas. A bit boisterous at weekends but friendly. Small family room. Darts and pool ☎ ◐

11.30–2.30; 6–10.30 (11 F, S & summer)
Wellington Arms
56 Park Road, Freemantle (off Shirley Road) ☎ (0703) 227356
Courage Directors; Gales HSB; Gibbs Mew Salisbury Best; Ringwood Best Bitter; Tetley Bitter; Wadworth 6X H
Popular, comfortable backstreet free house with 2 lounges. A veritable shrine to the Iron Duke – get there early to have a good look round!
⊛◐&

Try also: Southwestern, Priory Road (Free)

Stratfield Saye

11–2.30; 6–11
Four Horseshoes
West End Green
☎ (0734) 332320
Morland Mild, Bitter H**, Best Bitter** G
Friendly, unspoilt village local with an almost perpetual evening domino school. Close to Stratfield Saye house, a gift to Wellington for his victory at Waterloo 🏠⊛◐⊕&

11.30–2.30 (not winter Mon); 6 (6.30 winter)–11
New Inn
off A33 OS684616
☎ (0734) 332255
Burt 4X, VPA; Hook Norton Best Bitter, Old Hookey H
Remote pub with traditional games, bat and trap for garden drinkers. Guest beers. Nearby is Wellington Country Park and the National Dairy Museum 🏠☎⊛◐

Steep

11–2.30; 6–10.30 (11 F, S & summer)
Cricketers
1 Church Road ☎ (0730) 61035
Gales XXXD, BBB, XXXXX, HSB H
Lively thirties roadside local near Bedales School and popular walking area. 2 modern bars. Imaginative menu. Pub games
🏠⊛◐⊕&

10.30–2.30; 6–10.30 (11 F, S & summer)
Harrow Inn
off A272 ☎ (0703) 62685
Flowers Original; Fremlins Bitter; Whitbread Strong Country Bitter G
Classic, small 2-bar pub in pastoral setting, with its own country garden. Toilets are across the lane! Very busy at times 🏠Q⊛◐⊕&◐

Swanmore

10.30–2.30; 6–11
Bricklayers Arms
Church Road ☎ (048 93) 2461
Whitbread Strong Country Bitter, Pompey Royal H
Pleasant 1-bar village local near the church 🏠⊛◐&

Titchfield

10–2.30; 6–10.30 (11 F, S & summer)
West End Inn
24 West Street ☎ (0329) 42109
Flowers Original; Whitbread Strong Country Bitter H
Unspoilt friendly local with a games room
☎ (games room until 9)

Twyford

11.30–2.30; 6–10.30 (11 F, S & summer)
Phoenix Inn
(A333) ☎ (0962) 713322
Marston Mercian Mild, Burton Bitter, Pedigree H
Friendly village 1-bar pub. Good value food. Skittle alley
🏠⊛◐&⇌ (Shawford)

Upper Clatford

11–2.30; 6–11
Crook & Shears
In main street ☎ (0264) 61543
Flowers Original; Whitbread Strong Country Bitter H
365 year-old village pub; one of its famous customers was flier Amy Johnson. Folk club alternate Fri. Games room; intimate restaurant. Parking difficult 🏠Q⊛◐⊕⊕

Upton Grey

11–2.30; 6 (7 Sat)–11
Hoddington Arms
Off A32 ☎ (0256) 862371
Courage Best Bitter, Directors H
Located near pond in picturesque thatched village. Renowned for good food. Darts and dominoes
🏠☎⊛◐ (not Sun)⊕

Vernham Dean

11–2.30; 6–11
George Inn
4 miles N of A343
☎ (026 487) 279
Marston Burton Bitter, Pedigree H
16th-century unspoilt village inn, full of character. Occasional informal folk and jazz music. Inglenook fireplace. Pub games
🏠Q☎⊛◐ (not Sun)&

Vernham Street

12–2.30; 6–11 (closed Mon)
Boot
5 miles NW of Hurstbourne Tarrant OS581351
☎ (026 487) 213
Hall & Woodhouse Badger Best Bitter; Marston Burton Bitter, Pedigree G
Out-of-the-way thatched gem with welcoming atmosphere. Exceptional family facilities and separate dining room. Pub games 🏠Q☎⊛◐

Wallington

11–2.30; 6–10.30 (11 F, S & summer)
White Horse
44 North Wallington (off Delme Roundabout, A27/M27 Jct.11) ☎ (0329) 235197
Draught Bass G**; Charrington IPA** H
Small, friendly village local opposite river. No dogs. Darts, dominoes and cribbage. Patio
🏠 (Public) ⊛◐ (Mon–Fri)

Waterlooville

11–2.30; 6–10.30 (11 F, S & summer)
Woodpecker
179A, London Road (A3)
☎ (0705) 251012
Flowers Original; Whitbread Pompey Royal H
A Roast Inn, an unexpected oasis in a real ale desert
☎ (restaurant) ◐⊕&

Weyhill

10.30–2.30; 6 (7 Sat)–11
Weyhill Fair
on A342 (off A303)
☎ (026 477) 3631
Flowers Original H**; Morrell Dark Mild** G**, Bitter, Varsity** H
Popular free house with impressive record of imaginative guest beers and ciders. Mural of historic Weyhill Fair 🏠Q☎⊛◐⊕&

West Dean

10–2.30; 6–10.30 (11 F, S & summer)
Red Lion
Off A27/B3084 ☎ (0794) 40469
Flowers Original; Whitbread Strong Country Bitter, Pompey Royal H
Friendly village local, straddling 2 counties. Views over River Dun. Sunday roast lunches. Guest beers. Pub games 🏠Q☎⊛◐⊕&▲⇌

West End

11–2.30; 6–11
Master Builder

Hampshire

Swaythling Road (A27) ☎ (0703) 472426
Fuller London Pride; Theakston Best Bitter; Wadworth 6X H
Large comfortable roadside pub with many drinking areas including a non-smoking bar. Guest beers. No food Sun ᵹ⌑◖ (not Mon) ᴕ

11–2.30; 6–11
West End Brewery
High Street (B3035) ☎ (0703) 472214
Marston Mercian Mild, Burton Bitter, Pedigree, Owd Rodger (winter) H
Pleasant village pub with contrasting bars. Pub games ⌑ (patio) ◖ (not Sun) ⊞ᴕ

Whitchurch

10.30–2.30; 6–11
Bell
Bell Street (200 yds from town centre) ☎ (0256) 893120
Courage Best Bitter; Gales BBB, HSB H
Historic 16th-century timber-framed inn, renowned for its pizza selection. Pub games ᵹ⌑⊷◖⊞ᴕ≋

11–2.30; 6.30–11
Yeoman
Newbury Street (near Town Hall) ☎ (0256) 892304
Archers Best Bitter H or G
1-bar friendly local, reputedly haunted. Close to Britain's oldest apothecary (for hangover cures?) Town noted for its silk mill, fine trout and annual beer race. Folk festival Sept. Pub games ᵹ⌑⊷◗≋

Whitsbury

10.30–2.30; 6–10.30 (11 F, S & summer)
Cartwheel
Whitsbury Road (3 miles NW of Fordingbridge) ☎ (072 53) 362
Draught Bass; Bunces Benchmark; Eldridge Pope Dorset Original IPA; Miners Arms Guvnor's Special Brew Wadworth 6X H
Comfortable free house with previous incarnations as a barn, bakery and wheelwright – hence the name. Constantly changing beer range. Pub games ⌑ᵹ (weekend lunch) ⌑◖◗

Winchester

10.30–2.30; 6–10.30 (11 F, S & summer)
Bell
83 St Cross Road (A333, 1 mile S of city centre) ☎ (0962) 65284
Marston Mercian Mild, Burton Bitter, Pedigree H
Splendid old inn adjoining 12th-century "Hospital of St Cross" (England's oldest charity). Quiet lounge with huge display of miniature bottles. Garden playhouse. Pub games ⌑⌑◖⊞ᴕ

10.30–2.30; 6–10.30 (11 F, S & summer)
County Arms
85 Romsey Road (A3090) ☎ (0962) 51950
Marston Mercian Mild, Burton Bitter, Pedigree H
Pleasant out-of-town local near hospital and prison. Collection of enamel signs ⌑ᵹ⌑◖⊞ᴕ

10–2.30; 6–10.30 (11 F, S & summer)
Exchange
9 Southgate Street ☎ (0962) 54718
Courage Best Bitter, Directors; John Smith Bitter H
Busy city-centre pub. Smart and comfortable. One bar with games area. Often crowded, particularly with lunch trade.

Food discount for NUS members ᵹ⌑◖ᴕ≋

11–2.30; 6–10.30 (11 F, S & summer)
Fulflood Arms
28 Cheriton Road (300 yds off A272) ☎ (0962) 65356
Marston Burton Bitter, Pedigree H
Traditional, friendly street-corner local. Tiled sign still proclaims Winchester Brewery. ⌑⊞ᴕ≋

11–2.30; 6–10.30 (11 F, S & summer)
Green Man
53 Southgate Street ☎ (0962) 65429
Marston Mercian Mild, Border Mild, Burton Bitter, Pedigree, Merrie Monk H
Solid, corner, city-centre local popular with mild drinkers. Pub games include table skittles and skittle alley ◖⊞ᴕ≋

11–2.30; 6–10.30 (11 F, S & summer)
King Alfred
11 Saxon Road (off Hyde Street) ☎ (0962) 54370
Marston Mercian Mild, Burton Bitter, Pedigree H
Busy, traditional local in residential area; fine garden with barbecue for hire ᵹ⌑◖⊞ᴕ≋

10–2.30; 6–10.30 (11 F, S & summer)
White Swan
84 Hyde Street (A272/A3090 junction) ☎ (0962) 65526
Marston Burton Bitter, Pedigree, Merrie Monk, Owd Rodger H
Formerly the Winchester Brewery tap, now a listed town pub, given a new lease of life; particularly popular with younger drinkers. Bar billiards ᵹ⌑◖⊞ᴕ≋

KEY TO SYMBOLS

Facilities

- ⌑ real fire
- Q quiet pub – no electronic music, TV or obtrusive games
- ᵹ indoor room for children
- ⌑ garden or other outdoor drinking area
- ⊷ accommodation
- ◖ lunchtime meals
- ◗ evening meals
- ⊞ public bar
- ᴕ facilities for the disabled

- ▲ camping facilities close to the pub or part of the pub grounds
- ≋ near British Rail station
- ⊖ near Underground station
- ⌀ real cider

The facilities, beers and pub hours listed in the Good Beer Guide are liable to change but were correct when the Guide went to press.

Help keep real ale alive by joining CAMRA. Your voice helps encourage brewers big and small to brew cask beer and offer all beer drinkers a better choice.

Hereford & Worcester

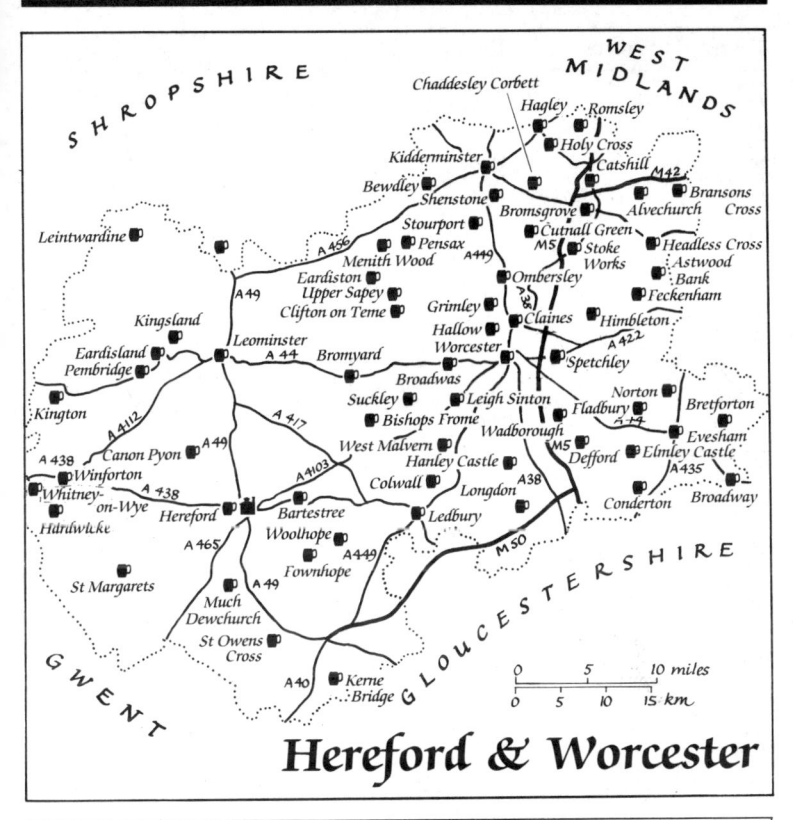

🏠 *Wye Valley*, Hereford

Alvechurch

11–2.30; 6–10.30 (11 F, S)

Coach & Horses
Weatheroak Hill OS056741
☎ (0564) 823386
Davenports Bitter; Everards Tiger; Holden Black Country Mild; Samuel Smith OBB; Woods Special H
Large, very popular pub on the old Roman road, Ryknild Street. Flagstoned bar; modern lounge and restaurant; large outdoor area
🚬 Q ❀ ◐ ▮ ⊕

Astwood Bank

12–2.30; 6–11

Oddfellows Arms
Foregate Street (off A441)
☎ (052 789) 2806
M&B Mild E**, Brew XI** H
Busy, welcoming local, tucked away in a back street. No food Sun 🚬 Q ❀ ◐ ⊕

Bartestree

10.30–2.30; 6–11

New Inn
On A438
Marston Burton Bitter, Pedigree H
Quiet, no-frills locals' pub housed in Victorian mock-Gothic edifice. A CAMRA favourite. Pub games 🚬 Q ❀ ⊕

Bewdley

11–2.30; 7–10.30 (11 F, S)

Black Boy
Wyre Hill (off A456)
☎ (0299) 3524
Banks's Mild, Bitter E
Unspoilt friendly local – a worthwhile ½ mile uphill walk from town centre. Several small rooms – 2 dart boards – pleasant gardens
Q ❀ ◐ ⊕

11–2.30; 7–10.30 (11 F, S)

Hop Pole
Cleobury Road (A456)
☎ (0299) 2127
Marston Burton Bitter, Pedigree H
Popular watering hole on main Tenbury Road. Carpeted bar with piano for impromptu sessions. Good food Tues–Sat eves Q ❀ ▮ ⊕

11–2.30; 7–10.30 (11 F, S)

Horn & Trumpet
Welchgate (A456/B4194)
Courage Directors; John Smith Bitter H
Popular lively inn which specialises in jazz sessions (Sat and Mon eves). Weekly folk club. Pool table in games room 🚬 ◐ ⊕

11–2.30; 7–10.30 (11 F, S)

Little Pack Horse
High Street ☎ (0299) 403762
Ansells Bitter; Ind Coope Burton Ale; Lumphammer H
Original of the Little Pub Company pubs. Appetising meals, try the generously filled jacket potatoes
🚬 Q ⊃ (for meals) ◐ ▮

11–2.30; 7–10.30 (11 F, S)

Rising Sun
Kidderminster Road (A456)
☎ (0299) 2336
Banks's Mild, Bitter E
Tiny, unspoilt local near safari park. Cosy, snug and extended bar which also serves draught cider; outdoor drinking areas front and rear
Q ❀ ◐ ⊕ ⌂

139

Hereford & Worcester

Bishop's Frome

12–2.30; 7–11

Green Dragon
100 yds off B4214, near Post Office ☎ (088 53) 607
Banks's Bitter E; Courage Directors H; Fuller ESB G; Robinson Best Bitter; Taylor Landlord H; Theakston Old Peculier G
Real ale, real food, real oak beams, real fires – this one's got the lot! Guest beers too
🏠 Q ⌛ ⊛ ( ) ⏣ &

Bransons Cross

11–2.30; 5.30–11

Cross & Bowling Green
Alcester Road (A435)
☎ (056 44) 2472
Ansells Mild, Bitter H
Site of a pub for 500 years, and a gibbet before that! Small lounge, larger restaurant/lounge. Playground in large garden. No food Sun
🏠 ⌛ ⊛ ( ) ⏣ ≷ (Wood End)

Bretforton

10.30–2.30; 6–11

Fleece
The Square (off B4035)
☎ (0386) 831173
Hook Norton Bitter; M&B Brew XI; Uley Old Spot H
Famous old inn owned by the National Trust. No outside signs are allowed. Interior untouched for many years; inglenook and antiques. Darts
🏠 ⊛ ( ) ⌂

Broadwas

11–2.30; 6–11

Royal Oak
On A44
Marston Border Mild, Burton Bitter, Pedigree H
Welcoming wayside tavern with fine views ⊛ ( ) ⏣

Broadway

10–2.30; 6–11

Crown & Trumpet
Church Street ☎ (0386) 853202
Flowers IPA, Original H
Fine house built of local Cotswold stone. Pleasant atmosphere complemented by an excellent range of traditional pub games
🏠 ⌛ ⊛ ⌘ ( ) ⌂

Bromsgrove

10.30–2.30; 5.30–10.30 (11 F, S)

Red Lion
73 High Street ☎ (0527) 35387
Banks's Mild, Bitter E
Busy 1-roomed, town-centre pub – a mild drinker's retreat!
⊛ ( ) (not Sun) ≷

Try also: Boars Head, Charford, Bromsgrove (Banks's)

Bromyard

11.30–2.30; 6.30–11

Crown & Sceptre
7 Sherford Street
☎ (0885) 82441
Flowers IPA, Original; Wood Parish Bitter or Special H
Comfortable town-centre pub, popular with visitors and locals alike. Pub games
🏠 Q ⌛ ⊛ ⌘ ( ) ▲

Canon Pyon

11–2.30; 6 (7 winter)–11

Nag's Head
On A4110 ☎ (043 271) 252
Marston Pedigree; Wye Valley Hereford Bitter, Supreme G
Large rambling inn which once brewed its own beer. 3 distinct drinking areas. Hereford Bitter sold as Pyon Bitter. Pub games
🏠 ⌛ ⌘ ( ) &

Try also: Plough Inn (Free)

Catshill

10.30–2.30; 7–10.30 (11 F, S)

Plough & Harrow
419 Stourbridge Road
☎ (0527) 78088
Ansells Mild, Bitter H
Cosy and comfortable roadside inn with restaurant. Noted for its mild
🏠 ⊛ ( ) (Tue–Sat) ⏣ ⌂

Chaddesley Corbett

11–2.30; 6.30–10.30 (11 F, S)

Swan
High Street ☎ (056 283) 302
Batham Mild E, Bitter H, Delph Strong Ale (Xmas) H
Country village local with bowling green and garden; children's room and dining room 🏠 Q ⌛ ⊛ ( ) ⏣ ⌂

Try also: Robin Hood (Ansells)

Claines

11–2.30; 6–11

Mug House
The Churchyard (off A449)
Banks's Mild, Bitter E
Ancient pub, virtually in the churchyard Q ⊛ ⏣

Clifton on Teme

11–2.30; 7–11

Lion
Batham Bitter; Flowers IPA; Hook Norton Bitter H
Busy, old village local with pleasant garden and interesting fireplaces. Good restaurant 🏠 Q ⊛ ( ) ⏣ ⏣

11–2.30; 7–11

New Inn
☎ (088 65) 226

Banks's Bitter H
Very old pub. One of few Banks's houses selling ale through handpump 🏠 ⊛ ( ) ⏣

Colwall

12–2.30; 6–11

Chase Inn
Chase Road, Upper Colwall (400 yds off Wyche Road)
☎ (0684) 40276
Donnington BB, SBA; Wye Valley Supreme H
Straightforward pub tucked away in backwater on slopes of the Malverns. "No children, no fruit machines" policy
Q ⊛ ( ) (until 8.30) ≷

Conderton

11–2.30; 7–11

Yew Tree
OS965372
Marston Burton Bitter, Pedigree H
Modernised and much altered old country pub with oak beams and flag floors. Off the beaten track 🏠 Q ⊛ ( ) ⌂

Cutnall Green

11–2.30; 6–11

New Inn
Cutnall Green (A442)
☎ (029) 923) 202
Marston Burton Bitter, Pedigree H
Popular country pub with oak beams and brasses ⊛ ⌘ ( )

Defford

11–2.30; 6.30–11

Defford Arms
On A4104
Davenports Bitter H
Roadside inn with through lounge. Cheerful atmosphere; pleasant garden ⌛ ( )

Eardisland

11–2.30; 6–11

White Swan
On A44 ☎ (054 47) 565
Marston Burton Bitter, Pedigree H
Large, comfortable lounge contrasts with small public bar in this pleasant village inn
🏠 ⊛ ( ) (not Tue) ⏣

Eardiston

12–2.30; 7–11

Nags Head
(A443, 1 mile W of village)
OS058470 ☎ (054 47) 234
Marston Burton Bitter, Pedigree H
Typical cosy country pub with large garden where the splendid smell of hops wafts from nearby fields Q ⊛ ( )

Elmley Castle

12–2.30; 6–11

140

Hereford & Worcester

Queen Elizabeth
Main Street ☎ (038 674) 209
Marston Burton Bitter, Pedigree H
16th-century hostelry, now village local of character. Busy weekends. Sign depicts visit of the Virgin Queen ▲⊛✿

Evesham

11–2.30; 6–11

Trumpet
Merstow Green ☎ (0386) 6227
Draught Bass; M&B Mild, Brew XI H
Town house near the main street, on the market square. Darts ⊛◐⇌

Feckenham

11–2.30; 6–11

Rose & Crown
High Street
Ansells Bitter H**; Banks's Mild** E**; Tetley Bitter** H
Welcoming village pub with high-backed settles in lounge ▲⊛◐✿

Fladbury

10–2.30; 6–11

Chequers
Chequers Lane (off village green) ☎ (0386) 860276
Banks's Bitter H
Friendly comfortable pub serving good food. Interesting aviary ▲☞⊛◐

Try also: Anchor

Fownhope

10.30–2.30; 6–11

Green Man Inn
On B4224 ☎ (043 277) 243
Hook Norton Best Bitter; Marston Pedigree; Samuel Smith OBB H
Historic roadside inn with 3 distinct drinking areas
▲Q☞⊛┅◐▶ (until 10)

Grimley

11–2.30; 6–11

Camp House Inn
Camp Lane
Flowers IPA, Original H**; Whitbread WCPA** H
Unspoilt riverside inn with spacious garden and home cooking ▲Q☞⊛◐▶✿A

Hagley

12–2.30; 6–10.30 (11 F, S)

Spencer Arms
Kidderminster Road (A456)
Banks's Mild, Bitter E
Pleasant, modern roadside hostelry offering a varied lunch menu Mon–Sat. Piano in small lounge is sometimes played ⊛◐✿

Hallow

11–2.30; 6–11

Crown Inn
Tenbury Road
☎ (0905) 640408
Younger Scotch, IPA H
Large pub with popular carvery restaurant ▲⊛◐▶✿

Hanley Castle

11–2.30; 6–11

Three Kings
Off B4211 ☎ (068 46) 2686
Butcombe Bitter; Theakston Best Bitter; Wadworth 6X H
Classic village pub. Small, cosy and friendly. Tiny parlour with old cooking range; adjoining cottage forms the lounge ▲Q☞⊛◐

Hardwicke

10.30–2.30; 6–11

Royal Oak
On B4348, 2 miles E of Hay
☎ (049 73) 248
Fuller ESB; Marston Pedigree H
Friendly village inn with unusual furnishings in lounge. Vegetarian meals. Pub games
▲Q☞⊛┅◐▶ (until 10) ✿

Headless Cross

12–2.30; 6–11

Gate Hangs Well
Evesham Road
☎ (0527) 401293
Ansells Mild, Bitter H
Large lounge-only pub with a lively atmosphere and convenient location ▲Q⊛◐

11–2.30; 5.30–11

Seven Stars
75 Birchfield Road
☎ (0527) 402138
Ruddles Best Bitter, County; Webster Yorkshire Bitter H
Locals' pub with games room and superb loos! ◐✿

Hereford

10.30–2.30; 6–11

Barrells Bar (Lamb Hotel)
69 St Owen's Street
☎ (0432) 274968
Wye Valley Hereford Bitter, Supreme, Brew 69 H
Lively and noisy, 2-bar local on edge of city centre. Beers brewed on the premises. Pub games ⊛◐⇌✿

11–3.00 (11 M–F); 6–11

Booth Hall Hotel
Hightown (entrance in precinct passageway)
Flowers IPA, Original H
Old city-centre hotel with 2 contrasting bars: real ale in 50s-style, right-hand bar. Monthly live jazz upstairs. Guest beers ⊛┅◐☆⇌

11–2.30; 6–11

Cock of Tupsley
Ledbury Road (A438, 2 miles E of centre) ☎ (0432) 274911
Banks's Mild, Bitter E
Large modern pub with a basic public bar and "pseudo-rustic" lounge. Pub games ⊛◐

11–2.30; 6–11

Saracen's Head Inn
1–5 St Martins Street
☎ (0432) 275480
Courage Directors; Marston Pedigree; Wye Valley Hereford Bitter H
Lively riverside inn. Former public bar has become a restaurant but lounge has unchanging atmosphere. Pub games ☞⊛◐▶⇌✿

Try also: Castle Pool Hotel (Free)

Himbleton

12–2.30; 6–11

Galton Arms
☎ (090 569) 672
Banks's Mild, Bitter E
Splendid village pub in very rural area Q☞⊛◐▶✿

Holy Cross

11–2.30; 6–10.30 (11 F, S)

Bell & Cross
Belbroughton Road, Clent
OS923788 ☎ (0527) 730319
M&B Mild, Brew XI H
Timeless pub with a warm welcome and 3 small, cosy rooms ▲Q⊛✿

Kerne Bridge

12–3; 6–11

Kerne Bridge Inn
On B4228 ☎ (0600) 890495
Draught Bass; Flowers Original; Whitbread Pompey Royal (summer) H
Simple roadside pub overlooking River Wye. Pub games ☞⊛◐▶✿A (1 mile)

Kidderminster

11–2.30; 6–10.30 (11 F, S)

Blue Bell
Hurcott Road (near Horsefair)
☎ (0562) 68009
Banks's Mild, Bitter
Comfortable oak-panelled lounge. Winner of a best-kept garden award. Good food Q⊛◐▶✿

11–2.30; 7–10.30 (11 F, S)

Little Tumbling Sailors
Mill Lane (off ring road, A442)
Ansells Bitter; Ind Coope Burton Ale; Lumphammer H
Another hostelry of the Little Pub Company. Nautical theme complete with lighthouse and wave machine! Seafood pies a speciality Q☞⊛◐▶

11–2.30; 7–10.30 (11 F, S)

141

Hereford & Worcester

Railway Train
Offmore Road (off A448)
☎ (0562) 740465
M&B Highgate Mild, Brew XI E
Peaceful local with cosy snug and friendly bar; alongside the railway Q ❀ ◖ ◗ ≠ (Town)

11–2.30; 6–10.30 (11 F, S)

Yew Tree
Chester Road North
☎ (0562) 751786
Banks's Mild, Bitter E
Lively local where visitors are treated as friends. Opposite Rose Theatre ◖ ◗ ⊟

Try also: King & Castle, Comberton Hill (Free)

Kingsland

12–2.30; 7 (6.30 summer)–11

Angel Inn
On B4360 ☎ (056 881) 355
Banks's Bitter E
Beautiful 16th-century black and white free house with oak beamed restaurant – good food (including vegetarian meals)
⌂ Q ♨ ❀ ◖ ◗ & ♿ (400 yds)

Kington

11–2.30 (not Mon–Fri); 7.30–11

Olde Tavern
Victoria Road (off A44)
Ansells Bitter H
Rare survival of a traditional urban pub. A warm welcome to strangers ensured! Pub games Q ♨ ⊟ ♿

11–2.30; 5.30–11 (open all day Tue & Thu)

Royal Oak
Church Street ☎ (0544) 230484
Marston Burton Bitter, Pedigree H
First and last pub in England. Bright and lively public bar contrasts with quieter lounge and restaurant. Games ♨ ❀ ⟋ ◖ ◗ (until 9) ⊟ ♿

Try also: Lamb Inn (Bass)

Ledbury

11–2.30; 7–11

Brewery Inn
Bye Street ☎ (0531) 4272
Marston Border Mild, Bitter H
Excellent town pub which predates the age of plastic. Probably the smallest bar in the country. Pub games
⌂ Q ♨ ❀ ◖ & ≠ ⟋

Try also: Seven Stars (Whitbread)

Leigh Sinton

11–2.30; 6–11

Somers Arms
On A4103 ☎ (0886) 32343
Banks's Mild, Bitter; Holdens Black Country Bitter; Hook Norton Bitter, Old Hookey; Wadworth 6X H
Busy village hostelry with traditional pub games. Jazz Tue; folk Fri. Guest beers ❀ ◖ ◗

Leintwardine

10.30–2.30; 6–11

Sun Inn
Rosemary Lane (off A4113)
Ansells Mild, Bitter G
Small converted house caught in a time-warp: beer fetched from living-quarters in a jug
⌂ Q ⊟

Leominster

10.30–2.30 (4.30 Fri); 6–11

Grape Vaults
Broad Street ☎ (0568) 611404
Marston Burton Bitter, Pedigree, Merrie Monk H
Superbly restored town pub, combining comfort with respect for tradition
⌂ ◖ ◗ (until 9) & ≠

10–2.30 (4.30 Fri); 6–11

Three Horseshoes
Corn Square ☎ (0568) 3019
Flowers IPA, Original H
Lively and friendly market pub popular with the young at weekends. Weaker beers are poor value. Guest beers. Pub games ◖ ⊟ ≠

Try also: Black Horse (Free)

Longdon

11–2.30; 7–11

Plough Inn
On B4211 ☎ (068 481) 324
Ansells Bitter; Hook Norton Bitter; Wadworth 6X H
Popular pub full of bric-a-brac. Games include a skittle alley. Gas mask collection. "Not so much a pub; more a way of life"! ⌂ ♨ ❀ ◖ ◗ ⊟

Try also: Drum & Monkey, B4211

Menith Wood

11–2.30; 7–11

Cross Keys
Between A443 and B4202 OS709690
Banks's Mild E; **Marston Burton Bitter, Pedigree** H
Isolated country pub in quiet surroundings, still manages to be busy – well worth seeking out! Guest beers ❀ ◖ ◗

Much Dewchurch

11–2.30; 6–11

Black Swan
On B4348 ☎ (0981) 540295
Buckleys Bitter; Flowers Original; Whitbread WCPA H
Friendly village pub with unusual internal layout and furnishings. Supper licence. Beer range may vary. Pub games
⌂ ♨ ❀ ◖ ◗ ⊟ & ♿ (1 mile)

Norton

10.30–2.30; 7–11

Norton Grange
A435/A439, 3 miles N of Evesham ☎ (0386) 870215
Marston Burton Bitter, Pedigree H
Small family-run hotel
⌂ ♨ ⟋ ◖ ♿

Ombersley

11–2.30; 6–11

Cross Keys
Main Road
Batham Bitter; Marston Border Mild, Burton Bitter, Pedigree H
Comfortable, cosy lounge; separate pool room with jukebox. Guest beers
⌂ ♨ ◖ ◗ & ♿ ⟋

Pembridge

11–2.30; 6–11

New Inn Hotel
On A44 ☎ (054 47) 427
Flowers IPA, Original H
Imposing 14th-century black and white inn with wooden settles in public bar. Food including a vegetarian dish. Guest beers
⌂ Q ♨ ❀ ◖ (patio) ⟋ ◖ ⊟

Pensax

11–2.30; 6–11

Bell
On B4202 ☎ (029 921) 677
Hook Norton Best Bitter; Taylor Landlord; Wadworth 6X; Wood Parish Bitter H
Extended village pub with parlour bar. Noted for its extensive menu of beers and food – worth searching for!
⌂ Q ♨ ◖ ◗

Romsley

11–2.30; 5.30–10.30 (11 F, S)

Manchester Inn
Bromsgrove Road
☎ (0562) 710242
M&B Highgate Mild, Springfield Bitter, Brew XI E
Popular roadside pub with small homely bar and larger comfortable lounge. Good summer pub with large garden. Next to North Worcestershire Path
Q ♨ ◖ ◗ ⊟

St Margarets

10.30–2.30; 6 (7 winter)–11

Sun Inn
St Margarets (signposted off Vowchurch–Michaelchurch road) OS354337
☎ (098 123) 223
Marston Pedigree (summer); **Wadworth 6X** (summer); **Uley**

142

Hereford & Worcester

Old Spot (winter) H or G
Unspoilt rural pub with 2 small rooms. Devil-amongst-the-tailors in lounge. Garden offers outstanding views. Guest beers ♿Q☺⊛🕿()🍴🅰

St Owens Cross

11–2.30; 6.30 (7 winter)–11
New Inn
A4137/B4521
Draught Bass; Courage Directors; Theakston Best Bitter H
Former coaching inn with comfortable lounge bar, beams and open fire. Large, more basic public bar. Pub games ♿⊛🕿()🍴🅰☺

Shenstone

10–2.30; 7–10.30 (11 F, S)
Plough
Off A450 OS863735
☎ (056 283) 340
Batham Bitter, Delph Strong Ale H
Superb, classic, country village inn. Large drinker's bar and 2 small snugs. Difficult to find but worth the effort ♿Q⊛()🍴🕿

Spetchley

11–2.30; 6–11
Berkley Knot
On B4084 ☎ (090 565) 654
Draught Bass; M&B Springfield Bitter H
Large lounge very popular with diners. (Slightly spartan modernisation) ☺⊛()

Stoke Works

11–2.30; 5.30–10.30 (11 F, S)
Boat & Railway
Shaw Lane ☎ (0527) 31065
Banks's Bitter; Hansons Mild E
Busy canalside village local. Welcome watering hole at the bottom of the infamous Tardebigge flight. Skittle room with bar for hire ♿⊛()🍴

Stourport

11–2.30; 6–10.30 (11 F, S)
Bell Inn
Lion Hill ☎ (029 93) 2483
Banks's Bitter; Hansons Mild E
Friendly and lively local a short stroll from pleasant riverside and canal walks ⊛()🍴

11–2.30; 5.30–10.30 (11 F, S)
Rock Tavern
Wilden Lane (off Hartlebury Road) ☎ (029 93) 2962
Banks's Mild, Bitter E; **Batham Bitter** H
Pleasant 1-roomed beamed local. Pub games

Suckley

11–2.30; 6–11
Cross Keys
OS715532
Marston Border Mild, Burton Bitter H
Basic rural local with pub games 🍴

Upper Sapey

12–2.30; 7–11
Baiting House
On B4203 ☎ (088 67) 201
Banks's Bitter; Hook Norton Best Bitter H
Cosy 2-bar village local with restaurant. Usually fairly quiet but can be busy in tourist season. Guest beers ♿☺⊛()🍴🅰 (pub grounds)

Wadborough

11–30–2.30; 7–11
Masons Arms
OS900478
Banks's Mild, Bitter E
Well-kept village pub. Only one for miles with public bar ⊛()🍴

West Malvern

10.30–2.30;; 6–11
Brewers Arms
West Malvern Road
Marston Burton Bitter, Pedigree, Merrie Monk (winter) H
Small rural pub with homely atmosphere. ½ mile from Worcestershire Beacon on Malverns. Folk evenings Q⊛()🍴🅰

Try also: Lamb Inn

Whitney-on-Wye

12–2.30; 6–11
Rhydspence Inn
Just off A438 ☎ (049 73) 262
Robinson Best Bitter; Wem Best Bitter H
Ancient drovers' inn with much period charm. The Welsh border runs through the garden! Excellent bar food includes a vegetarian dish. Pub games ♿Q☺ (lunch) ⊛🍽()🍴☺

Winforton

11–2.30; 6–11
Sun Inn
On A438 ☎ (054 46) 677
Wadworth 6X H
Sympathetically modernised village inn, still catering for the local trade. No food winter Tue ♿Q☺⊛()🍴

Woolhope

11.30–2.30 (not Mon); 7–11
Crown Inn
☎ (043 277) 468
Hook Norton Bitter; Smiles Best Bitter H
Quiet village pub, popular with locals. Pub games ♿☺⊛()🍴

Try also: Butcher's Arms (Free)

Worcester

11–2.30; 5.30–11
Bricklayers Arms
Park Street
Banks's Mild, Bitter E
Traditional 1-bar, back street friendly local 🍴🚉 (Shrub Hill)

10.30–2.30; 5.30–11
Dragon
The Tything
Draught Bass; Hook Norton Best Bitter; M&B Highgate Mild H
Quiet pub, recently refurbished Q☺⊛()🍴🚉 (Foregate St)

10.30–2.30; 5.30–11
Farriers Arms
9 Fish Street ☎ (0905) 27569
Courage Best Bitter, Directors H
Very busy old-world pub with traditional smoke room. Excellent home cooking ⊛()🍴🚉 (Foregate St)

11–2.30; 6–11
Herefordshire House
Bransford Road, St Johns
☎ (0905) 421585
M&B Mild, Brew XI H
Lively cheerful local ⊛()

10.30–2.30; 5.30–11
Jolly Roger Brewery & Tap
50 Lowesmoor
Jolly Roger Quaff Ale, Severn Bore Special, Old Lowesmoor H, **Winter Wobbler** G
Lively old English tavern. Frequent bands and folk groups. Tap to Worcester's only brewery ♿☺()🍴🚉 (Shrub Hill) ☺

10.30–2.30; 6–11
Lamb & Flag
30 The Tything (A38)
☎ (0905) 26894
Marston Burton Bitter, Pedigree H
Lively city hostelry with a superb atmosphere ⊛()🍴

11.30–2.30; 5.30–11 (7–11 Sat)
Mount Pleasant
London Road ☎ (0905) 351232
Flowers IPA, Original H
Superior roadside pub with 2 bars and imaginative use of space. Busy lunchtimes ♿()🚉 (Shrub Hill)

11–2.30; 6–11
Vine
Ombersley Road
☎ (0905) 56158
Davenports Mild, Bitter H
Well-run friendly pub ☺ (lunch) ⊛()🍴

143

Hertfordshire

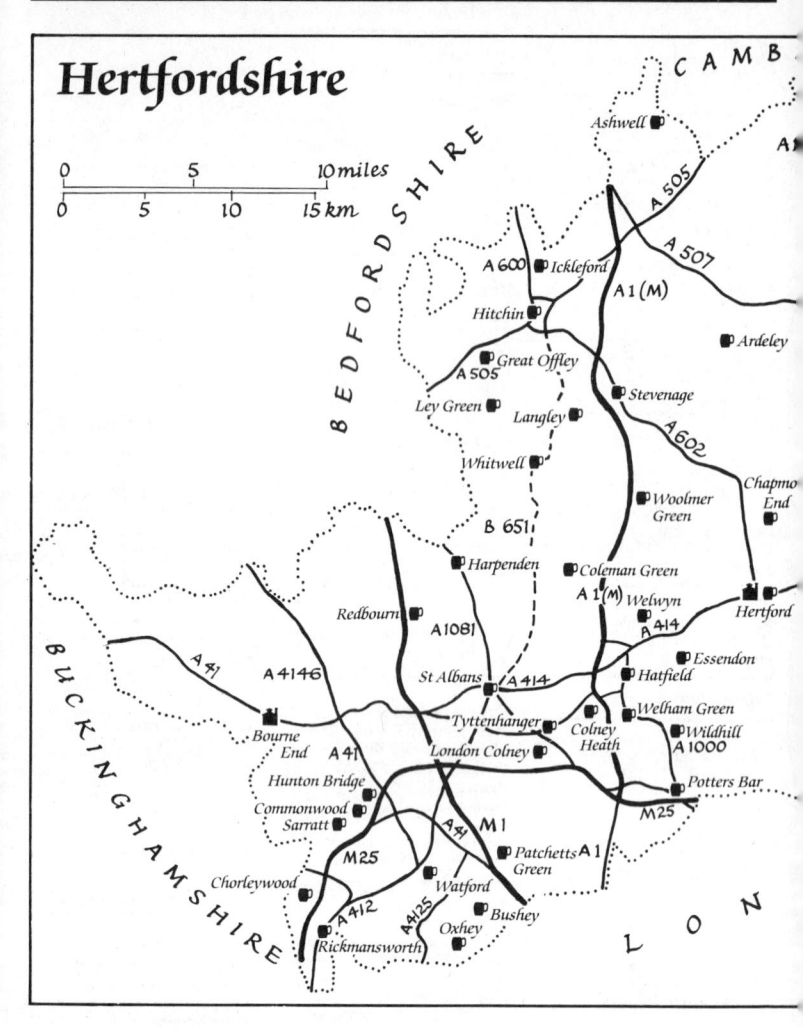

Berkhamsted, Bourne End; **McMullen**, Hertford

Ardeley

11.30–2.30; 6.30–11
Jolly Waggoner
Off B1037, 1 mile from village
OS310272 ☎ (043 886) 350
Greene King XX Mild, IPA, Abbot 🅖
Picturesque pink-washed former cottages in charming setting. 2 small intimate bars. Games
⌂⊛🍺🍽

Ashwell

10.30–2.30; 6–11
Rose & Crown
69 High Street
☎ (046 274) 2420
Greene King IPA, Abbot 🅗
Unspoilt late 15th-century timber-framed village pub
⌂Q⊛🍺

Barkway

10.30–2.30; 6–11
Chaise & Pair
High Street (B1368)
Adnams Bitter; Ringwood Best Bitter 🅗
Smart, comfortable pub
⌂⊛🍺

Barley

11–2.30; 6.30 (7 winter)–11
Fox & Hounds
High Street (B1368)
☎ (076 384) 459
Barley Nathaniels Special; Bateman XB; Courage Directors; Flowers IPA 🅗
Rare gallows sign spans road by 17th-century building now much extended. An early member of home-brew pub revival. Ale selection constantly varies ⌂⊛🍺🍽

Bishops Stortford

11–2.30; 6–11
Fox
Rye Street (B184) OS488222
Mauldon Fox Bitter; Greene King Rayment BBA; Courage Best Bitter 🅗
Small 3-bar pub ⌂Q⊛🍽🚆

Braughing

10.30–2.30; 5.30–11
Axe & Compasses
28 The Street (off B1368)
☎ (0920) 821610
Flowers IPA, Strong Country

Hertfordshire

Ale selection varies ⚏⚇🍺🍴

Bushey

11–3; 5.30–11

Swan
25 Park Road
Benskins Best Bitter; Ind Coope Burton Ale H
Small, public bar only. A survivor from a less flamboyant age. Games ⚏Q🍴

Chapmore End

12–2.30; 6–11

Woodman
Near B158 OS328163
☎ (0920) 3143
Greene King IPA; Abbot G
Pleasant cottage-style pub with a warm welcome; good conversation. Nice outside play area for children
⚏Q🍴⚇🍴

Chorleywood

11–3; 5.30–11

Old Shepherd
Chorleywood Bottom
OS029958 ☎ (092 78) 2740
Benskins Best Bitter; Ind Coope Burton Ale H
Small and friendly, set in a peaceful corner of Chorleywood Common. Darts and dominoes
🍴⚇🍺 (not Wed) ≠ ⊖

Coleman Green

11–2.30 (3 Sat); 6–11

John Bunyan
1 mile off B6129, near Wheathampstead OS189128
☎ (058 283) 2037
McMullen AK Mild, Country Bitter H
Isolated pub with a big welcome. Trivia debates can delay the traveller. Good, cheap fast food. Garden play area. Bunyan stayed nearby after release from Bedford jail
⚏Q🍴⚇🍺

Colney Heath

11–3; 5.30–11

Crooked Billet
88 High Street ☎ (0727) 22128
Adnams Bitter; Fullers ESB; Greene King Abbot; Wethered Bitter H
Old cottage-style pub Sidelines include book swaps, milk on draught and exotic cigarettes. Tue night folk music. Mini-zoo for children, and covered patio. Bikers welcome. Guest beers
🍴⚇🍺⚇&A⚲

Commonwood

11–3; 5.30–11

Cart & Horses
Quickmoor Lane OS047005
☎ (092 77) 63763
Benskins Best Bitter; Tetley Bitter H
Popular country pub. Cosy atmosphere, large garden plus hitch rail for horses
⚏🍴⚇🍺&

Essendon

11–2.30; 6–11

Rose & Crown
22 High Road (B158)
☎ (070 72) 61229
Benskins Bitter; Ind Coope Burton Ale H
2-bar Victorian local with a warm welcome in the public bar. Garden play area for children ⚏Q🍴⚇🍺&

Furneux Pelham

11–2.30; 6–11

Star
The Causeway (off main road through village)
☎ (027 978) 227
Greene King IPA, Rayment BBA, Abbot H
Friendly welcome in one of oldest buildings in picturesque village. No food Sun ⚏Q⚇🍺

Try also: Black Horse, Brent Pelham

Great Offley

10.30–2.30; 6–10.30 (11 F, S)

Green Man
The Green (off A505)
☎ (046 276) 256
Flowers IPA; Greene King IPA; Ruddles County; Webster's Yorkshire Bitter; Wethered Bitter; Whitbread Castle Eden Ale H
Big village pub with restaurant, always busy. Fine view over Hitchin ⚏Q🍴🍺

Harpenden

11–2.30; 5.30–11

Silver Cup
St Albans Road (A1081)
☎ (058 27) 3095/64694
Wells Eagle Bitter, Bombardier H
Old pub named after former local horse race. Plush saloon with a good fire; basic public with darts; outside tables overlooking common
⚏ (saloon) ⚇🍺⚇≠

Hatfield

10.30–2.30; 5.30–10.30

Wrestlers
89 Great North Road
☎ (070 72) 62116
Benskins Bitter; Ind Coope Burton Ale H
Landlord champion mastercellarman. Picturesque garden ⚏Q🍴⚇🍺&≠

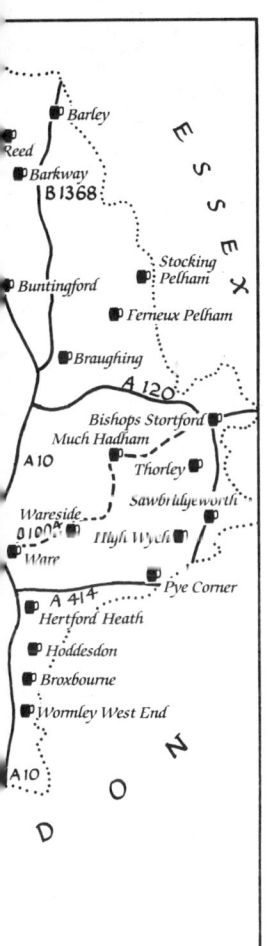

Bitter; Wethered Bitter H
Village pub with cricket field behind. Excellent food
⚏⚇🍺⚇

Broxbourne

11–2.30; 5–11

Anne of Cleves
95 High Road (A1010)
☎ (0992) 462053
Adnams Bitter; Greene King Rayments BBA, Abbot H
Lively and popular. Music Thu and Sat 🍺 (not Sun) ♦ ≠

Buntingford

11–2.30 (4 Mon); 5.30 (7 Sat)–11

Crown
High Street ☎ (0763) 71422
Adnams Bitter; Draught Bass; Greene King IPA H
Excellent small free house in quiet centre of recently by-passed town. No keg beers.

Hertfordshire

Hertford

10.30–2.30; 5.30–11
Duncombe Arms
24 Railway Street
☎ (0992) 581445
Greene King KK, IPA, Abbot Ⓔ
Drab exterior hides a well-run pub with 2 contrasting bars. Good value lunches. Bar billiards
🍺 🍴 (Mon–Sat) 🚭♿ ≠ (East)

10.30–2.30; 5.30–11
Great Eastern Tavern
29 Railway Place
☎ (0992) 583570
McMullens AK Best Mild, Country Bitter Ⓗ
Well renovated local. Beautifully-tended window boxes and hanging baskets
♿🍺 🍴 🚭≠ (East)

11.30–2.30; 5.45–11
Sportsman
117 Fore Street
☎ (0992) 551621
Greene King Rayments BBA, Abbot; Samuel Smith OBB; John Smith Yorkshire Bitter; Young Special; Adnams Bitter Ⓗ
Comfortable pub with good food. Once known as Blue Coat Boy after neighbouring school. Once the brewery tap of Youngs of Hertford. No pub games! 🐕 🍴 🍽 ≠ (East)

12–2.30; 5.30–11
White Horse
33 Castle Street
☎ (0992) 550127
Greene King IPA; Marston Pedigree; Mauldon Special Ⓗ
Tiny free house with warm welcome. Always 5 or more beers ♿🍺 🍴 (Mon–Fri) 🚭👶

Hertford Heath

11.30–2.30; 5.30–11
Townshend Arms
21 London Road
☎ (0992) 582241
Benskins Best Bitter Ⓗ**, Ind Coope Burton Ale** Ⓖ
Welcoming, comfortable pub – try the Burton 'from the wood.' Games 🍺 🍴🚭

Try also: East India College Arms

High Wych

10.30–2.30; 5.30–11
Rising Sun
High Wych Road (1 mile W of A1184) ☎ (0279) 726300
Courage Best Bitter, Directors Ⓖ
Very small basic and friendly village pub still known as Syd's even though Syd retired in 1987. In Good Beer Guide since 1975 ♿Q🚭

Hitchin

10.30–2.30; 6–10.30
Coopers Arms
Tilehouse Street (near priory)
☎ (0462) 59497
McMullen AK Mild, Country Bitter Ⓗ
Recently refurbished pub – now 1 large comfortable bar with plenty of beams. Near town centre but hard to find
Q🍴🍽

11–2.30; 6–10.30 (11 F, S)
Cricketers
Bedford Road (A600)
☎ (0462) 32116
Ind Coope Burton Ale; Benskins Best Bitter; Tetley Bitter Ⓗ
Pleasant 2 bar local, good for games. Once used as the changing rooms for Hitchin Town football club (nearby)
♿🚭

10.30–2.30; 5.30–11
Windmill
Charlton Lane, Charlton (off Priory bypass) ☎ (0462) 32096
Wells Eagle Bitter, Bombardier Ⓗ
Riverside setting. Small public bar and larger saloon. Venue for the annual duck race up the Hiz Q🍺 🍴🚭

Hoddesdon

11–2.30; 5.30–11
Rose & Crown
90 Amwell Street (A1170)
☎ (0992) 462553
Flowers IPA, Original; Wethered Bitter Ⓗ
Popular pub, just out of town centre. Pub sign beam still says Fordhams. Games ♿🍴🚭

11–2.30; 5–11
Salisbury Arms
High Street ☎ (0992) 462924
Benskins Best Bitter; Ind Coope Burton Ale; Tetley Bitter Ⓗ
Excellent town pub, pleasant and friendly. Good food at all times 🐕🏨🍴🍽🚭

Hunton Bridge

11–3; 6–11
Kings Head
Bridge Road (off A41 at Langleybury) OS082006
Benskins Best Bitter; Tetley Bitter Ⓗ
Pleasantly modernised old pub with a large garden. Old stable converted to children's room ♿🐕🍺 🍴🍽

Ickleford

11–2.30; 6–11
Cricketers
107 Arlesey Road (off A600)
☎ (0462) 32629
Adnams Bitter; Banks & Taylor SOS, SOD; Everards Tiger; Marston Pedigree; Samuel Smith OBB Ⓗ
Lively village alehouse. Warm and comfortable. Games
♿🐕🍺🏨 🍴 (not Sun)

Langley

11.30–2.30; 6 (7 Sat)–11
Farmers Boy
Off B656 ☎ (0438) 820436
Greene King IPA, Abbot Ⓗ
Warm and friendly country pub in quiet cul-de-sac. Listed building. Frequented by shooting enthusiasts. No food Sun 🍺 🍴🍽 🚭♿

Ley Green

11–2.30; 6–11
Plough
Plough Lane, Kings Walden (off Minor Road from Gt Offley) OS162243
☎ (043 887) 394
Greene King IPA, Abbot Ⓗ
Classic rural cottage local set in rolling countryside. Small and friendly yet in earshot of Luton Airport. No food Sun. Games 🍺 🍴🍽 🚭

London Colney

11–2.30 (3 F, S); 5.30–11
Bull
Barnet Road (½ mile from Jct 22 M25) ☎ (0727) 26364
Ind Coope Best Bitter, Burton Ale Ⓗ
Ancient, 2 roomed village pub. Comfortable lounge with huge open fire, busy public bar with accent on games
♿🍺 🍴 (not Sun) 🚭

Much Hadham

11–2.30; 6–11
Bull
High Street ☎ (027 984) 2668
Benskins Best Bitter; Ind Coope Burton Ale Ⓗ
Large old pub with family room, swings and zoo in garden. Good food. Darts
Q🍺 🍴🍽 🚭♿

Oxhey

11–3; 5.30–11
Haydon Arms
76 Upper Paddock Road
Benskins Best Bitter; Ind Coope Burton Ale Ⓗ
Thriving village-style pub with community atmosphere
🐕🍺 🍴 (not Sun)
🚭♿≠ (Bushey)

11.30–3; 6–11
Villiers Arms
108 Villiers Road
Benskins Best Bitter; Ind Coope Burton Ale; Tetley Bitter Ⓗ
Pleasant corner house;

Hertfordshire

landlord justifiably proud of his cellar. Games ⌂🍴🍺 (not Sun) ≠ (Bushey)

Patchetts Green

11–3; 5.30–11

Three Compasses
Hillfield Lane (near B462)
Benskins Best Bitter; Ind Coope Burton Ale; Tetley Bitter; Young IPA H
Deceptively large village pub with display of carpentry bric-a-brac ⌂🍴🍺 (till 9)

Potters Bar

10.30–3; 5.30–11

Artful Dodger
35 High Street
Draught Bass; Courage Directors; Younger IPA H
Converted shop – only free house in Potters Bar. Guest beers. Games 🍺🍴 &

10.30–3; 5.30–11

Chequers
Coopers Lane ☎ (0707) 56469
Courage Best Bitter, Directors H
Comfortable, recently renovated local. Exit from car park hazardous Q🍺🍴

Pye Corner

10.30–2.30; 6–11

Plume of Feathers
Old A414, 1 mile from Eastwick roundabout
☎ (0279) 24154
Courage Best Bitter, Directors H
Popular large pub on outskirts of Harlow. Occasional live music. Good bar food ⌂🍺🍴

Redbourn

11–2.30; 5.30–11

Cricketers
East Common
☎ (058 285) 2410
Benskins Best Bitter; Tetley Bitter H
Old pub facing the common. Comfortable saloon bar presided over by an African Grey parrot; lively and sporting public bar
🍺 (not Sun) 🍴 &

Reed

10.00–2.00; 5.00–11

Cabinet
High Street (off A10)
OS364361 ☎ (076 384) 366
Adnams Bitter; Bateman XB; Greene King IPA, Abbot; Tolly Cobbold XXXX G
Difficult to find, cosy weatherboarded building with large garden. Ale selection varies. Games ⌂🍺🍴 ⚘

Rickmansworth

11–3; 5.30–11

Halfway House
91 Uxbridge Road
☎ (0923) 772534
Courage Best Bitter, Directors; John Smith Bitter H
Long comfortable bar with garden fronting onto River Colne. No meals Sun. Games include shove ha'penny
⌂🍺🍴 & ⊖

St Albans

11–2.30 (3 S); 5.30–11

Farriers Arms
Lower Dagnall Street
McMullen AK Mild, Country Bitter H
No-nonsense drinking establishment and perennial entry in this guide Q 🍴⚘

11–2.30 (3 Sat); 5.30–11

Garibaldi
61 Albert Street (off Holywell Hill) ☎ (0727) 55046
Fuller Chiswick Bitter, London Pride, ESB H
Thriving side-street pub. Separate food area with good-value home-made food, including vegetarian meals. No chips!
🍺 🍴 (not Sun) ≠ (Abbey)

11.30–3; 5.30–11

Lower Red Lion
36 Fishpool Street
☎ (0727) 55669
Adnams Bitter; Fuller London Pride; Greene King IPA, Abbot; Young Special H
Unspoilt 2-bar pub in the conservation area. Atmosphere of its own – usually genteel and refined, but can get hectic in the evenings. Only genuine free house in town ⌂Q🍺⚘ (not Sun) 🍴 (Mon–Fri, 6–8)

11.30–2.30; 5.30–11

Rose & Crown
St Michaels Street (400 yds off A4147) ☎ (0727) 51903
Benskins Best Bitter; Ind Coope Burton Ale H
Very old pub with inglenook and oak beams. Darts. Near Verulam Park ⌂Q🍴⚘

11–2.30; 5.30–11

White Lion
91 Sopwell Lane (off Holywell Hill) ☎ (0727) 50540
Ind Coope Best Bitter, Burton Ale; Tetley Bitter H
Welcoming and unpretentious 2-roomed pub in conservation area. Large garden at rear with boules pitch
Q🍺🍴 (not Sun) ⚘≠

Sarratt

11–3; 5.30–11

Boot
The Green OS042996
☎ (092 77) 62247
Benskins Best Bitter; Ind Coope Burton Ale H
Popular village pub in nice setting by the green ⌂⌂🍺🍴&

11–3; 5.30–11

Cock
Church Lane OS040986
Benskins Best Bitter; Friary Meux Best H
Pleasant country pub opposite historic church ⌂Q⌂🍺🍴

Sawbridgeworth

10.30–2.30; 5.30–11

King William IV
8 Vantorts Road (off A1184)
☎ (0279) 722322
Courage Best Bitter, Directors H
Friendly and welcoming pub close to church at heart of original village Q⌂🍺🍴&≠

11–2.30; 5.00–11

White Lion Hotel
28 London Road (A1184)
☎ (0279) 726341
Greene King IPA, Rayments BBA, Abbot H
Well-run and deservedly popular. Formerly several small rooms; still retains the feel of separate areas. Good menu plus interesting daily specials
⌂Q⌂🍺🍴 (not Sun) ≠

Try also: Three Horseshoes, (McMullens)

Stevenage

11–2.30; 7–11

Two Diamonds
19 High Street, Old Town
☎ (0438) 354527
McMullen AK, Country Bitter H
Upholds all the traditional requirements of a good boozer. Pub games 🍺≠

Stocking Pelham

10.30–2.30; 6–11

Cock
Village centre ☎ (027 978) 217
Ind Coope Best Bitter, Burton Ale H
Idyllic thatched pub in very rural surroundings ⌂🍺&

Thorley

10.30–2.30; 5.30–11

Cellarman
Havers Lane (1 mile off A1184 SW of Bishops Stortford)
☎ (0279) 52802
Greene King BBA H
Spacious pub. Fine collection of vintage car pictures in lounge. Pub games Q⌂🍺⚘&

Hertfordshire

Tyttenhanger

11.30–2.30; 6–11

Plough
Tyttenhanger Green (off A414 via Highfield Lane) OS183059 ☎ (0727) 57777
Adnams Bitter; Brakspear Bitter; Fuller London Pride, ESB; McMullen Country Bitter; Wethered Bitter H
Popular free house on edge of open farmland, hosting a lively programme of social and sporting events. Varying range of real ales
🔥🍺 🕛 🍴 (not Sun) ♿

Ware

11.30–2.30; 5.30 (6.30 Sat)–11

Old Bulls Head
26 Baldock Street ☎ (0920) 2307
Benskins Best Bitter; Ind Coope Burton Ale; Tetley Bitter H
16th-century inn with some original timber and inglenook. Regulars keen on pub games, and charity fund-raising. Garden play area for children. Good food at reasonable prices 🔥👶🍺 🕛 🍴 (not Sun) ♿

10.30–2.30; 5.30–11

Spread Eagle
37 Amwell End ☎ (0920) 2784
McMullen AK Mild, Country Bitter H
Small local next to Ware level crossing. Now 1 bar in Mac's usual style, but nonetheless pleasant 🔥👶🍺 🕛 🚂

Wareside

10.30–2.30; 6–11

White Horse
On B1004 3 miles E of Ware ☎ (0920) 2582

Greene King Rayments BBA, Abbot H
Rural roadside pub
🔥Q👶🍺 🕛 🍴 🏛♿⛺ (phone)

Try also: Chequers

Watford

11–3; 5.30–11

Bedford Arms
26 Langley Road ☎ (0923) 226205
Benskins Best Bitter H
Small and cosy, well worth the 5 minute walk from the station. Darts
🔥 🕛 (Mon–Fri) 🚂

Welham Green

10.30–2.30; 5.30–11

Hope & Anchor
Station Road ☎ (070 72) 62939
Courage Best Bitter, Directors; John Smith Bitter H
Quiet, comfortable saloon and a lively public 🍺 🕛 🏛♿🚂

Welwyn

11–2.30; 5.30–10.30 (11 F, S)

Baron of Beef
11 Mill Lane (off B656) ☎ (043 871) 4739
McMullen AK Mild, Country Bitter H
True local with good atmosphere in historic coaching village. Hard to find
🔥 🕛🏛

11–2.30; 5.30 (7 Sat)–10.30 (11 F, S)

Rose & Crown
14 Church Street ☎ (043 871) 4190
Benskins Best Bitter; Tetley Bitter H
Fine 16th-century inn with old world charm. Van Gogh's sister slept here. Separate games and dining areas.

Lunches recommended; guest beers 🔥Q🍺 🕛 (not Sun) ♿

Whitwell

11.30–2.30; 6–11

Maidens Head
67 High Street (B651) OS185211 ☎ (043 887) 392
McMullen AK Mild, Country Bitter H
Attractive village local with lots of character. Landlord has a collection of keyrings and an insult for everyone. No food Sun 🔥👶🍺 🕛 🍴 (not Mon) 🏛

Wildhill

12–2.30; 5.30–11

Woodman
7 Wildhill Lane (between B158/A1000) OS263068 ☎ (0707) 42618
Greene King IPA, Abbot; McMullen AK Mild H
Village bar and snug in rural surroundings. A good value, no-nonsense pub. Games 🍺 🕛

Woolmer Green

11–2.30; 7–10.30 (11 F, S)

Fox
New Road (off B197) ☎ (0438) 813179
McMullen AK Mild, Country Bitter H
Cheerful 1-bar local, set off main road 🍺 🕛

Wormley West End

10.30–2.30; 5.30–11

Woodman
☎ (0992) 463719
McMullen AK Mild, Country Bitter H
Attractive pub on edge of Wormley woods
🔥Q🍺 🕛 🍴 🏛♿

KEY TO SYMBOLS

Facilities

- 🔥 real fire
- Q quiet pub – no electronic music, TV or obtrusive games
- 👶 indoor room for children
- 🍺 garden or other outdoor drinking area
- 🛏 accommodation
- 🕛 lunchtime meals
- 🍴 evening meals
- 🏛 public bar
- ♿ facilities for the disabled
- ⛺ camping facilities close to the pub or part of the pub grounds
- 🚂 near British Rail station
- ⊖ near Underground station
- ⚪ real cider

The facilities, beers and pub hours listed in the Good Beer Guide are liable to change but were correct when the Guide went to press.

Help keep real ale alive by joining CAMRA. Your voice helps encourage brewers big and small to brew cask beer and offer all beer drinkers a better choice.

Hertfordshire

landlord justifiably proud of his cellar. Games ☎🍴♣ (not Sun) ≠ (Bushey)

Patchetts Green

11–3; 5.30–11

Three Compasses
Hillfield Lane (near B462)
Benskins Best Bitter; Ind Coope Burton Ale; Tetley Bitter; Young Bitter H
Deceptively large village pub with display of carpentry bric-a-brac ☎🍴♣ (till 9)

Potters Bar

10.30–3; 5.30–11

Artful Dodger
35 High Street
Draught Bass; Courage Directors; Younger IPA H
Converted shop – only free house in Potters Bar. Guest beers. Games ♣♠♦

10.30–3; 5.30–11

Chequers
Coopers Lane ☎ (0707) 56469
Courage Best Bitter, Directors H
Comfortable, recently renovated local. Exit from car park hazardous Q♣♠

Pye Corner

10.30–2.30; 6–11

Plume of Feathers
Old A414, 1 mile from Eastwick roundabout
☎ (0279) 24154
Courage Best Bitter, Directors H
Popular large pub on outskirts of Harlow. Occasional live music. Good bar food ♠♣♦♪

Redbourn

11–2.30; 5.30–11

Cricketers
East Common
☎ (058 285) 2410
Benskins Best Bitter; Tetley Bitter H
Old pub facing the common. Comfortable saloon bar presided over by an African Grey parrot; lively and sporting public bar
♣ (not Sun) ♦♠

Reed

10.30–2.30; 5.30–11

Cabinet
High Street (off A10) OS364361 ☎ (076 384) 366
Adnams Bitter; Bateman XB; Greene King IPA, Abbot; Tolly Cobbold XXXX G
Difficult to find, very weatherboarded building with large garden. Ale selection varies. Games ♠♣♦♪

Rickmansworth

11–3; 5.30–11

Halfway House
91 Uxbridge Road
☎ (0923) 772534
Courage Best Bitter, Directors; John Smith Bitter H
Long comfortable bar with garden fronting onto River Colne. No meals Sun. Games include shove ha'penny
♠♣♦♠♪⊖

St Albans

11–2.30 (3 S); 5.30–11

Farriers Arms
Lower Dagnall Street
McMullen AK Mild, Country Bitter H
No-nonsense drinking establishment and perennial entry in this guide Q♣♦

11–2.30 (3 Sat); 5.30–11

Garibaldi
61 Albert Street (off Holywell Hill) ☎ (0727) 55046
Fuller Chiswick Bitter, London Pride, ESB H
Thriving side-street pub. Separate food area with good-value home-made food, including vegetarian meals. No chips!
♣♣♠ (not Sun) ≠ (Abbey)

11.30–3; 5.30–11

Lower Red Lion
36 Fishpool Street
☎ (0727) 55669
Adnams Bitter; Fuller London Pride; Greene King IPA, Abbot; Young Special H
Unspoilt 2-bar pub in the conservation area. Atmosphere of its own usually genteel and refined, but can get hectic in the evenings. Only genuine free house in the town ♠Q♣♠ (not Sun) ♠ (Mon–Fri, 6–8)

11.30–2.30; 5.30–11

Rose & Crown
St Michaels Street (400 yds off A4147) ☎ (0727) 51903
Benskins Best Bitter; Ind Coope Burton Ale H
Very old pub with inglenook and oak beams. Darts. Near Verulam Park ♠♣♠⊖

11–2.30; 5.30–11

White Lion
91 Sopwell Lane (off Holywell Hill) ☎ (0727) 50540
Ind Coope Best Bitter, Burton Ale; Tetley Bitter H
Welcoming and unpretentious 2-roomed pub in conservation area. Large garden at rear with boules pitch
Q♣♣ (not Sun) ♠≠

Sarratt

11–3; 5.30–11

Boot
The Green OS042996
☎ (092 77) 62247
Benskins Best Bitter; Ind Coope Burton Ale H
Popular village pub in nice setting by the green ♠♣♣♠♦

11–3; 5.30–11

Cock
Church Lane OS040986
Benskins Best Bitter; Friary Meux Best H
Pleasant country pub opposite historic church ♠Q♣♣♣♠

Sawbridgeworth

10.30–2.30; 5.30–11

King William IV
8 Vantorts Road (off A1184)
☎ (0279) 722322
Courage Best Bitter, Directors H
Friendly and welcoming pub close to church at heart of original village Q♣♣♠♦≠

11–2.30; 5.30–11

White Lion Hotel
28 London Road (A1184)
☎ (0279) 726341
Greene King IPA, Rayments BBA, Abbot H
Well-run and deservedly popular. Formerly several small rooms; still retains the feel of separate areas. Good menu plus interesting daily specials
♠Q♣♣♣ (not Sun) ≠

Try also: Three Horseshoes, (McMullens)

Stevenage

11–2.30; 7–11

Two Diamonds
19 High Street, Old Town
☎ (0438) 354527
McMullen AK, Country Bitter H
Upholds all the traditional requirements of a good boozer. Pub games ♣≠

Stocking Pelham

10.30–2.30; 6–11

Cock
Village centre ☎ (027 978) 217
Ind Coope Best Bitter, Burton Ale H
Idyllic thatched pub in very rural surroundings ♠♣♦

Thorley

10.30–2.30; 5.30–11

Cellarman
Havers Lane (1 mile off A1184 SW of Bishops Stortford)
☎ (0279) 52802
Greene King BBA H
Spacious pub. Fine collection of vintage car pictures in lounge. Pub games Q♣♣♣♠♦

Hertfordshire

Tyttenhanger

11.30–2.30; 6–11
Plough
Tyttenhanger Green (off A414 via Highfield Lane) OS183059 ☎ (0727) 57777
Adnams Bitter; Brakspear Bitter; Fuller London Pride, ESB; McMullen Country Bitter; Wethered Bitter ℍ
Popular free house on edge of open farmland, hosting a lively programme of social and sporting events. Varying range of real ales
🔥🍺 🌜 (not Sun) ♿

Ware

11.30–2.30; 5.30 (6.30 Sat)–11
Old Bulls Head
26 Baldock Street
☎ (0920) 2307
Benskins Best Bitter; Ind Coope Burton Ale; Tetley Bitter ℍ
16th-century inn with some original timber and inglenook. Regulars keen on pub games, and charity fund-raising. Garden play area for children. Good food at reasonable prices 🔥🛏🍺🌜 (not Sun) ♿

10.30–2.30; 5.30–11
Spread Eagle
37 Amwell End ☎ (0920) 2784
McMullen AK Mild, Country Bitter ℍ
Small local next to Ware level crossing. Now 1 bar in Mac's usual style, but nonetheless pleasant 🔥🛏🍺🌜🚆

Wareside

10.30–2.30; 6–11
White Horse
On B1004 3 miles E of Ware
☎ (0920) 2582
Greene King Rayments BBA, Abbot ℍ
Rural roadside pub
🔥Q🛏🍺🌜🍴♿🏕 (phone)

Try also: Chequers

Watford

11–3; 5.30–11
Bedford Arms
26 Langley Road
☎ (0923) 226205
Benskins Best Bitter ℍ
Small and cosy, well worth the 5 minute walk from the station. Darts
🔥🌜 (Mon–Fri) 🚆

Welham Green

10.30–2.30; 5.30–11
Hope & Anchor
Station Road ☎ (070 72) 62939
Courage Best Bitter, Directors; John Smith Bitter ℍ
Quiet, comfortable saloon and a lively public 🍺🌜♿🚆

Welwyn

11–2.30; 5.30–10.30 (11 F, S)
Baron of Beef
11 Mill Lane (off B656)
☎ (043 871) 4739
McMullen AK Mild, Country Bitter ℍ
True local with good atmosphere in historic coaching village. Hard to find
🔥🌜

11–2.30; 5.30 (7 Sat)–10.30 (11 F, S)
Rose & Crown
14 Church Street
☎ (043 871) 4190
Benskins Best Bitter; Tetley Bitter ℍ
Fine 16th-century inn with old world charm. Van Gogh's sister slept here. Separate games and dining areas. Lunches recommended; guest beers 🔥Q🍺🌜 (not Sun) ♿

Whitwell

11.30–2.30; 6–11
Maidens Head
67 High Street (B651)
OS185211 ☎ (043 887) 392
McMullen AK Mild, Country Bitter ℍ
Attractive village local with lots of character. Landlord has a collection of keyrings and an insult for everyone. No food Sun 🔥🛏🍺🌜 (not Mon) 🍴

Wildhill

12–2.30; 5.30–11
Woodman
7 Wildhill Lane (between B158/A1000) OS263068
☎ (0707) 42618
Greene King IPA, Abbot; McMullen AK Mild ℍ
Village bar and snug in rural surroundings. A good value, no-nonsense pub. Games 🍺🌜

Woolmer Green

11–2.30; 7–10.30 (11 F, S)
Fox
New Road (off B197)
☎ (0438) 813179
McMullen AK Mild, Country Bitter ℍ
Cheerful 1-bar local, set off main road 🍺🌜

Wormley West End

10.30–2.30; 5.30–11
Woodman
☎ (0992) 463719
McMullen AK Mild, Country Bitter ℍ
Attractive pub on edge of Wormley woods
🔥Q🍺🌜🍴♿

KEY TO SYMBOLS

Facilities

- 🔥 real fire
- Q quiet pub – no electronic music, TV or obtrusive games
- 🛏 indoor room for children
- 🍺 garden or other outdoor drinking area
- 🛌 accommodation
- 🌜 lunchtime meals
- 🍴 evening meals
- ♿ public bar
- 🪑 facilities for the disabled

- 🏕 camping facilities close to the pub or part of the pub grounds
- 🚆 near British Rail station
- ⊖ near Underground station
- Ȯ real cider

The facilities, beers and pub hours listed in the Good Beer Guide are liable to change but were correct when the Guide went to press.

Help keep real ale alive by joining CAMRA. Your voice helps encourage brewers big and small to brew cask beer and offer all beer drinkers a better choice.

148

Humberside

Humberside

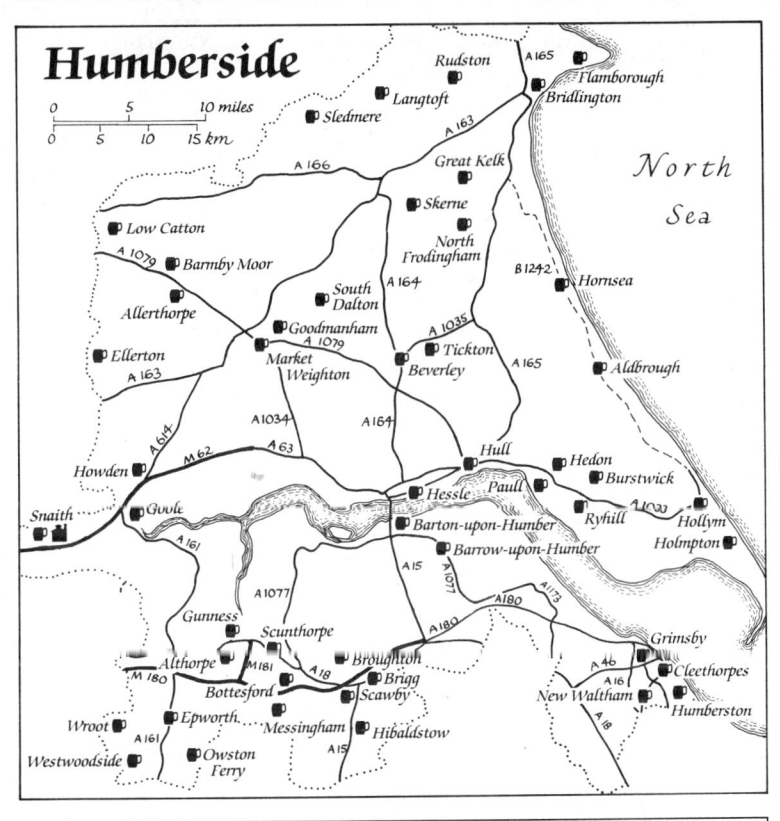

[Map of Humberside showing towns including Rudston, Langtoft, Sledmere, Flamborough, Bridlington, Great Kelk, Skerne, North Frodingham, Hornsea, Low Catton, Barmby Moor, Allerthorpe, South Dalton, Goodmanham, Tickton, Aldbrough, Ellerton, Market Weighton, Beverley, Howden, Hull, Hedon, Burstwick, Snaith, Goole, Hessle, Paull, Ryhill, Hollym, Barton-upon-Humber, Barrow-upon-Humber, Holmpton, Gunness, Scunthorpe, Broughton, Grimsby, Althorpe, Brigg, Cleethorpes, Bottesford, Scawby, New Waltham, Humberston, Wroot, Epworth, Messingham, Hibaldstow, Westwoodside, Owston Ferry]

Old Mill, Goole

Aldborough

12–3; 7–11

George & Dragon
1 High Street ☎ (0964) 527230
Younger Scotch, IPA, No.3 H
Modernised old country inn dating back 500 years. Tends to concentrate on the catering side of its business

Allerthorpe

12–3; 7–11

Plough
☎ (0759) 302349
Theakston Best Bitter, XB H
Pleasantly comfortable lounge with 2 separate drinking areas

Althorpe

11–3; 6–11

Dolphin
Main Road (A18)
☎ (0724) 783469
John Smith Bitter H
Pub increasingly noted for concentration on food. Small lounge

Barmby Moor

11–3; 7–11

Boot & Slipper
St Helens Square
☎ (0759) 303328
Younger Scotch, No.3 H
Large open-plan interior with pool room

Barrow-upon-Humber

11–3; 6.30–11

Royal Oak
High Street (off A1077)
☎ (0759) 30318
Bass Mild XXXX, Draught Bass; Stones Best Bitter H
Smart village pub. No meals

Barton-upon-Humber

10.30–3; 6–11

Coach & Horses
High Street ☎ (0759) 32161
Tetley Mild, Bitter H
Busy public bar. Lounge decorated in pre-war style. Jumbo sandwiches

10.30–3; 7–11

Wheatsheaf
Holydyke (A1077/B1218)
☎ (0759) 33175
Ward Darley Dark Mild, Sheffield Best Bitter H
Old pub with lounge/bar area and separate snug (lunch)
(Mon–Fri)

Try also: Steam Packet (Free)

Beverley

11–3; 6–10.30 (11 F,S)

Rose & Crown
North Bar Without
☎ (0482) 862532
Ward Darley Dark Mild, Thorne Best Bitter, Sheffield Best Bitter H
Large comfortable mock Tudor pub with friendly atmosphere close to Westwood and racecourse. Guest beers

11–3; 6–10.30 (11 F,S)

Royal Standard (Dollys)
North Bar Within (A164)
☎ (0482) 882434
Ward Darley Dark Mild, Darley Thorne Best Bitter H

149

Humberside

Small town pub with a superb front bar frequented by locals. Adjacent to Beverley's historic North Bar. Run by the same family for 97 years Q ち 🌫 ⊕

11–3; 7–10.30 (11 F,S)
Sun Inn
1 Flemingate ☎ (0482) 881547
Cameron Traditional Bitter, Strongarm H
Old local in the shadow of the magnificent Beverley Minster and handy for Army Transport Museum. Good value bar meals ち 🌫 ( ) ≢

11–3; 7–10.30 (11 F,S)
Tiger Inn
Lairgate (off A164)
☎ (0482) 869040
Ward Darley Dark Mild, Darley Thorne Best Bitter H
Traditional interesting pub within range of Beverley Minster. Popular with locals. Pub games ち 🌫 ( ) ⊕ ≢

11–3 (4 Wed, Sat); 7–10.30 (11 F,S)
White Horse Inn (Nellies)
Hengate (next to bus station)
☎ (0482) 861973
Samuel Smith OBB, Museum Ale H
Unique traditional pub with many gaslit rooms complete with stone-flagged floors. Victorian pictures and huge mirrors, iron ranges and an ancient and venerable gas cooker ≜ Q ち 🌫 ( ) ⊕ ≢

Bottesford

11.30–3; Bar 5–11; (Lounge M–Th 8–11; F & S 7–11)
Dolphin
Messingham Road (A159)
☎ (0724) 840906
Bass Special; Stones Best Bitter H
Popular large modern 2-room pub. Families welcome for meals ち 🌫 ( ) ⊕ &

Try also: Black Beauty (Mansfield)

Bridlington

10.30–3; 6–11
Albion Hotel
Hilderthorpe Road
☎ (0262) 676740
John Smith Bitter H
Cosy 2-roomer popular with locals ≜ 🌫 ( ) ⊕ ≢

10.30–3; 6–11
Hilderthorpe Hotel
Hilderthorpe Road
☎ (0262) 672205
Bass Mild XXXX, Draught Bass; Stones Best Bitter H
Basic local popular with fishermen ≜ ⋈ ⊕ ≢

10.30–3; 6–11
Old Ship Inn
90 St John's Street
☎ (0262) 670466
Ward Darley Dark Mild, Thorne Best Bitter H
Thriving local by the old town, retains traditional atmosphere ≜ Q ((Tue–Sat) ⊕

10.30–3; 6–11
Queens Hotel
High Street ☎ (0262) 672051
Tetley Mild, Bitter H
Basic, games oriented bar with comfy lounge, separate pool area 🌫 (⊕

Try also: The Ridings

Brigg

11–3; 6.30–11
Britannia Inn
Wrawby Street (A18)
☎ (0652) 52342
Mansfield Riding Bitter, Old Baily H
Friendly Victorian town pub on site of old brewery. Live trad jazz alternate Tues, piano sing-a-long Sats ≜ 🌫 ≢

10.30–3 (4 Th; closed Wed); 6.30–11
Dying Gladiator
Bigby Street (A18)
☎ (0652) 52110
Bass Mild XXXX; Webster Yorkshire Bitter H
A busy, welcoming open-plan town house near market place 🌫 ≢

10.30–2.30 (4 Thu); 6–11
White Horse
Wrawby Street (A15/A18)
☎ (0652) 52242
Ward Darley Dark Mild, Sheffield Best Bitter H
Welcoming old inn. Lunches popular 🌫 ((not Sun) ⊕ & ≢

Try also: Angel Hotel (Bass)

Broughton

10.30–3; 6–11
Red Lion
High Street ☎ (0652) 52560
Mansfield Riding Bitter H
Well kept pub with formal lounge and public bar at front; large plush games room with video juke box at rear. No food Mon 🌫 ( ) ⊕ & A

Try also: Thatche (Whitbread–Free)

Burstwick

11–3; 6–11
Hare & Hounds
Main Street (off B1362)
☎ (09644) 2318
Bass Mild XXXX, Draught Bass; Stones Best Bitter H
Old village local with very small public bar, lounge and separate dining room. Popular within the village and attracts a lot of passing trade ≜ ち 🌫 ( ) ⊕

Cleethorpes

11–3; 6–10.30 (11 F,S)
Crows Nest
Balmoral Road
☎ (0472) 698867
Samuel Smith OBB H
Large, popular and friendly local estate pub in the centre of the resort. A contrast with the flash seafront bars Q ち (Sat/Sun lunch) 🌫 ⋈ ( ) ⊕ &

11–3; 6–10.30 (11 F,S)
Fishermans Arms
25 Wardle Street
☎ (0472) 691811
Bass Mild XXXX E, **Draught Bass** H
Popular 2-roomed pub close to seafront. Live entertainment Wed eve. Pool and darts in the bar ⊕

11–3; 6–10.30 (11 F,S)
Number One Refreshment Room
Station Approach
☎ (0472) 691707
Marston Pedigree; Younger No.3 H
Situated in original 19th-century railway station. Although a listed building, expect no frills in here Q 🌫 ( ) ⊕

11–3; 7–10.30 (11 F,S)
Willy's
17 Highcliff Road
☎ (0472) 602145
Bateman XB; Ruddles County H
Modern seafront bar, offering good value food and regular guest beers ち (lunch) 🌫 (& ≢

Try also: Kings Royal (Tetley); **No.2 Refreshment Room** (Free)

Ellerton

12–3 (Sat & summer weekdays); 7–11
Boot & Shoe
Off B1228, 6 miles SW of York
☎ (075 785) 346
Old Mill Traditional Bitter; Tetley Bitter H
Out of the way village pub with several rooms in exposed brickwork and beamed ceilings. 4 real fires. Pub games. No lunches Mon–Fri ≜ ち 🌫 ( ) (not Mon)

Epworth

11–3; 7–11
Queens Head
Queen Street (off A161)
☎ (0427) 872306
John Smith Bitter H
Built in 1664 as a farmhouse, now a bustling open-plan local in the centre of Wesley's home town 🌫 ((Tue–Sat) &

Flamborough

10.30–3; 7–11

150

Humberside

Rose & Crown Hotel
High Street ☎ (0262) 850455
Cameron Traditional Bitter, Strongarm H
Comfortable but basic 1-roomer away from village centre. Popular with locals. Pub games

Goodmanham

11–3; 7–11

Goodmanham Arms
☎ (0696) 379
Theakston Best Bitter H
Small 1-roomed country inn opposite ancient Norman church on Wolds Way, long distance footpath

Goole

11–3; 6.30 (7 Sat)–11

Vikings
Airmyn Road ☎ (0405) 2875
Bass Light 5 Star, Draught Bass; Stones Best Bitter H
Large and lively roadhouse popular with the younger set. Pub games

10.30–3; 6–11

Woodlands
Rutland Road ☎ (0405) 2738
John Smith Bitter H
Friendly estate pub with snug

Try also: **Royal** (Younger)

Great Kelk

11–2.30; 6–11

Chestnut Horse
☎ (026 288) 263
John Smith Bitter; Younger Scotch H
Delightful well-cared for country cottage-styled village inn. Popular with folk from the surrounding villages. Pub games

Grimsby

11–3; 6–10.30 (11 F,S)

Angel
175 Freeman Street
☎ (0472) 42102
Younger IPA, No.3 H
Busy 3-roomed pub with pool darts and dominoes in bar (Docks)

11–3; 5.30–10.30 (11 F,S)

Kent Arms
Kent Street ☎ (0472) 354689
John Smith Bitter H
Typical 60s-style house with live music in the lounge most nights. Close to the docks and A180. Pub games (Docks)

11–3; 5.30 (7 Sat)–10.30 (11 F,S)

Lloyds Arms
76 Victoria Street
☎ (0472) 361872
Taylor Landlord; Tetley Bitter H
Converted bank, as the name suggests. Open plan with raised area and varied clientele. Bustling town centre pub
(not Sat) (Mon–Thu)

11–3; 5.30–10.30 (11 F,S)

Pestle & Mortar
Old Market Place
Bass Mild XXXX, Draught Bass; Stones Best Bitter H
Basic boisterous bar, with pool and juke box on ground floor. 1st floor lounge a peaceful oasis with 2 snooker tables

11–3; 6–10.30 (11 F,S)

Yarborough Vaults
Bethlehem Street
☎ (0472) 354159
John Smith Bitter H
2-roomed town centre pub with pool area off the public bar

Try also: **Friar Tuck** (Bass)

Gunness

11.30–3; 5–11

Jolly Sailor
Station Road ☎ (0724) 782423
Bass Special Bitter, Draught Bass H
3-roomed large basic public bar: mainly locals with a smattering of European mariners from nearby wharf. Pub games (Althorpe)

Hedon

11–3; 6–11

Shakespeare Inn
9 Baxtergate (off A1033)
☎ (0482) 898371
Vaux Bitter, Sampson; Ward Darley Dark Mild, Darley Thorne Best Bitter, Sheffield Best Bitter H
1-roomed cosy and friendly old inn. Over 3000 beer mats adorn the ceiling. Games include Yorkshire darts
(not Sun)

Hessle

11–3; 7–10.30 (11 F,S)

George Inn (Top House)
Prestongate (just off square)
☎ (0482) 648698
Bass Mild XXXX; Stones Best Bitter H
Welcoming and well-liked pub, with 3 contrasting rooms, in pedestrianised street off Hessle Square

Hibaldstow

11–2.30; 6–11

Wheatsheaf
Station Road (A15)
☎ (0652) 54056
Ward Darley Dark Mild E, **Sheffield Best Bitter** H
Popular pub with restaurant

Hollym

11–3; 6–11

Plough
Off A1033 ☎ (0964) 612049
John Smith Bitter; Tetley Mild, Bitter H
Friendly village pub, over 200 years old, facing the church. 3-rooms including games room

Holmpton

12–3; 6–11 (7–11 F,S)

George & Dragon
On B1242 ☎ (0964) 630478
Bass Mild XXXX; Stones Best Bitter; Tetley Mild, Bitter; Webster Green Label, Yorkshire Bitter H
Spacious free house with small hideaway corners. Very popular and busy. Used by tourists and good mix of customers

Hornsea

11–3; 6 (7 winter)–11

Marine
Marine Drive ☎ (0964) 532183
Tetley Mild, Bitter H
Large seafront pub with excellent sea views. Busy in summer

11–3; 6.30–11

Victoria
Market Place ☎ (0964) 533133
Bass Mild XXXX, Draught Bass; Stones Best Bitter H
Comfortable, well-run pub with restaurant and two public rooms frequented by locals (not Tue)

Howden

12–3 (closed Mon); 7 (6 Fri)–11

Barnes Wallis
Station Road (1 mile N on B1228) ☎ (0430) 430639
Old Mill Traditional Bitter; John Smith Bitter; Tetley Bitter; Younger IPA H
Clean, friendly rural pub built in 1860 and originally called The Station. Bright large bar with separate open space for eating. Used by local farmers. Barnes Wallis memorabilia in the bar
(not Mon)

11–3; 6–11

Cross Keys
2 Hull Road (A63)
Tetley Mild, Bitter H
Bustling no-frills local on the outskirts of town. Very popular with the local darts playing population

Hull

11–3; 5.30–10.30 (11 F,S)

Black Boy
150 High Street (old town)
☎ (0482) 26516

151

Humberside

Tetley Mild, Bitter H
Historic Heritage Inn which commemorates both the slave trade and the Hull man who outlawed it from Britain. 2 upstairs and 2 downstairs rooms. Beware the resident ghost!

11–3; 6–10.30 (11 F,S)

Duke of Wellington
104 Peel Street, Spring Bank
☎ (0482) 228185
Clarks Burglar Bill; Malton Pickwicks Porter; Taylor Landlord; Tetley Mild, Bitter, Imperial H
Back street restyled Victorian local featuring guest beers from throughout Yorkshire. The nearest thing to a free house in Hull

11–3; 6–10.30 (11 F,S)

East Riding
37 Cannon Street
☎ (0482) 29134
Tetley Mild, Bitter H
Small old fashioned industrial pub. Basic bar with Rugby League mementoes and cosy lounge. Retains old tradition of free Sunday lunch sandwiches and saveloys

11–3; 5.30–10.30 (11 F,S)

Gardeners Arms
Cottingham Road (B1233)
☎ (0482) 42396
Taylor Landlord; Tetley Mild, Bitter, Imperial H
Quiet, comfortable bar at the front of the building; a video juke box in larger lounge

11–3; 6–10.30 (11 F,S)

Green Bricks
Humber Dock Street
☎ (0482) 29502
Bass Mild XXXX, Draught Bass; Stones Best Bitter H
Small 1-roomed pub on eastern side of Hull Marina with impressive tiled frontage. Can be very crowded at weekends.

12–3; 6–10.30 (11 F,S)

Halfway House
595 Spring Bank West
☎ (0482) 53227
Bass Mild XXXX, Draught Bass; Stones Best Bitter H
Suburban pub with an unimpressive frontage which obscures 2 well-refurbished rooms. Popular with the locals

11–3; 6–10.30 (11 F,S)

Lockwood Arms
56 Green Lane ☎ (0482) 27661
Camerons Strongarm H
Old style pub in industrial area with separate games room. C and W nights and free and easys on the piano. Popular with older people (Mon–Fri)

11–3; 6–10.30 (11 F,S)

Minerva
Nelson Street (opposite Corporation Pier)
☎ (0482) 26909
Minerva Pilots Pride; Tetley Mild, Bitter H
Famous riverside pub with its own brewery and 4 contrasting rooms. Can get very busy at weekends. Handy for Hull Marina (lunch) (until 8)

11–3; 6–10.30 (11 F,S)

New Clarence
77–79 Clarence Street
☎ (0482) 20327
Tetley Mild, Bitter H
2-roomed back street pub: basic traditional bar with wooden floor and contrasting cheerful lounge. Handy for the New Theatre

11–3; 5.30–10.30 (11 F,S)

Oberon
Queen Street (near Corporation Pier)
☎ (0482) 24886
Bass Mild XXXX, Draught Bass; Stones Best Bitter H
Perennial Hull favourite. Fairly plain but always welcoming pub with a nautical flavour. Frequented by Humber pilots. Good weekend bet. Pub games Q

11–3; 7–10.30 (11 F,S)

Old Blue Bell
Market Place (old town)
☎ (0482) 24683
Samuel Smith OBB, Museum Ale H
Splendidly refurbished fine pub, down alley by market hall. 3 small rooms downstairs, plus upstairs concert room used by folk club Sun nights

11–3; 5.30–10.30 (11 F,S)

Olde White Harte
25 Silver Street (old town)
☎ (0482) 26363
Younger IPA, No.3 H
Largely 16th-century courtyard pub in heart of Hull's commercial centre. Played an important role in the Civil War. Don't miss the plotters room upstairs. 2 large sit-in fireplaces plus original timber and stained glass windows (Thu–Sat)

11–3; 5.30–10.30 (11 F,S)

Waterloo Tavern
Great Union Street (off A63)
☎ (0482) 228306
John Smith Bitter H
Boisterous rejuvenated 3-roomed pre-war pub across Drypool Bridge from old town. Live music Wed–Sun. Excellent value food. Pub games

Humberston

11–3; 6–10.30 (11 F,S)

Countryman
Fieldhouse Road
☎ (0472) 812402
Whitbread Castle Eden Ale H
Popular 2-roomed pub just a mile from the golf course, beach and caravan site. Pool and darts

Langtoft

11–2.30; 6–11 (midnight supper licence)

Ship Inn
Front Street (B1249)
☎ (0377) 87243
Cameron Traditional Bitter H
Cosy, friendly village local with dining room and pub games

Low Catton

11.30–3; 7–11

Gold Cup
Main Street
Old Mill Traditional Bitter; John Smith Bitter; Tetley Bitter H
Popular free house in tiny village. Good reputation for food. Cosy lounge with plainer pool room and small restaurant attached. Food Tue–Sat only (if eating)

Market Weighton

11–3; 7–11

Black Horse
Londesborough Road
Tetley Mild, Bitter; Younger Scotch Bitter H
Popular local with good meals trade. Friendly family-oriented pub. Guest beers (not Mon)

Messingham

11.30–3; 5–11

Green Tree
33 High Street ☎ (0724) 762395
Bass Mild XXXX, Special Bitter, Draught Bass H
1-roomed old village pub refurbished to modern cottage style. Good early evening trade. Good lunches and summertime barbecues. Pub games

New Waltham

11–3; 6–10.30 (11 F,S)

Cross Keys
Station Road ☎ (0472) 827933
Bass Mild XXXX, Draught Bass; Stones Best Bitter H
Spacious and comfortable modern pub with etched windows from the former Cleethorpes Cross Keys Q

North Frodingham

10.30–2.30; 7–11

Star
Main Street (B1249)
Cameron Traditional Bitter,

Humberside

Strongarm H
Pleasant and friendly rural free house serving the local community. Pub games ⌂☎⊛◖⌂

Owston Ferry

10.30–3; 7–11

Crooked Billet
Silver Street ☎ (042 772) 264
Ward Darley Mild, Bitter H
Trent-side village pub with pool, darts and boxing! Occasional live music. No food Mon ⌂☎⊛◖⊛

Paull

11–3; 7–11

Crown
Main Street (off A1033)
☎ (0482) 898383
Bass Mild XXXX, Draught Bass; Stones Best Bitter H
Bright, vastly-extended pub near bank of Humber. Low ceilings and lots of woodwork. Popular with office workers. Purpose built family room ⌂☎⊛◖⌂

Try also: Humber Tavern

Rudston

10.30–3; 6–11

Bosville Arms
B1253
Bass Mild XXXX; Stones Best Bitter H
Warm and welcoming pub with lots of brasswork ⌂Q☎⊛⌂▲

Ryhill

12–3 (Not Tue & Thu); 7–11

Crooked Billet
Pitt Lane (400 yds off A1033)
☎ (0964) 622303
Tetley Mild, Bitter H
Very popular old smugglers' haunt with large bar and split-level room used by farm workers and tourists alike, plus famous local character Wobbly Bob ⌂☎⊛◖⌂

Scawby

11–3; 6–11

Sutton Arms
West Street (B1207)
☎ (0652) 52430
Bass Mild XXXX; Old Mill Traditional Bitter; Stones Best Bitter H
Modernised old pub with real fire in public bar ⌂☎⊛⌂

Scunthorpe

11.30–3; 5–11

Queen Bess
Derwent Road (off B1501)
☎ (0724) 840827
Samuel Smith OBB H
50s estate pub with separate lounge; concert room used by C and W club. Pub games ⌂

11.30–3; 5.30 (6.30 Sat)–11

Riveter
50 Henderson Avenue
☎ (0724) 862701
Old Mill Dark Mild, Traditional Bitter, Bullion Bitter H
New open-plan 'Olde Worlde' split level pub with 2 lounge areas and games area. Owned by Old Mill brewery of Snaith ◖ (not Sun) ⊛⌂

Try also: Cocked Hat (Bass)

Skerne

11–2.30; 7–11

Eagle
Wansford Road
☎ (0377) 42178
Cameron Traditional Bitter H
Unspoilt country pubs like this are rare. Unpretentious, extremely welcoming and determined to keep it that way. No food ⌂Q☎ (lunch) ⊛⌂⌂

Sledmere

11.30–2.30; 7–11

Triton Inn
Jct B1252/B1253 ☎ (0377) 86644
Younger Scotch H
Splendid pub next to Sledmere House ⌂☎⌂◖⌂

Snaith

10.45–3; 6.45–11

Black Lion
Selby Road ☎ (0405) 860282
Tetley Mild, Bitter H
Friendly, popular, traditional pub. Games available ⌂&⇌

South Dalton

12–2.30; 7–10.30 (11 F,S)

Pipe & Glass
West End (off B1248)
OS964453 ☎ (069 64) 246
Ruddles County; Stones Best Bitter; Webster Choice H
Stylish, comfortable and relaxed pub on lane to Dalton Hall. Best bet in area for good food in a real ale pub. Games ⌂Q⊛◖◖ (not Sun)

Tickton

12–3; 7–10.30 (1 F,S)

New Inn
Main Street (just off A1035)
☎ (0964) 542371
Bass Mild XXXX; Stones Best Bitter H
Despite modern appearance a traditional layout. Mainly locals in unassuming, though comfortable bar. Families welcome until 9
⌂☎⊛◖⌂ (Caravan Club)

Westwoodside

10.30–3; 6–11

Park Drain Hotel
Off B1396 OS726988
☎ (0427) 752255
Bass Mild XXXX; Stones Best Bitter H
Unusual, remote Victorian pub. Large bar, comfortable lounge and excellent restaurant. Straw-fired central heating ⌂☎ (for meals) ⊛◖
◖ (not Mon) ⌂▲

Wroot

12–3; 7–11

Cross Keys
High Street (off B1396)
☎ (0302) 770231
Younger Scotch H
Pleasant 3-roomed inn in remote country village. Pub games ⌂☎⊛◖⌂

KEY TO SYMBOLS

- ⌂ real fire
- Q quiet pub – no electronic music, TV or obtrusive games
- ☎ indoor room for children
- ⊛ garden or other outdoor drinking area
- ⌂ accommodation
- ◖ lunchtime meals
- ◖ evening meals
- ⌂ public bar
- & facilities for the disabled
- ▲ camping facilities close to the pub or part of the pub grounds
- ⇌ near British Rail station
- ⊕ near Underground station
- ⌂ real cider

The facilities, beers and pub hours listed in the Good Beer Guide are liable to change but were correct when the Guide went to press.

Isle of Wight

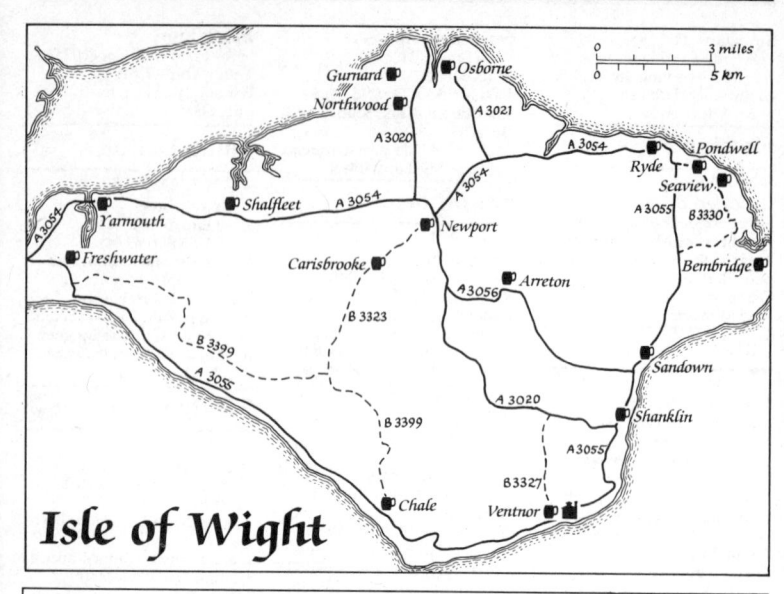

🏠 *Burt*, Ventnor

**General opening hours:
10.30–3; 6–11**

Arreton

Hare & Hounds
Downend (A3056)
Burt VPA H
Delightful ancient thatched pub of great character, next to Robin Hill Country Park

Try also: White Lion (Whitbread)

Bembridge

Crab & Lobster
Forelands (follow signs to Lane End & turn right into Field Road) ☎ (0983) 2244
Whitbread Strong Country Bitter, Pompey Royal H
Very pleasant, comfortable pub in yachting village; specialises in seafood

Carisbrooke

Shute Inn
Clatterford Shute
☎ (0983) 523393
Draught Bass; Burt VPA; Courage Directors H
Pleasant Georgian hotel in delightful setting beneath Carisbrooke Castle

Chale

Wight Mouse
Off A3055 ☎ (0983) 730431
Burt VPA; Flowers Original; Whitbread Strong Country Bitter H
Superb old stone-built pub attached to hotel: accent on food and families. Massive garden with playground and pets. Live music most evenings. Pub games. Nearby is Blackgang Chine and beach: popular with naturists

Freshwater

Royal Standard
School Green Road
☎ (0983) 753227
Burt Mild, VPA H
Homely town pub in hotel. Good value food. Pub games

Try also: Red Lion (Whitbread)

Gurnard

Woodvale
Woodvale Road
☎ (0983) 292037
Flowers Original; Whitbread Strong Country Bitter H
Large family pub on seashore with fine views: nearby clifftop walks and beach. Pub games

Try also: Empress Bars, Cowes (Free)

Newport

Swallowed Anchor
High Street
Tetley Bitter; Wadworth 6X H
Good town-centre free house, offering an alternative in the island's county town, which is dominated by a single brewer

Try also: George (Whitbread)

Northwood

Travellers Joy
Pallance Road (off A3020)
Burt VPA; Courage Best Bitter, Directors; Gibbs Mew Bishops Tipple; Ind Coope Burton Ale; Tetley Bitter H
Very popular country free house on the southern outskirts of Cowes. Pub games

Try also: Horseshoe (Whitbread)

Osborne

Prince of Wales
Whippingham Road
Flowers Original; Whitbread Strong Country Bitter H
Pleasant, comfortable town pub in East Cowes suburb, opposite Osborne House, Queen Victoria's favourite residence. Pub games

Try also: Victoria, East Cowes

Pondwell

Wishing Well
On Ryde-Seaview Road
☎ (0983) 3222
Burt Mild, VPA H
Popular large roadhouse. Pub games

154

Isle of Wight

Ryde

Yelfs Hotel
Union Street ☎ (0983) 64062
Draught Bass; Burt VPA H
Pleasant bar in large, plush town-centre THF hotel. Conveniently situated for Ryde Pier ferries. Ryde offers best choice of pubs and beers on the island
🍴🛏🍺 ⇌ (Esplanade)

Sandown

Commercial
15 St Johns Road
☎ (0983) 403848
Gales XXXL, BBB, XXXXX, HSB H
Superb, comfortable town pub with good, basic public bar. A welcome retreat from the tourist attractions and crowds.
Pub games ♟🍴🍺

Try also: **Castle** (Watney)

Seaview

Seaview Hotel
High Street ☎ (0983) 612711
Burt VPA H
An imposing and elegant seafront hotel in a pleasant yachting village. Superb public bar popular with locals and yellow wellies
🛏♟🍴🍺🍽♿

Try also: **Old Fort** (Free)

Shalfleet

New Inn
On A3054
Flowers Original; Wethered Bitter; Whitbread Strong Country Bitter G
Lovely old village pub, frequented by yellow wellies; adjacent to delightful quay and Newtown creek. Locally caught seafood is a speciality
🍴🍺

Shanklin

Crab
Old Village
Flowers Original; Whitbread Strong Country Bitter H
Very photogenic ancient thatched pub, very busy in summer. Close to 'The Chine', a tree-lined gorge leading down to the tranquil seafront.
Pub games ♟🍴🍺🍽⇌

Try also: **Longshoreman** (Free)

Ventnor

Mill Bay
Esplanade
Burt Mild, VPA H
Pleasant, basic seafront pub near foot of 'Cascade' in a Victorian setting overlooking the now defunct pier 🍴🍺

Try also: **Volunteer** (Burt)

Yarmouth

Kings Head
Quay Street
Flowers Original; Whitbread Pompey Royal H
Splendid, cosy pub near car ferry terminal, Tudor castle and picturesque harbour. The River Yar has an old tide mill
🛏♟🍴🍺

All Yarmouth pubs serve real ale

The Campaiging Year... (Oct. 87) the Rayments Battle Bus, driven round Bury St Edmunds by London campaigners. They closed it anyway ...

Kent

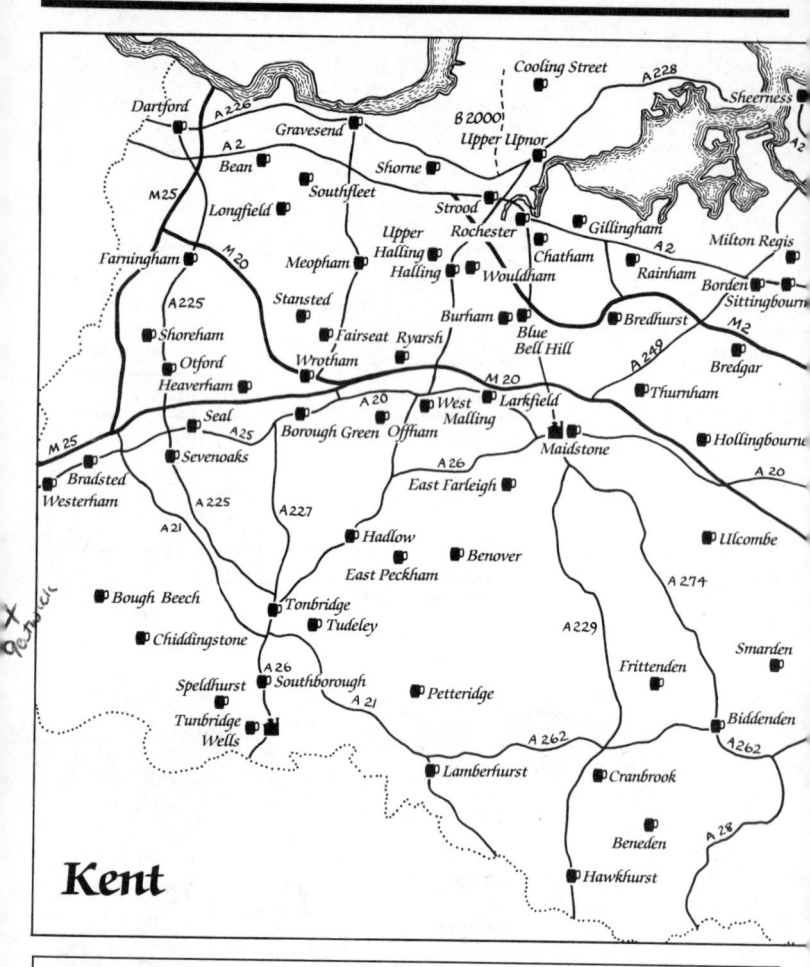

Canterbury, Canterbury; **Goacher's**, Bockingford; **Larkins**, Rusthall; **Martin**, Martin; **Shepherd Neame**, Faversham

Ash

10–2.30; 6–11

Volunteer
43 Guilton (A257)
☎ (0304) 812506
Adnams Bitter; Harvey XX; Young Special H
Popular, historic pub on edge of village. Bar billiards

Ashford

11–2.30; 6.30–11

Beaver
Beaver Road (A2070)
☎ (0233) 20264
Shepherd Neame Bitter H
2-bar pub catering for local trade. Spot the mistake in smoking room sign. Pub games

11–2.30; 6–11

Golden Ball
Canterbury Road, Kennington
Shepherd Neame Bitter H
Popular local. Darts and bat and trap teams

11–2.30; 6–11

Hare & Hounds
Potters Corner (A20)
☎ (0233) 21760
Courage Best Bitter, Directors H
Attractive, comfortable pub

11–2.30; 6–11

Prince Albert
109 New Street (A28/A292)
Bateman XB; Flowers Original; Fremlins Bitter H
Popular local trade. Darts. Guest beers

Bean

11–2.30; 6–11

Black Horse
High Street (B255)
☎ (04747) 2486
Ruddles Best Bitter, County; Truman Best Bitter; Webster Yorkshire Bitter H
Pub with a mini-zoo, barbecue and children's room. New restaurant. No food Sun

Benenden

11.30–2.30; 6–11

King William IV
The Street (B2086)
☎ (0580) 240636
Shepherd Neame Bitter H
Excellent village local in every

Kent

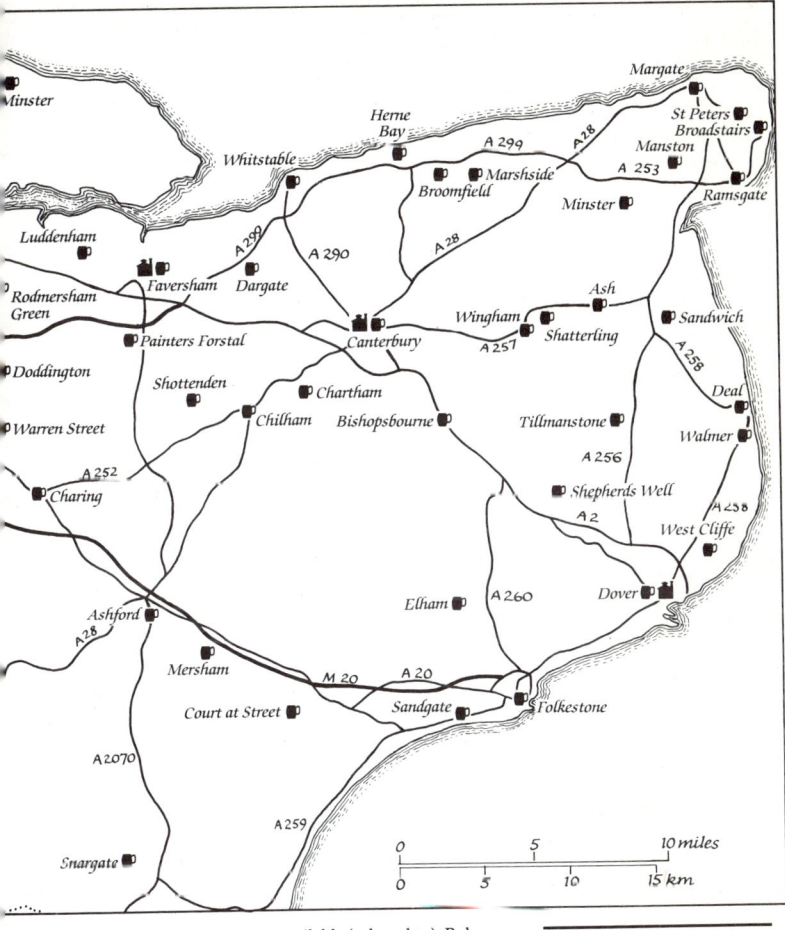

sense. No meals Sun. Pub games ▲⊜ ◐ (not Mon) ⊕

Benover

10.30–2.30; 6–11
Woolpack Inn
Benover Road (B2162 1 mile S of Yalding) ☎ (089 273) 356
Shepherd Neame Bitter H
Splendid 17th-century country pub; good food; family room – look out for the skeleton!
▲Q⊜⊜◐&

Biddenden

11–2.30; 6–11
Three Chimneys
Just off A262 towards Sissinghurst OS827387
☎ (0580) 291472
Adnams Bitter; Fremlins Bitter; Goacher's Light Maidstone Ale; Harvey BB; Hook Norton Old Hookey; Marston Pedigree H
Splendid old free house with traditional public bar. Interesting food always

available (saloon bar). Pub games ▲Q⊜⊜◐ ⊕

Bishopsbourne

11–2.30; 6–11
Mermaid Inn
The Street (½ mile off A2)
☎ (0227) 830581
Shepherd Neame Bitter H
Small, attractive pub with corkscrew collection. Games include shut-the-box ▲⊜⊜◐◑

Blue Bell Hill

10.30–2.30; 6–11
Robin Hood
Common Road, Chatham (1 mile W of A229)
☎ (0634) 61500
Courage Best Bitter, Directors H
Modernised 16th-century house with 3 bars and inglenook, in very isolated position
▲⊜⊜◐ (not Sun) ⊕&▲

Try also: **Upper Bell** (Whitbread)

Borden

11–2.30; 6.30–11
Plough & Harrow
Oad Street ☎ (0795) 843351
Greene King XX; Shepherd Neame Bitter H
Pleasant rural free house. Guest beers ▲⋈⊜◐

Borough Green

10–2.30; 6–11
Fox & Hounds
Maidstone Road (A25)
☎ (0732) 882334
Greene King Abbot; Harvey BB H
Old building with more character than at first glance; many photographs of earlier days ⊜◐ (not Sun) ⇌

Bough Beech

10–2.30; 6–11
Wheatsheaf
On Four Elms–Penshurst Road OS488468 ☎ (0732) 70254

157

Kent

Flowers Original; Fremlins Bitter ⒣
16th-century country pub with wood burning stove and delightful garden. Crowded on summer eves. Shove-ha'penny, backgammon and darts ⌂🛏🍴🍺▶ 🚇

Brasted

10.30–2.30; 6–11
Bull Inn
High Street (A25)
☎ (0959) 62551
Shepherd Neame Bitter, Best Bitter, Stock Ale (winter) ⒣
Friendly pub on edge of village. Mixture of local and passing trade. Darts and shove ha'penny
⌂Q🛏🍴▶ 🍴♿⛺ (ask landlord)

Bredgar

10.30–2.30; 6.30–11
Sun
The Street (B2163)
☎ (062 784) 221
Courage Best Bitter, Directors ⒣
Spacious country inn with good selection of food. Pub games ⌂🛏🍴▶

Bredhurst

10.30–2.30; 6.30–11
Bell
The Street (off M2 Jct 4)
☎ (0634) 32971
Courage Best Bitter, Directors ⒣
Large busy village local
⌂🛏🍴▶ (till 8.30 not Sun)

Broadstairs

11–2.30; 5.30–11
Brown Jug
Ramsgate Road, Dumpton Park (A255) ☎ (0843) 62788
Flowers Original; Fremlins Bitter ⒣
Collection of china jugs and animated musical clock. Colourful flower garden. Near the dogtrack ⌂Q (in public) 🛏🍴🚇 (Dumpton Pk)

11–2.30; 5.30–11
Neptunes Hall
1 Harbour Street
☎ (0843) 61400
Shepherd Neame Bitter ⒣
Large busy Victorian town pub, popular with musicians during Folk Week ⌂🛏🍴🚇

11–2.30; 5.30–11
Olde Crown
23 High Street ☎ (0843) 61747
Ruddles Best Bitter, County; Webster Yorkshire Bitter ⒣
2 contrasting bars – quiet and cosy lounge; lively public bar. Sun lounge and family room. Pub games 🛏🍴▶ 🚇

11–2.30; 5.30–11
Star
Margate Road (A254)
☎ (0843) 61245
Flowers Original; Fremlins Bitter ⒣
Popular and very friendly split-level pub. Four-pull beer engine in lower bar. Original Cobb and Co. windows. Guest beers. Pub games 🛏🍴♿

Broomfield

10–2.30; 6–11
Huntsman & Horn
Margate Road ☎ (0227) 375526
Fremlins Bitter ⒣
Genuine local with area's longest-serving landlord. Pub games ⌂🛏🍴♿

Burham

11–2.30; 7–11
Toastmasters
Church Street ☎ (0634) 61299
Boddingtons Bitter; Fuller London Pride, ESB; Hook Norton Old Hookey; Marston Pedigree; Young Special ⒣
Always a varied choice of beers, also draught cider. Bar has pews from demolished parish church 🛏🍴▶ ⌂

Try also: All 4 other pubs in Burham

Canterbury

11–2.30; 6.30–11
Gentil Knyght
Shipman Avenue, London Road Estate ☎ (0227) 65891
Shepherd Neame Bitter ⒣
Housing estate pub. Excellent for games 🛏🍴♿🚇 (E&W)

10–2.30; 6–11
Kentish Cricketers
14 St Peters Street
☎ (0227) 464227
Shepherd Neame Bitter ⒣
City-centre pub which caters for both locals and visitors. Cricketing theme. Pub games 🍴▶ (until 9) ♿🚇 (West)

11–2.30; 6–11
Maiden's Head
28 Wincheap (off ring road)
☎ (0227) 66362
Flowers Original; Fremlins Bitter ⒣
13th and 15th century houses knocked into one, popular with the younger set
🛏🍴▶ (early) ♿🚇 (East)

10.30 (10 Sat)–2.30; 6–11
New Inn
19 Havelock Street
☎ (0227) 464584
Bateman XB; Shepherd Neame Bitter; Theakston Old Peculier (winter); Wadworth 6X ⒣
Tiny and very popular with students. Darts 🛏🍴🚇 (East)

10–2.30; 6–11
Phoenix
67 Old Dover Road
☎ (0227) 464220
Adnams Bitter; Greene King IPA, Abbot; Young Bitter, Special ⒣
Cricket-oriented pub, handy for County ground
⌂Q🍴▶ ♿🚇 (East)

Try also: **Brewer's Delight**, Broad St. (Shepherd Neame)

Charing

10.30–2.30; 6–11
Kings Head
High Street
Fremlins Bitter ⒣
Large pub, formerly a hotel: very peaceful saloon contrasts with public bar. Darts and pool ⌂

Chartham

11–2.30; 6.30–11
Artichoke Inn
Rattington Street (off A28)
☎ (0227) 738316
Shepherd Neame Bitter ⒣
13th century Hall house with half-timbered "ladies"! Good for games ⌂🛏🍴▶ ⌂♿🚇

11–2.30; 6–11
George Inn
Shalmsford Street (off A28)
☎ (0227) 738253
Draught Bass; Goacher's Dark Maidstone Ale; Rayment BBA ⒣
Excellent real food. Try fruit curry with ice-cream! Family room. Darts and shut-the-box. Guest beers ⌂🛏🍴▶ ♿⌂
⛺ (in grounds) 🚇

Chatham

10–2.30; 6–11
Shipwrights Arms
29 Richard Street (behind Allders) ☎ (0634) 813684
Greene King IPA ⒣, **Abbot** ⒢
Friendly free house with original tiled fascia. Darts
⌂🍴 (not Sun) 🚇

Chiddingstone Hoath

11–2.30; 6–11
Rock Inn
About 2 miles from village on Penshurst Road OS497431
☎ (0892) 870296
Fremlins Bitter ⒣
Small characteful pub in open countryside. Wooden hand pumps in public bar. Darts and ring-the-bull ⌂Q🛏
🛏🍴▶ (not Wed) ♿⛺ (400 yds)

Chilham

11–2.30; 6–11
White Horse
Village Square

158

Kent

☎ (0227) 730355
Flowers Original; Fremlins Bitter H
Idyllic setting for this ancient, cosy house, which caters successfully for both locals and tourists. Darts; guest beers ⌂⏃ ◖▮ (not winter Tue) ▤⚐≹

Try also: Woolpack, High Street (Shepherd Neame)

Cooling Street

11–2.30; 6–11

Staff of Life
Turn into Merryboys Road from B2000 ☎ (0634) 221023
Everards Tiger, Old Original; Marston Pedigree; Wadworth 6X H
Large pub with restaurant and outside bar at weekends. Garden and children's play area ⏃⚐◖▮⚐

Court at Street

12–2.30; 6–11

Welcome Stranger
Court at Street (B2067)
☎ (023 372) 400
Harvey BB; Shepherd Neame Bitter H
Small 1-bar pub, ideal for a quiet drink and chat Q

Cranbrook

11–2.30; 6–11

Prince of Wales
High Street ☎ (0580) 713058
Harvey BB H
Popular town centre pub with 2 contrasting bars. Pub games. Guest beers ⌂⏃⚐◖▮ ▤⚐

All pubs in Cranbrook sell real ale

Dargate

11–3; 6–11 (restaurant licence to 12.30am)

Dove Inn
Plumpudding Lane (off A299)
☎ (0227) 751360
Shepherd Neame Bitter H
Mellow wood-panelled inn with attractive garden. Chess and dominoes
⌂⚐ (lunch) ⏃ ◖▮ ⚐

Dartford

10.30–2.30; 6–11

Malt Shovel
3 Darenth Road (off A226)
☎ (0322) 24791
Young Bitter, Special, Winter Warmer H
Pub of great character with unspoilt public bar. Table skittles
⌂Q (public) ⚐⏃ ◖▮ ▤⚐≹

10–2.30; 0–11

Victory
26 East Hill (A226)
☎ (0322) 24583
Shepherd Neame Bitter, Best Bitter, Stock Ale H
Very friendly street-corner local. Always busy. Popular with darts players ⏃≹

Deal

10–2.30; 6–11

Admiral Keppel
Manor Road (off A258)
Charrington IPA H
Out of the way pub ◖▮

10–2.30; 6–11

Clarendon Hotel
Beach Street ☎ (0304) 374748
Shepherd Neame Bitter H
Comfortable 2-bar hotel on seafront with view of pier
⌶◖▮▤≹

10–2.30; 6–11

Eagle
Queen Street ☎ (0304) 364295
Fremlins Bitter H
Busy pub close to station and taxi office; a popular 'first stop' in Deal ≹

10–2.30; 6–11

Ship
Middle Street (between High Street and beach)
☎ (0304) 372222
Draught Bass; Charrington IPA; Fuller ESB; Greene King Abbot; Shepherd Neame Bitter H
2 bar pub with naval theme
⌂◖▮≹

10–2.30; 6–11

Yew Tree
Mill Hill ☎ (0304) 373189
Fremlins Bitter H
Basic, working man's pub, out of the way in a residential area
▤≹ (Walmer)

Doddington

10.30–3; 6–11

Chequers
The Street ☎ (079 586) 269
Shepherd Neame Bitter H
Popular village inn with roaring log fire in winter. Pub games ⌂⏃ ◖▮ ▤

Dover

10–2.30; 6–11

Dublin Man o' War
Lower Road, Kearsney
☎ (0304) 822509
Flowers Original; Fremlins Bitter H
Near Kearsney Abbey Gardens ⚐ ◖▮ ≹ (Kearsney)

10–2.30; 6–11

Park Inn
1 Park Place, Ladywell
☎ (0304) 206471
Park Inn Castle Bitter H
Rambling unpretentious town centre free house. Other beers available. Darts
◖ (Mon–Fri) ≹ (Priory)

10–2.30; 6–11

White Horse Inn
St James Street (off A258)
☎ (0304) 202911
Flowers Original; Fremlins Bitter H
Multi-roomed with parts dating back to the 14th century. Handy for sports centre. Guest beers ⏃◖▮

10–2.30; 6–11

White Lion
35 Tower Street, Tower Hamlets ☎ (0304) 204754
Shepherd Neame Bitter H
Pleasant local in residential area ⏃≹ (Priory)

Try also: Royal Oak, Lower Rd, River (Shepherd Neame)

East Farleigh

11.30–2.30; 6–11

Walnut Tree
Forge Lane (½ mile off B2010 signed for Dean Street)
☎ (0622) 26368
Shepherd Neame Bitter, Stock Ale (winter) H
Unspoilt, cosy country local with easy chairs and real fires. Children's play area in garden. Pub games
⌂⚐⏃ ◖▮ ▤

East Peckham

11–2.30; 6–11

Bush, Blackbird & Thrush
Bush Road (off B2016, Peckham Bush)
☎ (0622) 871349
Fremlins Bitter G
Unspoilt and attractive tile-hung house in picturesque orchard setting ⌂⏃◖▤⚐

Elham

10.30–2.30; 6–11

Kings Arms
St Marys Road ☎ (030 384) 242
Flowers Original; Fremlins Bitter H
Popular pub with pleasant public bar and attractive saloon at rear. Bar billiards
⌂⏃ ◖▮ (not Sun) ⚐

Try also: New Inn, High St (Shepherd Neame)

Fairseat

12–2.30 (not Mon); 6–11

Vigo Inn
Gravesend Road (A227)
☎ (0732) 822547
Goacher's Vigo Bitter; Young Bitter, Special H
Very old travellers' inn, named after Battle of Vigo. A proper country ale house amidst the rising tide of trendy pubs. Daddlums table – a form of table skittles ⌂Q

Farningham

11–2.30; 6–11

Chequers

Kent

87 High Street ☎ (0322) 865222
Adnams Bitter; Everards Tiger; Fuller London Pride; Gibbs Mew GBH; Greene King IPA; Young Special H
Popular house at end of elongated picturesque village. Guest beers ⊛ ◖ ▶ (Wed–Sat)

Try also: Pied Bull, High St (Courage)

Faversham

10.30–3; 6–11
Bear
Market Place ☎ (0795) 532668
Shepherd Neame Bitter H
Friendly town pub with snug bar. Pub games ◖ ⊞ ⇌

10.30–3; 6–11
Bull
Tanners Street
☎ (0795) 534740
Flowers Original; Fremlins Bitter H
Spacious 14th-century inn, visited by Henry VIII in 1544. Pub games ▲⊛◖⊞⇌

10.30–3; 6–11
Mechanics Arms
44 West Street ☎ (0795) 532693
Shepherd Neame Bitter H
Small but splendid side street local near pedestrian precinct. Pub games Q⊞⇌

Folkestone

10–2.30; 6–11
Lifeboat
42 North Street ☎ (0303) 43958
Courage Directors; Fremlins Bitter; Hall & Woodhouse Badger Best Bitter; Hook Norton Best Bitter; Ind Coope Burton Ale; Taylor Landlord H
Small, bustling pub near harbour and fishmarket. Guest beers and ciders ⊛ ↻

10.30–2.30; 6–11 (7–11 Sat)
Richmond Tavern
1 Margaret Street
☎ (0303) 54857
Shepherd Neame Bitter H
Small, but lively locals' pub, off the beaten track ⊛

Frittenden

10–2.30; 6–11
Bell & Jorrocks
The Street ☎ (058 080) 415
Flowers Original; Fremlins Bitter H
Comfortable, friendly local in out of the way village. Guest beers. Pub games ▲⇗⊛◖▶&

Gillingham

10–2.30; 6–11
Golden Lion
18 High Street, Brompton (off A231) ☎ (0634) 44642
Courage Best Bitter H
Friendly house in centre of area with naval and military connections. Near Fort Amherst, historic dockyard, Heritage Centre and Royal Engineers Museum. No meals Sun ⇗◖▶⊞

Gravesend

10–2.30; 6–11
Bat & Ball
113 Wrotham Road
☎ (0474) 352097
Ruddles Best Bitter, County; Webster Yorkshire Bitter H
Spacious pub with very lively public bar. Overlooks the old Kent County cricket ground. Ideal for a summer drink and spot of spectating. Pub games ⊛◖⊞&⇌

11–2.30; 6–11
Jolly Drayman
1 Love Lane (off A226)
☎ (0474) 352355
Charrington IPA H
Old building with low ceilings, once the offices of a brewery. Games ⊛◖ (Mon–Fri) ⇌

10–2.30; 6–11
New Inn
1 Milton Road (A226)
☎ (0474) 66651
Fremlins Bitter H
Unpretentious little pub with strong local trade. Over 200 years old, the building was once part of a large private house ▲Q⇗⊛⊞&⇌

11–2.30; 6 (7 Sat)–11
Norfolk Arms
1 Norfolk Road (between A226 and Thames) ☎ (0474) 359158
Shepherd Neame Bitter, Best Bitter H
Unsophisticated pub, rather hidden away, with a strong local trade and its own video club. Pub games ◖

Hadlow

11–2.30; 6–11
Rose Revived
Ashes Lane (off A26)
☎ (0732) 850382
Fremlins Bitter; Harvey BB; King & Barnes Sussex Bitter, Old Ale H
Attractive and comfortable 15th-century inn. Note old keys in beams ▲⊛◖

Halling

11–2.30; 7–11
Homeward Bound
72 High Street (A228)
☎ (0634) 240743
Shepherd Neame Bitter H
1-bar local with pool and darts ▲◖ (not Sun) &⇌

Hawkhurst

10.30–2.30; 6–11
Oak & Ivy
Rye Road, Pipsden (A268)
☎ (058 05) 3293
Flowers Original G; **Fremlins Bitter** H
Popular roadside inn. Families welcome in dining area. Supper licence. Pub games ▲⇗⊛◖▶&

Heaverham

10–2.30; 6–11
Chequers
Watery Lane (2 miles N of A25) OS572587 ☎ (0732) 61413
Flowers Original; Fremlins Bitter H
Comfortable split-level saloon with inglenook. Public bar always lively. Restaurant, in a fine old barn, serves high quality food. Small menagerie with goats, ducks etc.
▲⊛◖▶⊞

Herne Bay

10–2.30; 6–11
Heron
Station Road ☎ (0227) 372991
Shepherd Neame Bitter H
Lively public – quiet smart saloon. Pub games ⇗⊛◖⊞⇌

10–2.30; 6–11
Prince of Wales
173 Mortimer Street
☎ (0227) 374205
Shepherd Neame Bitter H
Unspoilt, comfortable Victorian house between High Street and seafront. Pub games Q⊞

10–2.30; 7–11
Rose
111 Mortimer Street
Shepherd Neame Bitter H
Smart, cosy town-centre house Q◖⊞

Hollingbourne

11–2.30; 6–11
Park Gate
Ashford Road (A20)
☎ (062 780) 377
Fremlins Bitter; Goachers Dark Maidstone Ale; Ind Coope Burton Ale; Tetley Bitter H
Comfortable, friendly pub near Leeds Castle. Dates back to 1630; warm wood panelling in main bar. Table games ▲⇗⊛◖▶ (not Sun) &

10.30–2.30; 6–11
Windmill
Eyhorne Street (B2163)
☎ (062 780) 280
Flowers Original; Fremlins Bitter H
Cosy and popular 16th-century inn with extensive menu ▲⊛◖▶⇌

Lamberhurst

10.30–2.30; 6–11
Horse & Groom

160

Kent

High Street (B2100)
☎ (0892) 890302
Shepherd Neame Bitter, Best Bitter H
Attractive, friendly 2-bar village local with relaxed and comfortable saloon. Darts and Pool

Try also: Chequers (Fremlins)

Larkfield

10.30–2.30; 6–11
Monks Head
44 New Hythe Lane
☎ (0732) 842024
Courage Best Bitter, Directors H
Dates from 1540. A wealth of exposed timbers, large inglenook and galleried seating area. Pub games

Longfield

10.30–2.30; 6–11
Railway Tavern
2 Station Road ☎ (047 47) 2217
Ruddles Best Bitter, County; Truman Best Bitter, Sampson; Webster Yorkshire Bitter H
Village local offering friendly service and good value for money to a wide catchment area. Pub games

Luddenham

10.30–3; 6–11
Mounted Rifleman
Stone, near Stone railway crossing OS981627
Fremlins Bitter G
Beer carried up from the cellar. Well worth finding. Pub games

Maidstone

10–2.30; 6–11
Drakes Crab & Oyster House
9 Fairmeadow (off A229/A20 roundabout) ☎ (0622) 52531
Flowers IPA, Original; Fremlins Bitter H
Bare-boarded ale and wine house near river. Popular for lunches and with the young at night. Seafood a speciality
(West & East)

10–2.30, 0–11
First & Last
40 Bower Place (off A26)
☎ (0604) 51646
Flowers Original; Fremlins Bitter H
Recently reopened after minimum renovation. Guest beers. Pub games
(West & East)

10 2.30, 6–11
Greyhound
77 Wheeler Street
☎ (0604) 54032
Shepherd Neame Bitter H
Much improved corner local with small public bar. Pub games
Q (snug) (East)

10.30–2.30; 6–11
Hare & Hounds
45–47 Lower Boxley Road (A229 near prison)
☎ (0604) 678388
Fremlins Bitter H
Recent return to the real ale fold. Various games
(East)

11–2.30; 6–11
Wheelers Arms
1 Perry Street (off A229)
☎ (0604) 52229
Shepherd Neame Bitter, Best Bitter H
Excellent and popular pub. Folk club Sat eves. Darts, bar billiards (East)

Try also: Dog & Gun; Dragoon (Shepherd Neame)

Manston

11–2.30; 5.30–11
Jolly Farmer
3 High Street ☎ (0843) 823208
Fremlins Bitter H
Popular village local near RAF Manston and Spitfire Museum. Barbecues each summer weekend. Pub games
(not Sun)

Margate

11–2.30; 5.30–11
Duke of Edinburgh
Milton Avenue
☎ (0843) 221121
Shepherd Neame Bitter H
Popular local on corner of Victorian terrace. Pub games

11–2.30; 5.30–11
Orb
243 Ramsgate Road (A254)
☎ (0843) 220663
Shepherd Neame Bitter, Best Bitter H
14 consecutive years in Good Beer Guide – enough said? Pub games

11–2.30; 5.30–11
Spread Eagle
25 Victoria Road
☎ (0843) 293396
Brakspear Special; Burton Bridge Bitter; Hook Norton Old Hookey; Palmer IPA; Wadworth 6X; Young Special H
Probably the finest real ale outlet in these parts. Superb pub, not to be missed

Marshside

10.30–2.30; 6–11
Gate Inn
1½ miles up Chislet turning off A28 ☎ (0227) 86498
Shepherd Neame Bitter, Best Bitter, Stock Ale G
Lively country pub, superb value. Excellent snacks. Pub games

Meopham

10–2.30; 6–11
Cricketers
Wrotham Road
☎ (0474) 812163
Cricketers Bitter; Ind Coope Bitter, Burton Ale H
Characterful old pub on village green near cricket pitch. Ideal for Sunday lunch, a pint and a few overs. Preserved windmill next door

Mersham

11–2.30; 6.30–11
Farriers Arms
OS049341 ☎ (023 372) 444
Friary Meux Best H
Attractive pub with games area in what used to be the public bar

Milton Regis

10.30–2.30; 6–11
Forresters Arms
77 Charlotte Street (behind Bowaters factory)
☎ (0795) 72183
Fremlins Bitter H
Friendly back-street local. Pub games (Sittingbourne)

Minster (Sheppey)

11–2.30; 6–11
Prince of Waterloo
428 Minster Road (B2008)
☎ (0795) 872458
Ind Coope Burton Ale H
Popular village pub; various games

Minster (Thanet)

11–2.30; 5.30–11
Saddler
7–9 Monkton Road (B2047)
☎ (0843) 821331
Shepherd Neame Bitter H
Excellent 2-bar local in attractive village

Offham

10.30–2.30; 6–11
Kings Arms
The Green, Teston Road (off A20) ☎ (0732) 845208
Courage Best Bitter, Directors H
Overlooking the village green in this picturesque location, a warm welcome is assured. Hop-laden beams, bare ragstone walls and a fire in the inglenook. Darts
(not Sun) (not Mon)

Try also: Red Lion, Church Rd (Fremlins)

Otford

11–2.30; 6–11

161

Kent

Horns
66 High Street (near River Darent) ☎ (09592) 2604
Charrington IPA; Harvey BB; King & Barnes Sussex Bitter H
Friendly 15th-century inn with 2 comfortable bars and good food. Village has some fine old houses and ruined 16th-century archbishops' palace ▲Q✦(]►≠

Try also: All other pubs in village

Painters Forstal

10.30–3; 6–11

Alma
Painters Forstal Road (1½ miles S of A2 at Ospringe) ☎ (0795) 533835
Shepherd Neame Bitter H
Kentish weatherboard rural inn surrounded by hopfields. Pub games Q✦₠

Petteridge

11 (12 winter)–2.30; 6–11

Hopbine Inn
Petteridge Lane, Matfield (off A21 ½ mile S of Brenchley) OS667413 ☎ (0892) 722761
King & Barnes Sussex Mild, Sussex Bitter, Old Ale, Draught Festive H
Cosy, welcoming country pub in attractive and remote setting. Hard to find but worth the effort ▲✦(]

Rainham

10.30–2.30; 6.30–11

Green Lion
High Street (A2) ☎ (0634) 31938
Courage Best Bitter, Directors H
One-time coaching inn, simply "Lion" until this century ✦(]₠≠

Ramsgate

11–2.30; 5.30–11

Foy Boat Hotel
8 Sion Hill ☎ (0843) 591198
Flowers Original; Fremlins Bitter H
Plush single bar pub on clifftop overlooking Royal Harbour restaurant (]►

11–2.30; 5.30–11

Sportsman Inn
123 Sandwich Road (A256) ☎ (0843) 592175
Fremlins Bitter H
1-bar village pub on main road near Pegwell Bay Nature Reserve, Viking ship and old hoverport. Pub games; family room. No food Sun ▲ъ(]►

Rochester

11–2.30; 6–11

Coopers Arms
10 St. Margarets Street ☎ (0634) 404298
Courage Best Bitter, Directors; John Smith Bitter H
Very attractive and ancient 2-bar hostelry which has a warm and restful atmosphere. 100 yards from cathedral and castle, near the River Medway. Barbecues summer Fri eves ▲✦(] (not Sun) &≠

10–2.30; 6–11

Greyhound
68 Rochester Avenue ☎ (0634) 44120
Shepherd Neame Bitter H
Cosy, terraced tavern with Victorian furnishings and range in saloon. Various games ▲✦(]►₠≠

Try also: Britannia, High St (Free)

Rodmersham Green

10.30–2.30; 6–11

Fruiterers Arms
1½ miles SE of Sittingbourne ☎ (0795) 24198
Courage Best Bitter, Directors H
Thriving country inn with pleasant garden. Pub games ▲✦(]₠

Ryarsh

11–2.30; 6–11

Duke of Wellington
The Street (off A20) ☎ (0732) 842318
Flowers Original; Fremlins Bitter H
Old village inn with original wattle and daub wall, beams, brasses and inglenooks. 2 bars. Jazz and other live music weekly. Guest beers ▲ъ✦(]₠

St Peter's (Broadstairs)

9–2; 5–10.15

St Peter's (off licence)
68 Church Street ☎ (0843) 61524
Shepherd Neame Bitter H
Friendly service with cheap prices

Sandgate

10–2.30; 6–11

Ship
High Street
Ind Coope Burton Ale H
Seafront pub with small public and popular saloon bar ✦(]₠

Sandwich

10–2.30; 6–11

George & Dragon
24 Fisher Street ☎ (0304) 613106
Fremlins Bitter H
Busy backstreet pub with unfussy interior. Bar billiards ✦(]►

10–2.30; 6–11

New Inn
Harnet Street (corner of market square) ☎ (0304) 612335
Ruddles County; Webster Yorkshire Bitter H
Modernised, comfortable town-centre pub – bilingual pub sign offers 'Jeux de Pubs'! (]≠

All pubs in Sandwich sell real ale

Seal

10.30–2.30; 6–11

Five Bells
Church Road (100 yds N of A25) ☎ (0732) 61503
Charrington IPA; Harvey BB; Young Special H
Small, old pub in backstreet, beer range may vary. No food Sun ▲(]

Sevenoaks

10.30–2.30; 6–11

Royal Oak Tap
High Street (A225) ☎ (0732) 455664
Fremlins Bitter; Ruddles County; Webster Yorkshire Bitter H
Pleasant and comfortable 2-bar pub, in old part of town. Guest beers ▲✦(]

10.30–2.30; 6–11

Vine Tavern
11 Pound Lane (A225) ☎ (0732) 454641
Friary Meux Best; Ind Coope Burton Ale; Tetley Bitter H
Popular Victorian pub opposite second oldest cricket ground in country. Single bar on 3 different levels ▲✦(]≠

Try also: Anchor (Charrington)

Shatterling

10–2.30; 6–11

Green Man
Pedding Hill (A257 Ash–Wingham road) ☎ (0304) 812525
Adnams Bitter; Young Bitter, Special H
Comfortable, friendly pub with restaurant – descriptions of traditional pub games on walls ▲✦(]▲

Sheerness

12–2.30; 6–11

Red Lion
High Street, Bluetown ☎ (0795) 663165
Draught Bass; Brain Bitter; Felinfoel Double Dragon; Fremlins Bitter; Greene King

Kent

Abbot; Mansfield Old Baily ⓗ
Cosy real ale mecca, handy for ferry terminal. Pub games

11–2.30; 6–11

Seaview Hotel
Broadway ☎ (0795) 662003
Shepherd Neame Bitter ⓗ
Busy hotel with remains of windmill in car park. Pub games

Shepherds Well

10–2.30; 6–11

Bricklayers Arms
Coxhill ☎ (0304) 830323
Shepherd Neame Bitter ⓗ
Busy village local. Darts

Shoreham

10.30–2.30; 6–11

Royal Oak
High Street ☎ (095 92) 2903
Flowers Original; Fremlins Bitter ⓗ
Old village centre pub. Many teams; 2 darts boards prove that. Superb food. Guest beers

Shorne

10–2.30; 6–11

Rose & Crown
32 The Street (off A226)
☎ (047 482) 2373
Ruddles Best Bitter, County ⓗ
Most attractive and welcoming pub in pleasant surroundings
Q (not Sun)

Shottenden

10.30–2.00; 6–11

Plough
Shottenden Road (off A252, near Chilham) ☎ (022 773) 244
Adnams Bitter; Cornish Wessex Stud ⓖ**; Fremlins Bitter; Shepherd Neame Bitter** ⓗ
Comfortable country free house with large garden. Pub games

Sittingbourne

10.30–2.30; 7–11

Park Tavern
86 Park Road (off A?)
☎ (0795) 72486
Shepherd Neame Bitter ⓗ
Busy local near town centre. Pub games Q

10.30–2.30; 7–11

Red Lion
58 High Street (A2)
☎ (0795) 72706
Flowers Original; Fremlins Bitter ⓗ
Old 17th-century coaching house. Vegetarian food available. Guest beers

Smarden

11.30 (11 Sat)–2.30; 6–11

Bell
Bell Lane (off A274)
Flowers Original; Fremlins Bitter; Fuller London Pride; Goachers Light Maidstone Ale; Shepherd Neame Best Bitter; Theakston Best Bitter, Old Peculier ⓗ
Popular centuries-old pub with a good range of pub food. Family room

Snargate

11–2.30; 6–11

Red Lion
(B2080 Brenzett–Appledore road) ☎ (067 94) 648
Shepherd Neame Bitter ⓖ
Unspoilt, traditional pub with marble counter top in single bar. Pub holds key for village church. Toad in-the-hole game Q

Southborough

10.30–2.30; 6–11

Bat & Ball
London Road (A26)
Bateman XXXB; Flowers Original; Fremlins Bitter ⓗ
Comfortable and friendly 1-bar pub with low ceiling and cricketing mementos. Good value, well presented bar meals. Guest beers
(not Sun)

Southfleet

11–2.30; 6–11

Black Lion
Red Street ☎ (047 483) 2386
Ruddles Best Bitter, County; Truman Best Bitter; Webster Yorkshire Bitter ⓗ
Thatched building dates from 14th century; used as body store during the Great Plague! Excellent food; quiet country atmosphere (5) Q

10.30–2.30; 6–11

Wheatsheaf
8 High Cross Road, Westwood (1½ miles N of B260 at Longfield) ☎ (047 483) 3210
Courage Best Bitter, Directors ⓗ
Picturesque thatched inn of great character whose history can be traced back to 1408. Split-level bar
Q (Mon–Fri)

Speldhurst

10.30–2.30; 6–11

George & Dragon
Speldhurst Hill (off A26 at Southborough)
☎ (089 286) 3125
Flowers Original; Fremlins Bitter; Harvey PA, BB; Larkins Best Bitter, Porter ⓗ
Large, comfortable country pub which dates back to 1212. Cosy lounge and large stone-flagged public bar. Separate restaurant Q

Stansted

11–2.30; 7–11

Black Horse
Tumblefield Road (1 mile N of A20) ☎ (0732) 822355
Fremlins Bitter; Wethered Winter Royal; Whitbread Castle Eden Ale ⓗ
Rural pub popular with walkers, cyclists and travellers. Active participation in village life. Guest beers

Strood

10–2.30; 6–11

Horseshoe
51 Cuxton Road (A228)
☎ (0634) 718414
Ind Coope Burton Ale ⓗ
Lively 2-bar local. Pub games
(not Sun)

Thurnham

10.30–2.30; 6–11

Black Horse
Pilgrims Way (off A249 at Detling) OS806578
☎ (0622) 37185
Flowers Original; Fremlins Bitter ⓗ
Remote country pub with beer garden. Imaginative food. Guest beers
Q (not Sun) A

Tilmanstone

10–2.30; 6–11

Ravens
Upper Street (off A256)
☎ (0304) 617337
Fremlins Bitter ⓗ
Friendly local, popular with local farming community

Try also: **Plough & Harrow**, Dover Rd (Free)

Tonbridge

11–2.30; 6–11

Foresters Arms
Quarry Hill Road (A26)
☎ (0732) 354285
Shepherd Neame Bitter ⓗ**, Stock Ale (winter)** ⓖ
Friendly local with a lively public bar and quieter, cosy saloon (not Sun)

10.30–2.30; 6–11

Rose & Crown
125 High Street (A26) ☎ (0732) 357966
Fremlins Bitter; Larkins Best Bitter ⓗ
Small, comfortable bar in imposing and historic hotel
Q

163

Kent

11–2.30; 6–11
Uncle Tom's Cabin
Lavender Hill (off A2014)
☎ (0732) 365044
Crown SBB, Special H
Small, friendly free house in quiet terrace. Unusual choice of beers for the area 🍺 ⏵ ⇌

Try also: Chequers (Courage)

Tudeley

11–2.30; 7–11
George & Dragon
Five Oak Green Road (B2017)
☎ (0892) 832521
Courage Best Bitter, Directors H
Attractive, part weatherboarded pub dating back to 16th century. Traditional bar, comfortable saloon and dining room 🏨🍺 ⏵ ⇌

Tunbridge Wells

10.30–2.30; 6–11
Crystal Palace
69 Camden Road
☎ (0892) 22815
Harvey XX, Pale Ale, BB, XXXX H
2-bar pub with quiet, comfortable saloon, and down to earth public bar. Handy for Calverly Road shopping precinct ⏵ (not Sun) ⇌

10.30–2.30; 6–11
Duke of York
The Pantiles ☎ (0892) 30482
Flowers Original; Fremlins Bitter H
Extremely busy town pub frequented by young people. In middle of famous Pantiles area near 'the Waters'
🍺 (seats) ⚲

10.30–2.30; 6–11
George
29 Mount Ephraim (off A26)
☎ (0892) 20737
Flowers Original; Fremlins Bitter H
Former coaching inn, now a pleasant multi-roomed pub with ornate cut glass and Victorian and tiled fireplaces. Guest beers ⋈ ⏵ (not Sun) ⇌

Ulcombe

10.30–2.30; 6.30–11
Pepperbox
Windmill Hill Fairbourne Heath (1½ miles off A20)
☎ (0622) 842558
Shepherd Neame Bitter G
Charming 17th-century country pub with 2 real fires; free from modern pub games 🏨Q🍺⏵⚲

Upper Halling

12–2.30; 7–11
Robin Hood
The Street ☎ (0634) 240529
Fremlins Bitter H
Attractive and cosy pub with separate games and music area 🏨🍺⏵⚲

Upper Upnor

11–2.30; 7–11
Kings Arms
2 The High Street
☎ (0634) 717490
Courage Best Bitter, Directors H
Friendly village pub. No food Sun. Pub games 🏨🍺⏵⚲

11–2.30; 7–11
Tudor Rose
29 High Street ☎ (0634) 715305
Brain SA; Young Bitter, Special, Winter Warmer H
Friendly pub: quiet room with inglenook and separate games area. Near castle and river. No meals Sun 🏨🍺⏵⚲

Walmer

10–2.30; 6–11
Thompson Bell
Dover Road (A258)
☎ (0304) 361995
Charrington IPA H
Busy, convivial pub, named after Thompson's Brewery
🍺⏵⇌

Warren Street

11–2.30; 7–11
Harrow
1 mile NE of A20 at Lenham OS926529 ☎ (0622) 858727
Fremlins Bitter; Goachers Light Maidstone Ale; Shepherd Neame Bitter H
Spacious rural inn on North Downs with good restaurant. Guest beers 🏨🍺⋈⏵

West Cliffe

10–2.30; 6–11
Swingate Inn
Deal Road (A258)
☎ (0304) 204043
Draught Bass H
Cosy roadhouse – normal home of local CAMRA branch's daddlums table
🏨Q🍺

West Malling

10–2.30; 6–11
Bull
1 High Street ☎ (0732) 842753
Draught Bass; Charrington IPA; Everards Old Original H
Victorian exterior conceals a much altered 16th-century interior. Comfortable wood panelled single bar. Guest beers 🏨🍺⏵⇌

Try also: Swan Hotel (Charrington)

Westerham

10.30–2.30; 6–11
General Wolfe
High Street (A25)
☎ (0959) 62104
Friary Meux Best; Ind Coope Burton Ale H
Classic old weatherboard pub adjoining the former Westerham Brewery
🏨⏵ (Wed-Fri)

Whitstable

10–2.30; 6–11
Coach & Horses
Oxford Street (A290)
Shepherd Neame Bitter H
Busy high street local.
Pub games Q🍺⏵⚲⇌

10–2.30; 6–11
Rose in Bloom
69 Joy Lane (off A290)
Flowers Original; Fremlins Bitter H
Smart pub with sea views from gardens Q🏨🍺⏵⚲

10–2.30; 6–11 (supper licence extension)
Wall Tavern
Middle Wall
Flowers Original; Fremlins Bitter H
Weatherboarded pub behind the High Street 🏨🍺⏵

Wingham

10–2.30; 6–11
Anchor
High Street (A257)
☎ (0227) 720229
Fremlins Bitter H
Rambling old house – unusual variety of seating ⏵⏵

Try also: Red Lion, High St (Fremlins)

Wouldham

11–2.30; 6–11
Medway
2 High Street ☎ (0634) 666619
Fremlins Bitter H
Spacious village inn with a friendly relaxed atmosphere. No meals Sun. Darts and bar billiards 🏨🍺⏵⏵

Try also: Watermans Arms (Ind Coope)

Wrotham

10–2.30; 6–11
Three Post Boys
The Square (off A20)
☎ (0732) 883888
Courage Best Bitter H
Old coaching inn: first stop on London–Folkestone road. Royal Mails were sorted here for delivery to outlying villages by post boys who lived on the premises. Award-winning garden for children. No food Sun 🏨🍺⏵

Try also: Rose & Crown (Shepherd Neame)

THE ADVERTISING HYPE

TIME FOR A NATURAL BREAK?

Don Steele

The drinks industry is shy about its expenditure on advertising and now denies an annual figure of £200 million, which is based on a statement made by one of its own spokesmen two years ago. To be quite frank the actual amount hardly matters; whatever the outlay, the industry is getting a bargain, and it knows it. Not only has promotion almost reached saturation point, with the BBC apparently competing with ITV for booze exposure through soap operas and sponsored sport, but the content of advertisements goes virtually unchallenged. It is no coincidence that one of the first actions of the recently appointed Goverment Ministerial Alcohol Group (The Wakeham Committee) was to call on the IBA and ASA to get their act together. Both are now drawing up new codes of practice and it remains to be seen whether the ultimate outcome is anything other than cosmetic. On past evidence the brewers will continue to get a good deal, not least because the complaints procedure is so cumbersome that even those brave souls willing to negotiate it usually find that by the time their complaint is heard, the particular advertising campaign has come to an end anyway.

It is no surprise that a Government Committee (The Masham Committee – 1987) has now called for a ban on advertising. The industry laughed hysterically in 1986 when **Action on Alcohol Abuse** publicly predicted a ban by 1990. The laugh has now been reduced to a self-conscious smile. As usual the good old brand share argument has been wheeled out. Advertising, say its perpetrators, does not increase aggregate consumption – only encourage competition between brands. It is strange that the only products for which this argument is advanced are those which are under threat – alcohol and tobacco. Who would argue for one moment that brand advertising of motor cars did not contribute to the aggregate increase of vehicles on our roads? The trouble for the industry is that no-one believes them any more and, ominously, there are doubters within their own ranks. As David Abbot, Director of agency Abbott, Mead, Vickers said recently, 'I think arguments like shifting brands are just insulting in their shallowness'. Ouch!

Of course, no-one is denying that the brewers have problems. Most of their advertising spend goes on lager, and this is not surprising. It can't be easy promoting a product which is basically the same as that produced by the opposition. In such a war only the image counts – and in the world of the image makers hype is more important than reality. There can be no other explanation for the bizarre parade of improbables which is lager advertising.

Paul Hogan and his 'Amber Nectar' (if you don't laugh what else can you do?) sums up the whole charade. Nectar, the drink of mythology, ethereal, everything and nothing. Has there been any other substance in the history of the world which, on a single pub crawl could provide: **a manly image** (women don't get a look in except as the ogle factor – nectar is strictly for the boys);

acceptance by the in-crowd; refreshment of parts the drinker never knew he had; the ability to emulate Don Juan and at the same time keep the little woman in her place; **become a winner** in almost any sport or other pursuit which takes his fancy... and **pursue his fetish** for teddy bears, without facing ridicule?

And there is little doubt about the target audience of the Dream Merchants. The Advertising Agency brief for the Griff Rhys Jones (plus Marilyn Monroe) Holsten Pils commercials stated that its strategy was 'to woo 16–35 year old draught lager drinkers'. According to a growing mound of evidence – including that provided by the Government itself – 12 and 13 year olds also rather like lager advertisements (in several surveys Carling Black Label and Miller Lite beat Coca-Cola hands down) and are consuming the nectar to an unprecedented degree. 11% of 14 year olds interviewed in an Exeter University study were drinking 10 and a half pints or more of the stuff every week.

Advertising campaigns are obviously built on the assumption that there are large numbers of people around who will swallow anything. There is apparently no contradiction in the public mind between Jonathan Ross accepting public money on one day to warn the nation's children about the dangers of 'hard' drugs and his advertising Harp Lager on the next. Alcohol actually kills ten times more kids in one year than the so called 'dangerous' drugs will kill in ten; worth remembering the next time we are invited to 'Follow the Bear'.

Alongside lager, cider is increasingly being promoted for the teenage market. Bulmers 1080 ('Double fermented – **that** should blow the lid off the cider market') is typical of the current approach – get them young and make it **STRONG**. The explanation given by the Chairman of the Advertising Standards Authority for letting Bulmers get away with their audacious advert for Woodpecker ('Spend some Time out of Your Tree') was 'Our members didn't actually know what 'out of your tree' meant'. Rumour has it that a massage parlour in Notting Hill is about to produce a double page spread inviting pubescent sixth formers to enjoy 'an unforgettable Ugandan experience'. They shouldn't have too much difficulty.

The use of sex in advertisements has almost become a cliche and the injuction in the advertising code 'Advertisements must neither claim nor suggest that any drink can contribute toward sexual success' must be the best one-liner the Establishment has ever produced. Examples abound – Martini . . . Budweiser . . . Red Stripe . . . and of course, Smirnoff. At least Len Weinreich was honest enough when he described the Campaign as 'intended to show Smirnoff as "a good leg opener"!'

Drink and life-style are now inextricably linked and for most consumers the style seems to come first. Suggestive minimalism. The unsexy paraphernalia of drinking against a background of exotic sensuality. Tight jeans and easy living. Who really cares what's in the can – or for that matter, who in the end will have to carry it?

Don Steele is a director of ACTION ON ALCOHOL ABUSE and Secretary to the Parliamentary Alcohol Policy and Services Group.

CAMPAIGNING: WHY BOTHER?

Danny Blyth

CAMRA has been at it for years. Campaigning that is, constant hard work directed at those in power in the brewing industry and licensed trade, persuading them to act more in the interest of we, the consumers, rather than the accountants, admen and shareholders.

Let's face it, if the big national brewing combines had their way we'd all be drinking Fosters, Budweiser or some other "foreign" fizzy concoction at £2 a pint in a soulless, plastic, disco bar-cum eaterie that only our grannies would remember as having once been a warm and welcoming traditional British pub.

So it gives us a little cheer to look back at some of our successes:
- flexible pub opening hours coming at last to England and Wales in 1988, after hard lobbying by CAMRA
- the virtual death of keg beer (remember it?), the stuff the national brewers spent so many millions on forcing down our throats in the '70s
- breathing life into our small traditional brewers by creating a solid demand for real ale
- helping save several other independents from takeover, like Camerons of Hartlepool
- boosting real ale so much that since CAMRA started 200 new small breweries and 150 new brewpubs have started up.

But as we enter the 1990s, and the 20th year of CAMRA, some people are wondering out loud: "Why bother carrying on? Especially with so many pubs selling real ale these days – hasn't CAMRA outlived its usefulness?"

Well the truth is that there is more reason to step up campaigning pressure now than at any other time. So here is how to handle the doubting Thomas . . .

Why bother about the price of a pint?

Because drinkers in many areas are being ripped off. Only those lucky souls in the likes of Greater Manchester, – where a cluster of local independent brewers like Holts, Lees, Hydes and Robinson create the competition to keep prices down – are any different. Most areas are dominated by pubs of the Big Seven (now recoined The Voracious Eight), who bleed consumers for all they're worth for everything from soft drinks to strong ales.

Why bother about the independent brewers?

The independents give us the best quality beers at the cheapest prices. And they are much less prone to tarting up your local to look like a Californian bath house. But the Big Boys are on the prowl, buying them up, closing them down. This means less choice of beers, less competition and higher prices, along with more bland real ales, national brands like Websters Yorkshire Bitter from Watneys and Ind Coope Bitter from Allied. Ten years ago there were 100 independent brewers, now there are just 55 and if present trends continue there will be none left at all by the turn of the century. Imagine it – no Youngs, Holts, Maclays or Batemans.

Why bother about lager?

Lager has replaced keg beer as the national brewers' favourite son. It is poor quality stuff, often made from inferior ingredients and a poor imitation of what we can get on a holiday on the Rhine. It also sells for up to 20 per cent more than beer, so no wonder the big brewers are doing all they can to boost lager sales at the expense of traditional British beer. They are giving a thumping 70 per cent of their vast advertising budgets to lager,

The Campaigning Year . . . a funeral march to mark the passing of Wethered's Marlow brewery (April '88).

though it accounts for only 45 per cent of the market. The drinker deserves a better deal, and that includes the lager drinker.

Why bother about ingredients?
Though people don't exactly seem to be keeling over poisoned from what goes into their pints, there is growing concern at the way brewers seem to be shying away from telling the consumer exactly what it is that goes into what we drink. A recent CAMRA report on low alcohol beers found that a series of potentially harmful additives were being used: E150, E223, E224, E405 and other substances like Aspartame. The law, a particularly fat ass when it comes to beer, says that only beers under 1.2% alcohol by volume must list their ingredients. Only full ingredient listing, for all beer, no matter what strength, will allow us to choose what we want to consume with or without safety.

Why bother about monopolies?
Local monopolies – high concentrations of pubs belonging to one or two brewers, stifle competition and consumer choice. Birmingham, dominated by Ansells (Allied) and Mitchells & Butler (Bass), is a classic example of a city where takeovers and closures has left a city desperately short on choice. Monopolies are created by brewery takeovers, which if our brewing heritage is to survive into the next century, must be halted now. The prospect of Britain ending up like Canada or the USA with a handful of giant companies dominating the market with a handful of appallingly bland lagers is enough to make everyone cringe, with the possible exception of the manufacturers of home-brew kits.

So the fight is set to continue. We will keep the campaigning up and continue to:
- expose the ludicrous prices of the Voracious Eight in our surveys
- complain about sub-standard beer quality and praise the best when we find it
- back the independent brewers – those who give the consumer the best deal all round
- hit out at the millions spent on boosting sales of poor quality, high priced lager instead of traditional ale
- press the Government to legislate for an end to brewery takeovers and a break up of local monopolies

It will mean even more effort all round. There will be more work of all sorts put in by our 170 branches round the country, beavering away on a range of fronts at the grass roots level. More effort too by our national set-up, with the production of more and more reports and other publications to further the cause of good ales and good pubs. And it will mean greater work by our folk in parliament, both at home and on the European front.

It should be quite obvious from all this that CAMRA is far from a drinking club of old beer bores away in the back rooms of pubs swapping stories of ales gone by. We are determined to remain what we are – an active and vigorous consumer group dedicated to improving the lot of all drinkers and all pub users. There is a great social side to things too – but you'll have to join first to discover all about that. There is a form on page 384, fill it in and do the cause of good beer some good – we won't be able to do it all in our eighteenth year.

WOMEN AND THE PUB
THE BITTER TRUTH
Katherine Adams

You only have to glance down the opening page of this Good Beer Guide to know what passionate pub lovers rate as important. Pubs should, above all, be ⚜Q✤₠. For new readers unversed in the significance of these vital hieroglyphics, this means that pubs should, as well as serving good ale, be quiet ("no electronic music, TV or obtrusive games" admonishes the Guide, sternly), warmed by a **real** fire ("fuelled by coal, smokeless fuel or logs"), possess a "proper public bar", and a garden.

What people want from a pub, it seems, is a short breather from the strains and tedium of mass-produced modern convenience. It's true that some more modern pubs are to be found recommended in its pages ("excellent 60s decor", "real 50s ambience", whatever that might be) as fine examples of a particular, now defunct, **type**. But what seems to unite the real beer, real pubs campaigners is a desire for variety, distinctiveness, and good old fashioned hospitality.

This is, I am sure, 90% a Good Thing. And yet . . . let us consider for a moment what you might call the downside of this otherwise admirable urge to retain the finer parts of our long-standing and deeply rooted drinking heritage. Speaking personally, the biggest drawback with pubs is, to be blunt, that they were designed by and large for men. And I'm not thinking here of that well known, though thankfully increasingly rare, hazard, the outside ladies toilet; a convenience of dubious hygiene reached only by crossing a dark wet backyard containing two mysogynist Dobermen.

Nor am I referring to the inevitable little embarrassments attendant on an intrepid woman buying a round. Such as those times when I buy a pint for myself and a half of Guinness for an abstemious male companion, and he gets his half in a "lady's glass". This relic of a gentler age comes in various shapes and sizes; the essential feature though is that it should knock over easily and be difficult to drink out of, being designed, I suppose, for dainty sipping rather than full-blooded quaffing or sluicing.

This sort of thing is all part of the fun of pubs; just one of the hazards which would be intolerable anywhere else but which we positively embrace in the name of authenticity. The point of a pub, after all, is that its beery interior should remain impervious to the race of Progress outside. A really good pub will stand as a last bastion of a whole range of otherwise outmoded attitudes. Take that old dinosaur, class distinction, for example. The "proper public bar" (snug, smoke, bar) is the natural habitat of proles, students and others who can be relied upon to spit into the sawdust provided. The lounge (parlour, best end) is for the nobs, and, of course, the ladies.

The most rigid distinction in the minefield of pub etiquette, though, has to be that between the "locals" and the "foreigners". Many of the latter can tell you horror stories of the unresponsiveness, hostility or downright rudeness they have received at the hands of the local clique.

But if "foreign" men are only just tolerated, women have traditionally been beyond the pale in the hierarchy of pub life. The pub was, after all, the place where men went to escape their women, as we are nightly reminded by all those TV ads pushing the idea of boozy masculine bonhomie. Capturing a bigger market share may be the name of the corporate game, but the big breweries don't yet seem to have taken on board the fact that they'd all be chasing shares of a **bigger** market if they broadened their appeal to women too.

The real drawback of pubs as far as women are concerned is that we simply don't feel comfortable going into a pub alone. When a group of women plan to meet up in a pub, endless amounts of low

> "NAH! I DON'T ENCOURAGE WOMEN — IT'D RUIN THE ATMOSPHERE!"

cunning will be employed to avoid being the first to arrive. This may well involve hanging around a dark, wet bus stop in Brixton rather than risk being the first at a warm, well-lit hostelry. Is this one reason for the development of new style "fish-bowl" pubs, which you can see into from outside? They may be hideous, but they do have the advantage over the frosted glass and cosy claustrophobia of the old fashioned snug that you know exactly what you're getting into before chancing your arm.

But why don't women want to waltz into a strange pub unescorted, as men quite naturally do? Outright verbal abuse or hostility is thankfully quite rare in British pubs. But women who actually like pubs are familiar with the unspoken but quite palpable assumption of the assembled males that a woman who comes alone into a pub, or otherwise doesn't mind her ps and qs must be either a scarlet woman or a pint-swilling harridan.

Am I alone in thinking that this unwelcoming atmosphere might have something to do with lack of interest in real ale? In 1984, only 32% of women as opposed to 85% of men named beer or lager as their normal drink in a pub. And those figures don't reveal the whole story, since in that year only 24% of women regularly visited a pub, as opposed to 50% of men.

So what can be done to stop women being deterred from acquiring the peculiar pleasures of drinking beer in pubs? The answer is emphatically not to prettify pubs with mock Victoriana and hanging baskets. There are already plenty of wine bars, cocktail bars, and the like, where women are quite happy to venture alone. But we don't want to be consigned to these overdesigned backwaters of drinking life.

All the signs are that despite the pitfalls, more and more women will in future be summoning up their courage and walking into their local. In Scotland, the relaxation of the licensing laws ten years ago had very little effect on the amount of drinking done by men, but produced a 20% increase in women's consumption. And as CAMRA members have cause to know, more consumers mean more consumer power.

Lancashire

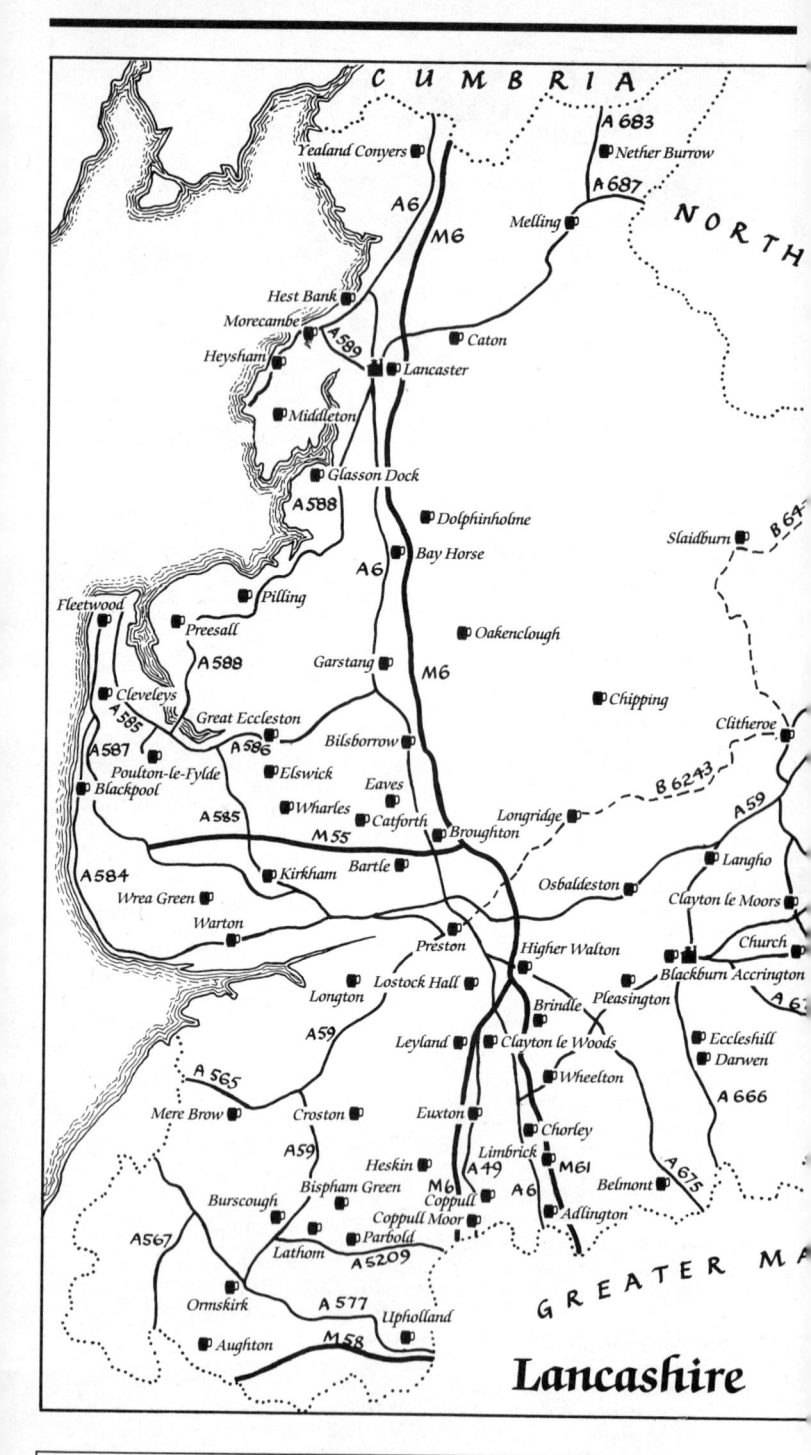

Matthew Brown, *Thwaites*; Blackburn, **Mitchells**, Lancaster; **Moorhouse's**, Burnley

Lancashire

Arnold Street (off A679)
☎ (0254) 34483
Thwaites Mild, Bitter H
Friendly local in improved part of town. Games

11.30–3; 6–11
New Brewery Inn
Maudsley Street
☎ (0254) 31503
John Smith Bitter H
Cosy local near town centre – watch out for the one-way system. Games

Adlington

11–3; 6–11
Cardwell
95 Chorley Road (A573)
☎ (0257) 480319
Vaux Samson; Ward Sheffield Best Bitter H
Much extended pub popular with young people. Open-plan lounge and separate games room. Regular guest beer

11–3; 6–11
White Bear
5a Market Street (A6)
☎ (0257) 482357
Matthew Brown Mild; Theakston Best Bitter, XB, Old Peculier H
Large, white-painted local pub with good food (not Mon) and a friendly welcome. Games

Aughton

11–3; 5.30 (6 Sat)–11
Dog & Gun
223 Long Lane (off A59)
☎ (0695) 423303
Burtonwood Dark Mild, Bitter H
Rural pub with bowling green, on edge of town

11–3; 5.30–11
Royal Oak
134 Liverpool Road
☎ (0695) 422121
Ind Coope Burton Ale; Walker Mild, Best Bitter H
Comfortable suburban local with distinctive U-shaped public bar. Pub games and teams (not Sun)

Bacup

11.30–3; 7–11
Waterworks
74 Market Street (A681)
☎ (0706) 878881
Chesters Mild; Hartley XB; Whitbread Castle Eden Ale, Trophy H
Tastefully decorated pub with 2 rooms at street level and sunken games room with pool table. Good food

Bartle

11–3; 6–11
Sitting Goose Inn
Sidgreaves Lane (A5085)
OS486329 ☎ (0772) 690344
Thwaites Best Mild, Bitter E
Very comfortable pub in wooded Fylde countryside. Good food

Bay Horse

11–3 (closed Mon); 6–11
Bay Horse
Between A6 and M6 S of Jct 33
OS492529 ☎ (0524) 791204
Mitchells Mild, Bitter H
Cosy lounge with attached pool room; small vault. Live music in large barn. Own Rugby Union team. Evening meals summer and weekends only

Belmont Village

12–3; 7–11
Black Dog Inn
Corner Church Street/A675
OS674158 ☎ (020 481) 218
Holt Mild, Bitter H
Popular moorland village pub. Landlord whistles the classics; occasional live orchestras
(not Mon)

Bispham Green

11–3; 5.30–11
Farmers Arms
Chorley Road OS497130
☎ (025 76) 2074
Burtonwood Dark Mild, Bitter H
Very popular country pub a mile from Parbold Hill. Large restaurant at rear (good food) and large garden
(till 8.30)

Bilsborrow

11–3; 6–11
Owd Nells Tavern
St Michaels Road (off A6)
☎ (0995) 40010
Boddingtons Bitter; Chesters Best Mild; Owd Nells Bitter; Whitbread Castle Eden Ale H
Brash canalside tavern with flag floors, wood beams, thatched roof. Good facilities for children

10.30–3; 6–11
White Bull
Garstang Road (A6)
☎ (0995) 40324
Matthew Brown Mild, Bitter H
Small, friendly canalside pub. Games

Blackburn

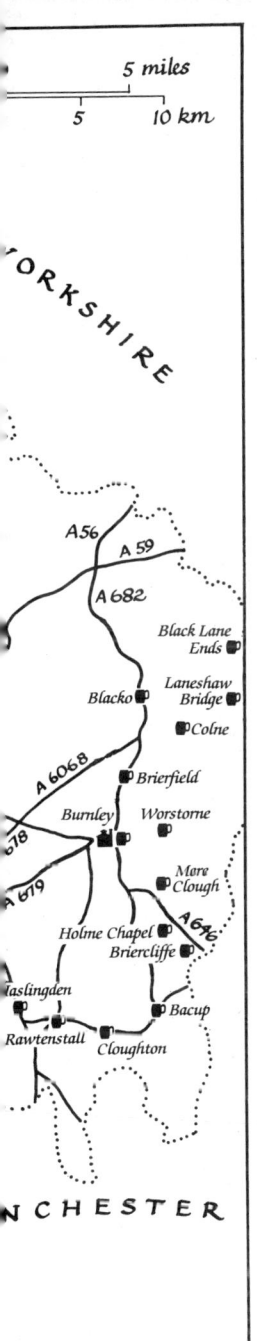

11–3; 6–11
Borough Arms
Exchange Street
Bass Mild XXXX, Special Bitter, Draught Bass H
Smart pub, handy for shopping centre and Lewis

Accrington

11.30–3; 6–11
Great Eastern

173

Lancashire

Textile Museum ([(not Sun) ⁂

11–3; 7–11

Brewers Arms
2 Great Bolton Street (A666)
☎ (0254) 52133
Boddingtons Bitter; Taylor Landlord; Thwaites Mild, Bitter H
Basic boozer between station and Blackburn Rovers football ground ⁂

11–3; 7–11

Corporation Park
Revidge Road (off A667)
☎ (0254) 53595
Thwaites Best Mild, Bitter H
Highest pub in town, near golf course and park ⌂

11–3; 6–11

Havelock Inn
Stancliffe Street (B6447)
☎ (0254) 53208
Thwaites Mild, Best Mild, Bitter H
Popular locals' pub; excellent value meals
⌂ ⁂ ⁑ (▶ ⁂ ⁂ (Mill Hill)

Black Lane Ends

11–3; 6.30–11

Hare & Hounds
Skipton Old Road OS928433
☎ (0282) 863070
Taylor Best Dark Mild, Bitter Ale H
Pennine hillside pub with panoramic views ⌂ ⁂ ⁑

Blacko

11–3; 5.30–11

Cross Gaits
Beverley Road (off A682)
OS866415 ☎ (0282) 66312
Burtonwood Mild, Bitter H
Friendly hillside inn with delightful views ⌂ ⁂ (⁑

Blackpool

11–3; 6–11

Bispham Hotel
Red Bank Road, Bispham (A584) ☎ (0253) 51752
Samuel Smith OBB H
Popular with locals and holiday makers. Games (⁂ ⁂

10.30–3; 6–11

Empress
59 Exchange Street, North Shore ☎ (0253) 20413
Thwaites Best Mild, Bitter H
Large Victorian hotel close to promenade; friendly welcome
⁑ ⁑ ⁂ (North)

10.30–3; 6–11

Mount Pleasant
103 High Street, North Shore ☎ (0253) 293335
Matthew Brown Mild, Bitter; Theakston Best Bitter, Old Peculier H
Small, friendly street corner local 200 yards from station ⁑ ⁂ (North)

11–3; 6–11

New Mariners
8 Norbreck Road, Bispham (off A584)
John Smith Bitter H
Tastefully furnished seaside pub. Games ⌂ (▶ ⁂

10.30–3; 6–11

Ramsden Arms
204 Talbot Road
Ind Coope Burton Ale; Jennings Bitter; Tetley Mild, Bitter H
Genuine locals' pub just a short distance from the hustle and bustle of the tourist trade
⌂ ⁑ (⁑ ⁂ (North)

11.30–3; 6–11

Saddle
286 Whitegate Drive, Marton (A583) ☎ (0253) 63065
Bass Mild XXXX, Special Bitter, Draught Bass H
Old inn of character, with a collection of old prints and photos ⌂ Q

10.30–3; 6–11

Wheatsheaf
192–194 Talbot Road
☎ (0253) 25062
Matthew Brown Mild; Theakston Best Bitter, XB, Old Peculier H
Basic, popular town local ⌂ ⁑ ⁂ (North)

Briercliffe

12–3; 7–11

Roggerham Gate Inn
Todmorden Road OS884337
☎ (0282) 22039
Younger IPA, No.3 H
Remote, well-appointed pub with restaurant, in attractive setting by reservoir Q ⌂ (if eating) ⁑ (▶ (not Mon) ⁑ ⁂

11–3; 5.30–11

Waggon & Horses
Colne Road (A56, off M65)
☎ (0282) 63962
Thwaites Best Mild, Bitter H
Popular main road pub. 1983 winner CAMRA award for best refurbishment ⌂ ⁑ (⁂

Brindle

11.30–3; 5.30–11

Cavendish Arms
Sandy Lane (B5256)
☎ (025 485) 2912
Burtonwood Dark Mild, Bitter H
Cosy old village pub with stained glass windows and à la carte restaurant (Wed–Sat). Opposite historic parish church ⌂ Q ⌂ ⁑ (▶ ⁑

Broughton

10.30–3; 6–11

Golden Ball
521 Garstang Road (A6 Jct B5269) ☎ (0772) 862756
Matthew Brown Mild, Bitter; Theakston Best Bitter H
Large multi-roomed pub at busy crossroads ⌂ ⁑ (⁂

Burnley

11–3; 7–11

General Scarlett
Accrington Road (A679)
☎ (0282) 831054
Moorhouse's Premier Bitter, Pendle Witches Brew; Thwaites Best Mild H
Small open-plan pub converted from a bookie's: Moorhouse's brewery tap and only tied house
⌂ (▶ ⁂ ⁑ (Rose Grove)

11–3; 7–11

Mechanics Institute Shuttle Bar
Manchester Road
☎ (0282) 30055
Moorhouse's Pendle Witches Brew; John Smith Bitter; Thwaites Bitter H
Social focus of new arts and entertainment complex. Usually crowded at night, often with disco
⌂ (lunch) (⁂

11–3; 7–11

Queens Head
Curzon Street ☎ (0282) 21077
Thwaites Mild, Bitter H
Marvellously restored Victorian style open-plan pub, handy for Central Station
⌂ Q ⁑ (⁂

11–3; 6–11

Woodman Hotel
129 Todmorden Road (A671)
☎ (0282) 24585
Bass Special Bitter H
Large popular corner pub with unusual layout; snug concealed by ornate wood-panelled bar. Well worth exploring ⌂ (▶ ⁑ ⁂

Try also: Grey Mare Inn (Bass); Lane Head (Thwaites)

Burscough

11–3; 5.30–11

Farmers Arms
New Lane via Higgins Lane off A59 ☎ (0704) 892168
Tetley Mild, Bitter; Walker Best Bitter H
Old, traditional and friendly 4-roomed pub on Leeds–Liverpool canal. Hard to find but worth the effort
⌂ Q ⁑ ⁂ (New Lane)

11–3; 5.30–11

Martin Inn
Martin Lane (off B5242)
☎ (0704) 892302
John Smith Bitter H
Remote pub with restaurant and good bar snacks; a good family pub for lunch. Near

174

Lancashire

Wildfowl Trust at Martin Mere ⛺🚆 (lunch) 🍴🍺🚬🍷🚻

Try also: Heatons Bridge (Tetley)

Catforth

10.30–3; 6–11

Running Pump
Catfort Road (off B5269)
☎ (0772) 690265
Robinson Best Mild, Bitter, Old Tom ᴴ
Deservedly popular country inn with a family room
⛺🚆🍴🍺🚬🍷🚻

Caton

11–3; 6–11

Station
Hornby Road (A683)
☎ (0524) 770323
Mitchells Mild, Bitter ᴴ
Solid sandstone pub predating railway. Knocked-through lounge has stained glass windows ⛺🚆🚬🍴🍺🚬🍷🚻

Try also: Ship (Thwaites)

Chipping

11–3; 6–11

Sun Inn
Windy Street ☎ (0995) 61206
Boddingtons Mild, Bitter ᴴ
Stone-built pub with staircase to front entrance. In same hands for 21 years. Games; Ring the Bull ⛺🚆 (family room) 🚬🍴 (Wed–Mon) 🍴🚻 🅰

11–3; 6–11

Talbot Hotel
Talbot Street ☎ (0995) 61260
Boddingtons Mild, Bitter ᴴ
Multi-roomed, friendly pub which draws people from a very wide area. Games ⛺🚆🚬🅰

Chorley

11–3; 7–11

Crown
46 Chapel Street
☎ (025 72) 75644
Matthew Brown Mild; Theakston Best Bitter, XB ᴴ
Clean, smart 1-roomed town centre pub with extensive lunch menu 🍴🚻🚆

11.30–3; 7–11

Market Tavern
21 Cleveland Street
☎ (025 72) 77991
Ind Coope Burton Ale; Walker Mild, Best Bitter ᴴ
Small busy town-centre pub with 4 small rooms, opposite market. Full of character
⛺Q🚆🚬🍷🚆

11–3; 6–11

Yates Wine Lodge
72 Market Street
☎ (025 72) 75700
Thwaites Mild, Bitter ᴴ
One of the few remaining unaltered Yates Wine Lodges, with bare floorboards and bar rails ⛺🚆🍷🚆

Try also: Bretherton (Brown)

Church

11.30–3; 5–11

Bridge
135 Henry Street (B6231)
☎ (0254) 32166
Bass Mild XXXX; Stones Best Bitter ᴴ
Cosy, double fronted pub with opened-out lounge and rear games room
⛺Q🚆🚬🍴🍺🚻

Clayton Le Moors

11–3; 6–11

Lamb
313 Whalley Road (A680)
☎ (0254) 34960
Whitbread Castle Eden Ale ᴴ
Set in a terrace of stone cottages. Strong on sports and games teams 🍷

11–3; 7–11

Old England Forever
13 Church Street (off A680)
☎ (0254) 33435
Matthew Brown Mild, Bitter ᴴ
Traditional 4-roomed local with unusual tiled hallway; near Leeds–Liverpool canal 🍷

Clayton Le Woods

11–3; 5.30–11

Halfway House Hotel
470 Preston Road (A6)
☎ (0772) 34477
Boddingtons Bitter; Stones Best Bitter; Thwaites Mild, Bitter ᴴ
Spacious pub halfway London–Glasgow. Family room and restaurant; Night club Wed–Mon ⛺🚆🚬🍴🍺🍷

Cleveleys

11–3; 6.30 (6 Sat)–11

Royal
North Promenade
☎ (0253) 852143
Boddingtons Bitter; Higsons Mild; Moorhouses Premier Bitter, Pendle Witches Brew ᴴ
Large seafront pub, popular all year round. Live music; family room; pub games; pizzas weekend eves 🚆🚬🍴🚬🚻

11.30–3; 6–11

Travellers Rest
90 Beach Road
☎ (0253) 853060
Boddingtons Mild, Bitter; Higsons Mild, Bitter ᴴ
Recently altered, spacious traditional style pub. Games 🚆🍴🚻

Clitheroe

11–3; 6–11

Buck
Lowergate ☎ (0200) 23299
Thwaites Best Mild, Bitter ᴴ
Fine building in centre of popular market town. Smart interior; busy with the young weekend eves 🍺

Try also: Cross Keys (Vaux)

Cloughfold

11.30–3; 7–11

Ashworth Arms
325 Bacup Road (A681)
☎ (0706) 215317
Bass Mild XXXX, Special Bitter ᴱ
Comfortable and friendly local with 4 small rooms. Near gas works 🍴

Try also: Crown

Colne

11–3; 7–11

Crown Hotel
Albert Road (A56)
Bass Mild XXXX, Special Bitter, Draught Bass; Stones Best Bitter ᴴ
Smart hotel with restaurant and separate games and snooker rooms ⛺🚆🍴🍴🚬🚻

11–3; 7–11

Golden Ball
Burnley Road (A56)
Tetley Mild, Bitter ᴴ
Cosy roadside pub with beer garden and sun lounge 🍺🍷

Try also: Spinners Arms (Tetley)

Coppull

11–3; 6–11

Alisons Arms
Preston Road ☎ (0257) 791262
Burtonwood Dark Mild, Bitter ᴴ
Small 1-roomed pub on main road, in old coal mining area. Large children's adventure playground ⛺🚆🍺🚬

Coppull Moor

12–3; 5.30–11

Plough & Harrow
Preston Road (A49)
Thwaites Best Mild, Bitter ᴱ
Small, friendly wayside local on Lancashire–Greater Manchester border. Family room 🚆🚬🍺🚬

Croston

11.30–3; 6–11

Lord Nelson
Out Lane (off A581)
☎ (0772) 600387
Boddingtons Bitter; Higsons Bitter ᴴ
Popular multi-roomed country local. Mind your head in the gents! Family room ⛺🚆🍴🚻

11–3; 6–11

175

Lancashire

Wheatsheaf
Town Road (A581)
☎ (0772) 600370
**Chesters Best Bitter;
Whitbread Castle Eden Ale,
Trophy** H
Comfortable locals' pub in
centre of village. No food
Mon. Separate games room

Darwen

11–3; 6–11
Alexander
Hindle Street
**Matthew Brown Mild, Bitter;
Theakston Old Peculier** H
Large open-plan pub with
separate snooker/darts room

11–3; 6–11
Entwistle Arms
15 Entwistle Street
☎ (0254) 73575
Thwaites Mild, Bitter H
Comfortable back street local

Try also: Golden Cup
(Thwaites)

Dolphinholme

12–3; 6–11
Fleece
Bay Horse OS509532
☎ (0524) 791233
Mitchells Mild, Bitter, ESB H
Former farmhouse on lonely
crossroads. Cosy lounge;
original little tap room;
dining/family room. Snacks
always available

Eaves

11.30–3; 6–11
Plough
Off B5269 OS494375
☎ (0772) 690233
Thwaites Mild, Bitter H
Attractive if isolated country
pub (Thu–Sun)

Eccleshill

11–3; 5.30 (6 Sat)–11
Handel's Arms
Roman Road OS701236
☎ (0254) 74110
**Matthew Brown Mild;
Theakston Bitter, XB** H
Friendly country pub with
good food and bowling green.
No meals Tue

Elswick

11.30–3; 6–11
Boot & Shoe
Beech Road (off A585)
☎ (0253) 70206
Thwaites Best Mild, Bitter H
Comfortable country pub with
summer barbecues

12–3; 6–11
Ship
High Street ☎ (0253) 70131

Boddingtons Bitter H
Lively, friendly comfortable
pub

Euxton

11–3; 6.30–11
Euxton Mills
Wigan Road (Jct A49/A581)
☎ (025 72) 64002
**Burtonwood Dark Mild,
Bitter** E
Very comfortable cosy pub
with excellent meals. Often
crowded weekends
(not Mon)

Fleetwood

10.30–3; 6–11
Fleetwood Arms
188 Dock Street
☎ (039 17) 2787
**Boddingtons Bitter; Higsons
Mild, Bitter** H
Basic Higson dockside tavern
with a reputation throughout
the seven seas

10.30–3; 6–11
Mount Hotel
Esplanade
Boddingtons Bitter H
Large pub with views over
Morecambe Bay

10.30–3; 6–11
North Euston
Esplanade ☎ (039 17) 6525
**Ruddles County; Webster
Yorkshire Bitter, Choice;
Wilson's Original Bitter** H
Large Victorian edifice 50
yards from sea. Large, elegant
public bars; family room

11–3; 6–11
Queens Hotel
Poulton Road ☎ (039 17) 6740
Thwaites Best Mild, Bitter H
Busy pub in residential area.
Games

Garstang

11–3; 6–11
Farmers' Arms
Church Street ☎ (099 52) 2195
**Jennings Bitter; Tetley Mild,
Bitter** H
Plush main bar with oak
beams and log fires; basic
games room; plainly-
furnished family room

Try also: Royal Oak
(Robinsons)

Glasson Dock

10.45–3; 5.45–11
Caribou
Victoria Terrace
☎ (0524) 751356
Thwaites Best Mild, Bitter H
Old pub, named after ship
skippered by former owner.
Spacious bar with cosy

corners, popular with young
locals

Try also: Victoria, Dalton
Arms

Great Eccleston

11.30–3; 6–11
White Bull
The Square ☎ (0253) 70203
**Bass Mild XXXX, Special
Bitter, Draught Bass** H
Pleasant village local with
stripped pine decor and 4 real
fires

Haslingden

11–30–3; 7–11
Foresters
12 Pleasant Street (off
Deardengate ☎ (0706) 216079
**Wilson's Original Mild,
Original Bitter** H
Local gem, hidden amongst
blocks of flats, 3 rooms and
unusual 3-sided bar

11–3; 5–11 (all day Thu)
Woolpack
488 Manchester Road
☎ (0706) 214195
**Ruddles County; Webster
Yorkshire Bitter, Choice;
Wilson's Original Bitter** H
Large open-plan pub
frequented by smart set. All
day licence Thu for local cattle
market

Heskin

12–3; 5.30–11
Farmers Arms
Wood Lane OS532154
☎ (0257) 451276
**Chesters Best Bitter; Hartley
XB** H
Small comfortable 2-roomed
country pub in prize-winning
village Q (lunch)
▲ (Park Hall)

Hest Bank

11–3; 6–11
Hest Bank
Hest Bank Lane (over canal
from A5105) ☎ (0524) 822226
Boddingtons Mild, Bitter H
In coaching days, the first or
last call for travellers crossing
the sands – the guiding light
can still be seen

Heysham

11–3; 6–11
Royal
7 Main Street, Morecambe
☎ (0524) 51475
Mitchells Mild, Bitter H
Multi-roomed pub in old
Heysham village; attracts both
locals and crowds of
holidaymakers

Higher Walton

11–3; 5.30–11

Lancashire

Mill Tavern
15 Cann Bridge Street (A675)
☎ (0772) 38462
Burtonwood Bitter H
Warm comfortable mill village pub at bottom of 2 hills. Jensen waiting to be rebuilt in yard. Games ((not Sun) &

Holme Chapel

11.30–3; 7–11

Queens Hotel
Burnley Road (A646)
☎ (0282) 36712
Burtonwood Dark Mild, Best Bitter H
Unaltered, cosy village local with unusual passageway entry. Morning coffee

Kirkham

10.30–3; 6–11

Queens Arms
Poulton Street ☎ (0772) 686705
Matthew Brown Mild;
Theakston Best Bitter, XB H
Popular small town pub opposite market square (not Sat)) (Thu–Sun) & ≷

Lancaster

11–3; 6–11

Golden Lion
Moor Lane ☎ (0524) 63196
Theakston Best Bitter, XB, Old Peculier H
Central bar serves several cosy drinking areas. Known locally as 'Whittle'. Bar billiards

11–3; 7–11

John O'Gaunt
55 Market Street
☎ (0524) 65356
Ind Coope Burton Ale;
Jennings Bitter; Tetley Mild, Bitter H
Handsome frontage with stained glass window hides lounge with much fake wood, odd apses and cut-glass lampshades. Live music Mon–Thu (and Sun lunch)
((not Sun) & ≷

12–3 (not Mon); 7–11 (10.30 Mon)

Moorlands
Quarry Road
Mitchells Mild, Bitter H
Thriving turn-of-the-century local

11–3; 5.45–11

Three Mariners
Bridge Lane ☎ (0524) 64877
Mitchells Mild, Bitter, ESB H
Alleged to be Lancaster's oldest pub, on old main road to Scotland. Antique decor and youngish clientele

Try also: **Brown Cow** (Thwaites); **Royal Oak** (Whitbread)

Laneshaw Bridge

11–3; 6.30–11

Alma
Hill Lane (off A6068)
☎ (0282) 863447
Tetley Mild, Bitter H
Pleasant pub in picturesque rural setting

Try also: **Hargreaves Arms** (John Smith)

Langho

11–3; 6–11

Lord Nelson
Whalley Old Road (off A666)
☎ (0254) 48387
Matthew Brown Mild, Bitter;
Theakston Old Peculier H
Perched on hillside overlooking the Ribble valley

Lathom

11–3; 5.30–11

Ship Inn
Wheat Lane (off A5209)
OS452115 ☎ (0704) 893117
Tetley Bitter; Theakston Best Bitter H
Known locally as The Blood Tub, this authentic free house has recently expanded into the cottage next door
Q ((not Sun)

Try also: **Ring o'Bells** (Higson)

Leyland

10.30–3; 6–11

Crofters Arms
Leyland Lane ☎ (0772) 42240
Matthew Brown Mild, Bitter;
Theakston Old Peculier H
Locals' pub with a formidable darts team (lunch)

11–3; 6–11

Original Ship
95 Towngate
Matthew Brown Mild, Bitter;
Theakston XB, Old Peculier H
Comfortable enlarged town-centre pub with large games area ((not Sun)

11–3; 5.30–11

Queens
1 Golden Hill Lane
☎ (0772) 421164
Matthew Brown Mild;
Theakston Best Bitter, XB, Old Peculier
Town-centre locals' pub near Leyland bus factory main entrance. Games (& ≷

Limbrick

11 (11.30 Sat)–3; 7–11

Black Horse
Long Lane OS602165
☎ (025 72) 64030
Matthew Brown Mild, Bitter;
Theakston XB; Younger IPA H
Popular rural stone-built pub with pleasant verandah by front door. Prize-winning black puddings available
Q ( )

Longridge

11–3; 6–11

Old Oak
111 Preston Road
☎ (077 478) 3648
Matthew Brown Mild;
Theakston Best Bitter, XB, Old Peculier H
Stone-built pub on road from Preston. Oak settees around the fire
(games room) &

11–3; 6–11

Towneley Arms
41 Berry Lane ☎ (077 478) 2219
Tetley Mild, Bitter H
Traditional warm and friendly local with wood-panelled rooms off main bar area Q &

Longton

12–3 (Sat, Sun only); 7.30–11

Dolphin (Flying Fish)
Marsh Lane OS459254
☎ (0772) 612032
Thwaites Best Mild, Bitter H
Remote farmhouse pub on the edge of Longton Marsh; haunt of wildfowlers and clay pigeon shooters. Traditional small tap room and lounge in modern extension Q &

11–3; 6–11

Longton Arms
2 Liverpool Old Road (off A59)
☎ (0772) 612335
Greenall Whitley Mild, Bitter H
Small terraced locals' pub with tiny snug and modernised lounge. Occasional live music

Lostock Hall

11–3; 6–11

Pleasant Retreat
Watkin Lane (A582)
☎ (0772) 35616
Boddingtons Bitter H & E
Large main road pub with lively vault. Bus stops outside
((not Sun) ≷

11–3; 6–11

Victoria
Watkin Lane (A582)
☎ (0772) 35338
John Smith Bitter H
Popular pub with large vault. Friendly welcome assured

Melling

11–3; 6–11

Melling Hall
☎ (052 42) 21298
Boddingtons Bitter; Marston

177

Lancashire

Pedigree; Hartley XB; Moorhouse's Premier Bitter H
Elegant hall, dated 1692 converted in the '60s to a well-appointed hotel. Locals' bar (door on left) and lounge

Mere Brow

11–3; 5.30–11
Legh Arms
The Gravel (just off A565) ☎ (077 473) 2225
Boddingtons Bitter; Higsons Mild, Bitter H
Cosy, well furnished and friendly village pub with as good a pint of Higsons as you could buy in Liverpool itself

Mereclough

11–3; 5.30–11
Kettledrum
302 Red Lees Road OS873306 ☎ (0282) 24591
Matthew Brown Mild, Bitter; Theakston Best Bitter, XB; Webster Yorkshire Bitter, Choice H
Attractive roadside inn with restaurant, overlooking town and country

Middleton

11–3; 6–11
Old Roof Tree
Middleton Road ☎ (0524) 52434
Thwaites Best Mild, Bitter E
Built in 1440 as grange of Cockersands Abbey. 5 linked rooms abounding in oak beams and exposed stonework

Morecambe

10.45–3; 6–11
George
Lancaster Road (Torrisholme Village) ☎ (0524) 418477
Thwaites Best Mild, Bitter H
Large 1936 Brewers'-Jacobean suburban local. Panelling in lounge. Games

11–3; 6–11
New Inn
Poulton Square ☎ (0524) 418179
Boddingtons Mild, Bitter H
Utterly basic, not a holidaymakers' pub, but strangers are welcome. Bring your own food!

Try also: Smugglers' Den (Jennings)

Nether Burrow

11–3; 6–11
Highwayman
On A683 ☎ (046 834) 249
Tetley Bitter; Theakston Best Bitter; Younger Scotch H
Turn-of-the-century pub built in country residence style with open-plan interior

Oakenclough

11–3; 6–11
Moorcock
☎ (099 52) 2130
Boddingtons Bitter; Tetley Mild, Bitter H
On the slopes of the Bowland Fells, so attracts day trippers. Thriving games teams

Ormskirk

11–3 (4 Thu); 5.30–11
Buck I' Th' Vine
35 Burscough Street ☎ (0695) 72647
Walker Mild, Bitter, Best Bitter H
Historic pub on pedestrian street. Unique sweetshop window bar counter (Tue–Sat)

11–3 (4 Thu); 5.30–11
Horse Shoe
24 Southport Road (A570) ☎ (0695) 72956
Tetley Mild; Walker Best Bitter H
Friendly alehouse opposite civic hall and famous tower-and-steeple parish church

11–3 (4 Thu); 5.30–11
Queen Inn
81 Aughton Street ☎ (0695) 72114
Vaux Bitter, Samson H
Handsome town pub with pleasant hall bar and several small rooms

Osbaldeston

11–3; 6–11
Bay Horse Inn
Longsight Road (A59) ☎ (025 481) 2203
Thwaites Mild, Bitter H
Welcoming rural inn on popular holiday route through the Ribble Valley

Parbold

11.30–3; 5.30–11
Railway Hotel
1 Station Road ☎ (025 76) 2917
Burtonwood Mild, Bitter H
Popular village pub, full of railway "numerasignia" (it says here!). Recent restaurant addition; daily newspapers provided; bar skittles

11.30–3; 5.30–11
Stocks Tavern
16 Alder Lane (A5209) ☎ (025 76) 2902
Tetley Mild, Bitter H
Eternally-busy local on edge of village. A Good Beer Guide regular

Try also: Windmill (Greenall Whitley)

Pilling

10.30–3; 6 (7 winter)–11
Golden Ball
School Lane ☎ (0253) 790212
Thwaites Best Mild, Bitter H
Large friendly local with 2 bowling greens and children's play area

Pleasington

11–3; 6–11
Railway
Off A674 ☎ (0254) 21520
Webster Yorkshire Bitter; Wilson's Original Mild, Original Bitter H
Homely, stone-built pub with own bowling green across the road

Poulton-Le-Fylde

10.30–3; 6–11
Queens
Higher Green ☎ (0253) 883471
Bass Special Bitter, Draught Bass H
Large Victorian pub opposite Poulton Park. Games

Preesall

12–3; 7–11
Saracen's Head
Park Lane (B5377) ☎ (0253) 810346
Thwaites Best Mild, Bitter H
Comfortable village local (Wed–Sun)

Preston

10.30–3; 6–11
Fox & Grapes
Fox Street ☎ (0772) 52448
Matthew Brown Mild, Bitter; Theakston XB H
Small popular town-centre pub, full of character

11.30–3; 7 (6.30 Sat)–11
George
39 Church Street ☎ (0772) 51529
Thwaites Mild, Best Mild, Bitter E; **Daniel's Hammer** (Christmas) G
Excellent multi-roomed town-centre pub; only one in Preston with both Thwaites milds. Games

11 (11.30 Sat)–3; 6–11
Greyhound
119 London Road (A6)
Boddingtons Bitter H
Basic local with tiled exterior

11.30–3; 6.30–11
Lamb & Packet
91a Friargate ☎ (0772) 51857
Thwaites Best Mild, Bitter H
Small pub near polytechnic;

178

Lancashire

often crowded term times
(Mon–Sat)

11–3; 6–11
Maudland
1 Pedder Street
☎ (0772) 726941
Matthew Brown Mild, Bitter
Small local next to St Walburgs church – third highest spire in England

12–3; 6–11
Mitre Tavern
90 Moor Lane ☎ (0772) 51918
Vaux Bitter, Samson; Ward Sheffield Best Bitter
Modern 2-bar pub in good drinking area. Ex-Wearside shipyard jumbo clock in vault. Friendly welcome assured (lunch & early eve)

11–3; 6 (6.30 Sat) 11
Royal Garrison
195 Watling Street Road, Fulwood (B6242)
☎ (0772) 794470
Matthew Brown Mild, Bitter; Theakston Best Bitter, XB
Large comfortable pub opposite Fulwood Barracks and near Preston North End football ground
(not Sun)

11–3; 6–11
Ship Inn
3 Fyde Road (A583)
☎ (0772) 51799
Matthew Brown Bitter; Theakston XB, Old Peculier
Comfortable pub near polytechnic; often crowded term time.
Games (Mon–Fri)

11–3; 6–11
Sumners
197 Watling Street Road, Fulwood (B6242)
☎ (0772) 705626
Boddingtons Mild, Bitter
Large new pub with spacious public bar, lounge with food counter and excellent wood-panelled snug. Can get very busy (disabled WC)

11–3; 6–11
Unicorn
378 North Road
☎ (0772) 57870
Matthew Brown Mild; Theakston Best Bitter, XB, Old Peculier

Comfortable pub on main road in good drinking area. Live music Sun; garden through pub at rear

11–3; 6–11
William IV
79 London Road
☎ (0772) 53339
Stones Best Bitter
Comfortable town pub on main road. Games

Rawtenstall

11.30–3; 7–11
Ashworth Arms
128 Burnley Road
☎ (0706) 216265
Bass Mild XXXX, Special Bitter
Friendly 3-roomed local with African mementoes on walls

Try also: Craven Heifer (John Smith)

Slaidburn

11–3; 5.30–11
Hark To Bounty Inn
Off B6478 ☎ (020 06) 246
John Smith Bitter; Moorhouse's Pendle Witches Brew
Village free house of great character; court sessions were once held here. Gateway to Trough of Bowland

Upholland

11–3; 5.30–11
White Lion
Church Street (off A577)
☎ (0695) 622593
Jennings Bitter; Tetley Mild, Bitter
Picturesque village pub opposite the parish church

Try also: Britannia (Greenall Whitley)

Warton

11.30–3; 6–11
Birley Arms
Bryning Lane ☎ (0772) 632201
Greenall Whitley Bitter, Original
Charming country pub with new dining area in conservatory

Wharles

12–3 (not Mon–Fri, whenever); 7–11

Eagle & Child
Church Road OS448356
☎ (0772) 312
Boddingtons Bitter; Clark Bitter; Eagle Special Bitter; Goose Eye Bitter
Country free house with thatched roof and beamed ceilings. Local CAMRA Pub of Year 1988. Guest beers

Wheelton

11–3; 5.30–11
Dressers Arms
Briers Brow (off A674)
☎ (0254) 830041
Boddingtons Bitter; Hartley XB; Matthew Brown Mild; Theakston Best Bitter, Old Peculier
Popular low beamed cottage pub with 3 rooms; Cantonese restaurant upstairs; family room. ½ mile from Leeds–Liverpool canal

Whittle-Le-Woods

12–3; 5.30 (7 Sat)–11
Royal Oak
216 Chorley Old Road
☎ (025 72) 76485
Matthew Brown Mild, Bitter
Small, friendly terraced pub with games

Worsthorne

11–3; 5.30–11
Crooked Billet
1 Smith Street
Tetley Mild, Bitter
Pleasant unspoilt village local with wood-panelled bar and lounge

Wrea Green

11–3; 6–1
Grapes
Station Road ☎ (0772) 682927
Boddingtons Bitter
Very popular pub at the centre of a prize-winning village

Yealand Conyers

11.30–3; 6–11
New Inn
Yealand Road ☎ (0524) 732938
Hartley XB
Archetypal village inn with interesting old fireplace, firearms and cash registers. Food recommended
(not Mon)

- real fire
- Q quiet pub – no electronic music, TV or obtrusive games
- indoor room for children
- garden or other outdoor drinking area
- accommodation
- lunchtime meals
- evening meals
- public bar
- facilities for the disabled
- camping facilities close to the pub or part of the pub grounds
- near British Rail station
- near Underground station
- real cider

The facilities, beers and pub hours listed in the Good Beer Guide are liable to change but were correct when the Guide went to press.

Leicestershire

Leicestershire

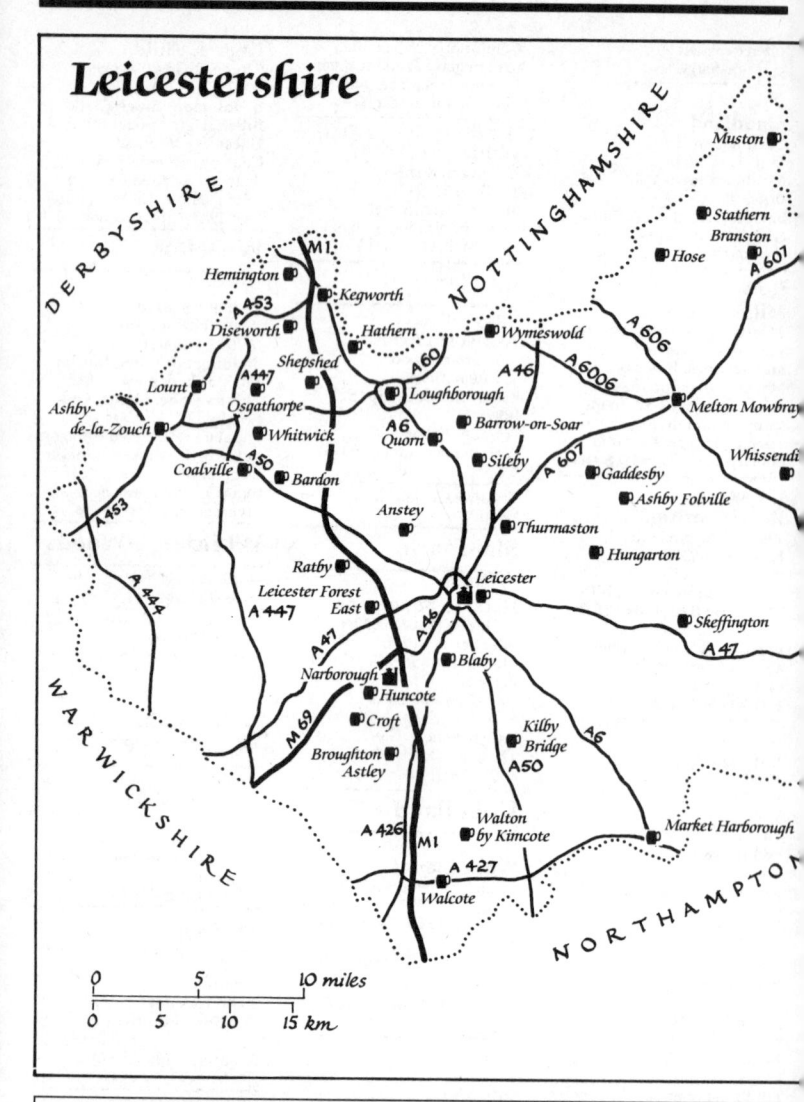

Everards, Narborough, Leicester; **Hoskins**, Leicester; **Hoskins & Oldfield**, Frog Island, Leicester

Anstey

11–2.30; 6.30–11

Old Hare & Hounds
34 Bradgate Road (B5327)
☎ (0533) 362496
Marston Burton Bitter, Merrie Monk, Pedigree H
Friendly village local opposite the church. Choice of many pub games ((not Sun) ⊕

Ashby-de-la-Zouch

10.30–2.30; 6.30–11

White Hart
Market Street ☎ (0530) 414531
Marston Pedigree H
Popular town centre pub with bar billiards ▲ ((not Sun)

Ashby Folville

10.30–2; 6–11

Carington Arms
Folville Street (B674)
☎ (0664) 840228
Adnams Bitter; Everards Beacon Bitter, Tiger, Old Original H
The prettiest pub in Leicestershire? Open bar and dining area. Long alley skittles and petanque track
▲ Q ✿ ⊛ (▶ & ✧

Bardon

11–2.30; 6–11

Birch Tree
on A50 ☎ (0530) 32134
Everards Burton Mild, Tiger, Old Original H
Friendly roadside pub with good garden. Evening meals in restaurant only. Pub games
⊛ (▶ (not Sun, Mon) ⊕ &

Barrow-on-Soar

10.30–2.30; 6–11

180

Leicestershire

Branston

10.30–2.30; 6–11

Wheel
Main Street ☎ (0476) 870376
Bateman XB
300 year-old 2-roomed pub with skittle alley and boules piste. No food Tues

Broughton Astley

11–2.30; 7–11

George & Dragon
18 Green Lane (off B581)
☎ (0455) 282256
Marston Border Mild, Burton Bitter, Pedigree
Popular, friendly village local with collection of walking sticks. Table skittles

Coalville

10.30–2.30; 5.30–11

Snibstone New Inn
Belvoir Road ☎ (0530) 33976
Marston Border Mild, Burton Bitter, Pedigree
Down-to-earth town local with bustling bar. Comfortable lounge with prints of old Coalville. Good home-made food. Shove ha'penny. Guest beers

Croft

11.30–2.30; 5.30–11

Heathcote Arms
Hill Street ☎ (0455) 282439
Adnams Bitter; Everards Mild, Beacon Bitter, Tiger, Old Original
Friendly 200 year-old village local set on hill overlooking Croft. Pub games

Diseworth

10.30–2.30; 5.30–11

Plough
Hall Gate ☎ (0332) 810333
Draught Bass
This pub is much older than it looks! It boasts some fine beams. Important local meeting place (not Sun)

Gaddesby

10.30–2.30; 6–11

Cheney Arms
Rearsby Lane (B674)
☎ (0664) 840260
Adnams Bitter; Everards Old Original
Friendly country local, popular with horsey set. Good quality snacks. Vintage car club meets here. Guest beers

Hathern

12–2.30; 7–11

Dew Drop
Loughborough Road (A6)
☎ (0509) 842438
Hardys & Hansons Best Mild, Best Bitter
Traditional 2-room pub; games available

Hemington

11–2.30; 6–11

Jolly Sailor
Main Street ☎ (0332) 810448
Draught Bass
Friendly village pub with outdoor skittle alley, bar skittles and shove ha'penny

Hose

10.30–2.30; 7–11

Black Horse
Bolton Lane ☎ (0949) 60336
Home Mild, Bitter
Characterful village local with 3 rooms. Bar very popular

12–2.30; 7–11

Rose & Crown
Bolton Lane ☎ (0949) 60424
Bateman Mild, XB
Comfortable 2-room pub with separate dining area. Constantly changing range of guest beers – usually 5 real ales. Pub games

Huncote

11–2.30; 5.30 (6 Sat)–11

Red Lion
Main Street ☎ (0533) 862233
Everards Mild, Beacon Bitter, Tiger, Old Original
Comfortable village local. Long alley skittles

Hungarton

10.30–2.30; 6–11

Black Boy
Main Street ☎ (053 750) 601
M&B Mild, Brew XI
Excellent 2-roomed pub, doubling as village sweet shop. No hot food Tue. Pub games

Kegworth

11.30–2.30; 6–11

Cap & Stocking
Borough Street
☎ (050 97) 4814
Draught Bass; M&B Mild
Traditional back-street pub; smoke room, tap room and snug. Ale is brought in jugs from the cellar
(7–8 pm)

Kilby Bridge

11.30–2.30; 5.30–11

Navigation
☎ (0533) 882280
Ind Coope Best Bitter, Burton Ale
Friendly canalside pub, families especially welcome. Pub games

---

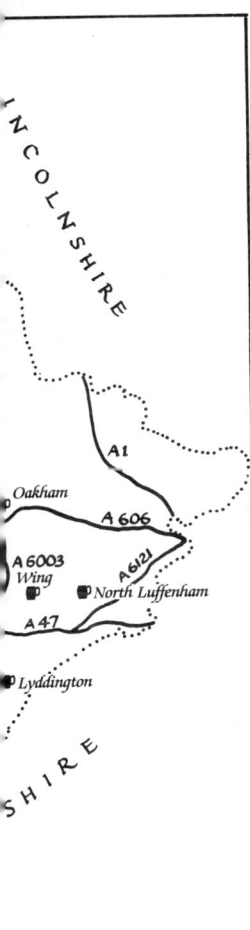

Navigation
Mill Lane (off B5328)
☎ (0509) 412842
Marston Pedigree; Shipstone Mild, Bitter; John Smith Bitter
Popular free house in an idyllic canalside location. Skittle alley (not Sun)
Try also: Three Crowns, Tap (Ind Coope)

Blaby

11–2.30; 5.30 (6 Sat)–11

Black Horse
Sycamore Street
☎ (0533) 771209
Shipstone Mild, Bitter
Small lively village local. Boisterous bar and (slightly) more laid back lounge

181

Leicestershire

Leicester

11–2.30; 5.30 (7 Sat)–11
Black Boy
35 Albion Street
☎ (0533) 540422
Draught Bass; M&B Mild E
Excellent pub tucked off main road behind Grand Hotel. Wood-panelled lounge with restored Victorian ceiling Q ✦ ❖ ❡ ▶ (on request) ❂ ⇌

11–2.30; 6–11
Black Horse
65 Narrow Lane, Alyestone (near A426 and Grand Union Canal) ☎ (0533) 832811
Everards Mild, Beacon Bitter, Tiger, Old Original
A pub since 1790, but in its early days it also functioned as a farm. Mainly a locals' pub. Guest beers. Chess and long alley skittles ⚿ Q ✦ ❖ ❡ ▶ ❂ ♿

11–2.30; 5.30–11
Bowlturners Arms
156–158 Belgrave Gate
Shipstone Mild, Bitter H
Traditional, basic town-centre boozer with accent on Mild drinking. Pub games Q ✦ ❖

11–2.30; 5.30–11
Rainbow & Dove
185 Charles Street
☎ (0533) 555916
Holden Black Country Mild; Hoskins Beaumanor Bitter, Penn's Ale, Premium, Old Nigel; Old Swan Bitter H
Large city-centre pub. Popular and lively. Jazz on Sun. Frequent guest beers ❡ ⇌

10.30–2.30; 5.30–11
Salmon Inn
Butt Close Lane
☎ (0533) 532301
Banks's Mild, Bitter E
Friendly locals' pub with quiet comfortable smoke room. Once a rent office. Handy for bus station
❖ ❡ (not Sun) ▶ (on request) ❂

11–2.30; 6–11
Shakespeares Head
Southgates (300 yds from A46/A47 jct) ☎ (0533) 24378
Shipstone Mild, Bitter H
2-roomed pub overlooking the underpass. Built in the 1960s on a semi-circular plan. Known locally as the library. Drinks also served in the foyer Q (lounge) ❖ ❡ ❂ ♿ ⇌

10.30–2.30; 5.30–11
Ship Inn
13 Soar Lane (off A50)
Shipstone Mild, Bitter
Small friendly locals' pub. Strong darts following. Near Grand Union Canal ❖ ❂

11.30–2.30; 5.30 (6 Sat)–11
Tom Hoskins
133 Beaumanor Road
☎ (0533) 681160
Hoskins Beaumanor Bitter, Penn's Ale, Premium, Old Nigel; Old Swan Bitter H
The brewery tap – a must. This friendly pub with its lively bar features a regular and varied guest beer list ❖ ❡ (not Sun) ❂

11–2.30; 6–11
Tudor
100 Tudor Road (off A47)
☎ (0533) 20087
Everards Mild, Beacon Bitter, Tiger, Old Original H
Pleasant Victorian corner pub. Cosy lounge and lively bar. Games room. Guest beers
✦ ❖ ❡ ▶ (not Sun) ❂ ⇌

11.30–2.30; 5.30–11
Union Inn
27 Middleton Street, Aylestone (off A426 and 300 yds E of Canal Bridge 106) ☎ (0533) 831796
Marston Mercian Mild, Burton Bitter, Merrie Monk (winter), Pedigree, Owd Rodger (winter) H
Popular and busy pub mainly used by locals. Near Grand Union Canal. Table skittles Q (lounge) ❖ ❡ ❂ ♿

Leicester Forest East

11–2.30; 6–11
Red Cow Inn
Hinckley Road (A47)
☎ (0533) 393021
Everards Mild, Beacon Bitter, Tiger, Old Original H
Impressive 18th-century 2-roomed roadside pub popular with younger set. Beer garden has own bar and children's play area ❖ ❡ ❂

Loughborough

11.30–2.30; 6–11
Duke of York
Nottingham Road
☎ (0509) 216234
Draught Bass; M&B Mild E
Locals' pub with basic public bar and tidy lounge. Handy for station; close to canal towpath. Pub games
❡ (not Sun) ❂ ⇌

11–2.30; 6–11
Maltings
Knightthorpe Road (just off ring road) ☎ (0509) 26857
Everards Mild, Beacon Bitter, Tiger, Old Original H
Modern suburban pub, consisting of a series of large lounge bars. Pub games ❖

11–2.30; 7–11
Old English Gentleman
Ashby Road ☎ (0509) 236890
Draught Bass; M&B Mild E
Small unobtrusive locals' pub with 3 drinking areas, including a quiet room with coal fire. Pub games ⚿ ❖ ❡

11–2.30; 5.30–11
Swan in the Rushes
The Rushes (A6)
☎ (0509) 217014
Banks's Mild, Bitter; Bateman XXXB; Marston Pedigree; Tetley Bitter H
Busy free house which attracts customers from far and wide. Good guest beer programme and range of naturally-conditioned bottled beers. Blues club Wed ❡ ▶ ❂ ♿

Try also: **Cotes Mill** (Free)

Lount

11–2.30; 6–11
Ferrers Arms
A453 ☎ (0530) 412982
Marston Pedigree H
Thriving inn, set back from main road. Close to Staunton Harold Estate. No meals weekends. Pub games ⚿ ❖ ❡ ❂

Lyddington

12–2.30; 6.30–11
Old White Hart
51 Main Street (near A6003)
☎ (0572) 823810
Greene King XX Mild, IPA, Abbot H
An 18th-century, oak-beamed pub; a popular and friendly village local. Good lunches. Pub games ⚿ Q ✦ ❖ ❡ ▶ ❂

Market Harborough

10.30–2.30; 6–11
Red Cow
High Street ☎
Ansells Bitter; Ind Coope Best Bitter, Burton Ale; Tetley Bitter H
One-roomed popular local; unpretentious and homely. Pub games available ❂

Melton Mowbray

11–2.30; 6.30–11
Cherry Tree
Valley Road (off A607)
☎ (0664) 65430
Draught Bass; M&B Mild H
Spacious estate pub
❖ ❡ (not Sun)

Try also: **Grapes** (Ind Coope)

Muston

10.30–2.30; 6–11
Gap
Muston Gap (on A52)

182

Leicestershire

Marston Pedigree H
Rambling roadside pub which has resident clay pigeon club. Popular with farming community

Try also: Red Lion, Bottesford (Hardys & Hansons)

North Luffenham

11–2.30; 6–11

Horse & Panniers
12 Church Street
☎ (0780) 720091
Adnams Bitter; Everards Beacon Bitter, Tiger H
Grade II Listed building dating back to 1640. Known as the Nag and Bag! Pub games

Oakham

10.30–2.30; 6–11

Wheatsheaf
2–4 Northgate (off A606)
☎ (0572) 3458
Adnams Bitter; Everards Beacon Bitter, Tiger, Old Original H
Popular market town pub. Guest beers

Osgathorpe

12–2.30; 7–11

Royal Oak
Main Street (off B5324)
☎ (0530) 222443
Draught Bass; M&B Mild; Marston Pedigree H
Characterful rural free house off the beaten track. Pub games

Quorn

11–2.30; 5.30–11

Blacksmiths Arms
Meeting Street (off A6)
☎ (0509) 412751
Marston Pedigree H
Bustling village local with friendly atmosphere. Pub games

11–2.30; 6–11

Bulls Head
High Street (A6)
☎ (0509) 412562
Draught Bass H
An imposing main road pub. Petanque and good garden amenities (not Sun)

11.30 (10.30 Sat)–2.00; 6.30–11

Royal Oak
High Street (A6)
☎ (0509) 413502
Draught Bass; M&B Mild H
Street-corner local with large L-shaped bar and smaller lounge. Pub games

Ratby

10.30–2.30; 5.30 (6 winter)–11

Plough Inn
Burroughs Lane
☎ (0533) 392103
Marston Burton Bitter, Merrie Monk, Pedigree H
Traditional village local. Piano singalong on Fri night. Pub games (Mon–Fri)

Shepshed

11–2.30; 7–11

Richmond Arms
Forest Street (off B5330)
☎ (0509) 503309
Draught Bass; M&B Mild H
Splendid friendly village local. Always someone to play dominoes with!

Try also: Railway (Marston)

Sileby

11–2.30; 5.30–11

Railway
37 King Street
☎ (050 981) 2447
Draught Bass; M&B Mild E
Busy 2-room local with a reputation for friendly service and value for money. Pub games

Skeffington

10.30–2.30; 6–11

Fox & Hounds
Uppingham Road (A47)
☎ (053 755) 250
Davenports Mild, Bitter H
Busy main road pub serving good food. Camping and caravan site in grounds. No meals Sun

Stathern

11.30–2.30; 6–11

Plough
Main Street ☎ (0949) 60411
Home Bitter E
Busy village inn with L-shaped bar, traditional wood-backed benches and roomy lounge. Pub games

Thurmaston

11–2.30; 6–11

Generous Briton
22 Garden Street
☎ (0533) 694112
Ruddles Best Bitter; Websters Yorkshire Bitter H
Friendly 2-roomed local, with large public bar, opposite playing fields. Oldest pub in village. Skittles

11–2.30; 5.30–11

Harrow Inn
635 Melton Road
☎ (0533) 620240
Shipstone Mild, Bitter H
Friendly 2-roomed local with pool room and skittles (not Sun)

Walcote

11–2.30; 5.30–11

Black Horse
Main Street (1 mile M1 jct 20)
☎ (045 55) 2684
Flowers Original; Hook Norton Best Bitter, Old Hookey; Hoskins & Oldfield HOB Bitter H
Quiet and friendly village local with large passing trade. Noted for its Oriental food and regular guest beers

Walton by Kimcote

12–2.30; 6 (7 winter)–11

Dog & Gun
Main Street ☎ (045 55) 2808
Banks's Mild, Bitter E
Friendly, old fashioned traditional village local. Pub games

Whissendine

10.30–2.30; 6–11

White Lion
Main Street ☎ (066 479) 233
Adnams Bitter; Everards Beacon Bitter, Tiger H, **Old Original** G
Old inn with large lounge and games area at one end. Devil-among-the-Tailors and outdoor skittles played. Separate restaurant

Whitwick

11–2.30; 6.30–11

Foresters Arms
Leicester Road (B587)
☎ (0530) 36180
Marston Pedigree H
Down-to-earth locals' pub with pool and darts

Wing

10.30–2.30; 6–11

Kings Arms
Top Street ☎ (057 285) 315
Bateman XXXB; Greene King IPA; Ruddles Best Bitter, County H
Popular stone-built village pub with separate restaurant. Near ancient turf maze. Boules played in summer (not Sun)

Wymeswold

11.30–2.30; 7–11

White Horse
Far Street (A6006)
☎ (0509) 880490
Home Mild, Bitter H
Welcoming village local with 3 small bars around a central servery. Skittles and games room

Try also: Three Crowns (Ind Coope)

183

Lincolnshire

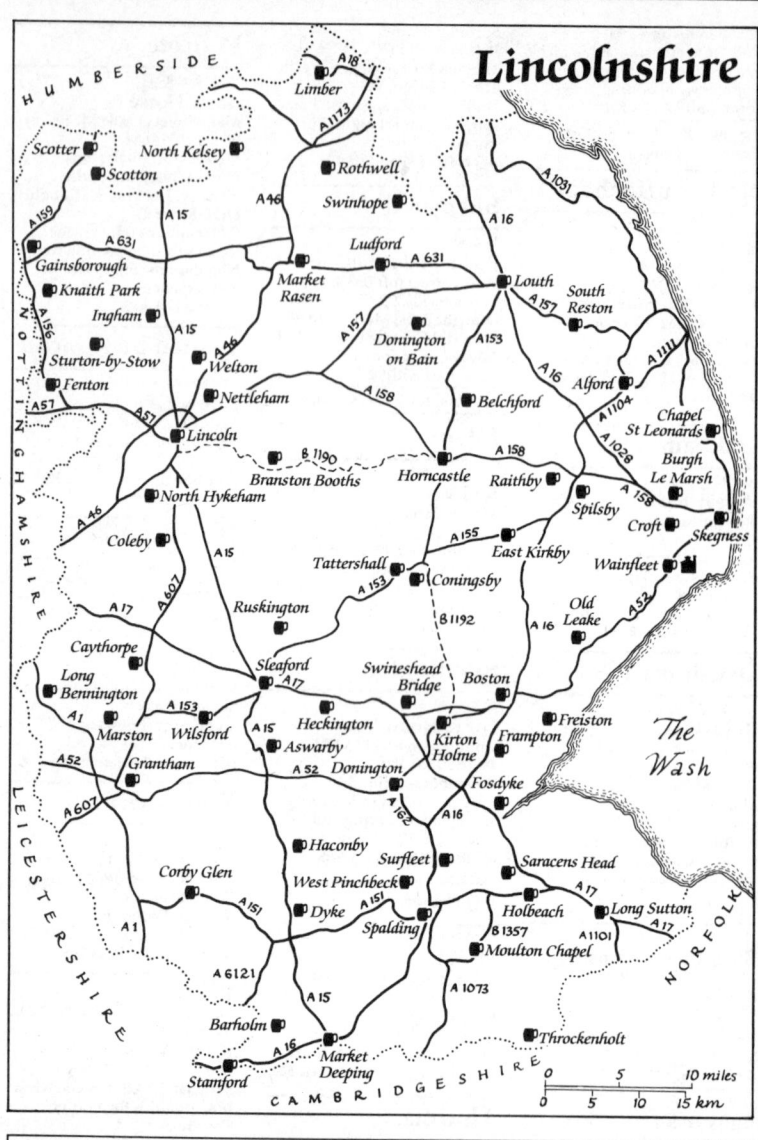

🏭 *Bateman, Wainfleet*

Alford

10–2.30; 6–10.30 (11 F,S)
Half Moon
West Street (A1104)
☎ (052 12) 3477
Bass Mild XXXX, Special Bitter, Draught Bass; Bateman XB, XXXB H
Busy and homely, this pub deserves an Oscar for its supporting role as home to the local Film Society. Guest beers always include a mild ⌂ (by arrangement) ⌘ ◐ ● (until 9) ⊞

Aswarby

12–2.30; 6–11
Tally Ho
On A15 ☎ (052 95) 205
Adnams Bitter; Bateman XB H
Comfortable and welcoming roadside pub. Guest beers. Accommodation in converted outhouses
⌂⌐ (if eating) ⌘≈ ◐ ●

Barholm

12–2 (not Mon); 7–11
Five Horseshoes
1 mile off A16 at Tallington
☎ (077 836) 238

Adnams Bitter; Bateman XXXB H
Fine stone-built pub in quiet village. Note the Javanese bed head board and old lamps over the bar! Guest beers
⌂⌐⌘♣

Lincolnshire

Belchford

11–2.30 (closed Mon & winter); 7–11
Blue Bell
Off A153 ☎ (0842) 602
Ind Coope Burton Ale H
Worthy member of Ind Coope Cellarman Guild. Handy for hikers and bikers, being close to both the Viking Way and Cadwell Park. Guest beers
♨Q⊛⊕▶

Boston

10.30–3; 7–11
Carpenters Arms
Witham Street (off Wormgate) ☎ (0205) 62804
Bateman Mild, XB, XXXB, Victory Ale H
Bustling back-street local with exotic lunch menu ♨☎⊛⋈⊕

10.30–3; 6.30–11
Eagle
144 West Street ☎ (0205) 61116
Adnams Bitter; Everards Old Original; Taylor Landlord H
Popular, traditional town pub with bustling public bar and quiet lounge. Good lunches. Draught off-sales service. Venue for folk club and games evenings. Guest beer (often mild) ♨⊛⊕⋈⇌⊙

10.30–3; 6–11
Mill Inn
Spilsby Road ☎ (0205) 52874
Bateman Mild, XB, XXXB H
Smart and comfortable with emphasis on good food. Handy for the hospital
☎⊛⊕▶&A

10.30–3; 6.30–11
Ropers Arms
Horncastle Road
Bateman Mild, XB H
Genuine street-corner local, welcoming and full of character. Popular with anglers. Pub games ⊕

10.30–3; 6.30–11
Town Pump
Craythorne Lane (off Market Place) ☎ (0205) 68594
Greene King IPA, Abbot H
Brash town pub. Popular with young people. Guest beers
⊕▶

Branston Booths

11–3; 7 (6 Sat)–11
Green Tree
Bardney Road (B1190, 6 miles E of Lincoln) ☎ (0522) 791208
Ward Darley Dark Mild, Thorne Best Bitter, Sheffield Best Bitter H
Cosy and welcoming rural local. Go steady on the long straight or you'll miss it. Guest beers ♨☎ (ask) ⊛⊕▶⊕

Burgh Le Marsh

10.30–3 (2.30 winter); 6–11
White Hart
High Street (A158) ☎ (0754) 810321
Bateman XB, XXXB; Ruddles County H
Contrasting bar and lounge in comfortable pub and restaurant. Pub games. Fine china displayed
♨☎⊛⋈⊕▶⊕&

Caythorpe

11–3; 6.30–11
Red Lion
62 High Street (off A607) ☎ (0400) 72632
Draught Bass; Greene King Abbot; Ind Coope Burton Ale; Marston Pedigree, Taylor Landlord H
Village local with live jazz Tue, folk jam session on Thu nights. Guest beers
♨☎⊛⋈⊕▶⊕A

Chapel St Leonards

10.30–3 (2.30 winter); 6–11
Ship
Sea Road ☎ (0754) 72975
Bateman XB, XXXB H
Cheerful pub catering for locals and holidaymakers alike. No food in winter. Pub games ♨⊛⊕▶

Coleby

10.30–2.30; 6–11
Bell Inn
Far Lane (off A607) ☎ (0522) 810240
Cameron Strongarm; Marston Pedigree H
Ever-popular village pub with increasing emphasis on food. A Melbourns' house
♨☎⊛⊕▶ (booking advised)

Coningsby

11.30–2.30; 6.30–11
Leagate Inn
Leagate Road/Boston Road (B1192) ☎ (0526) 42370
Taylor Landlord; Whitbread Trophy, Castle Eden Ale H
16th-century coaching inn. Excellent food; warm comfortable atmosphere. Children's play area outside. Jaguar Owners' Club and Koi Carp Club meeting place
♨Q⊛ (lunchtime meals) ⊕▶

Try also: Horse & Jockey (Free)

Corby Glen

10.30–2.30; 6.30–11
Woodhouse Arms
Main Street (A151)
Bateman Mild, XB, XXXB H
Roadside pub with attractive interior. Guest beers ⊛⊕▶⊕

Croft

10.30–3 (2.30 winter); 6–11
Old Chequers
Lymn Bank ☎ (0754) 880320
Bateman XB, XXXB E
An isolated former 16th-century post house with an old range. Reputedly haunted. Pub games ♨⊛⊕

Donington

11–3; 6–11
Queen Inn
49 Station Street (A52) ☎ (0775) 820281
Ruddles Best Bitter; Webster Yorkshire Bitter H
Popular village local, basic but comfortable. Pub games ♨⊕

Donington on Bain

11–2; 6.30–11
Black Horse
2 miles off A157 near Louth ☎ (0507) 84640
Adnams Bitter H
Delightful old village inn retaining its character through recent alterations
♨Q⊛⊕▶⊕A

Dyke

10.30–2; 6.30–11
Wishing Well
Main Street (off A15 1 mile N of Bourne) ☎ (0778) 423626
Adnams Extra G; **Greene King IPA, Abbot** H; **Marston Pedigree** G
Old village local with stone walls. Small bar. Pool table. Gravity-fed ales from room out back. Guest beers
♨☎⊛⋈⊕▶⊕&A (phone)

East Kirkby

10.30–2.30 (3 summer); 7–11
Red Lion
Main Road (A153) ☎ (079 03) 406
Bateman XB, XXXB H
Unspoilt village local close to World War II airfield, housing Lincolnshire Air Museum. Horological display grows by the minute! ♨☎⊛A

Fenton

11–2.30; 6.30–11
Carpenters Arms
on A156 ☎ (042 771) 633
Cameron Traditional Bitter, Strongarm H
Friendly roadside inn, very popular with local fishermen, also used by golfing fraternity
♨⊛⊕▶

Fosdyke

10.30–3; 7–11
Ship
Main Road (A17)

185

Lincolnshire

☎ (020 585) 628
Bateman Mild, XB H
Situated next to the infamous Fosdyke Bridge; a friendly pub with a nautical atmosphere 🏠 ( ) ▶ (summer)

Frampton

10.30–3; 6.30–11
Moores Arms
Church End ☎ (0205) 722408
Adnams Bitter; Draught Bass; Bateman XB; Tetley Bitter H
Cosy and busy pub opposite village church. Idyllic on a summer evening. Restaurant
🏠 ( ) ▶

Freiston

10.30–3; 6.30–11
Castle Inn
Wainfleet Road (A52)
☎ (0205) 760393
Bateman Mild, XB H
Attractive exterior; smart interior with adventure playground for children and adults! ♿ ☎ 🏠 ✉ ( ) ▶ ♣

Gainsborough

10.30–2.30; 6–11
Drovers Call
Lea Road (A156) ☎ (0427) 2044
Bass Mild XXXX, Special Bitter E, **Draught Bass; Stones Best Bitter** H
Large and cheerful estate pub. Electric pumps to be replaced by handpulls in near future
( ) ▶ ♣ ≉ (Lea Rd)

10.30–2.30; 6–11
Elm Cottage
Church Street ☎ (0427) 5474
Bass Mild XXXX, Special Bitter H
Popular and quiet – more like a village inn than a town pub
Q 🏠 ( )

Grantham

11–3; 6–11
Angel & Royal
High Street ☎ (0476) 65816
Adnams Bitter; Draught Bass; Greene King Abbot H
Historic coaching inn noted for its masonry, fireplace and tapestries. Excellent spit roasts in winter ♿ Q 🏠 ✉ ( ) ▶ ♣

11–3; 6–11
Blue Pig
Vine Street (off High Street)
☎ (0476) 63704
Flowers IPA; Whitbread Castle Eden Ale H
Very popular historic town pub, centrally located. Well maintained with lively and friendly atmosphere ( ) ▶ ♣

11–3; 6–11
Chequers
25 Market Place
☎ (0476) 76383
Everards Old Original;
Younger Scotch, IPA, No.3 H
Lively town centre alehouse
☎ (back room) ( ) ♣

11–3; 6–11
Five Bells
79 Brook Street ☎ (0476) 67152
Marston Pedigree; Shipstone Mild, Bitter H
Refurbished pub with high standard of beer and food
( ) ▶ ♣

Odd House
4 Fletcher Street (off Wharf Road)
Marston Mercian Mild, Pedigree; John Smith Bitter H
Warm, friendly backstreet pub. Excellent lunches. Guest beers ♿ 🏠 (♣ ≉

11–2.30; 6–11
Shirley Croft
Harrowby Road
Bateman XB, XXXB H
Victorian hotel in its own grounds. A centre for such diverse activities as chess tournaments, archery and small-bore shooting ☎ 🏠 ( ) ▶

Try also: Granby (Home); Waggon & Horses (Whitbread)

Haconby

10–2; 7–11
Sportsman
½ mile off A15 ☎ (077 837) 316
Bateman XB, XXXB H
Cheerful pub with restaurant and a reputation for home-made food. Children's garden. Pub games ☎ 🏠 ( ) ▶ ♣

Heckington

10.30–2.30; 6.30–11
Nags Head
High Street ☎ (0529) 60218
Ruddles Best Bitter, County; Webster Yorkshire Bitter H
Bustling village pub. Dick Turpin possibly stayed here after stealing horses nearby
🏠 ✉ ( ) ▶ ♣ ≉

Holbeach

10.30–3 (4 Thu); 6–11
Bell
High Street
Elgood Bitter H
Town centre pub with a warm and friendly welcome
♿ Q 🏠 ( ) ▶

Horncastle

11–2.30; 7–11
Red Lion
1 The Bull Ring
☎ (065 82) 3338
Shipstone Bitter H
Smart local, popular with arts and drama groups: theatre with own bar under construction ♿ Q ☎ (lunchtime meals) ✉ ( ) ▶ (book) ♣ ♿

10.30–2.30; 6–11
Rodney Hotel
North Street ☎ (065 82) 3583
Whitbread Castle Eden Ale H
Lively public bar and comfortable lounge. Excellent home-made food. Attractive snug ♿ Q (lounge) 🏠 ✉ ( ) ▶ ♣

Ingham

12–2.30; 7–11
Windmill
outside village on B1398
☎ (0522) 730249
Bass Mild XXXX, Draught Bass; Stones Best Bitter H
Isolated ridgetop roadhouse overlooking village; relaxed atmosphere. Pub games
♿ 🏠 ♣ ▲

Kirton Holme

10.30–3; 6.30–11
Four Crossroads
Swineshead Road (A52/B1192 Jct) ☎ (020 579) 283
Bateman XXXB; Marston Pedigree; Ruddles Best Bitter H
Comfortable pub offering excellent value meals in the restaurant 🏠 ( ) ▶

Knaith Park

11–2.30; 6–11
Stags Head
Willingham Road (B1241)
☎ (0427) 2917
Tetley Bitter; Ward Sheffield Best Bitter H
Unusual exterior hides this increasingly popular and welcoming village local. Strong emphasis on home-cooked food ☎ (ask) 🏠 ( ) ▶

Limber

10.30–2.30; 7–11
New Inn
High Street (A18)
☎ (0469) 60257
Bateman XXXB; Tetley Bitter; Ward Sheffield Best Bitter H
Friendly inn offering good value accommodation. Handy for Humberside Airport (3 miles). Guest beers ♿ Q ☎ 🏠 ✉ ((Mon–Fri) ▶ (residents) ♣ ♿

Lincoln

11–3; 6–11
City Vaults
Alfred Street (off High Street)
☎ (0522) 21035
Ward Darley Dark Mild, Sheffield Best Bitter H
Traditional ale house; once a police house – collection of old truncheons
( ) ▶ (phone) ♣ ≉

11–3; 6–11

Lincolnshire

Harvest Moon
(off A158) ☎ (0522) 36684
Younger Scotch, No.3 H
Old farmhouse converted into 1-roomed house on modern estate ⊛ ◑ &

11–3 (not Sun); 7–11
Jolly Brewer
Broadgate ☎ (0522) 28583
Draught Bass; Everards Tiger; Hardys & Hansons Best Bitter; Younger Scotch, No.3 H
1930s Art Deco style free house within easy reach of city centre. 60s jukebox. Guest beers ⊛ ◑ ≷

11–3; 6–11
Monks Abbey
Monks Road ☎ (0522) 44416
John Smith Bitter H
Friendly local. Lincoln's first John Smith's convert ⊛ ◑ ⇔ &

11–3; 5.30 (6 Sat)–11
Queen in the West
Moor Street (off A57, Carholme Road)
☎ (0522) 26169
Bateman XB; Marston Pedigree; Taylor Landlord; Theakston Old Peculier; Ward Sheffield Best Bitter H
Smart pub with comfortable lounge and friendly bar. Guest beers Q (lounge) ⋈ ◑ ⇔

10.30 am – 10.30 pm
Small Beer (off licence)
Newland Street West (off A57)
☎ (0522) 28628
Bateman XXXB; Taylor Landlord; Ward Sheffield Best Bitter H
Extensive range of bottled beers also available. Guest beers &

11–3; 7–11
Straits
The Strait ☎ (0522) 20814
Adnams Bitter; Everards Tiger, Old Original H
Pub on historic street in tourist area. Convenient stop en route to cathedral. Once a wine bar; still offers a good choice of wines Q ⋟ (for food) ⊛ ◑ ▶

11–3; 5.30 (6 Sat)–11
Strugglers
83 Westgate ☎ (0522) 24702
Bass Mild XXXX, Draught Bass H
Busy, basic and bursting with people – a little gem. Next to the castle Q ⇔ &

11–3; 5.30–11
Victoria
Union Road (behind castle)
☎ (0522) 36048
Bateman XB; Everards Old Original; Taylor Landlord; Ward Sheffield Best Bitter H
Busy pub. Clientele as amazingly varied as the guest beers (which usually include a mild). Excellent food Q ⋟ (ask) ⊛ ◑ ▶ (occasional) ⇔

Long Bennington

11–3; 6.30–11
Royal Oak
Main Street (off A1)
☎ (0406) 81733
Marston Burton Bitter, Pedigree H
Centrally located, welcoming watering-hole. Keen lunchtime domino players ⋒ ⋟ (lunch) ⊛ ◑

Try also: Wheatsheaf Inn (John Smith)

Long Sutton

10.30–3 (4 Fri); 7–111
Bull
Market Place (A17)
☎ (0406) 362258
Draught Bass H
400 year old hotel recently bought by the 84-year-old landlady who has lived here since 1920s. "I wanted a job for life" she said! Q ⋟ ⊛ ◑ ▶ ⇔

Louth

11–3 (4 W,F); 7–11
Olde Whyte Swanne
45 Eastgate ☎ (0507) 601312
Bass Mild XXXX, Draught Bass; Stones Best Bitter H
17th-century inn with low ceiling in the small front lounge; open fires make it a cosy place on cold winter evenings. Larger public bar ⋒ ⊛ ⇔

11–3; 6–11
Wheatsheaf
62 Westgate ☎ (0507) 603159
Draught Bass; Stones Best Bitter H
Situated in a quiet Georgian terrace, this superb inn, dating from 1625 is equally attractive inside and out. A must for any visitor ⋒ Q ◑ ▶ ⇔

11–3; 7–11
Woolpack
Riverhead Road
☎ (0507) 606568
Bateman Mild, XB, XXXB H
Traditional, friendly inn with universal appeal, typical of Bateman pubs. The short walk from the town centre will be well-rewarded. Pub games ⋒ ⊛ ⇔ &

Ludford

11–2.30; 6.30–11
Black Horse
Magna Mile (A631)
☎ (050 781) 645
Bateman Mild, XB; Marston Pedigree, Stones Best Bitter H
Relaxed and friendly atmosphere in a 250 year-old inn. Guest beers; pub games ⋒ ⊛ ◑ ▶ ⇔

Market Deeping

11–2; 5.30–11
Bull
19 Market Place (A16)
☎ (0778) 343320
Everards Beacon Bitter, Tiger, Old Original H
2-bar pub of ancient origin with public bar in old beer cellar, The Dugout, which has the casks on stillages. Increasing emphasis on food ⋟ ⊛ ⋈ ◑ ▶ (Tue–Sat) ⇔

Market Rasen

10.30–2.30 (4 Tue); 6–30–11
Red Lion
King Street ☎ (0673) 842424
Ruddles County; Ward Sheffield Best Bitter; Webster Yorkshire Bitter H
Friendly free house. Pool very popular ⋒ ◑ ⇔ ≷

Marston

11–3; 6.30–11
Thorald Arms
Main Street (off A1)
☎
Bateman XXXB; Marston Pedigree H
Rural pub with excellent value food. Beware of the pressurised Ruddles. Viking Way passes nearby ⋒ ⊛ ◑ ▶ ⇔

Moulton Chapel

11–3; 7–11
Wheatsheaf
4 Fengate (B1357)
☎ (0406) 380525
Elgood Bitter; Greene King XX Mild, IPA, Abbot H
300 year-old pub on site of former brewhouse. Pig and key collections ⋒ ⊛ ▶ (by arrangement) ⇔ ▲

Nettleham

11–2.30; 6 (7 Sat)–11
Plough
The Green ☎ (0522) 750275
Bateman Mild, XB H
Comfortable and welcoming, low-beamed village pub. Well deserves its 10th consecutive Good Beer Guide entry ⋟ (ask) ⊛ ◑

North Hykeham

11–2.30; 6–11
Harrows
Lincoln Road (off A46)
☎ (0522) 680088
Whitbread Castle Eden Ale H
Popular local with Air Force connections. Piano Sat ◑ ⇔ & ≷

North Kelsey

12–2.30; 7–11
Royal Oak
High Street ☎ (065 27) 544
Bateman XB; Stones Best

187

Lincolnshire

Bitter; Tetley Bitter; Ward Sheffield Best Bitter ⓗ
A warm and friendly, popular pub. Open-plan bar with separate games area and rear snug. Quiz night on Tue ▲☆⑧◖ (not Sun) ⊖&

Old Leake

11–3; 6.30–11

Bricklayers Arms
Wainfleet Road (A52)
☎ (0205) 870657
Bateman Mild, XB ⓗ
Large pub on edge of village. Children's play area; parking for caravans. Good restaurant open at weekends. Supper licence Mon–Sat to midnight ☆⑧◖▶ Å

Raithby

12–2.30 (not Mon–Fri); 7–11

Red Lion
Main Street ☎ (0790) 53727
Home Bitter; Ruddles County ⓗ
400 year-old pub with a cheerful welcome and good, home-made food
▲☆◖▶ (not Tue)

Rothwell

12–2.30; 7–11

Nickerson Arms
Hillrise ☎ (047 289) 300
Rothwell Village Bitter; Taylor Landlord; Tetley Bitter ⓗ
Deservedly popular Wolds pub with family room and excellent outdoor children's facilities. Guest beers. Village Bitter is by Hoskins & Oldfield
▲Q☆⑧◖ (Mon–Fri) ⊖&

Ruskington

10.30–2.30; 6.30–11

Black Bull
Rectory Road ☎ (0526) 832270
Bateman Mild, XB, XXXB ⓗ
Popular and comfortable village pub with growing reputation for its restaurant. Pub games ▶ ⊖&≠

Saracens Head

10.30–3; 6–11

Saracen's Head
Washway Road (A17)
☎ (0406) 22708
Greene King IPA Ⓖ
Situated on a sharp bend, this unspoilt pub always has a friendly welcome from the landlord and locals alike. Pub games ▲Q☆⑧⊮⊖

Scotter

11.30–2.30; 7–11

White Swan
9 The Green (off Gainsborough Road)
☎ (0724) 762342

Bateman XXXB; Ruddles County; Tetley Mild, Bitter; Webster Yorkshire Bitter ⓗ
Originally a village local, now extended to incorporate hotel and restaurant wing. Popular for night out at weekends. No food Mon Q⑧⊮◖

Scotton

10.30–2.30; 7–11

Three Horse Shoes
Westgate (off A159)
☎ (0724) 763129
Bass Mild XXXX, Special Bitter ⓗ
Warm and friendly village local off beaten track. 2 drinking rooms, separate games room. Folk music weekends ▲Q

Skegness

10.30–3 (2.30 winter); 6–11

Vine Hotel
Vine Road (1 mile S of town centre) ☎ (0754) 3018
Bateman XB, XXXB ⓗ
Secluded hotel with Tennyson connections ▲⑧⊮◖▶⊖

Sleaford

10.30–2.30; 6.30–11

Marquis of Granby
Westgate
Ind Coope Burton Ale; Tetley Bitter ⓗ
Delightful little pub with a warm welcome for all. A truly traditional pub. Games
▲☆⑧&≠

10.30–2.30; 6.30–11

Wagon & Horses
Eastgate
Draught Bass ⓗ
Busy and often crowded open-plan pub, popular with young people ⑧◖▶≠

South Reston

11.30–3 (closed winter Mon); 7–11

Waggon & Horses
Main Road ☎ (0521) 50364
Marston Pedigree; Whitbread Trophy; Castle Eden Ale ⓗ
Smart roadhouse. Just the place for a relaxing drink on the way home from the seaside ▲Q☆ (restaurant) ⑧◖▶ (not Mon) & Å

Spalding

10.30–3; 6 (7 winter)–11

Black Swan
New Road ☎ (0775) 2115
John Smith Bitter ⓗ
Traditional and comfortable hotel. Public bar with games and music for younger people. Quiet lounge Q☆⊮◖⊖&≠

10.30–3 (4 Tues); 7–11

Bull Inn
Churchgate ☎ (0775) 67749
Home Mild, Bitter Ⓔ

Large spacious pub next to River Welland. Comfortable lounge with L-shaped games room. Caravan park nearby ☆⑧◖⊖&≠

Try also: Olde White Horse (Samuel Smith)

Spilsby

11–3; 6.30–11

Red Lion
16 Market Street
☎ (0790) 53500
Bateman XB, XXXB ⓗ
Traditional 1-bar town pub. Warm welcome. Popular with pool players ☆⑧⊮ Å

Stamford

11–2.30; 6–11

Dolphin
60 East Street ☎ (0780) 55494
Wells Eagle Bitter, Bombardier ⓗ
One of the oldest pubs in Stamford; the original pub was just the smallest of the present 4 rooms ▲⑧◖⊖

10.30–2.30; 6–11

Green Man
29 Scotgate
Cameron Strongarm; Greene King Abbot; Ruddles County; Tolly Cobbold Original; Ward Sheffield Best Bitter ⓗ
Excellent free house; a modernised, single-bar pub ▲⑧⊮◖

11–2.30; 6.30–11

Hurdler
93 New Cross Road
☎ (0780) 63428
Adnams Bitter ⓗ**; Everards Mild** Ⓔ**, Beacon Bitter** ⓗ**, Tiger** Ⓔ**, Old Original** ⓗ
Lively estate pub. Football team and pub games including pool table. Guest beers. Entertainment Sat eves ⑧◖▶&

Sturton-by-Stow

11–2.30; 6.30–11

Plough
Tillbridge Lane (A1500)
☎ (0427) 788268
Ansells Bitter; Marston Pedigree; Tetley Bitter ⓗ
Modernised village pub. Guest beers ☆ (ask) ⑧◖▶ (booking advised) ⊖

Surfleet

11–3; 6.30–11

Mermaid
Gosberton Road (A16)
☎ (077 585) 466
Shipstone Bitter ⓗ
Comfortable, family-run riverside hotel with extensive garden which has children's playground. Children's room and large restaurant. Guest beers ▲☆⑧⊮◖▶&

Lincolnshire

Try also: **Crown** (Bateman)

Swineshead Bridge

10.30–3; 6.30–11

Barge
On A17 ☎ (0205) 820267
Home Bitter H
Large, busy pub serving good food in pleasant atmosphere. Good fishing nearby. Pub games

Swinhope

11.30–2.30; 7 (6 summer)–11

Clickem Inn
On B1203 3 miles from Binbrook ☎ (047 283) 253
Bateman Mild, XXXB; Marston Pedigree; Younger No.3 H
Isolated Wolds inn. Name is thought to derive from click of the gate to opposite field, into which farmers drove flocks when drinking at pub. Guest beers

Tattershall

11–2.30; 7–11

Fortescue Arms
The Square ☎ (0526) 42364
Draught Bass; Stones Best Bitter H
Large cheerful pub with popular games room. Good food. Close to leisure park, 15th-century castle and Battle of Britain Memorial Flight

Throckenholt

12–3 (Sat only); 7–11

Four Horseshoes
South Eau Bank (B1166) ☎ (0945) 700220
Elgood Bitter G
1-roomed, low ceilinged unspoilt pub in remote Fenland location. Time has passed this pub by. Devil-Among-the-Tailors game played

Wainfleet

10.30–3 (2.30 winter); 6–11

Jolly Sailor
19 St John Street ☎ (0754) 880275
Bateman Mild, XB H
Cheerful, friendly street-corner local. Pub games

Welton

10.30–2.30; 6.30–11

Black Bull
The Green (off A46) ☎ (0673) 60220
Ind Coope Best Bitter H
Large, busy coaching inn; only pub in ever-expanding village. Good reputation for food; serves mammoth steaks (booking advised)

West Pinchbeck

12–3; 7–11

Horse & Jockey
Six House Bank
Whitbread Castle Eden Ale H
Lively, friendly local with open plan lounge bar. Children's menu. Pub games

Wilsford

12–2 (not Mon); 7–11

Plough
Main Road ☎ (0400) 30304
Draught Bass H
Delightful country pub offering superb value-for-money meals (not Tue). Has a striking stone fireplace. Guest beers

Phil Evans

A TASTE OF LONDON

Roger Protz

It seemed a pleasant and undemanding task, to give serious consideration to the naturally-conditioned beers brewed in London. There are just a clutch of breweries left in what was once one of the great brewing centres, and one of the survivors is small enough to fit into the average potting shed.

Yet an evening pub crawl to evaluate the beers of Fuller, Guinness, Truman, Pitfield and Young turned out to be a major operation, tiring on both tastebuds and feet. It became a running debate not only about the brews on offer but also about the merits of the tied house system, the best temperature to serve beer and even such minor but not unimportant considerations as the cleanliness of the glasses.

The London tasting was the first in a series that will attempt to evaluate all the cask and bottle conditioned beers of Britain. Too many of us tip brown or black liquids down our throats and mutter "That's nice" or "Bit hoppy, that" without beginning to grasp the assorted tastes and aromas that go to make up the complex brews produced by master craftsmen.

The London tasting took place in pubs. The panel was determined to drink the beers that the punters were drinking. To organise special tasting sessions in the clinical surroundings of a brewery cellar would certainly produce perfect beer on every occasion. But that would miss the essence of a singular beer style which, in its draught form, comes to maturity in the pub cellar, not the brewery.

So to the pubs we went, with the aim of giving each beer a star rating from one to five. We began in a **Young's** pub near Kings Cross and started with the ordinary **Bitter**; Michael Jackson sternly telling us that with Young and Fuller we were dealing with two of the greatest ("grand cru") breweries in the world.

Both Andrea Gillies and Roger Protz felt that the bitter was a trifle too warm but Jackson felt that the traditional cellar temperature of 56 degrees Fahrenheit brought out the best aromatic qualities of cask beer. Protz countered with the belief that a slight reduction in cellar temperature might give cask beer greater appeal.

Rob Walker said Young's bitter was less hoppy than when he first came to London. Jackson said this was the result of a higher mashing temperature that left more residual sugars in the beer. He felt that it was a classic English bitter, fruity and with a long hoppy finish. All the judges felt the nose was disappointing, but that turned out to be a common theme of an evening which ended with the discovery that, unlike a good bottom-fermented Pilsner, where the toffee and citric nose bounces out of the glass, the aroma of an English beer is slow to develop.

The judges were impressed by the new version of Young's **Special Bitter**. Walker found it surprisingly dry for its gravity and Gillies praised its hoppy and citric overtones – "a pot pourri of flowers and herbs: wonderful!" (Did I really say that? Ed.) Protz liked the orange peel nose; Jackson would have preferred a shade more maltiness in the taste, but praised Young's determination to keep a strong hop character in their beers.

The panel moved on to a nearby **Fuller's** house. We were all disappointed by the sample of **Chiswick** bitter. The light, astringent and cleansing hoppiness was missing and was replaced by a heavy fruitiness that suggested the beer was past its best. Martin complained of a lack of finish. Although Jackson found it not up to standard, he praised the way in which British brewers pack so much flavour into low gravity beers.

There were wide divergencies of opinion on the sample of **London Pride**. Walker found it well-rounded but both Gillies and Martin thought the lack of finish disappointing. Jackson, however, declared himself stunned by the complexity of a beer that blended maltiness and hoppiness so skilfully. On **Extra Special Bitter**, however, the only disagreement was over the choice of superlatives. Martin was impressed by the "explosion of taste – full of fruit but not sweet. It's like marmalade – Cooper's of course!" Gillies found it rich and winey and Jackson thought it "perilously drinkable – the most complex of British beers, aromatic, fruity and hoppy".

Walker considered it surprisingly smooth and refreshing despite the strength and body. Protz extolled the soft, perfumey nose, malty taste but "stunningly dry hoppy finish".

A slow amble to a Truman pub in Smithfield helped refresh the palate. Watney's East London subsidiary is now down to just one cask beer, **Best Bitter**. The judges were pleased by its condition and appearance but surprised by the lack of body in a beer of its gravity. Jackson suspected that was due to the high level of adjuncts (non-malted ingredients) used. He pointed out that the American version of Budweiser has a similar gravity, a high level

The Assembled Company

of adjuncts – and virtually no taste. Gillies found it pleasant but a typical Big Seven beer, designed to please all tastes. Protz liked the earthy, blackcurrant nose but found the beer had no finish.

The judges called up taxis and headed for Bethnal Green and Hackney to find the brews of the **Pitfield** Brewery. The sample of **Hoxton Heavy** (to be renamed Hoxton Special) was sadly undrinkable, sour and vinegary. The judges decided not to award it a rating but came down against finding another outlet: like any other luckless drinker, they had chosen a free house offering the beer and had drawn the short straw. As we moved on to the final pub, there was general agreement that the strengths of the tied house tend to outweigh the weaknesses.

The Hackney pub, with both **Pitfield Bitter** and **Dark Star**, is another free house with a good range of cask beers. Gillies found the bitter two dimensional, rather like iced tea – "a refreshing summer beer but a bit flat." Protz found it in poor condition; no head, drinkable but with no finish. Walker, a devotee of the beer, was devastated by this "tired, fruity, flat" offering: "it is usually sharp, hoppy and lively." Jackson thought it a "refreshing, hearty beer but it falls away too quickly." Martin found it dull.

Dark Star created mixed feelings. Martin found it chocolatey but with little depth. Protz disliked the vinous nose and mouth-puckering dryness but Jackson thought it had "a good balance of raisiny fruitiness and bitter-chocolate notes – a good old ale." Walker, too, liked the chocolate malt smoothness but thought it was at a disadvantage as a result of poor keeping in a free house. Gillies was more upbeat: "Tons of flavour, rich and malty with a bitter aftertaste".

Bottle-conditioned **Guinness Extra Stout** is always prey to the vagaries of the free trade but it came up trumps as the judges' final beer. "Rich, fruity, amazing balance of malt, hops and roasted barley," said Protz, "why don't I drink it more often?" Gillies had to get through the natural fizz to find the taste but then found it "very more-ish – lovely stuff." Jackson praised the "wonderful balance of slight sourness, roastiness and hop bitterness; immensely complex". Walker liked the dry, malt taste but preferred the draught version as he found the bottled stout over-carbonated. Martin extolled the good nose, the balance of malt and hops and soft palate.

The ratings

Each beer was given a rating of one to five stars. There were no "half stars" so Pitfield Bitter, which scored 3,2,2,3,2 was rounded down to 2 while Guinness Extra Stout, which scored 5,4,5,4,5 was rounded up to 5.

Young Bitter (1036 Original Gravity): 3 stars
Young Special Bitter (1046 OG): 4 stars
Fuller Chiswick Bitter (1035 OG): 3 stars
Fuller London Pride (1041.5 OG): 4 stars
Fuller Extra Special Bitter (ESB) (1055.75 OG): 5 stars GB*
Truman Best Bitter (1045 OG): 3 stars
Pitfield Bitter (1038 OG): 2 stars
Pitfield Hoxton Heavy (1048 OG) —
Pitfield Dark Star (1050 OG): 3 stars
Guinness Extra Stout (1042 OG): 5 stars

*As ESB scored 5 stars from each judge, it was decided to rate it "5 stars Grand Brew" in line with a Grand Cru French wine.

The panel

Andrea Gillies, editor of the Good Beer Guide; Michael Jackson, author of the World Guide to Beer and chairman of the British Guild of Beer Writers; Peter Martin, managing editor of the Publican and Club Mirror; Roger Protz, compiler of Beer, Bed and Breakfast and author of the Great British Beer Book and Rob Walker, national chairman of CAMRA.

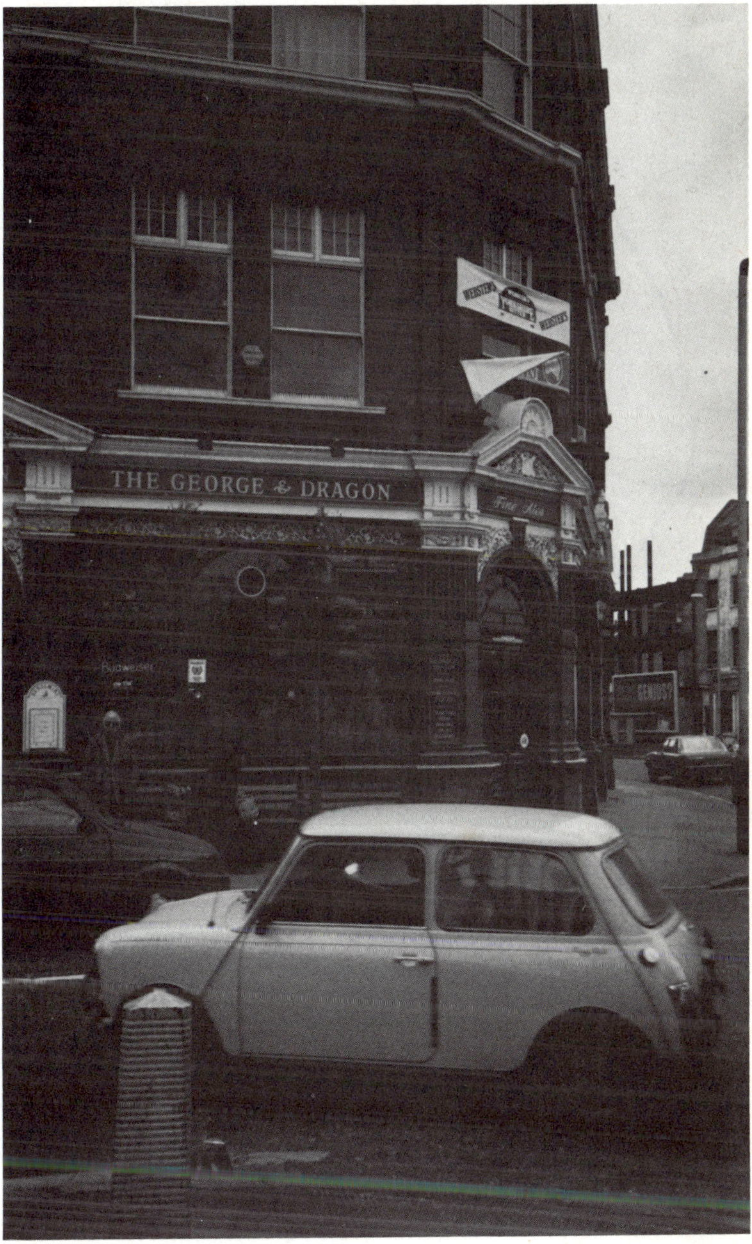
THE GEORGE & DRAGON
WEBSTERS
WEBSTERS

Greater London

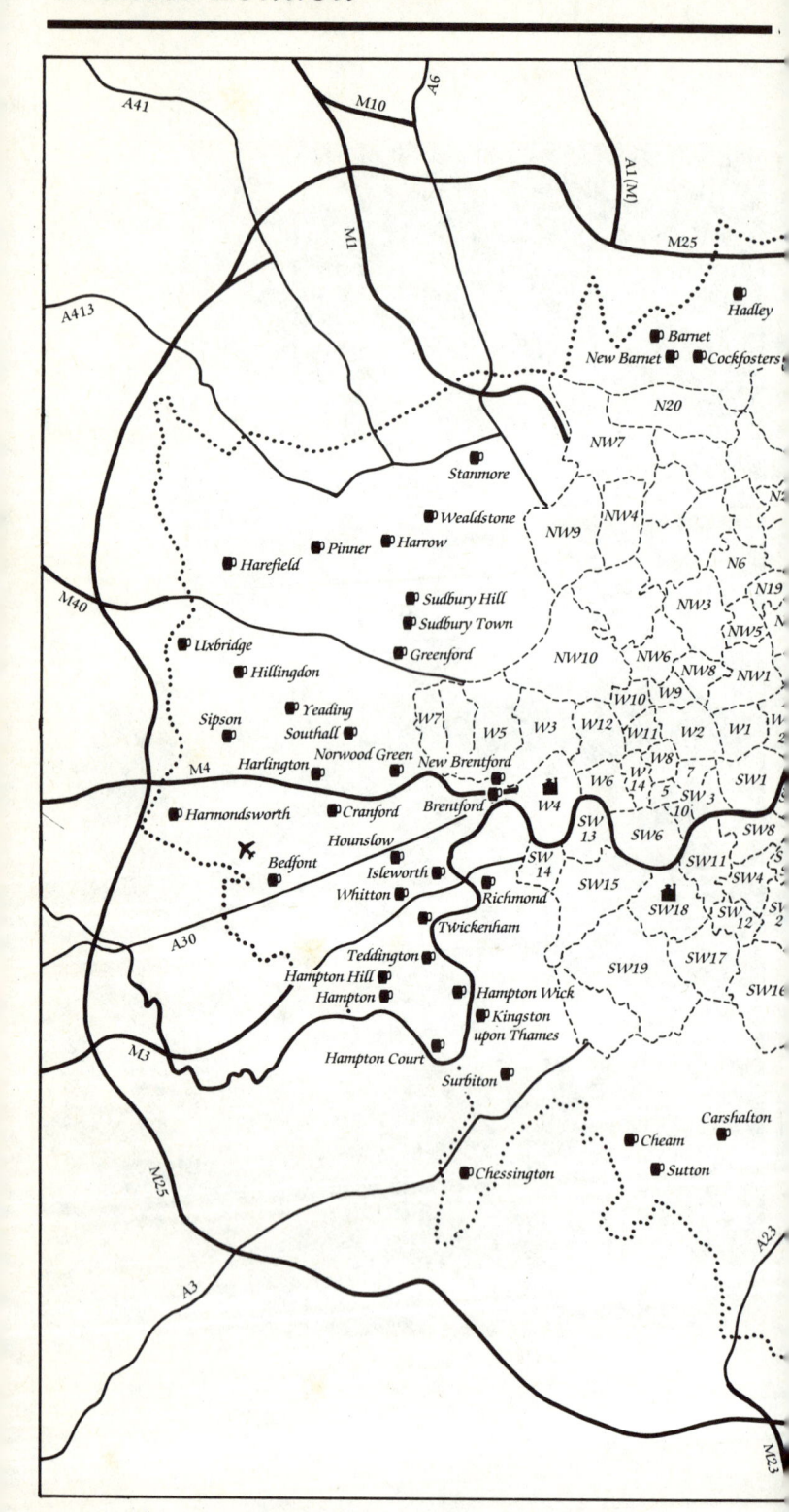

Greater London

Greater London

> *Fuller, Smith and Turner*, Chiswick W4; *Pitfield*, N1; *Young*, Wandsworth SW18

Central London

EC1: Clerkenwell

11–3; 5.30–11 (closed Sat eve)

City Pride
28 Farringdon Lane
**Fuller Chiswick Bitter,
London Pride, ESB** H
Attractive pub with modern stained glass windows
≜Q☎ (lunch) (] &
≠ (Farringdon) ⊖

11–3; 5–11 (closed Sun)

Eagle
159 Farringdon Road
☎ (01) 837 1353
Banks & Taylor Shefford Bitter, Eastcote Ale, SOS, SOD H
Crowded at lunchtime, quieter in the evenings (may close early). Occasional live music ([≠ (Farringdon)⊖

11–3; 5.30–11

Gunmakers Arms
13 Eyre Street Hill
☎ (01) 837 5026
Draught Bass; Charrington IPA H
Very small pub, so don't try to swing a cat. On 2 levels and both are often crowded
Q☎⬛ (] ≠ (Farringdon) ⊖

11–3; 5.30 (8 Sat)–11 (closed Sun eve)

Horseshoe
24 Clerkenwell Close
☎ (01) 253 6068
Courage Best Bitter, Directors H
Deceptively large pub with attractive glass frontage. Was alehouse in 1747. Quiet in the evening, very busy lunchtime
Q⬛ (] ▶ ⊖ (Farringdon) ⊖

EC1: Finsbury

11–3; 5 (5.30 Sat)–11

Artillery Arms
102 Bunhill Row
☎ (01) 253 4683
Fuller London Pride, ESB H
Small busy pub with island bar opposite the Bunhill cemetery and the artillery ground
☎ (] ≠ (Moorgate) ⊖

EC1: Holborn

11–3; 5.30–11 (closed weekends)

Olde Mitre Tavern
Ely Court, between Hatton Garden and Ely Place
☎ (01) 405 4751
Friary Meux Bitter; Tetley Bitter; Ind Coope Burton Ale H
Restful, wood-panelled, historic 16th-century pub with unusual little snug off rear bar.

See the preserved cherry tree that Sir Christopher Hatton and Queen Elizabeth I are supposed to have danced around Q⬛⬛⊖ (Holborn Viaduct) ⊖ (Chancery Lane)

EC1: Smithfield

11.30–3; 5–11 (closed weekends)

Hand & Shears
1 Middle Street
☎ (01) 600 0257
Courage Best Bitter, Directors H
A pub has been on this site since 1123; in Tudor times a centre for tailors and cloth merchants Q⊖ (Barbican)

11.30–3; 5–11

Rising Sun
Rising Sun Court, 38 Cloth Fair
Samuel Smith OBB, Museum Ale H
Re-established by the Yorkshire independent brewer, comfortable pub opposite the historic church of St. Bartolomew the Great
(] ▶ ⊖ (Barbican)

EC2: Finsbury

11–3; 5–9.30; 12–3 Sat (closed Sat eves Sun & bank hols)

Fleetwood
36 Wilson Street
☎ (01) 247 2242
Fuller Chiswick Bitter, London Pride, ESB H
Modern split-level pub at foot of modern office building. Unusually, serves cooked meals Sat lunchtime Q (] ≠ (Liverpool St) ⊖ (Moorgate)

11.30–3; 5–11 (closed weekends)

Sir Paul Pindar
213 Bishopsgate
☎ (01) 247 8275
Draught Bass; Charrington IPA H
Friendly local, threatened by redevelopment. 1 bar, with plush fittings
Q (]& ≠ (Liverpool St) ⊖

11.30–3; 5–9.30 (closed Sat eve, Sun eve & Bank Hols)

Woodins Shades
212 Bishopsgate
Draught Bass; Charrington IPA H
Typical medium-sized city pub with lots of polished wood and stained glass windows. Restaurant upstairs
(] ▶ (not Sat)
≠ (Liverpool St) ⊖

EC3: City

11.30–3; 5–9.30 (closed weekends)

East India Arms
67 Fenchurch Street

☎ (01) 480 6562
Young Bitter, Special H
Deservedly popular, 1-bar pub in heart of city; often crowded. Hot snacks Q≠ (Fenchurch St) ⊖ (Tower Hill)

11.30–3; 5–9 (closed Sat eve/Sun)

Lamb Tavern
10–12 Leadenhall Market
☎ (01) 626 2454
Young Bitter, Special, Winter Warmer H
3-tiered pub in Victorian covered market; includes dive bar. Very crowded at lunchtimes Q (]
≠ (Fenchurch St) ⊖ (Aldgate)

EC4: Blackfriars

11.30–3; 5–9.30 (closed weekends except Sat lunch summer)

Black Friar
174 Queen Victoria Street
☎ (01) 236 5650
Adnams Bitter; Arkells Best; Draught Bass; Boddington Bitter; Tetley Bitter H
Remarkable Art-Nouveau pub decorated with alabaster and marble. Mosaics depicting life in medieval friary
⬛≠ (Blackfriars) ⊖

EC4: City

11.30–3; 5–9.30 (closed weekends)

Banker
Cousin Lane
Fuller Chiswick Bitter, London Pride, ESB H
Tall split-level 1-bar pub with smart pine furnishing. Views of the Thames from south side
⬛ (] ▶ & ≠ (Cannon St) ⊖

11.30–3 (2.30 Sat); 5–10 (closed Sat eve & Sun)

Shades
5–6 Bucklersbury
☎ (01) 248 0523
Samuel Smith OBB, Museum Ale H
Spacious wood-panelled pub with subtle lighting and ample seating. Pleasant and peaceful; now threatened by redevelopment plans
Q (] ▶ ⊖ (Bank)

EC4: Fleet Street

11.30–3; 5–11 (closed Sun)

Ye Olde Cheshire Cheese
145 Fleet Street
☎ (01) 353 6170
Samuel Smith OBB, Museum Ale H
Famous pub rebuilt 1667 after Great Fire of London; not much changed. 4 bars on different levels, basic unpretentious furnishing. Good restaurant. Described in

Greater London

"A Tale of Two Cities"
♨Q☻⊷◑≠ (Blackfriars) ⊖
11.30–3; 5–11 (closed weekends)
Ye Olde Cock Tavern
22 Fleet Street ☎ (01) 353 9706
Ruddles Best Bitter, County; Truman Best Bitter; Webster's Yorkshire Bitter H
Another historic city pub known by many famous men of letters. Smart, heavily beamed single bar with bare floor, and low lighting
◑● ⊖ (Temple)

WC1: Bloomsbury

11–3; 5.30–1
Lamb
94 Lambs Conduit Street
Young's Bitter, Special, Winter Warmer
Popular and unspoilt, with snob screens and old theatrical photographs
Q❊◑&⇌ (Russell Sq)

WC1: Holborn

11–3; 5.30–11
Cittie of Yorke
22–23 High Holborn
Samuel Smith OBB, Museum Ale H
3-roomed former coffee house. Rear room has small compartments
Q◑&≠ (Holborn Viaduct)

WC1: Kings Cross

11.30–3; 5.30–11 (closed weekends)
Hansler Arms
133 Kings Cross Road
☎ (01) 837 4445
Brakspear Bitter; Flowers IPA; Whitbread Strong Country Bitter; Castle Eden Ale H
Quite small locals' pub. Beer range changes regularly ◑
(not Sun) ≠ (Kings Cross) ⊖

WC1: Mount Pleasant

11–3; 5.30–11
Calthorpe Arms
252 Grays Inn Road
☎ (01) 278 4732
Young Bitter, Special, Winter Warmer H
Straightforward and friendly pub with upstairs dining room; games room at back Q
☻❊◑&≠ (Kings Cross) ⊖

11–3; 5.30–11
Pakenham Arms
1 Pakenham Street
☎ (01) 837 6933
Adnams Bitter; Arkells Kingsdown Ale; Boddingtons Bitter; Brakspear Special; Flowers Original; Greene King Abbot H
Local serving the nearby postal sorting office. Sunday roast. Guest beers
◑●⇌ (Farringdon)
⊖ (Russell Sq)

WC2: Covent Garden

11–3; 5.30–11
Freemasons Arms
81 Long Acre ☎ (01) 836 3115
Samuel Smith OBB, Museum Ale H
Lofty, airy pub, often crowded
◑● (not Sun) ⊖ (Covent Gdn)

11–3; 5.30–11
Marquess of Anglesey
39 Bow Street ☎ (01) 240 3216
Young Bitter, Special, Winter Warmer
Busy corner pub near market hall and London Transport Museum. Upstairs bar and restaurant ◑≠ (Charing Cross) ⊖ (Covent Gdn)

11–3; 5.30–11
Nags Head
10 James Street
McMullen AK Mild, Country Bitter, Xmas Ale H
Large, often very busy pub near Royal Opera House
◑≠ (Charing Cross)
⊖ (Covent Gdn)

WC2: St Giles

11–3; 5.30–11
Angel
61 St Giles High Street
Courage Best Bitter, Directors H
Historic pub with reputedly haunted cellar; in the shadow of Centrepoint
◑⊖ (Tottenham Ct Rd)

WC2: Trafalgar Square

11–3; 5.30–11
Chandos
29 St Martins Lane
☎ (01) 836 2592
Samuel Smith OBB, Museum Ale H
Large popular, wood-panelled pub with upstairs bar and restaurant (open all day)
◑●≠ (Charing Cross) ⊖

E1: Spitalfields

11–2.30; 5–11 (closed weekends)
Gun
54 Brushfield Street
☎ (01) 247 7988
Ruddles County; Truman Best Bitter; Webster's Yorkshire Bitter H
Only pub in Spitalfields market – has 6am–9am early licence
♨◑&≠ (Liverpool St) ⊖

11–2.30; 5–11
Pride of Spitalfields
3 Heneage Street (just off Brick Lane) ☎ (01) 247 8933
Fuller London Pride, ESB; Marston Pedigree; Pitfield Dark Star; Young Special H
Popular side street pub

frequented by students and locals ♨❊◑●≠ (Liverpool St) ⊖ (Aldgate E)

E1: Stepney

11–2.30; 5 (6.15 Sat)–11
White Horse
48 White Horse Road
☎ (01) 790 1366
Charrington IPA H
Small old-fashioned, split-level, panelled 1-bar pub with peaceful atmosphere; all are made welcome Q☻◑&
≠ (Stepney E) ⊖ (DLR)

E1: Wapping

11–2.30; 5.30 (7 Sat)–11
Town of Ramsgate
62 Wapping High Street
☎ (01) 488 2685
Draught Bass; Charrington IPA H
Narrow historic grade II listed pub; cellars used to be dungeons. Ramsgate fishermen used to land catch here, hence name. Fine paved garden overlooks river
❊◑●&⊖ (Wapping)

N1: Canonbury

11–3; 5.30–11
Four Sisters
25 Canonbury Lane (off A1)
Courage Best Bitter, Directors H
1-bar pub with unusual mural
◑●≠ (Highbury & Islington) ⊖

11–3; 5.30–11
Marquess Tavern
32 Canonbury Street
Young Bitter, Special, Winter Warmer H
Impressive building dating from the 1850s; by the New River, North London's severed water supply artery
♨Q◑●≠ (Essex Rd)
⊖ (Highbury & Islington)

N1: Hoxton

11–3; 5.30 (7 Sat)–11
George & Vulture
63 Pitfield Street
☎ (01) 253 3988
Fuller London Pride, ESB H
Friendly to office workers and locals alike. Reputedly London's tallest pub
◑⊟≠ (Old St) ⊖

11–3; 5.30 (8 Sat)–11
Prince Arthur
49 Brunswick Place
☎ (01) 253 3187
Shepherd Neame Master Brew Bitter H
Small and basic back street local featuring race horse prints and East End atmosphere ≠ (Old St) ⊖

11–3; 5.30–12 (1 Fri/Sat)
Rosemary Branch

197

Greater London

2 Shepperton Road
Flowers Original; Greene King Abbot; Ruddles Best Bitter; Tetley Bitter; Tolly Cobbold Original H
Active pub with live music, regular fringe theatre and meeting room. Overlooks Regents Canal. Guest beers ♨☺()▮≠ (Essex Rd)

N1: Islington

11–3; 5.30–11
Albion
10 Thornhill Road
Ruddles County; Webster's Yorkshire Bitter H
Former coaching station, now much rebuilt. Many rooms, 2 bars and large garden ⚜()▮ ≠ (Caledonian Rd) ⊖ (Angel)

11–3; 5.30–11
Hemingford Arms
158 Hemingford Road
Adnams Bitter; Arkells BBB; Flowers Original; Greene King Abbot; Marston Pedigree; Palmer IPA H
Pleasant pub with splendid mahogany bar and fittings. Fringe perform on Sat nights in function room Q☺⚜()▮ & ⊖ (Caledonian Rd)

11–3; 5.30–11
Kings Head
59 Essex Road ☎ (01) 226 1825
Flowers Original; Wethered Bitter H
Well managed and recently refurbished pub close to the centre of Islington Q☺⚜()▮ &≠ (Essex Rd) ⊖ (Angel)

11–3; 5.30 (7 Sat)–11
Prince Albert
16 Elia Street ☎ (01) 837 5040
Charrington IPA H
Small 2-bar pub; traditional character in the old-fashioned public bar. Bar billiards Q☺()▮&⊖ (Angel)

11–3; 5.30–11
York
82 Islington High Street (A1)
Benskins Best Bitter; Ind Coope Burton Ale; Taylor Walker Best Bitter H
Attractive pub prominently situated near Camden Passage antiques market ()⊖ (Angel)

N1: Kings Cross

11–3; 5.30–11; 12–3; 7–11 Sat
Malt & Hops
33 Caledonian Road
☎ (01) 837 9558
Boddingtons Bitter; Flowers Original; Gibbs Mew Salisbury Best, Bishops Tipple; Malt & Hops Best; Marston Pedigree H
Conveniently situated for public transport interchange. Can be loud at times ()≠ (Kings Cross) ⊖

NW1: Marylebone

11–3; 5.30 (7 Sat)–11
Gloucester Arms
5 Ivor Place
Benskins Best Bitter; Ind Coope Burton Ale; Taylor Walker Best Bitter; Tetley Bitter H
Busy 1-bar corner pub in the Victorian style. Friendly service ()≠ (Marylebone) ⊖ (Baker St)

11–3; 5.30 (7 Sat)–11
Marquis of Anglesey
77 Ashmill Street (off B507)
Wells Eagle Bitter, Bombardier H
Small pub with pleasant atmosphere. Lounge bar was originally 3 rooms. No food weekends
()▮≠ (Marylebone) ⊖ (Edgware Rd)

NW1: Regents Park

11–3; 5.30–11
Prince Albert
11 Princess Road
☎ (01) 722 1886
Draught Bass; Charrington IPA; Fuller ESB (winter) H
Friendly 1-bar local specialising in food. Background music is fairly unobtrusive
⚜()≠ (Primrose Hill) ⊖ (Chalk Farm)

SE1: Bermondsey

11–3; 6–11
Sultan
238 St James Road (400 yds from Jct A2208/A2)
☎ (01) 237 4463
Shepherd Neame Master Brew Bitter, Stock Ale (winter) Best Bitter (summer) H
Popular large family pub with ornate interior reflecting its former glory as the 'Railway Hotel'. Barbecue every summer night ☺⚜()▮≠

SE1: Elephant & Castle

11–3; 5.30–11
Duke of Wellington
45 Tarn Street, Rockingham Street ☎ (01) 407 8560
Ind Coope Burton Ale; Taylor Walker Best Bitter; Tetley Bitter H
Imposing, but with an intimate and friendly interior. Busy lunch and early evening trade
()▮≠ (Elephant & Castle) ⊖

SE1: Southwark

11–3; 5.30–11
Bunch of Grapes
2 St Thomas Street
☎ (01) 403 2070
Brakspear Bitter; Young Bitter H
Wine-bar style pub near Guys Hospital; very busy lunchtimes ⚜()▮&
≠ (London Bridge) ⊖

11–5.30; 3–11
Founders Arms
52 Hopton Street, Bankside
Young Bitter, Special Bitter, Winter Warmer H
Modern riverside pub opened in 1976. Splendid views of the City and St Pauls. Restaurant and bar meals Q⚜() (not Sat) ▮ (not Sun) ≠ (Blackfriars) ⊖

SE1: Waterloo

11–3; 5.30–11
Kings Arms
25 Roupell Street
Ind Coope Burton Ale; Taylor Walker Best Bitter; Tetley Bitter H
One of finest 2-bar pubs of its kind in London; friendly and popular. Food weekdays only ()⊞&≠ (Waterloo E) ⊖

11–3; 5.30–11
Royal George
27 Carlisle Lane
☎ (01) 928 4163
Arkells Bitter; Brakspear Bitter; Greene King IPA; Ruddles Best Bitter; Young Special Bitter, Winter Warmer H
Busy friendly real ale pub due to be demolished in 1993 so channel tunnel terminal, so get there before it disappears! No food Sun
⚜()▮&≠ (Waterloo) ⊖

11–3; 5.30–11
Streets
121 Lower Marsh
Ruddles County; Webster's Yorkshire Bitter H
Spit and sawdust style downstairs bar, chesterfield lounge upstairs with a cast iron spiral staircase joining the two ⚜()≠ (Waterloo) ⊖

11–3; 5.30 (7 Sat)–11
Anchor & Hope
36 The Cut
Wells Eagle Bitter, Bombardier H
2 very clean and comfortable saloons; handy for the Old and Young Vic theatres Q()≠ (Waterloo)

SW1: Belgravia

11–3; 5.30–11
Antelope
22 Eaton Terrace
☎ (01) 730 7781
Adnams Bitter; Benskins Best Bitter; Ind Coope Burton Ale; Wadworth 6X H
Haven which has not been spoilt by refurbishment Q()⊖ (Sloane Sq)

11–3; 5.30–11

Greater London

(no meals Sun)
Q🕭🏠🍴🍽⊖ (Westferry DLR)

11–2.30; 5.30–11

Queens Head
8 Flamborough Street
☎ (01) 790 6481
Young Bitter; Special, Winter Warmer H
Grade II listed pub on corner of Georgian square in conservation area. Very popular with both visitors and locals 🍴≠ (Stepney E)
⊖ (Limehouse DLR)

11–2.30; 5.30–11

The House They Left Behind
27 Ropemaker's Fields, Narrow Street ☎ (01) 538 5102
Ruddles County; Webster's Yorkshire Bitter H
Rejuvenated real ale pub. Built 1857, it now stands alone; all around has been demolished. Good cooked meals
🍴🍽 ⊖ Westferry (DLR)

E15: Stratford

6am–8am; 11–3; 5.30–11

Railway Tavern
131 Angel Lane
☎ (01) 534 3123
Draught Bass; Charrington IPA H
Very pleasant Victorian-style corner pub with spacious bar and ample seating. Games room at rear ≠ (Stratford) ⊖

E16: Victoria Docks

11–3; 5.30–11

Essex Arms
92 Victoria Dock Road (off A13) ☎ (01) 476 2726
Courage Best Bitter, Directors H
Friendly between the wars pub, enjoying a renewed popularity with local and visiting drinkers. Disco weekends
🕭🍴🍽🏠⚘≠ (Canning Town)

11–3; 5.30–11

Tidal Basin Tavern
31 Tidal Basin Road
☎ (01) 476 0505
Fuller London Pride, ESB H
Could become an outstanding new era Docklands pub. 2 comfortable bars
🛏Q🕭🍴🍽🏠
≠ (Custom House)

E17: Walthamstow

11–3; 5.30–11

Coppermill
205 Coppermill Lane
☎ (01) 520 3709
Charrington IPA; Flowers Original; Fuller London Pride, ESB; Greene King Abbot; Marston Pedigree H
Friendly modern style, 1-bar pub with long bar. Popularity often means standing room only Q🏠≠ (St James Street)

11–3; 5.30–11

Flower Pot
128 Wood Street (off A503)
☎ (01) 520 7138
Draught Bass H
Handsome wood-panelled single bar pub, modern decor. Built 1863 as an Essex Brewery pub ≠ (Wood St)

E18: South Woodford

11–3; 5.30–11

Railway Bell
87 George Lane
☎ (01) 989 0229
Courage Best Bitter, Directors H
Large L-shaped 1-bar pub with a reputation for good jazz. Live music Thu/Sun. Meals till early eve 🍴🍽⊖

Barking

11–3; 5.30–10.30 (11 F, S)

Jolly Fisherman
108 North Street (off A124)
☎ (01) 594 2723
Truman Best Bitter; Webster's Yorkshire Bitter H
Small friendly family pub, once a coaching inn
🍴🍽 (Mon–Fri) ≠⊖

Try also: **Victoria**, 86 Axe Street (Charrington)

Barkingside

11–3; 5.30–10.30 (11 F, S)

Doctor Johnson
175 Longwood Gardens (near A406) ☎ (01) 550 0497
Courage Best Bitter, Directors H
Large impressive 3-bar pub with revolving door leading into saloon 🍴🏠⚘

Cranham

11–2.30; 6–10.30 (11 F, S)

Thatched House
St Marys Lane (B187)
☎ (040 22) 28080
Draught Bass; Charrington IPA H
Large 1930s 1-bar pub with family room. On fringe of countryside
🛏Q🕭🍴🍽 (not Sun) 🏠

Creekmouth

11–3; 5.30–10.30 (11 F, S)

Crooked Billet
113 River Road (1¼ miles S of A13) ☎ (01) 594 2623
Charrington IPA; Fuller ESB (winter) H
Traditional family pub with restaurant in saloon; singalongs Fri/Sat; quiet music Sun
Q🕭🍴🍽 (Mon–Fri) ⚘

Hornchurch

10–2.30; 6–10.30 (11 F, S)

Compasses
125 Abbs Cross Lane
☎ (040 24) 50240
Charrington IPA H
Large saloon bar with family room. Barbecue facilities in beer garden; children's shows summer
🕭🍴 (not Sun) 🍽🏠⚘

Ilford

11–3; 5.30–10.30 (11 F, S)

Angel
Station Road (near A123)
☎ (01) 478 3297
Charrington IPA H
Smart, new pub, built behind the original Angel
🍴 (Mon–Sat) 🏠≠

Try also: **Avenue** 902 Eastern Avenue, Newbury Park

Marks Gate

10.30–2.30; 6–10.30 (11 F, S)

Crooked Billet
Billet Road ☎ (01) 590 2630
Taylor-Walker Best Bitter H
Pleasant pub with comfortable wood-panelled saloon. Overlooks farmland and Hainault forest 🕭🍴⚘

North Ockendon

10.30–2.30; 6–10.30 (11 F, S)

Old White Horse
Ockendon Road (B186)
☎ (0708) 853111
Taylor Walker Best Bitter H
Traditional friendly country local 🍴⚘

Rainham

10.30–2.30; 6–10.30 (11 F, S)

Bell
Broadway (B1335, S of A13)
☎ (040 27) 20037
Ind Coope Burton Ale; Taylor Walker Best Bitter H
Large, well-decorated and upholstered bar with separate dining area
Q🕭🍴 (not Sun) 🍽🏠≠

Romford

10.30–2.30; 6–10.30 (11 F, S)

Crown
London Road (A118)
☎ (0708) 23935
Friary Meux Best Bitter; Ind Coope Burton Ale H
Massive mock-Tudor pub near dogtrack 🍴🍽

10.30–2.30; 6–10.30 (11 F, S)

Golden Lion Tavern
2 High Street (by Market Place, near A125)
☎ (0708) 40081
Ruddles County; Webster's Yorkshire Bitter H
Attractive 16th-century beamed pub at the centre of town
🍴 (Tue–Sun) 🍽 (Tue–Sat) ≠

Try also: **Royal Oak** Havering-Atte-Bower

201

Greater London

Upminster

11–2.30; 6–10.30 (11 F, S)

Huntsman & Hounds
Ockendon Road, Corbets Tey (B1421) ☎ (040 22) 20429
Friary Meux Best; Ind Coope Burton Ale; Taylor Walker Best; Tetley Bitter H
Traditional pub with family room, playground, small zoo, attractive beer garden and conservatory ☼☎🍺▷

10–2.30; 6–10.30 (11 F, S)

White Hart
Hacton Lane, Hacton Corner (1½ miles off A124) OS547851 ☎ (04022) 20252
Draught Bass; Charrington IPA H
Very popular country pub with children's play area ☎🍺▷ (Sat)

Woodford Bridge

11–3; 5.30–10.30 (11 F, S)

Crown & Crooked Billet
13 Cross Road (B173)
Draught Bass; Charrington IPA H
Friendly, comfortable split-level pub by the green ☎🍺▷

Woodford Green

11–3; 5.30–10.30 (11 F, S)

Cricketers
299/301 High Road (A11) ☎ (01) 504 2734
McMullen AK Mild, Country Bitter H
Excellent value traditional local. Rare mild outlet for area ☎🍺▷

11–3; 5.30–10.30 (11 F, S)

Travellers Friend
496/498 High Road (A104) ☎ (01) 504 2435
Courage Best Bitter; Marston Pedigree; Ridley PA; Young Special H
Traditional wood-panelled local with snob screens. Courage Best sold as "Webster's Wonderful Wallop" Q☎🍺

North London

N2: East Finchley

11–3; 5.30–11

Old White Lion
Great North Road (A1000)
Draught Bass; Charrington IPA H
Spacious but convivial brewers' Tudor pub next to LRT station ☎🍺▷⊖

11–3; 5.30–11

Windsor Castle
The Walks, Church Lane (off A1000)
Boddingtons Bitter; Greene King Abbot; McMullen AK Mild, Country Bitter; Marston Pedigree H
Enterprising and popular; can get quite crowded, but well worth the effort to seek out ☎🍺 (not Sun) ▷

N2: Fortis Green

11–3; 5.30–11

Clissold Arms
Courage Best Bitter, Directors H
Traditional atmosphere, French cuisine ☎🍺▷

N4: Crouch Hill

11–3; 5.30 (7 Sat)–11

Marlers Bar
29 Crouch Hill ☎ (01) 272 2076
Boddingtons Bitter; Marston Pedigree; James Paine XXX; Tolly Cobbold Bitter H
Pleasant pub with a warm welcome. Chess; guest beers Q🍺▷☼ ≠ (Crouch Hill) ⊖ (Finsbury Pk)

N4: Finsbury Park

11–3; 5.30–11

White Lion of Mortimer
125 Stroud Green Road
Greene King Abbot; Marston Pedigree; Wadworth 6X; Younger Scotch H
Large pub, formerly a car showroom. Guest beers 🍺▷≠⊖

N6: Highgate

11–3; 5.30–11

Red Lion & Sun
25 North Road
Draught Bass; Charrington IPA H
Traditional brewers' Tudor pub Q☎🍺 (Mon–Sat) ⊖

11–3; 5.30–11

Shepherds Tavern
312 Archway Road
Ruddles Best Bitter; Webster's Yorkshire Bitter H
Quiet and well kept, popular with local running teams Q⊖

N7: Barnsbury

11–3; 5.30–11

Railway
10 Roman Way ☎ (01) 607 0479
Fuller Chiswick Bitter, London Pride, ESB H
Excellent, characterful but tiny local ☎☼🍺▷≠⊖ (Highbury & Islington)

N9: Lower Edmonton

11–3; 5.30–11

Beehive
24 Little Bury Street (off B154)
Ind Coope Bitter, Burton Ale H
Well-run, friendly locals' pub. 1 bar divided into several drinking areas; separate darts corner Q☼☎🍺 (not Sun) ▷

N15: Tottenham

11–3; 5.30–11

Green Gate
492 West Green Road
Ruddles County; Webster's Yorkshire Bitter H
Large 1-bar pub with segregated areas ☼🍺▷≠ (Hornsey) ⊖ (Turnpike Lane)

N15: Turnpike Lane

11–3; 5.30–11

KK McCools
265 West Green Road ☎ (01) 889 2071
Marston Pedigree; Tolly Cobbold Bitter; Young Special H
Ex-Wetherspoon shop conversion with good atmosphere Q🍺 (not Sun) ▷

N16: Stoke Newington

11–3; 5.30–11

Prince of Wales
59 Kynaston Road (off Church Street)
Draught Bass; Charrington IPA; Fuller ESB (winter) H
First-rate community local ≠ (Rectory Rd)

11–3; 5.30–11

Rose & Crown
199 Stoke Newington Church Street
Ruddles Best Bitter, County; Truman Best Bitter H
Attractive period pub handy for Clissold Park Q🍺

N17: Tottenham

11–3; 5.30–11

Chequers
841–843 High Road ☎ (01) 808 3841
Draught Bass; Charrington IPA H
Busy friendly pub near Tottenham Hotspur football ground ☼☎🍺▷≠ (White Hart Lane)

N19: Upper Holloway

11–3; 5.30–11

Dog
17 Archway Road (A1)
Greene King Abbot; Marston Pedigree; Wadworth 6X; Younger Scotch, IPA H
Single bar with raised drinking areas Q🍺⊖ (Archway) ▷

N20: Whetstone

11–3; 5.30–11

Cavalier

202

Greater London

67 Russell Lane (off A109)
Courage Best Bitter, Directors H
Spacious public bar and large comfortable lounge featuring splendid station clock
Q🍴🍺🍷 (not Sun) ⊕

11–3; 5.30–11

York Arms
310 Oakleigh Road North (A109)
Ruddles Best Bitter; Webster's Yorkshire Bitter H
All that a locals' pub should be. Sat evening singalongs around the piano
🍺🍷 (not Sun)

N21: Winchmore Hill

11–3; 5.30–11

Dog & Duck
74 Hoppers Road
McMullen Country Bitter; Wethered Bitter H
Cosy, friendly neighbourhood pub, always busy. Shove ha'penny. Guest beers ⌂Q🍺🍷

11–3; 5.30–11

Green Dragon
889 Green Lanes (A105)
Courage Best Bitter, Directors H
Imposing, bustling pub with excellent facilities. Children's play area and barbecue in garden ⚘🍺🍷 (not Sun) ⊕🚆

N22: Wood Green

11–3; 5.30–11

Starting Gate
Station Road
Benskins Bitter; Ind Coope Burton Ale; Taylor Walker Bitter H
Large Victorian pub with central bar opposite Alexandra Palace station
⌂⚘🍷⊕ (Wood Green)

Barnet

11–3; 5.30–11

Albion
74 Union Street (off A1000)
Benskins Best Bitter; Ind Coope Burton Ale H
Down-to-earth, homely locals' pub tucked away off busy High Street
Q⚘🍺🍷 (not Sun)

11–3; 5.30–11

Alexandra
135 Wood Street (A411)
Ruddles Best Bitter, County; Truman Best Bitter H
Deservedly popular multi-award winning pub, although rather expensive for the area
Q🍺🍷 (Mon–Fri)

11–3; 5.30–11

Olde Monken Holt
193 High Street (A1000)
Courage Best Bitter, Directors H
Excellent wood-panelled pub of consistently high standard
Q🍺🍷

11–3; 5.30–11

Sebright Arms
3 Alston Road (between A1081/A411)
McMullen AK Mild, Country Bitter H
Back street pub with much character, despite recent alterations. Live jazz Thu
🍺🍷

Try also: **Moon Under Water**, 148 High Street (Free)

Cockfosters

11–3; 5.30–11

Trent Tavern
Cockfosters Road (A111)
Courage Best Bitter, Directors; John Smith Bitter H
Attractive comfortable 1950s pub in prominent position on main road Q🍺🍷⚘⊕

Enfield Highway

11–3; 5.30–11

Red Lion
371 Hertford Road (A1010)
Draught Bass; Charrington IPA H
Well-run, 2-bar pub on main road. Friendly and lively
🍺🍷 (not Sun) ⊕

Enfield Town

11–3; 5.30–11

Crown & Horseshoes
15 Horseshoe Lane (near A110)
Flowers Original; Wethered Bitter H
In secluded setting by New River; vast garden with children's play area
⚘🍺🍷 (not Sun) ⊕🚆

11–3; 5.30–11

Kings Head
Market Place (off A110)
Ind Coope Burton Ale; Taylor Walker Best Bitter; Tetley Bitter H
Fine Victorian town pub with equally fine neo Victorian interior. Upstairs games room
🍷 (Mon–Sat) 🚆

11–3; 5.30–11

Old Wheatsheaf
3 Windmill Hill (A110)
Ind Coope Burton Ale; Taylor Walker Best Bitter; Tetley Bitter H
Thriving 2-bar locals' pub noted for fine floral displays and good value lunches
🍺🍷 (not Sun) 🚆

Enfield Whitewebbs

11–3; 5.30–11

King & Tinker
Whitewebbs Lane (W of A10/M25 Jct 25) OS331998
Ind Coope Burton Ale; Taylor Walker Best Bitter; Tetley Bitter H
17th-century inn of genuine character in rural setting. Always busy ⌂Q⚘🍺🍷

Hadley

11–3; 5.30–11

Hadley Hotel
113 Hadley Road OS257967
Ruddles Best Bitter, County; Webster's Yorkshire Bitter H
Pleasant Victorian residential hotel with large public lounge bar ⚘🛏🍷 (Mon–Fri)

New Barnet

11–3; 5.30–11

Lord Kitchener
49 East Barnet Road (A110)
McMullen AK Mild, Country Bitter H
Traditional style 2-bar locals' pub. Unpretentious but welcoming. Opposite Sainsburys ⚘🍷🚆

Try also: **Builders Arms**

North West London

NW3: Belsize Park

11–3; 5.30–11

Sir Richard Steele
97 Haverstock Hill (A502)
☎ (01) 722 1003
Draught Bass; Charrington IPA H
Popular pub, especially with young; throbbing on weekend evenings. Pool and music upstairs ⌂🍷🚆 (Hampstead Heath) ⊕ (Belsize Park)

11–3; 5.30–11

Washington
50 Englands Lane
☎ (01) 722 6118
Ind Coope Burton Ale; Taylor Walker Best Bitter; Tetley Bitter H
Lively local with fine Victorian etched glass and mirrors
Q🍷 (Mon–Sat) ⊕ (Belsize Pk/Swiss Cottage)

Try also: **Load of Hay**, 93 Haverstock Hill

NW3: Hampstead

11–3; 5.30–11

Holly Bush
22 Holly Mount (via Holly Bush Steps) ☎ (01) 435 2892
Benskins Best Bitter; Ind Coope Burton Ale; Tetley Bitter H
Atmospheric ex-stables. Gets crowded. Loved by tourists and locals alike ⌂Q⚘🍷 (Tue–Sat) 🚆 (Hampstead Heath) ⊕

11–3; 5.30–11

Greater London

Rosslyn Arms
48 Rosslyn Hill
☎ (01) 435 0808
Courage Best Bitter, Directors
Basic pub which does not often attract the trendy set

Try also: Horse & Groom, 68 Heath Street

NW4: Hendon

11–3; 5.30–11

White Bear
56 The Burroughs (A504)
Ind Coope Burton Ale; Taylor Walker Best Bitter; Tetley Bitter
Multi-level, well-appointed 1-bar pub, home of Hendon's best behaved polar bear (for meals) (Mon–Sat)

NW5: Dartmouth Park

11–3; 5.30–11

Lord Palmerston
33 Dartmouth Park Hill
☎ (01) 485 1578
Courage Best Bitter, Directors
Compact and comfortable, with pleasant award-winning garden (Tufnell Pk)

NW5: Kentish Town

11–3; 5.30 (7 Sat)–11

Bull & Last
168 Highgate Road
☎ (01) 267 3641
Draught Bass; Charrington IPA
Opposite Parliament Hill Fields

NW6: Kilburn

11–3; 5.30–11

Queens Arms
1 Kilburn High Road
Young Bitter, Special, Winter Warmer
1950s pub with public bar and large lounge; local photos

NW7: Mill Hill

11–3; 5.30–11

Railway Tavern
129 Hale Lane (Jct A5100/A5109)
Ruddles County; Truman Best Bitter
Delightful cottage-style pub. The last train ran many years ago – but the memories remain (conservatory) (Broadway)

11–3; 5.30–11

Rising Sun
Highwood Hill (A5109)
Ind Coope Burton Ale; Taylor Walker Best Bitter
One of the oldest inns in Middlesex and also the most elevated. Outdoor loos! Q (until 9) (Mon–Sat)

NW8: Maida Vale

11–3; 5.30–11

Crocker's
24 Aberdeen Place (off A5)
Adnams Bitter; Greene King Abbot; Vaux Samson; Ward Sheffield Best Bitter
One of Britain's finest pub interiors, superbly restored. Name derives from the builder who believed Marylebone Station would be next door (Warwick Ave)

NW8: St Johns Wood

11–3; 5.30–11

Blenheim
21 Loudoun Road
Greene King XX Mild, IPA, Abbot
Comfortable L-shaped lounge; friendly staff and atmosphere Q (not Sun)

11–3; 5.30–11

Rossetti
23 Queens Grove
Fuller London Pride, ESB
Elegant split-level lounge bar with marble topped tables and tiled floors. Superb Italian restaurant upstairs (not Sun) Q

Try also: Ordnance Arms, 29 Ordnance Hill

NW9: Kingsbury

11–3; 5.30 (6.30 Sat)–11

George
234 Church Lane (B454)
☎ (01) 205 5153
Friary Meux Best; Ind Coope Burton Ale; Taylor Walker Best Bitter; Tetley Bitter
1930s suburban pub, tastefully decorated. No food Sun

NW10: Harlesden

11–3; 5.30–11

Fishermans Arms
50 Old Oak Lane (A4000)
Benskins Best Bitter; Ind Coope Burton Ale
Good value pub with 2 bars, near canal (Willesden Jct) (North Acton)

11–3; 5.30 (6 Sat)–11

Grand Junction Arms
Acton Lane (B4492)
☎ (01) 965 5670
Young Bitter, Special, Winter Warmer
4-bar pub with own moorings on Grand Union Canal. Basic public bar; large garden at rear (not Sun)

Harefield

11–3; 5.30–11

Plough
Hill End Road ☎ (0895) 822129
Ruddles Best Bitter, County; Chiltern Beechwood Bitter; Wadworth 6X
Excellent free house. Morris men perform occasionally

Harrow

11–3; 5.30–11

Castle
30 West Street (off A312)
☎ (01) 422 3155
Fuller London Pride, ESB
Little changed traditional and well-run pub, in conservation area Q

11–3; 5.30–11

Half Moon
1 Roxeth Hill (Jct A312/A4005)
☎ (01) 422 1353
Courage Best Bitter, Directors
3-bar pub with small quiet lounge. Trad jazz Wed and Sat eves

Pinner

10.30–3; 5.30–11

Hand in Hand
38 High Street ☎ (01) 866 2521
Greene King IPA, Abbot; Wethered Bitter
Popular "Roast Inn" with crowded front bar

11–3; 5.30–11

Queens Head
31 High Street ☎ (01) 868 4607
Benskins Best Bitter; Ind Coope Burton Ale
Historic 18th-century pub in picturesque setting; extremely popular

11–3; 5.30–11

Whittington
Cannon Lane
Flowers Original; Wethered Bitter, SPA, Winter Royal
Thirties estate pub popular with all ages. A genuine "local" Q

Stanmore

11–3; 5.30–11

Vine
154 Stanmore Hill
Benskins Best Bitter; Ind Coope Burton Ale
Cosy, spacious pub with family room

Sudbury Hill

11–3; 5.30–11

Black Horse
1018 Harrow Road (A4005)
☎ (01) 904 1013
Ind Coope Burton Ale; Taylor Walker Best Bitter; Tetley Bitter
Welcoming, friendly pub with large garden and family room. Evening meals on request

Greater London

Sudbury Town

11–3; 5.30–11
Sudbury Arms
Sudbury Heights Avenue
☎ (01) 902 5026
Courage Best Bitter, Directors H
Superb example of a 1930s Courage town pub. 3 separate bars, unspoilt by time
Q ◗ (Mon–Fri) ⊞ ⊖

Wealdstone

11–3; 5.30–11
Royal Oak
60 Peel Road (off A409)
☎ (01) 427 3122
Benskins Best Bitter; Ind Coope Burton Ale; Tetley Bitter; Young Bitter H
Comfortable local with long-established folk club
⊛ ◗ (Mon–Fri) ⊞ ≷ ⊖

South East London

SE3: Blackheath

11–3; 5.30–11
British Oak
109 Old Dover Road
Courage Best Bitter, Directors H
Large pub with 2 bars, renowned for good service
⌕ ⊛ ◗ ⊞

SE3: Lee Green

11–9; (Sun 12–2, 7–9)
Bitter Experience (off licence)
129 Lee Road (just off A20)
☎ (01) 852 8819
Fuller London Pride; King & Barnes Draught Festive; Shepherd Neame Master Brew Bitter G
Popular off-licence with beers kept in chilled room. Range of guest beers changes frequently ≷ ⌕

SE5: Camberwell

11–3, 5.30 (7 Sat)–11
Station Tavern
18 John Ruskin Street (off A215) ☎ (01) 703 3256
Charrington IPA H
Very traditional pub; usually quiet but can be lively weekends (pianist)
⊞ ≷ ⊖ (Kennington)

SE8: Deptford

11–3; 5.30–11
Dog & Bell
116 Prince Street
Fuller London Pride, ESB H
Tiny backstreet free house; if you think the bar is small try and find the snug! Guest beers ≷

11–3; 5.30–11
Royal George
85a Tanners Hill
Samuel Smith OBB, Museum Ale H
Recently renovated locals' pub. Games room upstairs
⌕ (lunch) ≷ ⊖ (New Cross)

SE9: Eltham

11–3; 5.30–11
Farmhouse
52 Jason Walk ☎ (01) 857 2422
Ind Coope Best Bitter, Burton Ale H
Popular 2-bar local with a relaxed country atmosphere
⌕ ⊛ ◗ ⊞ ≷

11–3; 5.30–11
White Hart
2 Eltham High Street
Courage Best Bitter, Directors H
Large mock-Tudor styled pub with collection of copper pots and pans. Family room; games
Q ⌕ ⊛ ◗ ⊞ ≷

SE10: Greenwich

11–3; 7–11
Ashburnham Arms
25 Ashburnham Grove
☎ (01) 692 2007
Shepherd Neame Master Brew Bitter H
Unspoilt back street local, old fashioned and friendly Q ⊛ ≷

11–3; 5.30–11
Cricketers
22 King William Walk
Charrington IPA H
Historic 2 bar pub close to Greenwich Hospital, Cutty Sark and museum
◗ (Mon–Fri) ⊛ ≷

11–3; 5.30–11
Richard I
52 Royal Hill ☎ (01) 692 2996
Young Bitter, Special, Winter Warmer H
Very popular, simply furnished pub; a good place for a chat ◐ ⊛ ◗ (not Sun) ⊞ ≷

11–3; 5.30 (Sat 7)–11
Vanbrugh Tavern
91 Colomb Street
☎ (01) 305 1007
Draught Bass; Charrington IPA H
Popular plush local with large garden. Excellent range of food (not Sun)
⊛ ◗ (not Sat) ≷ (Maze Hill)

SE11: Kennington

11–3; 5.30–11
Tankard
111 Kennington Road
☎ (01) 735 1517
Draught Bass; Charrington IPA H
Comfortable local with mock-Tudor exterior near Imperial War Museum ⊛ ◗ ⊞ ⌕ ≷ (Waterloo) ⊖ (Lambeth N)

SE12: Lee

11–3; 5.30–11
Crown
117 Burnt Ash Hill
☎ (01) 857 6607
Young Bitter, Special, Winter Warmer H
Pleasant pub with alcoves in large front bar Q ⊛ ◗ ⌕

SE13: Lewisham

11–3; 5.30–11
Royal Oak
1 Lee Church Street (off A20)
☎ (01) 852 0547
Courage Best Bitter, Directors; John Smith Bitter H
Old coaching house with 2 excellent bars ⊛ ◗ ⊞ ⌕

SE15: Peckham

11–3; 7–11
Beehive
122 Meeting House Lane
Shepherd Neame Master Brew Bitter, Stock Ale (winter) H
Pleasant, warm country style pub ⊛ ◗ ≷ (Queens Rd)

SE16: Rotherhithe

11–3; 5.30–11
Blacksmiths Arms
257 Rotherhithe Street
☎ (01) 237 1349
Fuller London Pride, ESB H
Comfortable, and isolated pub in up and coming Docklands area. Intimate restaurant; traditional English food ⌕ ⊛ ◗ (not Sat) ▶ (Wed–Sat) ⊞ ⊖

SE18: Woolwich

11–3; 5.30–11
Gatehouse
Leda Road (off A206)
☎ (01) 317 1052
Flowers Original; Wethered Bitter H
Large comfortable, lounge-style pub, on a nautical theme, at Woolwich Arsenal dockyard
⛵ ◗ ≷ (Dockyard)

11–3; 5.30–11
Princess of Wales
18 Wilmount Street
☎ (01) 854 1768
Flowers Original; Wethered Bitter H
Cosy old back street local, handy for Woolwich shopping centre. Guest beers. No food Sun ⛨ ⊛ ◗ ⊞ ≷ (Arsenal)

SE19: Upper Norwood

11–3; 5.30–11
Royal Albert
42 Westow Hill (A214)
☎ (01) 670 1208
Draught Bass; Charrington IPA H

205

Greater London

Front public bar and comfortable wood-panelled saloon; sells more real ale than lager Q⊛ ◖ (Mon–Fri) ⊖▲ ⇌ (Crystal Palace)

SE20: Penge

10.30–2.30; 5.30–10.30 (11 F, S)

Hop Exchange
149 Maple Road
Everard Tiger; Greene King Abbot; King & Barnes Draught Festive; Ruddles County; Wethered Bitter; Young Bitter, Special H
Pleasant, friendly local near market. Food area soon to be extended. Superb chilli, the landlord makes it himself ⊛ ◖ ⇌ (Penge E)

SE21: Dulwich Village

11–3; 5.30–11

Crown & Greyhound
73 Dulwich Village
Benskins Best Bitter; Ind Coope Burton Ale; Taylor Walker Best Bitter; Tetley Bitter H
Very popular public house in grand Edwardian style in centre of Dulwich village Q⊗⊛ ◖ (Wed–Sun) & ⇌ (N Dulwich)

SE22: East Dulwich

11–3; 5.30 (Sat 7)–11

Crystal Palace Tavern
193 Crystal Palace Road (A2216)
Ind Coope Burton Ale; Taylor Walker Best Bitter H
Friendly back street 2-bar Victorian local. Traditional interior; superb glasswork Q⊗⊛⊖⇌ (W Dulwich)

SE23: Forest Hill

11–3; 5.30–11

Prince of Wales
52 Perry Rise ☎ (01) 699 7591
Draught Bass; Charrington IPA; Fuller ESB (winter) H
Friendly local; conversation dominates the comfortable bar Q⊛ ◖ (Mon–Fri)

SE24: Herne Hill

11–3; 5.30–11

Commercial
210 Railton Road
Draught Bass; Charrington IPA; Fuller ESB (winter) H
Large 2-bar locals' pub with collection of rugby shirts. Friendly, bustling atmosphere ⊖⇌

SE25: South Norwood

11–3; 5.30–11

Albert Tavern
65–67 Harrington Road (off A215)
Courage Best Bitter, Directors; Young Special H
Modern pub, one of friendliest in the area. 2 cricket teams ⊛ ◖ (Mon–Fri) ⊖&⇌

11–3; 5.30–11

Prince of Denmark
152 Portland Road (A215)
☎ (01) 654 1769
Courage Best Bitter, Directors H
Large, traditional pub with convivial atmosphere in both bars ⊛ ◖ &⇌

11–3; 5.30–11

Ship
55 High Street ☎ (01) 653 2079
Brakspear Bitter; Everards Tiger; Greene King IPA, Abbot H
Fine old pub, run as a free house. Tiny snug; large noisy back bar with games ⊛ ◖ (Mon–Fri) ⇌

SE26: Sydenham

11–3; 5.30 (7 Sat)–11

Dolphin
121 Sydenham Road
☎ (01) 778 8728
Courage Best Bitter, Directors; John Smith Bitter H
Large popular mock-Tudor house with children's room, slides and menagerie. Imperial Russian Stout available ⊗ ◖ (not Sun) ⇌

11–3; 5.30–11

Dulwich Wood House
39 Sydenham Hill (A212)
☎ (01) 693 5666
Young Bitter, Special H & E, **Winter Warmer** H
Very popular with country atmosphere and extensive garden (garden bar served by electric pumps). No food Sun ⚓⊛ ◖▷ ⊖▲⇌

SE27: West Norwood

11–3; 5.30–11

Kings Head
82 Norwood High Street
☎ (01) 670 4056
Draught Bass H
Superb friendly pub. The old music hall is used as a family room (pool players quite harmless) ⊗⊖⇌

11–3; 5.30–11

Paxton
255 Gipsy Road (Jct A2199)
☎ (01) 670 0319
Draught Bass; Charrington IPA H
Attractive and relaxing saloon, large public bar. Games ⊛⊖▲⇌ (Gipsy Hill)

Addiscombe

11–3; 5.30–11

Claret Wine Bar
5a Bingham Corner
Eldridge Pope Dorchester Bitter, Royal Oak; King & Barnes Festive H
Despite the name, very much a pub, with a cosy bar catering for a wide range of people. Guest beers
Q⊛ ◖ (Mon–Fri) ⇌

11–3; 5.30–11

Cricketers
47 Shirley Road
Courage Best Bitter, Directors; Young Special H
Large, brewers-Tudor 1-bar pub with fake beams, but good atmosphere and very popular
⊛ ◖ (not Sun) ⇌ (Woodside)

Beckenham

10.30–2.30; 5.30–10.30 (11 F, S)

Coach & Horses
Burnhill Road (off A222)
Courage Best Bitter, Directors H
Excellent local ⊛ ◖ ⇌

10.30–2.30; 5.30–10.30 (11 F, S)

Jolly Woodman
Chancery Lane
Draught Bass; Charrington IPA H
Excellent back street local with sporting connections
⚓Q⊛ ◖⇌

Belvedere

10.30–2.30; 6–11

Royal Standard
39 Nuxley Road (off A206)
☎ (032 24) 33737
Draught Bass; Charrington IPA H
Pleasant family-run pub in centre of village
⊛ ◖ (Mon–Fri) ⊖

10–2.30; 6–11

Victoria
2 Victoria Street (near A206)
☎ (032 24) 33773
Draught Bass; Charrington IPA H
Pleasing back street local with strong following. Very friendly ⊛ ◖ (Mon–Fri)

Bexley

10.30–2.30; 6–11

Black Horse
63 Albert Road (off A223)
☎ (0322) 52337
Courage Best Bitter, Directors H
Busy back street local; true family pub of the highest order ⊛ ◖ (Mon–Fri) ⊖⇌

Bexleyheath

12–2; 5–9.30 (11–9.30 F, S)

Bitter Experience (off licence)
216 Broadway ☎ (01) 304 2839
Adnams Bitter; Bateman XB; King & Barnes Sussex Bitter;

206

Greater London

Marston Pedigree H
Off-licence providing much needed relief from the otherwise dominant Courage/Charrington duopoly ≠

10–2.30; 6–11

**Royal Oak
(Polly Clean Stairs)**
Mount Road/Alers Road (off A221) ☎ (01) 303 4454
Courage Best Bitter, Directors H
Cosy, weather-boarded local with superb atmosphere
Q ⊛ ◖ (Mon–Fri)

10.30–2.30; 6–11

Volunteer
46 Church Road (off A207) ☎ (01) 303 4910
Ruddles Best Bitter; Truman Sampson Ale; Webster's Yorkshire Bitter H
Thriving yet peaceful in old part of town. Attractive garden and warm welcome
⊛ ◖ (Mon–Fri) ≠

Blendon

10.30–2.30; 6–11

Three Blackbirds
Blendon Road (A2)
☎ (01) 303 4260
Draught Bass; Charrington IPA; Fullers ESB (winter) H
Unusual old inn with 2 contrasting bars. Good value food ⊛ ◖ (Mon–Fri) ⌐

Bromley

10.30–2.30; 5.30–10.30 (11 F, S)

Bricklayers
143 Masons Hill
Shepherd Neame Master Brew Bitter H
Superb local
Q ◖ ≠ (Bromley S)

10.30–2.30; 5.30–10.30 (11 F, S)

Freelands Tavern
31 Freelands Road
Courage Best Bitter, Directors H
Friendly suburban local with keen darts team
⊛ ◖ ≠ (Bromley N)

10.30–2.30; 5.30–10.30 (11 F, S)

Palace Tavern
1 Napier Road
Wethered Bitter H
Back street local with nautical theme ⊛ ◖ ≠ (Bromley S)

Bromley Common

10.30–2.30; 5.30–10.30 (11 F, S)

Bird in Hand
62 Gravel Lane
Courage Best Bitter, Directors H
Friendly back street local near bus garage; pleasant garden. Not easy to find ⊛ ◖

Chislehurst

10.30–2.30; 5.30–10.30 (11 F, S)

Imperial Arms
1 Old Hill (off the common)
Courage Best Bitter, Directors; John Smith Bitter H
Excellent hillside local ⊛ ◖ ≠

10.30–2.30; 5.30–10.30 (11 F, S)

Queens Head
High Street
Benskins Best Bitter; Ind Coope Bitter, Burton Ale; Taylor Walker Best Bitter; Tetley Bitter H
Friendly pub next to village pond. Attractive forecourt and garden ⊛ ◖

Crayford

10.30–2.30; 6–11

White Swan
143 Crayford Road (A207)
☎ (0322) 521115
Fuller London Pride, ESB; Felinfoel Double Dragon; Webster's Yorkshire Bitter H
Brash modern Swiss chalet-style establishment close to Crayford Stadium. Tends to attract the younger drinker
⊛ ◖ (Mon–Sat) ≠ ⌐

Croydon

11–3; 5.30–11

Dog & Bull
24 Surrey Street
Young Bitter, Special Bitter, Winter Warmer H
Old, traditional market pub with 1 very basic bar. Loads of atmosphere and noisy regulars ≠ (E Croydon)

11–3; 5.30–11

Golden Lion
144 Stanley Road
Courage Best Bitter, Directors H
Warm, friendly street corner local, improved by recent refurbishment. Keen darts teams ⊛ ⌐

11–3; 5.30–11

Lion
182 Pawsons Road (off A212)
☎ (01) 684 2978
Draught Bass, Everard Tiger; King & Barnes Mild, Sussex Bitter, Festive, Old H
Individualistic 2-bar free house. Disused pub brewery at rear; house bitter (real) brewed by Gibbs Mew. Other guest beers. No food Sun
Q ⊛ ◖

11–3; 5.30 (6 Sat)–11

Pitlake
7?? Waddon New Road
Fuller London Pride; Greene King IPA, Abbot; King & Barnes Sussex H
Lively pub with railway mementoes; ideal outside drinking area for those long summer evenings
⊛ ◖ (not Sun) ⌐ ≠

11–2.30; 6–11

Star
101 Southbridge Road
Charrington IPA H

Small pub with very friendly staff. Emphasis on charity events and darts
◖ ≠ (S Croydon)

11–3; 5.30–11

Tamworth Arms
62 Tamworth Road
☎ (01) 688 0397
Young Bitter, Special, Winter Warmer H
Friendly, cosy local, popular with both office workers and locals ⊛ ◖ (Mon–Fri)
≠ (W Croydon)

Downe

10.30–2.30; 5.30–10.30 (11 F, S)

George & Dragon
High Street
Draught Bass; Charrington IPA H
Charles Darwin lived at nearby Downe House
⌂ Q ⊛ ◖ ⌐

Foots Cray

10.30–2.30; 6–11

Seven Stars
40 High Street (A211)
☎ (01) 300 2057
Draught Bass; Charrington IPA; Fuller ESB (winter) H
Attractive 16th-century pub; friendly and good value for money ⊛ ◖ (not Sun) ⌂

Kenley

11–3; 5.30–11

Wattenden Arms
Old Lodge Lane (2 miles from A23) ☎ (01) 660 8638
Draught Bass; Charrington IPA; Fuller ESB (winter) H
Justifiably acclaimed up-market local with excellent food. Interior decor has a strongly patriotic theme
Q ⊛ ◖ (not Sun) ⌐ (Mon–Thu)

Keston

10.30–2.30; 5.30–10.30 (11 F, S)

Greyhound
Keston Common
Courage Best Bitter, Directors H
Superb pub on edge of common (pub garden); rural location with suitable welcome ⊛ ◖ ⌂

Orpington

10.30–2.30; 5.30–10.30 (11 F, S)

Cricketers
93 Chislehurst Road
Courage Best Bitter, Directors H
Back street pub with friendly welcome ⌂ ⊛ ◖

St Mary Cray

10.30–2.30; 5.30–10.30 (11 F, S)

Beech Tree
75 Wellington Road
Flowers Original H

207

Greater London

Excellent back street locals' pub, very friendly 🍺 🍴

Sidcup

10–2.30; 6–11

Charcoal Burner
Main Road (A211)
☎ (01) 300 2038
Courage Best Bitter, Directors; John Smith Bitter H
Large, smart old roadhouse for the more mature drinker
🍺 🍴 (not Sun) ⌂

Thornton Heath

11–3; 5.30–11

Fountain Head
114 Parchmore Road
Young Bitter, Special, Winter Warmer H
Detached pub set back from road. Large enclosed, well-equipped garden with swings, slides and boules. No food Sun ⌂🍺 🍴 ⌂≋

11–3; 5.30–11

Grange
23 Norbury Road (just off B273) ☎ (01) 653 3783
Wethered Bitter H
Large friendly back street pub with huge garden. Whitbread guest beers 🍺 🍴 (not Sun) ⌂

South West London

SW2: Brixton

11–3; 5.30–11

Hope & Anchor
123 Acre Lane (A2217)
☎ (01) 274 1787
Young Bitter, Special, Winter Warmer H
Large, plush roadhouse. Spacious garden with children's playground
⌂ Q 🍺 🍴 ⌂≋

SW3: Chelsea

11–3; 5.30–11

Princess of Wales
145 Dovehouse Street
Courage Best Bitter, Directors H
Small pub tucked behind Royal Marsden Hospital Q 🍴 (Mon–Fri) ⊖ (S Kensington)

11–3; 5.30–11

Rose
86 Fulham Road
Fuller Chiswick Bitter, London Pride, ESB H
Ornate ex-Watney house with theatre upstairs
🍴 ⊖ (S Kensington)

11–3; 5.30–11

Surprise
6 Christchurch Terrace
Draught Bass; Charrington IPA H
Genuine local with interesting frieze 🍴

SW4: Clapham

11–3; 5.30–11

Railway Tavern
18 Clapham High Street
☎ (01) 622 1696
Draught Bass; Charrington IPA; Fuller ESB H
Busy, comfortable pub with folk club ☎ (until 7) 🍴 (not Sun) ⌂≋⊖ (Clapham N)

SW5: Earls Court

11–3; 5.30–11

Drayton Arms
153 Old Brompton Road
☎ (01) 373 4089
Draught Bass; Charrington IPA; Fuller ESB (winter) H
Decorative cosmopolitan pub with arched terracotta frontage
🍴 ⊖ (Gloucester Rd)

SW6: Fulham

11–3; 5.30–11

Jolly Brewer
308 North End Road
Ruddles County; Webster's Yorkshire Bitter H
Busy street-market local
🍴⊖ (Bdwy)

SW6: Parsons Green

11–3; 5.30–11

White Horse
1 Parsons Green (off A308)
☎ (01) 736 2115
Draught Bass; Bateman Bitter; Charrington IPA; M&B Highgate Mild H
Large popular upmarket pub facing the green. Hearty weekend breakfasts and Sunday lunches 🍴 ⊖

SW6: West Brompton

11–3; 5.30–11

Atlas
16 Seagrave Road
Ruddles Best Bitter; Truman Best Bitter; Webster Yorkshire Bitter H
Popular local in side-street near Earls Court exhibition centre 🍺 🍴⊖

SW7: South Kensington

11–3; 5.30–11

Anglesea Arms
15 Selwood Terrace
☎ (01) 373 1207
Adnams Bitter; Boddingtons Bitter; Brakspear Special; Greene King Abbot; Theakston Old Peculier; Young Special H
Well-known, comfortable and popular free house Q 🍴 🍺 ⊖

SW8: South Lambeth

11–3; 5.30–11

Surprise
16 Southville (off Wandsworth Road)
Young Bitter, Special H
Very small friendly pub with outside seats next to Larkhall Park
⌂ Q 🍺 🍴≋ (Wandsworth Rd)

SW8: Vauxhall

11–3; 5.30–11

Burkes Freehouse (Nottingham Castle)
257 Wandsworth Road
☎ (01) 720 7243
Greene King Abbot; King & Barnes Sussex Bitter; Wethered Bitter; Young Bitter H
Enterprising free house with the keenest prices in the area
🍴 🍺≋

11–3; 5.30–11

Wheatsheaf
126 South Lambeth Road
☎ (01) 622 3602
Courage Best Bitter, Directors H
Fine traditional London street-corner pub with own golfing club. A welcome change from plastic interiors
🍴 (Mon–Fri) ⌂⊖

SW9: Brixton

11–3; 5.30–11

Trinity Arms
45 Trinity Gardens off Acre Lane (A2217) ☎ (01) 274 4544
Young Bitter, Special, Winter Warmer H
Lively back street local on quiet square near town hall and Ritzy Cinema
🍺 🍴 (not Sun) ⌂≋⊖

SW10: West Chelsea

11–3; 5.30–11

Chelsea Ram
32 Burnaby Street (off A3212)
Young Bitter, Special H
Comfortable pub built over 100 years ago but not licensed until 1984. No food weekends
🍴

SW11: Battersea

11–3; 5.30–11

Castle
115 Battersea High Street
☎ (01) 228 8181
Young Bitter, Special, Winter Warmer H
Newly refurbished; public bar as comfortable as lounge. Very friendly ⌂🍺 🍴 ⌂⌕

11–3; 5.30–11

Duke of Cambridge

Greater London

228 Battersea Bridge Road
☎ (01) 228 5064
Young Bitter, Special, Winter Warmer H
Good local, with excellent good value beers Q ❦ ◐ ⌂ ⚘

SW11: Clapham Junction

11–3; 5.30–11

Beehive
197 St Johns Hill
Fuller Chiswick Bitter, London Pride, ESB H
Award-winning, welcoming and unpretentious local. The only Fullers for miles. Good value lunches
Q ❦ (lunch) ◐ ⌂ ⚘

SW12: Balham

11–3; 5.30–11

Prince of Wales
270 Cavendish Road
Courage Best Bitter, Directors
Cosy saloon and friendly, boisterous public bar. Excellent lunches
Q ❦ ◐ (not Sun) ⌂ ⚘ ⊖

SW13: Barnes

11–3; 5.30–11

Red Lion
2 Castlenau
Fuller Chiswick Bitter, London Pride, ESB H
Superb, large pub with many rooms and a notable restaurant. Handy for Barne Elms sports ground
⌂ Q ❦ ◐ ⚘

SW14: Sheen

11–3; 5.30–11

Hare & Hounds
216 Upper Richmond Road West (A205) ☎ (01) 876 4304
Young Bitter, Special H
Large, busy pub with full-sized snooker table. Rejuvenated under present management
❦ ◐ ⚘ (Mortlake)

SW15: Putney

11–3; 5.30 (6.30 Sat)–11

Duke's Head
8 Lower Richmond Road
☎ (01) 788 2552
Young Bitter, Special, Winter Warmer
Famous pub overlooking the Thames. Etched screens and windows Q ❦ ◐ ⌂ ⚘ ⊖

11–3; 5.30–11

Fox & Hounds
167 Upper Richmond Road
☎ (01) 788 1912
Flowers IPA, Original; Wethered Bitter; Whitbread Castle Eden Ale H
Excellent pub with large comfortable bar and quieter back room. Regular guest beers ❦ ◐ (Mon–Sat)
⚘ ⊖ (E Putney)

11–3; 5.30–11

White Lion
14 High Street ☎ (01) 785 3081
Arkell Kingsdown Ale; Bateman XB; Brakspear Special; Greene King Abbot; Vaux Samson; Ward Sheffield Best Bitter H
Fine restored Victorian pub and "Lacy's" restaurant. A real ale paradise – regular guest beers ◐ (Mon–Sat) ▶
⚘ ⊖ (Putney Bridge)

SW16: Streatham

11–3; 5.30–11

Greyhound
151 Greyhound Lane (A24)
☎ (01) 677 9962
Greyhound Pedigree XXX, Special Bitter, Strong, Dynamite, Stout, Xmas Ale H
Bustling large roadside pub with own brewery. Very popular garden and new children's extension; indoor barbecue all year round
❦ ❀ ◐ ⌂ ⚘

11–3; 5.30–11

Pied Bull
498 Streatham High Road (A23) ☎ (01) 764 4006
Young Bitter, Special, Winter Warmer H
4-bar pub being refurbished at the time of going to press
⌂ ❀ ◐ ⌂ ⚘ (Streatham Common)

SW17: Tooting

11–3; 5.30–11

Castle
38 Tooting High Street (A24)
☎ (01) 672 7018
Young Bitter, Special, Winter Warmer H
Large town pub with excellent public bar
❀ ◐ ▶ ⌂ ⊖ (Tooting Bdwy)

11–3; 5.30–11

Gorringe Park Hotel
29 London Road
Young Bitter, Special, Winter Warmer H
Busy street-corner local; comfortably furnished. An oasis in a desert of nondescript pubs ❀ ◐ ▶ ⚘

11–3; 5.30–11

Prince of Wales
646 Garratt Lane
☎ (01) 946 2628
Young Bitter, Special H, **Winter Warmer** H
2-bar Victorian corner pub. Seafood stall outside Fri–Sun
❦ ❀ ◐ (not Sun) ⌂ ⚘ (Earlsfield) ⊖ (Tooting Bdwy)

SW18: Earlsfield

11–3; 5.30 (7 Sat)–11

Country House
4 Groton Road ☎ (01) 874 2715
Courage Best Bitter, Directors H
Immaculate pub that lives up to its name, opposite Earlsfield station ⌂ ⚘

SW18: Wandsworth

11.30–3; 5.30–11

County Arms
345 Trinity Road
☎ (01) 874 8532
Young Bitter, Special, Winter Warmer H
Traditional main road pub opposite common. Truly basic public bar; rambling warm saloon and lounge. Ideal for prison visitors and footballers. Non-smoking bar
⌂ Q ❀ ◐ ▶

11–3; 5.30 (7 Sat)–11

Grapes
39 Fairfield Street
Young Bitter, Special H
The best bet in Wandsworth, with a relaxed atmosphere. Especially recommended at Sun lunch ❦ ❀ ◐ (Mon–Fri) ⚘

11–3; 5.30–11

Old Sergeant
104 Garratt Lane
Young Bitter, Special H, **Winter Warmer** G
Basic, friendly pub. Sing along to piano Saturday evening
◐ (Mon–Fri) ⌂ ⚘

11–3; 5.30–11

Ship
41 Jews Row (off A217)
Young Bitter, Special H, **Winter Warmer** G
Traditional public bar; yuppies congregate in saloon. Riverside location, particularly nice in summer
⌂ ❀ ◐ ▶ ⌂ ⚘

SW19: Merton

11–3; 5.30–11

Grove Tavern
2 Morden Road (Jct A24/A238/A219) ☎ (01) 542 4822
Friary Meux Best; Ind Coope Burton Ale; Taylor Walker Best Bitter; Tetley Bitter H
Friendly, busy, 2-room pub opposite tube station. Live music Sun lunch and eve, and Thu eve ◐ (Mon–Fri) ⌂
⚘ (Morden Rd)
⊖ (Wimbledon)

11–3; 5.30–11

Prince of Wales
98 Morden Road (A24)
☎ (01) 542 0573
Young Bitter, Special, Winter Warmer H
Large, friendly 2-room pub near playing fields and Morden Road station.
No food Sun
⌂ ❀ ◐ ⌂ ⊖ (S Wimbledon)

11–3; 5.30 (6.30 Sat)–11

Princess Royal

209

Greater London

25 Abbey Road
☎ (01) 542 3273
Courage Best Bitter, Directors H
Small, well-run corner pub with great atmosphere; active for local charities ✱ ((not Sun) ⊕ ⊖ (S Wimbledon)

SW19: Wimbledon

11–3; 5.30–11
Alexandra
31 Wimbledon Hill Road
☎ (01) 947 7691
Young Bitter, Special, Winter Warmer H
Large wood-panelled pub with own restaurant and non-smoking bar. Occasional piano in public (▶ ⊕ ⊖

11–3; 5.30–11
Hand in Hand
7 Crooked Billet (just off B281)
☎ (01) 946 5720
Ruddles Best Bitter; Young Bitter, Special, Winter Warmer H
Large, popular 1-bar pub by common, often very busy in summer. Proper family room; good selection of country wines. Food till 9pm
⌂ Q ✱ (▶ (Mon–Fri)

11–3; 5.30–11
Rose & Crown
55 High Street (A219)
☎ (01) 947 4713
Young Bitter, Special, Winter Warmer H
Large village pub which in parts dates from 17th century. Large courtyard and small veranda area for children. Often busy ✎ ✱ (▶ (not Sun)

Carshalton

10.30–2.30; 5.30–10.30 (11 F, S)
Greyhound
2 High Street (A232)
☎ (01) 647 1511
Young Bitter, Special, Winter Warmer H
Distinctive 18th-century coaching inn overlooking Carshalton Ponds. 3 bars and restaurant ⌂ ⇨ ✱ ⊞ (▶ ⊕ ⇌

10.30–2.30; 5.30–10.30 (11 F, S)
Lord Palmerston
31 Mill Lane ☎ (01) 647 1222
Courage Best Bitter, Directors H
Small, bustling and friendly local ✱ ((not Sun) ⊕ ⇌

Cheam

10.30–2.30; 5.30–10.30 (11 F, S)
Prince of Wales
28 Malden Road (A2043)
☎ (01) 644 4464
Friary Meux Best; Ind Coope Burton Ale H
Spotless, friendly 2-bar local ✱ ((Mon–Fri) ⇌

Chessington

10.30–2.30; 5.30–11
North Star
271 Hook Road
☎ (01) 397 4227
Draught Bass; Charrington IPA; Fuller ESB (winter); M&B Highgate Mild H
Main road pub with both passing and local trade, and a rare mild outlet. Good lunchtime snacks and meals ✎ ✱ ((Mon–Fri)
⇌ (Chessington N)

Kingston upon Thames

11–2.30; 5.30 (6.30 Sat)–11
Bricklayers Arms
53 Hawks Road
Courage Best Bitter, Directors H
Homely in every sense of the word. Eve meals on request ✎ ✱ ((not Sun) ⇦

11–2.30; 5.30 (6 Sat)–11
Cocoanut
16 Mill Street
Fuller Chiswick Bitter, London Pride, ESB H
Refurbished early 1988 but retaining original glasswork and feel Q ✱ (

10.30–2.30; 5.30–11
Druids Head
3 Market Place
Wethered Bitter; Whitbread Castle Eden Ale H
A splendid example of market place haven. Games Q (▶

11–2.30; 5.30–11
Lamb
16 Acre Road (off A307)
Courage Best Bitter, Directors H
1-bar pub in side road; comfortable with good local trade ✱ ((Mon–Fri) ⇦

11–2.30; 5.30–11
Newt & Ferret
46 Fairfield South
Adnams Mild, Bitter; Hall & Woodhouse Badger Best Bitter, Tanglefoot; Wadworth 6X H
Popular pub; food a speciality; regular guest beers ✎ (⇦

10.30–2.30; 5.30–11
Willoughby Arms
47 Willoughby Road
☎ (01) 546 4236
Flowers Original; Wethered Bitter H
Small, friendly backstreet local Q ✱ ✱ (⊕ ⇦ ⇌

10.30–2.30; 5.30–11
Wych Elm
93 Elm Road
Fuller Chiswick Bitter, London Pride, ESB H
Warm and friendly atmosphere; popular with all Q ✱ (⊕ ⇦

Richmond

11–3; 5.30–11
Angel & Crown
5 Church Court
☎ (01) 940 1508
Fuller London Pride, ESB H
Historic pub in centre of town. Compact, attractive lounge bar; welcoming atmosphere. Good value food
✎ ✱ (▶ (not Sun) ⇦ ⇌ ⊖

11–3; 5.30–11
Orange Tree
45 Kew Road (A307)
☎ (01) 940 0944
Young Bitter, Special, Winter Warmer H
Extremely popular pub in large Victorian building, with fringe theatre upstairs. Good bar food and restaurant
⌂ Q ✱ (▶ (not Sun) ⇦ ⇌ ⊖

11–3; 5.30–11
White Cross Hotel
Water Lane ☎ (01) 940 0909
Young Bitter, Special, Winter Warmer H
150 year-old Thameside pub of character. Good bar food, à la carte restaurant menu. Outdoor riverside bar (summer) ⌂ Q ✱ (▶

Surbiton

10.30–2.30; 5.30–11
Black Lion
58 Brighton Road
Young Bitter, Special, Winter Warmer H
2-bar pub just off town centre ✱ ((not Sun) ⇌

10.30–2.30; 5.30–11
Waggon & Horses
1 Surbiton Hill Road (A240)
Young Bitter, Special H, **Winter Warmer** G
Large pub opposite Assembly Rooms; noted for many charity collections Q ✱ ((Mon–Fri) ⊕ ⇦

Sutton

10.30–2.30; 5.30–10.30 (11 F, S)
Lord Nelson
32 Lower Road
☎ (01) 642 4120
Young Bitter, Special, Winter Warmer G
Pub full of character and characters. Occasional evening meals
((not Sun) ⊕ ⇦

10.30–2.30; 5.30–10.30 (11 F, S)
New Town
7 Lind Road (off A232)
Young Bitter, Special, Winter Warmer H
Smart, split-level lounge and spacious public bar with games; bar billiards
Q ✱ ((Mon–Fri) ⊕ ⇦ ⇌

10.30–2.30; 5.30–10.30 (11 F, S)
Windsor Castle
13 Greyhound Road (off A232)
☎ (01) 643 2574
Fuller London Pride, ESB H

Greater London

Comfortable, busy 1-bar pub with clean air system
Q ⊛ ◑ (not Sun) ≠

Try also: Victory (Charrington)

West London

W2: Bayswater

11–3; 5.30–11

Heron
The Water Gardens, Norfolk Crescent
Adnams Bitter; Boddingtons Bitter; Fuller London Pride; Marston Pedigree; Young Special H
Pleasant free house in modern residential area. No meals weekends ⊛ ◑ ≠ (Paddington) ⊖ (Edgware Rd)

W2: Maida Vale

11–3; 5.30–11

Hero of Maida
435 Edgware Road
Benskins Bitter; Ind Coope Burton Ale H
Pleasant pub near Regents Canal; decorated with waterways prints and photographs ◑ ⊖ (Edgware Rd)

W2: Paddington

11–3; 5.30–11

Marquis of Clanricarde
36 Southwick Street (off Sussex Gardens)
Courage Best Bitter, Directors H
Large comfortable basic pub ◑ ≠ (Paddington) ⊖

11–3; 5.30–11

Queens Railway Tavern
15 Chilworth Street
Ind Coope Burton Ale; Taylor Walker Best Bitter; Tetley Bitter H
Side street pub, very handy for Paddington station ◑ ≠ ⊖

W3: Acton

11–3; 5.30–11

Kings Arms
The Vale
Fuller London Pride, ESB H
Large, imposing 3-bar pub with genuine public bar and large garden
⊛ ⊛ ◑ ≠ ⊖ (Acton Central)

11–3; 5.30–11

Red Lion & Pineapple
281 High Road
Fuller Chiswick Bitter, London Pride, ESB H
Spacious 2-bar pub. Name is a combination of 2 former pubs ◑ ⊖ (Acton Town)

W4: Chiswick

11–3; 5.30–11

Bell & Crown
72 Strand on the Green
☏ (01) 994 4164
Fuller Chiswick Bitter, London Pride, ESB H
Busy riverside pub with conservatory overlooking Thames; home cooking
Q ◑ ≠ (Kew Bridge) ⊖ (Gunnersbury)

11–3; 5.30–11

City Barge
27 Strand on the Green
Courage Best Bitter, Directors H
Riverside pub with 1 old bar and 1 modern bar
⊛ ◑ ≠ (Gunnersbury) ⊖

11–3; 5.30–11

George IV
184 Chiswick High Road
Fuller London Pride, ESB H
Spacious lounge; pub games in public bar
◑ ≠ (Turnham Green)

11–3; 5.30–11

Windmill
214 Chiswick High Road
Fuller Chiswick Bitter, London Pride, ESB H
Modern pub, often very busy
◑ ⊖ (Turnham Green)

W5: Ealing

11–3; 5.30 (6.30 Sat)–11

Fox & Goose
Hanger Lane ☏ (01) 997 2441
Fuller London Pride, ESB H
The only pub near the dreaded Hanger Lane gyratory system. Spacious and comfortable; lots of games
⊛ ◑ ≠ ⊖ (Hanger Lane)

11–3; 5.30–11

Greystoke
7 Queens Parade
☏ (01) 997 6388
Courage Best Bitter, Directors; John Smith Bitter H
Popular local serving both business and residential community. Games
⊛ ⊛ ◑ ⊛ ⊖ (Ealing)

11–3; 5.30–11

Plough
297 Northfield Avenue (B452)
☏ (01) 567 1416
Fuller Chiswick Bitter, London Pride, ESB H
Very popular 2-bar pub; attractive saloon has alcoves for a quieter drink. Good food
⊛ ◑ ◑ ⊖ (Northfields)

11–2.30 (3 Sat); 5.30 (7 Sat)–11

Red Lion
13 St Marys Road (A3001)
☏ (01) 587 2541
Fuller Chiswick Bitter, London Pride, ESB H
Lively popular 1-bar pub opposite Ealing studios, near technical college
Q ⊛ ◑ ♿ ≠ (Bdwy)

W6: Hammersmith

11–3; 5.30–11

Black Lion Tavern
2 South Black Lion Lane (off A4)
Ruddles County; Webster's Yorkshire Bitter H
Charming 17th-century inn. Pleasant garden with 300 year-old chestnut tree
⊛ ◑ ◑ ⊖ (Stamford Brook)

11–3; 5.30–11

Blue Anchor
13 Lower Mall
Courage Best Bitter, Directors H
Busy Thameside pub with pewter bar top ◑ ⊖

11–3; 5.30–11

Dove
19 Upper Mall ☏ (01) 748 5405
Fuller London Pride, ESB H
Historic 17th-century riverside inn with Charles I connections ◑ ⊛ ⊖

W7: Hanwell

11–3; 5.30–11

Fox
Green Lane (off A3002)
☏ (01) 567 3912
Courage Best Bitter, Directors H
Close to Grand Union Canal; popular with boat people and walkers. Excellent food
Q ⊛ ◑ ◑

11–3; 5.30–11

Royal Victoria
66 Boston Road (A3002)
☏ (01) 567 4389
Ruddles Best Bitter; Webster's Yorkshire Bitter H
Delightful old fashioned local with saloon bar like a living room. Ideal for a quiet pint and a chat Q ◑ ⊛

W8: Kensington

11–3; 5.30–11

Britannia
1 Allen Street (off A315)
Young Bitter, Special, Winter Warmer H
Busy pub ◑ ⊛ ⊖

11–3; 5.30–11

Windsor Castle
114 Campden Hill Road
☏ (01) 727 8491
Draught Bass; Charrington IPA H
3-bar pub, built 1845. Unspoiled cosy atmosphere; vine in back garden
Q ⊛ ◑ (not Sun)
⊖ (Notting Hill Gate)

W9: Little Venice

11–3; 5.30–11

Warwick Castle
6 Warwick Place
Draught Bass; Charrington IPA; Fuller ESB; Morrell Varsity H
Traditional pub near Canal

Greater London

basin 🏠Q ◐⊖ (Warwick Ave)

W9: Maida Vale

11–3; 5.30–11

Prince Alfred
5a Formosa Street
Adnams Bitter; Boddingtons Bitter; Ind Coope Burton Ale; Wadworth 6X ⒽⒷ
Large ornate multi-bar pub with magnificent windows and woodwork
◐ (not Sun) ⊖ (Warwick Ave)

11–3; 5.30–11

Robert Browning
15 Clifton Road
Samuel Smith OBB, Museum Ale ⒽⒷ
Ex-Truman pub revitalised by Sam Smiths. Food bar upstairs
◐ ▶ ⊖ (Warwick Ave)

11–3; 5.30–11

Warrington Hotel
93 Warrington Crescent
Arkells BBB; Brakspear Special; Fuller London Pride, ESB; Young Special ⒽⒷ
Enormous ornate Victorian gin palace with fantastic Art Nouveau decoration
◐ ⊖ (Warwick Ave)

W10: North Kensington

11–3; 5.30–11

Narrow Boat
346 Ladbroke Grove
Fuller London Pride, ESB ⒽⒷ
Small canalside local
⊖ (Ladbroke Grove)

W11: Holland Park

11–3; 5.30–11

Duke of Clarence
203 Holland Park Avenue
☎ (01) 603 5431
Draught Bass; Charrington IPA ⒽⒷ
Spacious pub with large heated conservatory
◐ ▶ ⊖ (Shepherds Bush)

W12: Shepherds Bush

11–3; 5.30–11

Crown & Sceptre
57 Melina Road
Fuller London Pride, ESB ⒽⒷ
Popular back street local
◐ ⊖ (Goldhawk Rd)

W14: West Kensington

11–3; 5.30–11

Britannia Tap
150 Warwick Road (A3228)
Young Bitter, Special ⒽⒷ
Friendly, narrow 1-bar pub
Q 🍴 ◐ ▶ ⊖ (Olympia)

11–3; 5.30–11

Warwick Arms
160 Warwick Road
Fuller Chiswick Bitter, London Pride, ESB ⒽⒷ
Popular 1-bar pub. No food Sun 🍴 ◐ ▶ ⇌ (Olympia) ⊖

Bedfont

11–3; 5.30–11

Beehive
333 Staines Road (A305)
☎ (01) 890 8086
Fuller London Pride, ESB ⒽⒷ
Excellent pub with friendly lively atmosphere. Attractive lounge; well kept garden, children's play area. Good value food 🐕 🍴 ◐ ▶ ♿

Brentford

11–3; 5.30–11

Beehive
227 High Street (A315/A3002)
Fuller London Pride, ESB ⒽⒷ
Popular roomy town-centre pub with wide selection of food (not Sun). Reduced prices to OAPs. Former brewery tap of Gomm's Beehive Brewery (closed 1908). No food Sun
🍴 ◐ ▶ ♿ ⇌ ⊖

11–3; 5.30–11

Griffin
57 Brook Road South
☎ (01) 560 8555
Fuller London Pride, ESB ⒽⒷ
Comfortable street corner family local opposite Brentford football club
🍴 ◐ (Mon–Fri) ⇌

11–3; 5.30 (7 Sat)–11

White Horse
24 Market Place (off A315)
☎ (01) 560 1522
Draught Bass; Charrington IPA ⒽⒷ
Comfortable pub tucked away off High Street with large conservatory and garden overlooking river
🏠Q 🐕 🍴 ◐ (Mon–Fri) ⇌

Cranford

11–3; 5.30–11

Queens Head
123 High Street (off A312)
Fuller London Pride, ESB ⒽⒷ
Lovely Tudor-style pub, busy but efficient 🏠 🍴 ◐

Greenford

11–3; 5.30–11

Black Horse
425 Oldfield Lane North
☎ (01) 578 1384
Fuller London Pride, ESB ⒽⒷ
Popular canalside pub with large garden. Beware of parrot in saloon bar!
Q 🍴 ◐ (Mon–Fri) ♿ ⇌ ⊖

Hampton

11–3; 5.30–11

White Hart
70 High Street (A304)
☎ (01) 979 5352
Boddingtons Bitter; Brakspear Bitter; Eldridge Pope Royal Oak; Flowers Original; Greene King Abbot Ale; King & Barnes Draught Festive ⒽⒷ
Comfortable, tasteful mock-Tudor free house with relaxed atmosphere and a dozen guest beers. Excellent lunches
🏠 🍴 ◐ (Mon–Fri) ♿ ⇌

Hampton Court

11–3; 5.30–11

Kings Arms
Lion Gate, Hampton Court Road (A308) ☎ (01) 977 1337
Adnams Mild, Bitter; Hall & Woodhouse Badger Best Bitter, Tanglefoot; Shepherd Neame Master Brew Best Bitter; Wadworth 6X ⒽⒷ
Imposing historic ex-hotel opposite Bushy Park, beside Palace grounds. Sawdust-floor public bar. Upstairs restaurant (closed Sun eve, Mon). Darts; bar billiards 🍴 ◐ ▶ ♿

Hampton Hill

11–3; 5.30–11

Windmill
80 Windmill Road
(just off A312)
Draught Bass; Charrington IPA ⒽⒷ
Small comfortable local with ornate terracotta frontage
🍴 ◐ (not Sun)

Hampton Wick

11–3; 5.30–11

White Hart
1 High Street (A310)
☎ (01) 977 1786
Fuller Chiswick Bitter, London Pride, ESB ⒽⒷ
Impressive pub with spacious oak-panelled lounge. Attractive award-winning garden with barbecue
🏠 🍴 ◐ ▶ (not Sun) ♿ ⇌

Harlington

11–3; 5.30–11

Crown
49 Bath Road (A4)
Courage Best Bitter, Directors ⒽⒷ
Excellent, friendly 2-bar pub, on the northern perimeter of Heathrow airport. Frequented by Concorde crews. Good food ◐ ▶ ♿

Harmondsworth

11–3; 5.30–11

Crown
High Street
☎ (01) 759 1007
Courage Best Bitter, Directors ⒽⒷ
Genuine village local in unspoilt village. Many nooks and crannies to explore. Genial hosts and staff. A must!

Greater London

Hillingdon

11–3; 5.30–11
Red Lion
Royal Lane (A4020)
☎ (0895) 34474
Fuller London Pride, ESB
Busy 500 year-old pub in village conservation area, steeped in history. No food Sun

11–3; 5.30–11
Star
Blenheim Parade, Uxbridge Road (A4020) ☎ (01) 573 1096
Draught Bass; Charrington IPA; Fuller ESB (winter)
Friendly and comfortable local with basic bar

Hounslow

11–3; 5.30 (6.30 Sat)–11
Chariot
34 High Street (A315)
☎ (01) 572 8044
Fuller London Pride, ESB
Very busy main street pub on site of former Kings Arms. Excellent home-made lunches (not Sun) ⊖ (Hounslow E)

11–3; 5.30 (7 Sat)–11
Earl Russell
274 Hanworth Road (A314)
☎ (01) 570 1560
Fuller London Pride, ESB
Traditional Victorian local with friendly atmosphere. Good value lunches (not Sun) ≠ (Hounslow Central)

11–3; 5.30–11
Jolly Farmer
177 Lampton Road
☎ (01) 570 1276
Courage Best Bitter, Directors
Popular, cosy family local 100 yards south of junction with Great West Road (Mon–Fri) ≠ (Hounslow Central)

Isleworth

11–3; 5.30–11
Castle
18 Upper Square
☎ (01) 560 3615
Young Bitter, Special, Winter Warmer
Roomy village pub with large conservatory area for families. Near river and Syon Park in old Isleworth conservation area. No food Sun

11–3; 5.30–11
Coach & Horses
183 London Road (A315)
☎ (01) 560 1447
Young Bitter, Special, Winter Warmer
Roomy comfortable coaching inn with dining room. Mentioned by Dickens in

Oliver Twist

11–3; 5.30–11
Town Wharf
Swan Street ☎ (01) 847 2287
Samel Smith OBB, Museum Ale
Splendid Thames pub with riverside terrace; traditional pub games in Terrace Bar. Comfortable upstairs lounge with balcony

New Brentford

11–3; 5.30–11
Globe
104 Windmill Road (B452)
☎ (01) 560 8932
Fuller London Pride, ESB
Comfortable local which has won many awards for its floral displays
≠ (Brentford Central)

11–3; 5.30–11
Lord Nelson
9 Enfield Road (off B452)
Fuller London Pride, ESB
Fine back street local, with strong Antipodean connections. Good public bar. 16oz steaks a speciality. Barbecues
≠ (Brentford Central)

Norwood Green

11–3; 5.30–11
Lamb
Norwood Road (A3005)
Courage Best Bitter, Directors
Cosy, low-ceilinged, 1-bar canalside pub with separate games room. No food Sun

11–3; 5.30–11
Wolf
170 Norwood Road (A3005)
Taylor Walker Best Bitter; Tetley Bitter
Recently lost its public bar; however, the atmosphere is still pleasant

Sipson

11–3; 5.30–11
King William IV
392 Sipson Road (A408)
Courage Best Bitter, Directors
Well-run, charming 16th-century inn with restaurant

Southall

11–3; 6–11
Old Oak Tree
The Common
Courage Best Bitter, Directors
Friendly pub with Grand Union Canal mooring right outside, 2 bars

Teddington

11–3; 5.30–11
Queen Dowager
49 North Lane
(100 yds S of A313)
Young Bitter, Special, Winter Warmer
Comfortable, usually quiet pub convenient for shopping centre Q (saloon)

Twickenham

11–3; 5.30–11
Eel Pie
9–11 Church Street (off A305)
Adnams Bitter; Hall & Woodhouse Badger Best Bitter, Tanglefoot; Shepherd Neame Best Bitter; Wadworth 6X, Old Timer
Popular ex-wine bar near riverside. Guest beers always available; traditional and Continental lunches ≠

11–3; 5.30–11
Pope's Grotto
Cross Deep (A310)
Young Bitter, Special, Winter Warmer
Large, imposing, comfortable pub overlooking Thames near St Mary's college. Excellent food Q (not Sun)
≠ (Strawberry Hill)

11–3; 5.30–11
Prince Albert
30 Hampton Road (A311)
Fuller Chiswick Bitter, London Pride, ESB
Small Victorian pub, locally famous for the excellence of its food. Gets very crowded
Q ≠ (Strawberry Hill)

Uxbridge

11–3; 5.30–11
Crown & Sceptre
135 High Street ☎ (0895) 36308
Courage Best Bitter, Directors
Traditional pub. Fruit machines and a jukebox but not obtrusive
(not Sun) ⊖

Whitton

11–3; 5.30–11
Admiral Nelson
127 Nelson Road
Fuller Chiswick Bitter, London Pride, ESB
Busy High Street pub, popular with Harlequins RFC. Varied menu (not Sun)

Yeading

11–3; 5.30–11
Walnut Tree
115 Willow Tree Lane (off A312) ☎ (01) 845 0849
Fuller London Pride, ESB
Smart locals' pub; busy but friendly. Parking a problem. No meals Sun
(until 9)

213

Greater Manchester

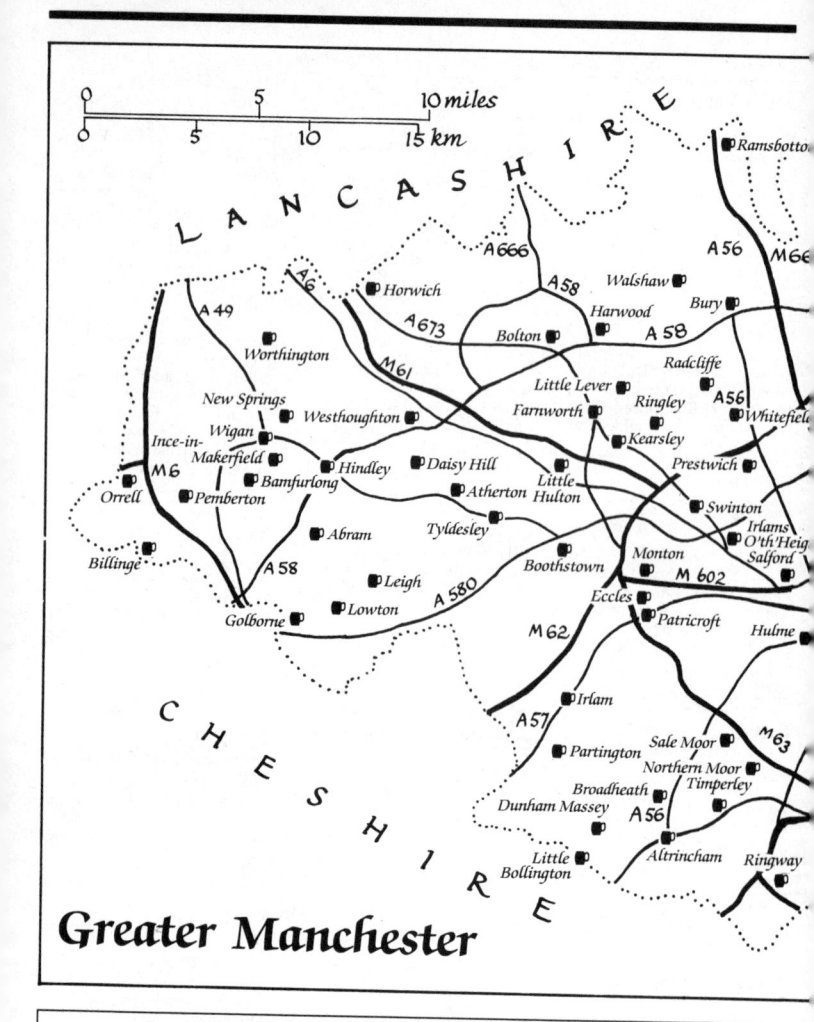

Boddingtons, Hydes, Manchester; **Holt,** Cheetham; **Lees,** Middleton Junction; **Robinson,** Stockport

Abram

11.30–3.30; 5.30–11

Red Lion (Dover Lock)
Warrington Road (A573)
☎ (0942) 866300
Greenall Whitley Mild, Bitter E
Popular, friendly canalside pub with collection of interesting artefacts, next to bridge No.4 on Leeds/Liverpool canal. Games (Mon–Fri)

Altrincham

11.30–3; 5.30 (6 Sat)–11

Bakers Arms
Pownell Road
☎ (061) 928 1411
Hydes Mild, Bitter E
Lively pub with live music and games

11.30–3; 5.30–11

Malt Shovels
Stamford Street (near old railway level crossing)
Samuel Smith OBB H
Tastefully renovated town-centre pub with live music every night

11–3; 5.30 (7 Sat)–11

Old Roebuck Inn
Victoria Street (off A56)
☎ (061) 928 2755
Webster Yorkshire Bitter; Wilson's Mild, Bitter H
Cosy multi-roomed pub with good homemade food. Games Q

11–3; 5.30 (7 Sat)–11

Tatton Arms
3–5 Tipping Street (off Lloyd Street) ☎ (061) 998 2281
Boddingtons Bitter H
What a Boddingtons pub used to be – a proper alehouse.
Games

Try also: Orange Tree (Wilson's)

Ancoats

12–3; 7–11

Cross Keys
95/97 Jersey Street
☎ (061) 202 4043
Tetley Mild, Bitter H
2-roomed traditional local in rundown industrial inner city location. Pub games (Piccadilly)

12–3; 5.30–11

White House

Greater Manchester

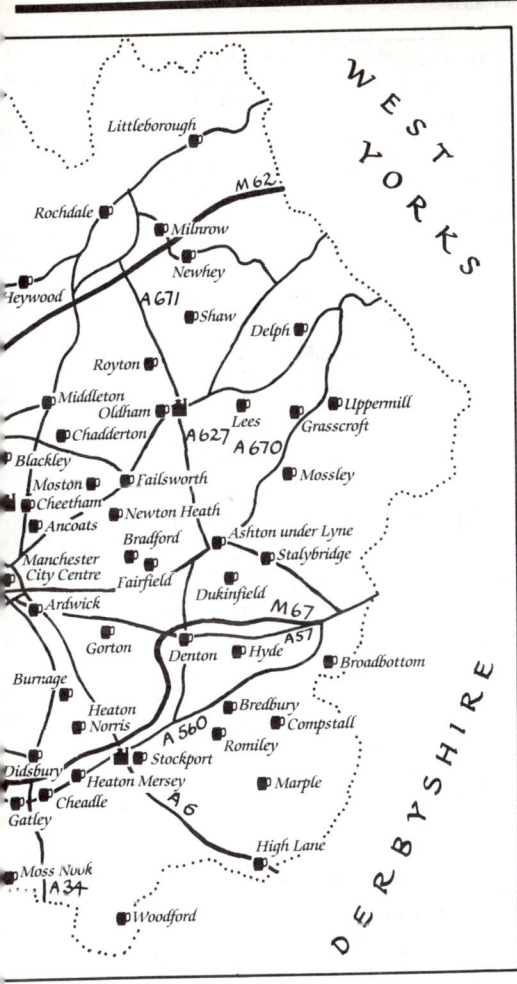

from town hall)
☎ (0942) 894814
Tetley Mild, Bitter H
Popular multi-roomed pub with very large lounge. Newton and Ridley breweriana on display

Bamfurlong

12–2.30; 7–11

Bamfurlong
Lily Lane (A58)
Tetley Walker Mild, Bitter H
Labyrinthine pub of character, with quiet lounges and busy public. Alongside West Coast main rail line Q

Billinge

11–3.30; 6–11

Hare & Hounds
142 Upholland Road (½ mile from hospital) ☎ (0695) 892843
Tetley Walker Mild, Bitter H
Large, comfortable pub near Greater Manchester/Merseyside boundary

12–3.30; 5.30–11

Holt Arms (Foot o' Causeway)
Crank Road (A580)
☎ (0695) 622705
Burtonwood Mild, Bitter H
Unpretentious country inn with bowling green; near Billinge Hill

Blackley

11.30–3; 5.30 (7 Sat)–11

Duke of Wellington
Weardale Road (behind garage on Victoria Avenue)
Holt Mild, Bitter H
Large 3-roomed pub, tucked away at end of old village; catering for locals

12–3; 7–11

Old House at Home
Bottomley side, off Crumpsall Vale (on track through ICI)
☎ (061) 740 7185
Wilson's Mild, Bitter H
Homely cottage style 3-roomed pub. Large vault with games area (until 8) (not Sun)

Bolton

11.30–3; 5.30–11

Ainsworth Arms
606 Halliwell Road
☎ (0204) 40671
Walker Mild, Bitter H
Busy comfortable local, popular with all types. Pub games

12–3; 5.30 (7 Sat)–11

Anchor
14 Union Buildings (off Bradshawgate) ☎ (0204) 26467
Bass XXXX Mild, Draught Bass H
Concealed back street local. Gets busy at weekends

122 Great Ancoats Street
☎ (061) 228 3231
Hanson Black Country Bitter; Holt Mild H
Small comfortable free house near Ashton canal. Games (Piccadilly)

Ardwick

11.30–3; 5.30 (7 Sat)–11

Seven Stars
163 Ashton Old Road (A635)
Holt Mild, Bitter H
A proper Holts pub, not totally unchanged but well renovated with 4 separate rooms, a no-nonsense atmosphere and a feared ladies' darts team (Mon–Fri lunch)

Ashton-Under-Lyne

11–3; 5.30–11

Buck & Hawthorn
Katherine Street
Robinson Best Mild, Best Bitter E
Traditional multi-roomed local near town centre. Nice wood panelling and tiles Q

11–3; 5.30–11

Oddfellows Arms
Kings Road, Hurst
Robinson Best Mild, Best Bitter H & E
Nicely furnished suburban local with welcoming atmosphere Q

Atherton

11.30–3.30; 5.30–11

Atherton Arms
6 Tyldesley Road (A577)
☎ (0942) 882885
Holt Mild, Bitter H
Well-refurbished ex-Labour club with large drinking areas. Full size snooker table in corner of vault

11.30–3.30; 7–11

Bay Horse
30 Bolton Old Road (100 yds

215

Greater Manchester

11.30–3; 7–11
Dog & Partridge
Manor Street (off A666)
☎ (0204) 388596
Thwaites Mild, Bitter H
Well-run, town-centre local. One of only a few in the vicinity not to have dress restrictions ♣&≠

11–3; 6–11
Howcroft Inn
Pool Street ☎ (0204) 26814
Walker Mild, Best Bitter H
Superb, award-winning pub with well-kept bowling green ♣♣♣

12–3; 7–11
Lodge Bank Tavern
264 Bridgeman Street
☎ (0204) 31946
Lees Mild, Bitter, Moonraker (winter) H
Popular 2-roomed pub, slightly off the beaten track. The only Lees pub in Bolton, and well worth finding. Games ♣≠

11.30–3; 5.30 (7 Sat)–11
York Hotel
112–114 Newport Street
☎ (0204) 383892
Burtonwood Dark Mild, Bitter H
Good Beer Guide regular, facing busy rail interchange – meeting place for many local societies ♣♣≠

Try also: **Anchor**, Bury Road; **Cross Guns**

Boothstown

11.30–3; 5.30–11
Royal Oak
20 Leigh Road
Wilson's Mild, Bitter H
Split-level, 3-roomed basic village pub, catering mainly for local trade. Games ♣♣♣

Bradford

11.30–3; 7–11
Duke of Edinburgh
366 Mill Street (between A635/A662) ☎ (061) 223 2170
Tetley Mild, Bitter H
Victorian monolith with attractive decorative features. Long narrow vault, larger lounge, and bar parlour turned pool room ♣ (lunch & early eve) ♣♣♣ (Ashburys)

Bredbury

11–3; 5.30–11
Arden Arms
Ashton Road (A6017)
Robinson Best Mild, Best Bitter E
Brick-built pub with good outdoors play area for children. Nice cosy atmosphere. Games ♣♣♣

Try also: **Horsfield Arms** (Robinson)

Broadheath

11–3; 5.30 (7 Sat)–11
Railway Inn
153 Manchester Road (A56)
☎ (061) 941 5383
Boddingtons Bitter H
Basic, former ale-only pub, next to railway bridge ♣

Broadbottom

11–3; 5.30–11
Shoulder of Mutton
138 Lower Market Street (off A57)
Marston Pedigree; Thwaites Mild, Bitter H
Unpretentious, popular pub which clings to hillside in Pennine village. Games ♣♣≠

Burnage

11–3; 5.30–11
Sun in September
Burnage Lane (100 yds Jct A34/Lane End Road)
☎ (061) 432 6162
Samuel Smith OBB H
Tastefully refurbished 2-roomed pub in pleasant city suburb ♣♣♣≠

Bury

11.30–3; 5–11
Blue Bell Hotel
Manchester Road, Sunnybank (A56) ☎ (061) 766 2496
Holt Mild, Bitter E
Typical Holt pub, with comfortable roomy lounge and thriving tap room. Well run with friendly atmosphere ♣♣

11.30–3; 5–11
Help Me Thro'
141 Crostons Road (off A56)
☎ (061) 764 6461
Thwaites Mild, Bitter H
Basic pub just outside the town centre. Large tap room (busy eves) plus 2 small lounges ♣Q♣♣

11.30–3; 5–11
Trafalgar Hotel
12 Manchester Old Road (off A56) ☎ (061) 764 5281
Burtonwood Mild, Bitter H
Friendly pub near town centre, with a thriving tap room and welcoming lounge. Games ♣♣♣♣

11.30–2 (3 Sat); 7–11
Walmersley Arms
741 Walmersley Road (A56)
☎ (061) 764 6676
Wilson's Mild, Bitter H
Large, attractive sandstone pub close to motorway. Former Chadwick's Walmersley brewery taps. 3-roomed pub ♣♣♣♣♣

Chadderton

11.30–3; 5.30–11
Sun Mill Inn
505 Middleton Road
☎ (061) 624 6232
Boddingtons Mild, OB Bitter H
Town-centre, street-corner local, handy for sports centre across the road. Games ♣♣

Cheadle

11.30–3; 5.30–11
Printers Arms
220 Stockport Road (A560 near M63 Jct 11) ☎ (061) 491 1448
Robinson Best Mild, Best Bitter E
Small, busy, family-run pub with strong local following. 3 rooms; lounge and vault separate from bar ♣♣

12–3; 5.30–11
Queens Arms
177 Stockport Road (A560)
☎ (061) 428 3081
Robinson Best Mild, Bitter H, **Old Tom** G
Rare outlet for Robinson's ordinary bitter. Families encouraged; swing and slide on the old bowling green ♣♣♣♣ (Mon–Fri)

All Cheadle pubs sell real ale

Cheetham

12–3; 7–11
Queens Arms
6 Honey Street, Red Bank
☎ (061) 834 4329
Taylor Landlord; Theakston Best Bitter, XB, Old Peculier H
Surprisingly pleasant single-roomed pub in inner city area, surrounded by factories and warehouses. Quality food; panoramic view of Irk Valley ♣♣♣≠ (Victoria)

Compstall

11–3; 5.30–11
Andrew Arms
George Street (off B6104)
☎ (061) 427 2281
Robinson Best Mild, Best Bitter H
Deservedly popular pub near Etherow Nature Reserve ♣Q♣♣

Daisy Hill

11–3; 5.30–11
Rose Hill Tavern (The Bug)
321 Leigh Road, Westhoughton (B5235)
☎ (0942) 811405
Holt Mild, Bitter H
Spacious locals' pub ♣≠

Delph

11.30–3; 5–11
Bulls Head
2 King Street
☎ (045 77) 458 4681
Bass Mild XXXX, Light 5 Star,

216

Greater Manchester

Special Bitter; Stones Best Bitter H
Homely stone-built local in pretty Pennine village

Denton

11–3; 5.30–11
Dog & Partridge
Ashton Road (A6017)
Robinson Best Mild, Bitter H
Small terraced local, very friendly. An outlet for the increasingly rare 'ordinary' bitter. Games

11–3; 5.30–11
Red Lion
Crown Point (Jct A57/A6017)
Hydes Best Mild, Best Bitter H
Spacious red-brick, Victorian-style pub; comfortable and welcoming

Didsbury

11.30–3; 5.30–11
Crown
770 Wilmslow Road
Davenports Bitter; Greenall Whitley Bitter, Original H
Open-plan multi-roomed pub with central bar. Many original features, including oven. Busy evenings

11–3; 5.30–11
Station
682 Wilmslow Road
☎ (061) 445 9761
Marston Burton Bitter, Pedigree H
Friendly small 3-roomed village local. Pub games

Dukinfield

11–3; 5.30–11
Lamb Hotel
Crescent Road
Boddingtons Bitter H
Locals' pub with good tap room and comfortable lounge

Dunham Massey

11.30–3; 7–11
Axe & Cleaver
School Lane ☎ (061) 928 3391
Ruddles County; Webster Yorkshire Bitter, Choice; Wilson's Mild, Bitter H
Large split-level pub with sofas, bar billiards table, and conservatory
(summer)

Try also: Rope & Anchor (Boddingtons)

Eccles

11–3; 5.30 (7 Sat)–11
Lamb
33 Regent Street (A57)
☎ (061) 789 3882
Holt Mild, Bitter H
4 rooms with etched glass and Edwardian woodwork, plus the last billiard table in Eccles.

Popular with older drinkers

Failsworth

11.30–3; 7–11
Black Horse
292 Oldham Road
☎ (061) 681 1490
Marston Border Mild, Burton Bitter H
Busy 'Rothwells' fronted hostelry, with a welcoming atmosphere. Darts

11.30–3; 7–11
Woodhouse Gardens Inn
Medlock Road, Woodhouses
☎ (061) 681 3782
Lees GB Mild, Bitter H
Recently extended, pleasant village pub with large open plan interior. Beer garden at rear has own serving hatch
(till 9)

Fairfield

11.30–3; 5.45–11
Railway
2 Manshaw Road (just off A635) ☎ (061) 370 2382
Holt Mild, Bitter H
Largely unspoilt multi-roomed Victorian boozer with impressive lamp over door. Pub games

Farnworth

11.45–3; 7–11
Britannia Inn
King Street ☎ (0204) 71629
Chesters Mild, Bitter; Whitbread Trophy, Castle Eden Ale H
Excellent town centre local, with pub games

Gatley

11.30–3; 5.30–11
Horse & Farrier
Gatley Road ☎ (061) 428 2080
Hydes Anvil Light, Anvil Bitter E, Anvil Strong Ale G
Busy, multi-roomed pub in centre of the village
Q (Mon–Fri)

Golborne

12–3.30; 5.30–11
Sir Charles Napier (Tippins)
69 High Street (A573)
☎ (0942) 726938
Ind Coope Burton Ale; Walker Mild, Best Bitter, Winter Warmer H
Large, friendly town-centre pub, popular in early evening. Split-level lounge; tap room with pool table

Gorton

11–3; 5.30 (7 Sat)–11
Hare & Hounds
187 Abbey Hey Lane

☎ (061) 370 1258
Boddingtons Bitter H
An unsuspected gem in urban Gorton – staunch old-fashioned vault, delightful front snug, and comfortable rear lounge plus the only beer garden for miles!

11–3; 5.30 (7 Sat)–11
Waggon & Horses
735 Hyde Road
Holt Mild, Bitter H
Imposing, successfully refurbished pub with some of the cheapest beer in the area. Unpretentious, caters for local tastes. Games (not Sun)

Grasscroft

11.30–3; 5–11
Farrars Arms
56 Oldham Road (Jct A669/A670) ☎ (045 77) 458 2124
Ruddles County; Webster Bitter, Choice; Wilson's Mild, Bitter H Handsome and comfortable 18th-century stone-built inn on outskirts of Oldham
(till 7.30)

Harwood

12–3; 5.30–11
Grey Mare
154 Tottington Road
☎ (0204) 50570
Bass Mild XXXX, Light 5 Star, Draught Bass H
Cosy 4-roomed local with a traditional tap room

Heaton Mersey

11.30–3; 5.30–11
Griffin
552 Didsbury Road (A5143)
Holt Mild, Bitter H
Multi-roomed "locals' local" with classic Victorian mahogany bar
(E Didsbury)

Heaton Norris

11.30–3; 5.30–11
Nursery
Green Lane (off A6)
☎ (061) 432 2044
Hydes Anvil Mild, Bitter E
Large, comfortable, well-hidden pub with good choice of rooms: fine wood-panelled lounge; superb bowling green
Q (Mon–Fri)

Heywood

11.30–3; 6–11
Engineers Arms
11–13 Aspinall Street
☎ (0706) 68365
Samuel Smith OBB H
Comfortable pub just outside town centre. Landlord proudly displays 2 Cellar of the Year Awards. Games

High Lane

217

Greater Manchester

11–3; 5.30–11
Royal Oak
Buxton Road (A6)
☎ (066 32) 2380
Burtonwood Mild, Bitter H
Comfortable roadside inn with occasional live music. Games

Try also: Bulls Head (Boddingtons)

Hindley

11.30–3.30; 5.30–11
Ellesmere Inn
Lancaster Road (off A58)
☎ (0942) 56922
Burtonwood Mild, Bitter H
Lively locals' pub with emphasis on traditional pub games

Horwich

11.30–3; 5.30 (7 Sat)–11
Bowling Green
175 Lee Lane ☎ (0204) 697502
Tetley Mild, Bitter H
Quite plush, but retains its character. Pub games

Hulme

11–3; 5.30 (7 Sat)–11
Pomona Palace
10 Cornbrook Road, St. Georges (just off A56)
☎ (061) 872 2786
Marston Burton Bitter H
Basic 2-bar pub with impressive trophy cabinet. Games

Hyde

11.30–3; 5.30–11
Bush Inn
278 Market Street
Robinson Best Mild, Best Bitter, Old Tom H
Pleasant 4-roomed local with panelling and attractive oak and stained-glass bar. A thriving social centre

11–3; 5.30–11
Cheshire Cheese
Market Street
Boddingtons Mild, Bitter H
Down-to-earth local meant for real drinking

11.30–3; 5.30–11
Crown Inn
173 Market Street
Robinson Best Mild, Best Bitter H, **Old Tom** G
4-roomed local with interesting snug/public bar on higher level at front of pub

Ince-in-Makerfield

11.30–3.30; 7–11
Walmesley Arms
465 Warrington Road, Spring View (A573)
Tetley Walker Mild, Bitter H
Comfortable, friendly pub with recently spruced-up exterior. Games

Irlam

11–3; 5.30–11
Boat House
Ferry Road
Boddingtons Mild, Bitter H
Thriving modern pub with pleasant garden; games and sporting teams

Irlams o'th' Height

11–3; 5.30–11
Red Lion
279 Bolton Road
☎ (061) 736 8690
Holt Mild, Bitter E
Pre-war, 3-roomed pub catering for the older drinker. One of 3 Holts pubs in the village. Games

Kearsley

11–3; 5.30–11
Clock Face
Old Hall Street ☎ (0204) 71912
Tetley Mild, Bitter H
No frills, well-lit local. A superb example of a traditional pub. Games

Lees

12–3 (weekend only); 7–11
Bridge Inn
616 Lees Road, Salem (A669)
☎ (061) 624 6055
Tetley-Walker Mild, Bitter H
Friendly local in shadow of Victorian textile mill. Games

Leigh

11.30–3.30; 7–11
Brewery Inn
Brewery Lane (off A572)
☎ (0942) 672974
Tetley Mild, Bitter H
Small cosy multi-roomed local with friendly atmosphere, next to former George Shaw's brewery

12–3.30; 7–11
Tamar
416 Wigan Road (A578)
☎ (0942) 679459
Walker Mild, Bitter H
Large, comfortable local with strong bowls following – once called The Bowling Green. Stained-glass windows depicting bowls match. No lunches winter

Little Bollington

11.30–3; 5.30–10.30 (11 F, S)
Swan with Two Necks
Park Lane (off A56)
Chesters Mild, Bitter; Whitbread Castle Eden Ale H
Typical country pub at back of Dunham Park, adjacent to Bridgewater canal

Try also: Wheatsheaf (Hydes)

Little Hulton

11.30–3; 5.30 (7 Sat)–11
Dukes Gate
Cleggs Lane, on Farnworth boundary near M61 (no direct access)
Holt Mild, Bitter H
New pub built on traditional Holts lines; very popular – busy and excellent value in pleasant surroundings

Little Lever

11.30–3; 7–11
Three Crowns Hotel
Fletcher Street ☎ (0204) 73433
Wilson's Mild, Bitter H
Unspoilt local, unusual in having 2 tap rooms. Games

Littleborough

12–3; 6–11
Railway Inn
1 Inghams Lane (off A58)
☎ (0706) 76250
Bass Special Bitter; Stones Best Bitter H
Popular multi-roomed village local. Games

Lowton

11.30–3.30; 5.30–11
Red Lion
Newton Road (A572)
☎ (0942) 601429
Grenall Whitley Mild, Bitter, Original E
Large pub with restaurant and conservatory leading to bowling green. HQ for San Miguel golf society
(till 9)

Manchester City Centre

11.30–3; 5.30–11
Beer House
6 Angel Street (just off A664)
☎ (061) 832 1452
Holt Mild, Bitter; Theakston Best Bitter, XB, Old Peculier
Newly acquired free house which is gradually gaining its own character. R & B jukebox
(Victoria)

11.30–3; 5.30 (8.30 Sat)–11
Circus Tavern
86 Portland Street
Tetley Walker Bitter H
Scarcely touched by time – tiny quadrant bar, narrow corridor, and 2 small side rooms, all with a tremendous atmosphere. Front door locked on busy nights; back door on Reyner Street Q (Piccadilly)

11.30–3 (not Sat); 5.30 (7 Sat)–11
Coach & Horses
8 London Road (A6)
☎ (061) 236 0245
Boddingtons Bitter; Burtonwood Bitter; Taylor

218

Greater Manchester

Landlord; Tetley Mild, Bitter
The city's first real-ale free house has seen rivals come and go, but carries on in its own inimitable style. No frills, no food, no nonsense but excellent Irish juke box (lunch) ≠ (Piccadilly)

11.30–3; 5.30–11
Harp & Shamrock
36 New Mount Street (just off Rochdale Road, A664)
☎ (061) 824 8579
Marston Border Mild, Burton Bitter, Pedigree
Basic unspoilt backstreet 2-roomer. Smallest gents loo in the city

11.30–3; 5.30–11
Jolly Angler
47 Ducie Street (off A665 behind station)
☎ (061) 236 5307
Hydes Anvil Light, Anvil Bitter, Anvil Strong Ale
Basic single-roomed small pub with some outside seats. Folk music Thu (Piccadilly)

11.30–3; 5.30–8; (Fri 5.30–11; Sat 7–11; closed Sun)
Mr Thomas Chop House
52 Cross Street
☎ (061) 832 5634
Chesters Mild, Bitter; Thwaites Bitter
Superb wall and floor tiling, ornate wood panelling with leaded glass panes – a Victorian masterpiece near St Anne's Square. Very busy, especially for good value lunches (Victoria)

11.30–3 (not Sun); 5.30 (7 Sat)–11
Peveril of the Peak
127 Great Bridgewater Street
Wilson's Mild, Bitter; Webster Yorkshire Bitter, Choice
Original tiles outside and stained glass inside – a classic town pub
(Oxford Road)

11.30–3; 5.30–11
Unicorn
26 Church Street (off A6)
☎ (061) 832 7938
Bass Light 5 Star, Draught Bass; Stones Best Bitter
Large oak-panelled pub of character in market area

11.30–3; 5.30–11 (8 Sat)
White Lion
43 Liverpool Road
☎ (061) 832 7373
Chesters Mild, Bitter
In the Castlefield conservation area, well placed for the museums and Roman remains. Games (Deansgate)

Marple

11–3; 5.30–11
Crown Inn
Hawk Green ☎ (061) 449 8533
Robinson Best Mild, Best Bitter
Smart restaurant-style pub in attractive building: a former farmers pub

11–3; 5.30–11
Hatters Arms
Church Lane
Robinson Best Mild, Best Bitter
Stone-built end of terrace local; small rooms and good vault

Middleton

11–3; 5–11
Gardeners
114 Sandy Lane (off A669)
☎ (061) 643 4438
Lees GB Mild, Bitter
Comfortable family local, HQ of the local pigeon fanciers club (Mills Hill)

11.30–3; 5–11
White Hart
86 Rochdale Road (A664)
Lees GB Mild, Bitter
Traditional local with busy vault. Pub games

Milnrow

11.30–3; 5–11
Waggon Inn
Butterworth Hall, via New Street (off B6225)
☎ (0706) 48313
Burtonwood Mild, Bitter
A warm welcome assured in this bustling 18th-century village pub. Family room

Monton

11–3; 5.30–11
Park Hotel
142 Monton Road (B5229)
Holt Mild, Bitter
Post-war pub in upmarket area of Eccles. Large vault, lounge and pleasant snug; games

Mossley

11.30–3; 5.30–11
Tollemache Arms
Manchester Road (A635)
Robinson Best Mild, Best Bitter
Deservedly popular local, cosy and welcoming, alongside the Huddersfield Canal

Try also: Britannia (Marston)

Moss Nook

11.30–3; 5.30–10.30
Tatton Arms
Trenchard Drive (B5166)
☎ (061) 437 2505
Robinson Best Mild, Best Bitter
Fine historic establishment used by residents and globetrotters alike. 17th-century carved fireplace (Mon–Fri)

Moston

11–3; 5.30–11
Dean Brook Inn
94–102 St Marys Road (off A62)
☎ (061) 682 4730
Marston Border Mild, Burton Bitter
Long terraced pub recently altered but still retaining its character as a thriving community local
(Dean Lane)

New Springs

12–3.30; 7–11
Colliers Arms
Wigan Road (B5238)
☎ (0942) 831171
Burtonwood Mild, Bitter
Old pub near Leeds–Liverpool canal. Games

Newton Heath

11–3; 5.30–11
Railway Hotel
82 Dean Lane (just off A62)
☎ (061) 681 8199
Holt Mild, Bitter
Monumental Victorian pub with original features; older customers; concert room crowded at weekends (lunch) (Dean Lane)

Newhey

11.30–3; 5–11
Bird in the Hand (Top Bird)
113 Huddersfield Road (A640)
☎ (0706) 847978
Samuel Smith OBB
Hospitable 2-roomed village pub with old photos and busy vault

Northern Moor

11–3; 5.30–11
Park Hotel
Moorcroft Road/Sledmore Road ☎ (061) 998 3078
Lees GB Mild, Bitter
Modern estate pub with large vault; Lees' busiest house, close to Wythenshawe Park and Hall

Oldham

11.30–3; 7–11
Bank Top Tavern
King Square, King Street (A627) ☎ (061) 620 5549
Lees GB Mild, Bitter
Busy town-centre pub with varied menu
(Werneth)

12–3; 7–11
Clarksfield Hotel
38 Ronald Street (off A669)
☎ (061) 624 1043

Greater Manchester

Boddingtons OB Mild, Mild, Bitter, OB Bitter H
Edwardian pub with strong local following. Well worth searching out. Games ⬛🍴🍺

11.30–3; 5.30 (7 Sat)–11
Gardeners
Dunham Street, Waterhead (off A62) ☎ (061) 624 0242
Robinson Best Mild, Best Bitter H, Old Tom G
Multi-roomed pub with tiled interior and excellent atmosphere ⬛🍴▶🍺

11.30–3; 5–11 (7 Sat)
Golden Buck
324 Manchester Road, Werneth (A62)
☎ (061) 624 4710
Boddingtons OB Mild, Bitter, OB Bitter H
Bustling roadside pub with large lounge, smaller busy vault. Games 🍺🚆 (Werneth)

11.30–3; 5–11
Westbourne Hotel
128 Middleton Road
☎ (061) 626 2566
Boddingtons OB Mild, OB Bitter H
Pleasantly decorated out-of-town pub with friendly locals 🐶🏨

Orrell

11.30–3.30; 5.30–11
Old Springs Inn
Springs Road, Kitt Green (off B5206) ☎ (0942) 211209
Burtonwood Mild, Bitter H
Named after local wells – a 20ft deep one is still behind the pub. Games include bowling 🍴⬛🍴🍺♿⚽

Partington

11–3; 5.30–11
King William IV
Manchester Road
☎ (061) 775 2840
Marston Mild E, Burton Bitter E & H, Pedigree H
Low-beamed village pub with separate "cocktail lounge". Pub games 🍴⬛🍺♿

Patricroft

11–3; 5.30–11
Stanley Arms
295 Liverpool Road (A57)
☎ (061) 788 8801
Holt Mild, Bitter H
Corner local with front vault best room and rear games room. Weekend singalongs 🐶🏨🍴🍺♿🚆

11–3; 5.30–11
White Lion
133 Liverpool Road (A57)
☎ (061) 707 5184
Holt Mild, Bitter H
3-roomed street corner local with piano singalongs at weekends 🍴🐶🍺♿🚆

Pemberton

11.30–3.30; 7–11
Dog & Partridge (Jem Lowe's)
30 Chapel Street, Pemberton (off A577)
Greenall Whitley Mild, Bitter E
Wonderful, unspoilt old boozer, worth searching for. Games 🍺

Prestwich

11.30–3; 5–11
Ostrich Hotel
163 Bury Old Road, Heaton Park (A665) ☎ (061) 773 2716
Holt Mild, Bitter E
Large 5-roomed pub near Heaton Park. Present darts room once used as a court room, and there's a secret tunnel connecting pub to nearby hall
🐶⬛🍴♿🚆 (Heaton Park)

Radcliffe

11.30–3; 5–11
Wellington
48 Stand Lane (A665)
☎ (061) 723 4423
Bass Mild XXXX H, Light 5 Star E; Stones Bitter H
Busy 4-room, town-centre pub with much original tilework and pool table 🍴⬛🍴♿🚆

Ramsbottom

11.30–3; 5–11
Old Dun Horse
Bolton Street (A676)
Thwaites Mild, Bitter E
Unspoilt, 1930s 4-roomed pub near town centre. Built in the distinctive former Bury Brewery style ⬛🍴🍺♿

Ringley

12–3; 7–11 (may vary summer)
Horseshoe Hotel
395 Ringley Road, Radcliffe
☎ (0204) 71714
Thwaites Mild, Bitter E
Attractive village local facing medieval bridge over the river Irwell 🐶🍴🚆 (Kearsley)

Try also: Lord Nelson (Thwaites)

Ringway

11–3; 5.30–11
Romper
Pinfold Lane (800 yds from Jct 6, M56) ☎ (061) 980 6806
Boddingtons Mild, Bitter H
Traditional gem near urban sprawl of airport. Multi-roomed, stone-flagged cosy pub with generous meals (not Sun) 🍴Q🐶🍴🍺

Rochdale

11.30–3; 7–11
Baths Hotel
42 Smith Street (near bus station) ☎ (0706) 48162
Boddingtons OB Mild, Bitter, OB Bitter H
Large town-centre pub with busy vault; pool table, live entertainment Thu
🐶 (lunch) 🍴 (not Sun) 🍺♿🚆

11.30–3; 7–11
Carters Rest Hotel
190 Spotland Road
☎ (0706) 59271
Webster Yorkshire Bitter; Wilson's Mild, Bitter H
Cosy, many-roomed local with splendid etched glass panels. Pub games 🐶🍺

11.30–3; 5–11
Cemetery
470 Bury Road (B6222)
☎ (0706) 43214
Boddingtons Bitter; Ruddles County; Taylor Dark Mild, Best Bitter, Landlord; Thwaites Bitter H
Unspoilt pub with tiled interior and small, comfortable rooms 🍴🍴

11.30–3; 6–11
Healey Hotel
172 Shawclough Road, Shawclough (B6377)
☎ (0706) 45453
Robinson Best Mild, Best Bitter H, Old Tom G
Stone-built terraced 1930s pub. Tiled lounge; games room with table football Q🍺

11.30–3; 5.30–11
Merry Monk
234 College Road (B6222)
☎ (0706) 46919
Marston Border Mild, Burton Bitter, Pedigree H
Popular free house with ring the bull game in lounge. Guest beers 🍴🍴

11.30–3; 5.30–11
Reed Hotel
Reed Hill (off Yorkshire Street)
☎ (0706) 46696
Bass Mild XXXX, Special Bitter H
Cosy town-centre hotel, built 1792 as coaching inn. Central open-plan staircase. Pub games Q♿🍴 (not Sun)

Romiley

11–3; 5.30–11
Duke of York
Stockport Road, (B6104)
☎ (061) 430 2806
John Smith Bitter H
Attractive, comfortable pub with long local history and excellent vault ⬛🍴▶🍺♿

11–3; 5.30–11
Forresters Arms
Sandy Lane, Greave
☎ (061) 494 6912
Boddingtons Mild, Bitter E

Greater Manchester

Low-ceilinged multi-roomed pub, known locally as 'Piggy'; comfortable and friendly

Royton

11.30–3; 5 (7 Sat)–11
Angel
230 Shaw Road (A663)
☎ (061) 624 2673
Lees GB Mild, Bitter
Warm welcome guaranteed

11.30–3; 7–11
Greyhound
1 Elly Clough, Holden Fold (off A663) ☎ (061) 624 4504
Lees GB Mild, Bitter
Friendly country pub atmosphere

Sale Moor

11.30–3; 5.30 (7 Sat)–10.45
Legh Arms
170 Northenden Road (Jct B5166/A6144)
Holt Mild, Bitter
Large many-roomed Edwardian pub, plainly furnished. Bowling green; games

Salford

11–3; 5.30–11
Braziers Arms
54 Hodson Street
☎ (061) 834 0203
Boddingtons Mild, Bitter
Unspoilt by time; locals out of Lowry paintings

11–3 (closed Sun); 5.30–11
Crescent
20 Crescent
Holt Mild, Bitter
Active local popular with students, plus a good mix of Salfordians. Multi-roomed with cheery atmosphere. Games (Crescent)

11.30–3; 5.30–11
Duke of York
97 Marlborough Road (between A665/A6010)
☎ (061) 792 6941
Holt Mild, Bitter
Hard to find, run down, but impressive large Edwardian Holt pub (lunch)

11.30–3; 5.30–11
Eagle Inn
15 Collier Street
☎ (061) 834 8957
Holt Mild, Bitter
Last beer house in Salford to convert to full licence. Well worth seeking out (Victoria)

11–3; 6.30–11
Prince of Wales
165 Oldfield Road
☎ (061) 832 5716
Boddingtons OB Mild, Bitter; Higson Bitter; Hydes Mild, Bitter
Popular 3-roomed free house with a growing reputation.

Pub games
11–3; 7–11
Union Tavern
105 Liverpool Street
☎ (061) 736 2885
Holt Mild, Bitter
Basic and remote enough to be sought out by its regular customers. Snacks available (Crescent)

Shaw

11–3; 5 (7 Sat)–11
Morning Star
109 Grains Road (off A663)
☎ (0706) 845347
Lees GB Mild, Bitter
Mullion-windowed pub on edge of moors. Large vault, games area, friendly service

Stalybridge

11.30–3; 5–11
Old Hunters Tavern
Acres Lane
Robinson Best Mild, Best Bitter
Country pub in town with much new brass. Yachting Monthly on cane table in award-winning gents!

11.30–3; 5–11
Station Buffet
Stalybridge Station (Platform 1)
Moorhouse's Premier Bitter
Station buffet with a style of its own, popular with both locals and passengers. Marble topped bar; folk club Sat. Guest beers

11.30–3; 5–11
White House
1 Water Street (opposite bus station)
Matthew Brown Mild; Theakston Best Bitter, XB, Old Peculier; Younger No.3
No frills former Cunningham brewery pub. Choice of malt whiskies

Stockport

11–3; 5.30–11
Arden Arms
Millgate ☎ (061) 480 2185
Robinson Best Mild, Best Bitter
Multi-roomed pub with relaxed atmosphere. Unusual snug accessible only through bar (Mon–Fri)

11.30–3; 5.30–11
Blossoms
2 Buxton Road, Heaviley
Robinson Mild, Best Bitter, Old Tom
Little gem with traditional bar area and lounge; darts room and separate pool room (until 9) (Mon–Fri)

11–3; 5 (7 Sat)–11 (closed Sun)
Boars Head
Market Place ☎ (061) 480 3878

Samuel Smith OBB, Museum Ale
Modernised, lively pub with interesting decor. Licensee notorious for his WC Fields impressions. Live music 6 nights a week with bar till midnight (lunch)

11.30–3; 5.30–11
Crown (Corner Cupboard)
14 Higher Hillgate
Wilson's Mild, Bitter
Small, unpretentious, but very welcoming corner pub with vault (TV) and small restful lounge

11.30–3; 5.30–11
Florist
100 Shaw Heath
Robinson Best Mild, Best Bitter
Fine old Victorian classic, a drink and chat pub. Difficult to spot: signs are high on front wall

11–3; 5.30–11
Grapes
1C Castle Street, Edgeley
Robinson Best Mild, Best Bitter, Old Tom
Busy, down-to-earth pub in shopping precinct. Basic vault, more comfortable lounge. Nice etched windows. Handy for football ground

11.30–3; 5.30–11
Manchester Arms
25 Wellington Road South (A6) ☎ (061) 480 2852
Robinson Best Mild, Best Bitter, Old Tom
Proudly proclaims "Bikers Welcome": a vibrant mix of punters in this good honest boozer. Live music every Tue; Jukebox a Top–40 free zone Pub games

12–3; 5.30–11
Olde Vic
1 Chatham Street, Edgeley
☎ (061) 480 2410
Taylor Landlord; Tetley Mild, Bitter
The only free house in Stockport. Friendly atmosphere; guest beers

11.30–3; 5.30–11
Swan with Two Necks
Princes Street (off A6)
Robinson Best Mild, Best Bitter
Wood-panelled pleasantly decorated pub popular with shoppers, often quieter at rear. Darts

Swinton

11–3; 5.30–11
Newmarket
621 Bolton Road, Pendlebury (A66)
Holt Mild, Bitter
Straight forward drinking

221

Greater Manchester

house with old fashioned atmosphere, opposite market. Games

11–3; 5.30–11
White Horse
Worsley Road
Boddingtons Mild, Bitter H
Popular local with excellent, good value lunches. Busy in the evenings

Timperley

11.30–3; 5.30–11
Quarry Bank Inn
151 Bloomsbury Lane
☎ (061) 980 4345
Hydes Mild, Bitter E
Thriving village local with lively vault and crown green bowling

Try also: Moss Trooper

Tyldesley

12–3.30; 5.30 (7 Sat)–11
Half Moon
115 Elliott Street
☎ (0942) 873206
Boddingtons Bitter; Holt Bitter H
Cosy, town-centre pub, licensed since 1781, but has only been a pub since 1984. Beware keg mild on handpump. Very popular weekends and with young. Games room

12–3.30; 5.30–11
Mort Arms
235 Elliott Street (A577)
☎ (0942) 883481
Holt Mild, Bitter H
Deservedly popular local with traditional Holt's bar. Piano in lounge; full of interesting characters. Games

12–3.30; 7–11
Welcome Traveller (Skennin' Bob's)
166 Elliott Street
☎ (0942) 891832
Webster Choice; Wilson's Mild, Bitter H
Busy town-centre pub with a boisterous atmosphere at weekends. Emphasis on pub games weekdays. Beer range likely to vary

Uppermill

11.30–3; 7–11
Cross Keys
Runninghill Gate (via Church Road) ☎ (045 77) 458 4626
Lees GB Mild, Bitter H
Pleasantly situated 18th-century inn. Folk club Wed. Pub games

Walshaw

11.30–3; 5–11
White Horse
18 Hall Street (off B6213)
☎ (0204) 883243

Thwaites Mild, Bitter H
Cosy, friendly village pub

Westhoughton

12–3; 7–11
Hartcommon Hotel
490 Wigan Road
☎ (0942) 813356
Matthew Brown Mild; Theakston Best Bitter, XB H
Small 3-roomed local of true character. Warm and friendly. Games

11–3; 5.30–11
White Lion Hotel
Market Street ☎ (0942) 813120
Holt Mild, Bitter H
Superb pub, oozes character. Games

Try also: Bridge (Whitbread)

Whitefield

11.30–3; 5–11
Coach & Horses
71 Bury Old Road (A665, Jct 17 M62)
Holt Mild, Bitter H
Traditional 1920s pub with waiter service. Games
(Besses o'th' Barn)

11.30–3; 5–11
Eagle & Child
Higher Lane (A665; Jct 17 M62) ☎ (061) 766 3024
Holt Mild, Bitter H
Imposing 1930s 4-roomed pub, with floodlit bowling green (lunch)
(Besses o'th' Barn)

Wigan

11.30–3.30; 6.30 (6 Sat)–11
Bird i' th' Hand (Th' 'en 'Ole)
102 Gidlow Lane (off B5375)
☎ (0942) 41004
Tetley-Walker Mild, Bitter H
Small and busy local with marvellous Peter Walker mosaic. Games

11.30–3.30; 5.30–11
Bold Hotel
161 Poolstock Lane (left at M6 Jct 25) ☎ (0942) 41095
Burtonwood Mild, Bitter H
Friendly locals' pub. Games

12–3.30; 5.30–11
Brickmakers Arms
49 Woodhouse Lane (off B5375) ☎ (0942) 42618
Greenall Whitley Mild, Bitter E
Friendly local, handy for Wigan Athletic FC

11.30–3.30; 6.15–11
Charles Dickens Hotel
14 Upper Dicconson Street
Tetley Mild, Bitter; Theakston Best Bitter, XB, Old Peculier H

Enterprising free house with quaint wine-bar atmosphere and piano player most nights. Beers likely to change
(not Sun) (Wallgate)

11.30–3.30; 5.30–11
Gem's
Upper Dicconson Street
Boddingtons Bitter; Holt Mild, Bitter H & E
The town centre's newest free house. Beers always changing. Pub games

11.30–3.30; 5.30–11
Old Pear Tree
Frog Lane ☎ (0942) 43677
Burtonwood Mild, Bitter H
A Good Beer Guide perennial. Traditional haunt of darts and dominoes fanatics

11.30–3.30; 7–11
Seven Stars Hotel
Wallgate (A49) ☎ (0942) 43126
Thwaites Best Mild, Bitter H
Roomy pub near Leeds–Liverpool canal. Meals on request; family room. Wigan CAMRA Pub of the year 1988
(Wallgate/North Western)

11.30–3.30; 7–11
Springfield Hotel
47 Springfield Road (off B5375)
☎ (0942) 42072
Walker Mild, Bitter, Best Bitter, Winter Warmer H
Ever-busy Peter Walker flagship pub, very close to football ground

12–3.30; 6–11
Swan & Railway
Wallgate (A49)
Bass Mild XXXX, Draught Bass; John Smith Bitter; Stones Best Bitter H
Bustling town-centre boozer; Wigan CAMRA Pub of the Year 1987 (North Western/Wallgate)

Woodford

11–3; 5.30–11
Davenport Arms
550 Chester Road (A5102)
Robinson Best Mild, Best Bitter H, **Old Tom** E
Unspoilt multi-roomed rural pub opposite aerodrome; full of flying memorabilia. Usually crowded, particularly with the wealthy young

Worthington

12–3 (3.30 Sat); 5.30–11
Crown Hotel
Platt Lane, Bradley (off A5106)
Draught Bass; Hydes Anvil Bitter; Theakston Best Bitter, XB, Old Peculier H
Country pub with antique furniture. Bowling green. Beer range varies

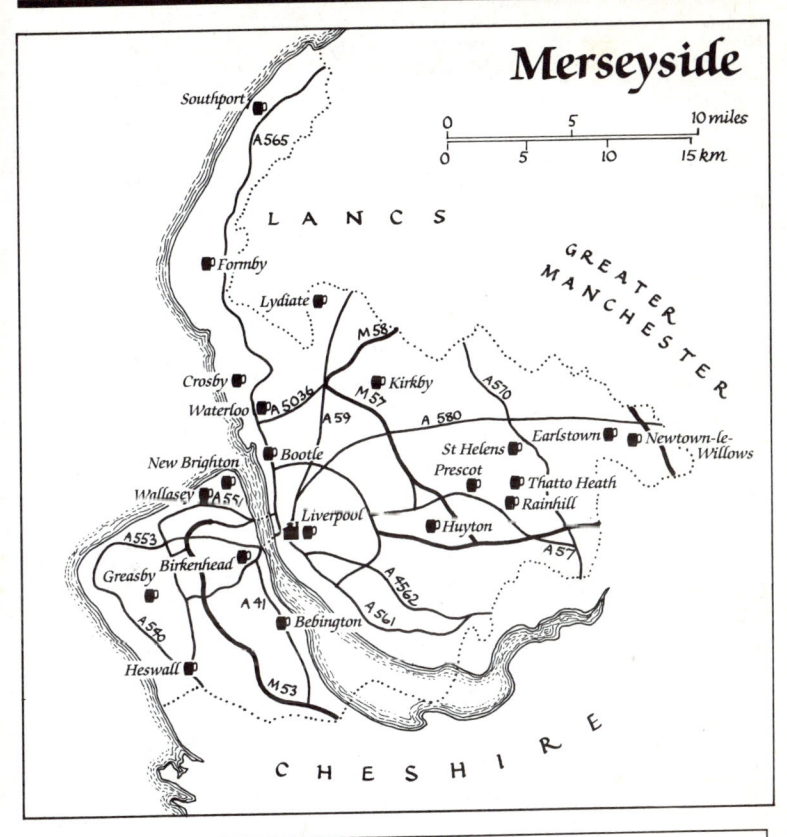

Merseyside

Bebington

11.30-3; 5-10.30 (11 F, S)

Cleveland Arms
31 Bebington Road, New Ferry
(in New Ferry Shopping Centre)
Thwaites Best Mild, Bitter H
Friendly town local

11.30-3; 5.30-10.30 (11 F, S)

Rose & Crown
57 The Village (B5148)
Thwaites Best Mild, Bitter H
Popular friendly village local
(Mon-Fri)

Birkenhead

11.30-3 (not Sun); 5-10.30 (11 F, S)

Copperfield
38 Market Street
John Smith Bitter H
Vibrant, lively pub, popular with office workers at lunchtime and with young people at night
(Hamilton Sq)

11.30-3; 5-10.30; (11 F, S)

George & Dragon
82 Grange Road

☎ (051) 647 4513
Walker Mild, Bitter H
Busy, friendly town centre pub. Traditional games
(not Sun) (Central)

11.30-3; 5-10.30 (11 F, S)

Lord Napier
St Paul's Road, Rock Ferry (off A41)
Boddingtons Mild, Bitter H
Comfortable, friendly 2-bar local. Pub games
(Rock Ferry)

11.30-3; 5.30-10.30 (11 F, S)

Shrewsbury Arms
38 Claughton Firs, Oxton
☎ (051) 652 1775
Boddingtons Bitter; Higsons Mild, Bitter H
Busy local in conservation area

11.30-3; 5-10.30 (11 F, S)

Vittoria Vaults
56 Vittoria Street (off A553)
☎ (051) 647 7617
Higsons Mild, Bitter H
Legendary local with table service in back lounge. Affectionately known as "The Piggy" (Park)

Bootle

11.30-3; 5.30-10.30 (11 F, S)

Strand
5 Strand Road (A5036 opposite Alexandra Dock)
Higsons Mild, Bitter H
Imposing pub with bustling lunch trade from what is left of Liverpool's dock workers. Quiet in evening
(New Strand)

Crosby

11.30-3; 5.30 (5 F, S)-10.30

Crow's Nest
61-63 Victoria Road
Boddingtons Bitter; Higsons Mild, Bitter H
Small traditional pub with comfortable lounge, lively bar and characterful snug. Very popular
(Blundellsands/Crosby)

Earlestown

12-3.30; 6.30-11

Houghton Arms
Houghton Close (off A572)

223

Merseyside

Burtonwood Dark Mild, Bitter H
Large pub, easier to see than find, situated in new housing development. Limited parking

Formby

11.30–3; 5–11
Bay Horse
Church Road (B5424)
☎ (070 48) 74229
Bass Mild XXXX, Draught Bass H
Warm, inviting and comfortable old pub with restaurant. The small lounge gets very crowded. Lively public (small)

11.30–3; 5–11
Pinewoods
Wicks Crescent
☎ (070 48) 72998
Boddingtons Bitter; Higsons Mild, Bitter H
Welcoming, well-furnished 2-room local. Only Higson outlet for miles

Greasby

11.30–3; 5.30–10.30 (11 F, S)
Irby Mill
Mill Lane (1 mile S of village centre) ☎ (051) 678 2565
Boddingtons Bitter; Higsons Bitter H
Stone-floored pub in Wirral countryside superbly converted from an old mill cottage. Close to Thurstaston Common (small) (not Sun) (till 7.30)

Heswall

11.30–3; 5–10.30 (11 F, S)
Black Horse
Village Road, Lower Heswall (off A541)
Bass Mild XXXX, Special Bitter, Draught Bass H
Popular pub with lounge, bar and snug catering for all ages (snug) (Mon–Sat)

Huyton

11.30–3; 5–10.30 (11 F, S)
Rose & Crown
Derby Road
Walkers Mild, Bitter H
Large between-the-wars pub on the site of Barkers Brewery. Large bar and chintzy lounges.

Kirkby

11.30–3; 5–10.30
Railway
Glovers Brow, Westvale
Higsons Mild, Bitter H
One of older buildings in mainly new town. Large bar and 3 chintzy lounges. Siu Mai is popular lunch snack (bar)

Liverpool: City Centre

11.30–3; 5–10.30 (11 F, S)
Blackburne Arms
24 Catharine Street, (near Women's Hospital)
Higsons Mild, Bitter H
Well-proportioned pub with wide mix of customers (Central)

11.30–3; 5–10.30 (11 F, S)
Cambridge
Mulberry Street, 7 (near University)
Burtonwood Dark Mild, Bitter H
Friendly corner pub frequented by students and locals alike. Busy all week (Central)

11.30–3; 5–10.30 (11 F, S)
Carnarvon Castle
5 Tarleton Street (off Church Street)
Boddingtons Bitter; Higsons Mild, Bitter H
Lovely little pub, handy for shoppers. Dinky Toy collection
Q (Lime St) (Central)

11.30–3; 5.30–10.30 (11 F, S)
Court House
3 Commutation Row, 1
Higsons Mild, Bitter H
Friendly local with unusual exterior. Near museum and St. George's Hall (Lime St)

11.30–3; 5–10.30 (11 F, S)
Cracke
Rice Street, 1 (off Hope Street)
Boddingtons Bitter; Marston Merrie Monk, Pedigree H
Characterful pub, popular with people from the arts (Lime St) (Central)

11.30–3; 5–10.30 (11 F, S); (closed Sun)
Excelsior
2 Dale Street, 2 (near Mersey Tunnel)
Boddingtons Bitter; Higsons Mild, Bitter H
City pub with local atmosphere. Folk club Fri offers the cream of local talent, including "Stormalong John" (early) (Lime St) (Moorfields)

11.30–3; 5–10.30 (11 F, S); (closed Sun)
Grapes
25 Mathew Street, 2 (opposite Cavern Walks)
Boddingtons Bitter; Higsons Mild, Bitter H
Cosy, but lively city centre pub of character (Lime St) (Moorfields)

11.30–3; 5–10.30 (11 F, S)
Lion Tavern
67 Moorfields, 2
Walkers Mild, Bitter
Cosy 3-roomed pub. Ornate tiles, woodwork, and unusual glass dome. Folk session Tue (Moorfields)

11.30–3; 5–10.30 (11 F, S)
Midland
25 Ranelagh Street, 1
Walker Mild, Bitter, Best Bitter H
Splendid, ornate little gin palace. Wide cross section of customers. Public bar not always open (Lime St) (Central)

11.30–3 (not Sun); 5–10.30 (11 F, S)
Railway
18 Tithebarn Street, 2
Boddingtons Bitter; Higsons Mild, Bitter H
Traditional 3-room city pub. Friendly atmosphere. Ornate leaded windows on railway theme. Watch out for groping hand! Darts, dominoes; jazz sessions (Moorfields)

11.30–3; 5–10.30 (11 F, S)
Roscoe Head
24 Roscoe Street, 1 (off Leece Street)
Jennings Bitter; Tetley Mild, Bitter H
Nothing fancy but a classic city pub Q (Lime St) (Central)

11.30–3; 5–10.30 (11 F, S)
White Star
2 Rainford Gardens, 2 (off Whitechapel)
Bass Special Bitter, Draught Bass H
Justifiably famous Bass outlet sandwiched between office and shop areas
Q (Lime St) (Moorfields)

Liverpool: East

11.30–3; 5–10.30 (11 F, S)
Halton Castle
86 Mill Lane, West Derby, 12
Higsons Mild, Bitter H
Cosy 4-room local, full of lively characters. Handy for Croxteth Country Park. Everton/Liverpool theme in bar. Darts

11.30–3; 6–10.30 (11 F, S)
Kensington
189 Kensington, 7 (200 yds A57/B5173 Jct)
Higsons Mild, Bitter H
Homely 2-room local with table service in lounge (lunch)

11.30–3; 5–10.30 (11 F, S)
Lord Nelson
East Prescot Road, Knotty Ash, 14 (A57)
Higsons Mild, Bitter H
Old style 2-room pub opposite Springfield Park. Bar has lively crowd; lounge small and welcoming

11.30–3; 5–10.30 (11 F, S)

Merseyside

Oxford
67 Oxford Street, 7
Boddingtons Bitter; Higsons Mild, Bitter H
Popular 2-roomed local attracting both locals and students (order)

11.30–3; 5–10.30 (11 F, S)

Prince Alfred
77 High Street, Wavertree, 15 (B5178)
Higsons Mild, Bitter H
Basic bar at front; cosy, old fashioned lounge at rear

11.30–3; 5–10.30 (11 F, S)

Rocket
Bowring Park Road
Boddingtons Bitter; Higsons Mild, Bitter H
Excellent modern 2-bar pub with Rocket locomotive theme. Children's room (Broadgreen)

11.30–3; 5–10.30 (11 F, S)

Royal Hotel
213 Smithdown Road, Wavertree, 15 (opposite Sefton General Hospital)
Ind Coope Burton Ale; Tetley Mild, Bitter H
Unusual gas-lit decor; lounge has cosy, wood-panelled alcoves (for meals)

11.30–3; 5–10.30 (11 F, S)

Royal Standard
1 Walker Street, 6
Draught Bass; Higsons Mild, Bitter H
The pub for which the phrase "warm friendly local" must have been coined. Darts, dominoes and cribbage

11.30–3; 5–10.30 (11 F, S)

Salisbury
Albany Road (off Derby Lane), 13
Higsons Mild, Bitter H
2-room local – part of a well cared for terrace (Sun lunch)

11.30–3; 5–10.30 (11 F, S)

Wheatsheaf
186 East Prescot Road, Knotty Ash, 14 (A57)
Higsons Mild, Bitter H
Comfortable 3-room pub. Lounges with waitress service. Lively bar. 14th year in Good Beer Guide Q

11.30–3; 5–10.30 (11 F, S)

Willowbank
329 Smithdown Road, Wavertree, 15 (A562 opposite Sefton General Hospital)
Walker Mild, Bitter, Best Bitter H
Pleasant, comfortable suburban pub with public bar, snug, lounge and 2 other drinking areas (Mon–Fri)

Liverpool: North

11.30–3; 5–10.30 (11 F, S)

Abbey
153 Walton Lane, 4 (opposite Stanley Park)
Walker Mild, Bitter H
Impressive half-timbered, maroon-tiled exterior. Cosy 2-roomed interior. Frequented by locals and well-behaved Everton/Liverpool supporters (lunch) (Kirkdale)

11.30–3; 5–10.30 (11 F, S)

Bull
2 Dublin Street, 3
Tetley Mild, Walker Best Bitter H
1-bar, street-corner Irish pub with a good mix of customers. Lively atmosphere

11.30–3; 5–10.30 (11 F, S)

Clock
167 Walton Road, 4 (A59)
Walker Mild, Bitter H
Bustling 2-room local, close to Everton FC. Darts (Kirkdale)

11.30–3; 5–10.30 (11 F, S)

Grove
145 Breckfield Road North, Anfield ☎ (051) 263 8825
Higsons Mild, Bitter H
Comfortably refurbished local providing a friendly welcome. Near Liverpool FC

11.30–3; 5–10.30 (11 F, S)

Melrose Abbey
331 Westminster Road, 4
Tetley Mild, Bitter H
Lively 3-room locals' pub. Popular with railmen and football fans. Live music Sat and Sun (Kirkdale)

11.30–3; 5–10.30 (11 F, S)

Orwell
46 Orwell Road, 4 (150 yds off A567)
Boddingtons Mild, Bitter H
The last pub built by the old Higsons. A perfect blend with adjacent streets. Interior is open-plan but with well defined "areas". In finals of CAMRA Best New Pub award (lunch) (Bank Hall)

11.30–3; 5.30–10.30 (11 F, S)

Rising Sun
124 Portland Street, 5
Tetley Mild, Bitter H
Spartan, spotless local, hard to find in middle of Vauxhall Estate

11.30–3; 5–10.30 (11 F, S)

Selwyn
106 Selwyn Street, 4
Tetley Mild, Bitter H
Bustling 3-room corner pub with mainly local trade. Handy for Everton FC. Games (lunch) (Kirkdale)

11.30–3; 5–10.30 (11 F, S)

Stanley Bar
99 Stanley Road, 5
Tetley Mild, Bitter H
3-room pub with impressive crest over corner. Survived local urban clearance but lost many customers. Darts and cribbage (parlour) (Sandhills)

11.30–3; 5–10.30 (11 F, S)

Top House
122 Walton Village, 4
Higsons Mild, Bitter H
Busy local, unspoilt by recent refurbishment. Handy for Everton FC

Try also: Queens Arms (Higsons)

Liverpool: South

11.30–3; 5–10.30 (11 F, S)

Anglesea Arms
36 Beresford Road, 8
Tetley Mild, Bitter H
Spotless but homely pub, catering mainly for local trade. Standard 2-room format

11.30–3; 5–10.30 (11 F, S)

Bleak House
131 Park Hill Road, 8
Higsons Mild, Bitter H
Popular 3-roomed local near River Mersey, in an area much loved by TV producers seeking authentic Merseyside "character"

11.30–3; 5–10.30 (11 F, S)

Cobden Vaults
89 Quarry Street, Woolton, 25
John Smith Bitter H
Busy, friendly local, tastefully decorated

11.30–3; 5–10.30 (11 F, S)

Croxteth
145 Lodge Lane, 8 (27 bus from town)
Tetley Mild, Bitter H
Lively, comfortable pub. Bingo Wed, live music most nights. Island bar (Edge Hill)

11.30–3; 5–10.30 (11 F, S)

King Street Vaults
74 King Street, 19
Walker Dark Mild, Bitter, Best Bitter H
Popular pub in centre of Garston's Dockland. Well known as darts centre (Garston)

11.30–3; 5–10.30 (11 F, S)

Mersey View
277 Grafton Street, 8
Tetley Mild, Bitter H
Comfortable local, near the river (although no view!) Pub games

11.30–3; 5–10.30 (11 F, S)

Mosley Arms
156 Mill Street, 8
Tetley Mild, Bitter H
Pleasant 2-room pub with ornate exterior sign (former Walker's ownership.)

11.30–3; 5–10.30 (11 F, S)

Poet's Corner
27 Parkhill Road, 8

225

Merseyside

Tetley Mild, Bitter ⊞
Popular family local – a friendly welcome ⌂⊟♿

Lydiate

11.30–3; 5.30–10.30 (11 F, S)
Running Horses
Bells Lane (off Southport Road by canal)
Ind Coope Burton Ale; Walker Dark Mild, Best Bitter, Winter Warmer ⊞
Extended pub with family room on banks of Leeds-Liverpool canal. Large outdoor drinking areas; barbecue – popular with coarse fishermen ⛺⊟⌂◑⊟

New Brighton

11.30–3; 5–10.30 (11 F, S)
Travellers Rest
Rowson Street, New Brighton (A554) ☎ (051) 691 1204
Draught Bass ⊞
2-tier pub with comfortable traditional lounge. No real ale in "Reflections" disco bar ◑≠

Newton-le-Willows

12–3.30; 7–11
Old Crow
248 Crow Lane East (A572)
Tetley Mild, Bitter ⊞
Large 2-roomed local with snug, well-lit lounge and games room. Smoky atmosphere
⊟◑♦ (on demand) ⊟

Prescot

11.30–3; 6–10.30 (11 F, S)
Clock Face
54 Derby Street (A57)
Thwaites Best Mild, Bitter ⊞
Well-furnished popular pub (ex-mansion!) with 4 separate drinking areas
Q⌂⊟◑ (not Sun) ♿

Rainhill

11.30–3; 5.30–11
Commercial
Station Road (off A57)
Higsons Mild, Bitter ⊞
4-roomed Victorian pub with windows of former Joseph Jones Brewery of Knotty Ash
⊟≠

St Helens

11.30–3; 7–11
Hope & Anchor
City Road
Boddingtons Mild, Bitter ⊞
Busy local with disco. Pub games ⊟

11.30–3; 7–11
Queens
Higher Parr Street

Boddingtons Mild, Bitter ⒺBoddingtons Mild, Bitter Ⓔ
Popular locals' pub with a collection of Victorian bottles from local glass industry. Pub games ⊟≠ (Central)

11.30–3; 5.30–11
Royal Alfred
Shaw Street
Boddingtons Mild, Bitter ⊞
Busy, comfortable town-centre pub handy for station. Pub games ⋈◑⊟♿≠ (Central)

11.30–3; 5.30–11
Sportsmans
Duke Street
Boddingtons Mild, Bitter ⊞
Pub renamed in 1984 because of long-standing sporting connections. Pub games ◑ (not Sun) ⊟♿≠ (Central)

11.30–3; 5.30–11; 7–11
Turks Head
Cooper Street
Tetley Mild, Bitter ⊞
Old pub in redevelopment area. Live groups several nights a week. Darts ⊟♿ (Central)

12–3.30; 7–11
Union
Hall Street
Boddingtons Mild, Bitter ⊞
Multi-roomed, street-corner local named after the old Union Plate Glass Works. Pub games ⊟♿≠ (Central)

Southport

11.30–3; 5–11
Bold Arms
Botanic Road, Churchtown (B5244) ☎ (0704) 28192
Ind Coope Burton Ale; Jennings Bitter; Tetley Mild, Bitter ⊞
Old coaching inn in beautiful area near Botanic Gardens. Strong quiz teams. Winner of 1987 Best Mild award ⛺⊟◑♿

11.30–3; 5–11
Portland Hotel
Bedford Road, Birkdale (7 and 3 bus routes from town)
☎ (0704) 69926
Tetley Mild, Bitter ⊞
Much improved, large local with friendly staff and a true public bar. Games ⊟

11.30–3; 5–11
Ship Inn
Cable Street (off Nevill Street)
☎ (0704) 30271
Bass Mild XXXX, Special Bitter, Draught Bass (summer) ⊞
Superb back-street gem with marvellous Walkden's windows. Good value snacks. Superb little snug with blazing fires ⛺⊟≠

11.30–3; 5–11

Zetland Hotel
Zetland Street ☎ (0704) 44541
Burtonwood Dark Mild, Bitter ⊞
Large suburban local within walking distance of town centre. Floodlit competition bowling green. Separate games room ⊟⊟

Try also: Blundell Arms (Tetley)

Thatto Heath

11.30–3; 6.15–11
Vine Tavern
Elephant Lane
Boddingtons Mild, Bitter Ⓔ
Busy pub with several games teams ⊟♿≠

Wallasey

11.30–3; 5.30–10.30 (11 F, S)
Brighton
133 Brighton Street (A554)
☎ (051) 638 1163
Higsons Mild, Bitter ⊞
Good locals' pub with attractive exterior. Pub games ⌂⊟

11.30–3; 5–10.30 (11 F, S)
Farmers Arms
☎ (051) 638 2110
Boddingtons Bitter; Higsons Mild, Bitter ⊞
Friendly locals' pub with traditional atmosphere; Bar, lounge and snug. Pub games ◑ (Mon–Fri) ⊟≠ (Grove Rd)

11.30–3; 5–10.30 (11 F, S)
Ferry
48 Tobin Street
☎ (051) 639 1753
Boddingtons Bitter; Higsons Mild, Bitter ⊞
Very popular hostelry overlooking the Mersey. Separate children's playroom. Pub games ⌂◑♦♿

11.30–3; 5–10.30 (11 F, S)
Nelson
Grove Road ☎ (051) 639 4402
Davenports Mild, Bitter Ⓔ
2-room pub with traditional bar. Lounge used by younger clientele. Pub games
⊟≠ (Grove Rd)

Waterloo

11.30–3; 5–11
Old Bank
43 South Road, 22 (off A565)
Marston Pedigree; Tetley Mild, Bitter; Whitbread Castle Eden Ale ⊞
Comfortable, spacious 1-bar pub with live Irish music Thur eves, jazz Sun lunch
⌂ (for lunch) ◑♦≠

Try also: Volunteer Canteen (Higsons)

226

The Licensing Act – A Layman's Guide

The Licensing Act 1988 makes a number of changes to existing law, which at the time of writing have not come into force, and there is provision for the Home Secretary to make Statutory Instruments bringing different aspects of the Act into force on different dates. One of the changes which will affect the average drinker is that drinking-up time is doubled from ten to twenty minutes. So what else is new?

On Sundays, Christmas Day and Good Friday, permitted hours are, following a Parliamentary "administrative cock-up", noon to 3pm with the evening session as before, 7–10.30. On all other days, off-licenses and clubs are permitted to sell from 11am, both closing by 11pm. Local licensing justices may modify the weekday hours in their district so as to begin at any time not earlier than 10 in the morning, so places used to opening at 10, half past 10, or even 10.45, may continue to do so. Local justices will now be able to make a "restriction order" relating to a particular pub, removing from its permitted hours any part of the time between half past two and half past five. The provisions remain for both the special order of exemption – as for a wedding reception or a birthday party – and the general order of exemption for cattle and other market days, or people following a special trade, but apart from allowing especially bibulous weddings to go on to midnight, there would seem to be little need for such orders: all those interesting noticeboards outside pubs about being open "until 5pm for the convenience of persons attending the cattle market" will be out of date.

The 1988 Act makes new provisions for on-licensed vineyard premises; their permitted hours may be at any times provided they do not exceed 5½ hours on Sunday (Christmas Day and Good Friday) afternoons and twelve hours on weekdays.

Extended hours orders (to 1am) are still available to restaurants providing entertainments, and special hours certificates (to 2am–3am in Central London) are still available for premises providing music, dancing and substantial refreshment. The actual permitted hours applying to the pub you want to be in will still depend on the licensee, the licensing justices, and upon what special orders are in force.

The "permitted hours" remain exactly that: the hours during which a pub is permitted to be open, and nothing in the law says a pub must be open all the permitted hours. The owner of a free house is beholden to no-one: it was, and will be, the brewery companies who are interested in ensuring that their tenanted and managed pubs are open for as long as possible, and until now such a stipulation was usually made in a licensee's contract. While the latest legislation was passing through Parliament, some brewery companies announced that they would not force licensees to be open all of the new hours; other companies have been more reticent, and it is impossible to estimate how many pubs will be open during the permitted hours.

It is to be expected that pub owners, private or corporate, will want to get maximum profits out of the new arrangements, and will be looking for more ways of making more profit during the increased opening hours. More pubs will place more emphasis on food, on video games, on juke boxes, on pool tables, and on anything else that gets money out of customers' pockets and purses. The large roadhouse and the bigger urban pubs are able to expand this way: the end-of-terrace corner local and the country cottage pub must either expand or be sold off. If we, the beer drinkers, are lucky, there will be individual entrepreneurs and small breweries willing to run these small pubs in the traditional way. If we are unlucky, the only pubs left in the land will be large, "total-leisure amenities", reeking of chips and vinegar, overrun with other people's shrieking children. Which is a very high price to pay for a few mid-afternoon bevvies.

Keith Greenhalgh

Norfolk

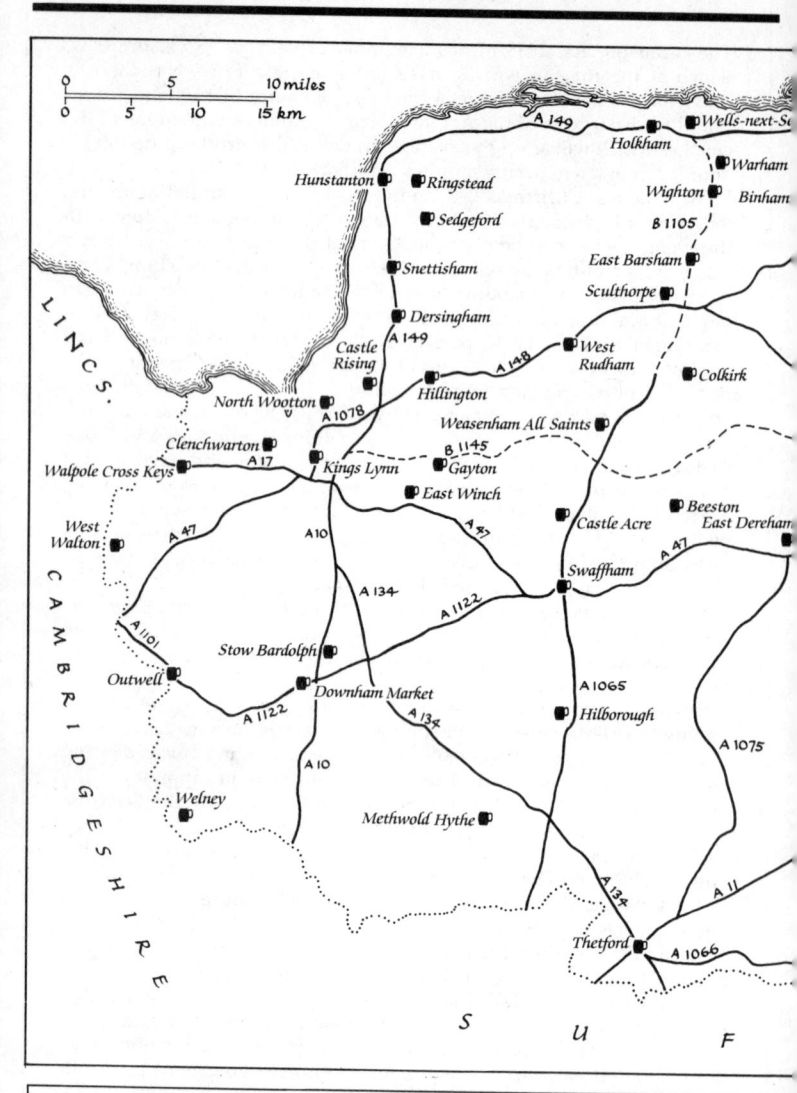

> **Reepham**, Reepham; **Woodforde's Norfolk Ales**, Erpingham

Acle

10.30–2.30; 6–11

Reba's Riverside Inn
Old Yarmouth Road (A1064)
☎ (0493) 750310
Courage Best Bitter; John Smith Bitter; Woodforde's Wherry Best Bitter H
Small modernised pub close to river. Homely atmosphere. Pub games

Attleborough

10.30–2.30; 5.30–11

Griffin Hotel
Church Street ☎ (0953) 452169
Greene King Abbot; Wethered Bitter H
Comfortable atmosphere in 16th-century pub with beamed walls and ceiling. Food served in bar and restaurant. Separate public bar. Family room. Guest beers

11–2.30; 6–11

White Lodge
London Road ☎ (0953) 452474
Adnams Bitter; Courage Directors; Wethered Bitter H
Comfortable roadside, thatched pub recently "by-passed." Old part of pub remains nicely unspoilt. New restaurant; family room.

Beeston

10.30–2.30; 6.30–11

Ploughshare
The Street (off A47)
☎ (0328) 701650
Adnams Bitter; Draught Bass; Greene King IPA, Abbot; Hall & Woodhouse Tanglefoot; Wadworth 6X H
Smart village pub with small restaurant. Large garden and bar

Norfolk

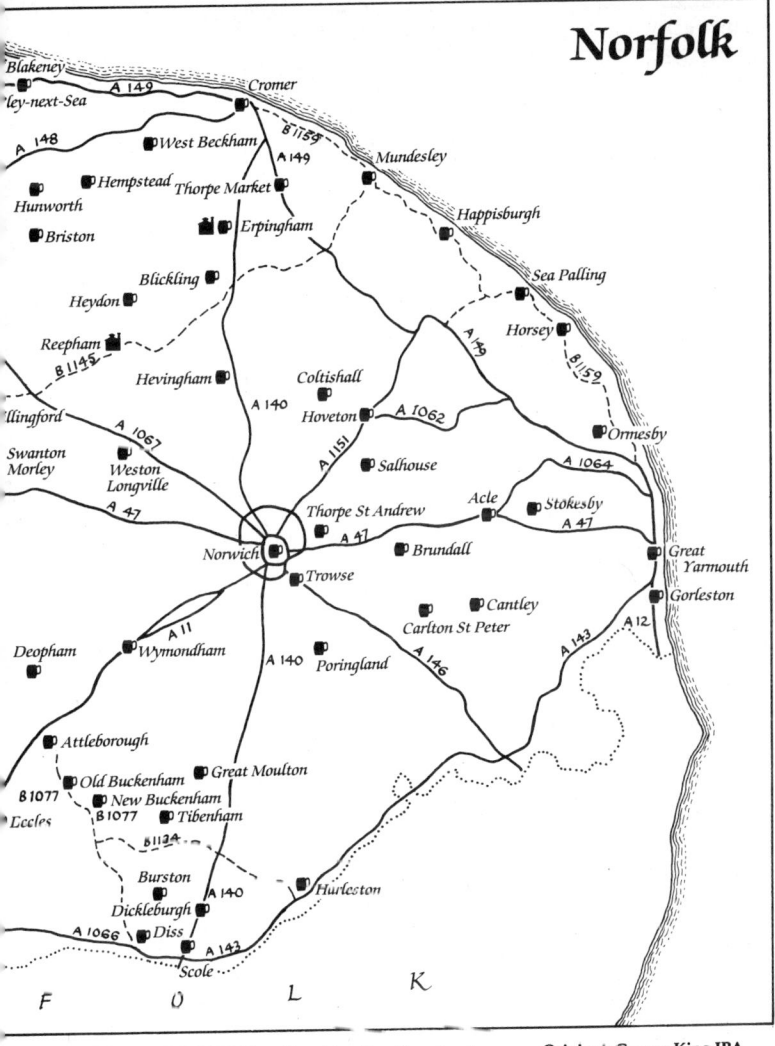

Billingford

12–2.30; 7–11

Forge
Bintree Road (300 yds off B1145) ☎ (036 281)486
Adnams Bitter; Greene King IPA, Abbot H
Former blacksmith's forge with a true rural atmosphere. Family room; pub games. Guest beers

Binham

11–2.30; 6–11

Chequers
Front Street (B1388)
☎ (032 875) 297
Bateman Mild, XB; Woodforde's Wherry Best Bitter H
Lovely old pub with open fire. Very friendly village local. Guest beers. Games available

Blakeney

11–2.30; 6.30–11

Manor Hotel
The Quay (off A149)
☎ (0263) 740376
Adnams Bitter H
Comfortable hotel bar with superb views over the salt marshes. Family room

Blickling

10.30–2.30; 6–11

Buckinghamshire Arms
Next to Blickling Hall
☎ (0263) 732133
Adnams Bitter; Flowers Original; Greene King IPA, Abbot H
Delightfully unspoilt 17th-century inn, 2 bars plus separate indoor room for children. Owned by the National Trust; on Blickling Hall estate

Try also: Greens, Aylsham (Free)

Briston

11–2.30; 6–11

Green Man
Hall Street (off B1354)
☎ (0263) 860993
Adnams Bitter; Greene King Rayment BBA, Abbot H
Village pub popular with locals. Superb log fire and real beams. Family room

229

Norfolk

Brundall

10.30–2.30; 5.30–11

Yare
Station Road (on River Yare)
☎ (0603) 713786
John Smith Bitter; Samuel Smith OBB; Wadworth 6X; Woodforde's Wherry Best Bitter, Phoenix H
Large refurbished Broadland pub, reflecting the history of the area in its decor. Family room. Pub games

Burston

11–2.30; 6–11

Crown
Crown Green ☎ (0379) 741257
Adnams Bitter; Greene King Abbot; Woodforde's Phoenix XXX H
Delightful, friendly 17th-century pub overlooking village green serving local ales. Pub offers bar meals and restaurant with à la carte menu. Pub games. Guest beers

Cantley

11–2.30; 6 (7 Sat)–11

Cock Tavern
Manor Road (A47)
☎ (0493) 700895
Draught Bass; Ind Coope Burton Ale; Tetley Bitter; Woodforde's Wherry Best Bitter, Phoenix XXX H
Friendly popular local with petanque pitch. Many separate rooms. Pub games

Carleton St Peter

11–2.30; 6–11 (closed winter Mon–Wed)

Beauchamp Arms
Buckenham Ferry (1 mile E of Claxton) OS350044
☎ (050 843) 247
Woodforde's Wherry Best Bitter, Phoenix XXX, Norfolk Nog, Headcracker H
Pleasant spot on River Yare. Former ferry inn with bars, restaurant, family room and games room

Castle Acre

11–2.30; 6–11

Ostrich Inn
Stocks Green ☎ (076 05) 398
Greene King XX, IPA, Abbot H
An attractive 16th-century coaching inn, the only one on Peddars Way. Good for food; caters for locals and tourists alike. Situated in an historic village with a ruined priory and castle

Castle Rising

10–2.30; 6–11

Black Horse Inn
½ mile from A149
☎ (0553) 87225
Adnams Bitter; Draught Bass; Charrington IPA H
Large inn situated between castle and church in an historic village. Guest beers. Live music Sun eves

11–2.30; 5.30–11

Farmers Arms/Village Inn
Knights Hill (A148)
☎ (0553) 875566
Adnams Bitter; Draught Bass; Bateman XXXB; Charrington IPA; Samuel Smith OBB H
Well-executed barn conversion, part of large former farm complex still under development. Good use of materials

Try also: Farmers Arms, South Wootton

Clenchwarton

11–3; 5.30–11

Victory
243 Main Road (off A17)
☎ (0553) 772377
Elgood Bitter H
Fine traditional, 2-bar pub, popular with locals. Snookerette and dominoes in public bar

Cley-Next-Sea

11–2.30; 6–11

George & Dragon Hotel
High Street (A149)
☎ (0263) 740652
Bateman XXXB; Greene King IPA, Abbot H
3 areas catering for local trade, tourists and ornithologists. Norfolk Naturalist Trust founded here. Fine stained glass window of George and Dragon. Pub games

Colkirk

10.30–2.30; 6–11

Crown
Crown Road (off B1146)
☎ (0328) 2172
Greene King XX, IPA, Abbot H
Very popular, 2-bar pub with separate restaurant serving good food. Range of games in good public bar. Bowling green

Coltishall

11–2.30; 6–11

Red Lion
Church Street
Flowers Original; Wethered Bitter; Whitbread; Castle Eden Ale H
Lovely 2-bar pub on two levels, top bar a classic. Close to river in this popular Broads area. Pub games

Try also: Jolly Farmers, Swanton Abbott (Free)

Cromer

10.30–2.30; 6–11

Wellington
New Street ☎ (0263) 511075
Adnams Bitter; Greene King Abbot; Samuel Smith OBB H
Large, single bar, locals' pub – unchanging. Pub games

Try also: Bath House; Red Lion (Free)

Deopham

11–2.30; 6 (7 winter)–11

Victoria Inn
Church Road ☎ (0953) 850783
Adnams Bitter; Greene King Abbot; Woodforde's Wherry Best Bitter H
Comfortable village pub; an oasis in a beer desert. Separate areas around a central bar. Darts

Dersingham

11–2.30 (3 summer); 5.30–11

Feathers
Manor Road (off A149)
☎ (0485) 40207
Adnams Bitter; Draught Bass; Charrington IPA H
Fine Carrstone building which rambles away through a series of separate rooms. Fine wood-panelled bar. Good value meals

Dickleburgh

12–2.30; 6.30–11

Crown
Norwich Road (A140)
☎ (0379) 741475
Bateman XXXB; Mauldon Bitter; Woodforde's Norfolk Pride H
Friendly roadside 16th-century pub with good atmosphere. One long bar area. Pub games. Guest beers

Diss

10–2.30; 6–11

White Elephant
Stuston Road (B1077)
☎ (0379) 651904
Adnams Bitter; Mauldon Bitter H
Friendly pub where all are welcome. Separate games area. Good value meals. Guest beers (pets too)

Downham Market

10.30–2; 6–11

Norfolk

Crown Hotel
Bridge Street ☎ (0366) 382322
Greene King Abbot; Tolly Cobbold Bitter, Original; Woodforde's Norfolk Nog H
Old beamed coaching inn in town centre. Very comfortable, unspoilt bar with 2 fine brick fireplaces
≜ ☎ ♨ ● ⊖ ♿

11–3; 6–11

Live & Let Live
22 London Road
☎ (0366) 383933
Adnams Bitter; Greene King Abbot H
Modernised pub with a small upper bar and large opened-out lower bar with games and video at far end. Popular with young people
☎ ♨ ● ● (Thu–Sat) ♿

East Barsham

11.30–2.30; 6 (7 winter)–11 (restaurant licence till 12)

White Horse Inn
Fakenham Road
☎ (032 872) 645
Adnams Bitter; Greene King Abbot; Tolly Cobbold Original; Woodforde's Wherry Best Bitter H
Lovely old beamed building with large fireplace. Separate restaurant with à la carte menu. Traditional country pub. Guest beers. Darts
≜ ☎ ♨ ● ● ♿

East Dereham

11 2.30 (3.30 Fri); 6 (7 Sat)–11

Bull
High Street ☎ (0362) 67771
Greene King XX, IPA, Rayment BBA, Abbot H
Bar divided into several anterooms and cubbyholes. Multi-coloured electronic notice board has to be seen to be appreciated! Pub games
≜ ☎ ♨ ● ♿

East Winch

11–2.30; 6–11

Carpenters Arms
On A47 ☎ (0553) 841228
Greene King XX, IPA, Abbot H
Comfortable pub – a welcome sight along a particularly 'dry' part of A47. Closed by Watneys and eventually reopened as a free house after a local campaign Q ☎ ♨ ● ♿

Eccles

11–2.30; 5.30–11

Old Railway Tavern
Eccles Road Station (E of A11)
☎ (095 387) 778
Adnams Old G; **Greene King IPA, Rayment BBA** H, **Abbot** G
Excellent friendly pub. Teams for darts, crib, petanque. Family room with pool table. Good varied menu (not Sun)
≜ Q ☎ ♨ ● ⊖ ♿

Erpingham

11–2.30; 6–11

Spread Eagle
1 mile off A140 (Cromer road)
☎ (0263) 761591
Woodforde's Eagle Bitter, Wherry Best Bitter, John Brown Special Bitter, Phoenix XXX, Norfolk Nog, Headcracker H
The original home of Woodforde's brewery. Comfortable country pub tucked away in quiet village setting. Children's room. Pub games ≜ Q ☎ ♨ ● ♿

Gayton

10 2; 6.30–11

Crown
Lynn Road (B1145)
☎ (055 386) 252
Greene King XX, IPA, Abbot H
Cosy old bar with low ceilings, separate restaurant area. A friendly traditional pub ≜ Q ♨ ● ●

Gorleston

11.30–2.30; 7–11

New Entertainer
80 Pier Plain (off A12)
☎ (0493) 653218
Adnams Old, Extra; Greene King Abbot; Marston Pedigree; Samuel Smith OBB H
An ordinary sort of pub serving locals and holidaymakers. Situated near the harbour mouth. Darts ●

10.30–2.30; 6.30 (6 summer)–11

Short Blue
47 High Street ☎ (0493) 602192
Adnams Bitter H
Pleasing pub with riverside views and good food. Guest beers ☎ ♨ ●

10.30–2.30; 6–11

Tramway
1 Lowestoft Road
Adnams Bitter, Old H
Plush lounge, basic town centre bar. Popular with locals. Darts and cards ⊖

Great Moulton

11–2.30; 6–11

Fox & Hounds
Frith Way ☎ (037 977) 506
Flowers Original; Wethered Bitter, Winter Royal H
Whitbread's oldest inn (500 years). A lovely beamed pub with warm welcome. Restaurant specialises in Spanish dishes (closed Mon/Tue). Guest beers in summer
≜ Q ☎ ♨ ● ● ♿

Great Yarmouth

10 (11 winter)–2.30; 6–11 (race-days opens after last race)

Avenue
Beatty Road (200 yds from race course) ☎ (0493) 842803
Adnams Extra; Flowers Original; Wethered Bitter H, **Winter Royal** G
Large Tudor-style pub with racing connections. Separate public bar and lounge
☎ ● ⊖ ▲

11–2.30; 7–11

Red Herring
24–25 Havelock Road
☎ (0493) 853384
Flowers Original; Wethered Bitter H
Friendly 1-room local in town with strong fishing links. Close to very old working smokehouse. Local guest beers. Pub games Q ♿

11–2.30; 7–11

Talbot
Howard Street North (behind Market Place) ☎ (0493) 843175
Bateman XXXB; Marston Owd Rodger; Reepham Brewhouse Ale; Woodforde's Wherry Best Bitter H
Small 1-roomed bar in historic row with interesting past (murder and pressgangs) and 'colourful' present-day customers. Beer range changes regularly ♿ ⇌

Happisburgh

11–2.30; 6 (7 winter)–11

Hill House
The Hill (off B1159)
☎ (0692) 650004
Adnams Bitter; Greene King Abbot; Woodforde's Wherry Best Bitter H
15th-century beamed building. Single long bar with separate restaurant à la carte meals. Fine, amusing tapestry in games area. Busy friendly pub. Family room, guest beers ≜ Q ☎ ♨ ● ● ♿

Harleston

10.30–2.30; 6–11

Cherry Tree
London Road ☎ (0379) 852345
Adnams Mild, Bitter, Old, Extra (summer) H
Excellent, friendly, unspoilt pub full of character with separate public bar and lounge. A quaint cooking range is used to heat the lounge
≜ Q (lounge) ☎ (lunch)
♨ ⊖ ▲ (1 mile)

11–2.30; 7–11

Duke William
28 Redenhall Road
☎ (0379) 853183

231

Norfolk

Adnams Bitter; Greene King Abbot H
Friendly, local 2-bar pub. Guest beers in summer. Darts and cards. Children welcome at lunch, if eating
Q (not bar) ⌂☎●◐ ⊞&A

Hempstead

11.30–2.30; 6 (7 winter)–11

Hare & Hounds
On Holt–Baconsthorpe Road
☎ (0263) 713285
Adnams Bitter; Draught Bass; Woodforde's Hobsons Choice H
Difficult to find and difficult to leave. Nicely converted interior has single bar. Popular with locals and tourists ⌂Q☎●◐⊞&A

Hevingham

10.30–2.30; 6–11

Marsham Arms
Holt Road (B1149 4 miles from Norwich Airport)
☎ (060 548) 268
Adnams Bitter; Draught Bass; Greene King Abbot; Wethered Bitter H
Pub for all the family. Very good food. Built in 1832 and extensively extended and modernised ⌂☎●◐&

Heydon

10.30–2.30; 6.30–11

Earle Arms
☎ (026 387) 376
Adnams Bitter; Greene King Abbot G
Comfortable, unspoilt free house in historic village. Pub in grounds of country estate opposite village green and church. Friendly atmosphere. Guest beers in summer. Pub games Q☎⌂⊞

Hilborough

11–2.30; 6–11

Swan
On A1065 ☎ (076 06) 380
Adnams Mild, Bitter; Greene King IPA, Abbot H
Popular, welcoming main road pub built in 1718. Little changed in recent years. Food is served in a separate restaurant area. Guest beers ⌂Q◐&

Hillington

10.30–2.30; 6–11

Ffolkes Arms
Main Road (A148)
☎ (0485) 600210
Adnams Bitter; Charrington IPA; Greene King Abbot H
Large open-plan pub with brick arches and alcoves.
⌂☎●◐&

Holkham

11–2.30; 6.30–11

Victoria Hotel
Park Road (A149)
☎ (0328) 710469
Tolly Cobbold Bitter H
Comfortable flint-faced Georgian hotel near beach and Holkham Hall. Separate restaurant. Guest beers in summer. Pub games
⌂☎●⌂◐⊞&

Horsey

10.30–2.30; 6–11

Nelsons Head
The Street (off B1159)
☎ (049 376) 378
Adnams Bitter, Old H
Friendly 1-bar country local with genuine family room. A comfortable and welcoming atmosphere. Popular with visitors to marshes and Horsey Mill (National Trust)
⌂Q☎●◐A

Hoveton

10–2.30; 5.30–11

Hotel Wroxham
☎ (060 53) 2061
Courage Best Bitter, Directors; John Smith Bitter; Woodforde's Wherry Best Bitter, Phoenix XXX, Norfolk Nog H
Large hotel with 2 bars on the river. Regular local trade all year. Games ☎●⌂◐⊞&≠

Hunstanton

11–2.30 (3 summer); 7 (6 summer)–11

Ancient Mariner, Le Strange Arms Hotel
Golf Course Road (off A149)
☎ (048 53) 34411
Adnams Bitter; Draught Bass; Charrington IPA; Greene King Abbot; Tolly Cobbold Old Strong H
An extension to the old hotel; old materials used to create a stables-effect interior
Q☎●◐

11–2.30; 6–11

Neptune
Old Hunstanton (on A149)
☎ (048 53) 2122
Adnams Bitter, Old; Greene King Abbot H
Old pub with 3 bars including a flagstone floored locals' bar. Antique shop at back of pub
Q⌂◐

Hunworth

11–2.30; 6–11

Bluebell
The Green ☎ (0263) 2300
Adnams Bitter; Woodforde's Wherry Best Bitter, Phoenix XXX, Norfolk Nog H
Comfortable village pub on the green. Good food and log fire. Pub games ⌂Q☎●◐&

Kings Lynn

12–2.30; 6–11

Bank House
King Staithe Square
Charrington IPA; Draught Bass H
Opulent lounge bar in smart hotel. Cellars worth a visit. They come complete with ghost called George searching for her lost baby!
⌂Q☎●⌂◐&≠

11–3; 6.30 (7 Sat)–11

Crossways
Valingers Road (off London Road) ☎ (0553) 771947
Greene King XX, IPA, Abbot H
Excellent local with good atmosphere. 1-bar pub, recently renovated. Pub games
☎◐&

11–2.30; 5.30–11

Tudor Rose
St Nicholas Street
☎ (0553) 762824
Adnams Bitter; Bateman XXXB; Draught Bass H
Fine, well restored 15th-century pub near market place. Good for food. Guest beers ☎●⌂◐≠

Try also: London Porterhouse (Greene King)

Methwold Hythe

11–2.30; 6–11

Green Man
Whiteplot Road
☎ (0366) 728357
Adnams Bitter; Greene King IPA, Abbot H
In Methwold itself Watneys have sold the last of 7 pubs. This 17th-century pub at nearby Methwold Hythe is in a rustic setting and has a good fireplace ⌂☎●◐

Mundesley

10.30–2.30; 6–11

Royal Hotel
Paston Road (B1159)
☎ (0263) 720096
Adnams Bitter; Draught Bass; Charrington IPA; Greene King Abbot H
Old beamed bar in hotel with Nelson connections. Serves excellent food at reasonable prices ⌂Q☎●⌂◐&

New Buckenham

11.30–2.30; 7–11

Kings Head
Market Place (B1113)
☎ (0953) 860487
Adnams Extra; Flowers Original H
Unspoilt pub overlooking picturesque village green on

Norfolk

which a May Day fair is held. Village also boasts a castle and 13th-century church

North Wootton

10.30–2.30; 6–11
Red Cat Hotel
Station Road ☎ (0553) 87244
Adnams Bitter; Greene King Abbot; Woodforde's Red Cat Special Bitter
Warm and welcoming pub. An interesting feature is a mummified red cat, which was presented by Globe Hotel, Kings Lynn after being found in attic.

Norwich

11–2.30; 5.30–11
Beehive
30 Leopold Road
☎ (0603) 51628
Courage Best Bitter, Directors
Popular local. Upstairs clubroom is well used (not Sun)

10.30–2.30; 7–11
Champion
101 Chapelfield Road
Wethered Bitter
A trip down Memory Lane – small corner local with cosy atmosphere. Pub games

11–2.30; 6–11
Freemasons Arms
27 Hall Road ☎ (0603) 623768
Courage Best Bitter, Directors
Busy single-bar local in good drinking area. Very friendly pub, popular at lunchtime. Pub games (not Sun)

10.30–2.30; 5.30–11
Gardeners Arms
2–4 Timber Hill
☎ (0603) 621447
Adnams Bitter; Draught Bass; Ind Coope Burton Ale; Tetley Bitter; Woodforde's Wherry Best Bitter, Norfolk Nog (winter)
Busy trendy city centre pub that has an alias – the Murderers, named after an historic misdeed at the pub (not eves)

11–2.30; 5.30–11
Golden Star
Duke Street ☎ (0603) 632447
Greene King XX, IPA, Abbot
Busy, sympathetically refurbished pub close to city centre. Has jazz Mon and folk Thu. Home of Golden Star Morris Men. Pub games (not Sun)

10.30–2.30; 5.30–11
Horse & Dray
Ber Street ☎ (0603) 624741
Adnams Mild, Bitter, Old, Extra, Broadside, Tally Ho (Xmas)
Popular city pub. Regular Friday garden barbecues in summer with live jazz. Roast chestnuts around the open fire in winter. Sun meals only by appointment. Pub games

12–2.30; 6.15–11 (Cannon Bar) 10.30–2.30; 5.30–11 (Quarterdeck Bar)
Hotel Nelson
Prince of Wales Road
Adnams Bitter
Quarterdeck upstairs more like a public bar. Cannon Bar downstairs quiet and serene (Thorpe)

10.30–2.30; 5.30–11
Lawyer
12–14 Wensum Street
☎ (0603) 629878
Adnams Bitter; Courage Directors
City pub near the cathedral. Mid-week disco and live music (jazz Sun). Popular with the young in evenings. Guest beers. Cribbage

10.30–2.30; 5.30–11
Lord Raglan
30 Bishop Bridge Road
☎ (0603) 623304
Flowers Original
Small cosy family boozer, very handy for yacht station. Whitbread guest beers. Pub games

11–2.30; 6 (5.30 summer)–11
Marlborough Arms
43 Spencer Road
☎ (0603) 623689
Courage Best Bitter, Directors
Victorian community pub which caters for all types. Pub games

10.30–2.30; 6–11
Mill Tavern
2 Millers Lane ☎ (0603) 410268
Adnams Mild, Bitter, Extra, Old (winter), **Tally Ho** (Xmas)
Traditional community pub with one single bar. Reasonably priced beer. Opposite Waterloo Park

10.30–2.30; 5.30–11
Plough
58 St Benedict's Street
☎ (0603) 626333
Courage Best Bitter, Directors
A pub full of character in a street full of same. One of the city's oldest buildings

11–2.30; 5.30–11
Pottergate Tavern
Pottergate ☎ (0603) 614589
Greene King IPA, Abbot; Woodforde's Wherry Best Bitter
Interesting city centre pub. Greene King tied house with good range of other beers. Pub games

10.30–2.30; 5.30–11
Prince of Denmark
140 Sprowston Road
☎ (0603) 45084
Courage Best Bitter
Warm, comfortable family pub with a huge plaque of Prince of Denmark

10.30–2.30; 5.30–11
Reindeer
10 Dereham Road
☎ (0603) 66821
Bateman Mild, XXXB; Elgood Bitter; Greyhound Special Bitter; Wadworth 6X
Norwich's only brewery! Popular ale house not to be missed. House-brewed beers stored under blanket pressure. Good value

11–2.30; 5.30–11
Rosary Tavern
95 Rosary Road
☎ (0603) 666287
Adnams Bitter; Bateman XXXB; Marston Pedigree; Woodforde's Wherry Best Bitter, New Rosary
Small, friendly, good value pub with caring staff. Close to Norwich Yacht station. Pub games. Other real ales available (Mon–Fri) (Thorpe)

10.30–2.30; 6–11
Rose Tavern
88 Rupert Street
☎ (0603) 625339
Flowers Original; Wethered Bitter
Friendly 2-bar pub, tucked away behind the hospital. Caters for wide age range. Whitbread guest beers. No food Sun

10.30–2.30; 5–11 (not Sun eve)
Sir Garnet Wolsey
36 Market Place
☎ (0603) 615892
Courage Best Bitter, Directors
Market pub of great character and charm. Just about all that is left worth visiting in a once magnificently pubbed area

10.30–2.30; 5.30–11
Vine
7 Dove Street ☎ (0603) 629258
Courage Best Bitter, Directors
Smallest pub in Norwich with warm friendly local atmosphere. Near tourist office and market. Pub games

10.30–2.30; 5.30–11
White Lion
Oak Street ☎ (0603) 620630
Adnams Mild, Bitter; Greene King Abbot; Woodforde's White Lion, Phoenix XXX
Excellent, basic pub. Popular

233

Norfolk

with wide range of people. Pub games. Guest beers 🍺 🍴

10.30–2.30; 5.30–11
Wild Man
29 Bedford Street
☎ (0603) 627686
Tolly Cobbold Bitter, Original, Old Strong, XXXX H
Attractive and comfortable city centre pub with 1 long bar 🍺 (if dining) 🍴 ♿

Try also: Lillie Langtry, Unthank Road (Greene King)

Old Buckenham

11–2.30; 6–11
Ox & Plough
The Green ☎ (0953) 860004
Adnams Bitter, Old H**, Tally Ho** G**; Charrington IPA; Courage Best Bitter; Woodforde's Wherry Best Bitter** H
This Edwardian pub overlooks the village green, to which the pub owners have rights 🏡 Q 🍴 🚭

Ormesby

11–2.30; 6 (7 winter)–11
Grange
☎ (0493) 731877
Adnams Bitter H
Fine Georgian building set in extensive grounds with farm animals and excellent facilities for children. Guest beers 🏡 🍺 🍴 🚭

Outwell

10.30–2.30; 6.30–11
Red Lion
Wisbech Road (on A1122)
Elgood Bitter H
Old beamed pub with 2 bars; large fireplace in lounge; overlooks the river 🏡 Q 🚭

Poringland

11–2.30; 6–11
Royal Oak
The Street (B1332)
☎ (050 86) 3734
Greene King IPA, Rayment BBA; Samuel Smith OBB; Wethered Winter Royal; Woodforde's Wherry Best Bitter H
Smart comfortable freehouse with extensive menu 🏡 🍴 🚭

Ringstead

11–3; 6.30–11
Gin Trap
☎ (048 525) 264
Adnams Bitter, Old; Woodforde's Gin Trap Bitter H
Formerly a Bullards pub called The Compasses; old traps in pub and stocks on the car park 🏡 🍴

Salhouse

10.30–2.30; 6–11
Lodge
Vicarage Road ☎ (060 53) 2828
Bateman XXXB; Greene King IPA, Abbot; Woodforde's Wherry Best Bitter, Phoenix XXX H
Converted Georgian rectory with delightful gardens. Guest beer. Pub games 🏡 🍺 🍴 ♿

Scole

11–2.30; 6–11
Crossways
Ipswich Road (A140)
☎ (0379) 740638
Adnams Bitter; Flowers Original; Wethered Bitter H
Large inn with many rooms, one being an excellent children's room. Cosy atmosphere 🏡 Q (fruit machine) 🍺 🍴 ♿ 🅿

10.30–2.30; 6–11
Scole Inn
Norwich Road (A140)
☎ (0379) 740481
Adnams Bitter; Broadside; Greene King Abbot H
Large, historic 2-bar free house. Strong emphasis on food. Unspoilt public bar with high backed wooden seats and large open log fire 🏡 Q (fruit machines) 🍺 🍴 ♿ 🅿

Sculthorpe

11–2.30; 6.30–11
Horse & Groom
The Street (off A148)
☎ (0328) 3145
Adnams Bitter, Old; Greene King IPA, Abbot H
Friendly village pub near air base. Long bar serves both lounge area and public bar/games area. Guest beers 🏡 🍺 🍴 ♿

Sea Palling

10.30–2.30; 5.30 (7 winter)–11
Hall Inn
Waxham Road (B1159)
☎ (069 261) 323
Adnams Bitter; Greene King Abbot H
Cosy pub in 16th-century building with pleasant atmosphere. Family room, guest beers, good food, reasonably priced. Tourist board approved. Crib, shove ha'penny 🏡 🍺 🍴 ♿ 🅿 (nearby)

Sedgeford

11–3; 6 (7 winter)–11
King William
☎ (0485) 71765
Adnams Bitter, Old; Draught Bass; Charrington IPA; Greene King Rayment BBA H
Last of 4 pubs in the village, sold off by Watneys. Friendly pub with 2 separate rooms 🍴

Try also: Docking Railway (Pilgrim)

Snettisham

11.30–2.30; 6–11
Rose & Crown
Old Church Road (off A149)
☎ (0485) 41382
Adnams Bitter, Old; Greene King IPA, Abbot; Woodforde's Wherry Best Bitter H
14th-century inn. Children's room and restaurant. Guest beers. Penny Seat played 🏡 Q 🍺 🍴 ♿

Stokesby

11–2.30; 6–11
Ferry
Adnams Extra; Flowers Original; Wethered Bitter H
By River Bure: extensive facilities for holidaymakers but kept local character. Whitbread guest beer. Pub games 🏡 🍺 🍴 ♿

Stow Bardolph

10.30–2.30; 6–11
Hare Arms
Off A10 ☎ (0366) 382229
Greene King IPA, Abbot H
Very busy pub in tiny village off main road. Has old fashioned wooden bar and brick fireplace with seated fender. Conservatory drinking area 🏡 🍺 🍴 ♿

Swaffham

10.30–2.30; 6–11
George Hotel
Station Street (A1065)
☎ (0760) 21238
Adnams Bitter; Greene King IPA, Abbot H
Substantial inn in market town known for historic local character, John Chapman, the Pedlar. Saturday markets are a Norfolk institution. Guest beers 🏡 Q 🍴 (restaurant) ♿

Swanton Morley

11–2.30; 6–11
Darby's
Elsing Road (B1147)
☎ (036 283) 647
Adnams Bitter, Broadside; Hall & Woodhouse Tanglefoot; Woodforde's Wherry Best Bitter H
Newest free house in Norfolk, converted from 2 derelict farm cottages. A place with a warm friendly feel. Children's room 🏡 Q 🍺 🍴

Thetford

11–2.30; 6–11

234

Norfolk

Albion
Castle Street ☎ (0842) 2796
Greene King IPA, Abbot H
Friendly locals' pub. Attractive flint and brick building; nice atmosphere. Pub games ⌂ (⌃

10.30–2.30; 6–11

Central Hotel
Market Place ☎ (0842) 2259
Draught Bass; Flowers Original H
Friendly, cosy, traditional pub with oak beams and photographs of old Thetford. Piano in bar. Guest beers Q ⌃ ⌂ ((not Sun))

11–2.30; 6–11

Chase
New Town (A11)
☎ (0842) 63609
Greene King IPA, Abbot E
New well designed pub on main Norwich–London road. Pub games ⌂ ( ) ⌃ ≠

Thorpe Market

10.30–2.30; 6–11

Suffield Arms
Church Road ☎ (026 379) 461
Adnams Bitter; Courage Best Bitter, Directors; Greene King Abbot H
Friendly country local with good rail access. Strongly seasonal trade, therefore greatly reduced beer range in winter ⌂ ⌃ ( ) ▲ ≠ (Gunton)

Thorpe St Andrew

11–2.30; 5.30–11

Kings Head
36 Yarmouth Road
☎ (0603) 33540
Flowers Original; Wethered Bitter H
Attractive riverside pub on main Norwich–Yarmouth road serving good food. Whitbread guest beers. Pub games ⌂ ⌃ ⌂ ( )

Tibenham

12–2.30 (not Mon–Fri); 7–11

Greyhound
The Street ☎ (037 977) 676
Woodforde's K9 H
Goat-milkers warmly welcomed! Hard to find but well worth the effort. Infamous soggy sandwiches. Guest beers. Pub games ⌂ ⌃ ⌂ ▣ ▲

Trowse

10.00–2.30; 6–11

Crown Point
Kirby Road (A146)
☎ (0603) 625689
Flowers Original; Wethered Bitter H
Popular 2-bar roadside pub with good food. Friendly public bar and comfortable lounge ⌂ ( ) ▣

Walpole Cross Keys

11.30–2.30; 5.30–11

Woolpack
Sutton Road (off A17)
Adnams Bitter; Flowers Original H
Delightful old pub with cosy lounge and separate public bar ⌂ ⌃ ⌂ ( ) ▣ ⌃

Warham

11–2.30; 6 (7 winter)–11

Horseshoes
☎ (0328) 710547
Greene King Abbot; Woodforde's Wherry Best Bitter G
Old, unspoilt pub with 1921 electric pianola and old gramophone (Sat nights). Pub games ⌂ Q ⌃ ⌂ (⌃

Weasenham All Saints

11–2.30; 6–11

Ostrich
On A1065 ☎ (032 874) 221
Adnams Extra H; **Tolly Original** G
Old pub, part of nearby Weasenham Hall Estate. Free house, serving as a charmingly simple village local. Fresh vegetables sold in bar. Pub games ⌂ Q ⌂ ( ) ⌃

Wells-Next-Sea

10.30–2.30; 6–11

Crown Hotel
Buttlands (near A149)
☎ (0328) 710209
Adnams Bitter; Ind Coope Burton Ale; Marston Pedigree H
This fine hotel facing the green is a Tudor building with a Georgian façade. Good food. Children's room. Darts ⌂ ⌃ ⌂ ▣ ( ) ⌃

Welney

10.30–2.30; 7–11

Three Tuns
Bedford Bank East
☎ (035 471) 861
Elgood Bitter H
Simple unchanged fenland local with good conversation. Spectacular riverside setting. A serious dominoes pub. Welney Wildlife Centre nearby ⌂ Q ⌃ ⌂ ⌃

West Beckham

11–2.30; 6–11

Wheatsheaf
The Street ☎ (0263) 822110
Greene King IPA, Abbot H
Converted farmhouse where large fireplace divides single bar area. Friendly atmosphere ⌂ ⌃ ⌂ ▣ ( ) (not Sun) ⌃

West Rudham

11–2.30; 7–11

Dukes Head
Lynn Road ☎ (048 522) 540
Adnams Bitter; Greene King Abbot; Woodforde's Wherry Best Bitter H
Cosy village pub with separate restaurant and public bar adjoining lounge bar. Building dates from 1663. Real beams ⌂ ⌃ ⌂ ( ) ▣ ⌃

West Walton

11–2.30; 6.30–11

King of Hearts
☎ (0945) 584785
Elgood Bitter H
Plush lounge bar, separate restaurant. Beer and food consistently high standard ⌂ ⌂ ( )

Try also: Princess Victoria, Walpole St Peter

Weston Longville

11.30–2.30; 6–11

Parson Woodforde
Church Lane ☎ (0603) 880106
Adnams Bitter; Flowers Original; Hall & Woodhouse Tanglefoot H
Beams a main feature. Friendly atmosphere. Pub games ⌂ Q ⌃ ( ) ⌃

Wighton

11–2.30; 6 (7 winter)–11

Sandpiper
55–57 The Street (off B1105)
☎ (032 872) 752
Samuel Smith OBB; Tolly Cobbold Original; Woodforde's Wherry Best Bitter H
Friendly pub with 3 separate areas for games, bar and quiet corner. Guest beers ⌂ Q ⌃ ⌂ ▣ ( ) ⌃

Wymondham

11–2.30; 7 (5.30 Fri)–11

Feathers
Town Green ☎ (0953) 605675
Adnams Bitter; Greene King Abbot; Marston Pedigree; Woodforde's Tickler Bitter, Wherry Best Bitter H
Town pub popular with young people, but it has quiet areas. Folk club upstairs Thu. Pub games Q ⌂ ( ) ⌃ ≠

235

Northamptonshire

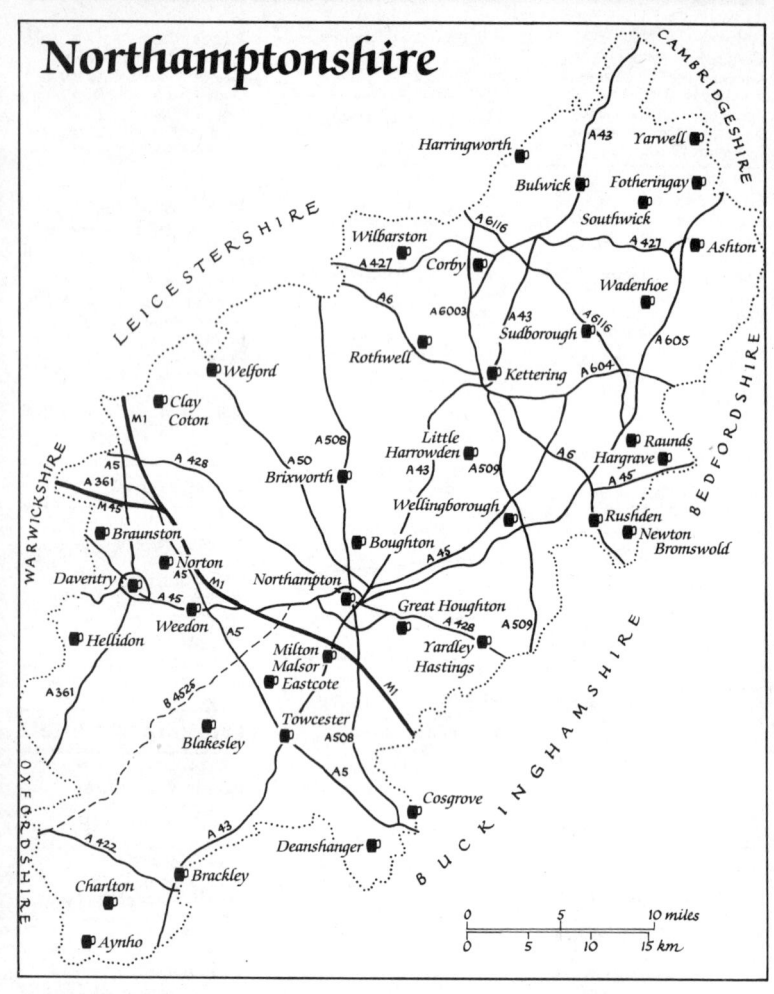

Ashton

11–2.30; 6 (7 winter)–11

Chequered Skipper
Village Green (off A605)
Adnams Bitter; Draught Bass; Hall & Woodhouse Tanglefoot H
Quaint thatched stone pub over looking village green where World Conker Championships are held
🏠⊗❶❷❸

Aynho

11–2.30; 6–11

Great Western Arms
Station Road (B4031)
Hook Norton Best Bitter; Old Hookey H
Old-world pub adjacent to Oxford Canal and on the edge of the Cotswolds. Large garden 🏠Q⊗❶❷❸♿▲⌂

Blakesley

11–2.30; 6.30–11

Bartholomew Arms
High Street ☎ (0327) 860292
Marston Pedigree H
Attractive village local complete with cricketing memorabilia. Annual Soap Box Derby in August
Q⊗▮❶❷❸

Boughton

11–2.30; 5.30–11

Whyte Melville Arms
Church Street (off A508)
Ruddles Best Bitter, County; Webster's Yorkshire Bitter H
Refurbished local retaining public bar. Friendly atmosphere. Occasional charity functions ⊗❶❷❸

Brackley

10.30–2.30; 5.30 (7 Sat)–11

Red Lion
Market Square
☎ (0280) 702228
Wells Eagle Bitter, Bombardier H
17th-century coaching inn with a range of home-cooked food 🏠❶❷❸

Try also: **Plumbers Arms** (Halls)

Braunston

11–2.30; 6–11

Old Plough
82 High Street (off A45)
Ansells Mild, Bitter; Ind Coope Burton Ale H
Comfortable lounge-cum-dining room with genuine wooden beams. Raised narrow garden. Good, reasonably-priced food. Table skittles 🏠⊗❶❷❸♿

Brixworth

236

Northamptonshire

10.30–2.30; 5.30–11
George
Northampton Road (A508)
Wells Eagle Bitter, Bombardier H
Busy village pub with many sports teams. Reputedly haunted ▲ ( ) &

Bulwick

11–2.30; 6–11
Queens Head Inn
Main Street (off A43)
Bateman XXXB; Marston Pedigree H
Pub of character dating from 17th century. Low-beamed ceiling. Good value meals
▲ Q ⊛ ⊛ ( ) (Wed–Sun) &

Clay Coton

12–2.30; 7–11
Fox & Hounds
OS593769 ☎ (0788) 860363
Adnams Bitter; Hook Norton Best Bitter, Old Hookey; Marston Pedigree H
Isolated country pub in pleasant surroundings. Beware keg Ansells bitter on handpump
▲ Q ⊛ ( ) (not Wed, Sun) &

Charlton

10.30–2.30; 5.30–11
Rose & Crown
Main Street ☎ (0295) 811317
Arkells BBB; Everards Tiger; Marston Burton Bitter, Pedigree; Tetley Bitter, Wadworth 6X H
Quiet local in rural conservation area. Non-smoking food bar ▲ Q ⊛ ( )

Corby

11–2.30; 6–11
Knights Lodge
Towerhill Road
Adnams Bitter; Everards Beacon Bitter, Tiger, Old Original H
Large ironstone pub surrounded by modern estates
▲ ⊛ ( ) ⊛ &

Cosgrove

11–2.30; 6.30–11
Barley Mow
7 The Stocks
Ruddles Best Bitter, County; Websters Yorkshire Bitter H
Canalside village pub. Pleasant lounge, separate restaurant and bar. Gun collection ▲ Q ⊛ ⊛ ( ) ▶ &

Daventry

11–2.30; 5.30–11
Coach & Horses
Warwick Street ☎ (0327) 76692
Ind Coope Burton Ale; Tetley Bitter H
Town-centre pub. Live jazz every other Tue ▲ ⊛ ( ) &

10.30–2.30; 5.30–11
Dun Cow
Brook Street ☎ (0327) 71545
Davenports Bitter H
Town-centre gem with hidden-away bar
▲ ( ) (not Sun) ⊛ &

11–2.30; 6–11
Pike & Eel
Tamar Square, Grange Estate
Ansells Mild, Bitter H
Modern split-level estate pub
( ) ▶ (not Sun) ⊛ &

Deanshanger

11.30–2.30; 6–11
Beehive
22 The Green (A422)
☎ (0908) 563441
Wells Eagle Bitter, Bombardier H
Single-room pub with pool table. Popular garden
Q ⊛ (lunch) ⊛ ≈ ( ) &

11–2.30; 6–11
Fox & Hounds
High Street (just off A422)
ABC Best Bitter; Draught Bass; Everards Tiger H
Busy 2-roomed pub with separate dining room. Good value bar and restaurant meals. Piano ▲ Q ⊛ ⊛ ( ) ▶ &

Eastcote

10.30–2.30 (not Mon); 6.30 (6 Mon)–10.30 (11 F, S)
Eastcote Arms
Gayton Road ☎ (0327) 830731
Banks & Taylor Eastcote Ale; Marston Pedigree; Samuel Smith OBB H
Cosy village pub with large collection of prints. Guest beers ▲ Q ⊛ ( ) (Tues–Sat) &

Fotheringay

10.30–2.30; 6 (7 Mon)–11
Falcon
Adnams Bitter; Elgood's Bitter, GSB Strong Bitter; Greene King IPA, Abbot H
18th-century village pub. Basic bar, busy lounge and dining room with good value meals. Near site of Fotheringay Castle
▲ Q ⊛ ⊛ ( ) ▶ (not Mon) ⊛ &

Great Houghton

11–2.30; 6–11
Old Cherry Tree
Cherry Tree Lane (off A423)
Wells Eagle Bitter, Bombardier H
Sympathetically extended 400 year-old whitewashed pub. Dress standards are observed Q ⊛

Hargrave

10.30–2.30; 6–11
Nags Head
Church Street (off A45)
Wells Eagle Bitter H
Quiet pub with plenty of horse brasses, thatched roof and inglenook ▲ Q ⊛ ( ) ⊛ ▲

Harringworth

12–2.30; 7–11
White Swan
Seaton Road ☎ (057 287) 543
Marston Pedigree; Ruddles Best Bitter, County H
Early 16th-century listed building with 2 lounge bars and carvery ▲ Q ≈ ▶

Hellidon

12–2.30; 7–11
Red Lion
Catesby Road ☎ (0327) 61200
Courage Best Bitter, Directors; Davenports Bitter H
Smart, spacious country local, on outskirts of attractive village ▲ Q ⊛ ⊛ ( ) ▶ &

Kettering

11–2.30; 7–11
Alexandra Arms
Victoria Street
Ruddles Best Bitter, County; Webster's Yorkshire Bitter H
Tidy town-centre pub. No food Sun ( ) (Fri & Sat) ⊛

10.30–2.30; 5.30–11
Cherry Tree
Sheep Street ☎ (0536) 514706
Wells Eagle Bitter, Bombardier H
Low-ceilinged pub with village atmosphere – a civilised refuge in the town ( ) ⊛ ≈

Little Harrowden

11–2.30; 7–11
Lamb
Orlingbury Road (off B547)
Wells Eagle Bitter, Bombardier H
Pub dating back to 1780 with cosy lounge ( ) ▶ (not Sun) ⊛

Milton Malsor

11–2.30; 6–11
Greyhound
Towcester Road (A43)
Ruddles Best Bitter; Webster Yorkshire Bitter H
Friendly roadside village pub with good games facilities. Large garden with children's games ▲ ⊛ ≈ ( ) ▶ &

Newton Bromswold

12–2.30; 7–11
Swan
6 Church Lane
Greene King IPA, Abbot H
Village local with 3 small rooms, a games room and a conservatory. Well worth finding. Northants skittles ⊛ ⊛

237

Northamptonshire

Northampton

11–2.30; 5.30 (6.30 winter)–11
Barn Owl
Olden Road, Rectory Farm
Greene King IPA, Abbot H
Popular estate pub with barn owl theme; winner of CAMRA Best New Pub of 1986 award
🍴 🍺 (not Sun) ♿

12–2.30; 5.30–11
Bat & Wickets
117 Bailiff Street
Courage Best Bitter, Directors H
Lively street corner local near the racecourse. Good value lunches 🍴 🍺 (not Sun) 🍷

10.30–2.30; 6–11
Queen Adelaide
50 Manor Road, Kingsthorpe (off A50) ☎ (0604) 714524
Ruddles Best Bitter, County; Webster Yorkshire Bitter H
Friendly village local with Domesday Book on display. Skittles popular Q 🍺 🍷

11.30–2.30; 6–11
Road to Morocco
Bridgewater Drive
Courage Best Bitter, Directors H
Twenty year-old estate pub near Weston Favell village suburb, decorated in Moorish style 🍺

10.30–2.30; 5.30–11
Spread Eagle
147 Wellingborough Road (A4500) ☎ (0604) 24386
Wells Eagle Bitter, Bombardier H
Welcoming pub for both old and young. Sing-a-long twice a week. Games area 🍺 ♿

10.30–2.30; 5.30–11
White Hart (Shipmans)
12 The Drapery ☎ (0604) 36739
Felinfoel Double Dragon H
Long-established town bar with character. Occasional guest beers Q 🍺 ⇌

Norton

12–2.30; 5.30–11
White Horse
Daventry Road
Wells Eagle Bitter, Bombardier H
Attractive country pub with comfortable lounges which tend to be full of diners (need to book). The bar is more games oriented
Q 🍽 🍺 🍷 A

Raunds

11–2.30; 6–11
World Upside Down
Marshalls Road (off A605)
Marston Burton Bitter, Pedigree, Merrie Monk, Owd Rodger H
2 small rooms: split level bar and penny-topped bar in the lounge. Bar billiards 🍺 🍴 🍷 ♿

Rothwell

11–2.30; 5.30–11
Red Lion
Market Square ☎ (0536) 710409
Wells Eagle Bitter, Bombardier H
Keen sports pub. Northants skittles played ⇌ 🍺 🍷

11–2.30; 5.30–11
Rowell Charter
Sun Hill, Kettering Road
Courage Directors; Greene King IPA; Hook Norton Best Bitter; Younger Scotch H
Popular with the younger drinker. Named after fair held Monday after Trinity Sunday. Beers may vary 🍴 🍺 🍷

Rushden

10.30–2.30; 5.30–11
King Edward VII
Queen Street (off A6 one-way)
Wells Eagle Bitter H;
Bombardier G
Back street local, popular with young. Piano in bar. Smaller comfortable lounge 🍺 🍷

Southwick

11–2.30; 6–11
Shuckburgh Arms
Main Street ☎ (0832) 74007
Adnams Bitter; Hook Norton Best Bitter H**; Old Hookey; Marston Pedigree; Wadworth 6X** G
16th-century thatched building with beer garden. Overlooks village cricket pitch
🍴 🍽 🍺 🍷 ♿ A

Sudborough

11.30–2.30; 6–11
Vane Arms
Main Street ☎ (080 12) 3223
Greene King IPA, Abbot; Samuel Smith OBB, Museum Ale H
Attractive, thatched 2-bar village pub. Upstairs dining room. Guest beers. Skittles
🍴 🍺 🍷 (not Sun) 🍷 ♿

Towcester

10.30–2.30; 5.30–11
Plough
Market Square ☎ (0327) 50738
Wells Eagle Bitter H
Pleasant lounge overlooking the Market Square with darker public bar to rear
🍴 Q 🍽 (for meals) 🍺 🍷

Wadenhoe

10.30–2.30; 7 (6 summer)–11
Kings Head
Church Street ☎ (080 15) 222
Adnams Bitter; Marston Pedigree H
16th-century stone-built pub with extensive gardens down to River Nene. Boat moorings. Meals served in summer only
🍴 Q 🍽 🍺 🍷 ♿ (summer)

Weedon

11–2.30; 6–11
Narrowboat Inn
Watling Street
Wells Eagle Bitter, Bombardier H
Busy canalside pub with large garden. Restaurant specialises in Oriental cuisine
🍽 🍺 ⇌ 🍺 ♿

Welford

12–2.30; 7–11
Shoulder of Mutton
12 High Street (A50)
Ruddles Best Bitter; Webster Yorkshire Bitter H
Welcoming 17th-century pub
🍴 🍺 🍺 🍷 ♿ A

Wellingborough

10.30–2.30; 7–11
Horseshoe
36 Sheep Street
Draught Bass; M&B Springfield Bitter H
Lively town-centre pub. Large lounge has stained glass windows 🍺 🍺 (not Sun) 🍷 ♿

10.30–2.30; 5.30–11
Vivian Arms
Knox Road ☎ (0933) 223660
Wells Eagle Bitter, Bombardier H
Excellent friendly back-street local, with small lounge, wood-panelled bar and separate games room
🍴 Q 🍺 🍺 (not Sun) 🍷 ♿ ⇌

Wilbarston

10.30–2.30; 6.30–11
Fox
2 Church Street (off A427)
Marston Border Bitter, Burton Bitter, Pedigree H
Characterful pub in pleasant village with comfortable lounge and Northants skittles in bar 🍴 🍺 🍺 🍷 (not Sun)

Yardley Hastings

11–2.30; 6–11
Red Lion
89 High Street ☎ (0604) 829210
Wells Eagle Bitter, Bombardier H
Neat, low-ceilinged pub in unspoilt village. Separate games room 🍴 Q 🍺 🍺 🍷 ♿

Yarwell

11.30–2.30; 6.30–11
Angel Inn
Main Street ☎ (0780) 782582
Bateman XXXB; Greene King IPA H
Built around 1670 with new room added for games and children 🍴 🍽 🍺 🍺 🍷

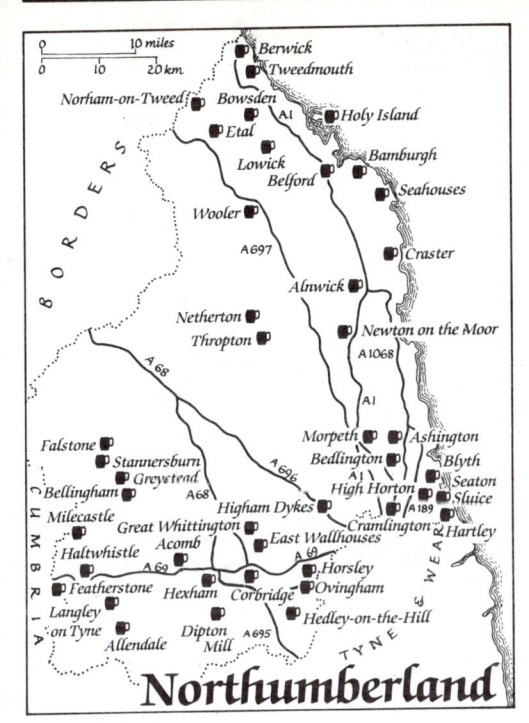

Northumberland

Bellingham

11-3; 6-11
Cheviot
Main Street
McEwan 80/-
Welcoming hostelry in centre of North Tyne Valley village

Berwick

11-3; 6-11
Free Trade Inn
Castlegate ☎ (0289) 806498
Vaux Lorimers Scotch
Bonnie Berwick boozer. Unspoilt interior; fine woodwork, glasswork and partitioning; matched in appeal by local banter!

11-3; 6-11
Meadow House
On A1
Vaux Lorimers Scotch
Most northerly pub in England. Welcoming roadside inn

11-3; 6-11
Pilot Inn
High Greens ☎ (0289) 304214
Broughton Greenmantle Ale
Strong nautical atmosphere in this friendly local

Blyth

11-3; 6-11
Top House
Marlow Street ☎ (0670) 356731
Theakston Best Bitter, XB, Old Peculier
Comfortable, street-corner lounge bar

Bowsden

11-3; 6-11
Black Bull
Off B6525 OS991418
McEwan 80/-
Surprisingly popular pub in isolated village

Corbridge

11-3; 6-11
Wheatsheaf
Watling Street
☎ (0434) 4712020
Vaux Bitter
Friendly hotel in historic town. Impromptu music sessions at weekends. Pub games
Try also: Lion of Corbridge

Craster

11-3; 6-10.30 (11 summer)
Jolly Fisherman
☎ (066 576) 218
Tetley Bitter
Excellent views of harbour and Dunstanburgh Castle; try the crab sandwiches!

Acomb

11-3; 5.30-11
Miners Arms
Main Street ☎ (0434) 603909
Miners Arms Own Ale; Morrels Varsity; Theakston Best Bitter
Friendly village inn

Allendale

11-3; 6-11
Allendale Hotel
☎ (043 483) 246
Theakston Best Bitter, Old Peculier
Stone-built pub in centre of village

Alnwick

11-3; 7-11
Oddfellows Arms
Narrowgate ☎ (0665) 602605
Vaux Samson
No odd fellows here; just friendly locals. Food and accommodation summer only

12-3; 7-11
Tanners Arms
Hotspur Street
☎ (0665) 602553
Taylor Best Bitter, Ram Tam; Belhaven 80/-
Small, stone built corner bar just outside town walls

Ashington

11-3; 5.30-10.30 (11 F, S & summer)
Great Oak
Woodhorn Road (near bus station) ☎ (0670) 811111
Theakston XB, Old Peculier
Small bar with disco extension – not a pub for a quiet drink

Bamburgh

11-3; 6-11
Castle Hotel
Main Street ☎ (066 84) 351
Vaux Lorimers Scotch, Samson
Village inn, in shadow of historic castle

Bedlington

11-3; 6-11
Northumberland Arms
112 Front Street East
☎ (0670) 822754
Greenall Whitley Original
Popular, well established street corner lounge bar in former mining village. Guest beers a speciality

Belford

11-3; 6-11
Salmon
31 High Street ☎ (066 83) 245
Vaux Lorimers Scotch
Long-serving real ale outlet, a short diversion off the A1

239

Northumberland

Dipton Mill

12–3; 6–11

Dipton Mill Inn
Dipton Mill Road (take Whitley Chapel Road from Hexham)
McEwan 80/-; Theakston Bitter, XB Ⓗ
Small country hostelry; with real fires and beams, miles from anywhere ⌂ (2) Q ☎ Å

East Wallhouses

11–3; 6–11

Robin Hood
Military Road ☎ (043 472) 273
Stones Best Bitter Ⓗ
Friendly and cosy free house in remote hamlet on Military Road. Near Hadrian's wall. Pub games ⌂ ☎ ⊛ ◐ ⚒

Etal

11–3; 6–11

Black Bull Inn
Off B6354 ☎ (089 082) 200
Vaux Lorimers Scotch, Samson Ⓗ
Thatched pub in picturesque village; attracts fox-hunting followers. Castle and working watermill nearby ⊛ ◐

Falstone

11–3; 6–11

Black Cock
☎ (0660) 40200
Vaux Samson Ⓗ
Inviting village local near Kielder Water ⌂ ⊛ ⋈ ◐ ⚒

Featherstone

11–3; 7–11 (winter variable)

Wallace Arms
☎ (0498) 21833
Ruddles Best Bitter; Theakston Best Bitter, XB Ⓗ
Secluded country inn with high class restaurant. Always a warm welcome. Guest beers ⌂ Q ☎ ⊛ ◐

Great Whittington

12–3; 6–11

Queens Head
OS005709 ☎ (043 472) 267
Marston Pedigree; Tetley Bitter Ⓗ
Welcoming village inn with cosy atmosphere. Pub games ⌂ ☎ ⊛ ◐ ⚒ &

Greystead

11–3; 6–11

Moorcock
Tarset ☎ (0660) 40269
Tetley Bitter Ⓗ
Friendly wayside inn on route to Kielder Water ⌂ ◐ ⚒

Haltwhistle

11–3; 6–11

Grey Bull
Main Street ☎ (0498) 20298
Theakston Best Bitter Ⓗ
Pleasant, stone-built, old town inn. Several interesting rooms ☎ ⋈ ⊛ ⚒ ≠

Try also: Spotted Cow, New Inn

Hartley

11–3; 6–11

Delaval Arms
A193, S of Seaton Sluice
McEwan 80/-; Younger No.3 Ⓗ
Large, many-roomed listed building; famous blue stone near entrance ⊛ ◐ ⚒

Hedley-on-the-Hill

11–3; 6–11

Feathers
2 miles S of Prudhoe
☎ (0661) 843607
Theakston Best Bitter, XB Ⓗ
Friendly and welcoming pub in hilltop village. Guest beers ⌂ Q ⊛ ◐

Hexham

11–3; 6–11

Coach & Horses
32 Priestpopple
☎ (0434) 603132
Tetley Bitter; Marston Pedigree Ⓗ
Old coaching inn. Unspoilt bar and comfortable lounge/dining area ☎ ◐ ⚒ & ≠

Higham Dykes

11–3; 6–11

Waggon Inn
Belsay Road (A696)
☎ (06 181) 666
Draught Bass Ⓗ
Inviting roadside inn on high road to Scotland Q ◐ ▶ ⚒

High Horton

11–3; 6–11

Three Horse Shoes
Hathery Lane, High Horton (off A189) ☎ (0670) 822410
Tetley Bitter Ⓗ
Surprisingly spacious but cosy pub. Always a warm welcome. Guest beers ⌂ ☎ ⊛ ◐

Holy Island

11–3; 7–11 (variable especially winter)

Northumberland Arms
Holy Island (in village)
☎ (0289) 89307
Tetley Bitter; Taylor Landlord; Younger Scotch; Whitbread Castle Eden Ale Ⓗ
Cosy and floorboarded free house situated on historic island – cut off from mainland at high tide. Meals summer only ⌂ ☎ ⊛ ◐

Horsley

11–3; 6–11

Crown & Anchor
☎ (0661) 853105
Vaux Lorimers Scotch, Samson Ⓗ
Fine views over Tyne valley with 2 good log fires. Pub games ⌂ ☎ ⊛ ◐ ⚒

Langley-on-Tyne

12–3; 7–11 (winter variable)

Carts Bog Inn
On A686 near Hexham
☎ (043 484) 338
Marston Pedigree; Tetley Bitter Ⓗ
Remote stone pub on edge of moors – its log fire is needed in winter. Listed camping and caravan site ⌂ ⊛ ◐ Å

Lowick

11–3; 6–11

Black Bull
On B6353 ☎ (0289) 88228
McEwan 70/-, 80/- Ⓗ
Renowned, quiet village inn. Good food and good service ⌂ ⊛ ⋈ ◐

Try also: White Swan

Milecastle

11–3; 6–11

Milecastle Inn
Military Road ☎ (0498) 20682
Theakston Best Bitter, XB Ⓗ
Small cosy pub on Military Road near Hadrian's Wall. Restaurant well known for its game dishes ⌂ Q ⊛ ◐

Morpeth

11–3; 6–11

Wansbeck
Abbey Meadows
☎ (0670) 512575
Bass Extra Light; Stones Best Bitter Ⓗ
Large 2-roomed estate pub above town. Pub games ⚒

Try also: Joiners Arms

Netherton

11–3; 6–10 (hours may vary)

Star Inn
OS989077 ☎ (0669) 30238
Whitbread Castle Eden Ale Ⓖ
Unspoilt gem in isolated village. Disused cock-fighting pit on hill opposite ⌂ Q ⚒

Newton on the Moor

11–3; 6–11

Cook & Barker
Off A1 ☎ (066 575) 234
McEwan 80/- Ⓗ
Warm, inviting country local with welcoming open fires. Separate sitting room ⌂ ⊛ ◐

240

Northumberland

Norham-on-Tweed

11–3; 6–11
Masons Arms
West Street (off B6470)
☎ (0289) 82326
Vaux Lorimers Scotch H
Excellent, traditional bar; a must. Fishing rights on the River Tweed

Ovingham

11–3; 6–11
Bridge End Inn
West Road ☎ (0661) 32219
Marston Pedigree; Tetley Bitter H
Comfortable old inn in picturesque Tyne Valley village. Pub games

Seahouses

11–3; 6–11
Black Swan
Union Street ☎ (0665) 720277
Vaux Lorimers Scotch, Samson H
Unpretentious pub above the harbour, hidden away from the amusement arcades and candyfloss (summer)

Seaton Sluice

11–3; 6–11
Waterford Arms
☎ (091 237) 0450
Vaux Samson H
Large pub off main road; fish a speciality. Local paintings in lounge

Stannersburn

11–3; 6–11
Pheasant Inn
☎ (0660) 40382
McEwan 80/– H
300 year-old coaching inn on road to Kielder Water

Thropton

11–3; 6–11
Cross Keys
☎ (0669) 20362
Draught Bass H
Old village pub in pleasant surroundings. Food summer only

Tweedmouth

11–3; 6–11
Harrow
Main Street ☎ (0289) 305451
Vaux Lorimers Scotch H
Convivial local near harbour; mellow panelled interior

Wooler

11–3; 6–10.30
Anchor Inn
Cheviot Street ☎ (0668) 81412
Vaux Samson H
Friendly pub in market town at foot of Cheviots

11–3; 6–10.30
Ryecroft Hotel
Ryecroft Way ☎ (0668) 81459
Marston Pedigree; Tetley Bitter; Yates Bitter H
Well-run family hotel with reputation for good food

ON THE PROFESSION ...

an alternative guide

Beer Bore someone who knows more about beer than you do

Beer Writer artist

Brewers' Society League of brewery owners. In recent years a tradition has emerged that during his term of office the Chairman of the Brewers Society will try to take over and/or close as many of his rivals' breweries as possible

Brewery Closure rubble without a cause

Pure Genius the ability to boost the value of your shares whilst escaping a spell in chokey

Free House theoretically allowed to sell the products of any brewery or other company. In practice the majority of so-called Free Houses have loans from large breweries which effectively ban the sale of rival beers

Manager licensee paid a wage to run a pub. Dying breed in many companies

Tenant licensee who pays a large rent to a brewer to run a tied house

Tied House pub owned by a brewery and thus allowed to sell only the products sanctioned (and usually produced) by its owner

Nottinghamshire

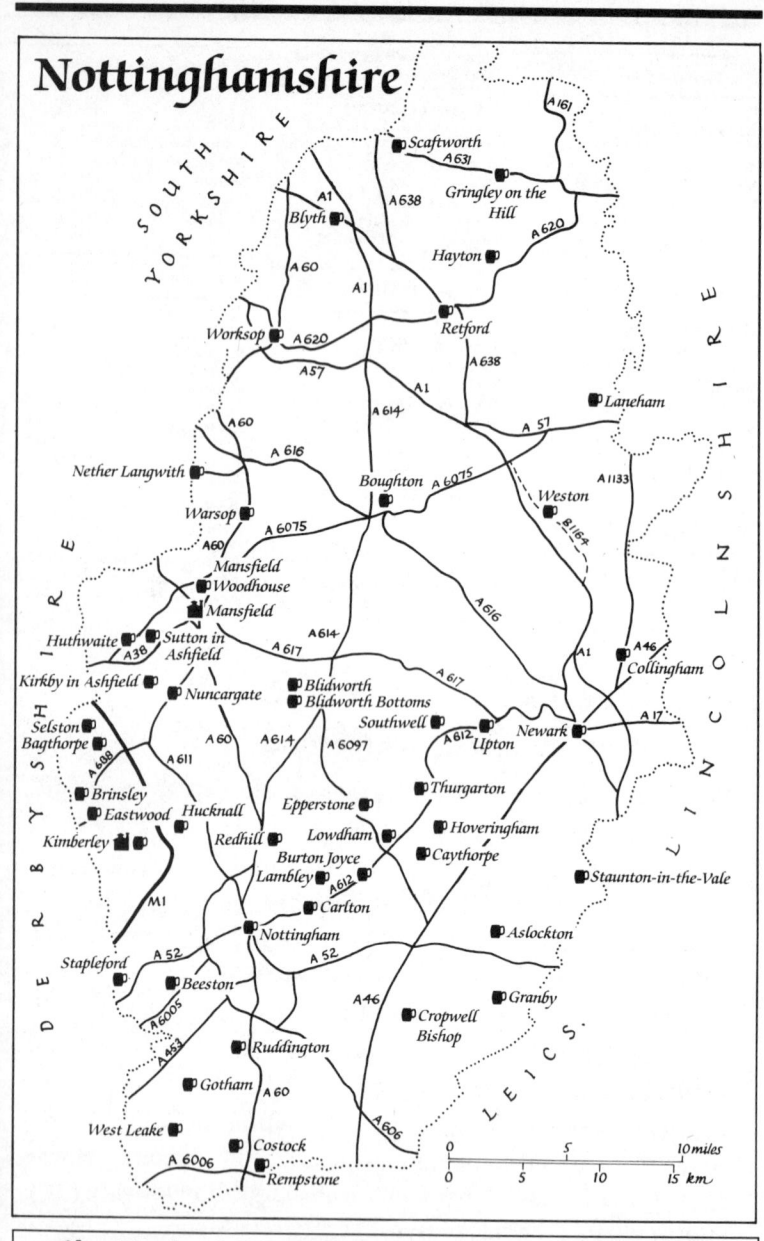

Hardys & Hansons, Kimberley; **Mansfield**, Mansfield

Aslockton

11–2.30; 6–11

Cranmer Arms
Main Street (near station)
☎ (0949) 50362
Home Bitter H
Cosy friendly village pub which holds many collections for charities. Winter meetings in lounge free. A genuine community centre. Long alley and table skittles

Bagthorpe

11–3; 6 (6.30 winter)–10.30 (11 F,S)

Dixies Arms
School Lane (off B600)
☎ (0773) 810505
Home Mild, Bitter H
Delightful country local in an attractive woodland setting. Extensive garden area and family room. Pub games

Beeston

10.30–2.30; 7–11 (summer eves – may open earlier)

Boat & Horses
Trent Road, Rylands
☎ (0602) 258589

242

Nottinghamshire

Home Mild, Bitter E
Convivial local; close to canal and catering for all sections of the community
⚫🍴 (Mon–Fri)

11–2.30; 6–11
Malt Shovel
Union Street ☎ (0602) 228551
Shipstone Mild, Bitter E
Modernised side-street pub, just off main shopping area. TV and pool table in bar; lounge more sedate. Landlord is winner of cellar-keeping award ⚫🍴 (Mon–Fri)

10.30–2.30; 5.30–11
Queens Hotel
Queens Road ☎ (0602) 225262
Shipstone Mild, Bitter E
Large and multi-roomed pub with all the facilities of a traditional community local, including pub games
⚫🍴 (not Sun) 🍺 (ask)

Blidworth

10.30–3; 6–10.30 (11 F,S)
Bird in Hand
Main Street ☎ (0623) 792356
Mansfield Riding Traditional Bitter, Old Baily H
This comfortable and friendly pub has the finest view in Nottinghamshire. Games available ⚫🍴

11–3; 6–10.30 (11 F, S)
Black Bull Inn
Main Street ☎ (0623) 792291
Shipstone Mild, Bitter H & E
Old village inn with a charm and appeal all its own. Pub games ⚫🍴

Blidworth Bottoms

11–3; 6–10.30 (11 F, S)
Fox & Hounds
Off A614 ☎ (0623) 792383
Hardys & Hansons Best Mild, Best Bitter H & E
Small village local in secluded hamlet. Family room and large garden. Pub games ⚫🍴 (till 1.30 Sun)

Blyth

11–3; 6.30–11
Angel
High Street (A634, off A1) ☎ (090 976) 213
Hardys & Hansons Best Bitter E
Oldest coaching inn in North Nottinghamshire. Huge fires all winter ⚫🍴

Boughton

11–3; 7–11
Harrow
Tuxford Road ☎ (0623) 860218
Whitbread Castle Eden Ale H
Very busy pub on edge of mining village ⚫🍴

Brinsley

10.30–2.30; 7–11
Durham Ox
High Street, New Brinsley ☎ (0773) 712659
Hardys & Hansons Best Mild, Best Bitter H
Mysterious village local dating from 1836. Old beer cooling well (beneath gents toilets). Pub games ⚫🍴

Burton Joyce

11–2.30; 5.30–11
Wheatsheaf Inn
Church Road (A612) ☎ (060 231) 3298
Home Mild, Bitter E
Large, traditional pub with excellent restaurant and bar meals. Pub games (restaurant) ⚫🍴

Carlton

11–2.30; 5.30–11
Fox & Hounds Hotel
Station Road (B686) ☎ (0602) 878681
Home Mild, Bitter E
Large traditional pub on city outskirts. 3-roomed local. Jocular landlord! Pub games ⚫🍴

Caythorpe

10.30–2.30; 6–11
Black Horse
Main Street ☎ (0602) 663520
Shipstone Bitter H
Unspoilt 18th-century inn. Reputedly a haunt of Dick Turpin whose secret cupboard may be viewed. Special occasion meals by arrangement
⚫🍴 (not Sun)

Try also: **Old Volunteer** (Hardys & Hansons)

Collingham

10.30–2.30; 6.30–11
Royal Oak
High Street
John Smith Bitter H
Multi-roomed local, popular with all ages, in centre of large village 🍴

Try also: **Grey Horse** (Home)

Costock

10.30–2.30; 6–11
Generous Briton
14 Main Street (off A60) ☎ (050 982) 2347
John Smith Bitter H
Former old coaching inn. Friendly local with good home-cooked food
⚫🍴

10.30–2.30; 6–11
Red Lion
Old Main Road (off A60) ☎ (050 982) 2535
Shipstone Mild, Bitter H
Mock-Tudor hostelry with cosy oak panelled lounge and convivial bar
⚫🍴 (not Sun)

Cropwell Bishop

11–2.30; 6–11
Lime Kiln
Kinoulton Road OS678345 ☎ (0949) 81540
Home Mild, Bitter E
Large coaching inn at rural crossroads. Pub games played
⚫🍴 (not Tues/Sun)

Eastwood

10.30–2.30; 6–11
New Inn
94 Newthorpe Common (off B6010) ☎ (0773) 713602
Home Mild, Bitter E
Unpretentious working class local. Pub games

Try also: **Lord Raglan** (Hardys & Hansons)

Epperstone

11–2.30; 6–11
Cross Keys
Main Street (just off A6097 N of Lowdham) ☎ (0602) 663033
Hardys & Hansons Best Mild, Best Bitter H & E
Very friendly old wayside inn. Always a good conversation or story-telling session in the bar. Jazz records on Tue; folk and Morris on Thu. Good food; pub games
⚫🍴

Gotham

11–2.30; 6–11
Sun Inn
The Square ☎ (0602) 830484
Everards Beacon Bitter, Tiger, Old Original H
Attractive, friendly village local. Food served in lounge; conversation in bar. Guest beers. Games ⚫🍴

Granby

10.30–2.30; 5.30–11
Boot & Shoe
Church Street ☎ (0949) 50354
Marston Pedigree; Theakston XB H
Hidden at the back of village. Country pub with small quiet room, plus popular lounge area. Skittle alley. Guest beers ⚫🍴

Try also: **Marquis of Granby** (Home)

Gringley on the Hill

11–3; 7–11
Blue Bell
High Street (off A621)

243

Nottinghamshire

☎ (0777) 817406
Bass Mild XXXX, Draught Bass H
Welcoming village pub with separate games room

Hayton

10.30–3; 6–11

Boat Inn
Main Street (B1403)
☎ (0777) 700158
John Smith Bitter; Whitbread Trophy, Castle Eden Ale H
Busy pub on the Chesterfield Canal with own moorings. Popular restaurant. Guest beers

Hoveringham

12–2.30; 6.30–11

Marquis of Granby
Main Street (off A612)
☎ (0602) 663080
Marston Pedigree H
Unspoilt country free house with lounge and cottage bars. Now family-owned. Near to River Trent. Popular with locals and tourists alike. Guest beers. No meals Sun

Try also: Reindeer (Mansfield)

Hucknall

10.30–2.30; 6–11

Red Lion
High Street ☎ (0602) 632174
Home Mild, Bitter E
Multi-roomed, town centre locals' pub. Spartan furnishings but a friendly welcome awaits. Pub games

Huthwaite

11–3; 6 (6.30 winter)–10.30

Miners Arms
Blackwell Road (B6026)
Home Bitter H
Quiet village inn which has remained relatively unspoilt. A landlady of long standing. Pub games played

Kimberley

10.30–2.30; 5.30–11

Lord Clyde
Main Street ☎ (0602) 384907
Hardys & Hansons Best Mild, Best Bitter H
Welcoming village pub; always busy. You will soon become convinced that Kimberley is an ideal place for a short pub crawl! Pub games

10.30–2.30; 5.30 (6 Sat)–11

Nelson & Railway
Station Road (opposite brewery) ☎ (0602) 382177
Hardys & Hansons Best Bitter H & E
Delightful village inn which retains its original character. Cheap B & B. Beware the mild which is not real. Cheap beer 5.30–7 Mon – Fri
(until 8)

10.30–2.30; 6–11

Queens Head
Main Street ☎ (0602) 382117
Hardys & Hansons Best Mild, Best Bitter E
Vibrant and lively local. Pub games played

10.30–2.30; 6–11

Stag Inn
67 Nottingham Road
☎ (0602) 383151
Shipstone Mild, Bitter E
Superb example of an old village inn dating back to 1537. Pub games
(early eve)

11–2.30; 6–11

White Lion
Swingate (off Main Street via Green Lane and High Street)
☎ (0602) 383687
Shipstone Mild, Bitter E
Fascinating little pub with a real local village atmosphere. Pub games available

Try also: Queen Adelaide (Hardys & Hansons)

Kirkby in Ashfield

11–3; 6–10.30 (11 F, S)

Ashfields Hotel
Sutton Road ☎ (0623) 554074
Home Mild, Bitter H
Friendly 3-roomed roadside hotel. Plain locals' bar with pool table. Warm, cosy lounge and smokeroom

Lambley

11–2.30; 6–11

Woodlark Inn
Church Street ☎ (0602) 312535
Home Bitter E
Friendly, quiet village pub. Upstairs room has pool table and juke box. Long alley skittles outside

Laneham

12–3; 7–11

Butchers Arms
Main Street (off A57)
☎ (077 785) 255
Ind Coope Burton Ale; Marston Pedigree H
Popular village free house. Games-oriented public bar, quieter traditional lounge. Separate family room

Lowdham

11–2.30; 5.30–11

Old Ship
Main Street (off A612)
☎ (0602) 663049
John Smith Bitter H
Pleasant pub situated in heart of village

11.30–2.30; 6.30–11

Worlds End
Plough Lane (off A6097)
Marston Burton Bitter, Pedigree H
Flagpole in car park helps to locate this interesting country pub. Games available
(not Sun)

Mansfield Woodhouse

11–3; 7–10.30 (11 F, S)

Greyhound Inn
82 High Street (off A60)
☎ (0623) 21047
Home Mild, Bitter E
Good honest popular local. Pub games played

Nether Langwith

11.30–3; 7–11

Jug & Glass
Queens Walk (A632)
☎ (0623) 742283
Hardys & Hansons Best Mild, Best Bitter E
Low stone pub on village green. Pub games

Newark

10.30–2.30; 6–11

Malt Shovel
Northgate (A46/A17)
Ward Sheffield Best Bitter H
Deservedly popular pub on edge of town centre. Stands out among other pubs in town. Guest beers
≉ (Castle & Northgate)

10.30–2.30; 6–11

Old Kings Arms
Kirkgate (off A46)
Marston Burton Bitter, Merrie Monk, Pedigree, Owd Rodger H
Workaday local which gets busy in evenings. Popular with younger clientele
≉ (Castle)

Try also: Newcastle Arms (Home)

Nottingham

11.30–2.30; 6–11

Castle
202 Lower Parliament Street (near ice stadium)
☎ (0602) 504601
ABC Best Bitter; Ind Coope Best Bitter, Burton Ale H
Modernised town pub on edge of city. Comfortably furnished. Pool table
(not Sun)

10.30–2.30; 6–11

Framesmiths Arms
287 Main Street, Bulwell
☎ (0602) 278394
Shipstone Bitter H & E
Locally known as the Monkey – many a tale as to why. Popular, long narrow bar; side

Nottinghamshire

passage and hatch service to the "best" room

11–2.30; 5.30–11
Loggerheads Inn
59 Cliff Road (behind Canal Street) ☎ (0602) 580653
Home Mild, Bitter
Located under an imposing cliff, this city pub has a cave at the rear which reputedly was used for cock-fighting. Long alley skittles. Handy for Broad Marsh shopping centre

11–2.30; 5.30–11
Magpies
Meadow Lane ☎ (0602) 863851
Home Mild, Bitter
Comfortable lounge complements more traditional bar (with pool). Close to Notts County and Forest football grounds, cricket ground, and Colwick Racecourse (Mon – Fri until 7.30)

10.30–2.30; 5.30–11
Milestone
Glaisdale Drive, Wollaton (off Trowell Road, A609) ☎ (0602) 296224
Banks's Mild, Bitter
Large modern building on light industrial estate. 'Olde barn'-style lounge; separate, more spartan but pleasant bar. The first Banks's pub to be built in the city

10.30–2.30; 5.30–11
Narrow Boat
Canal Street ☎ (0602) 501947
Shipstone Mild, Bitter
Comfortable pub near Broad Marsh shopping centre. Bar billiards (not Sun)

11–2.30; 5.30–11
Norfolk Hotel
68 London Road (near Trent Bridge in Meadows area) ☎ (0602) 863003
Home Mild, Bitter
Traditional local. Indoor long alley skittles in public bar. No food served at weekend

10.30–2.30; 5.30 (6 Sat)–11
Old Angel
7 Stoney Street ☎ (0602) 502303
Home Mild, Bitter
Unspoilt centuries-old pub in the historic lace market. Public bar extended to accommodate pool table

10.30–2.30; 5.30–11
Quorn Hotel
Hucknall Road, Sherwood ☎ (0602) 625267
Home Mild, Bitter
Typical town local, able to boast inclusion in every edition of Good Beer Guide

11.30–2.30; 5.30–11
Sir Charles Napier
North Sherwood Street ☎ (0602) 418197
Flowers IPA; Whitbread Castle Eden Ale
Comfortable one-roomer, decorated in Laura Ashley style. Vegetarian dishes on menu

11.30–2.30; 5.30–11
Stag & Pheasant
245 Lower Parliament Street ☎ (0602) 506414
Home Mild, Bitter
Expansive 4-roomed pub with something for all. One of the cheapest pints in town. Table and long alley skittles. Deservedly popular

11–2.30; 6 (5.30 Th, F, S)–11
Trip to Jerusalem
1 Brewhouse Yard, Castle Road (below Castle Rock) ☎ (0602) 473171
Draught Bass; Marston Pedigree; Ruddles Best Bitter; Samuel Smith OBB; Ward Sheffield Best Bitter
Nottingham's most famous inn; known throughout the world. The old-world atmosphere and cobwebs in the upstairs room have to be seen to be believed. The cellars are old caves. Guest beers weekly

10.30–2.30; 6–11
Vine
Handel Street, Sneinton (near market)
Home Mild, Bitter
Old-fashioned local, unaltered since '30s. Rare corner entrance. A 'no food, no frills' pub with conversation usually the only sound. Games

Nuncargate

11–3; 6–10.30 (11 F, S)
Cricketers Arms
Nuncargate Road (off A611)
Home Mild, Bitter
16th-century ex-farmhouse. Lounge has original low beams and is dedicated to Nuncargate's most famous son, Harold Larwood. Large drinking garden and children's playing field. Pub games

Redhill

10.30–2.30; 6–11
Ram Inn
244 Mansfield Road ☎ (0602) 267461
Shipstone Mild, Bitter &
Comfortable pub. Pool in bar, handpumps in smoke room. Family room

10.30–2.30; 5.30–11
Wagon & Horses
260 Mansfield Road ☎ (0602) 265212
Home Mild, Bitter
Very good traditional pub, unspoilt by pool, fruit machines or juke box, just traditional games. A good ale house. Run by ex-Forest footballer

Rempstone

11–2.30; 6–11
White Lion
Main Street (A6006) ☎ (0509) 880669
Shipstone Bitter
Small whitewashed village inn with beamed ceiling, quarry tile floor and much brassware

Retford

10.30–3; 7–11
Albert Hotel
Albert Road ☎ (0777) 708694
Webster Yorkshire Bitter; Whitbread Castle Eden Ale
Popular pub south of town centre, with good cheap food, bar billiards and darts

11–3; 6–11
Market Hotel
West Carr Road, Ordsall ☎ (0777) 703278
Adnams Bitter; Bateman XXXB; Cameron Strongarm; Tetley Bitter; Timothy Taylor Landlord
Friendly busy pub with good food; reached from railway station by footpath under tracks

10.30–3 (4 Sat); 7–11
New Sun
Spital Hill (on Ring Road) ☎ (0777) 703297
Ward Darley Dark Mild; Thorne Best Bitter
A pub with homely atmosphere; popular with older clientele

10.30–3; 6.30–11
Turks Head
Grove Street ☎ (0777) 702742
Ward Sheffield Best Bitter
Town centre pub with attractive oak panelling

Try also: Clinton Arms (John Smith)

Ruddington

11–2.30; 5.30–11
Red Lion
1 Easthorpe Street ☎ (0602) 844654
Home Mild, Bitter
Oldest pub in the village, dating from 1830. Typical 1970s brewery conversion. Known locally as "Tillos" after former landlord

10.30–2.30; 6–11
Three Crowns
23 Easthorpe Street

245

Nottinghamshire

☎ (0602) 213226
Shipstone Mild, Bitter H & E
Comfortable and friendly hostelry with separate games room

Scaftworth

12–2.30 (closed Mon – Thu); 7–11
King William
1 mile from Bawtry A63
☎ (0302) 710292
Cameron Strongarm; Everards Old Original; Whitbread Castle Eden Ale H
Scaftworth estate pub. Several small traditionally furnished rooms. Separate games room. Home-cooked food. New garden and barbecue area

Selston

11–3; 8.30–10.30 (11 F, S)
Horse & Jockey
Church Lane (off B600 and Commonside, Pinxton)
Shipstone Bitter H
Unspoilt rambling old alehouse on edge of village. Pub games played

11–3; 6–10.30 (11 F, S)
White Lion
Nottingham Road
☎ (0773) 810375
Shipstone Mild, Bitter H
Lively roadside local, offering good food. Popular with young people. Pub games (not Mon)

Southwell

10.30–2.30; 6–11
Newcastle Arms
Station Road (by Southwell Trail) ☎ (0636) 813094
Shipstone Mild, Bitter E
Homely traditional pub with the only real mild in Southwell

Try also: **Crown** (Mansfield)

Stapleford

10.30–2.30; 6–11
Old Cross
26 Church Street
☎ (0602) 394927
Shipstone Mild, Bitter E
Excellent, lively town centre local with friendly atmosphere. Island bar divides one large room into separate drinking areas. Noisy jukebox at times. Covered skittle alley at rear

Staunton-in-the-Vale

10.30–2.30; 6–11
Staunton Arms
Main Street (2½ miles W of A1 at Long Bennington, Lincs)
OS805435 ☎ (0400) 81062
Marston Pedigree; Tetley Bitter H
Friendly free house in isolated position near Vale of Belvoir. Guest beers

Sutton in Ashfield

11–3; 6–10.30 (11 F, S)
Cart & Horse Inn
Station Road ☎ (0623) 554570
Mansfield Riding Traditional Bitter H
Spacious roadside local with central bar. 2 distinct drinking areas. Family room. Pub games (not Sun)

11–3; 6–10.30 (11 F, S)
Duke of Sussex
Alfreton Road, Fulwood (A38 near M1 Jct 28)
☎ (0623) 552560
Hardys & Hansons Best Mild, Best Bitter E
Lively bar and smart lounge on outskirts of town. Good value food. Pub games. Has been in every edition of Good Beer Guide (not Mon)

10.30–3; 7–10.30 (11 F, S)
Market Hotel
Market Place ☎ (0623) 552961
Home Mild, Bitter H
Basic traditional boozer, built in 1905. Pub games played

11–3; 7–10.30 (11 F, S)
Railway Inn
High Pavement (off A615)
☎ (0623) 555476
John Smith Bitter H
Homely, popular town local. Unusually shaped interior. Attractively fitted. Popular with the young. Pub games

Thurgarton

10.30–2.30; 6–11
Coach & Horses
Main Street ☎ (0636) 830257
Home Mild, Bitter E
Excellent village local. Comfortable and spacious. Collection of bottled beer displayed in lounge. Table skittles

Upton

10.30–2.30; 6.30–11
Cross Keys
Main Street (A612)
☎ (0636) 813269
Flowers Original; Marston Border Bitter, Pedigree H
Interesting pub in conservation area. Popular with all ages. Regular live music

Try also: **French Horn** (John Smith)

Warsop

11–3; 6–11
Hare & Hounds
Church Street (off A60)
☎ (0623) 842440
Hardys & Hansons Best Mild, Best Bitter H
Town centre pub with bar and lounge to cater for all. Pub games

West Leake

10.30–2.30; 6–11
Star (Pit House)
Near M1 Jct 24
☎ (050 982) 2233
Draught Bass; M & B Springfield Bitter H
Fine old coaching inn – the epitome of the traditional English pub bar. Highly recommended for its weekday lunchtime buffet. Handy for East Midlands Airport
Q (Mon – Fri)

Weston

10.30–2.30; 6.30–11
Boot & Shoe
Old Great North Road (off A1)
☎ (0636) 821257
Younger Scotch H
Imposing pub on edge of village. Rooms to suit all tastes. Large garden. Beer choice subject to change

Worksop

11–3; 6–11
French Horn
Potter Street (opposite town hall) ☎ (0909) 472958
Stones Best Bitter E
With its tiled exterior, busy bars and quiet snug, this is how a town pub should be. Pub games played Q (snug)

11–3; 7–11
Greendale Oak
Norfolk Street (off A60)
☎ (0909) 481373
Stones Best Bitter E
Sandwiched in a terraced row. Has keen darts team

11–3; 7–11
White Lion
Park Street (B6005)
☎ (0909) 478125
Whitbread Castle Eden Ale H
Free House which has lost none of its character with recent conservatory-style extension Q

Oxfordshire

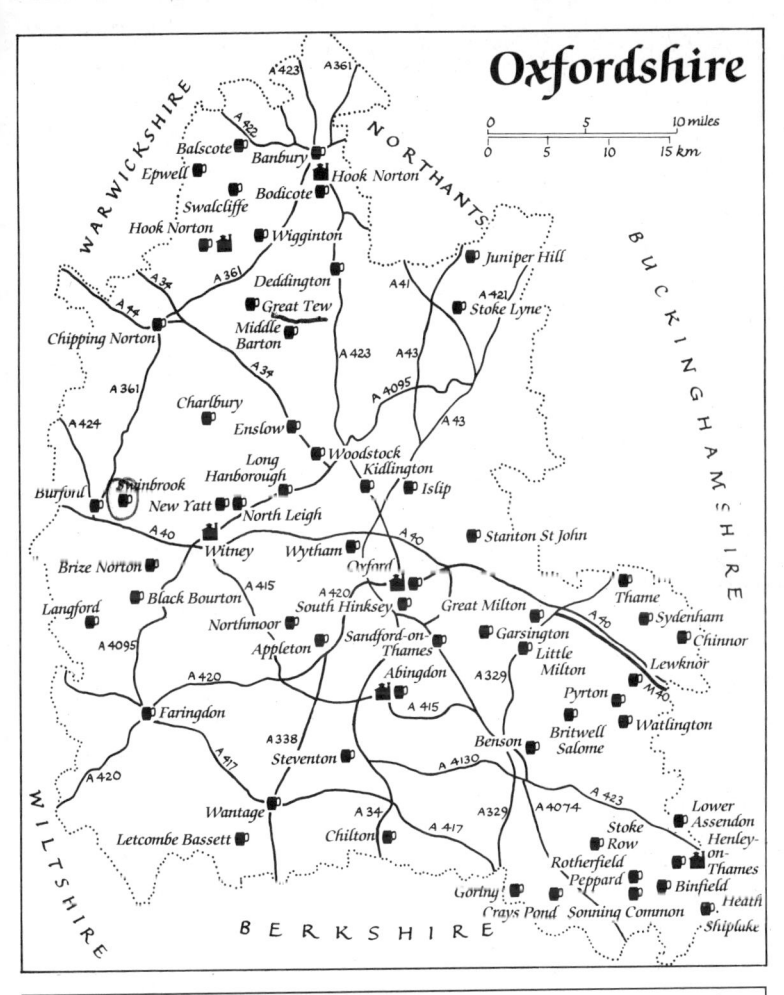

Brakspear, Henley-on-Thames; *Glenny*, Witney; *Hook Norton*, Hook Norton, Banbury; *Morland*, Abingdon; *Morrells*, Oxford

Abingdon

10–2.30; 6–11
Fitzharris Arms
Thornhill Walk, Wootton Road
☎ (0235) 23281
Morrell Dark Mild, Bitter H
Plain 1950s estate pub with 3 large bars. Disco Fri, country music Tue, and live music Sat. Aunt Sally pitch

10–2.30; 6–11
Old Anchor
St Helen's Wharf
☎ (0235) 21726
Morland Mild, Bitter H
Traditional old pub on the Thames between magnificent 15th-century almshouses and original junction of Wilts & Berks canal. Drink in 3 bars, the corridor, stand on the pavement or moor up

10–2.30; 6–11
Ox Inn
15 Oxford Road
☎ (0235) 20962
Morland Mild, Bitter, Best Bitter H
Popular town pub in residential area north of town centre. Busy but well-appointed public bar; extensive but inexpensive menu. Boots and overalls drink elsewhere. No food Sun

Appleton

10.30–2.30; 6–11
Plough
7 Eaton Road ☎ (0865) 862441
Morland Mild, Bitter H
Perfect example of a friendly traditional country local

Balscote

11–2.30; 6–11
Butchers Arms
Off A422, 4 miles from Banbury OS392418
☎ (029 573) 750
Hook Norton Mild G, **Best Bitter** H
Comfortable traditional

Oxfordshire

1-bar country pub
⌂Q☆⊛((summer) &

Banbury

10.30–2.30; 6–11

Elephant & Castle
6 Middleton Road
☎ (0295) 50258
Morrell Bitter H
Lively, popular down to earth pub ⊛⌂(&≠

10.30–2.30; 6–11

Lismore Hotel
Oxford Road (A423)
Bodicote Bitter G; **Hook Norton Bitter** H
Small, residential hotel; clean and smart ⌂Q⌂⊕

10.30–2.30; 6–11

Wheatsheaf
68 George Street (off High Street) ☎ (0295) 66525
M&B Mild, Springfield Bitter, Brew XI H
Popular town-centre pub, formerly a coaching inn
⌂⊕&≠

Benson

11–2.30; 6–11

Three Horseshoes
Oxford Road (off A423)
☎ (0491) 38242
Boddingtons Bitter; Brakspear Bitter, Special H
Friendly local with good food; separate dining room
⌂Q⊛(⊕&Å

Binfield Heath

11–2.30; 6–11

Bottle & Glass
Off A4155 OS743793
☎ (0491) 575755
Brakspear Bitter, Special, Old H
Popular thatched, low-beamed 17th-century pub with stone-flagged floors and scrubbed wooden tables. Large garden. Excellent home-cooked food, including vegetarian (not Sun)
⌂Q⊛(⊕&

Black Bourton

12–2.30; 7–11

Horse & Groom
Burford Road (off A4095)
☎ (0993) 842199
Morland Bitter; Wadworth 6X H
Large village pub with locals' bar and restaurant. Extensive grounds licensed for camping and caravanning
⌂☆⊛(⊕&Å

Bodicote

10.30–2.30; 6–11.30

Plough
9 High Street ☎ (0295) 62327
Bodicote Bitter, No.9, Triple X, Old English Porter (Xmas) H
Pleasant, friendly home-brew pub ⊛⌂(⊕&

Britwell Salome

11–2.30; 7 (6 summer)–11

Red Lion
On B4009 ☎ (049 161) 2304
Brakspear Mild (summer), Bitter, Special, Old (winter) H
Pleasant village pub with cosy lounge, good value food and accommodation. Within easy reach of Ridgeway long distance footpath and the Chilterns
☆⊛⌂(((not Wed) ⊕

Brize Norton

10–2.30; 6–11

Carpenters Arms
Station Road ☎ (0993) 842568
Morland Bitter H
Unpretentious but vibrant village local; no food but lots of conversation, Aunt Sally, bar billiards ⌂Q⊛

Burford

10.30–2; 6–11

Highway Hotel
117 High Street
☎ (099 382) 2136
Hook Norton Best Bitter; Wadworth 6X H
Fine old country hotel in picture postcard setting
⌂Q☆⊛⌂(►&

Try also: **Masons Arms**

11–2.30; 6–11

Lamb
Sheep Street ☎ (099 382) 3155
Wadworth IPA, 6X H, **Old Timer** G
15th-century Cotswold stone hotel with antique furniture and stone floors. Not a horsebrass or mantrap in sight! Dogs welcome
⌂Q☆⊛⌂(►&

Charlbury

11.30–2.30; 6–11

Charlbury Tavern
Market Street ☎ (0608) 810103
Hook Norton Bitter H
Town-centre, friendly local with many guest beers. Home-cooked food; live folk music every Thu. Beer garden
☆⊛(►&≠

Chilton

10.30–2.30; 7–11

Horse & Jockey
On A4185 near A34 Jct
☎ (0235) 834376
Morland Bitter, Best Bitter H
Quiet hotel, convenient for travellers on A34. Popular with ramblers from the Ridgeway Q⊛⌂(►

Chinnor

11–2.30; 6–11

Royal Oak
49 Lower Road ☎ (0844) 51307
Adnams Bitter; Glenny Witney Bitter; Hook Norton Best Bitter H
Friendly, comfortable and well-furnished 1-bar pub. Pizzas to eat in or take away. Range of beers constantly changes ⌂Q⊛(► (Thu–Sat)

Chipping Norton

11–2.30; 7–11

Red Lion
Cattle Market ☎ (0608) 41520
Hook Norton Best Bitter H
Small, friendly locals' pub
⌂Q☆⊛⊕&☉

Try also: **Crown & Cushion Hotel** (Free)

Crays Pond

10.30–2.30; 6–11

White Lion
Goring Road (Jct B471/B4526)
☎ (0491) 680471
Courage Best Bitter, Directors H
Cosy traditional pub. Large garden with children's play area ⌂Q⊛(►⊕&

Deddington

10.30–2.30; 6–11

Crown & Tuns
New Street (A423)
☎ (0869) 38343
Hook Norton Mild, Bitter, Old Hookey (winter) H
Friendly unpretentious old coaching inn. Knock if closed at above times ⌂⊛

Enslow

11–2.30; 6 (7 winter)–11

Rock of Gibraltar
On A4095 1½ miles from Bletchingdon ☎ (086 983) 223
Ruddles Best Bitter, County; Ushers Best Bitter; Webster's Yorkshire Bitter H
Friendly 1-bar, family canalside pub with garden. Small restaurant
⌂☆⊛(► (not Sun) &

Epwell

12–2.30; 7–11

Chandlers Arms
Bibford Road (B4035)
☎ (029 578) 344
Hook Norton Mild, Bitter H
Small, friendly pub in picturesque village. Dogs and children welcome Q☆⊛⊕&

Faringdon

10–2.30; 6–11

Folly
54 London Street

Oxfordshire

☎ (0367) 20620
Morrell Bitter, Varsity H
Charming little town pub with no frills, but beer served in lovingly polished glasses. CAMRA Oxford branch Pub of the Year 1985. Aunt Sally pitch ▲Q✤●

Garsington

11–2.30; 6–11

Plough Inn
1 Oxford Road ☎ (086 736) 395
Courage Best Bitter, Directors H
Busy welcoming local. Large enclosed garden with children's play area and Aunt Sally ▲✤●● (not Sun)✤●

Goring

10–2.30; 6–11

John Barleycorn
Manor Road (off B4009)
☎ (0491) 872509
Brakspear Bitter, Special H
Attractive 16th-century, low-beamed inn with cosy saloon, and good food. Close to River Thames and Ridgeway long distance footpath
Q✤●●●▲➝

Great Milton

12–2.30; 7–11

Bell
The Green (off A329)
☎ (084 46) 270
Brakspear Special; Glenny Wychwood Best; Uley Old Spot, Pigs Ear; Wethered SPA H
Typical country pub. Try the beef in Old Spot. Regular guest beers. ▲Q✤●●●▲

Great Tew

11.30–2.30 (closed Mon); 6–11

Falkland Arms
☎ (060 883) 653
Donnington BB; Hook Norton BB; Marston Pedigree; Morrell Celebration; Wadworth 6X H
Outstanding, classic pub in preserved village. Guest beers, home-made food, oak panels, settles, flagstones, oil lamps, clay pipes, snuff; thatched roof – a gem!
▲Q✤●●●●

Henley-on-Thames

11–2.30; 6–11

Royal Hotel
51 Station Road (off A4155)
☎ (0491) 577526
Brakspear Mild, Bitter H
Welcoming, spacious pub near river. A down-to-earth boozer with plenty of room, even with a pool table ✤ (for lunch)●●● (Mon–Fri)●▲➝

10–2.30; 6–11

Three Tuns
5 Market Place
☎ (0491) 573260
Brakspear Mild G, **Bitter, Special** H, **Old** G
Excellent old town-centre pub. Open throughout the day with a restaurant licence. Small public bar at front with traditional games; oak-beamed lounge with large fireplace ✤●●●●▲➝

Hook Norton

11–2.30; 7–11

Pear Tree
Scotland End (off A361/A34)
OS351333 ☎ (0608) 737482
Hook Norton Best Bitter, Old Hookey H
Cheerful, welcoming village pub near the brewery
▲Q✤●●

11.30–2.30, 7.30–11

Sun
High Street (Market Square)
☎ (0608) 737570
Hook Norton Mild, Best Bitter H
Unspoilt village local ▲Q✤●

Islip

10–2.30; 6–11

Swan
Lower Street (B4027)
Morrell Bitter, Varsity, Celebration, College Ale H
Comfortable 1-bar village local overlooking River Ray
Q✤●● (Tue–Sat)

Juniper Hill

10–2.30; 6–11

Fox Inn
Off A43 ☎ (0869) 810616
Hook Norton Best Bitter H, **Old Hookey** G
Friendly pub in centre of hamlet described in 'Lark Rise to Candleford' ▲Q✤●●

Kidlington

11–2.30; 7–11

Jolly Boatman
Banbury Road, Thrupp (A423)
☎ (086 75) 3775
Morrell Varsity H
Very friendly canalside pub, specialising in vegetarian meals Q✤●●●●

Langford

11–2.30; 6.30–11

Bell
Off A361 ☎ (036 786) 281
Morland Bitter; Wadworth 6X H
Quiet 17th-century inn and village local, difficult to find but worth the effort. Local guest beers. Aunt Sally
▲Q●● (not Sun) ● (not Mon)

Letcombe Bassett

10.30–2.30; 6–11

Yew Tree Inn
OS373851 ☎ (023 57) 3140
Archers Best Bitter G
Noisy village pub with intimate snug, a haven of peace from juke box and cigarette smoke. Books of local interest for sale. Limited food lunch, evenings only by arrangement ▲✤●●●

Lewknor

11–2.30; 6–11

Olde Leathern Bottel
1 High Street (off B4009)
☎ (0844) 51482
Brakspear Bitter, Special, Old H
Homely and welcoming low-beamed pub with Cromwellian connections. Good food ▲Q✤●●●●

Little Milton

11–2.30; 6–11

Lamb Inn
High Street (A329)
☎ (084 46) 527
Halls Harvest Bitter; Ind Coope Burton Ale H
Cosy, thatched, stone-built 17th-century inn in attractive village. Extensive and varied menu ▲✤●●

Long Hanborough

10.30–2.30; 6–11

Bell
A4095 ☎ (0993) 881324
Morrell Varsity G
Comfortable old pub with well-earned reputation for good, home cooked food
▲Q✤●●●➝

11–2.30; 6–11

Swan
Millwood End (off A4095)
Morrell Light Ale, Bitter H
Popular village pub. Large garden with pets and children's play area. Sun lunch barbecues ✤●●●●

Lower Assendon

11–2.30; 6–11

Golden Ball
On B480 ☎ (0491) 574157
Brakspear Bitter, Special H, **Old** G
Splendid, friendly country pub serving good value food. Popular and often busy
▲Q✤●●●

Middle Barton

10–2.30; 6–11

Carpenters Arms
Just off A34 ☎ (0869) 40378
Halls Harvest Bitter H
Comfortable thatched country

249

Oxfordshire

pub, popular with walkers. Good home-cooked food

Northmoor

10.30–2.30; 6–11

Dun Cow
Off A415 ☎ (086 731) 295
Morland Mild, Bitter G
Delightful, unspoilt traditional village local. No serving counter

New Yatt

11.30–2.30; 6–11

Saddlers Arms
Hailey Road ☎ (099 386) 368
Hook Norton Best Bitter, Old Hookey H
Pleasant country pub with large garden. Guest beers

North Leigh

11.30–2.30; 7–11

The Woodman
New Yatt Road
☎ (0993) 881790
Hook Norton Best Bitter; Glenny Wychwood Best, Witney Bitter; Wadworth 6X H
Actively supported village local. Guest beers

Oxford

10.30–2.30; 5.30–11

Bear
6 Alfred Street
☎ (0865) 244680
Ind Coope Burton Ale; Tetley Bitter H
Unspoilt 15th-century pub famous for its collection of ties. A Classic Town Pub

11–2.30; 6–11

Cricketers Arms
43 Iffley Road ☎ (0865) 726264
Morland Bitter, Best Bitter H
Traditional local pub. Try the veggie burgers

10.30–2.30; 5.30–11

Eagle & Child
49 St Giles Street
☎ (0865) 58085
Arkells BBB; Ind Coope Burton Ale; Wadworth 6X H
Multi-alcoved town pub with Tolkien and C.S. Lewis connections. Recently excellently restored

10.30–2.30; 5.30–11

Fairvew Inn
16 Glebelands ☎ (0865) 63448
Courage Best Bitter, Directors H
Comfortable 1950s estate pub hidden round the back of the Sunnyside estate

10.30–2.30; 6–11

Fir Tree Tavern
163 Iffley Road
☎ (0865) 247373
Morrell Bitter, Varsity H
Small local pub with large student following. No food Sun

10.30–2.30; 5.30–11

Globe
59–60 Cranham Street
☎ (0865) 57759
Morrell Light Ale, Bitter H
Pre-war town local in a predominantly Victorian suburb. Pub games popular (not Sun)

10.30–2.30; 10.30

Grog Shop (off licence)
13 Kingston Road
☎ (0865) 57088
Arkells Kingsdown Ale; Hook Norton Best Bitter, Old Hookey; Wadworth 6X, Farmers Glory H
Off-licence with varying range of real ales. Also sells unusual foreign bottled beers

10.30–2.30; 5.30–11

Old Tom
101 St Aldates ☎ (0865) 243034
Morrell Bitter, Varsity, Celebration H
Small city-centre pub with a pleasant secluded garden. Lunches a speciality. Popular with students, local residents and classical musicians

11–2.30; 7–11

Red White & Blue
47 James Street (off B480)
☎ (0865) 247127
Morland Mild, Bitter, Best Bitter H
Friendly local; comfortable lounge, bar with traditional pub games

11–2.30; 5.30 (6 Sat)–11

Rose & Crown
14 North Parade Avenue
☎ (0865) 510551
Halls Harvest Bitter; Ind Coope Burton Ale H
Students and professionals can meet in an atmosphere of Dickensian quaintness in this delightful and unspoilt tavern

12–2.30; 7–11

Temple Bar
21 Temple Street
☎ (0865) 243251
Hall & Woodhouse Tanglefoot; Wadworth 6X, Farmers Glory, Old Timer H
Busy and popular 2-bar pub. Regular live folk music

10.30–2.30; 5.30–11

Watermans Arms
7 South Street, Osney Island
☎ (0865) 248832
Morland Mild, Bitter, Best Bitter H
Riverside local popular with anglers

Pyrton

11–2.30; 6–11

Plough
Off B4009 OS687961
☎ (049 161) 2003
Adnams Bitter; Ringwood Fortyniner H
Attractive 17th-century thatched pub. Low beams and inglenook. Good food. Watch out for ghost of old man and his dog! Guest beers (not Sun)

Rotherfield Peppard

11–2.30; 6–11

Red Lion
On B481 ☎ (049 17) 329
Brakspear Mild, Bitter, Special H
Pleasant village pub overlooking large common. Extensive menu (not Sun)

Sandford-on-Thames

11–2.30; 6.30–11

Fox
25 Henley Road
☎ (0865) 777803
Morrell Light Ale, Dark Mild, Bitter G
Straight-forward roadside local, where the beer is among the cheapest in the area

Shiplake

11–2.30; 6–11

Baskerville Arms
Station Road (off A4155)
☎ (073 522) 3332
Flowers Original; Wethered Bitter, SPA, Winter Royal H
Smart and spacious inn which attracts a wide range of customers. Rowing theme in one bar. Separate restaurant; live jazz alternate Thu (Tue–Sat)

Sonning Common

11–2.30; 6–11

Bird in Hand
Reading Road (B481)
☎ (0734) 723230
Courage Best Bitter, Directors H
Cosy, low-beamed pub with very popular restaurant; bar meals also available. Attractive enclosed garden, ideal for children (not Tue)

Try also: Hare & Hounds

South Hinksey

10.30–2.30; 5.30–11

Oxfordshire

General Elliott
37 Manor Road
☎ (0865) 739369
Morrell Light Ale, Bitter, Varsity H
Village pub at the edge of the countryside, with easy access to riverside walks ち A

Stanton St John

11–2.30; 6.30–11

Star Inn
500 yds off B4027
☎ (086 735) 277
Hall & Woodhouse Tanglefoot (summer) H; **Wadworth, IPA, 6X, Farmers Glory, Old Timer (winter)** H
Friendly cosy village local with interesting collection of bottled beers. Helicopter parking available!
▲Q ち (if eating) 愛) 母 &

Steventon

10.30–2.30; 7–11 (10.30 Mon)

Cherry Tree
33 High Street ☎ (0235) 831222
Brakspear Bitter; Fuller London Pride; Hook Norton Best Bitter; Morland Bitter; Wadworth 6X H
Busy free house. Elegant lounge at one end; modernised bar and servery at the other. Splendid range of whisky. Guest beers
Q 愛) (Tue–Sat)

Stoke Lyne

10–2.30; 6–11

Peyton Arms
500 yds off A41 ☎ (086 96) 285
Hook Norton Best Bitter, Old Hookey (winter) G
Small village local unchanged by time – a rural gem
▲Q ち 愛 母 &

Stoke Row

10–2.30; 6–11

Cherry Tree
Off B481 ☎ (0491) 680430
Brakspear Mild, Bitter, Special, Old H
Picturesque, low-beamed village pub. Games room with pool; swings in the garden
▲ ち 愛 母

Swinbrook

11.30–2.30; 6–11

Swan
1 mile N of A40
☎ (099 382) 2165
Morland Bitter; Wadworth 6X H
Characterful country inn in the secluded Windrush valley, originally a 17th-century mill
▲Q ⇌) (not Tue)

Swalcliffe

10.30–2.30; 6.30 (5.30 summer)–11

Stags Head
Main Road (B4035)
☎ (0295) 232
Hook Norton Bitter; Ruddles Best Bitter; Webster's Yorkshire Bitter H
Pleasant, welcoming thatched pub ▲愛) 母

Sydenham

11–2.30; 6–11

Crown
Off B4445 ☎ (0844) 51634
Brakspear Bitter; Fuller London Pride; Wadworth 6X; Young Bitter H
17th-century free house in centre of village, with quiet and friendly atmosphere. Aunt Sally pitch in garden
▲Q 愛) (not Sun)

Thame

10.30–2.30; 6–11

Rising Sun
26 High Street
☎ (084 421) 4206
Hook Norton Best Bitter; Marston Merrie Monk, Pedigree H
Attractive 16th-century oak-beamed building with prominent sign and overhanging first floor. Friendly and cosy atmosphere heightened by low roof! No food Mon ▲) (not Sun)

Wantage

10.30–2.30; 6.30–11

Shoulder of Mutton
38 Wallingford Street
☎ (023 57) 2835
Morland Mild, Bitter H
Plain unspoilt town local frequented by rogues and characters. Intimate snug full of younger set, who enjoy a real pub. Not a place to impress your mother ▲Q 母

Watlington

11.30–2.30; 6–11

Chequers
Love Lane (off B4009)
☎ (049 161) 2874
Brakspear Bitter, Special H
Attractive old white-washed pub away from the town centre. A bit difficult to find but well worth it. Cosy interior; good food ▲Q 愛 ( )

Wigginton

12–2.30; 7–11

White Swan
Off A361 ☎ (0608) 737669
Hook Norton Best Bitter, Old Hookey E
Old country local with fine country views ▲Q 愛 母 &

Woodstock

10.30–2.30; 6.30–11

Black Prince
2 Manor Road (A34)
☎ (0993) 811530
Adnams Bitter; Archers Village Bitter; Ringwood Fortyniner; Ruddles County H
Very pleasant 16th-century pub. Mexican food and English bar snacks. Good local trade; beer garden by River Glyme ▲Q ち 愛 ( ) &

10.30–2.30; 6–11

Queens Own
59 Oxford Street (A34)
☎ (0993) 812414
Hook Norton Mild, Best Bitter, Old Hookey H
Friendly 1-bar pub offering good value simple fare. Try to work out the pictures! Parking can be difficult
Q ち ⇌ ( ) (not Mon)

Wytham

10.30–2.30; 5.30–11

White Hart
☎ (0865) 244372
Ind Coope Burton Ale; Tetley Bitter H
Popular 300 year-old pub in picture postcard village on the outskirts of Oxford. 16th-century dovecote stands in the garden ▲Q 愛 ( )

- ▲ real fire
- Q quiet pub – no electronic music, TV or obtrusive games
- ち indoor room for children
- 愛 garden or other outdoor drinking area
- ⇌ accommodation
- (lunchtime meals
-) evening meals
- 母 public bar
- & facilities for the disabled
- A camping facilities close to the pub or part of the pub grounds
- ⇜ near British Rail station
- ⊖ near Underground station
- ⊙ real cider

The facilities, beers and pub hours listed in the Good Beer Guide are liable to change but were correct when the Guide went to press.

251

Shropshire

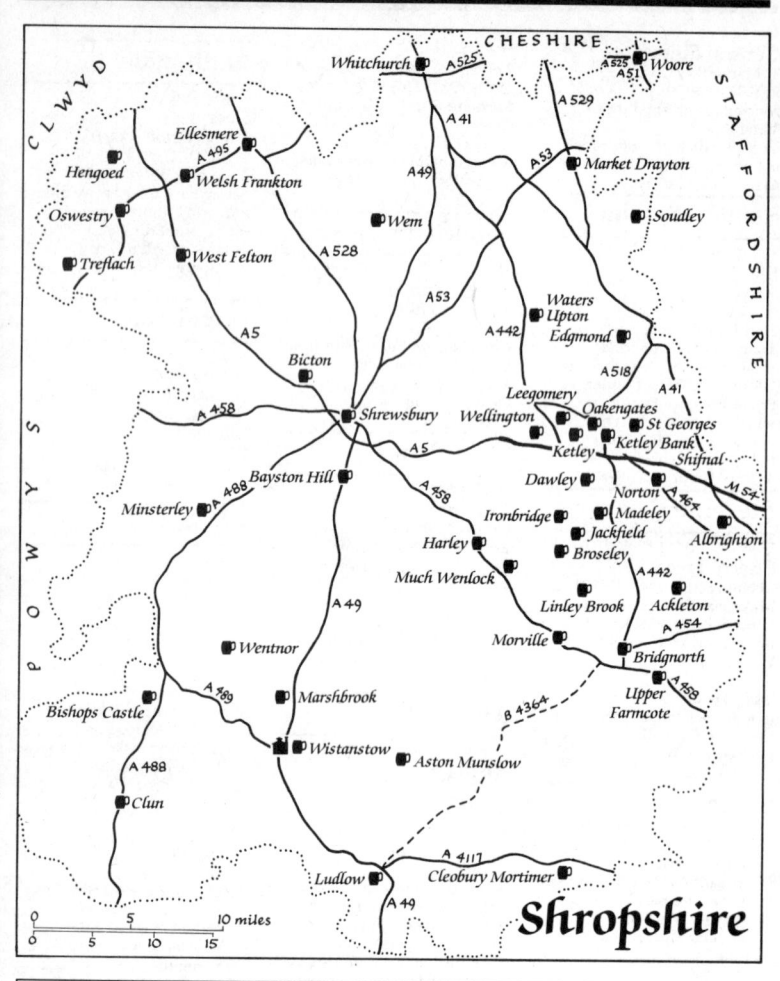

🏠 Wood, *Wistanstow*

Ackleton

11–2.30; 7–11

Folly Inn
On B4176
Banks's Mild, Bitter E
Pleasant open-plan pub with intimate ante-room. Large feature fireplace. A clean-air pub ♨Q☙⊛

Albrighton

11–2.30; 6–11

Crown Inn
High Street ☎ (090722) 2204
Banks's Mild, Bitter; Hanson's Black Country Bitter E
Large many-roomed local: basic bar, comfortable lounge and snug. Beer garden; children's play area
♨☙⊛≈()⊕&≷

Aston Munslow

12–2.30 (not Tue); 7–11

Swan Inn
On B4368, 6 miles NE of Craven Arms ☎ (058 476) 271
Draught Bass; M&B Mild, Brew XI H
1350 timber-framed inn, deserved winner of Shropshire Star's Perfect Pub award. Warm welcome and excellent home-made food
♨Q☙⊛()⊕&▲

Bayston Hill

10.30–3; 6–11

Compasses Inn
Hereford Road (A49)
☎ (0743) 722921
Draught Bass; M&B Highgate Mild, Springfield Bitter H
Friendly main road local with bar billiards table
♨☙⊛()⊕&

Try also: Pound (M&B)

Bicton

10.30–3; 6–11

Four Crosses Inn
☎ (0743) 850258
Draught Bass; M&B Mild, Springfield Bitter E
Convenient stopping off point on A5 (Telford route) into North Wales. Pub games
♨☙⊛≈()&

Bishops Castle

11.30–2.30; 6.30–11

Castle Hotel
Market Square
☎ (0588) 638403
Draught Bass; M&B Springfield Bitter E or H

252

Shropshire

Comfortable hotel, set in picturesque S. Shropshire hills. Its bowling green is at town's highest point ▲Q☎❀⋈◐❶▶

11.30–2.30; 6.30–11
Three Tuns
Salop Street ☎ (0588) 638797
Three Tuns Mild, XXX, Steamer H
Historic home-brew pub with coal-fired tower brewery; attracts a wide following. Home to rugby club and film society. Menu caters for vegetarians ▲❀◐❶❹❺

Bridgnorth

11.30–2.30; 6.30–11
Hare & Hounds
Bernard's Hill (on narrow lane climbing above A442)
☎ (094 62) 3043
Draught Bass H**; M&B Mild, Springfield Bitter** E
Small local with basic but comfortable facilities. New room for darts and dominoes ▲❀❀⋈◐❶❹

Try also: Friar's Inn (Free)

Broseley

10.30–2.30; 6–11
Cumberland Hotel
Queen Street ☎ (0952) 882301
Banks's Mild; Draught Bass H
Comfortable multi-roomed hotel, once a country residence. Basic bar contrasts with other smart rooms ▲❀❀◐❶❹❺▲

12–2.30; 7–11
Olde Tavern
High Street ☎ (0952) 883468
Banks's Mild, Bitter H
Friendly, basic town local. Can get busy in later part of evening. Darts and dominoes ▲❀❀

Cleobury Mortimer

10.30–2.30; 6–11
Bell
Lower Street ☎ (0299) 270305
Banks's Mild, Bitter E;
Courage Directors H
Unspoilt inn of character with a club room, situated in the middle of a sleepy town noted for its sloping church spire. Pub games ▲Q❹

Clun

11–2.30; 6–11
Sun Inn
High Street (B4368)
☎ (058 84) 559 or 277
Banks's Mild, Bitter; Woods Special H
Remote inn; a 15th-century listed Cruck building. Comfortable lounge and timeless public bar – note the "cash register" set of handpumps ▲Q☎❀⋈◐❶▶

Dawley

11–2.30; 7–11
Ring o' Bells
75 King Street ☎ (0952) 505142
Marston Burton Bitter, Pedigree
Small, basic local set back from narrow road. Clean-air pub ❀❹❺

Edgmond

11–2.30; 6–11
Lion Inn
Chetwynd Road (off B5062)
☎ (0952) 810346
Draught Bass; M&B Highgate Mild, Springfield Bitter H
Comfortable homely village local with award-winning garden and range of good value food. Games
❀❀◐❶ (not Sun) ❹

Ellesmere

10.30–3; 6.30–11
White Hart Inn
Birch Road ☎ (069 171) 2333
Marston Border Mild, Border Bitter, Pedigree H
Attractive old pub off main street, on canal side of a town at centre of Shropshire 'Lake District' ❀❀❀❹❺

Harley

12–3; 6–11
Plume of Feathers Hotel
On A458, 2 miles NW of Much Wenlock ☎ (0952) 727360
Flowers Original H
Attractive country roadside inn, between Wenlock Edge and Ironbridge World Heritage site. Guest beers
▲❀❀❹❺

Hengoed

closed lunch except Sun; 7–11
Last Inn
On back road, Oswestry–Weston Rhyn ☎ (0691) 659747
Marston Pedigree H**, Owd Rodger** G**; Woods Special; Younger Scotch** H
Large country pub with games and family rooms. Live entertainment Sun. Guest beers ▲❀◐❶❹❺

Ironbridge

12–2.30; 7 (6 summer)–11
Bird in Hand
Waterloo Street
☎ (095 245) 2226
Banks's Mild, Bitter E
Quaint old pub with view over River Severn. Excellent good-value food. Pub games ▲❀❀◐❶❹❺▲❺

Jackfield

11–2.30; 6 (7 winter)–11
Boat Inn
Ferry Road ☎ (0952) 882178
Banks's Mild, Bitter E
Fine riverside inn, once accessible by boat only! Now in Ironbridge World Heritage site. Footbridge from pub to unusual tar tunnel. Meals summer only
▲Q❀◐❶❹❺▲❺

Ketley

12–2.30; 6.30–11
Unicorn Inn
Holyhead Road (B5061/A518)
☎ (0952) 617250
Banks's Mild; Wrekin Bitter, Heavengate Bitter, Potter's Black Porter, Hellgate Special Bitter, Old Horny H
Roadside pub, producing a large range of beers from own brewery (visible from lounge). Good lunches
▲❀◐ (Mon–Sat) ❹❺

Ketley Bank

12–2.30; 7 (6.30 F, S)–11
Lord Hill Inn
Main Road ☎ (0952) 613070
Draught Bass; M&B Mild, Springfield Bitter H
Popular 2-room pub with active social scene next to former brewery. Cellar once acted as village bakery and mortuary! Guest beers
▲❀◐❶❹❺ (summer)

Leegomery

12–2.30; 6–11
Malt Shovel Inn
Hadley Park Road (off A442)
☎ (0952) 42963
Marston Pedigree H
Friendly atmosphere in workingman's bar; unusual brass collection in lounge. Popular for business lunches
▲Q◐ (Mon–Fri) ❹❺

Linley Brook

10.30–2.30; 6 (7 winter)–11
Pheasant Inn
Off B4373 (2½ miles S of Broseley) OS978680
☎ (074 62) 2260
Banks's Mild; Marston Burton Bitter; Holden Special Bitter H
Unspoilt rural free house on remote country lane. Amusing mural depicting caricatures of country life dominates the lounge. Guest beers; darts and dominoes ▲❀◐ (not Sun) ❶❹

Ludlow

10.30–2.30; 6–11
Bull Hotel
Bull Ring ☎ (0584) 3611

253

Shropshire

Marston Burton Bitter, Pedigree G or H
Classic coaching inn with covered entrance way leading to open half-timbered yard which hosts the Ludlow Festival's Fringe. Long comfortable bar ≜⏳() ▶ ⅋ ≢

10.30–2.30 (4 M, W, Sat); 6.30–11

George
Castle Square ☎ (0584) 2055
Ansells Mild, Bitter H
Tidy 2-room pub across square from Castle; reputedly haunted. Pub games
₩ (summer) ⅋ ≢

Madeley

12–2.30; 7–11

All Nations
Coalport Road
☎ (0952) 585747
All Nations Pale Ale H
Long-established home brewpub. A listed building overlooking the Ironbridge Gorge and Blists Hill Museum. Pub games Q⊛⅋

Market Drayton

11–3; 7–11

Coach & Horses
70 Shropshire Street (old A53)
☎ (0630) 2800
Marston Border Mild, Burton Bitter, Pedigree H
Small, 18th-century pub with beamed ceilings. Cosy lounge and friendly, locals' bar. Pub games ≜Q⊛⅋

11–3 (5 Wed); 7–11

Red Lion
Great Hale Street (A529)
☎ (0630) 2602
Draught Bass; M&B Springfield Bitter E
2-room pub with homely lounge and tiled floor in bar. Dominoes prize-winners! Open-air swimming pool just 2 minutes walk
≜Q (TV in bar) ⅋≢

Marshbrook

12–2.30 (not Mon); 7–11

Wayside Inn
Marshbrook (B4370)
☎ (069 46) 208
Banks's Bitter; Draught Bass; M&B Springfield Bitter H
1-roomed local with long bar. Old Guinness adverts and pictures by local artists (for sale) adorn walls. Pub games
≜⏳⊛₩() ⅋ ▲ (grounds)

Minsterley

12–3; 7–11

Crown & Sceptre
☎ (0743) 791260
Ansells Mild, Bitter H
Low-ceilinged local with bowling green and parrot (no connection) ≜⏳⊛₩()⅋

Morville

11–2.30; 6–11

Acton Arms
On A458 ☎ (074 631) 209
Banks's Mild, Bitter E
Large roadside pub. Strong equine connections in bar; comfortable lounge. Enclosed children's play area. Good food
≜⏳ (when eating) ⊛ ()
(12.30–2) ▶ (7–9.30, not Sun)
⅋≢

Much Wenlock

11–2.30; 6 (7 winter)–11

George & Dragon
2 High Street ☎ (0952) 727312
Hook Norton Bitter H
Excellent traditional local. Walls completely covered by brewery memorabilia; water jugs collection. Good food
Q⏳()▶ (Tue–Sat) ⅋

Oakengates

11.30–2.30; 7–11

Rose & Crown Inn
Holyhead Road (B5061)
☎ (0952) 614348
Ansells Mild, Bitter; Ind Coope Burton Ale H
Popular roadside inn with spacious beamed bar and comfortable lounge. Good lunches. Darts and dominoes. Guest beers
⏳⊛()(Mon–Fri)⅋≢

Oswestry

12–2.30; 6–11

Golden Lion
Upper Church Street
☎ (0691) 653747
Marston Border Exhibition, Pedigree, Merrie Monk H
Lively bar, comfortable lounge. Extended hours on market days – Wed and Sat. Pub games ≜⊛()▶⅋

11–3; 7–11

Oak Inn
Church Street
Draught Bass; M&B Mild, Brew XI E
Town-centre pub opposite church. Busy compact bar and spacious lounge. Extended hours market days – Wed and Sat. Pub games Q()⅋

St. Georges

12–2.30; 6 (7 Sat)–11

Albion Inn
Station Hill ☎ (0952) 614193
Marston Burton Bitter, Pedigree, Owd Rodger (winter) H
Superbly restored in Victorian style, complete with black-leaded range, stencilled ceiling and period furnishings. Good food
≜⏳⊛()▶≢

Shifnal

12–2.30; 7–11

Anvil
Aston Road
Banks's Mild, Bitter E
Traditional, unspoilt local: small cosy bar and small anteroom. Always busy at night
≜Q⅋≢

11–2.30; 7 (6 summer)–11

White Hart
4 High Street ☎ (0952) 461161
Ansells Mild, Bitter; Ind Coope Burton Ale H
Attractive old town pub with many exposed beams. Comfortable lounge. Darts. Guest beers () (not Sun) ⅋

Shrewsbury

11–3; 6.30–11

Boars Head
18 Belle Vue ☎ (0743) 50590
Banks's Mild, Bitter H
Homely, 15th-century pub near Shrewsbury Town FC. Pub games
⏳ (lunch and until 9) ⊛()▶⅋

11.30–3 (not Sun); 6–11

Castle Vaults
Castle Gates ☎ (0773) 58807
Marston Border Mild, Pedigree; Robinson Best Bitter H
In shadow of castle. Landlord exercises discretion over customers admitted. Mexican food a speciality. Non-smoking area ≜⏳⊛₩()▶⅋≢

10.30–3; 6–11

Dog & Pheasant
Severn Street, Castlefields
☎ (0743) 52835
Ansells Mild, Bitter; Ind Coope Burton Ale H
Terraced 2-room local tucked away in side street at back of prison and close to River Severn. Pub games ⅋≢

10.30–3; 6–11

Dolphin
St Michaels Street
Marston Border Mild, Border Exhibition, Merrie Monk, Pedigree H
Late Georgian symmetrical style pub with porticoed porch, 5 min walk from station. No keg beers or lager. No "policy" on dress or animals. Pub games ⅋≢

10.30–3; 6–11

Loggerheads
Church Street (off St Mary's Street) ☎ (0743) 55457
Draught Bass; M&B Mild E
Cosy side street pub with 4 rooms. Shove ha'penny board and strong sporting links. One of least spoilt town centre pubs around Q⏳₩()⅋≢

10.30–3; 6–11

Shropshire

Old Bell
115 Abbey Foregate
☎ (0743) 56041
Ansells Mild, Bitter; Ind Coope Burton Ale; Minera Nevilles Grog H
Public bar and snug with separate pool/bar billiards room; corridor drinking areas: this 18th century house serves all the local community

10.30–3; 6–11
Proud Salopian
Smithfield Road (50 yds off Welsh Bridge)
Whitbread Pompey Royal H
Thomas Southam, an old Shrewsbury brewer was the proud Salopian. One main bar; quiet at lunch, can be boisterous eves. Cellar occasionally floods due to proximity of river. Guest beers

10.30–3; 6–11
Swan Inn
Frankwell
Ansells Bitter; Ind Coope Burton Ale; Marston Pedigree; Wadworth 6X H
1 main room with pool room. Smart, attractive pub in restored group of buildings on Welsh side of Severn loop. Live piano music

Try also: Seven Stars, Coleham (M&B)

Soudley
12–2.30 (not winter); 6.30 (7.30 winter)–11
Wheatsheaf Inn
Off A41 ☎ (063 086) 311
Marston Burton Bitter, Pedigree; Owd Rodger H
Friendly, remote village pub dating back to 1784, on Staffordshire border. Games include bar skittles. No food Tue

Treflach
11–3; 7–11
Gibraltar Inn
☎ (0691) 650111
Ind Coope Burton Ale; Tetley Bitter H
17th-century pub in an attractive area, just a stone's throw from Offa's Dyke. Pub games

Try also: Efel, Trefonen (Marston)

Upper Farmcote
11–2.30; 7–11
Red Lion o' Morfe
Off A458, SE of Bridgnorth OS919770 ☎ (074 66) 678
Banks's Mild, Bitter; Wood's Special H
Excellent village pub converted from old farmhouse in pleasant rural setting. Superb traditional bar and smart modern lounge. Good lunches. Pub games (if eating)

Waters Upton
11–2.30; 6–11
Lion Inn
On A442 ☎ (0952) 83317
Flowers IPA; Whitbread Pompey Royal H
Multi-level pub with distinctly different areas. Strong pictorial links with "Lion" locomotive. Darts. Guest beers

Wellington
12–2.30; 7–11
Plough Inn
King Street ☎ (0952) 255981
Ansells Mild, Bitter; Ind Coope Burton Ale H
Modernised 18th century pub on perimeter of town centre. Smart, comfortable lounge. Darts and dominoes (lunch) (not Sun)

11.30–2.30; 7–11
Three Crowns Inn
7 High Street ☎ (0952) 223209
Ansells Mild, Bitter H
A relaxing pub, popular with lunchtime shoppers; good food. Darts and dominoes (not Sun)

Try also: Green Man (Free)

Welsh Frankton
11–3; 6–11 (restaurant & supper licence)
Narrow Boat Inn
Ellesmere Road, Whittington (A495) ☎ (0691) 661051
Draught Bass; Ruddles County; Wadworth 6X H
Modern canalside pub with boats for hire. Guest beers; varied menu; pub games

Wem
10.30–3 (5 Thu); 6.30–11
Dickin Arms
Noble Street ☎ (0939) 33085
Marston Mercian Mild, Burton Bitter, Pedigree H
Real ale oasis, since closure of Wem's brewery

Wentnor
11.30–2.30; 7–11
Crown Inn
Off A488/A489 OS385928 ☎ (058 861) 613
Draught Bass; Sam Powell Original Bitter, Samson H
Set in little village nestling below SW lip of the Long Mynd, it provides a haven for visitors to the South Shropshire hills

West Felton
11–3; 7–11 (supper licence)
Punchbowl Inn
On old A5 ☎ (0691) 88201
Banks's Mild, Bitter E
Old coaching inn on original Holyhead road. Pub games

Try also: Fox

Whitchurch
10.30–3; 6–11
Star
Watergate Street
Marston Burton Bitter, Pedigree H
Small friendly local with aquarium in lounge. Town is home to Joyce, the family clock-making firm whose work is found in public buildings, churches and cathedrals throughout the world

Wistanstow
12–2.30; 7–11
Plough Inn
½ mile W of A49
☎ (058 82) 3251
Wood's Parish Bitter, Special, Wonderful H
Village pub on 2 levels; public bar divided by huge log fire. Modern vaulted lounge has Royal Wedding bottle collection. Wood's brewery is at the rear

Woore
11.45–3; 5.45–11
Swan Hotel
Nantwich Road (A51)
☎ (063 081) 220
Wem Best Bitter, Special Bitter H
Former coaching inn, dating from 1539, with 3 comfortable lounges and pleasant restaurant. home-cooked buffet lunches. Bridgemere Garden Centre and Wildlife Park nearby. Pub games (right-hand door)

All pubs in Woore serve real ale

Worfield
11–2.30; 7–11
Davenport Arms (The Dog)
Banks's Mild, Bitter H & E; **Wadworth 6X; Wood's Special** H
Warm, friendly oak-beamed local in small village. Fine, traditional bar and comfortable lounge. Dominoes and darts

255

Somerset

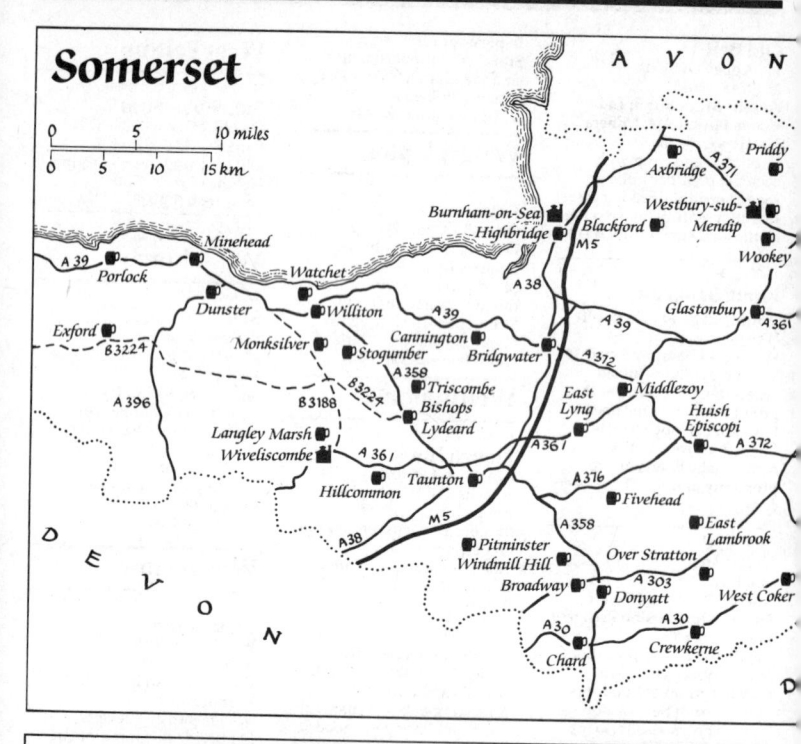

Somerset

Ash Vine, Frome; *Berrow*, Burnham-on-Sea; *Cotleigh* and *Golden Hill*, Wiveliscombe; *Miners Arms*, Westbury-sub-Mendip

Axbridge

11–2.30; 6.30–11

Lamb
The Square ☎ (0934) 732253
Butcombe Bitter; Flowers Original; Fuller London Pride H
Now owned by Butcombe Brewery. Bar made out of bottles. Large terraced beer garden ⌂♨⚭◐ (not Sun) ♿

Bishops Lydeard

10.30–2.30; 5.30–11

Bell Inn
Off A358 ☎ (0832) 432968
Cotleigh Tawny Bitter; Golden Hill Exmoor Ale; Webster Yorkshire Bitter H
Village pub catering for a wide range of clientele. Tile floored public bar with games room off. Wood fire and exposed stonework. Carpeted lounge and separate conservatory dining area. Guest beers
🏰⌂♨◐⚭♿♠♣

Blackford

11–2.30; 6.30–11

Sexey's Arms

☎ (0934) 712487
Courage Bitter Ale, Best Bitter H
13th-century village inn. Cosy oak beamed lounge – basic bar. Good food. Separate restaurant (which is closed Tue and Wed). Skittles and darts 🏰⌂♨⚭◐ ⚭♿

Bridgwater

10.30–2.30; 5.30–11

White Lion
29 High Street ☎ (0278) 429506
Courage Best Bitter, Directors H
Popular town-centre local with exposed wood beams and L-shaped bar. Occasional live music. Pinball machines – beware of the polaroid cameras! Darts
◐ (not Sun) ◐♿≈

11–2.30; 7–11

Fountain Inn
West Quay on River Parret's Bank ☎ (0278) 424115
Butcombe Bitter; Cotleigh Kingfisher Ale; Golden Hill Exmoor Ale H
Excellent town-centre, riverside pub. Wide range of customers providing a good

atmosphere. Darts a speciality (ladies and mens). Guest beers
Q⚭♿≈

10.30–2.30; 6–11

Quantock Gateway
95 Wembdon Road (A39)
☎ (0278) 423593
Draught Bass; Flowers IPA, Original H
Large comfortable pub where children are well catered for. Basic front bar, plush lounge with conservatory area where children can sit if unable to play outside. Guest beers
⌂♨◐ ◐♿♠

Broadway

11.30–2.30; 7–11

Bell Inn
Off A303 near Horton Cross
☎ (0460) 52343
Butcombe Bitter; Theakston Best Bitter; Wadworth 6X H
Thriving village pub with 2 bars and a dining room. Guest beer. Skittles and darts played
⌂♨◐ ◐♿♠♣

Bruton

11–2.30; 5.30–11

Castle Inn

256

Somerset

Chard

11–2.30; 5.30–11

Old Ship Inn
Furnham Road (A358)
☎ (04606) 3135
Golden Hill Exmoor Ale; Hall & Woodhouse Tanglefoot; Wadworth 6X
Cosy local, recently restored to 2 bars. Much exposed stonework. Skittles

Try also: Stumble Inn (Cotleigh)

Coleford

12–2.30 (not Mon); 7–11

Rose & Crown
High Street OS686488
☎ (0373) 812712
Butcombe Bitter
Friendly free house which displays the sources of its guest beers on a wall chart. Worth finding. Darts played

Cranmore

11.30–2.30; 6.30–11

Strode Arms
¼ mile off A361
☎ (074 988) 450
Draught Bass; Wadworth IPA, 6X
Village local next to duck pond, handy for East Somerset Railway

Crewkerne

12–2.30; 5.30 (6.30 Sat)–11

Kings Arms
Market Square (A30 behind Victoria Hall) ☎ (0460) 74927
Bass Hancocks HB; Flowers IPA; Golden Hill Exmoor Ale
Hamstone-built hostelry, popular with the young. Whimsical sign outside and painted frieze in bar. Skittles (yard)

Donyatt

11–2.30; 6–11

George Inn
On A358 ☎ (046 05) 52849
Eldridge Pope Dorchester Bitter, Royal Oak; Golden Hill Exmoor Ale
Tidy, genuine village stone pub offering darts, skittles and pool

Dunster

10–2; 6–11

Stags Head Inn
West Street ☎ (0643) 821229
Cotleigh Old Buzzard; Golden Hill Exmoor Gold; Hall & Woodhouse Badger Best Bitter
14th-century free house, well-used by locals, with interesting cruck beam construction. Wall mural satirising Henry VIII recently discovered in bedroom – now the honeymoon suite. Pub games. Beer range liable to change

Try also: Luttrell Arms Hotel

East Harptree

11–2.30; 6–11

Castle of Comfort
On B3134 ☎ (076 122) 221321
Draught Bass; Butcombe Bitter; Courage Best Bitter
Stone free house in Mendips; good food.

East Lambrook

11.30–2.30 (not Wed); 7–11

Rose & Crown
Off A303; 1½ miles N. of South Petherton
☎ (0460) 40433
Eldridge Pope Dorchester Bitter; Ind Coope Burton Ale; Tetley Bitter
Cosy oak-beamed pub with 2 bars and an attractive garden. Pub games played

East Lyng

10.30–2.30; 6.30–11

Rose & Crown
On A361 ☎ (082 369) 235
Butcombe Bitter; Cornish Wessex Stud; Eldridge Pope Royal Oak; Palmer IPA
Comfortable, civilised pub with stone fireplace. Well tended garden with fine view across Sedgemoor. Skittles and cards available

Emborough

11–2.30; 6.30–11

Old Down Inn
A37/B3139 Jct ☎ (0761) 232398
Draught Bass; Oakhill Farmers Ale
Former coaching inn, dating from 1640. Many rooms, some with old heavy furniture

Exford

11–2.30; 6–11

White Horse Hotel
On B3224 ☎ (064 383) 229
Draught Bass; Golden Hill Exmoor Dark
Rambling hotel in lovely village setting. Down to earth public bar with wood fire; smaller lounge. Both dominated by hunting theme. Darts

Try also: Simonsbath Inn (Cotleigh)

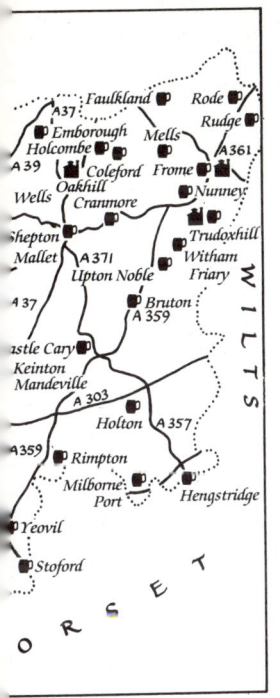

45 High Street (A359)
☎ (0749) 812211
Draught Bass; Butcombe Bitter; Palmer IPA; Young Special, Winter Warmer
Thriving 1-bar local, good food. Darts board

Cannington

11–2.30; 7–11

Malt Shovel
Blackmore Lane, Bradley Green ☎ (027867) 332
Butcombe Bitter; Golden Hill Exmoor Ale; Wadworth 6X
Country pub with small restaurant and large children's room, gardens and skittle alley

Castle Cary

10.30–2.30; 6–11

George Hotel
Market Place ☎ (0963) 50761
Butcombe Bitter; Young Special
15th-century coaching inn with comfortable, oak-beamed bar

10.30–2.30; 5.30–11

White Hart
Fore Street ☎ (0963) 50255
Courage Bitter Ale, Best Bitter, Directors
Cheerful town-centre pub. Darts and skittles played

257

Somerset

Faulkland

10.30–2.30; 6–11

Tuckers Grave Inn
Tuckers Grave (A366, ½ mile N.E. of village)
☎ (037 387) 230
Draught Bass; Butcombe Bitter G
The burial place of a 1747 suicide. A small farm cottage that has doubled as an inn for well over 200 years. Games include shove ha'penny and skittles ≜ Q ᛩ ⇔

Fivehead

11.30–2.30; 7–11

Crown Inn
Off A358 ☎ (046 08) 312
Butcombe Bitter; Courage Best Bitter, Directors H
Stone-built, 16th century extended pub with original fireplace and wattle ceiling. Separate restaurant (except Mon and Sun eves). plenty of games; family room
≜ ᛩ 8 ⋈ ( ) ⇔

Frome

10.30–2.30; 6–11

Angel
King Street (10 yards off A361)
☎ (0373) 62469
Courage Best Bitter, Directors H
300 year old former posting inn just off the Market Place
≜ ᛩ 8 ⋈ ( ) ⇔ ⇌ ⇔

10.30–2.30; 6–11

Sun
6 Catherine Street
☎ (0373) 73123
Marston Pedigree; Smiles Best Bitter; Wadworth 6X H
Comfortable, busy locals' pub with large central fireplace. Guest beers. Darts ≜ ⋈ (⇌

Glastonbury

11–2.30; 6–11

Beckets Inn
43 The High Street
☎ (0458) 32928
Wadworth Devizes Bitter, IPA, 6X, Farmers Glory (summer) Old Timer (winter) H
Situated in ancient and historic town, this pub serves beer from wooden casks. 3 character bars plus dining area. Beer garden and courtyard
Q (lounge & back bar) 8 (⇔

Try also: Crown Hotel (Free)

Henstridge

10.30–2.30; 5.30–11

Bird in Hand
Ash Walk (A357)
☎ (0963) 62255
Draught Bass; Butcombe Bitter H
Friendly village free house with public bar/games room and quiet bar with inglenook. Guest beers ≜ Q ᛩ 8 ⋈ (⇔ ⇔ ⇔

Highbridge

10.30–2.30; 5.30–11

Coopers Arms
Market Street ☎ (0278) 783562
Eldridge Pope Royal Oak; Palmer IPA E
Modernised pub very close to station. Popular town local – watch the blackboard for guest beers. Skittles, darts and pool
ᛩ 8 ⇔ ⇔ A ⇌

Hillcommon

11–2.30; 7–11

Royal Oak
On A361 ☎ (0823) 400295
Draught Bass; Golden Hill Exmoor Ale H
Friendly roadside pub with good local clientele. Comfortable lounge looking onto large garden. Fine view of Black Downs and Wellington Monument. Good down to earth public bar. Children welcome in skittle alley Q ᛩ 8 ⋈ ( ) ⇔

Holcombe

10.30–2.30; 6.30–11

Ring O' Roses
¾ mile off A367 at Stratton on the Fosse ☎ (0761) 232478
Butcombe Bitter; Oakhill Farmers Ale; Usher Best Bitter; Wadworth 6X H
Popular local by village football pitch. Darts
≜ ᛩ 8 ⋈ ( ) ⇔ ⇔

Holton

10.30–2.30; 5.30–11

Old Inn
½ mile from A357/B3149
☎ (0963) 32002
Butcombe Bitter; Wadworth 6X H
Old coaching inn and smithy, now a village pub with restaurant. Flagstone bar with piano and valve radio. No food Sun. Darts ≜ Q 8 ( ) ⇔

Huish Episcopi

11.30–2.30; 5.30–11

Rose & Crown (Eli's)
On A372 ☎ (0458) 25094
Draught Bass; Butcombe Bitter H
Many-roomed village local with flagstone floor in tap room. Known as Eli's after a member of family that owned it for over 50 years. Skittles, pool and darts ≜ ᛩ 8 ⋈ ⇔ ⇔

Keinton Mandeville

12–2.30; 6–11

Quarry Inn
High Street (B3153)
☎ (045 822) 3367
Oakhill Farmers Ale; Ruddles Best Bitter; Wadworth 6X H
Welcoming hostelry which used to be quarrymaster's house. Local stone building with vine clad frontage. Old maps and photos in bar. Separate dining area. Skittle alley ≜ ᛩ 8 ⋈ ( ) ⇔

Langley Marsh

12–2.30; 6–11

Three Horseshoes
Off A361 at Wiveliscombe
☎ (0984) 23763
Draught Bass G; **Cotleigh Tawny Bitter** H; **Fuller London Pride** G; **Hall & Woodhouse Tanglefoot** H; **Palmer IPA** G; **Theakston Best Bitter** H
Village pub with intimate atmosphere. Slate-floored traditional games room; lounge bar. Occasional live music ≜ Q ᛩ 8 ⋈ ( ) ⇔ ⇔

Mells

11–2.30; 6–11

Talbot Inn
2 miles SW of A362 at Buckland Dinham OS727493
☎ (0373) 812254
Boddingtons Bitter; Butcombe Bitter; Robinson Best Bitter; Wadworth 6X G
16th-century posting house with 3 bars leading off central courtyard. Guest beers. Darts and skittles
≜ ⋈ ( ) (not Sun) ⇔ ⇔

Middlezoy

12–2.30; 7–11

George Inn
Main Road (off A372)
☎ (0823) 69215
Butcombe Bitter; Cotleigh Tawny Bitter; Oakhill Farmers Ale H
17th-century free house close to site of Battle of Sedgemoor. Cosy lounge used mainly by diners. (No food Mon.) Wide age range. Occasional live music. Good selection of games. Guest beers
≜ ᛩ 8 ⋈ ( ) ⇔ ⇔ A

Milborne Port

11.30–2.30; 6.30–11

Queens Head
On A30 (Eastern end of town)
☎ (0963) 250314
Hook Norton Best Mild, Best Bitter; Smiles Best Bitter; Wadworth 6X H
Village pub with public bar/games room, quiet comfortable lounge and separate dining area
≜ Q (saloon) ᛩ 8 ⋈ (

258

Somerset

(not Sun) ✲&♿

Minehead

10.30–2.30; 5.30–11

Beach Hotel
The Avenue ☎ (0643) 2193
Draught Bass H
Hotel bar near the sea front and West Somerset Railway. Darts ♒✲⚓ ( )

11–2.30; 6–11

Old Ship Aground
Quay Street ☎ (0643) 2087
Ruddles County; Ushers Best Bitter H
Old inn by harbour noted for good bar meals. Pleasant courtyard bar open in summer. Ideal for children. Darts and pool
♒Q✲✿ ( )♿&

Monksilver

11–2.30; 6–11.30

Notley Arms
On B3188 between Washford and Wiveliscombe
☎ (0984) 56217
Ruddles County; Ushers Best Bitter H
400 year-old country inn noted for its menu and attractive gardens bordered by stream. Children's room
♒✲✿ ( )♿&

Nunney

10.30–2.30; 6–11

George Inn
½ mile N of A359/A361
☎ (037 384) 458
Draught Bass; Butcombe Bitter; Oakhill Farmers' Ale H
Comfortable former coaching inn and court house opposite remains of Nunney Castle. Darts ♒✲✿ ( ) ♿

Over Stratton

12–2.30; 7–11

Royal Oak
Off A303 ☎ (0460) 40906
Boddingtons Bitter (summer) H**; Butcombe Bitter; Wadworth 6X** H
Stone-built pub with large garden and play area. Noted for good food – busy at times
Q✲✿ ( )&

Pitminster

10.30–2.30; 5.30–11

Queens Arms
Off B3170 at Corfe OS219191
☎ (082 342) 529
Cotleigh Kingfisher Ale, Tawny Bitter, Old Buzzard; Golden Hill Exmoor Ale; Wadworth 6X H
Village free house off the beaten track. Mill bar part of a mill mentioned in Domesday Book. Pub games; guest beers
♒Q✲✿⚓ ( )▲

Porlock

10.30–2.30; 5.30–11

Ship Inn
High Street (A39)
☎ (0643) 862507
Draught Bass; Cotleigh Old Buzzard; Courage Best Bitter H
Welcoming old local with quaint public bar, updated lounge and family room, noted in Blackmore's 'Lorna Doone' as being Jan Ridd's local! Pub games
♒Q✲✿ ( )♿&▲♿

Try also: Castle Inn

Priddy

11 (12 winter)–2.30; 6 (7 winter)–11

New Inn
☎ (0749) 76465
Eldridge Pope Royal Oak; Marston Pedigree; Wadworth 6X H
15th-century farmhouse on the village green. Now a warm friendly pub with skittle alley, dining room and children's playground ♒✲ (Dining rm)
✲ ( )♿&▲ (500 yds) ♿

Rimpton

12 (11.30 summer)–2.30; 7 (6.30 summer)–11

White Post
B3148 2 miles S of Marston Magna ☎ (0935) 850717
Butcombe Bitter; Wadworth Devizes Bitter, 6X H
Excellent country inn where you are served in Somerset and can drink and eat in Dorset! Guest beers ( )

Rode

11–2.30; 6–11

Cross Keys
20 High Street ☎ (0373) 830354
Draught Bass; Charrington IPA H
Former brewery tap for now-defunct Fussells Brewery. Darts and skittles ✲♿

Rudge

11–2.30; 6–11

Full Moon
Lower Rudge (1 mile N of A36 at Standerwick)
☎ (0373) 830936
Butcombe Bitter; Wadworth 6X H
Small and friendly free house near Wiltshire border Q✲✿⚓

Shepton Mallet

10–2.30; 6–11

Kings Arms
Leg Square ☎ (0749) 3781
Halls Harvest Bitter; Ind Coope Burton Ale; Wadworth 6X H
17th-century pub of character

in northern part of town. Skittles ♒✲✿ ( )

Stoford

11–2.30; 6–11

Royal Oak
2 miles S of Yeovil
☎ (0935) 75071
Draught Bass H
Excellent friendly local on village green. Darts and bar billiards ♒Q (lounge) ✲✿
♿&⚓ (Yeovil Junction) ♿

Stogumber

11–2.30; 6–11

White Horse Hotel
Off A358 at Crowcombe
☎ (0984) 56277
Cotleigh Tawny Bitter; Golden Hill Exmoor Ale H
Interesting pub, with games room, in picturesque village setting. All food is home cooked. Guest beers
♒✲✿⚓ ( )♿&♿

Taunton

10.30–2.30; 5.30–11

Country Hotel
East Street ☎ (0823) 337651
Golden Hill Exmoor Ale; John Smith Bitter; Usher Best Bitter H
Plush bar in historic town-centre hotel. Excellent bar snacks ♒Q✲✿⚓ ( )&

10.30–2.30; 5.30–11

Harp Inn
Shoreditch Road (B3170, S of town centre) ☎ (0823) 272367
Courage Best Bitter; Directors H
Cosy suburban pub on road to racecourse. Pub games
✲✿ ( )♿

10.30–2.30; 5.30–11

Masons Arms
Magdalene Street
☎ (0823) 288916
Draught Bass; Golden Hill Exmoor Ale, Exmoor Dark; Wadworth 6X H
Comfortable back-street pub in town centre. Guest beers in winter Q✲ ( )♿⚓

11–2.30; 6–11

Old Ale House
The Parade
Cornish J D Dry Hop Bitter; Wessex Bitter; Marston Pedigree H
One of few Taunton pubs with real choice. In subterranean vault under old town hall. Can be noisy ( )⚓

10.30–2.30; 6–11 (10–4 Sat)

Royal Mail
Station Road ☎ (0823) 331567
Draught Bass H
One-bar pub near station and market. Games ⚓ ( )♿⚓

259

Somerset

10.30–2.30; 5.30–11
Wood Street Inn
Wood Street (off Bridge Street)
☎ (0823) 333011
Ruddles County; Usher Best Bitter H
Popular back-street local. Regular live rock music; skittles and darts 🍴🛏️🍺⇌

Try also: **Westgate**, Westgate Street (Whitbread)

Triscombe

11–2.30; 6 (7 winter)–11
Blue Ball
1 mile E of A358 OS157356
☎ (037 384) 324
Cotleigh Tawny Ale; Golden Hill Exmoor Ale H
17th-century thatched pub at the foot of the Quantock Hills; ideal for walkers. Extensive picturesque garden. Dominoes and skittles. Guest beers Q☆🍴🍺

Trudoxhill

12 (11.30 Sat)–2.30; 7–11
White Hart
½ mile S of A361 at Nunney Catch ☎ (037 384) 324
Adnams Bitter; Ash Vine Bitter H; **Butcombe Bitter** G; **Wadworth 6X** H
Welcoming inn with restaurant, Ash Vine Bitter from pub's own brewery
🏨🍴🍺⌛

Upton Noble

11.30–2.30; 6.30–11 (closed Mon)
Lamb Inn
⅓ mile A359 OS714395
☎ (074 985) 308
Butcombe Bitter; Wadworth 6X H
Former 17th-century cottages with fine views of Alfred's Tower and Wiltshire countryside
🏨Q☆ (restaurant) 🍴🍺

Watchet

10.30–2.30; 5.30–11
Bell Inn
Market Street ☎ (0984) 31387
Draught Bass; Golden Hill Exmoor Ale H
Ancient inn with old smuggling connections. Near working harbour and West Somerset railway station.

Local maritime community and visitors both treated with warm hospitality. Pub games
☆🍴⛵🅰⌛

Wells

10.30–2.30; 6–11
Star Hotel
High Street ☎ (0749) 72283
Draught Bass; Butcombe Bitter; Oakhill Farmers Ale; Wadworth 6X H
16th-century coaching inn near Market Place. 2 rooms lead off a courtyard, covered to provide all weather outdoor drinking.
Q🍴 (courtyard) 🛏️🍺

Try also: **Fountain**, St Thomas Street (Courage)

West Coker

11–2.30; 6–11
Royal George
11 High Street (A3)
☎ (093 586) 2334
Draught Bass; Charrington IPA; Hall & Woodhouse Tanglefoot H
16th-century pub with oak beamed ceiling; well supported by a wide range of pub lovers. Good range of games 🏨☆🍴🍺⌛

Williton

11.30–2.30; 5.30–11
Foresters Arms
Long Street (A39)
☎ (0984) 32508
Draught Bass; Charrington IPA; Cotleigh Tawny Ale H
17th-century coaching inn near West Somerset Railway Station. Ideal base for Quantocks, Brendons and coast. Darts. Guest beers
🏨☆🛏️🍴⛵🅰

Windmill Hill

11.30–2.30; 6.45–11 (closed Tue)
Square & Compass
Off A358 OS310165
☎ (0823) 480467
Butcombe Bitter H; **Wessex Stud** G
Homely pub off the beaten track. Garden with superb view. Children's playground and D.I.Y. barbecue. Reasonably priced bar menu and separate restaurant. Caravans to let. Pub games

🏨Q☆🛏️🍴🍺🅰 (in grounds) ⌛

Witham Friary

10–2.30; 6–11
Seymour Arms
OS745409
Usher Best Bitter G
Delightful locals' pub with serving hatch. Shove ha'penny and darts
🏨Q☆🛏️🍴⌛

Wookey

11–2.30; 6–11
Burcott Inn
On B3139 ☎ (0749) 73874
Butcombe Bitter H
Deservedly popular roadside pub with a friendly atmosphere. Over 40 different guest beers each year. Dining room and games room. Large garden with old cider press
Q☆ (lunch/early eve)
🍴🍺⛵🅰 (book)

Yeovil

10.30–2.30; 6–11
Great Lyde
Lyde Road (off A30)
☎ (0935) 29707
Palmer Bridport Bitter, IPA H
Pub converted from farm buildings. Plush lounge with indoor plants; large public with pool and darts in out-buildings 🍴🍺🍴⌛

11–2.30; 5.30–11
Armoury
1 The Park (opposite hospital)
☎ (0935) 71047
Butcombe Bitter; Smiles Best Bitter; Wadworth IPA, 6X, Farmers Glory, Old Timer (winter) H
Pub reputedly converted form an old armoury. Wood panelled eating area. Varied live music alternate Thu. eves. Open quizzes (Sun eves.) Darts
Q🍴🍺🍴⇌ (Pen Mill)

10.30–2.30; 5.30–11
Glovers Arms
Reckleford (next to ambulance station) ☎ (0935) 74223
Courage Best Bitter, Directors H
Oldest inn in town; comfortable lounge, busy bar. Darts and skittles
☆🍴🍺🍴⇌ (Pen Mill)

"I *hate* all the new fangled wineries, dineries, eateries etc. etc., which pass for British pubs these days. I did an LBC phone-in programme, where one of the subjects raised was the breakdown of marriages among people who run pubs. The calls came thick and fast and we all agreed that the basic problem was this new *stress* in today's pubs – pinball machines, fast foods etc. Pubs are no longer quiet places to retire to, they're just hell holes full of stress and smoke. Count me as an ardent supporter any day."

Sue Arnold *The Observer*

SMALL TOWNS, BIG TROUBLE

Tim Webb

On Friday night around the old market square, in the footsteps of the lamplighter's ghost, the lads gather for the last of the evening's entertainment. With the apparent collusion of brewery executives, licensing magistrates and disco bar licensees, the flower of British youth is once more about to kick hell out of itself and anything in its vicinity.

It's not Broadwater Farm or Toxteth or Lozells Road. It's Oxford and Aylesbury, Taunton and Yeovil, Ipswich and Bury St. Edmunds. This is the rich South, the agenda is strictly violence for pleasure and the fuel is alcohol.

Terry Morris, Professor of Criminology at the London School of Economics, cites two major causes for the upsurge in street violence over the past ten years. One: the emergence of a large group of high-spending, hard-drinking young people who do not share the suburban, middle class values that hold for much of U.K. society. Two: the willingness of alcohol traders and licensing justices to create and condone loosely-controlled drinking establishments aimed specifically at young drinkers.

Chief Inspector Rod Price of Somerset Constabulary agrees: "In the day these are hard-working respectable people. But with drink in their bellies they get the courage for a bit of aggro."

The traditional British Public House is not something that just happened. It evolved over 2,000 years in response to the demands of its customers and its legislators. Part of its fabric is the subtle control it exerts over drinking behaviour, by having a landlord or landlady whose home is on the premises; by being part of a community, with customers spanning the generations. In this way the young learn to drink sociably and within unstated but accepted conventions.

In recent years the development of fun pubs, disco bars and night clubs, run by absentee managers, targetted at the youth market and effectively excluding the more mature drinker, has been vigorously promoted by the big breweries at the expense of the traditional pub.

In Plymouth we have over 600 licensed premises, around a third of which are pubs. New pub licences, other than for redevelopments, are a rarity; stringent rules demand the proof of "need". Yet over the past ten years upwards of thirty licences have been granted to so-called "clubs" where teenagers can drink heavily until 2 am. It comes as little surprise to find that major street violence in the city is almost synonymous with clubland in the early hours of the morning.

If our community's use of alcohol is out of hand – and the increase in alcohol-related violence suggests it is – then surely there is an urgent need to comprehensively review our alcohol licensing practises. At present, magistrates seem afraid to use the powers of constraint vested in them. Big breweries for their part express unconvincing concern and then fight tooth-and-nail to supply the very outlets that are fuelling the problem.

In a recent interview John Lee, MD of Allied Breweries' new Parasol Corporation, a company set up to co-ordinate their foodier pubs, said that drinks outlets should be seen as "brands" which aim at "windows in the marketplace". I just hope for Mr. Lee's sake that his "windows in the marketplace" are not the same ones that my Friday night lads have their inebriated, bloodshot eyes on.

TIM WEBB is a Consultant Psychiatrist to Plymouth Health Authority, a director of the Plymouth Alcohol Advisory Service and a former director of **CAMRA**.

Staffordshire

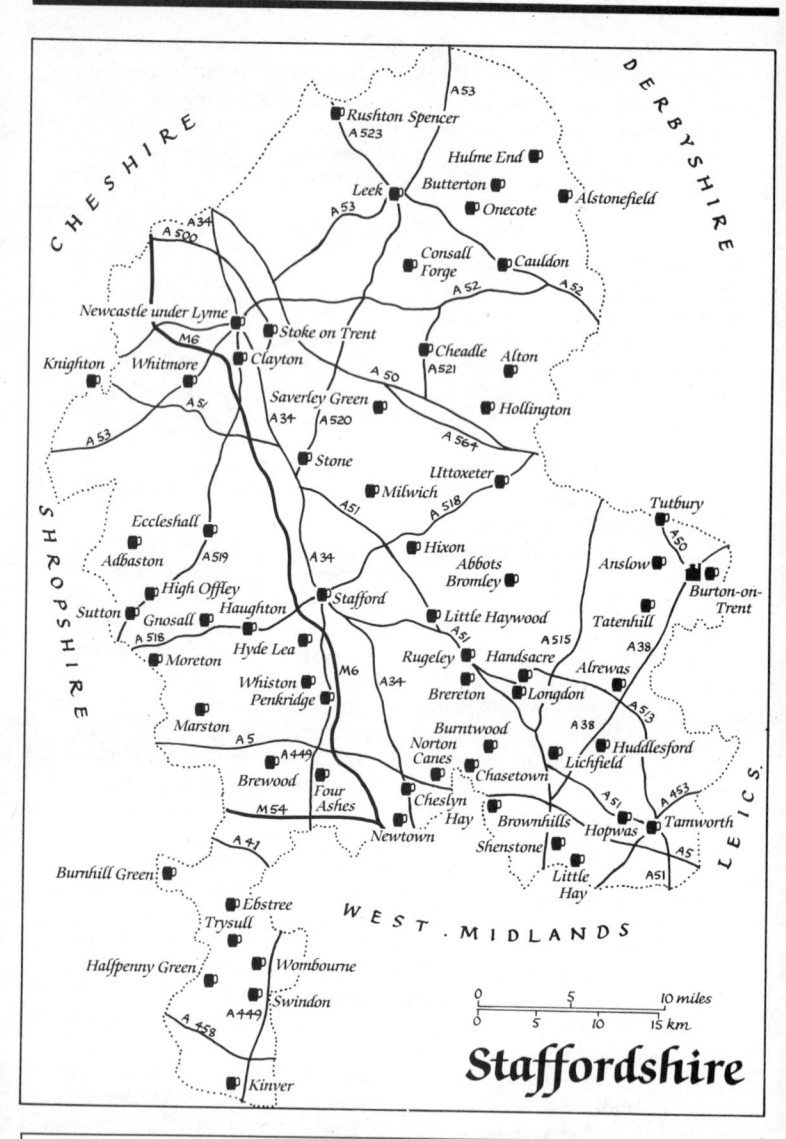

Burton Bridge, Marston, Burton-on-Trent

Abbots Bromley

10.30–2.30; 6–10.30 (11 F, S)

Bagot Arms
Bagot Street (B5014)
☎ (0283) 840371
Marston Pedigree H, **Owd Rodger (winter)** G
Traditional village pub with large bar

11–2.30; 6–10.30 (11 F, S)

Coach & Horses
High Street (B5014)
☎ (0283) 840256
Ind Coope Burton Ale H
Lively 16th-century pub. Bar billiards

Try also: Crown Inn

Adbaston

1 (12 Sat)–3; 6.340–11

Haberdashers Arms
Knighton OS753275
☎ (078 579) 339
Banks's Mild, Bitter; Hanson Black Country Bitter E
Unspoilt country local which sells home-grown produce

Alrewas

10.30–3; 5.30–11

George & Dragon
Main Street (off A38)
☎ (0283) 790202
Marston Pedigree H
Busy local with award-winning restaurant

Alstonefield

10.30–2.30; 6 (7 winter)–11

George
6 miles N of Ashbourne

262

Staffordshire

OS132556 ☎ (033 527) 205
Ind Coope Bitter, Burton Ale H
Attractive 18th-century village pub facing the village green. In spectacular countryside, very popular with walkers. Good food ≜ ⊛ ◐ ♦ Å

Alton

12–3 (2.30 winter); 6 (7 winter)–11
Talbot
Station Road ☎ (0538) 702767
Ind Coope Bitter, Burton Ale H
Warm friendly local in picturesque countryside near Alton Towers. Good value meals; games include Alton beer-tray dancing!
Q ≅ ⊛ ◐ ♦

Anslow

10.30–2.30; 5.30–11
Bell Inn
Main Street (off B5017)
Marston Merrie Monk, Pedigree H
Friendly village local with a good-sized beer garden. Mostly regulars, but friendly welcome. Piano in public
≜ Q ⊛ ⊕

Brereton

11–3; 6–11
Plough Inn
Main Road (A51)
Banks's Mild, Bitter E
Miners' pub on main road, looking over Lea Hall colliery and power station ⊕

Brewood

11–2.30; 6–11
Admiral Rodney
☎ (0902) 850583
HP & D Mild, Bitter, Entire H
Typical Holt Plant & Deakin-styled pub but with lots of Staffordshire oddments
≜ ≅ (lunch) ⊛ ◐ (6–8.30) ♦

Try also: **New Inns**, Kiddimore Green

Brownhills

11–3; 6–11
White Horse
White Horse Road, off A5
Banks's Mild, Bitter E
Comfortable 3-roomed pub overlooking Chasewater Reservoir. Games ⊕

Try also: **Prince of Wales** (A5)

Burnhill Green

11 (12 winter)–2.30; 6 (7 winter)–10.30 (11 F, S)
Dartmouth Arms
Snowden Road OS787006
☎ (074 65) 268
Ansells Bitter, Ind Coope Burton Ale H
Popular village pub with small restaurant area (book at busy times). Real Ansells Mild occasionally available (beware keg other times) ≜ Q ⊛ ◐ ♦ ⊕

Burntwood

11–3; 6–11
Trident
Chase Road
Marston Pedigree H
Basic 2-roomed local.
Games ⊕

Burton upon Trent

10.30–2.30; 5.30 (7 Sat)–11
Black Horse
72 Moor Street (B5017)
☎ (0283) 34187
Marston Pedigree H
Friendly town local with cosy lounge. Recommended as a port of call after Heritage Brewery visit Q ⊕ ♦ ⇌

11–2.30; 5.30–11
Burton Bridge
23 Bridge Street (A50)
☎ (0283) 36596
Burton Bridge XL Bitter, Bridge Bitter, Porter, Festival, Old Expensive H
Brewery with bar attached! Guest beers Sun. Very friendly; a must if visiting Burton ≜ Q ⊛ (back yard) ⊕ ♦

10.30–2.30; 5.30–11
Derby Inn
Derby Road A5121 (off A38)
☎ (0283) 43674
Marston Pedigree H, **Owd Rodger** (winter) G
Spartan but friendly 2-room pub. Landlord supplies weekend vegetables for locals, which can mean self-service when busy!
⊛ (back yard) ⊕ ♦ ⇌

10.30–2.30; 6–11
Elms Inn
Stapenhill Road (near Trent Bridge A444) ☎ (0283) 62272
Draught Bass H
Friendly 3-room local; deservedly popular ⊛ ⊕

Try also: **Duke of York** (Marston)

Butterton

12–2.30 (not Wed); 7–11
Black Lion
☎ (053 88) 232
McEwan 70/-; Younger No.3 H
Friendly, multi-roomed country inn in picturesque village near Manifold Valley, excellent food and accommodation; guest beers summer
≜ ≅ ⊛ ⋈ ◐ (not Wed) ♦ ⊕ ♦

Cauldon

10.30–2.30; 6–11
Yew Tree
Off A52/A523 ☎ (053 86) 348
Draught Bass; Burton Bridge XL Bitter; M&B Mild H
One of the finest pubs in the country, dating back to the late 17th century. Collections include working polyphonia, grandfather clocks and sundry Victoriana Q ≅ ⊛

Chasetown

11–3; 6–11
Crown
High Street ☎ (054 36) 6330
Banks's Mild, Bitter E
Friendly town local ⊕

Cheadle

11.30–3; 6–11
Miner's Rest
Froghall Road (A521)
☎ (0538) 756729
Burtonwood Bitter H
New pub, built round the original. Family room and children's play area in beer garden. Book for Sun lunch. No food Mon. Live music weekends ≅ ⊛ ◐ ♦

Cheslyn Hay

12–3; 7–11
Mary Rose
Moon Lane ☎ (0922) 415114
Ansells Mild, Bitter; Ind Coope Burton Ale; Tetley Bitter H
Converted farmhouse, with excellent food. Local CAMRA Pub of the Year 3 years running ≜ ⊛ ◐ ♦ (not Sun) ♦

Clayton

11.30–3; 6–11
Westbury Tavern
Westbury Park (off A519)
☎ (0782) 638766
Ansells Mild, Bitter; Ind Coope Burton Ale H
Pub of amazing contrasts: extremely popular "Yuppy" lounge, and traditional bar (with skittles) ⊛ ◐ ⊕

Consall Forge

10.30–2.30; 6–11
Black Lion
Consall village, follow signs to country park ☎ (0782) 550294
Marston Pedigree; Ruddles County H
Isolated basic country pub in picturesque countryside in the Churnet Valley. Recommended for a summer day out ≜ Q ≅ ⊛ ◐ ♦ ⊕ ♦ Å

Ebstree

11–2.30; 6–10.30 (11 F, S)

263

Staffordshire

Holly Bush
Ebstree Road, Trysull (1 mile off A454) OS854959
☎ (0902) 895587
Ansells Mild, Bitter; Ind Coope Burton Ale H
Pleasant country pub, half mile west of Staffs & Worcester canal. Lounge recently enlarged to form eating area

Eccleshall

11.30–3; 6–11
Bell
16 High Street (B5026)
☎ (0785) 850378
Draught Bass; M&B Springfield Bitter H
Popular small-town pub with attractive lounge fireplace (not Sun)

12–3; 7–11
Railway
Green Lane (off A519)
☎ (0785) 850564
Davenport Mild H
Friendly local on edge of town worth seeking out. Games

11–3; 6.30–11
Royal Oak
High Street (B5026)
☎ (0785) 850230
Burtonwood Bitter H
Large town-centre pub with separate restaurant; strong emphasis on food

Four Ashes

11–2.30; 5.30–11
Four Ashes
(A449) ☎ (0902) 822208
Banks's Mild, Bitter E
Large, busy roadside pub. Oak beamed ceiling, timber mostly original! Special garden service point (and playground). Industrial view in middle of rural Staffordshire

Gnosall

11–3 (12–3 winter); 7–11
Boat
Wharf Road ☎ (0785) 822208
Marston Burton Bitter, Pedigree H
Popular pub on Shropshire Union Canal, at Bridge 34. Bar billiards. No food Sun

Try also: Royal Oak

Halfpenny Green

11–2.30; 6–10.30 (11 F, S)
Royal Oak
On The Green OS825920
☎ (038 488) 318
Banks's Mild, Bitter E
Popular old country local on the crossroads, near Bobbington Aerodrome

Handsacre

11–3; 6–11
Crown
Jct of A513/canal
☎ (0543) 490239
Draught Bass H
Canalside pub with comfortable lounge and lively atmosphere, overlooking Staffordshire countryside

Haughton

11.30–3; 6–11
Bell
Newport Road (A518)
☎ (0785) 780301
Courage Best Bitter, Directors H
Modernised, main road village pub

High Offley

11–3; 6–11
(closed Sun eve – Thu lunch winter)
Anchor Inn
OS775255 ☎ (078 574) 569
Marston Pedigree, Owd Rodger; Wadworth 6X H
Famous unspoilt canalside pub. Camping by arrangement, plus impromptu folk singing

Hixon

12 (11.30 Sat)–3; 6–11
Green Man
Lea Road OS005262
☎ (0889) 270931
Draught Bass H
Village pub to north of High Street. No eve meals Sun/Mon

Hollington

closed Mon–Sat lunch; 7–11
Star
Off A50 on Tean–Rocester road OS059890
☎ (088 926) 250
ABC Best Bitter, Ansells Mild, Ind Coope Bitter, Burton Ale H
1-roomed stone cottage inn with separate games area, and convivial atmosphere 3 miles from Alton Towers. Railway memorabilia (Sun)

Hopwas

11.30–2.30; 6–11
Chequers
1 Mints Road ☎ (0827) 53361
Courage Best Bitter, Directors; John Smith Bitter H
Popular old-world pub by Coventry canal; beware the ghost of the dead cellarman! New restaurant; occasional live music

Try also: Red Lion

Huddlesford

11–2.30; 6–11
Plough
Huddlesford Lane (off A38)
☎ (0543) 432369
Ansells Mild, Bitter; Ind Coope Burton Ale H
Relaxing country pub alongside canal. Pleasantly furnished single L-shaped room has distinct bar type area; darts. No food Sun

Hulme End

11.30–2.30; 7–11
Manifold Valley Hotel
On B5054 ☎ (029884) 537
Ward Darley Dark Mild, Thorne Bitter, Sheffield Best Bitter H
Impressive stone-built hotel in picturesque countryside by River Manifold. Friendly atmosphere; excellent food, occasional live jazz/folk

Hyde Lea

11–3; 7–11
Crown
Off A449 ☎ (0785) 54240
Draught Bass; M&B Springfield Bitter H
Spick and span popular local with military theme in lounge. No meals Sun

Kinver

12–2.30; 6–10.30 (11 F, S)
Cross
Church Hill (off High Street)
☎ (0384) 872435
Banks's Bitter; Hanson Mild E
Popular local with smart lounge next to restored Tudor house (ex-Kinver grammar school)

12–2.30; 7–10.30 (11 F, S)
Elm Tree
183 Enville Road
☎ (0384) 872480
Davenports Bitter H
Pub at edge of village; garage was once a brewhouse. Children's swings; no food Mon–Sat

Try also: George & Dragon (Ansells)

Knighton

11–3; 5.30–11
White Lion
On B5026 ☎ (063 081) 300
Marston Burton Bitter, Pedigree H
Friendly inn, around 350 years old. Split-level public bar with low beams; small cosy lounge. Fine malt whisky range. Folknights (lunch)

Staffordshire

Leek

10–2.30; 6–11
Britannia
46 West Street ☎ (0538) 383178
Marston Mercian Mild, Pedigree H
Popular pub with large bar just out of the town centre. Games Q⊛⊕&

12–2.30 (10 Sat); 7–11 (6 Sat)
Flying Horse
130 Ashbourne Road
Marston Mercian Mild, Burton Bitter, Pedigree H
Small busy pub on the beaten track to Alton Towers. Games ⊛(&

11–2.30; 6–11
Merrie Monk
38 Compton Street
☎ (0538) 383624
Marston Border Mild, Burton Bitter H
Friendly local with regular ceilidhs. Pub 'question time' weekday nights; Frank Muir Appreciation Society
⊛⊛⊕&▲

Lichfield

12–3; 7–11
Carpenters Arms
Christchurch Lane
☎ (0543) 262098
Banks's Mild, Bitter E
Convivial 1-roomed local ⊛

12–3; 6–11
City Forge
St John Street
Draught Bass; M&B Highgate Mild H
Fun pub, noisy but perfectly acceptable during the week ⇌

11–3; 5.30–11
Duke of York
Church Street ☎ (0543) 255171
Davenport Bitter; Wem Special H
Lively drinking house with good views over the city and cathedral ⊛⊛⊕(♪⊕⇌

11.30–3; 7–11
Queens Head
Sandford Street
Marston Pedigree H
Unique small pub near Beacon Park; popular with sports people ⊕

Try also: Bald Buck

Little Hay

11–2.30; 6–11
Holly Bush
Off A5127/A38
☎ (0543) 481217
Ansells Mild, Bitter; Ind Coope Burton Ale; Tetley Bitter H
Friendly pub at end of small village. Good value public bar, trendy lounge cocktail bar, and excellent restaurant. Local CAMRA Pub of the Year 1987
⊛⊛⊕(♪⊕

Little Haywood

11–3; 6–11
Red Lion
Main Road (off A513)
OS007214 ☎ (0889) 881314
Ansells Bitter; Ind Coope Burton Ale H
Welcoming village local with friendly atmosphere
▲⊛⊛⊕(♪⊕&

Longdon

11.30–3; 6–11
Swan with Two Necks
Brooke End, Upper Longdon (off A51) ☎ (0543) 490251
ABC Bitter; Ansells Mild, Bitter; Ind Coope Burton Ale H
Authentic inn with stone floor, low beams and restaurant ⊛⊛⊕(♪

Marston

11–3; 7–11
Fox
OS835140 ☎ (0785) 840729
Lloyds Country Bitter; Marston Pedigree, Owd Rodger; Wadworth 6X; Woods Special Bitter H
Enterprising country free house with guest beers. Well worth a detour
▲Q⊛⊛⊕(♪⊕&▲⊘

Milwich

12–3; 6–11
Green Man
On B5027 ☎ (088 924) 310
Draught Bass H
Small friendly village pub by tiny 1833 schoolhouse. Games
▲Q⊛⊛⊕&

Moreton

11–3; 6 (7 winter)–11
Rising Sun
2 miles S of A518 OS799168
Marston Burton Bitter, Pedigree H
Friendly country pub, worth a visit ▲⊛⊛⊕(♪⊕&

Newcastle-under-Lyme

12–3; 7–11
Castle Mona
4 Victoria Street (off A34)
☎ (0782) 612849
Davenport Mild; Wem Best Bitter, Special H
2-roomed pub in quiet corner of town, a thriving sports and social fraternity ⊕

12–3; 7–11
Jolly Potters
Barracks Road ☎ (0782) 631736
Davenport Mild; Wem Best Bitter, Special H
Recently thoughtfully modernised 2-roomed pub which has survived the ravages of "road improvements" ⊛⊕

11–3; 5.30 (7 Sat)–11
Victoria
62 King Street ☎ (0782) 615569
Draught Bass H
Staunch traditionalists' pub with a strong games and quiz fraternity; handy for the new Victoria Theatre ⊕

Newtown

11–2.30; 7–11
Ivy House
Stafford Road (A34)
☎ (0922) 476607
Draught Bass; M&B Highgate Mild, Springfield Bitter H
Old low-ceilinged pub on main busy road. Children's garden ⊛⊛⊕

Norton Canes

12–3; 7–11
Railway
Norton Green Lane
Ansells Mild, Bitter H
Small 1-roomed pub Q

Onecote

12–2.30; 7–11
Jervis Arms
On B5053 2 miles from A523
☎ (053 88) 206
Draught Bass; McEwan 70/-; Marston Pedigree; Theakston Best Bitter, XB, Old Peculier H
Popular 17th-century inn in Peak District National Park. Beer garden with children's play area on banks of River Hamps. Excellent value food (including vegetarian) always available ▲⊛⊛⊕(♪⊕&

Penkridge

11–3; 5.30–11
Star
Market Place (B5013)
☎ (078 571) 2513
Banks's Mild, Bitter E
Re-opened after a century; not quite unspoilt by progress
⊛ (lunch) ⊛ ((not Sun) &⇌

10.30–3; 6.30–11
White Hart
Stone Cross (on A449, near B5012 Jct) ☎ (078 571) 2242
M&B Highgate Mild, Springfield Bitter, Brew XI E
Excellent village-centre hostelry ▲⊛⊛⊕(♪⊕&⇌

Rugeley

11–3; 6–11
Yorkshireman
On B5013
Courage Best Bitter, Directors H
Trendy up-market eating

265

Staffordshire

house next to main railway line 🏠 🍺 🚆

Try also: Red Lion

Rushton Spencer

10.30–2.30; 6–11

Crown Inn
Beat Lane (off A523) OS930616
☎ (026 06) 231
Younger Scotch, IPA H
Gem of a pub, friendly and welcoming, close to Cloud End (1200 feet): popular with hang-gliders 🍺 🍴 🚭

Saverley Green

12–3; 7–11

Hunter
Sandon Road (1 mile S of A50)
☎ (0782) 392067
ABC Bitter; Gibbs Mew Wiltshire Bitter; Ind Coope Burton Ale; Tetley Bitter H
Cosy, friendly atmosphere. Family room. Occasional beer festivals; guest beers
🏠 🍺 🍴 (Sun) 🍴 🚭 🏕

Shenstone

11–3; 5.30–11

Railway
Main Street (off A5127)
☎ (0543) 480803
Marston Burton Bitter, Pedigree, Merrie Monk H
Village pub with plenty going on. Split-level lounge with unobtrusive and relaxing feel 🍺 🚭 🚆

Stafford

11–3; 6 (7 Sat)–11

Bird in Hand
Victoria Square
☎ (0785) 52198
Courage Best Bitter, Directors; John Smith Bitter H
Popular, enterprising pub with bar, snug, lounge and games room 👶 🍺 🍴 🚭 🚆

11–3; 7 (6 Fri)–11

Coach & Horses
4 Mill Bank ☎ (0785) 223376
Draught Bass; M&B Springfield Bitter H
Straightforward town centre pub near Victoria Park 🚭 🚆

12–3; 7 (6 Fri)–11

Cottage by the Brook
59 Peel Terrace (off Sandon Road) ☎ (0785) 223563
ABC Best Bitter; Ansells Mild; Ind Coope Burton Ale; Tetley Bitter H
Large 4-roomed pub to suit all tastes. Variety of traditional pub games 🏠 👶 🍺 🍴 🚭

11–3; 6–11

Holmcroft
Holmcroft Road (off A5013) OS915244 ☎ (0785) 52634
Banks's Mild, Bitter E
Popular estate pub with long established landlord
🍺 🍴 (not Sun) 🚭

12–2.30; 7–11

Railway Inn
Castle Street, Castletown
☎ (0785) 42890
Ansells Bitter; Ind Coope Burton Ale H
Traditional Victorian local, with large whisky selection
🏠 👶 🍴 🚭

11–3; 6–11

Sun Inn
7 Lichfield Road (A34/A518 Jct)
☎ (0785) 42208
Draught Bass H
Old, modernised pub with variety of rooms, including restaurant. Reference library for crosswording and quizzing customers
🚗 👶 🍴 🍺 🚭 🚆

Stoke-on-Trent
Fenton:

12–3; 5.30–11

Malt 'n' Hops
295 King Street (A50)
☎ (0782) 313406
Burtonwood Dark Mild; Five Towns Bursley Bitter, Robinson Old Tom H
Single room lounge bar in Big 8 dominated area. Local CAMRA Pub of the Year 1988. An ever changing range of guest beers – at least 4 at any time. Packed at weekends
🚭 🚆 (Longton)

Hanley:

11.30–3; 7–11

Coachmakers
65 Lichfield Street
☎ (0782) 262158
Draught Bass H
Victorian 4-roomed pub with central drinking corridor; strong local loyalty. Skittles
🏠 🚭

12–3; 5.30 (7 Sat)–11

Globe
Bucknall New Road (A52)
☎ (0782) 25539
Draught Bass; Five Towns Bursley Bitter; Hook Norton Old Hookey H
Homely 2-roomed local; pub games in bar, regular quiz nights. Guest beers 🏠 🚭

11–3; 7–11

Northwood Inn
Botany Bay Road
☎ (0782) 271020
Ansells Mild; Ind Coope Burton Ale; Tetley Bitter H
Busy neighbourhood pub with smaller rooms leading off 1 bar 🏠 🍺 🚭

12–3; 7–11

Rose & Crown
Etruria Road (A53)
☎ (0782) 280503
Ansells Mild, Bitter; Gibbs Mew Wiltshire Bitter; Ind Coope Burton Ale H
Traditional bar and comfortable inviting lounge in former Parkers brewery showpiece pub. Good value home-cooked food (not Sun) Regular live music
🍺 🍴 🚭 🚆 (Etruria)

Longton:

11–3; 6–11

Rose Inn
Uttoxeter Road, Normacot (A50) ☎ (0782) 317689
Draught Bass H
Fairly small, busy friendly pub with separate bar and lounge with juke box 🏠 🚭 🍺 🚭

Stoke:

11–3; 5.30–11

Glebe
Glebe Street
Banks's Mild, Bitter E
Refurbished 2-room town pub. Bar with pool table; lounge popular with both locals and students 🍴 🚭 🚆

Tunstall:

11–3; 7–11

White Hart
Roundwell Street
☎ (0782) 85817
Marston Border Bitter, Pedigree H
Unpretentious unspoilt 1-roomed pub with Potteries characters. Only Marston's pub in town Q 🍺 🚭

12–3; 7–11

White Horse
143 Brownhills Road
☎ (0782) 85887
Draught Bass; M&B Springfield Bitter H
Old-fashioned, relaxing basic pub at lower end of town with genuine central heating by means of old stove pot
🏠 Q 🚭 🚆 (Longport)

Stone

11.30–3; 6–11

Pheasant
Old Road (off A520) OS902348
☎ (0785) 814603
Draught Bass; M&B Springfield Bitter H
Lively, street corner pub, a former Joules' House
🏠 Q 🍺 🍴 (not Sun) 🚭 🚆

Sutton

11–3; 6–11

Red Lion
On A519 ☎ (0952) 811048
Banks's Mild, Bitter E
Lively main road country pub; children's adventure playground 🏠 👶 🍺 🍴 🚭 🏕

266

Staffordshire

Swindon

10.30–2.30; 6–10.30 (11 F, S)

Green Man
High Street ☎ (0384) 287138
Banks's Mild, Bitter E
Friendly old village pub, once the butchers shop, at the edge of the village near the Staffs and Worcester canal
Q ☎ ((not Sun)) ⌑ ᛐ

Try also: Bush (Hanson) Greyhound (Banks's)

Tamworth

11–2.30; 7–11

Bulls Head
Watling Street, Two Gates (A5) ☎ (0827) 287820
Marston Mercian Mild, Pedigree H
Very popular local; twice recent winner of local CAMRA Pub of the Year Q ⊛ ((Tue–Fri) ⌑ ≋ (Wilnecote)

Try also: Railway

10–2.30; 7–11

Globe
Lower Gungate
☎ (0827) 63402
Draught Bass; M&B Mild H
Town pub from a byegone age; fascinating collection of memorabilia; look out for Churchill and the beehive
Q ⊛ ⋈ ⌑

10.30–2.30; 6.30–11

Hamlets Wine Bar
13–15 Lower Gungate
☎ (0827) 52277
Marston Mercian Mild, Pedigree; Samuel Smith OBB H
Bare-boards-and-sawdust busy town free house, popular with young locals. Regular guest beers; good home-cooked lunches (≋

11–2.30; 6.30–11
Tweedale Arms
Victoria Road ☎ (0827) 62748
Draught Bass; M&B Mild H
Popular locals' pub opposite railway station. Welcoming atmosphere ☎ ⌑ ᛐ ≋

Try also: Boot Inn; Tamworth Arms

Tatenhill

11.30–2.30; 5.30–11

Horseshoe Inn
1 mile from A38/A5121 Jct
☎ (0283) 64913
Marston Pedigree H, **Owd Rodger** (winter) G
Popular 18th-century village inn with unspoilt beamed lounge. Excellent food
Q ☎ ⊛ ( ) (Tue–Sat)

Trysull

11–2.30; 6–10.30 (11 F, S)

Plough
School Road ☎ (0902) 892254
Banks's Mild, Bitter E
15th-century halt-timbered farmhouse. Barbecues in summer. Pub games ⌑ ⊛ ( ) ᛐ

Tutbury

11–2.30; 7–11
(May open earlier summer)

Cross Keys
Burton Street (A50)
☎ (0283) 813677
Ind Coope Best Bitter, Burton Ale H
Small 2-room village local overlooking Dove Valley
☎ (early eve) ⊛ ⌑ A

Uttoxeter

12–2.30; 7–11

Roebuck
37 Dove Bank (A518)
☎ (0889) 565563
Burton Bridge Bitter H, **Porter** G; **John Smith Bitter; Marston Pedigree** H
Interesting, homely inn dating back to 1608. Oak-beamed inglenook fireplace
⌑ ☎ ⊛ ⋈ ( ) ⌑ ᛐ ᛗ (summer)

Whiston

11–3 (closed Tue); 6–11

Swan
Off A449 OS895144
☎ (078 571) 2460
Ansells Bitter; Ind Coope Burton Ale H
Reputable country pub with comfy lounge and popular bar. Electronic games in corridor
⌑ ☎ ⊛ ( ) ᛐ A

Whitmore

11–3; 5.30–11

Sheet Anchor
On A53, by railway bridge
☎ (0782) 680804
Davenports Mild, Bitter H
Large pub with island bar, nautical atmosphere and 4 distinct drinking areas. Good home-cooked food. Large patio and lawn with children's play area ⌑ ⊛ (ᛐ

Try also: Mainwaring Arms (Free)

Wombourne

11–2.30; 6–10.30 (11 F, S)

Red Lion
Old Stourbridge Road
(off A449) ☎ (0902) 892270
Draught Bass; Springfield Bitter E
Old coaching inn below the original main road
⌑ ☎ ⊛ ((not Sun)
) (Tue–Sat) ⌑ ᛐ A ᛗ

KEY TO SYMBOLS

Facilities

- ⌑ real fire
- Q quiet pub – no electronic music, TV or obtrusive games
- ☎ indoor room for children
- ⊛ garden or other outdoor drinking area
- ⋈ accommodation
- (lunchtime meals
-) evening meals
- ⌑ public bar
- ᛐ facilities for the disabled
- A camping facilities close to the pub or part of the pub grounds
- ≋ near British Rail station
- ⊖ near Underground station
- ᛗ real cider

The facilities, beers and pub hours listed in the Good Beer Guide are liable to change but were correct when the Guide went to press.

Help keep real ale alive by joining CAMRA. Your voice helps encourage brewers big and small to brew cask beer and offer all beer drinkers a better choice.

Suffolk

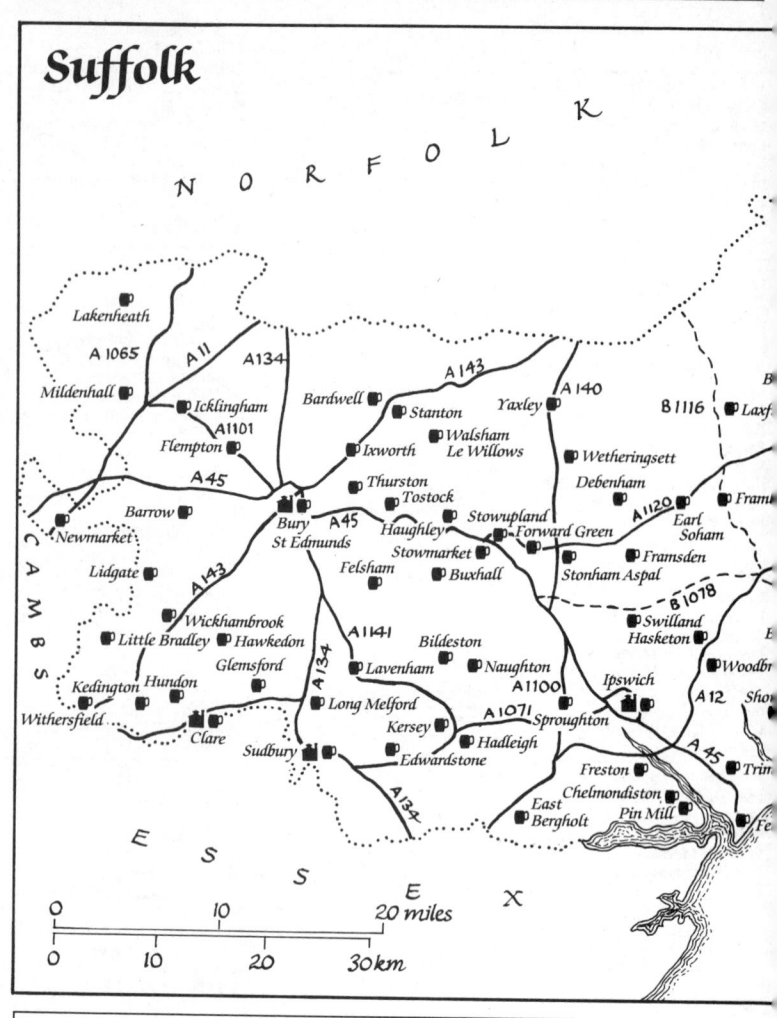

Adnams, Southwold; **Greene King**, Bury St. Edmunds; *Mauldon*, Sudbury; **Nethergate**, Clare; **Forbes Ales**, Lowestoft; **Tolly Cobbold**, Ipswich

Aldeburgh

10.30–2.30; 6–11
Mill Inn
Market Cross Place
☎ (072 885) 2563
Adnams Bitter, Old, Broadside H
Friendly seafront pub. Pub games
Q ≈ ( ) (not Sun, Wed) & A

All Aldeburgh pubs serve real ale

Bardwell

11–2.30; 5–11
Dun Cow
Up Street (off A143)
☎ (0359) 50806
Greene King XX, IPA, Abbot H
Welcoming village local with large plain bar, smart lounge and pool room Q & A

Try also: Six Bells (Free)

Barnby

11–2; 6.30–11
Swan Inn
Swan Lane ☎ (050 276) 646
Greene King IPA; Abbot H
Spacious country pub. Ask about the Barnby Giant. Live music – if you bring your own instrument. Games include shove ha'penny ≈ & ≈ ( ) & A

Barrow

11–2.30; 6–11
Willow
Bury Road ☎ (0284) 810492
Greene King XX, IPA, Abbot H
Pleasant country pub with oak-beamed lounge and bar. Good social life with many charity events. Butterfly farm nearby. Darts and cribbage
≈ & ≈ ( ) & &

Try also: Three Horseshoes (Greene King)

Suffolk

Bildeston

10.30 (12 winter) 2.30; 5-11

Kings Head
High Street ☎ (0449) 741434
Greene King IPA; Mauldon Fine Anglian Mild, Bildeston Bitter H
Fine old fluted, beamed pub with unusual carousel handpump system. Guest beers. Pub games; adventure playground

Bramfield

11-2.30; 6.30-11

Bell
On A144 ☎ (096 279) 395
Adnams Mild, Bitter H
Good Suffolk local with Ringing the Bull game

Bury St Edmunds

11-2.30; 5-11

Masons Arms
Whiting Street
☎ (0284) 753955
Greene King XX, IPA, Abbot H
17th-century posting house near Market Square

11-2.30; 6-11

Spread Eagle
Out Westgate (A143)
☎ (0284) 754523
Greene King XX, IPA, Abbot H
Popular town pub with thriving public bar and comfortable lounge. Pub games (not Sun)

Try also: Dog & Patridge (Greene King); Ipswich Arms; Suffolk Hotel (Free)

Butley

11-2.30; 6 (7 winter) 11

Oyster
On B1084 (Woodbridge–Orford Road)
Adnams Mild H, **Bitter, Old** G
Quaint old inn. Folk singing in lounge Sun eves. Parlour quoits; steel quoits played in village during summer

Buxhall

12-2.30; 7-11

Crown
Mill Lane ☎ (044 93) 521
Greene King XX, IPA, Abbot H
Traditional 2-bar pub. Informal atmosphere; home-cooked food; pub games

Chelmondiston

11-2.30; 6.30 (7 winter)-11

Red Lion
Main Road (B1456)
☎ (047 384) 327
Tolly Cobbold Bitter, Old Strong H
Family pub with strong darts following; also football and cribbage teams. Basic bar, smart lounge

Clare

11-2; 5-11

Bell
Market Hall (A1092/B1063)
☎ (0787) 277741
Greene King IPA · Nethergate Bitter H
Oak-beamed, 16th-century post house in a medieval weaving town. 2 restaurants and summer barbecues. Four-poster beds. Guest beers

Debenham

10.30-2.30; 5.45-11

Cherry Tree
Cherry Tree Green
☎ (0728) 860275
Tolly Cobbold Mild, Bitter H, **Old Strong** G
Large friendly village pub with its own bowling green, situated on edge of picturesque village. Excellent home-cooked food. Play area for children. Pub games Q (lounge)

Earl Soham

11.30-2.30; 5.30-11

Victoria
On A1120 ☎ (0728) 82758
Earl Soham Gannet Mild, Victoria Bitter, Albert Ale H, **Jolabrugg (winter)** G
Local country pub with friendly atmosphere. Brews all its own draught beers and serves home-made bar food. Local musicians often spontaneously entertain. Pub games

East Bergholt

11-2.30; 6-11

Royal Oak (Dickey)
East End ☎ (0206) 298221
Greene King IPA, Abbot H
Friendly, unspoilt village local. Large beer garden has a children's play area. Pub games

Edwardstone

11.30-2; 6.30-11

White Horse
Mill Green (A1071)
☎ (0787) 211211
Greene King XX, IPA H, **Abbot** G
Remote traditional village pub with 2 bars. Always a warm welcome. Various games including Shut-the-Box

Felixstowe

11-2.30; 6-11

Ferry Boat Inn
Felixstowe Ferry
☎ (0394) 284203
Tolly Cobbold Bitter, Original, Old Strong H
Old traditional pub, popular during high season. Water cooled casks at back of the bar. Backgammon (14+) (Tue–Fri 7-9)

Try also: Fludyer Arms Hotel (Tolly Cobbold)

Felsham

11-2.30; 6-11

Six Bells
Church Road (off A1141)
☎ (044 93) 268
Greene King XX, IPA, Abbot H
Village pub with a strong folk music tradition. Still has the rules for the Felsham Jolly

269

Suffolk

Boys' Society! Pub games
⌂Q⌘()⊕

Flempton

11–2.30; 7–11

Greyhound
The Green (off A1101)
☎ (028 484) 400
Greene King XX, IPA, Abbot H
Lively village pub tucked away behind church, so often unnoticed by travellers on main road. Pub games
⌂╳()⊕⌂

Forward Green

10.30–2.30; 5.30–11

Shepherd & Dog
On A1120 ☎ (0449) 711361
Greene King XX, IPA, Abbot H
Good, honest roadside ale house. Pub games ⌂⌘()

Framlingham

10.30–2.30; 5.30–11

Railway Inn
9 Station Road (B1116)
☎ (0728) 723693
Adnams Mild, Bitter, Old, Extra H
Traditional pub in historic town near 13th-century castle, reputedly haunted by the infamous Peter Read. Pub games ⌂Q⌘()⊕⌂

Framsden

11.30–2.30; 7–11

Dobermann
The Street ☎ (047 339) 461
Adnams Mild, Bitter, Broadside; Greene King IPA; Tolly Cobbold Bitter H
Old timber framed thatched inn with see-through fireplace. Extensive range of home-made food. Pub games. Guest beers ⌂Q⌘()⊕⌂

Freston

11–2.30; 6–11

Boot
Shotley Road (B1456)
☎ (047 384) 277
Tolly Cobbold Mild, Bitter, Original *or* **XXXX, Old Strong** H
Charming old-world pub, home of Freston Mummers who perform medieval plays. All home cooking; Fri fresh fish day. Pub games
⌂Q⌧⌘()⌂▲

Glemsford

11–2.30; 5–11

Angel
Egremont Street (B1065)
☎ (0787) 281671
Greene King XX, IPA, Abbot G
Carved angels feature on the exterior of this traditional pub in a former weaving village. George Cavendish, Cardinal Wolsey's secretary and biographer lived in the building. Pub games
Q⌘⌂()

Try also: Crown; Black Lion (Greene King)

Great Glemham

11–2.30; 6.30–11

Crown Inn
Off A12 ☎ (072 878) 693
Adnams Bitter; Draught Bass (summer); **Greene King IPA, Abbot; Mauldon Bitter** H
Homely 17th-century country pub in conservation area close to Heritage coast. Superior accommodation and home-cooked food. Pub games
⌂Q⌧⌘╳()

Hadleigh

11–2.30; 5 (6 Sat)–11

White Hart
46 Bridge Street (off A1071)
☎ (0473) 822206
Tolly Cobbold Mild, Bitter, Original H
Small, oak-beamed village-style pub catering for all tastes. Many pub games
⌂Q⌘╳()

Hasketon

11–3; 6 (6.30 winter)–11

Turks Head
Low Road ☎ (039 43) 2584
Tolly Cobbold Mild, Bitter H
Friendly country pub, with pub games, putting green and large children's play area
⌂⌧ (lounge) ⌘() (not Thu)
⊕▲ (caravans)

Haughley

11–2.30; 5.30–11

Railway Tavern
Station Road (off A45)
☎ (0449) 673577
Adnams Old; Greene King XX, IPA, Abbot; Mauldon Bitter H
Friendly 1-bar free house; guest beers ⌂Q⌧⌘()⌂

Try also: Kings Arms; White Horse

Hawkedon

11.30–2.30; 5.30–11.30 (closed Mon)

Queens Head
Off B1066 OS800531
☎ (028 489) 204
Greene King IPA H, **Abbot** G
Traditional pub set in rolling countryside. Pub games
⌂Q⌧()⌂

Hundon

12 (11 summer)–2.30; 5–11

Plough
Brockley Green OS722470
☎ (044 086) 248

Adnams Bitter; Mauldon Bitter; Nethergate Bitter H
Friendly beamed country pub in a hamlet. Cosy restaurant, also excellent bar food. Large garden with fine views
⌂Q⌧⌘()⌂

Icklingham

11–2.30; 7–11

Plough Inn
The Street (A1101)
☎ (0638) 713370
Bateman XXXB; Greene King IPA; Samuel Smith OBB H
Old flint cottages now a popular village local. Possibly originated as a pub for river traffic. Games room. Guest beers ⌂⌧⌘╳()⊕

Ipswich

11–2.30; 5 (7 Sat)–11

Arboretum
High Street ☎ (0473) 50711
Tolly Cobbold Mild (summer), **Bitter, Old Strong, XXXX** H
Happy town local with beer guide library. Shove ha'penny team includes ladies world champion! No food Sun
⌂⌘() (until 8) ⌂

11–2.30; 5.30 (5 F, S)–11

Blooming Fuschia
167 Foxhall Road
☎ (0473) 725874
Ind Coope Best Bitter, Burton Ale; Tetley Bitter H
Busy pub just outside town centre. England's only "Blooming Fuschia." Rare tiled sign. Good for families in summer. Pub games
⌧⌘() (not Sun) () (till 7) ⌂

11–2.30; 6–11

Lord Nelson
81 Fore Street ☎ (0473) 54072
Adnams Mild, Bitter, Extra, Old, Tally Ho (Xmas) H
Dates back to 1663; handy for swimming pool. Games include shove ha'penny
⌧╳⊕⌂

11–2.30; 5 (7 Sat)–11

Newt & Cucumber
24–26 Falcon Street (near bus station) ☎ (0473) 59181
Draught Bass; Greene King IPA, Rayment BBA, Abbot; Mauldon Bitter H
Modern pub popular for business lunches and with young people at weekends. Cards and dominoes ()⌀≈

11–2.30; 5–11

Rose & Crown
77 Norwich Road
☎ (0473) 58192
Tolly Cobbold Mild, Bitter, Original, XXXX, Old Strong H
Former brewery; pub dates back to 1685. Folk club Thu eves. Pub games ⌘()⊕

270

Suffolk

11–2.30; 5.30–11
Steamboat
78 New Cut West
☎ (0473) 601902
Tolly Cobbold Mild, Bitter H
Oldest dockside pub in Ipswich, very popular. Darts, cards and dominoes ⌘⌑

11–2.30; 6–11
Thrasher
Nacton Road (off A45 by airport) ☎ (0473) 723355
Greene King XX, IPA, Abbot H
Active pub with a good mix of local and passing customers. Comfortable lounge and public bar. Games include shove ha'penny; steel quoits in garden ⌘ ( ) ⌑⌃ A

11–2.30; 5.30–11
Water Lily
100 St Helens Street
☎ (0473) 57035
Tolly Cobbold Mild, Bitter, Old Strong G
Only Ipswich pub with beer straight from the barrel. Comfortable snug and spacious back garden. Pub games ⌘Q ( ) (not Sun) ⌑⌃

11–2.30; 5.30–11
Woolpack
1 Tuddenham Road
☎ (0473) 53059
Tolly Cobbold Mild, Bitter, Original, XXXX H
Country pub in the town. Pub games ⌘Q⌘ ( ) (not Sun) ⌑⌃

Try also: County (Adnams)

Ixworth

11–2.30; 5.30–11
Pickerel Inn
The Street (off A143)
☎ (0359) 30398
Greene King XX, IPA, Abbot H
Well-renovated and well-run 18th-century coaching inn. Excellent seafood. Pub games ⌘Q⌃⌘ ( ) ⌑

Kedington

11–2.30; 6.30–11
White Horse
Sturmer Road ☎ (0440) 63564
Greene King XX, IPA, Abbot H
A very popular village pub near a well-visited Saxon church. Large garden for summer barbecues. Excellent bar food. Pub games ⌃⌘ ( ) ⌑⌃

Kersey

11.30–2.30; 6.30–11
White Horse Inn
The Street ☎ (0473) 823353
Adnams Bitter, Extra, Old; Mauldon Special G
Traditional pub in picturesque village; visit the church and waterslash. Guest beers. Pub games ⌘Q⌃ (14+) ⌘ ( ) A

Lakenheath

11–2.30; 6–11
Plough
Mill Road (off B1112)
☎ (0842) 860285
Greene King XX, IPA, Abbot H
Fine Victorian flint building in centre of busy village. 2 bars – one a pool room ⌘ (⌑

Try also: Half Moon (Greene King)

Lavenham

11–2.30 (2 winter); 6–11
Swan Hotel
High Street ☎ (0787) 247477
Adnams Bitter; Greene King IPA, Abbot; Nethergate Bitter H
Large timbered hotel. Public bar has collection of army and air force memorabilia; airfields nearby. Dominoes ⌘Q⌃⌘⌘ ( ) ⌑⌃

Try also: Greyhound; Bush, Shimpling, (Greene King)

Laxfield

10.30–2.30; 6–11
Kings Head (Low House)
Gurams Mill Lane
☎ (098 683) 395
Adnams Bitter, Old, Broadside G
Unspoilt 600 year-old alehouse with its own bowls green in a small village, full of character. Pub games; guest beers ⌘Q⌃⌘ ( ) ⌑ A ⌃

Try also: Poacher, Cratfield

Lidgate

11–2.30; 7–11
Star
The Street (B1063)
☎ (063 879) 275
Greene King IPA, Abbot H
Centre of activity in pleasant village. Spit roast beef a speciality. Barbecues every summer weekend ⌘Q⌃⌘ ( ) (not Tue) ⌑⌃

Little Bradley

11–2.30; 5–11
Royal Oak
On A143, Haverhill to Bury St Edmunds Road
☎ (044 083) 229
Greene King IPA H
Small, friendly country free house with delicious food. Guest beers; pub games ⌘⌃⌘ ( ) ⌑⌃

Long Melford

11–2.30; 5–11

Swan
Hall Street (A134)
☎ (0787) 78740
Greene King XX, IPA, Abbot H
Good main street local with separate lounge at rear. Games; quiz team ⌃⌘ ( ) ⌑

Try also: Crown (Free)

Lowestoft

10.30–2.30; 5.30 (7 Sat)–11
Hearts of Oak
Raglan Street ☎ (0502) 61125
Flowers Original; Wethered Bitter H
Popular up-market catering house. Guest beers ⌘ ( ) ⌑⌃

Middleton

10.30–2.30; 6–11
Bell Inn
The Street (off B1122)
OS428678 ☎ (072 873) 286
Adnams Mild, Bitter, Old H
Very old listed building, near Minsmere, with large garden. Pony and traps frequent in summertime. Pub games ⌘Q⌃⌘ ( ) ⌑⌃ A

Mildenhall

11–2.30; 7–11
Queens Arms
42 Queensway
Greene King XX, IPA, Abbot H
Homely pub on outskirts of small town. Local trade of all ages. Home-made bar food. Pub games Q⌘⌃ ( )

Try also: Bell, Barton Mills (Greene King)

Naughton

11–2.30; 6–11
Wheelers Arms
Whatfield Road
☎ (0449) 740496
Tolly Cobbold Mild, Bitter, Original, Old Strong H
Thatched, picture postcard pub with cosy low-beamed interior. One of its 3 rooms was once a wheelwright's workshop. Pub games ⌘Q⌃⌘ ( ) ⌃

Newmarket

11–2.30; 6.15–11
Five Bells
16 St Marys Square (Rookery Shopping Precinct)
☎ (0638) 664961
Greene King XX, IPA, Abbot H
Good drinkers' pub with enthusiastic games players. 1 bar with traditional furnishings and pipe collection. Garden has an aviary and petanque pitch ⌘⌘⌃ A (1 mile)

271

Suffolk

Try also: **White Hart Hotel** (Tolly Cobbold)

Orford

11–2; 6.15–11
Jolly Sailor
Quay Street ☎ (0394) 450243
Adnams Bitter, Old H
16th-century quayside inn, long since deserted by the sea. Unusual collection of stuffed miniature dogs! Pub games

Pin Mill

11–2.30; 5 (7 winter)–11
Butt & Oyster
Off B1456 ☎ (047 384) 224
Tolly Cobbold Mild H **, Bitter** H **&** G**, Original** H**, Old Strong** G**, XXXX** H
Internationally known riverside inn, unchanging and unchanged. Family room. Pub games

Shadingfield

11.30 (11 summer)–2.30; 7–11
Fox
On A145 ☎ (0502) 79610
Adnams Mild (summer), Bitter, Old H
Cosy, roadside country pub just out of Beccles. Has 'non-smoking room. Meals summer only (not Sun or Wed) (on site)

Try also: **Huntsman & Hounds**, Spexhall (Free)

Shottisham

11–3; 6.30–11
Sorrel Horse
Off B1083 ☎ (0394) 411617
Tolly Cobbold Mild, Bitter G
Picturesque 500 year-old smugglers' inn, with collection of rural artefacts. Pub games

Somerleyton

11–2.30; 6–11
Dukes Head
Sluggs Lane (off B1074)
☎ (0502) 730281
Flowers Original; Wethered Bitter H
Broadland family pub in scenic village near River Waveney. Good children's room. Pub games

Southwold

10.30–2.30; 6–11
Red Lion
2 South Green ☎ (0502) 722385
Adnams Bitter, Broadside, Tally Ho (Christmas) H
1-bar pub with homely atmosphere and excellent family room
(summer) (Town)

All pubs in Southwold serve real ale

Sproughton

11–2.30; 5–11
Beagle
Old Hadleigh Road
☎ (047 385) 455
Adnams Mild, Bitter; Greene King IPA, Abbot; Mauldon Bitter; Younger Scotch H
A large free house converted from a row of whitewashed cottages. Good lunch trade. No food Sun or bank holidays. Pub games

Stanton

11–2.30; 7–11
Angel
The Street (off A143)
☎ (0359) 50119
Greene King XX, IPA, Abbot H
Popular village centre pub with large single bar. Bar billiards

Stonham Aspal

10.30–2.30; 6–11
Ten Bells
On A1120 ☎ (0449) 711601
Tolly Cobbold Mild, Bitter, Original H
Friendly, busy, roadside pub. Various games

Stowmarket

10.30–2.30; 5.30–11
Royal William
Union Street ☎ (0449) 674553
Greene King XX, IPA, Abbot H
A fine traditional old pub, off the main street. Games

Stowupland

11–2.30; 6.30–11
Crown
Church Street ☎ (0449) 674571
Tolly Cobbold Mild, Bitter H**, Old Strong** G
Attractive old thatched pub with good display of real flowers outside

Try also: **Retreat** (Greene King)

Sudbury

11–2.30; 6–11
Waggon & Horses
Acton Square ☎ (0787) 312147
Greene King XX, IPA, Abbot H
Sociable public bar; games room and restaurant

Swilland

11.30–2.30; 7 (6.30 F, S & summer)–11
Half Moon
High Road ☎ (0473) 85320

Tolly Cobbold Mild, Bitter, Original, Old H**, XXXX (occasional)** G
400 year-old rural village pub with exposed oak beams; popular with all ages. Near famous equestrian centre. Occasional live music. Pub games (until 10.30)

Thurston

12–2 (closed Tues & Thurs); 7–11
Black Fox
Barrells Road (approx. 1 mile outside village towards Norton) OS652939
☎ (0359) 30636
Adnams Bitter, Extra, Old; Greene King IPA, Abbot; Mauldon Bitter G
Remote basic beer house

Tostock

11–2.30; 7–11
Gardeners Arms
Church Road (off A45)
☎ (0359) 70460
Greene King IPA, Abbot H
Heavy black beams, inglenook and church pews. Pub games

Trimley St Martin

11–3; 5.30–11
Hand in Hand
High Road (old Ipswich Road A45) ☎ (0394) 275249
Tolly Cobbold Mild, Bitter, Old, XXXX H
Attractive timbered bar with red tile floor; comfortable lounge with emphasis on food (7.30–10.30)

Walberswick

11–2.30; 6–11
Bell
Ferry Road (off A12)
☎ (0502) 723109
Adnams Mild, Bitter, Extra H**, Old** G
Around 600 years-old; stone floors and oak beams. Bedrooms have sea or river views. Come and talk to the local fishermen. Pub games

Walsham Le Willows

11.30–2.30; 7–11
Six Bells
The Street (off A134)
☎ (035 98) 726
Greene King XX, IPA, Abbot H
Fine old beamed pub in pleasant village. Pub games

Wetheringsett

10.30–2.30; 5.30–11

Suffolk

Cat & Mouse
Pages Green (off A140, follow signs to Debenham)
☎ (0728) 860765
Adnams Old G; **Flowers Original** H; **Mauldon Fine Anglian Mild, Cat & Mouse, Special; Woodforde's Wherry Best Bitter** G
Traditional pub with low-beamed ceiling; homemade food, vegetarian meals available. Various games ▲Q❀⚫◐ (24hrs notice) ⊕

Wickhambrook

11–2.30; 5–11
Cloak
Off B1063 ☎ (0440) 820625
Greene King IPA H, **Abbot** G
Very welcoming, lively village pub serving excellent home-cooked food. Live music. England's only 'Cloak'
▲Q❀⚫◐ (until 9) ⊕&

Withersfield

11–2.30; 5–11
White Horse
Hollow Hill ☎ (0440) 706081
Greene King IPA; Nethergate Bitter H

17th-century thatched country inn, popular for business lunches; local trade eves and weekend and summer tourists. A la carte menu
▲Q❀◐⊕

Woodbridge

11.30 (11 Sat)–3.30; 6–11
Anchor
19 Quay Street ☎ (039 43) 2649
Tolly Cobbold Mild, Bitter, Original H
Original beams in back part of building date from 17th century. Friendly landlord and warm atmosphere. Pub games
▲Q❀⚫◐⊕&▲⇌

Try also: Olde Bell & Steelyard (Greene King)

11–3; 5.30–11
Seckford Arms
Seckford Street
☎ (039 43) 4446
Adnams Bitter, Extra; Mauldon Seckford Special H
Genuine free house with superb Mayan wood carvings and heated foot rail in bar! 4 real ales usually available
◐ (book) ⊕

Try also: Kings Head (Tolly Cobbold)

Wrentham

10.30–2.30; 6.30–11
Horse & Groom
London Road (A12)
☎ (0502 75) 279
Adnams Mild G, **Bitter** H, **Old** G
Excellent homely pub. Strangers made very welcome. Dominoes, darts and cards
▲❀◐

Try also: Five Bells, Southcove

Yaxley

10.30–2.30; 6–11
Bull Inn
Ipswich Road (A140/B1117)
☎ (037 983) 604
Adnams Bitter; Mauldon (house) Bitter H
16th-century high beamed village pub with large garden and children's play area. On busy main road but near Thornham Estate, thatched church and public walks. Pub games Q❀⚫◐▲

ON THE MECHANICS...
an alternative guide

Beer from the Wood increasingly rare with the decline of gravity dispense. Unlined wooden casks are said to flavour and preserve their beers. Wooden casks are much more heat resistant. Also prettier

Blanket Pressure low pressure layer of carbon dioxide, applied to real ale so as to suffocate the life out of it

Bottle Conditioned beer continues to mature in the bottle, usually because of the addition of a little yeast to the bottle at filling. Commonplace in Belgium, rare in the UK

Cask Breather the nearest that technology has come to imitating real ale. A valve system ensures a 100% carbon dioxide atmosphere fills the barrel without pressurising the beer. Beer often tastes unpleasantly "green" and inadvertent fizzing of the beer is commonplace

Electric pump popular in the North and Midlands, an electrically driven beer engine serves without gas pressured assistance. Often sounds like a dentists drill

Gravity Dispense the oldest, most natural and most efficient way of serving proper beer. Still in use in around 1000 pubs in the UK. A simple metal tap brings beer direct from barrel to glass

Handpump also known as Beer Engine, or Pull. Just what it says. There was an outcry about these newfangled dispense systems when they were introduced to Britain in the 19th century

Keg barrel which holds beer in a sealed canister prior to dispense under high pressure carbon dioxide gas

Surrey

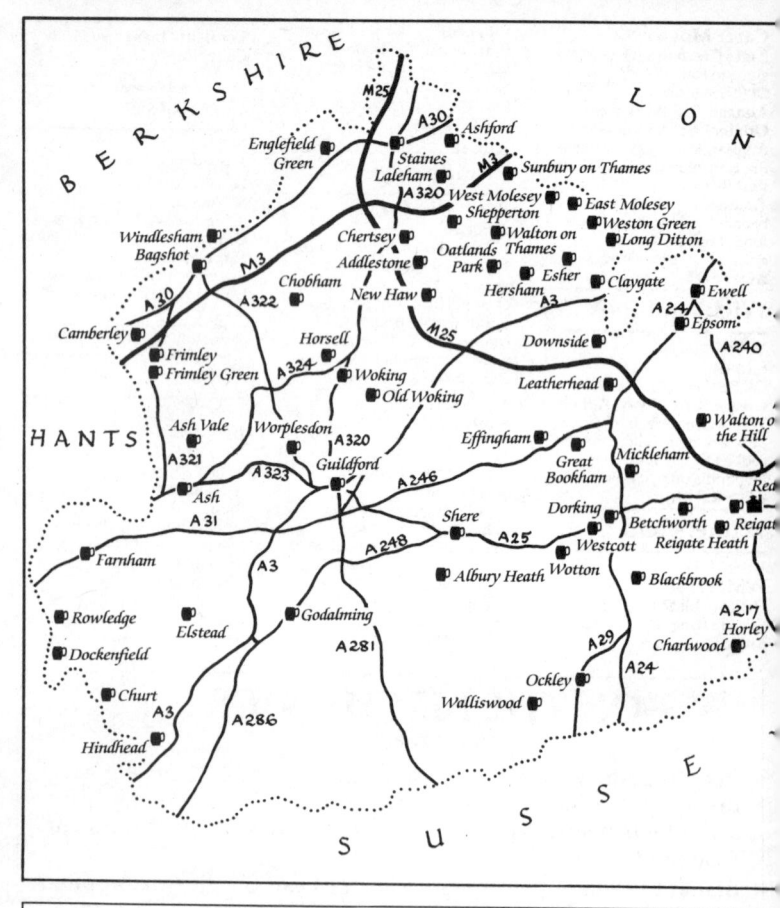

🏠 *Pilgrim*, Reigate

Addlestone

10.30–2.30; 5.30–11

Waggon & Horses
43 Simplemarsh Road
**Ruddles Best Bitter, County;
Webster Yorkshire Bitter** H
Smart pub, built in 1912 on site of a corrugated iron shack where beer was sold, hence locals' name for pub of 'The Tin House' ⌂ ⛳ ♿ ⓛ ⍾

Albury Heath

10.30–2.30; 5.30–11

William IV
Little London (off A25/A248)
OS066467 ☎ (048 641) 2685
**Courage Best Bitter,
Directors** H
Largely unspoilt pub deep in countryside with magnificent fireplace and flagstone floor. Darts and dominoes
⌂ Q ⛳ ♿ ⓛ ⍾ (not Sun)
🅰 (Edgley Park)

Ash

10.30–2.30; 5.30–11

Greyhound
1 Ash Street (A323)
☎ (0252) 22012
**Friary Meux Best; Gales HSB;
Ind Coope Burton Ale; Tetley
Bitter** H
Well modernised pub, often crowded. Good quality food in restaurant. Pub games ⛳ ⓛ ⍾ ⚡

Ashford

10.30–2.30; 5.30–11

District Arms
180 Woodthorpe Road
☎ (0784) 252160
**Courage Best Bitter,
Directors** H
Comfortably furnished pub near remand centre. Pub games Q ⛳ ♿ ⓛ (Mon–Fri) ♿ ⩰

Ash Vale

10.30–2.30; 6–11

Admiral Napier
72 Vale Road ☎ (0252) 25535
**Ind Coope Bitter; Tetley
Bitter** H
Cosily compact pub with wood panelling. Near Basingstoke Canal ⛳ ⓛ (not Sun) ⍾ (by request) ♿

Bagshot

10.30–2.30; 6–11

Foresters
173 London Road (A30, 400 yds W of village)
☎ (0276) 72038
**Courage Best Bitter,
Directors** H
Small, comfortable, welcoming locals' pub. Large garden suitable for families. Skittle alley Q ⛳ ♿ ⓛ ⍾ ⩰

Try also: Three Mariners

Betchworth

10.30–2.30; 5.30–11

274

Surrey

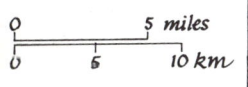

Surrey map

Comfortably furnished saloon opposite the Royal Military Academy. Military prints
🍴 🍺 (Mon–Fri) 🎯♿≠

Caterham

10.30–2.30; 6–11
Royal Oak
68 High Street (B2030)
Draught Bass; Charrington IPA; Fuller ESB (winter) 🅷
Small friendly 1-bar local 🍺♿

Try also: Golden Lion (Friary Meux)

Charlwood

10.30–2.30; 5.30–10.30 (11 F, S & summer)
Greyhound
The Street ☎ (0293) 862203
Draught Bass; Charrington IPA 🅷**; Gales HSB (winter)** 🅶
Comfortable 1-bar pub with non-smoking eating area and pleasant family room. Near Gatwick Airport 🏨🎯🍴🍺♿

Chertsey

11–2.30; 5.30–11
George
45 Guildford Street (A320)
☎ (0932) 562128
Courage Best Bitter, Directors 🅷
14th-century town pub mentioned in Oliver Twist and War of the Worlds. Allegedly haunted. No food Sun 🏨🅀🎯🍴🍺🎯🅰≠♻

10.30–2.30; 5.30–11
Golden Grove
St Anns Hill ☎ (0932) 562312/ 563762
Friary Meux Best; Gales HSB; Ind Coope Burton Ale 🅷
Attractive 15th-century pub on edge of town and near St Anns Hill public park
🏨🅀🎯🍴 (not Sun)

Chobham

11.30–2.30; 6–11
Red Lion
Red Lion Road, Burrowhill (off B383 N of village)
☎ (09905) 8813
Friary Meux Best; Ind Coope Burton Ale 🅷
Quiet relaxing pub slightly off the beaten track and handy for Chobham Common
🎯🍴 (not Sun) 🎯

11–2.30; 6–10.30 (11 F, S)
White Hart
High Street
Courage Best Bitter, Directors 🅷
Inviting village pub. Good food, friendly relaxed atmosphere ♿🎯🍴

Churt

11–2.30; 6–11
Crossways
Churt Road (A287)
Courage Best Bitter, Directors 🅷
An excellent village local with 2 good, contrasting bars
🎯🍴 (not Sun) 🎯♿

Claygate

10.30–2.30; 5.30–11
Griffin
Common Road
Ruddles Best Bitter, County; Webster Yorkshire Bitter 🅷
Friendly back-street pub which offers good lunches
♿🍴🎯♿

Copthorne

10.30–2.30; 5.30–11
Cherry Tree
Copthorne Bank (off B2037)
King & Barnes Sussex Mild (summer), Sussex Bitter, Old Ale; Draught Festive 🅷
400 year-old village local in easy reach of Gatwick Airport. Was once a library 🏨♿🎯🍴🎯

Dockenfield

11–2.30; 6–11
Blue Bell
Batts Corner (off A325)
OS820410 ☎ (025 125) 2801
Ballards Best Bitter, Wassail; Brakspear Special; Courage Best Bitter; Fuller ESB 🅶
Select cottage-style pub with large children's garden
🏨🅀🎯🍴♿

Dorking

10.30–2.30; 5.30–10.30 (11 F, S & summer)
Cricketers
81 South Street (A25)
Fuller Chiswick Bitter, London Pride, ESB 🅷
Deservedly popular 1-bar town-centre pub
🏨🅀🎯 (Mon–Fri)

10.30–2.30; 6–11
Falkland Arms
60 Falkland Road (off A2003)
☎ (0306) 889782
Friary Meux Best 🅷
Street-corner local with off-sales area. Cosy lounge bar has a living-room atmosphere, with real fire (and real till!)
🏨🎯🎯

10.30–2.30; 5.30–11
Spotted Dog
42–44 South Street (A25)
☎ (0306) 883729
Courage Best Bitter, Directors 🅷
Popular town-centre pub with large garden. Single L-shaped bar with 2 dartboards. Live music alternate Mon eves
🎯🍴 (not Sun) 🍴≠ (West)

275

Surrey

Dormansland

11–2.30; 6–11
Plough
44 Plough Road (off B2028)
☎ (0342) 832933
Flowers Original; Fremlins Bitter H
Popular pub with separate drinking and eating areas. Inglenook and large beer garden. Guest beers ▲ ☎ (if eating) ⑧ ( ) ▶ (not Mon)

Downside

10.30–2.30; 5.30–11
Plough
Plough Lane (½ mile from Cobham) ☎ (0932) 62514
Courage Best Bitter, Directors; John Smith Bitter H
Small lively rural pub with friendly, basic public bar. Limited parking. Darts and cribbage ▲ ☎ ⑧ (small) ( ) ▶ (until 9) ✠ ♿

East Molesey

10.30–2.30; 5.30–11
Bell
4 Bell Road (off B369)
☎ 01 941 0400
Courage Best Bitter, Directors; John Smith Bitter H
15th-century inn, known locally as Crooked House, with large garden. Stables at rear. Pub games Q ☎ ⑧ ( ) ♿

Effingham

11–2.30; 6–11
Plough
Orestan Lane (off A245)
Courage Best Bitter, Directors H
Pub with award-winning food Q ⑧ ( ) ▶ (before 8.30) ✠ ♿

Elstead

10.30–2.30; 5.30–11
Star
Milford Road (B3001)
☎ (0252) 703305
Courage Best Bitter, Directors H
Well cared-for village pub in good walking area. Darts ▲ ⑧ ( ) ▶ (not Wed) ✠ ♣

Englefield Green

10.30–2.30; 5.30–11
Beehive
34 Middle Hill (off A30)
☎ (0784) 31621
Brakspear Special; Gales XXXD, BBB, HSB; Hall & Woodhouse Badger Best Bitter H
Compact Gales-owned free house. Always busy, especially in local college term time. Pub games
▲ Q ☎ ⑧ ( ) ▶ (till 10) ♿

Epsom

10.30–2.30; 5.30–10.30 (11 F, S)
Barley Mow
12 Pikes Hill ☎ (037 27) 21044
Fuller London Pride, ESB H
Thriving little pub frequented mainly by the young. Piano in conservatory ⑧ ( )

Esher

10.30–2.30; 5.30–11
Claremont Arms
2 Church Street (A244 westbound) ☎ (0372) 64083
Courage Best Bitter, Directors H
Friendly side-street 1-bar pub with public and saloon areas ☎ ( ) (not Sun) ♿ ⇌

Ewell

10.30–2.30; 5.30–10.30 (11 F, S)
Green Man
71 High Street (off A24)
☎ 01 394 2923
Courage Best Bitter, Directors; John Smith Bitter H
Plushly furnished locals' pub with 3 separate drinking areas. Restaurant always popular. Pub games Q ☎ (restaurant) ( ) ▶ ✠ ♿

Farnham

10.30–2.30; 6–11 (closed Sun)
Bush Hotel (Vine Bar)
The Borough (A287/A325)
☎ (0252) 715237
Courage Best Bitter, Directors H
Hotel bar adjoining attractive cobbled courtyard. An enterprising choice of guest beers ▲ Q ☎ ⑧ ⛺ ( ) ▶ ♿ ⇌

11 (10.30 Sat)–2.30; 5.30–11
Queens Head
The Borough (A287/A325)
☎ (0252) 726524
Gales XXXD, BBB, HSB, XXXXX H
A deservedly popular and often crowded town-centre pub. Good Beer Guide regular ▲ Q ( ) ✠ ⇌

11–2.30; 6–11
Six Bells
55 Hale Road ☎ (0252) 716697
Ruddles Best Bitter, County; Webster Yorkshire Bitter H
One of Farnham's oldest pubs with bookable skittle alley ⑧ ( ) (not Sun) ✠ ♿

Frimley

10.30–2.30; 6–11
Railway Arms
78 High Street ☎ (0276) 23544
Gales HSB; Ind Coope Burton Ale; Tetley Bitter H
Attractively refurbished pub: a village local in an urban area. Darts ( ) (Mon–Fri) ✠ ⇌

Frimley Green

10.30–2.30; 5.30–11
Old Wheatsheaf
205 Frimley Green Road (A321) ☎ (0252) 835074
Morland Mild, Bitter, Best Bitter H
Wood-panelled, alcoved saloon with special shove ha'penny niche; also darts and cribbage ▲ Q ☎ ( ) ✠

Godalming

11–2.30; 5.30 (6 Sat)–11
Anchor
110 Ockford Road (A3100 south) ☎ (048 68) 7085
Adnams Bitter; Eldridge Pope Royal Oak; Fuller London Pride; Hall & Woodhouse Badger Best Bitter; Palmer IPA (summer), Tally Ho (winter) H
Busy, comfortable 1-bar pub. Beer range varies; guest beers; limited evening menu ☎ (lunch) ⑧ ( ) ▶ (Mon–Sat) ⇌

11–2.30; 5.30–11
Inn on the Lake
Ockford Road (A3100 south)
Flowers Original; Wethered Bitter, Winter Royal H
Comfortable hotel bar with restaurant and bar food. Innkeeper of the Year 1986–87
▲ Q ☎ ⑧ ⛺ ( ) ⇌

Great Bookham

10.30–2.30; 5.30–11
Royal Oak
16 High Street ☎ (0732) 52533
Friary Meux Best; Ind Coope Burton Ale H
Old pub set back off the High Street. The village, although a commuter area, retains its identity Q ☎ ( ) (not Sun) ✠

Guildford

10.30–2.30; 5.30–11
Clavadel Hotel (Chequers)
Epsom Road (A25 2 miles E of centre) ☎ (0483) 572064
Ballards Best Bitter; Bateman XXXB; Buckley Best Bitter; Fuller London Pride; Greene King Abbot H
Range of over 40 beers throughout the year in a city dominated by 2 breweries
Q ☎ ⑧ ⛺ (⇌ (London Rd) ♿

10.30–2.30; 5.30–11
Spread Eagle
46 Chertsey Street (A320)
☎ (0483) 35018
Courage Best Bitter, Directors H
Busy 1-bar town pub with friendly atmosphere. Recently extended into adjacent shop. Good lunches
☎ (lunch) ⑧ ( ) ♿ ⇌

Surrey

10.30–2.30; 5.30–10.30 (11 F, S)
Star
2 Quarry Street (off High Street) ☎ (0483) 32887
Friary Meux Best; Ind Coope Burton Ale H
Large character town pub, busy most evenings, mainly younger drinkers. Downstairs pool room Q ☎ (lunch) 🍴♿♿

Hersham

11–2.30; 5.30–11
Royal George
Hersham Road (off A244) ☎ (0932) 220910
Young Bitter, Special, Winter Warmer H
Pleasant and traditional pub with mixed clientele 🍴🍽 (▶

Hindhead

10.30–2.30; 5.30–11
Devils Punchbowl Hotel
London Road (A3) ☎ (042 873) 6565
Hall & Woodhouse Badger Best Bitter; King & Barnes Sussex Bitter; Draught Festive; Tetley Bitter; Wadworth 6X H
An excellent hotel bar opposite well-known beauty spot. Good walking country ☎🍴🛏 (▶ ♿

Horley

10.30–2.30; 5.30–10.30 (11 F, S & summer)
Gatwick
42 High Street ☎ (0293) 783801
King & Barnes Sussex Mild, Sussex Bitter, Old Ale, Draught Festive H
A popular 2-bar local with separate children's room and good food. Good choice of games ☎🍴 (▶ ⊞ ≠

Horsell

10.30–2.30; 6–11
Cricketers
Horsell Birch
Benskins Best Bitter; Friary Meux Best; Gales HSB; Ind Coope Burton Ale; Tetley Bitter H
A tastefully modernised pub with low beams 🍴Q☎🍽 (▶ ♿

10.30–2.30; 5.30–11
Plough
Cheapside (off South Road)
☎ (048 62) 4105
Benskins Best Bitter; Friary Meux Best; Gales HSB; Ind Coope Burton Ale; Tetley Bitter H
Friendly and efficient. A good mixture of drinkers and eaters amidst agricultural artefacts. Darts 🍽 (▶

Laleham

10.30–2.30; 5.30–11
Turks Head
The Broadway (B377)
☎ (0784) 54206
Courage Best Bitter, Directors H
Popular, friendly village local with 1 small "Tudorised" bar. Good range of games
🍴☎🍽 (benches) (

Leatherhead

10.30–2.30; 5.30–11
Running Horse
38 Bridge Street (off A2012)
☎ (0372) 372081
Friary Meux Best; Ind Coope Burton Ale; Tetley Bitter H
Historic lounge bar dates from c.1520. John Skelton (Poet Laureate to Henry VIII) wrote about Elinor Rumming brewing 'nappy ale' here. No food Sun 🍽 (▶ ⊞ ≠

Long Ditton

10.30–2.30; 5.30–11
New Inn
Rushett Road (off A307)
☎ 01 398 1893
Brakspear Special; Wethered Bitter; Whitbread Castle Eden Ale H
1-bar friendly side street pub, reputed to be haunted. Pub games (

Mickleham

summer: 11–2.30; 6–11; winter: 12–2.30; 7–10.30 (11 F, S)
King William IV
Byttom Hill (off A24 southbound) ☎ (0372) 372590
Flowers Original; Hall & Woodhouse Badger Best Bitter; King & Barnes Sussex Mild (summer), Sussex Bitter H
Charming pub perched on rocky hillside. Cosy public bar popular with all. Splendid garden can be a real sun trap
🍴Q☎🍽 (▶ (until 9) ⊞

New Haw

11–2.30; 5.30–11
White Hart
New Haw Road (A318/B385)
Courage Best Bitter, Directors H
Caters for local trade. Attractive canalside garden. Friendly and free of piped music in saloon 🍽 (⊞

Oatlands Park

11–2.30; 5.30–11
Prince of Wales
11 Cross Road (off A3050)
☎ (0932) 852082
Adnams Bitter; Boddingtons Bitter; Fuller London Pride; Gales HSB; Tetley Bitter; Young Special H
Traditional decor and cosy atmosphere: no electronic games or fruit machines. Good value restaurant (not Sat am or Sun pm) Q🍽 (▶

Old Woking

10.30–2.30; 5.30–11
White Hart
150 High Street (B382, off A247) ☎ (048 62) 63202
Courage Best Bitter, Directors; John Smith Bitter H
Lively public bar and contrasting lounge; bar billiards in lounge; live music Fri eves ☎ (lunch) 🍽 (▶ ⊞

Ockley

10.30–2.30; 5.30–11
Cricketers Arms
Stane Street (A29)
☎ (030 679) 205
Flowers Original; Fuller London Pride; Hall & Woodhouse Badger Best Bitter; King & Barnes Sussex Bitter H
Reasonably-priced 15th-century pub in pleasant village. Stone flagged bar, old beams and imposing fireplace. Restaurant. Darts
☎ (if eating) 🍽 (▶ ♿

Redhill

10.30–2.30; 5.30–10.30 (11 F, S & summer)
Home Cottage
3 Redstone Hill (A25)
Young Bitter, Special, Winter Warmer H
Large, busy pub with 2 contrasting drinking areas. Convenient for the station
🍴🍽 (▶ ≠

10.30–2.30; 5.30–10.30 (11 F, S & summer)
Plough
11 Church Road, St Johns (off A23) ☎ (0737) 766686
Friary Meux Best; Ind Coope Burton Ale; King & Barnes Old Ale; Tetley Bitter H
Comfortable and popular pub with separate eating and drinking areas. Next to Earlswood Common. No food Sun 🍴🍽 (▶ ♿ ≠ (Earlswood)

Try also: Flying Scud (Courage)

Reigate

10.30–2.30; 5.30–10.30 (11 F, S & summer)
Bulls Head
55 High Street (A25 westbound) ☎ (0737) 244004
Friary Meux Best; Ind Coope Bitter, Burton Ale H
Comfortable, split-level 1-bar pub with welcoming fire. Darts 🍴🍽≠

Reigate Heath

10.30–2.30; 5.30–10.30 (11 F, S & summer)

277

Surrey

Skimmington Castle
Bonny's Road OS237497
Friary Meux Best; Ind Coope Bitter, Burton Ale; Tetley Bitter H
Rambling, multi-roomed pub with interesting knick-knacks. Often busy. Very uneven road over heath ≜Q☎🕮 Ɫ (not Sun)

Rowledge

11–2.30; 6–10.30 (11 F, S & summer)

Hare & Hounds
2 The Square ☏ (025 125) 2287
Courage Best Bitter H
Village pub with small restaurant. Quiet locals' pub with bar billiards and darts
🕮 Ɫ ≜

Shepperton

11–2.30; 5.30–11

Barley Mow
67–69 Watersplash Road
Ruddles Best Bitter, County; Webster Yorkshire Bitter H
Tastefully modernised and extended pub with increased trade to match ≜☎🕮 Ɫ

Shere

10.30–2.30; 6–11

Prince of Wales
Shere Lane (off A25)
☏ (048 641) 2313
Young Bitter, Special, Winter Warmer H
Impressive building above road level. Games-based public bar, spacious lounge and excellent children's room ≜Q☎🕮 Ɫ Ɫ (Tue–Sat) ⊞≜

Staines

10.30–2.30; 5.30–11

Beehive
35 Edgell Road (off B376 south)
☏ (0784) 52663
Courage Best Bitter, Directors H
Splendid side-street local with public bar, games room and lounge ≜Q☎🕮 ƊƊ≜

10.30–2.30; 5.30–11

Bells
124 Church Street (off B376 north) ☏ (0784) 54240
Courage Best Bitter, Directors H
Lively 1-bar pub close to the river. The short walk from the town centre will be amply rewarded. Take your darts!
Q☎🕮 Ɫ

10.30–2.30; 5.30–11

Jolly Farmer
The Hythe ☏ (0784) 52807
Courage Best Bitter, Directors H
Well-run, long-established town pub with a welcoming atmosphere. Good Beer Guide regular. Pub games
Q☎🕮 Ɫ Ɫ≜

Sunbury-on-Thames

11–2.30; 5.30–11

Prince Albert
165 Staines Road, West Sunbury ☏ (0932) 787229
Ruddles Best Bitter, County; Webster Yorkshire Bitter H
Large refurbished roadhouse, attracts all sorts. Pub games
🕮 Ɫ Ɫ (early) ≜⇌

Tatsfield

10.30–2.30; 6–11

Old Ship
Ship Hill, Westmore Green
Charrington IPA H
Pleasant, comfortable pub with a relaxed atmosphere, overlooking the village pond
≜🕮 Ɫ (not Sun) ≜

Walliswood

11–2.30; 5.30–11

Scarlett Arms
OS119382 ☏ (030 679) 243
King & Barnes Sussex Mild, Sussex Bitter, Old Ale, Draught Festive H
Traditional, unspoilt old pub with 2 inglenooks and stone slab floors. Good choice of games. A classic country pub
≜🕮 Ɫ≜

Walton on Thames

10.30–2.30; 5.30–11

Swan
50 Manor Road (off A3050)
☏ (0932) 225964
Young Bitter, Special, Winter Warmer H
Impressive, multi-roomed pub next to river (swan upping takes place here). Restaurant in attached cottage (Tue–Sat, and Sun lunch). Pub games ≜☎🕮 Ɫ ⊞≜

Walton on the Hill

10.30–2.30; 5.30–10.30 (11 F, S)

Fox & Hounds
Walton Street (B2220)
☏ (073 781) 2090
Draught Bass; Charrington IPA H
Old-fashioned village pub
≜Q🕮 Ɫ

Try also: the other 3 village pubs

Westcott

10.30–2.30; 6–11

Cricketers
Guildford Road (A25)
☏ (0306) 883520
Hall & Woodhouse Badger Best Bitter, Tanglefoot; King & Barnes Sussex Bitter; Marston Pedigree; Pilgrim Progress H
Friendly 1-bar village free house. The open-plan bar is on 3 levels: eating upstairs; pool downstairs 🕮 (limited) Ɫ Ɫ (not Mon/Wed)

West Molesey

10.30–2.30; 5.30–11

Surveyor
Island Farm Road, East Molesey (off B369)
☏ 01 941 2075
Fuller Chiswick Bitter, London Pride, ESB H
Large welcoming pub with family atmosphere, behind trading estate Q☎🕮 Ɫ≜

Weston Green

10.30–2.30; 5.30–11

Alma Arms
Alma Road (off A309)
☏ 01 398 4444
Courage Best Bitter, Directors H
Cosy pub off beaten track, with friendly welcoming atmosphere. Pub games
≜Q🕮 Ɫ (not Sun) ≜⇌ (Esher)

Windlesham

10.30–2.30; 6–11

Surrey Cricketers
Chertsey Road (B386)
☏ (0276) 72192
Friary Meux Best; Gales HSB; Ind Coope Burton Ale H
Surprisingly roomy and comfortable, locals' 2-bar pub with good food. Dominoes
🕮 Ɫ Ɫ≜≜ A (Lightwater Pk)

Woking

11–2.30; 6–11

Star
Wych Hill, Hookheath (off A320) ☏ (048 62) 60526
Benskins Best Bitter; Friary Meux Best; Gales HSB; Ind Coope Burton Ale; Tetley Bitter H
Friendly and deservedly popular pub/restaurant with showbiz theme ☎🕮 Ɫ

Worplesdon

10.30–2.30; 5–11

Fox
Fox Corner (B380)
☏ (0483) 23250
Courage Best Bitter, Directors H
2 bar pub with friendly atmosphere. An excellent children's garden with marquee ≜☎🕮 Ɫ≜

Wotton

11–2.30; 5.30–11

Wotton Hatch
On A25 ☏ (0306) 885665
Fuller Chiswick Bitter, London Pride, ESB H
Country pub and restaurant with excellent food. Wonderful, old-fashioned public bar ≜Q🕮 Ɫ Ɫ≜

East Sussex

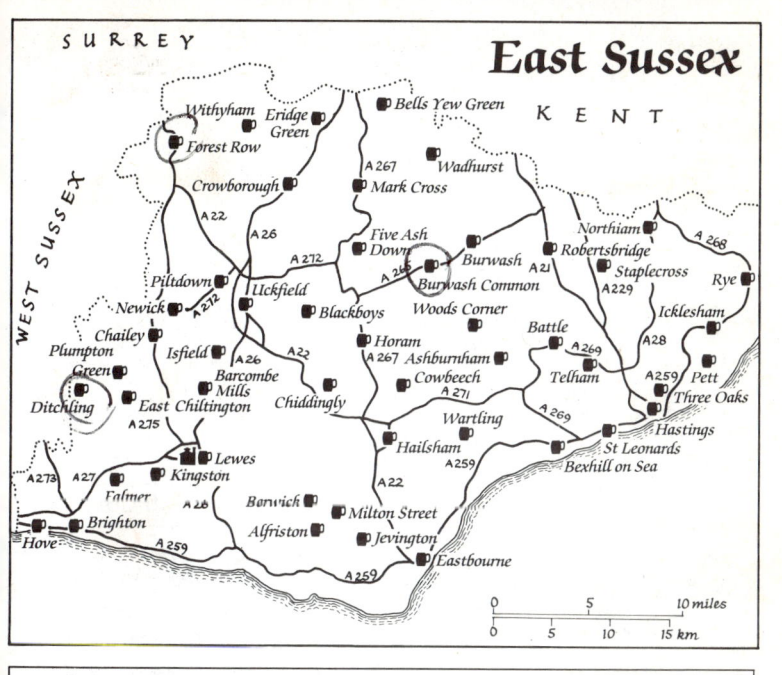

Harvey, Lewes

Alfriston

10–2.30; 6–11

Market Cross Inn (Smugglers)
Market Cross ☎ (0323) 870241
Courage Best Bitter, Directors Ⓗ
Pub with 2 ghosts, dating from 1358. Was a smugglers haunt. Lots of beams; cosy intimate atmosphere with hop festoons and a devil's step. Conservatory. Good food and picturesque village setting
Q ⇔ ✱ ◐ ▶ Å

Ashburnham

10.30–2.30; 6–11

Ash Tree Inn
Brownbread Street (N of B2204, about ½ mile S of Ponts Green) OS676149
☎ (0424) 892104
Wiltshire Stonehenge Bitter, Weedkiller Ⓗ
Hard-to-find country pub in the hamlet of Brownbread Street. Oak beams and inglenook; intimate atmosphere. Separate public bar. Darts, bar billiards. Guest beers ▲ Q ✱ ◐ ▶ ⊕

Barcombe Mills

10.30–2.30; 6–10.30 (11 F,S & summer)

Angler's Rest
1 mile W of A26 OS428150
☎ (0273) 400270
Cotleigh Tawny Bitter; Goachers Light Maidstone Ale; Hardington Somerset Best Bitter; Harvey BB Ⓗ
1-bar free house next door to the privately owned Barcombe Hills Station. 2 Toad in hole tables. Miniature bottle collection ⇔ ✱ ◐ ▶ Å

Battle

10.30–3; 6–11

Chequers
Lower Lake (just S of Battle on Hastings Road)
☎ (042 46) 2088
Flowers Original; Fremlins Bitter Ⓗ
Very smart and well-kept pub, dating from the 15th century. Has a very busy food trade. Handy for the abbey
▲ ✱ ⋈ ◐ ▶ & ≠

Bells Yew Green

10.30–2.30; 6–11

Brecknock Arms
Bayham Road (B2169)
☎ (089 275) 237
Harvey Pale Ale, BB, XXXX Ⓗ
2-bar Victorian country pub opposite the village green. Traditional public bar and comfortable saloon. Devil-amongst-the Tailors played
▲ Q ✱ ◐ ⊕ ≠ (Frant)

Berwick

11–2.30; 6–11

Cricketers
Off A27 OS519053
☎ (0323) 870469
Harvey XX, BB, XXXX Ⓖ
Timeless country pub with tiled floor, wood panelling and wooden furniture giving true rural atmosphere. Set in downland, the pub has attractive gardens ▲ Q ✱ ◐ ⊕

Bexhill on Sea

10.30–3; 6–11

Bell Hotel
Old Town ☎ (0424) 219654
Courage Best Bitter, Directors Ⓗ
Large, comfortable rambling pub in heart of old town. Various drinking areas to choose from. Very friendly and pleasant atmosphere. Beware of the fish!
⇔ ✱ ⋈ ◐ ▶ & ≠

10.30–2.30; 6–11

Sportsman
Sackville Road
☎ (0424) 214214
Adnams Bitter; Courage Directors; King & Barnes Draught Festive; Webster Yorkshire Bitter Ⓗ
A lively local, once a shop in the High Street. Warm comfortable atmosphere
✱ ◐ ▶ ≠

279

East Sussex

Blackboys

10–2.30; 6–10.30 (11 F,S & summer)

Blackboys Inn
Lewes Road (B2192)
☎ (082 582) 283
Harvey Pale Ale, BB, XXXX H
14th-century country inn of quality set in garden with duck pond. Games: Toad-in-the-Hole, Devil-Amongst-the-Tailors and Ring-the-Bull

Brighton

10–2.30; 5.30–11

Albion
28 Albion Hill ☎ (0273) 604439
Flowers Original; Fremlins Bitter; Whitbread Strong Country Bitter H
An unspoilt corner local with bar billiards: 4 teams play here. One of the cheapest pubs in town; a Good Beer Guide regular

10–2.30; 5.30–11

Evening Star
55 Surrey Street (outside station) ☎ (0273) 28931
Courage Best Bitter, Directors H
Attractive 1-bar pub, originally 2 cottages for railway construction workers

10–2.30; 5.30–11

Hand in Hand
33 Upper St James Street
☎ (0273) 602521
Bateman XXXB; Gale HSB; Hall & Woodhouse Badger Best Bitter, Tanglefoot; King & Barnes Draught Festive H
Small, compact corner house which is frequently crowded. Beer range may vary. ½ mile from Palace Pier

10.30–2.30; 5.30–11

Lamb & Flag
9 Cranbourne Street
☎ (0273) 26415
Charrington IPA H
Comfortable, spacious pub with good lunch trade due to proximity of shopping centre

10–2.30; 5.30–11

Lord Nelson
36 Trafalgar Street
☎ (0273) 682150
Harvey Pale Ale, BB, XXXX H
Busy town pub with 2 bars. Very popular at lunch times. Trafalgar Ale a strong draught beer available on Oct 21st. Dominoes and cribbage

10.30–2.30; 5.30–11

Pedestrians Arms
13–14 Foundry Street (off Queens Road/North Road)
☎ (0273) 697014
King & Barnes Draught Festive; Ruddles Best Bitter; Webster Yorkshire Bitter H
Thriving local with excellent mix of customers; popular with postal workers from nearby sorting office. Full of nooks and crannies. Darts, cards and dominoes

10.30–2.30; 5.30–11

Prince Albert
48 Trafalgar Street (below station) ☎ (0273) 28400
Gale HSB; Ruddles Best Bitter; Webster Yorkshire Bitter H
Grade II listed building with basic bar. Weekly folk sessions, jazz school, alternative/rock discos. Darts and shove ha'penny

10–2.30; 5.30–11

Queens Head
69 Queens Road (opposite station) ☎ (0273) 25284
Arkells Bitter; Boddingtons Bitter; Flowers Original; Higsons Bitter; Mitchell ESB; Tetley Bitter
Lively expansive free house with Victorian mirror behind bar. Unusual guest beers

10–2.30; 5.30–11

Robin Hood
3 Norfolk Place
Felinfoel Double Dragon; Greene King Abbot Ale; Hall & Woodhouse Badger Best Bitter; King & Barnes Sussex Bitter; Shepherd Neame Master Brew Bitter; Young Special H
Busy corner free house on border of Brighton and Hove. Interesting menu; occasional live music. Guest beers. Bar billiards

10–2.30; 5.30–11

Royal Exchange
58 Southover Street (near Queens Park) ☎ (0273) 601419
Gales HSB; Ruddles Best Bitter; Webster Yorkshire Bitter H
Deceptively spacious with side rooms for a good range of games. Reasonable prices. Beer range may change

10–2.30; 5.30–11

Sir Charles Napier
50 Southover Street
☎ (0273) 601413
Gales XXXL, BBB, XXXXX, HSB H
A lesson to breweries on how to enlarge a pub without loss of character. Often busy and prices reasonable. Darts

Try also: Nobles Bar (Free)

Burwash

11–2.30; 6–11

Bell
High Street (A265)
☎ (0435) 882304
Harvey BB; Fremlins Bitter H
Good atmosphere with plenty of beams and brickwork. Reputed to date back to 1609 and mentioned in "Puck of Pooks Hill". Fireplace equipped with mulling irons. Rare Ring-the-Bull game

10.30–2.30; 6–11

Rose & Crown
Ham Lane ☎ (0435) 882600
Bateman XXXB; Harvey BB; Hook Norton Old Hookey H
Large rambling pub with low beamed ceilings and a huge inglenook fireplace. Friendly relaxed atmosphere and a warm welcome. Very good food in restaurant. Darts

Burwash Common

11–3; 6–11

Kicking Donkey
Witherenden Hill (B2181)
OS647261 ☎ (0435) 883379
Harvey BB; Young Special H
A spotless rural gem next to hopfield, and enjoying a superb view. Friendly welcome. Home-made furniture and food. Morris dancing (Stonegate)

Chailey

11–2.30; 6–10.30

Horns Lodge
South Chailey (A275)
☎ (0273) 400422
Hall & Woodhouse Badger Best Bitter; Harvey BB H
Family-run pub with games and family areas. Steady local trade and travellers welcomed. Large garden with sandpit and games

Chiddingly

10.30–2.30; 6–11 (closed Mon)

Six Bells
☎ (0825) 872227
Courage Best Bitter, Directors H; **Harvey BB** G
Truly atmospheric, a treasure chest of paraphernalia on Wealden Way footpath. Has replica in Australia! Fine menu. Choice of games

Cowbeech

10.30–2.30; 6–11

Merry Harriers
OS619146 ☎ (0323) 833108
Charrington IPA; Flowers Original; Harvey XX, BB H
Village pub with oak beams, inglenook and settle in the public bar. Good food in lounge bar. Popular and often busy

280

East Sussex

Crowborough

10.30–2.30; 6–11

Boars Head Inn
A26 OS534326 ☎ (08926) 2412
Flowers Original; Fremlins Bitter G; Wethered Bitter H
Fine old country pub. The main bar is divided into several drinking areas; dining area attached. Huge stuffed boar's head above fireplace ⚫Q⊛◐

Ditchling

10.30–2.30; 6–11

Bull Hotel
2 High Street ☎ (07918) 3147
Flowers Original; Whitbread Strong Country Bitter, Pompey Royal H
Unspoilt village pub dating from 16th century. Low oak beams, large open fire and antique furnishings give a good atmosphere. Named after a Papal Edict – not the animal ⚫Q⊛⋈◐ (tiny snug)

Eastbourne

10.30–2.30; 5.30–11

Black Horse
220 Seaside ☎ (0323) 23143
Draught Bass; Charrington IPA H
A friendly, corner local with large, fairly basic public bar and smarter saloon. Darts and bar billiards. Family atmosphere; quiz team and many fund-raising activities ⊛⊛◐⊟♿

10–2.30; 6–11

Buccaneer
10 Compton Street (near Winter Garden)
☎ (0323) 32829
Benskins Best Bitter; Friary Meux Best; Ind Coope Burton Ale; Tetley Bitter H
Large busy pub of immense character. 2 totally contrasting bars with unusual beers for area. Handy for theatres and tennis ◐⊟

10.30–2.30; 5.45–11

Hurst Arms
76 Willingdon Road (in Ocklynge) ☎ (0323) 21762
Harvey XX, BB, XXXX H
Imposing Victorian local with bustling public bar and quieter saloon. Hampshire skittles. Recognised as selling the best Harveys in the area ⊛⊟

10.30–2.30; 5.30–11

Lamb
High Street, Old Town (A259) ☎ (0323) 20545
Harvey BB, XXXX H
Harveys showpiece; timbered exterior; full of antique furniture, 800 year-old cellar is commonly believed to have been a secret passage from pub to Norman church opposite ⊛⊛◐⊟

11–2.30; 6–11

Victoria
27 Latimer Road (off Seafront) ☎ (0323) 22673
Harvey XX, BB, XXXX H
Impressive Victorian local. Plush upholstery in saloon bar; magnificent dark wood full bar. Good atmosphere; popular with locals and holidaymakers alike ⊛⋈◐⊟

East Chiltington

10.30–2.30 (not winter Mon/Tue); 6–10.30 (11 F,S & summer)

Jolly Sportsman
Chapel Lane (off B2116) OS372153 ☎ (0273) 890400
Harvey BB, XXXX H
Small friendly ex-Beards pub in tiny village. Doubles as grocers shop, polling station and community centre. Off the beaten track but worth finding, popular with ramblers ⊛⊛◐▶

Eridge Green

10.30–2.30; 6–11

Huntsman
Eridge Road (A26 next to station) ☎ (089 276) 258
King & Barnes Sussex Bitter, Old Ale, Draught Festive H
Small and friendly 2-bar pub in attractive country setting. Darts and bar billiards ◐▶ (not Sun)⊟≠

Falmer

11–2.30; 6–11 (may close early in winter)

Swan Inn
Middle Lane (off A27/B2123) ☎ (0323) 681842
Hall & Woodhouse Badger Best Bitter; King & Barnes Old Ale, Draught Festive; Young Special H
3 bar free house close to Sussex University and very popular with students. Interesting range of bottled beers available. Occasional Morris dancing in summer ⊛◐≠

Five Ash Down

10–2.30; 6–10.30

Fishermans Arms
On old A26 ☎ (082 581) 2191
Harvey BB; Younger Scotch, IPA H
Run by Bluebell Steam Railway enthusiast. Traction engine meet January 1st. Good local trade and a welcome for visitors. Pub games. Guest beers ⚫≻⊛◐▶⊟

Forest Row

11–2.30; 6–11

Bramblethye Hotel
The Square
Harvey BB; Bateman XXXB; King & Barnes Sussex Bitter, Draught Festive H
Comfortable hotel with varied drinking areas. Emphasis on real ale. Relaxed atmosphere in picturesque village. Darts. Guest beers ⚫Q⊛⊛⋈◐▶♿▲

Hailsham

10–2.30; 6–11

Grenadier
High Street ☎ (0323) 842152
Harvey XX, BB, XXXX H
Traditional town pub. Popular with locals, mixed trade. Lively public bar, small odd-shaped saloon. Shove ha'penny and darts ⊛◐⊟♿

Hastings

11–3 (not Mon); 7 (6 Tue–Thu)–11

First In Last Out
14–15 High Street, Old Town ☎ (0424) 425079
St Clements Old Crofters, Cardinal H
Small friendly 18th-century home-brew pub. Window in bar overlooks full mash brewery. Magnificent open central fireplace. Darts. Guest beers ⚫♿▲ (½ mile)

11.30–3; 5.30–11

Palace Bars (Pigs in Paradise)
White Rock ☎ (0424) 439444
Draught Bass; Canterbury Ale; Ind Coope Burton Ale; King & Barnes Draught Festive H
Seafront 2-bar pub with a vast interior behind its small frontage. Boasts a fantastic bohemian atmosphere. All tastes catered for, including board game fans. Frequent live music ⚫◐≠

Horam

11–2.30; 6–11 (11am–11pm for food)

May Garland
Horam Road (½ mile S of village on A267) ☎ (04353) 2249
Harvey BB; King & Barnes Draught Festive; Ruddles County; Shepherd Neame Master Brew Bitter; Young Bitter H
Large country pub. Friendly and welcoming. Has 2 restaurants and good children's facilities. Large garden ⚫≻⊛◐▶

Hove

10–2.30; 6–11

Star of Brunswick
32 Brunswick Street West ☎ (0323) 771355
Flowers Original; Whitbread Strong Country Bitter H

281

East Sussex

Deservedly popular back-street pub. Unspoilt lounge, public bar with discos, jazz and extensions. Darts and pool

Icklesham

11–3; 6–11

Queens Head
Off A259 ☎ (0424) 814552
Cotleigh Tawny Bitter; Hook Norton Old Hookey; Mole's Cask Bitter; Moorhouses Pendle Witches Brew; Taylor Landlord H
Very attractive tile-hung country pub decorated with farm implements. Splendid views from the garden. Warm friendly atmosphere. Unusual wooden bar back. Guest beers

Isfield

10.30–2.30; 6–10.30 (11 F,S & summer)

Laughing Fish
Isfield Station, off A26 (Lavender Line) OS452172
☎ (082 575) 249
Harvey Pale Ale, BB, XXXX; King & Barnes Draught Festive H
Village inn adjacent to long disused but now re-opened station. Room at rear for children. Pub games

Try also: **Halfway House** (Harvey)

Jevington

10.30–2.30; 6–11

Eight Bells
High Street (B2109)
☎ (03212) 4442
Courage Best Bitter, Directors; John Smith Bitter H
A 600 year-old locals' village pub complete with wooden beams and window seats. A warm welcome is assured. Good value food. Paintings by local artists and locally-grown produce for sale

Kingston

10.30–2.30; 6–10.30 (11 F,S & summer)

Juggs Arms
Little Orchard, The Street (off A27) OS393083
☎ (0273) 472523
Harvey BB; King & Barnes Old Ale, Draught Festive H
15th-century pub with low beams and inglenook. Large garden with assault course for children. Off the beaten track but worth finding; popular in the summer

Lewes

10.30–2.30; 6–11

Black Horse Inn
55 Western Road
☎ (0273) 473653
Harvey BB; King & Barnes Old Ale, Draught Festive; Young Special H
Former coaching inn circa 1800. Photos of old Lewes pubs in public bar. Quiet saloon. Games include Toad-in-the-Hole. Guest beer

10.30–2.30; 6–11

Brewers Arms
91 High Street ☎ (0273) 479475
Hall & Woodhouse Tanglefoot; Harvey BB; Ind Coope Burton Ale; Ruddles Best Bitter, County; Shepherd Neame Master Brew Bitter H
Totally free house with 2 contrasting bars. Gents toilet used as wishing well for charity! Good choice of games

10.30–2.30; 6–11

Lansdown Arms
36 Lansdown Place
☎ (0273) 472807
Flowers Original; Fremlins Bitter
Friendly intimate 1-bar local with restored gas lights and fittings. Toad-in-the-Hole and other games. Guest beers

Mark Cross

10.30–2.30; 6–11

Mark Cross Inn
Off A267 OS583313
☎ (089 285) 2423
Flowers Original; Fremlins Bitter H
Comfortable pub with accent on food. Walls adorned with old photographs and brewery advertisements. Pool

Milton Street

10.30–2.30; 7–11 (6–11 in summer)

Sussex Ox
OS533039 ☎ (0323) 870840
Harvey Pale Ale, BB H
Rural pub at foot of South Downs. Old world charm; large children's room. Field with play equipment and for camping. Barbecues on summer Sats

Newick

10–2.30; 6–10.30

Royal Oak
Church Road (A272)
☎ (082 572) 2506
Flowers Original; Fremlins Bitter; Whitbread Strong Country Bitter, Pompey Royal H
Old oak-beamed public bar used by cricket club and locals. More comfortable saloon. Panel showing wattle and daub wall. Small garden.

Pub games. Whitbread guest beers

Try also: **Crown Hotel**, Church Road (Beards)

Northiam

10.30–3; 6–11

Six Bells Hotel
The Green (A28)
☎ (079 74) 2570
Flowers Original; Harvey BB; Marston Pedigree; Six Bells Bitter H
Comfortable welcoming pub with huge fireplace. Beer range may change. Pub games

Pett

11am–11pm

Two Sawyers
Pett Road
Flowers Original; Harveys BB H
17th-century farmhouse converted to pub. 3 bars including public. Bar food highly recommended. Unusual guest beers. Pub games

Piltdown

10–2.30; 6–10.30

Peacock
Shortbridge (B2102)
☎ (0825) 2463
Boddingtons Bitter; Draught Bass; Courage Directors; Harvey BB; King & Barnes Sussex Bitter H
Picturesque oak-beamed pub with separate restaurant. Inglenook in bar. Plenty of seating and pleasant garden

Plumpton Green

10.30–2.30; 6–10.30 (11 F,S & summer)

Fountain Inn
Station Road ☎ (0273) 890294
Young Bitter, Special H
Winter Warmer G
Young's only tied house in Sussex, deservedly popular. Large inglenook. Landlord runs cellar courses for Phoenix landlords. Good Beer Guide regular. Toad-in-the-Hole and darts

Robertsbridge

11–3; 6–11

George Inn
High Street (A21)
Flowers Original; Fremlins Bitter
Country-type pub with comfy settees, chairs to lounge in, books and magazines provided. Time has passed by leaving no ill effects. 5-star restaurant. Live music twice weekly; pool and shove ha'penny

282

East Sussex

Rye

10.30–3; 6–11

Standard Inn
The Mint (off A259)
☎ (0797) 223393
Hardington Cinque Ports Bitter; King & Barnes Draught Festive; Young Special H
Rebuilt 1420! All bare brick and wood beams plus a canonball in the wall! Smart family room with pool table and games. Lively pub
🔥 🛏 🍺 🍴 ⇌

11–3; 6–11

Ypres Castle Inn
Gun Gardens (off A259)
☎ (0797) 223248
Flowers Original; Fremlins Bitter; Whitbread Pompey Royal H
Family-run pub just behind castle, magnificent views of harbour and fishing port. Caters for all tastes. Reached by climbing 30 steps up from road. Welcoming atmosphere
🔥 🍺 🍴 ⇌

St Leonards

11.30–3; 5.30–11

Duke
48 Duke Road, Silverhill
☎ (0424) 436241
Benskins Best Bitter; Friary Meux Best Bitter; Ind Coope Bitter, Burton Ale; Taylor Walker Best Bitter; Tetley Bitter H
Unspoilt, traditional street corner local. Friendly cosy public bar, 1960s lounge. Wide range of superbly kept beer. Pub games 🍺 🍸

11–3; 6–11

Horse & Groom
Mercatoria (off London Road)
☎ (0424) 420612
Courage Directors; Harvey BB; XXXX; Hook Norton Old Hookey H
A smart, comfortable pub with intimate and pleasant atmosphere 🛏 🍴

Staplecross

11–3; 6–11

Cross Inn
On B2165 1 mile N of Cripps Corner ☎ (0626) 217
Draught Bass; Fremlins Bitter; Harvey BB H
Low ceilinged, unspoilt Sussex local. 15th-century building with big inglenook fireplace and stone floor. Good range of games 🔥 Q 🛏 🍺 🍸

Telham

10.30–3; 6–11

Black Horse
Hastings Road (A2100)
Flowers Original; Fremlins Bitter H
Friendly local with skittle alley, rare for area; Boules also played 🔥 Q 🛏 🍺 🍴 ⚓

Three Oaks

11–3; 6–11

Three Oaks
Butchers Lane (just off A259)
☎ (0424) 813303
Cotleigh Tawny Bitter; Wiltshire Old Devil; Weedkiller H
Friendly Victorian country pub, refitted using timber from local church. The hand pumps are in the old pulpit! Beer range liable to change.
Pub games 🔥 🛏 🍺 🍴 ⚓ A ⇌

Uckfield

10–2.30; 6–10.30

Alma Arms
Framfield Road (B2102)
☎ (0825) 2232
Harvey XX Pale Ale, BB, XXXX H
Traditional town pub in same family for generations. Beer served from wall mounted hand-pumps in public bar which has a good local trade. Worth finding. Small garden. Pub games Q 🍺 🍴 (not Tue, Sat, Sun) 🍸 ⚓ ⇌

Try also: Brickmakers Arms (Free)

Wadhurst

10.30–2.30; 6–11

Greyhound Hotel
St James Square, High Street (B2099) ☎ (089 28) 3224
Draught Bass; Charrington IPA H
Former posting inn, parts of which date back to 16th century. Has associations with infamous Hawkhurst gang of smugglers 🔥 🍺 🍴 ⚓

Wartling

11–2.30 (not winter Mon); 6–11

Lamb in Wartling
OS658092 ☎ (0323) 832116
King & Barnes Sussex Bitter, Draught Festive; Marston Pedigree H
Cosy, comfy pub in small village. Superb carvery. Real fires and low ceilings make it feel homely; always a warm welcome. Pub games
🔥 Q 🛏 🍺 🛌 🍴 ⚓

Withyham

10.30–2.30; 6–11

Dorset Arms
On B2110 OS496357
☎ (089 277) 278
Harvey XX, BB, XXXX (winter) H
Unspoilt pub in rural setting. Public bar has bare wooden floors and tables and is popular with agricultural workers. Restaurant 🔥 🍺 🍴 🍸

Woods Corner

11.30–2.30; 6–11

Swan
On B2096 ☎ (042 482) 242
Fremlins Bitter; Harveys BB; King & Barnes Sussex Bitter H
Built in 1399, a pub since the 16th century. Local community centre popular with horse and Land Rover set. Magnificent views to the south. Bar billiards
🔥 Q 🛏 🍺 🛌 🍴 ⚓

KEY TO SYMBOLS

- 🔥 real fire
- Q quiet pub – no electronic music, TV or obtrusive games
- 🛏 indoor room for children
- 🍺 garden or other outdoor drinking area
- 🛌 accommodation
- 🍴 lunchtime meals
- 🍴 evening meals
- 🍸 public bar
- ⚓ facilities for the disabled
- A camping facilities close to the pub or part of the pub grounds
- ⇌ near British Rail station
- ⊖ near Underground station
- ⚓ real cider

The facilities, beers and pub hours listed in the Good Beer Guide are liable to change but were correct when the Guide went to press.

West Sussex

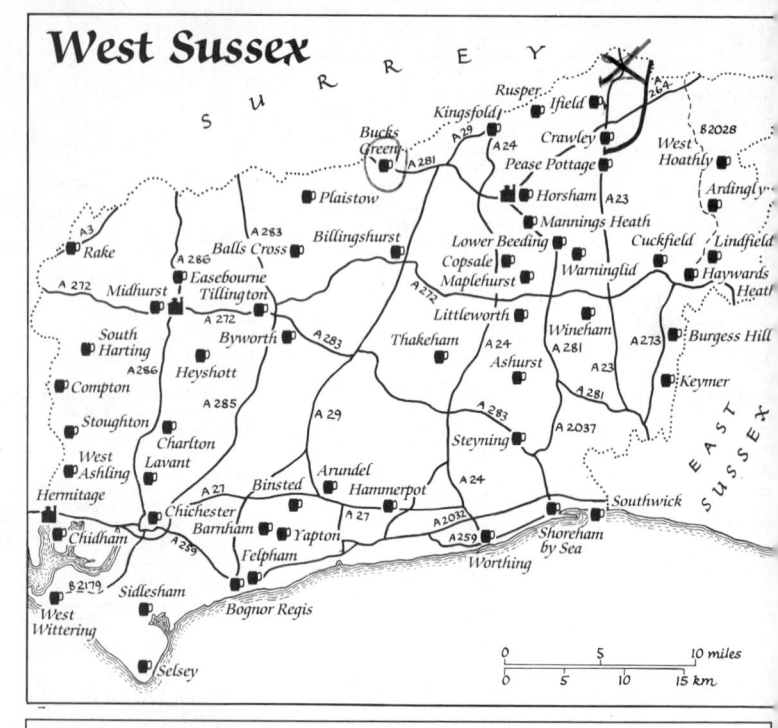

Ballards, Midhurst; **King & Barnes**, Horsham; **Sussex**, Hermitage

Ardingly

11–2.30; 6–11

Avins Bridge
College Road (off B2028)
☎ (0444) 892393
King & Barnes Sussex Mild, Sussex Bitter, Old Ale, Draught Festive H
Comfortable 2-bar pub near Ardingly College Q ❦ ⌘ ( ) &

Arundel

10.30–2.30; 6–11

Eagle
41 Tarrant Street (off Market Square) ☎ (0903) 882304
Bateman XXXB; Fuller London Pride, ESB H
A popular spot for the younger drinker; superb contemporary music. Can get very busy. Guest beers
( ) (Bistro) ≠

10.30–2.30; 6–11

White Hart
3 Queen Street
☎ (0903) 882374
Fuller London Pride; Greene King Abbot; Ruddles Best Bitter, County H
1 bar pub near river and castle; beer range varies. Pub games ⌘ Q ❦ ⌘ ( ) ≠

Ashurst

11–2.30; 6–11

Fountain
On B2135 ☎ (0403) 710219
Flowers Original; Fremlins Bitter; Whitbread Strong Country Bitter H**, Pompey Royal** G
Quaint 16th-century oak-beamed, stone-floored village pub, next to duck pond. Live music Mon and Sat. Up to 4 real ales served from stillage behind the bar ⌘ Q ❦ ⌘ ( ) & A

Balls Cross

10.30–2.30; 6–10.30 (11 F, S & summer)

Stag Inn
Off A283, 3 miles N of Petworth ☎ (040 377) 241
King & Barnes Sussex Mild, Sussex Bitter, Old Ale, Draught Festive H
Lively 16th-century pub. No food Sun
⌘ Q ❦ ⌘ ( ) (F, S or by arr)

Barnham

10.30–2.30; 6–11

Murrell Arms
Yapton Road (B2233)
☎ (0243) 553320
Friary Meux Best Bitter; Ind Coope Burton Ale G
3-bar local packed with drinking memorabilia. Vineyard; antiques auctions alternate Wed. Ring-the-Bull and Toad-in-the-Hole played
⌘ Q ❦ ⌘ ( ) & ≠

Billingshurst

10.30–2.30; 6–11

Olde Six Bells
76 High Street (A29)
☎ (040 381) 2124
King & Barnes Sussex Bitter, Old Ale, Draught Festive H
Recently extended oak-beamed pub with flagstone floor and Horsham slate roof. Darts and bar billiards
⌘ ⌘ ((not Sun)

Try also: Kings Head

Binsted

10.30–2.30; 6–11

Black Horse
Binsted Lane (off A27/B2132
OS980064 ☎ (0243) 551213
Gales BBB E**, XXXXX** G**, HSB** H
Unusual pub, hard to find but worth it, with reasonable prices. Fine garden and views. Games ⌘ Q ⌘ ❦ ( ) ⌘

West Sussex

Bognor Regis

11–2.30; 6–11

Claremont
Scott Street (off West Street)
☎ (0243) 865482
Friary Meux Best Bitter; Ind Coope Burton Ale H
Busy town centre pub. Landlord keen on live music (Thu, Fri, Sat). Pub games

10–2.30; 6–11

Terminus
26 Station Road
☎ (0243) 865674
Ind Coope Bitter, Burton Ale; Tetley Bitter H
Classic Victorian railway pub; oak-panelled saloon and popular public

Bucks Green

11–2.30; 6–11

Fox
Guildford Road (A281)
☎ (0403) 2386
King & Barnes Sussex Bitter, Old Ale, Draught Festive H
Typical rural village pub with pleasant garden. Dates back to 15th century. Pub games

Try also: **Queens Head** Rudgwick

Burgess Hill

10.30–2.30; 6–11

Watermill
Leylands Road
☎ (044 46) 5517
Gales HSB; Ruddles Best Bitter; Webster Yorkshire Bitter H
Single bar, locals' pub, situated in the "World's End" area of the town. Home-made food. Darts

Byworth

10.30–2.30; 6–10.30 (11 F, S & summer)

Black Horse Inn
Village Street (off A283)
☎ (0798) 42424
Ballards Wassail; Young Special H
Excellent village pub, a gem. Car parking a problem. Games

Charlton

10.30–2.30; 6–11

Fox Goes Free
Turn off the A286 towards E Dean at Singleton OS889133
☎ (024 363) 461
Ballards Best Bitter H, **Wassail** G; **Gales HSB; King & Barnes Chase Bitter, Draught Festive** H
16th-century inn set in pretty downland village. Recent improvements have carefully preserved its character. Darts

Chichester

10.30–2.30; 6–11

Chequers
203 Oving Road
☎ (0243) 786427
Flowers Original; Whitbread Strong Country Bitter H
Friendly local of character. Games room; comfortable lounge; busy public bar. Guest beers

10.30–2.30; 6–11

Four Chesnuts
234 Bognor Road (A259)
☎ (0243) 779974
Friary Meux Best Bitter; Ind Coope Burton Ale H
Friendly and busy local in middle of traffic island. The beer-swilling Jack Russell will pinch any dropped darts! Good value food

10.30–2.30; 6–11

Rainbow Inn
56 St Pauls Road (B2178)
☎ (0243) 785867
Friary Meux Best Bitter; Ind Coope Burton Ale; Tetley Bitter H
Small, well-run thriving local; monthly special food eves. Games

Chidham

10–2.30; 6–11

Old House at Home
Cot Lane (off old A27)
OS787704 ☎ (0243) 572477
Ballards Bitter; Ringwood Best Bitter, Old Thumper; Old House Bitter H
1-bar country pub with plenty of character. The 1987 hurricane revealed an old priest hole as it took the roof off!

Compton

10.30–2.30; 6–11

Coach & Horses
The Square (B2146)
☎ (070 131) 228
Adnams Bitter; Bateman XXXB; Buckley Best Bitter; Fuller ESB; King & Barnes Draught Festive; Palmer IPA H
A true local, at the heart of the village. Skittle alley in the old stables

Copsale

11–2.30; 6–11

Bridge House
Bar Lane (1 mile E of A24)
OS172249 ☎ (0403) 730383
King & Barnes Sussex Bitter, Old Ale, Draught Festive H
Delightful local in rural setting. Musician licensee so live jazz every Wed eve and country & western or folk on Fri eve (not Tue)

Crawley

10.30–2.30; 6–11

Maid of Sussex
89 Gales Drive, Three Bridges
☎ (0293) 25404
Courage Best Bitter, Directors H
Modernised town pub with friendly atmosphere. Darts (not Sun) (Three Bridges)

10–2.30; 6–10.30 (11 F, S)

Swan
1 Horsham Road, West Green
Flowers Original; Whitbread Strong Country Bitter, Pompey Royal H
Excellent Victorian street-corner pub

Cuckfield

11–2.30; 6–11

Kings Head
South Street ☎ (0444) 454006
Harvey BB; King & Barnes Sussex Bitter, Old Ale, Draught Festive; Marston Pedigree (summer) H
Popular 18th-century 2-bar coaching inn. Live music (Sat). Restaurant not always open but bar food available. Darts

Try also: **Wheatsheaf** (Free)

Easebourne

10.30–2.30; 6–10.30 (11 F, S & summer)

Rother
Lutener Road (off A286/A272)
☎ (073 081) 4024
King & Barnes Sussex Mild, Sussex Bitter, Old Ale, Draught Festive H
Pleasantly refurbished Victorian back street inn. Games

Felpham

10–2.30; 6–11

Old Barn
Felpham Road (off A259)
☎ (0243) 821564
Courage Directors; Fuller ESB; Gales HSB; Marston Pedigree; Owd Rodger; Pitfield Hoxton Best, Dark Star H
A much-needed free house on edge of Bognor. Extensively modernised 16th-century inn

Hammerpot

10.30–2.30; 6–11

Woodmans Arms
On A27 E of Arundel
☎ (090 674) 240
Ind Coope Bitter, Burton Ale H
Thatched pub on busy tourist route. Very popular for meals.

285

West Sussex

Take care to avoid a headache at the bar 🏠🍴🍺🌭🚻

Haywards Heath

10.30–2.30; 6–11

Fox & Hounds
Fox Hill (B2112)
☎ (0444) 413342
King & Barnes Draught Festive; Ruddles Best Bitter; Webster Yorkshire Bitter H
Large, comfortable pub which until mid-1800s was farm cottages. Ghost reputedly in ladies toilet, which was once the cellar
Q🍴🍺🌭

Heyshott

10.30–2.30; 6–10.30 (11 F, S & summer)

Unicorn
2 miles off A286
☎ (073 081) 3486
Ballards Best Bitter; Marston Pedigree H
Tranquil setting beneath South Downs. Good place for walkers. Darts 🏠🐕🍺🌭

Horsham

11–2.30; 6–11

Coot
Merryfield Drive (off A281)
☎ (0403) 65744
Charrington IPA H
Friendly pub on edge of town with customers of all ages.
Darts 🍴🍺 (not Sun) 🚻

11–2.30; 6–11

Nelson
25 Trafalgar Road
☎ (0403) 54029
King & Barnes Sussex Mild, Sussex Bitter, Old Ale, Draught Festive H
Popular and friendly street corner local; accent on pub games. Meat draw Fri 🍴🍺🌭🚻

11–2.30; 6–11

Rising Sun
Pondtail Road ☎ (0403) 53463
King & Barnes Sussex Mild, Sussex Bitter, Old Ale, Draught Festive H
Busy and friendly 2-bar pub; won a cellarmanship award in 1987. Pub games
Q🍴🍺 (not Sun) 🚻🌭

11–2.30; 6–11

Stout House
29 The Carfax ☎ (0403) 67777
King & Barnes Sussex Bitter, Old Ale, Draught Festive H
Very traditional town-centre pub, always welcoming. Best of King & Barnes. Darts 🍴🚻🚉

Ifield

11–2.30; 6–11

Gate Inn
Rusper Road
King & Barnes Sussex Bitter, Old Ale, Draught Festive H

Small, pleasant country pub with a friendly landlord; well worth a visit. No food Sun
Q🐕🍴🍺 (not Mon) 🚻🌭

10.30–2.30; 6–11

Royal Oak
Off A23 ☎ (0293) 26959
Draught Bass; Charrington IPA H
Country pub, with plenty of character near town and Gatwick airport. Games
🏠Q🍴🍺 🚻🌭

Try also Plough (King & Barnes)

Keymer

10.30–2.30; 6–11

Greyhound Inn
Keymer Road (B2116)
☎ (079 18) 2645
King & Barnes Draught Festive; Ruddles Best Bitter; Webster Yorkshire Bitter H
Popular village local with oak beams and inglenook. Collection of tankards in saloon bar. Varied menu.
Darts 🏠🍴🍺 (not Sun) 🚻

Kingsfold

11–2.30; 6–11

Dog & Duck
Durfold Hill (A24)
☎ (030 679) 295
King & Barnes Sussex Bitter, Old Ale, Draught Festive H
15th-century pub in easy reach of Warnham War Museum. Clay pigeon shooting and Morris dancing in pub grounds. Darts
🏠🍴🍺🌭

Lavant

10.30–2.30; 6–11

Earl of March
Mid Lavant (A286 2 miles N of Chichester) ☎ (0243) 774751
Courage Directors; King & Barnes Draught Festive; Marston Owd Rodger; Ringwood Old Thumper; Ruddles Best Bitter, County H
Deceptively large roadside pub, specialising in home-made food. Dogs welcome. Guest beers. Shove ha'penny and table skittles
Q🐕 (indoor area) 🍴🍺🌭

Lindfield

10.30–2.30; 6–11

Linden Tree
High Street (B2028)
☎ (044 47) 2295
Greene King Abbot; Harvey XXXX; Marston Merrie Monk, Pedigree; Young Special; Wadworth 6X H
Superior free house, with shoplike frontage in picturesque village. Friendly

welcome. Beer range may vary
🏠🍴

10.30–2.30; 6–11

Snowdrop Inn
Snowdrop Lane (between A272/B2111) ☎ (044 47) 2259
King & Barnes Sussex Bitter, Old Ale, Draught Festive H
Cosy post-war pub converted from farm cottages. Well-hidden, but friendly
Q🍴🍺🌭

Littleworth

11–2.30; 6–11

Windmill
Littleworth Lane (½ mile off A272) OS192206
☎ (0403) 710308
King & Barnes Sussex Bitter, Old Ale, Draught Festive H
Pleasant country local with cosy saloon bar. Winner of King & Barnes 1987 cellar competition. Bar billiards and darts 🏠Q🍴🍺🌭 🚻🌭

Lower Beeding

10.30–2.30; 6–11

Crabtree
Brighton Road (A281 1 mile S of village) ☎ (040 376) 257
King & Barnes Sussex Mild, Sussex Bitter, Old Ale, Draught Festive H
Large, smart roadhouse of 4 rooms, with a log fire in each. Popular with visitors to Leonardslee Gardens. Bar billards and darts
🏠🐕🍴🍺 (not Mon) 🚻

10–2.30; 6–11

Plough
Leech Pond, Hill Road (A279)
☎ (040 376) 277
King & Barnes Sussex Bitter, Old Ale, Draught Festive H
Friendly pub with good value pint, near Leonardslee Gardens 🏠🐕🍴🍺🌭

Mannings Heath

11–2.30; 6–10.30 (11 F, S & summer)

Dun Horse
Brighton Road (A281)
☎ (0403) 65783
Flowers Original; Whitbread Strong Country Bitter; Wethered Winter Royal H
Pleasant village pub with various games Q🐕🍴🍺🌭🍴🍺

Maplehurst

12 (11 summer)–2.30; 6–11

White Horse
Park Lane (between A281/A272) ☎ (0403) 76208
Brakspear Special; King & Barnes Sussex Bitter, Old Ale; Young Special H
Village local with spacious bar, large garden and excellent views. Live music Sun, and folk 1st Wed in month. Games
Q🐕🍴🍺 (not Sun) 🚻🌭

286

West Sussex

Midhurst

10.30–2.30; 6–10.30 (11 F, S & summer)

Crown Inn
Edinburgh Square
☎ (073 081) 3462
Gales HSB G**; Ruddles Best Bitter, County; Webster Yorkshire Bitter** H
Caters for all eccentrics! Pub games ▲ ▷ ⊛ ⇔ ◑ ▶ ⇦

10.30–2.30; 6–10.30 (11 F, S & summer)

Wheatsheaf Inn
North Street ☎ (073 081) 3450
King & Barnes Sussex Bitter, Old Ale, Draught Festive H
16th-century coaching inn.
Pub games ▲ ▷ ⊛ ⇔ ◑ ▶ ⇦

Pease Pottage

10.30–2.30; 6–11

Grapes
Brighton Road (400 yds from A23/M23) ☎ (0293) 26359
King & Barnes Sussex Bitter, Old Ale, Draught Festive H
Friendly and popular village local ▷ ⊛ ◑ ▶ ⇦ ♿

Plaistow

10.30–2.30; 6–10.30 (11 F, S & summer)

Sun Inn
☎ (040 388) 313
King & Barnes Draught Festive; Young Special H
Picturesque and homely ⊛ ◑ ▶

Rake

10.30–2.30; 6–10.30 (11 F, S & summer)

Sun Inn
On A3 ☎ (0730) 2115
Gales BBB, HSB H
Convivial homely pub. Games
▲ Q ▷ ⊛ ◑ ▶ ⇦

Rusper

11–2.30; 6–11

Star
High Street (off A264, 2 miles N of Faygate) ☎ (029 384) 264
Fremlins Bitter; Wethered Winter Royal; Whitbread Pompey Royal H
Old 16th-century coaching house, now a friendly and busy local. Rambling building with series of small comfortable rooms and large public bar. Darts ▲ ▷ ⊛ ◑ ⇦ ♿

Selsey

10.30–2.30; 6–11

Lifeboat
26 Albion Road (follow signs to lifeboat station)
☎ (0243) 603501
Ruddles Best Bitter, County; Webster Yorkshire Bitter H
Thriving fishermen's local with restaurant and large garden. Pub games
Q ▷ (restaurant) ⊛ ◑ (not winter Sun) ▶ (Tue–Sat) ⇦ ♿

Try also: Neptune (Ind Coope)

Shoreham By Sea

10–2.30; 6–11

Ferry Inn
East Street (A295)
☎ (0273) 464125
Courage Best Bitter, Directors H
Popular split-level pub opposite footbridge to beach.
Rare outlet for Russian Stout
Q ⇦ ⇌

11.30–2.30; 6–11

Red Lion
Old Shoreham
☎ (0273) 453171
Gales HSB; Ruddles Best Bitter; Webster Yorkshire Bitter H
Very popular pub with non-smoking area. Food very highly recommended
▲ Q ⊛ ◑ ▶ ♿ ☼

10.30–2.30; 6–11

Royal Sovereign
Middle Street ☎ (0273) 45318
Whitbread Strong Country Bitter, Pompey Royal H
Small, very popular local
Q ◑ ⇌

Try also: Marlipins (Bass)

Sidlesham

10.30–2.30; 6–11

Anchor
Street End Road (B2145)
☎ (024 356) 373
Friary Meux Best; Ind Coope Burton Ale H
Comfortable country pub with darts and dominoes
▲ ▷ ⊛ ◑ ▶ ♿

South Harting

10.30–2.30; 6–10.30 (11 F, S & summer)

Coach & Horses
☎ (073 085) 229
Flowers Original; Hall & Woodhouse Badger Best Bitter; Gales HSB H
Victorian atmosphere. Handy stop off from South Downs way. Pub games; guest beers
▲ ▷ ⊛ ◑ ▶

Southwick

10–2.30; 6–11

Romans Hotel
Manor Hall Road
☎ (0273) 592147
Draught Bass; Charrington IPA H
Well-run local with good facilities for children. Bar billiards. Reasonable prices
▷ ⊛ ⇦ ⇌

Steyning

10.30–2.30; 6–11

Chequers
High Street (A283)
☎ (0903) 814437
Wethered Winter Royal; Whitbread Strong Country Bitter H
Very old and cosy pub with several bars and many little rooms; one has a full-size snooker table. Beer range may vary ▲ Q ◑ ⇦

Try also: Star (Whitbread)

Stoughton

10.30–2.30; 6–11

Hare & Hounds
Off B2146 through Walderton OS791107 ☎ (070 131) 433
Fuller London Pride; Gales BBB, HSB; Hermitage Best Bitter H
A recent return to the free trade; warm welcome assured at this popular, remote pub, nestling in the folds of the South Downs ▲ ▷ ⊛ ◑ ▶ ⇦

Thakeham

11–2.30; 6–11

White Lion
The Street (400 yds off B2139)
☎ (079 83) 3141
Flowers Original; Whitbread Strong Country Bitter, Pompey Royal H
Timeless rural retreat in picturesque village. Good range of games ▲ ⊛ A

Tillington

10.30–2.30; 6–10.30 (11 F, S & summer)

Horseguards
Off A272 ☎ (0798) 42332
King & Barnes Sussex Mild, Sussex Bitter, Old Ale, Draught Festive H
Village pub near Petworth Park with view of Rother Valley. Games
▲ Q ⊛ ◑ ▶ (not Tue) ⇦

Warninglid

10.30–2.30; 6–11

Half Moon
The Street (B2115)
☎ (044 485) 227
Flowers Original; Fremlins Bitter; Whitbread Pompey Royal H
Friendly traditional 2-bar pub in village centre. Games
▷ ⊛ ◑ ▶ ⇦ ♿

West Ashling

10.30–2.30; 6–11

Richmond Arms
Mill Road (500 yds W of B2146)
OS806073 ☎ (0243) 575730
Adnams Bitter; Ballards Best Bitter; Fuller ESB; Harvey XX; King & Barnes Sussex Bitter; Taylor Landlord H
Probably the best real ale

West Sussex

choice in the south; unspoilt 10-pump village local. Serves good food. Games include skittles ♨ Q ⊛ ◐ ᚼ ▲

West Hoathly

11–2.30; 6–11

White Harte
Ardingly Road (B2028)
☎ (0342) 715217
Benskins Best Bitter; Ind Coope Burton Ale; King & Barnes Draught Festive; Tetley Bitter H
Busy free house with restaurant converted from a barn. Guest beers ♨ ⊛ ◐ ▶ ᚼ

West Wittering

10.30–2.30; 6–11

Lamb Inn
Chichester Road (B2179)
☎ (0243) 511105
Ballards Best Bitter, Wassail; Bunces Best Bitter; Ind Coope Burton Ale; King & Barnes Sussex Bitter; Young Special Bitter H
Very good, small pub with restaurant. Guest beers
♨ Q ⊛ ◐ ▶ ᚼ ▲

Wineham

10.30–2.30; 6–10.30 (11 F, S & summer)

Royal Oak
Wineham Lane (off B2116)
OS236206 ☎ (044 482) 252
Whitbread Pompey Royal G
Very traditional country pub; stone floor, inglenook and low beams. Worth finding. Shove ha'penny board ♨ Q ⊛ ▲

Worthing

10–2.30; 6–11

Chapmans
27 Railway Approach
☎ (0903) 30690
Gales HSB; Hall & Woodhouse Tanglefoot; Harvey BB; Wadworth 6X H
Lively, often crowded, main bar with music. 30s cocktail bar is plush and restful. Guest beers
♨ ⊛ ⇌ ◐ ▶ ᚼ ≢

10–2.30; 6–11

Seldon Arms
Lyndhurst Road (by hospital)
☎ (0903) 34854
Fuller ESB; Harvey BB H

Traditional, unspoilt 1-bar pub just out of town centre. Good value lunch. Guest beers
◐ ᚼ ≢

10.30–2.30; 6–11

Vine
29 High Street, Tarring
☎ (0903) 202891
Hall & Woodhouse Badger Best Bitter; Harvey BB; King & Barnes Sussex Bitter H
Popular haven in Tarring village conservation area. Large garden with Wendy house and swing. Guest beers
Q ⊛ ◐ ᚼ ≢

Yapton

10.30–2.30; 6–11

Maypole Inn
Maypole Lane (off B2132)
OS977042 ☎ (0243) 551417
Bateman XB; Flowers Original; Harvey XX, BB; Ringwood Best Bitter; Younger IPA H
Improved free house; hard to find but worth the effort. Games. Beer range varies
♨ Q ◐ (not Sun) ⊟

Try also: Lamb (Whitbread)

ON BEER...
an alternative guide

Best formerly meant better. Nowadays means only

Bitter traditionally straw coloured and benefiting from sackloads of hops. Now a generic term for anything brown coming out of a brewery

Heavy Scottish term for medium to stronger ales. Often called 80 shilling in memory of the day when 36 gallons cost a maximum four quid

Lager word adopted by large breweries in English speaking countries to describe a variety of light-coloured, heavily gassy and invariably over-priced beery fluids. Particularly popular with football crowds, who may travel abroad in search of exciting new brands. Unlike the German and Czech brews from which they take their name, most lagers are not in fact lagered ie. allowed to continue maturation in the brewery cellar at low temperatures

Mild Less bitterness, through lower hop rates. In areas of heavy industry, have tended to be sweet and dark; in non industrial areas, lighter coloured, weaker, of drier palate

Pils an imitation of the excellent beers that emanate from the town of Pilsen in western Czechoslovakia. In the UK the imitators are not exactly accomplished and the "l" tends to be silent

Porter invented around 1750 for London's market porters, a dark, bitter sweet ale now revived by a few smaller breweries

Special can still denote higher quality, eg. Youngs, but generally reserved for supermarket bitters of 'specially' low strength, which if called "light" would not sell as well

Stout strong dark porter that became fashionable in the mid 19th century

Tyne & Wear

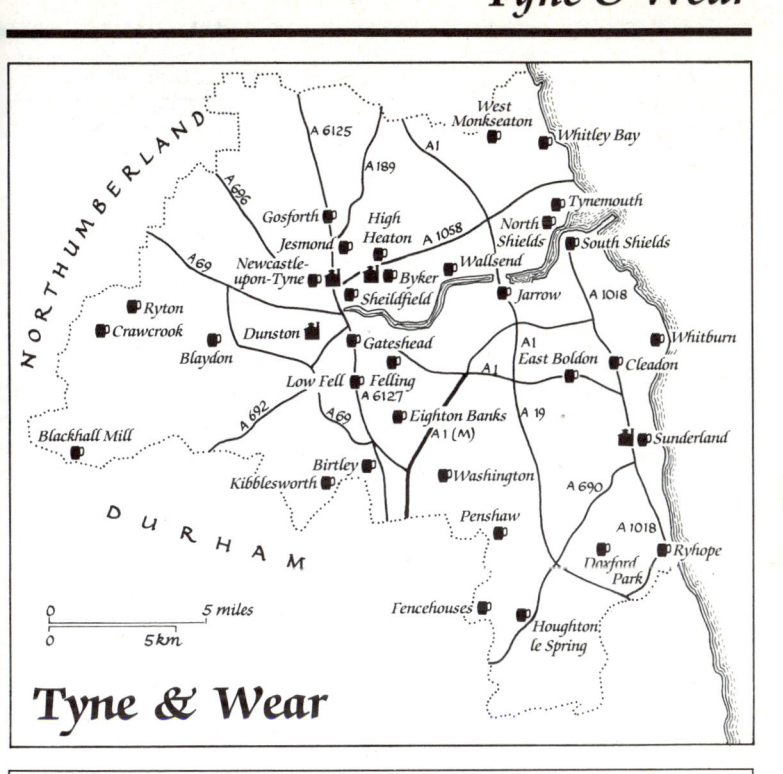

Big Lamp, Newcastle-upon-Tyne; **Federation**, Dunston; **Hadrian**, Byker; **Vaux**, Sunderland

Birtley

11–3; 6–10.30

Coach & Horses
Durham Road (A6127)
☎ (091) 410 2756
Bass Light 5 Star, Draught Bass; Stones Best Bitter H
Large roadhouse with restaurant at north end of town

Blackhall Mill

11–3; 6–10.30

Mill
River View (A694)
☎ (0207) 562207
Theakston Best Bitter, XB H
Large 3-roomed terraced free house overlooking River Derwent

Blaydon

11–3; 6–10.30

Black Bull
Bridge Street
Cameron Traditional Bitter, Strongarm; Everards Old Original H
A warm welcome assured. Photographs chart the demise of Old Blaydon

Byker

11–3; 5.30–10.30

Ship Inn
Stepney Bank (next to City Farm) ☎ (091) 232 4030
Whitbread Castle Eden Ale H
Friendly pub with character, and loyal clientele. Licensed for live music. Guest beers (Mon–Fri) (Manors)

11–3; 6–10.00

Tap & Spile
33 Shields Road
☎ (091) 276 1440
Robert Newton Bitter; Cameron Strongarm; Taylor Landlord H
Good renovation, good atmosphere, interesting nicknacks. Pub games
Q (Mon–Fri)

Cleadon

11–3.30; 6–11

New Ship
Sunderland Road (100 yds from A1018) ☎ (091) 456 0510
Vaux Samson H
Large popular roadside pub overlooking green belt. Plush interior on a nautical theme and excellent meals. Separate family room during lunch – a winner

Crawcrook

11–3; 6–10.30

Rising Sun
Bank Top ☎ (091) 413 3316
Whitbread Castle Eden Ale H
Comfortable, split-level hillside pub

Doxford Park

11–3; 6.30–10.30

Colonel Prior
1 Moorside Road, Moorside
☎ (091) 528 0098
Tetley Bitter H
Pleasant estate pub catering for the whole community. Abundant football memorabilia, named after local celebrity. Guest beers

11–3; 6.30–10.30

Doxford Lad
President Carter Shopping Centre ☎ (091) 528 0119
John Smith Bitter H
Modern estate pub catering for expanding conurbation

East Boldon

11–3; 6–11

289

Tyne & Wear

Black Bull
98 Front Street (A184)
Vaux Samson H
Open-plan with pleasant interior. Regular special evenings; good food; games ⌒⊛⌁▶ (not Sun)

11–3; 5.30–11

Grey Horse
Front Street (A184)
☎ (091) 536 4186
Vaux Samson H
Large roadside Tudor-style pub in heart of village; past winner of 'Pub in Bloom' competition. Dimly-lit interior lends itself to a cosy atmosphere. Smart dress for lounge. Guest beers ⌒⊛⌁▶ ⌬⇲

Eighton Banks

11–3; 6–10.30

Lambton Arms
☎ (091) 487 8137
Whitbread Castle Eden Ale H
Single-roomed lounge bar ⌁▶

Felling

11 (12 Sat)–3; 6–10.30

Old Fox
Carlisle Street
☎ (091) 438 0073
Ruddles County; Webster Green Label, Yorkshire Bitter, Choice H
Mid-terrace, L-shaped pub near Metro ⌂ ⌁▶ ⇲

11 (11.30 Sat)–3; 6–10.30

Wheatsheaf
Carlisle Street
☎ (091) 438 6633
Big Lamp Heroes Quaffing Bitter, Bitter, Stout, Old Genie H
2-room, street corner bar; Big Lamp's first Tyneside pub ⌂⌬⇲

Fencehouses

11–3; 6–10.30

Station
Morton Crescent (A1052)
☎ (091) 385 3363
Bass Light 5 Star E; **Stones Best Bitter** H
Friendly stone-built pub with huge hidden garden ⊛⌬

Gateshead

11–3; 6–10.30

Azure Blue
100 Eastbourne Avenue (near Leisure Centre)
☎ (091) 478 3772
Vaux Samson H
Residential pub with contrasting down-to-earth bar and 1980s style lounge ⌁▶⌬

11–3; 6–10.30

Five Wand Mill
201 Bensham Road (A692)
☎ (091) 478 1147
Tetley Bitter H
Large pub overlooking River Tyne. Named after sails of former windmill ⌬

11–3; 5.30 (6 Sat)–10.30

Queens Head
12 High Street (off A6127 near Tyne Bridge) ☎ (091) 478 3749
Draught Bass H
L-shaped bar and smaller lounge, impressive temperance shield above fire place ⌁▶⌬⇲

Gosforth

Gosforth Hotel
Salters Road ☎ (091) 285 6617
Marston Pedigree; Taylor Landlord; Tetley Bitter H
Unhurried service but worth waiting for in this street corner hostelry ⌁▶ (Mon–Fri) ⇲ (S. Gosforth)

High Heaton

11–3; 6 (5 in public ex Sat)–10.30

Corner House
Heaton Road (A1058)
☎ (091) 265 9602
McEwan 80/- A & H
Prominent and extensive pub, with numerous alcoves and conservatory. Jazz most days ⌂⊛⌁⌁▶⌬⇲

Houghton Le Spring

11–3; 6.30–10.30

Golden Lion
The Broadway (off A690)
☎ (091) 584 2460
Vaux Lorimers Best Scotch, Samson H
Superb old pub with 3 separate rooms. Excellent home cooking. Over 10 years in Good Beer Guide ⌒ (lunch) ⌁▶

Jarrow

11–3; 7–11

Western
Western Road (next to industrial estate)
☎ (091) 489 6243
Cameron Strongarm; Everards Old Original H
Basic but friendly boozer ⌒⌬⇲⇲

Try also: Royal Oak (Samuel Smith)

Jesmond

11–3; 6–10.30

Lonsdale
Lonsdale Terrace
McEwan 80/-; Younger No.3 H
Smart, popular with students and crowded at weekends. At closing time half the clientele are going to parties – the other half will gatecrash ⌁▶⌬⇲ (W Jesmond)

Kibblesworth

11–3; 6–10.30

Plough
☎ (091) 4410 2291
Draught Bass H
Comfortable pub in former mining village ⌁▶ (not Sun) ⌬

Low Fell

11–3; 6–10.30

Belle Vue
536 Durham Road
☎ (091) 487 0856
Draught Bass H
Busy pub in popular suburban drinking area ⌁▶⌬

Newcastle

11–3; 6–10.30

Bridge Hotel
Castle Square
☎ (091) 232 7780
Samuel Smith OBB; Theakston Best Bitter, XB H
Large former hotel near Castle Keep. Folk music venue. Guest beers ⊛⌬⇌⇲ (Central)

11–3; 5.30–10.30

Bacchus
High Bridge
McEwan 80/-; Samuel Smith OBB; Tetley Bitter H
Large 2-roomed pub in side street between business and shopping areas. Guest beers ⌁▶ (not Sun) ⇌⇲ (Monument)

11–3; 5.30–10.30

Duke of Wellington
High Bridge ☎ (091) 261 8852
Arrolls 70/-; Jennings Bitter; Tetley Bitter H
Often crowded lounge bar. Guest beers ⌁▶⇌⇲ (Monument)

11–3; 5.30–10.30

Old George
Old George Yard (off Cloth Market) ☎ (091) 232 3956
Draught Bass; Stones Best Bitter H
Former coaching inn, steeped in history. Fine wood panelling, beams and impressive fireplace ⌁▶⇌⇲ (Monument)

11–3; 5.30–10.30

Newcastle Arms
Darn Crook
Tetley Bitter H
Pub with narrow L-shaped bar; near coach station ⇲ (Haymarket)

11–3; 5.30–10.30

Strawberry
Strawberry Lane (opp. St James Park) ☎ (091) 232 6865
McEwan 80/-; Younger No.3 H
Unusual, basic pub threatened by road scheme. Next to football ground ⌬⇲ (St James)

Tyne & Wear

11–3; 5.30–10.30
Three Bulls Heads
Percy Street ☎ (091) 232 6798
Draught Bass; Stones Best Bitter H
Busy town centre 1-bar pub now surrounded by new shops development
((not Sun) ⊖ (Haymarket)

11–3; 5.30–10.30
Villa Victoria
Westmorland Road
☎ (091) 232 2460
Draught Bass; Stones Best Bitter H
1-room street corner local just west of city centre

North Shields

11–3; 5.30–10.30
Bell & Bucket
37 Norfolk Street
☎ (091) 257 1443
Theakston Best Bitter, XB, Old Peculier H
Pub converted from former fire station ⊖

11.30–3; 6–10.30
Chainlocker
Duke Street, New Quay
☎ (091) 258 0147
Matthew Brown Bitter; Theakston Best Bitter, XB, Old Peculier; Younger No.3 H
Compact friendly pub, handy for ferry. Good food, all homemade. Games
🅿Q (▶ & ⊖

11–3; 5.30–10.30
Tynemouth Lodge
Tynemouth Road (A193)
☎ (091) 257 7565
Belhaven 80/-; Marston Pedigree; Theakston Best Bitter, Old Peculier; Ward Sheffield Best Bitter H
Busy pub on road between North Shields and Tynemouth
🅿Q (⊖ (Tynemouth)

11–3; 6–10.30
Wolsington House
Burdon Main Row (by Smiths Dock) ☎ (091) 257 8487
Hartley XB; Robinson Best Bitter H
Large dockside pub now returning to its former glory
🅿⊕

11–3; 5.30–10.30
Wooden Doll
Hudson Street
☎ (091) 257 3747
Halls Harvest Bitter; Ind Coope Burton Ale; Ruddles County; Tetley Bitter; Younger No.3 H
Pub on a grand scale, with a grand piano, grand food and grand views over the Tyne
🅿 ☻ (▶ 🍴 & ⊖

Penshaw

11–3; 6.30–10.30
Grey Horse
Old Penshaw (off A183)
☎ (091) 584 4882
Tetley Bitter H
Cosy pub on old village green, in shadow of a famous folly and hill of 'Lambton Worm' fame 🍴 (&

Ryhope

11–3; 6–10.30
Albion
Village Green (A1018)
☎ (091) 521 0293
Whitbread Castle Eden Ale H
Large, Tudor-style popular pub. Games (▶

Ryton

11–3; 6–10.30
Jolly Fellows
☎ (091) 413 2604
Whitbread Castle Eden Ale H
Beautifully located pub in old village centre (

Try also: Half Moon

Shieldfield

11–3; 6–10.30
Globe
Wesley Street ☎ (091) 232 0901
Draught Bass; Stones Best Bitter H
Well-patronised local pub in inner-city suburb. Friendly atmosphere
🅿⊖ (Manors/Jesmond)

11–3; 6–10.30
Queens Arms
Shield Street/Simpson Street
☎ (091) 232 4101
Theakston Best Bitter, XB, Old Peculier H
Comfortable 1-roomed pub in residential area (⊖ (Manors)

South Shields

11–3; 5.30–11
Holborn Rose & Crown
East Holborn (Middle Dock Gates) ☎ (091) 455 2379
McEwan 80/-; Younger No.3 H
Large 1-roomed dockside pub, popular with dock workers at lunchtime. Etched windows and ornate bar; tastefully decorated in traditional style. Regular live music. Games
☻ (lunch) 🍴 & ⊖

11–3; 5.45–11
Railway Inn
Mill Dam (B1302/B1344)
☎ (091) 455 5227
Tetley Bitter H
Friendly pub near the revitalised riverside area, just out of market square. Dimly-lit, well-decorated lounge lends a cosy atmosphere. Good 'workingman's' bar; pub games; guest beers
☻ (lunch) 🍴 (summer) ⊕ & ⊖

11–3; 6–11

White Horse Inn
Quarry Lane (off A1300)
☎ (091) 456 2483
Draught Bass H
Large estate pub, named after local legend, beside golf course; difficult to find but worth it (always busy). Good walks to Marsden or Whitburn
☻ (lunch) 🍴 (▶ ⊕ &

Sunderland : North

11–3; 7 (5.30 F, S)–10.30
Pilot Cutter
Harbour View, Roker (A183)
☎ (091) 567 1402
Matthew Brown Bitter; Theakston Best Bitter, XB, Old Peculier H
Popular coast road pub, close to Roker Park, with a marine theme. Regular live music upstairs. Good sea views from outdoor drinking area. Guest beers ☻ (lunch) 🍴 ☻

11–3; 6–10.30
Sunderland Flying Boat
Sea Road, Fulwell (B1291)
☎ (091) 548 5961
Ind Coope Burton Ale; Marston Pedigree; Taylor Landlord; Tetley Bitter H
Immensely popular 1-roomed pub. Plenty of stained glass and brass decor; popular with the more mature drinker. Lots of flying boat memorabilia. Games
Q ☻ (lunch) (& ≠ (Seaburn)

11–3; 5.30–10.30
Wolseley
Harbour View, Roker (A183)
☎ (091) 567 2798
McEwan 80/- H
Popular pub with locals' bar and friendly lounge on coast road, near Roker Park; packed on match days. Pub games
🅿 ☻ (lunch) 🍴 (⊕ &

Sunderland : South

11–3; 6–10.30
Borough
Vine Place (opposite cinema)
☎ (091) 565 6316
Vaux Lorimer Best Scotch, Bitter, Samson; Ward Sheffield Best Bitter H
Victorian pub, popular with students. Bare floorboards and scrubbed island bar. Guest beers (≠

11–3; 6.30–10.30
Chesters
Chester Road (A183 to Chester Le Street) ☎ (091) 565 9952
Vaux Samson; Ward Sheffield Best Bitter H
Large roadside pub amongst local shops; friendly clean and airy with good meals; guest beers; games ☻ (lunch) 🍴 (⊕

11–3; 5.30–10.30
Saltgrass
Hanover Place, Ayres Quay,

291

Tyne & Wear

Deptford ☎ (091) 565 7229
Vaux Lorimer Best Scotch, Samson; Ward Sheffield Best Bitter H
Old friendly low-ceilinged pub tucked away among shipyards. Blazing fire and good bar snacks. Games 🏠🚭⌘🍴🍺🎮

11–3; 6.30–10.30
Shipwrights
Ferryboat Lane, North Hylton (under A19, Wear Bridge) ☎ (091) 549 5139
Vaux Samson; Ward Sheffield Best Bitter H
Comfortable pub overlooking River Wear, with 1st floor carvery restaurant 🚭⌘🍴🍺

Tynemouth

11–3; 6–10.30
Cumberland Arms
Front Street ☎ (091) 257 1802
McEwan 80/- H
Town-centre bar with nautical theme 🎮☺

11–3; 6–10.30
Dolphin
King Edward Road
☎ (091) 257 4342
Marston Pedigree; Tetley Bitter H
2-roomed suburban pub with friendly bar and plush lounge 🚭⌘🍴🎮

Wallsend

11–3; 6–10.30 (11 summer)
Rising Sun
Coast Road (A1058)
☎ (091) 262 3470
Stones Best Bitter H
Large busy pub named after former pit 🎮

Washington

11–3; 6.30–10.30
Duke of Albany
Albany Village Centre (off A1231) ☎ (091) 416 0019
Ward Sheffield Best Bitter H
Modern, well-decorated pub with sunken lounge area. Regular quiz nights; pub games; guest beers 🎮

West Monkseaton

11–3; 6–10.30

Shieling
Monkseaton Drive
Cameron Strongarm; Hadrian Gladiator Bitter H
Large modern estate pub with welcoming atmosphere ☺

Whitburn

11–3; 5.30–11
Jolly Sailor
East Street (A183)
☎ (091) 529 3221
Bass Light 5 Star, Draught Bass H
Reputedly haunted many-roomed pub with 'rabbit-warren' interior, cosy and lots of character. Pub games 🏠🚭⌘🍴🎮♿

Whitley Bay

11–3; 6–10.30
Victoria Hotel
Whitley Road
Marston Pedigree; Tetley Bitter H
Conspicuous town-centre pub with bars to suit all tastes Q🚭⌘🍴🎮☺

"At twenty, you recognise you will not win the Newdigate and stroke the Oxford shell through Hammersmith; at thirty, a small voice whispers that it is too late to take Joe Frazier in the third or baritone La Scala to its grateful knees; at forty, it is borne in upon you that you will neither charge the Russian guns nor, just as single-handedly, shatter the sexual taboos of Melanesia; by fifty, you have ceased to dream even of becoming Deputy Leader of the Labour Party or finding a gas lighter that works two days running.

But the dream of, someday, running a pub, shines on untarnished, like a good deed in a naughty world.

It is a good dream because it contains all the others: it is a fantasy that embraces power, pleasure, self-sufficiency, sexual possibility, money, notoriety, and social success. Great men will come whimpering to your door at 5.25, but their pleas shall not avail them. Beautiful women will beg to stay, at 11.15, and you will cast them into the night. You will subsidise this alcoholic poet, but not that; you will offer your authoritative advice to this adulterous bishop, but to his archiepiscopal sidekick you will curl the lip and ban the bottle; you will ignore the clamouring Chief Superintendent and his good lady, and serve the Hell's Angel and the Rastafarian first, you will tell the Prime Minister's husband he has had enough, you will stop Welshmen singing and kick out the millionaire's dog.

And nobody will be able to touch you, because you are the Landlord. You run the bridge, you preside over the bench, you command the army, you captain the team, you chair the board, you lead the pack and if the messiah comes again and wants a pink gin, you will draw His attention to the sign that says *Please Do Not Ask For Credit Since A Refusal Often Offends*."

An excerpt from 'Trapped Behind The Lounge Bar', by **Alan Coren**.
Reprinted from *Two Beers, My Friend Will Pay*
(order form, p.381)

Warwickshire

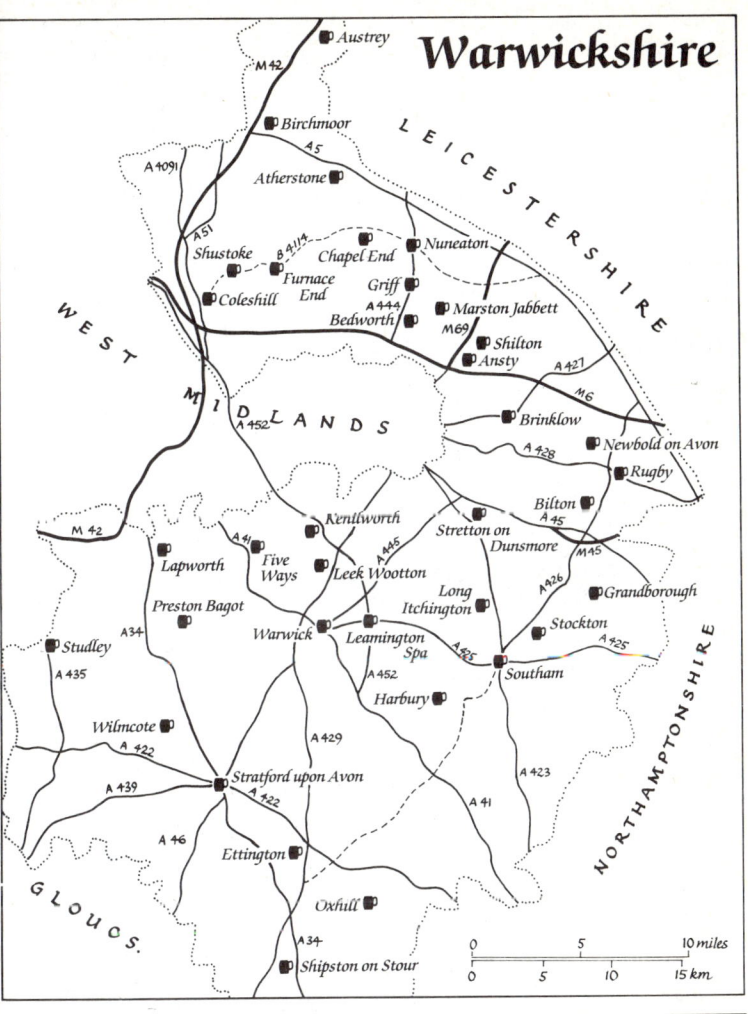

Ansty

11-2.30; 6-11

Sparrow Hall Hotel
Brinklow Road, Coombefields
☎ (0203) 611817
Draught Bass; Davenports Bitter; Ruddles County H
Country hotel with high class restaurant and lounge bar. Seating in garden

Atherstone

11.30-2.30; 7-11

Maid of the Mill
Coleshill Road (B4116)
☎ (0827) 713924
Davenports Mild, Bitter H
Very basic and very old, cramped pub with friendly atmosphere. Good drinking house; separate games room. Next to the old felt mill

11-2.30; 7-11

Square & Compass
Station Street ☎ (0827) 712544
Draught Bass; M&B Brew XI H
Large locals' pub in traditional, basic style. Various games
(not Wed, Sun)

Try also: Red Lion; White Horse

Austrey

12-2.30; 6-10.30

Bird in Hand
Church Lane (A453) 2 miles S of No Mans Heath
☎ (0827) 830260
Marston Pedigree H
Splendid old village inn dating back to the 17th century, with thatched roof. Next to old stone cross. No food Sun

Try also: Queens Head, Newton Regis

Bedworth

11-2.30; 8.30-11

Anchor Inn
64 Mill Street ☎ (0203) 312107
Marston Burton Bitter, Pedigree H
Friendly bar, popular with locals, small comfortable lounge and separate pool room

11-2.30; 6-11

Old Goose Inn
Orchard Street, Collycroft
☎ (0203) 313266
Ansells Mild, Bitter; Ind Coope Burton Ale H
Basic locals' bar and new comfortable lounge. Pleasant enclosed garden with children's play equipment. Small family room

293

Warwickshire

Try also: Cricketers Arms; Queens Head (M&B)

Bilton

11–2.30; 6–11

Black Horse
43 The Green (A4071)
☎ (0788) 811473
Ansells Mild, Bitter; Ind Coope Burton Ale; Tetley Bitter H
Large village local. Modernised but pleasant lounge; plain traditional bar. Usually very busy. Darts
⌕ (lunch) 🍴🍺🎯

Birchmoor

11–2.30; 7–11

Gamecock Inn
Cockspur Street (just past M42 bridge on Amington Road)
☎ (0827) 895144
Draught Bass; M&B Mild H
Locals' pub in old mining village. Characterful bar; quiet, bland lounge. Concert room. Difficult to find but worth the effort. Cards, darts and dominoes Q🍴🍺

Try also: Good Companions, Amington

Brinklow

11–2.30; 7 (6 summer)–11

Raven
Broad Street ☎ (0788) 832655
Ansells Mild, Bitter H
Oldest pub in village. Reputedly haunted – strange things often occur! Geese, rabbits, ducks in garden. Pub games 🎯⌕🍴↩🍺🎯🅰

Chapel End

12–2.30; 7–11

Salutation
Chancery Lane
Banks's Mild, Bitter
2-roomed pub with very comfortable lounge and locals' bar 🎯

Coleshill

11–2.30; 6–10.30

Swan Hotel
High Street ☎ (0675) 64107
Ansells Mild, Bitter; Tetley Bitter H
Old coaching inn near original centre of town (watch out for the stocks); now a very smart hotel ⌕↩🍴 (not Sun)
🍴 (restaurant)

Try also: Green Man; The Bell

Ettington

10.30–2.30; 6–11

Chequers
Banbury Road (A422)
☎ (0789) 740387
Adnams Bitter; Marston Pedigree; M&B Brew XI H
Free house with varied menu. Locals' bar with pub games. Lounge popular with both locals and tourists 🍺🍴🎯

Five Ways

11–2.30; 6–11

Case Is Altered
Rowington Road (off A41 near 5 Ways Island) OS225701
Ansells Mild, Bitter; Flowers Original; Ind Coope Burton Ale G
Charming old farmers' pub. Untouched for decades. Bar billiards take 6d pieces. Beer is served through unique cask pumps 🎯Q🎯

Furnace End

12–2.30; 7–11

Bulls Head
Coleshill Road (A47)
☎ (0675) 81602
Davenports Mild, Bitter; Wem Special Bitter H
Comfortable village inn. Good value food. Try the special menus. Varied games
🎯🍺🍴🎯

Grandborough

11.30–2.30; 7 (6 summer)–11

Shoulder of Mutton
Sawbridge Road
Flowers IPA H, **Original** E
Very much a village local with low-ceilinged panelled lounge and a basic bar/games/family room. Enormous garden with swings. Lovely and peaceful for summer lunch
⌕🍺🍴🎯🅰

Griff

11–2.30; 6–11

Griffin Inn
Nuneaton Road (B4102)
Draught Bass; M&B Brew XI H
Old coaching inn with several small rooms: very popular bar and snug. Live music in lounge most nights
🎯Q⌕🍺🍴🎯

Harbury

11.30–2.30; 7–11

Dog
The Bull Ring (off B4452)
☎ (0926) 612599
Ansells Bitter H
Purpose-built pub with plain bar, very popular with the locals; the lounge is 50s style
⌕🎯🅰

Kenilworth

11–2.30; 6–11

Clarendon Arms
Castle Hill ☎ (0926) 52017
Courage Best Bitter, Directors H
Pub opposite castle, ideally suited to the rather upmarket end of town; great emphasis on food. Pub atmosphere in the various nooks and crannies ⌕🍺🍴🎯

11–2.30; 6–11

Clarendon House Hotel
High Street (old town)
☎ (0926) 57668
Flowers IPA, Original; Hook Norton Best Bitter, Old Hookey H
Plush and friendly bar in a welcoming hotel. Full meals in restaurant only
Q⌕🍺 (patio) ↩🍴

Try also: Virgins & Castle

Lapworth

11–2.30; 5.30 (6 Sat)–11

Navigation
Old Warwick Road (B4439)
☎ (021) 528 3337
Draught Bass; M&B Mild, Brew XI H
Friendly village pub by Grand Union Canal 🎯⌕🍺🍴🎯⚓

Leamington Spa

10.30–2.30; 7.30 (5.30 by request)–11

Coach & Horses
4 Bedford Street (parallel to Parade) ☎ (0926) 24616
Davenports Bitter H
Pleasant, wood-panelled bar. Lounge has live music/disco in eves. A warm northern welcome in the Midlands!
Q (bar) 🍴 (not Sun) 🎯

11–2.30; 5.30–11

Coventry Arms
23 Guys Cliffe Road (Jct A445)
☎ (0926) 20390
Ansells Mild, Bitter; Ind Coope Burton Ale H
Attractive Regency-style pub recently refurbished as a Heritage Inn. Long single bar: lounge one end; public bar the other. Pub games Q🍴🍺 (early)

10.30–2.30; 5.30–11 (Mon–Sat)

Hope & Anchor
41 Hill Street ☎ (0926) 23031
Ansells Mild, Bitter H
A superb example of pub renovation – the best Ansells' Heritage Inn in the area. A pleasant Victorian feel has been created without going over the top. Darts and dominoes 🍴 (Mon–Fri) 🎯

11–2.30; 5.30 (7.30 winter)–11

Newbold Comyn Arms
Newbold Terrace East
☎ (0926) 38810
Marston Burton Bitter, Pedigree, Merrie Monk H
Ex-farmhouse on common, next to golf course, very popular in summer. The food is as excellent as the beer. Pub games. Guest beers 🎯Q🍺🍴🅰

11–2.30; 5.30–11

Red House
113 Radford Road

Warwickshire

raught Bass; M&B Mild,
pringfield Bitter H
 good, unspoilt local with
eparate bar and lounge
rinking areas. Attractive beer
ngines with porcelain
andles ▲Q✿◖ (not Sun) ⚐

1–2.30; 5.30–11

omerville Arms
ampion Terrace (off Holly
Valk) ☎ (0926) 26746
nsells Mild, Bitter; Ind
oope Burton Ale; Tetley
itter H
mall, friendly family local
vith "four ale bar" and small
rowded lounge. Darts and
ominoes ⚐&

1–2.30; 5.30–11

tar & Garter
 Warwick Street (near fire
tation)
Marston Burton Bitter,
edigree H
ictorian town pub with large
ront bar, originally 2 rooms.
mall lounge at the back has
opper-topped tables. Pool
s ◖ (Mon–Fri) ⚐&

Try also: Black Horse (Hook
Norton); Tavistock Inn
Davenports)

Leek Wootton

10.30–2.30; 6.30–11

Anchor
Warwick Road
Draught Bass; M&B Brew
XI H
Friendly village pub with a
basic locals' bar. Plusher
lounge has servery for the
excellent bar food. Dominoes
and darts
▲⚲✿◖ (not Sun) ⚐&♿

Long Itchington

10.30–2.30; 6–11

Harvester
5 Church Road
☎ (092 681) 2698
Hook Norton Bitter, Old
Hookey; Wadworth 6X H
Pleasant country pub with a
friendly welcome. Fairly plush
bar and comfortable lounge
with fish tank – better than
TV! Candlelit restaurant
excellent (and popular).
Various pub games
ᗐ✿◖⚐&⚜

Try also: Green Man
(Davenports)

Marston Jabbett

11–2.30; 6–11

Corner House Hotel
Nuneaton Road, Bulkington
(B4112, near canal)
☎ (0203) 383073
Marston Burton Bitter,
Pedigree, Owd Rodger
(winter) H
Large pub with busy public
and friendly lounge; games
and children's room. The
garden houses a collection of
unusual pets ▲Q✿◖⚐

Newbold on Avon

11–2.30; 6–11

Boat Inn
Main Street ☎ (0788) 76995
Davenports Mild, Bitter;
Wem Special H
Very popular canalside pub
decked out in narrow boat
regalia. Games room and
lunchtime dining area
ᗐ✿ (swings) ◖▶&

Nuneaton

11–2.30; 7–11

Hayrick
Meadowside ☎ (0203) 348181
Courage Best Bitter,
Directors H
Modern pub with 2 lounges
and children's room. Do not
miss the glass-walled toilets!
ᗐ✿◖

11–2.30; 6–11

Rose Inn
Coton Road (A444)
☎ (0203) 382983
Marston Burton Bitter,
Pedigree, Owd Rodger H
Basic public bar with friendly
local clientele. New plush
lounge geared towards food
◖▶⚐

Oxhill

11.30–2.30; 6.30–11

Peacock
1 mile off A422 ☎ (0295) 88301
Draught Bass E; Donnington
BB H
Cosy village inn with pleasant
garden, situated midway
between Stratford and
Banbury. Compton Winyates
stately home (not open to
public) is nearby ▲✿◖▶

Preston Bagot

11–2.30; 6.30–11

Crab Mill
On B4095, 2 miles from Henley
☎ (092 604) 3042
Flowers IPA, Original;
Marston Pedigree; Wadworth
6X H
300 year-old ex-cider mill.
Much emphasis on food.
Guest beers ▲Q✿▶◖▶

Rugby

10–2.30; 6–11

Engine
Bridget Street
M&B Mild, Brew XI E
Classic Victorian back-street
boozer with many rooms but
few frills. The small snug is
unusual for the town. Pool and
darts ◖⚐

11–2.30; 7–11

Raglan Arms
50 Dunchurch Road (A426
opposite Rugby School field
☎ (0788) 544441
Marston Burton Bitter,
Pedigree, Merrie Monk H
White-fronted terraced pub
with great traditional
atmosphere. Generally packed
with appreciative drinkers.
No loud music or food smells
to spoil the beer! Darts
Q✿⚐&

10.30–2.30; 7–11

Seven Stars
James Street ☎ (0788) 544789
M&B Mild, Brew XI H
Excellent old-style Victorian
boozer saved from developers.
Beers (unusually) on
handpumps. Good games
selection
ᗐ✿ (courtyard) ⚞⚐&≑

11–2.30; 7–11

Squirrel
33 Church Street (B5414)
☎ (0788) 543970
Marston Pedigree H
The smallest and most
unspoilt pub in town, with an
extremely low ceiling; very
picturesque. Popular with the
local Irish community. Darts
⚐&≑

Shilton

11–2.30; 7–11

Old Plough Inn
Leicester Road
☎ (0203) 612402
Draught Bass H
Pleasant locals' bar, and small
comfortable lounge Q◖⚐

Try also: Shilton Arms (Free)

Shipston-on-Stour

10.30–2.30; 5.30–11

George
High Street ☎ (0608) 61453
Donnington BB H
Old coaching inn dating back
to the 15th century with a
number of historical features
▲✿⚞◖▶

Try also: White Bear

Shustoke

12–2.30; 7–11

Griffin Inn
On B4114 ☎ (0675) 81205
Adnams Bitter; Everards Old
Original; Hook Norton Old
Hookey; Marston Pedigree;
M&B Mild; Theakston Old
Peculier H
Very popular 350 year-old
hostelry situated on
dangerous bend in road. Fine
inglenook and oak beamed
ceiling ▲Q✿◖▶

Try also: Plough Inn

Southam

11.30–2.30; 6.30–11

295

Warwickshire

Old Mint
Coventry Street (A423)
☎ (092 681) 2339
Adnams Bitter; Marston Pedigree; Samuel Smith OBB; Theakston XB, Old Peculier; Wadworth 6X H
15th-century stone pub rather like a small castle, built in 1420 by Cromwell as a mint. Real ale in the 'armoury', a small bar cluttered with old weapons. Popular with diners. Pleasant, cobbled courtyard. Dominoes ♨ ╘ ⊛ ⊲ ▮ ⊕ ♿

Try also: Bowling Green (Davenports)

Stockton

12–2.30; 7–11

Crown Inn
High Street (off A426)
☎ (092 681) 2255
Ansells Mild, Bitter H
18th-century village pub, much modernised but now mellowing. Unusual furniture in cluttered lounge. Good plain bar. Guest beers. Games include petanque
♨ ╘ ⊛ ⊲ ▮ ⊕ ♿

Stratford upon Avon

11–2.30; 6–11

Garrick
High Street ☎ (0789) 292186
Flowers IPA, Original H
Historic half-timbered inn. Next to Harvard House in town centre. Near the theatre (2 minutes' walk), river and several of the Shakespearian properties. Darts ♨ ⊲ ⇌

11–2.30; 6–11

Lamplighter
Rother Street ☎ (0789) 293071
Ansells Bitter; Courage Best Bitter; Tetley Bitter H
Recently renovated free house handy for market (Fri) ⊛ ⊲

11–2.30; 6–11

Old Tramway Inn
Shipston Road (A34)
☎ (0789) 297593
Davenports Bitter H
Modernised in Davenports Laura Ashley house style. A large garden with children's games, backs onto old tramway walk, which is ¾ mile from the town centre, passing the butterfly farm on the way. Darts ⊲ ▮ (early)

11–2.30; 6–11

Shakespeare Hotel
Chapel Street ☎ (0789) 294771
Courage Directors; Davenports Bitter; Donnington SBA; Hook Norton Bitter H
Smart THF hotel in town centre, near the theatre. Real ale in the Froth and Elbow bar. Bar billiards Q ╘ ⊛ ⋈ ⊲ ▮ ⇌

Try also: Cross Keys, Ely Street

Stretton on Dunsmore

11–2; 7–11

Shoulder of Mutton
Off A45 ☎ (0203) 542601
M&B Mild H
Marvellous old pub built in 1820 with a 1952 extension, since unmodernised. Tiny bar with old photographs; the extension has fancy tiled floor and 50s atmosphere. Hard to find at night. Darts
♨ ╘ ⊛ ⊕ ♿

Studley

11–2.30; 5.30–11

Railway Inn
Station Road (B4092 off A435)
☎ (052 785) 2597
Ansells Mild, Bitter; Tetley Bitter H
Lively L-shaped one-bar pub with darts area and snug. Railway theme ♨ ⊛ ⊲ ⇌

Try also: Green Dragon, Sambourne (M&B)

Warwick

11–2.30; 6–11

Simple Simon
Emscote Road (near canal)
☎ (0926) 491050
Chesters Mild; Flowers IPA, Original H
Popular 2-bar pub catering for most tastes. Name derives from the pie factory across the road. Darts and dominoes ♨ ⊛ (patio) ⊲ ▮ (most eves) ⊕ ♿ ⊘

11–2.30; 6–11

Vine
34 Vine Lane ☎ (0926) 493098
Ansells Mild, Bitter H
Unspoilt 100 year old pub tucked away in back streets, near hospital ⊛ ⊕ ⇌

10–2.30; 5.30–11

Zetland Arms Hotel
Church Street ☎ (0926) 491974
Davenports Bitter H
Unusual pub, normally busy. The garden is a must in summer Q ⊛ ⋈ ⊲

Wilmcote

11–2.30; 6–11

Swan House Hotel
☎ (0789) 67030
Hook Norton Bitter; Marston Pedigree H
Comfortable small hotel near Mary Arden's house and Stratford canal. Attracts a good local trade as well as visitors to Shakespeare country
⊛ ⋈ ⊲ ▮ ⇌

Try also: Masons Arms (Whitbread)

KEY TO SYMBOLS

Facilities

- ♨ real fire
- Q quiet pub – no electronic music, TV or obtrusive games
- ╘ indoor room for children
- ⊛ garden or other outdoor drinking area
- ⋈ accommodation
- ⊲ lunchtime meals
- ▮ evening meals
- ⊕ public bar
- ♿ facilities for the disabled
- ⛺ camping facilities close to the pub or part of the pub grounds
- ⇌ near British Rail station
- ⊖ near Underground station
- ⊘ real cider

The facilities, beers and pub hours listed in the Good Beer Guide are liable to change but were correct when the Guide went to press.

Help keep real ale alive by joining CAMRA. Your voice helps encourage brewers big and small to brew cask beer and offer all beer drinkers a better choice.

LETTERS PAGE

27, Wilmslow Gardens,

1st October 1988

Mrs. J. Partridge,
The Spotted Cow,
Amber.

Dear Joan,

By the time you read this you will already no doubt have heard the bad news. People don't keep secrets round this way. Believe me, I didn't want to hurt you, it's just that I don't think you're as good as you used to be.

It wasn't a bad run though, was it? Six years without a break. And who knows if things change I might take you back. But until then, love, I'm afraid the Spotted Cow is out of the Guide.

Looking back I guess we should have seen trouble coming when Master Simon became a Director at the brewery. His suggestions for the "improvements" in the public bar were certainly an innovation, if only in the use of the English language. Is it his cousin who does those Artex ceilings or is he the bloke who sells the beams you nail to the wall?

By the way, I'm sorry I wore my outdoor shoes in the Lounge last time I popped in. I could see it upset the wine waiter. I won't do it again.

Marvin, the Branch Secretary, wanted to know why you use so much wall space chalking up the 114 "Fresh Country Fare Specialities" on those blackboards. I explained it was more sophisticated than just photocopying the Freezer Centre order form and saying "add 150% to list price". No gourmet, Marvin.

At the selection meeting I thought the branch's comments about the new family room were a little harsh. I have no objection myself to boisterous children playing round my feet and spilling my pint. Provided they buy me another. And you're always so good about letting them do that, even if they are on their own.

In a sense this is probably a good year to be excluded, what with the name change and that. "Joe Brannigan's Brasserie" sounds like a New York brothel. You'd never guess it's just a small town pub run by a middle-aged woman from Cleethorpes, called Partridge.

I think the critical factor in dropping you from the Guide was the new Dunjohn Disco Bar. Whilst the branch recognises the pressing social need in the town for a place where the younger element can pursue their hobbies undisturbed by the Constabulary, we feel it was unfortunate that the greater part of the pub's cellar was made over to this purpose.

As a consequence of the above your beer now tastes like horsepiss and you stand as much chance of getting back in the Guide as Master Simon does of winning an Arts Council grant.

All the best,

Miles Brewster
Amber Valley Branch

P.S. Are you O.K. for the Branch Social a week on Friday?

All characters are entirely ficticious, and not intended to bear any resemblance to any persons living or dead.

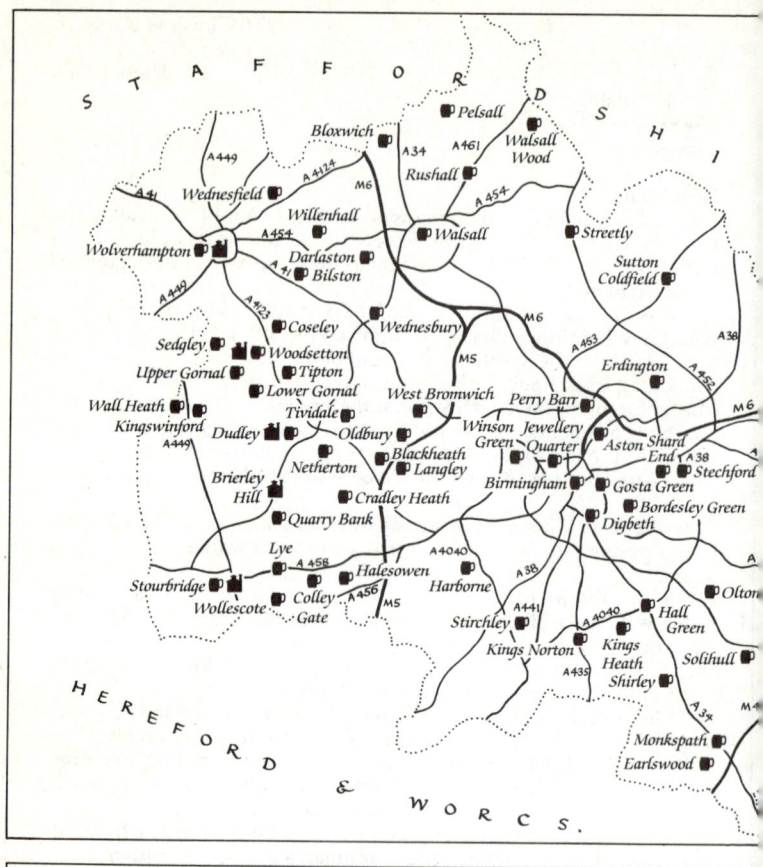

West Midlands

> **Banks's**, Wolverhampton; **Batham**, Brierley Hill; **Hansons**, Dudley; **Holden**, Woodsetton; **Premier Ales**, Stourbridge

Bilston

11–2.30; 6–10.30 (11 F, S)

Greyhound & Punchbowl
High Street (A4039)
Draught Bass; M&B Highgate Mild, Springfield Bitter E
Grand 15th-century former manor house. A ghost reputedly carries a glass of whisky from the ladies' to the bar!

10.30–2.30; 6–10.30 (11 F, S)

Swan Bank Tavern
Swan Bank, Lichfield Street (A41) ☎ (0902) 45790
Banks's Mild, Bitter E
Bright and basic friendly locals' bar

12 (11 Sat)–2.30; 8–10.30 (11 F, S)

Trumpet
58 High Street (A4039)
☎ (0902) 43723
Holden Mild, Black Country Bitter E, **Special** H
Popular 1-roomed jazz centre. Live groups nightly and Sun lunch (Mon–Fri)

Birmingham: Aston

11–2.30; 5.30–10.30 (11 F, S)

Bartons Arms
144 High Street
☎ (021) 359 0853
M&B Mild, Brew XI H
Large splendid Victorian bar. Still has 'snob screens'

Bordesley Green:

11–2.30; 6–10.30 (11 F, S)

Tipsy Gent
157 Cherrywood Road
Ansells Mild, Bitter; Banks's Mild Bitter H
Victorian inn in renovation area; run by chairman of Licensed Victuallers Association

City Centre:

10.30–2.30; 5.30–10.30 (11 F, S)

Bulls Head
Price Street
Ansells Mild, Bitter; Ind Coope BurtonAle H
Heritage Inn in the gunmaking quarter
(Snow Hill)

11–2.30; 5.30–10.30 (11 F, S)

Fox Hotel
Hurst Street (opposite Hippodrome)
Ansells Mild, Bitter; Ind Coope Burton Ale H
Genuine boozer in area earmarked for redevelopment

11–2.30; 5.30–10.30 (11 F, S)

Fountain
Wrentham Street

298

West Midlands

West Midlands

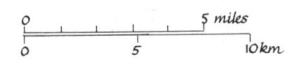

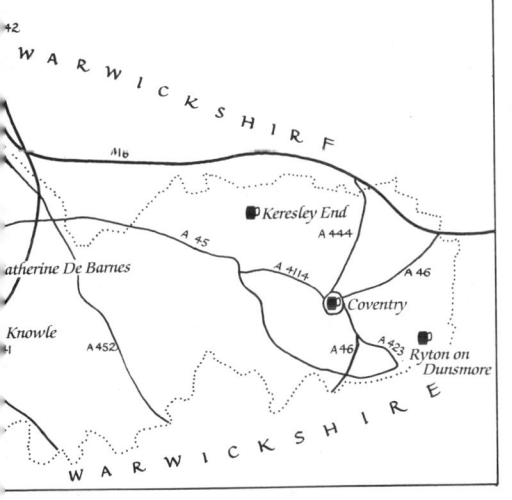

Ansells Mild, Bitter
Old corner pub with strong Irish flavour Q ≷

11–2.30; 5.30–10.30 (11 F, S)
Gough Arms
Upper Gough Street
Courage Best Bitter, Directors H
Compact pub just out of town, popular with post office workers and pool players ⌂≷

11–2.30; 6–10.30 (11 F, S)
Holloway
Holloway Road
Davenports Mild, Bitter H
Quietly comfortable pub near brewery. Games ⌂≷

10.30–2.30; 5.30–10.30 (11 F, S)
Lamp Tavern
Barford Street
Marston Pedigree; Taylor Landlord; Theakston Old Peculier H
City's smallest pub and one of its few free houses. Regular guest beers ()⌂

11–2.30; 5.30–10.30 (11 F, S)
Prince of Wales
Cambridge Street (off A456)
Ansells Mild, Bitter; Ind Coope Burton Ale; Tetley Bitter H
Popular Victorian pub. Handy for Birmingham Rep ⌂

12–2.30; 5.30–10.30 (11 F, S)
Queens Tavern
23 Essex Street (off Horsefair)
☎ (021) 622 3491
Courage Best Bitter, Directors H
Smart popular 1-roomed city-centre pub behind theatre
Q () ▶ ⌃ ≷

11–2.30; 5.30–10.30 (11 F, S)
Shakespeare
Lower Temple Street
Draught Bass; M&B Mild, Brew XI H
Busy pub frequented by both business people and shoppers. 200 yards from New Street station () ≷

10.30–2.30; 5.30–10.30 (11 F, S)
White Swan
116 Sherlock Street
☎ (021) 622 6717
Ansells Mild, Bitter H
Basic local with friendly welcome
⌃ () (Mon–Fri) ⌂⌃≷⌂

11–2.30; 5.30–10.30 (11 F, S)
Woodman
106 Albert Street
Ansells Mild, Bitter; Tetley Bitter H
Locals' pub with fine Irish welcome to visitors. Rare tiling; a listed building ⌂≷

Try also: British Oak

Digbeth:

11–2.30; 6–10.30 (11 F, S)
Market Tavern
Moseley Street (off A34/A45)
Ansells Mild, Bitter; Ind Coope Burton Ale H
Traditional tiled pub; in the back streets but well worth finding () ⌂

11–2.30; 5.30–10.30 (11 F, S)
Old Wharf
2 Oxford Street
☎ (021) 643 7339
Banks's Mild, Bitter E
Small cosy pub near city centre. No food after 8
() (not Sun) ▶ ⌂≷ (Moor St)

Erdington:

10.30–2.30; 5.30–10.30 (11 F, S)
Hare & Hounds
Marsh Hill (A4040)
☎ (021) 384 8047
Courage Best Bitter, Directors; John Smith Bitter H
Large roadhouse with beamed lounge; summer play area for children ⊛ () ⌂ ⌃

11–2.30; 6–10.30 (11 F, S)
Lad in the Lane
Bromford Lane (A4040)
Ansells Mild, Bitter; Ind Coope Burton Ale H
Reputedly Birmingham's oldest pub – now much altered. Children's playground () ⌂

10.30–2.30; 5.30–10.30 (11 F, S)
Safe Harbour
Moor Lane
Ansells Mild, Bitter; Ind Coope Burton Ale H
Also known as "Diggers" as opposite graveyard. Cosy lounge; spit and sawdust bar
⊛ () ⌂

Gosta Green:

5.30–10.30; 11–2.30 (11 F, S)
Sack of Potatoes
Lister Street ☎ (021) 359 6409
Draught Bass; M&B Mild, Springfield Bitter H
Lively students' pub near Aston University with a friendly welcome ⊛ () ▶ ⌂

Harborne:

11–2.30; 5.30–10.30 (11 F, S)
Kings Arms
352 High Street
☎ (021) 426 1048

West Midlands

Ansells Mild, Bitter; Tetley Bitter ⊞
Spacious 2-roomed pub, served by large horseshoe bar ⊕

Hall Green:

11–2.30; 5.30–10.30 (11 F, S)

Baldwin
Baldwins Lane
Courage Best Bitter, Directors; John Smith Bitter
Family pub with children's play area, bowls, skittles and bar games
☎ ⊞ ((not Sun) ⊕ & ≢

11–2.30; 6–10.30 (11 F, S)

Dog & Partridge
Priory Road ☎ (021) 474 2132
Ansells Mild, Bitter ⊞
Workingman's estate pub, backing onto river Cole. Bowling green and football pitch in grounds
☎ ⊞ (& ≢ (Yardley Wood)

Jewellery Quarter:

11–2.30; 6–10.30 (11 F, S)

St Pauls Tavern
Ludgate Hill, Hockley (off Queensway)
Draught Bass; M&B Mild, Brew XI ⊞
Small friendly corner of old Brum (⊕

Kings Heath:

11–2.30; 6–10.30 (11 F, S)

Hare & Hounds
High Street (A435)
☎ (021) 444 2081
Ansells Mild, Bitter; Ind Coope Burton Ale; Tetley Bitter ⊞
Edwardian pub popular with young
☎ ((Mon–Sat) ⊕ & (WC)

Kings Norton:

11–2.30; 5.30–10.30 (11 F, S)

Navigation
1a Wharf Road (off A441)
☎ (021) 458 1652
Davenports Mild, Bitter; Wem Special ⊞
Popular local near historic village green and canal.
Games ☎ ⊞ ( ) ⊕ & ≢

Perry Barr:

11–2.30; 6–10.30 (11 F, S)

Seventh Trap
Regina Drive
Banks's Mild, Bitter; Hanson Black Country Bitter ⊞
Typical Banks's pub with basic bar and large, comfortable lounge (⊕ ≢

11–2.30; 6–10.30 (11 F, S)

Wellhead Tavern
Franchise Street (off A38)
Ansells Mild, Bitter; Gibbs Mew Wiltshire Bitter; Ind Coope Burton Ale; Tetley Bitter ⊞
Heritage Inn, local CAMRA pub of the year 1987, popular with both students and locals (near Poly) (⊕ ≢

Shard End:

11–2.30; 6–10.30 (11 F, S)

Brook Meadow
Old Forest Way
Banks's Mild, Bitter ⊞
Suburban Banks's pub with large basic bar and comfortable lounge (⊕

Stetchford:

11–2.30; 5.30–10.30 (11 F, S)

Colehall Farm
Colehall Lane
☎ (021) 784 0155
Banks's Mild, Bitter; Hanson Black Country Bitter ⊞
Listed farmhouse converted in the early '80s. Very loud music
⊞ ( ) ⊕ &

Stirchley:

11–2.30; 5.30–10.30 (11 F, S)

Lifford Curve
Fordhouse Lane (A4040)
☎ (021) 451 1634
Banks's Mild, Bitter; Hanson Black Country Bitter ⊞
Popular modern pub with cosy rustic, split-level lounge
☎ ⊞ (⊕ &

Winson Green:

11–2.30; 6–10.30 (11 F, S)

Bricklayers Arms
218 Icknield Port Road (B4126)
☎ (021) 454 1828
Davenports Mild, Bitter ⊞
2-room pub in rundown area, with heavy Irish influence ⊕

11–2.30; 6–10.30 (11 F, S)

Bellefield Inn
36 Winson Street
☎ (021) 558 0647
Davenports Mild, Bitter ⊞
Former Samuel Whites brewhouse, now a thriving pub offering Asian food and a warm welcome ⊕ ○

Blackheath

12–2.30; 7–10.30 (11 F, S)

Beech Tree
Gorsty Hill Road (A4099)
☎ (021) 559 2170
H P & D Mild, Bitter, Entire ⊞
Cheerful locals' pub. Landlord keen music fan; excellent home cooking ≙ Q (⊕

12–2.30; 7–10.30 (11 F, S)

Waterfall
Waterfall Lane, Rowley Regis
☎ (021) 561 3499
Batham Bitter; Everards Tiger, Old Original; Hook Norton Old Hookey ⊞
Newly-opened free house. A wide choice of ales and hot meals; guest beers ≙ ⊞ ( ) ⊕

Bloxwich

11–2.30; 6 (7 Sat)–10.30 (11 F, S)

Station
Station Road (off A34)
☎ (0922) 477004
Ansells Mild, Bitter ⊞
Single U-shaped room with bar and lounge areas; bright and cheerful ⊞

Brierley Hill

11.30–2.30; 6–10.30 (11 F, S)

Bell
Delph Road (B4172, off A461)
☎ (0384) 72376
H P & D Mild, Bitter, Entire, Deakin's Downfall ⊞
Popular early Victorian pub at the bottom of the famous Delph Nine Locks. No meals Sun ≙ ⊞ ( ) ⊕ &

10.30–2.30; 6–10.30 (11 F, S)

New Inn
Dudley Road (A461)
☎ (0384) 73792
Davenports Bitter; Wem Best Bitter, Special Bitter ⊞
Friendly ex-Simpkiss local near town centre ≙ ☎ ⊕ &

11–2.30; 6–10.30 (11 F, S)

Vine (Bull & Bladder)
Delph Road (off A461)
☎ (0384) 77089
Batham Mild, Bitter, Delph Strong Ale ⊞
Famous basic Black Country brewery tap with brightly painted frontage. Irish folk music Sun ☎ ⊞ ⊕ &

Catherine De Barnes

11–2.30; 5.30–10.30 (11 F, S)

Boat Inn
Hampton Lane (B4102)
☎ (021) 705 0474
Davenports Mild, Bitter; Wem Special Bitter ⊞
Traditional canalside pub; tasteful bar, comfortable large lounge

Colley Gate

11–2.30; 6–10.30 (11 F, S)

Little White Lion
Windmill Hill (A458)
☎ (0384) 69314
Ansells Bitter, Mild; Ind Coope Burton Ale; Lumphammer ⊞
Little Pub Company owned; famed for Desperate Dan pies and sizzling bear steaks. Live music Tue ≙ (⊕

11–2.30; 6–10.30 (11 F, S)

Why Not
Whynot Lane, Two Gates
Batham Bitter; Everards Old Original; Hanson Mild; Marston Pedigree; Ringwood Forty-niner ⊞

West Midlands

ecently reopened free house; cosy lounges with alcoves, and a dining room
Q ( ) (not Sun)

Coseley

12–2.30; 6–10.30 (11 F, S)

New Inn
Ward Street (just off A4123)
☎ (090 73) 4511
Holden Mild, Bitter ⓔ, **Special Bitter, XL (winter)** Ⓗ
Extended local partly hidden by chapel, near Wolverhampton–Birmingham canal. Snacks

Coventry

11–3; 6–11

Biggin Hall Hotel
214 Binley Road, Copsewood (A427) ☎ (0203) 451056
Marston Mercian Mild, Burton Bitter, Pedigree, Owd Rodger Ⓗ
Not a hotel! Wood-panelled lounge; smart bar; games room at rear

10–2.30; 7–11

Black Horse
Spon End ☎ (0203) 77360
Draught Bass; M&B Mild, Brew XI Ⓗ
A popular old pub with indefinable character. Wood-panelled lounge; narrow locals' bar

11–2.30; 6–11

Boat Inn
Black Horse Road (off B4113) ☎ (0203) 361438
Ansells Mild, Bitter; Ind Coope Burton Ale Ⓗ
Splendid Heritage Inn near canal basin at Sutton Stop

11–2.30; 7–11

Boat Inn
31 Shilton Lane, Walsgrave ☎ (0203) 613686
Draught Bass; M&B Mild, Brew XI Ⓗ
Small multi-roomed pub on filled-in canal arm
(not Sun)

11–2.30; 6–11

Coombe Abbey Inn
Craven Street, Chapelfields ☎ (0203) 75743
Draught Bass; M&B Mild, Brew XI Ⓗ
Popular pub with basic bar and small lounge. Regular folk music sessions

11–2.30; 6–11

Earlsdon Cottage
Warwick Street ☎ (0203) 74745
Draught Bass; M&B Mild, Highgate Mild, Brew XI Ⓗ
Large popular pub, due for redecoration. Music in back room

11–2.30; 6.30–11

Elastic Inn
Lower Ford Street ☎ (0203) 27039
Ansells Mild, Bitter; Tetley Bitter Ⓗ
Single bar pub near bus station and leisure centre

11–2.30; 6–11

Greyhound Inn
Sutton Stop, Longford
Draught Bass ⓔ
Old canal pub in conservation area at Hawkesbury Junction; 2 rooms with outside drinking area. Famous for pies

11–2.30; 6–11

Haven
Dillotford Avenue ☎ (0203) 419029
Courage Best Bitter, Directors Ⓗ
Popular estate pub; games

11–2.30; 6 (7 Mon–Thu)–11

Malt Shovel
Spon End ☎ (0203) 20204
Ansells Mild, Bitter; Tetley Bitter Ⓗ
Heritage pub with genuine old beams. 1 room but several drinking areas

Try also: Jolly Colliers (Manns)

Cradley Heath

11.30–2.30; 6–10.30 (11 F, S)

Victoria Inn
Dudley Wood Road (off A4100) ☎ (0384) 62705
Banks's Bitter; Hanson Mild Ⓗ
Bright, comfortable old local next to speedway stadium. Bowling green
(not Sun)

11.30–2.30; 7–10.30 (11 F, S)

Waggon & Horses
Reddal Hill Road (A4100) ☎ (0384) 636035
Banks's Mild, Bitter ⓔ
Vibrant, main street Black Country pub with a strong affinity for the Staffordshire bull terrier. Games

Darlaston

11–2.30; 7–10.30 (11 F, S)

Green Dragon
55 Church Street ☎ (021) 526 3674
M&B Highgate Mild, Springfield Bitter Ⓗ
Friendly, homely pub with great emphasis on darts. Walsall CAMRA pub of the year

Dudley

11.30–2.30; 7–10.30 (11 F, S)

Lamp Tavern
High Street (A459) ☎ (0384) 54129
Batham Mild, Bitter, Delph Strong Ale Ⓗ
Busy pub with defunct brewery at rear

11–2.30; 6 (6.45 Sat)–10.30 (11 F, S)

Malt Shovel
Tower Street ☎ (0384) 52735
Banks's Mild, Bitter Ⓗ
Popular back street local overlooked by castle and zoo
(not Sun)

11.30–2.30; 6–10.30 (11 F, S)

Old Vic
King Street ☎ (0384) 236082
Flowers Original; Marston Pedigree; Wadworth 6X Ⓗ
Town-centre free house with guest beers; quality food

11–2.30; 6–10.30 (11 F, S)

Struggling Man
57 Salop Street (B4588) ☎ (0384) 231763
Banks's Bitter; Hanson Mild ⓔ
Quality old Black Country local serving mainly mild. Ex-farmhouse, 1 mile from town

Try also: British Oak (Free)

Earlswood

11–2.30; 5.30–10.30 (11 F, S)

Bulls Head
Lime Kiln Lane (off B4102) ☎ (021) 728 2335
Ansells Mild, Bitter; Ind Coope Burton Ale Ⓗ
Friendly public bar, very popular with Sunday cyclists. Water pump outside

Halesowen

12–2.30; 6–10.30 (11 F, S)

Beehive
Hagley Road ☎ (021) 550 1782
Banks's Bitter, Mild, Black Country Bitter ⓔ
Convivial 3-roomed local. A disco for the energetic – and a cosy lounge for relaxation. Pool table

11–2.30; 5.30–10.30 (11 F, S)

King Edward VII
Stourbridge Road (A458) ☎ (021) 550 4493
Ansells Mild, Bitter; Ind Coope Burton Ale Ⓗ
Popular local alongside football club. Noted for home cooking Q (meals)

12–2.30; 7–10.30 (11 F, S)

Waggon & Horses
Stourbridge Road (A458) ☎ (021) 550 4989
Banks's Mild; Marston Pedigree; Old Swan (Pardoe's) Bitter; Ruddles County; Samuel Smith OBB Ⓗ
Vibrant free house; basic bar with pool table; cosy snug.

301

West Midlands

Occasional live music. Guest beers 🏠 Q 🚭

Keresley End

11–2.30; 6–11

Golden Eagle
Howats Road (off Bennetts Road) ☎ (020 333) 3066
Banks's Mild, Bitter Ⓔ
Large estate pub in colliery village north of Coventry. Family room
🐕 ⊛ ◐ (not Sun) 🚭

Kingswinford

11.30–2.30; 6–10.30 (11 F, S)

Cross
High Street (Cross Roads) ☎ (0384) 287308
H P & D Mild, Bitter, Entire, Deakin's Downfall Ⓗ
Large 18th-century coaching house 🏠 ⊛ ◐ ▶

12 (11.30 Sat)–2.30; 6–10.30 (11 F, S)

Park Tavern
Barnett Lane ☎ (0384) 287178
Ansells Mild, Bitter; Batham Bitter; Ind Coope Burton Ale Ⓗ
Traditional local near Broadfield House Glass Museum 🐕 ⊛ 🚭 ♿

Try also: Old Court House

Knowle

11–2.30; 5.30–10.30 (11 F, S)

Red Lion
Warwick Road ☎ (056 45) 2461
Ansells Mild, Bitter; Ind Coope Burton Ale; Tetley Bitter Ⓗ
Bar with old wooden beams and open grate; comfortable lounge 🏠 Q 🐕 ◐ (not Sun) 🚭

Langley

11–2.30; 6–10.30 (11 F, S)

Brewery Inn
Station Road (B4182) ☎ (021) 544 6467
H P & D Mild, Bitter, Entire, Deakin's Downfall Ⓗ
Friendly and popular canalside pub with brewery attached. Snob screen and Black Country artefacts. Games 🏠 ◐ 🚭 ♿

11–2.30; 6–10.30 (11 F, S)

Crosswells
High Street (off B4182)
H P & D Mild, Bitter, Entire, Deakin's Downfall Ⓗ
Busy 2-roomed Victorian pub, close to Holt Plant and Deakin brewery 🏠 Q ◐ 🚭 ♿

Lower Gornal

11–2.30; 6–10.30 (11 F, S)

Red Cow
Grosvenor Road (off B4176) ☎ (0384) 53760
Banks's Bitter; Hanson Mild Ⓔ

Old Black Country local of character off the beaten track. Pub games 🐕 ⊛ 🚭 ♿

Try also: Miners Arms (Holden)

Lye

11–2.30; 6–10.30 (11 F, S)

Castle
Balds Lane (off A458) ☎ (038 482) 2799
Davenports Mild, Bitter; Wem Best Bitter Ⓗ
Country-style pub in an urban area. Bar billiards, unusual in the area; summer barbecues
🏠 ⊛ ◐ ▶

11–2.30; 6–10.30 (11 F, S)

Shovel
Pedmore Road ☎ (038 482) 2697
Banks's Mild; Batham Bitter; Everards Tiger, Old Original; Hook Norton Old Hookey Ⓗ
Busy free house known for its excellent range of fine ales and home-cooked meals. Guest beers 🏠 ⊛ (meals) ◐ ▶ 🚭 ♿

Monkspath

11–2.30; 5.30–10.30 (11 F, S)

Shelly Farm
Farmhouse Way (off A34)
Ansells Mild, Bitter; Ind Coope Burton Ale; Tetley Bitter Ⓗ
Converted 15th-century farmhouse with adjacent restaurant; open till 9 Mon–Sat
Q 🐕 ⊛ ◐ ▶

Netherton

11–2.30; 6–10.30 (11 F, S)

Elephant & Castle
Cradley Road (B4173) ☎ (0384) 636849
H P & D Mild, Bitter, Entire Ⓗ
Comfortable Black Country local with traction engine and forge in rear garden 🏠 ⊛ ◐ 🚭 ♿

Try also: Dry Dock (Little Pub Co.); Old Swan (Mrs Pardoe's)

Oldbury

11.30–2.30; 6–10.30 (11 F, S)

Railway
Bromford Road (A4034)
Draught Bass; M&B Mild, Springfield Bitter, Brew XI Ⓔ
Busy 2-roomed local opposite station. Sandwiches made to order
⊛ 🚭 ♿ (Sandwell & Dudley)

12 (11.30 Sat)–2.30; 6–10.30 (11 F, S)

Waggon & Horses
Church Street ☎ (021) 552 5467
Batham Bitter; Everard Tiger, Old Original; Marston Pedigree Ⓗ
Popular, listed Victorian town pub with original tiled walls, copper ceiling and Holt brewery window. Guest bee
🏠 ◐ 🚭 ♿ (Sandwell & Dudley)

Try also: White Swan (Banks

Olton

12–2.30; 6–10.30 (11 F, S)

Lyndon
Barn Lane ☎ (021) 743 2179
Ansells Mild, Bitter Ⓗ
Large, basic pub with excellent adventure playground 🏠 🐕 ⊛ ◐ ▶

Pelsall

10–2.30; 6–10.30 (11 F, S)

Free Trade
Wood Lane
Ansells Mild, Bitter Ⓗ
Bright friendly pub with live jazz Wed and new restaurant
◐ ▶ 🚭

10.30–2.30; 6–10.30 (11 F, S)

George & Dragon
High Street, Clayhanger
Ansells Mild, Bitter Ⓗ
Friendly estate pub with games room 🚭

10.30–2.30; 6–10.30 (11 F, S)

Old Bush
Walsall Road (B4155) ☎ (0922) 682806
Ansells Mild, Bitter; Holden Special Bitter Ⓗ
Popular pub, overlooking common. Guest beers
🐕 ⊛ ◐ ▶ 🚭

10.30–2.30; 6–10.30 (11 F, S)

Old House at Home
Walsall Road (B4154)
Banks's Mild, Bitter; Hanson Black Country Bitter Ⓔ
Popular pub near common

10.30–2.30; 6–10.30 (11 F, S)

Red Cow
Allens Lane ☎ (0922) 84743
Banks's Mild, Bitter Ⓔ
Cosy roadside pub, overlooking common

Quarry Bank

11–2.30; 6–10.30 (11 F, S)

Church Tavern
High Street (A4100) ☎ (0384) 68757
H P & D Mild, Bitter, Entire, Deakin's Downfall Ⓗ
Cheerful welcoming pub with Black Country society connections. Book for Sun lunch
🏠 🐕 ◐ ▶ 🚭 ♿ (Cradley Heath)

11–2.30; 7–10.30 (11 F, S)

Wagon & Horses
Just off A4100
Banks's Bitter; Hanson Mild Ⓔ
Basic 3-roomed locals' local. Barbecues in summer Q ◐ 🚭

302

West Midlands

Rushall

12 (11 Sat)–2.30; 6–10.30 (11 F, S)
Miners Arms
Lichfield Road (A461)
☎ (0922) 26184
M&B Highgate Mild, Springfield Bitter E
Traditional roadside local. Bright bar popular with darts players, and cosy small back room ☎ ( ) ⌂ ⚐

11–2.30; 6–10.30 (11 F, S)
Royal Oak
Daw End (B4154)
☎ (0922) 28859
M&B Highgate Mild, Springfield Bitter, Brew XI E
Bar with football mirrors; large family lounge; separate alcove with games machine
⌂ ( ) ⚐ &

Ryton-on-Dunsmore

11–2.30; 6–11
Blacksmiths Arms
19 High Street (off A45)
☎ (0203) 301818
Draught Bass; M&B Mild, Brew XI H
1-room village restaurant/pub near Peugeot factory. No food Sat lunch or Sun ⌂ ( ) &

Sedgley

12–2.30; 6.30–10.30 (11 F, S)
Mount Pleasant (Stump)
Wolverhampton Road (A459)
☎ (090 73) 72862
H P & D Mild, Bitter, Entire, Deakin's Downfall H
Popular local converted from 19th-century terraced house
☎ ( ) (not Sun) ⚐ &

11–2.30; 6–10.30 (11 F, S)
Beacon Hotel
Bilston Street (A463)
☎ (090 73) 3380
Burton Bridge Porter; Holden Special Bitter; Sarah Hughes Dark Ruby Mild; M&B Springfield Bitter H
Lovingly restored Victorian hostelry. 3-tier brewery reopened in 1987 after 30 years. Guest beers; family room ⌂ Q ⌂ ⚐ ⚐ &

Shirley

12–2 (closed Mon); 5.30–10
Bernies Real Ale Off Licence
266 Cranmore Boulevard (off A34) ☎ (021) 744 2827
Hoskins Oldfield EX5; Oakhill Farmers Ale; Taylor Landlord H; **Wadworth 6X** E
A wide and ever-changing range of unusual real ales. Small independent breweries encouraged ⌂

Solihull

10.30–2.30; 5.30 (6 Sat)–10.30 (11 F, S)
Golden Lion
Warwick Road
☎ (021) 704 9969
Courage Best Bitter, Directors; John Smith Yorkshire Bitter H
Town centre pub to satisfy all tastes. Games ⌂ ( ) ⚐ ⚐

Stourbridge

12–2.30; 7–10.30 (11 F, S)
Bulls Head
High Street, Wollaston (A461)
☎ (0384) 394073
Davenports Bitter H
Pleasing 3-roomed local with a panelled lounge and a small friendly bar Q ( ) ⚐

11–2.30; 6–10.30 (11 F, S)
Foresters Arms
Bridgnorth Road, Wollaston (A461) ☎ (0384) 394476
Ansells Bitter; Ind Coope Burton Ale; Tetley Bitter H
Overlooking rolling countryside; good food and summer barbecues Q ⌂ ( )

11–2.30; 6 (8 Sun & Mon)–10.30 (11 F, S)
Old Crispin Inn
Church Street ☎ (0384) 377581
Flowers Original; Marston Pedigree H
Excellent free house complete with sun lounge and upstairs restaurant. Newspapers to read. Whitbread beers sold as Crispin Special Q ⌂ ⌂ ( ) ⚐

11–2.30; 7–10.30 (11 F, S)
Plough
Bridgnorth Road (A458)
☎ (0384) 393414
M&B Mild, Springfield Bitter E
Popular roadside local with traditional atmosphere
⌂ ⌂ ( ) ⚐

11–2.30; 6–10.30 (11 F, S)
Red Lion
Lion Street ☎ (0384) 397563
Draught Bass H; **M&B Mild, Springfield Bitter** E
Comfortable pub with excellent atmosphere; cosy parlour offers good meals most of the day ⌂ ( ) ⚐ ⚐

Streetly

12–2; 5.30–10.30
Laurel Wines
63 Westwood Road
☎ (021) 353 0399
Batham Bitter; Donnington BB; Everards Old Original; Holden Bitter, Special Bitter G
Off-licence with large and varying selection of beers, and friendly licensee

Sutton Coldfield

11–2.30; 5.30–11
Blake Barn Inn
40 Shelley Drive, Four Oaks (off A5127) ☎ (021) 308 8421
Banks's Mild, Bitter; Hanson Black Country Bitter E
Large, popular modern pub in rustic-style in new estate. Popular with the young
⌂ ( ) (not Sun) & ⚐ (Blake St)

11–2.30; 5.30–11
Boot
Rectory Road ☎ (021) 378 0609
Courage Directors H
Very basic locals' public and younger lounge. Near Good Hope Hospital. Games
⌂ ( ) (Mon–Fri) ⚐

11–2.30; 5.30–11
Duke Inn
Duke Street (off Birmingham Road) ☎ (021) 355 3479
Ansells Mild, Bitter; Ind Coope Burton Ale; Tetley Bitter H
Friendly side-street local near town centre; many times winner of branch Pub of the Year Q ⌂ ⌂ ⚐ ⚐

11–2.30; 5.30–11
Four Oaks Carvery
62 Bellwell Lane, Mere Green
☎ (021) 308 1460
Ansells Mild, Bitter; Tetley Bitter H
Upmarket restaurant/pub with large comfortable lounge, near Sutton Park ⌂ ( ) &

11–2.30; 5.30–11
Plough & Harrow
Slade Road, Roughly
☎ (021) 308 1132
Banks's Mild, Bitter; Hanson Black Country Bitter E
Large comfortable pub with beer garden, good for children. Food recommended. Games ⌂ ( ) (not Sun) ⚐

10.30–2.30; 5.30–11
Station
Station Street ☎ (021) 355 3640
Draught Bass; M&B Mild, Brew XI E
Old railway tavern, busy at all hours. Large-screen satellite TV in lounge. Handy for station ⌂ ⌂ ( ) (not Sun) ⚐ & ⚐

Try also: New Inns, Lichfield Road; **Pint Pot**, Tower Road

Tipton

11–2.30; 6–10.30 (11 F, S)
M.A.D. O' Rourke's Pie Factory
Hurst Lane ☎ (021) 557 1402
Ansells Mild; Ind Coope Burton Ale; Lumphammer H
Not so much a pub, more an experience; cook room, butcher's shop and hanging room with the chief foreman –

303

West Midlands

a pig – presiding in his office

Try also: Old Court House (Free)

Tividale

11–2.30; 6–10.30 (11 F, S)

Barley Mow
City Road (off A4123)
☎ (0384) 54623
H P & D Mild, Bitter, Entire, Deakin's Downfall H
Extended farmhouse in urban setting on Rowley Hills, with panoramic Black Country views. Skittle alley

Upper Gornal

12–2.30; 7–10.30 (11 F, S)

Crown
Holloway Street, Ruiton (off A459) ☎ (09073) 4035
Banks's Bitter; Hanson Mild E
Friendly, popular old local at the top of the hill. Family room

Try also: Jolly Crispin (Davenports)

Wall Heath

12–2.30; 6–10.30 (11 F, S)

Wall Heath Inn
High Street (A449)
☎ (0384) 287319
Ansell's Mild, Bitter; Ind Coope Burton Ale H
Well-kept tidy pub at the edge of the village. Barbecues in beer garden in summer. Excellent food

Walsall

12–2.30; 6.30–10.30

Butts Tavern
Butts Street ☎ (0922) 29332
Ansells Mild, Bitter; Ind Coope Burton Ale H
Typical mid 1930s pub on site of 19th-century beerhouse. Regular live music in lounge

12 (11 Sat)–2.30; 5.30–10.30 (11 F, S)

Duke of Wellington
Birmingham Street
☎ (0922) 24209
M&B Highgate Mild, Springfield Bitter, Brew XI E
Popular local near St. Matthews church. Very pleasant step into the past

11–2.30 5.30 (6 weekends)–10.30 (11 F, S)

New Inns
John Street (off A34)
☎ (0922) 27660
Ansells Mild, Bitter; Ind Coope Burton Ale H
Small-roomed back street local. Traditional but warm and comfortable; a rare haven.

Excellent family lunches Sun (not Sun)

12–2.30; 5.30–10.30 (11 F, S)

Orange Tree
Wolverhampton Road (A454)
☎ (0922) 25119
Ansells Mild, Bitter; Tetley Bitter H
L-shaped pub with separate bar and lounge sections, popular with office workers and lorry drivers

12–2.30; 7–10.30 (11 F, S)

White Lion
Sandwell Street (off A4031)
☎ (0922) 28542
Ansells Mild, Bitter; Ind Coope Burton Ale H
Large, popular backstreet local with separate pool room. Students' haunt. Beware of sloping floor in bar

Walsall Wood

11.30–2.30; 5.30–10.30 (11 F, S)

Royal Exchange
Lichfield Road (A461)
☎ (0543) 372317
Ansells Mild, Bitter; Ind Coope Burton Ale H
Typical roadside pub with modern feel; well decorated but too bright in lounge

Wednesbury

11.30–2.30; 5.30–10.30 (11 F, S)

Horse & Jockey
Wood Green Road (A461)
☎ (021) 556 0464
Ansells Mild, Bitter; Ind Coope Burton Ale H
Pub restaurant: 24-ounce T-bone steak a speciality (book): happy hour 5.30–7 Mon–Fri

12–2.30; 6–10.30 (11 F, S)

Woodman
Wood Green Road (M6 near Jct 9) ☎ (021) 556 1637
Courage Directors H
Large, 3-roomed pub; handpump is in smoke room. Very easy to spot Directors drinkers! ⇌ (Bescot)

Wednesfield

10.30–2.30; 6–10.30 (11 F, S)

Broadway
Lichfield Road (A4124)
☎ (0922) 405872
Ansells Mild, Bitter; Holden Black Country Bitter; Ind Coope Burton Ale H
Pleasant multi-roomed pub with games (not Sun)

West Bromwich

11–2.30; 6–10.30 (11 F, S)

Merry Go Round
Garratt Street ☎ (021) 553 4338
Ansells Mild, Bitter; Ind Coope Burton Ale H
Large pub with bar and plush lounge; popular with dart

players. Singalong piano sessions in lounge

11–2.30; 6–10.30 (11 F, S)

Old Hop Pole
High Street (A41)
☎ (021) 525 6648
H P & D Mild, Bitter, Entire, Deakin's Downfall H
Comfortable 19th-century local. Succulent pork and beef sandwiches on fresh crusty bread a speciality

11.30–2.30; 6–10.30 (11 F, S)

Royal Oak
Newton Street
M&B Mild, Brew XI H
Small 2-roomed pub with basic bar and comfortable lounge Q

12–2.30; 6–10.30 (11 F, S)

Sow & Pigs
Hill Top (A41)
☎ (021) 553 3127
Banks's Bitter; Hanson Mild E
Compact 2-roomed 18th century local, little changed other than by intriguing wall paintings. Outside loos!

Try also: Wheatsheaf (Holden)

Willenhall

12–2.30; 6.30–10.30 (11 F, S)

Robin Hood
54 The Crescent (A462)
☎ (0902) 68006
Ansells Mild; Ind Coope Burton Ale; Tetley Bitter H
Deservedly popular pub which gets very crowded at times, but always friendly

Wollescote

11–2.30; 6–10.30 (11 F, S)

Top Bell
Belmont Road
Ansells Mild, Bitter; Holden Bitter; Ind Coope Burton Ale H
Transformed ex-keg house; value-for-money food

Wolverhampton

11–2.30; 6–10.30 (11 F, S)

Clarendon
Chapel Ash (A41)
☎ (0902) 20587
Banks's Mild, Bitter E
Banks's brewery tap; several varied rooms and rare corridor bar (Mon–Fri)

10.30–2.30; 6–10.30

Exchange
Exchange Street
Banks's Mild, Bitter E
Basic town centre pub. Lunchtime snacks (very busy) ⇌

304

West Midlands

11–2.30; 6–10.30 (11 F, S)
Great Western
Sun Street (off A4124)
☎ (0902) 351090
Batham Bitter; Holden Mild, Bitter, Special H
Revitalised pub next to the old low level station. Guest beers regularly ≜ ◐ ⇌

11.30–2.30; 6–10.30 (11 F, S)
Homestead
Lodge Road, Oxley (off A449)
Ansells Mild, Bitter; Holden Black Country Bitter; Ind Coope Burton Ale H
Large, pleasant suburban locals' pub with excellent children's playground and outdoor drinking area
≥ ≋ ◐ ⊞

12–2.30; 6–10.30 (11 F, S)
Lewisham Arms
Prosser Street, Park Village (off A460) ☎ (0902) 50429
Banks's Mild, Bitter E
Magnificent, unspoilt Victorian alehouse. Enormous bar area; tiny comfortable lounge Q ⊞

12–2.30; 6–10.30 (11 F, S)
Mitre
Lower Green, Tettenhall (off A41) ☎ (0902) 753487
Draught Bass; M&B Highgate Mild, Springfield Bitter E
Pleasant old pub by village green; deservedly popular
≋ ◐ ⊞

12–2.30; 6–10.30 (11 F, S)
Newhampton Inn
Riches Street, Whitmore Reans (off A41)
☎ (0902) 755565
Courage Best Bitter, Directors H
Bustling local; regular live Irish music ≋ ⊞

11–2.30; 6–10.30 (11 F, S)
Old Ash Tree
Dudley Road (A459)
☎ (0902) 342218
Banks's Mild, Bitter E
Large busy suburban pub on main road, a mile south of town. Floodlit bowling green at rear ≋ ⊞

11–2.30; 6–10.30 (11 F, S)
Paget Arms
Park Lane (off A460)
☎ (0902) 731136
Flowers Original; Ind Coope Burton Ale; Marston Pedigree; Owd Rodger; Thwaites Mild H
Popular pub with 3 spacious rooms and eating area. Regular guest beers and a variety of good food
≜ ≋ ◐ ▷ (Tue–Sat) ⊞ ♿

11–2.30; 6 (7 Sat)–10.30
Posada
Lichfield Street
☎ (0902) 710738
H P & D Mild, Bitter, Entire, Deakin's Downfall (winter) H
Town centre Victorian pub with original bar fittings and tiled front; popular with students ≜ ◐ (Mon–Fri) ⇌

11–2.30; 6–10.30 (11 F, S)
Queens Arms
Graisley Row (off A449)
☎ (0902) 26589
Ansells Mild, Bitter; Ind Coope Burton Ale H
Small, friendly pub hidden in industrial estate ≋

11–2.30; 6–10.30 (11 F, S)
Royal Oak
School Road, Tettenhall Wood
☎ (0902) 754396
M&B Highgate Mild, Springfield Bitter, Brew XI E
Charming pub with large games room and beautifully-kept garden ≜ ≋ ◐ ⊞

10.30–2.30; 6–10.30 (11 F, S)
Stamford Arms
Lime Street, Penn Fields
Banks's Mild, Bitter E
Victorian pub with award-winning garden; hidden gem in a run down area ≋ ⊞

11–2.30; 6–10.30 (11 F, S)
Swan
Lower Street, Lower Green (off A41) ☎ (0902) 755943
H P & D Mild, Bitter, Entire, Deakin's Downfall (winter) H
Pleasant and popular Holts-styled old world pub
≜ ≋ ◐ (Mon–Fri)

11 (10.30 Sat)–2.30; 6–10.30
Wheatsheaf
Market Street (opposite cinema) ☎ (0902) 24446
Banks's Mild, Bitter E
Busy town-centre pub with table service in lounge
≋ ≇ ⊞ ⇌

Try also: Old Ash Tree Dudley Road

Woodsetton

11.30–2.30; 6–10.30 (11 F, S)
Park Inn
George Street ☎ (090 73) 2843
Holden Mild E, **Bitter** H & E, **Special Bitter, XL (winter)** H
Holden's brewery tap; recently decorated. Summer barbecues ≜ ≥ ≋ ◐ (not Sun)
♿ ⇌ (Tipton)

Wiltshire

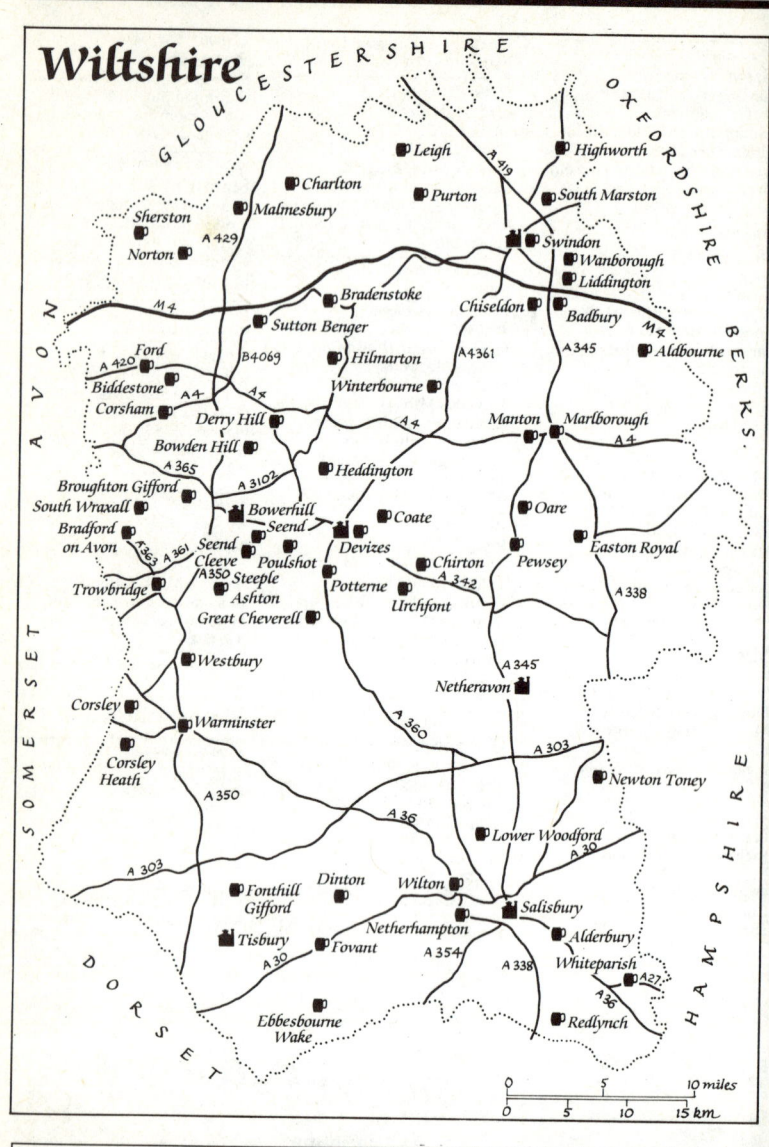

Archers, Arkell, Swindon; **Bunces,** Netheravon; **Gibbs Mew,** Salisbury; **Mole's,** Bowerhill; **Wadworth,** Devizes; **Wiltshire,** Tisbury

Aldbourne

11–2.30; 7–10.30 (11 F, S & summer)
Masons Arms
West Street (B4192)
Arkells Bitter, BBB H
Traditional, friendly village locals' local with small cosy bars. Pub games
☎ (lunch) ⊛ ◖⊟&

Alderbury

10–2.30; 6–10.30 (11 F, S & summer)
Green Dragon
Old Road (off A36)
☎ (0722) 710263
Courage Best Bitter H
14th-century Dickensian inn with small public bar, comfortable lounge, good garden. Snooker and other games Q⊛◖⊟

Badbury

11–2.30; 7–11
Bakers Arms
Off A345, ½ mile S of M4 Jct 15
☎ (0793) 740313
Arkells Bitter, BBB H
Neat little pub tucked away in

306

Wiltshire

a side road. Pub games 🚸⊛🌣🍴▶🎯

Biddestone

11–2.30; 6–10.30 (11 F, S)

White Horse
Off A420 ☎ (0249) 713305
Courage Bitter Ale, Best Bitter, Directors H
Characterful pub in picturesque village next to pond. Well organised despite small serving area. Pub games ৬⊛🍴▶

Bowden Hill

12–2.30 (not Tue); 7–10.30 (11 F, S)

Rising Sun
32 Bowden Hill (1 mile E of Lacock) ☎ (024 973) 363
Mole's PA, Cask Bitter, Landlord's Choice, 97 G;
Gibbs Mew Salisbury Best; Wadworth 6X H
Intimate pub with stone floors, settles and a terraced garden with extensive views over the Avon Valley. Pub games. Guest beers 🚸Q⊛🍴

Bradenstoke

12–2.30 (Fri–Mon); 7–10.30 (11 F, S)

Cross Keys
Off B4069 (formerly A420)
☎ (0249) 890279
Bunces Benchmark; Ind Coope Burton Ale; Wadworth 6X H
Traditional 200 year-old local in pretty village. RAF Lyneham at bottom of the garden! Pub games
🚸৬⊛🍴▶🎯▲

Bradford on Avon

11–2.30; 6.30–11

Bunch of Grapes
14 Silver Street
☎ (022 16) 3877
Hook Norton Best Bitter; Smiles Best Bitter H
Small, friendly town pub. Cosy front lounge, lively public. Guest beers. No food Tue. Darts and shove ha'penny 🍴▶ (not Sun) 🎯≠

10–2.30; 6–11

Dog & Fox
Ashley Road ☎ (022 16) 3257
Usher Best Bitter; Webster Yorkshire Bitter G
Country pub of character on northern fringe of town. Front parlour-style lounge; large sunny garden. No meals Sun. Darts 🚸🍴▶ (summer)🎯◯

Broughton Gifford

11–2.30; 6.30–11

Bell
The Common (off B3107)
☎ (0225) 782309
Wadworth IPA, 6X, Old Timer (winter) H

Fine old village pub on edge of common. Darts 🚸🍴▶🎯

Charlton

12–2.30; 7–10.30 (11 F, S & summer) (closed Sun eve & Monday)

Horse & Groom
On B4040 ☎ (0666) 823904
Archers Village Bitter; Moles Cask Bitter; Wadworth 6X H
Quiet, country pub with intimate restaurant – excellent food. Lovely garden. Pub games 🚸Q⊛🍴▶🎯

Chirton

10–2.30; 6–10.30 (11 F, S summer)

Wiltshire Yeoman
Andover Road (A342)
☎ (0380) 84665
Wadworth IPA, 6X H
Friendly main road pub with skittle alley 🚸৬🍴▶🎯🎯▲

Chiseldon

11–2.30; 6–11

Patriots Arms
New Road (B4005)
☎ (0793) 740331
Courage Best Bitter, Directors; John Smith Bitter H
Genuine family pub with good facilities for children. Pub games ৬⊛🍴▶🎯

Coate

11.30–2.30; 6.30–10.30 (11 F, S & summer)

New Inn
Off A361 OS040616
☎ (038 086) 644
Wadworth IPA, 6X G
Friendly traditional pub. Landlord is a member of the Society for the Preservation of Beers from the Wood. Pub games 🚸৬⊛🎯🎯

Try also: **Bridge Inn**, Horton

Corsham

10–2.30; 6–10.30 (11 F, S & summer)

Methuen Arms
2 High Street ☎ (0249) 714867
Draught Bass; Gibbs Mew Wiltshire Traditional Bitter, Salisbury Best, Bishops Tipple H
Family-run hotel with 2 bars and restaurant near Corsham Court. The long bar has skittle alley ৬⊛🎯🍴▶🎯▲

Corsley

11.30–2.30 (not Mon); 6.30–10.30 (11 F, S & summer)

Cross Keys
Lyes Green (off A362)
☎ (037 388) 406
Draught Bass; Moles Cask Bitter; Ruddles Best Bitter H
Welcoming free house near Cley Hill, well known for its 'UFOs'. Darts and shove ha'penny 🚸৬⊛🍴 (not Sun) ◯

Corsley

11.30–2.30 (not Mon); 6.30–10.30 (11 F, S & summer)

Cross Keys
Lyes Green (off A362)
☎ (037 388) 406
Draught Bass; Moles Cask Bitter; Ruddles Best Bitter H
Welcoming free house near Cley Hill, well known for its 'UFOs'. Darts and shove ha'penny 🚸৬⊛🍴 (not Sun) ◯

Corsley Heath

11–2.30; 6–11

Royal Oak
Corsley Heath (on A362)
☎ (037 388) 238
Draught Bass; Wadworth IPA, 6X, Farmers Glory (summer), Old Timer (winter) H
Busy roadside pub/restaurant near Longleat Estate. Family room. Darts 🚸৬⊛🍴▶🎯

Derry Hill

10.30–2.30; 6–10.30 (11 F, S)

Lansdowne Arms
On A342 ☎ (0249) 812422
Wadworth IPA, 6X, Farmers Glory, Old Timer (winter) H
Popular pleasant pub, good food. Home of Lansdowne Arms Formation Drinking Team 🚸⊛🍴▶🎯▲

Devizes

11–2.30 (4 Thu); 6–10.30 (11 F, S & summer)

Black Swan Hotel
Market Place ☎ (0380) 3259
Wadworth IPA, 6X H
Cosy L shaped bar in 1737 coaching inn. Popular with brewery workers and market traders who use the separate restaurant for business lunches Q🍴▶

11–2.30; 6.30–10.30 (11 F, S & summer)

Hare & Hounds
Hare & Hounds Street (off A361) ☎ (0380) 3231
Wadworth IPA, 6X H
Friendly, tucked-away pub with a relaxed atmosphere. Mainly used by locals. Pub games Q⊛🍴 (not Sun) 🎯🎯

Dinton

10–2.30 (not Tue); 6–10.30 (11 F, S & summer)

Penruddocke Arms
On B3089 (off A30)
☎ (072 276) 253
Usher Best Bitter; Wadworth 6X H
Thriving free house in the unspoilt Nadder Valley. Lounge with diner. Convivial locals' bar. Barbecues in summer. Guest beers
🚸৬⊛🍴▶🎯

307

Wiltshire

Easton Royal

12–2.30; 7–10.30 (11 F, S & summer)

Bruce Arms
On B3087
Whitbread Strong Country Bitter [G]
Completely unspoilt pub; part of a bygone age. Cheap ale and not a single keg. 82 year-old landlady. Pub games

Ebbsbourne Wake

11–2.30; 6–10.30 (11 F, S & summer)

Horseshoe Inn
Off A30 OS242993
☎ (0722) 780474
Wadworth 6X, Farmers Glory, Old Timer [G]
18th-century inn at foot of old ox drove. Stable-door entrance with tiny bars with farming and blacksmith's implements. Darts. Guest beers

Fonthill Gifford

10–2.30; 6–10.30 (11 F, S)

Beckford Arms
Off A303/B3089
☎ (0747) 870385
Wadworth IPA, 6X, Farmers Glory [G]
17th-century inn built from local stone, situated on the former Beckford's Fonthill estate with lakeside and woodland walks nearby. The bars have log fires and high ceilings

Ford

11–2.30; 6–10.30 (11 F, S)

White Hart
Off A420 ☎ (0249) 782213
Fullers London Pride, ESB; Hall & Woodhouse Badger Best Bitter; Marston Pedigree; Smiles Exhibition; Wadworth 6X [H]
Old inn by trout stream in lovely country setting. Outside seating. Expensive but excellent range of beers

Fovant

10–2.30; 6–10.30 (11 F, S & summer)

Cross Keys
On A30 ☎ (0722 270) 284
Wadworth 6X [G]
Fascinating 15th-century coaching inn of flint and stone, full of nooks and crannies. Views of Fovant chalk badges carved on local hills. Guest beers

Great Cheverell

12–2.30; 7–10.30 (11 F, S & summer)

Bell Inn
600 yds N of B3098

☎ (038 081) 3277
Mole's Cask Bitter; Wadworth IPA, 6X [H]
Rustic village local with friendly atmosphere. Family room. Guest beer; pub games. No food Mon

Try also: Owl Little Cheverell (Wadworth)

Heddington

10.30–2.30; 6–10.30 (11 F, S)

Ivy Inn
Off A4/A3102 ☎ (0380) 850276
Wadworth IPA, 6X, Old Timer (winter) [G]
Picturesque thatched village local with main bar and games/children's room. Small orchard for outside drinking

Highworth

11–2.30; 6–11

Saracens Head
Market Place (off A361)
☎ (0793) 762284
Arkells Bitter, BBB [H]
Smart (no T-shirts) lounge bar of considerable character. Very popular and often crowded

Try also: Globe (Courage)

Hilmarton

10–2.30; 6–10.30 (11 F, S)

Duke
On A3102 ☎ (024 976) 603
Arkells Bitter, BBB, Kingsdown Ale [H]
Single bar with lounge one end and public the other. Good value food. Singalong most Fri eves. Pub games

Leigh

12–2.30 (not Tue–Thu); 6–11

Foresters Arms
On B4040 ☎ (0793) 750901
Hall & Woodhouse Tanglefoot; Wadworth 6X, Old Timer [H]
Roadside pub with C&W evenings on Wed

Liddington

12–2.30; 6–11

Village Inn
Ham Road (off B4192)
☎ (0793) 790314
Flowers IPA, Original; Fuller ESB; Marston Pedigree; Wadworth 6X [H]
Busy, smart single bar

Lower Woodford

10–2.30; 6–10.30 (11 F, S)

Wheatsheaf
Off A345/A360 (3 miles from Salisbury) OS125350
☎ (072 273) 203

Hall & Woodhouse Badger Best Bitter, Tanglefoot [H]
Comfortable village pub with reputation for good food. Large garden with climbing games. Brewing began by Deare family when building was a farm in 1800s

Malmesbury

11–2.30; 6.30–10.30 (11 F, S & summer)

Red Bull
Sherston Road (B4040, 1½ miles W of town)
☎ (0666) 822108
Archers Village Bitter; Draught Bass [H]
Popular family pub with 3 gardens (swings) and children's room/skittle alley. Frequent skittles matches. Beware fake Whitbread WCPA handpump

Manton

11.30–2.30; 6.30–10.30 (11 F, S & summer)

Up The Garden Path
High Street (off A4)
☎ (0672) 52677
Arkells BBB; Archers Best Bitter; Hook Norton Best Bitter [H]
A cosy village inn with friendly, homely atmosphere. Pub games

Marlborough

10.30–2.30; 6–11

Lamb
The Parade ☎ (0672) 52668
Wadworth IPA, 6X [G]
Popular local, full of characters. Tucked away near the town hall. Occasional live music. Pub games

Netherhampton

10.30–2.30; 6–10.30 (11 F, S & summer)

Victoria & Albert
Off A3094 ☎ (0722) 743174
Usher Best Bitter; Webster Yorkshire Bitter [H]
Classic thatched country pub next to a farm. Long garden with fish ponds; popular with children. Pub games

Newton Toney

10.30–2.30; 6–10.30 (11 F, S & summer)

Malet Arms
Off A338 ☎ (098 064) 279
Hall & Woodhouse Badger Best Bitter; Wadworth 6X; Young Special [H]
Remote 17th-century local. Large public bar has original galleon window. Guest beers. Darts and bar billiards

308

Wiltshire

Norton

12–2.30; 7–10.30 (11 F, S & summer) (closed Tues)

Vine Tree
On the Foxley Road OS888846
☎ (0666) 837654
Archers Best Bitter, ASB (summer); Fuller London Pride; Wadworth 6X 🅗
Cosy remote pub offering a large menu. Watch out for 'young farmers' on Wed!
Guest beers ⚿Q☎⊛(]⊕&▲

Oare

11–2.30; 6–10.30 (11 F, S & summer)

White Hart
On A345 ☎ (0672) 62273
Wadworth IPA, 6X 🅗
Traditional local full of friendly villagers ⊛⊕&

Pewsey

12–2.00; 7–10.30 (11 F, S & summer)

Coopers Arms
Ball Road (off B3087)
☎ (0672) 62495
Ruddles County; Usher Best Bitter; Webster Yorkshire Bitter 🅗
Thatched country pub with restaurant. 3 acre field and outside seating. Pub games
⚿☎⊛(]▶&▲≉

Potterne

11.30–2.30; 6.30–10.30 (11 F, S & summer)

George & Dragon
High Street (A360)
☎ (0380) 2139
Wadworth IPA, 6X 🅗
Coaching inn with Civil War connections built by the Bishop of Salisbury circa 1500. Has an agricultural museum in the courtyard. Various pub games in the bar. No food Mon Q⊛☎(]

Poulshot

10.30–2.30; 6–10.30 (11 F, S & summer)

Raven
½ mile off A361
☎ (0380) 828271
Wadworth IPA, 6X, Farmers Glory (summer), Old Timer (winter) 🅖
Welcoming village pub, deservedly popular ⚿⊛(]▶

Purton

11–2.30; 6–11

Foresters Arms
Common Platt OS110868
☎ (0793) 770615
Courage Best Bitter, Directors 🅗
Friendly locals' pub, well hidden on the outskirts of Swindon
⊛(] (not Sun) ▶ (Wed–Sat) ⊕

Redlynch

11–2.30; 6–10.30 (11 F, S & summer)

Apple Tree Inn
Morgans Vale (off B3078)
☎ (0725) 20403
Draught Bass; Gibbs Mew Salisbury Best; Wadworth 6X 🅗
16th-century thatched country inn; originally a cider house
☎⊛(]▶⊕

Salisbury

10–2.30; 6–10.30 (11 F, S & summer)

Anchor
Gigant Street ☎ (0722) 330680
Gibbs Mew Wiltshire Traditional Bitter, Salisbury Best 🅗
Gibbs Mew brewery tap. Refurbished in Victorian style. Jovial company and warm atmosphere. The pub pre-dates the brewery which has grown up around it. Darts, bar billiards ☎(]&

10–2.30; 6–10.30 (11 F, S & summer)

George & Dragon
Castle Street ☎ (0722) 333942
Ruddles Best Bitter, County; Usher Best Bitter 🅗
16th-century low-ceilinged pub, formerly a brothel called 'The Silent Women'! Long rear garden down to the river. Barbecues in summer. Darts ☎⊛(]▶&

10–2.30; 6–10.30 (11 F, S & summer)

Haunch of Venison
Minster Street ☎ (0722) 22024
Courage Best Bitter, Directors 🅗
An old English chop house circa 1320. A busy city-centre pub with many historical features. Unusual pewter-topped bar
⚿Q☎(] (summer Sun) ≉

10–2.30; 6–10.30 (11 F, S & summer)

Railway Inn (Dust Hole)
Tollgate Road ☎ (0722) 24537
Gibbs Mew Salisbury Best, Chudley Local Line 🅗
Friendly corner local with railway theme. Popular with steam preservation enthusiasts. 2-sided pub sign shows the pub's dual name. Darts, cribbage and dominoes ☎⊛(]

11–2.30 (not Tue); 6–10.30 (11 F, S & summer)

Wyndham Arms
27 Escourt Road (near swimming pool)
☎ (0722) 28594
Hop Back GFB, Special, Entire Stout 🅗
Wiltshire's only pub brewery. Excellent value-for-money pub with home-cooked food. Pleasantly refurbished 1-bar, Victorian pub with adjoining front room. Darts and bar billiards ⚿(]&⊕

Seend

10.30–2.30; 6–10.30 (11 F, S & summer)

Bell Inn
Bell Hill (A361)
☎ (0380) 828338
Wadworth IPA, 6X 🅗
Well-run roadside inn with old brewhouse in the garden. Darts and cribbage
⚿☎⊛(] (not Sun) ⊕

Seend Cleeve

10.30–2.30; 6–10.30 (11 F, S & summer)

Brewery Inn
Seend Cleeve (near A361/A365) ☎ (0380) 828463
Ruddles County; Usher Best Bitter 🅗
Popular family pub near Kennet and Avon canal. Darts and pool ⚿Q☎⊛(]▶⊕&⊘

Sherston

11–2.30; 6–10.30 (11 F, S & summer)

Carpenters Arms
Eaton Town (B4040)
☎ (0666) 840665
Flowers Original; Whitbread WCPA 🅖
Friendly, oak-beamed pub with open fires. Recently extended; excellent small back room. Home-cooked food. As popular for its cider as beer. Guest beers. Pub games
⚿Q☎⊛(]▶&⊘

South Marston

11.30–2.30; 6–11

Carpenters Arms
Just off A420 ☎ (0793) 823179
Arkells Bitter, BBB, Kingsdown Ale 🅗
Deceptively large and comfortable beamed bar. Pub games ⚿Q☎⊛(]▶&▲

South Wraxall

11–2.30; 6–11

Longs Arms
½ mile W of B3109
☎ (022 16) 4450
Wadworth IPA, 6X, Old Timer (winter) 🅗
Warm and inviting village local. Darts ⚿⊛(]▶⊕

Steeple Ashton

10.00–3.00, 6–10.30 (11 F, S)

Longs Arms
1 mile E of A350
☎ (0380) 870245
Gibbs Mew Wiltshire Traditional Bitter, Salisbury Best 🅗
Old coaching inn in a pretty village; bar once used as a magistrates court. Pub games
⚿⊛(]⊕⊘

Wiltshire

Sutton Benger

10.30–2.30; 6–10.30 (11 F, S)

Wellesley Arms
10 High Street (B4069)
☎ (0249) 720251
Wadworth Devizes Bitter, IPA, 6X H, **Old Timer** G
Old stone building with 2 bars and skittle alley. Pool table in large public bar: quiet lounge bar ♨ Q ☻ ₰ ₳ ◐ ⌬ ὥ

Swindon

10.30–2.30; 5.30–11

Bakers Arms
Emlyn Square ☎ (0793) 35199
Arkells Bitter, BBB H
Genuine, old-fashioned local in heart of railway village. Basic public bar; quiet and cosy lounge ☻ ₰ ⌬ ≉

10.30–2.30 (3.30 Mon); 5.30–11

Railway Hotel
14 Newport Street
☎ (0793) 38048
Archers Village Bitter, Best Bitter, ASB; Cornish GBH H
Victorian hotel with courtyard. Skittle alley and other games. Guest beers
♨ ☎ ☻ ₳ ₰ ◐ ⌬ ὥ

10.30–2.30; 5.30–11

Wheatsheaf
Newport Street ☎ (0793) 23188
Wadworth IPA, 6X H
Characterful 2-bar inn. Bare boards in the bar; plush, new lounge. Can get very crowded
₳ ₰ ◐ ⌬

Trowbridge

11–2.30; 7–10.30 (11 F, S)

Ship
1 Frome Road (by football ground) ☎ (022 14) 3189
Halls Harvest Bitter, Ind Coope Burton Ale H
Comfortable split-level bar with nautical theme. Darts
☻ ₰ ⌬ ≉

Urchfont

11–2.30; 6–11

Lamb
The Street (off B3098)
☎ (038 084) 631
Wadworth IPA, 6X, Old Timer H
Excellent, unpretentious village local. A dedicated drinker's pub. Various games
♨ Q ☻ ⌬

Wanborough

10.30–2.30; 5.30–11

Black Horse
On Bishopstone road (former B4507) ☎ (0793) 790305
Arkells Bitter, BBB H, **Kingsdown Ale (winter)** G
Cheerful little local of character. Garden with aviary and children's games. Fine views of the Vale of White Horse. Occasional summer barbecues. Pub games
♨ ☻ ₰ (not Sun) ⌬ ὥ Å

11–2.30; 6–11

Plough
High Street
Draught Bass G
Listed thatched pub. Friendly public and quiet, beamed lounge. An old agreement allows this Whitbread house to sell Draught Bass, which is drawn in the cellar. Pub games
Q (lounge) ☻ ₰ (Mon–Fri) ⌬ ὥ

Try also: Harrow (Flowers)

Warminster

11–2.30; 6.30–10.30 (11 F, S & summer)

Weymouth Arms
12 Emwell Street (near A362)
☎ (0985) 218955
Ruddles Best Bitter, County; Usher Best Bitter; Webster Yorkshire Bitter H
Oak-panelled pub in narrow one-way street. Darts
♨ ☻ ₳ ₰ ◐ ⌬ ≉

Westbury

11–2.30; 6–10.30 (11 F, S & summer)

Crown Hotel
Market Place ☎ (0373) 822828
Wadworth IPA, 6X, Old Timer (winter) H
Bustling, small town local. Darts ☻ ₳ ⌬ ὥ

10–2.30; 6–10.30 (11 F, S & summer)

Ludlow Arms
3A Fore Street ☎ (0373) 822612
Hall & Woodhouse Tanglefoot; Marston Pedigree; Smiles Best Bitter; Wadworth 6X H
Popular, well-appointed, market-place local. Darts ☻ ⌬

Whiteparish

10.30–2.30; 6–10.30 (11 F, S & summer)

Kings Head
The Street (on A27)
☎ (079 48) 287
Flowers Original G; **Whitbread Strong Country Bitter** G & H
A proper English local in which to enjoy good company in a convivial atmosphere. Various games ♨ Q ☎ ☻ ₰ ◐ Å

Wilton

10.2.30; 6–10.30 (11 F, S & summer)

Bear
12 West Street (A30)
Hall & Woodhouse Badger Best Bitter H
Small local in ancient capital of Wessex. Wilton House and royal carpet factory nearby. Darts and pool ♨ ☻ ⌬

Winterbourne Monkton

10.30–2.30; 6–10.30

New Inn
Off A4361 OS099723
☎ (067 23) 240
Adnams Bitter; Wadworth 6X H
Small and friendly village local in remote area near Avebury stone circle. Guest beers. Pub games ☎ ☻ ₳ ₰ ◐

KEY TO SYMBOLS

- ♨ real fire
- Q quiet pub – no electronic music, TV or obtrusive games
- ☎ indoor room for children
- ☻ garden or other outdoor drinking area
- ₳ accommodation
- ₰ lunchtime meals
- ◐ evening meals
- ⌬ public bar
- ὥ facilities for the disabled
- Å camping facilities close to the pub or part of the pub grounds
- ≉ near British Rail station
- ⊖ near Underground station
- ὀ real cider

The facilities, beers and pub hours listed in the Good Beer Guide are liable to change but were correct when the Guide went to press.

BUSINESS FILE

Country Health Breweries plc (a subsidiary of Wombat International) announces the launch of a nationwide chain of wayside inns and hostelries, under the control of its new pub management division, the Taste Assembly.

TA Managing Director, Buzz Delacroix told GBG of his plans for the group in an exclusive interview:

"I don't see a pub as a place where beer is drunk, I see it as a total time occupation unit in the leisure mode. Once you've crossed that contextual barrier it's a lot easier to see things my way." Delacroix came to TA from male lingerie specialists "The Zip Corporation" where he had a reputation as a dawn raider.

"Beer retailing" he says "is irrelevant. We see the consumer as monarch of his domain and we try to actualise his destiny. And that way we will make a very great deal of money indeed."

Recent TA research has revealed that the majority of UK-based humans go to the pub "rarely" or "not at all". Delacroix believes it is the "image collage of pubness" that causes this and is determined to overcome it. He cites the presence of alcohol, cooking and bonhomie as three major facets of pub life which keeps customers away in their droves.

TA believes it has "found a pair of niches in the marketplace" which it plans to fill with two "new concepts in total occupation venues". "Shifters" and "Joby's".

The "Shifters" chain is designed to attract non-pub-users back to the pub. Features include a 28–inch flatscreen TV in every bar with armchairs turned towards it. Cans of Country Health Strong Organic Lager will be delivered to each table by waitresses specially trained to imitate fraught suburban housewives. When Sunday morning opening arrives each "Shifters" venue will have a car wash added.

The "Joby's" concept derives its name from "John Outside in the Back Yard". TA researchers found that the single aspect of modern pub design that most annoyed the consumers they surveyed was the practice of building inside toilets. "Joby's" bars are designed to appeal to "the sort of people who think Egon Ronay still writes his own pub guides". Features will include: CDs of Stockhausen piped to every room, computer chess games at 10p a move, Antabuse machines in the outside toilets, a choice of candle, gas or electric light at each table and bouncers on the door to keep out the unemployed.

The drinks policy in both chains will be an extension of the one that operates in existing CHB pubs. Customers ask for the brand of their choice, are given the chance to pick the right label and this is then applied to whichever CHB beer or wine is available. It is hoped that the handpumped Country Health Real Old Strong Ale will have a different name in each of the 5,000 planned developments.

Buzz Delacroix is 37.

Miles Brewster

North Yorkshire

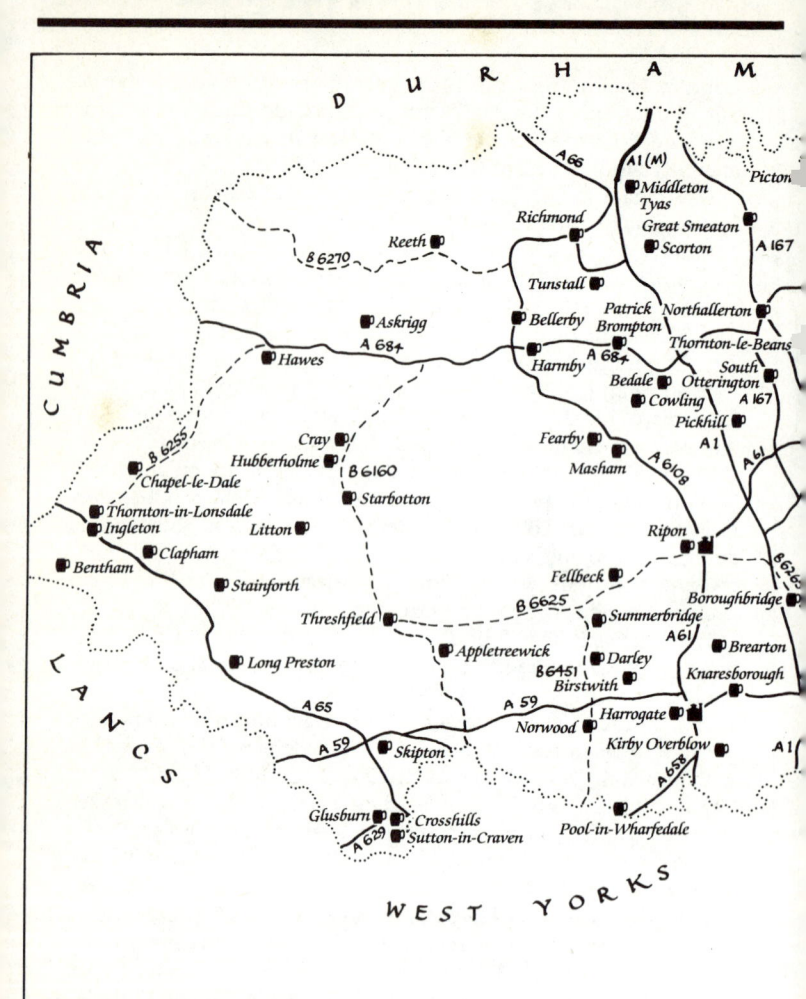

North Yorkshire

Cropton, Cropton; *Franklins*, Bilton; *Malton*, Malton; *Marston Moor*, Long Marston; *North & East Riding*, Scarborough; *Selby*, Selby; *Samuel Smith*, Tadcaster; *Whitby's Own*, Whitby

Ainthorpe

11–3; 6–11
Fox & Hounds
45 Brook Lane ☎ (0287) 60218
Theakston Best Bitter, XB, Old Peculier H
One of the county's oldest and most historic pubs. Ancient stone fireplace from Danby Castle. Quoits pitch
⌂☼⋈()▯⊟≅ (Danby)

Ampleforth

11–2.30; 6–11
White Horse Inn
West End (5 miles NE Easingwold) ☎ (043 93) 378
Tetley Bitter H
Deservedly popular and cosy village pub with main bar and dining room ⌂⊛⋈()▯

Appletreewick

11–3; 6 (7 winter)–11
New Inn
2 miles off B6160 at Burnsall
OS051601 ☎ (075 672) 252
John Smith Bitter; Younger Scotch, No.3 H
Clean and comfortable pub handy for walkers, anglers and canoeists. Foreign bottled beers ⌂Q☼⊛⋈()⌂⌂

Askrigg

11.30–3; 6.30–11
Kings Arms
Main Street ☎ (0969) 50258

North Yorkshire

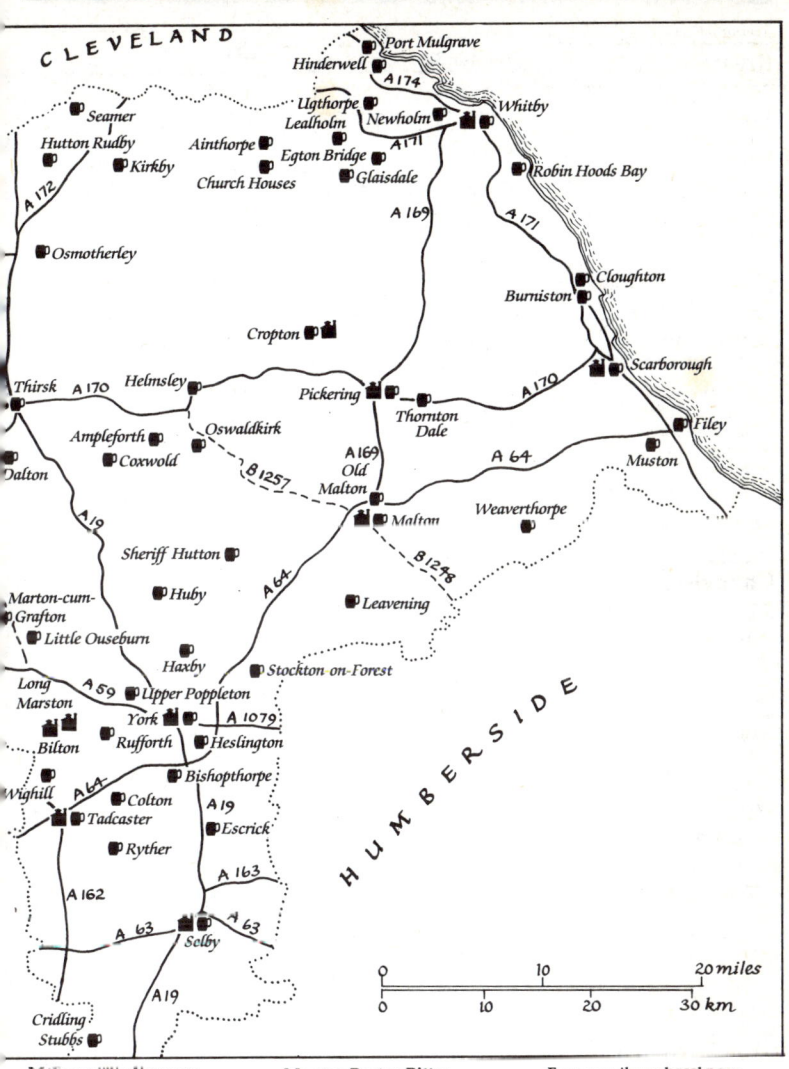

McEwan 80/-; Younger No.3 H
A truly English blend of informality and elegance pervades this small country hotel 🏰Q☎🛏🍴🍺

Try also: Crown

Bedale

11–3; 6–11 (all day Tue)

Green Dragon
Market Place ☎ (0677) 22902
Theakston Best Bitter, XB; Webster Yorkshire Bitter H
Popular main bar and a good restaurant
🏰Q☎ (restaurant) 🍴🍺

Bellerby

11–3; 5.30–11

Cross Keys
On A6108 ☎ (0969) 22256
Marston Burton Bitter, Pedigree H
Warm, unpretentious, but excellent village pub. Darts
🏰Q☎🛏🍴🍺🅰

Bentham

11–3; 7–11 (supper licence)

Sun Dial
Low Bentham, Lancaster
☎ (0468) 61532
Thwaites Bitter H
Delightful village-centre local built 18th century. Has bistro
☎🛏🍴 (not Mon)

Birstwith

11–3; 5 (6 winter)–11

Station
3 miles N of A59 OS245598
☎ (0423) 770254
Tetley Mild, Bitter H

Former railway hotel now with large lounge and small snug Q☎🛏🍴🚹

Bishopthorpe

10.30–3; 6–11

Ebor Hotel
Main Street ☎ (0904) 706190
Samuel Smith OBB, Museum Ale H
Comfortable local situated in village of the Archbishop of York's residence
☎🛏🍴 (Apr–Sep) 🍺

Boroughbridge

11–3; 5.30–11

Three Horseshoes
Bridge Street ☎ (090 12) 2314
Vaux Samson E
Impressive hotel of real character. Distinctive 1930s

313

North Yorkshire

flavour ▲Q☎⌂(|)⊕&▲

Brearton

12–3; 7–11 (closed Mon)

Malt Shovel
Off B6165 OS322608
☎ (0423) 862929
Old Mill Traditional Bitter; Theakston XB, Bitter, Old Peculier (summer); Ward Sheffield Best Bitter H
16th-century pub with stone walls and original oak beams. Local reputation for good food (not Mon) ▲Q⌂(|)&▲

Burniston

11.30–3; 6–11

Oak Wheel
Coastal Road (A165)
☎ (0723) 870230
Cameron Traditional Bitter, Strongarm H
Subdued but comfortable lounge; busy and basic public ▲☎⌂(|)⊕▲

Try also: Three Jolly Sailors

Chapel-le-Dale

11–3; 5.30–11 (supper licence)

Hill Inn
On B6255 OS743776
☎ (0468) 41256
John Smith Bitter; Theakston Best Bitter, XB, Old Peculier H
Isolated inn with dimly-lit public bar, built 1615. Cavers' and hikers' mecca
▲☎⌂(|)⊕▲

Church Houses (Farndale)

10.30–2.30; 7–10.30 (11 F, S) (5.30–11 summer)

Feversham Arms
Off A170 OS670974
☎ (0751) 33206
Tetley Bitter H
Old stone-built pub; bar has flagged floor and kitchen range ▲Q☎⌂(|)

Try also: Lion Inn, High Blakey

Clapham

12–3; 7–11 (supper licence)

Flying Horseshoe
OS733678 ☎ (046 685) 229
Moorhouse's Premier Bitter; Younger Scotch H
Country house hotel next to station with 1 comfortable bar and games room
▲☎⌂(|)&⇌

Cloughton

11–3; 6–11

Bryherstones Inn
½ mile N of village OS011955
☎ (0723) 870755
Cameron Traditional Bitter, Younger Scotch H
Families especially welcome during the day. Lively in the evening ▲☎⌂(|)

Try also: Shepherd's Arms

Colton

11.30–3; 6.30 (7 winter)–11

Olde Sun Inn
1 mile S of A64 ☎ (090 484) 261
Draught Bass; Stones Best Bitter H
17th-century inn in lovely village setting, 4 rooms, with low beamed ceilings ⌂(|)

Cowling

11–3; 7 (6 summer)–11

Black Bull
Colne Road ☎ (0535) 34060
Hartley XB; Whitbread Trophy H
Welcoming roadside pub. 3 rooms including spacious snooker and darts room. Good value food ☎⌂(|) (8–10)&▲

Coxwold

11–3; 6.30–11

Fauconberg Arms
Main Street ☎ (034 76) 214
Tetley Bitter; Theakston Best Bitter; Younger Scotch H
Beautifully-appointed old inn with lounge bar, oak room and restaurant (no food Mon). Very popular ▲(|)

Cray

11–3; 5.30–11

White Lion
On B6160 ☎ (075 676) 262
Goose Eye Bitter; Younger Scotch H
Classic 1-roomed stone flagged Dales inn, 1000 feet up at the head of Wharfedale. Popular with walkers. Ring the bull ▲Q☎⌂(|)▲

Cridling Stubbs

12–3 (not Sun/Mon); 7–11

Ancient Shepherd
Off A1/M62 (Jct 33/34)
☎ (0977) 83316
Taylor Best Bitter; Tetley Bitter H
Daunting exterior belies welcoming mellow Victorian interior with flagstone floors. Restaurant. No food Sun or Mon Q (| (Tue–Fri) ⊕&

Cropton

12–2.30; 7–10.30 (11 F, S) winter; 11–2.30; 5.30–11 summer

New Inn
Off A170 OS755889
☎ (075 15) 330
Cropton Two Pints, Special; Tetley Mild H
Imposing roadside inn at edge of village, with brewery in cellar. 1 bar; separate pool and dining rooms ▲☎⌂(|)&▲

Try also: Blacksmiths, Lastingham

Crosshills

11–3; 5.30–11

Dalesway
Skipton Road ☎ (0535) 33618
Bass Light 5 Star, Draught Bass; Stones Best Bitter H
Popular pub on busy road between Keighley and Skipton. Spacious, with cosy atmosphere. ☎⌂(|) (till 10) ⊕&

Dalton

11–3 (not Thu); 7 (7.30 winter)–11

Jolly Farmers of Olden Times
Between A1/A19 OS431762
☎ (0845) 577359
Ruddles County; Webster Yorkshire Bitter; Wilson's Original Bitter H
200 year-old beamed village pub. Traditional Sun lunches (book). Summer barbecues. Guest beers ▲☎⌂(|)&▲

Darley

11–3; 6–11

Wellington Inn
On B6451 ☎ (0423) 780362
Tetley Bitter, Imperial; Theakston Best Bitter, Old Peculier H
Cosy country pub in delightful Dales setting.
Games ▲Q⌂(|)⊕▲

Egton Bridge

11–3; 6–11 (summer); 12–3; 7–11 (winter)

Postgate Inn
Off A171 ☎ (0947) 85241
Cameron Traditional Bitter, Strongarm H
Small country pub by railway station; near River Esk
▲Q☎⌂(|)⊕⇌

Escrick

11–3; 6–11

Black Bull Hotel
Main Street ☎ (090 487) 245
John Smith Bitter H
Large wood-panelled lounge bar with locals' bar to rear. Separate cocktail room doubles as dining room
▲☎⌂(|) (until 10) ⊕

Fearby

11.30–3 (not Mon–Fri winter); 7.30–11

Kings Head
W of Masham off A6108
☎ (0765) 89448
Theakston Best Bitter, Old Peculier (summer) H
Small unspoilt pub known locally as The Cross. Family room open until 9pm in summer
▲Q☎⌂(|⊕&

Fellbeck

11.30 (12 winter)–3; 6 (7 winter)–11

314

North Yorkshire

Half Moon
On B6265 OS200662
Taylor Landlord; Theakston Best Bitter; Younger Scotch H
Roadside inn near Brimham Rocks with traditional public bar and large sunny lounge

Filey

11–3; 5.30–11

Grapes Inn
40 Queen Street
☎ (0723) 514700
John Smith Bitter H
Friendly locals' pub with pool room

Try also: Foords

Glaisdale

10–3; 6–11

Anglers Rest
Top of hill off A171
☎ (0947) 87261
Cropton Two Pints; Theakston Best Bitter, Old Peculier H
Very friendly old hilltop pub formerly called the 3 Blast Furnaces. Live music

Glusburn

11–3; 5.30 (6 Sat)–11

Dog & Gun Inn
On A6068 ☎ (0535) 33855
Taylor Dark Mild, Golden Best, Bitter, Landlord H
Popular spacious roadside inn. Open-plan lounge with large stone pillars. Live jazz Mon

Great Smeaton

12–3; 6.30–11

Day House
On A167 ☎ (060 981) 466
Marston Pedigree; Tetley Bitter H
Small old free house in centre of pleasant village. Busy locals' bar, largish lounge. Guest beers

Try also: Grange Arms, Hornby (Free)

Harmby

11–3; 6–11

Pheasant
On A684 ☎ (0969) 22223
Tetley Bitter H
Popular rural inn at Gateway to Wensleydale

Try also: Richard III, Middleham

Harrogate

11–3; 5.30–11

Coach & Horses
16 West Park
John Smith Bitter H
Welcoming town pub overlooking The Stray

Dragon
Skipton Road
John Smith Bitter H
Large corner local subjected to an expensive but successful refit. Small, wood-panelled snug; large popular lounge

11–3; 5.45–11

Hales Bar
1 Crescent Road (opposite Valley Gardens)
Draught Bass; Stones Best Bitter H
Fascinating, comfortable old pub with gas lights, mirrors and stuffed birds

12–3; 6.30–11

Pump Rooms
51 Parliament Street
Tetley Bitter H
Recently renamed, popular town-centre local. Real ale in downstairs bar only

10.30–3; 5.30–11

Woodlands Hotel
Wetherby Road
☎ (0423) 883396
Webster Yorkshire Bitter, Choice; Wilson's Mild H
Imposing building on busy junction near Yorkshire Showground. Modernised, with conservatory; pub games (Mon–Fri)

Hawes

11–3; 6–11 (all day Tue)

Board Hotel
Market Place ☎ (096 97) 223
Marston Burton Bitter, Pedigree H
Recently modernised but retains unpretentious market pub atmosphere

Haxby

11–3; 6–11

Tiger
The Village ☎ (0904) 768355
Samuel Smith OBB H
Well-appointed pub in commuter village. Busy, noisy bar and quieter lounge

Helmsley

10.30–2.30; 6–10.30 (11 F, S & summer); market day extension

Feathers Hotel
Market Place ☎ (0439) 70275
Theakston XB; Younger No.3 H
Old market town hotel. Public bar has 'Mousey' Thompson fitments and real ale

Try also: Brown Hotel (Cameron)

Heslington

11–3; 6–11

Deramore Arms
Main Street ☎ (0904) 413433
Tetley Bitter H
Traditional 2-roomed pub, popular with locals and students. Pub games (not Wed, Sun)

Hinderwell

11–3; 7–11

Badger Hounds
High Street (A174)
Tetley Bitter H
Busy road house on Whitby road. Excellent food

Hubberholme

11.30–3; 6.30–11

George Inn
Kirk Gill ☎ (075 676) 223
Younger Scotch Bitter, IPA H
Ancient inn in rural surroundings of great beauty. Stone-clad throughout; flagged floor, low oak beams and warm atmosphere. Superb food

Huby

12–3; 6–11

Queen of Trumps
Main Street (near B1363)
☎ (0347) 810358
Tetley Mild, Bitter H
Pleasant brick building typical of the area. Pleasant lounge and busy public bar

12–3; 6–10.30 (11 F, S)

Kings Head
36 Northside ☎ (0642) 700342
Cameron Strongarm H
The pick of 4 pubs in a 100% real ale village. Read a book from the landlord's library and sup your pint round a roaring fire

Ingleton

11–3; 5.30–11

Craven Heifer
Main Street ☎ (052 42) 41427
Thwaites Best Mild (summer), Bitter, Daniel's Hammer (winter) H
2 contrasting bars, each once the ground floors of 2 cottages. In season vault is full of cavers and hikers

Kirkby Overblow

11.30–3; 5.30–11

Shoulder of Mutton
Main Street ☎ (0423) 871205
Tetley Mild, Bitter H
A stone-built village inn with varied customers. Games. No food Sun
(Tues–Sat)

Knaresborough

11–3 (4 Wed); 5.30–11

Cross Keys

315

North Yorkshire

17 Cheapside ☎ (0423) 862163
Tetley Bitter H
Busy pre-war local with distinct Tetley touch, in town's historic core near Castle ruins ⌂ ◐ ⌁ ⇌

11–3 (4 Wed); 5.30–11
Groves
Market Place ☎ (0423) 863022
Younger Scotch, No.3 H
18th-century stuccoed pub overlooking market square
◐ ⌁ ⇌

11–3 (4 Wed); 5.30–11
Old Royal Oak
Market Place ☎ (0423) 863139
John Smith Bitter H
17th-century pub overlooking market place. Small bar and lounge ⊷ ◐ ⌁ ⇌

Lealholm

11.30–3; 7–11
Board Inn
Village Green ☎ (0947) 87276
Cameron Strongarm H
Unspoilt local set in idyllic surroundings next to river
⌂ ⌂ ◐ ⌁ ⇌

Leavening

10.30–2.30; 5.30–10.30 (11 F, S)
Jolly Farmer
5 miles S of Malton OS785630
☎ (065 385) 276
Cameron Strongarm; Tetley Bitter; Whitbread Trophy H
Unpretentious cosy village pub, popular with farmers. Games ⌂ ⌂ ⌂ ⊷ ◐ ⌁

Little Ouseburn

11–3; 6–11
Green Tree
Off B6265
Taylor Landlord; Tetley Mild, Bitter H
Roadside country inn with wood panelling and plush upholstery. Friendly atmosphere ⌂ Q ⌂ ◐ ⌁ ⌃

Litton

11–3; 6–11
Queens Arms
☎ (075 677) 208
Younger Scotch H
17th-century unspoilt stone-built Dales pub in beautiful countryside. Quality food; receives regular awards for cellarmanship
⌂ Q ⌂ ⌂ ⊷ ◐ ⌁ ⌃ A

Long Preston

11–3; 6.30 (5.30 Sat)–11
Maypole Inn
☎ (072 94) 219
Hartley XB; Whitbread Castle Eden Ale H
Welcoming village local on busy A65 Skipton–Settle road. Lounge and taproom. Good value food ⌂ ⌂ ⌂ ⊷ ◐ ⌁ ⇌

Malton

10.30–2.30; 5.30–10.30 (11 F, S & summer) market extension Fri
Crown Hotel (Suddaby's)
12 Wheelgate ☎ (0653) 692038
Malton Pale Ale, Double Chance, Porter, Owd Bob; Tetley Bitter H
Unpretentious locals' bar in tidy hotel with brewery in Double Chance's stable at rear. Family room
⌂ ⌂ ⊷ ◐ ⌁ ⌃

Try also: Blue Ball

Old Malton

10.30–2.30; 5.30–10.30 (11 F, S & summer)
Royal Oak
Town Street (B1257)
☎ (0653) 692503
Cameron Strongarm; Tetley Bitter H
250 year-old building haunted by cobblers! Keen games school and fishing close by
⌂ ⌂ ⊷ ◐ ⌁ ⌃

Try also: Wentworth Arms

10.30–2.30; 5.30–10.30 (11 F, S & summer) market extension Tue
Spotted Cow
Cattle Market ☎ (0653) 692100
Tetley Bitter H
Many-roomed old drovers' pub popular with marketeers
⌂ Q ⌁ ⇌

Marton-cum-Grafton

12.30–3; 7–11
Punch Bowl
OS416634 ☎ (0423) 322519
Tetley Bitter; Younger Scotch, IPA, No.3 H
Picturesque village pub with exposed timbers, panelled snug and recently opened restaurant ⌂ Q ⊷ ⌂ ◐ ⌁ ⌃

Masham

11–3; 6–11
White Bear
Old Brewery Yard
☎ (0765)89319
Matthew Brown Mild; Theakston Best Bitter, XB, Old Peculier H
Excellent brewery tap with comfortable atmosphere
⊷ ◐ ⌁

Middleton Tyas

12–3; 6.30–11
Shoulder of Mutton
1 mile from A1, Scotch Corner
☎ (032 577) 271
Vaux Samson; Ward Sheffield Best Bitter H
The 'Top House' attractively fills 3 old stone cottages – a variety of rooms and spaces. Bustling traditional bar (must specify cask beer); upstairs restaurant. Quoits pitches at rear ⌂ ⌂ ⊷ ◐ ⌁ ⌃ ⌃

Muston

11–3; 6–1
Ship Inn
West Street ☎ (0723) 512722
Cameron Traditional Bitter H
Smart 1-room lounge style village centre pub ⌂ ⌂ ◐ ⌁ A

Newholm

11.30–3; 7–11
Olde Beehive Inn
Off A171 OS867115
☎ (0947) 602703
McEwan 80/-; Younger No.3 H
Village pub of great character. Listed duck pond, oak beams. Pub sign with verse
⌂ Q ⊷ ⌂ ⊷ ◐ ⌁ A

Northallerton

11–3 (5 Wed); 7–11
County Arms
219A High Street
☎ (0609) 70610
John Smith Bitter; Tetley Bitter H
Northallerton's newest pub. Main bar downstairs, lounge upstairs ⊷ (upstairs) ◐ (not Sun) ⌁ (Fri–Sat) ⌃ ⇌

Try also: Nags Head (John Smith)

Norwood

10.30–3; 5.30–11
Sun Inn
On B6451 OS207538
☎ (094 388) 220
Younger Scotch, IPA, No.3 H
Popular spacious pub near Fewston–Swinsty reservoir. Good walks ⌂ ⌂ ⌂ ◐ ⌁

Osmotherley

12–3; 6–11
Three Tuns
9 South End ☎ (060 983) 301
McEwan 80/-; John Smith Bitter; Younger No.3 H
17th-century local, splendidly located by village square
⌂ Q ⊷ ⌂ ◐ A

Oswaldkirk

11–2.30; 6.30–11
Malt Shovel
Off B1363 ☎ (043 93) 461
Samuel Smith OBB H
Beautifully restored interior, with 17th-century staircase and imposing large open fire; warm and welcoming
⌂ ⊷ ⌂ ⊷ ◐ ⌁ (not Mon)

Patrick Brompton

12–3 (not Tue winter); 6–11
Green Tree
On A684 ☎ (0677) 50262
Cameron Strongarm;

North Yorkshire

Theakston Best Bitter, XB ⓗ
Entrance hall divides the bar reserved for darts and good conversation, from the dining room on the right ⌂Q☎⌇✉◐ ◗ (not winter Sun) ⌘

Pickering

10.30–2.30; 5.30–10.30 (11 F, S)

Black Bull
Malton Road (A169)
☎ (0751) 75258
Tetley Mild, Bitter, Imperial; Theakston Best Bitter, XB, Old Peculier ⓗ
Large friendly roadside pub. C&W music evenings
⌂☎⌇◐ ◗ A

Try also: White Swan Hotel

Pickhill

10.30–2.30; 5.30–11

Nags Head
1 mile off A1 ☎ (0845) 567391
Tetley Bitter; Theakston Best Bitter, XB, Old Peculier; Younger Scotch ⓗ
Restaurant and accommodation of a very high standard. Public bar popular with locals
⌂Q☎⌇✉◐ ◗ ⌘&

Picton

12–3; 7–11

Station Hotel
☎ (0642) 700067
Cameron Strongarm ⓗ
Red brick 1860s railway hotel with cosy and welcoming open-plan interior ☎⌇ ◗ & A

Pool-in-Wharfedale

11–3; 6–11

Hunters Inn
Harrogate Road
☎ (0532) 842298
Theakston Best Bitter, XB; Younger Scotch ⓗ
Multi-roomed pub with restaurant and games room which has a round pool table. Guest beers Q☎⌇◐ ◗ A

Port Mulgrave

11.30–3; 6.30–11

Ship
20 Rosedale Lane, Staithes & Hinderwell (off A174)
☎ (0947) 840303
Younger Scotch, No.3 ⓗ
Old terraced pub, ¼ mile from high cliffs. Caters for children
⌂Q☎⌇◐ A

Reeth

11–3; 6–11

Buck
On B6270 ☎ (0748) 84210
Webster Yorkshire Bitter, Choice ⓗ
Imposing building overlooking village green
⌂Q☎⌇◐ ◗ A

Richmond

10.30–3; 6–11

Black Lion Hotel
Finkle Street (just off Market Square) ☎ (0748) 3121
Cameron Strongarm; Everards Old Original ⓗ
Hotel with warm, friendly public bar and non-smoking lounge serving bar meals. Restaurant upstairs
⌂Q☎⌇◐ ◗ ⌘

Try also: Holly Hill Inn, Sleagill

Ripon

11–3 (4 Thu); 6–11

Black Bull
Old Market Place
☎ (0765) 2755
Theakston Best Bitter, XB, Old Peculier ⓗ
Historic coaching inn with 16th and 18th-century features. Large rambling bar, quiet lounge ◐

11–3; 6–11

Lamb & Flag
High Skellgate ☎ (0765) 2895
Vaux Lorimers Scotch, Bitter; Ward Sheffield Best Bitter ⓗ
Old coaching inn on steep hill leading to market place
⌂Q◐ ⌘&

11–3; 6–11

Turks Head
Low Skellgate (A61 approaching market place)
☎ (0765) 4876
Vaux Lorimers Scotch, Bitter; Ward Sheffield Best Bitter ⓗ
Very old and friendly pub with snug and games room ⌘

11–3; 6–11

Wheatsheaf
Harrogate Road
Vaux Bitter, Samson; Ward Darley Thorne Bitter, Sheffield Best Bitter ⓗ
Old inn with intricate carving in the bar, and a sunken garden with peacocks
⌂Q☎⌇◐⌘&

Robin Hood's Bay

10.30 (11 winter)–3; 6 (7 winter)–11

Bay Hotel
The Dock ☎ (0947) 880278
Cameron Traditional Bitter, Strongarm; Everards Old Original ⓗ
Listed building at bottom of village with superb views of bay and surrounding countryside ⌂☎⌇✉◐

10.30 (11.30 winter)–3; 6–11

Laurel Inn
☎ (0947) 880400
John Smith Bitter; Tetley Bitter ⓗ
Small, friendly corner local in picturesque cliffside village. Folk club Fri night Q☎⌇✉A

Rufforth

11–3; 6–11

Tankard Inn
Main Street ☎ (090 483) 621
Samuel Smith OBB ⓗ
Rebuilt in 1937, with white exterior in the brewery style. Pleasant lounge and bar; good darts following. No eve meals winter ⌂☎ (if eating) ⌇✉ ◐ (not Mon) ◗ (not Sun) ⌘

Ryther

12–3 (Sat only); 7–11

Rythre Arms
☎ (075 786) 372
John Smith Bitter; Tetley Bitter ⓗ; Theakston Old Peculier ⓖ
Old stone-built, country pub with excellent reputation for food, especially steaks (try the 38 oz T-bone!) ⌂☎⌇◐ (Sat & Sun) ◗⌘A (within 1 mile)

Scarborough

11–3; 6–11

Archives
51 Valley Road
☎ (0723) 375311
McEwan 80/-; Theakston Best Bitter; Younger Scotch, No.3 ⓗ
Pleasant lounge style bar in hotel complex ⌇✉◐ ◗ ⇌

Try also: Angel, Crown Tavern

11–3; 5.30–11

Golden Ball
31 Sandside (by harbour)
☎ (0723) 362181
Samuel Smith OBB ⓗ
Very popular in the summer. Excellent sea views from the Harbour Lounge ☎⌇◐ ◗ ⌘

Try also: Criterion

11–3; 5.30–11

Highlander Bar
Stresa Hotel, Esplanade, South Cliff ☎ (0723) 365627
Wm Clark Mild; Thistle, EXB, 68; Tetley Bitter; Younger IPA ⓗ
Home-brew pub whose strong Scottish flavour is enhanced by reputedly the largest whisky collection in the North
⌂☎⌇✉◐&

11.30–3; 7–11

Hole in the Wall
Vernon Road
Theakston Best Bitter, XB, Old Peculier ⓗ
Thriving ale house featuring guest beers, live music and traditional games. Food includes vegetarian ◐⇌

11.30–3; 7–11

Leeds Arms
St Mary's Street (old town)
☎ (0723) 361699
Draught Bass ⓗ

317

North Yorkshire

Subdued old town gem with a nautical atmosphere 🏠

11–3; 6–11

North Riding Hotel
North Marine Road (by Floral Hall) ☎ (0723) 362386
Cameron Traditional Bitter H
Locals' bar dominated by pool table; quieter lounge with TV

11–3; 6–11

Spa Hotel
Victoria Road ☎ (0723) 372907
Tetley Mild; Bitter H
Games oriented local: Yorkshire Super League darts champions for the last 3 years

11–3; 5.30–11

Trafalgar Hotel
Trafalgar Street West ☎ (0723) 372054
Cameron Traditional Bitter; Strongarm H
Bustling games-oriented bar; less hectic but popular lounge

Scorton

11–3; 6–11

White Heifer
On B1263 ☎ (0748) 811357
Theakston Best Bitter, XB H
Smart, friendly free house facing the raised village green. 2 tastefully-appointed rooms

Try also: Farmers (Tetley); **Royal** (Cameron)

Seamer

12–3; 7–10.30 (11 F, S & summer)

Kings Head
12 Hilton Road
McEwan 80/-; Younger Scotch, No.3 H
Been a pub since 1760. Many older features include solid oak tables. 'Tally Ho Jack' from Hunter Hill once rode his horse into the pub for a bet

Selby

10.30–3 (4.30 Mon); 6–11

New Inn
Gowthorpe (near Market Place) ☎ (0757) 703429
Tetley Mild, Bitter H
Has a separate wood-panelled smoke room with bowed and glazed serving hatch. Weekend disco in back room

10.30–3; 6–11

Station
Ousegate (near toll bridge) ☎ (0757) 702186
Tetley Mild, Bitter H
Overlooks water front between toll and railway bridges. Old-time singalongs Sat eves

Sheriff Hutton

11–3; 6–11

Highwayman Inn
Finkle Street ☎ (034 77) 328
Tetley Bitter H
White-painted inn with large welcoming porch, lounge, dining area and small bar

Skipton

11–3; 5.30–11

Royal Shepherd
Canal Street ☎ (0756) 3178
Chesters Bitter; Hartley XB; Whitbread Trophy, Castle Eden Ale H
A pub revered by ale buffs far and wide! Very friendly. Lots of photos of old Skipton and large original Bentleys mirror. Pub games

South Otterington

12–2; 7–11

Otterington Shorthorn
On A167 4 miles S of Northallerton ☎ (0609) 3816
Tetley Bitter; Younger Scotch H
Well-appointed rural inn with lounge bar and games room

Stainforth

11–3; 5.30–11

Craven Heifer
Main Street (just off B6479) ☎ (072 92) 2599
Thwaites Best Mild, Bitter H
Multi-roomed village inn amidst dramatic scenery of Upper Ribblesdale. Family room; pool table

Starbotton

11–3; 5.30–11

Fox & Hounds
On B6160, Kettlewell–Buckden road ☎ (075 676) 269
Taylor Landlord; Theakston Best Bitter, Old Peculier; Younger Scotch Bitter H
Set in spectacular walking country, a homely Dales inn of great character. Quality food. Busy in summer

Stockton-on-Forest

11–3; 6–11

Fox Inn
The village (off A64) ☎ (0904) 400359
Tetley Bitter H
An attractive village pub, noted for its food. 2 lounge bars and dining area

Summerbridge

11.45–3; 6–11

Flying Dutchman
On B6165 ☎ (0423) 780361
Samuel Smith OBB H
A Nidderdale village inn named after 1849 racehorse. Brimham Rocks nearby

Sutton in Craven

11–3; 5.30–11

Kings Arms
High Street, Crosshills ☎ (0535) 32332
Whitbread Castle Eden Ale H
Small friendly village local. 2 lounges and separate tap room

Tadcaster

10.30–3; 6–11

Angel & White Horse
Bridge Street ☎ (0937) 835470
Samuel Smith OBB H
Brewery tap in large Georgian coaching inn with fine wood panelling. Rear view of brewery yard and its shire horses (not Sat)

Thirsk

11–3 (5 Mon); 6–11

Olde Three Tuns
15 Finkle Street (just off square) ☎ (0845) 23291
Tetley Bitter H
Late 16th-century building, sympathetically restored (lunch) (not Sun)

Try also: Lord Nelson

Thornton Dale

11–2.30; 6.30–10.30 (11 F, S)

Buck Hotel
☎ (0751) 74212
Cameron Traditional Bitter H
Comfortable lounge with separate restaurant; large games oriented bar

Thornton-in-Lonsdale

12–3; 6–11 (closed Sun and winter Mon lunch)

Marton Arms
Westhouse, Carnforth (off A65) ☎ (052 42) 41281
Matthew Brown Mild; Moorhouse's Pendle Witches Brew; Theakston Old Peculier H
Pre-turnpike coaching inn, dated 1679 but reputedly older. Comfortable, large oak-beamed lounge. Guest beers

Thornton-le-Beans

10.30–3 (not winter Tue); 6–11

Crosby
½ mile off A168 ☎ (0609) 2776
Webster Yorkshire Bitter H
Large, well-appointed village pub. 'Ringing the Bull' played

318

North Yorkshire

Threshfield

11–3; 5.30–11

Old Hall Inn
Side of B6265 at Jct with Grassington road
☎ (0756) 752441
Taylor Best Bitter, Landlord; Younger Scotch H
Recently upgraded, popular roadside Dales inn with fine wood panelling. Games

Tunstall

12–3 (not Mon, Tue); 7–11

Bay Horse Inn
2 miles off A1 ☎ (0748) 818564
Samuel Smith OBB H
200 year-old local with a great enthusiasm for pub games
(Tue–Sat)

Ugthorpe

11–3; 7–11

Black Bull
Off A171 ☎ (0947) 840286
Cameron Strongarm; Tetley Bitter; Theakston Best Bitter, XB, Old Peculier H
Excellent village pub set in row of cottages

Upper Poppleton

11–3; 6.30 (5.30 F, 7 S)–11

Lord Collingwood
Hodgson Lane
☎ (0904) 794388
Younger Scotch, IPA, No.3
Attractive white 19th-century pub overlooking village green. Large L-shaped lounge with wood beams
(lunch) (not Sun) (until 8.30) (Poppleton)

Weaverthorpe

11–3; 6–11

Star Inn
☎ (094 43) 273
Theakston Best Bitter, XB, Old Peculier H
Welcoming village pub with pool room

Try also: Blue Bell Hotel

Whitby

11–3; 7–11

Black Horse
91 Church Street
☎ (0947) 602906
Tetley Bitter H
Small busy pub of character. Games

11–3; 6.30–11

Fleece
Church Street ☎ (0947) 603649
Tetley Bitter H
1930s harbourside pub with balcony view of marina. Games

11–3; 6.45–11

Jolly Sailors
St Annes Staith
☎ (0947) 605999
Samuel Smith OBB H
Popular quayside pub with comfortable lounge. Live music during Folk Week. Games

Wighill

12–3; 6–11

White Swan
Main Street ☎ (0937) 832217
Stones Best Bitter; Theakston Best Bitter, XB, Old Peculier
Popular with both locals and visitors. Many small rooms with real character. Pub games (by request)

York

11–3; 5.30–11

Acorn
St Martins Lane (off Micklegate) ☎ (0904) 29820
Cameron Traditional Bitter, Strongarm; Everards Old Original H
Surprise local tucked away in a quiet street. 2 cosy rooms; darts and quiz teams

11–3; 5.30–11

Bootham Tavern
29 Bootham (near Bootham Bar) ☎ (0904) 31093
Tetley Bitter H
Compact and usually busy 2-roomed local

11–3; 5.30–11

Brown Cow
36 Hope Street ☎ (0904) 34010
Taylor Best Bitter, Landlord; Porter, Ram Tam H
Homely, friendly locals' pub. Lively games-oriented bar and quieter, cosy lounge

11.30–3; 5.30–11

Crystal Palace
66 Holgate Road
☎ (0904) 25305
Samuel Smith OBB H
Pleasant pub with comfortable lounge and public bar with pool table. Darts (Sat)

11–3; 5.30–11

Fox Inn
168 Holgate Road (A59)
☎ (0904) 798341
Tetley Bitter H
Nicely furnished Tetley Heritage Inn with 4 separate drinking areas. Outside play area for children

11–3; 5.30–11

Golden Ball
Cromwell Road
☎ (0904) 52211
Courage Directors; John Smith Bitter H
Unspoilt, traditional 5-room pub, a fine, friendly servant to the local community, away from tourist haunts

11–3; 5.30–11

John Bull
Layerthorpe (continuation of Stonebow) ☎ (0904) 21593
Franklins Bitter; Taylor Best Bitter, Landlord; Ward Sheffield Best Bitter H
Superb ex-John Smith's pub. 30s decor; live music nights
Q (lunch)

11–3; 5.30–11

Minster Inn
24 Marygate (off Bootham)
Draught Bass; Stones Best Bitter H
Excellent little terraced pub with bar and 2 side-lounges. Close to ruins of St Marys Abbey

11–3; 5.30–11

Royal Oak
50 Goodramgate (Monk Bar end) ☎ (0904) 653856
Cameron Traditional Bitter; Everards Old Original H
Attractive 3 room pub, which manages to cater well for both tourists and locals

11–3; 5.30–11

Spread Eagle
98 Walmgate ☎ (0904) 35868
Draught Bass; Taylor Best Bitter, Landlord; Tetley Bitter; Theakston XB, Old Peculier H
Busy, basic pub with eclectic clientele. Always the chance of unusual guest beers. Live music Sun lunch

11–3; 5.30–11

Swan
Bishopgate Street, Clementhorpe
☎ (0904) 655746
Tetley Bitter H
Traditional street-corner local. Entrance lobby with counter service, and hatches to 2 lounge bars. Games

11–3; 5.30–11

Walkers Bar
47 Micklegate ☎ (0904) 28501
Theakston Best Bitter, XB, Old Peculier H
Busy pub with a narrow chain of interesting rooms adorned with mirrors and ornaments

11–3; 6.30–11

Wellington Inn
47 Alma Terrace (off Fulford Road) ☎ (0904) 645642
Samuel Smith OBB H
Cosy back-street terraced local with stone-flag floor; main bar and 2 side rooms. Pool

11–3; 5.30–11

York Arms
26 High Petergate
☎ (0904) 624508
Samuel Smith OBB, Museum Ale H
Splendid pub in shadow of Minster. Public bar and 2 comfortable lounges
Q (summer)

319

South Yorkshire

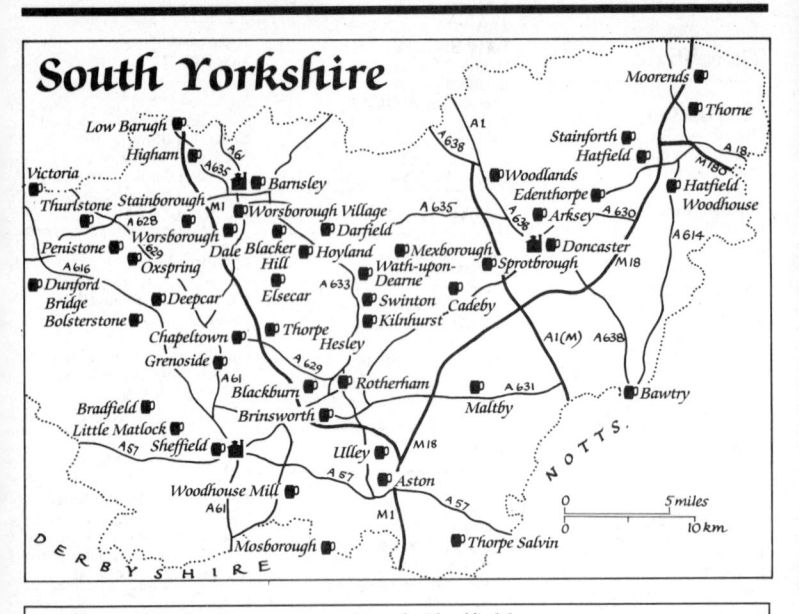

Stocks, Doncaster; **Ward**, Sheffield

Arksey

11–3; 7–11
Plough
2 High Street ☎ (0302) 872472
John Smith Bitter H
Comfortable local in village threatened with "yuppiefication". Traditional tap room for darts and dominoes and larger lounge with commemorative plates

Aston

10.30–3; 6–10.30 (11 F, S)
Blue Bell
Worksop Road
☎ (0742) 872302
Stones Best Bitter E
Large roadhouse on old A57 which still caters for a strong local trade

Barnsley

11–3; 7–11
Manx Arms
Sheffield Road (A61 roundabout)
Draught Bass; Ind Coope Burton Ale; Stones Best Bitter; Tetley Bitter; Taylor Landlord H
Deservedly popular town centre pub (not Sun)

12–3; 7–11 (6–11 Sat)
Wheatsheaf
Towend A628
Tetley Bitter; Ind Coope Burton Ale H
Revitalised local, popular with clubs and societies but threatened by unnecessary roundabout (not Sun)

Bawtry

11–3; 6–11
Turnpike
28–30 High Street (A614)
☎ (0302) 711960
Stocks Best Bitter, Select, Old Horizontal H
Former wine bar and shop. Tastefully decorated. Popular with all ages
(Mon–Thu)

Blackburn

10.30–3; 6–10.30 (11 F, S)
Crown Inn
Blackburn Road (M1 Jct 34)
Tetley Bitter H
Family pub with pool table. Split-level garden houses aviary and children's games. No meals weekends

Blacker Hill

11–3; 5.30–11
Royal Albert
Barnsley Road (500 yds off B6096) ☎ (0226) 742193
Ward Sheffield Best Bitter H
Hub of village life. Cosy wood-panelled lounge. Busy public bar. Games

Bolsterstone

11–3; 6–10.30 (11 F, S)
Castle
Off A616 at Deepcar Crossroads ☎ (0742) 882145
Stones Best Bitter E
Old stone-built locals' pub in Pennine foothills. Comfortable lounge and public bar with friendly atmosphere. Frequented by local (famous) male voice choir

Bradfield

7.30–10.30 (11 F, S)
Haychatter Inn
Bradfield Dale (Strines Road off B6077) ☎ (0742) 81332
Greene King IPA H
Remote 3-roomed country inn with pleasant atmosphere. Very busy in summer. Guest beers only. No regular real ales. Closed lunch ex Sun

Brinsworth

12–3; 6–10.30 (11 F, S)
Waverley
☎ (0709) 360906
Ruddles County; Webster Yorkshire Bitter H
New estate pub with facilities for children. Range of beers may vary

Cadeby

10.30–3; 6–11
Cadeby Inn
Main Street ☎ (0709) 864009
Samuel Smith OBB, Museum Ale; Tetley Bitter H
Ex-farmhouse in quiet village. Retains character and charm. Guest beers. Pub games

Chapeltown

11–3; 5.30–10.30 (11 F, S)

South Yorkshire

Prince of Wales
80 Burncross Road (A629)
☎ (0742) 467725
Ward Sheffield Best Bitter H
& E
A late 19th-century locals' pub with a small comfortable lounge and smaller public bar. Friendly atmosphere. Pub games

Darfield

12–3; 6 (7 winter)–11

Hewer & Brewer
77 Snape Hill Road (B6096)
Rockside Barnsley Bitter; Tetley Bitter; Whitbread Castle Eden Ale; Taylor Landlord; Ram Tam H
Friendly 2-room pub. Plush lounge, quiet tap room with collection of old brewery prints. Guest beers. Pub games

Try also: Cross Keys

Deepcar

11.30–3; 5.30–10.30 (11 F, S)

Royal Oak
Manchester Road (A616)
☎ (0742) 882205
Tetley Bitter H
Busy village local with warm atmosphere. Live music 3 nights; pool room and 2 comfortable drinking areas. Separate accommodation (lunch) (by request)

Doncaster

11.30–3; 6–11

Corner Pin
145 St Sepulchre Gate West
☎ (0302) 323142
John Smith Bitter H
Street corner local just away from the town centre, a minute's walk from the station

11–3; 7–11

Corporation Brewery Taps
Cleveland Street
☎ (0302) 63715
Samuel Smith OBB H
Popular and friendly local. Large concert room with clubland atmosphere. No lunches at weekends. Pub games

11–3; 6–11

Hallcross
33 Hallgate ☎ (0302) 328213
Hallcross Best Bitter, Stiletto, Old Horizontal H
Busy, cosmopolitan home-brew pub, impressively decorated with mirrors. Has been a pub for just 7 years although the building used to house the family bakery

11 (10.30 Tu, F, S)–3 (4 Tu); 7–11

Masons Arms
Market Place ☎ (0302) 64391
Tetley Bitter H
Traditional market tavern which has retained much of its character. Over 200 years old and formerly a brew-pub

10.30–3; 7–11

St Leger Tavern
8 Silver Street ☎ (0302) 64556
Shipstone Bitter H
Attractive town centre tavern named after an obscure French Bishop murdered in the 7th century. Family room

11–3; 6–11

White Swan
34A Frenchgate
☎ (0302) 66573
Ward Sheffield Best Bitter H & E
Narrow frontage belies the length of the lounge. Tiny tap room at the front boasts the tallest bar in Britain. Families welcome if eating

Dunford Bridge

11–3; 7–11

Stanhope Arms
Windle Edge Lane (off A628)
☎ (0226) 763104
John Smith Bitter H
Originally built as a shooting lodge; has several rooms interlinked with bar and separate dining room. Breakfast available for walkers

Edenthorpe

11–3; 6–11

Ridgewood Hotel
Thorne Road (A18)
☎ (0302) 882841
Samuel Smith OBB H
Spacious, comfortably decorated lounge; separate public bar, and extensive beer garden. Pub games

Elsecar

11–3; 5.30–11

Market Hotel
Wentworth Road
(off B6097)
Stones Best Bitter H & E
Multi-roomed local in historic mining village

Grenoside

11–3; 5.30–10.30 (11 F, S)

Cow & Calf
Skew Hill Lane (off A61)
☎ (0742) 46891
Samuel Smith OBB E
This sprawling hostelry was previously a farmhouse and there has been a building on the site since c1100. Traditionally furnished lounge. Meals till 8pm

Hatfield

11–3; 6–11

Blue Bell
Manor Road
John Smith Bitter H
Basic, unchanged, friendly local in centre of the village

Hatfield Woodhouse

10.30–3; 6–11

Green Tree
Bearswood Green (A18/A614)
☎ (0302) 840305
Ward Darley Thorne Best Bitter, Sheffield Best Bitter H
Very welcoming 17th-century posting house; emphasis on food

10.30–3; 6–11

Robin Hood & Little John
Main Street (A614)
☎ (0302) 840213
Stones Best Bitter H
Friendly, comfortable village local very busy at weekends

Higham

11–3; 6.30–11

Engineers Inn
Higham Common Road (off A628) ☎ (0226) 384204
Samuel Smith OBB H
Busy village local. Wed quiz night. Families welcome lunchtimes. Pub games (Mon–Sat)

Try also: Spencers Arms, A635

Hoyland

11–3; 6.30–11

Furnace Inn
Milton Road (off B6097)
☎ (0226) 742000
Ward Darley Thorne Best Bitter, Sheffield Best Bitter H
Welcoming stone-built inn by old forge pond

Kilnhurst

11–3; 6–10.30 (11 F, S)

Ship Inn
1 Hooton Road (B6090)
☎ (0709) 584322
Whitbread Castle Eden Ale H
Oldest building in village, perilously close to railway and canalside. Comfortable and homely atmosphere; upstairs restaurant (not Sun)

10.30–3; 6–10.30 (11 F, S)

Terrace
Hooton Road (B6090)
☎ (0709) 582014
Stones Best Bitter E
Welcoming mining village pub full of local characters, and unspoilt by

321

South Yorkshire

refurbishment. Occasional live music ⚫ ◖ (Mon–Fri) ⌑ ♿

Little Matlock

11–3; 7–10.30 (11 S)

Robin Hood
Off B6076 OS893312
☎ (0742) 344565
Stones Best Bitter Ⓔ
This near 200 year-old building was originally a rest house for travelling gentlemen. Close to the alleged birthplace of Robin Hood. Split-level lounge. Pub games ⚫ ◖ ▶ ⌑

Low Barugh

11–3; 7–11

Millers Inn
Dearnehall Road (B6428)
☎ (0226) 382888
Ruddles County; Taylor Landlord; Tetley Bitter Ⓗ
Busy pub on site of old watermill. Small taproom with dart board. Good value food served in lounge
⛲ ⚫ ◖ ▶ ⌑ ↺ (Darton)

Maltby

11.30–3; 6–10.30 (11 F, S)

Toll Bar
Rotherham Road (A631)
☎ (0709) 812339
Stones Best Bitter Ⓔ
Popular 2-roomed locals' pub with games oriented bar ⌑ ♿

Mexborough

11–3; 7–11

Concertina Band
9A Dolcliffe Road (off Main Street) ☎ (0709) 580841
John Smith Bitter; Ward Sheffield Best Bitter Ⓗ
Recently re-opened private club. Comfortable, friendly; visitors welcome. Guest beers
♿ ↺

Moorends

10.30–3; 6–11

Winning Post
Marshland Road
☎ (0405) 813159
Ward Darley Thorne Best Bitter Ⓗ
Vast, imposing multi-roomed local in mining village. 2 snooker tables at rear ⛴ ⌑

Mosbrough

11–3; 5.30–10.30

British Oak
High Stret (on A616)
☎ (0742) 486442
Shipstone Bitter Ⓔ
Traditional pub with strong local following on main road. Games room and comfortable lounge ⚫ ⌑ ▷

Oxspring

12–3; 6 (7 winter)–11

Travellers Inn
Four Lane Ends (A629)
☎ (0226) 762518
Ward Sheffield Best Bitter Ⓔ & Ⓗ
Cosy pub with open bar. Overlooks Penistone Moors
⛴ Q ⛲ ⚫ ◖

Penistone

11–3; 6–11

Cubley Hall
Mortimor Road, Cubley
Clark Traditional Bitter; Ind Coope Burton Ale; Tetley Bitter, Imperial Ⓗ
Former country house. Fine interior decor and gardens. Try the food. Family room
⛴ ⚫ ◖ ▶ ♿

Rotherham

10.30–3; 6–10.30 (11 F, S)

Bridge
Greasbrough Road
☎ (0709) 363683
Stones Best Bitter Ⓔ
Many-roomed pub next to the famous chapel on the bridge. Maps of the pubs of Rotherham at the turn of the century adorn the walls ◖ ⌑ ↺

10.30–3; 6–10.30 (11 F, S)

Butchers Arms
Midland Road, Masbrough
☎ (0709) 560037
Cameron Traditional Bitter, Strongarm Ⓗ
Small cosy pub with lounge and supper room. Near football ground ◖ ↺

10.30–3; 6–10.30 (11 F, S)

Limes Hotel
38 Broom Lane
☎ (0709) 382446
Younger Scotch Bitter, IPA, No. 3 Ⓗ
17-bedroom hotel with a very comfortable bar lounge. Emphasis on meals (served till 9.30) ⛲ ⚫ ◖ ▶ ♿

11–3; 6–10.30 (11 F, S)

Stags Head
1 Tenter Street (B6089 just off A629) ☎ (0709) 377336
John Smith Bitter Ⓗ
Old pub with friendly atmosphere, comfortable lounge and more basic public bar. Surrounded by works and industrial units ◖ ⌑ ↺

10.30–3; 6–10.30 (11 F, S)

Turners Arms
53 Psalters Lane
☎ (0709) 558937
Ward Darley Thorne Best Bitter, Sheffield Best Bitter Ⓔ
Friendly local known as "The Green Bricks" ⚫ ◖ ⌑

12–3; 7–10.30 (11 F, S)

Woodman
Midland Road, Masbrough (off A629) ☎ (0709) 561486
Stones Best Bitter Ⓗ
Friendly pub with a comfortable lounge and more basic public bar. Snooker table upstairs ⚫ ⌑ ↺

Sheffield: Central

11.30 (12 Sat)–3; 5.30 (7.30 Sat, Sun)–10.30 (11 F, S)

Bath Hotel
66 Victoria Street
☎ (0742) 729017
Tetley Mild, Bitter Ⓗ
Small 2-roomed local, popular with students. Occasional live folk music. A Tetley Heritage pub converted from mid-Victorian cottages ⚫ ◖ ⌑ ♿

11–3; 5.30–10.30 (11 F, S)

Fagan's
69 Broad Lane (off A61)
☎ (0742) 728430
Ind Coope Burton Ale; Tetley Bitter Ⓗ
Friendly local close to city centre. Lively meeting place for folk musicians. Popular quiz Thu Q ⚫ ◖ ♿ ↺

11–3; 5.30–10.30 (11 F, S)

Fat Cat
23 Alma Street (off A61)
☎ (0742) 728195
Marston Merrie Monk, Pedigree, Owd Rodger; Taylor Landlord; Theakston Old Peculier Ⓗ
Sheffield's first real ale free house, recently renovated as part of conservation scheme. 2 comfortable rooms (one non-smoking) and corridor drinking area
⛴ Q ⛲ ⚫ ◖ ▶ (till 7pm) ↻

12–3; 6.30–10.30 (11 F, S)

Grapes
80–82 Trippett Lane
☎ (0742) 720230
Ind Coope Burton Ale; Tetley Bitter Ⓗ
Heritage pub with a warm and friendly atmosphere. 2 rooms on ground floor; snooker room upstairs. Quiz on Tue nights. Games ⚫ ◖ ⌑ ♿ ↺

11–3; 5.30–10.30 (11 F, S)

Lord Nelson
166 Arundel Street
☎ (0742) 722650
Stones Best Bitter Ⓗ
Basic, but clean and welcoming, back street local in area of small workshops on edge of town centre. Lunch trade mainly factory workers. In evenings, thriving local trade of all ages
⛲ (lunch) ⌑ ♿ ↺

11–3; 5.30–10.30 (11 F,S)

Red Deer
18 Pitt Street ☎ (0742) 722890
Ind Coope Burton Ale; Tetley Mild, Bitter Ⓗ

322

South Yorkshire

Small one-roomed pub popular with students and professionals. Friendly and traditional. Active folk club; Quiz Sun. Excellent food ⛴🕮 (

11–3; 5.30–10.30 (11 F, S)
Red House
168 Solly Street
☎ (0742) 727926
Ward Darley Thorne Best Bitter, Sheffield Best Bitter H
Comfortably refurbished local retaining 3 distinct drinking areas around central bar. Live folk music most Sundays. Popular with students
Q ⛄ (&

11.30–3; 5.30–10.30 (11 F, S)
Red Lion
109 Charles Street
☎ (0742) 724997
Ward Sheffield Best Bitter H & E
Ward's town-centre showpiece pub with small tap-room, large lounge and conservatory. Busy with office staff lunchtimes. Cosmopolitan trade in evenings (⛃ & ≠

11–3; 5.30–10.30 (11 F, S)
Royal Standard
156 St Marys Road
☎ (0742) 722883
Ward Darley Dark Mild, Sheffield Best Bitter H & E; **Vaux Samson** H
Busy pub popular with students and business community. Pool room, snug and lounge. Fine wood panelled bar
⛄ (lunch) 🕮 (⛃ & ≠

11.30–3 (not Sun); 5.30–10.30 (11 F, S)
Rutland Arms
86 Brown Street
☎ (0742) 729003
Tetley Bitter H
Comfortably refurbished 2-roomed corner pub. Unusual tiled frontage. Pub games
Q ⛄ 🕮 (🍺 (till 7.30) ⛃ ≠

11–3; 5.30–10.30 (11 F, S)
Washington
79 Fitzwilliam Street
☎ (0742) 754937
Ind Coope Burton Ale; Tetley Mild, Bitter H
2 comfortably furnished rooms with large display of teapots. Taproom has regular trade; lounge especially popular with students Q ⛄ (⛃

Sheffield: East

11–3; 5.30–10.30 (11 F, S)
Cocked Hat
75 Worksop Road
☎ (0742) 448332
Marston Burton Bitter, Pedigree H
Warm and welcoming hostelry in Attercliffe environmental corridor. Noted for its lunches. Pub games ⛴ (&

11.30–3; 5.30–10.30 (11 F, S)
Cross Keys
400 Handsworth Road (A57)
☎ (0742) 694413
Stones Best Bitter E
Popular village local set in the corner of the parish church graveyard. An outstanding example of an unspoilt and friendly watering hole ⛃

11.30–3; 5.30–10.30 (11 F, S)
Excelsior
1 Carbrook Street
☎ (0742) 444152
Ward Sheffield Best Bitter H & E
Thriving street-corner local with lively atmosphere. Regular organ music. Large enclosed grassed beer garden. Pub games 🕮 ((Mon–Fri)

11.30–3; 6.30–10.30 (11 F, S)
Foundry Arms
Barrow Road, Wincobank
☎ (0742) 426498
Tetley Bitter E
With a history dating back to the late 19th century, this thriving pub is well worth a visit. Landlord has many documents tracing history 🕮 &

12–3; 5.30–10.30 (11 F, S)
Manor Castle
239 Manor Lane
☎ (0742) 724768
Tetley Bitter H
Built on the site of Sheffield Castle, the original lodge was used as a prison for both Cardinal Wolsey and Mary Queen of Scots. Tap room and lounge ⛴ ⛄ 🕮 (&

Sheffield: North

11–3; 7–10.30 (11 F, S)
Denison Arms
33 Watery Street
☎ (0742) 727845
Stones Best Bitter E
Traditional and pleasant pub in industrial area. Warm friendly atmosphere; lively clientele. Pub games 🕮 &

11–3; 5.30–10.30 (11 F, S)
Golden Perch
2–4 Earnshaw Street, Burngreave
Shipstone Mild, Bitter; Taylor Landlord H
Traditional ale house with no smoking room and taped classical music. Guest beers ⛃ ⛄

11.30–3; 7–10.30 (11 F, S)
Norfolk Arms
195–199 Carlisle Street
☎ (0742) 752469
Ind Coope Burton Ale; Tetley Bitter H
A Tetley 'Heritage' pub amongst disused steelworks. Lavish exterior and interior, with unusual roundabout bar

and magnificent staircase ((Mon–Fri) &

Sheffield: South

11–3; 6–10.30 (11 F, S)
Byron House
16 Nether Edge Road
☎ (0742) 551811
Draught Bass; Stones Best Bitter E
Friendly 2-roomed suburban local with plush lounge and traditional tap room. Pub games ⛃

11–3; 5.30–10.30 (11 F, S)
Shakespeare
106 Well Road (off A61)
☎ (0742) 553995
Tetley Bitter H
Popular, clean, well-appointed locals' pub with 3 separate drinking areas. Warm atmosphere. Pub games 🕮 &

12–3; 5.30–10.30 (11 F, S)
White Hart
27 Greenhill Main Road (off A61) ☎ (0742) 377343
Ind Coope Burton Ale; Tetley Bitter H
Popular locals' pub with village atmosphere. Large busy tap room and comfortable lounge. Attracts young people. Pub games
⛄ 🕮 (⛃ &

11–3; 5.30–10.30 (11 F, S)
White Swan
57 Greenhill Main Road
☎ (0742) 377851
Whitbread Trophy, Castle Eden Ale H
Large rambling village local with charm and character. Very friendly pub catering for all ages. Pianist most nights. Pub games 🕮 (&

Sheffield: West

11–3; 5.30–10.30 (11 F, S)
Banner Cross
971 Ecclesall Road (A625)
☎ (0742) 661479
Ind Coope Burton Ale; Tetley Bitter H
Busy suburban local with large comfortable taproom and lounge. Separate snooker room upstairs. Good outdoor family facilities 🕮 (⛃

11–3; 5.30–10.30 (11 F, S)
Bulls Head
396 Fulwood Road
☎ (0742) 302008
Draught Bass; Stones Best Bitter H
1-room lounge with tap room atmosphere and comfortable sofas Q 🕮 (&

11.30–3; 6–10.30 (11 F, S)
Firwood Cottage
279 Whitehouse Lane
☎ (0742) 346057
Tetley Bitter H
Small and friendly local, with

323

South Yorkshire

comfortable bar, warm atmosphere and lively games nights 🍺 🍴

11–3; 5.30–10.30 (11 F, S)
Noah's Ark
94 Crookes ☎ (0742) 663300
Whitbread Trophy, Castle Eden Ale H
Excellent local, popular with all ages, variety of home-cooked meals 🍺 🍴&

11–3; 5.30–10.30 (11 F, S)
Pomona
255 Ecclesall Road (A625) ☎ (0742) 665922
Home Bitter E
Modern 2-roomed estate-type pub with conservatory leading off large lounge. Pub games Q 🍺 🍴

11–3; 5.30–10.30 (11 F, S)
Sportsman
57 Benty Lane (A57) ☎ (0742) 660502
Draught Bass; Stones Best Bitter H
Large split-level lounge with smaller games room; both well-furnished. Pub games 🍺 🍴 (Mon–Fri) &

Sprotbrough

11–3; 6–11
Ivanhoe
Melton Road ☎ (0302) 853130
Samuel Smith OBB H & E
Large pub near village cricket pitch. Refurbished showpiece with conservatory. Snooker table in bar
🍺 🍴 (not Mon) &

Stainborough

12–3; 7–11
Strafford Arms
Park Drive (off B6099) ☎ (0226) 287488
John Smith Bitter H
Country pub with traditional Yorkshire range in open bar. Adjoining quaint local cricket ground. Try the food
🏨 Q 🍺 🍴 & ♿

Try also: Horse & Jockey, Dodworth

Stainforth

11–3; 6.30–11
Harvester
Thorne Road ☎ (0302) 841660
John Smith Bitter H
Pleasant comfortable well-established estate pub in typical John Smith style. Pub games 🍺 🍴 &

Swinton

11.20–3; 6.20–10.30 (11 F, S)
Sportsmans
149 Fitzwilliam Street ☎ (0709) 582537

Stones Best Bitter E
Popular sports-oriented local 🍺 🍴 &

Thorne

10.30–3; 6–11
Rising Sun
Hatfield Road (close to A614) ☎ (0405) 740016
Ward Darley Thorne Best Bitter E
Friendly traditional 2-room local 🍺 🍴

Thorpe Hesley

12–3; 6–10.30 (11 F, S)
Ball Inn
Hesley Bar (just off M1 Jct 35) ☎ (0742) 467681
Tetley Mild E, **Bitter** H
Originally 3 cottages, has been a pub for over 100 years. Comfortable lounge and public bar. Has Rawsons panelled windows. Snooker 🏨 🍺 🍴 &

Thorpe Salvin

11–3; 5.30–10.30 (11 F, S)
Old Parish Oven
Worksop Road (off B6059) ☎ (0909) 760685
Younger Scotch Bitter, No.3 H
Family oriented pub, modern but built in traditional style. Separate family room, Large play area to rear and good parking 🍺 🍴 &

Thurlstone

12.30–3 (closed Mon–Fri); 7–11
Huntsman
136 Manchester Road (A628) ☎ (0226) 764892
Greene King Abbot; Marston Pedigree, Oak Porter; Ruddles County; Stones Best Bitter H
Popular roadside local in ancient weavers' village. Oak beamed open bar. Separate pool room. Guest beers 🏨 &

Ulley

11–3; 6–10.30 (11 F, S)
Royal Oak
(off A618) ☎ (0742) 872464
Samuel Smith OBB H
Very popular pub with purpose-built family lounge and separate restaurant. Excellent food at reasonable prices. Beer garden with play equipment
🍺 🍴 (not Sun) &

Victoria

12–3; 7–11
Victoria Inn
Hepworth (A616) ☎ (0484) 682785
Tetley Bitter; Youngers IPA H

Welcoming Pennine pub. Lobby bar and comfortable lounge Q

Try also: Pratty Flowers, Crow Edge

Wath-upon-Dearne

10.30–3; 7–10.30 (11 F, S)
New Inn
West Street ☎ (0709) 872347
John Smith Bitter H
Busy 2-roomed inn with an upstairs restaurant (lunch times only) 🍺 🍴

10.30–3; 7–10.30 (11 F, S)
Sandygate House Hotel
Sandygate ☎ (0709) 877827
Youngers Scotch Bitter, IPA, No.3 H
Large, imposing old house decorated and furnished to a high standard
🏨 Q 🍺 🍴 &

Woodhouse Mill

10.30–3; 6–10.30 (11 F, S)
Princess Royal
680 Retford Road (A57) ☎ (0742) 692615
Tetley Bitter H
Large pub with several rooms including concert lounge 🍺 🍴 ≠

Woodlands

10.30–3; 6–11
Woodlands Hotel
Great North Road (A638) ☎ (0302) 723207
Tetley Bitter H
Huge mining village institution with rough and ready taproom ≠ 🍴

Worsborough Dale

12–2 (12–3 Sat); 7–11
Boatmans Rest
Edmunds Road (off B6100)
Ind Coope Burton Ale; Tetley Bitter H
Pleasant local with games room, lounge and separate dining room. Knockout pool competitions and regular quiz nights 🍺 🍴

Try also: Masons Arms, B6100

Worsborough Village

11–3; 7–11
Edmunds Arms
Off A61 ☎ (0226) 206865
Samuel Smith OBB H
Splendid village inn near historic mill and country park. Good value food
Q 🍺 (restaurant, lunch) 🍴 (not Mon–Wed) 🍴

324

DEATH OF A YOUNG CONSERVATIVE

Residents here do not associate the Dogwater Park Estate with national disasters. But that is exactly what happened a year ago last Tuesday. The pub that had been a home for many of us during the black years of the 1980s was sold off by Wombat Breweries only to be savagely renovated by its new owners without any regard for the opinions of the regulars.

"Jumpers" was a great place with a really great atmosphere. The fact that it had a new manager every six weeks meant that it never got stale. There was always more fun on the horizon. But the new owners, Yeabsley & Co., family brewers from the Cotswolds, have completely wrecked it.

It is now called "The Old Red Lion". What a stupid name for a pub. I reckon it must be named after one of those things Mr Yeabsley senior sees crawling up the wall before his breakfast pint of Old Incorrigible.

They ripped out the Budweiser glass-fronted standing fridge to make space for some sideways-pointing barrels. Don't they realise that Bud tastes like rubbish if it comes from the wrong fridge. And I can't imagine it's healthy to drink beer out of wooden containers. Someone said they wash them out with Sanilav before they fill them. Something makes the stuff taste all bitter, anyway.

The removal of the four-screen video was totally uncalled for. They could at least have kept the synchronised laser show. Now there's nothing. Just the odd background tape of Julian Lloyd Webber playing Brahms and Liszt and stuff like that. You can hardly hear yourself think for people *talking* everywhere. I don't need it. Some of us go out to relax, OK?

The big bar is ruined. It used to be enormous. We had some great fights in there. But this Yeabsley lot have made it into a load of separate rooms. One for families, one for geriatrics, one for social workers etc, etc. Now there isn't room to breakdance even if you bring your own Walkman.

The new gaffer is dead boring. He fills the glasses and gives you the right change. It isn't like a proper pub at all. And he's made up this new over-18s rule. Doesn't he realise the kids of today are the lunchtime-gallon men of tomorrow?

Needless to say the regulars hate it and don't drink there any more. You should see the crowd he's got in there now. Some of them are old enough to have children. "All terribly Radio Four" my mate Den calls them.

Anyway, what I mean is, if you CAMRA lot are on about freedom of choice, howsabout freeing "Jumpers" from these cultural vandals. I enclose a load of machine tokens as my subscription to the Pub Preservation Group.

Darren Hatchback
Dogwater Park Residents Association

(As told to **Miles Brewster**.)

West Yorkshire

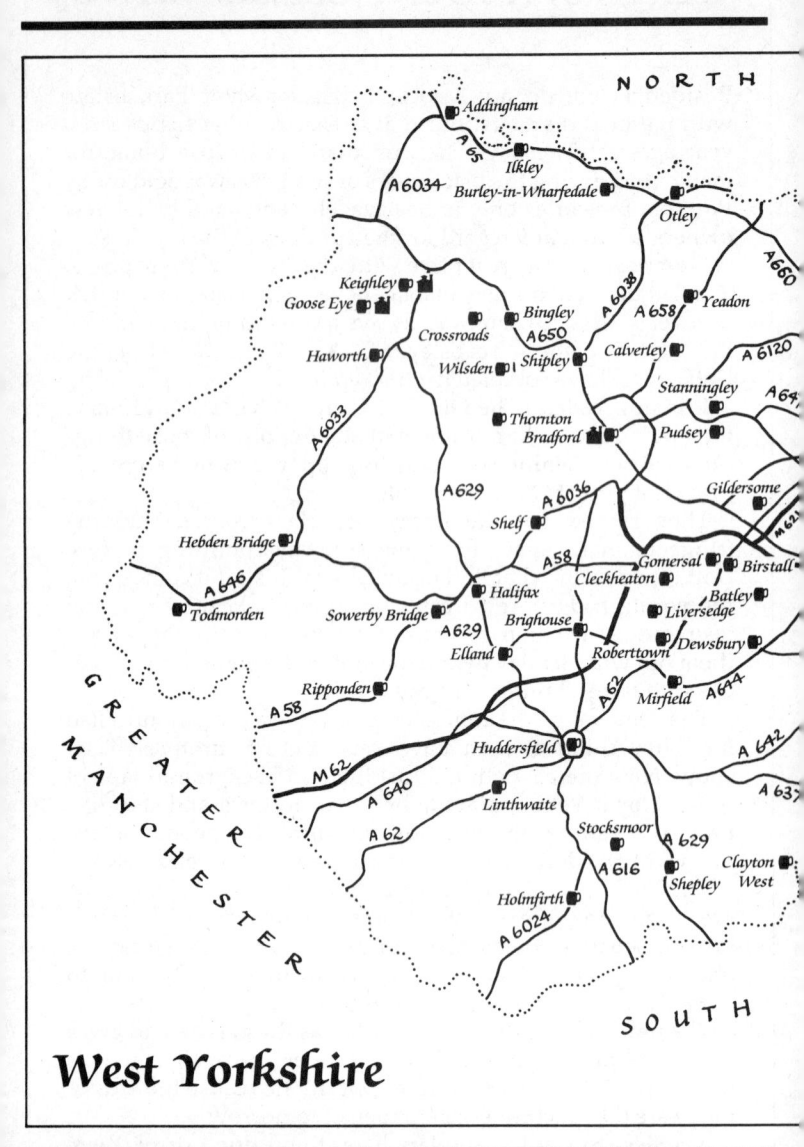

Clark, Wakefield; *Goose Eye*, Timothy Taylor, Keighley; **Trough**, Bradford

Addingham

11.30–3; 5.30–11

Swan
Main Street ☎ (0943) 830375
Bass Light 5 Star, Draught Bass; Stones Best Bitter H
Survivor of a bygone era: 4 small rooms plus central stand-up drinking area. Unusually peaceful atmosphere. Unused room at back was a mortuary
♣ Q ъ (Mon–Fri lunch) (日

Barwick-in-Elmet

11–3; 5.30–11

New Inn
Main Street (1 mile S of A64)
John Smith Bitter H
Former village alehouse that still retains its character.
Pub games ⚑ (日 &

Batley

11–3; 5.30–11

Wilton Arms
4 Commercial Street (off A652)
☎ (0924) 479996
Bass Mild XXXX, Bass Light 5 Star, Draught Bass; Stones Best Bitter H
3-roomed comfortable high street pub. B&B accommodation available
⋈ ((Mon–Fri) 日 & ≉

Bingley

11.45–3; 7–11

West Yorkshire

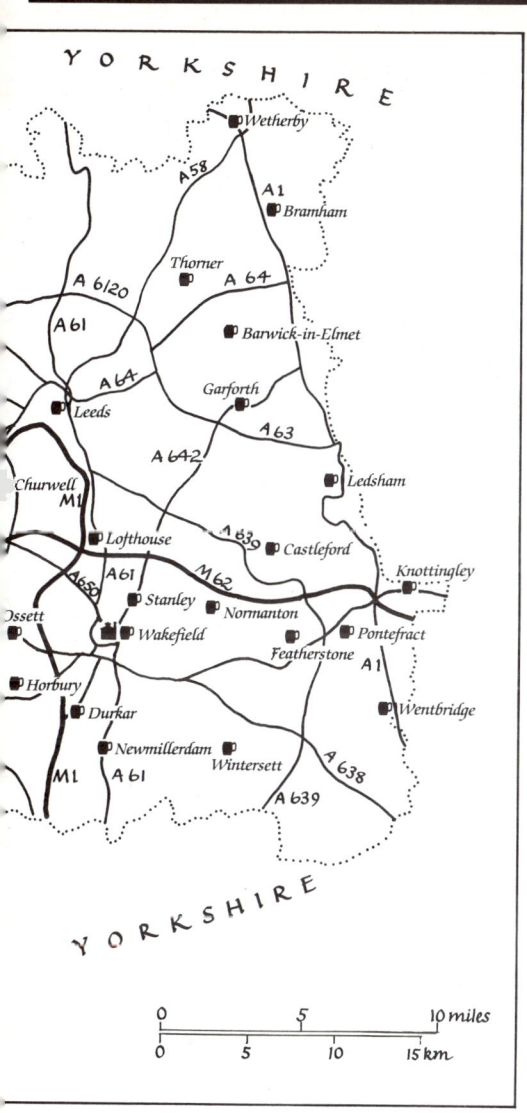

Brown Cow Inn
Ireland Bridge (B6429)
☎ (0274) 569482
Taylor Golden Best, Best Bitter, Landlord, Ram Tam H
Wood panelling and comfortable armchairs give a cosy rural feel to this pleasant riverside pub. Excellent meals; popular with business community. Jazz Mon ✱ (patio) ⛬ ( ) (Tues–Sat) & ≋

Birstall

11.30–3; 7–11
Black Bull
Kirkgate (near A643/A652)
☎ (0274) 873039
Whitbread Trophy, Castle Eden Ale H
350 year-old pub still has courtroom upstairs – last trial in 1839. Folk Fri; singalong Mon (

Bradford

11–3; 6–11
Barrack Tavern
Killinghall Road (ring road, E of centre) ☎ (0274) 66495?
Cameron Traditional Bitter H
Large multi-roomed pub. Live music (

12–3; 7–11
Blue Pig
Fagley Road, Fagley OS193351
☎ (0532) 562738
Old Mill Traditional Bitter; Taylor Landlord; Tetley Bitter; Theakston Best Bitter, Old Peculier H
Split-level pub with separate eating area. Rural location near the Leeds Country Way. Handy for Bradford Industrial Museum ✇ ⛬ ( ) &

11.30–3; 6.30 (7 Sat)–11
Brewery Tap
51 Albion Road, Idle
☎ (0274) 613936
Trough Bitter, Wild Boar Bitter H
300 yards through village from brewery (note Brewery Arms next door), a locals' pub with central bar in single stone-walled room with fireplace. Rock bands Tue ✱ (

12–3; 7–11
Brown Cow
886 Little Horton Lane
☎ (0274) 574040
Samuel Smith OBB H
Small pub extended into adjoining cottage to create comfortable split-level lounge separate from busy locals' tap room ⛬&

11–3; 6–11
Cock & Bottle
93 Barkerend Road
☎ (0274) 722403
Tetley Mild, Bitter H
Heritage inn with splendid glass and woodwork, 200 yards from cathedral. Thriving taproom; live music and pub pianist (⛬ ≋ (Forster Sq)

11.30–3; 5.30–11
Fighting Cock
21–23 Preston Street (off B6145) ☎ (0274) 726907
Bateman XXXB; Boddingtons Bitter; Marston Pedigree; Old Mill Traditional Bitter; Taylor Landlord H
Back-to-basics, bare floorboard alehouse, popular with students and workers. Overlooks large development site. Several guest beers and ciders plus biggest sandwiches in Bradford (& ⌂

11–3; 6–11
Jacobs Well
Kent Street (off A641)
Tetley Mild, Bitter H
Oldest pub in Bradford. Started life as a water house and was one of the last to gain a spirit licence. History reflected in mural. Now dwarfed by office blocks (⛬ ≋ (Interchange)

12–3; 5.30 (7 Sat)–11
Macrorys Bar (Beechfield Hotel)
4 Easby Road (400 yds from Alhambra Theatre)
☎ (0274) 729524
Draught Bass; Stones Best Bitter; Taylor Landlord H
Hotel cellar bar. Solid wood tables and bare boards with

327

West Yorkshire

interesting home-cooked menu; excellent resident R&B bands Sat ⋈ (till 7.30) ⧫ ≉ (Interchange)

12–3; 6 (7 Sat)–11

Oakleigh Hotel
4 Oak Avenue, Manningham (off A650) ☎ (0274) 544307
Marston Pedigree; Old Mill Traditional Bitter; Taylor Best Bitter, Landlord; Theakston XB; Thwaites Best Bitter H
One of the first genuine free houses in Bradford. A former hotel, popular with the young at weekends – but no juke box. Large beer garden
Q ⊛ ⧫ ≉ (Frizinghall)

11–3; 6.30–11

Peel
52 Richmond Road (behind university) ☎ (0274) 391739
Ruddles County; Webster Yorkshire Bitter, Choice; Wilson Original Bitter H
Welcoming family-run pub, full of students. Good value lunches; live music outside in summer with barbecue
⊛ ⧫ ▶ (till 8) ⧫

11–3; 5.30 (7 Sat)–11

Rams Revenge
Opposite Kirkgate shopping centre ☎ (0274) 720283
Clark Traditional Bitter; Taylor Best Bitter, Landlord; Tetley Bitter; Theakston XB H
Owned by Tetleys but with a better range of beers than most free houses. Former Berni Inn now restored to traditional style. Folk music Thu and Sun ⧫ (not Sun) ≉

11–3; 5.30 (7 Sat)–11

Red Lion
589 Thornton Road, Four Lane Ends (B6145) ☎ (0274) 496684
Samuel Smith OBB H
Comfortable lounge with sewing machine tables and thriving taproom. Pub games
⚒ ⧫ (Mon–Fri) ⧫

11.30–3; 5.30 (7 Sat)–11

Ring o' Bells
18 Bolton Road (off Forster Square)
Tetley Mild, Bitter H
As the name suggests, near the cathedral. Some fine glass and woodwork. Separate snug at the rear. Comfortable lounge and good value food attract local workers. Live music Sat ⧫ ▶ ≉ (Forster Sq)

11–3; 5.30 (7 Sat)–11

Royal Oak
32 Sticker Lane (ring road) ☎ (0274) 665265
Matthew Brown Mild, Bitter; Theakston Best Bitter, XB, Old Peculier H
Pleasant local with comfortable seating and separate games area. Darts, dominoes and pool ⊛ ⧫ ⧫

11–3; 5.30–11

Shoulder of Mutton
Kirkgate ☎ (0274) 726038
Samuel Smith OBB H
18th-century pub with snug and tap room. Award-winning patio garden at rear has high walls; office workers enjoy good value lunch outdoors in the heart of the city ⊛ ⧫ ≉ (Forster Sq)

11–3; 5.30 (6.30 Sat)–11

Smiling Mule
171 Moorside Road, Eccleshill ☎ (0274) 637803
Tetley Mild, Bitter H
Cosy low-beamed den, over 200 years-old, now officially known by the local nickname. Handy for the Industrial Museum ⊛ ⧫ (Mon–Fri) ⧫

11–3; 5.30 (6.30 Sat)–11

White Hart
44 Victoria Road, Eccleshill ☎ (0274) 639546
Whitbread Trophy, Castle Eden Ale H
Comfortable local with separate area for darts. Country & Western Mon, when landlord often sports six shooter and star! ⊛ ⧫

Try also: Brewery Arms, Idle (Trough); **Victoria** (Free)

Bramham

11.30–3; 6–11

Red Lion
The Square ☎ (0937) 843524
Samuel Smith OBB H
One-time coaching inn in attractive village square; racehorse theme
⊛ ⧫ ▶ (Wed–Sat) ⧫

Brighouse

11.30–3; 5 (6 Sat)–11

Black Horse
6 Westgate, Clifton (off A643) ☎ (0484) 713862
Whitbread Trophy, Castle Eden Ale H
3 cosy drinking areas around L-shaped bar. Renowned for food and accommodation. Charming walled garden
⚒ ⊛ ⋈ ⧫ ▶

11.30–3; 5–11

Dusty Miller
290 Halifax Road (A644) ☎ (0484) 712390
Tetley Mild, Bitter, Imperial H
Popular roadhouse with small lounge and large games room. Can be very busy at weekends
⊛ ⧫ (not Sun) ⧫

12–3; 6–11

Old White Beare
Village Street, Norwood Green (3 miles N of Brighouse) ☎ (0274) 676645
Whitbread Trophy, Castle Eden Ale H

Elizabethan village inn. Dining area and cocktail bar added, but many of oldest features remain
⚒ ⊛ ⋈ ⧫ (Mon–Sat) ⧫

11.30–3; 5 (7 Sat)–11

Star
29 Bridge End, Rastrick (A643) ☎ (0484) 714499
Tetley Mild, Bitter H
Tucked in next to railway viaduct. Large, busy tap room. Comfy unusually shaped lounge ⧫

Burley-in-Wharedale

12 (11 Sat)–3; 5.30–11

White Horse
Main Street ☎ (0943) 863113
Tetley Bitter H
Tiny pub of character with 2 rooms. Array of old bottles; pub games ⚒ ⧫ ≉

Calverley

11.30–3; 6–11

Thornhill Arms Tavern
Towngate (A657) ☎ (0532) 565492
Webster Green Label, Yorkshire Bitter, Choice H
Fine stone-built pub dating back to the 17th century
⊛ ⧫ (not Sun) ⧫

Castleford

11–3.30; 6–11

Rock Inn
Rock Hill, Glasshoughton (off B6136) ☎ (0977) 552985
Ward Darley Dark Mild, Thorne Best Bitter H
Welcoming traditional local with cosy lounge and tidy tap room. Pub games ⚒ ⧫

11–3.30; 6–11

Ship Inn
Aire Street (next to bridge)
Tetley Bitter, Imperial H
Vast imposing town pub with original multi-roomed layout; popular with all ages ⚒ ⧫ ⧫ ≉

Try also: Eagle (Tetley)

Churwell

11–3; 5.30 (7 Sat)–11

Commercial Inn
78 Elland Road (A643) ☎ (0532) 532776
Tetley Mild, Bitter H
5-roomed former coaching inn on several levels. Known locally as "Top 'Ole" due to its position on Churwell's steep hill ⚒ ⊛ ⊛ ⧫ ⧫ ⧫

Clayton West

11.30–3; 5–11

Junction
Wakefield Road (A636) ☎ (0484) 865117
Whitbread Trophy H

328

West Yorkshire

Village pub with coal mining connections. Games 🚶☺🍺🍃

Cleckheaton

11–3; 5.30 (7 Sat)–11

Rose & Crown
Westgate (A643)
☎ (0274) 872785
Tetley Mild, Bitter, Imperial H
Close to bus station, comfortable games room and busy lounge 🍺🍃

Try also: Talbot

Crossroads

12–3; 7–11 (11.30 if eating; 12 Sun)

Quarry House Inn
Ringley Road (1 mile from A629) ☎ (0535) 42239
Bass Light 5 Star, Special Bitter, Draught Bass; Stones Best Bitter H
Converted farmhouse with small cosy public bar (formerly pulpit) and welcoming sheep dog. Family-run pub in open countryside. Good food 🚶Q☺🍺🍃🍻🍃♿

Dewsbury

11.30–3; 7–11

Aletasters
22 Brewery Lane, Thornhill Lees ☎ (0924) 463866
Thwaites Best Mild, Bitter H
Unusual pine and heraldic decor in an otherwise all-as-usual local
Q☺🍺 (not Tue) 🍻 (not Wed)

12–3; 5.30–11

Alma Inn
Combs Hill, Thornhill (B6117)
☎ (0924) 450237
Matthew Brown Mild, Bitter; Theakston Best Bitter, XB, Old Peculier H
Village pub near 15th-century church and site of 1893 mine disaster, details recorded in bar Q☺🍺🍻 (Mon–Fri) ♿

12–3 Sat (closed weekdays); 7–11

John F. Kennedy
2 Webster Hill (A644 inner ring road) ☎ (0924) 461519
Taylor Landlord; Ram Tam (winter); **Tetley Bitter** H
Town-centre location with heavy metal juke-box. Parking awkward (even for motorbikes) 🚂

11–3; 5.30–11

Ravensthorpe
Huddersfield Road (A644)
🍴 (0924) 494173
John Smith Bitter H
Softer decor does not disguise strong Rugby League affections or role as community local
☺🍃🚂 (Ravensthorpe)

Durkar

11–3; 7–11

New Inn
Denby Dale Road East (off A636) ☎ (0924) 255897
Tetley Mild, Bitter H
Popular village inn, with traditional tap room, pleasant L-shaped lounge
☺🍺 (not Sun) 🍃

Elland

11.30–3; 5–11

Barge & Barrel
Park Road (A6025)
☎ (0422) 73623
Marston Burton Bitter, Pedigree; Oak Best Bitter, Tyke Bitter, Old Oak; Taylor Landlord H
Plush Victorian style pub with polished wood and leaded glass. Fine fireplace in front room; large children's room; bar billiards. Guest beers
🚶☺🍺🍻♿

11.30–3; 5–11

Colliers Arms
66 Park Road (A6025)
☎ (0422) 72007
Samuel Smith OBB H
Low-ceilinged cottage pub next to canal; 2 smart rooms
🚶☺🍺

11.30–3 (not Mon–Wed); 7 (5 Fri & winter Sat)–11

Druids Arms
2–4 Spring Lane, Greetland (just S of B6113)
☎ (0422) 72465
Bass Light 5 Star; Old Mill Traditional Bitter; Stones Best Bitter H
Comfortably furnished, mainly locals because difficult to find. Known as 'The Rat'
🚶☺

11.30–3; 6.30–11 summer; 12–2.30 (not Mon); 7.30–11 winter

Duke of York
On B6112, Stainland Village
☎ (0422) 76928
Old Mill Traditional Bitter; Taylor Landlord; Tetley Falstaff Best, Bitter H
Cosy local in main street of hilltop village. Meeting place of local cricket and bowling clubs. Bar billiards in back room 🚶☺🍺🍻

Featherstone

11–3.30; 6–11

White House
Pontefract Road, Purston (A645) ☎ (0977) 708659
Samuel Smith OBB H
Pleasant whitewashed pub with stylish L-shaped lounge
🍺🍻

Garforth

11–3; 5.30–11

Gaping Goose
Selby Road (A63)
☎ (0532) 862127
Tetley Mild, Bitter,

Imperial H
Oldest pub in Garforth, in imposing position on main road. Fine woodwork, glass and brass Q☺🍺🍃

Try also: Miners Arms

Gildersome

11–3; 5.30 (6.30 Sat)–11

New Inn
Church Street (between A58 & A62) ☎ (0532) 534821
Samuel Smith OBB H
Friendly, active village local; air-raid warning siren base for Gildersome. Limited number of tickets for fishing club available ☺🍺🍻🍃♿

Gomersal

11.30–3; 5.30–11

West End
Latham Lane (off A651)
☎ (0274) 871809
Ruddles County; Webster Best; Wilson's Bitter H
Friendly local hidden behind Burnley's Mill. Small restaurant 🚶☺🍺🍻🍃

Goose Eye

11.30–3; 7 (8 winter)–11 closed Mon

Goose Eye Hotel (Mint Bar)
On Oakworth–Laycock road
☎ (0535) 605807
Goose Eye White Rose Bitter, Porter, Pommies Revenge; Thwaites Bitter H
Relaxed and friendly brewery tap in former high-security paper-mill. Meals in bar or Owls Nest restaurant. Brewery visits by arrangement. Supper licence 🚶🍻

Halifax

11.30–3; 5.30–11 (7–11 Sat)

Dean Clough Inn
36 Lee Bridge (under A629)
☎ (0422) 46708
Draught Bass; Stones Bitter; Tetley Bitter H
Refurbished Edwardian pub with single arrowhead-shaped bar. Popular for lunch (pizzas good) 🍺🍻 (Mon)

11.30–3; 7 (7.30 winter)–11

Shears Inn
Paris Gates, Boys Lane
☎ (0422) 62936
Taylor Best Bitter, Landlord; Younger Scotch, No.3 H
Tucked into valley bottom and dwarfed by dark satanic mills, a deservedly popular free house and clubs' meeting place. But not easy to find!
🚶☺🍺🚂♿

12–2.30 (3 Sat); 6 (7 Sat)–11 (supper licence)

Sportsman Inn
Lee Lane, Shibden (off A647)
OS093272 ☎ (0422) 67000

329

West Yorkshire

Old Mill Traditional Bitter; Ruddles County; Taylor Landlord; Tetley Bitter; Theakston Old Peculier H
Popular hilltop freehouse with expansive views. Squash court, solarium, sauna, and all weather ski-slope attached. Folk club Thu
🏠🌳🍴🍺🍻 (not Mon)

11.30–3; 5–11
Union Cross
12 Old Market ☎ (0422) 69620
Ruddles County; Webster Green Label, Yorkshire Bitter, Choice H
Busy town centre pub – probably town's oldest – restyled on a Victorian theme, including gas lighting
🍺 (small) 🍴♿

11.30–3; 5–11
William IV
247 King Cross Road (off A58) ☎ (0422) 54889
Tetley Falstaff Best, Bitter H
In out-of-town shopping street. Lunches popular. Split-level bar 🍺 🍴♿

Haworth

11.30–3; 7–11
Fleece Inn
Main Street ☎ (0535) 42172
Taylor Golden Best, Best Bitter, Landlord, Ram Tam (winter) H
Ancient coaching inn, popular with all ages. Visitors welcome; stone-flagged floor. Heaving in summer 🏠🌳 🍴♿ A

11–3; 5.30–11
Haworth Old Hall
Sun Street ☎ (0535) 42709
Bass Dark Mild XXXX, Draught Bass; Stones Best Bitter; Tetley Bitter H
Friendly, pleasant 17th-century pub with open stonework, oak beams and mullioned windows. Large beer garden; children welcome. Restaurant
🌳🍺🛏 🍴♿ A

Hebden Bridge

11.30–3; 7–11
Cross Inn
46 Towngate, Heptonstall ☎ (0422) 843833
Taylor Golden Best, Best Bitter H
Simple and welcoming inn built in 1617, with Victorian frontage, in centre of historic hilltop village 🌳🛏 🍴♿ A

11.30–3; 5–11
Railway
12 New Road (A646) ☎ (0422) 844088
Tetley Mild, Bitter H
Traditionally arranged local: 2 cosy bars and splendid tap room. Opposite newly restored canal basin
🏠🌳🍺🍴♿🚆

11.30–3; 7–11
Shoulder of Mutton
38 New Road, Mytholmroyd (B6138) ☎ (0422) 883165
Hartley XB; Whitbread Trophy, Castle Eden Ale H
Popular roadside local. Recently extended and partly opened up but retains character 🌳🍺 🍴♿🚆

Holmfirth

11.30–3; 7–11
Elephant & Castle
Hollowgate (just off A635 behind garage) ☎ (0484) 683178
Bass Mild XXXX, Bass Light 5 Star, Draught Bass; Stones Best Bitter H
Former coaching inn now famed for proximity to the home of the wrinkled stocking!
🌳 🍴 (Mon-Fri) ♿♿ A

11.30–3; 5–11
Rose & Crown (Nook)
Victoria Square ☎ (0484) 683960
Samuel Smith OBB; Stones Best Bitter; Taylor Landlord; Tetley Mild, Bitter; Younger No.3 H
Basic boozer. Lacks trappings but provides succour. Should be visited – but difficult to find! 🏠🌳♿

Horbury

11–3; 7–11
Old Halfway House
Westfield Road (B6128) ☎ (0924) 262090
Tetley Mild, Bitter H
Suburban stone-built inn. Attractive lounge, family room, small tap room and children's playground. Regular summer barbecues
🌳🍺🍴🍻

Try also: Shepherds Arms (Younger)

Huddersfield

11.30–3; 5.30–11
College Arms
33 Queensgate ☎ (0484) 21410
Ruddles County; Webster Yorkshire Bitter, Choice; Wilson's Mild, Bitter H
Unconventional interior in an old established pub. Convenient for polytechnic
🍴♿🚆

11.30–3; 5–11
Grey Horse
Halifax Road (A629) ☎ (0422) 72549
Bass Mild XXXX, Light 5 Star, Draught Bass; Stones Best Bitter H
Plush local with live jazz Mon; country & western Tue 🏠🍺 🍴♿

11.30–3; 5 (7 Sat)–11
Jug & Bottle
62 New Street (near bus station) ☎ (0484) 516216
Samuel Smith OBB, Museum Ale H
Town-centre pub popular with all ages. Taped music; no juke-box. Tobacconist shop memorabilia 🍴 (not Sun)♿🚆

11.30–3; 5 (6 Sat)–11
Rat & Ratchet
40 Chapel Hill (A616, near ring road) ☎ (0484) 516734
Marston Pedigree; Old Mill Traditional Bitter; Taylor Landlord, Ram Tam; Tetley Bitter; Thwaites Mild H
Large pub geared to students on edge of town centre. Folk music Sun lunch. Always 3 guest beers 🍺🍻♿

12–3 (not Mon–Fri); 7–11
Shoulder of Mutton
Neale Road, Lockwood (off B6108) ☎ (0484) 24835
Taylor Landlord; Tetley Mild, Bitter; Theakston XB; Thwaites Bitter H
Old fashioned multi-roomed pub, at head of cobbled street, with authentic walnut panelling, subdued lighting and legendary juke box. Parking can be difficult
🌳🍺 🍴 (curries)

11.30–3; 6.30 (7 Sat)–11
Slubbers Arms
1 Halifax Old Road (near Jct with A641)
Marston Border Mild, Pedigree; Taylor Best Bitter H
Wedge-shaped pub with central bar. Guest beers can be expensive. Pub games 🏠🍻♿

12–3; 7–11
Warren House
Manchester Road, Milnsbridge (A62) ☎ (0484) 650220
Matthew Brown Mild; Theakston Best Bitter, XB, Old Peculier H
Opened-out pub with separate pool-room
🌳 🍴 (not Mon)

Ilkley

11–3; 5.30–11
Ilkley Moor Vaults
Stockeld Road (off A65) ☎ (0943) 607012
Taylor Best Bitter, Landlord; Tetley Mild, Bitter, Imperial H
Stone-flagged floors and wood panelling give a rural feel, in this leafy setting on edge of town near the start of Dalesway 🏠Q🍺 🍴

11–3; 5.30 (6.30 winter)–11
Wharfe Cottage
Leeds Road (A65) ☎ (0943) 607323
Ruddles County; Tetley Mild,

West Yorkshire

Imperial; Theakston XB, Old Peculier; Webster Choice ⒽⒽ
9 beers available at all times in this small but welcoming Dales-type pub on the edge of town. Extensive menu ♨☺ (play area) ⑧◖▮ (till 8.30) ⇌
Try also: Wharfedale Gate (Whitbread)

Keighley

11–3; 7–11
Albert Hotel
Bridge Street ☏ (0535) 602306
Taylor Golden Best, Best Dark Mild, Best Bitter, Landlord (summer), Ram Tam (winter) Ⓗ
Spacious Victorian pub with large pool room. Friendly and popular ☺ (lunch) ⇌

11–3; 5.30 (6.30 Sat)–11
Boltmakers Arms
117 East Parade
☏ (0535) 661936
Taylor Golden Best, Best Bitter, Landlord Ⓗ
Town's smallest pub with 1 split-level room, popular with locals of all ages
◖ (Fri only) ⇌

11–3; 7–11
Brown Cow
Leeds Street (200 yds from A629) ☏ (0535) 602577
Taylor Golden Best, Best Bitter, Ram Tam (winter) Ⓗ
L-shaped comfortable lounge; separate taproom/games room. Friendly staff, welcoming atmosphere
☺⑧⇌

11–3; 5.30–11
Cricketers Arms
Coney Lane ☏ (0535) 669912
Taylor Golden Best, Best Bitter, Landlord (summer), Ram Tam (winter) Ⓗ
Cosy local, sandwiched between mills near town centre ☺ (lunch) ◖☆⇌

11–3; 5.30 (6.30 Wed, Fri)–11
Grinning Rat
Church Street ☏ (0535) 609717
Marston Pedigree; Old Mill Traditional Bitter; Taylor Landlord; Theakston XB Ⓗ
Former run-down Tetley pub, now a friendly alehouse owned by 5 CAMRA members. 2 main rooms and central stand-up drinking area: more rooms to open when funds permit
◖▮ (on request) ⓭⇌

11–3; 8.30–11
Royal Hotel
Damside, Oakworth Road
☏ (0535) 604347
Taylor Golden Best, Best Bitter Ⓗ
Popular pub with large L-shaped front room and large tap room, both with a pool table ☺ (lunch) ⑧◖⓭☆

11–3; 5.30 (6.30 Mon, Fri, Sat)–11 closed Sun
Volunteers Arms
Lawkholme Lane
☏ (0535) 600173
Taylor Golden Best, Best Bitter, Ram Tam (winter) Ⓗ
Tidy local with 2 rooms downstairs, 1 room upstairs, with pool table and bar ⓭⇌

11.30–3; 7–11
Worth Valley Inn
1 Wesley Place, Ingrow (A629)
☏ (0535) 603539
Whitbread Trophy, Castle Eden Ale Ⓗ
Small friendly pub with pleasant decor. Popular with office workers at lunchtime
☺⑧◖☆

Knottingley

11–3.30; 6–11
Green Bottle
Spawdbone Lane (off A645)
☏ (0977) 82391
Younger Scotch, IPA, No.3 Ⓗ
Country-style pub on edge of industrial town. 2 cheerful lounges; children's play area in garden. Summer barbecues
♨⑧◖▮☆⇌

Ledsham

11–3; 5.30–11; closed Sun
Chequers Inn
1 mile from Selby Fork, off A1
☏ (0977) 683135
Younger Scotch, IPA, No.3 Ⓗ
Classic local dating from 15th century, scenic rural village setting. Originally an undertakers! ♨Q☺⑧◖▮☆

Leeds

11–3; 5.30–10.30 (7.30–11 Sat)
Adelphi
Hunslet Road, Leeds Bridge
Tetley Mild, Bitter Ⓗ
Heritage inn. Restored Edwardian pub with choice of rooms; beautiful woodwork, glass and tiles. Live pop music Fri and live jazz Sat
☺◖(Mon–Fri) ⓭⇌

11.30–3; 5.30 (7 Sat)–10.30 (11 F, S)
Albion
Armley Road (opposite jail)
☏ (0532) 456729
Tetley Mild, Bitter Ⓗ
In the Good Beer Guide for the 16th time, and deservedly so. A prizewinning gem that was once 2 pubs
♨⑧◖(Mon–Fri) ⓭☆

11–3; 5.30–10.30 (11 F, S)
Cardigan Arms
364 Kirkstall Road
☏ (0532) 742000
Tetley Mild, Bitter Ⓗ
Excellent stone-faced pub with several rooms. Long history of Rugby League connections. Games ◖⓭☆

11–3; 5.30–10.30 (11 F, S)
City of Mabgate
Mabgate (just off A58)
☏ (0532) 457789
Whitbread Trophy, Castle Eden Ale Ⓗ
Attractive back street pub with fine tiled façade and pleasant bar. Games ♨⑧◖⓭

11–3; 5.30–10.30 (11 F, S)
Cobourg
1 Claypit Lane
Ind Coope Burton Ale; Tetley Mild, Bitter Ⓗ
Fine, friendly pub with a good mix, from students to navvies
◖⇌

11.30–3; 5.30 (6.30 Sat)–10.30 (11 F, S)
Eagle Tavern
North Street, Sheepscar (A61)
☏ (0532) 457146
Taylor Best Bitter, Landlord, Porter, Ram Tam Ⓗ
Splendid Georgian building popular for its live music
☺⑧♨◖⓭☆

11–3; 5.30–10.30 (11 F, S)
Fishermans Hut
2 Ellerby Lane (off East Street)
☏ (0532) 459421
Tetley Mild, Bitter, Imperial Ⓗ
Fine establishment in an area of redevelopment. Maintains separate rooms and regular customers ⑧◖(not Sun) ⓭☆

11–3; 5.30 (6.30 Sat)–10.30 (11 F, S)
Fox & Newt
Burley Street (near inner ring road) ☏ (0532) 432612
Chesters Best Bitter; Fox & Newt Burley Bitter, Old Willow, Rutland Mild, Kirkstall Ruin; Whitbread Castle Eden Ale Ⓗ
Home-brew house with simple yet interesting traditional style interior. Popular with students
◖(not Sat)

11.30–3; 5.30–10.30 (11 F, S)
Gardeners Arms
33 Beza Street, Hunslet (off A61)
Tetley Mild, Bitter Ⓗ
Simple 3-roomed corridor pub in industrial Hunslett ⑧⓭

11–3; 5.30–10.30 (11 F, S)
Garden Gate
37 Waterloo Road, Hunslet
☏ (0532) 700379
Tetley Mild, Bitter Ⓗ
Victorian palace, totally unspoilt with tiles, woodwork – the lot. 4 rooms all with their own unique atmosphere
♨⓭☆

11–3; 5.30–10.30 (11 F, S)
General Elliott
Vicar Lane (opposite City Market Buildings)
☏ (0532) 442663
Samuel Smith OBB Ⓗ
Small city centre pub with basic groundfloor bar and

331

West Yorkshire

comfortable upstairs lounge, (only open lunchtimes) ♦ (not Sun) 🍴≠

11–3; 5.30–10.30 (11 F, S)
Nelson
Armley Road, Armley
☎ (0532) 638505
Younger Scotch, No.3 🅷
Pleasant main road pub, once the HQ of Yorkshire's first independent bus company – Samuel Ledgard's, who also brewed his own beer here ♦🍴&

11.30–3; 5.30–10.30 (11 F, S)
Old Red Lion
49 Thwaite Gate, Hunslet
☎ (0532) 701910
Tetley Mild, Bitter 🅷
Noisy lounge with young clientele, and smashing tap room with lots of old Rugby League photos. Games 🍴&

11–3; 5.30 (7 Sat)–10.30 (11 F, S)
Old Unicorn
Town Street, Bramley (A657)
Tetley Mild, Bitter; Younger No.3 🅷
Congenial old Bramley free house with opened out interior. Games 🏠 ♦ 🍴

11–3; 5.30–10.30 (11 F, S)
Pig & Whistle
Merrion Centre (Woodhouse Lane) ☎ (0532) 445354
Cameron Traditional Bitter, Strongarm; Everard Old Original 🅷
Modern pub next to music college – impromptu sessions a speciality ♦&≠ (City)

11–3; 5.30 (6 Sat)–10.30 (11 F, S)
Queen
102 Burley Road
☎ (0532) 459024
Tetley Mild, Bitter 🅷
Neo-Edwardian establishment with public bar. Popular and busy 🏠 ♦ 🍴

11–3; 5.30–10.30 (11 F, S)
Skinners Arms
Sheepscar Street (A61)
☎ (0532) 623820
Tetley Mild, Bitter 🅷
Large welcoming locals' pub, regular winner of Tetley's best-kept cellar competition. Takeaways available from nearby famous corner curry house ఆ&

11–3; 5.30–10.30 (11 F, S)
Three Horseshoes
98 Otley Road, Headingley (A660) ☎ (0532) 757222
Tetley Mild, Bitter, Imperial 🅷
Fine 19th-century pub, frequented by students. Good meals. Outside tables Q 🏠 ♦ ▶ (until 7) 🍴

11–3; 5.30 (Sat)–10.30 (11 F, S)
Town Hall Tavern
17 Westgate (opposite town hall) ☎ (0532) 453966

Tetley Mild, Bitter; Whitbread Castle Eden Ale; Younger No.3 🅷
Popular cosmopolitan city centre pub with choice of comfortable lounge drinking areas ≠

11–3; 5.30–10.30 (11 F, S)
Victoria
Great George Street (rear of town hall) ☎ (0532) 451386
Tetley Mild, Bitter 🅷
Victorian style interior with side rooms; a popular meeting place. Live jazz at weekends ♦≠

11–3; 5.30–10.30 (11 F, S)
Whitelocks
Turks Head Yard, Briggate
☎ (0532) 453950
McEwan 80/-; Younger Scotch, IPA, No.3 🅷
Deservedly popular city-centre watering hole dating from 1715, originally called Turks Head. Ale is drawn from cellars 200 yds away ≞Q ᴥ (in restaurant) 🏠 ♦ ▶ (until 8) ≠

11–3; 5.30–10.30 (11 F, S)
Wrens
61A New Briggate
☎ (0532) 458888
Ind Coope Burton Ale; Tetley Mild, Bitter 🅷
Pleasant street corner pub, popular with theatre-goers (close to The Grand) ♦ (not Sun) 🍴≠

Linthwaite

12–3; 7–11 (closed weekday lunch ex hols)
Sair
139 Lane Top (off A62)
OS100143 ☎ (0484) 842370
Linfit Mild, Bitter, English Guineas, Old Eli, Leadboiler, Enoch's Hammer 🅷
Multi-roomed home-brew pub with a history of brewing in 19th century, recommended in 1982. Overlooks Colne Valley & Huddersfield Narrow Canal, now under reconstruction ≞Qᴥ🏠🍴▲

Liversedge

11–3; 5.30–11
Black Bull
Halifax Road, Millbridge (A649) ☎ (0924) 408779
Clark Traditional Bitter; Old Mill Traditional Bitter; Stones Best Bitter; Taylor Landlord; Tetley Bitter 🅷
Rejuvenated, no frills local. Guest beers 🍴

Lofthouse

12–3; 6.30–11
Gardeners Arms
383 Leeds Road (A61)
☎ (0924) 822673
Tetley Mild, Bitter 🅷

Well-renovated Tetley house with well used tap room and smart lounge 🏠 ♦🍴&

Mirfield

11.30–3; 5.30–11
White Gate
105 Leeds Road
☎ (0924) 490471
Draught Bass; Stones Best Bitter 🅷
Successfully extended and redesigned in Bass Victorian style ≞ ♦🍴&

Newmillerdam

11–3; 7–11
Pledwick Well Inn
Barnsley Road (on A61)
☎ (0924) 255088
Cameron Traditional Bitter, Strongarm 🅷
Quaint old inn near beauty spot. Tiny front bar with good antique collection, larger lounge extension and attractive garden 🏠 ♦ ▶

Normanton

11–3; 7–11
Lee Brigg Hotel
Lee Brigg, Altofts
☎ (0924) 895046
Ward Darley Thorne Best Bitter 🅷
Comfortable 2-roomed local mainly popular with the older generation 🍴≠

11–3; 5.30–11
Talbot
Talbot Street ☎ (0924) 892032
Tetley Mild, Bitter 🅷
Large improved local, retaining most of original character. Fine Victorian bar, snug, lounge and pool room 🍴≠

Ossett

11–3; 7–11
Boon's End
Low Mill Road, Healey Road
☎ (0924) 273865
Clark Garthwaite Special, Traditional Bitter, Hammerhead; Taylor Landlord; Tetley Bitter 🅷
Old stone fronted pub in industrial area. Brewery artefacts; cosy atmosphere ♦

11–3; 7–11
Commercial
Dewsbury Road
☎ (0924) 274197
Stones Best Bitter 🅷
Tidy traditional local retaining separate rooms 🏠

11–3; 5.30–11
Crown
Horbury Road
☎ (0924) 274197
Tetley Mild, Bitter 🅷
Popular stone terrace pub with cheerful wood-panelled

West Yorkshire

lounge and separate side rooms. Summer barbecues on rear patio. Renowned for good-value lunches 🍴🛏🍺🍺

Try also: George (Tetley); **Thorn Tree** (Younger)

Otley

11–3 (4 Mon & Fri, ex hols); 5.30–11

Bay Horse
Market Place (A659)
☎ (0943) 461122
Tetley Mild, Bitter H
Small and fascinating traditional pub of character
🍺 (Mon–Fri) 🏛

11–3, (4 Mon & Fri, ex hols); 5.30–11

Junction
Bondgate/Charles Street (off A660) ☎ (0943) 463233
Taylor Best Bitter, Landlord; Tetley Mild, Bitter; Theakston XB, Old Peculier H
Convivial pub with lively atmosphere, popular with younger people. Always busy
🛏 🍺 (not Sun)

Pontefract

11–3.30; 6–11

Fox Inn
South Baileygate (A645)
☎ (0977) 780619
Wilson's Original Bitter H
Friendly local in sight of ruined castle. Family room
🛏🐕🍴🍺🛏🏛♿🚂 (Monkhill/Baghill)

Pudsey

11–3; 5.30 (6.30 Sat)–11

Masons Arms
64 Lowtown ☎ (0532) 577857
Whitbread Trophy, Castle Eden Ale H
Robust town centre local with taproom, lounge and corridor. Some attractive glass
🐕 (lunch) 🍴🏛

Ripponden

12–3 (closed Tue); 7–11

Blue Ball Inn
Blue Ball Lane, Soyland (off A58) ☎ (0422) 823603
Marston Pedigree; Taylor Golden Best, Dark Mild, Landlord; Theakston Best Bitter, Old Peculier H
Homely moorland inn dating from 1672. Fine views. Folk music Mon. Singalong Fri
🛏🐕🍴🍺🍺 (not Tue) 🍺♿

11.30–3; 5.30–11

Bridge Inn
Priest Lane (off A58)
☎ (0422) 822595
Marston Pedigree; Taylor Golden Best, Best Bitter; Younger Scotch H
Ancient hostelry with splendid interior timber structure. Daniel Defoe reputed former patron. Beer pumps unlabelled
🛏Q🍺 (book) 🍺 (Mon–Fri) ♿

12–3; 5–11 (supper licence)

New Inn
Rochdale Road (A58)
☎ (0422) 822575
Boddingtons Bitter; Stones Best Bitter; Tetley Bitter; Thwaites Bitter H
Amply proportioned former coaching house with sundial on wall. Picturesque setting overlooking reservoir
🛏🐕🍴🍺🍺🅰

Roberttown

11–3; 6.15–11 (restaurant licence to 12)

New Inn
Child Lane ☎ (0924) 402069
Webster Yorkshire Bitter H
Almost as many plates on the walls as there are on the tables in this catering-oriented pub
🍴🍺🍺🏛

Shelf

11.30–3; 5–11

Bottomleys Arms
Wade House Road (A6036)
☎ (0274) 678649
Clark Bitter; Whitbread Trophy H
Roadside pub catering for both local and passing trade. Games 🐕 (lunch) 🍴

11.30–3; 5–11

Brown Horse
Denholme Gate Road, Coley (A644) ☎ (0422) 202112
Ruddles County; Webster Yorkshire Bitter, Choice; Wilson's Original Bitter H
Smart and busy roadhouse, adorned with brass, copper, and china. The Choice and Ruddles alternate 🐕 (lunch) 🍴🍺🍺 (some eves) ♿

11.30–3; 5–11

Duke of York
West Street, Stone Chair (A644) ☎ (0422) 202056
Whitbread Trophy, Castle Eden Ale H
Ancient inn with remarkable roofscape. Refurbished within but remains cosy and comfortable. Popular and good for food 🐕🍴🛏🍺🅰

Shepley

11.30–3; 5–11

Outfitters
Abbey Road (A629)
☎ (0484) 607238
Taylor Landlord; Tetley Mild, Bitter; Younger Scotch, IPA H
Revamped local with emphasis on food
Q🐕🍴🍺🍺 (not Sun) ♿🚂

Shipley

11–3; 5.30 (7 Sat)–11

New Inn
Otley Road, Charlestown (A6038) ☎ (0274) 586530
Whitbread Trophy, Castle Eden Ale H
Formerly a row of weavers cottages, now a smart local with a series of discreet areas from the music room at one end to games room at the other. Good food
🍺🍺 (till 10) ♿🚂 (Baildon)

11–3; 5.30 (7 Sat)–11

Oddfellows Hall
125 Otley Road (A6038)
☎ (0274) 584568
John Smith Bitter H
Comfortable 19th-century local with L-shaped lounge and darts in small tap room
🍺🏛

Try also: Ring o' Bells (Tetley)

Sowerby Bridge

11.30–3; 7 (6 F, S)–11

Ash Tree
75 Wharf Street (A58)
☎ (0422) 831654
Old Mill Traditional Bitter; Stones Best Bitter; Taylor Best Bitter, Landlord H
Large roadside free house with a stylish, up-market bar in the restaurant: authentic Indonesian cuisine (booking recommended) 🛏Q🐕🍴🍺🚂

12–3; 6.30–11

Moorings
No.1 Warehouse, Canal Basin (off A58) ☎ (0422) 833940
McEwan 80/-; Moorhouse's Premier Bitter; Younger Scotch, No.3 H
Successful conversion from canal warehouse to distinctive free house with upstairs cellar and restaurant. Wide range of bar meals, plus Belgian bottled beers 🐕🍴🍺🍺♿🚂

11.30–3; 5–11 M–F (7–11 Sat)

Puzzle Hall
Hollins Lane (off A58)
☎ (0422) 831983
Ward Darley Mild, Thorne Best Bitter, Sheffield Best Bitter H
Compact traditional pub between canal and river. Odd assortment of architectural styles including small brewery tower 🛏🍴♿🅰🚂

Stanley

11–3; 7–11

Thatched House
Aberford Road (A642)
☎ (0924) 823361
Stones Best Bitter H
Remodelled roadside pub, with Victorian-style lounge, tap room, family room and attractive garden overlooking river valley 🐕🍴🍺🏛

333

West Yorkshire

Stanningley

11.30–3; 5.30 (6.30 Sat)–11
Sun
153 Town Street (A647)
☎ (0532) 574894
Tetley Mild, Bitter H
Busy Victorian pub with several rooms, all with different appeal ᕗ (lunch) ✿ (yard) ♫ (not Sun) ⊖ &

Stocksmoor

11.30–3; 5.30–11
Clothiers Arms
Station Road (off A629)
☎ (0484) 602752
Tetley Mild, Bitter; Taylor Bitter, Landlord; Younger Scotch H
Large village pub with barn restaurant and large children's play area
Q ᕗ ✿ ♫ ▶ (Thu–Sat) & ≠

Thorner

11–3; 5.30–10.30 (11 F, S)
Fox
2 miles W of A1 from Bramham
Tetley Mild, Bitter H
Village inn with lounge, snug and tap room. Comfortable and friendly. Pub games ✿ ♫ ⊖

Thornton

11–3; 6–11
Blue Boar
Thornton Road (B6145)
☎ (0274) 833298
Taylor Golden Best, Best Bitter, Landlord H
Former Trough pub overlooking green valley. Friendly local with separate pool room. Live music Sun
♫ ⊖

Try also: Great Northern (Thwaites)

Todmorden

11.30–3; 7–11 (supper licence)
Bird I' Th' Hand
Rochdale Road, Walsden (A6033) ☎ (0706) 78145
Chesters Mild, Bitter; Whitbread Trophy, Castle Eden Ale H
Cosy 3-roomed roadside inn, in Pennine Gorge near Lancs border. Good local trade; noted for food. Keen quiz team Q ᕗ ♫ ▶

12–3; 5–11 (7.30–11 Sat)
Masons Arms
1 Bacup Road ☎ (0706) 812180
John Smith Bitter; Thwaites Best Mild, Bitter H
Refurbished house with relaxed intimate atmosphere. Lounge area plus triangular snug with fine fireplace and scrubbed tables
ᕗ ᕗ (lunch) ♫ ▶

12–3; 7–11
Staff of Life
550 Burnley Road, Knotts (A646) ☎ (0706) 812929
Moorhouse's Premier Bitter; Robinwood Bitter, XB, Old Fart; Taylor Landlord H
Idiosyncratic and atmospheric free house in wooded gorge with stone walls and flag floors. Small seafood restaurant
ᕗ ᕗ (lunch) ✿ ⌇ ♫ ▶ ▲ ♡

Wakefield

11–3; 7–11
Albion
Stanley Road (A642)
☎ (0924) 376206
Samuel Smith OBB H
1930s estate pub with typical Sam Smith's stylish refurbished interior ⊖

11–3; 5.30–11
Blue Light
Green Lane, Alverthorpe
☎ (0924) 373041
Tetley Mild, Bitter H
Mock-Tudor-fronted suburban local with smart lounge and basic tap room ✿ ⊖

11–3; 5.30–11
Cock Inn
Batley Road, Alverthorpe
☎ (0924) 373649
Stones Best Bitter H
Cheerful thriving traditional 1930s local ⊖

11–3; 5.30–11
Henry Boon's
Westgate ☎ (0924) 378126
Clark Garthwaite Special, Traditional Bitter, Burglar Bills, Hammerhead; Taylor Landlord; Tetley Bitter H
Busy town pub with brewery artefacts and Victoriana. Live jazz Sun–Tue; local rock bands Thu ✿ ♫ ≠

11–3; 5.30–11
Jockey
Northgate ☎ (0924) 376302
Tetley Mild, Bitter, Imperial H
Spacious 3-roomed town pub catering for all ⊖ ≠ (Westgate)

11–3; 7–11
Kings Arms
Heath Village (off A655)
Theakston Best Bitter, XB, Old Peculier H
Piece of history in beautiful conserved village. Gas lighting, wood panelling.
Adjoining restaurant
ᕗ Q ✿ ♫ ▶ ⊖

11–3; 5.30–11
Redoubt
Horbury Road (Jct A638/A642)
☎ (0924) 377085
Tetley Mild, Bitter H
Well-preserved Yorkshire local with 4 small rooms and plenty of atmosphere
⊖ ≠ (Westgate)

Try also: Roundabout (Watney)

Wentbridge

11–3; 7–11
Blue Bell
Off A1 ☎ (0977) 620697
Taylor Best Bitter; Tetley Bitter H
Former 17th-century coaching inn in picturesque village. Attractive open-plan lounge areas have accent on food. Family room and children's play area ᕗ ✿ ♫ ▶

Wetherby

11–3 (4 Mon); 6–11
George & Dragon
8 High Street (next to bridge)
☎ (0937) 62888
John Smith Bitter H
The only pub in Wetherby with a view. Choice of rooms. Sells fishing licences ✿ ♫ ⊖ ▲

Wilsden

11.30–3; 5.30–11
New Inn
114 Main Street (off B6144)
☎ (0535) 272551
Bass Light 5 Star, Draught Bass; Stones Best Bitter H
Popular village local; comfortable lounge with games area at one end. Good homemade food ✿ ♫

Wintersett

11–3; 7–11
Anglers Retreat
A638 through Crofton
Tetley Bitter; Theakston Best Bitter H
Small unspoilt country village inn. Family beer garden with lovely view over reservoir ✿

Yeadon

11–3; 5.30–11
Oddfellows (The Rag)
The Green ☎ (0532) 503819
Tetley Mild, Bitter H
Delightful and friendly traditional village pub. A local doss house in Victorian times, hence the nickname ⊖

WALES *Clwyd*

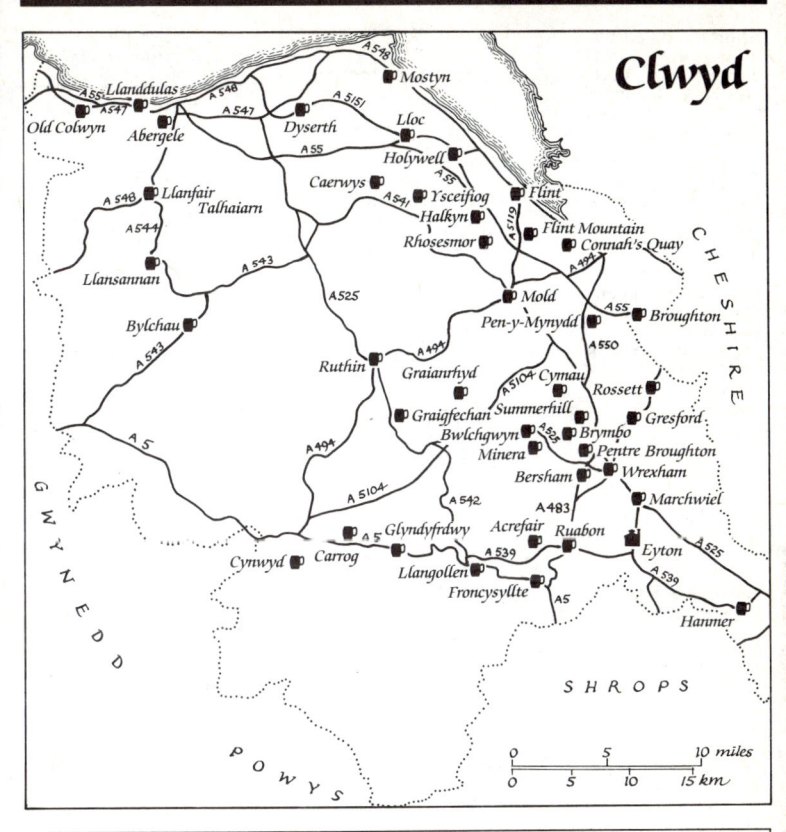

Plassey, Eyton

Abergele

11–3; 5.30–11 (open all day Mon)
Gwindy
Market Street
Marston Mercian Mild, Burton Bitter, Merrie Monk, Pedigree H
Typical town pub with nice quiet lounge

11–3; 5.30–11
Harp
Market Street ☎ (0745) 824080
Higsons Mild, Bitter H
700 year-old jail converted 200 years ago to a pub. Lots of character

Try also: George & Dragon

Acrefair

11.30–3; 7–11
Hampden Arms
Llangollen Road (A539)
☎ (0978) 821734
Banks's Mild, Bitter E
Large busy locals' bar with an interest in the turf. Friendly cosy lounge

Bersham

11–3; 6.30–11
Black Lion Inn
Off Bersham Road (B5099)
OS312492 ☎ (0978) 365588
Hydes Anvil Mild, Anvil Bitter E
Known locally as the Hole in the Wall. Village pub near Industrial Heritage Centre. Pub games

Broughton

1.15–3; 7.15–11
Kings Head
Main Road (A5104, off A55)
Greenall Whitley Mild, Bitter H
Unspoilt traditional local with original rooms, renowned for its mild. Parking difficult

Brymbo

11–3; 5.30–11
Black Lion
Railway Road (B5101)
☎ (0978) 758307
Burtonwood Dark Mild, Bitter H
Welcoming village pub in an area full of interest for the industrial archaeologist. The ladies darts team boasts 2 Welsh internationals

12–3; 7–11
Miners Arms
High Street (off B5101)
☎ (0978) 757809
Minera Bitter; Tetley Bitter H
Pit winding wheel in public bar; canal relics in the cavernous lounge. Otherwise a modernised industrial local

Bwlchgwyn

12–3; 5.30–11
Kings Head
On A525, Wrexham–Ruthin road ☎ (0978) 755961
Hydes Anvil Mild, Anvil Bitter E
Hilltop locals' pub with friendly welcome

Bylchau

11–3; 7 (6 Sat)–11

335

Clwyd

Sportsmans Arms
Bryntrillyn (opposite Llyn Brenig) ☎ (074 570) 214
Lees GB Mild, Bitter H
Reputedly the highest pub in Wales. Pub games

Caerwys

12–3; 7–11
Travellers Inn
Pen-y-Cefn (A55)
☎ (0352) 720252
Marston Border Mild, Border Bitter, Pedigree H
Good atmosphere for locals and travellers

Carrog

12–3; 7–11
Grouse Inn
On B5437, off A5
Lees Bitter H
Simple, pleasant pub overlooking a beautiful section of the Dee Valley.
(till 9)

Connah's Quay

11.30–3; 5.30–11
Sir Gawain & the Green Knight
Golftyn Lane (500 yds from A548 Jct)
Samuel Smith OBB H
Former farmhouse with a split lounge; an oasis in a real ale desert

Cymau

11.30–3; 7–11
Olde Talbot
Off A541 OS297562
Hydes Anvil Mild, Anvil Bitter E
Frequented by keen dominoes players. Elevated position offers fine views

Cynwyd

12–3; 6–11
Blue Lion
On B4401
Marston Border Mild, Border Exhibition H
One of 2 village locals – 3 real milds, no real bitters! Rare outlet for Border Exhibition

Try also: **Prince of Wales** (Burtonwood)

Dyserth

11–3; 5.30–11
Red Lion
Waterfall Road (opposite waterfall, off A5151)
☎ (0745) 570404
Greenall Whitley Bitter H
Popular with the older pub-goer. Near local beauty spot

Flint

11–3; 5.30–11
Dee Inn
Chester Street (A548)
☎ (035 26) 2144
Draught Bass H
Popular town-centre pub. Alterations to interior have not spoilt the atmosphere.

Flint Mountain

11.30–3; 5.30–11
Coach & Horses
Northop Road (A5119)
☎ (035 26) 1371
Greenall Whitley Mild, Bitter H
Very popular village local. Darts and dominoes

Froncysyllte

11–3; 5.30–11
Britannia
Holyhead Road (A5)
☎ (0691) 772246
Marston Border Bitter, Pedigree H
Small cheerful pub on holiday routes of canal and road to the coast

Glyndyfrdwy

11–3; 6–11
Berwyn Arms Hotel
On A5
Burtonwood Bitter H
Intimate residential pub with 3 small drinking rooms, one with a great view over the River Dee

Graianrhyd

11.30–3; 6–11
Rose & Crown
B5430, off A494
Marston Burton Bitter, Pedigree H
Rural pub in fine surroundings. Impressive range of home-cooked food including vegetarian dishes. Pub games

Graigfechan

12–2 (3 Sat, closed winter); 7–10.30 (11 Sat)
Three Pigeons Inn
B5429, 3 miles S of Ruthin
☎ (082 42) 3178
Stones Best Bitter G & H
Popular pub in Vale of Clwyd's attractive countryside. Pub games

Gresford

12–3; 6.30–11
Griffin
The Green (B5373, off A483)
Greenall Whitley Mild, Bitter H
Bustling village local close to parish church, housing one of the Seven Wonders of Wales – the Gresford Bells

Halkyn

11.30–3; 7–11
Britannia Inn
Pentre Road (200 yds from A55) ☎ (0352) 780272
Lees GB Mild, Bitter H, **Moonraker (winter)** G
500 year-old pub catering for locals and travellers alike
(lunch)

Hanmer

11.30–3; 5.30–11
Hanmer Arms
Just off A539, 6 miles W of Whitchurch ☎ (094 874) 532
Marston Border Mild, Pedigree; Stones Bitter; Tetley Bitter H
Attractive coaching inn and hotel of high standard set in peaceful rolling landscape within pretty Mereside village

Holywell

11.30–3; 7–11
Feathers Inn
Whitford Street
☎ (0352) 714792
Banks's Bitter H
Popular town-centre pub with separate public bar

Try also: **Boars Head** (Wilsons)

Llanddulas

12–3; 5.30–11
Valentine
Mill Street (B5443)
Draught Bass; M & B Mild
Small friendly pub

Llanfair Talhaiarn

11–3; 5.30–11
Swan Inn
Swan Square ☎ (0492) 233
Marston Mercian Mild, Burton Bitter, Pedigree H
Unspoilt traditional village local

Llangollen

12–3; 6.30–11
Cambrian Hotel
Berwyn Street (A5)
☎ (0978) 860686
Younger Scotch H
Simple hotel with small bar where the locals drink
≠ (Llangollen Rly)

11–2; 5.30–11
Hand Hotel
Bridge Street (A5)
☎ (0978) 860303
McEwan 70/- H
Smart hotel overlooking river. Good spot in Eisteddfod week

336

Clwyd

Q ⋈ ()&▲⇌ (Llangollen Rly)

Try also: **Grapes** (Burtonwood)

Llansannan

12–3.30; 6–11

Red Lion
☎ (074 577) 256
Lees GB Mild, Bitter H
14th-century popular local.
Pub games ▲Q❀⋈()⊞&▲

Try also: **Saracens Head**

Lloc

11–3; 5.30–11

Rock Inn
On A5026 ☎ (0352) 710049
Burtonwood Dark Mild, Bitter H
Excellent pub with a welcome for locals and strangers
▲ ⊼ ❀ ()) (not Tue) ⊞ &

Marchwiel

11–3; 5.30–11

Red Lion
On A525/A528
☎ (0978) 262317
Marston Border Mild, Border Bitter, Pedigree, H **Owd Rodger** (winter) G
Smart roadside pub, handy for Erddig Hall, owned by National Trust ⊼ ❀ ( ) ⊞ & ▲

Minera

11.30–3; 6–11

City Arms
Wern Road (B5426) OS275512
☎ (0978) 758890
Minera Bitter, Premium, Winter Warmer; Tetley Mild, Bitter H
Popular family pub with restaurant standing in the lee of Minera Mountain. Minera beers brewed on the premises
⊼ ❀ ( ) ⊞ &

Mold

11.30–3; 6.30–11

Ruthin Castle
New Street (A494)
Whitbread Castle Eden Ale H
Warm and cosy 3-room local near town centre
⊼ (lunch) ((not Sun) ⊞ &

Mostyn

11.30–3; 5.30–11

Lletty Hotel
Coast Road (A548)
☎ (0745) 560292
Burtonwood Dark Mild, Bitter H
Old smugglers inn once known as The Honest Man
⊼ ( ) ⊞

Old Colwyn

11.30–3; 6–11

Red Lion Hotel
Abergele Road (off A55)
☎ (0492) 515042
Flowers IPA; Whitbread Trophy H
▲❀⋈ ( ) ⊞ &

11–3; 5.30–11

Ship Hotel
Abergele Road (off A55)
Draught Bass; Stones Best Bitter H
⊼ ❀ (⊞ & ⇌

11.30–3; 6–11

Sun Inn
Abergele Road (off A55)
Marston Burton Bitter, Pedigree H
Good friendly pub; pool table and darts ▲ ⊼ ❀ ⊞

Try also: **Plough**

Pentre Broughton

11–3; 5.30–11

Cross Foxes
High Street (B5433)
☎ (0978) 755973
Burtonwood Dark Mild, Bitter H
Popular village pub, pleasant surroundings. Meeting place of local pigeon club ⊼ ❀ ⊞ &

Pen-y-Mynydd

12–3; 7–11

White Lion Inn
On A5104
Marston Border Bitter H
Unspoilt homely pub with no modern distractions.
Landlady a contender for oldest licensee in country. Best value beer for miles ▲Q ⊞

Rhosesmor

12–3; 6–11

Red Lion
On B5123 Mold to Holywell Road OS213681
☎ (0352) 780570
Burtonwood Dark Mild, Bitter H
Popular friendly unspoilt local, worth finding. Pub games ▲Q ⊼ ❀ (⊞ ▲

Rossett

11.30–3; 5.30–11

Butchers Arms
Chester Road (A483/B5102 Jct)
☎ (0244) 570233
Burtonwood Dark Mild, Bitter H
Revitalised village local. Good range of excellent value food
⊼ ❀ ( ) ⊞ &

Ruabon

12–3; 7–11

Duke of Wellington
50 yds off the High Street (B5606) ☎ (0978) 820381
Marston Border Mild, Pedigree H
Handsome old pub set in a hollow by a stream.
Traditional bar and relaxing lounge. Keg bitter on false handpump Q ❀ ( ) ⊞ ⇌

Ruthin

12–3; 5.30–11

Wine Vaults
St Peters Square
☎ (082 42) 2067
Robinson Best Bitter H, **Old Tom** G
Friendly 2-bar pub. Open all day 1st Tue of month and Wed June–Sept Q ⊼ ❀ ⋈ ⊞ & ▲

Summerhill

11–3; 7–11

Crown Inn
Top Road (off A541) OS312535
☎ (0978) 755788
Hydes Anvil Mild, Anvil Bitter E
One of a number of Hyde's pubs in old industrial area.
Public has boisterous atmosphere; 60s lounge more sedate ⊼ (if eating) ▲

Wrexham

11–3 (4 Mon); 5.30–11

Cross Foxes
15 Abbot Street
☎ (0978) 261456
Minera Bitter; Tetley Bitter H
Thriving traditional town local
▲⊼ ❀ ( ) ⊞ & ⇌

11.30–3 (4 Mon); 5.30–11

Nags Head
Mount Street ☎ (0978) 261177
Marston Border Bitter, Pedigree, Merrie Monk, Owd Rodger H
Unspoilt old pub, formerly the Border brewery tap. Pub games ⊼ ( ) ⊞ & ⇌ (Central)

12–3; 6.30–11

Oak Tree
Ruabon Road (A5152)
☎ (0978) 261450
Marston Border Mild, Burton Bitter, Pedigree H
Friendly local with many fund raising activities ❀ ⊞

11.30–3; 5.30–11

Turf
Mold Road (A541)
☎ (0978) 261484
Marston Burton Bitter, Pedigree H & G
Busy 2-bar pub built into Wrexham F.C. ground. Ask for real ale ( ) ⊞ & ⇌ (General)

Try also: **Seven Stars** (Whitbread)

Ysceifiog

12–3; 5.30–11

Fox
½ mile from A541 OS152715
☎ (0352) 720241
Greenall Whitley Mild, Bitter H
Step back in time in a real old-fashioned local. Welsh sing-song Fri eves ▲Q ⊼

337

Dyfed

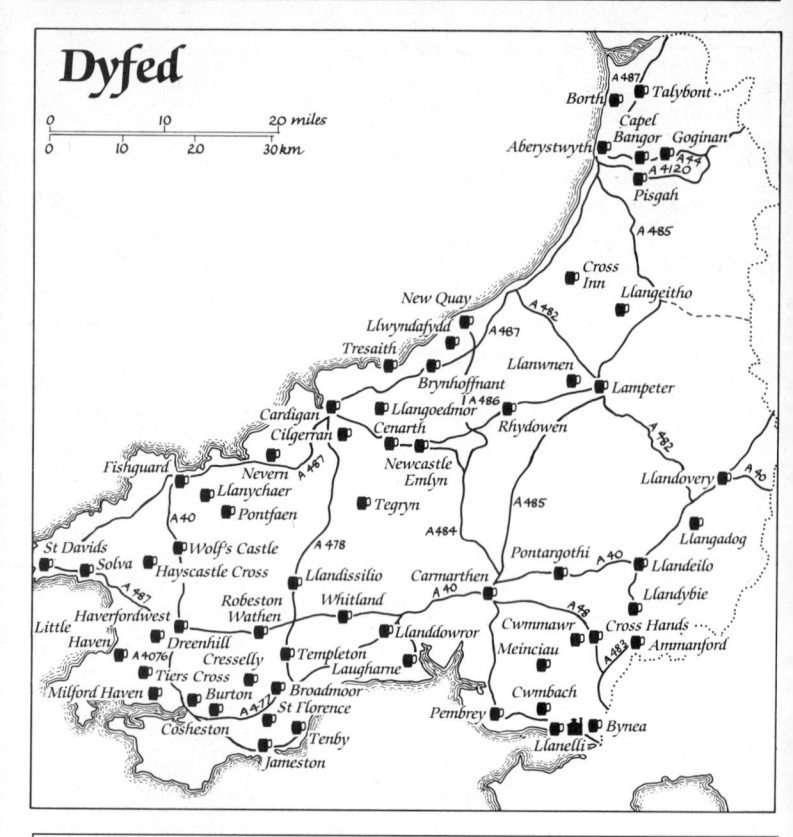

🏭 *Buckley, Felinfoel*; Llanelli, **Pembrokeshire Own Ales**; Llanteg, Amroth

* closed all day Sunday

Aberystwyth

11–3; 5.30–11
Downies Vaults*
Eastgate Street (A487)
☎ (0970) 624748
Banks's Mild, Bitter E
Popular and vibrant 2-bar town centre pub

11–3; 5.30–11
Nags Head*
Bridge Street (A487)
☎ (0970) 614725
Banks's Mild, Bitter E
Cosy, quiet local just outside the main shopping area

11–3; 5.30–11
Pier Hotel*
Pier Street (B4346)
☎ (0970) 615126
Banks's Mild, Bitter E
Small, 2-room pub near sea front. Pool table

11–3; 5.30–11
Ship & Castle*
High Street
Courage Directors; Ind Coope Burton Ale; Tetley Bitter H
Crowded 1-bar pub particularly popular with the young

Ammanford

11.30–4; 6–11 (closed Sun eve)
Cross Inn
Quay Street ☎ (0269) 2657
Buckley Mild, Best Bitter H
Friendly locals' bar with comfortable lounge

Borth

11–3; 5.30–11
Friendship*
On B4353
Burtonwood Bitter H
Friendly pub of character in main street of resort village. Piano

Broadmoor

11.30–3; 5.30–11
Cross Inn
On A477 ☎ (0834) 812287
Welsh Brewers HB H
Welcoming family pub with playground

Try also: White Horse, Kilgetty

Brynhoffnant

11–3; 5.30–11
New Inn
On A487 ½ mile N of village
OS338521 ☎ (023 978) 285
Ushers Best Bitter H
Exceptionally comfortable wood-panelled public bar; rather plain lounge

Burton

11–3; 5.30–11
Jolly Sailor
½ mile off A477
Draught Bass; Ind Coope Burton Ale H
Pleasant shoreline pub with good meals

Bynea

338

Dyfed

11–3; 5–10.30 (11 F, S)
Lewis Arms
90 Yspitty Road (A484)
Felinfoel Mild, Bitter, Double Dragon H
Friendly local close to Loughor Estuary ⊛ (🏠 ⇌

Capel Bangor

11–3; 5.30–11
Tynllidart Arms
On A44 ☎ (097 084) 248
Draught Bass; Flowers IPA, Original; Welsh Brewers HB H
Stone-built village pub popular with both locals and tourists ⌂ ⛺ ⊛ (🏠 ♿ A

Cardigan

11–3; 5.30–11 (all day Mon & Sat)
Lamb*
Finch Square (A484)
Buckley Best Bitter H
Friendly, attractive, straightforward local beside the bus terminus Q 🏠 ♿

Carmarthen

11–11 (closes 3–5.30 Tues & Fri)
Queens
Queens Street ☎ (0267) 231800
Draught Bass; Welsh Brewers Dark H
First class pub with good service; very reliable ⊛ (🏠 ⇌

Cenarth

11–3; 5.30–11
Three Horseshoes
On A484 ☎ (0239) 710217
Buckley Best Bitter; Flowers Original H
Large, popular village pub by the famous falls ⛺ ⊛ (🏠 ♿

Cilgerran

11–3; 5.30–11
Pendre Inn
High Street ☎ (0239) 614223
Draught Bass; Welsh Brewers BB H
Ancient stone-built pub of great character. Occasional guest beers ⌂ ⛺ ⊛ (🏠 ♿ A

Cosheston

11.30–3; 6.30–11
Brewery Inn
Off A477 ☎ (0646) 686678
Ind Coope Burton Ale; Welsh Brewers BB H
200 year-old pub. Wales in Bloom winner '91. Family room ⌂ Q ⛺ ⊛ (🏠 ♿ A

Cresselly

11–3; 5.30–11
Cresselly Arms
Off A4075 ☎ (064 67) 210
Welsh Brewers HB G
Unspoilt village pub. On beautiful estuary with mooring places ⌂ ⊛ Q ♿

Cross Hands

11.30–3; 5.30–11
Cross Hands Hotel
Carmarthen Road (A48/A476) ☎ (0269) 842235
Felinfoel Mild, Bitter, Double Dragon H
Very hospitable pub with locals' bar and comfortable lounge ⛺ ⊛ ⌂ (🏠

Cross Inn

11–3; 5.30–11
(midnight supper licence)
Rhos Yr Hafod*
B4337/B4577 Jct ☎ (097 46) 644
Flowers IPA; Sam Powell Best Bitter H
Comfortable, traditional pub in hilltop crossroads village. Stables converted into restaurant ⌂ Q ⛺ ⊛ (🏠 ♿ A

Cwmbach

12–3; 7 (6 Sat)–11
Farriers Arms
On B4308 ☎ (0554) 4256
Felinfoel Double Dragon; Marston pedigree H
Busy and attractive country pub with many individual features. Guest beers ⊛ (🏠 ♿

Cwmmawr

11–3; 5.30–11
Gwendraeth Arms
On B4310 ☎ (0269) 843737
Felinfoel Mild, Bitter, Double Dragon H
Welcoming, well appointed village pub (🏠

Dreenhill

11–3; 6–11
Denant Mill
B4327 from Haverfordwest; left at Masons Arms ☎ (0437) 66569
A medieval gem and a mecca for ale connoisseurs – serves a merry-go-round of different beers ⛺ ⊛ ⌂ (🏠 ♿ A

11–3 (closed Mon winter); 6–11
Masons Arms
Dale Road (B4327 2 miles SW of Haverfordwest)
Draught Bass; Courage Directors; Welsh Brewers BB H
The last cottage pub in Dyfed; small homely front parlour ⌂ Q ⛺ ⊛ (🏠 ♿ A

Fishguard

11–3; 5.30–11
Fishguard Arms
24 Main Street (A487) ☎ (0348) 872763
Felinfoel Double Dragon; Marston Pedigree; Welsh Brewers BB G
Cosy and original; occasional live music and singing ⌂ Q

11–3; 7–11
Ship Inn
Newport Road (A487)
Welsh Brewers Dark, BB G
Friendly and popular pub near picturesque harbour. Maritime curios ⌂ Q ⛺

Goginan

11–3; 5.30–11
Druid Inn*
On A44 ☎ (097 084) 650
Usher Best Bitter; Marston Pedigree; Webster Yorkshire Bitter H
Friendly village pub with attractively decorated bar and a pool room. Spectacular view across the Melindwr Valley ⌂ ⛺ (🏠

Haverfordwest

11–3; 6–11 (all day Mon/Tues)
County Hotel
Salutation Square ☎ (0437) 3542
Draught Bass; Welsh Brewers BB H
Beautifully refurbished, lively town-centre pub where all are welcome ⌂ (🏠 ⇌

11.30–3; 7–11
Dragon
Hill Street ☎ (0437) 66122
Draught Bass; Courage Directors H; **McEwan 80/-** E; **Welsh Brewers BB** H
Pleasant local with relaxed and comfortable atmosphere. Games ⌂ Q ⛺ 🏠

11–3; 6–11
George's Inn
24 Market Street
Ind Coope Burton Ale H
Modernised with originality. Good food; guest beers Q (⇌

Hayscastle Cross

11–3; 6.30–11
Cross Inn
On B4330 ☎ (0348) 840216
Courage Directors; Felinfoel Double Dragon; Ind Coope Burton Ale; Welsh Brewers BB H
Popular country village inn with games and family rooms ⌂ ⛺ ⊛ (🏠 ♿

Jameston

11–3; 5.30–11
Swan Lake Inn
Off A4139
Draught Bass; Courage Directors; Welsh Brewers BB, HB H
Old world, comfortable village inn ⌂ Q ⛺ ⊛ (🏠 ♿ A

Lampeter

11–3; 5.30–11 (all day markets days)

Dyfed

Kings Head*
14 Bridge Street (A482/A485)
Buckley Best Bitter; Marston Pedigree H
Excellent, colourful, town-centre local with small front bar and larger lounge

Laugharne

11–3; 5.30–11
New Three Mariners
Victoria Street (A4066)
☎ (099 421) 426
Buckley Best Bitter; Crown 1041 H
Former home-brew pub built around 1703. 2 old established bars; a third recently opened on the site of the former brewery

Little Haven

11–3; 5.30–11
Castle Inn
Off B4341 ☎ (0437) 781251
Brain Dark, SA; Welsh Brewers BB H
Comfortable, well-kept pub facing sea in small inlet. 2 delightful bars. Food summer only

11–3; 6.30–11
St Brides Inn
Off B4341 ☎ (0437) 781266
Welsh Brewers BB H
Comfortable, well-kept pub with a collection of horse brasses

11–3; 6.30–11
Swan Inn
Draught Bass; Welsh Brewers BB H
Old coastal pub overlooking rocky inlet; steeped in tradition. Restaurant

Llandeilo

11–3; 5.30–11 (all day market days)
Three Tuns
Market Street (off A483)
☎ (0558) 2667
Everards Old Original; Felinfoel Double Dragon; Fuller ESB H
Small, friendly pub tucked away in centre. 2 guest beers usually available

11–3; 5.30–11 (all day market days)
White Horse
Rhosmaen Street (off A483)
Draught Bass; Welsh Brewers BB H
Excellent pub with guest beers at weekends; no food Sun

Llanddowror

11–3; 6–11 (may vary in winter)
Coopers Arms
A477 ☎ (0994) 230793
Buckley Best Bitter H
Cosy, friendly pub on main holiday route

Llandissilio

11–3; 5.30–11
Bush
A478 ☎ (099 16) 626
Crown SBB, 1041 G
Old fashioned village pub with comfortable, cosy bar and 2 dining rooms

Llandovery

11–3; 5.30–11 (all day Tue, Fri & fair days)
White Swan
47 High Street (A40)
Marston Pedigree H; **Wadworth 6X** G
Friendly pub just on eastern edge of town. Guest beers

Llandybie

11.30–4; 6–11
Red Lion Hotel
Off A483
Flowers Original H
Pleasantly situated, with many rooms to explore. Nice drinking area outside

Llanelli

11–3; 5–10.30 (11 F, S & summer); open all day Thu, Sat
Clarence
42 Murray Street
Draught Bass; Welsh Brewers Dark, BB H
Well-appointed and friendly pub. Good lunches

Llangadog

11–3; 5.30–11
Castle Hotel
Queens Square
Flowers IPA; Marston Pedigree H
Welcoming village local

Llangeitho

11–3; 5.30–11
Three Horseshoes*
On B4342 ☎ (097 423) 244
Sam Powell Original H
Friendly pub in quiet village. Games room, public bar with occasional sing-songs (electric organ) and a small intimate lounge. Beer range may vary

Llangoedmor

11.30–3 (closed Mon & Tue winter); 5.45 (6 winter)–11
Penllwyn-du*
On B4570 OS241458
Felinfoel Double Dragon H
Ex-home-brew pub, ex-courthouse, now a comfortable, traditional country pub with fine views to Mynydd Presceli

Llanwnen

11–3; 5.30–11
Fish & Anchor
On B4337 1 mile N of village
Greenall Whitley Bitter H
Modernised country pub, popular for its food

Llanychaer

11–3; 5.30–11
Bridgend Inn
1½ miles from A487 on B4313
Draught Bass; Courage Directors; Flowers Original; Ind Coope Burton Ale; Marston Pedigree G
Extensive family lounge with quaint agricultural implements. Range of beers liable to vary; always guest ales on offer

Llwyndafydd

11.30–2.30; 5.30–11
Crown Inn
Draught Bass; Flowers IPA, Original H
Attractive and comfortable pub in a quiet, rural valley. Extremely popular place to eat

Meinciau

11–3; 5.30–11
Black Horse
On B4309
Buckley Mild; Felinfoel Bitter G
Exceptionally homely local in Welsh-speaking village

Milford Haven

11–3; 5.30–11
Priory Inn
OS904072 ☎ (064 62) 5231
Draught Bass; Welsh Brewers HB H
Delightful historic pub originally part of old priory, near stream. Children's play area; bowls and boules!

Nevern

11–3; 6 (5.30 summer)–11
Trewern Arms
½ mile off A487
☎ (0239) 820395
Draught Bass; Flowers IPA, Original H
A complex of rooms in traditional stone and timber; good restaurant and bar food

Newcastle Emlyn

11.30–3; 5.30–11 (all day Fri)
Bunch of Grapes
Bridge Street ☎ (0239) 711185
Courage Best Bitter, Directors H

Dyfed

17th-century building, now opened out, with pine floors and furniture. Guest beers usually available 🏠🛏🍴🕭 🕪 🍺

11–3; 5.30 (7 Sat)–11; open all day Fri

Penguin
Sycamore Street (A475)
☎ (0239) 710606
Felinfoel Double Dragon; Ind Coope Burton Ale H
Popular, split-level pub in main shopping street. Guest beers in summer
🏠 Q 🛏 🍴 🕭 🕪 🍺

Try also: Red Cow (Bass)

New Quay

11–3; 5.30–11

Black Lion*
☎ (0545) 560209
Marston Pedigree; Ruddles Best Bitter H
Attractively furnished popular hotel bar with a superb view of the harbour 🏠 🛏 🍴 🕭 🕪 🍺

Pembrey

11–3; 5.30–11

Butchers Arms
On A484 ☎ (0554) 890473
Felinfoel Mild, Bitter, Double Dragon H
Friendly village local 🍴 🕪 🍺

Pisgah

12–3; 6–11

Halfway Inn
on A4120 OS673777
Isolated but lively pub overlooking Rheidol Valley. Customers can serve themselves from the casks. Beer range changes daily; up to 8 ales always on offer
🏠 Q 🛏 🍴 🕭 🕪 🍺
⇌ (Nantyronen summer only)

Pontargothi

11–3; 5.30–11

Cresselly Arms
On A40 ☎ (026 788) 221
Brain Dark, Bitter H
Superbly situated next to river, delightful restaurant specialising in seafood
🏠 🍴 🕪

11–3; 5.30–11; closed Mon

Salutation
On A40 ☎ (026 788) 336
Felinfoel Double Dragon H
Interesting, friendly pub with varied menu 🏠 🍴 🕪

Pontfaen

11–3; 5.30–11

Dyffryn Arms
Off B4313 OS025341
Draught Bass; Ind Coope Burton Ale G
Old fashioned pub with warm friendly atmosphere; family room 🏠 Q 🛏 🍴 🕭 🕪 🍺

Rhydowen

11–3; 5.30–11

Alltyrodyn Arms*
On A475 ☎ (054 555) 363
Buckley Best Bitter; Marston Pedigree H
Wayside pub with public bar, lounge and games room
🏠 🛏 🍴 🕭 🕪 🍺

Robeston Wathen

11–3; 5.30–11

Bush
On A40
Draught Bass H
Family pub with children's room and good outdoor facilities; very welcoming, not too modern 🛏 🍴 🕭 🕪 🍺

St Davids

11–3; 5.30–11

St Nons Hotel
Goat Street ☎ (0137) 720239
Draught Bass; Welsh Brewers HB H
Friendly pub-cum-hotel with bar meals and restaurant
🏠 🛏 🍴 🕭 🕪

St Florence

11–3; 5.30–11

New Inn
High Street (off B4318)
Brain SA H
Welcoming village pub with animals in garden. Games
🏠 🛏 🍴 🕭 🕪 🍺

Solva

11–3; 5.30–11

Ship Inn
St Davids Road (A487)
Draught Bass; Brain Dark; Courage Directors H
Small quiet pub in attractive coastal village. Restaurant in summer; family room
🏠 Q 🛏 🍴 🕭 🕪

Try also: Harbour House

Talybont

11–3; 5.30–11

White Lion
On A487 ☎ (097 086) 245
Banks's Mild, Bitter E
Inn on the village green, with a bustling, slate-floored public bar and quiet attractive lounge
🏠 🛏 🍴 🕭 🕪 🍺

Tegryn

11–3; 5.30–11

Butchers Arms
☎ (023 977) 680
Buckley Best Bitter H
Remote village pub with attractive, comfortable interior and spectacular views
🏠 🛏 🍴 🕭 🕪 🍺

Templeton

11–3; 5.30–11

Boars Head
A478/A4115 Jct
Ushers Best Bitter; Webster Yorkshire Bitter H
Good traditional pub with stone walls, wood beams, tiled bar and hanging hops. Full à la carte eating 🛏 🍴 🕭 🕪 🍺

Tenby

11–3; 5.30–11

Lamb Inn
High Street ☎ (0834) 2154
Brain Dark, SA; Felinfoel Double Dragon; McEwan 80/-; Welsh Brewers BB H
Refurbished Victorian pub with carved figurines. Live music in summer 🍴 🕪 ⇌

11–3; 5.30–11

Lifeboat Tavern
St Julians Street, Tudor Square
Welsh Brewers BB H
Lively pub with good jukebox, popular with the young
🍴 🕪 ⇌

Try also: Tenby House, Mariners

Tiers Cross

11–3; 6–11

Welcome Traveller
Old Hakin Road
☎ (0437) 891398
Brain Bitter; Greenall Whitley Bitter H
Stone-built pub with beamed ceilings; extensive à la carte restaurant menu, Sun roast a speciality. Children's play area. Barbecue facility. Guest beers 🏠 🛏 🍴 🕭 🕪 🍺

Tresaith

11–?; 5.20 (6.30 winter)–11

Ship Inn*
Buckley Best Bitter H
Comfortable, small pub just a few yards from the beach. Regular guest beers
🏠 🛏 🍴 🕭 🕪 🍺

Whitland

11–3; 5.30–11 (supper licence till 12)

Fishers Hotel
Spring Gardens (A40)
☎ (0994) 240371
Felinfoel Bitter, Double Dragon H
Traditional and comfortable town pub with 3 rooms including lounge and pool room 🏠 🛏 🍴 🕭 🕪 🍺 ⇌

Wolf's Castle

11–3; 6–11

Wolf Inn
On A40 ☎ (0437) 87662
Felinfoel Double Dragon H
250 year-old stone inn with beamed ceilings. Excellent restaurant, occasional live music 🏠 🛏 🍴 🕭 🕪 🍺

Mid Glamorgan

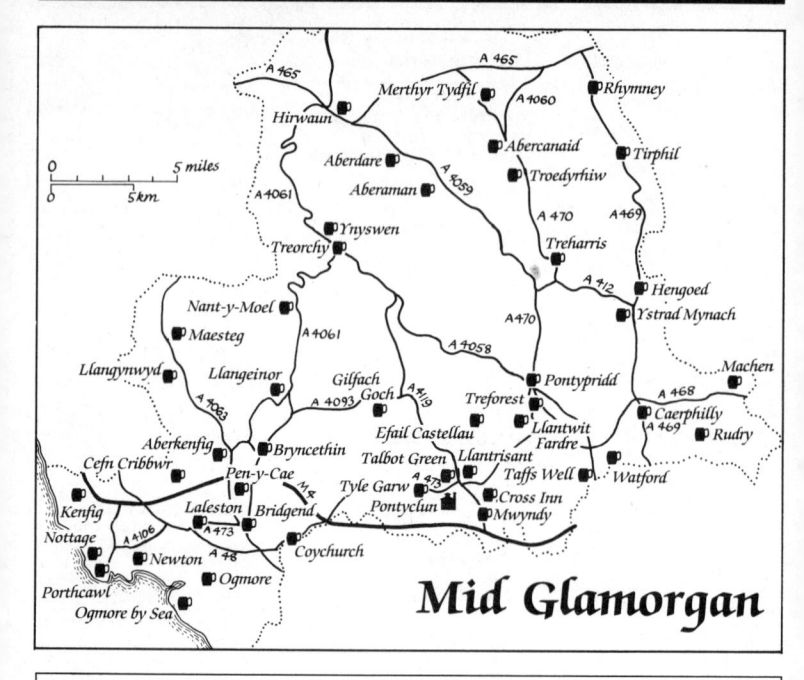

🏠 *Crown*, Pontyclun

Aberaman

11.30–4; 6–11
Rock Inn
167 Cardiff Road (A4224)
☎ (0685) 872906
Draught Bass; Wadworth 6X H
Small and friendly free house. Beer range may vary
⊛ ◑ ▶ ⊞ &

11.30–4; 6–11
Temple Bar
Cardiff Road (A4224)
☎ (0685) 876137
Brain Dark; Felinfoel Double Dragon; Samuel Smith OBB H
Homely local with a bar library and an unobtrusive games room ♨ Q ⊞

Abercanaid

11.30–4; 7–11
Colliers Arms
Nightingale Street (off A470)
☎ (0443) 690376
Flowers IPA H
Comfortable village pub
⊞ ⇌ (Pentrebach)

Aberdare

11.30–4; 6–11
Conway
Cardiff Road ☎ (0685) 883666
Courage Best Bitter, Directors H
Comfortable and lively town centre pub ◑ ⇌

11.30–4; 6–11
Glandover Arms
Gadlys Road (A4059)
☎ (0685) 872923
Ansells Bitter H; **Ind Coope Burton Ale** E
Comfortable local near town centre ⊛ ◑ ▶ ⊞ ⇌

Aberkenfig

11.30–4; 6–11
Swan Inn
128 Bridgend Road
☎ (0656) 725612
Brain Bitter; Flowers Original H
Pleasant village pub. Outstanding meals. Beer range may change. Darts ⚐ ⊛ ◑ ▶ (Wed–Sat) ⊞ &

Bridgend

11.30–4; 6–11
Five Bells
Five Bells Road (A473/B4265)
☎ (0656) 68188
Draught Bass; Welsh Brewers BB H
Busy pub at edge of town centre. Darts, pool and cards available Q ◑ ⊞ ⇌

11.30–4; 6–11
Victoria
Adare Street ☎ (0656) 67667

Courage Best Bitter, Directors H
Comfortable busy town-centre pub. Darts ⚐ (upstairs) ◑ ⇌

Bryncethin

11.30–4; 6–11
Masons Arms
Bridgend Road (A4061)
☎ (0656) 720253
Draught Bass; Brain Dark; Welsh Brewers BB H
Unspoilt bar and plush lounge/restaurant ♨⊛ ◑ ▶ ⊞ &

Caerphilly

11.30–4; 6–11
Court House
Cardiff Road ☎ (0222) 888120
Courage Best Bitter, Directors; John Smith Bitter H
Stone-roofed 14th-century building near the castle. Smart lounges with exposed stone walls and beams. Caerphilly cheese made on the premises. Expensive
♨⊛ ◑ ▶ (not Sun) & ⇌

Cefn Cribbwr

11.30–4; 6–11
Farmers Arms
Cefn Road (B4281)
☎ (0656) 743648
Draught Bass H
Unspoilt village local with mining memorabilia in bar.

Mid Glamorgan

Darts and table skittles

Coychurch

11.30–4; 6–11

Prince of Wales
400 yds from A473/B4181 jct
☎ (0656) 860600
Draught Bass; Welsh Brewers BB, HB H
Comfortable unpretentious village pub. Exposed stone walls inside and out Q

Cross Inn

11.30–4; 6–11

Cross Inn
On A473
Flowers IPA H
Small well kept village local. Guest beers

Efail Castellau

11.30–4; 6.30–11

Lamb & Flag
Castellau Road, Castellau (½ mile off B4595 on edge of Llantrisant Common) OS051856
Flowers IPA, Original H
Attractive pub in lovely countryside. Unspoilt bar with collection of porcelain ornaments. Childrens playground
(bar) (Thu–Sat)

Gilfach Goch

11.30–4; 6–11

Griffin
600 yds off A4093 OS988875
Brain SA H
Excellent old-fashioned local remotely situated in small valley bottom at end of narrow bumpy lane. Much rural bric-a-brac and antique furniture. Peacocks and assorted poultry! Q

Hengoed

11.30–4; 6–11

Junction
King's Hill (off A469)
☎ (0443) 814499
Brain SA; Flowers Original H
Smart pub near famous viaduct. No food Sun

Hirwaun

11.30–4; 6–11

Glancynon Inn
Swansea Road (400 yds from A4059) OS960055
☎ (0685) 811043
Felinfoel Double Dragon; Fuller London Pride, ESB H
Large comfortable popular free house, easy to miss as there's no pub sign. Games room

Kenfig

11.30–4; 6–11

Prince of Wales
Ton Kenfig (Off B4283)
☎ (0656) 740356
Draught Bass; Marston Pedigree G; **Sam Powell Original Bitter** H; **Robinson Old Tom; Theakston Old Peculier** G; **Welsh Brewers BB** H
Old pub linked with historic Kenfig buried under sand dunes. Large main bar with exposed stone walls. Cards and dominoes

Try also: Angel (Whitbread)

Laleston

11.30–4; 6–11

Laleston Inn
Wind Street (off A473)
☎ (0656) 652946
Draught Bass; Welsh Brewers BB H
15th-century free house. Exposed stone walls and beams. Smart and comfortable. Live music Weds (C&W), Jazz 1st Sunday in month

Llangeinor

11.30–4; 6–11

Llangeinor Arms
Off A4093, next to church OS925879 ☎ (0656) 870344
Draught Bass; Welsh Brewers BB H
Isolated hilltop free house with superb views. Restaurant; children welcome in conservatory (12–2) (Tue–Fri & Sun 7–9.30)

Llangynwyd

11.30–4; 6–11

Old House (Yr Hen Dy)
Off A4063 opposite church
☎ (0656) 733310
Flowers IPA, Original H
Picturesque thatched pub full of atmosphere. One of Wales' oldest pubs. Guest beers

Try also: Tylers Arms (Whitbread)

Llantrisant

11.30–4; 6–11

Bear Inn
Bullring (100 yds from B4595)
☎ (0443) 222271
Draught Bass; Welsh Brewers BB H
Typical town-centre local with comfortable lounge and large public. Separate pool and darts room

Llantwit Fardre

11.30–4; 6.30–11

Crown Inn
Main Road (A473)
☎ (0443) 208531
Brain Dark, Bitter; Flowers Original H
Large, lively, open-plan pub with games annexe. Popular with younger crowd

Machen

12–4; 6–11

White Hart
Nant-y-ceisiad
Off A468 OS203892
☎ (0633) 441005
Brain Bitter E
Curiously extended 200 year-old cottage hidden by railway embankment. Bar lined with ships' oak panelling. Compact dining room offers extensive menu. Guest beer Q

Maesteg

11.30–4; 6–11

Beethoven's
Castle Street ☎ (0656) 738848
Crown SBB H
Plush local with 2 family rooms

Merthyr Tydfil

11.30–4; 6–11

Anchor
High Street ☎ (0685) 3840
Draught Bass H
Welcoming one-bar town pub
≠

Mwyndy

11.30–4; 6–11

Castell Mynach
Cardiff Road (A4119)
☎ (0443) 222298
Draught Bass; Welsh Brewers PA, HB H
Smart, comfortable and popular with all types. Good food Q (patio) (Mon–Fri)

Nant-y-moel

11.30–4; 6–11

Nant-Y-Moel
Commercial Street (off A4061)
☎ (0656) 840384
Draught Bass; Welsh Brewers BB H
Valley local. Large lively bar and comfortable lounge. Darts and pool

Newton

11.30–4; 6–11

Jolly Sailor
Church Street (off A4106)
☎ (065 671) 2403
Brain Dark, Bitter, SA H
Village green pub with a nautical flavour. Cards and dominoes

Nottage

11.30–4; 6–11

Rose & Crown
Heol-y-capel (off A4229)
☎ (0656) 714850
Ruddles Best Bitter, County;

343

Mid Glamorgan

Usher Best Bitter H
Smart local Q ❄ ⓑ ⌇ ◐ 〗 ⅍

Ogmore

11.30–4; 6–11

Pelican
On B4524 ☎ (0656) 880049
Courage Best Bitter, Directors H
Smart, comfortable country pub overlooking ruins of Ogmore Castle. Restaurant Q ⓑ ◐ 〗

Ogmore by Sea

11.30–4; 6–11

Sea Lawns Hotel
Off B4524 ☎ (0656) 880311
Draught Bass; Welsh Brewers BB H
Seaside hotel with 3 contrasting bars offering superb views of Devon and Somerset coast. Comfortable lounge with sunroom; large garden ⌇ ❄ (sun room) ⓑ ⌇ ◐ 〗 ⅍

Pen-y-cae

11.30–4; 6–11

Tyr Isha
Off A4061, behind Sarn motorway service area
☎ (0656) 725287
Draught Bass; Welsh Brewers HB H
Converted farmhouse; plush and popular. Darts
⌇ ❄ ⓑ ◐ 〗 ⅍

Pontypridd

11.30–4; 6–11

Bunch of Grapes
Ynysangharad Road (400 yds from A470/A4054 jct)
☎ (0443) 402934
Brain Dark, SA; Welsh Brewers HB H
Popular local with famous vine growing in restaurant
❄ ⓑ ◐ 〗 ⇌

11.30–4; 6–11

Greyhound
The Broadway (A4058)
☎ (0443) 402350
Draught Bass H
Small and charismatic pub opposite station ⓑ ⅍ ⇌

Try also: **Llanover** (Brain)

Porthcawl

11.30–4; 6–11

Rock Hotel
John Street (opposite police station) ☎ (065671) 2340
Draught Bass; Welsh Brewers BB H
Town pub with basic bar and comfortable lounge. Darts
❄ ⓑ ◐ 〗 ⅍ ⅍

Try also: **Royal Oak** (Welsh Brewers)

Rhymney

11.30–4; 7–11

Farmers Arms
Off A469 ☎ (0685) 840257
Flowers IPA H
Traditional pub ⓑ ◐ 〗 ⅍ ⇌

Rudry

11.30–4; 6–11

Griffin Inn
Off A468 OS143865
☎ (0222) 883396
Brain Bitter; Marston Pedigree H
Country inn in attractive area. Part of a small hotel with restaurant ⌇ ❄ ⓑ ⌇ ◐ 〗 ⅍

Taffs Well

11.30–4; 6–11

Taffs Well Inn
Cardiff Road (A4054)
☎ (0222) 810324
Ansells Bitter; Ind Coope Burton Ale H
Comfortable, open-plan pub with lively atmosphere ⓑ ◐ ⇌

Talbot Green

11.30–4; 6–11

Pinkies
Talbot Road
Brain Dark, Bitter; Flowers IPA H
Recently converted from pair of terraced cottages. Exposed stone walls and flagstone floor. Caters for all age groups
◐ 〗 ⅍

Tirphil

11.30–4; 6–11

Dynevor Arms
The Square (A469)
☎ (0443) 834219
Welsh Brewers PA H
Small village pub ⅍ ⇌

Treforest

11.30–4; 6–11

Otley Arms
Forest Road (A473)
☎ (0443) 402033
Draught Bass; H **Brain Dark** H & E, **SA; Crown SBB; Welsh Brewers HB** H
Bustling Polytechnic local
◐ 〗 ⅍ ⇌

Treharris

11.30–4; 6.30–11

Perrot Inn
Suzannah Place (A470)
☎ (0443) 412401
Brain Dark, Bitter, SA; Flowers Original; Welsh Brewers BB H
Friendly local. Live music Sat. nights ◐ 〗 ⇌ (Quakers Yard)

Treorchy

11.30–4; 6–11

Prince of Wales
High Street (A4058)
☎ (0443) 773121
Flowers IPA H
Pleasant town-centre local with pool oriented public bar
◐ ⅍

Troedyrhiw

11.30–4; 6–11

Green Meadow
28 Bridge Street (off A470)
☎ (0443) 690028
Brain Bitter, SA H
Friendly local, cosy lounge bar. Guest beers ⌇ ⓑ ⅍ ⇌

Tyle Garw

11.30–4; 6–11

Boars Head
Coed Cae Lane (½ mile off A473)
Draught Bass; Welsh Brewers HB H
Small, plain, unspoilt local; quiet and friendly. Forest walks opposite ⓑ ⅍

Watford

11.30–4; 6–11

Black Cock
Caerphilly Mountain Road (off A468) OS145848
Draught Bass; Welsh Brewers HB H
Popular country inn frequented by horse riders. Comfortable lounge ⌇ Q ⓑ ◐ ⅍

Ynyswen

11.30–4; 6–11

Crown
Ynyswen Road (A4061)
Brain SA; Fuller London Pride; Welsh Brewers BB H
Busy, lively local. Large public bar dominated by open stone fireplace and old red telephone kiosk. Guest beers
⌇ ⅍

Ystrad Mynach

11.30–4; 6–11

Olde Royal Oak
Commercial Street (A469)
☎ (0443) 814196
Draught Bass H
Comfortable pub on crossroads. No food Sun
Q ◐ 〗 ⅍ ⇌

South Glamorgan

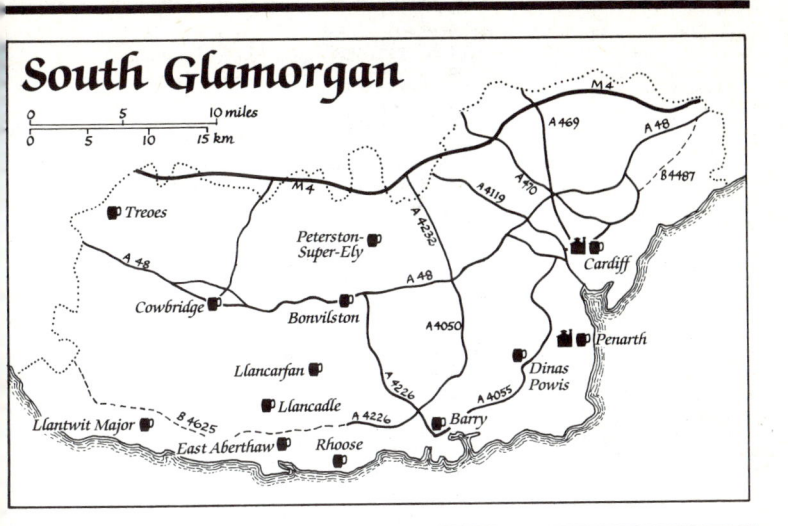

Brain, Cardiff; **Bullmastiff**, Penarth

Barry

11.30–3.30; 5.30–11

Three Bells
Coldbrook Road, Cadoxton (off A4231)
Flowers IPA, Original H
Popular village-style pub in an urban area; comfortable and welcoming with lively bar and pub games. Whitbread guest beer scheme. No food Sun
(lunch if eating) (Cadoxton)

Bonvilston

11.30–3.30; 5.30–11

Red Lion
On A48 ☎ (044 68) 208
Brain Dark, Bitter, SA H
Cosy, stone-walled village pub on the main road. Dartboard in separate room. Basket meals

Cardiff

11–3; 5.30–11

Blue Bell
High Street ☎ (0222) 25543
Brain Dark, Bitter, SA H
Comfortable city centre lounge adjacent to castle and main shopping area (Mon–Sat) (Queen St or Central)

11–3; 5.30–11

Bulldog
Plasmawr Road, Fairwater
☎ (0222) 564129
Brain Dark, Bitter, SA H
Sizeable 2-bar estate pub with darts and skittles
(Fairwater)

11–3; 5.30–11

Butchers Arms
High Street, Llandaff
Off A4119 ☎ (0222) 561898
Draught Bass; Welsh Brewers HB H
Unspoilt welcoming local near Llandaff Cathedral. Small front bar and comfortable lounge. Pub games
(lunch) (Mon–Fri)

11–3 (not Sat); 5.30–11

Coach House
Station Terrace, Ely
☎ (0222) 555573
Ruddles County H
Cosy, attractively decorated lounge bar with attached restaurant. Guest beers
(Waun-Gron Road)

11–3; 5.30–11

Crown
37 Bute Street ☎ (0222) 463945
Ansells Dark, Best Bitter; Ind Coope Burton Ale E
Pleasant, easy going local rebuilt in the 1970s but retaining a fine traditional pub atmosphere
(Central)

12.30–3; 6.30–11 (7–2 Th,F,S) closed Sun

Golden Cross
Hayes Bridge Road
☎ (0222) 394556
Brain Dark, Bitter, SA H
Splendidly preserved Victorian city pub. Admission £1 after 11pm Thu–Sat! Disco late evenings. Video juke-box. Opens Sun eve if ice hockey match played at adjacent ice-rink (lunch) (Thu–Sat)
(Central)

11–3; 5.30–11

Hollybush
Pendwyallt Road (A4054)
☎ (0222) 625037
Draught Bass; Welsh Brewers HB H
Comfortable suburban pub with Toby Carving Room
(Coryton)

11–3; 5.30–11

Old Ton
Merthyr Road, Tongwynlais (off A470 near M4 Jct)
☎ (0222) 811865
Flowers IPA, Original H
Stone-built terraced village pub overlooked by Castell Coch. Table skittles
(Mon–Sat)

11–3; 5.30–11

Packet
92 Bute Street ☎ (0222) 492677
Brain Dark, Bitter, SA H
Superbly modernised dockland pub opposite Industrial and Maritime Museum (Bute Rd)

11–3; 5.30–11

Plough
Merthyr Road, Whitchurch
☎ (0222) 623017
Brain Dark, Bitter, SA H
Busy, friendly, multi-roomed local. Skittles
(Whitchurch)

11–3; 5.30–11

Quarry House
St Fagans Rise, Fairwater
☎ (0222) 565577
Courage Best Bitter, Directors H
Comfortable suburban local tucked away up a cul-de-sac. Pub games

11–3; 5.30–11

Royal Oak
Jct Broadway/Newport Road
☎ (0222) 491933
Brain Dark, Bitter H **SA** G

345

South Glamorgan

Shrine to Peerless Jim Driscoll, and full of sporting memorabilia. Regular live music in lounge. Possibly the only Brains pub to have been pictured on an LP sleeve! 🏠 🍺

11–3; 5.30–11

Three Horseshoes
Merthyr Road, Gabalfa ☎ (0222) 625703
Brain Dark, Bitter, SA 🅗
Friendly local with good food. The bar and lounge are equally comfortable and welcoming to everyone 🏠 🍴 (Mon–Fri) 🍺 &

11–3; 5.30–11

Westgate
Cowbridge Road East, Riverside ☎ (0222) 26945
Brain Dark, Bitter, SA 🅗
A basic street-corner local near Sophia Gardens. Note the rugby mural and the newspaper cuttings which proves this is the only pub in Cardiff to allow elephants in the public bar! 🍴 🍺 &

Try also: Lewis Arms, Tongwynlais; Maltsters Cardiff Road, Landaff (Brain)

Cowbridge

12–3; 5.30–11

Bear Hotel
High Street ☎ (044 63) 4814
Brain Dark, Bitter, SA; Buckley Best Bitter; Flowers IPA, Usher Best Bitter 🅗
Large, well-appointed town-centre hotel. Always 1 extra guest beer available
Q 🛏 🏠 🍴 🍺 &

Try also: Duke of Wellington (Brain)

Dinas Powys

11.30–3.30; 5.30–11

Star
Station Road ☎ (0222) 512176
Brain Dark, Bitter, SA 🅗
Spacious village pub catering for everyone. Good lunches. Live jazz Thu eve and Sun lunch. Children welcome in dining area at lunch
🔥 🏠 🍴 (Mon–Sat) 🍺 ⇌

East Aberthaw

11.30–3.30; 5.30 (6 Sat)–11

Blue Anchor
Off B4265 ☎ (0446) 750329
Brain Dark, SA; Buckley Best Bitter; Flowers IPA; Marston Pedigree 🅗 **Theakston Old Peculier** 🅖 **Wadworth 6X** 🅗
14th century thatched inn, reputed to be smugglers haunt. Beware of low oak beams as you explore the 6 connecting rooms around the central bar. 2 guest beers. Family room
🔥 Q 🛏 🏠 🍴 (not Sun) 🍺

Llancadle

11.30–3.30; 6–11

Green Dragon
Off B4265 ☎ (0446) 750367
Courage Best Bitter, Directors 🅗
Quaint, thatched village pub, offering 3 guest beers which change regularly 🔥 Q 🏠 🍴 (not Mon) 🍺 (Tue–Sat) 🍺

Llancarfan

11.30–3.30; 6.30–11

Fox & Hounds
3 miles down country lanes from Bonvilston on A48 ☎ (044 68) 297
Brain Dark, Bitter; Felinfoel Double Dragon; Wadworth 6X 🅗
Award-winning 16th-century village pub with restaurant (must book Sats). Guest beers. Darts 🔥 🛏 🏠 🍴 🍺 &

Llantwit Major

11.30–3.30; 5.30–11

Tudor Tavern
Church Street ☎ (04465) 2290
Welsh Brewers HB 🅗
Next to the Town Hall, this is a popular, stone-built pub with split-level public areas, interesting photographs; pub games 🛏 &

Try also: Old Swan (Ansells)

Penarth

11.30–3.30; 5.30–11

Pilot
67 Queens Road ☎ (0222) 702340
Brain Dark, Bitter, SA 🅗
2-bar local in residential area overlooking Cardiff Bay. Well-behaved children welcome at lunchtime Q 🛏 🏠 🍴 & ⇌

11.30–3.30; 5.30–11

Royal Hotel
Queens Road ☎ (0222) 708048
Brain Dark, Bitter; Bullmastiff Ebony Dark, Son Of A Bitch; Welsh Brewers HB 🅗
Comfortable, recently restored hotel in a side street just off the town centre. Darts
🛏 🏠 🍺 & ⇌ (Dingle Rd)

Try also: Albion, Glebe Street (Brain)

Peterston-Super-Ely

11.30–3.30; 6–11

Three Horseshoes
2 miles N A4226/A48 Jct OS085765 ☎ (0446) 760388
Brain Dark, Bitter, SA 🅗
Cosy, traditional 2-bar village local in a quiet corner of the Vale of Glamorgan. Just beyond the outskirts of the city of Cardiff. Darts. Must book for Sun lunch 🔥 Q 🛏 (lunch) 🏠 🍴 🍺 (not Sun) 🍺 & ⛺

Rhoose

12–3; 7 (6 summer)–11

Highwayman
Fonmon ☎ (0446) 710205
Ruddles Best Bitter, County; Webster Yorkshire Bitter 🅗
Large comfortable bar with adjoining restaurant
🔥 🛏 (lunch) 🍴 🍺

Treoes

11.30–3.30; 5.30–11

Star
Off A473 (behind Waterton Industrial Estate) ☎ (0656) 58458
Crown SBB, 1041 🅗
Comfortable thatched village local. Separate dining and games area (table skittles, darts and boules)
🔥 🛏 🏠 🍴 🍺 & (ramps & wc)

KEY TO SYMBOLS

- 🔥 real fire
- Q quiet pub – no electronic music, TV or obtrusive games
- 🛏 indoor room for children
- 🏠 garden or other outdoor drinking area
- 🛌 accommodation
- 🍴 lunchtime meals
- 🍺 evening meals
- 🍺 public bar
- & facilities for the disabled
- ⛺ camping facilities close to the pub or part of the pub grounds
- ⇌ near British Rail station
- ⊖ near Underground station
- ○ real cider

The facilities, beers and pub hours listed in the Good Beer Guide are liable to change but were correct when the Guide went to press.

West Glamorgan

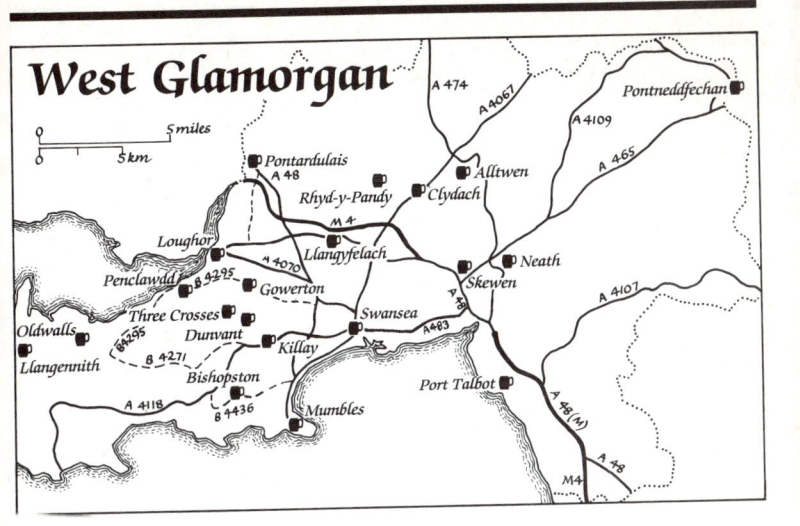

Alltwen

11.30–4; 6–10.30 (11 F, S)

Butchers
Off A474 ☎ (0792) 863100
Everards Old Original H
Well-appointed free house with at least 3 guest beers. Restaurant at rear overlooks Swansea valley ♨☎ (▶

Bishopston

11.30–3; 5.30–10.30 (11 F, S)

Bishopston Valley Hotel
Bishopston Road (off B4436)
☎ (044 128) 42937
Welsh Brewers Dark, BB H
2-bar village pub with friendly atmosphere ☎ ((not Sun) ⊕

Try also: Plough & Harrow (Free)

Clydach

11.30–4; 6–10.30 (11 F, S)

Old Glais
On B4291 ☎ (0792) 843316
Ruddles Best Bitter, County; Webster Yorkshire Bitter H
Friendly village local; pool table in bar, comfortable lounge ☎⊕

Dunvant

11.30–3.30; 5.30–10.30 (11 F, S)

Found Out
Killan Road ☎ (0792) 203596
Flowers IPA, Original H
Pleasant pub, very popular for lunch ☎ (⊕

Gowerton

11.30–4; 6–10.30 (11 F, S)

Berthlwydd
On B4295 W of Gowerton
☎ (0792) 873454
Courage Directors; Felinfoel Double Dragon; John Smith Bitter H
Comfortable 1-roomed pub with restaurant. Pleasant beer garden overlooks Loughor Estuary Q ☎ (▶ ⊕ ≈

11.30–4; 6–10.30 (11 F, S) open all day Tue

Commercial
Station Road ☎ (0792) 873496
Buckley Best Bitter H
Very popular bar, especially Tue. Smart lounge and pleasant outdoor area. Pool, darts, caravan club ☎ (⊕≈

11.30–4; 6–10.30 (11 F, S)

Welcome to Gower
Mount Street (B4295/B4296)
☎ (0792) 872611
Buckley Mild, Best Bitter H
Well-furnished village pub
☎ (⊕≈

Killay

11.30–3.30; 5.30–10.30 (11 F, S)

Railway Inn
Gower Road (A4118)
☎ (0792) 203946
Draught Bass; Welsh Brewers Dark, HB H
Popular 3-roomed former station house, adjacent to Clyne Valley walk ☎⊕

Llangennith

11.30–3.30; 5.30–10.30 (11 F, S)

Kings Head
☎ (044 127) 212
Wadworth 6X H
Pub near seaside with large bar, small lounge, separate electronic games room
Q ☎ ☎ (⊕ ⚒

Llangyfelach

11.30–4; 6–10.30 (11 F, S)

Plough & Harrow
Off Jct 46 M4, on B4489
☎ (0792) 71816
Courage Best Bitter, Directors; John Smith Bitter H
Spacious, comfortable 1-roomed pub with views of Penllergaer Forest ☎ (

Loughor

11.30–4; 6–10.30 (11 F, S)

Red Lion
80 Glebe Road (A4070)
☎ (0792) 892893
Felinfoel Mild, Bitter, Double Dragon H
Rare outlet for Felinfoel real ales in area. Large, comfortable lounge; smaller, locals' bar ☎ (⊕

Mumbles

11.30–3.30; 5.30–10.30 (11 F, S)

Beaufort Arms
Castle Road, Norton
☎ (0792) 404886
Draught Bass; Welsh Brewers Dark, BB H
Atractive village pub 400 yds from coast ♨☎ (▶ (book) ⊕

11.30–3.30; 5.30–10.30 (11 F, S)

Waterloo
2 Western Lane
☎ (0792) 362133
Draught Bass H & G
Seafront pub with friendly atmosphere

11.30–3.30; 5.30–10.30 (11 F, S)

White Rose
1 Newton Road
☎ (0792) 361164
Draught Bass; Welsh Brewers Dark, HB E
Extremely busy pub with consistently good service and good food ☎ (⊕

Neath

11.30–4; 6 (7 Sat)–10.30 (11 F, S)

Three Cranes
55 Wind Street ☎ (0639) 57207
Courage Best Bitter, Directors; John Smith Bitter H

347

West Glamorgan

Busy friendly pub in main shopping area ()⊞&≥

Oldwalls

11.30–3.30; 5.30–10.30 (11 F, S)

Greyhound
☎ (0795) 391027
Draught Bass; Welsh Brewers HB H
True free house: a welcoming atmosphere in pleasant countryside. Guest beers
▲⊛()⊞

Penclawdd

11.30–3.30; 5.30–10.30 (11 F, S)

Royal Oak
On B4295 ☎ (0792) 850642
Welsh Brewers Dark E
Friendly 2-bar village local overlooking Loughor Estuary
⊛()⊞

Pontardulais

11.30–4; 6–10.30 (11 F, S)

Wheatsheaf
St. Teilo Street (A48)
☎ (0792) 882683
Felinfoel Mild, Bitter H
Small popular locals' pub ⊞≥

11.30–4; 6–10.30 (11 F, S)

Farmers Arms
152 St Teilo Street (A48)
☎ (0792) 882450
Draught Bass; Welsh Brewers Dark H
Large friendly pub with live music at weekends ⊛()▶⊞

Pontneddfechan

11.30–4; 6–10.30 (11 F, S)

Angel Hotel
On B4242 ☎ (0639) 722013
Flowers Original H
Attractive country pub at gateway to waterfalls ()⊞

Port Talbot

11.30–4; 6–11

St Oswalds
6 Station Road
☎ (0639) 899200
Crown SBB, 1041 H
Well-appointed, comfortable 1-bar pub with adjoining restaurant ()▶≥

Rhyd-Y-Pandy

11.30–4; 6–10.30 (11 F, S)

Masons Arms
2 miles N of M4 Jct 46
☎ (0792) 842535
Courage Best Bitter H

Isolated pub frequented by DVLC office workers. Pleasant surroundings ▲⊛()

Skewen

11.30–4; 6–10.30 (11 F, S)

Crown
216 New Road
☎ (0792) 813309
Brain Dark, MA, SA H
Regulars' bar and comfortable lounge. Only outlet for MA, a brewery mix of dark and bitter – ask for light ⊞

Swansea

11.30–3.30; 5.30–10.30 (11 F, S)

Adam & Eve
207 High Street ☎ (0792) 55913
Brain Dark, Bitter, SA H
Traditional local unspoilt by modern trends. Certificate of excellence for cellarmanship
⊞≥

11.30–3.30; 5.30–10.30 (11 F, S)

Bryn-Y-Mor
Bryn-Y-Mor Road
☎ (0792) 466650
Ansells Dark Best Bitter; Ind Coope Burton Ale E
Locals' bar with games area; comfortable lounge with live music Sun ⊛()⊞

11.30–3.30; 5.30–10.30 (11 F, S)

Cockett Inn
Waunarlydd Road, Cockett (A4216) ☎ (0792) 582083
Buckley XD Mild, Best Bitter H
Village local with spacious bar and games area ⊛()⊞

11.30–3.30; 5.30–10.30 (11 F, S)

Cricketers
King Edward Road
Ansells Dark, Best Bitter; Ind Coope Burton Ale E
Energetic, young peoples pub with cricketing theme ⊛()

11.30–3.30; 5.30–10.30 (11 F, S)

Duke Hotel
Wind Street ☎ (0792) 54567
Draught Bass; Welsh Brewers Dark, BB H
Locals' bar, usually busy, especially weekends when entrance may be limited
()⊞≥

11.30–3.30; 5.30–10.30 (11 F, S)

Glamorgan Hotel
88 Argyle Street
☎ (0792) 53389
Draught Bass H
Friendly seafront pub; good food in comfortable surroundings ⊛()

11.30–3.30; 5.30–10.30 (11 F, S)

Jersey Arms
On A4067, just N of Swansea
Welsh Brewers Dark E
Lively locals' bar with separate pool room ⊞

11.30–3.30; 5.30–10.30 (11 F, S)

Kings Arms
26 High Street ☎ (0792) 42216
Ruddles Best Bitter, County; Webster Yorkshire Bitter H
Attractive, well-appointed pub near city centre ()≥

11.30–3.30; 5.30–10.30 (11 F, S)

Rhyddings Hotel
Brynmill Avenue, Brynmill
☎ (0792) 466545
Ansells Dark, Best Bitter; Ind Coope Burton Ale H
Attractive turreted building; unusually large airy bar and split-level comfortable lounge. Good food ⊛() (not Sat) ⊞

11.30–3.30; 5.30–10.30 (11 F, S)

Singleton Hotel
1 Dillwyn Street
☎ (0792) 54409
Ruddles Best Bitter, County; Webster Yorkshire Bitter H
Well-appointed pub with separate area for live music (most evenings); beer expensive but entertainment free from around 8.30 ()

11.30–3.30; 5.30–10.30 (11 F, S)

Star Inn
1070 Carmarthen Road, Fforestfach (A4070)
☎ (0792) 586910
Buckley XD Mild, Best Bitter E
Popular local serving nearby industrial estate ⊛()⊞

11.30–3.30; 5.30–10.30 (11 F, S)

Westbourne Hotel
Bryn-Y-Mor Road
☎ (0792) 54952
Draught Bass; Welsh Brewers Dark, HB H
Popular pub with comfortable lounge. Excellent menu ⊛()⊞

Three Crosses

11.30–3.30; 5.30–10.30 (11 F, S)

Joiners
Joiners Road ☎ (0792) 873479
Ruddles Best Bitter, County; Webster Yorkshire Bitter H
Popular village local with pool and darts in bar ⊛()▶⊞

- ▲ real fire
- Q quiet pub – no electronic music, TV or obtrusive games
- ╆ indoor room for children
- ⊛ garden or other outdoor drinking area
- ⨇ accommodation
- () lunchtime meals
- ▶ evening meals
- ⊞ public bar
- & facilities for the disabled
- A camping facilities close to the pub or part of the pub grounds
- ≥ near British Rail station
- ⊖ near Underground station
- ⌀ real cider

The facilities, beers and pub hours listed in the Good Beer Guide are liable to change but were correct when the Guide went to press.

Gwent

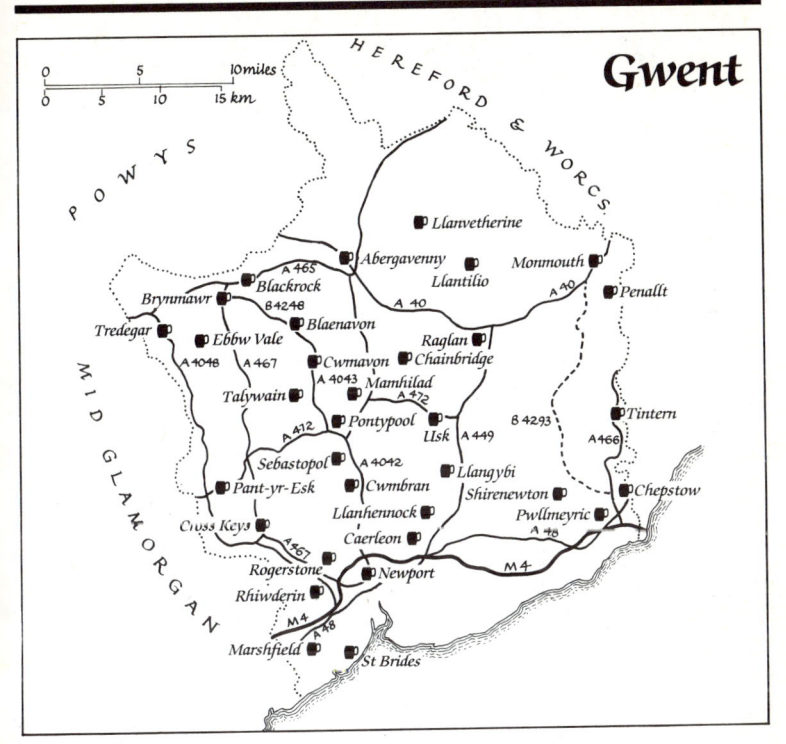

Abergavenny

11–3 (10.30–4 Tue); 6–11

Hen & Chickens Hotel
Flannel Street ☎ (0873) 3613
Draught Bass H
Good old-fashioned pub, a short walk from castle. The doorstep sandwiches are popular lunchtimes. Entrance via the Rotary Club Q ☎ (ask)

10–3; 6–11

Station Hotel
37 Brecon Road (NW of town on A40) ☎ (0873) 4759
**Draught Bass, Brain SA;
Davenports Bitter** H
A great combination of well lived-in comfort, character and a bit of railway nostalgia. Guest beers; pub games

11–3 (4 Tue); 7–11 (6.30 F, S; 6 summer)

Victoria Hotel
Hereford Road ☎ (0873) 3568
Davenports Bitter H
Friendly 1-room pub: functional bar and comfortable lounge areas. Meals are popular. Near cattle market and Bailey Park

Blaenavon

11.30–4; 6.30–11

Cambrian Inn
Llanover Road
☎ (0495) 790327
Brain Bitter, SA E
Traditional local near old mining community. Car park nearby. Pub games Q

Blackrock

12–4.30; 7–11

Old Drum & Monkey
On A465 ☎ (0873) 830542
Draught Bass; Brain Bitter, SA H
Open-plan pub in a small village in the narrow, steep sided Clydach Gorge between Abergavenny and Brynmawr. Carvery Sat nights and Sun lunch

Try also: Rock & Fountain

Brynmawr

11.30–4.30; 6.30–11

Goose & Firkin
33 Bailey Street
☎ (0495) 311171
**Butcombe Bitter; Gales HSB;
Hall & Woodhouse
Tanglefoot** H
Friendly, noisy town pub. Guest beers. Pub games

Try also: Hobby Horse

Caerleon

11.3; 5.30–11

Old Bull Inn
High Street ☎ (0633) 420583
Ansells Dark, Best Bitter; Ind Coope Burton Ale H
15th-century pub in the town square, restored 1983. Plenty of old stonework remains. Close to local Roman sites

11–3; 5.30–11

Rising Sun Inn
Ponthir Road ☎ (0633) 420534
Brain SA H
Snug 17th-century inn with cosy lounge bar and adjoining dining area. A wide range of ales during the year but watch out for up-market prices

Chainbridge

11–3; 6–11

Bridge Inn
On B4598 ☎ (0873) 880243
Davenports Bitter E
Excellent riverside pub with own campsite. Idyllic for outside summer drinking

Chepstow

11–3; 5.30–11

Beaufort Hotel
Saint Mary Street
☎ (029 12) 2497
Draught Bass H
Plush comfortable hotel bar with excellent meals

11–3; 6–11

Coach & Horses
Welsh Street (B4293)
☎ (029 12) 2626

349

Gwent

Brain SA; Ruddles Best Bitter, County; Usher Best Bitter H
Lively free house with warm atmosphere. Split-level bar. Guest beers. Near beginning (or end) of Offa's Dyke
☼ (lunch) ⚭ ◐ (not Sun) ≹

11–3; 5.30–11

White Lion
Bank Street ☎ (029 12) 2854
Draught Bass, Welsh Brewers PA E
Oldest pub in town. 17th-century building includes part of the old Port Wall. Skittles very popular here (alley doubles as family room)
Q ☼ ⚇ ◐ ⊞ ≹

Cross Keys

12–4.30; 7–11

Eagle
High Street (400 yds off A467) ☎ (0495) 270643
Draught Bass; Welsh Brewers PA, HB H
Friendly valley local popular with rugby enthusiasts. Pub games Q ◐ ▶ ⊞ ♣

Cwmavon

12–4; 6–11

Westlakes Arms
On A4043 ☎ (0495) 772123
Draught Bass; Brain Bitter; Robinson Best Bitter; Shepherd Neame Master Brew Bitter H
A superb little local with interesting paraphernalia. Guest beers. Gwent CAMRA Pub of the Year 1987. Pub games Q ⚇ ◐ ▶ ⊞

Cwmbran

11–3; 5.30–11

Blinkin' Owl
Henllys Way, Coed Eva ☎ (063 33) 4749
Brain Dark, Bitter, SA H
An established favourite in the area: modern estate pub with standard bar facilities and quiet lounge
Q ☼ ⚇ ◐ ▶ ⊞ ⚒

11–3; 7(6 S)–11

Bush Inn
Graig Road, Upper Cwmbran ☎ (063 33) 3764
Courage Best Bitter; John Smith Bitter H
Charming hillside pub overlooking Cwmbran. Homely lounge bar in which to relax; candlelit in evenings, warm fires in winter. Worth a detour ⚏ ☼ ⚇ ◐ ▶ (book)

11–3; 5.30–11

Crows Nest
Llangorse Road, Llanyravon (off A4042) ☎ (063 33) 4404
Draught Bass; Welsh Brewers HB, BB H
Large estate pub in pleasant residential area. Basic bar, skittle alley/bar and open-plan lounge. Boules also available. Family room ☼ ⚇ ◐ ⊞

11–3; 5.30–11

Upper Cock Inn
The Highway, Croesyceiliog (alongside A4042) ☎ (063 33) 3218
Ansells Best Bitter; Ind Coope Burton Ale H
Smart roadside inn attracting passing trade and locals. Spacious lounge includes dining area. Short drive from Llandegvedd reservoir ◐ ▶ ⊞

Ebbw Vale

12–4.30; 7–11

Beaufort Arms
Beaufort Road
Courage Best Bitter H
Large friendly valley pub, recently decorated in traditional style. On the outskirts of town ⚇ ◐ ▶ ⊞ ⚒

Llangibby

11–3; 6–11

White Hart Inn
On B4596 ☎ (063 349) 258
Marston Pedigree; Theakston Best Bitter H
Comfortable coaching inn built 12–14th century as a monastery. Originally formed part of Jane Seymour's wedding dowry to Henry VIII. Bar meals, and grill room-restaurant
⚏ Q ☼ ⚇ ⚭ ◐ (book Sun) ▶ ⚒

Llanhennock

11–3; 5.30–11

Wheatsheaf Inn
1 mile off B4596 ☎ (0633) 420468
Draught Bass; Welsh Brewers BB; Samuel Smith OBB H
Traditional country pub in attractive rural surroundings. Pub games ⚏ Q ⚇ ⊞ ♣

Llantilio Crossenny

12–3; 6–11

Hostry Inn
Off B4233 ☎ (060 085) 278
Draught Bass; Smiles Best Bitter, Exhibition H
Excellent 15th-century village pub with good food (including vegetarian). Situated on Offa's Dyke path
☼ ⚭ ◐ ▶ ⚒

Llanvetherine

12–3; 6–11

Kings Arms
On B4521 ☎ (087 386) 221
Ruddles County; Usher Best Bitter H
Rustic local with cheery wood stove. Offa's Dyke path and White Castle nearby. Home cooking ⚏ Q ☼ (till 8) ⚇ ◐ ▶

Mamhilad

11–3; 5.30–11

Horseshoe Inn
2 miles from A4042 ☎ (0873) 880542
Brain Bitter; Felinfoel Double Dragon; Flowers Original H
Former staging post for the Royal Mail, close to Monmouth and Brecon canal. Restaurant ⚏ ⚇ ◐ ▶

Marshfield

11.30–3; 5.30–11

Port o'Call
Marshfield Road, 2 miles S of A48 ☎ (0633) 680171
Courage Best Bitter H; **Directors** G **and** H; **John Smith Bitter** H
Solitary pub with a welcoming atmosphere and excellent meals. Family room separate from the pub. Games
☼ ⚇ ◐ ▶ ⊞

Monmouth

11–3 (4 M, F & S); 6–11

Punch House
Agincourt Square ☎ (0600) 3855
Draught Bass; Wadworth 6X; Welsh Brewers BB H
Historic pub overlooking the town square, justly famous for the substantial meals served in the upstairs restaurant
Q ☼ ⚇ ◐ ▶ ♣

11–3; 6–11

Queens Head Hotel
St James Street (next to A449) ☎ (0600) 2767
Draught Bass; Flowers IPA H
Built circa 1630. Comfortable lounge: part of ceiling covered with leather. Small bar with pool table. Guest beers
☼ ⚭ ◐ ▶ ⊞

Newport

11–3; 5.30–11

Riverside Tavern
Clarence Place (next to bridge) ☎ (0633) 67499
Courage Best Bitter, Directors H
Modern nautical theme pub with views of Newport Castle and the River Usk. Popular with the younger set ⚇ ◐ ≹

11.30–3; 7–11

Black Horse
Somerton Road ☎ (0633) 273058
Ansells Best Bitter H
Popular local, a goal kick from Newport County football ground. Once run by 3-times county manager, Billy Lucas. The pub still has strong links with the club ⚇ ◐ ▶ ⊞

11–3; 5.30–11

Globe Inn

Gwent

32 Chepstow Road (A48)
☎ (0633) 213062
Courage Best Bitter H
Quiet local in heart of
Maindee shopping area Q ⌂ ✿ ⌑

1–3; 5.30–11
Lyceum Tavern
110 Malpas Road (near M4 Jct
26) ☎ (0633) 858636
**Courage Best Bitter,
Directors** H
Popular local. Folk music Thu
✿ ⌑

11.30–3; 6.30–11
Orange Tree
25 St. Michael's Street,
Pillgwenlly ☎ (0633) 58569
Brain SA; Taylor Landlord H
Real ale mecca off main road to
docks. Live music on Tue ⌑

11–3; 5.30–11
Simpson's
12–13 High Street
☎ (0633) 67801
Flowers Original H
Decorative bar in town centre.
Bedecked in greenery,
mirrors, and signs depicting
Newport's past. Live music
some eves. Upstairs lounge
open weekends only
⌂ (ask) ⇌

Pant-Yr-Esk

11.30–4.30; 7–11
Pant-Yr-Esk Inn
Pant-Yr-Esk Road OS202956
Crown SBB H
The proverbial gem; the pub
that time forgot Q ⌑

Penallt

11–3; 6–11
Boat
Lone Lane (off A466)
☎ (0600) 2615
**Greene King Abbot Ale;
Marston Pedigree; Taylor
Landlord; Theakston Best
Bitter, Old Peculier;
Wadworth 6X** G
Small friendly pub on the
bank of the River Wye. Live
music – folk and jazz nights.
Good value food. The only
pub in Wales with its car park
in England ⌂ ⌂ ✿ ⌑ ⌂

Pontypool

11.30–4; 7–11
George Hotel
Commercial Street
☎ (049 55) 4734
**Courage Best Bitter, Directors;
John Smith Bitter** H
Popular single-room
Victorian-style pub in town
centre, featuring pictures on
the 'George' theme. Dining
room upstairs. Favoured by
young. Near Pontypool park
⌂ ⇌ ⌑

Pwllmeyric

11–3; 5.30–11
New Inn
On A48, just W of Chepstow
☎ (029 12) 2670
**Draught Bass E; Flowers IPA;
Usher Best Bitter** H
Large old coaching inn with
atmospheric lounge,
comfortable bar, genial host.
Well worth a visit
⌂ Q ⌂ ✿ ⌑ ⌂

Raglan

11–3; 7–11
Crown Inn
Usk Road ☎ (0291) 690232
Flowers IPA, Original H
Welcoming village local
convenient for Raglan Castle
✿ ⌑

Try also: Ship

Rhiwderin

11–3; 5.30–11
Rhiwderin Inn
Caerphilly Road (A468)
☎ (0633) 893234
**Draught Bass; Welsh Brewers
BB, HB** H
Comfortable local with family
room ✿ ⌂

Rogerstone

11–3; 6–11
Tredegar Arms
Cefn Road
**Courage Best Bitter, Directors;
John Smith Bitter** H
Busy, comfortable pub on the
old main valleys road
✿ ⌑ (Mon–Fri) ⌂

Sebastopol

11.30–3; 6–11
Open Hearth
Wern Road (off A4051)
☎ (049 55) 3752
**Boddingtons Bitter; Courage
Best Bitter; Davenports Bitter;
Marston Pedigree** H
A friendly oasis by the Brecon
and Monmouth canal. Cosy
tree house and restaurant. A
varied range of guest beers
Q ✿ ⌑ ⌂

Shirenewton

11–3; 7–11
Tredegar Arms
☎ (029 17) 274
**Smiles Best Bitter; Wadworth
6X; Welsh Brewers PA** H
Welcoming village inn with
renowned selection of malt
whiskies. Guest beers
Families welcome if eating
⌂ ⌂ ✿ ⌑ ⌂

Try also: Carpenters

St Brides Wentlooge

11–3; 5.30 (6.30 winter)–11
Church House Inn
On B4239 ☎ (0633) 680807

Brain Dark, Bitter, SA H
Old country pub with lounge,
speparate children's room, and
pleasant garden. Pub games
⌂ ✿ ⌑ ⌂

Talywain

12–4; 6.30–11
Globe
Commercial Road (B4246)
☎ (0495) 772053
Brain Dark, Bitter H
A friendly local. Check lunch
opening times midweek. Pub
games ⌂ ✿ ⌂

Tintern

11–3; 7–11
Cherry Tree
Devauden Road (off A466)
Welsh Brewers PA G
Small cosy local, untouched by
the passage of time ⌂ Q ⌂ ✿ ⌂

Tredegar

12–4.30; 7–11
Cambrian Hotel
The Circle ☎ (0495) 711107
**Brain Bitter, SA; Courage Best
Bitter** E
Busy pub in town centre
⌂ ✿ ⇌ ⌑

Usk

11–3; 5.30–11
Kings Head
Old Market Street
☎ (029 13) 2963
**Brain SA; Flowers Original;
Tetley Bitter** H
Large comfortable pub with
impressive fireplace in lounge,
pool table in bar ⌂ ⇌ ⌑ ⌂

12–2 (not Mon/Tue); 6.30–11
Olway
800 yds from square on old
Chepstow Rd ☎ (029 13) 2047
**Davenports Bitter; Felinfoel
Double Dragon** H
Small friendly pub with
excellent food ⌂ Q ✿ ⌑ ⌂

Help keep real ale alive by
joining CAMRA Your voice
helps encourage brewers big
and small to brew cask beer
and offer all beer drinkers a
better choice.

351

Gwynedd

Gwynedd

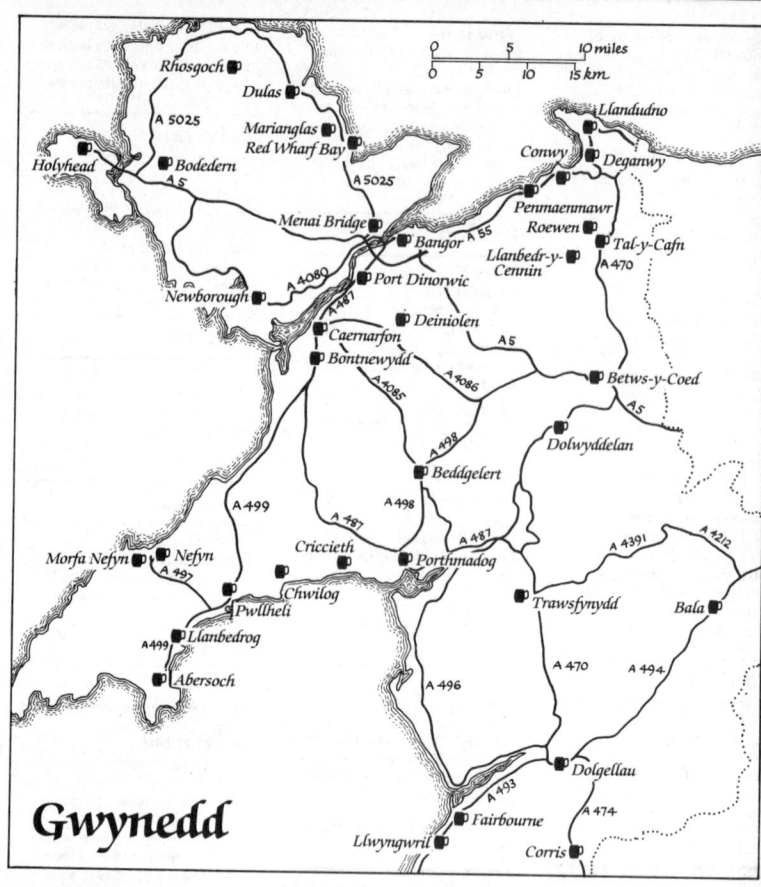

* closed all day Sunday

Abersoch

11–3; 5.30–10.30 (11 summer F,S)
St Tudwal's Hotel*
Main Street ☎ (075 881) 2539
Robinson Best Mild E, **Best Bitter** H, **Old Tom** G
Friendly pub with excellent accommodation and meals. Near beautiful beach. Pub games ♨ Q ざ ⊛ ⋈ ◑ ▶ ⊖ & Å

Bala

11–3; 6–10.30 (11 summer F,S)
White Lion Royal Hotel
66 High Street (A494)
☎ (0678) 520314
Younger No.3 H
Welcoming residential hotel. Comfortable lounge bar, with beamed ceilings and inglenook. The smaller Poachers Bar has adjacent pool room. Traditional Welsh cooking ♨ ざ ⊛ ⋈ ◑ ▶ ⊖ &

Bangor

11–3; 5.30–10.30 (11 summer F,S)

Union Hotel
Garth Road (off A5)
☎ (0248) 2462
Burtonwood Bitter H
Backing onto a bay near Bangor pier. Various small rooms with collections of glass, china, brass & copper
ざ ⊛ ⋈ ◑ ⇌

11–3; 5.30–10.30 (11 summer F,S)
White Lion
289 High Street
☎ (0248) 353394
Draught Bass; M & B Mild H
Friendly 1-room pub in Bangor centre. Good reasonably priced food and excellent beer ◑ ⇌

Beddgelert

11–3; 5.30–10.30 (11 summer F,S)
Prince Llewelyn Hotel*
A498 by river bridge
☎ (076 686) 242
Robinson Best Mild, Best Bitter E
Comfortable hotel in picturesque mountain village. Peaceful atmosphere and good food ♨ ざ ⊛ ⋈ ◑ ▶ ⊖ & Å

Betws-y-Coed

11–3 (summer & winter Sat); 6–11
Pont-y-Pair Hotel
On A5 opposite bridge on Trefriw Road ☎ (069 02) 407
Younger Scotch Bitter, IPA, No.3 H
Small, stone-built hotel with island lounge bar, family room and games area. Quizzes, live music, bingo ♨ ざ ⊛ ⋈ ◑ (Sat, Sun & summer) ▶ Å ⇌

Bodedern

11–3.30; 6–10.30 (11 summer F,S)
Crown Hotel
B5109, 1 mile off A5025
☎ (0407) 740734
Burtonwood Bitter H
Fine example of a village pub with accommodation, popular with locals and visitors alike. Good range of reasonably priced food. Pub games
♨ ざ ⊛ ⋈ ◑ ▶ ⊖

Bontnewydd

11–3; 5.30–10.30 (11 summer F,S)

352

Gwynedd

Newborough Arms
Main Street (A487)
☎ (0286) 3126
Ansells Mild, Bitter; Ind Coope Burton Ale; Tetley Bitter H
Popular riverside local with excellent food and friendly service ▲❀⬛ ( ) ⊞ ▲

Caernarfon

11–3; 5.30–10.30 (11 summer F,S)

Alexandra
North Road ☎ (0286) 2871
M & B Mild, Draught Bass H
Suburban local on outskirts, with home-made food; good value accommodation; views across to Anglesey
Q ❀⬛ ⊞ ⇌

11–3; 5.30–10.30 (11 summer F,S)

Palace Vaults
Castle Ditch (opposite Castle)
☎ (0286) 2093
Marston Burton Bitter, Pedigree, Owd Rodger (winter) H
Busy pub, modernised in neo-Victorian style, with library, old posters and prints. Good food Q ⬛ ⬥ ⚓

Try also: Anglesey (Marston)

Chwilog

11–3; 5.30–10.30 (11 summer F,S)

Madryn Arms*
High Street (A4354)
☎ (076 668) 250
Burtonwood Dark Mild, Bitter H
120 year-old pub of character. Lively local trade and popular with Butlins holidaymakers. Good bar meals. Family room
▲ ❀⬛ ⬥ ⚓ ▲

Conwy

11–3; 5.30–11 (11 summer F,S)

Albion Vaults
Upper Castle Street
☎ (019 263) 2494
Ind Coope Bitter; Tetley Mild, Bitter H
Town centre pub with rooms in 3 different styles and wood burning stoves ▲❀⬛⊞

Corris

11–3; 6–10.30 (11 F,S)

Slater's Arms
Lower Corris (off A487)
Banks's Mild, Bitter E
2-room pub with outside toilets, real fire and piano, in this tiny, former slating community. YHA hostel nearby ▲Q⊞

Criccieth

11–3; 5.30–10.30 (11 summer F,S)

Castle[d]
Station Square
☎ (076 671) 2624
Draught Bass; Stones Best Bitter H
Warm, friendly, popular town pub by the station. Cosy lounge. Meals in summer only. Pub games
▲ ❀⬛ ⬥ ⊞ ⚓ ▲ ⇌

Try also: Brynhir Arms (Greenall)

Deganwy

11–3; 5.30–11

Farmers Arms
Towyn Hill (off the Conwy–Deganwy Road)
☎ (0492) 83197
Ansells Mild; Ind Coope Bitter, Burton Ale; Tetley Bitter H
Busy, roomy pub decorated with old farming implements. Pub games ▲❀⬛ ⬥ ⊞⚓⇌

Deiniolen

11–3; 5.30–10.30 (11 summer F,S)

Bull Inn
High Street (1 mile off B4547)
☎ (0286) 870231
Greenall Whitley Mild, Bitter H
Pleasant, popular pub with mountain views. Inexpensive snacks. Friendly staff and good community spirit. Pub games Q❀⬛⬥⊞⚓▲

Dolgellau

10.30–3 (4 F); 6–10.30 (11 F,S)

Stag
Bridge Street
Burtonwood Dark Mild, Bitter H
Lively 1-roomed town pub with larger-than-life landlord. The by-pass has helped recover its timeless Welsh character ▲❀⬛⊞⚓

Dolwyddelan

11–3 (12–2.30 winter); 6–10.30 (11 summer F,S)

Gwydyr
On A470 ☎ (069 06) 209
Banks's Bitter H
Village pub with cosy bar and good atmosphere, on Llandudno Junction to Blaenau Ffestiniog rail route ▲❀⚓⬛⊞⚓⇌

Dulas

11 (winter 11.30)–3.30; 6 (winter 7)–10.30 (11 summer F,S)

Pilot Boat
On A5025 ☎ (024 888) 205
Robinson Best Mild, Best Bitter E
Old country pub with low-beamed bar, stone fireplace and nautical items – bar front is a small wooden boat. Smart lounge and separate pool room. Good value food
▲❀⬛⬥⊞▲

Fairbourne

10–3; 6–10.30 (11 F,S)

Fairbourne Hotel
Off A493, 100 yards from station ☎ (0341) 250203
Draught Bass; McEwan 70/-; Younger IPA H
300 year-old hotel standing in own grounds. Excellent food in lounge bar; separate restaurant. Games room
▲❀⬛⚓⬥⊞⚓▲⇌

Holyhead

11–3.30; 6–10.30 (11 summer F,S)

Boston
London Road (A5)
☎ (0407) 2449
Ansells Mild; Ind Coope Bitter H
Busy open-plan local on the outskirts of town, with separate areas for pool, darts and small lounge ⊞⇌

Llanbedrog

11–3; 5.30–10.30 (11 summer F,S)

Glyn-y-Weddw Arms*
Lower Village ☎ (0758) 240212
Robinson Best Mild, Best Bitter E, **Old Tom (winter)** G
One of the most popular pubs on Lleyn Peninsula, with pleasant outside seating area near sheltered beach
▲❀⬛⬥⊞⚓▲

11–3; 5.30–10.30 (11 summer F,S)

Ship*
Bryn-y-Gro (B4413)
☎ (0758) 740270
Burtonwood Dark Mild, Bitter H
Cosy, friendly old pub very popular with visitors. Food good. 2 bars and sunny garden area. Pub games
▲Q❀⬛⬥⊞⚓▲

Llanbedr-y-Cennin

11.30 (12 winter Mon–Fri)–3; 6–11

Olde Bull Inn
About ½ mile off B5106
☎ (049 269) 508
Lees GB Mild, Bitter H
Lovely old Welsh inn with magnificent views of the Conwy Valley and mountains beyond. Cosy dining-room has timbers from an Armada wreck. Extensive menu and comfortable accommodation
▲❀⬛⚓⬥⊞▲

Llandudno

11–3; 7 (5.30 summer)–11

Kings Arms
17 Mostyn Street
☎ (0492) 75882
Ansells Mild; Ind Coope Burton Ale; Tetley Bitter H
Large 1-room pub with wooden floorboards. Walls decorated with old motoring

353

Gwynedd

signs. Guest beers
⌂⊛◐▮ (summer) ♿⇌

11.30–3; 5.30–11
London Hotel
131 Upper Mostyn Street
☎ (0492) 75515
Burtonwood Bitter 🅗
Unusual design. London theme includes an old red telephone box inside. Folk club each Sun
⌂⋈ (summer) ♿

12–3; 7–11
Snowdon Hotel
11 Tudno Street
☎ (0492) 76740
Draught Bass 🅗
Large open-plan lounge with a section reserved for the RNLI. Original large Victorian etched window. Small public bar
Q (TV occasionally) ⋈ ◐♿

Try also: Cottage Loaf (Free); **Kings Head** (Allied); **Links Hotel** (Lees)

Llwyngwril

11.30–3; 6–10.30 (11 summer F,S)
Garthangarad
On A493 ☎ (0341) 250240
Banks's Mild, Bitter 🅔
Old pub of character in small coastal village. Good food; pleasant, friendly atmosphere
Q⌂⋈◐▮♿⇌

Marianglas

11–3.30; 6–10.30 (11 summer F,S)
Parciau Arms
On B5110 ☎ (0248) 853766
Banks's Bitter; Draught Bass 🅗
Welcoming pub in own grounds. Comfortable lounge, family dining room and separate public bar. Well-equipped play area
⌂⊛◐▮♿

Menai Bridge

11–3.30; 6–10.30 (11 summer F,S)
Liverpool Arms
St Georges Pier (off A545)
☎ (0248) 712453
Greenall Whitley Bitter, Original 🅗
Comfortable, interesting old pub with 2 cosy bars. Separate lounge; sun-trap conservatory. Good food and fine wines Q⌂⊛◐▮♿

Morfa Nefyn

11–3; 6–10.30 (11 summer F,S)
Cliffs Inn*
Beach Road ☎ (0758) 720356
Whitbread Castle Eden Ale 🅗
Welcoming pub, highly recommended for bar meals. Lovely position by sea
⌂⊛⋈◐▮♿

Nefyn

11–3; 5.30–10.30 (11 summer F,S)

Sportsman*
Stryd Fawr (B4417)
☎ (0758) 720205
Ind Coope Bitter, Burton Ale 🅗
Friendly pub, popular with visitors and locals. Celebrations on saints days. Huge wood fire
⌂Q⊛◐▮♿

Newborough

11 (12 winter)–3.30; 6 (6.30 winter)–10.30 (11 summer F,S)
White Lion
Malltraeth Street (A4080)
☎ (024 879) 236
Marston Mercian Mild; Burton Bitter 🅗
Friendly local pub in a small village near Anglesey's south coast. Small lounge and fairly spartan bar. Pub games ⊛♿

Penmaenmawr

11–3; 5.30–11
Alexandra
High Street (A55 towards Bangor) ☎ (0492) 622484
Ansell's Mild; Draught Bass; M & B Mild 🅗
1-bar, no-frills, friendly local, small snug, pool room and lounge. Sea view from back window ♿

11–3; 5.30–11
Bron Eryri
Bangor Road (A55)
☎ (0492) 622211
Marston Mercian Mild; Burton Bitter; Pedigree 🅗
Village pub with basic bar and comfortable lounge ⊛♿⇌

Try also: Mountain View (Allied)

Port Dinorwic

11.30–3; 5.30–10.30 (11 summer F,S)
Gardd Fôn
Beach Road (off A487)
☎ (0248) 670359
Burtonwood Bitter 🅗
Small local pub situated on the Menai Strait. Unofficial home of the local sailing club
⌂⊛◐▮♿

Porthmadog

11–3; 5.30–10.30 (11 summer F,S)
Queens Hotel*
Station Road ☎ (0766) 2583
Burtonwood Dark Mild, Bitter 🅗
Large residential hotel with mountain views from bedrooms. Comfortable with warm welcome
⌂⊛⋈◐▮♿⇌

Try also: Station Buffet (Bass)

Pwllheli

11–3; 5.30–10.30 (11 summer F,S)
Penlan Fawr*

Penlan Street (100 yds from station) ☎ (0492) 612486
Ind Coope Bitter; Tetley Bitter 🅗
Old pub popular with young. Tasty bar meals; barbecue area for families. Pub games
⌂⌂⊛◐▮♿⇌

Try also: Victoria (Free)

Red Wharf Bay

11 (12 winter)–3.30; 6 (7 winter)–10.30 (11 summer F,S)
Ship
1 mile off A5025
☎ (0248) 852568
Banks's Bitter; Tetley Bitter 🅗
Pub of character, almost on the beach, with wood beamed ceilings, flagged floors and stone fireplaces. Superb food.
⌂⌂⋈ (S/C) ◐▮♿

Rhosgoch

11–3.30; 6–10.30 (11 summer F,S)
Rhosgoch Hotel (The Ring)
2 miles off B5111
☎ (0407) 830720
Stones Best Bitter 🅗
Hospitable country pub with friendly atmosphere. Good-value food; community singing Fri and Sat. "Last orders" rung on Anglesey's biggest ship's bell
⌂Q⌂⊛◐▮♿

Roewen

11–3; 6.30–11
Ty Gwyn
1 mile off B5106 (Conway Valley Road) OS759720
☎ (0492)650232
Lees GB Mild, Bitter 🅗
Old Welsh inn in quiet backwater in foothills of Snowdonia National Park. Featured in TV "Home-Brew" series ⌂Q⌂⊛⋈◐▮♿

Tal-y-Cafn

12–3; 7–11
Tal-y-Cafn Hotel
Llanwrst Road (A470)
☎ (0492) 650203
Greenall Whitley Bitter 🅗
Comfortably furnished bar with low beams; wide range of food and garden with play area. Near Llandudno Junction – Blaenau Ffestiniog Railway
⌂⋈ (Easter–Oct) ◐▮⇌

Trawsfynydd

10.30–3; 6–10.30 (11 summer F,S)
White Lion
Main Street (off A470)
☎ (076 687) 277
Burtonwood Dark Mild, Bitter 🅗
Cosy, unspoilt village pub in lovely mountain area. Pub games ⌂Q⌂⊛⋈◐▮♿

354

Powys

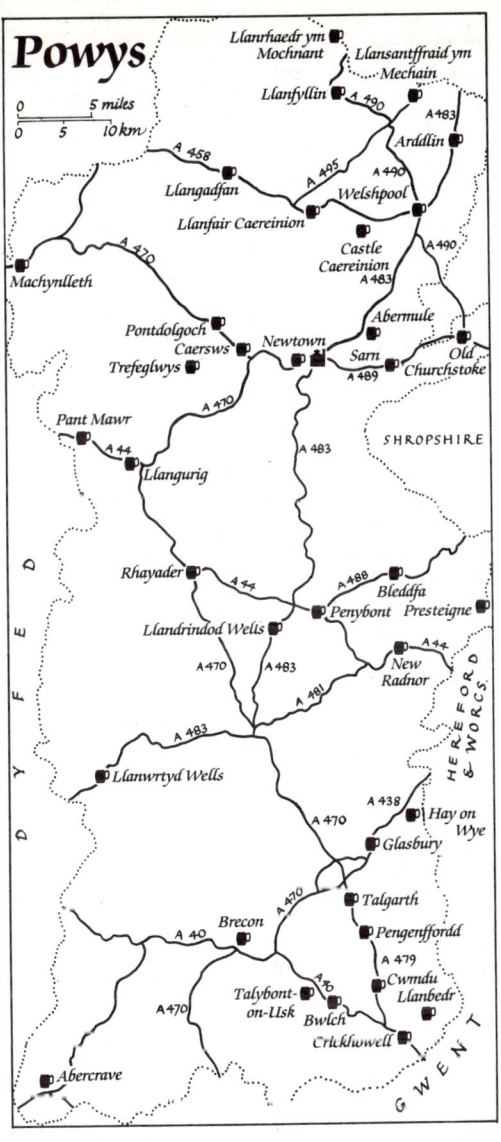

and Offa's Dyke. Guest beers in summer. Games

Bleddfa

11–3; 6–11

Hundred House
On A488 ☎ (054 781) 225
Marston Pedigree; Wood's Special
Comfortable village pub with several rooms and a restaurant. Guest beers. Darts

Brecon

11–3; 5.30–11

Gremlin Hotel
The Watton (A40)
☎ (0874) 3829
Draught Bass; Everards Old Original; Robinson Best Bitter; Wadworth 6X
Roadside pub with comfortable lounge. Very busy and popular, particularly eves Games include quoits

11–3; 5.30–11 (all day Tue & Fri)

Olde Boars Head
Ship Street, Watergate (A40)
☎ (0874) 2856
Draught Bass; Boddingtons Bitter; Courage Directors; Davenports Bitter; Fuller ESB; Wadworth 6X
Popular roadside pub with busy front bar, and comfortable lounge serving light lunches. Car park has seats overlooking river with views of Brecon Beacons

Bwlch

12–3; 7–11

Morning Star Inn
On A40 ☎ (0874) 730080
Courage Best Bitter, Directors
Small welcoming roadside pub. Excellent meals and snacks in a separate eating area. Very friendly, good service

Try also: Coach & Horses, Llangynidr

Caersws

11–2.30; 7–11

Red Lion
3 Main Street (off A470)
☎ (068 684) 606
Tetley Bitter
Comfortable 2-bar village local with a warm welcome for tourists

Castle Caereinion

11–3; 6–11

Red Lion
Off A458 ☎ (093 883) 233
Wood's Parish Bitter
Well modernised village pub, ½ mile from narrow gauge

Powell, Newtown

Abercrave

12–4; 6–11

Copper Beech
Off A4067 ☎ (0639) 730269
Courage Best Bitter; Theakston XB
Excellent pub in fine setting. Good food always available. Guest beers

Abermule

11–2.30; 6–11

Abermule Hotel
On B4386 ☎ (068 686) 273
Marston Pedigree; Tetley Bitter
Well-kept 2-bar village local

Arddlin

11–3; 5.30–11

Horseshoe
A483/B4392 ☎ (093 875) 318
Marston Burton Bitter, Pedigree
Well-restored pub on canal

355

Powys

railway station. Guest beers in summer. Games
⌂ ☼ ⊛ ⋈ ( ) ⇌ (summer)

Crickhowell

11–3; 6–11

Bear
Beaufort Street (A40)
☎ (0873) 810408
Draught Bass; Ruddles County; Webster Yorkshire Bitter H
A 15th-century coaching inn on the main square. A comfortable bar with good food and à la carte restaurant
⌂ Q ☼ ⊛ ⋈ ( ) (until 10) ⊕

Try also: Bridge End

Cwmdu

11–3; 6–11

Farmers Arms
On A479 6 miles S of Talgarth
☎ (0874) 730464
Brain SA; Wadworth 6X; Younger IPA H
Friendly busy country pub; families welcome. Large wholesome meals a speciality
⌂ ☼ ⊛ ⋈ ( ) ⊕ Å ⌀

Glasbury

11–3; 6–11

Harp Inn
On B4350 ☎ (049 74) 373
Flowers IPA, Original; Robinson Best Bitter H
Busy pub overlooking the Wye. A warm welcome for families ⌂ Q ☼ ⊛ ⋈ ( ) ⊕ &

Hay on Wye

11–3; 7–11 (all day Thu)

Blue Boar
Castle Street ☎ (0497) 820884
Flowers IPA, Original H
Traditional pub with comfortable, no-frills public bar ⌂ Q ☼ ( ) ⊕ ⌀

Try also: Kilvert

Llanbedr

12–3; 6.30–11

Red Lion
☎ (0873) 810754
Draught Bass; Welsh Brewers BB H
Friendly country pub, an ideal watering-hole after a day on the mountains. Children's room ⌂ Q ☼ ⊛ ( ) Å

Try also: Dragons Head, Llangenny

Llandrindod Wells

11.30–3; 6–11

Llanerch Inn
Waterloo Road (behind police station) ☎ (0597) 2086
Draught Bass; Robinson Best Bitter; Welsh Brewers BB H
Comfortable 16th-century coaching inn. Boules played
☼ ⊛ ⋈ ((12–2)) (6–9) ⇌

Llanfair Caereinion

11–3; 6–11

Goat Hotel
High Street ☎ (0938 810) 428
Felinfoel Double Dragon; Welsh Brewers HB H
Comfortable old pub of great character. Excellent accommodation. Games
⌂ ☼ ⊛ ⋈ ( )

11–3; 6–11

Wynnstay Hotel
☎ (0938 810) 203
Ansells Mild; Marston Pedigree; Tetley Bitter H
Friendly old pub with pub games ⌂ ( ) ⊕

Try also: Black Lion

Llanfyllin

11–3; 5.30–11

Cain Valley Hotel
High Street (A490)
☎ (069 184) 366
Draught Bass; Marston Burton Bitter, Pedigree H
Superb 17th-century coaching inn ⌂ Q ⋈ ( ) ⊕

Llangadfan

12–3; 7–11

Cann Office Hotel
On A458 ☎ (093 888) 202
Marston Pedigree H
Large, well-kept pub with fishing rights. Mainly Welsh speaking. Pub games
⌂ ⊛ ⋈ ( ) ⊕ Å

Llangurig

10.30–2.30; 5.30–11

Blue Bell
On A44 ☎ (055 15) 254
Flowers Original; Sam Powell Original Bitter H
16th-century hotel with fine slate-floored bar and inglenook; pool room, 2 dining rooms and a family room ⌂ Q ☼ ⋈ ( ) ⊕ & Å

Llanrhaedr Ym Mochnant

7–11

Plough
On B4580
Draught Bass G
Totally unspoilt small village pub. Games ⌂ Q

Llansantffraid Ym Mechain

11.30–3; 6.30–11

Sun
On A495 ☎ (069 181) 214
Marston Border Mild, Border Bitter, Pedigree H
Friendly village pub with good restaurant ⊛ ⋈ ( ) ⊕

Llanwrtyd Wells

11–3; 6–11

Neuadd Arms Hotel
On A483 ☎ (059 13) 236
Felinfoel Double Dragon; Greene King Abbot H
Traditional, comfortable hotel with 3 log fires. Near the Cambrian mountains, it is famous for its walking weekends, also for "bog snorkelling" and the Mid-Wales beer festival in Nov
⌂ ☼ ⊛ ⋈ ( ) ⊕ Å ⇌

Machynlleth

11.30–2.30 (4 Wed); 5.30–10.30 (11 F, S & summer)

Skinners Arms
Main Street (A487)
☎ (0654) 2354
Burtonwood Bitter H
Wood-beamed town centre pub with a comfortable lounge and friendly atmosphere. Public bar has rock concert memorabilia
⌂ ☼ (upstairs) ( ) ⊕ & ⇌

New Radnor

11–3; 6–11

Radnor Arms Hotel
Broad Street (B4372)
☎ (054 421) 232
Flowers IPA H
Bustling modernised pub in the centre of the village. Family room. Guest beers
⌂ ☼ ( ) ⊕ & Å

Newtown

11–2.30; 5–11 (all day Tue)

Pheasant
Market Street ☎ (0686) 27054
Burtonwood Bitter H
Friendly, timbered old pub with a separate children's room and a games room. Public bar has walking sticks collection ⌂ ☼ ⊛ ( ) ⇌

11–2.30; 5–11 (all day Tue)

Sportsman
Severn Street (off A483)
☎ (0686) 25885
Ansells Mild; Ind Coope Burton Ale; Minera Sportsman Special Bitter; Tetley Bitter H
Comfortable, modernised town-centre local with original beams. Games area. Friendly lively atmosphere
Q ⇌

10.30–2.30; 5.30–11 (all day Tue)

Wagon & Horses
Lower Canal Road (off B4568)
☎ (0686) 25790
Marston Border Exhibition, Pedigree H
Pleasant edge-of-town locals' pub with separate games room. Pub stands by former Shropshire Union Canal basin
⊛ ⊕ & (ramps)

Powys

Old Churchstoke

11–2.30; 6–10.30 (11 F, S & summer)

Oak Inn
Off A489 ☎ (058 85) 574
Sam Powell Original Bitter H
Delightful small, stone-walled, wooden-beamed 16th-century inn. Occasional live music and games room in outbuilding
🏠 ☎ 🍴 ( ) 🍺

Pant Mawr

10.30–2.30; 6.30–11

Glansevern Arms
On A44, 4½ miles W of Llangurig ☎ (055 15) 240
Draught Bass H
2 impeccable, quiet, comfortable bars in hotel high up in the Wye Valley. Must book for meals 🏠 Q ⇌ ( )

Pengenffordd

11–3; 6–11

Castle Inn
On A479 3 miles S of Talgarth ☎ (0874) 711353
Wadworth 6X H
Friendly country local, popular with trekkers and walkers, high up in the heart of the Black Mountains
🏠 ☎ 🍴 ( ) 🍺 A

Penybont

11–3; 6–11

Severn Arms Hotel
On A44 ☎ (059 787) 224
Draught Bass H
Large hotel with fishing rights. Traditional bar adorned with farming bric a brac and sporting trophies. Quoits played
🏠 ☎ 🍴 ⇌ ( ) 🍺 A

Pontdolgoch

11–2.30; 6–11

Mytton Arms
A489, 1 mile outside Caersws ☎ (0686) 848919
Sam Powell Original Bitter, Samson H
17th-century coaching inn, now a comfortable pub with bright modern interior but a traditional feel. Games room
🏠 ☎ 🍴 ( ) 🍺

Presteigne

11–3; 7–11

Farmers Arms
Hereford Street (B4362)
☎ (0554) 267389
Ansells Bitter; Draught Bass H
A small town pub with a big, friendly welcome. Quoits and darts ☎ 🍺 A

Rhayader

11–3; 6–11

Royal Oak Hotel
On A44 ☎ (0597) 810315
M&B Mild H
Well-kept bar with excellent old fashioned atmosphere
🏠 Q 🍺

11–3; 6–11

Triangle Inn
Cwmdauddwr (off Bridge Street, B4518) ☎ (0597) 810537
Draught Bass; Welsh Brewers HB H
A beautiful little, old, weatherboard pub with a lounge overlooking the River Wye. Impeccably kept bar was not designed with tall people in mind!
☎ (not late eve) ☎ ⇌ ( ) 🍺 A

Sarn

11–2.30; 6–11

Sarn Inn
On A489 ☎ (0686) 88601
Burtonwood Best Bitter E
Welcoming, well-kept village pub with games area. Food in lounge. Garden has a play area for children ☎ ( ) 🍺 A

Talgarth

11–3; 7–11

Tower Hotel
The Square ☎ (0874) 711253
Flowers IPA, Original H
Popular town-centre pub that dominates the square alongside the Town Hall
🏠 ☎ 🍴 ⇌ 🍺

Talybont-on-Usk

11–3; 5.30–11 (all day Thu and alt Sat)

Star Inn
½ mile off A40
☎ (087 487) 635
Adnams Bitter; Flowers Original; Robinson Old Tom; Wadworth 6X; Younger IPA H
Immensely popular canalside pub, very welcoming and comfortable. Large drinking area to rear. Coach parties welcome. At least 14 real ales
🏠 ☎ 🍴 ( ) 🍺 ♻

Trefeglwys

11–2.30; 6–11

Red Lion
On B4569, Llanidloes–Caersws road ☎ (055 16) 255
Burtonwood Dark Mild, Best Bitter H
Excellent, comfortable village pub with old village photographs displayed. Good reputation for bar meals 🏠 ☎ (lounge/pool room) ☎ ( ) 🍺

Welshpool

11–3; 5.30–11

Talbot
High Street ☎ (0938) 3711
Banks Mild E, **Bitter** H
Small, well-kept pub. Games
☎ ( ) 🍺 ⇌

Try also: **Mermaid; Raven**

KEY TO SYMBOLS

Facilities

- 🏠 real fire
- Q quiet pub – no electronic music, TV or obtrusive games
- ⊔ indoor room for children
- ☎ garden or other outdoor drinking area
- ⇌ accommodation
- (lunchtime meals
-) evening meals
- 🍺 public bar
- ♻ facilities for the disabled
- A camping facilities close to the pub or part of the pub grounds
- ⇌ near British Rail station
- ⊖ near Underground station
- ↻ real cider

The facilities, beers and pub hours listed in the Guide are liable to change but were correct when the Guide went to press.

Help keep real ale alive by joining CAMRA. Your voice helps encourage brewers big and small to brew cask beer and offer all beer drinkers a better choice.

Borders

SCOTLAND — Borders

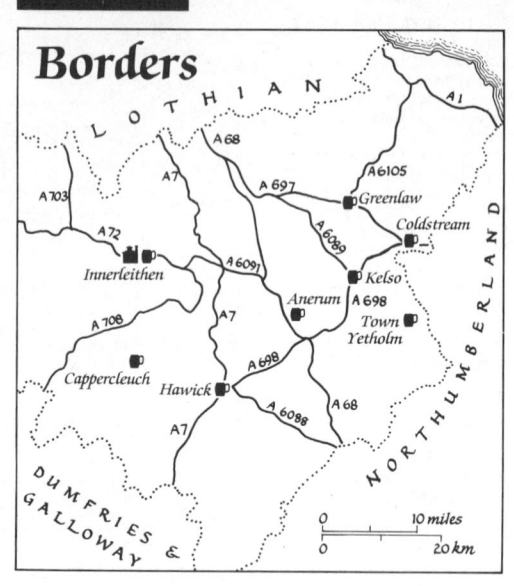

Traquair House, Innerleithen

Ancrum

11–2.30; 6–11 (12 F); 12.30–2.30; 7.30–11 Sun

Cross Keys Inn
Off A68, on B6400
☎ (083 53) 344
Arrols 70/-, 80/- H
Superb wee bar in village local thankfully untouched by brewery improvements Q ⌑

Cappercleuch

11–11 (winter: 11–2.30; 6.30–11); 12.30–11 Sun

Tibbie Shiels Inn
St Mary's Loch, Selkirk (on A708) ☎ (0750) 42231
Belhaven 60/-, 80/- H
Wonderful isolated lochside Howff on the southern upland way. Closed winter Mon
Q ⌑ ⌑ ⌑ ⌑ ⌑

Coldstream

11–12 (11.30 Sat); 12.30–12 Sun

Newcastle Arms Hotel
50 High Street (A697)
☎ (0890) 2376
Arrols 70/-, 80/- E
Bustling borders lounge bar, bedecked with model motors. Family room ⌑ ⌑ ⌑

Greenlaw

11–2.30; 5–11; (11–11 summer) 12.30–11 (Sun)

Cross Keys Hotel
3 The Square (A697)
☎ (036 16) 247
Arrols 70/- H
Unpretentious wee front-room bar ⌑ ⌑ ⌑ ⌑ ⌑

Hawick

11–2.30; 5–11 (closed Sun)

High Level
Green Terrace
McEwan 80/- A
Bonny Borders backstreet boozer ⌑

Innerleithen

11–12; 12.30–11 Sun

Traquair Arms Hotel
Traquair Road (off A72, on B709) ☎ (0896) 830229
Broughton Greenmantle Ale; Traquair Bear Ale H
Comfortable lounge bar in friendly 18th-century family run hotel near Traquair House brewery ⌑ ⌑ ⌑ ⌑ ⌑ ⌑

Kelso

11–11; 12.30–11 Sun

Black Swan Hotel
Horsemarket (just off Square)
☎ (0573) 24563
Tennent 80/- H
Robust public bar with boisterous customers. Meals served in comfortable lounge ⌑ ⌑ ⌑ ⌑ ⌑

Town Yetholm

11–11; 12.30–11 Sun

Plough Hotel
Main Street (B6352)
Arrols 70/- H
Friendly rural inn in deepest Borders arcadia, near England ⌑ ⌑ ⌑ ⌑ ⌑ ⌑

The magnificent Traquair House, Innerleithen

Central

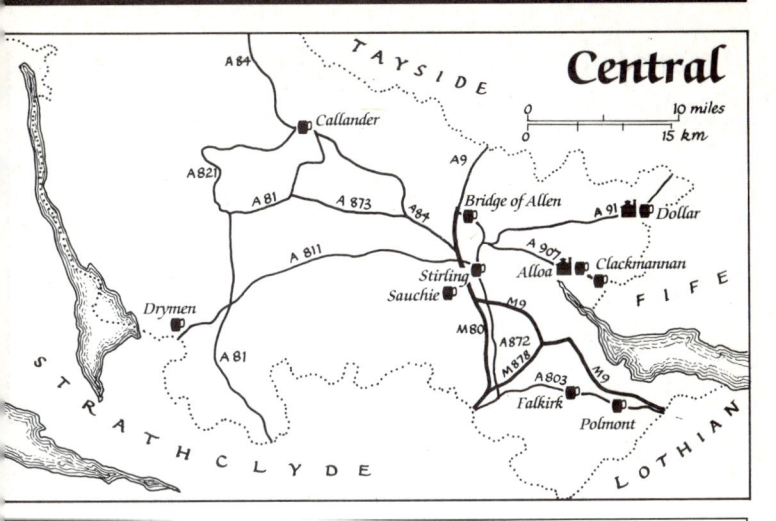

Harviestoun, Dollar; **Maclay**, Alloa

Alloa

11–11 (12.30–2.30; 7–11 Sun)
Crams Bar
Candleriggs ☎ (0259) 722019
Maclay 80/-; Tennent 80/- Ⓐ
Small homely pub Q ⊖

11–2.30; 5–11 (11–midnight Th–Sat)
12–2.30; 7–11 Sun
Thistle Bar
1 Junction Place
☎ (0259) 723933
Maclay 60/-, 80/- Ⓐ
Popular lounge and bar;
Maclay's brewery tap ( ) ⊖

Bridge of Allan

11–1am (12.30–1 Sun)
Queens Hotel
Henderson Street
☎ (0786) 833268
**Arrols 70/-, 80/-; Younger
IPA** Ⓐ
Renowned for its IPA. Hot
meals till midnight; beer
garden ⊛ ⋈ ( ) 🛌 ⇌

11–1am (midnight Sat) 12.30–2.30;
6–10.30 Sun
Westerton Arms
Henderson Street
Younger No.3, IPA Ⓐ
Large bar; open-plan lounge
with copper pots and guns
⊛ ⊛ ( ) ⊖ ⇌

Callander

11.30–2.30; 5–11 (1am Fri) 11.30–1 Sat
(12.30–11 Sun)
Bridgend House Hotel
Bridgend ☎ (0877) 30130
**Broughton Greenmantle
Ale** Ⓐ
Friendly family-run hotel on
the banks of the River Teith.
Popular with walkers and
climbers ⊛ ⊛ ⋈ ( ) ⊖ 🛌

Clackmannan

11–11 (midnight Sat); (12.30–2.30;
6.30–11 Sun
County Hotel
Main Street
Maclay 80/- Ⓐ
Excellent village local; historic
Clack outside ⊛ ⊖

Dollar

11–2.30; 5–11 (midnight Th–Sat)
(12.30–2.30; 5–11 Sun)
Kings Seat
19–23 Bridge Street
☎ (025 94) 2515
Belhaven 70/-, 80/- Ⓗ
Cosy pub with a friendly
atmosphere ⊛ Q ⊛ ( ) 🛌

11–1am (12.30–midnight Sun)
Strathallan Hotel
Chapel Place
Harviestoun 80/- Ⓗ
Busy family-run hotel with
intimate atmosphere ⊛ ⊛ ⋈ ( )

Drymen

11.30–1am (12.30–12 Sun)
Salmon Leap Inn
19 Main Street ☎ (0360) 60357
Belhaven 80/- Ⓐ
Friendly wood panelled bar in
old hotel. Handy for West
Highland Way
⊛ ⊛ ⊛ ⋈ ( ) ⊖ 🛌

Falkirk

11–midnight (12.45 F, Sat); 12.30–
2.30; 6.30–11.30 Sun
Behind the Wall
14 Melville Street
☎ (0324) 33338
Whitbread Castle Eden Ale Ⓗ
Large lively bar and bistro
built in old Playtex bra factory
⊛ ⊛ ⊛ ( ) ⇌ (Grahamston)

11–11.45 (12.45 F, S); 12.30–2.30;
6.30–11 Sun
Crossbow
Union Road, Camelon
☎ (0324) 24414
Tennent 80/- Ⓗ
Uninspiring modern exterior
conceals friendly and well-
kept interior ( ) ⊖

11–midnight (12.30–2.30; 6.30–
midnight Sun)
Woodside
76 High Station Road
☎ (0324) 29393
McEwan 80/- Ⓐ
Fine panelled bar with old
Campbell Hope and King
windows ⇌ (High)

Polmont

11–11 (11.45 F, Sat) 12.30–2.30;
6.30–11 Sun
Claremont Inn
Main Street
McEwan 80/- Ⓐ
Large open-plan modern pub
with raised lounge and
partitioned family room
⊛ ( ) 🛌 ⇌

Sauchie

11–11 (12.30–4; 6.30–11 Sun)
Mansfield Arms
7 Main Street
Arrols 70/-; Harviestoun 80/- Ⓐ
Basic bar, well-patronised
lounge ( ) 🛌 ⊖

Stirling

11–11 (12 Th–Sat); 12.30–2.30,
6.30–11 Sun
Settle Inn
91 St Marys Wynd **Maclay
70/-, 80/-, Porter** Ⓐ
Maclays make it, McNally sells
it, beer drinkers love it ⊛ ⇌

359

Dumfries

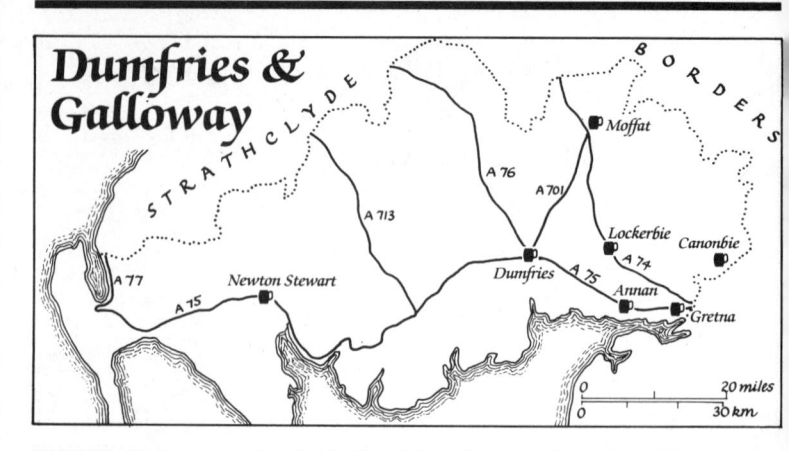

Dumfries & Galloway

Annan

Blue Bell
High Street (A75)
☎ (046 12) 2385
McEwan 70/-, 80/-; Younger No.3 Ⓐ; Theakston Best Bitter Ⓗ
Lively ex-State Brewery pub. Bar billiards Q❀⊞≉

Canonbie

Riverside Inn
A7 ☎ (054 15) 295
Broughton Merlin's Ale; Theakston Best Bitter Ⓗ
Pleasant country inn with good food Q❀⇥◐▶

Dumfries

Ship Inn
97 St Michaels Street
McEwan 70/-, 80/- Ⓐ
A real collector's item; fine Toby jugs Q⊞

12.30–2.30 (6.30–11 Sun)
Tam O'Shanter
117 Queensberry Street
McEwan 80/-; Younger No.3 Ⓐ
Homely pub near town centre
Q⊞≉

Gretna

Solway Lodge Hotel
Annan Road ☎ (0461) 38266
Broughton Greenmantle Ale; Jennings Bitter Ⓗ
Comfortable lounge bar with restaurant ⌂❀⇥◐▶♿▲

Lockerbie

Kings Arms Hotel
29 High Street ☎ (057 62) 2410
McEwan 80/- Ⓐ
17th-century town centre coaching inn ⌂❀◐▶▲≉

Moffat

Black Bull Hotel
1 Church Gate (A708)
☎ (0683) 20206
Broughton Greenmantle Ale; Merlin's Ale Ⓗ; McEwan 80/-; Younger No.3 Ⓐ; Theakston Best Bitter Ⓗ
Bar adorned with railway memorabilia from defunct local line. Large range of malt whisky ⇥◐▶⊞

Newton Stewart

12–2.30; 6–11; 12.30–2; 7–11 Sun
Creebridge House Hotel
Minigaff Road (B7079)
☎ (0671) 2121
Broughton Special; Theakston Best Bitter; Old Peculier Ⓗ
Comfortable hotel, close to town centre. Good food
♨Q⌂❀⇥◐▶♿

Down Memory Lane . . . the 1910 Shrove Tuesday Atherstone ball game contestants pause for a little refreshment.

360

Fife

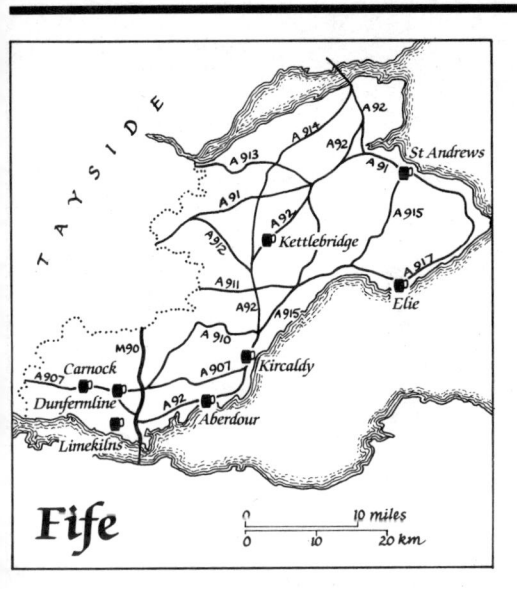

Aberdour

11–2.30; 5–11 (11–11 Sat) 12.30–11 Sun

Aberdour Hotel
High Street (A92)
Belhaven 70/-, 80/- H
Cosy, friendly bar in old coaching inn. Good food
🏠 ☎ ⛺ ( ) 🍺 ≈

Carnock

11–11 summer. Winter: 11–3; 5–11 (11–11 F, S); 12.30–2.30; 6.30–11 Sun

Old Inn
6 Main Street (A907)
☎ (0383) 850381
Maclay 70/-, 80/- H, **Porter** A
Welcoming village pub with large bar, comfortable lounge and separate restaurant
🍺 ( ) 🍺 &

Dunfermline

11–11 (12.30–2.30; 6.30–11 Sun)

Old Inn
Kirkgate ☎ (0383) 736652
McEwan 80/-; Younger No.3 A
Oldest pub in city; busy traditional bar popular with both locals and tourists. Vast range of malt whisky; good food ( ) 🍺

Elie

11–midnight (12.30–2.30; 6.30–11 Sun)

Ship Inn
The Toft (by sailing club)
☎ (0333) 330246
Belhaven 80/- H
Quaint waterfront bar with strong nautical features. Pub games. Barbour and green wellies optional! 🏠 Q ⛺ 🍺 🍺 &

Kettlebridge

11–2.30; 5–11 (11–11 Sat) 12.30–11 Sun

Kettlebridge Inn
9 Cupar Road (A92)
☎ (0337) 30323
Arrols 70/-; Ind Coope Burton Ale H

Friendly country inn with tiny bar, lounge and games room
🏠 ⛺ ☎ ( ) (ex winter Sun)) (Thu–Sat) 🍺 & ⚑

Kirkcaldy

11–2.30; 5–11 (11–11 Th–Sat) 12.30–2.30; 6.30–11 Sun

Novar Bar
17 Nicol Street
☎ (0592) 260545
McEwan 80/-; Younger No.3 A
Large wood-panelled modern pub built on the site of the old Novar Bar. In the same family for 3 generations. Good value meals. Worthington White Shield available ( ) 🍺 & ≈

Limekilns

11–2.30; 5–11 (11–11 Sat) 12.30–2.30; 6.30–11 Sun

Ship Inn
Halketts Hall (off A985)
☎ (0383) 872247
Belhaven 60/-, 70/-, 80/- H
1-roomed lounge bar on the waterfront, with splendid view of the River Forth ( )

St Andrews

12–2.30; 5–11 (11.45 Th–Sat) 12.30–2.30; 6.30–11 Sun

Ardgowan Hotel
2 Playfair Terrace
☎ (0334) 72970
McEwan 80/-; Younger No.3 A
Comfortable hotel lounge with prints of old St Andrews and its golfing worthies
⛺ (not Jan) ( ))

11–11 (midnight Th–Sat); 6.30–11 Sun

St Andrews Wine Bar (Cellar Bar)
32 Bell Street ☎ (0334) 77425
Belhaven 70/-, 80/- H
Small, comfortable and popular. The copper bar was made from boiler of the Oceanic, sister ship of the Titanic. Food may be brought down from wine bar upstairs. Very busy weekends term time ⛺ ( ))

KEY TO SYMBOLS

- 🏠 real fire
- Q quiet pub – no electronic music, TV or obtrusive games
- ⛺ indoor room for children
- 🍺 garden or other outdoor drinking area
- ☎ accommodation
- ( ) lunchtime meals
-) evening meals
- 🍺 public bar
- & facilities for the disabled
- A camping facilities close to the pub or part of the pub grounds
- ≈ near British Rail station
- ⊖ near Underground station
- ◇ real cider

The facilities, beers and pub hours listed in the Good Beer Guide are liable to change but were correct when the Guide went to press.

Grampian

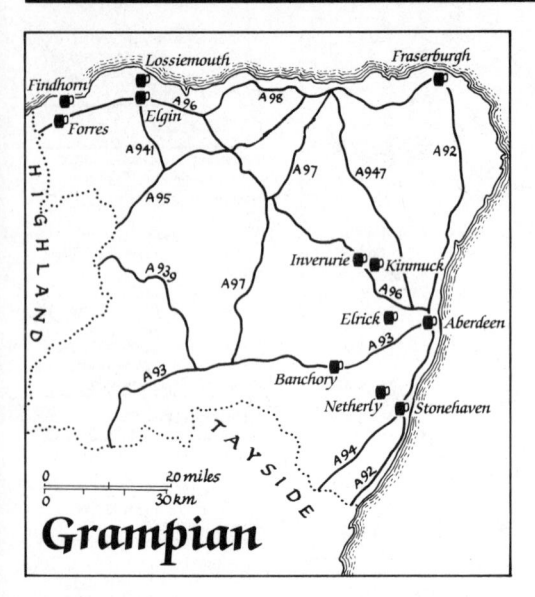

Aberdeen

11–11
Albyn
1 Queens Cross
Ind Coope Burton Ale H
Dizzy, popular night spot, good for rhythm and Burton or a pint 'n' pizza

11–11 (11.45 F, Sat)
Blue Lamp
121 Gallowgate
☎ (0224) 647472
Belhaven 80/-; Taylor Landlord H
Excellent 60s/70s juke box, lively locals and friendly bar staff

11–2.30; 5–11 (12.30–2.30; 6.30–11 Sun)
Carriages
101 Crown Street
☎ (0224) 595440
Wethered Bitter; Whitbread Castle Eden Ale H
Comfortable lounge bar with excellent value food and friendly service. Large piazza-type room off main bar area

11–11; 11–2.30; 5–11 Sat; 12.30–2.30; 6.30–11 Sun
Craighaar Hotel
Waterton Road, Bucksburn (W of A947) ☎ (0224) 712275
Tennent Heriot 80/- H
Popular wood-panelled suburban lounge

11–11 (11–midnight Th–Sat); 7.30–11 Sun
Grill
213 Union Street
McEwan 80/- A
Superb Edwardian pub with magnificent loos and super service. 24-hour clock and splendid wood panelling

11–10.30; open Sun
Kirkgate Bar
18 Upperkirkgate
☎ (0224) 640515
Belhaven 80/- H
Basic local bar, popular with students. Beware of Old George!

11–11.30 (11.45 F, S) 12.30–2.30; 6.30–10.50 Sun
Moorings
2 Trinity Quay
☎ (0224) 587602
Theakston Best Bitter H
Dimly-lit harbour bar; rock and bikers' bar

11–11; open Sun
Prince of Wales
7 St Nicholas Lane
☎ (0224) 640597
Caledonian 80/-; Theakston Best Bitter, Old Peculier H; **Younger No.3** A
Rare example of a traditional Scottish long bar. Mecca of the North, a joy, not to be missed. Guest beers

Banchory

11–11 (12.30–2.30; 6.30–10.30 Sun)
Tor-Na-Coille
Inchmarlo Road
☎ (033 02)2242
Theakston Best Bitter H
Large hotel on west side of town with expansive gardens. Excellent sports facilities nearby

Elgin

12–2.30; 5–11 (11.45 F, S); 12.30–2.30; 7–11 Sun

Braelossie Hotel
2 Sheriffmill Road (off A96)
☎ (0343) 7181
McEwan 80/- E
Hotel lounge in quiet and secluded surroundings on west of town

11–2.30; 5–11 (11.45 F, S); 12.30–2.30; 6.30–11 Sun
Sunninghill Hotel
Hay Street ☎ (0343) 7799
Ind Coope Burton Ale H
Comfortable and friendly lounge bar

11–11 (11.45 Sat); 6.30–11 Sun
Thunderton House
Thunderton Place
☎ (0343) 48767
Belhaven 80/-; Maclay 80/-; Tennent Heriot 80/-; Thunderton House Ale H
Superb bar, reclaimed from the dead, follow in Charlie's footsteps and have a pint before going on to Culloden (not too many though – or you too could be over the sea)

Elrick

11–2.30; 5–11 (11–midnight F, S); 12.30–11 Sun
Broadstraik Inn
On A944 ☎ (0224) 743217
Tennent Heriot 80/- H
Pleasant old coaching inn, popular for its bar lunches and suppers (lunch)

Findhorn

11–11 (11.45 F, S); noon–11 Sun
Crown & Anchor
Near yacht club
☎ (0309) 30243
Brakspear Bitter; Tennent Heriot 80/- H
Beautiful setting, excellent choice of beers – what more could one want? Only one way to find out

Forres

11–11 (11.45 F, S); 12.30–11 Sun
Red Lion Hotel
Tolbooth Street
☎ (0309) 72716
McEwan 70/- H
Known as the 'Red Beastie', a welcoming and popular spot; no-frills public and comfortable lounge bar. The oldest outlet in the region

11–11 (12.30–11 Sun)
Royal Hotel
Tytler Street ☎ (0309) 7261
Younger No.3 A
100 year-old hotel on western edge of town. Large garden with play area for children. Magnificent, stupendous gents' loo!

Grampian

Fraserburgh

11–11; open Sun
Crown Bar
45 Broad Street ☎ (0346) 24941
McEwan 80/-
Friendly homely bar with long wooden bar top; oasis in a great desert

Inverurie

11–11 (12.30–11 Sun)
Thainstone House Hotel
Thainstone (A96)
☎ (0467) 21643
Tennent Heriot 80/-
Imposing country house set back off road. Very friendly atmosphere in the large upstairs bar. Barbecues on the lawn summer Sun

Kinmuck

11–2.30; 5–11 (12.30–2.30; 7–11 Sun)
Boars Head
Off B993 ☎ (0224) 791235
Broughton Greenmantle Ale
Small rural pub with possibly the cheeriest landlord in the world! 14 different pub games and always full of local couthy characters. Real mince toasties! Many guest beers: why not try the beer from the cupboard?

Lossiemouth

11–2.30; 5–11 (11–11 Sat); 12.30–2.30; 6.30–11 Sun
Clifton
Clifton Road ☎ (034 381) 2100
McEwan 80/-, Younger No.3
Friendly bar near harbour. Guest beers

11–11 (11.45 F, S); 12–10.45 Sun
Huntly House Hotel
Stotfield Road
☎ (034 381) 2085
Broughton Greenmantle Ale; McEwan 80/-
Comfortable hotel with grand view across Moray Firth

Netherly

11–11 (12.30–2.30; 6.30–10.30 Sun)

Lairhillock

On B979
Theakston Best Bitter
Friendly, remote bar, cosy and comfortable

Stonehaven

11–11 (noon–11 Sun)
Heugh Hotel
Westfield Road ☎ (0569) 62379
Tennent Heriot 80/-
Imposing Baronial style hotel

11–midnight (noon–11 Sun)
Marine Hotel
9–10 Shorehead (opposite North Sea!) ☎ (0569) 62155
McEwan 80/-; Theakston Best Bitter
Popular pub beside picturesque harbour. Special harbour swim 4pm summer Sundays

11–11 Fri/Sat
Market Bar
Allardyce Street
☎ (0569) 63642
Belhaven 80/-
Marvellous market bar; mince and tattie pies are a must

AGM '89: A WEEKEND IN ABERDEEN!

CAMRA's 1989 Annual General Meeting will be held in Aberdeen on the weekend of 8/9 April. And it's well worth the trip, for those of us who live far away. The two days of official business (broken up, naturally, by a good deal of socialising) will take place in the cloistered hall of ancient Aberdeen University, in old Aberdeen. The venue is only 15–20 minutes walk from the city centre; accommodation is in any case available in university halls of residence. Aberdeen itself is a fascinating city, well worth a visit, and there's lots to see and do in the surrounding countryside; Balmoral, for instance, is just 50 miles away. Going on a whisky trail may be more your cup of tea. For those driving up from the south, your journey will take you through superb scenery, along the edge of the Grampian mountains, or along the coast road. For skiing fans, there should still be some sport in early April. Come for a few days and make a holiday of it!

Terry Lock, who's organising the AGM, promises there'll be a few surprises too, including "a special way of getting people up on the Sunday morning..." – more than this he is unprepared to divulge!

If you're not yet a member of CAMRA, now is the time to join (you'll find a form on page 384); come to the 1989 Annual General Meeting, it's the best way to find out what the campaign's all about.

FLY THERE, DRIVE THERE, TRAIN THERE ... BUT BE THERE!

ABERDEEN '89

Highland

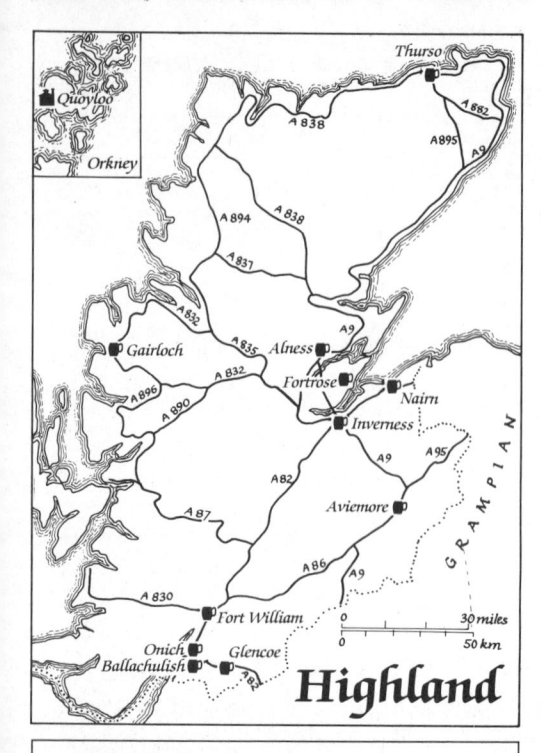

Orkney, Sandwick, Orkney

Alness

11–2.30; 5–11 (1am Fri); 12.30–11 Sun
Morven House Hotel
Novar Road ☎ (0349) 882323
Younger No.3 Ⓐ
Family-run hotel with distinctive tartan carpet in lounge and a very unusual heating system

Aviemore

11–11 (open Sun)
Tavern Bistro
Grampian Road
Arrols 70/-, 80/- Ⓗ
Cabin style split-level bar; Italian food menu (good value); occasional live entertainment

11–11; open Sun
Winking Owl
Grampian Road
Arolls 70/-, 80/- Ⓗ
Nest bar popular with the après-skier and tourist. Split-level, with skiing theme on walls

Ballachulish

12.30–2am
Ballachulish Hotel
On Oban Road
Arrols 70/-, 80/- Ⓗ
Friendly hotel. Live music at weekends

Fortrose

11–2.30; 5–11 (12.30–2.30; 6.30–11 Sun)
Royal Hotel
High Street ☎ (0381) 20236
McEwan 80/-; Younger No.3 Ⓐ
Popular hotel lounge overlooking ruins of medieval cathedral. Mini beer festival in August at town's St Boniface Fayre

Fort William

12.30–11
Nevis Bank Hotel
Belford Road (Glen Nevis Jct)
McEwan 80/-; Younger No.3 Ⓐ
Good finishing point for survivors of Ben Nevis. Occasional live music

Gairloch

11–1am (11.45 Sat); 12.30–11 Sun
Old Inn
The Harbour ☎ (0445) 2066
Tennent Heriot 80/- Ⓐ
Popular family-run hotel with lively, traditional atmosphere. Beautiful views of lochs and mountains

Glencoe

12.30–2am
Clachaig Inn
Off A82
McEwan 80/-; Younger No.3 Ⓐ
Set in the midst of Britain's most spectacular scenery. Often busy with hill walkers and rock climbers

12.30–2am
Kingshouse Hotel
Off A82
McEwan 80/- Ⓐ
The oldest inn in the area. Popular with climbers and skiers

Inverness

11–11 (midnight Th, F, 11.45 Sat); 12.30–2.30; 6.30–11 Sun
Clachnaharry Inn
19 High Street, Clachnaharry ☎ (0463) 239806
McEwan 80/-; Younger No.3 Ⓐ
Unspoilt horse shoe bar with sawdust on the floor and marble trough; original beer engine on the wall

11–2.30; 5–11 (12.30–2.30; 6.30–11 Sun)
Glen Mhor Hotel
10 Ness Bank ☎ (0463) 234308
Ind Coope Burton Ale Ⓗ
Nicky Tam's bar at the rear of the hotel, converted from the old stables

11–11 (12.30am Th, Fri); 12.30–11 Sun
Heathmount Hotel
Kingsmills Road
☎ (0463) 235877
McEwan 80/-; Younger No.3 Ⓐ
Lively comfortable hotel bar with a reputation for excellent food. Well worth a visit!

11–2.30; 5–11 (12.30–2.30; 6.30–11 Sun)
Kingsmills Hotel
Culcabock Road
☎ (0463) 237166
McEwan 80/-; Younger No.3 Ⓐ
Very comfortable hotel on the edge of the town near the hospital

11–11 (1am Fri, 11.45 Sat); 12.30–11 Sun
Muirtown Motel
11 Clachnaharry Road
Caledonian 80/- Ⓐ
Lounge bar popular with locals and those who sail the canal, which goes from East Scotland to the West through Loch Ness

Highland

11–2.30; 5–11 (12.30–2.30; 6.30–11 Sun)
Raigmore Motel
Perth Road (just off A9)
☎ (0463) 221546
Ind Coope Burton Ale H
Modern busy bar near town's Raigmore Hospital, and popular with army families at nearby barracks ⌂ ◐

Nairn

11–2.30; 5–11 (winter: eves only); 12.30–2.30; 6.30–11 Sun

Invernairn Hotel
Thurlow Road ☎ (0667) 52039
Younger No.3 A
Pleasant lounge bar with large open fire; live jazz every Mon. Some no-smoking tables
⌂ Q ☎ ⊞ ⌂ ◐ ▶ ≉

Onich

12.30–2am
Onich Hotel
On A82
Arrols 70/-, 80/- H
Peaceful setting amid glorious scenery Q ☎ ⊞ ⌂ ◐ ▶ & Å

Thurso

11–2.30; 5–10 (closed Sun)
Station Bar
Princes Street
McEwan 80/-; Younger No.3 A
Plain but friendly traditional Scottish bar, with a number of large old brewery mirrors
⌂ ⊕ Å ≉

Question: Where will you find this typical British pub?
Answer: Southern California!

365

Lothian

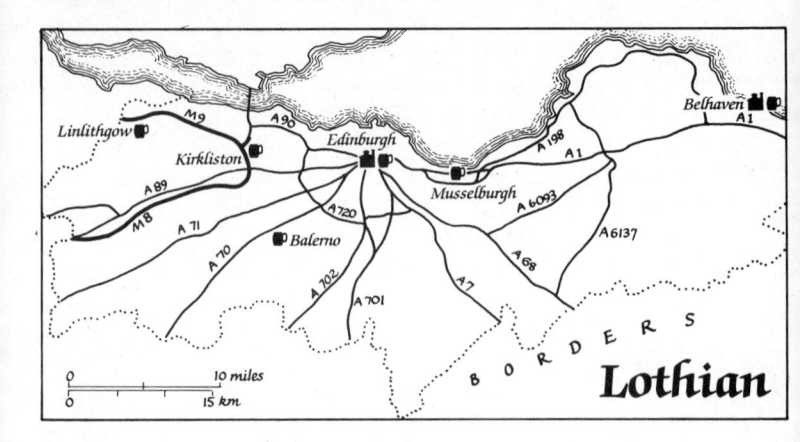

Belhaven, Dunbar; **Caledonian**, Edinburgh

Balerno

11–2.30; 5.–10.30 (closed Sun)

Grey Horse Inn
22 Main Street (off A70)
☎ (031) 449 3092
Belhaven 60/-, 80/- H
Gem of a pub set in old part of village on the western outskirts of Edinburgh 🍺

11–2.30 (4.30 Sat); 6–12 (12.30–4.30; 6.30–11 Sun)

Marchbank Hotel
Mansfield Road (off A70)
☎ (031) 449 3970
Caledonian 70/-, 80/- H
Well-appointed bar and restaurant with 2 log fires in beautiful wooded surroundings 🏨 Q ❦ ⛴ 🍴 🍺 ♿

Belhaven

11–2.30; 5–11 (12.30–2.30; 6.30–11 Sun)

Masons Arms
Off A1, on A1087
☎ (0368) 63700
Belhaven 80/- H
Functional bar at the brewery gates. Handy for beach; to the west of historic town of Dunbar 🏨 🍺

Edinburgh

11–2.30; 5–10.30 (closed Sun)

Athletic Arms
1–3 Angle Park Terrace
☎ (031) 337 3822
McEwan 80/- A
Probably the city's most famous beer shop, dedicated to the Scottish art of perpendicular drinking 🍺 ≠ (Haymarket)

11–12; (1am F; midnight S) 12.30–2.30; 6.30–11 Sun

Bannermans
53–57 Niddry Street (Cowgate)
☎ (031) 556 3254
Arrols 80/-; Caledonian 70/-;
Ind Coope Burton Ale H
Superb stone-vaulted catacomb bar buried in the city's old town. Cooked breakfast Sun from 11am
Q 🍴 🍺 ≠

11–2.30; 5–11

Bennet's Bar
11 Maxwell Street, Morningside ☎ (031) 447 1903
Belhaven 70/-, 80/-; Taylor Landlord A
Modest but engaging little bar in tenement area. 60/- is keg Q

11–2.30; 5–11; (midnight F)
11–midnight Sat & summer Fri (12.30–2.30 Sun)

Cramond Inn
Glebe Road (off A90)
☎ (031) 336 2035
Belhaven 80/-; Caledonian 80/-; Maclay 70/-; Taylor Best Bitter A
Much altered 1670 building close to river and remains of Roman fort. Very popular with both locals and tourists. Good restaurant 🍴 🍺

11–11

Doric Tavern
15 Market Street
☎ (031) 225 5243
Caledonian 80/- A
Basic beer shop with smart upstairs bistro. Excellent food. 'Wine bar' upstairs also has beer; very popular with students and trendies
🍺 🍴 ≠

11–11 (12.30–2.30; 6.30–11 Sun)

Guildford Arms
1 West Register Street
☎ (031) 556 4312
Belhaven 80/-; Caledonian 80/- H
Magnificent Edwardian palace with ornate ceiling and unusual balcony 🍺 ≠

11–2.30; 5–11; open Sun

Hampton Hotel
14 Corstorphine Road
☎ (031) 337 1130
Belhaven 80/-; McEwan 80/- A
Exceedingly well-run lounge bar near Murrayfield Q ❦ 🍺

11–11 (11.30 Fri; 11.45 Sat);
12.30–2.30; 6.30–11 Sun

Leslie's Bar
45 Ratcliffe Terrace
☎ (031) 667 5957
Caledonian 70/-, 80/-; Younger No.3 A
Outstanding Victorian pub with carved snob screens, superb ceiling and panelling 🏨

12–11.30 (12 F, 11.45 S); 12–2.30;
6.30–11 Sun

Malt Shovel
11–15 Cockburn Street
☎ (031) 225 6843
Caledonian 70/- H; **McEwan 80/-** A; **Mitchells Bitter** H
Busy city-centre lounge bar with large range of malt whiskies and guest beers. Handy for bus and railway stations. Breakfasts on Sun
❦ 🍺 ≠

11–midnight (11.45 Sat) 12.30–2.30;
6.30–11 Sun

Minders
14 Causewayside
Caledonian 80/- H; **Maclay 80/-** A
Dark modern interior; attracts young people. Guest beers

noon–midnight (11 Mon) 12.30–2.30;
6.30–11 Sun

Navaar House Hotel
12 Mayfield Gardens (A7)
☎ (031) 667 2828
Caledonian 80/-; McEwan 80/-; Maclay 70/-, 80/- A
Comfortable suburban hotel lounge. Guest beers ❦ 🍺

11–11 (closed M–Th winter)
12.30–2.30; 6.30–11 Sun

Lothian

Olde Inn
25 Main Street, Davidson
Mains ☏ (031) 336 2437
Arrols 80/- Ⓐ; **Ind Coope Burton Ale** Ⓗ
Suburban local in what was once the village of Muttonhole. Outdoor drinking area

11–2am (11.45 Sat) 12.30–2.30; 6.30–11 Sun

Oxford Bar
8 Young Street (near Charlotte Square) ☏ (031) 225 4262
Caledonian 80/-;
McEwan 80/- Ⓐ
Vibrant new town drinking shop, retains original early 19th-century parlour arrangement. Traditional pub music Q

11–11 (11.45 Th, F, Sat)

Piershill Tavern (Porter's)
7 Piershill Place
☏ (031) 661 6661
Belhaven 80/- Ⓐ
Traditional local near Meadowbank Stadium. Games room at rear

11–11.45 (12.30–2.30; 6.30–11.45 Sun)

Smithie's Ale House
49–51 Eyre Place, Canonmills
☏ (031) 556 9805
Caledonian 70/-, 80/-; Ind Coope Burton Ale; McEwan 80/- Taylor Landlord Ⓐ
19 specially commissioned mirrors adorn this 1-room, late Edwardian style lounge. Gas lighting Q

Kirkliston

11–11 (midnight F, Sat;) 12.30–11 Sun

Newliston Arms Hotel
Main Street ☏ (031) 333 3214
McEwan 70/-, 80/- Ⓐ
Large busy public bar in hotel once on busy village crossroads – now by-passed by motorway

Linlithgow

12–2.30; 5–11; noon–11 Sat (12.30–2.30; 7–11 Sun)

Four Marys
65 High Street ☏ (0506) 842171
Belhaven 70/-, 80/-, 90/- Ⓗ
Attractive lounge bar with antique furniture, reflecting town's historic past. Good selection of malt whisky
(till early eve)

11–2.30; 5–11 (11–11 Th, Fri, Sat)
12.30–2.30; 6.30–11 Sun

Red Lion
50 High Street ☏ (0506) 842348
McEwan 80/- Ⓐ
Small friendly bar, popular for pool and darts; petanque piste in garden area
(till early eve)

Musselburgh

11–2.30; 5–11

Volunteer Arms (Staggs)
79–81 North High Street
☏ (031) 665 6481
Caledonian 70/-;
McEwan 80/- Ⓐ
Busy local with Whitelaw mirror and wood-panelled interior. Superb gantry. White Shield available

A taste of how things used to be ... the now sadly defunct Coulsons Scotch Ale, once brewed in Edinburgh and sold in cans like this!

Strathclyde

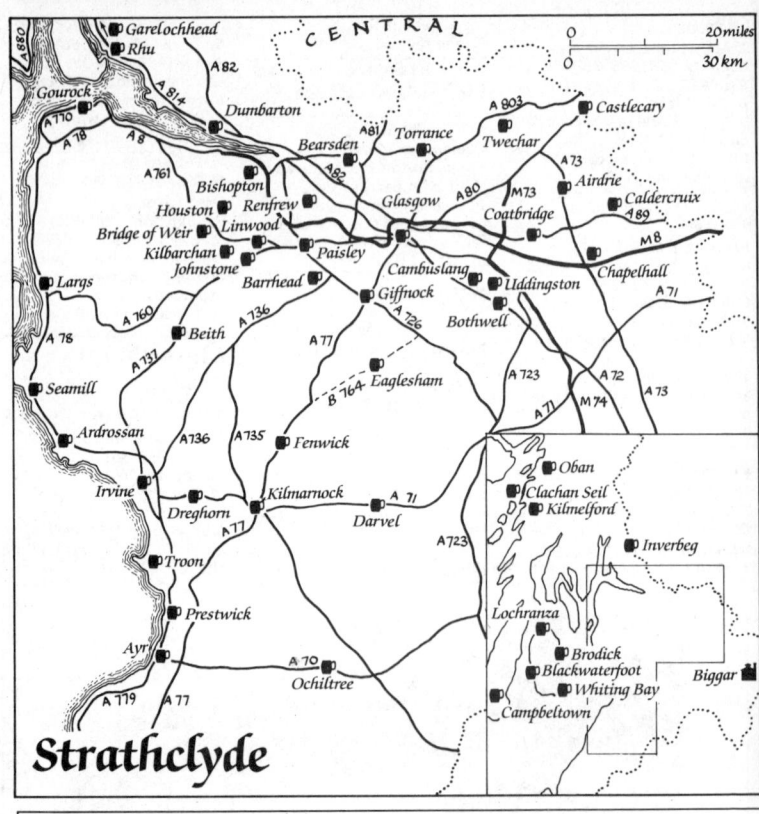

Broughton, Biggar

---

* closed all day Sunday

Airdrie

closed lunch; 6–11 (12 Sat, 1am Fri)
**Tudor Hotel
(Elizabethan Lounge)**
39 Alexander Street
☎ (0236) 64144
Ind Coope Burton Ale Ⓐ
Large hotel serving ale only in comfortable wood-panelled lounge bar

Ardrossan

11 (12.30 Sun)–11 (12 Thu)
High Tide
23 Parkhouse Road (A78)
☎ (0294) 61527
McEwan 80/- Ⓐ
Modern hotel ½ mile from sea. Front public bar with games; large lounge has live music Thu–Sun; quiz (for meals) (South Beach)

Ayr

11–12 (12.30 F & S); 12–12 Sun
Old Racecourse Hotel
2 Victoria Park (off A719)
☎ (0292) 262873
McEwan 70/- Younger No.3 Ⓗ
Plush sandstone hotel close to the shore. First Ayr Gold Cup presented here 1804: Jockeys' colours decorate the bar

Barrhead

11–midnight (11.45 Sat); 12.30–2.30; 6.30–11 Sun
Brig Inn
145 Cross Arthurlie Street
☎ (041) 881 1677
Belhaven 70/-, 80/- Ⓐ
Popular local with 2 lounges, one quiet, one not. Regular folk and country music. Golf, angling and chess clubs

Bearsden

11–2.30; 6.30–11 (11–11 F; 11.45 S open Sun)
Brae Bar, Burnbrae Hotel
Milngavie Road
☎ (041) 942 5951
Broughton Merlin; McEwan 70/-, 80/-; Younger No.3 Ⓐ
Well-run bar in modern hotel, used by locals and refugees from nearby sports centre
(hotel) (Hillfoot)

Beith

11–2.30; 5–11 (12 Th, Fri) 11am–midnight Sat; 6.30–11 Sun (closed lunch)
Eglinton Arms
48–50 Eglinton Street (B7049)
☎ (05055) 2736
McEwan 80/- Ⓐ
2-bar friendly pub with lively, welcoming atmosphere

Bishopton

11–2.30; 5–11 (12.30–2.30; 5.30–11 Sun)
Golf Inn
28–30 Old Greenock Road
☎ (0505) 862303
Belhaven 80/-; Broughton Greenmantle Ale; Caledonian 70/- Ⓐ
Basic drinking shop, with well in cellar still used to this day. Well stocked off-licence

Blackwaterfoot, Isle of Arran

12–1am (shuts in afternoon if quiet)

368

Strathclyde

Kinloch Hotel
On front, at end of String Road
☎ (0770) 86444
Younger No.3 Ⓐ
Modern sea-front hotel (49 rooms) with busy public bar and separate lounge ☎⛵⏠

Bothwell

11–2.30; 5–11 (11–11 Fri, Sat); 12.30–2.30; 6.30–11 Sun

Camphill Vaults
Main Street
McEwan 80/- Ⓐ
Multi-roomed, friendly gem in conservation area Q⏠

Bridge of Weir

11–11 (midnight Th, F; 11.45 Sat); 12.30–2.30; 6.30–11 Sun

Railway Tavern/Jacksons
Main Street
Maclay 80/- Ⓐ
Popular village pub with a modern lounge upstairs ⏠⛵⏠

Brodick, Isle of Arran

11–11 (midnight Th–S); 12.30–2.30; 8–11 Sun

Brodick Bar
Invercloy (beside post office)
☎ (0770) 2169
McEwan 70/- 80/- Ⓐ
Lively pub in relatively new single-storey whitewashed building. Evening meals summer only ☎ (lunch) ⏠⛵⏠

12–2.30; 4.30–12 (12–12 Sat; 12.30–12 Sun) (closed M–Thu winter)

Ormidale Hotel
past golf course at west end of village ☎ (0770) 2293
McEwan 70/- Ⓐ
Attractive sandstone hotel, with boat-shaped bar; sun lounge
⏠☎⛵ ⏠ (summer) ⏠⛵

Caldercruix

11–2.30; 5–11 (11–11 Fri, Sat); 12.30–2.30; 6.30–11 Sun

Railway Tavern
67–69 Main Street (off A89)
☎ (0236) 842429
Belhaven 60/- Ⓐ
Out of the way pub in old mining village; owned by the same family for over 60 years. Superb Robert Youngers mirror in bar ⏠⛵⏠

Cambuslang

11–11; 12.30–2.30 (6.30–11 Sun)

Sefton Bar
40 Main Street
☎ (041) 641 3463
Belhaven 60/- Ⓐ
Locals' bar with fine Art Deco interior ⏠⛵⏠

Cambeltown

11–2.30; 5–12 (12.30–2.30; 6.30–11 Sun)

Ardsheil Hotel
Kilkerran Road, 50 yds from harbour (New Quay)
Arrols 70/- Ⓐ
Cocktail bar in family-run hotel on quiet periphery of town ⏠Q☎⛵⏠ ⏠

Castlecary

11–11 (12.30–3.30; 6.30–11 Sun)

Castlecary House Hotel
Near railway viaduct over A80
☎ (0324) 840233
Belhaven 80/- Ⓐ; **Broughton Greenmantle Ale** Ⓗ, **Merlin's Ale** Ⓐ; **Harviestoun 80/-**; **Theakston Best Bitter, Old Peculier** Ⓗ
Small, popular village hotel; quiet lounge, busy in public and snugs ⏠⛵ ⏠ ⏠⛵

Chapelhall

11–2.30; 5–11

Tavern★
70 Main Street (A73)
Broughton Greenmantle Ale Ⓗ
Small unpretentious 2-roomed village local ⏠☎⛵⏠

Clachan Seil

11–11 May–Sept; closed weekday afternoons winter

Tigh an Truish
Across bridge over Atlantic on B844 ☎ (085 23) 242
McEwan 80/- Ⓗ
Traditional West Highland pub with vibrant atmosphere. Beer and meals only available in summer ⏠☎⛵⛵ ⏠ ⏠

Coatbridge

11–11 (12.30–2.30; 6.30–11 Sun)

Carsons
Main Street, Whifflet
Broughton Greenmantle Ale Ⓗ; **McEwan 80/-** Ⓐ
Busy pub with tasteful mural interior ⏠

Darvel

11–2.30; 5–11 (11–11 Fri, Sat); 12–11 Sun

Loudounhill Inn
On A71, 2 miles E of Darvel
☎ (0560) 20275
Broughton Greenmantle Ale Ⓗ
Friendly roadside inn facing Loudoun Hill, a local landmark and scene of a famous battle
⏠☎ (until 8) ⏠⛵⏠

Dreghorn

11–11 (11.30 Th, F, S); 12.30–2.30; 6.30–11 Sun

Dreghorn Inn
39 Main Street (B7081, Old A71) ☎ (0294) 211557
Younger No.3 Ⓐ
Modernised 1-lounge bar in conservation area within Irvine New Town

Dumbarton

11–11 (1am Th, F, S) 12.30–2.30; 6.30–11 Sun

Stags Head
116 Glasgow Road (A814)
☎ (0389) 32642
Arrols 80/- Ⓐ
Friendly modern bar next to station. Only real ale in town. Pool, darts, dominoes
☎⏠ ⏠⛵≉ (Dumbarton E)

Eaglesham

11–2.30; 5–11 (11.30 Th); 11–midnight Sat (12.30–2.30; 5.30–11 Sun)

Cross Keys
Montgomery Street
Broughton Greenmantle Ale Ⓗ
Large bar with pool table; spacious lounge; restaurant next door ⏠ ⏠ ⏠

11–2.30; 5–11 (midnight Th–Sat) 12.30–11 Sun

Eglinton Arms Hotel
Gilmour Street
☎ (035 53) 2631
McEwan 80/-; Younger No.3 Ⓐ
Popular village hotel on the borders of Renfrewshire. Now serves cask beer in both public bar and lounge ⛵ ⏠ ⏠ ⏠

11–2.30; 5–11; (midnight Th, F; 11.45 Sat) 12.30–2.30; 6.30–11 Sun

Swan
23 Polndon Street
McEwan 80/- Ⓐ
Busy local pub with loyal regulars ⏠

Fenwick

11–2.30; 5–11.30 (11–11.30 Fri, Sat) 12.30 –2.30; 6.30–11 Sun

Kings Arms
89 Main Road (off A77)
☎ (056 06) 276
Younger No.3 Ⓐ
Busy village local just off main Kilmarnock–Glasgow road. Walls of public bar decorated with cartoons by McCormick (a regular) ☎⏠⏠⛵⏠

Garelochhead

11–11; 12.30–11 Sun

Garelochhead Hotel
On A814 in village
☎ (0436) 810263
McEwan 80/- Ⓐ
Traditional hotel with pine lodge saloon and modernised lounge. Views over the loch
⛵ ⏠ ⏠ ⏠

Giffnock

11–11 (midnight Th–Sat); 12.30–5; 6.30–11 Sun

MacDonald Hotel
Eastwood Toll
Younger No.3 Ⓐ
Comfortable bar in corner of Thistle Hotel. Separate games

369

Strathclyde

room with own entrance
⋈ ◑ ◗ ⊞ ≅ (White Craigs)

Glasgow

11–2.30; 5–11 (12.30–2.30; 6.30–11 Sun)

Athena Greek Taverna
780 Pollockshaws Road
☎ (041) 424 0858
Belhaven 80/-; Caldeonian 80/- H
Popular family pub/diner. Guest beers
Q ๛ (till 8) ◑ ◗ ≅ (Queens Pk)

11–midnight (12.30–2.30; 6.30–11 Sun)

Blackfriars
36 Bell Street ☎ (041) 552 2932
Arrols 80/-; Belhaven 70/-; Taylor Landlord A
Merchant city local given kiss of life by new owners; Live jazz/blues and folk club downstairs
๛ (lunch) ◑ ◗ ᏺ ≅ (Argyle St)

11–2.30; 5–11 (12.30–2.30; 6.30–11 Sun)

Bon Accord
153 North Street (just off M8)
☎ (041) 248 4427
Belhaven 60/- A; **Broughton Greenmantle Ale; Caledonian 70/-** H; **Maclay 70/-** A; **Marston Pedigree; Theakston Best Bitter** H
Renowned throughout Glasgow as a veritable cornucopia of beery delights. Guest beers. Trivial Pursuit
Q ◑ ◗ ⊞ ≅ (Charing Cross)
⊖ (St Georges Cross)

11–11 (12.30–2.30; 6.30–11 Sun)

Gables
6 Baillieston Road
☎ (041) 778 9655
Belhaven 80/-
Small local bar on Glasgow city boundary. Stained glass windows ⊞ ᏺ ≅ (Garrowhill)

11–11 (12.30–2.30; 7–11 Sun)

Hayfield
148 Old Dalmarnock Road
☎ (041) 554 7452
Belhaven 80/-
Friendly local pub east of city centre ◑ ⊞ ≅ (Dalmarnock)

11–11 (12.30–2.30; 6.30–11 Sun)

Lock 27
1100 Crow Road North
☎ (041) 958 0853
McEwan 80/- A
New canalside bar designed in traditional style ⊛ ◑ (until 9) ᏺ ≅ (Anniesland)

11–11

Mitre*
12 Brunswick Street
☎ (041) 552 3764
Maclay 80/- H
Fine, small Victorian pub just off main shopping thoroughfare. Meals until 7pm; beer in public only ◑ ◗ ⊞
≅ (Argyle St) ⊖ (St Enoch)

11–11 (12.30–2.30; 6.30–11 Sun)

Orwells
70 Elderslie Street
Belhaven 80/- H
Small local pub with Orwellian artefacts around the walls Q ◑ ᏺ ≅ (Charing Cross)

11–11; (7–11 Sun)

Outside Inn
1256 Argyle Street
☎ (041) 334 8907
Belhaven 60/-, 70/-, 80/-; Broughton Greenmantle Ale A
Spacious, comfortable modern pub 800 yds from Kelvin Hall. Live music mid-week. Displays of local photography and art
◑ ◗ ᏺ ≅ (Exhibition Centre) ⊖

11–11 (11–2.30; 6.30–11 Sun)

Quaich
52 Coulstonholm Road, Shawlands
Belhaven 80/-; Broughton Greenmantle Ale H
Busy local pub with smart lounge. Old pictures of Glasgow adorn the walls
◑ (Mon–Fri) ⊞ ᏺ
≅ (Pollockshaws E)

11–midnight (12.30–2.30; 6.30–11 Sun)

Victoria
157–159 Bridgegate
☎ (041) 552 6040
Broughton Greenmantle Ale, Merlin Ale; Maclay 70/-, 80/-; Theakston Best Bitter H
Friendly, old-fashioned pub frequented by students and folk musicians; music at weekends Q ◑ ⊞ ≅ (Argyle St) ⊖ (St Enoch)

Gourock

11.30–11 (midnight Th, Fri; 11.45 Sat) 12.30–2.30; 5.30–11 Sun

Spinnaker Hotel
121 Albert Road (A8 coastal route) ☎ (0475) 33107
Belhaven 80/- A
Small family hotel on sea front, with splendid views over the Firth of Clyde. Renowned for its food
Q ๛ ⋈ ◑ ◗ ᏺ

Houston

11–midnight (12.30–2.30; 6.30–11 Sun)

Cross Keys
Main Street ☎ (0505) 612209
McEwan 80/- A
Olde worlde inn. Quality bar meals and full à la carte restaurant, with personal service by owners
ᛉ ๛ ⊛ ◑ ◗ ⊞ ᏺ

11–midnight (11.45 Sat); 12.30–2.30; 6.30–11 Sun

Fox & Hounds
Main Street ☎ (0505) 612448
Broughton Merlin's Ale; McEwan 70/- A
Comfortable lounge plus stables bar for the younger customer. Restaurant bar upstairs serving à la carte and good quality bar meals
◑ ◗ ⊞ᏺ

11–midnight (11.45 Sat) 12.30–2.30; 6.30–11 Sun

Houston Inn
North Street (off Main Street)
☎ (0505) 614315
McEwan 80/- A
The oldest pub in Houston. Enjoy a drink outside in summer ๛ ⊛ ⋈ ⊞ᏺ

Inverbeg

11–11 (midnight summer) 12.30–11 Sun

Inverbeg Inn
On A82 Luss–Tarbet road
☎ (043 686) 678
Younger No.3 A
Small friendly family hotel on banks of Loch Lomond
ᛉ Q ๛ ⊛ ⋈ ◑ ◗ ⊞ᏺ ▲

Irvine

11–11 (midnight Th, 12.15 F, S); open Sun

Crown Inn
162 High Street ☎ (0294) 79715
Younger No.3 A
Rare example of renovation improving a pub. Deceptively large behind narrow frontage, the single bar is well divided up by walls and screens. Lively ◑ ≅

Johnstone

11–11 (midnight F; 11.45 Sat) 12.30–2.30; 6.30–11 Sun

Coanes
26 High Street ☎ (0505) 22925
Broughton Greenmantle Ale; Marston Pedigree; Tennent 80/- A
Cosy town-centre pub with relaxed atmosphere. Guest beers
◑ ⊞ᏺ ≅ (Johnstone High)

11–2.30; 5–11 (12.30–2.30; 6.30–11 Sun)

Lynhurst Hotel
Park Road ☎ (0505) 24331
Younger No.3
Residential hotel ⋈ ◑ ◗

Kilbarchan

11–2.30; 5–11 (11–midnight Th, Fri; 11.45 Sat) 12.30–2.30; 6.30–11 Sun

Trust Inn
8 Low Barholm (Main Street)
☎ (050 57) 2401
Arrols 80/- E; **Ind Coope Burton Ale** H
Cosy village local. Weavers cottage nearby is worth a visit
◑ ◗ ᏺ

Kilmarnock

11–11

Gordon's Lounge*
17 Fowlds Street
☎ (0563) 42122
Belhaven 80/- H
Converted grain store; attractive lounge bar with

370

Strathclyde

vaulted ceiling and adjacent restaurant. Live music some evenings ()▶≉

Kilmelford

11–2.30; 5–12 (12.30–2.30; 6.30–11 Sun)

Culfail Hotel
16 miles S of Oban on A816
Younger No.3 Ⓐ
Cosy bar in hotel offering excellent food; a favourite meeting place for locals and sailing people ♨Q☎⋈()▶

Largs

11–midnight (12.30–2.30; 6.30–11 Sun)

Clachan
Bath Street (just off A78
☎ (0475) 672224
Belhaven 70/-, 80/- Ⓐ
Cheery and popular 1-bar pub in side street just behind seafront. Vast whisky selection ()&≉

11–11 (midnight Th–Sat); 12.30–2.30; 7–11 Sun

Sheiling
144 Main Street (off A78)
☎ (0475) 672079
Belhaven 80/- Ⓗ
Busy pub with small lounge. Photographs of Clyde Puffers adorn the walls of the public bar ⊟&≉

Linwood

11–11 (12.30–2.30; 6.30–11 Sun)

Venture
Bridge Street (off A761)
☎ (0505) 22496
Arrols 70/- Ⓐ
Lounge bar with nautical theme. Vast range of whisky (also from barrel). Superb view from bay window () (not Sun) ⊟&

Lochranza (Isle of Arran)

summer 11–1am; 12.30–1 Sun; winter 11–2.30, 5.00–11; 12.30–2.30; 6.30–11 Sun

Lochranza Hotel
On front between castle and pier ☎ (0770) 83223
McEwan 70/- (summer), 80/- Ⓐ
Comfortable bar and lounge in family hotel with sea views across to Loch Fyne
♨Q☎ (until 8) ☷⋈()▶⊟

Oban

11–1am

Oban Inn
Stafford Street (next to harbour) ☎ (0631) 62484
McEwan 80/-; Younger No.3 Ⓐ
The pub that put Oban on the real ale map. Medieval stained glass panels in lounge
☎ (for meals) ⋈()⊟&≉

Ochiltree

11–2.30 (3.30 Sat); 5–11 (midnight Sat)

Commercial Inn
1 Mill Street (A70)
☎ (029 07) 432
Maclay 60/- Ⓐ
Friendly well-run local in conservation village near Ayrshire's only remaining colliery. The only outlet for 60/- in the county. New upstairs lounge ♨☎⊟

Paisley

11–2.30; 5–11 (11–midnight Fri; 11.45 Sat); 12.30–2.30; 6.30–11 Sun

Bar Point
42 Wellmeadow Street
☎ (041) 889 5188
Whitbread Castle Eden Ale Ⓐ
Friendly pub with backgammon and occasional live music ☷ ()

11–11; (midnight Th, F; 11.45 Sat) open Sun

Buddies
23 Broomlands Street
☎ (041) 889 5314
Belhaven 80/- Ⓐ
Friendly welcome assured in this fine corner pub west of town centre. Library, chess, and angling clubs () ⊟&

11–11; (12 Th, F; 11.45 Sat) open Sun

Waverley Inn
29 Abercorn Street
☎ (041) 889 3156
McEwan 80/- Ⓗ
New pub with Clyde paddle steamer and other craft models on wall. Darts, dominoes in public bar; spacious yet homely lounge
☷ ()▶⊟&≉ (Gilmour St)

11–11 (11.30 F, Sat)

Wee Howff*
53 High Street
☎ (041) 889 2095
Arrols 70/-; Ind Coope Burton Ale Ⓗ
Traditional town centre Scottish bar near art gallery ≉

Prestwick

11–2.30; 5–12.30 (1am F, S); 12.30–12.30 Sun

Parkstone Hotel
Central Esplanade
☎ (0292) 77286
Belhaven 80/- Ⓗ
Seafront hotel with modernised lounge bar. Popular with locals and airline pilots ♨Q☎☷⋈()▶≉

Renfrew

11–11 (12.30–2.30; 6.30–11 Sun)

Ferry Inn
1 Clyde Street
☎ (041) 886 2104
Belhaven 80/- Ⓗ
Pictures of the heyday of the Clyde shipyards and previous Renfrew ferries adorn the walls. Non-smoking lounge ♨

11–11 (12.30–2.30; 6.30–11 Sun)

Pickwicks
7 Meadowside Street
☎ (041) 886 6552
Caledonian 80/- Ⓗ
Circular bar with large TV, popular with darts teams. Plenty of characters on both sides of the bar ()

Rhu

11–11.45 (12.30–11 Sun)

Ardencaple Hotel
Shore Road (A814)
☎ (0436) 820200
Arrols 80/- Ⓗ
Old hotel with traditional bar, smart lounge and much activity ♨☎☷⋈()▶⊟&

Seamill

11–1 (12.30–midnight Sun)

Glenboyd Hotel
7 Glenbryde Road (off A78)
Broughton Greenmantle Ale Ⓗ
Converted mill hidden from main road. Small public bar; fine view from garden
☎☷⋈()▶ (book)

Torrance

11–midnight; open Sun

Wheatsheaf Inn
77 Main Street (A807)
☎ (0360) 20374
Maclay 70/-; McEwan 80/- Ⓗ
Pleasant wood-panelled village pub with interior stained glass windows
♨Q☎☎()▶⊟&

Troon

11–12 (1, F S)

Anchorage Hotel
149 Templehill (B749)
☎ (0292) 317448
Broughton Greenmantle Ale, Merlin's Ale; Maclay 60/-; Theakston Old Peculier Ⓐ
Stone interior walls and catamaran-shaped bar counter in this old harbourside inn. Fish nets, creels add to the nautical flavour. Guest beers
♨☎⋈()▶&

winter: 11–2.30; 5–11 (12 F,S); summer: 11–11 (12 F,S) (12.30–2.30; 6.30–11 Sun)

Lookout
Marina, Harbour Road (B749)
☎ (0292) 311523
Broughton Greenmantle Ale Ⓐ
Modern lounge bar on 1st floor of marina building. Grey brick and painted block walls, soft seating; balcony overlooking marina. Separate restaurant. A little unusual
Q☎☷()▶▲ (Marina)

371

Strathclyde

Twechar

11–11 (1am F; 11.30 S) (12.30–2.30; 6.30–11 Sun)

Quarry Inn
Main Street OS700755
☎ (0236) 821496
Belhaven 70/-; Maclay 60/-, 70/-, 80/- H
Classic unspoilt local in one-time mining village; full of character ♨ 🄴

Uddingston

11–11 (midnight Th–Sat); 12.30–2.30; 7–11 Sun

Rowan Tree
60 Old Mill Road
☎ (0698) 812678
Maclay 70/-, 80/-, Porter A
Fine old public bar (the best architecture in the Maclays estate) with small lounge attached ♨ (& ≠

Whiting Bay (Isle of Arran)

11–1 (12.30 Sun) (shuts in afternoon and at 11 if quiet)

Cameronia Hotel
North end of village
☎ (07707) 254

Broughton Greenmantle Ale H
Small comfortable lounge with adjacent dining area. Fine view across the Clyde
Q ☎ (until 8) 🍴 ≠ ( )

11 (4.30 winter)–1am M–Th (12.30–1am Sun)

Nags Inn
South end of village
☎ (07707) 283
McEwan 70/-; Younger No.3 A
Pleasant modernised lounge in annexe to old hotel. Evening meals till 8pm
♨ ☎ (until 8) 🍴 ( ) 🄴

Real ale's ups and downs

This invention from the prolific output of Arthur Paul Pedrick is one of his minor works, but nevertheless demonstrates his attention to detail and his desire to add to the sum of human happiness.

British Patent 1 153 249 is entitled Tower with Revolving Restaurant and Other Amenities, and was issued in 1969.

You might well point out that another rather famous tower with revolving restaurant was built well before 1969 – the Post Office Tower, now known as the Telecom London Tower, and unfortunately without the revolving restaurant since the IRA bombed it.

What might have broken London's skyline.

Pedrick's patent shows what might have been had the Post Office had the vision to do the job properly.

His tower not only has a revolving restaurant but also tv aerials (well, the Telecom Tower does have quite a lot of those) and a mooring mast for airships and a transparent globe for transcendental meditation and tanks of beer under gravity for supplying local houses.

The lifts work on an ingenious principle. The centre of the tower is filled with beer, and the lift is arranged to be slightly buoyant with the right number of people in it. So in they get, and it bobs to the top. How do they get down?

According to Pedrick: "Because the lift is arranged to be just buoyant when it is in operation for raising people to the restaurant, if exactly the same number of people step into it for going down it will be clear that, having a meal inside them, they will be slightly heavier, the lift will have some 'negative buoyancy', and will sink slowly in the liquid in the tower."

JACK PLUG.

Reprinted from ELECTRONIC TIMES

Tayside

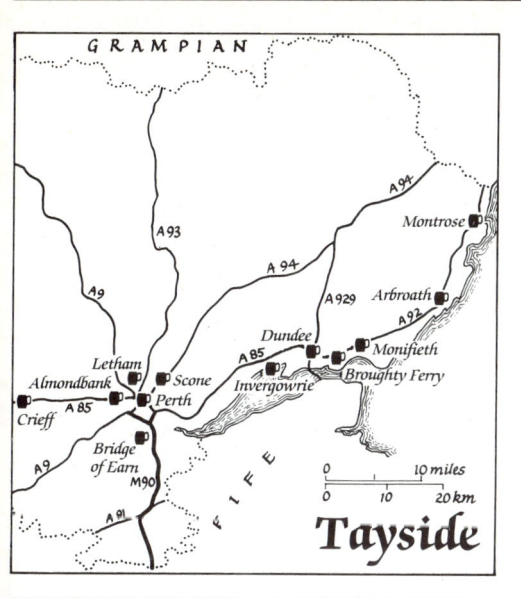

Almondbank

11–11; 12.30–2.30; 6.30–11 Sun

Almondbank Inn
Main Street (off A85)
Broughton Greenmantle Ale H
Country pub with family room ♨︎☎⊛ ◑ (Fri/Sat) ⊕

Arbroath

11–11; 12.30–2.30 Sun

Lochlands Bar
14 Lochlands Street
McEwan 80/-; Younger No.3 A
Traditional panelled pub with friendly atmosphere ⊕≷

Bridge of Earn

11–11 (11.45 F, S); 12.30–2.30; 6.30–11 Sun

Cyprus Inn
Back Street (off Main Street)
Belhaven 80/- A; **Broughton Greenmantle Ale** H
200 year-old inn ♨︎ ◑ ⊕&

Broughty Ferry

11–11 (12 Th, F, S); 12.30–2.30; 6.30–11 Sun

Fisherman's Tavern
12 Fort Street ☎ (0382) 75941
Belhaven 80/-; McEwan 70/-, 80/-; Maclay 80/-; Theakston Best Bitter H, **Younger No.3** A
Small and welcoming. Guest beers Q⊕≷

Crieff

11–2.30; 5–11 (11.45 F, S; all day summer); (12.30–2.30; 6.30–11 Sun)

Oakbank Inn
Turret Bridge (off A822)
Arrols 70/- H
Smart, modern lounge
☎ (till 8) ⊛ ◑ &

Dundee

11–11 (12.30–2.30; 6.30–11 Sun)

Balmore
47 Dura Street ☎ (0382) 453992
McEwan 80/-
Fine Victorian interior ⊕

11–12 (12.30–2.30; 6.30–11 Sun)

McGonagalls
Perth Road ☎ (0382) 22392
McEwan 70/-, 80/- A
Would surely have won Sir William's praise? ◑ ◗ ≷

11–12 (12.30–2.30; 6.30–11 Sun)

Pentland
105 Logie Street
Arrols 80/- A
Good value, friendly local ⊕&

11–12; 12.30–2.30; 6.30–11 Sun

Phoenix
105 Nethergate
Broughton Greenmantle Ale; McEwan 80/-; Taylor Best Bitter, Landlord, Porter A; **Theakston Old Peculier** H
Deservedly popular pub. Regular guest beers ◑ & ≷

11–midnight; open Sun

Shakespeare Bar
267 Hilltown ☎ (0382) 21454
Belhaven 80/- A
Basic public bar; comfortable lounge ◑ (not Sun) ⊕

11–2.30; 5–11 (11–11 F, S) 12.30–2.30; 6.30–11 Sun

Speedwell Bar (Mennies)
165 Perth Road ☎ (0382) 67783
Belhaven 80/-; Ind Coope Burton Ale H; **McEwan 80/-** A
Splendid Edwardian bar with sitting rooms Q ⊕

11–11.30 (midnight F, S;) 7–11 Sun

Tally Ho
7–13 Old Hawkhill
Taylor Landlord; Younger No.3 A
Bric-a-brac and hunting souvenirs. No food Sun
♨︎ ◑ ◗ ⊕&≷ (Taybridge St)

11–11.30 (12.30–2.30; 6.30–11 Sun)

Weavers Arms
27 Princes Street
Broughton Greenmantle Ale A
Tally Ho clone opposite old jute mill. No food Sun ◑ ◗

Invergowrie

11–11

Swallow Hotel
Kingsway West (off A972)
☎ (0382) 641122
Belhaven 80/- A
Elegant cocktail lounge with potted palms ☎⊛⋈ ◑ ◗ &

Letham

11–midnight (12.30–2.30; 6.30–11 Sun)

Commercial Inn
2 The Square ☎ (030 781) 245
Caledonian 70/- H
Very friendly rural local with active social life ♨︎☎⊛ ◑⊕&♿

Monifieth

11–midnight (12.30 Sun)

Panmure Hotel
Princess Street
McEwan 80/- A
Busy village hotel with family room ☎⊛⋈ ◑⊕&♿≷

Montrose

11–11

Salutation Inn
71 Bridge Street (A92)
Younger No.3 A
Comfortable well furnished local Q ◑⊕&♿≷

Perth

11–11 (closed Sun)

Auld Hoose
83 South Street ☎ (0738) 24136
Arrols 80/- H
Victorian-style pub with large island bar Q&≷

11–2.30; 5–11 (11–11 F, S); not Sun

Old Ship Inn
Skinnergate (off High Street)
Arrols 70/- H
Historic pub; a must. Meals till 7pm Thu–Sat ◑≷

11–11 (12.30–2.30; 6.30–11 Sun)

Robert Burns
County Place ☎ (0738) 33724
Belhaven 80/- A
Compact modern lounge bar
◑ ◗ &≷

Scone

11–11 (12.30–2.30; 6.30–11 Sun)

Scone Arms
Perth Road (A94)
McEwan 80/-; Younger No.3 A
Renowned for meals; coffee and all-day salad bar
♨︎☎ ◑ ◗ (weekend)⊕&

373

Isle of Man

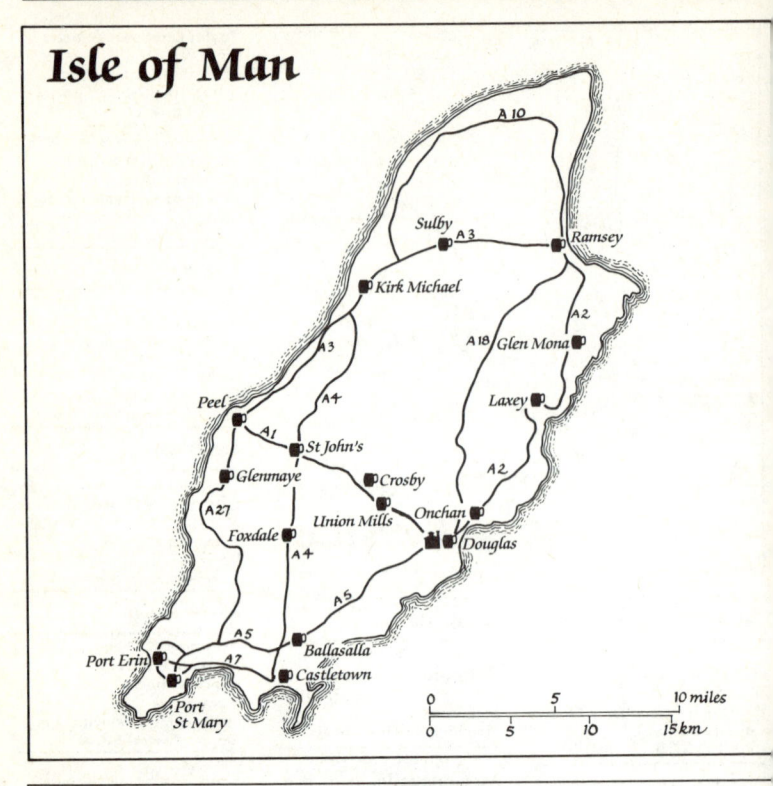

Isle of Man

Isle of Man Breweries, Douglas

Ballasalla

noon–10.45pm
Whitestone Inn
☎ (0624) 822334
Okell Mild, Bitter H
Village centre pub. Lounge large and comfortable, but often crowded. Dedicated ale drinkers are probably more at home in the bar. Darts ♨ ◐ ⌂ ≉ (IMR)

Try also: Rushen Abbey Hotel

Castletown

noon–10.45pm
Duck's Nest Hotel
Station Road ☎ (0624) 823282
Castletown Bitter H
Large, but basic bar, which boasts a lively evening trade from nearby housing estates. Live music Fri. Darts ♨⌂≉ (IMR)

11.30am–10.45pm
Union Hotel
The Square ☎ (0624) 823214
Castletown Bitter H
Large town-centre pub and home of the Castletown Ale Drinkers Society, the charitable organisation which holds the annual world tin bath races! Darts ⌂

noon–10.45pm
Victoria Hotel
Malew Street ☎ (0624) 823529
Castletown Bitter H
Small, comfortable pub, a few minutes' walk from the town centre. Darts ♨ Q

Try also: Castle Hotel; Ship Inn (Okell)

Crosby

noon–10.45pm
Crosby Hotel
Main Road
Okell Mild, Bitter H
Located on the T.T. course, the hotel displays motor cycle racing photographs as well as a racing machine. Darts ♨ (public bar) ◐⌂

Try also: Waggon & Horses (Okell)

Douglas

11.30am–10.45pm
Bridge Inn
North Quay ☎ (0624) 75268
Castletown Bitter H
Imaginative range of cooked meals. Popular with office-workers. Darts ◐▶⌂≉ (IMR)

noon–10.45pm
Bushy's Brewpub
Victoria Street (on promenade) ☎ (0624) 75139
Bushy's Bitter, Old Bushy Tail H
Beers are brewed by the licensee. Vegetarian dishes feature on the menu. Vibrant atmosphere at night. Pub games ♨ ◐

11.30am–10.45pm
Manor Hotel
Willaston (centre of Corporation Estate)
Okell Mild; Castletown Bitter H
Former manor house. Spacious bar and fine wood-panelled lounge. Popular with students and staff of nearby college. Darts ♨ ◐⌂

noon–10.45pm
Queen's Hotel
Queen's Promenade
☎ (0624) 75543
Okell Mild, Bitter H
Large seafront pub which can be reached by horse tram from town centre. Darts ♨▶≈ ◐⌂≉ (MER)

Isle of Man

11.30am–10.45pm
Waterloo
Strand Street ☎ (0624) 76833
Okell Mild, Bitter H
Delightful pub; a welcome retreat from the busy, pedestrianised shopping street

11.30am–10.45pm
Wheatsheaf Hotel
Ridgeway Street
☎ (0624) 73144
Okell Mild, Bitter H
Large town pub with lively atmosphere in the evening. Darts (IMR)

noon–10.45pm; Sun 12–1.30; 8–10
Woodbourne Hotel
Alexander Drive (Upper Douglas) ☎ (0624) 21766
Okell Mild, Bitter H
Friendly local with a splendid Edwardian façade. Has a men-only bar! Pub games Q

Try also: **Albert Hotel**; **Saddle Inn** (Okell)

Foxdale

noon–10.45pm
Foxdale Hotel (Baltic)
Main Road, Higher Foxdale (off A24) ☎ (062 471) 305
Castletown Bitter H
Extremely friendly local in centre of old mining village. Vegetarians catered for. Pub games Q

Glenmaye

noon–10.45pm
Waterfall Hotel
Village centre
☎ (062 484) 2238
Castletown Bitter H
Situated at the entrance to a well-known glen, the Waterfall offers somewhat upmarket pub catering. Darts

Glen Mona

noon–10.45pm
Glen Mona Hotel
On main road ☎ (0624) 781263
Okell Mild, Bitter H
The only relief for the thirsty traveller between Laxey and Ramsey. Good facilities for holidaymakers. Darts (MER)

Kirk Michael

noon–10.45pm
Mitre Hotel
Main Road
Castletown Bitter; Okell Mild H
Situated at the Peel end of the village. This is said to be the oldest pub on the island (Glen Wyllin)

Laxey

noon–10.45pm
Mines Tavern
Captain's Hill
Okell Mild, Bitter H
Beautifully situated in the sylvan setting of Laxey MER station. Mining and railway themes. (MER)

noon–10.45pm
New Inn
New Road ☎ (0624) 781077
Okell Bitter H
Well-supported village local with varied lunch menu. Darts (MER)

noon–10.45pm
Queens Hotel
New Road ☎ (0624) 781195
Castletown Bitter H
Comfortable pub with motor-cycling theme. Darts (MER)

Onchan

noon–10.45pm
Keppel Gate Hotel
Creg Ny Baa ☎ (0624) 76948
Castletown Bitter H
Friendly country pub situated on well known corner of the TT course. Darts Q

noon–10.45pm
Manx Arms
Main Road (A2)
Okell Mild, Bitter H
Large village hostelry

Try also: **Liverpool Arms** (Castletown)

Peel

noon–10.45pm
Central Hotel
Castle Street ☎ (0624) 842473
Okell Mild; Castletown Bitter H
Backstreet local off the tourist track. Folk music some weekends. Darts

11am–10.45pm
Creek Inn
Station Place ☎ (0624) 843594
Okell Mild, Bitter H
Situated close to Peel's picturesque quayside. Extensive range of cooked meals always available. Darts

Try also: **Marine** (Okell); **Royal** (Castletown)

Port Erin

noon–10.45pm
Station Hotel
Station Road ☎ (0624) 832236
Okell Bitter H
Large, sometimes noisy bar, and comfortable lounge with more sedate atmosphere. Darts (holiday season) (IMR)

Try also: **Avon** (Castletown)

Port St Mary

noon–10.45pm
Bay View Hotel
Bay View Road
☎ (0624) 832234
Okell Bitter H
Children admitted to pool room at landlord's discretion. Popular yachting harbour nearby. The garden is across road – be careful!

noon–10.45pm
Station Hotel
☎ (0624) 832234
Castletown Bitter H
Comfortable pub outside the village (holiday season) (IMR)

Ramsey

11.30am–10.45pm
Bridge Inn
Bowring Road
☎ (0624) 813248
Okell Mild, Bitter H
Bar has panoramic photographs and restored cast iron tables. Darts

11am–10.45pm
Plough Hotel
Parliament Street
☎ (0624) 813323
Okell Mild, Bitter H
Small pub in town's main shopping street

St John's

noon–10.45
Tynwald Hill Inn
☎ (062 471) 249
Okell Bitter H
Pub near historic Tynwald Hill, ancient centre of Manx Government. Darts

Sulby

noon–2; 5–10.45; 12–10.45 (F, S) May open all day in summer
Ginger Hall Hotel
☎ (062 489) 7231
Castletown Bitter H
Fine, unspoilt pub with imposing vintage bar counter, cast iron tables and brass handpumps. Motor-cycling photographs displayed. Darts

Union Mills

12–2 (5.30 Sat); 8 (9 Sat)–10.30
Railway Inn
Peel Road (Lhergy Crippety)
Okell Mild; Castletown Bitter G
Although tracks disappeared 20 years ago, this small village pub still commemorates the age of the train. Opening hours can vary. Darts Q

Channel Islands

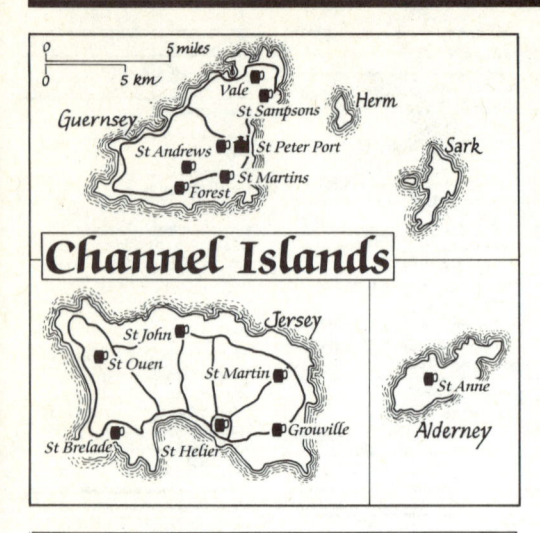

Guernsey; Randall,
St. Peter Port

* closed all day Sunday

Alderney

St Anne

10am–1am (midnight Sat & winter);
Sun 12–2, 8–midnight

Coronation Inn
36 High Street
☎ (048 182) 2630
Randall Best Bitter G
Friendly town local

Guernsey

Forest

10.30–2; 5–11

Deerhound Inn
Le Bourg (200 yds from airport) ☎ (0481) 38585
Guernsey Draught Bitter H
Cosy country hotel of character. Restaurant

St Andrews

10.30am–11pm

Last Post*
St Andrews Road
☎ (0481) 36353
Randall Best Mild, Best Bitter E
Popular country pub with large bar and comfortable lounge. Pub games

St Martins

10.30am–11pm

Captains Hotel
La Fosse ☎ (0481) 38990
Guernsey LBA Mild, Draught Bitter H
Attractive country hotel near Moulin Huet and Saints Bays. Unusual handpump in lounge. Restaurant upstairs

10.30am–11pm

Greenacres Hotel
Les Hubits ☎ (0481) 35711
Guernsey Draught Bitter H
Comfortable country hotel with outdoor swimming pool. Bar meals recommended

10.30am–11pm

L'Auberge Divette*
Jerbourg Road (below Jerbourg Monument)
☎ (0481) 38485
Guernsey LBA Mild, Draught Bitter H
Popular friendly pub with spectacular view from lounge and garden. Near South Coast Cliff Path. Family room. Pub games

St Peter Port

11–2.30; 4.30–11 (11am–11pm F, S)

Britannia Inn*
Trinity Square ☎ (0481) 21082
Guernsey Draught Bitter H
Pleasant pub with single lounge bar, near old quarter of town

10.30am–11pm

Crown (Ship & Crown)*
North Esplanade
☎ (0481) 21368
Guernsey Draught Bitter H
Popular single lounge bar overlooking marina

10.30am–11pm

Kosy Korner (Albion Hotel)*
Church Square ☎ (0481) 23518
Guernsey Draught Bitter G
Very busy pub overlooking harbour, near bus terminus. Cellar in roof! Restaurant. Pub games

10.30–2; 4.30–11 (10.30am–11pm Sat)

Plough Inn*
25 Vauvert ☎ (0481) 20599
Guernsey LBA Mild H
Established local in old quarter of town. Pub games

10.30am–11pm

Rohais Inn*
Rohais ☎ (0481) 20060
Guernsey LBA Mild G
Friendly local with large bar, on western outskirts of town. Pub games

10.30am–11pm

Salerie Inn*
Salerie Corner ☎ (0481) 24484
Guernsey LBA Mild H
Small, cosy, friendly pub opposite new marina. Popular with runners. Pub games

10.30am–11pm

Victoria Arms*
Victoria Road ☎ (0481) 25049
Guernsey LBA Mild G
Busy local high above town. Pub games

St Sampsons

10.30am–11pm

London House*
New Road ☎ (0481) 47988
Randall Best Mild, Best Bitter H
Pleasant local, handy for Bridge shopping centre. Pub games

10.30am–11pm

Pony Inn*
Les Capelles ☎ (0481) 44374
Guernsey LBA Mild, Draught Bitter H
Friendly 3-bar local close to Guernsey Candles and Oatlands Craft Centre. Pub games. Children welcome in lounge for lunch

Vale

10.30am–11pm

Hampshire Lodge*
Rue Mainguy ☎ (0481) 57230
Guernsey LBA Mild H
Comfortable pub with an emphasis on games

10.30am–11pm

Trafalgar Inn (Parrot)*
Trafalgar Road, Northside
☎ (0481) 46380

Channel Islands

Guernsey LBA Mild, Draught Bitter G
Basic and sociable local near Vale Castle Q

Jersey

Grouville

9am–11pm; Sun 11–1; 4.30–11

Pembroke Hotel
Grouville Coast Road
Draught Bass H
Friendly local bar with spacious lounge adjacent to Royal Jersey Golf Club. Near the beach and 1 mile from Mont Orgueil Castle
Q (12–2 M–S) (6–8.30 M–S)

St Brelade

9am–11pm; Sun 11–1; 4.30–11

La Pulente Hotel
On B35 (bus no. 12A)
Draught Bass H
Unspoilt bar with bar billiards and cosy lounge. At southern end of St Ouen's Bay overlooking the beach. Evening meals summer only
(12.30–2 M–S) (6.30–8)

9am–11pm; Sun 11–1; 4.30–11

Old Portelet Inn
Portelet Bay ☎ (0534) 41899
Draught Bass H
farm house with 4 separate bars. Large children's area. Friendly local above Portelet Bay beach Q (12–2.30) (6–8.30)

Try also: **Smugglers Inn**, Ouaisne Bay

St Helier

10am–11pm; Sun 11–1; 6–11

Esplanade Bars
Esplanade ☎ (0534) 22925
Draught Bass H
Spacious pub close to bus station. Friendly atmosphere and a varied clientele. Pub games (12–2.30 M–S)

10am–11pm; Sun 11–1; 5–11

Peirson
Royal Square ☎ (0534) 22726
Draught Bass H
Historic pub opposite seat of Government in town square. Scars of the Battle of Jersey on wall. Occasional live music
(not Sun)

Try also: **Dog & Sausage**; **Lamplighter**

St John

11am–11pm; Sun 11–1; 4.30–11

Les Fontaines Tavern
Route du Nord ☎ (0534) 62707
Draught Bass H
14th-century timber-beamed pub, one of the few pubs where Jersey patois is spoken. Friendly local. Ideal for families (games room)
(12–2 M–S) (6–8.30)

St Martin

11–2.30; 5–11 (11–11 Sat); Sun 11–1; 4.30–11

Anne Port Bay Hotel
Anne Port (200 yds from Anne Port Bay) ☎ (0534) 53515
Draught Bass G
Convivial and friendly hotel at east end of the island. Snug bar (12–2.15 M–S)

10am–11pm; Sun 11–2; 4.30–11

Rozel Bay Inn
Rozel
Draught Bass H
Cosy pub at bottom of picturesque valley in attractive old fishing village by quaint harbour. Pub games Q (not Sun)

Try also: **Castle Green**, Gorey

St Ouen

11am–11pm; Sun 11–1; 4.30–11

Le Moulin de Lecq
Greve de Lecq ☎ (0534) 82818
Draught Bass H
16th-century working watermill, close to beach. Popular Jersey dishes served (not Sun). Children's play area
Q (12–2.30) (6–8)

Peter Martin sampling the Guinness. See A Taste of London, *p. 190*

377

Northern Ireland

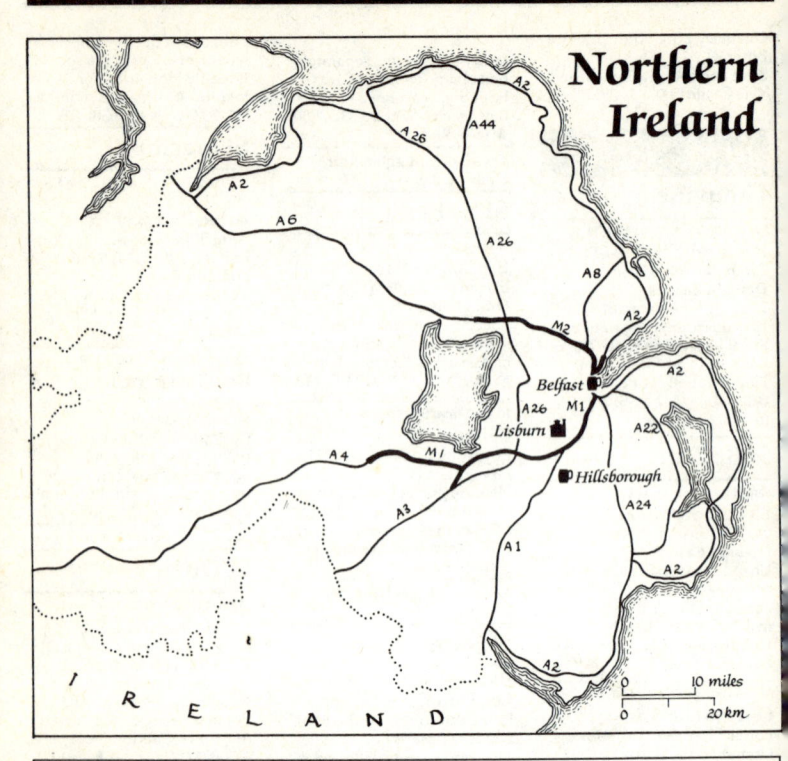

🏭 *Hilden, Lisburn*

Belfast

11.30–11 (12.30–2.30; 7–10 Sun)
Botanic Inn
23 Malone Road (off B23)
☎ (0232) 660460
Hilden Ale 🄴
Busy pub in heart of university district
🔥🍽🍺🚉 (Botanic)

11.30–11 (12.30–2.30; 7–10 Sun)
Kings Head
Lisburn Road, Balmoral (A1)
☎ (0232) 667805
Hilden Ale, Special Reserve 🄷

Plush establishment with impressive lounges, good public bar and restaurant. Opposite Exhibition Centre
🔥🍽🍺 (Balmoral)

11.30–11 (12.30–2.30; 7–10 Sun)
Linen Hall
9 Clarence Street
☎ (0232) 248458
Hilden Special Reserve 🄷
Friendly Edwardian-style bar near City Hall. Regular live music in rear lounge. Good lunches; popular with business community and musicians. Hilden Ale also on sale, but dispensed under pressure 🍽🍺🚉 (Botanic)

Hillsborough

11.30–11 (12.30–2.30; 7–10 Sun)
Hillside Bar
21 Main Street (off A1)
☎ (0846) 682765
Hilden Ale 🄷
Comfortable country-town pub with spacious bar and cosy lounge 'snug'. On the steep main street which offers good views of the hills around Belfast. (The town has many points of interest for the visitor) 🔥🌳🍽🍺♿

KEY TO SYMBOLS

- 🔥 real fire
- Q quiet pub – no electronic music, TV or obtrusive games
- 👶 indoor room for children
- 🌳 garden or other outdoor drinking area
- 🛏 accommodation
- 🍽 lunchtime meals
- 🍴 evening meals
- 🍺 public bar
- ♿ facilities for the disabled
- ⛺ camping facilities close to the pub or part of the pub grounds
- 🚉 near British Rail station
- Ⓞ near Underground station
- 🍏 real cider

The facilities, beers and pub hours listed in the Good Beer Guide are liable to change but were correct when the Guide went to press.

378